Collins Gem

BRADFORD'S
CROSSWORD
SOLVER'S
DICTIONARY

n Imprint of HarperCollins

first edition 2004

© Anne R. Bradford 2004

The Author hereby asserts her moral rights to be identified
as the author of this work.

HarperCollins Publishers
Westerhill Road, Bishopbriggs, Glasgow G64 2QT
Great Britain

www.collins.co.uk

Collins Gem® is a registered trademark of HarperCollins
Publishers Limited

ISBN 0-00-717780-1

Note

A catalogue record for this book is available from
the British Library

Computing support and typesetting by Thomas Call

Printed in Italy by Amadeus S.p.A.

Author's preface

Every word has a definition – an identity. If it has only one definition we can look at it and know it for what it is, but some words are like cut stones with many facets; they can mean different things according to the way in which we use them. These are the words which add spice to the cryptic crossword puzzle – the setter plays with them and tries to deceive his solvers into believing he means what he does not. They are the basis of puns and word-play. Introduced to crossword puzzles at an early age, it soon became clear to me that some words are beloved of setters – rivers Po and Dee; the town of Diss in Norfolk; the diocesan 'see' of Ely. These and many more quickly became familiar, but now and again the odd one would elude the memory. It seemed logical then to write these down, and by a natural progression to start to turn the normal dictionary inside out – if 'flummery' is defined as a blancmange, then why not list it under 'blancmange' alongside other words which can be defined as such? Not a new idea, of course, but why stop at synonyms? There are words which have recognised associations with other words – descriptive words or words with literary connections, foreign words, archaic words, technical words and even folkloric words – all highly collectable. And so this crossword dictionary began to evolve. Every puzzle I have laid hands on in the past forty-five years has been scrutinised, the clues broken down into definitions and cryptic parts; words indicating anagrams, reversals, puns, etc. all carefully recorded and stored.

I wish all who use this book the satisfaction that comes with completing a challenging puzzle.

A.R.B. 2004

Solving crossword clues

Crossword puzzles tend to be basically 'quick' or 'cryptic'. A 'quick' crossword usually relies on a one or two-word clue which is a simple definition of the answer required. As has been stated, many words have different meanings, so that the clue 'ball' could equally well lead to the answer 'sphere', 'orb' or 'dance'. The way to solve 'quick' crosswords is to press on until probable answers begin to interlink, which is a good sign that you are on the right track.

'Cryptic' crosswords are another matter. Here the clue usually consists of a basic definition, given at either the beginning or end of the clue, together with one or more definitions of parts of the answer. Here are some examples taken from all-time favourites recorded over the years:

1. '*Tradesman who bursts into tears*' (**Stationer**)

Tradesman is a definition of stationer. Bursts is cleverly used as an indication of an anagram, which into tears is of stationer.

2. '*Sunday school tune*' (**Strain**)

Here Sunday is used to define its abbreviation S, school is a synonym for train, and put together they give strain, which is a synonym of tune.

3. '*Result for everyone when head gets at bottom*' (**Ache**) (used as a 'down' clue)

This is what is known as an '& lit' clue, meaning that the setter has hit on a happy composition which could literally be true. Everyone here is a synonym for each, move the head (first letter) of the word to the bottom, and the answer is revealed, the whole clue being the definition of the answer in this case.

4. '*Tin out East*' (**Sen**)

In this example, tin, implying 'money', requires its chemical symbol Sn to go out(side) East, or its abbreviation, E, the whole clue being a definition of a currency (sen) used in the East.

5. '*Information given to communist in return for sex*' (**Gender**)

Information can be defined as gen; communist is almost always red, in return indicates 'reversed', leading to gen-der, a synonym for sex.

6. '*Row about no enclosure of this with sardines*' (**Tin-opener**)

Row is a synonym for tier, about indicates 'surrounding', no enclosure can be no pen, leading to ti-no pen-er, and another '& lit' clue.

7. '*Cake-sandwiches-meat, at Uncle Sam's party*' (**Clambake**)

Meat here is lamb, sandwiches is used as a verb, so we have C-lamb-ake, which is a kind of party in America. Uncle Sam or US is often used to indicate America.

8. '*Initially passionate meeting of boy and girl could result in it*' (**Pregnancy**)

Initially is usually a sign of a first letter, in this case 'p' for passionate + Reg (a boy) and Nancy (a girl), and another clever '& lit'.

With 'cryptic' clues the solver needs to try to analyse the parts to see what he or she is looking for – which word or words can be the straight definition, and which refer to the parts or hint at anagrams or other subterfuges. Whilst it would be unrealistic to claim total infallibility, practice has shown that in most crosswords a large percentage of the answers are to be found in this work.

Anne R Bradford

How to use the dictionary

This dictionary is the result of over forty-five years' analysis of some 300,000 crossword clues, ranging from plain 'quick' crosswords requiring only synonyms to the different level of cryptic puzzles. Therefore the words listed at each entry may be connected to the keyword in various ways, such as:

– a straightforward synonym

– a commonly-associated adjective

– an associated or proper noun

– a pun or other devious play on words

Keywords are listed alphabetically; in cases where the heading consists of more than one word, the first of these words is taken to be the keyword, and in cases where the end of a word is bracketed, the material up to the opening bracket is taken to be the keyword. Keywords marked with the symbol ▸ refer the user to other entries where additional information may be found. Keywords marked with the symbol ▷ give leads to anagrams and other ploys used by crossword setters. If the keywords found in the clue do not lead directly to the required answer, the solver should look under words given as cross-references to other entries. These are indicated by the symbol ▸, with the cross-referenced word shown in capitals.

About the Author

Anne Bradford's love of words began to make itself evident even in her schooldays, when, as Head Girl of her school, she instituted a novel punishment – instead of making rulebreakers write lines, she had them write out pages from a dictionary, on the grounds that this was a more useful exercise. Little did she know this was soon to be her own daily routine!

In time, crosswords became a magnificent obsession for Anne. All lovers of crosswords can understand the irresistible lure of solving them, but Anne's interest went much deeper than most people's, and when she stopped work in 1957 to have her first child, she found herself starting to note down answers to particularly tricky clues as an aid to memory, in case she should come across them again in another puzzle. It was from this simple beginning that this crossword dictionary evolved.

Over the space of 25 years, Anne continued to build on her collection of solutions, analysing every crossword clue as she solved it and adding it to her steadily growing bank of entries. This unique body of material eventually reached such proportions that she had the idea of offering it to her fellow crossword-solvers as a reference book, and since then, the book has gone from strength to strength, providing valuable help to countless cruciverbalists over a number of editions. This new Gem offers crossword-solvers Anne's bestselling brand of instant crossword help in a handy portable format.

Anne Bradford continues to devote time each day to solving crosswords, averaging some 20 a week – both quick and cryptic – and still avidly collects new solutions for her Crossword Solver's Dictionary at a rate of around 150 a week, compiling each solution by hand (without the use of a computer!) This book therefore includes much new material, gleaned by a true crossword lover who not only solves crosswords but, as an active member of the Crossword Club, can offer the user an insight into the mind of a cunning crossword compiler.

The Crossword Club

If you are interested in crosswords, you might like to consider joining the Crossword Club. Membership is open to all who enjoy tackling challenging crosswords and who appreciate the finer points of clue-writing and grid-construction. The Club's magazine, Crossword, contains two prize puzzles each month. A sample issue and full details are available on request.

The Crossword Club
Coombe Farm
Awbridge
Romsey, Hants.
SO51 0HN
UK

email: bh@thecrosswordclub.co.uk
website address: www.crosswordclub.demon.co.uk

Aa

A, An Ack, Adult, Ae, Alpha, Angstrom, Argon, D, Ein, Her, If, L, One, Per, They

Abandon(ed), Abandonment Abnegate, Abort, Amoral, Apostasy, Back down, Cancel, Castaway, Corrupt, Decommission, Defect, Derelict, ➤ DESERT, Desuetude, Discard, Disown, Dissolute, Ditch, Drop, Dump, Elan, Expose, Flagrant, Forhoo(ie), Forlend, Forsake, Gomorra, Immoral, Jack(-in), Jettison, Jilt, Loose, Louche, Maroon, Old, Orgiastic, Profligate, Quit, Rat, Renounce, Reprobate, Scrap, Shed, Sink, Strand, Waive, Wanton

Abase Degrade, Demean, Disgrace, Grovel, ➤ HUMBLE, Kowtow, Lessen

Abate(ment) Allay, Appal, Decrescent, Diminish, Lyse, Lysis, Moderate, Reduce, Remit, ➤ SUBSIDE

▷**Abate** may indicate a contention

Abbey Abbacy, Bath, Buckfast, Cloister, Downside, Fonthills, Fountains, Glastonbury, Je(r)vaulx, Medmenham, Melrose, Nightmare, Northanger, Priory, Tintern, Westminster, Whitby, Woburn

Abbot Aelfric, Archimandrite, Brother, Friar

Abbreviate, Abbreviation Abridge, Ampersand, Compendium, Condense, Curtail, ➤ SHORTEN, Sigla

Abdicate Cede, Disclaim, Disown, Resign

Abdomen Belly, C(o)eliac, Epigastrium, Gaster, Hypochondrium, Paunch, Pleon, ➤ STOMACH, Tummy, Venter

Abduct(ed), Abduction Enlèvement, Kidnap, Rapt, Ravish, Shanghai, Steal

Abet(tor) Aid, Back, Candle-holder, Second

Abeyance, Abeyant Dormant, Shelved, Sleeping, Store

Abhor(rent) ➤ DETEST, ➤ HATE, Loathe, Shun

Abide Dwell, Inhere, ➤ LAST, Lie, Live, Observe, Remain, Stand, Tarry

Ability Aptitude, Calibre, Capacity, Cocum, ➤ COMPETENCE, ESP, Facility, Faculty, Ingine, Lights, Prowess, Savey, Savv(e)y, Skill, Talent

Abject Base, Craven, Grovel, Humble, Servile, Slave

Able Ablins, ➤ ADEPT, Aiblins, Apt, Capable, ➤ COMPETENT, Fere, Seaman, Yibbles

Abnormal(ity) Anomalous, Atypical, ➤ DEVIANT, Dysfunction, Ectopic, Erratic, Etypical, Freakish, Odd, Preternatural, ➤ QUEER, Sport, Unnatural, Varus

Abode Domicile, Dwelling, Habitat, ➤ HOME, Lain, Libken, Midgard, Remain

Abolish, Abolition(ist) Annihilate, Annul, Axe, ➤ BAN, D, Delete, Destroy, Eradicate, Erase, Extirpate, John Brown, Nullify, Repeal, Rescind

Abominable, Abominate, Abomination Bane, Cursed, ➤ HATE, Nefandous, Nefast, Revolting, Snowman, Vile, Yeti

Aborigine, Aboriginal Boong, Bushmen, Gin, Indigenous, Lubra, Maori, Mary, Myall, Siwash, Vedda(h)

Abound(ing) Bristle, Copious, Enorm, Rife, Teem

About A, Almost, Anent, Around, C, Ca, Circa, Circiter, Concerning, Encompass, Environs, Going, Near, Of, On, Over, Re, Regarding, Soon at

▷ **About** may indicate one word around another

Above Abune, Over, Overhead, Overtop, Owre, Sopra, Superior, Supra-, Upon

Abrade, Abrasive Carborundum®, Chafe, Emery, Erode, File, Garnet paper, ➤ GRATE, Rub, Sand, Scrape

Abreast Alongside, Au courant, Au fait, Beside, Level, Up

Abridge(ment) Audley, Compress, Condense, Cut, Digest, Dock, Epitome, Pot, Shorten, Trim

Abroad Afield, Away, Distant, Forth, Out, Overseas

▷ **Abroad** may indicate an anagram

▷ **Abrupt** may indicate a shortened word

Abrupt(ly) Bold, Brusque, Curt, Gruff, Offhand, Premorse, Prerupt, Short, Staccato, Terse

Abscond Decamp, Desert, Elope, Flee, Levant, Welch

Absence, Absent(ee), Absent-minded(ness) Abs, Abstracted, Away, Distant, Distracted, Distrait, Exile, Hookey, Mitch, Scatty, Skip, Truant, Vacuity, Void, Wool-gathering

Absolute(ly) Bang, Complete, Dead, Downright, Implicit, Ipso facto, Just, Mere, Mondo, Plumb, Quite, Real, Sheer, Total, Unmitigated, Unqualified, Utter, Veritable, Very

Absolve Clear, Exculpate, Excuse, Pardon, Shrive

Absorb(ed), Absorbent, Absorbing, Absorption
Assimilate, Autism, Blot, Consume, Desiccant, Devour, Digest, Dope, Drink, ➤ ENGROSS, Imbibe, Ingest, Intent, Merge(r), Occlude, Occupy, Porous, Preoccupation, Rapt, Sorbefacient, Spongy, Unputdownable

Abstain(er), Abstemious, Abstinence, Abstinent
Band of Hope, Celibacy, Chastity, Continent, Desist, Eschew, Forbear, Forgo, Maigre, Nazarite, Nephalism, Rechab(ite), Refrain, Resist, Sober, Temperate, TT

Abstract(ed), Abstraction Abrege, Abridge, Academic, Appropriate, Brief, Deduct, Digest, Discrete, Epitome, Essence, Metaphysical, Musing, Notional, Précis, Prepossessed, Prescind, Resumé, Reverie, Stable, Steal, Summary, Tachism

Absurd(ity) Apagoge, Fantastic, Farcical, Folly, Inept, Irrational, Laputan, Ludicrous, Nonsense, Paradox, Preposterous, Ridiculous, Silly, Solecism, Stupid, Toshy

Abundance, Abundant A-gogo, Bounty, Copious, Flood, Flush, Fouth, Fowth, Fruitful, Galore, Lashings, Mickle, Mine, Mint, Oodles, Opulent, Over, Plenitude, Plenteous, ➤ PLENTIFUL, Pleroma, Prolific, Replete, Rich, Rife, Routh, Rowth, Sonce, Sonse, Store, Tallents, Teeming, Uberous

Abuse Assail, Billingsgate, Blackguard, Flak, Fustilarian, Fustil(l)irian, Hail, Insult, Invective, Limehouse, Maltreat, Miscall, ➤ MISTREAT, Misuse, Obloquy, Opprobrium, Philippic, Rail, Rampallian, Rate, Rayle, Revile, Satire, Scarab(ee), Scurrilous, Slang, Slate, Sledging, Snash, Solvent, Tirade, Vilify, Violate, Vituperation

Abut Adjoin, Border, Touch

Academic(ian) A, Della-Cruscan, Don, Erudite, Fellow, Hypothetic(al), Immortals, Literati, Master, Pedantic, PRA, RA, Reader, Rector

Academy Athenaeum, Dollar, Loretto, Lyceum, Military, Sandhurst, Seminary, St Cyr, West Point

Accelerate, Acceleration, Accelerator Bevatron, Collider, Cyclotron, G, Gal, Gun, Hasten, Increase, Linac, Linear, Rev, Speed, Stringendo, Synchrotron

Accent(ed), Accentuate Acute, Beat, Breve, Brogue, Bur(r), Circumflex, Cut-glass, Doric, Drawl, Enclitic, Enhance, Grave, Hacek, Intonation, Kelvinside, Long, Macron, Martelé,

Morningside, Mummerset, Nasal, Orthotone, Oxford, Oxytone, Pitch, Rhythm, Stress, Tittle, Tone, Twang

Accept(able), Acceptance, Accepted A, Accede, Admit, Adopt, Agree, Allow, Approbate, Bar, Believe, Buy, Can-do, Common, Consent, Cosher, Done, Grant, Kosher, Obey, On, Pocket, Putative, Stand, Swallow, Take, Tolerate, U, Wear

Access(ible) Avenue, Card, Come-at-able, Credit, Door, Entrée, ➤ ENTRY, Fit, Ingo, Key, Passe-partout, Password, Random, Recourse, Remote, Sequential, Spasm, Wayleave

Accessory, Accessories Abettor, Addition, Aide, Ally, Ancillary, Appendage, Appurtenance, Attribute, Bandanna, Bells and whistles, Cribellum, Findings, Staffage, Trappings, Trimming

Accident(al) Adventitious, Bechance, Blowdown, Blunder, Calamity, ➤ CHANCE, Circumstance, Contingency, Contretemps, Crash, Disaster, Fall, Fluke, Hap, Hit and run, Mischance, Mishap, Promiscuous, Rear-ender, Shunt, Smash, Smash-up, Spill, Stramash, Wreck

Acclaim Accolade, Applaud, Brava, Bravo, Cheer, Eclat, Fame, Fanfare, Hail, Kudos, Ovation, Praise, Salute

Accolade Award, Honour, Palm, Token

Accommodate, Accommodation Adapt, B and B, Bedsit, Berth, Board, Botel, Bunkhouse, Camp, Chalet, Compromise, Crashpad, Flotel, Gaff, Gite, Grace and favour, Homestay, Hostel, Hotel, House, Lend, Loan, Lodge, Lodgement, Motel, ➤ OBLIGE, Parador, Pension, Quarters, Rapprochement, Recurve, Room, Sorehon, Stabling, Stateroom, Steerage, Storage, Wharepuni

▷**Accommodating** may indicate one word inside another

Accompany(ing), Accompanied (by), Accompaniment, Accompanist Accessory, Alberti, And, Attend, Chaperone, Chum, Concomitant, Consort, Continuo, Descant, ➤ ESCORT, Harmonise, Herewith, Obbligato, Obligate, Obligato, Trimmings, Vamp

Accomplice Abettor, Aide, ➤ ALLY, Collaborator, Confederate, Federarie, Partner, Shill, Stale

Accomplish(ed) Able, ➤ ACHIEVE, Arch, Attain, Clever, Complete, Done, Effect, Master, Over, Perform, Polished, Realise, Ripe, Savant

Accord(ingly), According to After, Agree, Ala, Allow, As per, Attune, Chime, Consensus, Give, Grant, Harmony, Jibe, Meet, Sort, Thus

Accost Abord, Approach, Greet, Hail, Importune, Molest, Solicit, Tackle

Account(s) AC, Audit, Battels, Behalf, Bill, Cause, Charge, Chronicle, Current, Deposit, Discretionary, Enarration, Expense, Explain, Exposition, Ledger, Long, Memoir, Narration, Procès-verbal, Reason, Recital, Regest, Register, ➤ REPORT, Repute, Resumé, Sake, Suspense, Swindlesheet, Tab, Tale, Thesis, Version

Accountant Auditor, CA, Cost, Liquidator, Reckoner

Accumulate, Accumulation Adsorb, Aggregate, ➤ AMASS, Augment, Backlog, Collect, Gather, Hoard, Lodg(e)ment, Pile, Uplay

Accuracy, Accurate(ly) Bang-on, Cocker, ➤ CORRECT, Dead-on, Fair, Fidelity, Minute, Precise, Right, Spot-on, True, Word-perfect

Accusation, Accuse(d) Allege, Arraign, Attaint, Bill, Blame, Censure, Challenge, Charge, Criminate, Denounce, Dite, Gravamen, Impeach, Incriminate, Panel, Suspect, Tax, Threap, Threep, Traduce, Wight, Wite, Wyte

Accustom(ed) Acquaint, Attune, Enure, General, Habituate, Inure, Wont, Woon

Ace(s) Basto, Dinger, ➤ EXPERT, Jot, Master, Mournival, One, Quatorze, Spadille, Spadill(i)o, Spot, Tib, Virtuoso, Wonderful

Ache, Aching Aitch, Die, Long, Mulligrubs, Nag, Otalgia, Pain, Stitch, Yearn, Yen

Achieve(ment) Accomplish, Acquisition, Attain, Come, Compass, ➤ EFFECT, Exploit, Feat, Fulfil, Gain, Hatchment, Realise, Satisfice, Statify, Stroke, Succeed, Triumph, Trock, Troke, Truck

Acid(ity) Acrimony, Acrylic, Corrosive, Drop, Etchant, LSD, Reaction, Solvent, Sour, Tart, Vinegar, Vitriol

Acknowledge(ment) Accept, Admit, Allow, Answer, Avow, Confess, Grant, Mea culpa, Nod, Own, Receipt, Recognise, Respect, Righto, Roger, Salute, Ta, Touché, Wilco

Acoustic(s) Harmonics, Sonics

Acquaint(ance), Acquainted Advise, Cognisant, Enlighten, Familiar, ➤ INFORM, Knowledge, Nodding, Notify, Tell, Versed

Acquire, Acquisition Acquest, Earn, Ern, Gain, ➤ GET, Land, Obtain, Procure, Purchase, Steal, Take-over, Usucap(t)ion

Acquit(tal) Assoil, Cleanse, Clear, Exonerate, Free, Loose, Loste, Pardon

Acrid, Acrimony Bitter(ness), Empyreuma, Rough, Sour, Surly

Acrobat(ic)s Equilibrist, Gymnast, Ropedancer, Splits, Trampoline, Tumbler

Across A, Ac, Athwart, Opposite, Over, Through

Act(ing), Action A, Antic, Assist, Auto, Barnstorm, Behave, Business, Camp, Case, Cause, Conduct, Deal, ➤ DEED, Do, Excitement, Exert, Exploit, Feat, Feign, Function, Impersonate, Industrial, Litigate, Measure, Method, Movement, Perform(ance), Play, Practice, Pretence, Procedure, Process, Reflex, Represent, Rising, Serve, Simulate, Suit, Test, Treat, Turn, Union, War

Activate Arm, Goad, Spark, Spur, Stur, Styre, Trigger

Active, Activist, Activity A, Alert, At, Athletic, Brisk, Busy, Cadre, Deedy, ➤ DIY, Do(ing), Dynamited, Ecowarrior, Effectual, Energetic, Energic, Extra-curricular, Floruit, Fluster, Go-go, Goings-on, Hum, Hyper, Leish, Licht, Live, Mobile, Motile, Nimble, Ongo, Operant, Play, Rambunctious, Sprightly, Springe, Spry, Voice, Wimble

Actor(-like) Agent, Alleyn, Artist, Ashe, Barnstormer, Benson, Betterton, Burbage, Cast, Character, Company, Diseur, Donat, Gable, Garrick, Gielgud, Guiser, Ham, Hamfatter, Heavy, Histrio(n), Jay, Juve(nile), Kean, Luvvie, MacReady, Mime, Mummer, Olivier, Performer, Player, Playfair, Roscian, Roscius, Savoyard, Sim, Stager, Strolling, Super, Thespian, Tragedian, Tree, Tritagonist, Trouper, Understudy, Wolfit

Actress Bankhead, Duse, Ingenue, Pierrette, Siddons, Soubrette, Terry, West

Actual(ity), Actually De facto, Entelechy, Literal, Live, Material, Real, Real-life, True, Very

Acute Astute, Dire, Fitché, ➤ INTENSE, Keen, Quick-witted

Adage Aphorism, Gnome, Maxim, Motto, Paroemia, Proverb, Saw, Saying, Truism

Adamant Inexorable, Obdurate, Rigid, Unbending

Add(ed), Addendum Accrue, Adscititious, ➤ APPENDIX, Attach, Cast, Coopt, Dub, Ech(e), Eik, Eke, Elaborate, Embroider, Enhance, Fortify, Insert, Lace, Reckon, Score, Spike, Sum, Summate, Tot(e), Total

Addict(ion) Abuser, Acidhead, Buff, Devotee, Etheromaniac, Fan, Fiend, Freak, Hophead, Hype, Jones, Joypopper, Junkie, Mainliner, Mania, Need, Pillhead, Pillpopper, Pothead, Shithead, Slave, Space-cadet, Speedfreak, User, Wino

Addition(al) Also, And, Codicil, Encore, Etc, ➤ EXTRA, ➤ IN ADDITION, Increment, New, Odd, On, Other, Padding, Plus, PS, Rider, Spare, Suffix, Supplementary, Top-up

Address, Address system Accommodation, ➤ ATLAS, Call, Dedication, Delivery, Diatribe, Discourse, Lecture, Orate, Poste-restante, Salute, Sermon, Speech, Tannoy®

Adept Able, Adroit, Dab, Deacon, Don, ➤ EXPERT, Fit, Handy, Mahatma

Adequate Condign, Does, Due, Egal, Equal, Ere-now, Passable, Proper, ➤ SUFFICIENT, Tolerable, Valid

Adhere(nt), Adhesive Allegiance, Ally, Bond, Burr, Child, Cling, Conform, Dextrin, Disciple, Epoxy, Follower, Glue, Gum, Jain(a), Mucilage, Partisan, Resin, Sectator, Servitor, Sticker, Supporter, Slave, Synechia, Waterglass

Adjacent, Adjoining Bordering, Conterminous, Contiguous, Handy, Nigh

Adjourn(ment) Abeyance, Delay, ➤ POSTPONE, Prorogate, Recess, Rise, Suspend

Adjunct Addition, Aid, Ancillary, Rider

Adjust(able), Adjustment Accommodate, Adapt, Attune, Coapt, Dress, Ease, Fit, Gang, Gauge, J'adoube, Modify, Modulate, Orientate, Prepare, Reduce, Regulate, Scantle, Sliding, Suit, Tram, Trim, True, Tune, Tweak

▷**Adjust** may indicate an anagram

Administer, Administration, Administrator Adhibit, Anele, Apply, Arrondissement, Bairiki, Control, ➤ DIRECT, Dispence, Dispense, Executive, Intendant, Intinction, ➤ MANAGE, Regime, Registrar, Run, Secretariat, Steward

Admirable, Admiration, Admire(d), Admirer Clinker, Clipper, Conquest, Crichton, Esteem, Estimable, ➤ EXCELLENT,

Flame, Fureur, Ho, Iconise, Idolater, Laudable, Partisan, Regard, Ripping, Toast, Tribute, Venerate, Wonder

Admission, Admit(ting), Admittance Access, Agree, Allow, Avow, Concede, ➤ CONFESS, Enter, Entrée, Entry, Estoppel, Grant, Ingress, Initiate, Intromit, Ordain, Owe, Own, Recognise, Tho(ugh), Yield

Admonish, Admonition Chide, Lecture, Moralise, Rebuke, ➤ SCOLD, Tip, Warn

Ado Bother, Bustle, Fuss

Adolescent Developer, Grower, Halflin, Juvenile, Neanic, Teenager, Veal, Youth

Adopt Accept, Affiliate, Assume, Embrace, Espouse, Father, Foster, Mother

Adoration, Adore Homage, Love, Pooja(h), Puja, Revere, Venerate, Worship

Adorn(ed), Adornment Attrap, Banderol, Bedeck, Bedight, Bejewel, Caparison, Clinquant, Deck, Dight, Drape, Embellish, Emblaze, Emblazon, Embroider, Enchase, Equip, Festoon, Flourish, Furnish, Garnish, Grace, Graste, Ornament, Riband, Tattoo, Tatu, Tinsel

Adulate, Adulation Flatter(y), Praise, ➤ WORSHIP

Adult Amadoda, Grown-up, Man, Mature, Upgrown, X

Advance(d) A, Abord, Accelerate, Ante, Approach, Assert, Charge, Develop, Extreme, Fore, Forge, Forward, Get on, Haut(e), Impress, Imprest, Incede, Late, Lend, ➤ LOAN, March, Mortgage, Overture, Pass, Piaffe, Posit, Postulate, Precocious, Prefer, Prest, Process, Progress, ➤ PROMOTE, Propose, Propound, Ripe, Rise, Sub, Submit, Tiptoe

Advantage(ous) Accrual, Aid, ➤ ASSET, Avail, Batten, Benefit, Bisque, Boot, Edge, Emolument, Expedient, Exploit, Favour, Fruit, Gain, Grouter, Handicap, Handle, Head-start, Help, Interess, Interest, Lever(age), Odds, One-up, Percentage, Plus, Privilege, Prize, Purchase, Salutary, Strength, Toe-hold, Use, Van, Whiphand

Adventure(r), Adventuress Argonaut, Assay, Buccaneer, Casanova, Conquistador, Emprise, Enterprise, Escapade, ➤ EXPLOIT, Filibuster, Gest, Lark, Mata Hari, Mercenary, Merchant, Picaresque, Picaro, Risk, Routier, Rutter, Swashbuckler, Vamp, Voyage

Adversary Cope(s)mate, Enemy, Foe

Adverse, Adversity Calamity, Cross, Down, Harrow, Misery, Reversal, Setback, Untoward, Woe

Advert(ise), Advertisement Ad, Allude, Bark, Bill, Circular, Classified, Coign(e), Coin, Commercial, Copy, Display, Dodger, Flysheet, Hype, Jingle, Madison Avenue, Mailshot, Noise, ► NOTICE, Parade, Placard, Plug, ► POSTER, Promo, Promote, Promulgate, Prospectus, Puff, Quoin, Refer, Sky-write, Splash, Stunt, Subliminal, Teaser, Throwaway, Tout, Trailer, Trawl

Advice Conseil, Counsel, ► GUIDANCE, Guideline, Information, Invoice, Opinion, Read, Recommendation, Re(e)de

Advise(d), Adviser, Advisable Acquaint, CAB, Counsel, Enlighten, Expedient, Inform, Instruct, Mentor, Oracle, Peritus, Prudent, ► RECOMMEND, Tutor, Urge, Wise

Advocate(d) Agent, Argue, Attorney, Back, Devil's, Exponent, Gospel, Lawyer, Move, Paraclete, Peat, Peddle, Pleader, Pragmatist, Preach, Proponent, Syndic, Urge

Aerial Antenna, Dipole, Dish, Ethereal, Loop, Parabolic

►**Aeroplane** see AIRCRAFT

Affable Amiable, Avuncular, Benign, Suave, Urbane

Affair(s) Amour, Business, Concern, Current, Event, Fight, Go, Intrigue, Matter, Pash, Pidgin, Pi(d)geon, Ploy, Relationship, Res, Romance, Shebang, Subject, Thing

Affect(ed), Affectation(ate), Affection(ate) Air, Alter, Breast, Camp, Chi-chi, Concern, Crazy, Endearment, Euphuism, Foppery, Hit, Ladida, Lovey-dovey, Mimmick, Minnick, Minnock, Mouth-made, Phoney, ► POSE, Poseur, Precieuse, Preciosity, Pretence, Spoilt, Stag(e)y, Storge, Susceptible, Sway, Tender, Twee, Unction, Unnatural

Affiliate, Affiliation Adopt, Associate, Merge, Unite

Affinity Bro, Kin(ship), Penchant, Rapport, Tie

Affirm(ative), Affirmation Assert, Attest, Maintain, Predicate, Protestation, Uh-huh, ► VERIFY

Afflict(ed), Affliction Asthma, Cross, Cup, Curse, Disease, Furnace, Harass, Hurt, Lumbago, Molest, Nosology, Palsy, Persecute, Pester, Plague, Scourge, Smit, Sore, ► SORROW, Stricken, Teen, Tene, Tic, Tribulation, ► TROUBLE, Unweal, Visitation, Woe

Affluence Abundance, Fortune, Opulence, Wealth

Afford Bear, Manage, Offer, Provide, Spare

Affront Assault, Defy, Facer, ➤ INSULT, ➤ OFFEND, Outrage, Scandal, Slight, Slur

Afraid Adrad, Alarmed, Chicken, Fearful, Funk, Rad, Regretful, Scared, Timorous, Windy, Yellow

Africa(n) Abyssinian, Ashanti, Bantu, Barbary, Basuto, Berber, Black, Boer, Botswana, Cairene, Carthaginian, Congolese, Eritrean, Ethiopian, Fanti, Gambian, Hausa, Herero, Hottentot, Ibo, Kaf(f)ir, Kenyan, Kikuyu, Lesotho, Liberian, Libyan, Lowveld, Malawi, Malian, Masai, Matabele, Moor, Moroccan, Mozambican, Namibian, Negro, Nilot(e), Nubian, Rastafarian, Rhodesian, Shona, Somali, Sudanese, Swahili, Transkei, Transvaal, Tuareg, Tutsi, X(h)osa , Yoruban, Zairean, Zulu

After(wards) About, At, Behind, Beyond, Eft, Epi-, ➤ LATER, On, Past, Rear, Since, Sine, Subsequent

▷ **After injury** may indicate an anagram

Afternoon A, Arvo, PM, Postmeridian, Undern

Afterpiece, Afterthought Addendum, Codicil, Epimetheus, Exode, Footnote, Note, PS, Supplement

Again Afresh, Agen, Anew, Back, Bis, De novo, Ditto, Do, Eft, Eftsoons, Encore, Iterum, More, Moreover, Over, Re-, Recurrence, Reprise, Than, Then

Against A, Anti, Beside, Con, Counter, Gainsayer, Into, Nigh, On, Opposing, To, V, Versus

Age(d), Ages, Aging Ae, Aeon, Antique, Chellean, Cycle, Dark, Eon, Epact, Epoch(a), Era, Eternity, Generation, Golden, Heroic, Ice, Iron, Jurassic, Kalpa, Mature, Middle, Millennium, Neolithic, New, Paleolithic, Period, Senescence, Space, Stone

Agency, Agent Ambassador, Bailiff, Broker, Catalyst, Cat's paw, Consul, Doer, Double, Emissary, Envoy, Estate, Factor, Free, G-man, Go-between, Hand, Influence, Instrument, Legate, Literary, Means, Medium, Mole, Narco, Pinkerton, Proxy, Rep(resentative), Runner, Salesman, Secret (service), Solvent, Spy, Tass, Travel, Voice

Agenda Business, Programme, Remit, Schedule

Aggravate Annoy, Inflame, Irk, Needle, Nettle, Provoke, Try, Vex

Aggression, Aggressive, Aggressor Attack, Belligerent, Bullish, Butch, Defiant, Enemy, Feisty, Foe, Gungho, Hawk,

Invader, Militant, On-setter, Pushing, Rambo, Rampant, Shirty, Truculent, Wild

Agile Acrobatic, Deft, Lissom(e), Nifty, Nimble, Quick, Spry, Supple, Swank

Agitate(d), Agitation, Agitator Activist, Ado, Agitprop, Boil, Bolshie, Bother, Churn, Commotion, Convulse, Distraught, ➤ DISTURB, Ebullient, Emotion, Excite, Extremist, Fan, Ferment, Firebrand, Fluster, Frenzy, Fuss, Goad, Heat, Hectic, Lather, Militant, Perturb, Pother, Rattle, Restless, Rouse, Ruffle, Seethed, Stir(-up), Tailspin, Tizzy, Toss, Tremor, Trouble, Turmoil, Twitchy, Welter, Whisk

▷**Agitate** may indicate an anagram

Agony Ache, Anguish, Ecstasy, Heartache, ➤ PAIN, Torment, Torture

Agree(ing), Agreed, Agreement Accede, Accept, Accord, Acquiescence, Allow, Amen, Analogy, Assent, Aye, Chime, Coincide, Compact, Comply, Concert, Concord(at), Concur, Conform, ➤ CONSENT, Contract, Covenant, Deal, Entente, Equate, League, Nod, Okay, Pact, Right(o), Roger, Sanction, Side, Square, Suit, Sympathy, Synchronise, Tally, Trade, Treaty, Union, Unison, Wilco, Yea, Yes

Agreeable Amene, Harmonious, Pleasant, Sapid, Sweet, Well-disposed, Willing, Winsome

▷**Ague(ish)** may indicate an anagram

Ahead Anterior, Before, Foreship, Forward, Frontwards, Onward, Up

Aid(s), Aide Accessory, Adjutant, Assist, Decca, ➤ DEPUTY, Galloper, Grant, Help, Key, Legal, Lend-lease, Monitor, Optophone, PA, Relief, Serve, Slim, Succour, Support, Visual

Ail(ment) Affect, Afflict(ion), Complaint, Croup, Disease, Malady, Narks, Pink-eye, Pip, Sickness

Aim Approach, Aspire, Bead, Bend, End, Ettle, Eye, Goal, Hub, Intent, Level, Mark, Mission, Object, Plan, Plank, Point, Purpose, Reason, Sake, Seek, Sight(s), Target, Tee, Telos, Train, View, Visie, Vizy, Vizzie

Aimless Drifting, Erratic, Haphazard, Random, Unmotivated

Air(s), Airer, Airy Ambience, Atmosphere, Attitude, Aura, Bearing, Ether(eal), Expose, Inflate, Lift, Lullaby, Madrigal,

Manner, Melody, Mien, Ozone, Parade, Screen, Serenade, Shanty, ▶ TUNE, Ventilate, Wind

Aircraft, Airship Autogiro, Biplane, Blimp, Camel, Chopper, Concorde, Crate, Dirigible, Doodlebug, Glider, Harrier, Helicopter, Hurricane, Jumbo, Jump-jet, Kite, Lancaster, Messerschmitt, Mosquito, Moth, Parasol, ▶ PLANE, Spitfire, Trident, Turbo-prop, Viscount, Zeppelin

Aircraftsman, Airman AC, Aeronaut, Kiwi, LAC, RAF

Airline, Airway Aeroflot, Anthem, BAC, BEA, Duct, Larynx, Lot, SAS, S(ch)norkel, TWA, Weasand(-pipe), Windpipe

Airport Drome, Entebbe, Faro, Gander, Gatwick, Heliport, Idlewild, Kennedy, Landing strip, Lod, Luton, Lympne, Orly, Runway, Shannon, Stansted, Stolport, Vertiport, Wick

Air-tight Hermetic, Indisputable, Sealed

Akin Alike, Cognate, Congener, Kindred

Alarm Alert, Arouse, Bell, Bleep, Caution, Dismay, False, Fricht, Fright, Ghast, Larum, Panic, Perturb, Rouse, Siren, Smoke, Startle, Tirrit, Tocsin, Warn, Yike(s)

Alas Ah, Alack, Ay, Eheu, Ha, Haro, Harrow, Io, Lackadaisy, Lackaday, O, Oh, Ohone, O me, Waesucks, Waly, Well-a-day, Wellanear, Wel(l)away, Woe

Albatross Alcatras, Golf, Gooney(-bird), Omen, Onus

Alchemic, Alchemist, Alchemy Adept, Brimstone, Faust(us), Hermetic(s), Multiplier, Quicksilver, Sal ammoniac, Sorcery, Spagyric, Spagyrist, Witchcraft

Alcohol(ic) Bibulous, Booze, Chaptalise, Dipsomaniac, Drinker, Firewater, Grain, Hard, Inebriate, Rotgut, Rubbing, Spirits, Wino

Alcove Apse, Bay, Bole, Dinette, Niche, Recess

Ale, Alehouse Audit, Barleybree, Beer, Humpty-dumpty, Lamb's wool, Light, Morocco, Nappy, Nog, Nogg, October, Purl, Real, Stout, Swats, Tiddleywink, Tipper, Whitsun, Wort, Yard, Yill

Alert Arrect, Astir, Attentive, Aware, Gleg, Gogo, Intelligent, Qui vive, Red, Scramble, Sharp, Sprack, Sprag, Stand-to, Vigilant, Volable, Wary, Watchful

Alga(e) Anabaena, Blanketweed, Chlorella, Conferva, Desmid, Diatom, Dulse, Heterocontae, Isokont, Jelly, Nostoc, Pleuston, Pond scum, Prokaryon, Protococcus, Seaweed, Spirogyra,

Star-jelly, Stonewort, Ulothrix, Ulotrichales, Valonia, Volvox, Zooxanthella

Algebra Boolean, Linear, Quadratics

Alias Aka, Epithet, Moni(c)ker, Pen-name, Pseudonym

Alibi Excuse, Watertight

Alien(ate), Alienation A-effect, Amortise, Disaffect, Ecstasy, Estrange, ET, Exotic, External, Foreign, Hostile, Martian, Metic, Outlandish, Philistine, Repugnant, Strange(r)

Alight Alowe, Availe, Detrain, Disembark, Dismount, In, Lambent, Land, Lit, Perch, Pitch, Rest, Settle

Align Arrange, Associate, Collimate, Dress, Juxtapose, Marshal, Orient

▶**Alike** see LIKE

Alive Alert, Animated, Breathing, Extant, Quick

Alkali(ne), Alkaloid Antacid, Base, Lye, Soda

All A, ▶ ENTIRE, Entity, Finis, Omni, Pan, Quite, Sum, ▶ TOTAL, Toto, Tutti, Whole

Allay Calm, Lessen, Quieten, Soothe

Allegation, Allege Assert, Aver, Claim, Obtend, Plead, Purport, Represent, Smear

Allegiance Faith, Foy, Loyalty

Allegory, Allegorical Apologue, Fable, Mystic, Myth, Parable

Alleviate Allege, Calm, Mitigate, Mollify, Palliate, ▶ RELIEVE, Temper

Alley Aisle, Blind, Bonce, Bowling, Corridor, Ginnel, Lane, Laura, Marble, Passage, Tinpan, Vennel, Walk, Wynd

Alliance Agnation, Axis, Bloc, Cartel, Coalition, Combine, Compact, Federacy, ▶ LEAGUE, Marriage, NATO, Syndicate, Union

Alligator Al(l)igarta, Avocado, Cayman

Allocate, Allocation Allot, Apportion(ment), Earmark, Placement, Ration, Share, Zone

Allot(ment), Allow(ance), Allowed, Allowing Alimony, Allocation, Although, Award, Budget, Confess, Discount, Excuse, Grant, Indulge, Latitude, Let, Licit, Pension, ▶ PERMIT, Portion, Quota, Ration, Rebate, Sanction, Share(-out), Stipend, Suffer, Though, Tolerance, Yield

▶**Allow** SEE ALLOT

Alloy Amalgam, Compound, Mix, Solder

▷**Alloy** may indicate an anagram

All-right A1, Assuredly, Fit, Hale, Hunky(-dory), OK, Safe, Tickety-boo, Well

Allude, Allusion Hint, Imply, Innuendo, Mention, Refer, Reference, Suggest

Allure, Alluring Agaçant(e), Charm, Circe, Decoy, Glam, Glamour, Magnet(ic), SA, Seduce, Seductive, Tempt, Trap, Trepan, Vamp

Ally, Allied Accomplice, Agnate, Aide, Alley, Alliance, Backer, Belamy, Cognate, Colleague, Dual, German(e), Holy, Marble, Marmoreal, Partner, Plonker, Related, Taw, Unholy

Almanac Calendar, Clog, Ephemeris, Nostradamus, Whitaker's, Wisden, Zadkiel

Almost Anear, Anigh, Most, Near, Nigh(ly), Ripe, Une(a)th, Virtually, Well-nigh, Welly

Alms Awmous, Charity, Dole, Handout

Alone Hat, Jack, Lee-lane, Onely, Secco, Separate, Single, Singly, Sola, Solo, Solus, Unaccompanied, Unaided, Unholpen

Along, Alongside Abeam, Aboard, Abreast, Apposed, Beside, By, Parallel

Alphabet ABC, Brahmi, Braille, Cyrillic, Devanagari, Estrang(h)elo, Futhark, Futhorc, Futhork, Glagol, Glagolitic, Glossic, Grantha, Hangul, Horn-book, ITA, Kana, Kanji, Katakana, Kufic, Manual, Nagari, Og(h)am, Pangram, Phonetic, Pinyin, Romaji, Roman, Signary, Syllabary

Alpine, Alps Bernese, Cottian, Dinaric, Gentian, Graian, Laburnum, Lepontine, Matterhorn, Transylvanian, Tyrol

Also Add, And, Eke, Item, Likewise, Moreover, Too, Und

Altar, Altar-cloth, Altarpiece Dossal, Dossel, Polyptych, Retable, Shrine, Tabula

Alter Adapt, Adjust, Bushel, Change, Correct, Customise, Evolve, Falsify, Lib, Modify, Modulate, Mutate, Recast, Revise, Transpose, Up-end, ▶VARY

Alternate, Alternating, Alternation, Alternative Boustrophedon, Bypass, Exchange, Instead, Metagenesis, ▶OPTION, Ossia, Other, Rotate, Solidus, Staggered, Systaltic, Tertian, Variant

▷**Alter(native)** may indicate an anagram

▷**Alternately** may indicate every other letter

Although Admitting, Albe(e), All-be, But, Even, Howsomever, Whereas, While

Altitude Elevation, Height

▷**Altogether** may indicate words to be joined

Altruistic Heroic, Humane, Philanthropic, Selfless, Unselfish

Alumnus Graduate, OB

Always Algate(s), Ay(e), Constant, E'er, Eternal, Ever(more), Forever, I, Immer, Sempre, Still

Amass Accumulate, Assemble, Collect, Heap, Hoard, Pile, Upheap

Amateur(s) A, AA, Armchair, Beginner, Corinthian, Dilettante, Diy, Ham, Inexpert, L, Lay, Novice, Tiro, Tyro

Amaze(d), Amazement, Amazing Astonish, Astound, Awhape, Cor, Criv(v)ens, Dumbfound, Flabbergast, Gobsmack, Goodnow, Grace, Incredible, Magical, Monumental, O, Open-eyed, Open-mouthed, Perplex, Poleaxe, Pop-eyed, Stagger, Stupefaction, Stupendous, Thunderstruck

Ambassador Diplomat, Elchee, Elchi, Eltchi, Envoy, HE, Internuncio, Ledger, Legate, Leiger, Minister, Nuncio, Plenipo, Plenipotentiary

Ambience Aura, Milieu, Setting

Ambiguous, Ambiguity Amphibology, Cryptic, Delphic, Double, Enigmatic, Epicene, Equivocal, Loophole, Weasel words

Ambition, Ambitious Aim, Aspiring, Careerism, Drive, Emulate, Goal, Go-getter, High-flier, Keen, Office-hunter, Purpose, Pushy, Rome-runner

Amble Meander, Mosey, Pace, Saunter, Stroll

Ambulance, Ambulance-men Blood-wagon, Pannier, Van, Yellow-flag, Zambu(c)k

Ambush(ed) Ambuscade, Bushwhack, Embusque, Latitant, Lurch, Perdu(e), Trap, Waylay

Amen Ammon, Approval, Inshallah, Verify

Amend(ment) Alter, Change, Expiate, Fifth, Redress, Reform, Repair, Restore, ➤ REVISE, Satisfy

▷**Amend** may indicate an anagram

America(n) Algonki(a)n, Algonqu(i)an, Am, Caddo, Cajun, Carib, Chicano, Chickasaw, Copperskin, Digger, Doughface, Down-easter, Federalist, Flathead, Fox, Gringo, Interior, Jonathan, Latino, Mistec, Mixtec, Norteno, Olmec, Paisano, Salish, Stateside, Statesman, Statist, Tar-heel, Tico, Tupi, US(A), Yankee, Yanqui

Amiable Friendly, Genial, Gentle, Inquiline, Sweet, Warm

Amid(st) Among, Atween, Between, Inter, Twixt

Amiss Awry, Ill, Up, Wrong

Ammunition Ammo, Buckshot, Bullets, Chain-shot, Grenade, Round, Shot, Slug, Tracer

Among Amid(st), In, Within

Amorous(ly) Erotic, Fervent, Lustful, Warm

Amount Come, Dose, Element, Figure, Levy, Lot, Number, Pot(s), Price, Quantity, Quantum, Span, Stint, Throughput, Whale, Wheel

Amphibian, Amphibious Amb(l)ystoma, Amtrack, Anura, Axolotl, Batrachian, Caecilia, Caecilian, Desman, Eft, Frog, Guana, Hassar, Mermaid, Mudpuppy, Newt, Olm, Proteus, Rana, Salamander, Salientia, Seal, Tadpole, Urodela(n), Urodele, Weasel

Amphitheatre Bowl, Coliseum, Colosseum, Ring, Stage

Ample Bellyful, Copious, Enough, Generous, Good, Large, Opulent, Profuse, Rich, Roomy, Round, Uberous, Voluminous

Amplifier, Amplify Booster, Double, Eke, Enlarge, Hailer, Laser, Loud hailer, Maser, Megaphone, Push-pull, Solion, Transistor, Treble

Amulet Charm, Fetish, Pentacle, Talisman, Tiki, Token

Amuse(ment), Amusing(ly) Caution, Disport, Diversion, Divert, Drole, Droll, Game, Gas, Glee, Hoot, Killing, Levity, Light, Occupy, Pleasure, Popjoy, Priceless, Rich, Scream, Slay, Solace, ▶ SPORT, Tickle, Titillate

▶**An** see A

Anaesthetic, Anaesthetise, Anaesthetist Analgesic, Avertin®, Benzocaine, Bupivacaine, Chloroform, Cocaine, Epidural, Ether, Eucain(e), Freeze, Gas, General, Halothane, Jabber, Ketamine, Lignocaine, Local, Metopryl, Morphia, Novocaine, Number, Opium, Orthocaine, Procaine, Stovaine, Trike, Urethan(e)

Analogous, Analogy Akin, Corresponding, Like, Parallel, Similar

Analyse(r), Analysis Alligate, Anagoge, Anatomy, Assess, Breakdown, Construe, Emic, Eudiometer, Examine, Fourier, Harmonic, Parse, Process, Qualitative, Quantative, Quantitative, Rundown, Scan(sion), Semantics, Sift, Spectral, Systems, Test

▷ **Analysis** may indicate an anagram

Analyst Alienist, Jung, Psychiatrist, Shrink, Trick cyclist

Anarchist, Anarchy Black Hand, Bolshevist, Chaos, Kropotkin, Provo, Rebel, Revolutionary, Trotskyite

Anatomy, Anatomist Bones, Framework, Histology

Ancestor, Ancestral, Ancestry Adam, Avital, Descent, Extraction, For(e)bear, Gastraea, Humanoid, Lin(e)age, Parent, Proband, Profectitious, Progenitor, Propositus, Roots, Sire, Tree

Anchor(age) Atrip, Bower, Cell, Deadman, Drag, Eremite, Grapnel, Hawse, Hermit, Kedge, Killick, Killock, Laura, Mud-hook, Nail, Ride, Roads(tead), Root, Scapa Flow, Sheet, Spithead, Stock

Ancient Antediluvian, Archaic, Auld-warld, Early, Gonfanoner, Historic, Hoary, Iago, Immemorial, Lights, Neolithic, Ogygian, ► OLD(EN), Old-world, Primeval, Primitive, Pristine, Ur, Veteran

And Als(o), Ampassy, Ampersand, Amperzand, Ampussyand, Besides, Et, Furthermore, 'n', Plus, Und

Anecdote(s) Ana, Exemplum, Story, Tale, Yarn

Angel(s) Abdiel, Adramelech, Apollyon, Archangel, Ariel, Arioch, Asmadai, Azrael, Backer, Banker, Beelzebub, Belial, Benefactor, Cake, Cherub, Clare, Deva, Dominion, Dust, Eblis, Falls, Gabriel, Guardian, Hierarchy, Host, Investor, Israfel, Ithuriel, Lucifer, Power, Principality, Raphael, Recording, Rimmon, Seraph, Spirit, St, Throne, Uriel, Uzziel, Virtue, Watcher, Zadkiel, Zephiel

Anger, Angry ► ANNOY, Bristle, Choler(ic), Conniption, Cross, Dander, Dudgeon, Enrage, Exasperation, Face, Fury, Gram, Heat, Horn-mad, Incense, Infuriate, Iracund, Irascible, Ire, Kippage, Livid, Mad, Monkey, Moody, Nettle, Pique, Radge, Rage, Rampant, Ratty, Renfierst, Rile, Roil, Rouse, Sore, Steam, Tantrum, Tarnation, Teen(e), Tene, Vex, Vies, Waspish, Waxy, Wrath, Wroth, Yond

Angle(d), Angular Acute, Altitude, Argument, Aspect, Axil, Azimuthal, Canthus, Cast, Catch, Chiliagon, Coign, Complementary, Conjugate, Contrapposto, Corner, Cos, Critical, Deidre, Diedral, Diedre, Dihedral, Elbow, Elevation, Ell, Fish, Fish-hook, Fork, Geometry, Gonion, Hade, Hip, In, L, Laggen, Laggin, Mitre, Oblique, Obtuse, Parallax, Pediculate, Perigon, Piend, Pitch, Plane, Quoin, Radian, Rake, Re-entrant, Reflex, Right, Sally, Sine, Sinical, Solid, Steeve, Steradian, Supplementary, Sweepback, Trotline, Vertical, Viewpoint, Washin, Weather

Anglican(s) CE-men, Conformist, Episcopal

Angora Goat, Mohair, Rabbit

Anguish(ed) Agony, Distress, Gip, Gyp, Hag-ridden, Heartache, Misery, ➤ PAIN, Pang, Sorrow, Throes, ➤ TORMENT, Torture, Woe

Animal(s) Bag, Beast, Bestial, Brute, Carnal, Creature, Critter, Fauna, Herd, Mammal, Menagerie, Pet, Sensual, Sloth, Stud, Zoo

Animate(d), Animation Activate, Actuate, Arouse, Biophor, Ensoul, Excite, Fire, Hot, Inspire, Live, Morph, Mosso, Rouse, Spritely, Verve

Animosity Enmity, Friction, Hostility, Malice, Pique, Rancour

Ankle Coot, Cuit, Cute, Hock, Hucklebone, Knee, Malleolus

Annal(s) Acta, Archives, Chronicles, Register

Annex(e) Acquire, Add, Affiliate, Attach, Codicil, Extension, Subjoin

Annihilate Destroy, Erase, Exterminate, Slay

Anniversary Birthday, Feast, Jubilee, Obit, Yahrzeit

Announce(r), Announcement Banns, Bellman, Biil(ing), Blazon, Bulletin, Communiqué, Decree, Divulgate, Gazette, Herald, Hermes, Inform, Intimate, Meld, Newsflash, Post, Preconise, Proclaim, Promulgate, Pronunciamente, Publish, Release, ➤ REPORT, Speaker(ine), State, Trumpet

Annoy(ance), Annoyed, Annoying Aggravate, Aggrieve, Anger, Antagonise, Badger, Bother, Bug, Bugbear, Chagrin, Disturb, Drat, Fash, Fleabite, Frab, Fumed, Gall, Harass, Hatter, Hector, Hip, Huff, Hump, Incense, Irk, ➤ IRRITATE, Miff, Mischief, Molest, Nag, Nark, Nettle, Noisome, Peeve, Pesky,

Pester, Pipsqueak, Pique, Rankle, Rats, Resentful, Ride, Rile, Roil, Rub, Shirty, Tiresome, Tracasserie, Try, Vex

Annual, Annuity Book, Etesian, ➤ FLOWER, Half-hardy, Hardy, Pension, Perpetuity, Rente, Tontine, Yearbook, Yearly

Annul(ment) Abolish, Abrogate, Cashier, Cassation, Dissolution, Irritate, Negate, Repeal, Rescind, Reversal, Revoke, Vacatur, ➤ VOID

▷**Anomaly** may indicate an anagram

Anon Again, Anew, Later, Soon

Anonymous Adespota, Anon, A.N.Other, Faceless, Grey, Impersonal, Somebody, Unnamed

Answer(ing), Answer(s) Acknowledge, Amoebaean, Ans, Antiphon, Because, Comeback, Crib (sheet), Defence, Echo, Key, Lemon, Light, No, Oracle, Rebuttal, Rebutter, Rein, Rejoin(der), Repartee, Reply, Rescript, Respond, Response, Retort, Return, Riposte, Serve, Sol, Solution, Solve, Verdict, Yes

Ant(s), Anthill Amazon, Army, Bull(dog), Carpenter, Colony, Driver, Dulosis, Emmet, Ergataner, Ergates, Fire, Formic, Formicary, Myrmecoid, Myrmidon, Nasute, Neuter, Pharaoh, Pismire, Sauba, Soldier, Termite, Thief, Velvet, White, Wood

Ante Bet, Punt, Stake

Ant-eater Aardvark, Echidna, Edental, Manis, Numbat, Pangolin, S(e)ladang, Spiny, Tamandu, Tamandua, Tapir

Antelope Addax, Blackbuck, Bluebuck, Bongo, Bushbuck, Chamois, Dikdik, Eland, Elk, Gazelle, Gnu, Hartebeest, Impala, Kid, Klipspringer, Oribi, Reebok, Saiga, Steinbock, Waterbuck , Wildebeest

Antenna Aerial, Dipole, Dish, Horn, Sensillum, TVRO

Anterior Anticous, Earlier, Front, Prior

Anthem Hymn, Introit, Isodica, Marseillaise, Motet(t), National, Psalm, Responsory, Song, Theme, Tract

Anthology Album, Ana, Chrestomathy, Digest, Divan, Florilegium, Garland, Pick, Spicilege

Anti Against, Agin, Con, Hostile

Anti-bacterial, Antibiotic Drug, Interferon, Penicillin

Antibody Agglutinin, Amboceptor, Antitoxin, Blocker, Isoagglutinin, Lysin, Monoclonal, Precipitin, Reagin

Antic(s) Caper, Dido, Frolic, Gambado, Hay, Prank, Shenanigan, Stunt

Anticipate, Anticipation Antedate, Augur, Await, Drool,
➤ EXPECT, Forecast, Foresee, Forestall, Foretaste, Hope,
Intuition, Prevenancy, Prolepsis, Prospect, Type

Anticlimax Bathos, Deflation, Letdown

Antidote Adder's wort, Alexipharmic, Angelica, Antivenin,
Bezoar, Contrayerva, Cure, Emetic, Guaco, Mithridate,
Nostrum, Orvietan, Remedy, Ribavirin, Senega, Theriac(a),
(Venice)-Treacle

Antipathy Allergy, Aversion, Detest, ➤ DISLIKE, Enmity,
Repugnance

Antiquated, Antique, Antiquarian Ancient, Archaic,
A(u)stringer, Bibelot, Curio, Dryasdust, FAS, Fogram(ite),
Fog(e)y, Fossil, Old-fangled, Ostreger, Relic

Antiseptic Acriflavine, Carbolic, Cassareep, Creosote,
Disinfectant, Eupad, Eusol, Formaldehyde, Guaiacol, Iodine,
Phenol, Sterile, Thymol, Tutty

Antisocial Hostile, Ishmaelitish, Misanthropic

Antithesis Contrary, Converse, Opposite

Anvil Bick-iron, Block, Incus, Stiddie, Stithy

Anxiety, Anxious Angst, Brood, Care(ful), Cark, Concern,
Disquiet, Dysthymia, Fanteeg, Fantigue, Fantod, Fraught,
Grave, Heebie-jeebies, Hypochondria, Inquietude, Jimjams,
Jumpy, Reck, Restless, Scruple, Solicitous, Suspense, Sweat,
Tension, Twitchy, Unease, Unquiet, Upset, Uptight, Worriment

Any Arrow, Ary, Some

Anybody, Anyone One, Whoso, You

Anyhow Anyway, Leastways

Anything Aught, Ought, Owt, Whatnot

▷**Anyway** may indicate an anagram

Apart Aloof, Aside, Asunder, Atwain, Beside, Separate

Apartment Ben, Condominium, Digs, Duplex, Flat, Insula,
Mansion, Paradise, Penthouse, Pied-a-terre, Quarters, Room,
Simplex, Solitude, Suite, Unit

Apathetic, Apathy Accidie, Acedia, Incurious, Languid,
Lethargic, Listless, Lobotomized, Pococurante, Torpid

Ape(-like), Apeman Anthropoid, Barbary, Big-foot,
Catarrhine, Copy, Dryopithecine, Gelada, Gibbon, Gorilla,
➤ IMITATE, Magot, Mimic, Orang, Paranthropus, Pongo,
Proconsul, Simian, Simulate, Yowie

Apex Acme, Culmen, Keystone, Knoll, Knowe, Summit, Vortex

Aphorism Adage, Epigram, Gnome, Proverb, Sutra

Aphrodisiac, Aphrodite Cytherean, Erotic, Idalian, Paphian, Philter, Philtre, Spanish fly, Urania, Yohimbine

Apology Excuse, Justifier, Mockery, Oops, Pardon, Scuse

Apostle, Apostolic Cuthbert, ➤ DISCIPLE, Evangelist, Johannine, Jude, Matthew, Pauline, Spoon, Twelve

Appal(ling) Abysmal, Affear(e), Dismay, Egregious, Frighten, Horrify, Piacular, Tragic

▷**Appallingly** may indicate an anagram

Apparatus Appliance, Condenser, Device, Equipment, Gadget, Incubator, Instrument, Retort, Set, Snorkel, Still

Apparel Attire, Besee, ➤ COSTUME, Garb, Raiment, Wardrobe, Wardrop

Apparent(ly) Ap, Detectable, Ostensible, Outward, Overt, Plain, Prima facie, Semblance, Visible

▷**Apparent** may indicate a hidden word

Apparition Dream, Eidolon, Fetch, Ghost, ➤ ILLUSION, Phantom, Shade, Spectre, Visitant, Wraith

Appeal(ing) Ad, Beg, Cachet, Catchpenny, Charisma, Charm, Cri de coeur, Cry, Entreat, Entreaty, Epirrhema, Fetching, Invocation, It, O, Oomph, Plead, SA, Screeve, Solicit, SOS, Suit

Appear(ance) Advent, Air, Arrival, Aspect, Brow, Debut, Emerge, Enter, Facade, Feature, Garb, Guise, Hue, Image, Loom, ➤ MANNER, Mien, Occur, Outward, Phenomenon, Physiognomy, Presence, Represent, Rise, Seem, Semblance, Show, Spring, View, Visitation

Appease(ment) Allay, Calm, Danegeld, Mitigate, ➤ MOLLIFY, Munichism, Pacify, Placate, Propitiate, Satisfy, Soothe, Sop

Appendage Adjunct, Codpiece, Hanger-on, Lobe, Lug, Tail, Tentacle, Uvula

Appendix Addendum, Apocrypha, Codicil, Grumbling, Label, Pendant, Pendent, Rider, Schedule, Vermiform

Appetite, Appetitive, Appetize(r) Antepast, Antipasto, Aperitif, Appestat, Bhagee, Bhajee, Bulimia, Bulimy, Canapé, Concupiscence, Concupy, Crudités, Dim-sum, Entremes(se), Entremets, Flesh, Hunger, Limosis, Malacia, Meze, Nacho, Orectic, Orexis, Passion, Pica, Polyphagia, Relish, Tapa(s), Titillate, Twist, Yerd-hunger, Yird-hunger

Applaud, Applause Bravo, ➤ CHEER, Clap, Claque, Eclat, Encore, Extol, Olé, Ovation, Praise, Root, Tribute

Apple Blenheim orange, Bramley, Codlin(g), Cooker, Costard, Crab, Custard, Granny Smith, Jonathan, Pearmain, Pippin, Pyrus, Russet, Toffee, Winesap

Application, Apply, Appliance(s) Address, Adhibit, Appeal, Appose, Assiduity, Barrage, Blender, Diligence, Dressing, Exercise, Foment, Implement, Inlay, Lay, Lotion, Ointment, Petition, Plaster, Poultice, Put, Resort, Rub, Sinapism, Stupe, Truss, ➤ USE, White goods

Appoint(ee), Appointment Advowson, Assign, Berth, Date, Delegate, Depute, Designate, Dew, Due, Executor, Induction, Installation, Make, Name, ➤ NOMINATE, Nominee, Office, Ordain, Position, Post, Posting, Rendezvous, Room, Set, Tryst

▷**Appointed** may indicate an anagram

Appraise, Appraisal Analyse, ➤ EVALUATE, Gauge, Judge, Tape, ➤ VALUE, Vet

Appreciate, Appreciation Acknowledgement, Cherish, Clap, Dig, Endear, Esteem, Gratefulness, Increase, Prize, Realise, Regard, Relish, Rise, Sense, Thank you, Treasure, ➤ VALUE

Apprehend, Apprehension Afears, Alarm, Arrest, ➤ CATCH, Fear, Grasp, Insight, Intuit, Perceive, See, Take, Trepidation, Uh-oh, Unease, Uptake

Apprehensive Jumpy, Nervous, Uneasy

Apprentice(ship) Article, Cub, Devil, Garzone, Improver, Indent(ure), Jockey, Learner, L, Lehrjahre, Novice, Noviciate, Novitiate, Printer's devil, Pupillage, Trainee, Turnover

Approach(ing) Abord, Access, Accost, Advance, Anear, Appropinquate, Appulse, Avenue, Close, Come, Converge, Cost(e), Drive, Driveway, Fairway, Feeler, Gate, Imminent, Line, Near, Nie, Overture, Pitch, Procedure, Road, Run-up, Verge

Appropriate Abduct, Abstract, Annex, Apposite, Apt, Asport, Assign, Bag, Borrow, Collar, Commandeer, Commensurate, Confiscate, Convenient, Due, Embezzle, Expedient, Fit, Germane, Good, Happy, Hijack, Hog, Jump, Just, Meet, Nick, Pilfer, Pocket, Pre-empt, Proper, Right, Seize, Sequester, Sink, Snaffle, Steal, Suit, Swipe, Take, Timely, Trouser, Usurp

Approval, Approve(d) Adopt, Allow, Amen, Applaud, Attaboy, Aye, Blessing, ➤ COUNTENANCE, Credit, Dig, Endorse, Hubba-bubba, Imprimatur, Kitemark, Laud, Nod, Okay, Olé, Orthodox, Plaudit, Rah, Ratify, Rubber-stamp, Sanction, Stotter, Thumbs-up, Tick, Tribute, Yes

Approximate(ly), Approximation Almost, Circa, Close, Coarse, Estimate, Guess, Imprecise, Near, Roughly

Apron Barm-cloth, Bib, Blacktop, Brat, Bunt, Canvas, Fig-leaf, Pinafore, Pinny, Placket, Stage, Tablier, Tier

Apt(ly) Apposite, Appropriate, Apropos, Ben trovato, Capable, Evincive, Fit, Gleg, Happy, Liable, Prone, Suitable, Tends

Aptitude Ability, Bent, Faculty, Flair, Gift, Skill, Talent, Tendency

Aqueduct Canal, Channel, Conduit, Hadrome, Xylem

Arab(ian), Arabia Abdul, Algorism, Ali, Baathist, Bahraini, Bahrein, Bedouin, Druse, Druz(e), Effendi, Fedayee(n), Gamin, Geber, Hashemite, Himyarite, Horse, Iraqi, Jawi, Lawrence, Mudlark, Nabat(h)ean, Omani, PLO, Rag(head), Saba, Sab(a)ean, Saracen, Semitic, Sheikh, UAR, Urchin, Yemen

Arbiter, Arbitrator ACAS, Censor, Daysman, Judge, Ombudsman, Ref(eree), Umpire

Arbitrary Despotic, Random, Wanton

Arboreal, Arbour Bower, Dendroid, Pergola, Trellis

Arc Azimuth, Bow, Carbon, ➤ CURVE, Flashover, Fogbow, Halo, Octant, Quadrant, Rainbow, Reflex, Trajectory

Arcade Amusement, Burlington, Cloister, Gallery, Loggia, Triforium

Arcane Esoteric, Obscure, Occult, Orphism, Recherché, Rune, Secret

Arch(ed) Admiralty, Arcade, Camber, Chief, Crafty, Cross-rib, ➤ CUNNING, Curve, Fallen, Gothic, Instep, Keystone, Lierne, Marble, Ogee, Ogive, Portal, Proscenium, Roguish, Saucy, Span, Triumphal, Vault

Archaeological, Archaeologist Carter, Dater, Dig, Evans, Layard, Leakey, Mycenae, Petrie, Pothunter, Wheeler, Woolley

Archangel Azrael, Gabriel, Israfeel, Israfel, Israfil, Jerahmeel, Michael, Raguel, Raphael, Sariel, Satan, Uriel

Archbishop Anselm, Augustine, Cosmo, Cranmer, Davidson, Dunstan, Ebor, Elector, Hatto, Lanfranc, Lang, Langton, Laud, Metropolitan, Primate, Temple, Trench, Tutu, Whitgift

Archer Acestes, Bow-boy, ► BOWMAN, Cupid, Eros, Hood, Philoctetes, Sagittary, Tell, Toxophilite

Archetype Avatar, Model, Pattern

Architect(ure), Architectural Baroque, Bauhaus, Byzantine, Composite, Corinthian, Doric, Flamboyant, Gothic, Ionic, Landscape, Neoclassical, Norman, Palladian, Perpendicular, Planner, Romanesque, Saxon, Tuscan

Archive(s) Muniment, PRO, Records, Register

Arctic Estotiland, Frigid, Hyperborean, In(n)uit, Inupiat, Polar, Tundra

Ardent, Ardour Aflame, Aglow, Boil, Broiling, Burning, Fervent, Fervid, Fiery, Flagrant, Heat, Het, ► HOT, In, Mettled, Mettlesome, Passion(ate), Perfervid, Rage, Spiritous, Vehement, Warm-blooded, Zealous, Zeloso

Are A

Area Acre, Are, Bailiwick, Belt, Catchment, Centare, Centre, Development, Disaster, District, Extent, Hectare, Hide, Landmass, Latitude, Locality, Milieu, No-go, Place, Plot, Precinct, Province, Quad, Quarter, Range, ► REGION, Sector, Shire, Terrain, Territory, Theatre, Tract, Yard, Zone

Arena Circus, Cockpit, Dohyo, Field, Maidan, Olympia, ► RING, Stadium, Tiltyard, Venue

Argue, Argument Altercation, Argy-bargy, Bandy, Beef, Conflict, Contend, Debate, Difference, Dilemma, Dispute, Exchange, Expostulate, Free-for-all, Logic, Moot, Patter, Plead, Quibble, ► REASON, Remonstrate, Run-in, Spar, Tiff, Wrangle

Aria Ballad, Cabaletta, Melody, Song

Arise Appear, Develop, Emanate, Emerge, Upgo, Wax

Aristocracy, Aristocrat(ic) Blood, Classy, Debrett, Duc, Elite, Gentry, Grandee, High-hat, Nob, Noble, Optimate, Patrician, Tony, U-men, Upper-crust, Well-born

Arm(ed), Arms Akimbo, Arsenal, Bearing, Brachial, Branch, Cove, Crest, Embattle, Equip, Escutcheon, Fin, Firth, Frith, Halbert, Hatchment, Heel, Heraldic, Inlet, Jib, Krupp, Limb, Loch, Member, Olecranon, Quillon, Radius, Ramous, Rotor,

SAA, Small, Tappet, Tentacle, Timer, Transept, Tremolo, Ulnar, ➤ WEAPON, Whip

▷**Arm** may indicate an army regiment, etc.

Armadillo Dasypod, Dasypus, Pangolin, Peba, Pichiciago, Tatou(ay), Xenurus

Armour(ed) Armet, Buckler, Cannon, Chain, Cors(e)let, Cuirass, Culet, Defence, Gear, Gorget, Greave, Jack, Mail, Panoply, Panzer, Poleyn, Secret, ➤ SHIELD, Tace, Tank, Taslet, Tasse(t), Thorax, Tuille, Vambrace, Visor

Army Arrière-ban, BEF, Church, Colours, Confederate, Crowd, Federal, Fyrd, Golden (Horde), Horde, Host, IRA, Land, Landwehr, Legion, Line, Military, Militia, Multitude, Para-military, Red, SA, Sabaoth, Salvation, Sena, Service, Soldiers, Standing, Swarm, TA, Territorial, Volunteer, War, Wehrmacht

▷**Army** may indicate having arms

Aroma(tic) Allspice, Aniseed, Aryl, Balmy, Coriander, Fenugreek, Fragrant, Odorous, Pomander, Spicy, Vanillin, Wintergreen

Around About, Ambient, Circa, Near, Peri-, Skirt, Tour

▷**Around** may indicate one word around another

Arouse, Arousal Alarm, ➤ EXCITE, Fan, Fire, Incite, Inflame, Must(h), Needle, Provoke, Stole, Urolagnia, Waken

Arrange(r), Arrangement Adjust, Array, Attune, Bandobast, Bundobast, Concert, Concinnity, Design, Dispose, Do, Edit, Engineer, Foreordain, Formation, Grade, Ikebana, Layout, Marshal, Modus vivendi, Orchestrate, Orchestration, Ordain, ➤ ORDER, Ordnance, Organise, Pack, Pattern, Perm, Permutation, Plan, Prepare, Prepense, Quincunx, Redactor, Regulate, Run, Schedule, Scheme, Set, Settle, Sort, Stow, Straighten, System, Tactic, Taxis, Transcribe

▷**Arrange** may indicate an anagram

Array(ed) Attire, Deck, Herse, Marshal, Muster

Arrear(s) Aft, Ahint, Backlog, Behind, Debt, Owing

Arrest(ed), Arresting Abort, Alguacil, Alguazil, Ament, Apprehend, Attach, Attract, Blin, Bust, Caption, Capture, Cardiac, Catch, Check, Citizen's, Collar, Hold, Knock, Nab, Nail, Nip, Pinch, Pull, Restrain, Retard, Riveting, Round-up, Run-in, Sease, Seize, Stasis, Stop, Sus(s)

Arrival, Arrive, Arriving Accede, Advent, Attain, Come, Get, Happen, Hit, Inbound, Influx, Johnny-come-lately, Land, Natal, Nativity, Reach, Strike

Arrogance, Arrogant Assumption, Bold, Bravado, Cavalier, Cocksure, Disdain, Dogmatic, Effrontery, Haughty, Haut(eur), High, Hogen-mogen, Hoity-toity, Hubris, Imperious, Morgue, Overweening, Presumption, Proud, Side, Surquedry, Toploftical, Uppity, Upstart

Arrow, Arrow-head Acestes, Any, Ary, Bolt, Dart, Filter, Flechette, Missile, Pheon, Pointer, Quarrel, Reed, Sagittate, Shaft, Sheaf

Arsenal Ammo, Armo(u)ry, Depot, Magazine, Side

Arson(ist) Firebug, Pyromania

Art(s), Arty, Art school, Art style Abstract, Bauhaus, Bloomsbury, Chiaroscuro, Commercial, Conceptual, Craft, Cubism, Cunning, Dada, Deco, Decorative, Diptych, Expressionism, Fauvism, Feat, Finesse, Flemish, Genre, Impressionist, Kinetic, Kitsch, Knack, Mannerism, Martial, New Wave, Performance, Pop, Postmodern, Pre-Raphaelite, Primitive, Relievo, ➤ SKILL, Still-life, Surrealism, Trecento, Trompe l'oeil, Trouvé, Virtu, Visual

▷ **Art** may indicate an -est ending

▷ **Artefact** may indicate an anagram

Artery Aorta, Carotid, Coronary, Duct, Femoral, Iliac, Innominate, M1, Pulmonary, Route

Artful Cute, Dodger, Foxy, Ingenious, Quirky, Sly, Subtle, Tactician

Article(s) A, An, Apprentice, Column, Commodity, Definite, Feature, Indefinite, Indenture, Item, Leader, Paper, Piece, Pot-boiler, Sidebar, Specify, The, Thing, Thirty-nine, Treatise, Ware

Articulation, Articulate(d) Clear, Diarthrosis, Distinct, Eloquent, Enounce, Express, Fluent, Gimmal, Hinged, Jointed, Lenis, Limbed, Lisp, Pretty-spoken, Pronounce, Utter, Vertebrae, Voice

Artifice(r), Artificial Bogus, Chouse, Dodge, Ersatz, Factitious, Finesse, Guile, Hoax, In vitro, Logodaedaly, Man-made, Mannered, Opificer, Pretence, Prosthetic, Pseudo,

Reach, Ruse, Sell, Sham, Spurious, Stratagem, ➤ STRATEGY, Synthetic, Theatric, ➤ TRICK, Unnatural, Wile, Wright

Artillery Battery, Cannon, Fougade, Fougasse, Guns, Mortar, Ordnance, Pyroballogy, RA, Rafale, Ramose, Ramus, Train

Artisan Craftsman, Joiner, Journeyman, Mechanic, Pioner, Pyoner, Workman

Artist(ic) Bohemian, Cartoonist, Colourist, Cubist, Dadaist, Daedal(e), Decorator, Deccie, Etcher, Fine, Gentle, Gilder, ICA, Impressionist, Limner, Linear, Maestro, Master, Miniaturist, ➤ MUSICIAN, Nazarene, Oeuvre, Orphism, ➤ PAINTER, Pavement, Paysagist, Piss, Plein-airist, Primitive, RA, Romantic, Screever, ➤ SCULPTOR, Sien(n)ese, Tachisme, Trapeze, Trecentist, Virtuose, Virtuoso

Artless Candid, Ingenuous, Innocent, Naive, Open, Seely

As Aesir, Als, Arsenic, Coin, Eg, Forasmuch, Kame, Qua, Ridge, 's, Since, So, Thus, Ut, While

As before Anew, Ditto, Do, Stet

Ascend(ant), Ascent Anabasis, Climb, Dominant, Escalate, Gradient, Pull, Ramp, Rise, Sclim, Sklim, Slope, Up, Upgang, Uphill, Uprise, Zoom

Ascertain Determine, Discover, ➤ ESTABLISH, Prove

Ascribe Assign, ➤ ATTRIBUTE, Blame, Imply, Impute

As good as Equal, Tantamount

Ash(es), Ashy Aesc, Aizle, Cinders, Cinereal, Clinker(s), Easle, Embers, Kali, Pallor, Pearl, Pozz(u)olana, Prickly, Rowan, Ruins, Sorb, Tephra, Urn, Varec, Wednesday, Witchen, Yg(g)drasil(l)

Ashamed Abashed, Embarrassed, Hangdog, Mortified, Repentant, Shent

Ashore Aland, Beached, Grounded, Stranded

Asia(n), Asiatic Balinese, Bengali, Cantonese, E, Evenki, Ewenki, Gook, Hun, Hyksos, Indian, Korean, Kurd, Lao, Malay, Mongol, Naga, Negrito, Nepalese, Pushtu, Samo(y)ed, Shan, Siamese, Sogdian, Tamil, Tibetan, Turanian, Turk(o)man

Aside Apart, By, Despite, Private, Separate, Shelved, Sotto voce

Ask Beg, Beseech, Cadge, Demand, Desire, Entreat, Enquire, Evet, Implore, Intreat, Invite, Korean, Newt, Petition, Prithee, Pump, Quiz, Request, Rogation, Seek, Solicit, Speer, Speir, Touch

Askance Asconce, Askew, Oblique, Sideways

Asleep Dormant, Inactive, Napping

Aspect Angle, Bearing, Brow, Face, Facet, Facies, Feature, Look, Mien, Nature, Outlook, Perfective, Perspective, Side, ➤ VIEW, Visage, Vista

Aspersion Calumny, Innuendo, Libel, Slander, Slur, Smear

Asphalt Bitumen, Blacktop, Gilsonite®, Pitch, Uinta(h)ite

Aspirant, Aspirate, Aspiration, Aspire Ambition, Breath, Buckeen, Challenger, Desire, Dream, Ettle, Goal, H, Hope(ful), Pretend, Pursue, Rough, Spiritus, Wannabe(e)

Assail Assault, Batter, Bego, Belabour, Bepelt, Beset, Bombard, Impugn, Oppugn, Pillory, Ply, Revile

Assassin(ate), Assassination Booth, Brave, Bravo, Brutus, Casca, Frag, Gunman, Highbinder, Hitman, Killer, Ninja, Sword, Thuggee, Tyrannicide

Assault Assail, Assay, Attack, Battery, Bombard, Hamesucken, Indecent, Invasion, Mug, ➤ RAID, Stoor, Storm, Stour, Stowre

Assemble, Assembly Audience, Ball, Chapter, ➤ COLLECTION, Company, Conclave, Convention, Convoke, Council, Court, Diet, Forgather, Gather(ing), Group, Levee, Mass, ➤ MEETING, Moot, Muster, National, Parliament, Quorum, Rally, Resort, Senate, Society, Synod, Tribunal, Troop, Unlawful

Assent Accede, Acquiesce, Agree, Amen, Aye, Comply, Concur, Nod, Placet, Sanction, Yea, Yield

Assert(ing), Assertion Affirm, Allege, Constate, Contend, ➤ DECLARE, Ipse-dixit, ➤ MAINTAIN, Pose, Predicate, Proclaim, Protest, Thetical

Assess(ment) Affeer, Appraise, Estimate, Evaluate, Gauge, Guesstimate, ➤ JUDGE, Levy, Measure, Perspective, Rating, Referee, Scot and lot, Tax, Value, Weigh

Asset(s) Advantage, Capital, Chattel, Fixed, Intangible, Liquid, Plant, Property, Resource, Talent, Virtue

Assign(ation), Assignment Allocate, ➤ ALLOT, Apply, Aret, Ascribe, Attribute, Award, Date, Dedicate, Duty, Errand, Fix, Grant, Impute, Point, Quota, Refer, Transfer, Tryst

Assimilate(d) Absorb, Blend, Digest, Esculent, Fuse, Imbibe, Incorporate, Merge

Assist(ance), Assistant Acolyte, Adjunct, Aid(e), Ally, Alms, Attaché, Busboy, Cad, Collaborate, Counterhand, Dresser, Facilitate, Factotum, Famulus, Gofer, ➤ HAND, Help,

Henchman, Legal aid, Offsider, Omnibus, Relief, Reinforce,
Second, Server, Servitor, Sidesman, Stead, Subsidiary,
Suffragan, ► SUPPORT, Usher

Associate, Association Accomplice, Affiliate, Alliance,
Attach, Bedfellow, Brotherhood, Cartel, Chapel, Club,
Combine, Comrade, ► CONNECT, Consort(ium), Correlate,
Crony, Fellow, Fraternise, Guild, Hobnob, Join, League, Liaison,
Member, Mix, Partner, Relate, Ring, Stablemate, Syndicate,
Trade, Union, Word

▷**Assorted** may indicate an anagram

Assuage Allay, Appease, Beet, Calm, Ease, Mease, Mitigate,
Mollify, Slake, Soften

Assume, Assuming, Assumption Adopt, Affect, Arrogate,
Attire, Axiom, Believe, Don, Donné(e), Feign, Hypothesis,
Lemma, Occam's Razor, Posit, Postulate, Preconception,
Premise, Premiss, Presuppose, Pretentious, Principle, Putative,
Saltus, Suppose, Surmise, Take

▷**Assumption** may mean attire

Assure(d), Assurance Aplomb, Aver, Belief, Calm,
► CERTAIN, Confidence, Confirm, Earnest, Gall, Guarantee,
Pledge, Poise, Warranty

Asteroid Ceres, Eros, Hermes, Hygiea, Juno, Pallas, Star,
Starfish

Astonish(ed), Astonishing, Astonishment, Astound
Abash, Admiraunce, Amaze, Banjax, Bewilder, Confound,
Corker, Crikey, Daze, Donnert, Dum(b)found, Dumbstruck,
Flabbergast, Gobsmack, Open-eyed, Open-mouthed, Phew,
Rouse, Singular, Stagger, Startle, Stupefaction, Stupefy,
Stupendous, Surprise, Thunderstruck, Wow

Astray Abord, Amiss, Errant, Lost, Will, Wull

Astride Athwart, Spanning, Straddle-back

Astringent Acerbic, Alum, Catechu, Gambi(e)r, Harsh, Kino,
Rhatany, Sept-foil, Severe, Sour, Styptic, Tormentil, Witch-hazel

Astrologer Archgenethliac, Chaldean, Culpeper, Faust,
Figure-caster, Genethliac, Lilly, Moore, Nostradamus,
Soothsayer, Starmonger, Zadkiel

Astronaut Cosmonaut, Gagarin, Glenn, Lunarnaut,
Spaceman, Spacer

Astronomer, Astronomy Planetology, Radio, Urania

Astute Acute, Canny, Crafty, Cunning, Downy, Perspicacious, Shrewd, Subtle, Wide, Wily

As well Additionally, Also, Both, Even, Forby, Too

Asylum Bedlam, Bin, Bughouse, Frithsoken, Funny-farm, Girth, Grith, Haven, Institution, Magdalene, Refuge, Retreat, Sanctuary, Shelter, Snake-pit

Asymmetric(al) Lopsided, Skew

Atheist Doubter, Godless, Infidel, Sceptic

Athlete, Athletic(s) Agile, Agonist, Blue, Coe, Discobolus, Field, Gymnast, Jock, Leish, Miler, Milo, Nurmi, Olympian, Pacemaker, Runner, Sportsman, Sprinter, Track

Atlas Linguistic, Maps, Range, Silk

▷**At last** may indicate a cobbler

Atmosphere Aeropause, Air, Ambience, Aura, Chemosphere, Elements, Epedaphic, Ether, F-layer, Geocorona, Ionosphere, Lid, Magnetosphere, Mesophere, Meteorology, Miasma, Ozone, Thermosphere, Tropopause, Troposphere, Upper, Vibe(s)

Atom(ic), Atoms Boson, Electron, Excimer, Gram, Ion, Iota, Isobare, Isotone, Isotope, Ligand, Molecule, Monad, Monovalent, Muonic, Nuclide, Particle, Pile, Radionuclide, Side-chain, Steric, Substituent

Atone(ment) Aby(e), Acceptilation, Appease, Expiate, Redeem, Redemption, Yom Kippur

▷**At random** may indicate an anagram

Atrocious, Atrocity Abominable, Brutal, Diabolical, Flagitious, Heinous, Horrible, Monstrous, Outrage, Vile

▷**At sea** may indicate an anagram

Attach(ed), Attachment Accessory, Adhesion, Adhibition, Adnate, Adnation, Adscript, Affix, Allonge, Bolt, Bro, Byssus, Covermount, Devote ment, Devotion, Distrain, Glue, ▶ JOIN, Obconic, Pin, Snell, Stick, Tie, Weld

Attack(ing) Airstrike, Alert, Apoplexy, Assail, Assault, Batten, Belabour, Beset, Blitz(krieg), Bombard, Bout, Broadside, Campaign, Charge, Clobber, Counteroffensive, Feint, Fit, Foray, Incursion, Inroad, Invade, Inveigh, Lampoon, Maraud, Mug, Offensive, Onrush, Onset, Onslaught, Oppugn, Pillage, Pre-emptive, Push, Raid, Savage, Seizure, Siege, Snipe, Sortie, Storm, Strafe, Strike, Thrust, Tilt, Vituperate, Wage, Zap

Attain(ment) Accomplish, Arrive, Earn, Fruition, Get, Land, Reach

Attempt Bash, Bid, Burl, Crack, Debut, Effort, Endeavour, Essay, Go, Mint, Nisus, Seek, Shot, Shy, Stab, Strive, ➤ TRY, Venture, Whack, Whirl

Attend(ance), Attendant Accompany, Batman, Bearer, Chaperone, Courtier, Entourage, Equerry, Escort, Esquire, Footman, Gillie, Hear, ➤ HEED, ➤ LISTEN, Marshal, Note, Outrider, Page, Presence, Respect, Satellite, Second, Steward, Trainbearer, Valet, Visit, Wait, Watch, Zambuck

Attention, Attentive Achtung, Assiduity, Court, Coverage, Dutiful, Ear, Gallant, Gaum, Gorm, Heed, Mind, Notice, Present, Punctilio, Qui vive, ➤ REGARD, Tenty, Thought

Attest Affirm, Certify, Depose, Guarantee, Notarise, Swear, ➤ WITNESS

Attic Bee-bird, Garret, Greek, Koine, Loft, Mansard, Muse, Salt, Solar, Soler, Sollar, Soller, Tallat, Tallet, Tallot

Attire Accoutre, Adorn, Apparel, Clobber, ➤ DRESS, Garb, Habit

Attitude Air, Aspect, Behaviour, Demeanour, Light, ➤ MANNER, Mindset, Nimby, Pose, Posture, Sense, Stance, Tone

Attorney Advocate, Counsellor, DA, Lawyer, Proctor, Prosecutor

Attract(ion), Attractive Bait, Becoming, Bewitch, Bonny, Catchy, Charisma, ➤ CHARM, Cute, Dish(y), ➤ DRAW, Engaging, Entice, Eye-catching, Fascinate, Fetching, Heartthrob, Hunky, Inviting, Loadstone, Looker, Luscious, Magnet(ism), Photogenic, Picturesque, Sexpot, Sideshow, Striking, Taking, Tasteful, Winning, Winsome

Attribute Accredit, Allot, Ap(p)anage, Ascribe, Asset, Credit, Gift, Impute, Lay, Metonym, Owe, Refer, Shtick

Aubergine Brinjal, Brown Jolly, Egg-plant, Mad-apple

Auburn Abram, Chestnut, Copper, Vill(age)

Auction(eer) Barter, Bridge, Cant, Dutch, Hammer, Outcry, Outro(o)per, Roup, Sale, Subhastation, Tattersall, Vendue

Audacious, Audacity Bold, Brash, Cheek, Der-doing, Effrontery, Face, Hardihood, Indiscreet, Insolence, Intrepid, Neck, Nerve, Sauce

Audience, Auditorium Assembly, Court, Durbar, Gate, House, Interview, Pit, Sphendone, Tribunal

Audit(or) Accountant, Check, Ear, Examine, Inspect, Listener

Augment(ed) Boost, Eche, Eke, Ich, Increase, Supplement, Swell, Tritone

Aunt(ie) Agony, Augusta, Beeb, Giddy, Naunt, Sainted, Tia

Aura Aroma, Mystique, Nimbus, Odour, Vibrations

Austere, Austerity Astringent, Bleak, Dantean, Hard, ➤ HARSH, Moral, Plain, Rigour, Stern, Stoic, Stoor, Strict, Vaudois, Waldensian

Australia(n) Alf, Antipodean, Aussie, Balt, Banana-bender, Bananalander, Billjim, Canecutter, Cobber, Currency, Darwinian, Digger, Gin, Godzone, Gumsucker, Gurindji, Koori, Larrikin, Myall, Norm, Ocker, Oz, Pintupi, Roy, Sandgroper, Strine, Wallaby, Yarra-yabbies

Austrian Cisleithan, Tyrolean

Authentic(ate) Certify, Echt, Genuine, Honest, Notarise, Official, Real, Sign, Test, True, Validate

Author(ess) Anarch, Auctorial, Inventor, Me, Parent, Volumist, Wordsmith, ➤ WRITER

▷**Author** may refer to author of puzzle

Authorise(d), Authorisation Accredit, Clearance, Empower, Enable, Exequatur, Imprimatur, Legal, Legit, ➤ LICENCE, Official, OK, Passport, ➤ PERMIT, Plenipotentiary, Sanction, Sign, Stamp, Warrant

Authority, Authoritarian, Authoritative Canon, Charter, Circar, Cocker, Commission, Commune, Crisp, Dominion, Ex cathedra, Expert, Gravitas, Hegemony, Inquirendo, Jackboot, Licence, Magisterial, Mandate, Mastery, Name, Oracle, Permit, ➤ POWER, Prefect, Prestige, Pundit, Remit, Right, Rod, Say-so, Sceptre, Sircar, Sirkar, Source, Warrant

Autobiography Memoir

Autocrat(ic) Absolute, Caesar, Cham, Despot, Neronian, Tsar, Tyrant

Automatic, Automaton Android, Aut, Browning, Deskill, Instinctive, Machine, Mechanical, Pistol, Reflex, Robot, RUR, Zombi

Auxiliary Adjunct, Adjuvant, Adminicle, Aide, Be, Feldsher, Have, Helper, Ido

Avail(able) Benefit, Dow, Eligible, Going, Handy, On call, Open, Pickings, ➤ READY, Serve, Use, Utilise

Avalanche Deluge, Landfall, Landslide, Landslip, Lauwine, Slide, Slip, Snowdrop

Avarice, Avaricious Cupidity, Golddigger, Greed, Money-grubbing, Pleonexia, Sordid

Avenge(r) Eriny(e)s, Eumenides, Goel, Kurdaitcha, Punish, Redress, Requite, ➤ REVENGE, Wreak

Avenue Alley, Arcade, Channel, Corso, Cradle-walk, Hall, Mall, Passage, Vista, Way, Xyst(us)

Average Adjustment, Av, Batting, Dow Jones, Mean, Mediocre, Middle-brow, Middling, Moderate, Norm, Par, Run, Soso, Standard

Averse, Aversion Against, Antipathy, Apositia, Disgust, Distaste, Hatred, Horror, Opposed, Phobic, Scunner

Avert Avoid, ➤ DEFLECT, Forfend, Parry, Ward

Aviator Airman, Alcock, Bleriot, Brown, Earhart, Flier, Hinkler, Icarus, Johnson, Lindbergh, Pilot

Avid ➤ EAGER, Greedy, Keen

Avoid(er), Avoidance Ba(u)lk, Boycott, Bypass, Cop-out, Cut, Dodge, Duck, Elude, Escape, Eschew, Evade, Evitate, Evite, Fly, Forbear, Gallio, Hedge, Miss, Parry, Prevaricate, Scutage, Secede, Shelve, Shun, Sidestep, Skirt, Spare, Spurn, Waive

Avow(ed) Acknowledged, Affirm, Declare, Own, Swear

Await Abide, Bide, Expect, Tarry

Awake(ning) Aware, Conscious, Conversion, Fly, Rouse, Vigilant

Award Academy, Accolade, Addoom, Allot, Alpha, Aret(t), Bafta, Bestow, Bursary, Cap, Clasp, Clio, Crown, Emmy, Exhibition, Grammy, Grant, Medal, Meed, Mete, Oscar, Palme d'or, Premium, Present(ation), ➤ PRIZE, Scholarship, Tony, Trophy, Yuko

Aware(ness) Alert, Cognisant, Conscious, Conversant, ESP, Est, Hep, Hip, Informed, Liminal, Onto, Panaesthesia, Prajna, Presentiment, Samadhi, Scienter, Sensible, Sensile, Sensitive, Sentience, Streetwise, Vigilant, Wot

Away Absent, Afield, Apage, Avaunt, By, For-, Fro(m), Go, Hence, Off, Out, Past

▷**Away** may indicate a word to be omitted

Awe(d) Dread, D(o)ulia, Fear, Intimidate, Loch, Overcome, Popeyed, Regard, Respect, Reverent, Scare, Solemn

Awful(ly) Alas, Deare, Dere, Dire, Fearful, Horrendous, O so, Piacular, Terrible

▷**Awfully** may indicate an anagram

Awkward Angular, Bumpkin, Complicated, Clumsy, Corner, Crabby, Cubbish, Cumbersome, Embarrassing, Farouche, Fiddly, Fix, Gauche, Gawky, Handless, Howdy-do, Inconvenient, Inept, Lanky, Loutish, Lurdan(e), Lurden, Mauther, Mawr, Nasty, Ornery, Perverse, Refractory, Slummock, Spot, Sticky, Stroppy, Stumbledon, Swainish, Uneasy, Ungainly, Wry

Awry Agley, Askew, Cam, Kam(me), Wonky

Axe Abolish, Adz(e), Bill, Celt, Chop(per), Cleaver, Gisarme, Gurlet, Halberd, Halbert, Hatchet, Ice, Partisan, Palstaff, Palstave, Piolet, Retrench, Sax, Sparth(e), Sperthe, Spontoon, Thunderbolt, Tomahawk, Twibill

Axiom Adage, Motto, Peano's, Proverb, Saw, Saying

Aye Eer, Ever, Yea, Yes

Bb

B Bachelor, Black, Book, Born, Boron, Bowled, Bravo

Babble(r) Blather, Chatter, Gibber, Haver, Lallation, Lurry, Prate, Prattle, Runnel, Tonguester, Twattle, Waffle

Baboon Ape, Bobbejaan, Chacma, Dog-ape, Drill, Gelada, Hamadryas, Mandrill, Sphinx

Baby(hood) Bairn, Blue, Bub, Bunting, Duck, Grand, Infant, Jelly, Neonate, Nursling, Pamper, Papoose, Preverbal, Sis, Small, Sook, Suckling, Tar, Test tube, Tot, Wean

Bachelor BA, Bach, Benedict, Budge, Celibate, En garçon, Pantagamy, Parti, Single, Stag

Bacillus Comma, Germ, Micrococcus, Virus

Back(ing), Backward Abet, Accompany, Addorse, Again,
Ago, Anticlockwise, Arear, Assist, Backare, Bankroll, Buckram,
Consent, Defender, Dorsal, Dorse, Dos, Ebb, Empatron,
Encourage, Endorse, Finance, Frae, Fro, Gaff, Help, Hind,
Historic, La-la, Late, Notaeum, Notal, Notum, On, Patronise,
Poop, Pronotum, Punt, Rear(most), Retral, Retro(grade),
Retrogress, Retrorse, Return, Rev, Ridge, Root, Shy, Spinal,
Sponsor, Stern, ➤ SUPPORT, Sweeper, Tail, Telson, Tergum,
Third, Thrae, Tonneau, Ulu, Uphold, Verso, Vie, Vo, Wager

▷ **Back(ing)** may indicate a word spelt backwards

Backbone Chine, Grit, Guts, Mettle

Backchat Lip, Mouth, Sass

Backer Angel, Benefactor, Patron, Punter, Seconder, Sponsor

Backgammon Acey-deucy, Lurch, Tick-tack, Tric-trac,
Trick-track, Verquere

Background Antecedence, Fond, History, Horizon, Setting,
Ulterior

Backslide(r), Backsliding Apostate, Lapse, Regress,
Relapse, Revert

Bacon Danish, Essayist, Flitch, Francis, Gammon, Lardo(o)n,
Pancetta, Pig, Pork, Rasher, Roger, Spec(k), Streaky, Verulam

Bacteria, Bacterium Bacteriological, ➤ BUG, Culture,
➤ GERM, Intestinal flora, Microbe, Mother, Packet, Proteus, Pus,
Septic, Serotype, Serum, Spore, Superbug

Bad(ly), Badness Addled, Chronic, Crook, Defective,
Diabolic, Dud, Duff, Egregious, Execrable, Faulty, Heinous, Ill,
Immoral, Inferior, Injurious, Lither, Mal, Naughty, Nefandrous,
Nefarious, Nice, Off, Ominous, Oncus, Onkus, Piacular, Poor,
Rank, Ropy, Scampish, Scoundrel, Sinful, Spoiled, Turpitude,
Useless, Wack, Wick, ➤ WICKED

▷ **Bad(ly)** may indicate an anagram

Badge Brassard, Brooch, Button, Chevron, Cockade, Crest,
Emblem, Ensign, Epaulet, Episemon, Fáinne, Flash, Garter,
Gorget, ID, Insignia, Kikumon, Mark, Mon, Rosette, Scallop,
➤ SIGN, Symbol, Token, Vernicle, Wings

Badger ➤ ANNOY, Bait, Bedevil, Beset, Brock, Browbeat, Bug,
Bullyrag, Cete, Dassi(e), Ferret, Gray, Grey, ➤ HARASS, Hassle,
Hog, Honey, Hound, Nag, Pester, Plague, Provoke, Ratel, Ride,
Roil, Sow, Teledu, Wisconsin

Bad luck Ambs-ace, Ames-ace, Deuce-ace, Hoodoo, Jinx, Jonah, Shame, Voodoo

Bad-tempered Carnaptious, Curmudgeon, Curnaptious, Curst, Grouchy, Grum(py), Irritable, Moody, Patch, Splenetic, Stroppy

Baffle(d), Baffling Anan, Balk, Bemuse, Bewilder, Confound, Confuse, Elude, Evade, Floor, Flummox, Foil, Fox, Get, Hush-kit, Mate, Muse, Mystify, Nark, Nonplus, Pose, Puzzle, Stump, Throw, Thwart

Bag(s), Baggage Besom, Bladder, Body, Bulse, Caba(s), Caecum, Capture, Carpet, Carrier, Carryall, Cecum, Cly, Cod, Cool, Corduroy, Crone, Cyst, Daypack, Dilli, Dilly, Dime, Diplomatic, Ditty, Doggy, Dorothy, Duffel, Dunnage, ➤ EFFECTS, Excess, Flannels, Follicle, ➤ GEAR, Gladstone, Grip, Holdall, Ice, Impedimenta, Jelly, Jiffy®, Kill, Minx, Mixed, Nap, Net, Overnight, Oxford, Pantaloons, Pochette, Pock(et), Poke, Port(manteau), Pot, Pouch, Purse, Rake, Reticule, Rucksack, Sac(cule), Sachet, Sack, Saddle, Satchel, Scrip, Scrotum, Shopper, Slattern, Sleeping, Sponge, Sporran, Stacks, Survival, Tea, Tote, ➤ TRAP, Trews, Trollop, Trouse(r), Udder, Unmentionables, Valise, Vanity, Wallet, Weekend, Win

Bagpipe Chorus, Cornemuse, Drone, Musette, Pibroch, Piffero, Skirl, Sourdeline, Uillean, Zampogna

Bail(er), Bailment Bond, Ladle, Mainpernor, Mainprise, Mutuum, Scoop

Bailiff Adam, Beagle, Bum, Factor, Grieve, Land-agent, Philistine, Reeve, Steward, Tipstaff, Water

Bait Badger, Berley, Brandling, Burley, Chum, Dap, Decoy, Entice, Gentle, Harass, Incentive, Lobworm, Lug(worm), Lure, Mawk, ➤ RAG, Ragworm, Teagle, Tease

Bake(r), Baked, Baking Alaska, Batch, Baxter, ➤ COOK, Fire, Kiln-dry, Roast, Scorch, Shirr

Balance(d) Account, Beam, Counterpoise, Counterweight, Equate, Equilibrium, Equipoise, Equiponderate, Even, Gyroscope, Gyrostat, Isostasy, Launce, Libra, Librate, Meet, Otolith, Peise, Perch, Peyse, Poise, ➤ REMAINDER, Remnant, Residual, Rest, Scale, Spring, Stand, Steelyard, Symmetry, ➤ TOTAL, Trial, Trim, Tron(e)

Balcony Circle, Gallery, Loggia, Mirador, Moucharaby, Porch, Sundeck, Tarras, Terrace, Veranda(h)

Bald(ing), Baldness Alopecia, Apterium, Awnless, Barren, Calvities, Coot, Crude, Egghead, Fox-evil, Glabrous, Hairless, Madarosis, Open, Peelgarlic, Pilgarlic(k), Pollard, Psilosis, Slaphead, Smoothpate, Tonsured

Bale Bl, Bundle, Evil, Pack, Truss

Ball(s) Agglomerate, Alley, Ally, Ammo, Aniseed, Beach, Bead, Beamer, Bobble, Bolus, Bosey, Bouncer, Break, Cap, Cherry, Chinaman, Clew, Clue, Cotill(i)on, Cramp, Croquette, Crystal, Cue, Curve, Daisy-cutter, ➤ DANCE, Delivery, Dollydrop, Gazunder,' ➤ GLOBE, Glomerate, Googly, Gool(e)ys, Goolies, Grub, Gutta, Gutter, Hank, Hop, Inswinger, Ivory, Knur(r), Leather, Leg-break, Lob, Long-hop, Marble, Masque(rade), Medicine, Minié, Moth, Nur(r), O, Off-break, Off-spin, Outswinger, Overarm, Pea, Pellet, Pill, Pompom, Prom, Puck, Quenelle, Rissole, Rover, Rundle, Seamer, Sneak, Sphere, Spinner, Testes, Tice, Witches, Wood, Yorker

Ballast Kentledge, Makeweight, Stabiliser, Trim, Weight

Ballerina Coryphee, Dancer, Pavlova

Ballet, Ballet movement, Ballet-system Bolshoi, Checkmate, Développé, Écarté, Firebird, Giselle, Kirov, Laban

Balloon(ist) Aeronaut, Aerostat, Airship, Bag, Barrage, Billow, Blimp, Bloat, Dirigible, Dumont, Fumetto, Hot air, Lead, Montgolfier, Pilot, Rawinsonde, Weather, Zeppelin

Ballot Election, ➤ POLL, Referendum, Suffrage, Ticket, Vote

Balm(y) Anetic, Arnica, Balsam, Calamint, Fragrant, Garjan, Gilead, Gurjun, Lemon, Lenitive, ➤ MILD, Mirbane, Myrbane, Nard, Oil, Opobalsam, Ottar, Redolent, Remedy, Soothe, Spikenard, Tolu, Unguent

Balsam Canada, Copaiba, Copaiva, Nard, Peruvian, Resin, Spikenard, Tamanu, Tolu(ic), Touch-me-not, Tous-les-mois, Turpentine

Ban Abolish, Accurse, Anathema, Black(ing), Censor, D-notice, Debar, Embargo, Excommunicate, For(e)say, For(e)speak, Gate, Moratorium, No, Prohibit, Proscribe, Taboo, Tabu, Veto

Banal Corny, Flat, Hackneyed, Jejune, Mundane, Platitudinous, ➤ TRITE, Trivial

Banana(s) Abaca, Hand, ➤ MAD, Musa, Plantain, Split

Band(s) Alice, Anadem, Armlet, Belt, Border, Braid, Brass, Brassard, Brassart, Caravan, CB, Channel, Circlet, Citizen's,

Cohort, Collar, Collet, Combo, Company, Corslet, Coterie, Crew, Elastic, Endorse, Facia, Falling, Fascia, Ferret, Ferrule, Filament, Fillet, Frieze, Frog, Frontlet, Galloon, Gamelan, ➤ GANG, Garland, Garter, Gasket, Gaskin, Geneva, Gird, Girth, ➤ HOOP, Hope, Iron, Jazz, Jug, Kitchen, Label, Massed, Noise, One-man, Orchestra, Pack, Pass, Patte, Pipe, Plinth, Puttee, Rib, Ribbon, Rim, Ring, Robbers, Rubber, Sash, Scarf, Screed, Sect, Shoe, Snood, Steel, Strake, Strap, Stratum, String, Stripe, Swath(e), Tape, Tendon, Tie, Tippet, Tourniquet, Train, Troop, Troupe, Turm, Tyre, Unite, Vitrain, Vitta, Wanty, Weeper, Welt, With(e), Wristlet, Zona, Zone

Bandage Bind, Dressing, Fillet, Lint, Pledget, Roller, Sling, Spina, Swaddle, Swathe, T, Tape, Truss, Wadding

Bandit Apache, Bravo, Brigand, Desperado, Outlaw, Pirate, Rapparee, ➤ ROBBER, Turpin

Bane Curse, Evil, Harm, Poison

Bang(er) Amorce, Big, Cap, Chipolata, Clap, Cracker, Crock, Explode, Flivver, Fringe, Haircut, Heap, Implode, Jalopy, Maroon, Rattletrap, Report, Sausage, Sizzler, Slam, Thrill, Wurst

Bangle Anklet, Armlet, Bracelet, Kara

Banish(ment) Ban, Deport, Depose, Exile, Expatriate, Expel, Extradition, Forsay, Maroon, Ostracise, ➤ OUTLAW, Relegate, Rusticate

Bank(s) An(n)icut, Asar, Backs, Bar, Bay, Bk, Blood, Bluff, Bottle, Brae, Brim, Bund, Camber, Cay, Central, Chesil, Clearing, Cloud, Data, Depend, Deposit, Dogger, Down, Dune, Dyke, Earthwork, Escarp, Gene, Giro, Glacis, Gradient, Gradin(e), Hele, Hill, Jodrell, Left, Levee, Link, Merchant, Mound, Nap, Nore, Overslaugh, Parapet, Piggy, Rake, Ramp, Rampart, Reef, ➤ RELY, Reserve, Rivage, Riverside, Rodham, Row, Sandbar, Shallow, Shelf, Side, Slope, Sperm, Staithe, Sunk, Terrace, Terreplein, Tier, Vault, World

Banker Agent, Financial, Fugger, Gnome, Lombard, Medici, ➤ RIVER, Rothschild, Shroff

Bankrupt(cy) Break, Broke, Bung, Bust, Cadaver, Carey Street, Crash, Debtor, Deplete, Duck, Dyvour, Fail, Fold, Insolvent, Receivership, Ruin, Rump, Scat, Sequestration, Skatt, Smash

▷**Bankrupt** may indicate 'red' around another word

Banner Banderole, Bandrol, Bannerol, ➤ FLAG, Gumphion, Labarum, Oriflamme, Sign, Streamer

Banquet Beanfeast, Dine, Feast, Junket, Spread

Banter Badinage, Borak, Chaff, Dicacity, Dieter, Jest, ➤ JOKE, Persiflage, Picong, Rag, ➤ RAILLERY, Rally, Ribaldry, Roast, Tease

Baptise(d), Baptism, Baptist Affusion, Amrit, Christen, Dip, Dipper, Dopper, Dunker, Illuminati, Immersion, Sprinkle, Tinker

Bar(s) Angle-iron, Bail, Ban, Baulk, Beam, Bilboes, Billet, Bistro, Blackball, Blacklist, Block(ade), Bloom, Bolt, Boom, Bottega, Brasserie, Buffet, Bull, But, Buvette, ➤ CAGE, Came, Cantina, Capo, Capstan, Colour, Counter, Cramp(on), Crow, Crush, Dive, Espresso, Estop(pel), Except, Exclude, Fen, Fid, Flinders, Forbid, Foreclose, Forestall, Gad, Grate, Grid, Hame, Handspike, Heck, ➤ HINDRANCE, Horizontal, Hound, Impediment, Ingot, Inn, Inner, Judder, Juice, Karaoke, Kickstand, Knuckleduster, Latch, Let, Lever, Line, Local, Lounge, Macron, Mandrel, Mandril, Measure, Milk, Mullion, No-go, Norman, Obstacle, Onely, Parallel, Pile, Pinch, Pole, Prohibit, Pub, Public, Rabble, Rack, Rail, Ramrod, Rance, Restrict, Rib, Risp, Rod, Roo, Rung, Salad, Saloon, Sans, Save, Saving, Scroll, Shaft, Shanty, Shet, Shut, Singles, Skewer, Slot, Snack, Snug, Spacer, Spar, Speakeasy, Spit, Sprag, Stave, Stick, Stretcher, Stripe, Swee, T, Tap(-room), Tapas, Taphouse, Tavern(a), Temple, Toll, Tombolo, Tommy, Torsion, Tow, Trace, Trangle, Transom, Trapeze, Vinculum, Ward, Whisker, Wine, Z, Zed ·

Barb(ed) Bur(r), Fluke, Harl, Herl, ➤ HOOK, Jag(g), Jibe, Pheon, Prickle, Ramus, Tang, Vexillum

Barbarian, Barbaric Boor, Fifteen, Foreigner, Goth, Heathen, Hottentot, Hun, Inhuman, Lowbrow, Outlandish, Philistine, Rude, Savage, Tatar(ic), Tartar

Barbecue Braai vleis, Cook-out, Flame-grill, Grill, Hangi, Hibachi, Roast, Spit

Barber Epilate, Figaro, Scrape(r), Shaver, Strap, Todd, Tonsor, Trimmer

Bare, Bare-headed Adamic, Aphyllous, Bald, Barren, Blank, Bodkin, Cere, Décolleté, Denude, Hush, Lewd, Marginal, Moon, ➤ NAKED, Open, Plain, Scant, Sear, Stark, Uncase, Uncover, Unveil

Barely Hardly, Just, Merely, Scarcely, Scrimp

Bargain(ing) Barter, Chaffer, Champerty, ➤ CHEAP, Collective, Coup, Deal, Dicker, Find, Go, Haggle, Higgle,

Horse-trade, Huckster, Option, ➤ PACT, Plea, Scoop, Snip, Steal, Trade, Trock, Troke, Truck, Wanworth, Wheeler-dealing

Barge Birlinn, Bucentaur, Budgero(w), Butty, Gabbard, Gabbart, Galley-foist, Hopper, Intrude, Jostle, Keel, Lighter, Nudge, Obtrude, Pra(a)m, Ram, Scow, ➤ SHIP, Trow, Wherry

▷**Barge** may indicate an anagram

Bark(ing) Angostura, Ayelp, Bass, Bast, Bay, Bowwow, Canella, Cascara, Cassia, China, Cinchona, Cinnamon, Cork, Cortex, Honduras, Kina, Kinakina, Liber, Myrica, Peel, Pereira, Peruvian, Quebracho, Quest, Quillai, Quina, Quinquina, Rind, Salian, Sassafras; Scrape, ➤ SHIP, Skin, Tan, Tap(p)a, Waff, Waugh, Woof, Wow, Yaff, ➤ YAP, Yelp, Yip

Bar-keeper, Barmaid, Barman Advocate, Ale-wife, Bencher, Hebe, Luckie, Lucky, Tapster, Underskinker

Barley Awn, Bear, Bere, Bigg, Malt, Pearl, Truce

Barn Bank, Byre, Cowshed, Dutch, Grange, Skipper, Tithe

Barnacle Acorn, Cypris, Goose(neck), Limpet

Baroque Gothic, Ornate, Rococo

▷**Baroque** may indicate an anagram

Barrack(s), Barracking Asteism, Boo, Cantonment, Casern(e), Cat-call, Garrison, Heckle, Irony, Quarters

Barrage Balloon, Fusillade, Heat, Salvo

Barrel(-stand) Bl, Butt, Cade, Capstan, Cascabel, Cask, Clavie, Drum, Hogshead, Keg, Kibble, Morris-tube, Organ, Pièce, Run(d)let, Tan-vat, Thrall, Tierce, Tun, Vat, Wood

Barren Addle, Arid, Badlands, Blind, Blunt, Clear, Dry, Eild, ➤ EMPTY, Farrow, Hirstie, Jejune, Sterile, Unbearing, Waste, Wasteland, Wilderness, Yeld, Yell

Barricade, Barrier Bail, Barrage, Bayle, Block, Breakwater, Cauld, Cheval de frise, Chicane, Cordon (sanitaire), Crash, Crush, ➤ DAM, Defence, Drawgate, Dyke, Fence, Fraise, Gate, Hedge, Hurdle, Mach, Obstruct, Rail(-fence), Rampart, Restraint, Revetment, Roadblock, Sonic, Sound, Spina, Stockade, Tollgate, Turnpike, Turnstile, ➤ WALL

Barrister Advocate, Attorney, Counsel, Devil, Lawyer, Rumpole, Serjeant(-at-law), Silk, Templar, Utter

Barrow Dolly, Handcart, Henge, How, Hurley, Kurgan, Molehill, Mound, Pushcart, Tram, Trolley, Truck, Tumulus

Barter Chaffer, Chop, Dicker, ➤ EXCHANGE, Haggle, Hawk, Niffer, Sco(u)rse, Swap, ➤ TRADE, Traffic, Truck

Base(ness) Alkali, Bed, Beggarly, Billon, Bottom, Camp, Degenerate, Degraded, Dog, Down, E, ➤ ESTABLISH, Floor, Foot, Foothold, Footstall, Found, Fundus, Harlot, Ignoble, Infamous, Install, Lewis, ➤ LOW, ➤ MEAN, Nefarious, Nook, Partite, Patten, Platform, Plinth, Podium, Premise, Ptomaine, Purin(e), Rascally, Rests, Ribald, Root, Servile, Shameful, Shand, Sheeny, Socle, Soda, Staddle, ➤ STAND, Station, Substrate, Ten, Torus, Turpitude, Unworthy, Vile

Bash Belt, Clout, Go, Hit, Rave, Shot, Slog, Strike, Swat, Swipe

Bashful Awed, Blate, Coy, Modest, Retiring, Shamefast, Sheep-faced, Sheepish, ➤ SHY

Basic(s), Basis ABC, Abcee, Alkaline, Aquamanale, Aquamanile, Crude, ➤ ESSENTIAL, Fiducial, Fond, Fundamental, Ground(work), Gut, Integral, Intrinsic, Logic, Nitty-gritty, No-nonsense, Primordial, Principle, Radical, Rudimentary, Spit-and-sawdust, Staple, Substance, Underlying, Uracil

Basin Artesian, Bidet, Bowl, Canning, Catch, Cirque, Corrie, Cwm, Dish, Dock, Great, Lavabo, Laver, Minas, Monteith, Pan, Park, Piscina, Playa, Porringer, Reservoir, Scapa Flow, Slop, Stoop, Stoup, Tank, Tidal

Bask Apricate, Revel, Sun, ➤ WALLOW

Basket, Basket-work Bass, Bassinet, Bread, Buck, Cabas, Car, Cob, Coop, Corbeil(le), Corf, Creel, Cresset, Dosser, Fan, Flasket, Frail, Gabian, Hamper, Hask, Junket, Kipe, Kit, Leap, Maund, Mocuck, Moses, Murlain, Murlan, Murlin, Osiery, Pannier, Ped, Petara, Pottle, Punnet, Rip, Scull, Scuttle, Seed-lip, Skep, Skull, Trug, Van, Wagger-pagger(-bagger), Waste(-paper), Wicker(-work), Will(e), Wisket

Bass Alberti, Ale, Alfie, B, Continuo, Deep, El-a-mi, Fish, Low, Ostinato, Serran

▷**Bastard** may indicate an anagram

Bat(ter), Bats, Batting, Batsman, Batty Ames, Assail, Barbastelle, Baton, Blink, Close, Cosh, Crackers, Dad, Die Fledermaus, Eyelid, Flittermouse, Grace, Hatter, Haywire, Hit, Hobbs, Hook, Horseshoe, In, Ink mouse, Kalong, Language, Man, Mastiff, Maul, May, Mormops, Myopic, Nictate, Nictitate, Night, Nightwatchman, Noctilio, Nora, Opener, Pinch-hit, Pipistrel(le), Poke, Pummel, Racket, Racquet, Ram, Rearmouse,

Ruin, Sauch, Serotine, Sledge, Stick, Stonewall, Striker, Swat, Vampire, Viv, Whacky, Willow, Wood

Batch Bake, Bunch

Bath(room) Aeson's, Bagnio, Bain-marie, Bed, Blanket, Bubble, Caldarium, Cor, En suite, Epha, Foam, Hammam, Hip, Hummaum, Hummum, Jacuzzi®, Laver, Mik vah, Mustard, Piscina, Plunge, Sauna, Sitz, Slipper, Spa, Steam, Stew, Stop, Tepidarium, Therm, Tub, Turkish, Tye, Whirlpool, Wife

Bathe, Bathing Bay(e), Beath, Bogey, Bogie, Dip, Dook, Embay, Foment, Immerse, Lave, Lip, Skinny-dip, Souse, Splash, Stupe, ➤ SWIM, Tub, ➤ WASH

Baton Mace, Rod, Sceptre, Staff, Truncheon

▷**Bats, Batting** may indicate an anagram

Batter(ed) Bombard, Bruise, Buffet, Decrepit, Pound

Battery Artillery, Drycell, Field, Henhouse, Nicad, Pra(a)m, Solar, Troop, Voltaic

Battle, Battleground Action, Affair, Ben, Clash, Cockpit, Combat, ➤ CONFLICT, Encounter, Engagement, Field, ➤ FIGHT, Fray, Front, Joust, Royal, Sarah, Sciamachy, Skiamachy, Spurs, Stoor, Stour, Stowre, Theatre, Wage, ➤ WAR

Battle-axe Amazon, Bill, Gorgon, Halberd, Ogress, Sparth(e), Termagant, Termagent, Turmagant, Turmagent

Battlement Barmkin, Crenellate, Merlon, Rampart

Battleship Carrier, Destroyer, Dreadnought, Gunboat, Man-o'-war, Potemkin

Bauble Bagatelle, Gaud, Gewgaw, Trifle

Bawl Bellow, Gollar, Howl, Weep

Bay Arm, Bark, Bell, Bight, Cove, Covelet, Creek, Harbour, ➤ HOWL, Inlet, Laura, Laurel, Niche, Oleander, Oriel, Recess, Red, Roan, Sick, Vae, Voe, Waff, Wash, Yowl

Bazaar Alcaiceria, Emporium, Fair, Fete, Market, Pantechnicon, Sale, Sook, Souk

Beach Bondi, Coast, Ground, Hard, Lido, Littoral, Machair, Miami, Plage, Sand, Seaside, Shingle, Shore, Strand, Waikiki

Beacon Belisha, Fanal, Lightship, Need-fire, Pharos, Racon, Radar, Radio, Signal

Bead(s) Aggri, Aggry, Baily's, Bauble, Blob, Bugle, Chaplet, Crab-stones, Drop, Droplet, Gaud, Paternoster, Poppet, Poppit, Prayer, Rosary, Tear, Wampum(peag), Worry

Beak AMA, Bailie, Bill, Cad, Cere, Coronoid, Gar, JP, Kip(p), Magistrate, Master, Metagnathous, Mittimus, Nasute, Neb, Nose, Pecker, Prow, Ram, Rostellum, Rostrum

Beam(ing) Arbor, Balance, Bar, Boom, Bowstring, Breastsummer, Broadcast, Bum(p)kin, Cantilever, Carling, Cathead, Collar, Deck, Girder, Grin, Hammer, I, Irradiate, Joist, Ke(e)lson, Laser, Lentel, Lintel, Manteltree, Needle, Outrigger, Particle, Pencil, Principal, Purlin, ➤ RAFTER, ➤ RAY, Rayon, Refulgent, Rident, Ridgepole, Rood, Searchlight, Shaft, Shine, Sleeper, Smile, Stanchion, Stemson, Sternpost, Streamer, Stringer, Summer, Support, Tie, Timber, Transom, Trave, Trimmer, Truss, Universal, Yard

Bean(s) Abrus, Adsuki, Arabica, Berry, Black, Black-eye, Borlotti, Broad, Bush, Butter, Cacao, Calabar, Castor, Cocoa, Coffee, Cow-pea, Fabaceous, Fava, Flageolet, French, Frijol(e), Garbanzo, Gram, Haricot, Harmala, Head, Horse, Jack, Jumping, Kidney, Lablab, Lentil, Lima, Locust, Molucca, Moth, Mung, Nelumbo, Nib, Noddle, Ordeal, Pichurim, Pinto, Runner, Snap, Soy(a), String, Sugar, Tonga, Tonka, Tonquin, Urd, Wax, Winged

Bear(er), Bearish Abide, Andean, Arctic, Baloo, Balu, Beer, Bigg, Brenda, Brook, Brown, Bruin, Brunt, ➤ CARRY, Churl, Cinnamon, Coati-mondi, Coati-mundi, Demean, Dree, Ean, ➤ ENDURE, Engender, Exert, Fur-seal, Gonfalonier, Grizzly, Hack, Ham(m)al, Have, Hold, Honey, Humf, Hump(h), Jampani, Keb, Koala, Kinkajou, Kodiak, Koolah, Lioncel(le), Lionel, Lug, Mother, Nandi, Owe, Paddington, Panda, Polar, Pooh, Rac(c)oon, Rupert, Russia, Sackerson, Seller, Shoulder, Sit, Sloth, Spectacled, Stand, Stay, Stomach, ➤ SUFFER, Sunbear, Sustain, Targeteer, Teddy, Teem, Thole, Throw, Tolerate, Tote, Undergo, Upstay, Ursine, Whelp, Wield, Woolly, Yield

Beard(ed) Arista, Awn, Balaclava, Barb, Beaver, Charley, Charlie, Confront, Defy, Face, Five o'clock shadow, Fungus, Goatee, Hair(ie), Hairy, Hear(ie), Imperial, Kesh, Mephistopheles, Outface, Peak, Rivet, Stubble, Vandyke, Whiskerando, Whiskery, Ziff

▷ **Bearhug** may indicate Teddy or similar around a word

Bearing(s) Air, Aspect, Babbitt, Ball, Behaviour, Bush, Carriage, Deportment, Direction, E, Endurance, Gait, Hatchment, Manner, Mascle, Mien, N, Nor, Port, Presence, Reference, Relevant, S, Tenue, Thrust, W, Yielding

▷**Bearing** may indicate compass points

Beast(ly) ➤ ANIMAL, Behemoth, Brute, Caliban, Caribou, ➤ CREATURE, Dieb, Dragon, Dzeren, Gayal, Genet, Grampus, Hog, Hy(a)ena, Jumart, Kinkajou, Lion, Mammoth, Marmot, Mastodon, Mhorr, Oliphant, Oryx, Panda, Potto, Quagga, Rac(c)oon, Rhytina, Rother, Sassaby, Steer, Sumpter, Teg, Wart-hog, Yahoo, Yak, Yale, Zizel

Beat(er), Beaten, Beating Anoint, Arsis, Athrob, Bandy, Bang, Baste, Bastinado, Batter, Battue, Belabour, Belt, Bepat, Best, Blatter, Bless, Cadence, Cane, Chastise, Clobber, Club, Clump, Conquer, Cream, Cuff, Curry, Debel, ➤ DEFEAT, Ding, Donder, Dress, Drub, Excel, Fatigue, Faze, Feague, Feeze, Fibbed, Flagellate, Flail, Flam, Float, Flog, Floor, Flush, Fly, Fustigate, Hollow, Horsewhip, Ictus, Knock, Knubble, Lace, Laidy, Lambast(e), Larrup, Lash, Laveer, Lay, Lick, Lilt, Lounder, Mall, Malleate, Mersey, Nubble, Outclass, Outdo, Outflank, Outstrip, Palpitate, Pash, Paste, Pommel, Pound, Prat, Pug, Pulsate, Pulse, Pummel, Pun, Quop, Raddle, Ram, Ratten, Resolve, Retreat, Rhythm, Ribroast, Round, Ruff(le), Scourge, Slat, Smite, Soak, Sock, Strike, Swinge, Systole, Taber, Tabor, Tact, Tala, Tattoo, Thesis, Thrash, Thresh, Throb, Thud, Thump, Thwack, Tick, Tired, Top, Torture, Trounce, Tuck, Verberate, Vibrate, Wallop, Wappend, Welt, Wham, Whip, Whisk, Whitewash, Wraught, Ybet, Yerk, Yirk

▷**Beaten-up** may indicate an anagram

Beaut(y) Advantage, Belle, Camberwell, Charmer, Colleen, Corker, Dish, Glory, Houri, Hyperion, Lana, Monism, Picture, Pride, Pulchritude, Purler, Sheen, Smicker, Smasher, Stunner

Beautiful, Beautify Bonny, Bright, Embellish, Enhance, Fair, Fine, Ornament, Pink, Smicker, Specious, To kalon

Beaver Beard, Castor, Eager, Grind, Oregon, Rodent, Sewellel

Because (of) As, Forasmuch, Forwhy, Hence, In, Inasmuch, Sens, Since

Beckon Gesture, Nod, Summons, Waft, Wave

Become, Becoming Apt, Besort, Decent, Decorous, Enter, Fall, Fit, Flatter, Get, Go, Grow, Happen, Occur, Seemly, Suit, Wax, Worth

Bed(ding), Bedstead Air, Allotment, Amenity, Apple-pie, Arroyo, Base, Bassinet, Berth, Bottom, Box, Bunk, Caliche, Camp, Carrycot, Channel, Charpoy, Cill, Cot(t), Couch(ette), Cradle, Crib, Cul(t)ch, Day, Divan, Doona, Doss, Duvet, Erf, Filter, Flying, Four-poster, Futon, Gault, Greensand, Hammock, Inlay, Kang, Kip, Knot, Layer, Lilo®, Litter, Mat, Matrix, Mattress, Nap, Nest, Nookie, Pad, Paillasse, Pallet, Palliasse, Pan, Parterre, Pavement, Plant, Plot, Procrustean, Quilt, Retire, Roost, Sack, Scalp, Shakedown, Sill, Sitter, Sleep, Sofa, Stratum, Stretcher, Tanning, Test, Thill, Trough, Truckle, Trundle, Wadi, Wady, Ware, Water, Wealden

Bed-bug B, B flat, Chinch, Flea, Louse, Vermin

Bedchamber, Bedroom Boudoir, Chamber, Cubicle, Dormer, Dorm(itory), Ruelle, Ward

▷**Bedevilled** may indicate an anagram

Bee Athenia, Bumble, Carpenter, Cuckoo, Deseret, Drone, Drumbledor, Dumbledore, Group, Hiver, Honey, Humble, Killer, King, Lapidary, Leaf-cutter, Mason, Queen, Solitary, Spell, Spell-down, Swarm, Worker

Beech Hornbeam, Mast, Tree

Beef(y) Baron, Bleat, Brawny, Bresaola, Bull(y), Bullock, Carpaccio, Charqui, Chateaubriand, Chuck, Complain, Corned, Filet mignon, Groan, Grouse, Hough, Jerk, Liebig, Mart, Mice, Mousepiece, Muscle, Neat, Ox, Pastrami, Peeve, Porterhouse, Rother, Sauerbraten, Sey, Silverside, Sirloin, Stolid, Stroganoff, Tournedos, Tranche, Undercut, Vaccine

Beer Ale, Alegar, Bantu, Bitter, Bock, Chaser, Drink, Entire, Export, Gill, Ginger, Granny, Grog, Heavy, Kaffir, Keg, Kvass, Lager, Lambic, Lush, Malt, March, Middy, Mild, Mum, Near, Nog, October, Pils(e)ner, Pint, Pony, Porter, Root, Saki, Scoobs, Sherbet, Skeechan, Small, Spruce, Stingo, Stout, Swanky, Swats, Swipes, Switchel, Taplash, Tinnie, Tipper, Tshwala, Tube, Wallop, Zythum

Beet Blite, Chard, Fat-hen, Goosefoot, Mangel(wurzel), Spinach

Beetle Bug, Bustle, Hangover, Impend, Overhang, Project, Protrude, Scurry, VW

Before(hand) A, Advance, Ante, Avant, By, Coram, Earlier, Early, Ere, Erst(while), ➤ FORMER, Or, Pre, Previously, Prior, Pro, Sooner, Till, To, Until, Van, Zeroth

Befriend Assist, Cotton, Fraternise, Support

Beg(gar), Beggarly, Begging Ask, Badgeman, Beseech, Bey, Blighter, Blue-gown, Cadge, Calendar, Crave, ➤ ENTREAT, Exoration, Flagitate, Fleech, Gaberlunzie, Gangrel, Hallan-shaker, Implore, Impoverish, Lackall, Lazar(us), Lazzarone, Maund, Mendicant, Mump, Niggardly, Panhandle, Pauper, Penniless, ➤ PLEAD, Pled, Pray, Prig, Prog, Rag, Randy, Ruffler, Schnorr(er), Screeve, Scrounge, Shool(e), Skelder, Skell, Solicit, Sue, Supplicate, Thig(ger), Toe-rag, Touch, Undo, Whipjack

Begin(ning), Begun Ab ovo, Alpha, B, Cause, Clapdash, Commence, Daw, Dawn, Debut, Embryo, Enter, Exordium, Fall-to, Genesis, Germ, Go, Inaugural, Inception, Inchoate, Incipient, Incipit, Initial, Initiate, Intro, Lead, Learn, Logos, Nascent, Onset, Ope(n), Ord, ➤ ORIGIN, Outbreak, Pose, Prelim(inary), Seed, Set, ➤ START, Startup, Takeoff, To-fall, Yearn

Beginner Author, Black, Deb, Greenhorn, L, Learner, Neophyte, ➤ NOVICE, Primer, Rookie, Tenderfoot, Tiro, Tyro

Behave, Behaviour Act, Conduct, Convenance, Decorum, Demean, Do, Etepimeletic, Ethics, Horme, ➤ MANNER, Nature, Netiquette, Noblesse oblige, Obey, Praxeology, Quit, React, Response, Strong meat, Tribalism

Behind(hand) Abaft, Aft(er), Ahind, Ahint, Apoop, Arear, Arere, Arrear, Astern, Beneath, Bottom, Bum, Buttocks, Croup, Derrière, Fud, Late, Overdue, Prat, ➤ REAR, Slow, Tushie

Being Cratur, Creature, Ens, Entia, Entity, Esse, Essence, Existence, Human, Man, Metaphysics, Mode, Nature, Omneity, Ontology, ➤ PERSON, Saul, Soul, Subsistent, Substance, Wight

Belch Boak, Boke, Brash, Burp, Emit, Eruct, Rift, Spew, Yex

Belgian Flemish, Walloon

Belief, Believe(r), Believed, Believing Accredit, Bigot, Buy, Conviction, Credence, Credit, Creed, Cult, Culture, Deism, Deist, Doctrine, Doxy, Faith, Gnostic, Heterodoxy, Hold, Holist, Idea, Islam, Ism, Ludism, Messianist, Methink, Notion, ➤ OPINION, Ovist, Pantheism, Persuasion, Physicism, Pluralism, Presumption, Religion, Reputed, Seeing, Superstition, Tenet,

Theist, Think, Threap, Threep, Trinitarian, Trow, Trust, Unitarian, Wear, Wis(t)

Belittle Cheapen, Decry, Depreciate, Derogate, Discredit, Disparage, Humble, Slight

Bell(s) Angelus, Ben, Bob, Bow, Bronte, Cachecope, Canterbury, Carillon, Chime, Crotal, Curfew, Daisy, Diving, Division, Gong, Grandsire, Jar, Low, Lutine, Passing, Pavilion, Peal, Peter, Pinger, Ring, Roar, Sacring, Sanctus, Tailor, Tantony, Tenor, Tent, Tintinnabulum, Toll, Tom, Triple, Tubular, Vair

Bellow(s) Buller, Holla, Holler, Moo, Rant, Rave, Roar, Saul, Thunder, Troat, Tromp(e), Trumpet, Windbag

Belly Abdomen, Alvine, Bag, Beer, Bunt, Calipee, Celiac, Coeliac, Kite, Kyte, Pod, ➤ STOMACH, Swell, Tum(my), Venter, Wame, Weamb, Wem(b), Womb

Belonging(s) Apply, Appurtenant, Chattels, Effects, Inhere, Intrinsic, Paraphernalia, Pertain, ➤ PROPERTY, Relate, Traps

Beloved Alder-lief, David, Dear, Esme, Inamorata, Joy, Lief, Pet, Popular, Precious

Below Beneath, Inf(erior), Infra, Nether, Sub, Under, Unneath

Belt(ed) Baldric(k), Band, Bandoleer, Bandolier, Baudric(k), Bible, Black, Cartridge, Chastity, Clitellum, Clobber, Commuter, Conveyor, Copper, Cotton, Crios, Equator, Fan, Gird(le), Girt, Inertial, Kuiper, Judoka, Larrup, Life, Lonsdale, Mitre, Orion's, Orogenic, Polt, Pound, Roller, Safety, Sam Browne, Sash, Seat, Speed, Stockbroker, Storm, Strap, Surcingle, Stratosphere, Suspender, Swipe, Taiga, Tear, Tore, Tract, Van Allen, Wanty, Webbing, Wing, Zodiac, Zone, Zoster

Bemoan ➤ LAMENT, Mourn, Sigh, Wail

Bemuse Infatuate, Stonn(e), Stun, Stupefy, Throw

Bench Banc, Bink, Counter, Court, Cross, Exedra, Form, Knifeboard, Magistrates, Pew, Rusbank, ➤ SEAT, Settle, Siege, Stillage, Thoft, Thwart, Treasury, Trestle

Bend(er), Bending, Bends Angle, Arc, Arch, Articular, Bight, Binge, Buck(le), Bust, Camber, Carrick, Chicane, Circumflect, Corner, Crank(le), Cringe, ➤ CROOK, Curl, Curve, Diffraction, Dog-leg, Elbow, Engouled, Epinasty, Es(s), Falcate, Fawn, Flex(ural), Flexion, Flexure, Fold, Gebur, Geniculate, Genu, Genuflect, Grecian, Hairpin, Hinge, Hook, Horseshoe, Hunch, Inflect, Knee(cap), Kneel, Knot, Kowtow, Mould,

Nutant, Ox-bow, Plash, Plié, Ply, Recline, Reflex, Retorsion, Retortion, Retroflex, Riband, S, Scarp, Souse, Spree, Spring, Stave, Stoop, Swan-neck, Twist, U, Ups(e)y, Uri, Wale, Warp, ➤ YIELD, Z

▷ **Bendy** may indicate an anagram

Beneath Below, Sub, Under, Unworthy

Benefactor Angel, Backer, Barmecide, Carnegie, Donor, Maecenas, ➤ PATRON, Promoter

Benefice, Beneficial, Beneficiary, Benefit ➤ AID, Avail, Behalf, Behoof, Behove, Boon, Boot, Charity, Collature, Commendam, Commensal, Devisee, Dole, Donee, Endorsee, Enure, FIS, Fringe, Incumbent, Inure, Invalidity, Living, Ménage, Neckverse, Pay, Perk, Perquisite, Portioner, Postulate, Prebend, Profit, Sake, Salutary, Sanative, Sinecure, Spin-off, Stipend, Supplementary, Unemployment, Use, Usufruct

Benevolence, Benevolent Charitable, Clement, Humanitarian, Kind, Liberal, Philanthropy

Benign Affable, Altruistic, Gracious, Kindly, Trinal

Bent Akimbo, Bowed, Brae, Coudé, Courb, Crooked, Curb, Determined, Dorsiflex, Falcate, Fiorin, Flair, Habit, Heath, Inclination, Ingenium, Intent, Leant, Peccant, Penchant, Ply, Reclinate, Redtop, Scoliotic, Talent, Taste

▷ **Bent** may indicate an anagram

Bequeath, Bequest Bestow, Chantr(e)y, Demise, Endow, Heirloom, ➤ LEAVE, Legacy, Mortification, Pittance, Transmit, Will

Berate Censure, Chide, Jaw, Reproach, Scold, Slate, Vilify

Bereave(d), Bereavement Deprive, Loss, Mourning, Orb, Sorrow, Strip, Widow

Berry Allspice, Bacca, Cubeb, Fruit, Goosegog, Haw, Pepo, Pimento, Pottage, Rhein, Rhine, Sal(l)al, Slae, Sloe, Sop, Tomatillo

Berserk Amok, Baresark, Frenzy, Gungho, Rage

Berth Anchorage, Bunk, Cabin, Couchette, Dock, Moor, Seat, Space

Beseech Beg, Crave, Entreat, Implore, Invoke, Obsecrate

Beset Amidst, Assail, Assiege, Badger, Bego, Environ, Harry, Perplex, Scabrid, Siege

Beside(s) Adjacent, Alone, And, At, Au reste, Else, Forby, Moreover, Next, On, Withal

Besiege(d) Beset, Best(ed), Blockade, Gherao, Girt, Invest, Obsess, Plague, Surround

▷**Besiege** may indicate one word around another

Besot(ted) Dotard, Infatuate, Intoxicate, Lovesick, Stupefy

Best A1, Ace, Aristocrat, Beat, Choice, Cream, Creme, Damnedest, Deluxe, Elite, Eximious, Finest, Flower, Foremost, Greatest, Ideal, Optima, Outdo, Outwit, Overcome, Peak, Peerless, Pick, Pink, Plum, Purler, Ream, Super, The, Tiptop, Top, Topper, Transcend, Wale

Bet, Betting System A cheval, Ante, Back, Banco, Double, Flutter, Gaff, Gamble, Go, Hedge, Impone, Lay, Long shot, Martingale, Mise, Note, Pari-mutuel, Perfecta, Pip, Punt, Quadrella, Quinella, Ring, Risk, Saver, Set, Spec, Stake, Tattersalls, Tatts, Totalisator, Totalise, Tote, Treble, Triella, Trifecta, ➤ WAGE(R), Yankee

Betray(al), Betrayer Abandon, Abuse, Belewe, Cornuto, Desert, Divulge, Dob, Double-cross, Giveaway, Grass, Judas, Renegade, Renege, Rumble, Sell, Sellout, Shop, Sing, Sinon, Stab, Traditor, Traitor, Treachery, Treason, Turncoat

Betroth(ed), Betrothal Assure, Engage, Ensure, Espouse, Fiancé(e), Pledge, Subarr(h)ation

Better Abler, Amend, Apter, Bigger, Buck, Cap, Fairer, Gambler, Gamester, Imponent, Improve, Meliorate, Mend, Outdo, Outpoint, Preponderate, Punter, Race-goer, Reform, Superior, Surpass, Throw, Top, Turfite, Worst

Between Amid, Bet, Betwixt, Inter, Interjacent, Linking, Mesne, Twixt

Beverage Ale, Cocoa, Coffee, Cordial, Cup, ➤ DRINK, Nectar, Tea

Bevy Flock, Group, Herd, Host

Beware Cave, Fore, Heed, Mind, Mistrust

Bewilder(ed), Bewilderment Amaze, Baffle, Buffalo, Confuse, Consternation, Daze, Flummox, Mate, Maze, Mystify, Perplex, Stun, Taivert, Will, Wull

Beyond Above, Ayont, Besides, Farther, Outwith, Over, Thule, Trans, Ulterior

Bias(ed) Angle, Bent, Discriminatory, Imbalance, One-sided, Partial, Parti pris, Partisan, Penchant, Predilection, ➤ PREJUDICE, Prepossess, Skew, Slope, Tendency, Warp

Bible Alcoran, Alkoran, Apocrypha, Authority, AV, Avesta, Bamberg, Book, Breeches, Coverdale, Cramer, Cromwell, Douai, Douay, Family, Gemara, Geneva, Gideon, Good book, Goose, Gospel, Hexapla, Itala, Italic, King James (version), Leda, Mazarin(e), Midrash, Missal, Murderer, NT, Omasum, OT, Pentateuch, Peshito, Polyglot, Psalter, Revised Version, ➤ RSV, RV, Scriptures, Stomach, Talmud, Tantra, Targum, Taverners, Tyndale, Vinegar, Vulgate, Wig, Wyclif(fe), Zurich

Bicker Argue, Bowl, Brawl, Coggie, Dispute, Tiff, Wrangle

Bicycle, Bike Bone-shaker, Coaster, Dandy-horse, Draisene, Draisine, Hobby, Mixte, Moped, Mount, Mountain, Ordinary, Pedal, Penny-farthing, Raleigh®, Roadster, Safety, Scooter, Spin, Tandem, Velocipede

Bid(der), Bidding system Acol, Apply, Call, Canape, Command, Contract, Declare, Double, Gone, Invite, Misère, Nod, NT, ➤ OFFER, Order, Pass, Pre-empt, Proposal, Puffer, Redouble, Summon, Take-over, Tell, Tender, Vied

Big Beamy, Bulky, Bumper, Burly, Cob, Enormous, Fat, Ginormous, Gross, ➤ LARGE, Loud, Massive, Mighty, Obese, Stonker, Thumping, Tidy, Vast, Whacker, Whopper

Bigot(ed) Chauvinist, Dogmatist, Fanatic, Hide-bound, Intolerant, Racialist, Wowser, Zealot

Bigshot, Bigwig Cheese, Nob, Swell, ➤ VIP

Bile, Bilious(ness) Cholaemia, Choler, Gall, Icteric, Melancholy, Scholaemia, Venom

Bilge Leak, Pump, Rot, Waste

Bill(y) Ac(c), Accompt, Account, Act, Ad, Addition, Barnacle, Beak, Becke, Budd, Buffalo, Can, Carte, Chit(ty), Cody, Coo, Coronoid, Dixy, Docket, Double, Exactment, Fin, Finance, Goat, Hybrid, Invoice, Kaiser, ➤ LAW, Lawin(g), Legislation, Liam, Liar, List, Measure, Menu, Neb, Ness, Nib, ➤ NOTE, Notice, Poster, Private, Programme, Public, Reckoning, Reform, Rostral, Rostrum, Score, Shot, Sickle, Silly, Sparth(e), Sperthe, Spoon, Sticker, Tab, Tomium, Treasury, Willy

Billiards, Billiards player, Billiards stroke Bar, Cueist, Jenny, Massé, Pool, Potter, Pyramids, Snooker, Whitechapel

Billow Roil, Roller, Rule, Surge, Swell, Wave

Bin Bing, Box, Container, Crib, Hell, Receptacle, Snake-pit, Stall, Wagger-pagger, Wheelie, Wheely

Bind(er), Binding Adherent, Apprentice, Astrict, Astringent, Bale, Bandage, Bandeau, Bandster, Bias, Brail, Calf, Chain, Cinch, Clamp, Colligate, Complain, Cord, Cummerbund, Drag, Edge, Embale, Enchain, Engage, ➤ FASTEN, Fetter, Gird, Girdle, Hay-wire, Hold, Incumbent, Indenture, Keckle, Lash(er), Leash, Ligament, Ligature, Mail, Marl, Morocco, Muslin, Obi, Obligate, Oblige, Oop, Organdie, Oup, Parpen, Pinion, Raffia, Restrict, ➤ ROPE, Sheaf, Strap, Stringent, Swathe, Tether, Thirl, Thong, Three-quarter, Tie, Tree-calf, Truss, Twine, Valid, Whip, Withe, Yapp, Yerk, Yoke

Binge Bat, Beano, Bend(er), Blind, Carouse, ➤ DRINK, Drinking-bout, Party, Riot, Soak, Souse, Spree, Toot, Tout

Bingo Beano, Housey-housey, Lotto, Tombola

Binocular(s) Glasses, OO, Stereoscope

Biographer, Biography Boswell, CV, Hagiography, History, Life, Memoir, Plutarch, Potted, Prosopography, Suetonius, Vita

Biologist, Biology Cladistics, Mendel, Phenetics

Birch Birk, Cane, Cow, Flog, Hazel, Kow, Larch, Reis, Rice, Rod, Silver, Swish, Twig, Whip, Withe

Bird Al(l)erion, Bertram, Brood, Damsel, Doll, Early, Flier, Fowl, Gal, ➤ GIRL, Grip, Hen, Left, Pecker, Pen, Poultry, Quod, Raptor, Roaster, Sis, Skirt

▷**Bird** may indicate a prison sentence

Bird-watcher Augur, Twitcher

Birth Burden, Congenital, Delivery, Drop, Extraction, Genesis, Jataka, Lineage, Nativity, Origin, Parage

Birthday Anniversary, Genethliac

Birthmark Blemish, Mole, Mother-spot, Naevus, Stigmata

Birthright Heritage, Mess, Patrimony

Biscuit Abernethy, Bath-oliver, Bourbon, Butterbake, Charcoal, Cookie, Cracker, Cracknel, Crispbread, Dandyfunk, Digestive, Dunderfunk, Fairing, Flapjack, Florentine, Garibaldi, Gingersnap, Hardtack, Kiss, Lebkuchen, Macaroon, Marie, Mattress, Nut, Oliver, Osborne, Parkin, Perkin, Petit four, Pig's ear, Poppadom, Poppadum, Pretzel, Ratafia, Rusk, Shortbread, Sweetmeal, Tack, Wafer, Zwieback

Bishop Aaronic, Abba, Aidan, Ambrose, Bench, Berkeley, Bp, Cambrensis, Cantuar, Chad, Coverdale, Diocesan, Dunelm, Ely, Eparch, Episcopate, Eusebian, Exon, Golias, Hatto, Henson, Latimer, Lord, Magpie, Metropolitan, Norvic, Odo, Ordainer, Patriarch, Peter, Piece, Polycarp, Pontiff, Prelate, Priest, Primate, Primus, Proudie, RR, Sleeve, Suffragan, Titular, Tulchan, Weed

Bison Bonas(s)us, Buffalo, Ox, Wisent

Bit(s) Baud, Cantle(t), Chad, Cheesecake, Chip, Crumb, Curb, Curn, Drib, Excerpt, Fraction, Haet, Hate, Ion, Jaw, Jot, Mite, Modicum, Morsel, Mote, Mu, Nit, Ort, Ounce, Pelham, Peni, Penny, ▶ PIECE, Port, Rap, Rare, Ratherish, Scintilla, Scrap, Section, Shaving, Shiver, Shred, Smidgen, Snaffle, Snatch, Snippet, Soupcon, Spale, Speck, Splinter, Spot, Suspicion, Tad, Tait, Tate, Threepenny, Trace, Unce, Whit

Bite(r), Biting, Bitten Caustic, Chelicera, Chew, Eat, Engouled, Erose, Etch, Gnash, Gnat, Hickey, Hickie, Incisor, Knap, Masticate, Midge, Molar, Mordacious, Mordant, Morsel, Morsure, Nibble, Nip(py), Occlude, Pium, Rabid, Remorse, Sarcastic, Sharp, Shrewd, Snap, Tart

Bitter(ness) Absinth, Acerb, Acid, Acrimonious, Ale, Aloe, Angostura, Bile, Caustic, Eager, Ers, Fell, Gall, Keen, Marah, Maror, Myrrh, Pique, Rancorous, Rankle, Resentful, Sarcastic, Sardonic, Snell, Sore, Spleen, Tart(aric), Venom, Verjuice, Virulent, Vitriolic, Wersh, Wormwood

Bizarre Antic, Curious, Eccentric, Exotic, Fantastic, Gonzo, Grotesque, Odd, Off-the-wall, Outlandish, Outré, Pythonesque, Queer, Strange, Surreal, Weird

Black(ness), Blacken(ing), Black-out Atramental, B, BB, Bess, Blae, Carbon, Charcoal, Cilla, Coloured, Coon, Cypress, Darkie, Darky, Death, Denigrate, Dinge, Dwale, Ebon(y), Eclipse, Ethiop, Fuzzy-wuzzy, Geechee, Graphite, Heben, Hole, Ink(y), Ivory, Japan, Jeat, Jet, Jim Crow, Kohl, Malign, Market, Melanic, Melano, Moke, Moor, Muntu, Myall, Negritude, Negro, Niello, Niger, Nigrescent, Nigritude, Obliterate, Obscure, Outage, Oxford, Piceous, Pitch, Platinum, Pongo, Prince, Pudding, Quashee, Raven, Sable, Sambo, Scab, School, Sheep, Sloe, Solvent, Sombre, Soot, Sooterkin, Spode, Spook, Stygian, Swart(y), Swarth(y), Tar, Uncle Tom, Weeds

Blackberry Acini, Bramble, Mooch, Mouch

Blackbird Crow, Jackdaw, Ousel, Raven

Blackjack Billie, Billy, Cosh, Flag, Sphalerite, Tankard, Truncheon, Vingt(-et)-un

Blackmail(er) Bleed, Chantage, Chout, Exact, Extort, Ransom, Strike, Vampire

Blackout ARP, Eclipse, Faint, Swoon

Black sheep Neer-do-well, Reprobate

Blacksmith Brontes, Burn-the-wind, Farrier, Forger, Harmonious, Shoer, Vulcan

Blade Acrospire, Bilbo, Brand, Brown Bill, Cleaver, Co(u)lter, Cutlass, Dandy, Espada, Faible, Feable, Foible, Forte, Gleave, Gouge, Guillotine, Hydrofoil, Lance, Leaf, Man, Mouldboard, Oar, Palmetto, Peel, Propellor, Rachilla, Rapier, Razor, Rip, Rotor, Scimitar, Scull, Skate, Spade-, Spatula, Spatule, Spear, Spoon, Stiletto, Stock, ➤ SWORD, Symitar, Toledo, Vane, Vorpal, Web

Blame Accuse, Censure, Condemn, Confound, Decry, Fault, Guilt, Inculpate, Odium, Rap, Reproach, Reprove, Stick, Thank, Twit, Wight, Wite, Wyte

Blameless Innocent, Irreproachable

Blanch Bleach, Etiolate, Scaud, Whiten

Bland Anodyne, Mild, Pigling, Sleek, Smooth, Suave, Unctuous

Blank Cartridge, Empty, Erase, Flan, Lacuna, Mistigris, Planchet, Shot, Space, Tabula rasa, ➤ VACANT

Blanket Afghan, Bluey, Chilkat, Counterpane, Cover, General, Kaross, Mackinaw, Manta, Obscure, Overall, Poncho, Quilt, Rug, Saddle, Sarape, Security, Serape, Shabrack, Smog, Space, Stroud, Wagga, Wet, Whittle

Blast(ed) Blight, Blore, Blow, Bombard, Dang, Darn, Dee, Drat, Dynamite, Explode, Fanfare, Flaming, Flurry, Fo(e)hn, Gale, Gust, Parp, Pryse, Rats, Scarth, Scath(e), Sere, Shot, Sideration, Skarth, Tantara, Toot, Tromp(e), Trump(et), Volley

Blatant Flagrant, Hard-core, Noticeable, Strident, Vulgar

Blaze(r) Beacon, Bonfire, Burn, Cannel, Conflagration, Firestorm, ➤ FLAME, Flare, Glare, Jacket, Low(e), Lunt, Palatinate, Race, Ratch, Star, Sun, Tead(e)

Bleach(er) Agene, Blanch, Chemic, Chloride, Decolorate, Etiolate, Keir, Kier, Peroxide, Whiten, Whitster

Bleak Ablet, Bare, Blay, Bley, Dour, Dreary, Dreich, Raw, Wintry

Bleed(er), Bleeding Cup, Ecchymosis, Epistaxis, Extravasate, Fleam, Haemorrhage, Leech, Menorrh(o)ea, Menorrhagia, Metrorrhagia, Milk, Purpura, Root-pressure

Blemish Birthmark, Blot, Blotch, Blur, Botch, Defect, Flaw, Mackle, Mark, Mote, Naevus, Scar, Smirch, Spot, Sully, Taint, Tash, Vice, Wart, Wen

Blend(ing) Amalgam, Coalesce, Commix, Contemper, Contrapuntal, Counterpoint, Electrum, Fuse, Go, Harmonize, Hydrate, Interfuse, Interlace, Liquidise, Meld, Melt, ➤ MERGE, Mingle, Mix, Osmose, Portmanteau, Scumble, Sfumato, Synalepha

▷**Blend** may indicate an anagram

Bless(ed), Blessedness, Blessing Amen, Approval, Asset, Beatitude, Benedicite, Benediction, Benison, Benitier, Bensh, Bismillah, Boon, Brachah, Brocho, Consecrate, Cup, Damosel, Darshan, Elysium, Ethereal, Felicity, Gesundheit, Gwyneth, Holy (dam), Kiddush, Luck, Macarise, Mercy, Mixed, Sain, Saint, Sanctify, Sanctity, Urbi et orbi, Xenium

Blight Afflict, Ague, Bespot, Blast, Destroy, Eyesore, Rot, ➤ RUIN, Rust, Shadow, Viticide, Wither

Blimey Coo, Cor, Crimini, O'Riley, Strewth

Blind(ness), Blind spot Amaurosis, Amblyopia, Artifice, Austrian, Beesome, Bisson, Blend, Blotto, Carousal, Cecity, Chi(c)k, Cop, Concealed, Dazzle, Eyeless, Feint, Festoon, Gravel, Hemeralopia, Hood, Jalousie, Legless, Mole, Meropia, Nyctalopia, Onchocerciasis, Persian, Persiennes, Pew, Prestriction, Rash, Roller, Scotoma, Seel, Shade, Shutter, Stimie, Stimy, Stymie, Sun, Snow, Teichopsia, Typhlology, Venetian, Word, Yblent

Blindfold Bandage, Hoodwink, Muffle, Seal, Wimple

Blink(er), Blinkered, Blinking Bat, Bluff, Broken, Flash, Haw, Idiot, Insular, Nictate, Owl-eyed, Owly, Twink, Wapper, Wink

Bliss(ful) Beatitude, Bouyan, Composer, Delight, ➤ ECSTASY, Eden, Happy, Ignorance, Married, Millenium, Nirvana, Paradise, Rapture, Sion, Tir-na-nog, Valhalla, Walhalla, Wedded

Blister(ed), Blistering Blab, Blain, Bleb, Bubble, Bullate, Epispastic, Herpes, Pemphigus, Phlyctena, Scorching, Tetter, Vesicant, Vesicle

Blitz Attack, Bombard, Onslaught, Raid

Blizzard Buran, Gale, Snowstorm, Whiteout

Bloat(er) Buckling, Puff, Strout, Swell, Tumefy

Blob Bead, Bioblast, Drop, Globule, O, Spot, Tear

Bloc Alliance, Cabal, Cartel, Party

Block(ade), Blockage, Blocked Altar, Anvil, Ashlar, ➤ BAR, Barricade, Barrier, Brake, Breeze, Brick, Briquette, Building, Bung, Bunt, Choke, Chunk, Clint, Clog, Clot, Cloy, Compass, Congest, Constipated, Cylinder, ➤ DAM, Dead-eye, Debar, Dentel, Dentil, Die, Dit, Embolism, Encompass, Fipple, Hack-log, High-rise, Hunk, Ileus, Impasse, Impede, Impost, Ingot, Insula, Interrupt, Interclude, Jam, Lingot, Lodgment, Log-jam, Lump, Ministroke, Nog, Oasis®, Obstacle, ➤ OBSTRUCT, Occlude, Pad, Page, Parry, Pile-up, Plinth, Pre-empt, Prevent, Ram, Scotch, Sett, Siege, Stalemate, Stap, Starting, Stenosis, Stimie, Stimy, Stone, Stonewall, Stop, Stumbling, Stymie, Tamp, Thwart, Tower, Tranche, Trig, Triglyph, Writer's

Bloke Beggar, Chap, Cove, Fellow, Gent, Man, Oik

Blonde Ash, Cendré, Fair, Goldilocks, Platinised, Platinum, Strawberry, Tallent, Towhead

Blood(y) Ancestry, Bally, Blue, Blut, Claret, Clot, Cruor, Cup, Ecchymosis, Ensanguine, Epigons, Factor, ➤ GORE, Haemal, Ichor, Introduce, Kin, Knut, Menses, Nut, Opsonin, Parentage, Persue, Pigeon's, Plasma, Platelet, Properdin, Pup, Race, Rare, Red, Rh negative, Rh positive, Ruby, Sang, Serum, Show, Stroma, Toff, Welter

Bloodless Anaemic, Isch(a)emic, Wan, White

Blood-sucker Asp, Dracula, Flea, Gnat, Ked, Leech, Louse, Mosquito, Parasite, Reduviid, Sponger, Tick, Vampire(-bat)

Bloom(er), Blooming Anthesis, Bally, Blossom, Blow, Blush, Boner, Dew, Error, Film, Florescent, Flowery, Flush, Gaffe, Glaucous, Heyday, Knickers, Loaf, Miscalculation, Out, Pruina, Rationals, Reh, Remontant, Rosy, Underwear

▷**Bloomer** may indicate a flower

Blossom Blow, Burgeon, Festoon, Flourish, Flower, May, Orange, Pip

Blot Atomy, Blob, Cartel, Delete, Disgrace, Eyesore, Obscure, Smear, Smudge, Southern, Splodge, Splotch

Blotch(y) Blemish, Giraffe, Monk, Mottle(d), Spot, Stain

Blouse Choli, Garibaldi, Gimp, Guimpe, Middy, Sailor, Shirtwaist, Smock, Tunic, Windjammer

Blow(er) Bang, Bash, Bat, Bellows, Biff, Billow, Blip, Bloom, Brag, Breeze, Buffet, Burst, Calamity, Clap, Clat, Claut, Clip, Clout, Clump, Conk, Coup, Cuff, Dad, Daud, Dev(v)el, Dint, Douse, Dowse, Etesian, Facer, Fan, Gale, Grampus, Gust, Haymaker, Hit, Hook, Ictus, Impact, Insufflate, Karate, Kibosh, Knuckle sandwich, KO, Lame, Lander, Lick, Muff, Northerly, Noser, Oner, One-two, Pash, Phone, Piledriver, Plague, Plug, Plump(er), Polt, Pow, Puff, Punch, Purler, Rattler, Rats, Rib-roaster, Sas(s)arara, Scat, Settler, Sideswipe, Side-winder, Sis(s)erary, Skiff, Skite, Skyte, Slat, Slog, Slug, Snot, Sock, Sockdolager, Southwester, Spanking, Spat, Spout, Squander, Stripe, Stroke, Stunning, Supercharger, Swash, Swat, Swinger, Telephone, Thump, Thwack, Tingler, Tootle, Trump(et), Upper-cut, Waft, Wallop, Wap, Waste, Welt, Whammy, Whang, Whap, Wheeze, Whiffle, Whirret, ➤ WIND, Winder, Wipe

Blow-out Binge, Bloat, Exhale, Feast, Feed, Flat, Lava, Nosh-up, Snuff, Spiracle, ➤ SPREAD

Bludgeon Bully, Club, Cosh, Cudgel, Sap

Blue(s) Adult, Anil, Aquamarine, Azure, Beard, Berlin, Bice, Blow, Bottle, Butterfly, Cambridge, Cantab, Celeste, Cerulean, Cobalt, Copenhagen, Cornflower, Cyan, Danish, Danube, Dejected, Dirty, Disconsolate, Doldrums, ➤ DOWN, Duck-egg, Eatanswill, Eggshell, Electric, Firmament, Fritter, Gentian, Germander, Glum, Hump, Indecent, Indigo, Indol(e), Iron, Isatin(e), Lapis lazuli, Lavender, Lewd, Lionel, Low, Mazarine, Methylene, Midnight, Mope, Morose, Murder, Nattier, Naughty, Navy, Nile, Oxford, Peacock, Perse, Petrol, Porn, Powder, Prussian, Rabbi, Ribald, Riband, Right, Ripe, Robin's egg, Royal, Sad, Sapphire, Saxe, Saxon(y), Scurrilous, ➤ SEA, Shocking, Sky, Slate, Smalt(o), Smutty, Sordid, Splurge, Squander, Stafford, Steel, Stocking, Teal, Tony, Tory, Trist, True, Ultramarine, Unhappy, Wedgwood®, Welkin, Woad

▷ **Blue** may indicate an anagram

Bluebell Blawort, Blewart, Campanula, Harebell

Bluebottle Blawort, Blewart, Blowfly, Blowie, Brommer, Brummer, Cop, Cornflower, Fly, Policeman

Blueprint Cyanotype, Draft, Plan, Recipe

Bluff(ing) Blunt, Cle(e)ve, Cliff, Clift, Crag, Fake, Flannel, Frank, Hal, Headland, Height, Hoodwink, Kidology, Pose, Precipice, Steep, Trick

Blunder(er), Blundering Betise, Bévue, Bish, Bloomer, Blooper, Boob, Bull, Bumble, Clanger, Clinker, Cock-up, Err, Faux pas, Floater, Flub, Fluff, Gaff(e), Goof, Howler, Inexactitude, Irish, Josser, Malapropism, ➤ MISTAKE, Mumpsimus, Slip, Solecism, Stumble, Trip

Blunt(ed), Bluntly Abrupt, Alleviate, Bate, Bayt, Brusque, Candid, Deaden, Disedge, Forthright, Hebetate, Mole, Morned, Obtund, Obtuse, Outspoken, Pointblank, Rebate, Retund, Retuse, Roundly, Snub, Straight-out, Stubby

Blur(ring) Cloud, Confuse, Fog, Fuzz, Halation, Mackle, Macule, ➤ SMUDGE, Stump, Tortillon

Blush(ing) Colour, Cramoisy, Crimson, Erubescent, Erythema, Incarnadine, ➤ REDDEN, Rouge, Ruby, Rutilant

Bluster(er), Blustery Arrogance, Bellow, Blore, Hector, Rage, Rant, Rodomontade, Roister, Sabre-rattler, Squash, Swagger, Vapour, Wuthering

Boar Barrow, Calydonian, Erymanthian, Hog, Pentheus, Sanglier, Sounder, Tusker

Board(s), Boarding Abat-voix, Admiralty, Banker, Beaver, Billet, Bristol, Bulletin, Cheese, Chevron, Committee, Counter, Dart, Deal, Directors, Diving, Draft, Embark, Embus, Enter, Entrain, Fare, Fascia, Featheredge, Fibro, Gibraltar, Hack, Hawk, Hoarding, Idiot, Kip, Lag, Ledger, Lodge, Malibu, Notice, Otter, Ouija, Palette, Pallet, Panel, Particle, Pension, Planch(ette), Scaleboard, Plank, Ply(wood), Quango, Sandwich, Sarking, Screed, Shelf, Shingle, Side-table, Sign, Skirting, Sounding, Stage, Strickle, Stringboard, Surf, ➤ TABLE, Theatre, Trencher, Wainscot, Wobble

▷ **Board** may refer to chess or draughts

Boarder Interne, PG, Roomer

Boarding house Digs, Lodgings, Pension

Boast(er), Boasting Big-note, Blow, Blew, Blowhard, Bluster, Bobadil, Bounce, Brag, Braggadocio, Breeze, Crake, Crow, Fanfaronade, Gas, Gascon(nade), Glory, Hot air, Jactitation, Line, Ostent(atious), Prate, Rodomontade, Scaramouch, Skite, Swagger, Swank, Tall, Thrasonic, Vainglory, Vaunt, Yelp

Boat Canal, Dragon, Eight, Four, Foyboat, Gravy, Hooker, Jolly, Lapstrake, Launch, Lymphad, Mackinaw, Monohull, Narrow, Outrigger, Pair-oar, Pedalo, Pont, Puffer, Sailer, Sauce, Shallop, ➤ SHIP, Skiff, Slogger, Swing, Tender, Torpid, Vaporetto, ➤ VESSEL, Weekender

Boatman Bargee, Charon, Cockswain, Coxswain, George, Gondolier, Harris, Hoveller, Phaon, Voyageur, Waterman, Wet-bob

Bob Acres, Beck, Curtsey, Deaner, Dip, Dock, Dop, Duck, Float, Hod, Hog, Jerk, Page-boy, Peal, Plumb, Plummet, Popple, Rob, S, Shingle

Bobby Bluebottle, Busy, Copper, Flatfoot, Patrolman, Peeler, Pig, ➤ POLICEMAN

Body, Bodies, Bodily Administration, Amount, Anatomic, Astral, Barr, Board, Bouk, Buke, Bulk, Cadaver, Cadre, Carcase, Carnal, Caucas, Chapel, Chapter, Chassis, Clay, Cohort, Column, Comet, Committee, Contingent, Corpor(e)al, Corps, Corpse, Corpus, Corse, Cytode, Detail, Earth, Flesh, Frame, Fuselage, Goner, ➤ GROUP, Hull, Inclusion, Lich, Like, Lithites, ➤ MASS, Militia, Moit, Mote, Mummy, Nacelle, Nucleole, Nucleolus, Pack, Personal, Phalanx, Pineal, Plant, Platelet, Platoon, Politic, Posse, Purview, Quango, Relic(t), Ruck, Senate, Solid, Soma, Sound-box, Spinar, Spore, Squadron, Square, Staff, Stiff, Syndicate, Torso, Trunk, Turm, Ulema

▷ **Body** may indicate an anagram

Bodyguard Amulet, ➤ ESCORT, Gentleman-at-arms, House-carl, Minder, Praetorian, Protector, Retinue, Schutzstaffel, ➤ SHIELD, SS, Triggerman, Varangian, Yeomen

Bog(gy) Allen, Can, Carr, Clabber, Fen, Gents, Glaur, Hag, Lair, Loo, Machair, Marsh, Mire, Morass, Moss(-flow), Mud, Muskeg, Peat, Petary, Quag, Serbonian, Slack, Slade, Slough, Spew, Spouty, Stodge, Sump, Vlei, Washroom, WC, Yarfa, Yarpha

Bog(e)y Boggart, Bug(aboo), Bugbear, Chimera, Eagle, Poker, Scarer, Spectre, Troll

Bohemian Arty, Beatnik, Gypsy, Hippy

Boil(er), Boiled, Boiling point Anthrax, Blain, Botch, Brew, Bubble, C, Coction, Cook, Cree, Dartre, Decoct, Ebullient, Feruncle, Foam, Furuncle, Gathering, Hen, Herpes, Kettle, Leep, Ligroin, Pimple, Poach, Poule, Rage, Reflux, Samovar, Seethe, Simmer, Sod, Sore, Stew, Stye, Tea-kettle

Boister(ous) Gilp(e)y, Gusty, Hoo, Knockabout, Noisy, Rambunctious, Randy, Riotous, Rorty, Rough, Stormy, Termagant, Turbulent, Wild

Bold(ly), Boldness Brash, Brass, Bravado, Bravery, Bravura, Brazen, Crust, Daredevil, Defiant, Derring-do, Familiar, Free, Hardihood, Heroics, High-spirited, Impudent, Intrepid, Malapert, Mature, Outspoken, Pert, Plucky, Presumptive, Rash, Sassy, Temerity, Unshrinking

Bolt Arrow, Cuphead, Dash, Dead, Eat, Elope, Flee, Gobble, Gollop, Gorge, Gulp, Latch, Levant, Levin, Lightning, Lock, Missile, Pig, Pintle, Ragbolt, Rivet, Roll, Scoff, Slot, Snib, Sperre, Thunder, Toggle, U, Wolf

Bomb(er), Bombing Atom, Attack, B, Blockbuster, Borer, Buzz, Carpet, Cluster, Daisycutter, Deterrent, Doodlebug, Egg, Fission, Flop, Fusion, Grenade, H, Hydrogen, Lancaster, Land-mine, Letter, Liberator, Logic, Megaton, Mills, Minnie, Mint, Molotov cocktail, Mortar, Nail, Napalm, Neutron, Nuclear, Nuke, Parcel, Petar, Petard, Petrol, Pineapple, Pipe, Plaster, Plastic, Prang, Ransom, Robot, Shell, Smoke, Stealth, Stick, Stink, Stuka, Tactical, Terrorist, Time, Torpedo, V1

Bombard(ment) Attack, Battery, Blitz, Cannonade, Drum-fire, Mortar, Pelt, Shell, Stone, Stonk, Strafe, Straff

Bond(age) Adhesive, Agent, Bail, Cement, Chain, Compact, Connect, Copula, Corporate, Duty, Escrow, Flemish, Gilt, Hyphen, Ionic, James, Knot, Liaise, Ligament, Link(age), Manacle, Mortar, Nexus, Noose, ➤ PLEDGE, Rapport, Shackle, Starr, ➤ TIE, Valence, Vinculum, Yearling, Yoke

Bond(s), Bondsman Bail, Bearer, Consols, Coordinate, Covalent, Covenant, Dative, English, Ernie, Esne, Fetter, Fleming, Flemish, Geasa, Granny, Income, Junk, Pair, Premium, Recognisance, Relationship, Revenue, Running, Serf, Slave, Stacked, Thete, Treasury, Vassal

Bone(s), Bony Catacomb, Coffin, Coral, Crane, Fillet, Gaunt, Horn, Ivory, Orthopaedics, Relic, Skeleton, Splint, ➤ STEAL, Tot, Wish

Bonfire Bale-fire, Beltane, Blaze, Clavie, Pyre

Bonny Blithe, Gay, Merry, Sonsy, Weelfar'd

Bonus Bounty, Bye, Dividend, Hand-out, Lagniappe, No-claim, ➤ PREMIUM, Reward, Scrip, Spin-off, Windfall

Book(ish), Books, Bookwork Academic, Acts, Album, Amos, Apocalypse, Atlas, Audio, B, Backlist, Bestiary, Bible, Black, Blue, Bodice-ripper, Breviary, Caxton, Chron(icles), Classic, Commonplace, Compendium, Cookery, Corinthians, Course, Cyclopedia, Dan(iel), Deuteronomy, Diary, Dictionary, Digest, Directory, Domesday, Doomsday, Eccles, Edda, Encyclopedia, Engage, Enter, Eph, Ephesians, Erudite, Ezek(iel), Esther, Exercise, Exeter, Exodus, Ezra, Folio, Gal, Galatians, Genesis, Good, Gradual, Guide, Hag(gai), Haggadah, Hardback, Heptameron, Herbal, Hosea, I Ching, Imprint, Incunabula, Isaiah, Issue, John, Joshua, Jude, Jud(ges), Kells, Kings, Lam(entations), Ledger, Leviticus, Lib, Liber, Libretto, Literary, Log, Luke, Macc, Manual, Mark, Martyrs, Matthew, Micah, Missal, Monograph, Nahum, NT, Numbers, Octavo, Omnibus, Open, Order, Ordinal, OT, Page-turner, Paperback, Pedantic, Penny dreadful, Pharmacopoeia, Philippians, Phrase, Pica, Plug, Porteous, Potboiler, Primer, Proverbs, Psalms, Psalter, Publication, Quarto, Quire, Ration, Reader, Remainder, ► RESERVE, Revelations, Romans, Script, Scroll, Sir, Snobs, Softback, Statute, Studious, Study, Tablet, Text(ual), Thriller, Title, Titule, To-bit, Tome, Twelvemo, Vade-mecum, Veda, Vol(ume), Work, Year, Zephadiah

Bookbinder, Bookbinding Fanfare, Grolier, Mutton-thumper, Organdie

Book-case Credenza, Press, Satchel

Bookie(s), Bookmaker John, Layer, Librettist, Luke, Mark, Matthew, Printer, Ringman, To-bit

Bookkeeper, Bookkeeping Clerk, Double entry, Librarian, Posting, Recorder, Satchel, Single-entry

Booklet B, Brochure, Folder

Boom(ing) Baby, Beam, Boost, Bowsprit, Bump, Increase, Jib, Orotund, Prosper, Roar, Sonic, Spar, Thrive, Wishbone

Boon Bene, Benefit, Blessing, Bounty, Cumshaw, Gift, Godsend, Mills, Mitzvah, Prayer, Windfall

Boor(ish) Bosthoon, Chuffy, Churl, Clodhopper, Crass, Goth, Grobian, Hog, Ill-bred, Jack, Keelie, Kern(e), Kernish, Kill-courtesy, Lob, Lout, Lumpen, Ocker, Peasant, Philistine, Trog, Uncouth, Yahoo, Yob

Boost(er) Afterburner, Bolster, Encourage, Fillip, Help, Hoist, Impetus, Increase, Injection, Lift, Promote, Raise, Reheat, Reinforce, Reinvigorate, Spike, Supercharge, Tonic

Boot(s) Addition, Adelaide, Avail, Balmoral, Beetle-crushers, Benefit, Blucher, Bottine, Bovver, Brogan, Brogue, Buskin, Chukka, Cold, Combat, Concern, Cowboy, Denver, Derby, Desert, Dismiss, Field, Finn(e)sko, Finsko, Fire, Galage, Galosh, Gambado, Go-go, Granny, Gum, Hessian, Hip, Jack, Jemima, Lace-up, Last, Mitten, Muchie, Muc(k)luc(k), Pac, Para, Profit, Sabot, ► SACK, ► SHOE, Surgical, Toe, Tonneau, Tops, Trunk, Ugh, Vibs, Wader, Warm, Weller, Wellie, Wellington, Welly

Booth Assassin, Crame, Kiosk, Polling, Stall, Stand, Voting

Bootlegger Cooper, Coper, Runner

Booty Creach, Creagh, Haul, Loot, Prey, Prize, Spoil(s), Spolia optima, Swag

Booze ► DRINK, Liquor, Spree, Tipple

Border(land), Borderline Abut, Adjoin, Apron, Bed, Bind, Bound, Checkpoint, Coast, Cot(t)ise, Dado, Dentelle, ► EDGE, Engrail, Fimbria, Frieze, Fringe, Frontier, Furbelow, Head-rig, Hedgerow, Hem, Herbaceous, Impale, Kerb, Limb, Limbo, Limes, Limit, Lip, List, March, Marchland, ► MARGIN, Mat, Mattoid, Meith, Mete, Mount, Neighbour, Orle, Pand, Pelmet, Perimeter, Purfle, Purlieu, Rand, Rim, Roadside, Roon, Royne, Rund, Selvage, Side, Skirt, Strand, Strip, Surround, Swage, The Marches, Trench, Valance, Valence, ► VERGE

▷ **Borders** may indicate first and last letters

Bore(d), Boredom, Borer, Boring Aiguille, Anorak, Apathy, Auger, Awl, Beetle, Bind, Bit, Broach, Brog, Bromide, Calibre, Deadly, Drag, ► DRILL, Dry, Eagre, Eat, Eger, Elshin, Elsin, Endured, Ennui, Ennuye, Foozle, Gim(b)let, Gouge, Gribble, Grind, Had, Heigh-ho, Ho-hum, Irk, Listless, Longicorn, Longueur, Miser, Mole, Nerd, Nuisance, Pall, Penetrate, Perforate, Pest, Pierce, Pill, Probe, Prosaic, Prosy, Punch, Ream(ingbit), Rime, Sat, Screw, Severn, Snooze, Snore, Sondage, Spleen, Sting, Stob, Tedious, Tedium, Termes, Termite, Thirl, Tire, Trocar, Tunnel, ► WEARY, Well, Wimble, Windbag, Wonk, Woodworm, Worldweary, Yawn

Born B, Free, Great, Nascent, Nat(us), Né(e)

Borough Borgo, Pocket, Port, Quarter, Rotten, Township, Wick

Borrow(ed), Borrowing Adopt, Appropriate, Cadge, Copy, Eclectic, George, Hum, Scunge, Straunge, ➤ TAKE, Touch

Boss(ed), Bossy Blooper, Burr, Cacique, Director, Dominate, Gadroon, Headman, Honcho, Hump, Inian, Inion, Jewel, Knob, Knop, Knot, ➤ MISTAKE, Maestro, ➤ MANAGER, Massa, Mistress, Netsuke, Noop, Nose-led, Omphalos, Overlord, Overseer, Owner, Pellet, Protuberance, Ruler, Run, Stud, Superintendent, Taskmaster, Umbo(nate)

Bother Ado, Aggro, Care, Deave, Deeve, Disturb, Drat, Fash, Fluster, Fuss, Get, Hector, Incommode, Irritate, Moither, Nuisance, Perturb, Pest(er), Pickle, Rile, Todo, ➤ TROUBLE

Bottle(s) Ampul(la), Balthasar, Balthazar, Belshazzar, Bundle, Carafe, Carboy, Cock, Cork, Costrel, Courage, Cruet, Cruse, Cucurbital, Cutter, Dead-men, Decanter, Demijohn, Fearlessness, Feeding, Fiasco, Flacket, Flagon, Flask, Goatskin, Gourd, Hen, Imperial, Jeroboam, Klein, Lachrymal, Lagena, Magnum, Matrass, Medicine, Methuselah, Mettle, Nebuchadnezzar, Phial, Pitcher, Rehoboam, Resource, Retort, Salmanazar, Siphon, Split, Vial, Vinaigret(te), Wad, Water, Winchester, Woulfe

▷ **Bottle(d)** may indicate an anagram or a hidden word

Bottom(ness) Anus, Aris, Arse, Ass, Base, Beauty, Bed, Benthos, Bilge, Breech, Bum, Butt, Buttocks, Croup(e), Croupon, Demersal, Derrière, Doup, Fanny, Floor, Foot, Foundation, Fud, Fundus, Haunches, Hunkers, Hurdies, Keel(son), Kick, Nadir, Podex, Posterior, Pottle-deep, Prat, Pyramus, Rear, Rock, Root, Rump, Seat, Sill, Ship, Sole, Staddle, Tail, Tush, Weaver

Bounce(r), Bouncy Bang, Blague, Bound, Caper, Dap, Dead-cat, Doorman, Dop, Dud, Eject, Evict, Jounce, Kite, Lie, Lilt, Resilient, Ricochet, Spiccato, Spring, Stot, Tale, Tamp, Verve, Vitality, Yorker, Yump

▷ **Bouncing** may indicate an anagram

Bound(er), Boundary Adipose, Apprenticed, Articled, Bad, Barrier, Beholden, Border, Bourn(e), Cad, Cavort, Certain, Circumference, Curvet, Decreed, Demarcation, Demarkation, Duty, End, Engirt, Entrechat, Erub, Eruv, Fence, Four, Galumph, Gambado, Gambol, Girt, Hedge, Heel, Held, Hoarstone, Hops, Hourstone, Interface, Jump, Kangaroo, ➤ LEAP, Limes, Limit, Linch, Lollop, Lope, Meare, Meer, Mere, Merestone, Mete,

Muscle, Obliged, Outward, Pale, Parameter, Perimeter,
Periphery, Plate, Prance, Precinct, Purlieu, Redound, Ring-fence,
Roller, Roo, Roped, Rubicon, Scoup, Side, Sideline, Six(er), Skip,
Spang, Spring, Sten(d), Stoit, T(h)alweg, Tied, Touchline,
Upstart, Vault, Verge, Wallaby

▷**Bounds** may indicate outside letters

Bountiful, Bounty Aid, Bligh, Boon, Christian, Generosity,
➤ GIFT, Goodness, Grant, Head money, Honorarium,
Largess(e), Lavish

Bouquet Aroma, Attar, Aura, Compliment, Corsage, Fragrancy,
Garni, Nose, Nosegay, Plaudit, Posy, Spiritual, Spray

Bout Bender, Bust, Contest, Dose, Go, Jag, Match, Spell, Spree,
Turn, Venery, Venewe, Venue

Bow(er), Bowing, Bowman Alcove, Arbour, Arc, Arch,
➤ ARCHER, Arco, Arson, Beck, Bend, Boudoir, Clara, Congé(e),
Crescent, Crook, Cupid, ➤ CURVE, Defer, Dicky, Droop, Duck,
Eros, Eye, Fiddle(r), Fiddlestick, Foredeck, Halse, Hawse, Jouk,
Kneel, Kotow, Lean, Lout, Nod, Nutate, Obeisance, Paganini,
Pergola, Quarrel, Reverence, Salaam, Seamer, Shelter, Slope,
Spiccato, Stick, ➤ SUBMIT, Tie, Yew, Yield

Bowels Entrails, Guts, Innards, Viscera

▷**Bower** may indicate using a bow

Bowl(er), Bowling, Bowl over, Bowls B, Basin, Begging,
Bicker, Bodyline, Bool, Bosey, Bouncer, Cage-cup, Calabash,
Cap, Carpet, Caup, Chalice, Cheese, Chinaman, Christie,
Christy, Cog(g)ie, Crater, Cup, Derby, ➤ DISH, Dismiss, Dome,
Drake, Dumbfound, Dust, Ecuelle, End, Finger, Goldfish,
Googly, Grub, Hog, Hoop, Jack, Jeroboam, Jorum, Lavabo,
Laver, Leg-spin, Lightweight, Lob, Locke, Monteith, Night,
Offbreak, Old, Over-arm, Pace, Pan, Pétanque, Porringer,
Pot-hat, Pottinger, Punch, Raku, Rink, Roll, Roundarm,
Seam(er), Skip, Skittle(s), Spare, Spinner, Stadium, Stagger,
Super, Ten-pin, Tom, Underarm, Underhand, Voce, Wassail,
Wood, York(er)

Box(ing) Baignoire, Bandbox, Bareknuckle, Bijou, Binnacle,
Black, Bonk, Bunk, Bush, Caddy, Call, Camera, Canister, Case,
Cash, Chest, Chinese, Christmas, Coach, Coffer, Coffret,
Confessional, Cool, Crate, Cuff, Deed, Dialogue, Dispatch,
Drawer, Enclose, ➤ FIGHT, File, Fist, Fund, Fuse, Glory, Go-kart,
Hedge, Honesty, Humidor, Hutch, Inro, Journal, Junction, Jury,

Kiosk, Kite, Knevell, Ladle, Locker, Lodge, Loge, Mill, Mocuck, Musical, Package, Pandora's, Peepshow, Penalty, Pew, Phylactery, Pillar, Pix, Press, Prompt, Protector, Pyxis, Register, Ring, Saggar(d), Sagger, Savate, Scrap, Seggar, Sentry, Shoe, Signal, Skinner, Skip(pet), Slipcase, Solander, ➤ SPAR, Swell, Telephone, Telly, Tube, Tuck, TV, Voice, Witness

Boxer Ali, Bantamweight, Bruiser, Bruno, Canine, Carnera, Carpentier, Carthorse, Chinaman, Cooper, Crater, Cruiserweight, Dog, Eryx, Farr, Featherweight, Flyweight, Ham, Heavyweight, Middleweight, Pandora, Pug, Pugil(ist), Rebellion, Rocky, Shadow, Welterweight

Boy(s) Apprentice, Ball, Bevin, Blue-eyed, Breeches, Bub(by), Cabin, Chiel(d), ➤CHILD, Chummy, Cub, Callant, Champagne, Galopin, Garçon, Groom, Ha, Jack, Kid, Klonkie, Knave, Lackbeard, ➤ LAD, Loblolly's, Loon(ie), Minstrel, Nibs, Nipper, Page, Prentice, Principal, Putto, Rent, Roaring, Shaver, Son, Spalpeen, Sprig, Stripling, Tad, Ted(dy), Tiger, Toy, Urchin, Whipping, ➤ YOUTH

▷**Boy** may indicate an abbreviated name

Boycott Avoid, Bat, Black, Blacklist, Exclude, Hartal, Isolate, Ostracise, Shun

Brace(s), Bracing Accolade, Couple, Crosstree, Gallace, Gallows, Gallus(es), Gird, Hound, Invigorate, Pair, Pr, Rear-arch, Rere-arch, Skeg, Splint, Steady, Stiffener, Strut, ➤ SUPPORT, Suspenders, Tauten, Tone, Two

Bracelet Armil(la), Armlet, Bangle, Cuff, Darbies, Handcuff, Manacle, Manilla

Bracken Brake, Fern, Pteridium, Tara

Bracket(s) Angle-iron, Bibb, Brace, Cantilever, Console, Corbel, Couple, Cripple, Misericord(e), Modillion, Mutule, Parenthesis, Potence, Pylon, Rigger, Sconce, Straddle, Strata, ➤ STRUT, Trivet, Truss

Brag(gart), Bragging Birkie, Bluster, Boast, Bobadil, Braggadocio, Bull, Cockalorum, Crow, Falstaff, Fanfaronade, Gab, Gascon, Hot-air, Loudmouth, Puff, Rodomontader, Skite, Slam, Swagger, Vainglorious, Vaunt

Braid A(i)glet, Aiguillette, Frog, Galloon, Lacet, Plait, Plat, Rickrack, Ricrac, Rick-rack, Seaming-lace, Sennet, Sennit, Sinnet, Soutache, Tress, Trim, Twist, Weave

▷**Brain(s)** may indicate an anagram

Brain(y), Brain disease, Brain-power Appestat, Bean, Bright, Cerebellum, Cerebrum, Cortex, Dura mater, Encephalon, Fornix, Genius, Gyrus, Harn(s), Head, Hippocampus, Hypothalamus, Insula, Intelligence, IQ, Loaf, Lobe, Mater, Medulla, Mind, Noddle, Noesis, Nous, Peduncle, Pericranium, Pia mater, Pons, Pontile, Sconce, Sense, Sensorium, Striatum, Subcortex, Thalamus

Brake Adiantum, Air, Bracken, Curb, Disc, Drag, Drum, Fern, Grove, Hydraulic, Nemoral, Overrun, Ratchet, Rein, Shoe, ➤ SLOW, Spinney, Sprag, Tara, Thicket, Vacuum

Bramble, Brambly Batology, Blackberry, Boysenberry, Brier, Cloudberry, Rubus, Thorn, Wait-a-bit

Bran Cereal, Chesil, Chisel, Oats, Pollard

Branch(ed), Branches, Branching, Branch Office Affiliate, Antler, Arm, BO, Bough, Cladode, Cow, Dendron, Dept, Diversify, Diverticulum, Divide, Filiate, Fork, Grain, Kow, Jump, Lateral, Limb, Lobe, Loop, Lye, Lylum, Offshoot, Olive, Patulous, Raguly, Ramate, Ramulus, Reis, Rice, Shroud, Special, Spray(ey), Sprig, Spur, Tributary, Turning, Turn-off, Twig, Wattle, Yard

Brand Broadsword, Buist, Burn, Cauterise, Chop, Class, Denounce, Earmark, Ember, Excalibur, Falchion, Faulchin, Faulchion, Idiograph, Iron, Label, Line, ➤ MARK, Marque, Sear, Stigma, Sweard, Sword, Torch, Wipe

Brandy Aguardiente, Applejack, Aqua vitae, Armagnac, Bingo, Calvados, Cape smoke, Cold without, Dop, Eau de vie, Fine, Framboise, Grappa, Marc, Mampoer, Nantes, Nantz, Napoleon, Quetsch, Slivovic(a), Slivovitz, Smoke

Brash Impudent, Pushy, Rain, Rash

Brass(ware), Brassy Benares, Brazen, Cheek, Corinthian, Cornet, Dinanderie, Face, Front, Harsh, Horn, Horse, Latten, Lip, Loot, Lota(h), Loud, Matrix, ➤ MONEY, Moola(h), Pyrites, Sopranino, Sass, Snash, Talus, Top, Trombone

Brat Bairn, Gait(t), Gamin, Imp, Lad, Terror, Urchin

Brave(ry) Amerind, Apache, Bold, Conan, Corragio, Courage, Creek, Dare, ➤ DEFY, Doughty, Dress, Face, Gallant, Game, Gamy, Gutsy, Hardy, Heroism, Indian, Injun, Intrepid, Lion, Manful, Manly, Nannup, Plucky, Prow(ess), Sannup, Stout, Uncas, Valiant, Valour, Wight

Bravo Acclaim, Bandit, Bully, Desperado, Euge, Murderer, Olé, Spadassin, Villain

Brawl Affray, Bagarre, Bicker, Brabble, Donnybrook, Dust, Fight, Flite, Flyte, Fracas, Fratch, Fray, Melee, Prawl, Rammy, Roughhouse, Scuffle, Set-to, Shindig, Stoush, Tar, Wrangle

Brawn(y) Beef, Burliness, Headcheese, He-man, Muscle, Power, Rillettes, Sinew

Bray Cry, Heehaw, Stamp, Vicar, Whinny

Brazen Bold, Brassy, Flagrant, Impudent, Shameless, Unabashed

Breach Assault, Break, Chasm, Cleft, Gap(e), Infraction, Redan, Rupture, Saltus, Schism, Solution, Trespass, Violate

Bread Azym(e), Bagel, Baguette, Bannock, Bap, Barmbrack, Batch, Brewis, Brioche, Brownie, Bun, Cash, Chal(l)ah, Chametz, Chapati, Cheat, Ciabatta, Cob, Coburg, Corn, Corsned, Croute, Crouton, Crumpet, Crust, Damper, Dibs, Dika, Doorstep, Flatbread, Focaccia, French, Garlic, Gluten, Graham, Grissino, Guarana, Host, Indian, Jannock, Johnny-cake, Laver, Leavened, Loaf, Long tin, Manchet, ➤ MONEY, Na(a)n, Panada, Panary, Paneity, Paratha, Pikelet, Pit(t)a, Pone, Poultice, Pumpernickel, Puri, Ravel, Roll, Rooty, Roti, Rusk, Rye, Sally Lunn, Sippet, Smor(re)brod, Soda, Sourdough, Staff of life, Stollen, Sugar, Sweet, Tartine, Tommy, Wastel

Break(ing), Break-down, Break-in, Break-up, Broken Adjourn, Bait, Breach, Caesura, Caesure, Cark, Cesure, Chinaman, Chip, Cleave, Comb, Comma, Commercial, Comminute, Compost, Crack, Crock, Crumble, Debacle, Demob, Destroy, Diffract, Disintegrate, Disperse, Disrupt, Erupt, Exeat, Fast, Fault, Four, ➤ FRACT(URE), Fritter, Frush, Gaffe, Half-time, Half-term, Hernia, Holiday, Infringe, Interim, Interlude, Intermission, Interrupt, ➤ INTERVAL, Irrupt, Knap, Lacuna, Lapse, Leave, Moratorium, Outage, Pause, Polarise, Recess, Relief, Rend, Respite, Rest, Rift, Ruin, Rupture, Saltus, Schism(a), Secede, Shatter, Shiver, Smash, Snap, Stave, Stop, Stove, Sunder, Tame, Tea-ho, Tear, Time-out, Torn, Transgress, Truce, Vacation, Violate

Breakable Brittle, Delicate, Fissile, Frail, Friable

Breakdown Analyse, Autolysis, Cataclasm, Collapse, Conk, Glitch, Glycolosis, Histolysis, Lyse, Lysis, Ruin

Breaker Billow, Comber, Ice, Roller, Smasher, Surf

Breakfast B, Brunch, Chota-hazri, Continental, Disjune, Kipper, Wedding

Breakwater Groyne, Jetty, Mole, Pier, Tetrapod

Bream Fish, Porgy, Sar(gus), Tai

Breast(bone), Breasts, Breastwork Bazuma, Blob, Bosom, Brave, Brisket, Bust, Counter, Diddy, Duddy, Dug, Garbonza, Gazunga, Heart-spoon, Jubbies, Jugs, Knockers, Norg, Nork, Rampart, Redan, Sangar, Sungar, Stem, Sternum, Supreme, Tit, Xiphisternum

Breastplate Armour, Byrnie, Curat, Curiet, Pectoral, Plastron, Rational, Rest, Shield, Thorax, Xiphiplastron

Breath(ing), Breathe(r) Aerobe, Aspirate, Exhalation, Expiration, Flatus, Gasp, Gill, H, Halitosis, Hauriant, Inhale, Inspiration, Lung, Nares, Nostril, Oxygenator, Pant, Pneuma, Prana, Pulmo, Rale, Respire, Respite, Rest, Rhonchus, Scuba, Snorkel, Snuffle, Spiracle, Spirit, Vent, Wheeze, Whiff, Whisper, Whift, Whist, Wind, Windpipe

Breathless(ness) Anhelation, Apnoea, Asthma, Dyspnoea, Emphysema, Orthopnoea, Puffed-out, Tachypnoea, Wheezing

Breech(es) Bible, Buckskin, Chaps, Flog, Galligaskins, Hose, Jodhpurs, Kneecords, Knickerbockers, Plushes, Smallclothes, Smalls, Trews, Trouse(rs), Trusses

Breed(ing), Breeding-place Bear, Beget, Engender, Eugenics, Lineage, ➤ MANNERS, Origin, Procreate, Pullulate, Race, Rear, Seminary, Sire, Species, Stock, Strain, Stud, Tribe

Breeze, Breezy Air, Breath, Brisk, Catspaw, Chipper, Doctor, Gust, Mackerel, Slant, Sniffler, Tiff, Zephyr

Brew(er), Brewery, Brewing Ale, Billycan, Brose, Browst, Bummock, ➤ CONCOCT, Contrive, Dictionary, Ferment, Infusion, Liquor, Malt, Potion, Steep, Yeast, Yill, Zymurgy

Bribe(ry) Backhander, Bonus, Boodle, Bung, Dash, Embracery, Get at, Graft, Grease, Hush-money, Insult, Kickback, Oil, Palm, Payola, Schmear, Slush, Soap, Sop, Square, Straightener, Suborn, Sweeten(er), Tempt, Tenderloin, Vail, Vales

Brick(s), Brickwork Adobe, Bat, Bath, Boob, Bullnose, Bur(r), Clanger, Clinker, Closer, Course, Fletton, Gaffe, Gault, Header, Ingot, Klinker, Lateritious, Lego®, Malm, Nogging, Red, Soldier, Sport, Stalwart, Stretcher, Terra-cotta, Testaceous, Tile, Trojan, Trump

Bride(s) Bartered, Danaides, Ellen, Spouse, War, Wife, Ximena

Bridge(head), Bridge player Acol, Aqueduct, Auction, Bailey, Balance, Barre, Bascule, Bestride, Brooklyn, Cantilever, Capo, Capodastro, Capotasto, Catwalk, Chicago, Chicane, Clapper, Clifton, Contract, Counterpoise, Cross, Cut-throat, Deck, Declarer, Drawbridge, Duplicate, Gangplank, Gangway, Gantry, Hog's back, Humpback, Humpbacked, Jigger, Ligger, Link, London, Menai, Overpass, Pivot, Pontoon, Rialto, Rubber, Sighs, ➤ SPAN, Spanner, Stamford, Straddle, Suspension, Swing, Tay, Tête-de-pont, Transporter, Trestle, Truss, Vertical lift, Viaduct, Waterloo, Wheatstone

Bridle Bit, Branks, Bridoon, Bristle, Browband, Curb, Hackamore, Halter, Headstall, Musrol, Noseband, Rein

Brief(s), Briefing, Briefly, Brevity Awhile, Bluette, Brachylogy, Breviate, Cape, Compact, ➤ CONCISE, Curt, Dossier, Fleeting, Instruct, Laconic, Nearly, Pants, Pennorth, Pithy, Prime, Scant, Short-term, Short-winded, ➤ SHORT(EN), Sitrep, Succinct, Summing, Tanga, Terse, Transient, Undies, Update, Watching

Brigade Boys', Corps, Fire, International, Red, Troop

Bright(en), Brightness Afterglow, Alert, Brainy, Breezy, Brilliant, Brisk, Cheery, Cla(i)re, Clear, Clever, Effulgent, Elaine, Fair, Floodlit, Florid, Garish, Gay, Glad, Glow, Hono(u)r, Light, Lit, Loud, Lucid, Luculent, Lustre, Net(t), Nit, Radiant, Rosy, Scintillating, Sematic, Sharp, Sheeny, Sheer, Shere, Skyre, Smart, Stilb, Sunlit, Sunny, Vive, Vivid, White

Brilliance, Brilliant Ace, Blaze, Brainy, Def, Effulgent, Flashy, Galaxy, Gay, Gemmy, Glossy, Inspired, Lambent, Lustre, Mega-, Meteoric, Nitid, Pear, ➤ RADIANT, Refulgent, Resplendent, Shiny, Spangle, Splendour, Star, ➤ VIVID, Virtuoso, Water

Brim Edge, Lip, Rim, Ugly

Brine Muriatic, Ozone, Pickle, Saline, Salt

Bring(ing) Afferent, Bear, Carry, Cause, Conduct, Convey, Earn, Evoke, Fet, Fetch, Hatch, Induce, Land, Produce, Wreak

Bring up Breed, Educate, Exhume, Foster, Nurture, Raise, ➤ REAR

Brisk(ness) Active, Alacrity, Alert, Allegro, Breezy, Busy, Chipper, Crank, Crisp, Crouse, Fresh, Gaillard, Galliard, Jaunty, Kedge, Kedgy, Kidge, Lively, Perk, Pert, Rattling, Roaring,

Scherzo, Sharp, Smart, Snappy, Spanking, Spirited, Sprightly, Vivace, Yare, Zippy

Bristle(d), Bristling, Bristly Arista, Awn, Barb, Birse, Bridle, Chaeta, Flurry, Fraught, Frenulum, Gooseflesh, Hackles, Hair, Hérissé, Horripilation, Seta, Setose, Striga, Strigose, Stubble, Whisker, Vibraculum, Villus

Britain Alban(y), Albion

Brit(ish), Briton(s) Anglo, Herring, Iceni, Insular, Isles, Limey, Pict, Pom, Rooinek, Saxon, Silurian, UK

Brittle Bruckle, Crackly, Crimp, Crisp, Delicate, ➤ FRAGILE, Frush, Redsear, Shivery, Spall, Spalt

▷ **Brittle** may indicate an anagram

Broach Approach, Open, Raise, Spit, Suggest, Tap, Widen

Broad(ly) Crumpet, Dame, Doll, Doxy, Drab, General, Generic, Largo, Latitudinous, Loose, Outspoken, Ovate, Pro, Roomy, Spatulate, Thick, Tolerant, Wide, Woman

Broadcast(er), Broadcasting Ad(vertise), Air, Announce, Beam, Breaker, B4, Disperse, Disseminate, Emission, Ham, IBA, OB, On, Outside, Pirate, Programme, Promulgate, Radiate, Radio, Relay, ➤ SCATTER, Scattershot, Screen(ed), SECAM, Seed, Sky, Sow, Sperse, Spread, Sprinkle, Transmission, Ventilate, Wavelength

Brochure Leaflet, Pamphlet, Tract

Broke(n) Bankrupt, Bust(ed), Duff, Evans, Fritz, Insolvent, Kaput, Puckeroo, Shattered, Skint, Stony, Stove, Strapped

▷ **Broken** may indicate an anagram

Broker Agent, Banian, Banyan, Jobber, Go-between, Mediator, ➤ MERCHANT, Shadchan, Uncle

Bronze, Bronze age Bell, Bras(s), Brown, Gunmetal, Hallstatt(ian), Helladic, Minoan, Mycenean, Ormolu, Phosphor, Schillerspar, Sextans, Talos, Tan, Third

Brooch Cameo, Clasp, Fibula, Luckenbooth, Ouch, Owche, Pin, Preen, Prop, Spang, Sunburst

Brood Clock, Clutch, Cogitate, Covey, Eye, Eyrie, Hatch, Hover, Incubate, Introspect, Kindle, Litter, Meditate, Mill, Mull, Nest, Nid, Perch, Pet, ➤ PONDER, Repine, Roost, Sit, Sulk, Team

Brook Babbling, Beck, Branch, Burn, Countenance, Creek, Endure, Ghyll, Gill, Kerith, Kill, Pirl, Purl, Rill(et), River, Rivulet, Runlet, Runnel, Stand, Stomach, Stream, Suffer, Tolerate

Broom Besom, Brush, Cow, Genista, Gorse, Greenweed, Knee-holly, Kow, Orobranche, Retama, Spart, Sweeper, Whisk

Broth Bouillon, Brew(is), Cullis, Dashi, Kail, Kale, Muslin-kale, Pottage, Scotch, Skilly, ➤ SOUP, Stock

Brothel Bagnio, Bordel(lo), Cathouse, Corinth, Crib, Den, Honkytonk, Hothouse, Kip, Knocking shop, Seraglio, Stew

Brother Ally, Bhai, Billie, Billy, Blood, Brethren, Bro, Bud, Comrade, Fellow, Fra, Freemason, Lay, ➤ MONK, Moose, Sib(ling), Theatine, Trappist, Worker

Brow Crest, Forehead, Glabella, Ridge, Sinciput, Tump-line

Brown Abram, Adust, Amber, Auburn, Bay, Biscuit, Bisque, Bister, Bistre, Bole, Br, Braise, Brindle, Bronzed, Brunette, Burnet, Capability, Caramel, Caromel, Cinnamon, Cook, Coromandel, Dun, Fallow, Filemot, Fulvous, Fusc(ous), Grill, Hazel, Ivor, John, Khaki, Liver, Meadow, Mocha, Mousy, Philamot, Rufous, Rugbeian, Russet, Rust, Scorch, Sepia, Sienna, Soare, Sore, Sorrel, Tan, Tawny, Tenné, Testaceous, Toast, Tom, Umber, Vandyke, Wholemeal, Windsor

Browse Graze, Pasture, Read, Scan, Stall-read, Surf

Bruise Contund, Contuse, Crush, Damage, Ding, Ecchymosis, Frush, Golp(e), Hurt, Intuse, Livedo, Lividity, Mark, Mouse, Pound, Purpure, Rainbow, Shiner, Ston(n), Stun, Surbate

Brush (off), Brushwood Bavin, Brake, Broom, Carbon, Chaparral, Clash, Dandy, Dismiss, Dust, Encounter, Fan, Filbert, Filecard, Firth, Fitch, Frith, Grainer, Hag, Hog, Kiss, Liner, Loofah, Mop, Paint, Pig, Pope's head, Putois, Rebuff, Rice, Rigger, Sable, Scrub, Scuff, Skim, Striper, Thicket, Touch

Brutal, Brute Animal, Beast, Bête, Caesar, Caliban, Cruel, Hun, Iguanodon, Inhuman, Nazi, Nero, Ostrogoth, Pitiless, Quagga, Roughshod, Ruffian, Thresher-whale, Yahoo

Bubble(s), Bubbly Air-bell, Air-lock, Barmy, Bead(ed), Bell, Bleb, Blister, Boil, Buller, Cavitate, Champagne, Cissing, Ebullition, Effervesce, Embolus, Enthuse, Espumoso, Foam, ➤ FROTH, Gassy, Globule, Gurgle, Head, Mantle, Mississippi, Popple, Rale, Reputation, Roundel, Rowndell, Seed, Seethe, Simmer, South Sea, Vesicle, Widow

Buck (up) Bongo, Brace, Cheer, Dandy, Deer, Dollar, Elate, Encheer, Hart, Jerk, Leash, Male, Ourebi, Pitch, Pricket, Ram, Rusa, Sore, Sorel(l), Sorrel, Spade, Spay(a)d, ➤ STAG, Staggard, Stud, Wheel

Bucket(s) Bail, Bale, Clamshell, Ice, Kibble, Noria, Pail, Piggin, Scuttle, Situla, Stoop(e), Stope, Stoup, Tub

Buckle Artois, Clasp, Contort, Crumple, Deform, Dent, Fasten, Warp

▷ **Buckle** may indicate an anagram

▷ **Bucks** may indicate an anagram

Bucolic Aeglogue, Eglogue, Idyllic, Pastoral, Rural, Rustic

Bud(ding), Buddy Botoné, Bottony, Bulbil, Burgeon, Clove, Cobber, Deb, Eye, Gem(ma), Germinate, Knosp, Knot, Nascent, Pal, Scion, Serial, Shoot, Sprout, Taste, Turion

Buddha, Buddhism, Buddhist Abhidhamma, Ahimsa, Amitabha, Anata, Anicca, Arhat, Asoka, Bodhisattva, Dalai Lama, Gautama, Hinayana, Jain, Jataka, Jodo, Mahatma, Mahayana, Maya, Pali, Pitaka, Pure Land, Sakya-muni, Sila, Soka Gakkai, Theravada, Tripitaka, Triratna, Zen(o)

Budge Jee, Move, Stir, Submit

Budget Estimate, Plan, Programme, Shoestring

Buff Beige, Birthday suit, Eatanswill, Fan, Fawn, Nankeen, Nude, Nut, Polish, ► RUB, Streak

Buffalo African, Anoa, Arna, Asiatic, Bison, Bonasus, Bugle, Cap, Cape, Carabao, Ox, Perplex, Takin, Tamarao, Tamarau, Timarau, Water, Zamouse

Buffer Bootblack, Cofferdam, Cutwater, Fender

Buffet Bang, Blow, Box, Counter, Cuff, Hit, Lam, Maltreat, Perpendicular, Shove, Sideboard, Smorgasborg, Strike, Strook(e)

Bug(s) Arthropod, Assassin, Bacteria, Beetle, Capsid, Chinch, Cimex, Cockchafer, Croton, Damsel, Debris, Dictograph®, Eavesdrop, Harlequin, Hassle, ► INSECT, Jitter, June, Kissing, Lace, May, Mealy, Micrococcus, Mike, Milkweed, Millennium, Mite, Squash, Tap, Vex, Wheel, Wiretap

Buggy Beach, Car, Cart, Shay, Tipcart, Trap

Bugle, Bugle call Chamade, Clarion, Cornet, Hallali, Last post, Ox, Reveille, Taps, ► TRUMPET, Urus

Build(ing), Building site Ar(a)eostyle, Accrue, Assemble, Big, Capitol, Colosseum, Commons, Cot, ► CREATE, Cruck, Curia, Develop, Drystone, Duplex, Edifice, Edify, Erect, Fabric, Hut, Infill, Insula, Kaaba, Ken, Linhay, Listed, Low-rise, Lyceum, Minaret, Mould, Observatory, Outhouse, Palazzo, Phalanx, Pile,

Portakabin®, Premises, Quonset®, Raise, Rotunda, Skyscraper, Stance, Structure, Synthesis, Tectonic, Telecottage, Temple, Tenement, Tower

▷ **Building** may indicate an anagram

Bulb Camas(h), Chive, Cive, Corm, Globe, Lamp, Light, Pearl, Scallion, Set, Shallot, Squill

Bulge, Bulging Astrut, Bag, Bias, Biconvex, Bug, Bulbous, Bunchy, Cockle, Entasis, Expand, Exsert, Inion, Protrude, Relievo, Rotund, Strout, Strut, ➤ SWELL, Tumid

Bulk(y) Aggregate, Ample, Big, Body, Corpulent, Extent, Gross, Hull, Massive, Preponderance, Roughage, Scalar, ➤ SIZE, Stout, Vol(ume), Weight

Bull(ock), Bully Anoa, Apis, Beef, Blarney, Bluster, Bovine, Brag, Brave, Browbeat, Bucko, Despot, Dragoon, Drawcansir, Englishman, Fancyman, Farnese, Flashman, Flatter, Gold, Gosh, Hapi, Harass, Haze(r), Hector, Hoodlum, Huff, Intimidate, Investor, Irish(ism), John, Killcow, Lambast, Maltreat, Mick(e)(y), Mistake, Mithraism, Mohock, Neat, Papal, Piker, Pistol, Placet, Poler, Rhodian, Roarer, Rot, Ruffian, Sitting, Stag, Strong-arm, Swash-buckler, Taurine, Taurus, Tommy-rot, Tosh, Trash, Twaddle, Tyran(ne), Tyrannise, Tyrant, Zo(bo)

Bulldoze(r) Coerce, Earthmover, Leveller, Overturn

Bullet Balata, Ball, Biscayan, Dumdum, Fusillade, Minié, Minié ball, Missile, Pellet, Plastic, Round, Rubber, Shot, Slug, Tracer

Bulletin Memo, Newsletter, Report, Summary

Bull-fight(er) Banderillero, Banderillo, Corrida, Cuadrilla, Escamillo, Matador, Picador, Rejoneador, Tauromachy, Toreador, Torero

Bulwark Bastion, Defence, Rampart, Resistor

Bum Ass, Beg, Prat, Sponge, Thumb, Tramp, Vagabond

Bumble Beadle, Bedel(l)

▷ **Bumble** may indicate an anagram

Bump(er), Bumps Big, Blow, Bucket, Clour, Collide, Dunch, Fender, Hillock, Immense, Inian, Inion, Joll, Jo(u)le, Jowl, Keltie, Kelty, Knar, Knock, Mamilla, Mogul, Organ, Phrenology, Reveille, Rouse, Speed, Thump

Bumpkin Bucolic, Bushwhacker, Clodhopper, Hawbuck, Hayseed, Hick, Jock, Lout, Oaf, Put(t), Rube, Rustic, Yokel, Zany

Bun Barmbrack, Bath, Chelsea, Chignon, Chou, Hot-cross, Huffkin, Mosbolletjie, Roll, Teacake, Toorie, Wad

Bunch Acinus, Anthology, Bob, Botryoid, Cluster, Fascicle, Finial, Flock, ➤ GROUP, Hand, Handful, Lot, Lump, Panicle, Raceme, Spray, Staphyline, Tassel, Tee, Truss, Tuft

Bundle Axoneme, Bale, Bavin, Bluey, Bottle, Byssus, Desmoid, Dorlach, Drum, Fag(g)ot, Fascicle, Fascine, Fibre, Fibrovascular, Kemple, Knitch, Lemniscus, Matilda, ➤ PACK(AGE), Parcel, Sack, Sheaf, Shiralee, Shock, Shook, Stook, Swag, Tie, Top, Trousseau, Truss, Vascular, Wad, Wadge, Wap

Bungle(r) Blunder, Blunk, Bodge, Boob, Botch, Bumble, Bummle, Duff, Fluff, Foozle, Foul, Goof, Mess, Mis(h)guggle, Muddle, Muff, Mull, Prat, Screw, Spoil

Bunk(er), Bunkum Abscond, Absquatulate, Balderdash, Baloney, Berth, Blah, Bolt, Casemate, Claptrap, Clio, Entrap, Guy, Hazard, History, Hokum, Humbug, Malarky, Rot, Scuttle, Tosh, Trap, Tripe

Bunting Bird, Cirl, Flag, Fringilline, Ortolan, Snow, Streamer, Yellow-hammer, Yowley

Buoy Bell, Breeches, Can, Dan, Daymark, Dolphin, Float, Marker, Nun, Raft, Ring, Seamark, Sonar, Sustain

Buoyant Blithe, Floaty, Resilient

Burden(ed) Albatross, Beare, Bob, Cargo, Cark, Chant, Chorus, Cross, Cumber, Drone, Droore, Encumber, Encumbrance, Fa-la, Fardel, Folderol, Fraught, Freight, Gist, Handicap, Hum, Lade, ➤ LOAD, Lumber, Millstone, Monkey, Oercome, Onus, Oppress, Put-upon, Refrain, Rumbelow, Saddle, Servitude, Shanty, Substance, Tax, Tenor, Torch, Trouble, Weight, Woe, Yoke

Burdensome Irksome, Onerous, Oppressive, Weighty

Bureau Agency, Agitprop, Cominform, Davenport, Desk, Interpol, Kominform, Marriage, ➤ OFFICE

Bureaucracy, Bureaucrat(ic) CS, Impersonal, Jack-in-office, Mandarin, Red tape, Tapist, Wallah

Burgeon(ing) Asprout, Bud, Grow, Sprout

Burglar, Burgle Area-sneak, Cat, Crack(sman), Intruder, Peterman, Picklock, Raffles, Robber, Screw, Thief, Yegg

Burial, Burial place Catacomb, Charnel, Committal, Crypt, Darga, Funeral, Golgotha, Grave, Interment, Kurgan, Lair, Last rites, Sepulture, Tomb, Vault, Zoothapsis

Burlesque Caricatura, Caricature, Comedy, Farce, Heroicomical, Hudibrastic(s), Hurlo-thrumbo, Lampoon, Macaronic, Parody, Satire, Skimmington, Skit, Spoof, Travesty

Burmese Karen(ni), Naga, Shan

Burn(er), Burning, Burnt Adust, Afire, Alow(e), Ardent, Argand, Arson, Ash, Auto-da-fé, Bats-wing, Beck, Bishop, Blaze, Blister, Brand, Brent, Brook, Bunsen, Caustic, Cauterise, Char, Chark, Chinese, Cinder, Coal, Coke, Combust, Conflagration, Cremate, Cruciai, Destruct, Eilding, Ember, Emboil, Fervid, ➤ FIRE, Fishtail, Flagrant, Flare, Flash, Fresh(et), Gleed, Gut, Holocaust, Ignite, In, Incendiary, Incinerate, Inure, Inust(ion), Kill, Live, Lunt, Offering, On, Rill, Sati, Scald, Scorch, Scouther, Scowder, Scowther, Sear, Sienna, Singe, Smart, Smoulder, Suttee, Swale, Thurible, Torch, Umber, Urent, Ustion, Wick

Burrow(er), Burrowing Dig, Earth, Fossorial, Gopher, Groundhog, Hole, How, Howk, Mole, Nuzzle, Sett, Tunnel, Viscacha, Warren, Wombat, Worm

Bursar(y) Camerlengo, Camerlingo, Coffers, Grant, Purser, Scholarship, Treasurer

Burst(ing) Blowout, Brast, Break, Dehisce, Disrupt, Dissilient, Ebullient, Erumpent, Erupt, ➤ EXPLODE, Fly, Implode, Pop, Sforzato, Shatter, Spasm, Spirt, Split, Sprint, Spurt, Stave, Tetterous

Bury Cover, Eard, Earth, Embowel, Engrave, Enhearse, Graff, Graft, Imbed, Inhearse, Inhume, Inter, Inurn, Landfill, Repress, Sepulture, Sink, Ye(a)rd, Yird

Bus Aero, Bandwagon, Car, Charabanc, Coach, Double-decker, Hondey, Hopper, ISA, Jitney, Mammy-wagon, Rattletrap, Single-decker, Tramcar, Trolley

Bush(y) Bramble, Brier, Bullace, Busket, Clump, Dumose, Firethorn, Hawthorn, Hibiscus, Kapok, Mallee, Matagouri, Mulberry, Outback, Poinsettia, Poly-poly, Sallee, Shepherd, Shrub, Thicket, Tire, Tod(de)

Bushel Co(o)mb, Homer, Peck, Weight, Wey

Business Affair, Agency, Biz, Bus, Cartel, Cerne, Co, Commerce, Company, Concern, Conglomerate, Craft, Duty, Enterprise, Ergon, Establishment, Exchange, Fasti, Firm, Funny,

Game, Gear, Hong, Industry, Line, Métier, Monkey, Office, Palaver, Pi(d)geon, Pidgin, Practice, Professional, Shebang, Shop, To-do, Trade, Traffic, Transaction, Tread, Turnover, Vocation, Zaikai

Businessman Babbitt, City, Realtor, Taipan, Trader, Tycoon

Busk(er) Bodice, Corset, Entertainer, German-band

Bust Beano, Brast, Boob, Break, Chest, Falsies, Herm(a), Sculp, Shatter(ed), Spree, Statue, Term(inus), To-tear, To-torne, Ups(e)y

▷**Bust** may indicate an anagram

Bustle Ado, Do, Flap, Pad, Scurry, ➤ STIR, Swarm, Tournure, Whew

Busy Active, At (it), ➤ DETECTIVE, Deedy, Detective, Dick, Eident, Employ, Ergate, Eye, Goer, Hectic, Hive, Humming, Occupied, Ornate, Prodnose, Stir, Tec, Throng, Worksome

Busybody Bustler, Meddler, Snooper, Trout, Yenta

But Aber, Bar, Except, However, Merely, Nay, Only, Save, Sed, Simply, Tun

Butcher(y) Cumberland, Decko, Dekko, Flesher, Kill, Killcow, Look, Massacre, Ovicide, Sever, Shambles, Shochet, Shufti, Slaughter, Slay

Butler Bedivere, Bread-chipper, Jeeves, RAB, Rhett, Samuel, Servant, Sewer, Sommelier, Steward

Butt (in) Aris, Barrel, Bunt, Clara, Enter, Geck, Glasgow kiss, Goat, Header, Horn, Jesting-stock, Laughing-stock, Mark, Outspeckle, Pantaloon, Pipe, Push, Ram, Roach, Scapegoat, Snipe, ➤ STOOGE, Straight man, Stump, Target, Tun, Ups

Butter Adulation, Billy, Brandy, Butyric, Cocoa, Coconut, Drawn, Flatter, Galam, Garcinia, Ghee, Ghi, Goat, Illipi, Illupi, Kokum, Mahua, Mahwa, Mow(r)a, Nutter, Pat, Peanut, Print, Ram, Scrape, Shea, Spread

▷**Butter** may indicate a goat or such

Buttercup Crow-foot, Crow-toe, Goldilocks, Ranunculus, Reate, Thalictrum

Butterfly Dilettante, Eclosion, Imaginal, Nerves

Buttock(s) Arse, Ass, Bahookie, Bottom, Coit, Derrière, Doup, Duff, Fundament, Gluteus maximus, Hinderlan(d)s, Hurdies, Jacksie, Jacksy, Keester, Keister, Nates, Prat, Quoit, Seat

Button(s) Barrel, Bellboy, Fastener, Frog, Hot, Knob, Netsuke, Olivet, Page(boy), Panic, Snooze, Stud, Switch, Toggle

Buttonhole Accost, Detain, Eye, Flower

Buttress Brace, Counterfort, Pier, Prop, Stay, Support

Buy(er), Buying Believe, Bribe, Coff, Corner, Customer, Emption, Engross, Monopsonist, Purchase, Shop, Shout, Spend, Take, Trade, Vendee

▷**Buyer** may indicate money

Buzz(er) Bee, Bombilate, Bombinate, Button, Fly, Hum, Rumour, Scram, Whirr, Whisper, Zed, Zing, Zoom

Buzzard Bee-kite, Bird, Buteo, Hawk, Pern, Puttock, Vulture

By Alongside, At, Gin, Gone, In, Near, Neighbouring, Nigh, Of, Past, Per, Through, With, X

Bye-bye Adieu, Farewell, Tata

Bygone Dead, Departed, Past, Yore

Bypass Avoid, Circuit, Coronary, ➤ DETOUR, Evade, Ignore, Omit, Shunt, Skirt

By-product Epiphenomenon, Spin-off

Byre Cowshed, Manger, Stable, Trough

By the way Incidentally, Obiter

Byway Alley, Lane, Path

Byword Ayword, Phrase, Proverb, Slogan

Cc

C Around, Caught, Celsius, Cent, Centigrade, Charlie, Conservative, San

Cab Boneshaker, Crawler, Drosky, Fiacre, Growler, Hackney, Hansom, Mini, Noddy, Taxi, Vettura

Cabbage(-head), Cabbage soup Book choy, Borecole, Brassica, Castock, Cauliflower, Chinese, Choucroute, Cole, Collard, Crout, Kohlrabi, Kraut, Loaf, Loave, Pak-choi, Pamphrey, Sauerkraut, Savoy, Thieve, Turnip, Wort

Cabin Berth, Bibby, Bothy, Box, Cabana, Caboose, Camboose, Coach, Cottage, Crannog, Crib, Cuddy, Den, Gondola, Hovel,

Hut, Izba, Lodge, Log, Long-house, Room, Roundhouse, Saloon, Shanty, Stateroom

Cabinet Bahut, Cabale, Case, Closet, Commode, Console, Cupboard, Kitchen, Ministry, Secretaire, Shadow, Shrinal, Vitrine

Cable(way) Coax(ial), Extension, Flex, Halser, Hawser, Jump leads, Junk, Landline, Lead, Lead-in, Lifeline, Outhaul, Rope, Slatch, Téléférique, ➤ TELEGRAM, Telpher(age), Wire

Cackle Cluck, Gaggle, Gas, Haw, Snicker, Titter

Cactus, Cactus-like Alhagi, Barel, Cereus, Cholla, Christmas, Dildo, Easter, Echino-, Hedgehog, Jojoba, Maguey, Mescal, Nopal, Ocotillo, Opuntia, Organ-pipe, Peyote, Prickly pear, Retama, Saguaro, Star, Torch-thistle, Tuna, Xerophytic

Cad Base, Boor, Bounder, Churl, Cocoa, Heel, Oik, Rascal, Rotter, Skunk

Cadaver(ous) Body, Corpse, Ghastly, Haggard, Stiff

Cadence Beat, Close, Fa-do, Flow, Lilt, Meter, Plagal, Rhythm

Cadet(s) Junior, OTC, Scion, Syen, Trainee

Cafe(teria) Automat, Brasserie, Bistro, Buvette, Canteen, Commissary, Diner, Dinette, Donko, Estaminet, Filtré, Greasy spoon, Juke joint, Pizzeria, Pull-in, Tearoom, Transport

Cage Bar, Battery, Box, Cavie, Confine, Coop, Corf, Dray, Drey, Enmew, Faraday, Fold, Frame, Grate, Hutch, Mew, Pen, ➤ PRISON, Trave

Cake Clot, Filter, ➤ HARDEN, Mud, Pat, Patty, ➤ PLASTER, Wad

▷ **Cake** may indicate an anagram

Calculate(d), Calculation, Calculator Abacus, Actuary, Compute(r), Cost, Design, Estimate, Extrapolate, Log, Prorate, Quip(p)u, Rate, ➤ RECKON, Slide-rule, Sofar, Soroban, Tactical, Tell

Calendar Advent, Agenda, Almanac, Chinese, Diary, Fasti, Gregorian, Intercalary, Jewish, Journal, Julian, Luach, Menology, Newgate, New Style, Ordo, Perpetual, Revolutionary, Roman, Sothic

Calf Ass, Bobby, Box, Cf, Deacon, Dogie, Dogy, Freemartin, Golden, Leg, Poddy, Stirk, Sural, Tollie, Tolly, Veal, Vitular

Call(ed), Calling, Call on, Call up Adhan, Appeal, Arraign, Art, Awaken, Azan, Banco, Bawl, Beck, Behote, Bevy, Bid, Business, Buzz, Career, Chamade, Cite, Claim, Clang, Clarion,

Cleep, Clepe, Close, Cold, Conference, Conscript, Convene, Convoke, Cooee, Cry, Curtain, Dial, Drift, Dub, Evoke, Gam, Go, Hallali, Haro, Heads, Hech, Hete, Hey, Hight, Ho, Hot(e), Howzat, Huddup, Hurra(h), Job, Junk, Last (post), Line, Local, Métier, Misère, Mobilise, Mot, Name, Nap, Need, Nempt, Nominate, Olé, Page, Phone, Photo, Post, Proo, Pruh, Pursuit, Rechate, Recheat, Retreat, Reveille, Ring, Roll, Rort, Route, SOS, Sa-sa, Sennet, ➤ SHOUT, Shut-out, Slam, Slander, Slogan, Soho, Sola, STD, Style, Subpoena, Summon(s), Tails, Tantivy, Taps, Telephone, Term, Toho, Toll, Trumpet, Trunk, Visit, Vocation, Wake-up, Waken, Whoa-ho-ho, Wo ha ho, Yell, Yo, Yodel, Yodle, Yo-ho(-ho), Yoicks, Yoo-hoo

Caller Fresh, Guest, Herring, Inspector, Muezzin, Rep, Traveller, ➤ VISITOR

Calm Abate, Allay, Allege, Appease, Ataraxy, Composed, Cool, Doldrums, Easy, Equable, Equanimity, Even, Eye, Flat, Glassy, Halcyon, Loun(d), Lown(d), Lull, Mellow, Mild, Milden, Millpond, Nonchalant, Pacify, Peaceful, Philosophical, Phlegmatic, Placate, Placid, Quell, Quiet, Relax(ed), Repose, Seraphic, Serene, Settle, Sleek, ➤ SOOTHE, Still, Stilly, Subside, Tranquil(lise), Windless

Camel, Camel train Arabian, Artiodactyla, Bactrian, Caisson, Colt, Dromedary, Kafila, Llama, Oont, Sopwith, Tulu

Camera Box, Brownie®, Camcorder, Candid, Chambers, Cine, Compact, Disc, Flash, Gamma, Iconoscope, Kodak®, Obscura, Orthicon, Palmcorder, Panoramic, Pantoscope, Pinhole, Polaroid®, Reflex, Schmidt, SLR, Somascope, Speed, Steadican®, Video

Camouflage Conceal, ➤ DISGUISE, Mark, Maskirovka, War-dress

▷**Camouflaged** may indicate an anagram

Camp(er) Affectation, Aldershot, Banal, Belsen, Bivouac, Boma, Boot, Caerleon, Castral, Colditz, Concentration, David, Depot, D(o)uar, Dumdum, Faction, Flaunt, Gulag, Holiday, L(a)ager, Lashkar, Leaguer, Manyat(t)a, Oflag, Outlie, Peace, Side, Stagey, Stalag, Stative, Swagman, Tent, Theatrical, Transit, Work, Zare(e)ba, Zariba, Zereba, Ziriba

Campaign(er) Barnstorm, Battle, Blitz, Blitzkreig, Canvass, Crusade, Drive, Field, Jihad, Lobby, Mission, Promotion, Run,

Satyagraha, Smear, Stint, Strategist, Venture, Veteran, War, Warray, Warrey, Whistle-stop

Can(s) Able, Billy, Bog, Capable, Churn, Cooler, Dow, Gaol, Gents, Headphones, Is able, Jug, Karsy, Loo, May, Nick, Pail, Pot, Preserve, ➤ PRISON, Privy, Stir, Tin

Canada, Canadian Abenaki, Acadian, Canuck, Dene, Herring choker, Inuit, Johnny Canuck, Quebeccer, Quebecker, Québecois

Canal Alimentary, Ampul, Birth, Caledonian, Channel, Conduit, Corinth, Duct, Duodenum, Ea, Erie, Foss(e), Gota, Grand (Trunk), Grand Union, Groove, Gut, Haversian, Kiel, Klong, Lode, Meatus, Midi, Navigation, Panama, Pipe, Pound, Resin, Root, Scala, Schlemm's, Semi-circular, Ship, Soo, Spinal, Suez, Urethra, Waterway, Welland, Zanja

Canal-boat Barge, Fly-boat, Gondola, Vaporetto

Canary Bird, Grass, Roller, Serin, Singer, Yellow

Cancel Abrogate, Adeem, Annul, Counteract, Countermand, Cross, Delete, Destroy, Erase, Kill, Negate, Nullify, Obliterate, Override, Remit, Repeal, Rescind, Retrait, Revoke, Scrub, Undo, Unmake, Void, Wipe

Cancer(ous) Big C, Carcinoma, Crab, Curse, Kaposi's Sarcoma, Leukaemia, Oat-cell, Tropic, Tumour, Wolf

Candid, Candour Albedo, Blunt, Camera, Franchise, Frank, Honesty, Open, Round, Upfront

Candidate(s) Applicant, Aspirant, Contestant, Entrant, Field, Nominee, Ordinand, Postulant, Testee

Candied, Candy Caramel, Eryngo, Glace, Snow, Succade, Sweet

Candle(stick), Candelabra Amandine, Bougie, C(i)erge, Dip, Fetch, Girandole, Hanukiah, Jesse, Lampadary, Light, Menorah, Padella, Paschal, Pricket, Roman, Rushlight, Sconce, Serge, Shammas, Shammes, Slut, Sperm, Tace, Tallow, Tallow-dip, Taper, Torchère, Tricerion, Wax

Cane Arrow, Baculine, Bamboo, Baste, Beat, Birk, Dari, Dhurra, Doura, Dur(r)a, Ferula, Ferule, Goor, Gur, Jambee, Malacca, Narthex, Penang-lawyer, Pointer, Rat(t)an, Rod, Stick, Sugar, Swagger-stick, Swish, Switch, Swordstick, Tan, Tickler, Vare, Wand, Whangee, Wicker(-work)

Canine Biter, C, Dog, Eye-tooth

Cannibal Anthropophagus, Heathen, Long pig, Ogre, Thyestean

Cannon Amusette, Barrage, Basilisk, Bombard, Breechloader, Carom, Carronade, Chaser, Collide, Criterion, Culverin, Drake, Falcon, Gun, Howitzer, Kiss, Long-tom, Monkey, Nursery, Saker, Stern-chaser, Water, Zamboorak, Zomboruk, Zumbooru(c)k

Canny Careful, Frugal, Prudent, Scot, Shrewd, Slee, Sly, Thrifty, Wice, Wily, Wise

Canoe(ist) Bidarka, Bidarkee, Canader, Dugout, Faltboat, Kayak, Monoxylon, Montaria, Oomiack, Paddler, Piragua, Pirogue, Rob Roy, Woodskin

Canon Austin, Brocard, Camera, Chapter, Chasuble, Code, Crab, Isodorian, ➤ LAW, Line, Mathurin(e), Nocturn, Nursery, Pitaka, Polyphony, Prebendary, Premonstratensian, Rota, Round, Rule, Square, Squier, Standard, Tenet, Unity

Canopy Awning, Baldachin, Baldaquin, Chuppah, Ciborium, Dais, He(a)rse, Huppah, Majesty, Marquee, Marquise, Pavilion, Shamiana(h), State, Tabernacle, Tent, Tester

Canvas Awning, Burlap, Dra(b)bler, Lug-sail, Mainsail, Marquee, Oil-cloth, Paint, Raven's-duck, Reef, ➤ SAIL, Staysail, Stunsail, Tent, Trysail, Wigan

Canvass(er) Agent, Doorstep, Drum, Poll, Solicit

▷ **Canvasser** may indicate a painter or a camper

Canyon Box, Canada, Defile, Grand, Nal(l)a, Nallah

Cap(ped) Amorce, Balaclava, Balmoral, Barret, Baseball, Bathing, Bellhop, Bendigo, Ber(r)et, Biggin, Biretta, Blue, Bonnet-rouge, Call, Calotte, Capeline, Caul, Chaco, Chapeau, Chaperon, Chapka, Chechia, Cheese-cutter, Cloth, Cockernony, Coif, Cope, Cornet, Cowl, Cradle, ➤ CROWN, Czapka, Davy Crockett, Deerstalker, Dunce's, Dutch, Fatigue, Ferrule, Flat, Forage, Gandhi, Garrison, Glengarry, Grannie, Granny, Havelock, ➤ HAT, Iceberg, International, Jockey, Juliet, Kalpak, Kepi, Kilmarnock, Kippa, Kippoth, Kipput, Kiss-me(-quick), Knee, Liberty, Lid, Mob, Monmouth, Monteer, Montero, Mor(r)ion, Mortar-board, Mutch, Newsboy, Outdo, Pagri, Patellar, Percussion, Perplex, Phrygian, Pileus, Pinner, Polar, Puggaree, Quoif, Schapska, Shako, Skullcap, Square, Stocking, Summit, ➤ SURPASS, Taj, Tam(-o'-shanter), Thinking, Toe, Toorie, Top, Toque, Toy, Trenchard, Trencher, Tuque, Turk's, Yarmulka, Yarmulke, Zuchetto

Capable, Capability Able, Brown, Capacity, Competent, Deft, Effectual, Efficient, Firepower, Qualified, Skilled, Susceptible, Up to

Capacitance, Capacity Ability, Aptitude, C, Cab, Competence, Content, Cor, Cubic, Endowment, Function, Limit, Log, Power, Qua, Receipt, Scope, Size, Tonnage, Valence, Vital, Volume

Cape Cloak, Faldetta, Fanion, Fanon, Fichu, Head(land), Mant(e)let, Mantilla, Mantle, Mo(z)zetta, Muleta, Ness, Peninsula, Point, Poncho, Ruana, Talma, Tippet, Waterproof

Capitals A1, Assets, Block, Boodle, Bravo, Cap, Chapiter, Chaptrel, Doric, Euge, Excellent, Float, Floating, Fonds, Great, Helix, Initial, Ionic, Lethal, Lulu, Metropolis, Principal, Rustic, Seat, Splendid, Sport, Stock, Super, Topping, UC, Upper case, Working

▷**Capitalist** may indicate one living in a capital

▷**Capless** may indicate first letter missing

▷**Capriccioso** may indicate an anagram

Caprice, Capricious Arbitrary, Boutade, Capernoitie, Conceit, Desultory, Erratic, Fancy, Fitful, Freak, Humoresk, Humoresque, Irony, Mood, Perverse, Quirk, Vagary, Wayward, Whim(sy)

Capsize Overbalance, Purl, Tip, Turn turtle, Upset, Whemmle, Whomble

▷**Capsized** may indicate a word upside down

Capsule Amp(o)ule, Bowman's, Cachet, Habitat, Ootheca, Orbiter, Ovisac, Pill, Spacecraft, Spermatophore, Time, Urn

Captain Ahab, Bligh, Bobadil, Bones, Brassbound, Capt, Chief, Cid, Commander, Condottiere, Cook, Copper, Cuttle, Flint, Group, Hornblower, Kettle, Kidd, Leader, Macheath, Master, Nemo, Old man, Owner, Patroon, Post, Privateer, Protospatharius, Skip(per), Standish, Subah(dar), Subedar, Swing, Trierarch

Caption Heading, Headline, Inscription, Masthead, Sub-title, Title

Captivate(d), Captivating Beguile, Bewitch, Charm, Enamour, Enthrall, Epris(e), Take, Winsome

Captive, Captivity Bonds, Duress, POW, Prisoner, Slave

Capture Abduct, Annex, Bag, Catch, Collar, Cop, Grab, Land, Net, Prize, Rush, Seize, Snabble, Snaffle, Snare, ➤ TAKE

Car Astra, Audi, Auto, Banger, Beetle, Biza, BL, Bomb, Brake, Bubble, Buffet, Bugatti, Buick, Bumper, Bus, Cab(riolet), Cadillac, Catafalco, Catafalque, Chariot, Coach, Company, Convertible, Cortina, Coupé, Crate, Daimler, Diner, Dodgem®, Drag(ster), Drophead, Elf, Estate, Fastback, Fiat, Flivver, Ford, Formula, Freight, Gondola, GT, Hardtop, Hatchback, Heap, Hearse, Hillman, Hot-rod, Jalop(p)y, Jamjar, Jammy, Jaunting, Kart, Lada, Lagonda, Lancia, Landaulet, Landrover, Limo, Limousine, Merc(edes), MG, Mini, Morris, Nacelle, Notchback, Observation, Opel, Panda, Patrol, Prowl, Racer, Ragtop, Rattletrap, Restaurant, Roadster, Roller, Rolls, RR, Runabout, Rust bucket, Sedan, Skoda, Sleeper, Sports, Squad, Station wagon, Stock, Stretch-limo, Subcompact, Sunbeam, Tank, Telepherique, Telpher, Three-wheeler, Tin Lizzie, Tonneau, Tourer, Tram, Trolley, Turbo, Two-seater, Vehicle, Veteran, Vintage, VW, Wheeler, Wheels

Caravan Caf(f)ila, Convoy, Fleet, Kafila, Safari, Trailer

Carbohydrate Agarose, Carrageenan, Cellulose, Chitin, Dextran, Disaccharide, Glycogen, Heptose, Hexose, Inulin, Ketose, Laminarin, Mannan, Pectin, Pentosan(e), Pentose, Saccharide, Sorbitol, Starch, Sucrose, Sugar

Carcase, Carcass Body, Cadaver, Carrion, Corpse, Cutter, Krang, Kreng, Morkin, Mor(t)ling

Card(s), Cardboard Ace, Affinity, Amex®, Baccarat, Basto, Bill, Birthday, Bower, Business, Calling, Canasta, Cartes, Cash, Caution, Charge, Chicane, Club, Comb, Compass, Court(esy), Credit, Cue, Dance, Debit, Deck, Deuce, Diamond, Donor, Ecarté, Eccentric, Euchre, Expansion, Flaught, Flush, ➤ GAME, Green, Hand, Heart, Honour, Identity, Jack, Jambone, Joker, Kanban, Key, King, Loo, Loyalty, Manille, Matador, Meishi, Mise, Mistigris, Mogul, Mournival, Oddity, Ombre, Pack, Pasteboard, PC, Picture, Placard, Plastic, Playing, Proximity, Quatorze, Queen, Quiz, Red, Rippler, Rove, Scribble, Singleton, Smart, Soda, Solo, Sound, Spade, Spadille, Squeezer, Store, Strawboard, Swab, Swipe, Swish, Switch, Swob, Swot, Talon, Tarok, Tarot, Tease(r), Tenace, Test, Thaumatrope, Ticket, Tose, Toze, Trading, Trey, Trump, Valentine, Visiting, Wag, Weirdie, Wild, Yellow, Zener

Cardigan Jacket, Wam(m)us, Wampus, Woolly

Cardinal Camerlingo, Chief, College, Eight, Eminence, Eminent, Grosbeak, Hat, HE, Hume, Legate, Manning, Mazarin, Newman, Number, Pivotal, Polar, Prelate, Radical, Red, Red-hat, Richelieu, Sacred college, Sin, Spellman, Virtue, Vital, Ximenes

Care(r), Caring Attention, Burden, Cark, Caution, Cerne, Cherish, ➤ CONCERN, Cosset, Grief, Heed, Intensive, Kaugh, Keep, Kiaugh, Maternal, Mind, Pains, Palliative, Parabolanus, Reck(e), Reke, Respite, Retch, Solicitude, ➤ TEND, Tenty, Worry

Career Course, Hurtle, Life, Line, Run, Rush, Speed, Start, Tear, Vocation

▷ **Career** may indicate an anagram

Careful(ly) Canny, Chary, Discreet, Gentle, Hooly, Meticulous, Mindful, Pernickety, Provident, Prudent, Scrimp, Studious, Tentie, Tenty, Thorough, Vigilant, Ware, Wary

Careless(ly) Casual, Cheery, Debonair, Easy, Free-minded, Gallio, Improvident, Imprudent, Inadvertent, Insouciance, Lax, Lighthearted, Négligé, ➤ NEGLIGENT, Nonchalant, Oversight, Raffish, Rash, Remiss, Resigned, Riley, Slam-bang, Slapdash, Slaphappy, Slipshod, Sloven(ly), Slubber, Taupie, Tawpie, Unguarded, Unmindful, Untenty, Unwary

▷ **Carelessly** may indicate an anagram

Caress Bill, Coy, Embrace, Fondle, Kiss, Lallygag, Lollygag, Noursle, Nursle, Pet, Touch

Caretaker Concierge, Curator, Custodian, Guardian, Janitor, Nightwatchman, Sexton, Shammash, Shammes, Superintendent, Verger, Warden

Careworn Haggard, Lined, Tired, Weary

Cargo Bulk, Burden, Fraught, Freight, Lading, Last, ➤ LOAD, Payload, Shipment

Caribbean Belonger, Puerto Rican, Soca, Sokah, Taino, WI

Caricature, Caricaturist Ape, Beerbohm, Burlesque, Caron d'Ache, Cartoon, Cruikshank, Doyle, Farce, Gillray, Rowlandson, Skit, Spy, Travesty

Carnation Dianthus, Malmaison, Picotee, Pink

Carnival Fair, Festival, Fete, Moomba, Revelry

Carol Noel, Sing, Song, Wassail, Yodel

Carousal, Carouse Bend, Birl(e), Bouse, Bride-ale, Compotation, Drink, Mallemaroking, Mollie, Orge, Orgy, ➤ REVEL, Roist, Screed, Spree, Upsee, Upsey, Upsy, Wassail

Carp(er) Beef, Censure, Complain, Crab, Critic, Crucian, Crusian, Gibel, Goldfish, Id(e), Kvetch, Mirror, Mome, Nag, Nibble, Roach, Roundfish, Scold, Twitch, Yerk, Yirk

Carpenter Cabinet-maker, Carfindo, Chips, Fitter, Joiner, Joseph, Menuisier, Quince, Tenoner, Wright

▷ **Carpenter** may indicate an anagram

Carpet Aubusson, Axminster, Beetle, Berate, Bessarabian, Broadloom, Brussels, Castigate, Chide, Drugget, Durrie, Kali, Kelim, Khilim, Kidderminster, Kilim, Kirman, Lecture, Lino, Mat, Moquette, Persian, Rate, Red, Reprimand, Reproach, Rug, Runner, Shagpile, Shark, Turkey, Wall-to-wall, Wig, Wilton

Carriage Air, Bandy, Barouche, Bearing, Berlin(e), Bier, Brake, Brit(sch)ka, Britska, Britzka, Brougham, Buckboard, Buggy, Cab, Calash, Calèche, Car, Cariole, Caroche, Carriole, Carryall, Cartage, Chaise, Charet, Chariot, Chassis, Chay, Clarence, Coach, Coch, Conveyance, Coupé, Curricle, Demeanour, Dennet, Deportment, Désobligeante, Diner, Dos-a-dos, Do-si-do, Drag, Dros(h)ky, Ekka, Equipage, Fiacre, Fly, Four-in-hand, Gait, Gig, Gladstone, Go-cart, Growler, Haulage, Herdic, Horseless, Hurly-hacket, Landau(let), Limber, Non-smoker, Norimon, Phaeton, Pick-a-back, Pochaise, Pochay, Poise, Port(age), Portance, Postchaise, Posture, Poyse, Pram, Pullman, Railcar, Randem, Ratha, Remise, Rickshaw, Rockaway, Shay, Sled, Sleeper, Smoker, Sociable, Spider, Stanhope, Sulky, Surrey, Tarantas(s), Taxi, Tender, Tenue, Tilbury, Tim-whiskey, Tonga, Trail, Trap, Vetture, Victoria, Voiture, Wagonette, Waterage, Whirligig, Whisk(e)y

Carrier Airline, Arm, Baldric, Barkis, Barrow, Bomb-ketch, Caddy, Cadge, Camel, Coaster, Conveyor, Fomes, Fomites, Frog, Grid, Hamper, Haversack, Hod, Janker, Jill, Nosebag, Noyade, Packhorse, Pigeon, Porter, Rucksack, Satchel, Schistosoma, Semantide, Sling, Stretcher, ➤ TRAY, Vector

Carrion Cadaver, Carcase, Carcass, Flesh, Ket, Stapelia

Carry(ing) Bear, Chair, Convey, Enlevé, Ferry, Frogmarch, Hawk, Hent, Hump, Land, Pack, Pickaback, Port, Stock, Sustain, Tote, ➤ TRANSPORT, Trant, Wage, With, Yank

Cart Bandy, Barrow, Bogey, Buck, Car(r)iole, Chapel, Dog, Dolly, Dray, Furphy, Gambo, Gill, Governess, Gurney, Hackery, Jag, Jill, Lead, Mail, Rickshaw, Shandry, T, Telega, Trolley, Tumbrel, Tumbril, Wag(g)on, Wain, Whitechapel

Cartel Duopoly, Ring, Syndicate

Carton Box, Case, Crate, Sydney, Tub

Cartoon(ist) Animated, Caricature, Comic, Disney, Drawn, Emmet, Garland, Leech, Low, Manga, Mel, Partridge, Popeye, Short, Spy, Strip, Tenniel, Tintin, Trog

Cartridge Blank, Bullet, Cartouche, Doppie, Shell

Carve(d), Carver, Carving Bas relief, Cameo, Chisel, Cilery, Crocket, Cut, Dismember, Doone, Enchase, Engrave, Entail, Entayle, Fiddlehead, Gibbons, Glyptic, Hew, Incise, Inscribe, Insculp, Intaglio, Netsuke, Nick, Petroglyph, Scrimshaw, Sculp(t), Slice, Tondo, Truncheon, Whittle

Cascade Cataract, Fall, Lin(n), Stream, Waterfall

Case(s), Casing Ablative, Accusative, Action, Allative, Altered, Appeal, Aril, Ascus, Assumpsit, Attaché, Basket, Beer, Bere, Blimp, Box, Brief, Bundwall, Burse, C, Ca, Cabinet, Calyx, Canister, Canterbury, Capsule, Cartouch(e), Cartridge, Cellaret, Chase, Chitin, Chrysalis, Cocoon, Compact, Crate, Croustade, Crust, Dative, Declension, Detinue, Dispatch, Dossier, Elytron, Etui, Etwee, Example, Flan, Flapjack, Frame, Genitive, Grip, Hanaper, Hard, Hold-all, Housewife, Hull, Humidor, Husk, ➤ IN CASE, Instance, Keister, Locative, Locket, Lorica, Manche, Matter, Nacelle, Nominative, Non-suit, Nutshell, Objective, Ochrea, Ocrea, Papeterie, Patient, Phylactery, Plight, Plummer-block, Pod, Port, Possessive, Prima facie, Quiver, Recce, Reconnoitre, Sabretache, Scabbard, Sheath(e), Situation, Six-pack, Sporran, Stead, Subjunctive, Suit, Tantalus, Tea-chest, Test, Theca, Tichborne, Trunk, Valise, Vasculum, Vocative, Volva, Walise, Wallet, Wardian

Cash Blunt, Bonus, Bounty, Change, Coin, Dosh, Dot, Float, Imprest, Lolly, ➤ MONEY, Needful, Ochre, Pence, Petty, Ready, Realise, Rhino, Spondulicks, Stumpy, Tender, Tin, Wampum, Wherewithal

Cashier Annul, Break, Depose, Disbar, Dismiss, Teller, Treasurer

Cask(et) Armet, Barrel, Barrico, Bas(i)net, Box, Breaker, Butt, Cade, Casque, Cassette, Drum, Firkin, Galeate, Harness, Heaume, Hogshead, Keg, Leaguer, Octave, Pin, Pipe,

Puncheon, Pyxis, Run(d)let, Salade, Sallet, Sarcophagus, Shrine, Solera, Tierce, Tun

Casserole Diable, Osso bucco, Pot, Salmi, Terrine, Tzimmes

Cassette Cartridge, Tape, Video

Cast (down, off, out), Casting Abattu, Actors, Add, Appearance, Bung, Die, Discard, Ecdysis, Eject, Exorcise, Exuvial, Exuviae, Fling, Found, Fusil, Heave, Hob, Hue, Hurl, Impression, Ingo(w)es, Keb, Look, Lose, Mew, Molt, Moulage, Mould, Plaster(stone), Players, Put, Reject, Shed, Shoot, Sling, Slive, Slough, Spoil, Stookie, Tailstock, ➤ THROW, Toss, Tot, Warp, Wax, Ytost

▷**Cast** may indicate an anagram or a piece of a word missing

Castaway Adrift, Crusoe, Gunn, Left, Outcast, Selkirk, Stranded

▷**Cast by** may indicate surrounded by

Castle(d) Adamant, Bouncy, Broch, C, Casbah, Chateau, Citadel, Fastness, Fort, Kasba(h), Mot(t)e, Perilous, Rook, Stronghold, Villa

Casual Accidental, Adventitious, Airy, Blasé, Chance, Flippant, Grass, Haphazard, Idle, Incidental, Informal, Jaunty, Lackadaisical, Odd(ment), Offhand, Orra, Passing, Promiscuous, Random, Sporadic, Stray, Temp, Throwaway

Cat Abyssinian, Alley, Angora, Asparagus, Balinese, Baudrons, Bluepoint, Bobcat, Burmese, Cacomistle, Cacomixl, Caracal, Cheetah, Cheshire, Civet, Clowder, Colourpoint, Cop, Cougar, Dandy, Eyra, Fat, Felid, Feline, Felix, Foss(a), Foumart, Foussa, Genet(te), Gib, Gossip, Grimalkin, Gus, Himalayan, Hipster, Hodge, Jazzer, Kilkenny, Kit, Korat, Lair, Lash, Leopard, Linsang, Lion, Long-hair, Lynx, Maine coon, Malkin, Maltese, Manul, Manx, Margay, Marmalade, Mehitabel, Mewer, Mog, Mouser, Musang, Nandine, Neuter, Nib, Ocelot, Ounce, Painter, Panther, Pard, Pardal, Persian, Pharaoh, Polecat, Practical, Puma, Puss, Race, Rex, Ringtail, Rumpy, Russian blue, Scourge, Sealpoint, Serval, Shorthair, Siamese, Sick, Spew, Spue, Swinger, Tabby, Tibert, Tiger, Tigon, Tigress, Tobermory, Tom, Tortoise-shell, Tybalt, Weasel

Catalogue Dewey, Index, Inventory, List, Litany, Magalog, Messier, Ragman, Ragment, Raisonné, Record, Register, Table, Tabulate

Catalyst Accelerator, Agent, Influence, Unicase, Ziegler

Catapult Ballista, Ging, Launch, Mangon(el), Perrier, Petrary, Propel, Scorpion, Shanghai, Sling, Slingshot, Stone-bow, Tormentum, Trebuchet, Wye, Y

Catastrophe Calamity, ➤ DISASTER, Doom, Epitasis, Fiasco, Meltdown

Catch(y), Caught Air, Apprehend, Attract, Bag, Benet, Bone, C, Capture, Chape, Clasp, Cog, Collar, Contract, Cop, Corner, Ct, Deprehend, Detent, Dolly, Engage, Enmesh, Ensnare, Entoil, Entrap, Fang, Field, Fumble, Gaper, Get, Glee(some), Grasp, Had, Hank, Haud, Haul, Hear, Hold, Hook, Inmesh, Keddah, Keight, Kep(pit), Kheda, Kill, Land, Lapse, Lasso, Latch, Lime, Lock, Morse, Nab, Nail, Net, Nick, Nim, Nobble, Noose, Overhear, Overhent, Overtake, Parti, Pawl, Rap, Release, Rope, Round, Rub, Safety, Sean, Sear, See(n), Seize, ➤ SNAG, Snap, Snare, Snig, ➤ SONG, Surprise, Swindle, Tack, Take, Trammel, Trap, Trawl, Trick, Tripwire, Troll, Twig, Understand, Wrestle

Categorise, Category ➤ CLASS, Etic, Genus, Label, Order, Pigeonhole, Range, Taxon

Cater(er) Acatour, Cellarer, Feed, Manciple, ➤ PROVIDE, Serve, Steward, Supply, Victualler, Vivandière

Caterpillar Aweto, Boll worm, Cotton-worm, Cutworm, Eruciform, Geometer, Hop-dog, Hornworm, Inchworm, Larva, Looper, Osmeterium, Palmer, Tent, Webworm, Woolly-bear

Cathedral Basilica, Chartres, Chester, Cologne, Dome, Duomo, Ely, Lateran, Minster, Notre Dame, Rheims, Sens, St Paul's, Wells, Westminster, Winchester

Catholic Broad, Defenders, Doolan, Ecumenical, Fenian, General, Irvingism, Jebusite, Latin, Left-footer, Liberal, Marian, Ostiary, Papalist, Papaprelatist, Papist, Recusant, Redemptionist, Roman, Salesian, Spike, Taig, Te(a)gue, Teigne, Thomist, Tory, Tridentine, Universal, Ursuline, Wide

Cattle(pen) Beefalo, Buffalo, Carabao, Drove, Fee, Gaur, Gayal, Herd, Kine, Ky(e), Oxen, Rabble, Steer, Stock

Caucus Assembly, Cell, Gathering, Race

Caulk Fill, Pitch, Snooze

Causation, Cause(d), Causes Aetiology, Agent, Beget, Breed, Bring, Compel, Create, Crusade, Determinant, Due, Effect, Efficient, Factor, Flag-day, Formal, Gar(re), Generate, Ideal, Induce, Lead, Lost, Make, Material, Motive,

➤ OCCASION, Parent, Provoke, Reason, Root, Sake, Source, Teleology, Topic, Ultimate, Wreak

Caustic Acid, Acrimonious, Alkaline, Burning, Erodent, Escharotic, Moxa, Pungent, Sarcastic, Scathing, Seare, Tart, Vitriol, Waspish, Withering

Caution, Cautious (person) Achitophel, Admonish, Ahithophel, Alert, Amber, Awarn, Beware, Cagey, Care, Cave, Caveat, Chary, Circumspect, Credence, Cure, Deliberate, Defensive, Discretion, Fabian, Gingerly, Guard(ed), Heedful, Leery, Prudent, Rum, Skite, Tentative, Vigilant, Ware, ➤ WARN, Wary, Yellow card

Cave(rn), Caves, Cave-dwelling Acherusia, Altamira, Antar, Antre, Beware, Cellar, Collapse, Corycian, Den, Domdaniel, Erebus, Fingal's, Fore, Grot(to), Hollow, Jenolan, Lascaux, Look-out, Lupercal, Mammoth, Nix, Pot-hole, Proteus, Sepulchre, Spel(a)ean, Speleology, Spelunker, Speos, Tassili, Vault, Waitomo, Ware, Weem

Caveman Adullam, Aladdin, Fingal, Neanderthal, Primitive, Troglodyte, Troll

Caviare Beluga, Roe, Sevruga, Sturgeon

Cavity Acetabulum, Amygdale, Atrial, Camera, Celom, Chamber, Coelom(e), Concepticle, Concha, Countermark, Crater, Crypt, Dent, Druse, Enteron, Follicle, Foss, Gap, Geode, Glenoid, Hold, Hole, Lacuna, Locule, Orbita, Mediastinum, Orifice, Pocket, Sinus, Tear, Tympanum, Vacuole, Vein, Ventricle, Vesicle, Vitta, Vomica, Vug, Well

Cease(fire) Abate, Blin, Cut, Desist, Die, Disappear, Halt, Intermit, Lin, Lose, Pass, Refrain, Sessa, ➤ STOP, Truce

Cedar(wood) Arolla, Atlas, Deodar, Incense, Toon

Ceiling Absolute, Barrel, Coffered, Cove, Cupola, Dome, Glass, Lacunar, Laqueatia, Limit, Plafond, Roof, Soffit

Celebrate(d), Celebration, Celebrity Ale, Beanfeast, Besung, Bigwig, Binge, Carnival, Chant, Commemorate, Distinguished, Do, Emblazon, Encaenia, Epithalamion, Epithalamium, Fame, Feast, Fest, Festivity, Fete, Fiesta, Gala, Gaudeamus, Gaudy, Glorify, Grog-up, Harvest home, Hold, Holiday, Honour, Jamboree, Jollifications, Jollities, Jubilee, Keep, Laud, Legend, Lion, Loosing, Lowsening, Maffick, Mardi gras, Mawlid al-Nabi, Monstre sacre, Name, Noted, Nuptials, Observe, Occasion, Orgy, Panathenaea, Praise, Randan, Rejoice,

Renown, Repute, Revel, Roister, Saturnalia, Sing, Spree, Star, Storied, Sung, Triumph, Wassail, Wet

Celestial Chinese, Divine, Ethereal, Heavenly, Supernal, Uranic

Celibate, Celibacy Bachelor, Chaste, Paterin(e), Rappist, Rappite, Shakers, Single, Spinster

Cell(s), Cellular Arthrospore, Astrocyte, Athrocyte, Ascus, Basal, Basidium, Battery, Blasteme, Blastula, Bullpen, Button, Cadre, Cambium, Cathode, Censor, Chamber, Chapel, Chromosome, Clark, Coenocyte, Comb, Companion, Cone, Congenic, Corpuscle, Crypt, Cubicle, Cybrid, Cyte, Cytoid, Cytology, Daniell, Daughter, Death, Defensin, Dry, Dungeon, Ectomere, Ectoplasm, Electrolytic, Embryo-sac, Endoderm, Endosarc, Epiblast, Fibroblast, Fibroma, Flame, Fuel, Gad, Gamete, Gemmule, Gland, Goblet, Gonidium, Group, Guard, Haematoblast, Hair, Hapteron, Helper T, Histiocyte, Idioblast, Interneuron, Internode, Iridocyte, Killer, Laura, Leucoblast, Leukoblast, Linin, Lithite, Mast, Meristem, Microcyte, Microgamete, Microvillus, Monocyte, Morula, Motor neuron, Myeloblast, Myelocyte, Myoblast, Neoblast, Neurite, Neuroblast, Neuron, Neurone, Neutron, Neutrophil, Oocyte, Organelle, Osteoclast, Padded, Palisade, Parietal, Pec, Periplasm, Periplast, Peter, Photoelectric, Photoreceptor, Plasma, Plastid, Primary, ► PRISON, Proembryo, Protoplast, Receptor, Retinula, Secondary, Selenium, Sensor, Seredium, Sickle, Solar, Soma(tic), Somite, Spermatocyte, Spongioblast, Spore, Sporocyte, Sporule, Squamous, Standard, Stem, Stone, Storage, Suspensor, Swarm, Sweatbox, Symplast, Synergid, T, Tapetum, Thymocyte, Trabecula, Unipolar, Unit, Vesicle, Voltaic, Wet, X-body, Zeta, Zoosperm, Zoospore, Zygote

Cellar Basement, Coalhole, Storm, Vault, Vaut

Celt(ic) Breton, Brython, Druid, Gadhel, Gael, Goidel, Helvetii, Kelt, Taffy, Welsh

Cement Araldite®, Compo, Concrete, Fix, Flaunch, Glue, Grout, Lute, Maltha, Mastic, Mortar, Paste, Pointing, Portland, Putty, Rubber, ► STICK, Trass

Cemetery Aceldama, Arenarium, Arlington, Boneyard, Boot Hill, Campo santo, Catacomb, God's Acre, Golgotha, Graveyard, Musall, Necropolis, Père Lachaise, Saqqara, Urnfield

Censor(ious), Censure Accuse, Admonition, Animadvert, Appeach, Ban, Banner, Berate, Blame, Blue-pencil, Bowdler,

Braid, Cato, Comstockery, ➤ CONDEMN, Critical, Criticise, Damn, Dang, Decry, Dispraise, Edit, Excommunicate, Excoriate, Expurgate, Gag, Obloquy, Rap, Reprimand, Repress, Reproach, Reprobate, Reprove, Satirise, Slam, Slate, Suppress, Tax, Tirade, Traduce, Wig

Cent Bean, Coin, Ct, Penny, Red

Central, Centre Amid, Attendance, Axis, Bunt, Cardinal, Chakra, Civic, Core, Day, Dead, Detention, Deuteron, Deuton, Downtown, Epergne, Eye, Focus, Frontal, Garden, Health, Heart, Hotbed, Hothouse, Hub, Inmost, Internal, Kernel, Kingpin, Leisure, Lincoln, Main, Mecca, Medulla, Mid(st), Nave, Nucleus, Pompidou, Reception, Rehabilitation, Remand, Storm, Waist, Weather

▷ **Centre** may indicate middle letters

Century Age, C, Era, Magdeburg, Period, Ton

Ceramic(s) Arcanist, China, Earthen, Ferrite, Porcelain, Pottery, Sialon, Tiles

Cereal Amelcorn, Barley, Blé, Bran, Buckwheat, Bulgar, Bulg(h)ur, Cassava, Corn, Couscous, Emmer, Farina, Gnocchi, Grain, Granola, Hominy, Maize, Mandioc(a), Mandiocca, Mani(h)oc, Manihot, Mealie, Millet, Muesli, Oats, Paddy, Popcorn, Rye(corn), Sago, Samp, Seed, Semolina, Sorghum, Spelt, Tapioca, Tef(f), Triticale, Wheat, Zea

Ceremonial, Ceremony Amrit, Barmitzvah, Chanoyu, Common Riding, Coronation, Doseh, Durbar, Encaenia, Enthronement, Eucharist, Flypast, Form(al), Habdalah, Havdalah, Havdoloh, Heraldry, Investiture, Matsuri, Maundy, Mummery, Observance, Ordination, Pageantry, Parade, Pomp, Powwow, Protocol, Rite, Ritual, Sacrament, Seder, Service, State, Tea, Usage

Cert(ain), Certainty Absolute, Actual, Assured, Banker, Bound, Cast-iron, Cinch, Cocksure, Confident, Convinced, Decided, Exact, Fact, Fate, Indubitable, Inevitable, Infallible, Monte, Nap, One, Positive, Poz, Precise, Shoo-in, Siccar, Sicker, Some, Snip, ➤ SURE, Sure-fire, Truth, Yes

Certificate, Certified, Certify Affirm, Attest, Bond, Chit, Cocket, Confirm, Credential, Debenture, Depose, Diploma, Docket, Document, Enseal, Guarantee, Licence, Lines, MOT, Paper, Patent, Proven, Scrip, Sworn, Testamur, Testimonial, U, Voucher, Warrant

Chafe, Chafing Chunter, Fray, Fret, Harass, Intertrigo, Irritate, ► RUB, Seethe, Worry

Chain(ed) Acre's-breadth, Albert, Anklet, Bind, Bond, Bracelet, Bucket, Cable, Catena, Choke, Cistron, Daisy, Decca, Drive, Dynasty, Engineer's, Esses, Fanfarona, Fetter, Fob, Food, Furlong, Gleipnir, Gunter's, Gyve, Markov, Mayor, Micella(r), Micelle, Noria, Pennine, Pitch, Range, Roller, Seal, ► SERIES, Shackle, Slang, Sprocket, String, Strobila, Team, Tug, Watch

Chair Basket, Bath, Bench, Berbice, Bergère, Birthing, Bosun's, Butterfly, Captain's, Carver, Club, Curule, Deck, Easy, Electric, Estate, Fauteuil, Fiddle-back, Gestatorial, Guérite, Jampan, Jampanee, Jampani, Ladder-back, Lounger, Morris, Pew, Preside, Recliner, Rocker, ► SEAT, Sedan, Stool, Swivel, Throne, Wainscot, Windsor, Wing

Chairman Convener, Emeritus, Mao, MC, Pr(a)eses, Prof, Prolocutor, Sheraton, Speaker

Chalk(y) Calcareous, Cauk, Cawk, Crayon, Credit, Cretaceous, French, Soapstone, White(n), Whit(en)ing

Challenge(r), Challenging Acock, Assay, Call, Cartel, Champion, Confront, Contest, Dare, Defy, Gage, Gauntlet, Glove, Hazard, Hen(ner), Iconoclasm, Impugn, Oppugn, Provoke, Query, Question, Recuse, Sconce, Shuttle, Tackle, Taker, Tall order, Tank, Threat, Vie, Whynot

Chamber(s) Atrium, Auricle, Camarilla, Camera, Casemate, Cavern, Cavitation, Cavity, Cell(a), Chanty, Cloud, Cofferdam, Combustion, Cubicle, Decompression, Dene-hole, Dolmen, Echo, Float, Gas, Gazunder, Hall, Horrors, Hypogea, Ionization, Jerry, Jordan, Kiva, Lethal, Locule, Mattamore, Po(t), Privy, Roum, Serdab, Silo, Spark, Star, Swell-box, Synod, Thalamus, Undercroft, Upper, Utricle, Vault, Ventricle, Zeta

Champ Bite, Chafe, Chew, Chomp, Eat, Gnash, Gnaw, Mash, Morsure, Munch

Champagne Boy, Bubbly, Charlie, Fizz, Gigglewater, Pop, Sillery, Simkin, Simpkin, Stillery, Troyes, Widow

Champion Ace, Adopt, Ali, Apostle, Belt, Campeador, Cid, Cock, Defend, Don Quixote, Doucepere, Douzeper, Dymoke, Enoch, Espouse, Gladiator, Harry, ► HERO, Horse, Kemp, Kemper(yman), King, Knight, Maintain, Matchless, Messiah, Messias, Neil, Paladin, Palmerin, Peerless, Perseus, Promachos, Proponent, Protagonist, Roland, St Anthony, St David, St Denis,

St George, St James, St Patrick, Spiffing, Spokesman, Star, Support, Tribune, Upholder, Victor, Wardog, ➤ WINNER, Yokozuna

Chance, Chancy Accident, Aleatory, Aunter, Bet, Break, Buckley's, Cast, Casual, Cavel, Contingent, Dice, Earthly, Even, ➤ FATE, Fluke, Fortuity, Fortuitous, Fortune, ➤ GAMBLE, Game, Hap, Happenstance, Hobnob, Iffy, Kevel, Light, Look-in, Lot, ➤ LOTTERY, Luck, Meet, Mercy, Occur, Odds, Opening, Opportunity, Posse, Potluck, Probability, Prospect, Random, Rise, Risk, Serendipity, Slant, Spec, Stake, Stochastic, Sweep, Toss-up, Treble, Turn, Tychism, Ventre, Venture, Wager

Change(able), Changing Adapt, Adjust, Agio, ➤ ALTER, Amendment, Attorn, Backtrack, Barter, Become, Bob-major, Capricious, Cash, Catalysis, Chop, Cline, Commute, Convert, Coppers, Denature, Departure, Edit, Enallage, Eustatic, Exchange, Find, Flighty, Fluctuate, Float, Flux, Guard, Gybe, Inflect, Innovate, Killcrop, Labile, Make-over, Metabolic, Metabolise, Metamorphosis, Mobile, Modify, Mutable, Mutation, Parallax, Peal, Permute, Protean, Realise, Recant, Rectify, Reform, Refraction, Rest, Revise, Rework, Sandhi, Sd, Seesaw, Shake-out, Shake-up, Shift, Silver, Small, Substitute, Swap, Swing, Switch, Tolsel, Tolsey, Tolzey, Transfer, Transfiguration, Transform, Transition, Transmute, Transpose, Transubstantial, Turn, Uncertain, Upheaval, U-turn, Vagary, Variant, Variation, Vary, Veer, Volatile, Volte-face, Wheel, Wow

▷**Change(d)** may indicate an anagram

Channel Access, Aqueduct, Artery, Beagle, Bed, Billabong, Bristol, Canal, Chimb, Chime, Chine, Chute, Conduit, Culvert, Cut, Ditch, Drain, Duct, Dyke, Ea, Euripus, Fairway, Flume, Foss, Funnel, Furrow, Gat, Geo, Gio, Glyph, Gully, Gut, Gutter, Head-race, Ingate, Katavothron, Khor, Kill, Lane, Leat, Leet, Limber, Major, Meatus, Medium, Minch, Moat, Narrows, North, Penstock, Pipeline, Qanat, Race, Rebate, Rigol(l), Rivulet, Sea-gate, Seaway, Sewer, Sinus, Sloot, Sluice, Sluit, Sny(e), Solent, Solway Firth, Sound, Sow, Spillway, Sprue, Strait, Suez, Sure, Swash, Tailrace, Tideway, Trough, Ureter

Chant Anthem, Antiphon, Cantillate, Cantus, Chaunt, Decantate, Euouae, Evovae, Gregorian, Haka, Harambee, Hymn, Intone, Introit, Motet, Pennillion-singing, Psalm, Sing, Slogan, Te deum, Yell

Chaos, Chaotic Abyss, Anarchy, Confusion, Disorder, Fractal, Hun-tun, Jumble, Mess, Muss, Shambles, Snafu, Tohu bohu
▷**Chaotic** may indicate an anagram
▷**Chaps** may indicate an anagram

Chapel Bethel, Bethesda, Beulah, Cha(u)ntry, Ebenezer, Feretory, Galilee, Lady, Oratory, Sacellum, Sistine

Chapter Accidents, C, Canon, Cap, Capitular, Ch, Chap, Cr, Division, Episode, Lodge, Phase, Section, Social, Sura(h), Verse

Character(s) Aesc, Alphabet, Ampersand, Ampussyand, Aura, Backslash, Brand, Calibre, Case, Cipher, Clef, Cliff, Climate, Complexion, Contour, Credit, Digamma, Dramatis personae, Eta, Ethos, ➤ FEATURE, Fish, Fist, Form, Grain, Grit, Hieroglyphic, Ideogram, Ideograph, Italic, Kern, Kind, La(m)bda, Letter, Logogram, Make-up, Mark, Mu, Nagari, ➤ NATURE, Nu, Ogam, Ogham, Pahlavi, Pantaloon, Part, Pehlevi, Person(a), Personage, ➤ PERSONALITY, Phonogram, Physiognomy, Protagonist, Psi, Reference, Repute, Rho, Role, Rune, Runic, Sampi, San, Self, Sirvente, Slash, Sonancy, Stamp, Subscript, Superscript(ion), Swung dash, Syllabary, Symbol, Testimonial, Ton(e), Trait, Uncial, Vav, Vee, Waw, Wen

Characterise(d), Characterism, Characteristic Attribute, Aura, Cast, Colour, Distinctive, Ethos, Facies, Feature, Hair, Hallmark, Has, Headmark, Idiomatic, Idiosyncrasy, Jizz, Lineament, Mien, Nature, Notate, Peculiar, Persona, Point, Property, Quality, Stigma, Strangeness, Streak, Style, ➤ TRAIT, Typical, Vein

Charge(s), Charged, Charger Accuse, Agist, Allege, Annulet, Arraign, Ascribe, Baton, Bear, Behest, Blame, Brassage, Brush, Buckshot, Care, Cathexis, Commission, Complaint, Cost, Count, Cover, Criminate, Damage, Debit, Delate, Delf, Delph, Demurrage, Depth, Depute, Directive, Dittay, Due, Duty, Electron, Entrust, Expense, Fare, Fee, Fill, Flock, Freight, Fullage, Gazump, Gravamen, Heraldic, Hot, Hypothec, Impeach, Impute, Indict, Inescutcheon, Inform, Instinct, Ion, Isoelectric, Last, Lien, Lioncel(le), Lionel, Live, Load, Mandate, Mine, Mount, Objure, Obtest, Onrush, Onus, Ordinary, Orle, Overhead, Pervade, Plaint, Positive, Premium, Prime, Q, Rack-rent, Rap, Rate, Red-dog, Rent, Report, Reprise, Roundel, Run, ➤ RUSH, Saddle, Service, Specific, Steed, Tariff, Tax, Tear,

Terms, Tilt, ➤ TRAY, Tressure, Trickle, Trust, Upfill, Verdoy, Vigorish, Ward, Wharfage

Charitable, Charity Alms, Awmous, Benign, Caritas, Dole, Dorcas, Eleemosynary, Largesse, Leniency, Liberal, Lion, Love, Mercy, Oddfellow, Openhanded, Oxfam, Pelican, Zakat

Charm(er), Charming Abracadabra, Abrasax, Abraxas, Allure, Amulet, Appeal, Aroma, Attraction, Beguile, Bewitch, Captivate, Charisma, Circe, Comether, Cute, Cutie, Emerods, Enamour, Enchant, Engaging, ➤ ENTRANCE, Fascinate, Fay, Fetish, Grace, Greegree, Gri(s)gris, Hand of glory, Houri, Juju, Magnetic, Mascot, Mojo, Obeah, Obi(a), Periapt, Phylactery, Porte-bonheur, Prince, Quaint, Quark, Ravish, Siren, Smoothie, Spellbind, Suave, Sweetness, Taking, Talisman, Telesm, Tiki, Trinket, Unction, Voodoo, Winsome

▷ **Charming** may indicate an anagram

Chart(ed), Charting Abac, Bar, Breakeven, Card, Diagram, Eye, Flip, Flow, Gantt, Graph, Histogram, Hydrography, Isogram, Isopleth, List, Magna Carta, ➤ MAP, Mappemond, Nomogram, Plot, Portolano, Ringelmann, Social, Table, Timetable, Waggoner, Weather

Charter Book, Covenant, Hire, Lease, Novodamus, Rent

Chase(r), Chasing Cannock, Chace, Chevy, Chivy, Ciseleur, Ciselure, Course, Cranbome, Decorate, Drink, Game, Harass, Hound, ➤ HUNT, Jumper, Oxo, Pursuit, Race, Scorse, Sic(k), Steeple, Sue, Suit, Wild-goose

Chasm Abyss, Gap, Gorge, Fissure, Gulf, Schism, Yawn

Chaste, Chastity Agnes, Attic, Celibate, Classic, Clean, Florimell, Ines, Innocent, Modesty, Nessa, ➤ PURE, Vestal, Virginal, Virtue

Chat, Chatter(box) Babble, Bavardage, Blab(ber), Blether, Campanero, Causerie, Chelp, Chinwag, Clack, Clishmaclaver, Confab(ulate), Converse, Cosher, Coze, Crack, Dialogue, Froth, Gab(ble), Gas, Gossip, Gup, Hobnob, Jabber, Jargon, Jaw, Kilfud, Madge, Mag(pie), Natter, Patter, Pie, Pourparler, Prate, Prattle, Rabbit, Rabble, Rap, Rattle, Scuttlebutt, Shmoose, Talk, Talkee-talkee, Tattle, Twattle, Waffle, Windbag, Witter, Wongi, Yacketyyak, Yak, Yarn, Yatter, Yoking

Cheap Bargain, Base, Catchpenny, Cheesy, Chintzy, Cut-price, Downmarket, Giveaway, Knockdown, Low, Off-peak, Poor,

Sacrifice, Shoddy, Stingy, Tatty, Tawdry, Ticky-tacky, Tinpot, Tinselly, Trivial, Undear, Vile

▷**Cheap** may indicate a d- or p- start to a word

Cheat(ers), Cheating Bam, Bamboozle, Beguile, Bilk, Bite(r), Bob, Bonnet, Bullock, Bucket, Cardsharp(er), Charlatan, Chiaus, Chicane(ry), Chisel, Chouse, Clip, Cod, Cog(ger), Colt, Con, Cozen, Crib, Cross, Cross-bite(r), Cuckold, Cully, Defraud, Delude, Diddle, Dingo, Dish, Do, Doublecross, Duckshove, Dupe, Escroc, Faitor, Fiddle, Finagle, Flam, Fleece, Fob, Foister, Fox, Fraud, Gaff, Gip, Glasses, Gum, Gyp, Hoax, Hocus, Hoodwink, Hornswoggle, Horse, Intake, Jockey, Magsman, Mulct, Mump, Nick, Pasteboard, Picaro(on), Poop, Queer, Rib, Rig, Rogue, Rook, Rush, Scam, Screw, Shaft, Sharper, Short-change, Slur, Smouch, Snap, Stack, Stiff, Sting, Swindle, Thimble-rigging, Trepan, Trim, Two-time, Welsh, Wheedle

Check Arrest, Audit, Ba(u)lk, Bauk, Bill, Bridle, Collate, Compesce, Control, Count, Cramp, Curb, Dam, Damp, Detent, Dogs-tooth, Examine, Foil, Frustrate, Halt, Hamper, Hobble, Houndstooth, Inhibit, Jerk, Jerque, Let, Limit, Mate, Monitor, Observe, Overhaul, Prevent, Rebuff, Rebuke, Rein, Repress, Reprime, Repulse, Reread, ➤ RESTRAIN, Revoke, Saccade, Screen, Service, Setback, Shepherd's, Sit-upon, Sneap, Sneb, Snib, Snub, Spot, ➤ STEM, Stop, Stunt, Tab, Tally, Tartan, Tattersall, Test, Thwart, Tick, Trash, Verify, Vet

Cheek(y) Alforja, Audacity, Buccal, Chap, Chollers, Chutzpah, Crust, Flippant, Fresh, Gum, Hussy, Jowl, Lip, Malapert, Malar, Masseter, Neck, Nerve, Noma, Pert, Presumption, Quean, Sass, Sauce, Sideburns, Wang, Yankie, Zygoma

Cheer(s), Cheerful(ness), Cheering Acclaim, Agrin, Applaud, Banzai, Barrack, Blithe, Bonnie, Bravo, Bright, Bronx, Bubbly, Buck, Buoy, Cadgy, Canty, Cherry, Chin-chin, Chipper, ➤ COMFORT, Crouse, Debonair, Drink, Ease, Elate, Elevate, Enliven, Exhilarate, Festive, Genial, Gladden, Happy-go-lucky, Hearten, Hilarity, Holiday, Hooch, Hoorah, Huzzah, Insouciance, Jocund, Jovial, Kia-ora, Lightsome, Lively, Ovate, Peart, Please, Praise, Prosit, Rah, Riant, Rivo, Root, Rumbustious, Shout, Sko(a)l, Slainte, Sonsie, Sunny, Ta, Tata, Tiger, Toodle-oo, Winsome, Yell

Cheese, Cheesy American, Amsterdam, Appenzell, Bel Paese, Blue, Boursin, Brie, Caboc, Caerphilly, Camembert, Cantal,

Chef → **Chest(y)** (cont.)

Casein, Caseous, Cheddar, Cheshire, Chessel, Chèvre, Cottage, Cream, Crowdie, Curd, Damson, Derby, Dolcelatte, Dunlop, Edam, Emmental(er), Emmenthal(er), Ermite, Esrom, Ewe, Fet(a), Fontina, Fromage frais, Gloucester, Goat, Gouda, Gruyère, Haloumi, Hard, Havarti, Huntsman, Ilchester, Islay, Jarlsberg®, Junket, Kenno, Killarney, Leicester, Limburg(er), Lymeswold, Mascarpone, Mousetrap, Mozzarella, Mu(e)nster, Mycella, Neuchatel, Orkney, Parmesan, Pecorino, Port Salut, Quark, Raclette, Rarebit, Rennet, Ricotta, Romano, Roquefort, Sage Derby, Samso, Sapsago, Skyr, Stilton®, Tofu, Truckle, Vacherin, VIP, Wensleydale

Chef Commis, Escoffier

Chemical Acid, Acrolein, Adrenalin®, Alar, Aldehyde, Alkali, Alum, Amide, Barilla, Bute, Carbide, Caseose, Catalyst, Cephalin, Developer, Dopamine, Encephalin, Fixer, Fluoride, Formyl, Fungicide, Glutamine, Glycol, Halon, Harmin, Heptane, Hexylene, Histamine, Hypo, ICI, Imine, Indican, Interleukin, Natron, Nitre, Oestregen, Olein, Olefin, Oxide, Oxysalt, Pentane, Pentene, Pentyl, Peptide, Phenol, Phenyl, Pheromone, Potash, Potassa, Ptomaine, Reagent, Resorcin, Soup, Strontia, Sulphide, Thio-salt, Trimer, Weedkiller

Chemist(ry) Alchemy, Alchymy, Analyst, Apothecary, Bunsen, Butenandt, Cavendish, Davy, Debye, Dispenser, Druggist, Drugstore, FCS, Gahn, Hevesy, Inorganic, Lavoisier, Liebig, LSA, MPS, Nernst, Newlands, Nobel, Organic, Paracelsus, Pasteur, Pothecary, Pharmacist, Physical, Pottingar, Proust, Prout, RIC, Sabatier, Sanger, Spageric, Spagiric, Spagyric

Cheque Blank, Giro, Gregory, Stumer, Tab, Traveller's

Cherry (tree) Amarelle, Ball, Bigaroon, Bigarreau, Blackheart, Cerise, Cornelian, Gean, Ground, Heart, Jerusalem, Kearton, Kermes, Kermesite, Malpighia, Marasca, Maraschino, May-duke, Maz(z)ard, Merry, Morel(lo), Red, Whiteheart

Chessman Bishop, Black, Castle, Horse, King, Knight, Pawn, Pin, Queen, Rook, White

Chest(y) Ark, Bahut, Bosom, Box, Breast, Buist, Bunker, Bureau, Bust, Caisson, Cap-case, Cassone, Chapel, Chiffonier, Coffer, Coffin, Coffret, Commode, Cub, Hope, Inro, Kist, Larnax, Locker, Lowboy, Medicine, Ottoman, Pectoral, Pereion, Pigeon, Pleural, Safe, Scrine, Scryne, Shrine, Sternum, Tallboy, Tea, Thorax, Toolbox, Trunk, Wangun, Wanigan, War

Chestnut Auburn, Badious, Ch, Chincapin, Chinese, Chinkapin, Chinquapin, Cliché, Conker, Favel(l), Hoary, Marron, Marron glacé, Moreton Bay, Russet, Saligot, Soare, Sorrel, Spanish, Sweet, Water

Chew Bite, Champ, Chaw, Cud, Gnaw, Gum, Manducate, Masticate, Maul, Meditate, Moop, Mou(p), Munch, Ruminate, Siri(h), Spearmint

Chic Dapper, Elegant, In, Kick, Modish, Posh, Smart, Soigné, Stylish, Swish, Tonish, Trim

Chick(en) Battery, Biddy, Broiler, Cheeper, Chittagong, Chuckie, Clutch, Cochin, Coward, Cowherd, Eirack, Gutless, Hen, Howtowdie, Kiev, Layer, Marengo, Minorca, Niderling, Poltroon, Poot, Poult, Pout, Prairie, Precocial, Quitter, Roaster, Spatchcock, Spring, Squab, Supreme, Timorous, Unheroic, Windy, Wyandotte, Yellow

Chief(tain) Arch, Ardrigh, Boss, Caboceer, Cacique, Calif, Caliph, Capital, Capitan, Capitayn, Capo, Caradoc, Cazique, Ch, Chagan, Dat(t)o, Dominant, Emir, First, Foremost, Geronimo, Grand, Haggis, ➤ HEAD, Hereward, Jarl, Kaid, King, Leader, ➤ MAIN, Mass, Mugwump, Nizam, Oba, Overlord, Pendragon, Premier, Primal, Prime, Principal, Quanah, Raja(h), Rajpramukh, Rangatira, Ratoo, Ratu, Sachem, Sagamore, Sarpanch, Sudder, Supreme, Tanist, Tank, Top

Child(ish), Children Aerie, Alannah, Babe, Baby, Badger, Bairn, Bambino, Bantling, Boy, Brat, Brood, Butter-print, Ch, Changeling, Cherub, Chick, Chickabiddy, Chit, Collop, Cub, Dream, Elfin, Eyas, Foundling, Gangrel, Ge(i)t, Girl, Gyte, Heir, Hurcheon, Imp, Infant, Issue, It, Jailbait, Jejune, Juvenile, Kid(die), Kiddie(wink), Kiddy, Kinder, Lad, Limb, Litter, Littlie, Mamzer, Minion, Minor, Mite, Munchkin, Naive, Nipper, Nursling, Offspring, Papoose, Piccaninny, Pickin, Progeny, Puerile, Puss, Putto, Ragamuffin, Rip, Rug rat, Scion, Smout, Smowt, Sprog, Street arab, Subteen, Ted, Tike, Toddle(r), Tot(tie), Totty, Trot, Tyke, Urchin, Wean, Weanel, Weanling, Weeny-bopper, Whelp, Younker, Youth

Chill(er), Chilly Bleak, ➤ COLD, Frappé, Freeze, Freon®, Frigid, Frosty, Gelid, Ice, Iciness, Mimi, Oorie, Ourie, Owrie, Parky, Raw, Refrigerate, Rigor, Scare

Chime(s) Bell, Cymar, Jingle, Peal, Semantron, Tink, ➤ TOLL

Chimney (pot), Chimney corner Can, Cow(l), Femerall, Flare stack, Flue, Funnel, Lug, Lum, Smokestack, Stack, Stalk, Tallboy, Tunnel

China(man), Chinese Ami, Amoy, Boxer, Cameoware, Cantonese, Cathay, Celestial, Ch, Chelsea, Chow, Coalport, Cochin, Cock, Confucius, Crackle, Crockery, Delft, Derby, Dresden, Eggshell, Etrurian, Hakka, Han, Hizen, Hmong, Imari, Kanji, Kaolin, Kuo-yu, Limoges, Manchu, Mandarin, Mangi, Maoist, Mate, Meissen, Ming, Minton, Oppo, Pal, Pareoean, Pekingese, Pe-tsai, Pinyin, Porcelain, ➤ POTTERY, Putonghua, Rockingham, Seric, Sèvres, Shanghai, Sinic, Spode®, Sun Yat-sen, Tai-ping, Taoist, Teng, Tocharian, Tungus, Uigur, Wal(l)y, Ware, Wedgwood®, Willowware, Worcester, Wu

Chip(s) Bo(a)st, Carpenter, Counter, Cut, Deep-fried, Fish, Flake, Fragment, Hack, Knap, Nacho(s), Nick, Pin, Shaving, Silicon, Spale, Spall, Tortilla, Transputer

▷ **Chip** may indicate an anagram

Chirp(y), Chirrup Cheep, Cherup, Chirm, Chirr, Cicada, Peep, Pip, Pipe, Pitter, Stridulate, Trill, Tweet, Twitter

Chisel(ler), Chisel-like Bam, Boaster, Bolster, Bur, Burin, Carve, Cheat, Clip, Drove, Firmer, Gad, ➤ GOUGE, Mason, Scalpriform, Scauper, Scorper, Sculpt, Sting

Chit Docket, Girl, Note, Voucher

Chivalry, Chivalrous Brave, Bushido, Courtly, Gallant

Chocolate Aero, Brown, Cacao, Carob, Cocoa, Dragee, Ganache, Neapolitan, Noisette, Pinole, Truffle

Choice, Choose, Choosy, Chosen Adopt, Anthology, Appoint, Aryan, Cherry-pick, Cull, Dainty, Decide, Druthers, Eclectic, Elect, Elite, Esnecy, Fine, Fork, Free will, Hobson's, Leet, Leve, Lief, List, Opt, Option, Or, Ossian, Peach, Peculiar, ➤ PICK, Picking, Plum(p), Precious, Predilect, Prefer, Proairesis, Rare, Recherché, ➤ SELECT, Superb, Try(e), Via media, Volition, Wale

Choir, Choral, Chorister, Chorus Antiphony, Antistrophe, Anvil, Apse, Burden, Dawn, Decani, Faburden, Fauxbourdon, Group, Hallelujah, Harmony, Hymeneal, Motet, Parabasis, Precentor, ➤ REFRAIN, Singing, Strophe, Treble, Triad, ➤ UNISON

Choke(r) Block, Clog, Gag, Silence, Smoor, Smore, Smother, Stifle, Stop, Strangle(hold), Strangulate, ➤ THROTTLE

Chop(per), Chops, Chopper(s), Choppy Adze, Ax(e), Celt, Charge, Cheek, Chump, Cleave, Côtelette, Cuff, Cutlet, Dice, Fell(er), Flew, Hack, Helicopter, Hew, Ivory, Karate, Lop, Mince, Mouth, Rotaplane, Rough, Suey, Teeth, Wang

Chord Arpeggio, Barré, Common, Diameter, Harmony, Intonator, Nerve, Triad, Vocal

Christ Ecce homo, ➤ CHRIST, Messiah, Saviour, X

Christen(ing) Baptise, Launch, Name-day

Christian Adventist, Albigenses, Beghard, Believer, Cathar(ist), Coptic, D(o)ukhobor, Dior, Donatist, Ebionite, Galilean, Giaour, Gilbertine, Gnostic, Goy, Holy roller, Homo(i)ousian, Jehovah's Witness, Marrano, Melchite, Melkite, Moral, Mozarab, Mutineer, Nazarene, Nestorian, Phalange, Pilgrim, Protestant, RC, Quartodeciman, Sabotier, Scientist, SCM, Traditor, Uniat(e), Unitarian, Waldensian, Wesleyan, Xian, Zwinglian

Christmas(time) Dec, Island, Nativity, Noel, Yuletide

Chronicle(r) Anglo-Saxon, Annal, Brut, Calendar, Diary, Froissart, Hall, History, Holinshed, Logographer, Paralipomena, Parian, ➤ RECORD, Register, Stow

Church Abbey, Armenian, Autocephalous, Basilica, Bethel, Bethesda, Brood, Byzantine, CE, Ch, Chapel, Chevet, Clergy, Collegiate, Congregational, Coptic, Delubrum, EC, Ecumenical, Episcopal, Episcopalian, Established, Faith, Fold, Free, High, Kirk, Lateran, Low, Lutheran, Maronite, Methodist, Minster, Moravian, Mormon, Orthodox, Prebendal, Presbyterian, RC, Reformed, Rome, Shrine, Smyrna, Stave, Steeple, Temple, Unification, Wee Free, Western

Cider Drink, Perry, Scrumpy

Cigar(ette), Cigarette cards Beedi(e), Bumper, Cancer stick, Caporal, Cartophily, Cheroot, Claro, Coffin nail, Conch, Concha, Corona, Dog-end, Durry, Fag, Filter-tip, Gasper, Giggle(-stick), Havana, Joint, Locofoco, Long-nine, Maduro, Manilla, Panatella, Perfecto, Regalia, Roach, Roll-up, Smoke, Snout, Splif(f), Stogie, Stog(e)y, Stompie, Weed, Whiff, Zol

Cinema(s) Biograph, Bioscope, Circuit, Drive-in, Films, Fleapit, Flicks, Movies, Multiplex, Mutoscope, Nickelodeon, Nouvelle Vague, Odeon, Plaza, Theatre, Tivoli

Cinnamon, Cinnamon stone Canella, Cassia(bark), Essonite, Spice

Circle Almacantar, Almucantar, Annulet, Antarctic, Arctic, Circassian, Co, Colure, Company, Compass, Corolla, Coterie, Cromlech, Crop, Cycloid, Cyclolith, Dip, Disc, Dress, Eccentric, Embail, Enclose, Epicyclic, Equant, Equator, Equinoctal, Euler's, Family, Fraternity, Full, Galactic, Girdle, Gyre, Halo, Hoop, Horizon, Inner, Inorb, Lap, Longitude, Loop, Malebolge, Mandala, Meridian, O, Orbit, Parhelic, Penannular, Peristalith, Polar, Rigol, ➤ RING, Rotate, Roundure, Set, Setting, Sphere, Stemme, Surround, Tinchel, Tropic, Turning, Umbel, Upper, Vertical, Vicious, Vienna, Volt, Wheel

Circuit(ous) AND, Ambit, Autodyne, Bypass, Closed, Comparator, Daughterboard, Diocese, Dolby®, Eyre, IC, Integrated, Lap, Limiter, Logic, Loop, Motherboard, NAND, NOR, NOT, OR, Perimeter, Phase, Reactance, Ring, Round, Scaler, Series, Short, Tour, Windlass

Circular Annular, Court, Folder, Leaflet, Mailshot, Orby, Spiral, Unending, Wheely

Circulate, Circulation Astir, Bloodstream, Cyclosis, Disseminate, Flow, Gyre, Issue, Mix, Orbit, Pass, Publish, Revolve, Rotate, Scope, Spread, Stir, Troll, Utter

▷**Circulating** may indicate an anagram

Circumference Boundary, Girth, Perimeter, Size

Circumstance, Circumstantial Case, Detail, Event, Fact, Formal, ➤ INCIDENT, Precise

Circus, Circus boy Arena, Big top, Flying, Hippodrome, Marquee, Maximus, Media, Monty Python, Ring, Three-ring

Citation, Cite Adduce, Allegation, Mention, Name, Quote, Recall, Reference, Repeat, Sist, Summon

Citizen(ship) Burgess, Burgher, Civism, Cleruch, Denizen, Dicast, Ephebe, Franchise, Freeman, Jus sanguinis, Jus soli, Kane, National, Oppidan, Patrial, People, Quirites, Resident, Roman, Senior, Snob, Subject, Venireman, Voter

Citrus Acid, Calamondin, Cedrate, Lemon, Lime, Mandarin, Min(n)eola, Orange, Pomelo, Tangerine, Ugli

City Agra, Athens, Atlantis, Babylon, Burgh, Carthage, Cosmopolis, Ctesiphon, EC, Empire, Eternal, Forbidden, Gath, Holy, Inner, LA, Leonine, Medina, Megalopolis, Metropolis, Micropolis, Mycenae, NY, Petra, Pompeii, Rhodes, Smoke, Sparta, Tech, Town, Ur, Vatican, Weldstadt

Civil(ian), Civilisation, Civilised, Civility Amenity, Christian, Citizen, Civ(vy), Comity, Courtesy, Culture, Fertile crescent, Humane, Indus Valley, Maya, Municipal, Nok, Polite, Politesse, Secular, Temporal, Urbane

Claim Appeal, Arrogate, Assert, Bag, Challenge, Charge, Darraign(e), Darrain(e), Darrayn, Demand, Deraign, Droit, Encumbrance, Haro, Harrow, Lien, List, Maintain, Nochel, Plea, Pose, Posit, Postulate, Pretence, Pretend, Profess, Pulture, Purport, Puture, Revendicate, Right, Set-off, Sue, Title

Claimant Irredentist, Petitioner, Pot-waller, Pretender, Prospector, Tichborne, Usurper

Clam Bivalve, Cohog, Geoduck, Giant, Gweduc, Littleneck, Mollusc, Mya, Quahang, Quahog, Tridacna, Venus

Clammy Algid, Damp, Dank, Moist, Sticky, Sweaty

Clamp Clinch, Denver boot, Fasten, Grip, Holdfast, Jumar, Pinchcock, Potato-pit, Stirrup, Tread, Vice, Wheel

Clan(sman) Cameron, Clique, Gens, Gentile, Group, Horde, Kiltie, Kindred, Name, Phratry, Phyle, Sect, Sept, Society, Stewart, Stuart, Tribe

Clap(per), Clapping Applaud, Blow, Castanet, Chop, Crotal, Dose, Jinglet, Peal, Thunder, Tonant

Clarify, Clarifier Clear, Despumate, Dilucidate, Explain, Explicate, Finings, Purge, Refine, Render, Simplify

Clash(ing) Bang, Clangour, Clank, Claver, Coincide, Collide, Conflict, Friction, Gossip, ➤ IMPACT, Incident, Jar, Loud, Missuit, Shock, Showdown, Strike, Swash

Clasp(ing) Adpress, Agraffe, Barrette, Brooch, Button, Catch, Chape, Clip, Embrace, Fibula, Grasp, Hasp, Hesp, Hook, Hug, Link, Morse, Ochreate, Ouch, Tach(e), Unite

Class(ify), Classification, Classy Acorn, Arrange, Assort, Bourgeois(ie), Bracket, Brand, Breed, Business, Cabin, Canaille, Caste, ➤ CATEGORY, Cheder, Cl, Clan, Clerisy, Clinic, Club, Course, Criminal, Dewey, Division, Economy, Estate, Evening, Faction, Form, Genera, Genus, Gentry, ➤ GRADE, Group, Heder, Hubble, Ilk, Keep-fit, League, Linn(a)ean, List, Lower, Mammal, Master, Middle, Number, Order, Phylum, Pigeon-hole, Race, Range, Rank, Rate, Rating, Remove, Salariat, Seminar, Shell, Siege, Sort(ation), Steerage, Stratum, Stream, Syntax, Taxonomy, Teach-in, Third, Tourist, Tribe, ➤ TYPE, U, Upper, Varna, Water, Working, World, Year

Classic(al), Classics, Classicist Ageless, Ancient, Basic, Derby, Elzevir, Grecian, Greek, Humane, Leger, Literature, Pliny, Purist, Roman, Standard, Traditional, Vintage

Clause Apodosis, Article, Condition, Escalator, Escape, Filioque, Four, Golden parachute, Grandfather, Member, Poison-pill, Protasis, Proviso, Reddendum, Reservation, Rider, Salvo, Sentence, Subordinate, Tenendum, Testatum

Claw Chela, Claut, Crab, Dewclaw, Edate, Falcula, Grapple, Griff(e), Hook, Nail, Nipper, Pounce, Scrab, Sere, Talent, ➤ TALON, Tear, Telson, Unguis

Clay Argil, Blaes, Blaise, Blaize, Bole, Calm, Cam, Caum, Ceramic, China, Charoset(h), Cloam, Clunch, Cob, Earth, Engobe, Fango, Figuline, Fuller's earth, Gault, Glei, Gley, Hardpan, Haroset(h), Illite, Kaolin, Laterite, Lithomarge, Loam, Lute, Malm, Marl, Meerschaum, Mire, Mortal, Mud, Papa, Pipeclay, Pise, Potter's, Pottery, Pug, Saggar(d), Sagger, Seggar, Slip, Slurry, Thill, Till(ite), Varve, Warrant, Warren, Wax

Clean(se), Cleansing, Cleaner Absterge, Besom, Bleach, Bream, Broom, Careen, Catharise, Catharsis, Chaste, Clear, Daily, Debride, Depurate, Deterge(nt), Dhobi, Dialysis, Douche, Dust(er), Eluant, Emunge, Enema, Erase, Ethnic, Evacuant, Evacuate, Expurgate, Fay, Fettle, Fey, Floss, Flush, Full, Grave, Groom, Gut, Heels, Hoover®, Hygienic, Immaculate, Innocent, Launder, Lave, Lustrum, Lye, Mouthwash, Mrs Mop(p), Mundify, Net, Overhaul, Porge, Pull-through, Pumice, Pure, Purgative, Purge, Ramrod, Rebite, Rub, Rump, Scaffie, Scavenge, Scour, Scrub, Shampoo, Snow-white, Soap, Soogee, Soogie, Soojey, Sponge, Spotless, Squeaky, Squeegee, Sterile, Sujee, Swab, Sweep, Vac(uum), Valet, ➤ WASH, Whistle, Wipe

Clear(ance), Clearly Absolve, Acquit, Aloof, Apparent, Bell, Berth, Bold, Bore, Brighten, Bus, Clarify, Crystal, Decode, Definite, Diaphanous, Dispel, Distinct, Downright, Eidetic, Evacuate, Evident, Exculpate, Exonerate, Explicit, Fair, Gain, Headroom, Hyaline, Intelligible, Iron, Laund, Leap, Legible, Limpid, Lucid, Luculent, Manifest, Mop, Neat, Negotiate, Net(t), ➤ NOT CLEAR, Observable, Obvious, Ope(n), Overlap, Palpable, Pellucid, Perspicuous, Plain, Play, Pratique, Predy, Pure, Quit, Rack, Realise, Remble, Rid, Ripple, Serene, Sheer, Shere, Slum, Sweep, Thro(ugh), Thwaite, Transire, Translucent, Transparent, Unblock, Vault, Vivid, Well, Windage, Wipe

Clearing Assart, Glade, Opening, Shire, Slash

Clergy(man), Cleric(al) Abbé, Canon, Cantor, Cardinal, Chaplain, Cleric, Clerk, Cloth, Curate, Curé, Deacon, Dean, Ecclesiast(ic), Goliard, Incumbent, Josser, Levite, Ministerial, Ministry, Non-juror, Non-usager, Notarial, Parson, Pastor, Pontifex, Pontiff, Preacher, Prebendary, Precentor, Prelate, Presbyter, Presenter, Priest, Primate, Prior, Proctor, Rabbi, Rector, Red-hat, Reverend, Rome-runner, Scribal, Secretarial, Shaveling, Shepherd, Slope, Spin-text, Squarson, Subdeacon, Theologian, Vartabed, Vicar

Clerk(s) Actuary, Baboo, Babu, Basoche, Cleric, Cratchit, Cursitor, Limb, Notary, Penman, Penpusher, Poster, Protocolist, Prot(h)onotary, Recorder, Scribe, Secretariat, Tally, Vicar, Writer

Clever(ness) Able, Adroit, Astute, Brainy, Bright, Canny, Cute, Daedal(e), Deft, Gleg, Ingenious, Natty, Sage(ness), Shrewd, Skilful, Smart(y), Smarty-pants, Souple, Subtle

Cliché Banality, Boilerplate, Commonplace, Corn, Platitude, Saying, Tag

Click(er), Clicking Castanet, Catch, Forge, Pawl, Ratch(et), Snick, Succeed, Tchick, Ticktack

Client Customer, Gonk, John, Patron, Trick

Cliff(s) Beachy Head, Bluff, Cleve, Crag, Craig, Escarp, Palisade, Precipice, Sca(u)r

Climate Atmosphere, Attitude, Continental, Mood, Sun, Temperament, Temperature, Weather

Climax Apex, Apogee, Catastasis, Come, Crescendo, Crest, Crisis, Edaphic, End, Head, Heyday, Orgasm, Top, Zenith

Climb(er) Alpinist, Aralia, Aristolochia, Ascend, Breast, Briony, Bryony, Bugle, Clematis, Clusia, Cowage, Cowhage, Cowitch, Crampon, Creeper, Cucumber, Dodder, Heart-pea, Hedera, Ivy, Kie-kie, Kudzu, Lawyer, Layback, Liana, Liane, ► MOUNT, Pareira, Parvenu, Prusik, Rat(t)an, Rise, Scale, Scan, Scandent, Scansores, Sclim, Shin, Shinny, Smilax, Social, Speel, Steeplejack, Sty(e), Swarm, Timbo, Tuft-hunter, Udo, Up(hill), Uprun, Vine, Wistaria, With(y)wind, Zoom

Clinch Attach, Ensure, Fix, Rivet, Secure, Settle

Cling(er), Clinging Adhere, Bur(r), Cherish, Cleave, Embrace, Hold, Hug, Ring, Tendril

Clinic Dispensary, Hospital, Hospitium, Mayo

Clip(ped), Clipper, Clipping Barrette, Brash, Bulldog, Butterfly, Clasp, Crocodile, Crop-ear, Crutch, Curt, Curtail, Cut, Cutty Sark, Dag, Dock, Dod, Excerpt, Fleece, Jubilee, Jumar, Krab, Lop, Pace, Pare, Prerupt, Prune, Scissel, Secateur, Shear, Ship, Shore, Shorn, Snip, Staccato, Tie, Tie-tack, Tinsnips, Topiarist, Trim

Clique Cabal, Clan, Club, Coterie, Faction, Gang, Ring, Set

Cloak(room), Cloaks Aba, Abaya, Abba, Abolla, Amice, Bathroom, Burnous, Capa, Cape, Capote, Caracalla, Cardinal, Cassock, Chasuble, Chimer(e), Chlamydes, Chlamys, Chuddah, Chuddar, Conceal, Cope, Cover, Disguise, Dissemble, Djellaba(h), Domino, Gabardine, Gaberdine, Gal(l)abea(h), Gal(l)abi(y)ah), Gal(l)abi(y)eh, Gentlemen, Gents, Hall-robe, Heal, Hele, Himation, Hood, Inverness, Jelab, Jellaba, Joseph, Kaross, Manta, Manteel, Mant(e)let, Mantle, ➤ MASK, Mousquetaire, Mozetta, Paenula, Paletot, Pallium, Paludamentum, Pelisse, Pilch, Poncho, Rail, Revestry, Rocklay, Rokelay, Roquelaure, Sagum, Sarafan, Scapular, ➤ SCREEN, Shroud, Swathe, Talma, Toga, Vestiary, Vestry, Visite

Clock Alarm, Ammonia, Analogue, Astronomical, Atomic, Beetle, Big Ben, Biological, Blowball, Body, Bracket, Bundy, Caesium, Carriage, Clepsydra, Cuckoo, Dandelion, Floral, Grandfather, Grandmother, Hit, Knock, Long case, Meter, Repeater, Solarium, Speaking, Speedo, Strike, Sundial, Tell-tale, Time(r), Wag at the wa', Water

Clog Ball, Block, Clam, Crowd, Dance, Fur, Galosh, Golosh, Hamper, Jam, Lump, Mire, Obstruct, Overshoe, Patten

Close(d), Closing, Closure Airless, Atresia, Block, Boon, By, Cadence, Clammy, Clench, Complete, Dear, Debar, Dense, ➤ END, Epilogue, Ewest, Finale, Gare, Grapple, Handy, Hard, Imminent, Inbye, Infibulate, Intent, Intimate, Lock, Lucken, Mean, Miserly, Muggy, Mure, Narre, Narrow, Near, Neist, Nie, Nigh, Niggardly, Nip and tuck, Obturate, Occlusion, Oppressive, Parochial, Precinct, Reserved, Reticent, Seal, Secret, Serre, Serried, Serry, Shet, Shut(ter), Shutdown, Silly, Slam, Snug, Stap, Stuffy, Sultry, Tailgate, Temenos, Tight, Uproll, Warm, Yard

Closet Cabinet, Confine, Cubicle, Cupboard, Earth, Locker, Safe, Wardrobe, WC, Zeta

Close-up Detail, Fill, Shut, Stop, Zoom

Cloth Carmelite, Clergy, Cloot, Clout, ➤ FABRIC, ➤ FELT, Frocking, Frontal, Loin, Lungi, ➤ MATERIAL, Nap, Napery, Napje, Nappie, Needlework, Netting, Pall, Pane, Panel, Pilch, Priesthood, Print(er), Puke, Rag, Raiment, Roll, Sashing, Scarlet, Serviette, Sheet, Sheeting, Shoddy, Stripe, Tapestry, Tea, ➤ TEXTILE, Throw, Tissue, Veronica

Clothe(s), Clothing, Clothed Apparel, Array, Attire, Baggies, Besee, Cape, Casuals, Choli, Cits, Clad, Clericals, Clobber, Combinations, Coordinates, Costume, Cover, Cover, Croptop, Dicht, Dight, Don, Drag, ➤ DRESS, Duds, Emboss, Endue, Finery, Frippery, Garb, Garments, Gear, Gere, Get-up, Glad rags, Habit, Haute couture, Innerwear, Judogi, Jumps, Layette, Outfit, Pannicle, Raiment, Rami, Rigout, Robes, Samfoo, Samfu, Schmutter, Scungies, Shroud, Slops, Swaddling, Swathe, Swothling, Tackle, Togs, Tracksuit, Trappings, Trousseau, Tweeds, Vernicle, Vestiary, Vestiture, Vestment, Wardrobe, Watteau, Weeds, Workwear, Yclad, Ycled

Cloud(ed), Cloudiness, Cloudy Altocumulus, Altostratus, Benight, Cirrocumulus, Cirrostratus, Cirrus, Coalsack, Coma, Crab Nebula, Cumulonimbus, Cumulus, Dim, Dull, Emission nebula, Fog, Fractostratus, Funnel, Goat's hair, Haze, Horsehead Nebula, Infuscate, Magellanic, Mare's tail, Milky, Mist, Mushroom, Nacreous, Nephele, Nephelometer, Nepho-, Nimbostratus, Nimbus, Nubecula, Nubilous, Nuée ardente, Obscure, Oort, Overcast, Pall, Pother, Rack, Stain, Storm, Stratocumulus, Stratus, Thunderhead, Turbid, Virga, War, Water-dog, Woolpack, Zero-zero

Clove Chive, Eugenia, Rose-apple, Split

Clover Alfalfa, Alsike, Berseem, Calvary, Cinque, Cow-grass, Hare's foot, Japan, Ladino, Lespedeza, Medic(k), Melilot, Owl's, Rabbit-foot, Serradella, Serradilla, Shamrock, Souple, Suckling, Trefoil, Trilobe

Clown(ish) Antic, Antick, August(e), Boor, Bor(r)el, Buffoon, Carl, Chough, Chuff, Coco, Clout-shoe, ➤ COMEDIAN, Comic, Costard, Daff, Feste, Froth, Girner, Gobbo, Goon, Gracioso, Grimaldi, Harlequin, Hob, Jack-pudding, Jester, Joey, Joker, Joskin, Leno, Merry Andrew, Mountebank, Nedda, Nervo, Peasant, Pickle-herring, Pierrot, Put, Rustic, Slouch, Thalian, Touchstone, Trinculo, Wag, Zany

Club(s), Club-like Adelphi, Airn, Almack's, Alpeen, Artel, Association, Athen(a)eum, Baffy, Band(y), Basto, Bat, Beefsteak, Blackjack, Blaster, Bludgeon, Boodles, Bourdon, Brassie, Brook's, Bulger, C, Card, Carlton, Caterpillar, Cavalry, Cleek, Clip-joint, Combine, Cosh, Cotton, Country, Crockford's, Cudgel, Disco(theque), Driver, Driving iron, Drones, Fan, Fascio, Garrick, Glee, Golf, Guild, Hampden, Hell-fire, Honky-tonk, Indian, Iron, Jacobin, Jigger, Jockey, Kierie, Kiri, Kitcat, Kiwanis, Knobkerrie, League, Leander, Lofter, Mace, Mallet, Mashie, Maul, Mell, Mere, Meri, Mess, Midiron, Monday, Niblick, Night(stick), Nitery, Oddfellows, Patu, Polt, Priest, Pudding, Putter, RAC, Reform, Ring, Rota, Rotarian, Rotary, Savage's, Shillelagh, Slate, Society, Sorosis, Spoon, Spot, Spurs, Strike, Strip, Trefoil, Truncheon, Trunnion, Union, Variety, Waddy, Wedge, White's, Wood, Youth

Clue Across, Anagram, Ball, Charade, Clave, Dabs, Down, ▶ HINT, Inkling, Key, Lead, Light, Rebus, Scent, Signpost, Thread, Tip

Clump Cluster, Finial, Knot, Mass, Mot(te), Patch, Plump, Tread, Tuft, Tump, Tussock

▷**Clumsily** may indicate an anagram

Clumsy Artless, Awkward, Bauchle, Bungling, Butterfingers, Calf, Chuckle, Clatch, Clodhopper, Cumbersome, Dub, Dutch, Galoot, Gauche, Gimp, Ham(-fisted), Heavy-handed, Inapt, Inelegant, Klutz, Lob, Loutish, Lubbard, Lubber, Lummox, Lumpish, Maladroit, Mauther, Mawr, Mawther, Messy, Mor, Nerd, Nurd, Palooka, Rough, Schlemihl, S(c)hlemiel, Squab, Stot, Swab, Swob, Two-fisted, Ungain, Unwieldy

Clutch Battery, Brood, Chickens, Clasp, Cling, Eggs, Glaum, Grab, ▶ GRASP, Gripe, Nest, Seize, Sitting, Squeeze

Clutter Confusion, Litter, Mess, Rummage

Coach Battlebus, Berlin, Bogie, Bus, Car, Carriage, Chara, Clerestory, Crammer, Diligence, Dilly, Double-decker, Drag, Edifier, Fly, Gig, Hackney, Landau(let), Microbus, Phaeton, Pullman, Railcar, Rattler, Repetiteur, Saloon, Shay, Sleeper, Stage, Surrey, Tally-(ho), Teach(er), Thoroughbrace, Train(er), Tutor, Voiture

Coal Anthracite, Bituminous, Burgee, Cannel, Cherry, Clinker, Coom, Crow, Culm, Eldin, Ember, Fusain, Gathering, Jud, Knob,

Lignite, Open-cast, Purse, Sapropelite, Score, Slack, Splint, Vitrain, Wallsend

Coalition Alliance, Bloc, Janata, Merger, Tie

Coarse(ness) Base, Blowzy, Bran, Broad, Common, Crude, Earthy, Fisherman, Foul, Grained, Gross, Ham, Illbred, Indelicate, Low-bred, Plebeian, Rank, Raunchy, Ribald, Rough, Rudas, Rude, Sackcloth, Slob, Sotadic, Vulgar

Coast(al) Barbary, Beach, Causeway, Coromandel, Costa, Drift, Freewheel, Glide, Hard, Ivory, Littoral, Longshore, Maritime, Orarian, Riviera, Seaboard, Seafront, Seaside, ➤ SHORE, Sledge, Strand, Toboggan

Coaster Beermat, Drog(h)er, Mat, Ship

Coat(ing) Ab(b)a, Abaya, Acton, Admiral, Anarak, Anodise, Anorak, Barathea, Bathrobe, Belton, Benjamin, Blazer, Box, Buff, Car, Chesterfield, Cladding, Claw-hammer, Clearcole, Cloak, Clutch, Cocoon, Coolie, Cover, Covert, Creosote, Crust(a), Cutaway, Dress, Duffel, Duster, Enamel, Encrust, Extine, Film, Fleece, Frock, Fur, Gabardine, Galvanise, Gambeson, Glaze, Grego, Ground, Ha(c)queton, Hair, Happi, Impasto, Inverness, Jack(et), Jemmy, Jerkin, Jodhpuri, Joseph, Jump, Jupon, Lacquer, Lammie, Lammy, Layer, Mac, Mackinaw, Matinee, Metallise, Morning, Newmarket, ➤ OVERCOAT, Paint, Paletot, Palla, Parka, Parkee, Patinate, Pebbledash, Pelage, Pelisse, Perfuse, Petersham, Plate, Polo, Pos(h)teen, Primer, Prince Albert, Raglan, Redingote, Resin, Resist, Riding, Sack, Saque, Seal, Sheepskin, Shellac, Silver, Spencer, Stadium, Surtout, Swagger, Tabard, Taglioni, Tail, Tar, Teflon, Tent, Top, Trench, Truss, Trusty, Tunic, Tuxedo, Ulster(ette), Veneer, Verdigris, Warm, Wash, Windjammer, Wool, Zamarro, Zinc

Coax Blandish, Blarney, Cajole, Carn(e)y, Cuittle, Flatter, Lure, Persuade, Wheedle, Whilly(wha), Whillywhaw

Cobble(rs) Cosier, Cozier, Mend, Patch, Rot, Snob, Soutar, Souter, Sowter, Stone, Sutor, Twaddle, Vamp

Cobweb(by) Arachnoid, Araneous, Gossamer, Snare, Trap

Cock(y) Alectryon, Ball, Capon, Chanticleer, Chaparral, Erect, Flip, Fowl, France, Fugie, Half, Hay, Jack-the-lad, Jaunty, Penis, Roadrunner, Robin, Rooster, Snook, Strut, Swaggering, Tilt, Turkey, Valve, Vain, Vane

Cockatoo Bird, Corella, Galah, Major Mitchell, Parrot

▷**Cockle(s)** may indicate an anagram

Cockney 'Arriet, 'Arry, Bow, Londoner, Londonese
▷**Cockney** may indicate a missing h
Cocktail Alexander, Aperitif, Atomic, Bloody Mary, Buck's fizz, Bumbo, Cape, Cold duck, Crusta, Daiquiri, Drink, Egg-flip, Fustian, Gibson, Gimlet, Manhattan, Margarita, Martini®, Mix, Molotov, Old-fashioned, Piña colada, Pink lady, Prawn, Rickey, Rusty nail, Sazerac®, Screwdriver, Side-car, Stengah, Stinger, Swizzle, Tom Collins, Twist, White-lady
Cod Bag, Cape, Coalfish, Fish, Gade, Gadus, Haberdine, Keeling, Kid, Lob, Man, Morrhua, Saith, Stockfish, Torsk, Tusk, Whiting
Code Access, Alphanumeric, Amalfitan, Bar, Binary, Bushido, Canon, Cipher, City, Civil, Clarendon, Codex, Cryptogram, Disciplinary, Dogma, Dress, ➤ EBCDIC, Error, Escape, Ethics, Fuero, Genetic, Gray, Hammurabic, Highway, Justinian, Morse, Napoleon, Object, Omerta, Penal, ➤ PGP, Postal, Rulebook, Scytale, Signal, Source, Talmud, Zip
Coffee, Coffee beans, Coffee pot Arabica, Brazil, Cafetiere, Cappuccino, Decaff, Demi-tasse, Espresso, Expresso, Filter, Gaelic, Gloria, Granules, Instant, Irish, Java, Latte, Mocha, Peaberry, Robusta, Tan, Triage, Turkish
Coffin Bier, Casket, Hearse, Sarcophagus, Shell
Cog(ged) Contrate, Mitre-wheel, Nog, Pinion, Tooth
Cogent Compelling, Forceful, Good, Sound, Telling
Cohere(nt) Agglutinate, Clear, Cleave, Cling, Logical, Stick
Cohort Colleague, Crony, Soldier
Coil(ed) Bight, Bought, Choke, Clew, Clue, Curl, Fake, Fank, Furl, Hank, Helix, Induction, Mortal, Rouleau, Scorpioid, Solenoid, Spark, Spiral, Spiraster, Spire, Tesla, Tickler, Toroid, Twine, Twirl, ➤ WIND, Wound, Wreath, Writhe
Coin Base, Bean, Bit, Cash, Change, Copper, Create, Doctor, Dump(s), Fiver, Han(d)sel, Imperial, Invent, Make, Mint, Mite, ➤ MONEY, Neoterise, Numismatic, Nummary, Piece, Plate, Proof, Shiner, Slip, Smelt, Specie, Stamp, Strike, Tenner, Unite, Unity
Coincide(nt), Coincidence Accident, Chance, Consilience, Fit, Fluke, Overlap, Rabat(to), Simultaneous, Synastry, Synchronise, Tally
Cold(-blooded) Ague, Algid, Arctic, Austere, Biting, Bitter, Bleak, C, Catarrh, Cauld(rife), Chill(y), Colubrine, Common,

Coryza, Ectotherm, Frem(d), Fremit, Frigid, Frost(y), Gelid, Glacial, Hiemal, Icy, Impersonal, Jeel, Nippy, Nirlit, Parky, Passionless, Perishing, Poikilotherm(ic), Polar, Psychro-, Remote, Rheumy, Rigor, Rume, Snap, Snell, Sour, Streamer, Subzero, Taters, Weed, Wintry

Collapse Apoplexy, Cave, Conk, Crash, Crumble, Crumple, Debacle, Downfall, Fail(ure), Fall, Fold, Founder, Give, Implode, Inburst, Landslide, Meltdown, Phut, Purler, Rot, Ruin, Scat(ter), Sink, Slump, Stroke, Subside, Sunstroke, Swoon, Telescope, Tumble, Wilt, Zonk

▷ **Collapsing** may indicate an anagram

Collar(ed) Arrest, Astrakhan, Bermuda, Bertha, Berthe, Bib, Bishop, Brecham, Butterfly, Button-down, Buttonhole, Capture, Carcanet, Chevesaile, Choke(r), Clerical, Collet, Dog, Esses, Eton, Falling-band, Flea, Gorget, Grandad, Hame, Holderbat, Jabot, Jampot, Karenni, Mandarin, Moran, Mousquetaire, Nab, Nail, Neckband, Necklet, Ox-bow, Peter Pan, Piccadell, Piccadillo, Piccadilly, Pikadell, Polo, Puritan, Rabato, Rebater, Rebato, Revers, Rollneck, Roman, Ruff, Sailor, Seize, Tackle, Tappet, Tie-neck, Torque, Turndown, Turtleneck, Vandyke, Whisk, Wing, Yoke

Colleague Associate, Bedfellow, Confrère, Mate, Oppo, Partner

Collect(ed), Collection, Collector Accrue, Agglomerate, Aggregate, Album, Alms, Amass, Ana, Anthology, Assemble, Bank, Bow, Budget, Bundle, Burrell, Caboodle, Calm, Cap, Clowder, Compendium, Compile, Congeries, Conglomerate, Covey, Cull, Dossier, Dustman, Earn, Egger, Exaltation, Exordial, Fest, Gaggle, Garner, Gather, Gilbert, Glean, Glossary, Grice, Heap, Herd, Hive, Idant, Jingbang, Kit, Kitty, Levy, Magpie, Meal, Meet, Menagerie, Miscellany, Mish-mash, Montem, Murmuration, Museum, Muster, Nide, Offertory, Omnibus, Paddling, Pile, Plate, Pod, Post, Prayer, Quest, Raft, Raise, Recheat, Sedge, Serene, Set, Shoe, Siege, Skein, Smytrie, Sord, Sottisier, Sounder, Spring, Stand, Team, Troop, Unkindness, Watch, Whipround, Wisp

▷ **Collection** may indicate an anagram

College(s) Academy, Ampleforth, All Souls, Balliol, Brasenose, Business, C, Caius, Campus, CAT, Cheltenham, Clare, Classical, Commercial, Community, Corpus, Downing, Electoral, Emmanuel, Eton, Exeter, Foundation, Girton, Hall, Herald's, Jail,

Keble, King's, Lancing, Linacre, Lincoln, LSE, Lycée, Lyceum, Madras(s)a(h), Madressah, Magdalen(e), Medresseh, Merton, Newnham, Nuffield, Oriel, Poly, Polytechnic, Protonotariat, Queen's, Ruskin, St. Johns, Saliens, Selwyn, Seminary, Sixth-form, Somerville, Sorbonne, Staff, Tech(nical), Tertiary, Theologate, Training, Trinity, Tug, UMIST, Up, Village, Wadham, Winchester, Yeshwa(h)

Collide, Collision Afoul, Barge, Bird-strike, Bump, Cannon, Carom(bole), Clash, Dash, Fender-bender, Foul, Head-on, Impact, Into, Kiss, Meet, Pile-up, Strike, Thwack

Colony Aden, Cleruchy, Crown, Dependency, Hongkong, Nudist, Penal, Presidio, Proprietary, Rookery, Settlement, Swarm, Termitarium, Zambia

Colour(ed), Colouring Alizarin(e), Anil, Anthocyan, An(n)atta, An(n)atto, Arnotto, Aquamarine, Auburn, Bay, Bedye, Bice, Bister, Bistre, Blee, Blue, Blush, Buff, C, Camel, Cap, Cappagh-brown, Cardinal, Cerise, Chica, Chromatic, Chrome, Complementary, Complexion, Coral, Crayon, Criant, Cyan, Day-Glo®, Distort, Dye, Ecru, Eosin, False, Filemot, Flag, Florid, Gamboge, Gouache, Gules, Haem, ► HUE, Ink, Isabel, Jet, Kalamkari, Lake, Leer, Lemon, Lilac, Lime, Local, Lovat, Lutein, Magenta, Maroon, Mauve, Metif, Nankeen, Oatmeal, Ochre, Olive, Or, Orange, Orpiment, Palette, Pastel, Peach, Philamot, Philomot, Pied, Pigment, Pochoir, Polychrome, Primary, Prism, Puke, Reddle, Reseda, Rince, Riot, Roucou, Rouge, Ruddle, Sand, Sepia, Shade, Sienna, Solferino, Spectrum, Startle, Tartrazine, Taupe, Tinc(ture), Tinge, Tint, Titian, Tone, Ultramarine, Umber, Umbrage, Uvea, Vert

▷**Coloured** may indicate an anagram

Colourful Abloom, Brave, Flamboyant, Flowery, Iridescent, Kaleidoscope, Opalescent, Splashy, Vivid

Colourless Albino, Bleak, Drab, Dull, Hyalite, Pallid, Pallor, Wan, White

Column(s), Column foot Agony, Anta, Atlantes, Commentary, Corinthian, Correspondence, Cylinder, Decastyle, Diastyle, Doric, Editorial, Eustyle, Fifth, File, Gossip, Hypostyle, Impost, Lat, Lonelyhearts, Monolith, Nelson's, Newel, Obelisk, Pericycle, Peristyle, Persian, Personal, Pilaster, ► PILLAR, Pilotis, Prostyle, Rouleau, Row, Spina, Spinal, Spine,

Stalactite, Stalagmite, Steering, Stylobate, Systyle, Tabulate, Telamone, Third, Tige, Tore, Torus, Trajan's

Comb(er), Combed, Combing Alveolate, Beehive, Breaker, Card, Copple, Crest, Curry, Dredge, Fine-tooth, Hackle, Heckle, Hot, Kaim, Kame, Kangha, Kemb, Noils, Pecten, Rake, Red(d), Ripple(r), Scribble, Search, Smooth, Tease(l), Toaze, Tose, Toze, Trawl, Wave

Combination, Combine(d), Combining Accrete, Alligate, Ally, Amalgam, Associate, Axis, Bloc, Cartel, Cleave, Clique, Coalesce, Coalition, Concoction, Conflated, Conglomerate, Consortium, Coordinate, Crasis, Fuse, Group, Harvester, Integration, Join, Junta, Kartell, League, Meld, Merge(r), Mingle, Mixture, Perm(utation), Piece, Pool, Quill, Ring, Solvate, Splice, Syncretize, Synthesis, Terrace, Trona, Unite, Valency, Wed

▷**Combustible** may indicate an anagram

Come, Coming (back), Coming out Advent, Anear, Anon, Appear, Approach, Ar(r), Arise, Arrive, Attend, Debouch, Derive, Future, Happen, Iceman, Issue, Millenarian, Orgasm, Parousia, Pass, Pop, Respond, Second, Via

Comedian Benny, Buffoon, Chaplin, ➤ CLOWN, Comic, Durante, Emery, Goon, Groucho, Joker, Karno, Leno, Quipster, Robey, Scream, Screwball, Tate, Tati, Wag, Wise, Yell

Comedy Com, Drama, Errors, Farce, Humour, Millamant, Situation, Slapstick, Thalia, Travesty

Comet Geminid, Halley's, Kohoutek, Meteor

Comfort(er), Comforting Amenity, Analeptic, Balm, Bildad, Calm, Cheer, Cherish, Cold, Consolation, Console, Creature, Crumb, Dummy, Ease, Eliphaz, Featherbed, Reassure, Relief, Relieve, Scarf, Solace, Soothe, Succour, Zophar

Comfortable, Comfy Bein, Canny, Cose, Cosh, Cosy, Couthie, Couthy, Cushy, Easy, Gemutlich, Heeled, Homely, Mumsy, Relaxed, Rug, Snug, Tosh, Trig, Warm, Well, Well-to-do

Comic(al) Beano, Buff, Buffo(on), Bumpkin, Buster, Chaplin, Clown, ➤ COMEDIAN, Dandy, Droll, Eagle, Facetious, Fields, ➤ FUNNY, Gagster, Hardy, Horror, Jester, Knock-about, Laurel, Leno, Mag, Manga, Quizzical, Robey, Strip, Tati, Trial, Zany

Command(ing), Commander, Commandment(s) Behest, Bid, Categorical imperative, Charge, Coerce, Control, Decalogue, Direction, Dominate, Easy, Edict, Fiat, Fighter,

Firman, Haw, Hest, Imperious, Instruction, Jussive, Mandate, Mastery, Mitzvah, ▶ ORDER, Precept, Press, Requisition, Rule, Seize, Ukase, Warn, Warrant, Will, Wish, Writ

Commander Ag(h)a, Barleycorn, Bey, Bloke, Blucher, Boss, Brennus, Brig, Caliph, Centurion, Cid, Decurion, Emir, Emperor, Field cornet, Generalissimo, Hetman, Hipparch, Imperator, Killadar, Leader, Manager, Marshal, Master, Meer, Moore, Officer, Overlord, Pendragon, Raglan, Shogun, Sirdar, Taxiarch, Trierarch, Warlord

Commemorate, Commemoration Encaenia, Epitaph, Eulogy, Keep, Memorial, Monument, Plaque

Comment(ary), Commentator Analyst, Animadvert, Annotate, Comm, Coryphaeus, Critic, Descant, Discuss, Editorial, Essay, Explain, Exposition, Expound, Footnote, Gemara, Gloss(ographer), Glosser, Hakam, Kibitz, Margin, Midrashim, Note, Par, Platitude, Postil, Remark, Scholiast

Commerce, Commercial Ad, Barter, Cabotage, Jingle, Marketable, Mercantile, Mercenary, Merchant, Shoppy, Simony, Trade, Traffic

Commission(er), Commissioned Brevet, Brokerage, Charge, Charity, Countryside, Delegation, Depute, ECE, Employ, Engage, Envoy, Errand, Factor, High, Husbandage, Job, Kickback, Magistrate, Mandate, Office(r), Official, Ombudsman, Order, Percentage, Perpetration, Place, Poundage, Rake-off, Roskill, Task, Task force, Trust

Commit(al), Commitment Consign, Contract, Decision, Dedication, Delegate, Depute, Devotion, Do, Engage, Entrust, Enure, Perpetrate, Pledge, Rubicon

Committee Board, Body, Commission, Council, Group, Joint, Junta, Politburo, Presidium, Propaganda, Samiti, Select, Standing, Steering, Syndicate, Table, Vigilance, Watch

Common(s), Commoner, Commonly Average, Cad, Conventional, Diet, Dirt, Ealing, Eatables, Enclosure, Epicene, Everyday, Familiar, Fare, Folk, General, Green, House, Law, Lay, Low, Mark, Mere, MP, Mutual, Naff, Non-U, Normal, People, Pleb, Prevalent, Prole, Public, Related, Rife, Roturier, Ryfe, Scran, Sense, Shared, Stray, Tie, Trite, Tritical, Tuft, Tye, Use, ▶ USUAL, Vile, Vul(gar), Vulgo, Vulgus, Widespread, Wimbledon

Commonsense Gumption, Nous, Smeddum, Wit

Communal, Commune Agapemone, Collective, Com, Meditate, Mir, Phalanstery, Public, Talk, Township

Communicate, Communication Ampex, Announce, Baud, Boyau, Cable, Channelling, Conversation, Convey, Cybernetic, E-mail, Expansive, Impart, Infobahn, Inform, Intelsat, Internet, Message, Note, Oracy, Prestel®, Proxemics, Reach, Road, Semiotics, Signal, Tannoy®, Telepathy, Telex, Telstar, Tieline, Transmit, Utraquist

Communism, Communist Apparat(chik), Aspheterism, Bolshevist, Com, Comecon, Cominform, Comintern, Commo, Comsomol, Deviationist, Essene, Fourier, Khmer Rouge, Komsomol, Leninite, Maoist, Nomenklatura, Perfectionist, Pinko, Politburo, Red, Revisionism, Soviet, Spartacist, Tanky, Titoist, Trot, Vietcong, Vietminh

Communities, Community Alterne, Ashram, Biome, Body, Brotherhood, Clachan, Climax, Coenobitism, Coenobium, Colonia, Colony, Consocies, Ecosystem, EEC, Enclave, European, Frat(e)ry, Kahal, Kibbutz, Mesarch, Neighbourhood, People, Phyle, Public, Pueblo, Seral, Sere, Shtetl, Sisterhood, Society, Street, Town, Tribe, Ujamaa, Village, Virtual, Zupa

Commute(r) Change, Convert, Reduce, Straphanger, Travel

Compact Agreement, Cement, Concise, Conglobe, Covenant, Covin, Coyne, Dense, Entente, Fast, Firm, Flapjack, Hard, Knit, League, Match, Neat, Pledge, Powder, Solid, Terse, Tight, Treaty, Well-knit

Companion(able) Achates, Arm candy, Associate, Attender, Barnacle, Bedfellow, Bonhomie, Bud(dy), Butty, CH, China, Comate, Comrade, Consort, Contubernal, Crony, Cupman, Duenna, Ephesian, Escort, Felibre, ➤ FELLOW, Fere, Handbook, Mate, Pal, Pard, Sidekick, Thane, Thegn, Vade-mecum

Company, Companies Actors, Artel, Ass, Assembly, Band, Bank, Battalion, Bevy, ➤ BUSINESS, Bv, Cahoot, Cartel, Cast, Cavalcade, CIA, Circle, Club, Co, Conger, Consort, Cordwainers, Core, Corporation, Corps, Coy, Crew, Crowd, Decury, East India, Enterprise, Faction, Financer, ➤ FIRM, Flock, Gang, Garrison, Ging, Guild, Haberdashers, Heap, Holding, Hudson's Bay, ICI, In-house, Inc, Indie, Intercourse, Investment, Joint-stock, Limited, Listed, Livery, Maniple, Muster, Order, Organisation, Plc, Private, Public, Rep(ertory), SA, Set, Shell,

Siege, Sort, Syndicate, Team, Troop, Troupe, Twa, Two(some),
SpА, Stock, Table, Touring, Trust, Visitor, White

Compare(d), Comparison Analogy, Beside, Bracket,
Collate, Confront, Contrast, Correspond, Cp, Equate, Liken,
Match, Odious, Parallel, Relation, Simile, Weigh

Compartment Bay, Booth, Box, Carriage, Casemate, Cell,
Chamber, Cubbyhole, Cubicle, Dog box, Locellate,
Loculament, Loculus, Panel, Partition, Pigeonhole, Pocket,
Room, Room(ette), Severy, Stall, Till

Compass Ambit, Area, Beam, Bounds, Bow, Gamut,
Goniometer, Gyro, Gyroscope, Infold, Magnetic, Needle, Orbit,
Perimeter, ➤ RANGE, Reach, Rhumb, Room, Scale

Compassion(ate) Aroha, Clemency, Commiseration,
Empathy, Humane, Mercy, Pity, Samaritan, Sympathy

Compel(led), Compulsion, Compulsive, Compulsory
Addiction, Coact, Coerce, Command, Constrain, Dragoon,
Duress, Enforce, Extort, Fain, ➤ FORCE, Gar, Make, Mandatory,
Oblige, Pathological, Steamroller, Strongarm, Tyrannise

Compensate, Compensation Amend(s), Balance, Boot,
Comp, Counterbalance, Counterpoise, Damages, Demurrage,
Guerdon, Offset, Payment, Recoup, Redress, Reparation,
Reprisal, Requital, Restitution, Restore, Retaliation, Salvage,
Satisfaction, Solatium, Wergild, X-factor

Compete Contend, Enter, Match, Play, Rival, Vie

Competence, Competent Ability, Able, Adequate, Can,
Capacity, Dab, Efficient, Fit, Responsible, Sui juris, Worthy

Competition, Competitive, Competitor Agonist, Bee,
Biathlon, Contest, Cup, Drive, Entrant, Event, Field, Gymkhana,
Heptathlon, Match, Open, Opponent, Pairs, Panellist,
Pentathlon, Player, Puissance, Race, Rally, Repechage, Rival(ise),
Rodeo, Show-jumping, Tension, Test, Tiger, Tournament,
Tourney, Trial, Triallist, Wap(p)enshaw

Compile(r), Compilation Anthology, Arrange, Collect, Edit,
Prepare, Zadkiel

Complain(t), Complainer Adenoids, Affection, Affliction,
Alas, Alopecia, Anaemia, Angina, Asthma, BSE, Barrack, Beef,
Bellyache, Bitch, Bleat, Carp, Charge, Chorea, Colic, Crab,
Cramp, Criticise, Diatribe, Disorder, Dropsy, Epidemic, Ergot,
Exanthema, Girn, Gout, Gravamen, Groan, Grouch, Grouse,
Growl, Grudge, Grumble, Grutch, Harangue, Hives, Hone,

Hypochondria, ➤ ILLNESS, Jeremiad, Lupus, Malady, Mange, Mean(e), Mein, Mene, Moan, Morphew, Mumps, Murmur, Nag, Natter, Neuralgia, Pertussis, Plica, Poor-mouth, Protest, Pyelitis, Rail, Remonstrate, Repine, Rickets, Sapego, Sciatica, Scold, Sigh, Silicosis, Squawk, Staggers, Thrush, Tic, Tinea, Upset, Whimper, Whine, Whinge, Yammer, Yawp

Complete(ly) Absolute, Accomplish, All, Arrant, Attain, Clean, Congenital, Consummate, Crown, Do, End, Entire, Finalise, Finish, Fruition, Fulfil, Full, Full-blown, Hollow, Incept, Integral, In toto, One, Out, Out and out, Perfect, Plenary, Quite, Sheer, Spang, Sum, Teetotal, Thorough, Total, Uncut, Unequivocal, Unmitigated, Whole (hog)

Complex(ity) Abstruse, Compound, Difficult, Electra, Hard, Inferiority, Intricate, Intrince, Involute, Knot, Manifold, Mixed, Multinucleate, Nest, Network, Obsession, Oedipus, Paranoid, Phaedra, Superiority, Syndrome, Web

Complexion Aspect, Blee, Hue, Leer, Temper, Tint, View

Compliance, Compliant, Complicit, Comply Agree, Assent, Conform, Deference, Hand-in-glove, Obey, Observe, Sequacious, Surrender, Wilco

Complicate(d), Complication Bewilder, Complex, Deep, Elaborate, Embroil, Implex, Intricate, Involve, Inweave, Node, Nodus, Perplex, Ramification, Rigmarole, Tangle, Tirlie-wirlie

▷**Complicated** may indicate an anagram

Compliment(s) Baisemain, Bouquet, Congratulate, Devoirs, Douceur, Encomium, Flatter, Flummery, Praise, Soap, Tribute

Compose(d), Composure Aplomb, Arrange, Calm, Consist, Cool, ➤ CREATE, Equanimity, Even, Face, Improvise, Indite, Lull, Notate, Placid, Poise, Produce, Reconcile, Sangfroid, Sedate, Serenity, Settle, Soothe, Tranquil

Composer Contrapuntist, Inventor, Maker, Melodist, Musician, Serialist, Symphonist, Triadist, Tunesmith, Writer

▷**Composing** may indicate an anagram

Composition, Compositor Aleatory, Beaumontage, Capriccio, Caprice, Cob, Concerto, Creation, Dite, Essay, Etude, Fantasia, Ingredient, Inditement, Loam, Met, Montage, Morceau, Nonet(te), Opus, Oratorio, Pastiche, Piece, Poem, Polyphony, Printer, Quartette, Raga, Rhapsody, Ship, Sing, Smoot, Sonata, Sonatina, Structure, Symphony, Synthesis, Terracotta, Texture, Toccata, Treatise, Typesetter, Work

Compound Amalgam, Bahuvrihi, Blend, ➤ CAMP, Composite, Constitute, Cpd, Derivative, Mix, Multiply, Racemate, Type

▷ **Compound(ed)** may indicate an anagram

Comprehend, Comprehensive All-in, Catch-all, Catholic, Compass, Compendious, Contain, Exhaustive, Fathom, Follow, General, Global, Grasp, Include, Indepth, Ken, Large, Omnibus, Panoramic, Perceive, School, Sweeping, Thoroughgoing, ➤ UNDERSTAND, Wide

Compress(ed), Compression Astrict, Bale, Coarctate, Contract, Solidify, Squeeze, Stupe, Thlipsis

Compromise Avoision, Brule, Commit, Concession, Endanger, Involve, Settlement, Time-server, Trade off

Computation, Computer (language), Computer term, Computer user Apple, Cyberpunk, Cybersurfer, Digerati, Hacker, HAL, Hardware, Internet, Laptop, Modem, On-line, Personal, Software, Spreadsheet

Con(man) Against, Anti, Bunco, Diddle, Dupe, Jacob, Learn, Peruse, Read, Scam, Scan, Steer, Sucker, Swindle

Concede, Concession Acknowledge, Admit, Allow, Carta, Charter, Compromise, Confess, Favour, Forfeit, Franchise, Munich, Ou, Owe, Own, Privilege, Sop, Synchoresis

Conceit(ed) Bumptious, Caprice, Carriwitchet, Concetto, Crank, Crotchet, Device, Dicty, Egomania, Fancy, Fastuous, Fop, Fume, Hauteur, Idea, Notion, Podsnappery, Prig, Princock, Princox, Puppyism, Quiblin, Side, Snotty, Stuck-up, Swellhead, Toffee-nose, Vain(glory), Wind

Conceive, Conceivable Beget, Create, Credible, Imagine, Possible, Surmise

Concentrate(d), Concentration Aim, Bunch, Centre, Collect, Condense, Dephlegmate, Distil, Elliptical, Essence, Extract, Focalise, Focus, Intense, Listen, Major, Mantra, Mass, Molality, Molarity, Potted, Rivet, Samadhi, Titrate, Titre

Concern(ing) About, After, Ail, Altruism, Anent, As to, Business, Care, Cerne, Company, Disturb, Firm, In re, Intéressé, Interest, Into, Lookout, ➤ MATTER, Mell, Misease, Over, Pidgin, Part, Pigeon, Re, Reck, Regard, Reke, Respect, Retch, Solicitude, Touch, Trouble

▷ **Concerned** may indicate an anagram

Concert (place) Agreement, Benefit, Charivari, Cooperation, Device, Gig, Hootananny, Hootenanny, Hootnannie, Odeon, Odeum, Pop, Prom(enade), Recital, Singsong, Smoker, Symphony, Together, Unity, Wit

Concise Compact, Curt, Laconic, Short, Succinct, Terse, Tight

Conclude(d), Conclusion, Conclusive Achieve, A fortiori, Afterward, Amen, Binding, Cease, Clinch, Close, Complete, Dead, Decide, Deduce, ➤ END, Envoi, Explicit, Finding, Fine, Finis, ➤ FINISH, Foregone, Gather, Illation, Infer, Limit, Omega, Peroration, Point, Postlude, Punchline, Reason, Resolve, Settle, Summary, Upshot, Uptie

Concrete, Concretion Actual, Aggregate, Beton, Bezoar, Cake, Calculus, Clot, Dogger, Gunite, Hard, Mass, Minkstone, No-fines, Pile-cap, Positive, Reify, Siporex, Solid, Tangible, Tremie

Condemn(ation) Blame, Blast, Cast, Censor, Censure, Convict, Damn, Decry, Denounce, Deprecate, Doom, Judge, Kest, Obelise, Proscribe, Sentence, Theta, Upbraid

Condense(r), Condensation Abbreviate, Abridge, Capacitator, Compress, Contract, Distil, Encapsulate, Epitomise, Liebig, Précis, Rectifier, Reduce, Shorten, Shrink, Summarise

Condescend Deign, Patronise, Stoop, Vouchsafe

Condiment Caraway, Cayenne, Chutney, Flavour, Kava, Relish, Sambal, Sambol, Sauce, Tracklement, Turmeric, Vinegar

Condition(al), Conditioning Circ(s), Connote, Fettle, Going, Hammertoe, Hood, If, ➤ IN GOOD CONDITION, Kelter, Kilter, Nick, Order, Pass, Pavlovian, Plight, Pliskie, Ply, Point, Position, Predicament, Prepare, Prerequisite, Presupposition, Protasis, Proviso, Provisory, Repair, Reservation, Reserve, Rider, Ropes, Sine qua non, Sis, Standing, Sted, Stipulation, String, Term, Tid, Tox(a)emia, Trim, Trisomy, Unless

Condom Cap, Gumboot, Johnny, Letter, Prophylactic, Rubber, Safe, Sheath

Conduct(or), Conductress Accompany, Anode, Arm, Arrester, Bearing, Behaviour, Bus-bar, Cad, Clippie, Coil, Comport, Demean(our), Deportment, Direct, Drive, Editor, Electrode, Escort, Fetch, Hallé, Ignitron, 1ark, Klemperer, Lead, Liber, Lightning, Maestro, Mho, Microchip, Nerve, Officiate, Outer, Parts, ➤ PILOT, Previn, Prosecute, Rattle, Safe, Sargent,

Scudaller, Scudler, Solicit, Solti, Tao, Thermistor, Toscanini, Transact, ➤ USHER, Wire, Wood

▷ **Conducting** may indicate an '-ic' ending

Conduit Aqueduct, Canal, Carrier, Duct, Main, Pipe, Tube

Cone, Conical Cappie, Fir, Moxa, Pastille, Peeoy, Pineal, Pingo, Pioy(e), Puy, Pyramid, Spire, Storm, Strobilus, Taper, Tee, Traffic, Volcanic, Windsock

Confederal, Confederacy, Confederate, Confederation Accessory, Alliance, Ally, Association, Body, Bund, Bunkosteerer, Cover, Illinois, League, Partner, Union

Confer(ence) Bestow, Cf, Collogue, Colloqium, Colloquy, Congress, Council, Diet, Do, Dub, Fest, Forum, Grant, Huddle, Imparlance, Indaba, Intercommune, Lambeth, Meeting, Munich, Negotiate, Palaver, Parley, Pawaw, Pear, Potsdam, Pourparler, Powwow, Press, Pugwash, Quadrant, Seminar, Settle, Summit, Symposium, Synod, ➤ TALK, Vouchsafe, Yalta

Confess(or), Confession Acknowledge, Admit, Agnise, Avowal, Concede, Declare, Disclose, Edward, Own, Recant, Shrift, Shriver, Sing, Whittle

Confide(nce), Confident(ial), Confidant Aplomb, Aside, Assertive, Assured, Bedpost, Belief, Cocksure, Cred, Crouse, Entre nous, Entrust, Faith, Feisty, Gatepost, Hardy, Hope, Hush-hush, Intimate, Morale, Pack, Private, Privy, Sanguine, Secret, Self-possessed, Sub rosa, Sure, Tell, Trust, Unbosom, Under the rose, Vaulting

Confine(d), Confines, Confinement Ambit, Bail, Bale, Cage, CB, Chain, Constrain, Cramp, Crib, Detain, Emmew, Encase, Enclose, Endemic, Enmew, Ensheath, Gate, Immanacle, Immew, Immure, Impound, ➤ IMPRISON, Incommunicado, Inhoop, Intern, Local, March, Mail, Mew, Mure, Narrow, Pen, Pent, Pinion, Poky, Restrict, Rules, Solitary, Trammel

Confirm(ed), Confirmation Addict, Assure, Attest, Bear, Certify, Chrisom, Christen, Chronic, Clinch, Corroborate, Endorse, Homologate, Obsign, OK, Ratify, Sacrament, Sanction, Seal, Strengthen, Ten-four, Tie, Validate, Vouch

Conflict(ing) Agon, Armageddon, Battle, Camp, Clash, Contend, Contravene, Controversy, Disharmony, Encounter, Feud, Fray, Inconsistent, Jar, Lists, Mêlée, Muss, Oppose, Rift, Strife, ➤ STRUGGLE, Tergiversate, War

Conform(ity) Accord, Adjust, Comply, Consistence, Correspond, Normalise, Obey, Observe, Propriety, Standardize, Stereotype(d), Suit, Trimmer, Yield

Confound(ed) Abash, Amaze, Astound, Awhape, Baffle, Bewilder, Blamed, Blasted, Blest, Bumbaze, Contradict, Darn, Drat, Dumbfound, Elude, Floor, Jigger, Mate, Murrain, Nonplus, Perishing, Perplex, Rabbit, Spif(f)licate, Stump, Throw

▷ **Confound** may indicate an anagram

Confront(ation) Appose, Beard, Breast, Eyeball, Face, Mau-mau, Meet, Nose, Oppose, Showdown, Tackle

Confuse(d), Confusion Addle, Anarchy, Astonishment, Babel, Baffle, Bedevil, Befog, Befuddle, Bemuse, Bewilder, Blur, Burble, Bustle, Chaos, Cloud, Clutter, Complicate, Debacle, Didder, Disconcert, Disorient, Distract, Dither, Dizzy, Dudder, Dust, Embrangle, Embroglio, Embroil, Farrago, Flap, Flummox, Flurry, Fluster, Fog, Fox, Fuddle, Galley-west, Hash, Havoc, Hazy, Huddle, Hugger-mugger, Hurly-burly, Hurry-skurry, Imbrangle, Imbroglio, ► IN CONFUSION, Indistinct, Litter, Lost, Lurry, Maelstrom, Maffled, Mayhem, Maze, Melange, Melee, Mess, Mingle, Mish-mash, Mixtie-maxtie, Mizzle, Moider, Moither, Moonstruck, ► MUDDLE, Mudge, Muzzy, Overset, Pellmell, Perplex, Pi(e), Pose, Ravel, Razzle-dazzle, Razzmatazz, Rout, Snafu, Spin, Stump, Stupefy, Tangle, Throw, Topsy-turvy, Tzimmes, Welter, Whomble, Woolly, Woozy

▷ **Confuse(d)** may indicate an anagram

Congratulate, Congratulation Applaud, Felicitate, Laud, Mazeltov, Preen, Salute

Congregate, Congregation(alist) Assembly, Barnabite, Body, Brownist, Class, Community, Conclave, Ecclesia, Flock, Fold, Gathering, Host, Laity, Oratory, Propaganda, Synagogue

Congress(man) Assembly, Conclave, Council, Eisteddfod, Intercourse, Legislature, Rally, Senator, Solon, Synod, Vienna

Conjunction Alligation, Ampersand, And, Combination, Consort, Synod, Syzygy, Together, Union

Connect(ed), Connection, Connector Accolade, Adaptor, Affinity, Agnate, Anastomosis, And, Associate, Attach, Band, Bind, Bridge, Bridle, Cable, Clientele, Coherent, Colligate, Conjugate, Couple, Cross-link, Delta, Dovetail, Drawbar, Fishplate, Fistula, ► IN CONNECTION WITH, Interlink, Interlock, Join, Jumper, Kinship, Liaison, Lifeline, Link, Marry, Merge,

Nexus, On, Online, Pons, Raphe, Rapport, Relate, Relative, Respect, S-R, Shuttle, Splice, Tendon, Through, Tie, Tie-in, Union, Yoke, Zygon

Connive, Connivance Abet, Cahoots, Collude, Condone, Conspire, Plot

Connoisseur Aesthete, Cognoscente, Epicure, Expert, Fancier, Gourmet, Judge, Oenophil

Conquer(or), Conquest Beat, Conquistador, Crush, Debel, Genghis Khan, Hereward, ► MASTER, Moor, Norman, Ostrogoth, Overcome, Overpower, Overrun, Pizarro, Subjugate, Tame, Tamerlane, Vanquish, Victor

Conscience, Conscientious Casuistic, Heart, Inwit, Morals, Painstaking, Pang, Remorse, Scruple(s), Sense, Superego, Syneidesis, Synteresis, Thorough, Twinge

Conscious(ness) Awake, Aware, Limen, Sensible, Sentient

Consent Accord, Affo(o)rd, Agree, Approbate, Comply, Concur, Grant, Informed, Permit, Ratify, Volens, Yes-but, Yield

Consequence, Consequent(ial) Aftermath, Consectaneous, Corollary, Effect, End, Importance, Issue, Karma, Knock-on, Moment, Outcome, Ramification, Repercussion, ► RESULT, Sequel

Conservative Blimpish, Blue, C, Cautious, Diehard, Disraeli, Fabian, Hard-hat, Hunker, Old guard, Rearguard, Right(-wing), Square, Thrifty, Tory, True blue, Unionist

Conserve, Conservation(ist) Comfiture, Husband(ry), Jam, Jelly, Maintain, Maintenance, Protect, NT, Save

Consider(able), Consideration Animadvert, Attention, Avizandum, By-end, Case, Cogitate, Contemplate, Count, Courtesy, Debate, Deem, Deliberate, Entertain, Envisage, Factor, Fair, Feel, Heed, Importance, Inasmuch, Judge, Many, Meditate, Muse, Pay, Perpend, Poise, Ponder, Pretty, Rate, Reckon, Reflect, Regard, Respect, See, Several, Solicitous, Song, Speculate, Steem, Study, Substantial, Think, Tidy, Vast, View, Ween, Weigh

Consign(ment) Allot, Award, Batch, Bequeath, Delegate, Deliver, Entrust, Lading, Ship, Transfer

Consist(ent), Consistency Coherent, Comprise, Enduring, Liaison, Rely, Steady

Consolation, Console Ancon, Appease, Balm, Comfort, Relief, Solace

Conspicuous Arresting, Blatant, Clear, Eminent, Glaring, Kenspeck(le), Landmark, Light, Manifest, Patent, Salient, Signal, Striking

Conspiracy, Conspirator, Conspire, Conspiring Cabal, Casca, Cassius, Catiline, Cato St, Cinna, Collaborate, Colleague, Collogue, Collude, Complot, Connive, Covin, Covyne, Guy, In cahoots, Intrigue, Oates, Omerta, ➤ PLOT, Ring, Scheme

Constancy, Constant Abiding, Boltzmann, C, Chronic, Coefficient, Devotion, Dirac, Eccentricity, Faith, G, H, Honesty, Hubble's, K, Lambert, Leal(ty), Logical, Loyal, Often, Parameter, ➤ PERPETUAL, Planck's, Pole star, Resolute, Sad, Staunch, Steadfast, Steady, True, Unfailing, Uniform, Usual

Constellation Galaxy, ➤ PLANET, ➤ STAR, Twins, Unicorn, Virgo, Volans

Constituency, Constituent Borough, Component, Element, Part, Seat, Voter

▷**Constituents** may indicate an anagram

Constitute, Constitution(al) Appoint, Charter, Compose, Comprise, Congenital, Creature, Establishment, Form, Fuero, Health, Physique, Policy, Polity, Seat, State, Synthesis

Constrain(ed), Constraint Bind, Bondage, Coerce, Confine, Coop, Curb, Duress(e), Hard, Oblige, Pressure, Repress, Stenosis, Taboo

Constrict(ed), Constriction Bottleneck, Choke, Coarctate, Contract, Cramp, Hour-glass, Impede, Limit, Phimosis, Squeeze, Stegnosis, Stenosis, Thlipsis, Tighten, Venturi

Construct(ion), Constructor, Constructive Build, Compile, Engineer, Erect, Fabricate, Facture, Fashion, Form, Frame, Make, Manufacture, Seabee, Tectonic, Weave

Consult(ant), Consultation Confer, Deliberate, Discuss, Imparl, Peritus, See, Surgery

Consume(r), Consumption, Consumptive Bolt, Burn, Caterpillar®, Decay, Devour, Diner, Eat, Engross, Exhaust, Expend, Feed, Glutton, Hectic, Mainline, Scoff, Spend, Swallow, TB, Use, Waste, Wear

Contact Abut, Adpress, Contingence, Hook-up, Lens, Liaise, Liaison, Meet, Reach, Shoe, ➤ TOUCH

Contagious, Contagion Infection, Noxious, Poison, Taint, Variola, Viral

Contain(er) Amphora, Ampulla, Aquafer, Aquifer, Bass, Bidon, Bin, Bottle, Box, Buddle, Cachepot, Can, Canakin, Canikin, Canister, Cannikin, Cantharus, Capsule, Carboy, Carry, Carton, Case, Cask, Cassette, Chase, Chest, Churn, Coffer, Comprise, Coolamon, Crate, Crater, Crucible, Cup, Cupel, Dracone, Dredger, Enclose, Encompass, Enseam, Esky®, Feretory, ► HOLD, House, Igloo, Include, Incubator, Jerrican, Jerrycan, Kirbeh, Leaguer, Lekythos, Monkey, Monstrance, Mould, Olpe, Pail, Piscina, Pithos, Pod, Pottle, Reliquary, Repository, Restrain, Saggar, Scyphus, Shaker, Skin, Skip, Spittoon, Stamnos, Tank, Terrarium, Tinaja, Tub, Tun, Tupperware®, Urn, Vessel, Vinaigrette, Woolpack

Contaminate(d) Corrupt, Defile, Flyblown, Impure, Infect, Soil, Stain, Tarnish

Contemporary AD, Coetaneous, Current, Equal, Fellow, Modern, Present, Verism

Contempt(ible), Contemptuous Abject, Ageism, Aha, Arsehole, Bah, BEF, Cheap, Contumely, Crud, Crumb, Cullion, Cynical, Derision, Disparaging, Dog-bolt, Fig, Ignominious, Low, Mean, Measly, Misprision, Paltry, Phooey, Pish, Poxy, Pshaw, Rats, Razoo, Scabby, Scarab, ► SCORN, Scumbag, Sexism, Shabby, Shithead, Sneeze, Sniff, Snooty, Snot, Soldier, Sorry, Squirt, Squit, Supercilious, Toad, Toerag, Weed, Wretched

Contend(er) Candidate, Claim, Clash, Compete, Cope, Debate, Dispute, Fight, Grapple, Oppose, Stickle, ► STRIVE, Struggle, Submit, ► VIE, Wrestle

Content Apaid, Apay, Appay, Blissful, Happy, Inside, Please, Satisfy, Volume

▷ **Content** may indicate a hidden word

Contention, Contentious Argument, Bellicose, Case, Cantankerous, Combat, Competitive, Perverse, Polemical, Rivalry, Strife, Struggle, Sturt

Contest(ant) Agon, Battle, Bout, Catchweight, Challenge, Combat, Competition, Concours, Decathlon, Defend, Duel(lo), Entrant, Eurovision, Examinee, Fronde, Heptathlon, Kriegspiel, Lampadephoria, Match, Matchplay, Olympiad, Pentathlon,

Pingle, Prizer, Race, Roadeo, Rodeo, Set-to, Skirmish, Slugfest, Strife, Struggle, Tenson, Tournament, Triathlon, Vie, War, With

Continent(al) Abstinent, Asia, Atlantis, Austere, Chaste, Epeirogeny, Euro, Gallic, Gondwanaland, Laurasia, Lemuria, Mainland, Moderate, Pang(a)ea, Shelf, Teetotal, Temperate, Walloon

Continual(ly), Continuous Adjoining, Away, Chronic, Connected, Eer, Endlong, Eternal, Ever, Frequent, Incessant, On(going)

Continue, Continuation, Continuing, Continuity Abye, Duration, Dure, During, Enduring, Enjamb(e)ment, Hold, Keep, Last, Link, Onward, Persevere, Persist, Proceed, Prolong, Resume, Sequence, Stand, Subsist, Survive, Sustain, Tenor

▷ **Continuously** may indicate previous words to be linked

Contraception, Contraceptive Cap, Coil, Condom, Diaphragm, IU(C)D, Minipill, Oral, Pessary, Pill, Prophylactic, Loop, Sheath, Vimule®

Contract(ion), Contractor Abbreviate, Abridge, Agreement, Astringency, Bargain, Biceps, Bridge, Builder, Catch, Champerty, Charter, Clonus, Condense, Constringe, Contrahent, Covenant, Cramp, Curtail, Debt, Dwindle, Engage, Entrepreneur, Escrow, Gainsay, Gooseflesh, Guarantee, Hire, Incur, Indenture, Jerk, Knit, Lease, Levator, Make, Miosis, Myosis, Narrow, Party, Promise, Pucker, Purse, Restriction, Shrink, Shrivel, Sign, Slam, Social, Spasm, Specialty, Stenosis, Stipulation, Supplier, Sweetheart, Systole, Tetanie, Tetanus, Tic, Tighten, Tonicity, Treaty, Triceps, Yellow-dog, Wrinkle, Z

Contradict(ion), Contradictory Ambivalent, Antilogy, Antinomy, Bull, Contrary, Counter, Dementi, Deny, Disaffirm, Disprove, Dissent, ► GAINSAY, Negate, Oxymoron, Paradox, Sot, Stultify, Sublate, Threap, Threep, Traverse

Contrarily, Contrary Adverse, A rebours, Arsy-versy, But, Captious, Converse, Counter, Crosscurrent, Froward, Hostile, Inverse, Mary, Opposite, Ornery, Perverse, Rebuttal, Retrograde, Wayward, Withershins

Contrast Chiaroscuro, Clash, Compare, Differ, Foil, Relief

Contribute, Contribution Abet, Add, Assist, Conduce, Donate, Dub, Furnish, Go, Help, Input, Mite, Offering, Share, Sub, Subscribe, Whack

▷ **Contributing to** may indicate a hidden word

Contrive(r) Chicaner, Cook, Devise, Engineer, Frame, Hatch, Intrigue, Machinate, Manage, Manoeuvre, Plan, Procure, Scheme, Secure, Stage, Trump, Weave

Control(ler), Controllable Ada, Appestat, Big Brother, Birth, Boss, Bridle, Cabotage, Chair, Check, Christmas tree, Corner, Corset, Cybernetics, Dirigible, Dirigism(e), Dominion, Fet(ch), Finger, Gerent, Govern, Gubernation, Harness, Have, Heck, Helm, Influence, Influx, Joystick, Knee-swell, Lead, Lever, ➤ MANAGE, Martinet, Mastery, Moderate, Mouse, Nipple, Pilot, Police, Possess, Power, Preside, Puppeteer, Quality, Regulate, Regulo®, Rein, Remote, Repress, Restrain, Rheostat, Ride, Rule, Run, School, Servo, Snail, Solion, Steady, Steer, Stop, Stranglehold, Stringent, Subdue, Subject, Subjugate, Supervise, Suzerain, Sway, Takeover, Thermostat, Throttle, Tiller, Valve, Weld, Wield, Zapper

Controversial, Controversy Argument, Contention, Debate, Dispute, Eristic(al), Furore, Hot potato

Convenience, Convenient Behoof, Eft, Expedient, Facility, Gain, Gents, ➤ HANDY, Hend, Lav, Leisure, Near, Opportune, Pat, Privy, Public, Suitable, Toilet, Use, Well

Convent Cloister, Fratry, Friary, House, Motherhouse, Nunnery, Port-royal, Priory, Retreat

Convention(al) Academic, Accepted, Babbitt, Blackwood, Bourgeois, Caucus, Conclave, ➤ CUSTOMARY, Diet, Done, Formal, Geneva, Iconic, Meeting, More, Nomic, Orthodox, Pompier, Staid, Starchy, Stereotyped, Stock, Synod, Uptight, Usage, Warsaw

Conversation(alist), Converse, Conversant Abreast, Antithesis, Board, Buck, Cackle, Causerie, Chat, Chitchat, Colloquy, Commune, Deipnosophist, Dialogue, Discourse, Eutrapelia, Eutrapely, Hobnob, Interlocution, Jaw-jaw, Opposite, Palaver, Parley, Rap, Rhubarb, Shop, Socialise, ➤ TALK, Transpose, Wongi, Word

Conversion, Converter, Convert(ible) Adapt, Alter, Assimilate, Bessemer, Catalytic, Catechumen, Change, Commute, Cyanise, Diagenesis, Disciple, Encash, Exchange, Expropriate, Fixation, Liquid, Marrano, Metanoia, Neophyte, Noviciate, Novitiate, Persuade, Proselyte, Put, Ragtop, Realise, Rebirth, Recycle, Revamp, Souper, Tablet, Transduce, Transmute, Try

▷**Conversion, Converted** may indicate an anagram

Convey(ance) Assign, BS, Carousel, Carry, Charter, Coach, Conduct, Cycle, Deed, Eloi(g)n, Enfeoffment, Grant, Guide, Lease, Litter, Lorry, Mailcar(t), Re-lease, Sac and soc, Tip, Title deed, Tote, Tram, Transfer, Transit, Transmit, Transport, Vehicle

Convict(ion) Attaint, Belief, Bushranger, Certitude, Cockatoo, Cogence, Crawler, Credo, Creed, Criminal, Demon, Dogma, Faith, Felon, Forçat, Lag, Magwitch, ➤ PERSUASION, Plerophory, Ring, Trusty, Vehemence, Yardbird

Convince(d), Convincing Assure, Cogent, Doubtless, Luculent, Persuade, Satisfy, Sold, Sure

Convulsion(s), Convulsive Agitate, Clonic, Commotion, Disturb, DT, Eclampsia, ➤ FIT, Galvanic, Paroxysm, Spasm, Throe, Tic

Cook(s), Cooker, Cooking Aga®, Babbler, Bake, Balti, Beeton, Benghazi, Bhindi, Bouche, Braise, Broil, Cacciatore, Calabash, Captain, Charbroil, Chargrill, Chef, Coddle, Concoct, Cordon bleu, Cuisine, Devil, Do, Doctor, Dumple, Edit, Escoffier, Fake, Falsify, Fiddle, Flambé, Forge, Fricassee, Fry, Fudge, Greasy, Grill, Haute cuisine, Haybox, Marinière, Meunière, Microwave, Poach, Prepare, Pressure, Ring, Roast, Roger, Sous-chef, Spit, Steam, Stew, Stir-fry, Tandoori, Tire

▷**Cook** may indicate an anagram

Cool(er), Coolness Aloof, Aplomb, Calm, Can, Chill, Collected, Composed, Cryogen, Cryostat, Defervescence, Dispassionate, Distant, Esky®, Fan, Frappé, Fridge, Frigid, Frosty, Gaol, Goglet, Ice(box), Jail, Jug, Keel, Phlegm, Prison, Quad, Quod, Refresh, Reserved, Sangfroid, Serene, Skeigh, Stir, Temperate, Thou(sand), Unruffled

Coop Cage, Cavie, Confine, Gaol, Hutch, Mew, Pen, Rip

Cooperate, Cooperation, Cooperative Collaborate, Combine, Conspire, Contribute, Coop, Liaise, Teamwork, Together

Coordinate(d), Coordination Abscissa, Abscisse, Agile, Arrange, Cartesian, Ensemble, Harmony, Nabla, Orchestrate, Ordonnance, Peer, Polar, Synergy, X, Y, Z

Cop(s) Bag, Bull, Catch, Dick, Keystone, Peeler, Peon, ➤ POLICEMAN

Cope Chlamys, Deal, Face, Handle, ➤ MANAGE, Mantle, Meet, Negotiate, Pallium, Poncho

Copy(ing), Copier, Copyist Aemule, Ape, Apograph, Autotype, Calk, Calque, Carbon, Clerk, Clone, Counterpart, Crib, Cyclostyle, Diazo, Ditto, Dyeline, Echo, Echopraxia, Ectype, Edition, Eidograph, Electro, Emulate, Engross, Estreat, Example, Facsimile, Fair, Fax, Flimsy, Forge, ➤ IMITATE, Issue, Manifold, Manuscript, Match, Me-tooer, Milline, Mimeograph®, Mimic, Mirror, MS, Parrot, Photostat®, Plagiarism, Read-out, Replica, Repro, Reproduce, Roneo®, Scribe, Script, Scrivener, Sedulous, Simulate, Spit, Stencil, Stuff, Tenor, Tenure, Trace, Transcribe, Transume, Vidimus, Xerox®

Coral (reef) Alcyonaria, Aldabra, Atoll, Brain, Gorgonia(n), Laccadives, Madrepore, Millepore, Pink, Reef, Sea fan, Sea ginger, Sea whip, Sea-pen, Zoothome

Cord, Cord-like Aiguillette, Band, Bedford, Bind, Boondoggle, Cat-gut, Chenille, Communication, Creance, Drawstring, Flex, Fourragère, Funicle, Gasket, Heddle, Laniard, Lanyard, Ligature, Line, Moreen, Myelon, Net, Ocnus, Piping, Quipo, Quipu, Rep(s), Restiform, Rip, Rope, Sash, Sennit, Service, Spermatic, Spinal, ➤ STRING, Tendon, Tie, Twine, Umbilical, Vocal

Cordon Picket, Ring, Surround

Core Barysphere, Calandria, Campana, Centre, Essence, Filament, Heart, Hub, Nife, Plerome, Quintessence

Cork(ed), Corker Balsa, Bouché, Bung, Float(er), Humdinger, Oner, Phellem, Phellogen, Plug, Seal, Shive, Stopper, Suber(ate)

Corkscrew Bore, Opening, Spiral

Cormorant Duiker, Duyker, Scart(h), Skart(h)

Corn(y) Bajr(a), Banal, Blé, Cereal, Cob, Emmer, Epha, Flint, Gait, Graddan, Grain, Grist, Icker, Indian, Kaffir, Mabela, Maize, Mealie, Muid, Nubbin, Pickle, Pinole, Posho, Rabi, Shock, Stitch, Straw, Thrave, Trite, Zea

Corner Amen, Angle, Bend, Cantle, Canton, Cranny, Dangerous, Dièdre, Elbow, Entrap, Hole, Hospital, Lug, Monopoly, NE, Niche, Nook, NW, Predicament, Quoin, SE, Spot, Speaker's, SW, Tack, Trap, Tree, Vertex

Corporation Belly, Body, Commune, Company, Conglomerate, Guild, Kite, Kyte, Paunch, Stomach, Swag-belly, Tum, Wame, Wem

Corps Body, C, Crew, Diplomatic, Peace, RAC, REME, Unit

Corpse Blob, Body, Cadaver, Carcass, Carrion, Goner, Like, Mort, Relic, Remains, Stiff, Zombi(e)

Correct(ing), Correctly, Correctness, Correction, Corrector Accurate, Alexander, Align, Amend, Aright, Bodkin, Castigate, Chasten, Chastise, Check, Decorous, Diorthortic, Emend, Exact, Fair, Grammatical, Legit, Mend, Preterition, Probity, Proofread, Proper, Propriety, Punctilious, Punish, Rebuke, Rectify, Redress, Remedial, Reprove, Revise, Right(en), Scold, Spot-on, Sumpsimus, Trew, True, U

▷ **Corrected** may indicate an anagram

Correspond(ence), Corresponding Accord, Agree, Analogy, Assonance, Coincident, Communicate, Congruence, Counterpart, Equate, Eye-rhyme, Fit, Homolog(ue), Identical, Match, On all fours, One to one, Par, Parallel, Relate, Symmetry, Tally, Veridical, Write

Corridor Air, Aisle, Gallery, Lobby, Passage

Corrode(d), Corrosion, Corrosive Acid, Brinelling, Burn, Canker, Decay, Eat, Erode, Etch, Fret, Gnaw, Hydrazine, Mordant, ➤ ROT, Rubiginous, Rust, Waste

Corrupt(er), Corrupting, Corruption Adulterate, Bent, Canker, Debase, Debauch, Decadent, Defile, Depravity, Dissolute, Dry rot, Emancipate, Embrace(o)r, Embrasor, Empoison, Etch, Fester, Gangrene, Graft(er), Immoral, Impure, Inquinate, Jobbery, Leprosy, Malversation, Nefarious, Obelus, Payola, Perverse, Poison, Pollute, Power, Ret(t), Rigged, Rot, Scrofulous, Seduce, Sepsis, Septic, Sleaze, Sodom, Sophisticate, Spoil, Suborn, Tammany, Twist, Venal, Vice, Vitiate

Cosmetic Beautifier, Blusher, Eye-black, Eyeliner, Eye-shadow, Foundation, Fucus, Kohl, Lip gloss, Lip liner, Lipstick, Lotion, Maquillage, Mascara, Paint, Powder, Reface, Rouge, Talcum, Toner

Cosmos, Cosmic Globe, Heaven, Infinite, Nature, Universe, World

Cost(ly) Bomb, Carriage, Charge, Damage, Earth, Escuage, Estimate, Exes, ➤ EXPENSE, Hire, Loss, Marginal, Outlay, Overhead, Precious, Price, Quotation, Rate, Sacrifice, Sumptuous, Toll, Unit, Upkeep, Usurious

Costume Apparel, Attire, Camagnole, Cossie, Dress, Ensemble, Get-up, Gi(e), Guise, Judogi, Livery, Maillot, Motley, Nebris, Polonaise, Rig, Surcoat, Tanga, Uniform

Cosy Cosh, Intime, Snug

Cottage(r) Bach, Bordar, Bothie, Bothy, Box, Bungalow, Cabin, Chalet, Cot, Crib, Dacha, Hut, Lodge, Mailer

Cotton Agree, AL, Alabama, Balbriggan, Batiste, Batting, Calico, Candlewick, Ceiba, Chambray, Chino, Chintz, Collodion, Coutil(le), Cretonne, Denim, Dho(o)ti, Dimity, Ducks, Fustian, Galatea, Gossypine, Gossypium, Humhum, Ihram, Jaconet, Lawn, Lea, Lille, Lint, Lisle, Manchester, Marcella, Muslin, Nainsook, Nankeen, Nankin, Pongee, Sea-island, Seersucker, Silesia, Stranded, Surat, T-cloth, Thread, Twig, Upland

Couch Bed, Davenport, Daybed, ➤ DIVAN, Express, Grass, Lurk, Palanquin, Palkee, Palki, Quick, Recamier, Sedan, Settee, Sofa, Studio, Triclinium, Word

Cough(ing) Bark, Croup, Expectorate, Hack, Hawk, Hem, Hoast, Kink, Rale, Tisick, Tussis, Ugh, Whooping

Council (meeting), Councillor, Counsel(lor) Achitophel, Admonish, Admonitor, Advice, Advocate, Ahithophel, Alfred, Aread, Assembly, Attorney, Aulic, Board, Body, Boule, Bundesrat, Burgess, Cabinet, Casemate, Committee, Consistory, Corporation, County, Cr, Decurion, Devil, Divan, Douma, Duma, Egeria, Exhort, Greenbag, Hebdomadal, Indaba, Induna, Info, Jirga, Junta, Kabele, Kebele, Kite, Landst(h)ing, Lateran, Leader, Legislative, Majlis, Mentor, Nestor, Nicene, Panchayat, Parish, Powwow, Privy, Provincial, Rede, Reichsrat, Samaritan, Sanhedrim, Sanhedrin, Security, Senate, Shura, Sobranje, Sobranye, Soviet, Syndicate, Synod, Thing, Trent, Tridentine, Trullan, Volost, Whitley, Witan, Witenagemot, Works, Zila, Zillah

Count(ed), Counter, Counting Abacus, Add, Algoriam, Anti, Bar, Basie, Buck, Buffet, Calculate, Cavour, Census, Chip, Compute, Coost, Desk, Dracula, Dump, Earl, Enumerate, Fish, Geiger, Geiger-Muller, Graf(in), Grave, Itemise, Jet(t)on, Landgrave, Margrave, Matter, Merel(l), Meril, Number, Obviate, Olivia, Oppose, Palatine, Palsgrave, Paris, Pollen, Presume, Rebut, ➤ RECKON, Refute, Rejoinder, Rely, Retaliate, Retort, Rhinegrave, Scintillation, Score, Sperm, Squail,

Statistician, Stop, Sum, Table, Tally, Tell, Tiddleywink, Ugolino, Weigh, Zeppelin

Counterfeit(er) Belie, Bogus, Boodle, Brum, Coiner, Duffer, Dummy, Fantasm, Flash, Forge, Imitant, Phantasm, Phoney, Pseudo, Queer, Rap, Sham, Schlenter, Shan(d), Simulate, Slang, Slip, Smasher, Snide, Spurious

Countless Infinite, Innumerable, Myriad, Umpteen, Untold

Country Annam, Bangladesh, Boondocks, Bucolic, Champaign, Clime, Colchis, Edom, Enchorial, Fatherland, Karoo, Karroo, ➤ LAND, Lea, Lee, Mongolia, Motherland, Nation, Parish, Paysage, People, Province, Realm, Region, Republic, Rural, Satellite, Soil, State, Tundra, Weald, Wold, Yemen

County Co, Comital, District, Palatine, Parish, Seat, Shire

Coup Blow, Deal, KO, Move, Putsch, Scoop, Stroke

Couple(r), Coupling Ally, Band, Brace, Bracket, Connect, Duet, Duo, Dyad, Fishplate, Gemini, Geminy, Hitch, Item, ➤ JOIN, Marry, Mate, Meng(e), Ment, Ming, Pair, Pr, Relate, Shackle, Tie, Tirasse, Turnbuckle, Tway, Union, Universal, Voltaic, Wed, Yoke

Coupon(s) Ration, Ticket, Voucher

Courage(ous) Balls, Bottle, Bravado, Bravery, Bulldog, Dutch, Fortitude, Gallantry, Game, Gimp, Grit, Gumption, Guts, Heart, Heroism, Lion-heart, Macho, Mettle, Moxie, Nerve, Pluck, Rum, Spirit, Spunk, Stalwart, Steel, Valiant, Valour, Wight

Course(s) Afters, Aim, Aintree, Antipasto, Appetiser, Arroyo, Ascot, Assault, Atlantic, Bearing, Beat, Canal, Career, Chantilly, Chase, Circuit, Consommé, Correspondence, Crash, Current, Curriculum, Cursus, Dessert, Diadrom, Dish, Dromic, Entrée, Fish, Food, Foundation, Going, Goodwood, Greats, Heat, Lane, Lap, Layer, Leat, Leet, Line, Lingfield, Links, Longchamp, Meal, Meat, Mess, Newbury, Newmarket, Nine-hole, Nulla, ➤ OF COURSE, Orbit, Period, Policy, PPE, Procedure, Process, Programme, Progress, Pursue, Race, Raik, Refresher, Regimen, Rhumb, Ride, Ring, Rink, Road, Rota, Route, Routine, Run, Rut, Sandown, Sandwich, Semester, Series, Soup, Starter, Stearage, Steerage, Step(s), Stratum, Streak, Stretch, String, Syllabus, Tack, Tanride, Tenor, Track, Trade, Troon, Way

Court(ier) Address, Arches, Atrium, Attention, Audience, Audiencia, Aula, Banc, Bar, Basecourt, Bench, Beth Din, Boondock, Caravanserai, Cassation, Centre, Chancery, Chase,

Clay, Consistory, County, Crown, CS, Ct, Curia, Curia Regis, Curtilage, Dale, Dedans, Diplock, District, Doctor's Commons, Duchy, Durbar, Dusty Feet, En tout cas, Eyre, Federal, Fehm(gericht), Forensic, Forest, Forum, Fronton, Galleria, Garth, Grass, Guildenstern, Halimot(e), Hampton, Hard, High, Hof, Hustings, Intermediate, Invite, Jack, Kacheri, Kangaroo, Keys, King, King's Bench, Kirk Session, Knave, Law, Leet, Lobby, Marshalsea, Moot, Old Bailey, Parvis, Patio, Peristyle, Philander, Piepowder, Porte, Presbytery, Probate, Provincial, Quad, Queen, Queen's Bench, Retinue, Royal, Sanhedrin, See, Session, Shire-moot, Spoon, Stannary, Star Chamber, Sue, Supreme, Swanimote, Sweetheart, Thane, Thegn, Tribunal, Vehm, Vestibulum, Ward, Wench, Woo, Wow, Yard

Courteous, Courtesy Affable, Agrement, Bow, Comity, Devoir, Etiquette, Genteel, Gracious, Hend, Polite, Refined, Urbanity

Courtly Chivalrous, Cringing, Dignified, Flattering, Refined

Courtyard Area, Cortile, Marae, Patio, Quad

Cousin(s) Bette, Cater, Country, Coz, Cross, German, Kin, Kissing, Robin, Skater

Cover(ed), Covering A l'abri, Adventitia, Amnion, Antependium, Antimacassar, Apron, Aril, Attire, Awning, Barb, Bard(s), Bark, Bedspread, Bestrew, Bind, Blanket, Bodice, Brood, Bubblewrap, Camouflage, Canopy, Cap, Caparison, Cape, Casing, Casque, Catch-all, Caul, Ceil, Ciborium, Cladding, Clapboard, Cleithral, Clithral, Coat, Cocoon, Coleorhiza, Conceal, Cope, Copyright, Cosy, Counterpane, Cour, Covert, Cowl, Curtain, Deck, Deputise, Dome, Drape(t), Dripstone, Dust-sheet, Duvet, Eiderdown, Encase, Endue, Enguard, Enlace, Enshroud, Envelop(e), Exoderm(is), Exoskeleton, Extra, Face, Falx, Fanfare, Felting, Fielder, Figleaf, First-day, Flashing, Fother, Front, Gaiter, Gambado, Grolier, Ground, Hap, Harl, Hat, Hatch, Havelock, Heal, Heel, Hejab, Hele, Hell, Helmet, Hood, Housing, Hubcap, Immerse, Incase, Indusium, Insulate, Insurance, Insure, Jacket, Lag, Lay, Leap, Leep, Legging, Legwarmer, Lid, Manche, Mantle, Mount, Mulch, Notum, Numnah, OC, Occlude, On, Operculum, Orillion, Orlop, Overlay, Palampore, Palempore, Pall, Pand, Parcel, Pasties, Patch, Pebbledash, Pelmet, Periderm, Plaster, Plate, Pleura, Point, Pseudonym, Pullover, Quilt, Radome, Regolith, Robe, Roof, Roughcast, Rug,

Sally, Screen, Serviette, Setting, Sheath, Sheet, Shell, Shelter, Shield, Shrink-wrap, Shroud, Shuck, Skin, Smokescreen, Span, Spat, Stand-by, Stifle, Swathe, Tampian, Tampion, Tapis, Tarpaulin, Teacosy, Tectorial, Tegmen, Tegument, Tent, Test(a), Tester, Thatch, Thimble, Tick(ing), Tilt, Top, Trapper, Trench, Trip, Turtleback, Twill, Twilt, Umbrella, Upholster, Valance, Veil, Vele, Veneer, Ventail, Vesperal, Vest, Visor, Volva, Wainscot, Whelm, Whitewash, Wrap, Yapp

Covet(ed), Covetous Avaricious, Crave, Desiderata, Desire, Eager, Envy, Greedy, Hanker, Yearn

Cow Adaw, Alderney, Amate, Appal, Awe, Bovine, Browbeat, Cash, Charolais, Colly, Crummy, Danton, Daunt, Dexter, Dsomo, Dun, Galloway, Gally, Goujal, Guernsey, Hawkey, Hawkie, Heifer, Hereford, Intimidate, Jersey, Kouprey, Kyloe, Mart, Milch, Mog(gie), Moggy, Mooly, Muley, Mulley, Overawe, Red Sindhi, Redpoll, Rother(-beast), Sacred, Santa Gertrudis, Scare, Simmental, Stirk, Subact, Teeswater, Threaten, Unnerve, Vaccine, Zebu, Z(h)o

Coward(ly) Bessus, Cat, Chicken, Cocoa, Craven, Cuthbert, Dastard, Dingo, Dunghill, Fraidy-cat, Fugie, Funk, Gutless, Hen, Hilding, Lily-livered, Meacock, Niddering, Nidderling, Nidering, Niderling, Niding, Nithing, Noel, Panty-waist, Poltroon, Pusillanimous, Recreant, Scaramouch, Sganarelle, Slag, Sook, Viliaco, Viliago, Villagio, Villiago, Yellow, Yellow-belly

Cowboy, Cowgirl Buckaroo, Gaucho, Inexpert, Io, Jerrybuilder, Leger, Llanero, Puncher, Ranchero, Ritter, Roper, Vaquero, Waddy, Wrangler

Coy Arch, Coquettish, Mim, Shamefast, ➤ SHY, Skittish

Crab(by), Crablike Apple, Attercop, Cancer, Cancroid, Cantankerous, Capernoity, Cock, Coconut, Daddy, Decapoda, Diogenes, Ethercap, Ettercap, Fiddler, Ghost, Grouch, Hard-shell, Hermit, Horseman, Horseshoe, King, Land, Limulus, Mantis, Mitten, Nebula, Ochidore, Oyster, Pagurian, Partan, Perverse, Podite, Roast, Robber, Rock, Saucepan-fish, Scrawl, Sentinel, Sidle, Soft-shell, Soldier, Spider, Xiphosura, Zoea

▷ **Crab** may indicate an anagram

Crack(ed), Cracker(s), Cracking Ad-lib, Admirable, Bananas, Biscuit, Bonbon, Break, Cat, Catalytic, Chap, Chasm, Chat, Chink, Chip, Chop, Clap, Cleave, Cleft, Cloff, Confab, Cranny, Craquelure, Craqueture, Craze, Cream, Crepitate,

Crevasse, Crevice, Crispbread, Dawn, Decode, Doom, Dunt, Elite, Fatiscent, Fent, Firework, First-rate, Fisgig, Fissure, Fizgig, Flaw, Flip-flop, Fracture, Go, Graham, Grike, Gryke, Gully, Hairline, Hit, Jibe, Joint, Leak, Liar, Little-endian, Matzo, Moulin, Oner, Peterman, Pore, Praise, Prawn, Quip, Rap, Report, Rhagades, Rictus, Rift, Rille, Rima, Rime, Rimous, Rive, Rock, Saltine, Seam, Snap, Soda, Solve, Split, Squib, Sulcus, Top, Try, Waterloo, Yegg

Cradle Bassinet, Berceau, Cat's, Cot, Crib, Cunabula, Hammock, Knife, Nestle, Rocker

Craft(y) Arch, Art, Aviette, Barbola, Boat, Canal boat, Cautel, Cunning, Disingenuous, Finesse, Fly, Guile, Hydroplane, Ice-breaker, Insidious, Kontiki, Landing, Machiavellian, Mister, Mystery, Oomiack, Reynard, Saic, Shallop, Ship, Shuttle, ► SKILL, Slee, Sleeveen, Slim, Slippy, Sly, Slyboots, State, Subdolous, Subtil(e), Subtle, Suttle, Triphibian, Umiak, Underhand, Versute, ► VESSEL, Wile, Workmanship

Craftsman AB, Artificer, Artisan, Artist, Chippy, Cutler, Ebonist, Fabergé, Finisher, Gondolier, Guild, Hand, Joiner, Journeyman, Mason, Mechanic, Morris, Opificer, Wainwright, Wright

Cram(mer) Bag, Candle-waster, Cluster, Craig, Fill, Gag, Gavage, Neck, Pang, Prime, Rugged, Scar(p), Spur, Stap, Stodge, Stow, Swat, Tuck

Cramp(ed) Agraffe, Charleyhorse, Confine, Constrict, Crick, Hamper, Hamstring, Incommodious, Myalgia, Pinch, Poky, Potbound, Restrict, Rigor, Squeeze, Stunt, Tetany, Writer's

Crane Cherry picker, Davit, Demoiselle, Derrick, Gantry, Herd, Heron, Hooper, Ichabod, Jib, Jigger, Rail, Sarus, Sedge, Shears, Sheer, Siege, Stork, Stretch, Whooper, Winch

Crash Bingle, Collapse, Dush, Fail, Fall, Fragor, Intrude, Linen, Nosedive, Prang, Rack, Ram, Rote, Shunt, Slam, Smash, Thunderclap, Topple

▷ **Crashes** may indicate an anagram

Crate Biplane, Box, Case, Ceroon, Crib, Hamper, Tube

Crave, Craving Appetite, Aspire, Beg, Beseech, Covet, Desire, Entreat, Hanker, Hunger, Itch, Libido, Long, Lust, Malacia, Methomania, Orexis, Pica, Polyphagia, Sitomania, The munchies, Thirst, Yearn, Yen

Crayfish Astacology, Gilgie, Jilgie, Yabbie, Yabby

Crayon Chalk, Colour, Conté, Pastel, Pencil

Craze(d), Crazy Absurd, Ape, Barmy, Bats, Batty, Berserk, Bonkers, Break, Cornflake, Crack(ers), Crackpot, Cult, Daffy, Dement, Derange, Dingbats, Dippy, Distraught, Doiled, Doilt, Doolally, Dottle, Dotty, Fad, Flake, Flaw, Folie, Frantic, Furious, Furore, Gaga, Geld, Gonzo, Gyte, Haywire, Headbanger, Insane, Loco, Loony, Lunatic, Madden, Maenad(ic), Mania, Manic, Mattoid, Meshug(g)a, Nuts, Porangi, Potty, Psycho(path), Rage, Rave, Scatty, Screwball, Skivie, Stunt, Unhinge, Wacko, Wacky, Wet, W(h)acky, Whim, Wowf, Zany

Creak(y) Cry, Grate, Grind, Rheumatic, Scraich, Scraigh, Scroop, Seam, Squeak

Cream(y) Barrier, Bavarian, Best, Chantilly, Cold, Crème fraiche, Devonshire, Double, Elite, Foundation, Glacier, Lanolin, Liniment, Lotion, Mousse, Off-white, Ointment, Opal, Paragon, Pick, Ream, Rich, Salad, Single, Skim, Vanishing

Crease Crumple, ➤ FOLD, Lirk, Pitch, Pleat, Popping, Ridge, Ruck(le), Ruga, Rugose, Wrinkle

Create, Creation Build, Coin, Compose, Devise, Dreamtime, Engender, Establish, Fabricate, Forgetive, Form, Found, Generate, Genesis, Godhead, Ideate, ➤ INVENT, Oratorio, Originate, Produce, Shape, Universe

Creature Animal, Ankole, Basilisk, Beast, Being, Chevrotain, Cratur, Critter, Crittur, Man, Nekton, Sasquatch, Sphinx, Whiskey, Wight

Credible, Credit(or) Ascribe, Attribute, Belief, Byline, Esteem, Honour, HP, Kite, Kudos, LC, Lender, Mense, Probable, Reliable, Renown, Shylock, Strap, Tally, Tick, Title, Trust, Weight

Creep(er), Creeping, Creeps Ai, Aseismic, Cleavers, Crawl, Grew, Grovel, Grue, Heebie-jeebies, Heeby-jeebies, Herpetic, Inch, Insect, Ivy, Nerd, Nuthatch, Pussyfoot, Repent, Reptant, Sarmentous, Sittine, Skulk, Slink, Snake, Sobole(s), Toad, Truckle, Vine, Virginia, Willies

Crepe Blini, Blintz(e), Canton, Pancake

Crescent Barchan(e), Bark(h)an, Fertile, Lune(tte), Lunulate, Lunule, Meniscus, Moon, Red, Sickle, Waxing

Crest(ed) Acme, Chine, Cimier, Cockscomb, Comb, Copple, Crista, Height, Kirimon, Knap, Mon, Peak, Pileate, Pinnacle, Plume, Ridge, Summit, Tappit, Tee, ➤ TOP

Crew Boasted, Company, Core, Eight, Four, Lot, Manners, Men, Oars, Sailors, Salts, Seamen, Team, Teme

Crib Cheat, Cot, Cowhouse, Cratch, Filch, Horse, ➤ KEY, Manger, Pony, Purloin, Putz, Shack, Stall, Steal, Trot

Crime Attentat, Barratry, Caper, Chantage, Chaud-mellé, Computer, Corpus delicti, Ecocide, Fact, Felony, Fraud, Graft, Heist, Iniquity, Malefaction, Mayhem, Misdeed, Misdemeanour, ➤ OFFENCE, Organised, Ovicide, Peccadillo, Perjury, Pilferage, Rap, Rape, Rebellion, ➤ SIN, Tort, Transgression, Treason, Wrong

Criminal Bent, Bushranger, Con, Cosa Nostra, Counterfeiter, Crack-rope, ➤ CROOK, Culpable, Culprit, Delinquent, Escroc, Felon, Flagitious, Forensic, Gangster, Heavy, Heinous, Highbinder, Hood(lum), Jailbird, Ladrone, Lag, Larcener, Looter, Lowlife, Maf(f)ia, Malefactor, Maleficent, Mob(ster), Mobster, Ndrangheta, Nefarious, Nefast, Outlaw, Perp(etrator), Racketeer, Receiver, Recidivist, Rustler, Triad, Underworld, Villain, Wicked, Wire, Yakuza, Yardie, Yegg

▷ **Criminal** may indicate an anagram

Cringe, Cringing Cower, Creep, Crouch, Fawn, Grovel, Shrink, Sneaksby, Truckle

Cripple(d) Damage, Disable, Game, Hamstring, Handicap, Injure, ➤ LAME, Lameter, Lamiter, Maim, Paralyse, Polio, Scotch, Spoil

Crisis Acme, Crunch, Drama, Emergency, Exigency, Fastigium, Fit, Flap, Head, Identity, Make or break, Mid-life, Panic, Pass, Shake-out, Solution, Test

Crisp Brisk, Clear, Crimp, Crunchy, Fresh, Sharp, Short, Succinct, Terse

Critic(al), Criticism, Criticize Acute, Agate, Armchair, Arnold, Attack, Badmouth, Barrack, Bird, Blame, Boileau, Captious, Carp, Castigate, Cavil, Censor(ious), ➤ CENSURE, Clobber, Comment, Condemn, Connoisseur, Crab, ➤ CRUCIAL, Crunch, Dangle, Decisive, Denigrate, Denounce, Deprecate, Desperate, Diatribe, Exacting, Excoriate, Fastidious, Fateful, Flak, Flay, Harrumph, Important, Impugn, Inge, Inveigh, Judge, Knock(er), Lash, Leavis, Masora(h), Mas(s)orete, Nag, Nasute, Nibble, Nice, Niggle, Pan, Pater, Puff, Pundit, Quibble, Rap, Rebuke, Reprehend, Review(er), Rip, Roast, Ruskin, Scalp, Scarify, Scathe, Scorn, Serious, Severe, Shaw, Sideswipe, Slag,

Slam, Slashing, Slate, Sneer, Snipe, Stick, Stricture, Strop, Tense, Textual, Threap, Touch and go, Urgent, Vet

Croak Creak, Crow, Die, Grumble, Gutturalise

Crockery Ceramics, China, Dishes, Earthenware, Ware

▷ **Crocks** may indicate an anagram

Crocodile Cayman, File, Garial, Gavial, Gharial, Line, Mugger, River-dragon, Saltwater, Sebek, Teleosaur(ian)

Crook(ed) Adunc, Ajee, Awry, Bad, Bend, Bow, Cam, Camsho(ch), Camsheugh, Criminal, Cromb, Crome, Crosier, Crummack, Crummock, Crump, Curve, Elbow, Fraud, Heister, Hook, Indirect, Kam(me), Kebbie, Lituus, Malpractitioner, Shyster, Sick, Skew(whiff), Slick(er), Staff, Swindler, Thraward, Thrawart, Thrawn, Twister, Wonky, Yeggman

▷ **Crooked** may indicate an anagram

Crop(s), Cropped Basset, Browse, Cash, Catch, Clip, Craw, Cut, Distress, Dock, Emblements, Epilate, Eton, Foison, Forage, Harvest, Hog, Not(t), Plant, Poll, Produce, Riding, Rod, Root, Shingle, Stow, Succession, Top, Truncate

Cross(ing), Crossbred Angry, Ankh, Ansate, Basta(a)rd, Beefalo, Burden, Calvary, Cantankerous, Capital, Cattalo, Celtic, Channel, Chi, Chiasm(a), Clover-leaf, Compital, Constantine, Crosslet, Crotchety, Crucifix, Crux, Decussate, Demi-wolf, Dihybrid, Dso(mo), Dzobo, Eleanor, Faun, Fiery, Fitché, Fleury, Foil, Footbridge, Ford, Frabbit, Fractious, Frampold, Franzy, Funnel, Fylfot, Geneva, George, Grade, Greek, Holy rood, Hybrid, Ill, Imp, Indignant, Interbreed, Intersect, Intervein, Iracund, Irate, Irked, Iron, Jerusalem, Jomo, Jumart, Ladino, Latin, Level, Liger, Lorraine, Lurcher, Maltese, Mameluco, Mermaid, Military, Mix, Moline, Mongrel, Mule, Narky, Nattery, Node, Northern, Nuisance, Ordinary, Orthodox, Overpass, Overthwart, Papal, Patonce, Patriarchal, Patté, Pectoral, Pelican, Plus, Pommé, Potence, Potent, Quadrate, Ratty, Red, Rood, Rouen, Rouge, Rubicon, Sain, St Andrew's, St Anthony's, St George's, Saltier, Saltire, Satyr, Shirty, Sign, Snappy, Southern, Strid, Swastika, Tangelo, Tau, Ten, Testy, Thraw, Thwart, Tiglon, Tigon, Times, Transit, Transom, Transverse, Traverse, Tree, Urdé, Vexed, Vext, Victoria, ➤ VOTE, Weeping, Whippet, Wry, X, Zebra(ss), Z(h)o, Zobu

▷ **Cross** may indicate an anagram

Cross-examine Grill, Interrogate, Question, Targe

Crossword Cryptic, Grid, Puzzle, Quickie

Crouch Bend, Cringe, Falcade, Fancy, Lordosis, Ruck, Set, Squat, Squinch

Crow Boast, Brag, Carrion, Chewet, Chough, Corbie, Corvus, Crake, Currawong, Daw, Gorcrow, Hooded, Hoodie, Huia, Jackdaw, Jim(my), Murder, Raven, Rook, Skite, Squawk, Swagger, Vaunt

Crowd(ed) Abound, Army, Bike, Boodle, Bumper, Bunch, Byke, Caboodle, Clutter, Concourse, Congest(ed), Cram, Crush, Crwth, Dedans, Doughnut, Drove, Fill, Flock, Galere, Gate, Gathering, Herd, Horde, ➤ HOST, Huddle, Jam, Lot, Meinie, Mein(e)y, Menyie, Mob, Mong, Ochlo-, Pack, Pang, Press, Rabble, Raft, Ram, Ratpack, Ring, Ruck, Scrooge, Scrouge, Scrowdge, Scrum, Serr(é), Shoal, Shove, Slew, Slue, Squeeze, Stuff, Swarm, Swell, Three, Throng, Trinity, Varletry

Crown Acme, Bays, Bull, Camp, Cantle, Cap, Capernoity, Cidaris, Civic, Coma, Corona, Cr, Diadem, Ecu, Engarland, Enthrone, Fillet, Garland, Gloria, Haku, Head, Headdress, Instal, Iron, Ivy, Krantz, Laurel, Monarch, Mural, Naval, Nole, Noll, Noul(e), Nowl, Olive, Ore, Ovation, Pate, Peak, Pschent, Sconce, Taj, Tiara, ➤ TOP, Triple, Triumphal, Trophy, Vallary, Vertex

Crucial Acute, Critical, Essential, Key, Pivotal, Vital, Watershed

Crude Bald, Brash, Brute, Earthy, Halfbaked, Immature, Incondite, Primitive, Raw, Rough, Rough and ready, Rough-hewn, Rough-wrought, Tutty, Uncouth, Vulgar, Yahoo

Cruel Barbarous, Bloody, Brutal, Dastardly, De Sade, Draconian, Fell, Fiendish, Flinty, Hard, Heartless, Immane, Inhuman, Machiavellian, Neronic, Pitiless, Raw, Remorseless, Sadist(ic), Stern, Tormentor, Vicious

▷ **Cruel** may indicate an anagram

Cruise(r) Busk, Cabin, Nuke, Prowl, Sail, Ship, Tom, Travel, Trip, Voyager

Crumb(le), Crumbly, Crumbs Coo, Decay, Disintegrate, Ee, Fragment, Friable, Law, Leavings, Moulder, Mull, Murl, Nesh, Nirl, Ort, Particle, Ped, Raspings, Rot

Crunch(y) Chew, Craunch, Crisp, Gnash, Grind, Munch, Occlude, Scranch

Crush(ed), Crusher Acis, Anaconda, Annihilate, Bow,
Champ, Comminute, Conquer, Contuse, Cranch, Crunch,
Destroy, Graunch, Grind, Hug, Jam, Knapper, Levigate, Mangle,
Mash, Molar, Oppress, Overcome, Overwhelm, Pash,
Policeman, Pound, Press, Pulp, Pulverise, Quash, Ruin,
Schwarmerei, Scotch, Scrum, Smash, Squabash, Squash,
Squeeze, Squelch, Squish, Stamp, Stave, Steam-roll, Stove,
Suppress, Telescope, Trample

Crust(y) Argol, Beeswing, Cake, Coating, Coffin, Continental,
Cover, Crabby, Craton, Fur, Gratin, Heel, Horst, Kissing, Kraton,
Lithosphere, Osteocolla, Pie, Reh, Rind, Rine, Sal, Salband, Scab,
Shell, Sial, Sima, Sinter, Surly, Tartar, Teachie, Terrane, Tetchy,
Upper, Wine-stone

Crustacea(n) Amphipod, Barnacle, Cirriped, Copepod, Crab,
Crayfish, Cyclops, Cyprid, Cypris, Decapod(a), Entomostraca,
Fishlouse, Foot-jaw, Gribble, Isopod, Krill, Lobster, Maron,
Nauplius, Ostracoda, Prawn, Sand-hopper, Scampi, Shrimp,
Slater, Squilla, Woodlouse

Cry(ing) Aha, Alalagmus, Alew, Banzai, Bark, Battle, Bawl, Bell,
Blat, Bleat, Bleb, Blub(ber), Boo, Boohoo, Bray, Bump,
Caramba, Caw, Cheer, Chevy, Chirm, Chivy, Clang, Crake,
Croak, Crow, Dire, Euoi, Eureka, Evoe, Exclaim, Fall, Field-holler,
Gardyloo, Geronimo, Gowl, Greet, Halloo, Harambee, Haro,
Harrow, Havoc, Heigh, Hemitrope, Herald, Hinny, Holler, Hoo,
Hoop, Hosanna, Hout(s)-tout(s), Howl, Humph, Io, Kaw, Low,
Mewl, Miaou, Miau(l), Miserere, Mourn, Night-shriek,
O(c)hone, Oi, Olé, Ow, Pugh, Rivo, Sab, Scape, Scream,
Screech, Sell, Sese(y), Sessa, ➤ SHOUT, Shriek, Slogan, Snivel,
Snotter, Sob, Soho, Sola, Squall, Squawk, Tantivy, Umph,
Vagitus, Vivat, Vociferate, Wail, War, Watchword, Waul, Wawl,
Weep, Westward ho, Whee(ple), Whimper, Whine, Whinny,
Whoa, Whoop, Winge, Wolf, Yammer, Yelp, Yikker, Yippee,
Yodel, Yoick, Yoop, Yowl

Crypt(ic) Catacomb, Cavern, Chamber, Crowde, Encoded,
Favissa, Grotto, Hidden, Obscure, Occult, Secret, Sepulchre,
Short, Steganographic, Tomb, Unclear, Undercroft, Vault

Crystal(s), Crystal-gazer, Crystalline, Crystallise
Baccara(t), Beryl, Candy, Clear, Copperas, Coumarin, Cumarin,
Dendrite, Druse, Epitaxy, Geode, Glass, Hemitrope, Ice-stone,
Lead, Liquid, Love-arrow, Macle, Melamine, Nicol, Orthogonal,

Pellucid, Piezo, Prism, Pseudomorph, Purin(e), Quartz, R(h)aphide, R(h)aphis, Rhinestone, Rock, Rotenone, Scryer, Shoot, Skryer, Snowflake, Sorbitol, Spar, Table

Cub Baby, Kit, Novice, Pup, Whelp

Cubicle Alcove, Booth, Carrel(l), Stall

Cuckoo Ament, Ani, April fool, Bird, Gouk, Gowk, Inquiline, Insane, Koel, ➤ MAD, Mental, Piet-my-vrou, Stupid

▷**Cuckoo** may indicate an anagram

Cuddle Canoodle, Caress, Clinch, Embrace, Fondle, Hug, Nooky, Smooch, Smuggle, Snuggle

Cue Cannonade, Catchword, Feed, Half-butt, Hint, Mace, ➤ PROMPT, Reminder, Rod, Sign, Signal, Wink

Cuisine Cookery, Food, Menu, Nouvelle

Cult Cabiri, Cargo, Creed, Sect, Worship

Cultivate(d), Cultivation Agronomy, Arty, Civilise, Dig, Dress, Farm, Genteel, Grow, Hoe, Hydroponics, Improve, Labour, Pursue, Raise, Refine, Sative, Sophisticated, Tame, Tasteful, Till, Tilth

Culture(d), Cultural Acheulean, Acheulian, Agar, Art(y), Aurignacian, Azilian, Bel esprit, Brahmin, Capsian, Civil(isation), Ethnic, Experiment, Explant, Gel, Grecian, Hallstatt, Hip-hop, Humanism, Kultur(kreis), La Tène, Learning, Mousterian, Polish, Refinement, Solutrean, Sophisticated, Strepyan, Tissue

Cunning Arch, Art, Artifice, Cautel, Craft(y), Deceit, Deep, Devious, Down, Finesse, Foxy, Insidious, Leery, Machiavellian, Quaint, Skill, Slee(kit), Sleight, Slim, Sly(boots), Smart, Sneaky, Subtle, Vulpine, Wile

Cup(s), Cupped Aecidium, America's, Beaker, Calcutta, Calix, Calyculus, Cantharus, Chalice, Claret, Cotyle, Cruse, Cupule, Cyathus, Cylix, Davis, Demitasse, Dish, Dop, Final, Fingan, Finjan, Glenoid, Goblet, Grace, Hanap, Horn, Kylix, Loving, Melbourne, Merry, Monstrance, Moustache, Mug, Noggin, Nut, Pannikin, Planchet, Plate, Pot, Procoelous, Quaich, Quaigh, Rhyton, Rider, Ryder, Sangrado, Scyphus, Stirrup, Tantalus, Tass(ie), Tastevin, Tazza, Tea-dish, Tig, Tot, ➤ TROPHY, Tyg, Volva, World

Cupboard Almery, Almirah, A(u)mbry, Beauf(f)et, Cabinet, Chiffonier, Chiff(o)robe, Closet, Court, Credenza, Dresser, Locker, Press

Cupid Amoretto, Amorino, Archer, Blind, Cherub, Dan, Eros, Love, Putto

Curb Bit, Brake, Bridle, Check, Clamp, Coaming, Dam, Edge, Puteal, Rein, Restrain, Rim, Snub

Cure(d), Curative Amend, Antidote, Antirachitic, Bloater, Cold turkey, Dry-salt, Euphrasy, Ginseng, Hobday, Heal, Jadeite, Jerk, Kipper, Medicinal, Nostrum, Panacea, Park-leaves, ➤ PRESERVE, Recover, Recower, Reest, Remede, Remedy, Restore, Salt, Salve, Serum, Smoke, Smoke-dry, Tan, ➤ TREATMENT, Tutsan

▷ **Cure** may indicate an anagram

Curfew Gate, Prohibit, Proscribe

Curio, Curiosity, Curious Agog, Bibelot, Freak, Inquisitive, Meddlesome, Nos(e)y, Objet d'art, Objet de vertu, Odd, Peculiar, Prurience, Rarity, Rum, ➤ STRANGE

▷ **Curious(ly)** may indicate an anagram

Curl(er), Curling, Curly Bonspiel, Cirrus, Coil, Crimp, Crimple, Crinkle, Crisp, Crocket, Earlock, Friz(z), Frizzle, Heart-breaker, Hog, Inwick, Kiss, Leaf, Loop, Love-lock, Outwick, Perm, Pin, Quiff, Repenter, Ringlet, Roll, Roulette, Shaving, Spiral, Spit, Twiddle, ➤ TWIST, Wave, Wind

Currant Berry, Raisin, Rizard, Rizzar(t), Rizzer

Currency Cash, Circulation, ➤ COIN, Coinage, Decimal, Euro, Finance, Jiao, Kip, Koruna, Monetary, ➤ MONEY, Prevalence

▷ **Currency** may indicate a river

Current Abroad, AC, Actual, Alternating, Amperage, Amp(ere), California, Canary, Contemporaneous, Cromwell, DC, Direct, Draught, Drift, Dynamo, Ebbtide, Electric, El Nino, Equatorial, Euripus, Existent, Flow, Foucault, Going, Humboldt, I, Immediate, Inst, Intermittent, Japan, Kuroshio, Labrador, Millrace, Modern, Newsy, Now, Ongoing, Present, Prevalent, Race, Rapid, Rife, Rip, Roost, Running, Stream, Thames, Thermal, Thermionic, Tide, Topical, Torrent, Turbidity, Underset, Undertow

Curry Bhuna, Brush, Comb, Cuittle, Dhansak, Fawn, Groom, Ingratiate, Korma, Spice, Tan, Turmeric, Vindaloo

Curse Abuse, Anathema, Badmouth, Ban, Bane, Beshrew, ➤ BLASPHEME, Blast, Chide, Dam(me), Damn, Dee, Drat, Excommunicate, Execrate, Heck, Hex, Imprecate, Jinx, Malison,

Maranatha, Mau(l)gré, Mockers, Moz(z), Mozzle, Oath, Pize, Plague, Rant, Rats, Scourge, Spell, Swear, Upbraid, Weary, Winze, Wo(e)

Curtain(s), Curtain-rod Arras, Backdrop, Bamboo, Canopy, Caudle, Cloth, Death, Demise, Drape, Drop, Dropcloth, Dropscene, Fatal, Hanging, Iron, Louvre, Net, Pall, Portière, Purdah, Safety, Scene, Screen, Scrim, Tab, Tormentor, Tringle, Vail, Valance, Veil, Vitrage

Curtsey Bob, Bow, Dip, Dop

Curve(d), Curvy, Curvature, Curvaceous Aduncate, Arc, Arch, Archivolt, Axoid, Bend, Bow, Camber, Catacaustic, Catenary, Caustic, Cissoid, Conchoid, Contrapposto, Crescent, Cycloid, Entasis, Epinastic, Ess, Evolute, Exponental, Extrados, Felloe, Felly, Geodesic, Gooseneck, Growth, Hance, Helix, Hodograph, Hyperbola, Inswing, Intrados, Isochor, J, Jordan, Laffer, Learning, Lemniscate, Limacon, Lituus, Lordosis, Loxodrome, Nowy, Ogee, Parabola, Pothook, Rhumb, Roach, Rotundate, Scoliosis, Sheer, Sinuate, Spiral, Spiric, Strophoid, Swayback, Tie, Trajectory, Trochoid, Twist, Witch

Cushion Air, Allege, Bolster, Buffer, Hassock, ➤ PAD, Pillow, Pouf(fe), Pulvillus, Soften, Squab, Upholster, Whoopee

Custodian, Custody Care, Claviger, Guard, Hold, Janitor, Keeping, Sacrist, Steward, Trust, Ward

Custom(ary), Customs Agriology, Coast-waiters, Consuetude, Conventional, Couvade, De règle, Douane, Exciseman, Familiar, Fashion, Folklore, ➤ HABIT, Lore, Manner, Montem, Mores, Nomic, Octroi, Ordinary, Practice, Praxis, Relic, Rite, Routine, Rule, Sororate, Sunna, Tax, Thew, Tidesman, Tradition, Unwritten, Usance, Used, Usual, Won, Wont, Woon, Zollverein

Customer Client, Cove, Patron, Prospect, Purchaser, Shillaber, Shopper, Smooth, Trade, Trick

Cut(ter), Cutting Abate, Abjoint, Abridge, Abscond, Acute, Adeem, Adze, Aftermath, Ali Baba, Amputate, Axe, Bang, Bisect, Bit, Bite, Bowdlerise, Boycott, Brilliant, Broach, Caesarean, Caique, Canal, Cantle, Caper, Carve, Castrate, Caustic, Censor, Chap, Chisel, Chop, Circumscribe, Clinker-built, Clip, Colter, Commission, Concise, Coulter, Coupé, Crew, Crop, Cruel, Curtail, Deadhead, Decrease, Dice, Die, Discide, Disengage, Dismember, Dissect, Division, Divorce, Dock, Dod, Edge, Edit,

Embankment, Engrave, Entail, Epistolary, Epitomise, Eschew, Excalibur, Excide, Excise, Exscind, Exsect, Exude, Fashion, Fell, Fillet, Flench, Flense, Flinch, Form, Froe, Frow, Garb, Gash, Grate, Graven, Gride, Gryde, Hack, Handsaw, Hew(er), Ignore, Incision, Incisor, Indent, Intersect, Jigsaw, Joint, Junk, Kerf, Kern, Kirn, Lacerate, Lance, Leat, Lesion, Lin, Lop, Math, Medallion, Microtome, Milling, Mohel, Mortice, Mortise, Mow, Nick, Not, Notch, Nott, Occlude, Omit, Open, Operate, Oxyacetylene, Padsaw, Pare, Pink, Plant, Pliers, Ploughshare, Pollard, Pone, Power, Precisive, Proin, Quota, Race, Rake off, Rase, Razor, Re-enter, Reap, Rebate, Reduction, Resect, Retrench, Revenue, Ring, Ripsaw, Roach, Rose, Rout, Saddle, Sarcastic, Saw(n), Scarf, Scathing, Scion, Scission, Scissor, Score, Sculpt, Scye, Scythe, Secant, Secateurs, Sect, Sever, Sey, Share(out), Shave, Shear, Shingle, Ship, Shorn, Short, Shred, Shun, Sickle, Sirloin, Skip, Slave, Slash, Slice, Slip, Slit, Sloop, Sned, Snee, Snib, Snick, Snip, Snub, Spade, Spin, Spud, Steak, Stencil, Stir, Stramazon, Style, Surgeon, Tailor(ess), Tart, Tenderloin, Tomial, Tonsure, Tooth, Topside, Transect, Trash, Trench, Trenchant, Trepan, Trim, Truant, Truncate, Urchin, Whang, Whittle

▷ **Cut** may indicate an anagram

▷ **Cutback** may indicate a reversed word

Cute Ankle, Pert, Pretty, Taking

Cutlery Canteen, Flatware, Fork, Knife, Setting, Silver, Spoon, Tableware, Trifid

Cycle, Cyclist Anicca, Arthurian, Bike, Biorhythm, Cal(l)ippic, Calvin, Carbon, Carnot, Cell, Circadian, Daisy, Eon, Era, Fairy, Frequency, Heterogony, Indiction, Ko, Krebs, Life, Metonic, Oestrus, Orb, Otto, Pedal, Peloton, Period, Repulp, Revolution, Ride, Roadster, Rota, Round, Samsara, Saros, Scorch, Series, Sheng, Solar, Song, Sonnet, Sothic, Spin, TCA, Trike, Turn, UCI, Water, Wheeler, Wheelman, Wu

Cyclone Storm, Tornado, Typhoon, Willy-willy

Cylinder, Cylindrical Clave, Column, Drum, Pipe, Roll, Rotor, Slave, Spool, Steal, Stele, Terete, Torose, Treadmill, Tube

Cyst Atheroma, Bag, Blister, Chalazion, Dermoid, Hydatid, Impost(h)ume, Meibomian, Ranula, Sac, Vesicle, Wen

Dd

Dab(s) Bit, Daub, Fish, Flounder, Pat, Print, Ringer, Smear, Spot, Stupe, Whorl

Dad(dy) Blow, Dev(v)el, Father, Generator, Hit, Male, Pa(pa), Pater, Polt, Pop, Slam, Sugar, Thump

Daffodil Asphodel, Jonquil, Lent-lily, Narcissus

Daft Absurd, Crazy, Potty, Ridiculous, Silly, Simple, Stupid

Dagger(s) An(e)lace, Ataghan, Baselard, Bayonet, Bodkin, Crease, Creese, Da(h), Diesis, Dirk, Double, Dudgeon, Han(d)jar, Hanger, Jambiya(h), Katar, Kindjahl, Kirpan, Kreese, Kris, Lath, Misericord(e), Obelisk, Obelus, Poi(g)nado, Poniard, Puncheon, Sgian-dubh, Skean, Skene(-occle), Stiletto, Whiniard, Whinyard, W(h)inger, Yatag(h)an

Daily Adays, Char, Circadian, Diurnal, Domestic, Guardian, Help, Journal, Mail, Mirror, Paper, Per diem, Quotidian, Rag, Regular, Scotsman, Sun, Tabloid

Dainty Cate(s), Cute, Delicacy, Elegant, Elfin, Entremesse, Entremets, Exquisite, Junket, Lickerish, Liquorish, Mignon(ne), ➤ MORSEL, Neat, Nice, Particular, Petite, Pussy, Sunket, Twee

Dairy Creamery, Loan, Parlour

Daisy African, Bell, Felicia, Gowan, Hen and chickens, Livingstone, Michaelmas, Ox-eye, Shasta, Transvaal

Dale Dell, Dene, Dingle, Glen, Vale, Valley

Dam An(n)icut, Aswan, Bar, Barrage, Barrier, Block, Boulder, Bund, Cauld, Check, Hoover, Kariba, Kielder, Ma, Mater, Obstacle, Obstruct, Pen, ➤ STEM, Sudd, Weir

Damage(d), Damages Bane, Banjax, Bruise, Buckle, Charge, Contuse, Cost, Cripple, Dent, Desecrate, Detriment, Devastate, Devastavit, Estrepe, Fault, Flea-bite, Harm, Havoc, Hit, Hole, Hurt, Impair, Injury, Loss, Mar, Mayhem, Moth-eaten, Nobble, Prang, Price, Retree, Sabotage, Scaith, Scath(e), Scotch, Scratch, Skaith, Smirch, Solatium, ➤ SPOIL, Tangle, Toll, Value, Vandalise, Violate, Wear and tear, Wing, Wound, Wreak, Wreck

Dame Crone, Dowager, Edna, Gammer, Lady, Matron, Nature, Naunt, Partlet, Peacherino, Sis, Title(d), Trot, Woman

Damn(ed), Damnation Accurst, Attack, Blame, Condemn, Curse, Cuss, Darn, Dee, Execrate, Faust, Hell, Hoot, Jigger, Malgre, Perdition, Predoom, Sink, Swear, Very

Damp(ness) Aslake, Black, Check, Clam(my), Dank, Dewy, Fousty, Humid, Moist, Muggy, Raw, Rheumy, Rising, Roric, Soggy, Sordo, Sultry, Unaired, ➤ WET

Dance(r), Dancing Astaire, Ballerina, Boogie, Bop, Chorus-girl, Dervish, Diaghilev, Figurant, Formation, Glide, Headbang, Hoofer, Hop, Kick-up, Knees-up, Leap, Loup, Measure, Nureyev, Nijinsky, Partner, Paul Jones, Pavlova, Progressive, Routine, Rug-cutting, Sir Roger de Coverley, Smooch, Salome, Taglioni, Thé dansant, Tread

▷**Dancing** may indicate an anagram

Danger(ous) Apperil, Breakneck, Crisis, Dic(e)y, Dire, Emprise, Fear, Hairy, Hazard, Hearie, Hot, Insecure, Jeopardy, Lethal, Menace, Mine, Nettle, Nocuous, Parlous, ➤ PERIL, Pitfall, Precarious, Quicksand, Risk, Serious, Severe, Snag, Tight, Trap

Dangle A(i)glet, Aiguillette, Critic, Flourish, Hang, Loll, Swing

Dank Clammy, Damp, Humid, Moist, Wet, Wormy

Dare, Daring Adventure, Bold, Brave, Challenge, Courage, Da(u)nton, Defy, Durst, Emprise, Face, Gallant, Gallus, Hardihood, Hazard, Hen, Prowess, Racy, Taunt, Venture

Dark(en), Darkie, Darkness Aphelia, Aphotic, Apophis, Black, Blind, Cimmerian, Cloud, Depth, Dim, Dingy, Dirk(e), Dusky, Eclipse, Erebus, Evil, Gloom, Glum, Inumbrate, Mare, Maria, Melanous, Mulatto, Murk(y), Negro, Night, Obfuscate, Obscure, Ominous, Ousel, Ouzel, Pall, Phaeic, Pitch-black, Pit-mirk, Rooky, Sable, Sad, Secret, Shady, Shuttered, Sinister, Solein, Sombre, Sooty, Sphacelate, Sullen, Swarthy, Tar, Tenebr(i)ous, Tenebrose, Unfair, Unlit, Wog, Woosel, Yellowboy, Yellowgirl

Darling Acushla, Alannah, Asthore, Beloved, Charlie, Cher, Chéri(e), Chick-a-biddy, Chick-a-diddle, Chuck-a-diddle, Dear, Dilling, Do(a)ting-piece, Duck(s), Favourite, Grace, Honey, Idol, Jarta, Jo(e), Lal, Love, Luv, Mavourneen, Mavournin, Minikin, Minion, Oarswoman, Own, Peat, Pet, Poppet, Precious, Sugar, Sweetheart, Yarta, Yarto

Dart(er) Abaris, Arrow, Banderilla, Dace, Dash, Deadener, Dodge, Fleat, Fléchette, Flit, Harpoon, Javelin, Launch, Leap, Scoot, Skrim, Speck, Spiculum, Strike, Thrust, Wheech

Dash(ed), Dashing Backhander, Bally, Blade, Blight, Blow, Buck, Charge, Collide, Cut, Dad, Dah, Damn, Dapper, Dart(le), Daud, Debonair, Ding, Elan, Flair, Fly, Go-ahead, Hang, Hurl, ➤ HURRY, Hustle, Hyphen, Impetuous, Jabble, Jaw, Jigger, Lace, Line, Minus, Natty, Nip, Panache, Pebble, Ramp, Rash, Rule, Rush, Run, Sally, Scamp(er), Scart, Scoot, Scrattle, Scurry, Scuttle, Shatter, Showy, Soupçon, Souse, Spang, Speed, Splash, Splatter, Sprint, Strack, Streak, Stroke, ➤ STYLE, Throw, Touch

Data, Database Archie, Evidence, Facts, Fiche, File, Floating-point, Gen, Info, Input, Material, Matrix, News

Date(d), Dates, Dating AD, Age, AH, Almanac, Appointment, Blind, Boyfriend, Calendar, Carbon, Carbon-14, Computer, Court, Deadline, Engagement, Epoch, Equinox, Era, Escort, Exergue, Expiry, Fixture, Girlfriend, Ides, Julian, Meet, Outmoded, ➤ OUT OF DATE, Passé, Past, Radio-carbon, Rubidium-strontium, See, System, ➤ TRYST, Ult(imo)

Daunt Adaw, Amate, Awe, Deter, Dishearten, Intimidate, Overawe, Quail, Stun, Stupefy, Subdue

Dawdle(r) Dally, Draggle, Drawl, Idle, ➤ LOITER, Potter, Shirk, Slowcoach, Troke, Truck

Dawn Aurora, Cockcrow, Daw, Daybreak, Day-peep, Dayspring, Eoan, Eos, False, Light, Morrow, Occur, Prime, Start, Sunrise

Day(s) All Fools', All Hallows', All Saints', All Souls', Anniversary, Annunciation, Anzac, April Fool's, Armistice, Ascension, Australia, Bad hair, Banian, Bastille, Boxing, Calends, Calpa, Canada, Columbus, Commonwealth, D, Date, Distaff, Dog, Ember, Empire, Fasti, Father's, Feast, Ferial, Field, Flag, Fri, Groundhog, Guy Fawkes', Halcyon, Hogmanay, Holy Innocents', Hundred, Ides, Inauguration, Independence, Intercalary, Judgment, Kalends, Kalpa, Labo(u)r, Lady, Lammas, Lay, Mardi, May, Memorial, Midsummer, Mon, Morrow, Mother's, Mufti, New year's, Nones, Oak-apple, Octave, Open, Pancake, Poppy, Present, Primrose, Quarter, Remembrance, Robin, Rock, Rogation, Rood, Rosh Chodesh, St Swithin's, St Valentine's, Salad, Sat, Settling, Sidereal, Solar, Solstice, Speech, Sun, Tag, Thanksgiving, Thurs, Ticket, Time, Tues, Twelfth, Utas, VE, Veterans', Victoria, VJ, Wed

Daydream(er) Brown study, Dwam, Fancy, Imagine, Mitty, Muse, Reverie, Rêveur

Daze(d) Amaze, Bemuse, Confuse, Dwaal, Gally, Muddle, Muzzy, Reeling, ➤ STUN, Stupefy, Stupor, Trance

Dazzle(d), Dazzling Bewilder, Blend, Blind, Eclipse, Foudroyant, Glare, Meteoric, Outshine, Radiance, Resplendent, Splendour, Yblent

Dead(en) Abrupt, Accurate, Alamort, Asgard, Asleep, Blunt, Bung, Cert, Cold, Complete, D, Deceased, Defunct, Doggo, Expired, Extinct, Gone(r), Inert, Infarct, Late, Lifeless, Muffle, Mute, Napoo, Numb, Obsolete, Obtund, Ringer, She'ol, Smother, Stillborn, True, Utter, Waned

Dead end, Deadlock Cut-off, Dilemma, Impasse, Logjam, Stalemate, Stoppage

Deadline Date, Epitaph, Limit

Deadly Baleful, Dull, Fell, Funest, Internecine, ➤ LETHAL, Malign, Mortal, Pestilent, Unerring, Venomous

Deal(er), Dealings Agent, Agreement, Allot(ment), Arb, Arbitrageur, Bargain, Brinjarry, Broker, Business, Cambist, Chandler, Chapman, Commerce, Cope, Coup, Cover, Croupier, Dispense, Distributor, Do, Dole, Eggler, Exchange, Fripper, Goulash, Hand(le), Help, Inflict, Insider, Jiggery-pokery, Jobber, Lashing, Let, Manage, Mercer, Merchant, Mickle, Middleman, Monger, Mort, Negotiate, New, Operator, Package, Pine, Raft, Raw, Sale, Serve, Sort, Spicer, Square, Stockjobber, Takeover, Tape, Timber, Tout(er), ➤ TRADE, Traffic, Transaction, Treat, Truck, Wheeler, Wield, Woolstapler, Yardie

Dear(er), Dearest, Dear me Ay, Bach, Beloved, Cara, Caro, Cher(e), Cherie, Chuckie, Darling, Duck(s), Expensive, High, Honey(bun), Lamb, Leve, Lief, Lieve, Loor, Love, Machree, Mouse, My, Pet, Steep, Sweet, Toots(ie), Up

Death(ly) Bane, Bargaist, Barg(h)est, Black, Cataplexis, Charnel, Curtains, Cypress, Demise, Departure, Dormition, End, Eschatology, Euthanasia, Exit, Extinction, Fatality, Funeral, Gangrene, Grim Reaper, Hallal, Infarction, Jordan, Lethee, Leveller, Necrosis, Nemesis, Night, Obit, Quietus, Reaper, Sati, Sergeant, SIDS, Small-back, Strae, Sudden, Suttee, Terminal, Thanatism, Thanatopsis, Thanatos

Deathless(ness) Athanasy, Eternal, Eterne, Immortal, Struldberg, Timeless, Undying

Debase(d) Adulterate, Allay, Bemean, Corrupt, Demean, Depreciate, Dialectician, Dirty, Grotesque, Hedge, Lower, Pervert, Traduce, Vitiate

Debate(r) Argue, Combat, Contention, Contest, Deliberate, Dialectic, Discept, Discuss(ion), ► DISPUTE, Flyte, Forensics, Moot, Polemics, Reason, Teach-in, Warsle, Wrangle, Wrestle

Debris Bahada, Bajada, Detritus, Eluvium, Moraine, Moslings, Refuse, ► RUBBLE, Ruins, Tephra, Waste

▷**Debris** may indicate an anagram

Debt(or) Alsatia, Arrears, Arrestee, Dr, Due, Insolvent, IOU, Liability, Moratoria, National, Obligation, Score, Tie

Debt-collector Bailiff, Forfaiter, Remembrancer

Decadence, Decadent Babylonian, Decaying, Degeneration, Dissolute, Effete, Fin-de-siècle, Libertine

▷**Decapitated** may indicate first letter removed

Decay(ed), Decaying Alpha, Appair, Beta, Biodegrade, Blet, Canker, Caries, Caseation, Crumble, Decadent, Declension, Decline, Decompose, Decrepit, Dieback, Disintegrate, Doat, Doddard, Doddered, Dote, Dricksie, Druxy, Dry rot, F(o)etid, Fail, Forfair, Gangrene, Heart-rot, Impair, Moulder, Pair(e), Plaque, Putrefy, Ret, Rot, Saprogenic, Sap-rot, Seedy, Sepsis, Spoil, Tabes, Wet-rot

Decease(d) Death, Decedent, Demise, Die, Stiff

Deceit(ful), Deceive(r) Abuse, Artifice, Bamboozle, Befool, Bitten, Blind, Bluff, ► CHEAT, Chicane, Chouse, Cozen, Cuckold, Defraud, Delude, Diddle, Dissemble, Double-cross, Dupe, Duplicity, False(r), Fast-talk, Fiddle, Flam, Fox, Fraud, Gag, Guile, Gull, Hoax, Hoodwink, Humbug, Hype, Imposition, Inveigle, Invention, Kid, Mislead, Poop, Poupe, Pretence, Punic, Rig, Ruse, Sell, Sham, Sinon, Spruce, Stratagem, Swindle, Swizzle, Trick, Trump, Two-time, Wile

Decency, Decent Chaste, Decorum, Fitting, Healsome, Honest, Kind, Modest, Seemly, Sporting, Wholesome

Deception, Deceptive Artifice, Catchpenny, Catchy, Cheat, Chicanery, ► DECEIT, Disguise, Dupe, Duplicity, Eyewash, Fallacious, False, Flam, Fraud, Gag, Gammon, Guile, Have-on, Hocus-pocus, Hokey-pokey, Hum, Hunt-the-gowks, Ignes-fatui, Ignis-fatuus, Illusion, Insidious, Lie, Moodies, Ruse, Sell, Specious, ► TRICK, Trompe l'oeil, Two-timing

Decide(d), Decider Addeem, Agree, Ballot, Barrage, Cast, Clinch, Conclude, ➤ DECISION, Deem, Definite, Determine, Distinct, Firm, Fix, Jump-off, Mediate, Opt, Parti, Predestination, Pronounced, Rescript, ➤ RESOLVE, Rule, Run-off, See, Settle, Tiebreaker, Try

Decipher(ing) Cryptanalysis, Decode, Decrypt, Descramble, Discover, Interpret

▷**Decipher(ed)** may indicate an 'o' removed

Decision Arbitrium, Arrêt, Crossroads, Crunch, Decree, Fatwa, Fetwa, Firman, Judg(e)ment, Placit(um), Referendum, Resolution, Resolve, Responsa, Ruling, Sentence, Verdict

Decisive Climactic, Clincher, Critical, Crux, Definite, Final, Pivotal

Deck Adorn, Array, Attrap, Bejewel, Boat, Cards, Clad, Daiker, Daub, Decorate, Dizen, Embellish, Equip, Flight, Focsle, Forecastle, Garland, Hang, Helideck, Hurricane, Lower, Orlop, Pack, Platform, Poop, Prim, Promenade, Quarter, Sun, Tape, Upper, Void

Declaim, Declare, Declaration, Decree Absolute, Affidavit, Affirm, Air, Allege, Announce, Assert, Asseverate, Aver, Avow, Balfour, Bann(s), Breda, Dictum, Diktat, Doom, Edict, Enact, Fatwa(h), Fiat, Firman, Go, Grace, Harangue, Insist, Interlocutory, Irade, Law, Mandate, Manifesto, Meld, Mou(th), Nisi, Noncupate, Novel(la), Nullity, Orate, Ordain, Order, Ordinance, Parlando, Pontificate, Proclaim, Profess, Promulgate, Pronounce, Protest, Publish, Rant, Recite, Resolve, Rescript, Rights, Rule, Ruling, SC, Sed, Signify, Speak, Spout, State, Testimony, Testify, UDI, Ultimatum, Unilateral, Vie, Voice, Vouch, Word

▷**Declaring** may indicate a word beginning 'Im'

Decline, Declining Age, Comedown, Decadent, Degringoler, Deny, Descend, Deteriorate, Devall, Die, Dip, Dissent, Downtrend, Downturn, Droop, Dwindle, Ebb, Fade, Fall, Flag, Forbear, Paracme, Quail, Recede, Recession, Refuse, Retrogression, Rot, Rust, Sag, Senile, Set, Sink, Slump, Stoop, Wane, Welke, ➤ WILT, Withdraw, Wither

Decorate(d), Decoration, Decorative Adorn, Angelica, Attrap, Award, Baroque, Beaux-arts, Bordure, Braid, Brooch, Cartouche, Champlevé, Centrepiece, Chinoiserie, Christingle, Cinquefoil, Cloissoné, Crocket, Dentelle, Diamante, Doodad,

Dragée, Emblazon, Emboss, Embrave, Enrich, Epergne, Etch,
Fancy, Festoon, Filigree, Finial, Fleuron, Floriated, Frieze, Frill,
Frog, Furbish, Garniture, Gaud, Goffer, Gradino, Guilloche, Ice,
Illuminate, Impearl, Inlay, Intarsia, Intarsio, Interior, Knotwork,
Linen-fold, Marquetry, MC, Medal(lion), Moulding, Oath, OBE,
Order, ► ORNAMENT, Ornate, Orphrey, Ovolo, Paint, Paper,
Parament, Pokerwork, Prettify, Prink, Purfle, Rag-rolling,
Rangoli, Repoussé, Rich, Ruche, Scallop, Scrimshaw, Set-off,
Sgraffito, Soutache, Spangle, Staffage, Stomacher, Strapwork,
Tailpiece, Tattoo, TD, Titivate, Tool, Topiary, Trim, Wallpaper

Decoy Allure, Bait, Bonnet, Button, Call-bird, Coach, Crimp,
Entice, Lure, Piper, Roper, Ruse, Shill, Stale, Stalking-horse,
Stool-pigeon, Tole, Toll, Trap, Trepan

Decrease Decrew, Diminish, Dwindle, Iron, Lessen, Press,
Reduce, Rollback, Step-down, Subside, Wane, Wanze

►**Decree** see DECLAIM

Decrepit Dilapidated, Doddery, Failing, Feeble, Frail,
Moth-eaten, Tumbledown, Warby, Weak

Dedicate(d), Dedication Corban, Devote, Endoss, Hallow,
Inscribe, Oblate, Pious, Sacred, Votive

Deduce, Deduction, Deductive A priori, Assume,
Conclude, Consectary, Corollary, Derive, Discount, Gather,
Illation, Infer(ence), Reason, Rebate, Recoup, Reprise, Stoppage,
Surmise, Syllogism

Deed(s) Achievement, Act(ion), Atweel, Backbond, Charta,
Charter, Derring-do, Escrol(l), Escrow, Exploit, Fact(um),
Indeed, Indenture, Manoeuvre, Mitzvah, Muniments, Specialty,
Starr, ► TITLE

Deep(en), Deeply Abstruse, Bass(o), Brine, Briny, Enhance,
Excavate, Grum, Gulf, Hadal, Intense, Low, Mindanao,
Mysterious, ► OCEAN, Profound, Re-enter, Rich, Sea, Sonorous,
Throaty, Upsee, Ups(e)y

Deer(-like) Axis, Bambi, Barasing(h)a, Barking, Brocket, Buck,
Cariacou, Carjacou, Cervine, Chevrotain, Chital, Doe, Elaphine,
Elk, Fallow, Gazelle, Hart, Moose, Mouse, Mule, Muntjac,
Muntjak, Musk, Père David's, Pricket, Pudu, Red, Rein, Roe,
Rusa, Sambar, Sambur, Selenodont, Sika, Sorel(l), Spade,
Spay(d), Spayad, Spitter, Spottie, Stag(gard), Tragule,
Ungulate, Virginia, Wapiti

▷**Defaced** may indicate first letter missing

Defame, Defamatory, Defamation Abase, Blacken, Calumny, Cloud, Denigrate, Detract, Dishonour, Impugn, Libel, Mud, Mudslinging, Scurrilous, Slander, Smear, Stigmatise, Traduce, Vilify

Default(er) Absentee, Bilk, Dando, Delinquent, Flit, Levant, Neglect, Omission, Waddle, Welsh

Defeat(ed), Defeatist Beat, Best, Caning, Capot, Codille, Conquer, Counteract, Debel, Defeasance, Demolish, Discomfit, Dish, Ditch, Fatalist, Floor, Foil, Foyle, Hammer, Hiding, Lick, Loss, Lurch, Marmelize, Master, Mate, Negative, Out, Outclass, Outdo, Outplay, ➤ OVERCOME, Overpower, Overreach, Overthrow, Pip, Reverse, Rout, Rubicon, Scupper, Set, Shellacking, Sisera, Stump, Tank, Thrash, Thwart, Tonk, Trounce, Vanquish, War, Waterloo, Whap, Whip, Whitewash, Whop, Whup, Wipe-out, Worst

Defect(ion), Defective, Defector Abandon, Amateur, Apostasy, Bug, Coma, Faulty, Flaw, ➤ FORSAKE, Frenkel, Halt, Hamartia, Kink, Manky, Mote, Natural, Renegade, Renegate, Ridgel, Ridgil, Rig, Rogue, Runagate, Shortcoming, Spina bifida, Terrace, Treason, Trick, Want, Weakness

Defence, Defend(er) Abat(t)is, Alibi, Antibody, Antidote, Antihistamine, Apologia, Back, Bailey, Barbican, Barmkin, Barricade, Bastion, Battery, Battlement, Berm, Bridgehead, Bulwark, Calt(h)rop, CD, Champion, Civil, Curtain, Demibastion, Embrasure, Hedgehog, Herisson, Hold, J(i)u-jitsu, Justify, Kaim, Keeper, Laager, Laer, Maintain, Martello Tower, Miniment, Moat, Muniment, Outwork, Palisade, Parapet, Rampart, Redan, Redoubt, Resist, Ringwall, ➤ SHELTER, Shield, Stonewall, Support, Tenail(le), Testudo, Tower, Trench, Trou-de-loup, Uphold, Vallation, Vallum, Vindicate, Wall, Warran(t)

Defenceless Helpless, Inerm, Naked, Sitting duck, Vulnerable

Defendant Accused, Apologist, Respondent, Richard Roe

Defer(ence), Deferential Bow, Delay, Dutiful, Homage, Morigerous, Obeisant, Pace, Polite, Postpone, Procrastinate, Protocol, Respect, Shelve, Submit, Suspend, Waive, Yield

Defiance, Defiant, Defy Acock, Bold, Brave, Dare, Daring, Disregard, Do or die, Outbrave, Outdare, Recusant, Stubborn, Titanism, Truculent, Unruly

Deficiency, Deficient Absence, Acapnia, Anaemia, Beriberi, Defect, Inadequate, Incomplete, Lack, SCID, Scant, Scarcity, Shortage, Spanaemia, Want

▷**Deficient** may indicate an anagram

Deficit Anaplerotic, Arrears, Defective, Ischemia, Loss, Poor, Shortfall

Define(d), Definition, Definitive Decide, Demarcate, Determine, Diorism, Distinct, Explain, Fix, Limit, Parameter, Set, Tangible, Term

Definite(ly) Classic, Clear, Emphatic, Firm, Hard, Positive, Precise, Specific, Sure, Yes

Deflate Burst, Collapse, Flatten, Lower, Prick

Deflect(or), Deflection Avert, Bend, Detour, Diverge, Divert, Glance, Otter, Paravane, Refract, Snick, Swerve, Throw, Trochotron, Veer, Windage

Deform(ed), Deformity Anamorphosis, Blemish, Crooked, Disfigure, Distort, Gammy, Hammer-toe, Harelip, Mishapt, Mutilate, Polt-foot, Stenosed, Talipes, Valgus, Warp

▷**Deformed** may indicate an anagram

Defraud Bilk, Cheat, Cozen, Gyp, Mulct, Sting, Swindle, Trick

Degrade, Degradation Abase, Cheapen, Culvertage, Debase, Demote, Diminish, Disennoble, Humble, Imbase, Lessen, Lower, ➤ SHAME, Waterloo

Degree(s) Aegrotat, As, Azimuthal, B es S, BA, Baccalaureate, BCom, BD, C, Class, D, Desmond, Doctoral, Engler, Extent, External, F, First, German, Gradation, Grade, Grece, Gree(s), Greece, Gre(e)se, Grice, Griece, Grize, ➤ IN A HIGH DEGREE, K, Lambeth, Latitude, Letters, Level, Licentiate, MA, Measure, Mediant, Nuance, Peg, PhD, Pin, Poll, Rate, Remove, Second, Stage, Status, Step, Third, Water

Dejected, Dejection Abase, Abattu, Alamort, Amort, Chap-fallen, Crab, Crestfallen, Despondent, Dismay, Dispirited, Downcast, Gloomy, Hangdog, Humble, Melancholy

Delay(ed) Ambage, Avizandum, Behindhand, Check, Cunctator, Defer, Demurrage, Detention, Fabian, Filibuster, For(e)slow, Forsloe, Frist, Hesitate, Hinder, Hitch, Hold up, Hysteresis, Impede, Laches, Lag, Late, Laten, Let, Linger, Mora(torium), Obstruct, Procrastinate, Prolong, Prorogue,

Remanet, Reprieve, Respite, Retard, Setback, Slippage, Sloth, Slow, ➤ STALL, Stand-over, Stay, Stonewall, Temporise, Wait

Delegate, Delegation Agent, Amphictyon, Appoint, Assign, Decentralise, Depute, Devolution, Mission, Nuncio, Representative, Transfer, Vicarial

Delete Cancel, Cut, Erase, Expunge, Purge, Rase, Scratch, Scrub

Deliberate(ly) Adagio, Consider, Debate, Intentional, Meditate, Moderate, Prepensely, Ponder, Studied, Voulu, Weigh, Witting

Delicacy, Delicate Airy-fairy, Beccafico, Canape, Cate, Caviare, Dainty, Difficult, Discreet, Ectomorph, Eggshell, Elfin, Ethereal, Fastidious, Finespun, Flimsy, Fine, Finesse, Fragile, ➤ FRAIL, Friand, Gossamer, Guga, Hothouse, Inconie, Incony, Ladylike, Light, Lobster, Nesh, Nicety, Niminy-piminy, Oyster, Reedy, Roe, Sensitive, Soft, Subtle(ty), Sunket, Taste, Tender, Tenuous, Ticklish, Tidbit, Titbit, Truffle

Delicious Ambrosia, Delectable, Exquisite, Fragrant, Goloptious, Goluptious, Gorgeous, Lekker, Lip-smacking, Mor(e)ish, Mouthwatering, Scrummy, Scrumptious, Tasty, Toothsome, Yummy, Yum-yum

▷**Delight** may indicate 'darken'

Delight(ed), Delightful Bliss, Chuff, Delice, Dreamy, Elated, Enamour, Enjoyable, Enrapture, Exuberant, Felicity, Fetching, Frabjous, Gas, Glad, Glee, Gratify, Honey, Joy, Overjoy, Please, Pleasure, ➤ RAPTURE, Regale, Scrummy, Super, Taking, Turkish, Whacko, Whee, Whoopee, Yippee, Yum-yum

Delinquent Bodgie, Criminal, Halbstarker, Negligent, Offender, Ted

Delirious, Delirium Deranged, DT, Frenetic, Frenzy, Insanity, Mania, Phrenetic, Spazz, Wild

Deliver(ance), Deliverer, Delivery Accouchement, Ball, Birth, Bowl, Caesarean, Consign, Convey, Deal, Escape, Give, Lead, Liberate, Orate, Over, Pronounce, Recorded, Redeem, Release, Relieve, Render, Rendition, ➤ RESCUE, Rid, Round(sman), Salvation, Save, Say, Seamer, Sell, Shipment, Speak, Special, Tice, Transfer, Underarm, Underhand, Utter, Wide, Yorker

Dell Dale, Dargle, Dene, Dimble, Dingle, Dingl(e)y, Glen, Valley

Delude, Delusion Bilk, Cheat, Deceive, Fallacy, Fool, Hoax, ➤ MISLEAD, Trick

Delve Burrow, Dig, Excavate, Exhume, Explore, Probe, Search

Demand(ing) Appetite, Call, Claim, Cry, Dun, Exact, Exigent, Fastidious, Final, Hest, ➤ INSIST, Market, Need, Order, Postulate, Pressure, Request, Requisition, Rush, Sale, Stern, Stipulate, Stringent, Summon, Ultimatum, Want

Demean(ing) Comport, Debase, Degrade, Lower, Maltreat

Demented Crazy, Hysterical, Insane, Mad

Demo March, Parade, Protest, Rally, Sit-in

Democracy, Democrat D, Locofoco, Montagnard, Popular, Republic, Sansculotte, Social, Tammany

Demolish, Demolition Bulldoze, Devastate, Devour, Floor, KO, Level, Rack, ➤ RAZE, Smash, Wreck

➤**Demon** see DEVIL

Demonstrate, Demonstration, Demonstrator Agitate, Barrack, Display, Endeictic, Evènement, Explain, Evince, Maffick, Manifest, March, Morcha, Ostensible, Portray, Protest, Prove, Provo, ➤ SHOW, Sit-in, Touchy-feely

Demoralize Bewilder, Corrupt, Destroy, Shatter, Unman, Weaken

Demote, Demotion Comedown, Degrade, Disbench, Embace, Embase, Reduce, Relegate, Stellenbosch

Demure Coy, Mim, Modest, Prenzie, Primsie, Sedate, Shy

Den Dive, Domdaniel, Earth, Hide-away, Hell, Holt, Home, Lair, Lie, Room, Shebeen, Study, Sty, Wurley

➤**Denial** see DENY

Denote Import, Indicate, Mean, Signify

Denounce, Denunciation Ban, Commination, Condemn, Criticise, Decry, Diatribe, Hatchet job, Hereticate, Proclaim, Proscribe, Shop, Stigmatise, Upbraid

Density Compact, D, Firm, Opaque, Relative, Solid, Spissitude, Tesla, Thick, Woofy

Dent Batter, Dancette, Depress, Dimple, Dinge, Dint, Nock, V

Dental, Dentist DDS, Extractor, Kindhart, LDS, Odontic, Periodontic, Toothy

Deny, Denial, Denier Abnegate, Antinomian, Aspheterism, Bar, Contradict, Démenti, Disavow, Disenfranchise, Disown, Forswear, ➤ GAINSAY, Nay, Negate, Nick, Protest, Refuse,

Refute, Renague, Renay, Reneg(e), Renegue, Reney, Renig, Renounce, Reny, Repudiate, Sublate, Withhold

Depart(ed), Departing, Departure Abscond, Absquatulate, Bunk, D, Dead, Decession, Defunct, Die, Digress, Divergence, Exit, Exodus, Flight, ➤ GO, Leave, Lucky, Outbound, Remue, Vade, Vamoose, Walkout

Department Achaea, Ain, Aisne, Allier, Angers, Arcadia, Ardeche, Ardennes, Argo, Arrondissement, Arta, Attica, Aube, Aude, Belfort, Branch, Bureau, Calvados, Cantal, Cher, Commissariat, Cote d'Or, Cotes d'Armor, Cotes du Nord, Creuse, Deme, Deux-Sevres, Division, Dordogne, Essonne, Faculty, Finistere, FO, Gard, Gironde, Greencloth, Guadeloupe, Gulag, Hanaper, Isere, Jura, Loire, Lot, Lot-et-Garonne, Ministry, Nome, Nomos, Office, Oise, Orne, Province, Region, Savoie, Secretariat(e), Section, Somme, Sphere, State, Treasury, Tuscany, Var, Vienne, Wardrobe, Yonne

Depend(ant), Dependency, Dependent Addicted, Child, Client, Colony, Conditional, Contingent, Count, Dangle, Fief, Habit, Hang, Hinge, Icicle, Lean, Minion, Pensioner, Relier, Rely, Retainer, Sponge, Subject, Trust, Turn on, Vassal

Dependable Reliable, Reliant, Secure, Solid, Sound, Staunch, Sure, ➤ TRUSTWORTHY

▷**Deploy(ment)** may indicate an anagram

Deport(ment) Address, Air, Banish, ➤ BEARING, Carriage, Demeanour, Mien, Renvoi, Renvoy

Depose, Deposition Affirm, Banish, Dethrone, Displace, Dispossess, Overthrow, Pieta, Testify

Deposit Alluvial, Alluvium, Arcus, Argol, Atheroma, Bank, Bathybius, Bergmehl, Calc-sinter, Calc-tuff, Caliche, Cave-earth, Coral, Crag, Delta, Depone, Diluvium, Evaporite, Fan, File, Firn, Fur, Gyttja, Kieselguhr, Land, Lay, Lodge(ment), Loess, Löss, Measure, Natron, Outwatch, Park, Placer, Plank, Plaque, Put, Repose, Residuum, Saburra, Saprolite, ➤ SEDIMENT, Silt, Sinter, Sludge, Stockwork, Stratum, Surety, Tartar, Terramara, Terramare, Tophus, Turbidite

Depot Barracoon, Base, Camp, Depository, Station, Terminus, Treasure-city, Warehouse

Depraved, Depravity Bestial, Cachexia, Cachexy, ➤ CORRUPT, Dissolute, Evil, Immoral, Low, Rotten, Sodom, Turpitude, Ugly, Vice, Vicious, Vile

Depress(ed), Depressing, Depression Alamort, Amort, Black dog, Blight, Blues, Cafard, Canada, Canyon, Chill, Col, Combe, Couch, Crab, Crush, Cyclone, Dampen, Deject, Despair, Dell, Dene, Dent, ➤ DIMPLE, Dip, Dismal, Dispirit, Drear, Drere, Dumpish, Exanimate, Flatten, Foss(ula), Fossa, Glen, Gloom, Ha-ha, Hammer, Hilar, Hilum, Hilus, Hollow, Howe, Hyp, Joes, Kettle, Kick(-up), Lacuna, Leaden, Low-spirited, Low(ness), Moping, Neck, Pit, Postnatal, Prostrate, Recession, Re-entrant, Sad, Saddle, Salt-cellar, Salt-pan, Sink, Sinkhole, Sinus, Slot, ➤ SLUMP, Soakaway, Spiritless, Sump, Swag, Swale, Trench, Trough, Vale, Valley, Wallow

Deprive(d), Deprivation Bereft, Deny, Disenfranchise, Disfrock, Disseise, Disseize, Expropriate, Geld, Have-not, Hunger, Reduce, Remove, Rob, Withhold

Depth F, Fathom, Gravity, Intensity, Isobath, Pit, Profundity

Deputise, Deputy Act, Agent, Aide, Assistant, Commis(sary), Delegate, Legate, Lieutenant, Locum, Loot, Number two, Proxy, Represent, Secondary, Standby, Sub, Substitute, Succentor, Surrogate, Vicar, Vice, Viceregent, Vidame

Derange(d) Craze, Détraqué, Disturb, Insane, Manic, Troppo, Unhinge, Unsettle

Derelict Abandoned, ➤ DECREPIT, Deserted, Negligent, Outcast, Ramshackle

Deride, Derision, Derisive Contempt, Gup, Guy, Hoot, Jeer, Mock, Nominal, Raspberry, ➤ RIDICULE, Sardonic, Scoff, Scorn, Snifty, Snort, Yah, Ya(h)boo

Derive, Derivation, Derivative Ancestry, Creosote, Deduce, Descend, Extract, Get, Kinone, Of, Offshoot, Origin, Pedigree, Secondary

Descend(ant), Descent Ancestry, Avail, Avale, Bathos, Blood, Chute, Cion, Decline, Degenerate, Derive, Dismount, Dive, Drop, Epigon, Extraction, Heir, Heraclid, ➤ LINEAGE, Offspring, Pedigree, Prone, Rappel, Said, Say(y)id, Scarp, Scion, Seed, Shelve, Sien(t), Sink, Stock, Syen, Vest, Volplane

Describe, Description Blurb, Define, Delineate, Depict, Designate, Epithet, Exposition, Expound, Narrate, Outline, Paint, Portray, Recount, Relate, Report, Sea-letter, Sketch, Specification, Term, Trace

▷**Describing** may indicate 'around'

Desecrate, Desecration Abuse, Defile, Dishallow, Profane, Sacrilege, Unhallow

▷**Desecrated** may indicate an anagram

Desert(s), Deserted, Deserter, Dissident Abandon, Apostasy, Arabian, Arid, Arunta, Atacama, AWOL, Badland, Barren, Bug, Bunk, D, Defect, Desolate, Dissident, Due, Empty, Eremic, Factious, Fail, Foresay, Forhoo, Forhow, Forlorn, Forsake, Forsay, Gibson, Gila, Gobi, Great Basin, Great Sandy, Great Victoria, Heterodox, Kalahari, Libyan, Lurch, Merit, Mojave, Nafud, Namib, Negev, Nubia, Ogaden, Painted, Pategonian, Pindan, Rat, Refus(e)nik, Reg, ➤ RENEGADE, Reward, Run, Sahara, Sands, Secede, Simpson, Sinai, Sonoran, Sturt, Syrian, Tergiversate, Turncoat, Void, Wadi, Waste, Worthiness

Deserve(d) Condign, Earn, ➤ MERIT, Well-earned, Worthy

Design(er) Adam, Aim, Architect, Ashley, Batik, Broider, Cardin, Cartoon, Chop, Cloisonné, Create, Cul de lampe, Damascene, Decor, Depict, Devise, Dévoré, Dior, Draft, Embroidery, End, Engine(r), Engineer, Erté, Etch, Fashion, Former, Hepplewhite, Hitech, Iconic, Impresa, Imprese, Intend(ment), Intent(ion), Interior, Layout, Linocut, Logo, Marquetry, Mean, Meander, Modiste, Monogram, Morris, Mosaic, Motif, ➤ PLAN, Plot, Propose, Pyrography, Quant, Ruse, Schema, Scheme, Seal, Sheraton, Sketch, Specification, Stencil, Stubble, Tatow, Tattoo, Tatu, Think, Tooling, Trigram, Vignette, Watermark, Whittle

Desirable, Desire, Desirous Ambition, Appetite, Aspire, Avid, Best, Cama, Conation, Concupiscence, Covet, Crave, Cupidity, Dreamboat, Earn, Epithymetic, Fancy, Gasp, Hanker, Hope, Hunger, Itch, Kama(deva), Le(t)ch, Libido, Long, Luscious, Lust, Mania, Owlcar, Reck, Request, Residence, Salt, Streetcar, Thirst, Velleity, Vote, Wanderlust, Want, Whim, Will, Wish, Yearn, Yen

Desk Almemar, Ambo, Bureau, Carrel(l), Cash, Check-in, Cheveret, City, Desse, Davenport, Devonport, E(s)critoire, Faldstool, Lectern, Lettern, Pedestal, Prie-dieu, Pulpit, Roll-top, Vargueno

Desolate, Desolation Bare, Barren, Desert, Devastate, Disconsolate, Forlorn, Gaunt, Gousty, Moonscape, Waste, Woebegone

Despair, Desperate Acharne, De profundis, Despond, Dire, Extreme, Frantic, Gagging, Giant, Gloom, Hairless, Headlong, Reckless, Unhopeful, Urgent, Wanhope

▶**Despatch** see DISPATCH

Despise Condemn, Contemn, Forhow, Hate, Ignore, Scorn, Spurn, Vilify, Vilipend

Despite For, Malgré, Notwithstanding, Pace, Though, Venom

Despot(ism) Autarchy, Autocrat, Caesar, Darius, Dictator, Napoleon, Nero, Satrap, Stratocrat, Tsar, Tyrant, Tzar

Dessert Afters, Baked Alaska, Baklava, Bavarois, Bombe, Charlotte, Charlotte russe, Cobbler, Compote, Coupe, Crème brulée, Crème caramel, Entremets, Flummery, Fool, Junket, Kissel, Knickerbocker glory, Kulfi, Marquise, Mousse, Nesselrode, Parfait, Pashka, Pavlova, Pud(ding) Sawine, Pudding, Strudel, Sundae, Syllabub, Tiramisu, Trifle, Vacherin, Zabaglione

Destination, Destine Design, End, Fate, Foredoom, Goal, Home, Intend, Joss, Port, Purpose, Weird

Destiny Doom, ▶ FATE, Karma, Kismet, Lot, Manifest, Moira, Yang, Yin

Destroy(er) Annihilate, Apollyon, Atomise, Blight, D, Decimate, Deface, Delete, Demolish, Denature, Destruct, Dish, Dismember, Dissolve, Eat, Efface, End, Eradicate, Erase, Exterminate, Extirpate, Fordo, Harry, Iconoclast, ▶ KILL, Murder, Obliterate, Overkill, Perish, Predator, Ravage, Raze, Ruin, Saboteur, Scuttle, Slash, Smash, Spiflicate, Sterilize, Stew-can, Stonker, Subvert, Undo, Uproot, Vandal, Vitiate, Whelm, Wreck, Zap

Destruction, Destructive Adverse, Bane, Can, Collapse, Deathblow, Deleterious, Devastation, Doom, Downfall, End, Götterdämmerung, Grave, Havoc, Holocaust, Insidious, Internecine, Kali, Lethal, Loss, Pernicious, Rack, Ragnarok, Ravage, Sabotage, Stroy, Wrack

Detach(ed), Detachment Abstract, Alienate, Aloof, Body, Calve, Clinical, Cut, Detail, Discrete, Isolate, Loose, Outlying, Outpost, Patrol, Separate, Sever, Staccato, Stoic, Unfasten, Unhinge

Detail(s), Detailed Dock, Elaborate, Embroider, Expatiate, Explicit, Expound, Instance, ▶ ITEM, Minutiae, Nicety,

Particular(ise), Pedantry, Point, Recite, Relate, Respect, Send, Spec, Special, Specification, Technicality

▷**Detailed** may indicate last letter missing

Detain(ee), Detention Arrest, Buttonhole, Collar, Custody, Delay, Detinue, Gate, Glasshouse, Hinder, Intern, Keep, POW, Retard, Stay, ➤ WITHHOLD

Detect(ive), Detector Agent, Arsène, Asdic, Bloodhound, Brown, Bucket, Busy, Catch, Chan, CID, Cuff, Dick, Discover, Divine, Doodlebug, Dupin, Espy, Eye, Fed, Find, Flambeau, Flic, Fortune, French, Geigercounter, Geophone, Gumshoe, Hanaud, Hercule, Holmes, Interpol, Investigator, Jack, Lecoq, Lupin, Maigret, Minitrack®, Nose, Peeper, PI, Pinkerton, Plant, Poirot, Private eye, Prodnose, Radar, Reagent, Rumble, Scent, Scerne, Sense, Sensor, Shadow, Shamus, Sherlock, ➤ SLEUTH, Sofar, Sonar, Sonobuoy, Spot, Tabaret, Take, Tec, Thorndyke, Toff, Trace, Trent, Vance, Wimsey, Yard

Deter(rent) Block, Check, Daunt, Dehort, Delay, Dissuade, Prevent, Restrain, Turn-off

Detergent Cleaner, Solvent, Surfactant, Syndet, Tepol, Whitener

Deteriorate, Deterioration Decadence, Degenerate, Derogate, Pejoration, Rust, Worsen

▷**Deterioration** may indicate an anagram

Determination, Determine(d) Arbitrament, Ascertain, Assign, Assoil, Bent, Condition, Dead-set, ➤ DECIDE, Define, Doctrinaire, Dogged, Dour, Drive, Earnest, Fix, Govern, Grit(ty), Headstrong, Hell-bent, Indomitable, Influence, Intent, Judgement, Law, Out, Point, Purpose, Quantify, ➤ RESOLUTE, Resolve, Rigwiddie, Rigwoodie, Self-will, Set, Settle, Shape, Stalwart, Type, Weigh

▷**Determination** may indicate 'last letter'

Detest(able) Abhor, Despise, Execrable, Execrate, Hate, Loathsome, Pestful, Vile

Detonate, Detonator Blast, Explode, Fire, Fuse, Fuze, Ignite, Kindle, Plunger, Primer, Saucisse, Saucisson, Tetryl, Trip-wire

Detour Bypass, Deviate, Divert

Detract Belittle, Decry, Diminish, Discount, Disparage

Devalue Debase, Reduce, Undermine

Devastate Demolish, Destroy, Overwhelm, Ravage, Sack, Waste

Develop(ed), Developer, Development Advance, Breed, Build, Educe, Elaborate, Enlarge, Escalate, Evolve, Expand, Expatriate, Fulminant, Germinate, Gestate, Grow, Hatch, Hypo, Imago, Improve, Incubate, Larva, Mature, Metamorphose, Metol, Pathogeny, Pullulate, Pupa, Pyro, Quinol, Ribbon, Ripe(n), Shape, Soup, Sprawl, Unfold, Upgrow

▷**Develop** may indicate an anagram

Deviant, Deviate, Deviation Aberrance, Abnormal, Anomaly, Brisure, Deflect, Depart, Derogate, Digress, Diverge, Divert, Error, Kurtosis, Pervert, Quartile, Sheer, Solecism, Sport, Stray, Swerve, ➤ TURN, Valgus, Varus, Veer, Wander, Wend

Device Afterburner, Appliance, Artifice, Aspirator, Atomiser, Audio, Bearing, Bootjack, Bug, Bungee, Buzzer, Capacitor, Capo, Carburettor, Centrifuge, Chaff, Charge, Cleat, Cleaver, Clicker, Commutator, Compass, Compasses, Contraption, Contrivance, Converter, Conveyor, Counter, Coupler, Cramp, Dasher, Deckle, Descendeur, Detector, Detent, Detonator, Diode, Divider, Dodge, Dongle, Doubler, Ecraseur, Elevon, Emblem, Engine, Enlarger, Episcope, Episemon, Etalon, Excelsior, Expedient, Frame, Fret, Fuse, Gadget, Generator, Geophone, Gimbals, Gimmick, Gizmo, Gland, Gobo, Grapnel, Gubbins, Hendiadys, Imprese, Inhaler, Instrument, Interferometer, Jetpack, LED, Lighter, Logo, Machine, Maser, Metronome, Microphone, Microscope, Mnemonic, Modem, Monogram, Mouse, Nebuliser, Optic®, Orle, Pacemaker, Pager, Paravane, Pattern, Petar(d), Phonoscope, Pickoff, Plan, Polygraph, Possum, Prism, Ratchet, Relay, Resister, Rest, Roller, Satellite, Scanner, Scart, Scrambler, Sensor, Servo, Shoehorn, Shut-off, Siderostat, Smokejack, Snow-eyes, Snowplough, Snuffer, Solenoid, Sonde, Sonograph, Spectograph, Sprag, Spreader, Squeegee, Stabiliser, ➤ STRATAGEM, Subterfuge, Swellbox, Switch, Synchro, Tachograph, Tachometer, Tactic, Tag, Temple, Thermistor, Thermopile, Thermostat, Timer, Tipple, Tonepad, Tourniquet, Trademark, Transducer, Transformer, Transistor, Tremie, Trick, Triode, Tromp(e), Tympan, Valve, Ventilator, Videophone, Viewer, Viewfinder, Widget

Devil(ish) Abaddon, Afrit, Apollyon, Asmodeus, Auld Hornie, Beelzebub, Belial, Buckra, Clootie, Cloots, Deev, Deil, Demon, Deuce, Diable, Diabolic, Dickens, Div, Drudge, Familiar, Fiend, Ghoul, Hornie, Iblis, Imp, Incubus, Infernal, Lucifer, Mahoun(d), Mephisto(pheles), Mischief, Nick, Old Nick, Rahu, Ralph, Satan, Satyr, Succubine, Succubus, Tasmanian, Tempter, Wicked, Worricow

Devious Braide, Cunning, Deep, Eel(y), Erroneous, Implex, Indirect, Scheming, Shifty, Subtle, Tortuous, Tricky

Devise(d) Arrange, Contrive, Decoct, Hit-on, Imagine, Invenit, Invent, Plot

Devote(e), Devotion(al), Devoted Addiction, Aficionado, Angelus, Attached, Bhakti, Consecrate, Corban, Dedicate, Employ, Fan, Fervid, Fiend, Holy, Hound, Loyalty, Novena, Passion, Pious, Puja, Religioso, Solemn, True, Zealous

Devour Consume, Eat, Engorge, Engulf, Manducate, Moth-eat, Scarf, Scoff, ➤ SWALLOW

▷ **Devour** may indicate one word inside another

Devout Holy, Pious, Reverent, Sant, Sincere

Dew(y) Bloom, Moist, Mountain, Rime, Roral, Roric, Rorid, Roscid, Serene, Tranter

Diagnose, Diagnosis Findings, Identify, Scan, Scintigraphy

Diagonal Bias, Cater(-corner), Counter, Oblique, Slant, Solidus, Twill

Diagram Argand, Butterfly, Chart, Compass rose, Decision tree, Drawing, Feynman, Figure, Graph, Graphics, Grid, Map, Plan, Plat, Scatter, Schema, Stemma, Stereogram, Venn

Dial(ling) Card, Face, Mug, Phiz, Phone, STD, Visage

Dialect Accent, Burr, Eldin, Erse, Eye, Franconian, Gascon, Geordie, Idiom, Ionic, Isogloss, Jargon, Jockney, Ladin, Lallans, Landsmaal, Langue d'oui, Lingo, Low German, Norman, Norn, Parsee, Patois, Prakrit, Romansch, Scouse, Taal, Tongue, Yenglish, Yinglish

Dialogue Colloquy, Conversation, Critias, Discussion, Exchange, Lazzo, Pastourelle, Speech, Stichomythia, Talk, Upspeak

Diameter Breadth, Calibre, Gauge, Width

Diamond(s), Diamond-shaped Adamant, Black, Boart, Brilliant, Bristol, Carbonado, Cullinan, D, DE, Delaware, Eustace,

Florentine, Hope, Ice, Isomer, Jim, Koh-i-noor, Lasque, Lattice,
Lozenge, Paragon, Pick, Pitch, Pitt, Rhinestone, Rhomb, Rock,
Rose-cut, Rosser, Rough, Sancy, Solitaire, Spark, Sparklers,
Squarial, Suit

Diary, Diarist Chronicle, Dale, Day-book, Evelyn, Hickey,
Journal, Kilvert, Log, Nobody, Pepys, Pooter, Record

Dice(y) Aleatory, Astragals, Bale, Bones, Chop, Craps, Cube,
Dodgy, Fulham, Fullams, Fullans, Gourd(s), Highman, Jeff,
Shoot, Snake-eyes, Tallmen

▷**Dick** may indicate a dictionary

▷**Dicky** may indicate an anagram

Dictate, Dictator(ial) Amin, Autocrat, Caesar, Castro,
Cham, Command, Czar, Decree, Demagogue, Despot, Duce,
Franco, Fu(e)hrer, Gauleiter, Hitler, Impose, Lenin, Ordain,
Peremptory, Peron, Salazar, Shogun, Stalin, Tell, Tito,
Totalitarian, Tsar, Tyrant, Tzar

Dictionary Alveary, Calepin, Chambers, Etymologicon, Fowler,
Gazetteer, Glossary, Gradus, Hobson-Jobson, Johnson's,
Idioticon, Larousse, Lexicon, Lexis, OED, Onomasticon,
Thesaurus, Webster, Wordbook

Die(d), Dying Ache, Cark, Choke, Crater, Croak, Cube, D,
Decadent, Desire, End, Evanish, Exit, Expire, Fade, Fail, Forfair,
Fulham, Fulhan, Fullam, Go, Highman, Hop, Kark, Long,
Morendo, Moribund, Ob(iit), Orb, Pass, Perdendosi, Perish,
Peter, Snuff, Solidum, Sphacelation, Stamp, Sterve, Succumb,
Suffer, Swage, Swelt, Tine, Wane

Diet(er) Assembly, Bant(ing), Council, Dail, Eat, Fare, Hay,
Intake, Landtag, Lent, Macrobiotic, Parliament, Reduce,
Regimen, Reichstag, Slim, Solid, Sprat, Staple, Strict, Tynwald,
Vegan, Vegetarian, Weightwatcher, Worms

Differ(ence), Differing, Different(ly) Allo, Barney,
Change, Cline, Contrast, Deviant, Diesis, Disagree, Discord,
Discrepant, Disparate, Dispute, Dissent, Distinct, Diverge,
Diverse, Else, Elsewise, Nuance, Omnifarious, Other,
Othergates, Otherguess, Otherness, Otherwise, Separate,
Several, Tiff, Unlike, Various, Vary

Difficult(y) Abstruseness, Ado, Aporia, Arduous, Augean,
Badass, Balky, Ballbuster, Block, Bolshie, Bother, Catch, Choosy,
Complication, Corner, Deep, Depth, Dysphagia, Fiddly,
Formidable, Gordian, ➤ HARD, Hassle, Hazard, Hiccup, Hobble,

Hole, Ill, Impasse, Indocile, Kink, Knot, Lurch, Mulish, Net,
Nodus, Obstacle, Pig, Plight, Quandary, Recalcitrant, Rough,
Rub, Scrape, Scrub, Setaceous, Shlep, Snag, Soup, Steep, Stick,
Sticky, Stiff, Strait, Stubborn, Ticklish, Trial, Tricky, Troublous,
Une(a)th, Uphill, Via dolorosa

Diffuse, Diffusion Disperse, Disseminate, Endosmosis,
Exude, Osmosis, Pervade, Radiate, Spread

Dig(ger), Digging, Digs, Dig up Antipodean, Australian,
Backhoe, Beadle, Bed(e)ral, Billet, Bot, Burrow, Costean, Delve,
Enjoy, Excavate, Flea-bag, Fossorial, Gaulter, Gibe, Gird, Graip,
Grub, Howk, Jab, Kip, Lair, Like, Lodgings, Mine, Navvy, Nervy,
Nudge, Pad, Pioneer, Probe, Prod, Raddleman, Resurrect, Root,
Ruddleman, Sap, See, Spade, Spit, Spud, Star-nose, Taunt,
Tonnell, Trench, Tunnel, Undermine, Unearth

Digest(ible), Digestion, Digestive Abridgement, Absorb,
Abstract, Aperçu, Archenteron, Assimilate, Codify, Concoct,
Endue, Epitome, Eupepsia, Eupepsy, Gastric, Index, Indue,
Light, Pandect, Pem(m)ican, Pepsin(e), Peptic, Précis, Salt-cat,
➤ SUMMARY

Dignified, Dignify August, Elevate, Exalt, Handsome,
Honour, Lordly, Majestic, Manly, Proud, Stately

Dignity Aplomb, Bearing, Cathedra, Decorum, Face, Glory,
Grandeur, Majesty, Nobility, Poise, Presence, Scarf

Digress(ion) Deviate, Diverge, Ecbole, Episode, Excurse,
Excursus, Maunder, Veer, Wander

Dilate(d), Dilation, Dilatation Amplify, Develop, Diastole,
Ecstasis, Enlarge, Expand, Increase, Mydriasis, Sinus, Tent, Varix

Dilemma Casuistry, Choice, Cleft, Dulcarnon, Fix, Horn,
Predicament, Quandary, Why-not

Diligence, Diligent Active, Application, Assiduous, Coach,
Conscience, Eident, Industry, Intent, Painstaking, Sedulous,
Studious

Dilute, Dilution Adulterate, Delay, Diluent, Lavage, Simpson,
Thin, Water, Weaken

Dim(ness), Dimming, Dimwit Becloud, Blear, Blur,
Brownout, Caligo, Clueless, Crepuscular, Dense, Dusk, Eclipse,
Fade, Faint, Feint, Gormless, Ill-lit, Indistinct, Mist, Nebulous,
Ninny, Obscure, Overcast, Owl, Pale, Shadow, Unsmart

Dimension Area, Breadth, Extent, Height, Length, Measure, Size, Volume, Width

Diminish(ed), Diminuendo, Diminution, Diminutive Abatement, Assuage, Baby, Calando, Contract, Cot(t)ise, Deactivate, Decrease, Détente, Detract, Disparage, Dissipate, Dwarf, Dwindle, Erode, Fourth, Hypocorism(a), Lessen, Lilliputian, Minify, Minus, Mitigate, Petite, Pigmy, Scarp, Small, Stultify, Subside, Toy, Trangle, Wane, Whittle

Dingy Crummy, Dark, Dirty, Drear, Dun, Fusc(ous), Grimy, Isabel(la), Isabelline, Lurid, Oorie, Ourie, Owrie, Shabby, Smoky

Dining-room Cafeteria, Cenacle, Commons, Frater, Hall, Langar, Refectory, Restaurant, Triclinium

Dinner Banquet, Collation, Feast, Hall, Kail, Kale, Meal, Prandial, Repast

Dinosaur Allosaurus, Brachiosaurus, Brontosaurus, Diplodocus, Hadrosaur, Ichthyosaur(us), Iguanodon, Megalosaur, Plesiosaur, Prehistoric, Pterodactyl, Pterosaur, Sauropod, Smilodon, Stegosaur, Teleosaurus, Titanosaurus, Triceratops, Tyrannosaurus

Diocese Bishopric, District, Eparchate, See

Dip(per) Baptise, Basin, Bathe, Bob, Brantub, Dabble, Dap, Dean, Dib, Diver, Dop, Duck, Dunk, Foveola, Geosyncline, Guacomole, Houmous, H(o)ummus, Hum(m)us, Immerse, Intinction, Ladle, Lucky, Ouzel, Paddle, Rinse, Rollercoaster, Salute, Star, Submerge, Tzatziki, Ursa

Diploma Charter, Parchment, Qualification, Scroll, Sheepskin

Diplomacy, Diplomat(ic) Altemat, Ambassador, Attaché, CD, Chargé d'affaires, Consul, DA, Dean, Doyen, El(t)chi, Envoy, Fanariot, Finesse, Gunboat, Legation, Lei(d)ger, Phanariot, Suave, ➤ TACT

▷**Dippy** may indicate a bather

Dire Dreadful, Fatal, Fell, Hateful, Ominous, Urgent

Direct(ly), Director Administer, Advert, Aim, Airt, Auteur, Board, Boss, Cann, Channel, Charge, Command, Compere, Con(n), Conduct, Control, Cox, Dead, Due, Enjoin, Explicit, Fellini, First-hand, Forthright, Frontal, Guide, Helm, Hitchcock, Immediate, Impresario, Instruct, Kappelmeister, Lead, Lean, Manager, Navigate, Outright, Pilot, Play, Point-blank, Ready,

Refer, Régisseur, Rudder, Set, Signpost, Stear, ➤ STEER, Straight,
Teach, Tell, Truffaut, Vector

Direction Aim, Airt, Arrow, Astern, Bearings, Course,
Cross-reference, E, End-on, Guidance, Guide, Heading, Keblah,
L, Line, N, Orders, Passim, R, Route, Rubric, S, Sanction, Send,
Sense, Side, Slap, Tack, Tenor, Thataway, Trend, W, Way

Directory Crockford, Debrett, Encyclop(a)edia, Kelly, List, Red
book, Register

Dirge Ballant, Coronach, Dirige, Epicedium, Knell, Monody,
Requiem, Song, Threnody

Dirigible Airship, Balloon, Blimp, Zeppelin

Dirk Dagger, Skean, Whinger, Whiniard, Whinyard

Dirt(y) Begrime, Bemoil, Chatty, Clag, Clarty, Colly,
Contaminate, Coom, Crock, Crud, Draggle, Dung, Dust, Earth,
Filth, Foul, Gore, Grime, Grufted, Grungy, Impure, Manky,
Moit, Mote, Muck, Obscene, Ordure, Pay, Ray, Sculdudd(e)ry,
Scum, Scuzzy, Skulduddery, Smirch, Smut(ch), Sordor, Squalid,
Soil, Stain, Trash, Unclean, Yucky, Yukky

Disable, Disability Cripple, Lame, Maim, Paralyse, Scotch,
Wreck

Disadvantage Detriment, Drawback, Handicap, Mischief,
Out, Penalise, Penalty, Supercherie, Upstage, Wrongfoot,
Zugswang

Disagree(ing), Disagreeable, Disagreement Argue,
Argy-bargy, Bad, Clash, Conflict, Contest, Debate, Differ,
Discrepant, Dispute, Dissent, Dissonant, Evil, Fiddlesticks,
Friction, Heterodoxy, Pace, Rift

Disappear(ing) Cook, Dispel, Evanesce, Evanish, Evaporate,
Fade, Kook, Latescent, Melt, Occult, Pass, Skedaddle, Slope,
➤ VANISH

Disappoint(ed), Disappointment Anticlimax, Balk,
Chagrin, Crestfallen, Comedown, Delude, Disgruntle, Frustrate,
Gutted, Heartsick, Lemon, Letdown, Regret, Sell, Shucks, Sick,
Suck-in, Sucks, Swiz(zle), Thwart

Disapproval, Disapprove Ach, Animadvert, Boo, Catcall,
Censure, Deplore, Deprecate, Expostulate, Frown, Harrumph,
Hiss, Napoo, Object, Pejorative, Po-faced, Raspberry, Reject,
Reproach, Reprobate, Squint, Tush, Tut, Umph, Veto, Whiss

Disarm(ament), Disarming Bluff, Defuse, Demobilise, Nuclear, Winsome

Disarray Disorder, Mess, Rifle, Tash, Undress

Disaster, Disastrous Adversity, Apocalypse, Bale, Calamity, Cataclysm(ic), Catastrophe, Debacle, Dire, Doom, Evil, Fatal, Fiasco, Flop, Impostor, Meltdown, Mishap, Pitfall, Rout, Ruin, Shipwreck, Titanic, Tragedy, Wipeout

Disbelief, Disbelieve(r) Acosmism, Anythingarian, Atheism, Incredulity, Mistrust, Nothingarianism, Occamist, Phew, Phooey, Puh-lease, Puh-leeze, Question, Sceptic, Voetsak

Disc, Disk Bursting, Button, Compact, Coulter, Counter, Diaphragm, Dogtag, EP, Epiphragm, Floppy, Frisbee®, Gold, Gong, Hard, Harrow, Intervertebral, Laser, LP, Magnetic, Mono, O, Optical, Paten, Patin, Planchet, Plate, Platinum, Puck, Rayleigh, Record, Rosette, Roundel, Rowel, Slipped, Slug, Stereo, Tax, Token, Video, Wafer, Whorl, Wink

Discard(ed) Abandon, Crib, Dele, Jettison, Kill, Leave, Obsolete, Off, Offload, Oust, ➤ REJECT, Scrap, Shuck, Slough, Sluff, Supersede

Discern(ing), Discernment Acumen, Acute, Descry, Discrimination, Flair, Insight, Perceive, Percipient, Perspicacity, Realise, Sapient, Scry, See, Skry, ➤ TASTE, Tell, Wate

Discharge Acquit, Arc, Assoil, Brush, Cashier, Catarrh, Conditional, Corona, Demob, Disembogue, Disgorge, Dismiss, Dump, Efflux, Egest, Ejaculate, Eject, Emission, Emit, Effusion, Enfilade, Evacuate, Excrete, Execute, Exemption, Expulsion, Exude, Fire, Flower, Flux, Free, Glow, Lava, Lay off, Leak, Loose, Maturate, Menses, Mute, Offload, Oust, Pay, Perform, Period, Purulence, Pus, Pyorrhoea, Quietus, Rheum, Sack, Salvo, Sanies, Secretion, Show, Shrive, Snarler, Spark, Suppurate, Teem, Unload, Vent, Void

Disciple Adherent, Apostle, Catechumen, Follower, John, Judas, Luke, Mark, Matthew, Peter, Simon, Son, Student, Thomist, Votary

Discipline, Disciplinarian Apollonian, Ascesis, Chasten, Chastise, Correct, Despot, Drill, Exercise, Feng Shui, Inure, Martinet, Mathesis, Punish, Regimentation, Regulate, School, Science, Spartan, Stickler, Subject, Train, Tutor

Disclaim(er) Deny, Disown, No(t)chel, Recant, Renounce, ➤ REPUDIATE, Voetstoots

Disclose, Disclosure Apocalypse, Confess, Divulge, Expose, Impart, Leak, Manifest, Propale, ► PUBLISH, Report, Reveal, Spill, Tell, Unheal, Unhele, Unrip, Unveil

Discomfort Ache, Angst, Dysphoria, Gyp, Heartburn, Pain, Unease

Disconcert Abash, Confuse, Disturb, Embarrass, Faze, Feeze, Flurry, Nonplus, Phase, Pheese, Pheeze, Phese, ► RATTLE, Shatter, Throw, Upset, Wrong-foot

▷**Disconcert(ed)** may indicate an anagram

Disconnect(ed) Asynartete, Detach, Disjointed, Off-line, Sever, Staccato, Uncouple, Undo, Unplug

Discontent(ed) Disquiet, Dissatisfied, Repined, Sour

Discord(ant) Absonant, Ajar, Conflict, Din, Dispute, Eris, Faction, Hoarse, Jangle, Jar, Raucous, Ruction, Strife

▷**Discord(ant)** may indicate an anagram

Discount Agio, Cashback, Deduct, Disregard, Forfaiting, Invalidate, ► REBATE, Trade

Discourage(ment) Caution, Chill, Dampen, Dash, Daunt, Demoralise, Deter, Dishearten, Disincentive, Dismay, Dissuade, Enervate, Frustrate, Opposition, Stifle

Discourse Address, Argument, Conversation, Descant, Diatribe, Dissertate, Eulogy, Expound, Homily, Lecture, Lucubrate, Orate, Preach, Relate, Rigmarole, Sermon

Discover(er), Discovery Amundsen, Anagnorisis, Ascertain, Betray, Breakthrough, Columbus, Cook, Descry, Detect, Discern, Discure, Eureka, ► FIND, Heureka, Heuristic, Learn, Locate, Manifest, Moresby, Protege, Rumble, Serendip, Serendipity, Spy, Tasman, Trace, Unearth, Unhale, Unmask, Unveil

▷**Discovered in** may indicate an anagram or a hidden word

Discredit(able) Debunk, Decry, Disgrace, Explode, Infamy, Scandal, Unworthy

Discreet, Discretion Cautious, Circumspect, Freedom, Option, Polite, Politic, Prudence, Prudent, Trait, Wise

Discrepancy Difference, Gap, Lack, Shortfall, Variance

Discriminate, Discriminating, Discrimination Ag(e)ism, Colour bar, Diacritic, Differentiate, Discern, Distinguish, Elitism, Invidious, Nasute, Racism, Secern, Segregate, Select, Sexism, Siz(e)ism, Speciesism, Subtle, Taste

Discuss(ing), Discussion Agitate, Air, Canvass, Commune, Conf(erence), Debate, Dialectic, Dialogue, Dicker, Disquisition, Examine, Handle, Hob and nob, Interlocution, Korero, Moot, Over, Palaver, Parley, Pourparler, Prolegomenon, Quodlibet, Rap, Re, Symposium, Talk, Tapis, Treatment

Disdain(ful) Belittle, Contempt, Coy, Deride, Despise, Geck, Poof, Pooh-pooh, Puh, Sassy, ➤ SCORN, Scout, Sniffy, Spurn, Supercilious

Disease(d) Affection, Ailment, Contagion, Deficiency, Dread, Endemic, English, Epidemic, Fever, Flu, Iatrogenic, Infection, Malady, Nosography, Nosology, Pandemic, Pathogen, Pneumo(no)coniosis, Rabid, Scourge, Sickness, Social, ➤ STD, Zymosis

▷**Diseased** may indicate an anagram

Disengage(d), Disengagement Clear, Divorce, Liberate, Loosen, Release, Untie

▷**Disfigured** may indicate an anagram

Disgrace Atimy, Attaint, Baffle, Blot, Contempt, Contumely, Degrade, Discredit, Dishonour, Dog-house, Ignominy, Indignity, Infamy, Obloquy, Opprobrium, Scandal, Shame, Shend, Slur, Soil, Stain, Stigma, Yshend

Disgraceful Ignoble, Ignominious, Indign, Infamous, Mean, Notorious, Shameful, Turpitude

▷**Disgruntled** may indicate an anagram

Disguise(d) Alias, Blessing, Camouflage, Cloak, Colour, Conceal, Cover, Covert, Dissemble, Hide, Hood, Incog(nito), Mantle, Mask, Masquerade, Obscure, Peruke, Pretence, Pseudonym, Ring, Travesty, Veil, Vele, Veneer, Visagiste, Vizard

▷**Disguised** may indicate an anagram

Disgust(ing) Ach-y-fi, Ad nauseam, Aversion, Aw, Bah, Cloy, Discomfort, Execrable, Faugh, Fie, Foh, Fulsome, Grody, Irk, Loathsome, Manky, Nauseous, Noisome, Obscene, Odium, Oughly, Ouglie, Pah, Pho(h), Pish, Repel, Repugnant, ➤ REVOLT, Revulsion, Scomfish, Scumfish, Scunner, Scuzz, ➤ SICKEN, Squalid, Tush, Ugsome, Vile, Yech, Yu(c)k

Dish(es) Adobo, Allot, Ashet, Basin, Bowl, Dreamboat, Grail, Kitchen, Petri, Pilau, Plate, Platter, Porringer, Receptacle, Regale, Sangraal, Sangreal, Sangrail, Satellite, Saucer, Serve, Service, Side, Smasher, Special, Squarial, Watchglass, White-pot

Dishevel(led) Blowsy, Blowzy, Daggy, Mess, Rumpled, Touse, Tousle, Touzle, Tumble, Uncombed, Unkempt, Windswept

Dishonest(y) Bent, Crooked, Cross, Dodgy, False, Fraud, Graft, Hooky, Hot, Knavery, Malpractice, Malversation, Shonky, Stink, Twister, Underhand, Venal

Dishonour Defile, Disgrace, Disparage, Ignominy, Seduce, ➤ SHAME, Violate, Wrong

Disinfect(ant) Acriflavin(e), Carbolic, Cineol(e), Cleanse, Eucalyptole, Formalin, Fumigate, Fuchsine, Lysol®, Phenol, Purify, Sheep-dip, Terebene

Disjointed Bitty, Incoherent, Rambling, Scrappy

▶**Disk** see DISC

Dislike(d) Allergy, Animosity, Animus, Antipathy, Aversion, Derry, Disesteem, Displeasure, Distaste, Lump, Mind

Dislocate, Dislocation Break, Diastasis, Displace, Fault, Luxate, Slip

Dislodge Budge, Displace, Expel, Oust, Rear, Uproot

Disloyal(ty) False, Treason, Unfaithful, Untrue

Dismal Black, Bleak, Cheerless, Dark, Dowie, Drack, Dreary, Funereal, ➤ GLOOMY, Grey, Morne, Obital, Sepulchral, Sombre, Sullen, Trist(e), Wae

Dismantle(d), Dismantling Derig, Divest, Get-out, Sheer-hulk, Strike, Strip, Unrig

Dismay Amate, Appal, Confound, Consternation, Coo, Daunt, Ha, Horrify, Lumme, Qualms

Dismiss(al) Annul, Ax, Boot, Bounce, Bowl(er), Bum's rush, Cancel, Cashier, Catch, Chuck, Congé, Daff, Discard, Discharge, Expulsion, Fire, Heave-ho, Lay off, Marching orders, Mitten, Och, Prorogue, Push, Recall, Reform, Remove, Road, Sack, Scout, Send, Shoo, Spit, Stump, Via, Walking papers, York

Disobedience, Disobedient, Disobey Contumacy, Defy, Flout, Insubordination, Rebel, Wayward

Disorder(ed), Disorderly Ague, Ailment, Anarchy, Ariot, Asthma, Ataxia, Catatonia, Chaos, Clutter, Confuse, Contracture, Defuse, Derange, Deray, Diabetes, Dishevel, Dystrophy, Echolalia, Entropy, Farrago, Grippe, Haemophilia, Huntingdon's chorea, Hypallage, Inordinate, Irregular, ME, Mess, Mistemper, ➤ MUDDLE, Muss(y), Neurosis, Oncus, Onkus, Pandemonium, Para-, Psychomatic, Psychosis, Rile, SAD,

Seborrh(o)ea, Shell-shock, Slovenly, Thalass(a)emia, Tousle, Unhinge, Unruly, Upset, Virilism

▷**Disorder(ed)** may indicate an anagram

Dispatch Bowl, Celerity, Consign, Destroy, Dismiss, Expede, Expedite, Express, Gazette, Kibosh, Kill, Missive, Post, Pronto, Remit, Report, ➤ SEND, Ship, Slaughter, Slay

Dispensation, Dispense(r), Dispense with Absolve, Administer, Ax(e), Cashpoint, Chemist, Container, Distribute, Dose, Dropper, Exempt, Handout, Indult, Scrap

Displace(ment), Displaced Antevert, Blueshift, Depose, Disturb, Ectopia, Ectopy, Fault, Heterotopia, Luxate, Move, Oust, Proptosis, Ptosis, Reffo, Stir, Subluxation, Unsettle, Uproot, Valgus, Varus

Display, Display ground Air, Array, Blaze, Blazon, Brandish, Bravura, Depict, Eclat, Epideictic, Etalage, Evidence, Evince, Exhibition, Exposition, Express, Extend, Exude, Fireworks, Flaunt, Float, Gondola, Hang, LED, Lek, Liquid crystal, Manifest, Mount, Muster, Ostentation, Outlay, Overdress, Pageant, Parade, Paraf(f)le, Peepshow, Pixel, Pomp, Propale, Pyrotechnics, Rodeo, Scene, Shaw, ➤ SHOW, Sight, Spectacle, Splash, Splurge, Sport, Spree, State, Stunt, Tableau, Tattoo, Tournament, Up, Vaunt, Wear

Displease(d), Displeasure Anger, Dischuffed, Humph, Irritate, Provoke, Umbrage

Dispose(d), Disposal Arrange, Bestow, Cast, Despatch, Dump, Eighty-six, Lay(-out), Prone, Sale, Sell, Service, Settle, Stagger

▷**Disposed, Disposition** may indicate an anagram

Disposition Affectation, Attitude, Bent, Bias, Humour, Inclination, Kidney, Lie, Nature, Penchant, Talent, Temper(ament), Trim

Disprove Debunk, Discredit, Negate, Rebut, Redargue, Refel, Refute

Dispute(d), Disputant Argue, Barney, Brangle, Cangle, Case, Chaffer, Chorizont(ist), Contend, Contest, Contretemps, Controversy, Debate, Deny, Differ, Discept, Discuss, Eristic, Fray, Haggle, Kilfud-yoking, Lock-out, Militate, Ob and soller, Odds, Oppugn, Plea, Polemic, Pro-and-con, ➤ QUESTION, Resist, Rag, Spar, Stickle, Threap(it), Threep(it), Tiff, Tissue, Variance, Wrangle

Disqualify Debar, Incapacitate, Recuse, Reject, Unfit

Disregard(ed) Anomie, Anomy, Contempt, Disfavour, Flout, Forget, Ignore, Oblivion, Omit, Overlook, Oversee, Pass, Pretermit, Slight, Spare, Violate, Waive

Disreputable, Disrepute Base, Disgrace, Louche, Low, Lowlife, Raffish, Ragamuffin, Rip, Seamy, Shameful, Shy, Sleazy

Disrespect(ful) Contempt, Discourtesy, Impiety, Impolite, Irreverent, Profane, Slight, Uncivil

Disrupt(ion) Breach, Cataclasm, Disorder, Distract, Hamper, Interrupt, Jetlag, Mayhem, Perturb, Quonk, Screw, Upheaval

▷**Disruption** may indicate an anagram

Dissatisfaction Displeasure, Distaste, Humph, Umph

Dissension, Dissent(er), Dissenting Contend, Differ, Disagree, Discord, Dissident, Faction, Heretic, Jain, Lollard, Noes, Non-CE, Non-con(formist), Pantile, Protest, Raskolnik, Recusant, Splinter group, ► STRIFE, Vary

Dissertation Essay, Excursus, Lecture, Thesis, Treatise

Dissipate(d) Debauch, Diffuse, Disperse, Dissolute, Gay, Revel, Scatter, Shatter, Squander, Waste

▷**Dissipated** may indicate an anagram

Dissolute Degenerate, Hell, Lax, Libertine, Licentious, Loose, Rake-helly, Rakish, Rip, Roué

▷**Dissolute** may indicate an anagram

Dissolve Deliquesce, Digest, Disband, Disunite, Liquesce, Melt, Terminate, Thaw

Distance Absciss(a), Afield, Apothem, Breadth, Coss, Declination, Eloi(g)n, Farness, Foot, Headreach, Height, Interval, Klick, Kos(s), Latitude, League, Length, Mean, Mileage, Parasang, Parsec, Range, Reserve, Rod, Span, Spitting, Stade, Striking, Way, Yojan

Distant Aloof, Far, Frosty, Icy, Long, Offish, Remote, Tele-, Timbuctoo, Yonder

Distaste(ful) Repugnant, Ropy, Scunner, Unpalatable, Unpleasant, Unsavoury

Distil(late), Distillation, Distiller, Distilling Alcohol, Alembic, Anthracine, Azeotrope, Brew, Condense, Drip, Pelican, Pyrene, Pyroligneous, Rosin, Turps, Vapour

▷**Distillation** may indicate an anagram

Distinct(ive) Apparent, Characteristic, Clear, Different, Evident, Grand, Individual, Peculiar, Plain, Separate, Several, Signal, ➤ SPECIAL, Stylistic, Vivid

Distinction Beaut(y), Blue, Cachet, Credit, Diacritic, Difference, Dignity, Diorism, Disparity, Division, Eclat, Eminence, Honour, Lustre, Mark, Mystique, Note, Nuance, OM, Prominence, Quiddity, Rank, Renown, Speciality, Style, Title

Distinguish(ed), Distinguishing Classify, Demarcate, Denote, Diacritic, Different(iate), Discern, Discriminate, Divide, Elevate, Mark, Notable, Perceive, Prestigious, Prominent

Distort(ed), Distortion Anamorphosis, Bend, Colour, Contort, Deface, Deform, Dent, Fudge, Misshapen, Jaundiced, Mangle, Misshapen, Pervert, Rubato, Thraw, Twist, ➤ WARP, Wow, Wrest, Wring, Wry

▷ **Distort(ed)** may indicate an anagram

Distract(ed), Distraction Absent, Agitate, Amuse, Avocation, Bewilder, Divert, Nepenthe, Éperdu, Forhaile, Frenetic, Lost, Madden, Mental, Perplex, Upstage

▷ **Distract(ed)** may indicate an anagram

Distress(ed), Distressing Afflict, All, Alack, Anger, Anguish, Antique, Distraint, Dolour, Exigence, Extremity, Grieve, Harass, Harrow, Hurt, Ill, ➤ IN DISTRESS, Irk, Misease, Misfortune, Need, Oppress, Pain, Poignant, Prey, Sad, Shorn, Sore, SOS, Straits, Traumatic, ➤ TROUBLE, Une(a)th

Distribute(d), Distribution Allocate, Allot, Binomial, Busbar, Carve, Chi-square, Colportage, Deal, Deliver(y), Deploy, Dish, Dispense, Dispose, Issue, Lie, Lot, Mete, Out, Pattern, Poisson's, Prorate, Repartition, Serve, Share

▷ **Distributed** may indicate an anagram

District Alsatia, Amhara, Arcadia, Ards, Area, Bail(l)iwick, Banat, Barrio, Belt, Canton, Cantred, Classis, Community, Diocese, End, Exurb, Federal, Gau, Ghetto, Hundred, Lathe, Liberty, Locality, Loin, Manor, Metropolitan, ➤ NEIGHBOURHOOD, Oblast, Pachalic, Pale, Parish(en), Paroch, Pashalik, Patch, Province, Quarter, Quartier, Rape, ➤ REGION, Ride, Riding, Ruhr, Sanjak, Section, Sheading, Sircar, Soc, Soke(n), Stannary, Suburb, Sucken, Talooka, Taluk, Tender, Township, Venue, Vicinage, Walk, Wapentake, Way, Zila, Zillah, Zone

Disturb(ance), Disturbed Ado, Aerate, Affray, Agitate, Atmospherics, Autism, Betoss, Brabble, Brainstorm, Brash,

Brawl, Broil, Carfuffle, Collieshangie, Concuss, Delirium, Dementia, Derange, Desecrate, Disquiet, Dust, Feeze, Firestorm, Fray, Fret, Harass, Hoopla, Incommode, Infest, Interrupt, Jee, Kerfuffle, Kick-up, Kurfuffle, Muss, Outbreak, Prabble, Ramp, Ripple, Romage, Rook, Roughhouse, Rouse, Ruckus, Ruction, Ruffle, Rumpus, Shake, Shindy, Shook-up, Stashie, Static, Steer, Stir, Sturt, Tremor, Trouble, Turbulent, Unquiet, Unrest, Unsettle, Upheaval, Uproot, ➤ UPSET, Vex

▷ **Disturb(ed)** may indicate an anagram

Ditch Barathron, Barathrum, Channel, Cunette, Delf, Delph, Dike, Discard, Donga, Drainage, Drop, Dyke, Euripus, Foss(e), Graft, Grip, Gully, Ha(w)-ha(w), Haw-haw, Jettison, Khor, Level, Lode, Moat, Na(l)la(h), Nulla(h), Rean, Reen, Rhine, Rid, Sea, Sheuch, Sheugh, Sike, Sloot, Sluit, Spruit, Stank, Syke, Trench

Dive(s), Diving Belly-flop, Duck, Half-gainer, Header, Honkytonk, Jackknife, Joint, Ken, Nitery, Nose, Plummet, Plunge, Plutocrat, Power, Scoter, Skin, Sound, Stoop, Submerge, Swallow, Swoop, Urinant

Diver(s) Didapper, Duck, Embergoose, Flop, Frogman, Gainer, Grebe, Guillemot, Loom, Loon, Lungie, Many, Merganser, Pearl, Pike, Plong(e), Pochard, Poker, Puffin, Sawbill, Scuba, Snake-bird, Speakeasy, Sundry, Urinator, Various, Zoom

Diverge(nce) Branch, Deviate, Spread, Swerve, Variant, Veer

Diverse, Diversify Alter, Dapple, Different, Interlard, Intersperse, Manifold, Motley, Multifarious, Separate, Variegate, Various, Vary

Diversion, Divert(ing) Amuse, Avocation, Beguile, Deflect, Disport, Dissuade, Distract, Entertain, Game, Hare, Hobby, Interlude, Pastime, Pleasure, Prolepsis, Ramp, Red-herring, Refract, Reroute, Ruse, Shunt, Sideshow, Sidetrack, Sport, Stalking-horse, Stratagem, Sway, Switch, Upstage, Yaw

▷ **Diverting** may indicate an anagram

Divide(d) Apportion, Band, Bipartite, Bisect, Branch, Cantle, Cleft, Comminute, Commot(e), Continental, Counter-pale, Cut, Deal, Demerge, Dimidiate, Estrange, Fork, Great, Indent, Parcel, Part, Polarise, Rend, Rift, Separate, Sever, Share, ➤ SPLIT, Sunder, Watershed, Zone

Dividend Bonus, Div, Interim, Into, Share

Divine, Divine presence, Divinity Acoemeti, Atman, Avatar, Beatific, Clergyman, Conjecture, Curate, DD, Deduce,

Deity, Douse, Dowse, Ecclesiastic, Forecast, Foretell, Fuller,
► GOD, ► GODDESS, Godhead, Guess, Hariolate, Heavenly,
Holy, Immortal, Inge, Isiac, Mantic, Numen, Olympian, Pontiff,
Predestinate, Predict, Presage, Priest, RE, RI, Rector, Rimmon,
Scry, Sense, Seraphic, Shechinah, Shekinah, Spae, Supernal,
Theanthropic, Theologise, Theology, Triune

Divisible, Division Arcana, Arm, Arrondissement, Banat(e),
Bar, Branch, Caesura, Canton, Cantred, Cantref, Caste,
Category, Chapter, Classification, Cleft, Cloison, Clove,
Commune, Compartment, Corps, County, Crevasse, Curia,
Department, Dichotomy, Disagreement, Disunity, Fork,
Grisons, Gulf, Hedge, Hide, Hundred, Inning, Lathe, Leet,
Legion, List, Lobe, Nome, Part, Partition, Period, Pipe, Pitaka,
Platoon, Polarisation, Presidency, Quotition, Rape, Region,
Reservation, Riding, Schism, Section, Sector, Segment,
Sept(ate), Sever, Share, Shed, Shire, Stage, Subheading, Tahsil,
Trichotomy, Trio, Troop, Unit, Wapentake, Ward

Divorce(d) Diffarreation, Dissolve, Disunion, Div, Estrange,
Get(t), Part, Separate, Sequester, ► SUNDER, Talak, Talaq

Divulge Confess, Disclose, Expose, Publish, Reveal, Split, Tell,
Unveil, Utter

Dizziness, Dizzy Beaconsfield, Ben, Capricious, Dinic, Disraeli,
Giddy, Giglot, Lightheaded, Mirligoes, Swimming, Vertiginous,
► VERTIGO, Woozy

Do(es), Doing Accomplish, Achieve, Act, Anent, Beano, Char,
Cheat, Chisel, Cod, Con, Cozen, Deed, Dich, Dish, Div, Doth,
Dupe, Effectuate, Enact, Execute, Function, Gull, Handiwork,
Hoax, Mill, Perform, Same, Serve, Settle, Shindig, Spif(f)licate,
Suffice, Thrash, Ut

▷ **Do** may indicate an anagram

Dock(er), Docked, Docks Abridge, Barber, Basin, Bistort,
Bob, Camber, Canaigre, Clip, Curta(i)l, Cut, Deduct, De-tail,
Dry, Floating, Grapetree, Knotweed, Lop, Marina, Moor,
Off-end, Pare, Patience, Pen, Pier, Quay, Rhubarb, Rumex,
Rump, Seagull, Shorten, Snakeweed, Sorrel, Sourock,
Stevedore, Tilbury, Watersider, Wet, Wharf, Yard

Doctor(s) Arnold, Barefoot, Bleeder, BMA, Bones, Breeze,
Bright, Brighton, Brown, Caius, Castrate, Clinician, Cook,
Cup(per), Cure(r), Dale, Diagnose, Dr, Erasmus, Extern(e), Fake,
Falsify, Faustus, Fell, Finlay, Flying, Foster, Galen, GP, Healer,

Homeopath, Houseman, Hyde, Intern, Internist, Jekyll, Jenner, Johnson, Kildare, Lace, Leach, Leech, Load, Locum, Luke, Manette, Massage, MB, MD, Medicate, Medico, Minister, Misrepresent, MO, MOH, Molla(h), Moreau, Mulla(h), Neuter, No, Ollamh, Ollav, Panel, Pangloss, Paracelsus, Pedro, PhD, Physician, Pill(s), Practitioner, Quack, Quacksalver, Rabbi, RAMC, Registrar, Resident, Rig, Salk, Sawbones, Slop, Spin, Surgeon, Syn, Thorne, Treat, Vet, Watson, Who, Witch

▷ **Doctor(ed)** may indicate an anagram

Doctrine Adoptionism, Archology, Cab(b)ala, Calvanism, Chiliasm, Creed, Credo, Dogma, Doxie, Doxy, Esotery, Federalism, Gnosticism, Gospel, Holism, Islam, Ism, Jansenism, Lore, Malthusian, Monroe, Pragmatism, Reformism, Sheria, Shibboleth, Subjectivism, Substantialism, Syndicalism, Synergism, System, ➤ TENET, Theory, Thomism, Transubstantiation

Document(s), Documentary Bumph, Carta, Certificate, Charter, Contract, Conveyance, Covenant, Daftar, Deed, Diploma, Doco, Docket, Dompass, Dossier, Form, Holograph, Latitat, Logbook, Mandamus, Papers, Production, Ragman, Ragment, Roll, Roul(e), Screed, Waybill, Writ

Dodge(r) Artful, Avoid, Column, Elude, Evade, Evasion, Jink, Jook, Jouk, Racket, Ruse, Shirk, Sidestep, Skip, Slalom, Slinter, Tip, Trick, Twist, Urchin, Weave, Welsh, Wheeze, Wire, Wrinkle

Dog(s) Andiron, Argos, Barker, Bird, Bitser, Bobbery, Boots, Bowler, Bowwow, Bounce, Brak, Caesar, Canes, Canidae, Canine, Cant, Cerberus, Dangle, Dhole, Dingo, Eye, Feet, Fido, Gelert, Guard, Guide, Gun, Harlequin, Haunt, Hearing, Heel(er), Hot, Hound, Hyena, Iron, Jackal, Katmir, Kennel, Kennet, Ketmir, Kratim, Kurre, Laika, Lassie, Lorel, Luath, Mauthe, Moera, Montmorency, Moppet, Mutt, Oath, Orthrus, Pluto, Pooch, Pursue, Queue, Rab, Raccoon, Rach(e), Ranger, Reynard, Rover, Shadow, Shaggy, Shin-barker, Shock, Sirius, Sled, Sniffer, Sothic, Stalk, Starter, Tag, Tail, Tike, Toby, Top, Touser, Towser, Tracker, Trail, Tray, Trendle-tail, Trindle-tail, Turnspit, Tyke, Whelp, Whiffet, Wishtonwish, Wolf, Yap(per), Yapster, Zorro

Dogma(tic) Assertive, Belief, Conviction, Creed, Doctrinal, Opinionative, Ideology, Pedagogic, Peremptory, Pontifical, Positive, ➤ TENET

Dole Alms, Batta, B(u)roo, Give, Grief, Maundy, Payment, Pittance, Ration, ➤ SHARE, Tichborne, Vail, Vales

Doll(y) Barbie®, Bimbo, Common, Corn, Crumpet, Dress, Dutch, Golliwog, Kachina, Kewpie®, Maiden, Marionette, Matryoshka, Maumet, Mommet, Mummet, Ookpik®, Ornament, Parton, Poppet, Puppet, Ragdoll, Russian, Sis(ter), Sitter, Toy, Tearsheet, Trolley, Varden, Washboard

Dollar(s) Balboa, Boliviano, Buck, Cob, Euro, Fin, Greenback, Iron man, Peso, Piastre, Pink, S, Sand, Sawbuck, Sawhorse, Scrip, Smacker, Spin, Wheel

▷ **Dolly** may indicate an anagram

Dolphin Amazon, Arion, Beluga, Bottlenose, Cetacean, Coryphene, Delphinus, Grampus, Lampuka, Lampuki, Meer-swine, Porpess(e), Risso's, River, Sea-pig

Dome(-shaped) Cap, Cupola, Dagoba, Geodesic, Head, Imperial, Louvre, Millennium, Onion, Periclinal, Rotunda, Stupa, Tee, Tholos, Tholus, Tope, Vault

Domestic(ate) Char, Cleaner, Dom, Esne, Familiar, Home-keeping, Homely, House, Housetrain, Humanise, Interior, Internal, Intestine, Maid, Menial, ➤ SERVANT, Tame, Woman

Dominate, Dominance, Dominant Ascendancy, Baasskap, Bethrall, Clou, Coerce, Control, Henpeck, Maisterdome, Mesmerise, Monopolise, O(v)ergang, Override, Overshadow, Power, Preponderant, Preside, Rule, Soh, ➤ SUBDUE, Subjugate, Tower

Dominion Dom, Empire, Khanate, NZ, Realm, Reame, Reign, ➤ RULE, Supremacy, Sway, Territory

Domino(es) Card, Fats, Mask, Matador

Don Academic, Address, Assume, Caballero, Endue, Fellow, Garb, Giovanni, Indew, Juan, Lecturer, Prof, Quixote, Reader, Senor, Spaniard, Tutor, Wear

Donate, Donation Aid, Bestow, Contribution, Gift, Give

Done Achieved, Complete, Crisp, Ended, Executed, Had, Over, Spitcher, Tired, Weary

Donkey Ass, Burro, Cardophagus, Cuddie, Cuddy, Dapple, Dick(e)y, Eeyore, Fussock, Genet(te), Jennet, Jerusalem pony, Kulan, Modestine, Moke, Mule, Neddy, Onager, Stupid, Years

Donor Benefactor, Bestower, Settlor

Doom(ed) Condemned, Date, Destine, Destiny, ➤ FATE, Fay, Fey, Fie, Goner, Ill-starred, Lot, Predestine, Preordain, Ragnarok, Ruined, Sentence, Star-crossed, Weird

Door(way) Aperture, Dutch, Entry, Exit, French, Haik, Hake, Hatch, Heck, Ingress, Jib, Lintel, Oak, Portal, Postern, Revolving, Rory, Sliding, Stable, Stage, Storm, Swing, Up and over, Vomitory, Wicket, Yett

Doorkeeper, Doorman Bouncer, Commissionaire, Guardian, Janitor, Ostiary, Porter, Tiler, Tyler, Usher

Dope Acid, Amulet, Bang, Coke, Crack, ➤ DRUG, Gen, Goose, Info, Narcotic, Nobble, Rutin, ➤ STUPID PERSON, Sedate

Dormitory Barrack, Dorter, Dortour, Hall, Hostel, Quarters

Dose(age) Administer, Cascara, Draught, Drug, Kilogray, ➤ MEASURE, Physic, Posology, Potion, Powder

Dot(s), Dotted, Dotty Absurd, Bullet, Criblé, Dit, Dower, Dowry, Engrailed, Leader, Lentiginose, Limp, Micro, Occult, Or, Particle, Pixel, ➤ POINT, Polka, Precise, Punctuate, Punctuate, Punctum, Schwa, Semé(e), Set, Speck, Spot, Sprinkle, Stigme, Stipple, Stud, Tap, Tittle, Trema, Umlaut

Dote, Dotage, Doting, Dotard Adore, Anile, Anility, Cocker, Dobbie, Idolise, Imbecile, Pet, Prize, Senile, Tendre, Twichild

Double(s) Amphibious, Ancipital, Bi-, Bifold, Binate, Counterpart, Crease, Dimeric, Doppel-ganger, Dual, Duo, Duple(x), Duplicate, Equivocal, Fetch, Fold, Foursome, Geminate, Gimp, Image, Ingeminate, Ka, Look-alike, Loop, Martingale, Pair, Parlay, Polyseme, Reflex, Replica, Ringer, Run, Similitude, Spit, Trot, Turnback, Twae, ➤ TWIN, Two(fold)

Doubt(ful), Doubter Ambiguous, Aporia, Askance, But, Debatable, Distrust, Dubiety, Dubitate, Hesitate, Hum, Iffy, Incertitude, Misgiving, Mistrust, ➤ NO DOUBT, Precarious, Qualm, Query, ➤ QUESTION, Rack, Scepsis, Sceptic, Scruple, Shady, Shy, Sic, Skepsis, Sus, Suspect, Suss, Thomas, Thos, Umph, Uncertain, Unsure, Waver

Dough(y) Boodle, Cake, Calzone, Cash, Duff, Hush-puppy, Knish, Loot, Magma, Masa, Money, Paste, Pop(p)adum, Ready, Sad, Spondulicks

Doughnut Cruller, Knish, Sinker, Torus

Dour Glum, Hard, Mirthless, Morose, Reest, Reist, Sinister, Sullen, Taciturn

Douse Dip, Drench, Extinguish, Snuff, Splash

Dove Collared, Columbine, Culver, Cushat, Diamond, Doo, Ice-bird, Mourning, Pacifist, ► PIGEON, Ring, Rock, Stock, Turtle

Dowdy Frumpish, Mums(e)y, Shabby, Sloppy, Slovenly

Down(beat), Downs, Downward, Downy A bas, Abase, Abattu, Alow, Amort, Bank, Below, Blue, Cast, Catabasis, Chapfallen, Comous, Cottony, Crouch, Darling, Dejected, Dowl(e), Drink, Epsom, Feather, Fledge, Flue, Floccus, Fluff, Fly, Fuzz, Goonhilly, Ground, Hair, Hill, Humble, Humiliate, Lanugo, Losing, Low, Lower, Nap, Oose, Ooze, Owing, Pappus, Pennae, Pile, Plumage, Quash, Repress, Sebum, Thesis, Thistle, Tomentum, Vail, Wretched

Downcast Abject, Chapfallen, Despondent, Disconsolate, Dumpish, Hopeless, Melancholy, Woebegone

Downfall, Downpour Cataract, Collapse, Deluge, Fate, Flood, Hail, Onding, Overthrow, Rain, Ruin, Thunder-plump, Torrent, Undoing, Waterspout

Downright Absolute, Arrant, Bluff, Candid, Clear, Complete, Flat, Plumb, Plump, Pure, Rank, Sheer, Stark, Utter

Dowry Dot, Dower, Lobola, Lobolo, Merchet, Portion, Settlement, Tocher

Doze Ca(u)lk, Dove(r), Nap, Nod, Semi-coma, Sleep, Slip, Slumber

Drab Cloth, Dell, Dingy, Dull, Dun, Isabel(line), Lifeless, Livor, Prosaic, Pussel, Quaker-colour, Rig, Road, Slattern, Sloven, Subfusc, Tart, Trull, Wanton, Whore

Draft Cheque, Draw, Ebauche, Essay, Landsturm, Minute, MS, Outline, Plan, Press, Rough, Scheme, Scroll, Scrowle, ► SKETCH

Drag Car, Drail, Dredge, Drogue, Elicit, Eonism, Epicene, Extort, Hale, Harl, ► HAUL, Keelhaul, La Rue, Lug, Puff, Pull, Rash, Sag, Schlep, Shoe, Skidpan, Sled, Snig, Sweep, Toke, Tote, Trail, Train, Travail, Travois, Trawl, Treck, Trek, Tump

Dragon Basilisk, Bel, Bellemère, Chaperon(e), Chindit, Draco, Drake, Komodo, Kung-kung, Ladon, Lindworm, Opinicus, Python, Rouge, Wantley, Wivern, Worm, Wyvern

Drain(age), Draining, Drainpipe Bleed, Brain, Buzz, Catchment, Catchwater, Channel, Cloaca, Cundy, Delf, Delph, Dewater, Ditch, Dry, Ea(u), ➤ EMPTY, Emulge(nt), Exhaust, Fleet, Grating, Grip, Gully, Gutter, Kotabothron, Ketavothron, Lade, Leach, Leech, Limber, Lose, Milk, Pump, Rack, Rone, Sap, Scupper, Seton, Sew(er), Sheuch, Sheugh, Sink, Silver, Siver, Sluice, Sluse, Soakaway, Sough, Spend, Stank, Sump, Sure, Syver, Tile, Trench, Trocar, Unwater, Ureter, U-trap

Dram Drink, Drop, Portion, Snifter, Tickler, Tiff, Tot, Wet

Drama(tic), Drama school Charade, Comedy, Farce, Heroic, Histrionic, Kabuki, Kathakali, Kitchen sink, Legit, Mask, Masque, Mime, Moralities, No, Nogaku, Noh, Piece, Play, RADA, Scenic, Sensational, Singspiel, Stagy, Striking, Tetralogy, Theatric, Thespian, Tragedy, Unities, Wagnerian, Wild

Drape Adorn, Coverlet, Coverlid, Curtain, Festoon, Fold, Hang, Swathe, Valance, Veil, Vest

Draught(s), Draughtsman Aloetic, Breeze, Dam, Design, Drench, Drink, Fish, Gulp, Gust, Haal, Hippocrene, King, Men, Nightcap, Outline, Plan, Potation, Potion, Pull, Quaff, Sketch, Sleeping, Slug, Swig, Tracer, Veronal, Waucht

▷**Draught** may refer to fishing

Draw(er), Drawing, Drawn, Drawers, Draw off Adduct, Allure, Attract, Bottom, Cock, Crayon, Dead-heat, Delineate, Derivation, Describe, Doodle, Dr, Draft, Drag, Dress, Educe, Entice, Equalise, Evaginate, Extract, Fetch, Gather, Gaunt, Glorybox, Gut, Haggard, Hale, Halve, Haul, Induce, Indue, Inhale, Lengthen, Limn, Longbow, Lottery, Pantalet(te)s, Panty, Perpetual check, Petroglyph, Protract, Pull, Rack, Raffle, Remark, Scent, Sesquipedalian, Shottle, Shuttle, Siphon, Sketch, Slub, Stalemate, Snig, Spin, Stumps, Sweepstake, Syphon, Tap, Taut, Technical, Tempt, Tenniel, Tie, Till, Toke, Tole, Tombola, Top, Tose, Tow(age), Toze, Trice, Troll, Tug, Unsheathe, Uplift

▷**Draw** may indicate something to smoke

Drawing Cartoon, Charcoal, Crayon, Dentistry, Elevation, Freehand, Fusain, Graphics, Indraft, Monotint, Orthograph, Pastel, Profile, Seductive, Sepia, Silver-point, Study, Traction

▷**Drawn** may indicate an anagram

Dread Angst, Anxiety, Awe, Fear, ➤ HORROR, Redoubt, Thing

Dreadful Awful, Chronic, Dearn, Dire, Formidable, Ghastly, Horrendous, Penny, Sorry, Terrible

Dream(er), Dreamy, Dream state Alchera, Alcheringa, Aspire, Desire, Drowsy, Dwa(u)m, Fantast, Fantasy, Faraway, Idealise, Illusion, Imagine, Languor, Mare, Mirth, Moon, Morpheus, Muse, Nightmare, On(e)iric, Pensive, Pipe, ➤ REVERIE, Rêveur, Romantic, Somniate, Stargazer, Surreal, Sweven, Trance, Trauma, Vague, Vision, Walter Mitty, Wet

Dreary Bleak, Desolate, Dismal, Doleful, Dreich, Dull, Gloom, Gray, Grey, Oorie, Ourie, Owrie, Sad

Dress(ed), Dressing Adorn, Align, Array, Attire, Attrap, Bandage, Black-tie, Bloomer, Blouson, Boast, Bodice, Busk, Caftan, Cheongsam, Chimer, Cimar, Clad, ➤ CLOTHING, Coat, Cocktail, Comb, Compost, Compress, Corsage, Corset, Costume, Court, Curry, Cymar, Deck, Deshabille, Dirndl, Dolly Varden, Dolman, Don, Drag, Dirndl, Dub, Dubbin, Empire, Enrobe, Evening, Fancy, Farthingale, Fatigues, Fertiliser, Fig, Finery, French, Frock, Garb, Garnish, Gauze, Girt, Gown, Gymslip, ➤ HABIT, Italian, Jaconet, Ketchup, Kimono, Line, Lint, Lounger, Mayonnaise, Mob, Morning, Mother Hubbard, Mufti, Mulch, Muu-muu, Oil, Patch, Pinafore, Plaster, Pledget, ▹ Plumage, Pomade, Poultice, Prank, Preen, Prepare, Rag, Raiment, Rehearsal, Rémoulade, Rig, Robe, Russet, Sack, Salad, Sari, Sarong, Sartorial, Sauce, Separates, Sheath, Shift, Shirt, Shirtwaister, Smock, Sterile, Stole, Subfusc, Suit, Sundress, Symar, Tasar, Taw, Tent, Thousand Island, Tiff, Tire, Tog, Toga, Toilet, Top, Treat, Trick, Trim, Tunic, Tusser, Tussore, Tuxedo, Uniform, Vest, Vinaigrette, Wear, Wedding, White-tie, Wig

▹**Dressed up, Dressing** may indicate an anagram

Dresser Adze, Almery, Bureau, Chest, Couturier, Deuddarn, Dior, Lair, Lowboy, Sideboard, Transvestite, Tridarn, Welsh

Dribble Drip, Drivel, Drop, Slaver, Slop, Trickle

Drift(er), Drifting Becalmed, Continental, Cruise, Current, Digress, Float, Heap, Impulse, Maunder, North Atlantic, Plankton, Purport, Rorke, Slide, Tendence, Tendency, ➤ TENOR, Waft, Wander

Drill Auger, Bore, Burr, Close order, Educate, Exercise, Form, Hammer, Jackhammer, Jerks, Monkey, Pack, PE, Pierce, Pneumatic, PT, Reamer, Ridge, Seeder, Sow, Square-bashing, Teach, Train, Twill, Twist, Usage, Wildcat

Drink(er), Drunk(enness) AA, Absorb, Alky, Aperitif, Bacchian, Bender, Beverage, Bev(v)y, Binge, Blind, Blitzed,

Bloat, Blotto, Bombed, Boose, Booze, Bosky, Bottled, Bouse, Bracer, Bumper, Carafe, Carousal, Cat-lap, Chaser, Corked, Crapulous, Crocked, Cuppa, Cut, Demitasse, Dipsomaniac, Double, Down, Drain, Draught, Drop, Ebriate, Elixir, Entire, Eye-opener, Finger, Fou, Fuddled, Full, Half-seas-over, High, Hogshead, Hoo(t)ch, Hophead, Imbibe, Indulge, Intemperate, Irrigate, Jag, Jar, Lap, Legless, Lethean, Lit, Loaded, Lord, Lower, Lush(y), Maggoty, Maudlin, Merry, Mortal, Mug, Nightcap, Nog(gin), Obfuscated, Oiled, One, Overshot, Paid, Paint, Partake, Particular, Pickled, Pick-me-up, Pie-eyed, Pint(a), Piss-artist, Pissed, Pisshead, Pisspot, Pixil(l)ated, Potion, Primed, Quaff, Rat-arsed, Ratted, Refresher, Reviver, Rolling, Rotgut, Rotten, Rummer, Screwed, Sea, Shebeen, Short, Shotover, Sip(ple), Skinned, Slake, Slewed, Sloshed, Slug, Slurp, Smashed, Snifter, Snort, Soak, Soused, Sponge, Squiffy, Stewed, Stimulant, Stinko, Stoned, Sup, Swacked, Swallow, Swig, Swill, Tank, Tiddl(e)y, Tiff, Tight, Tipple, Tipsy, Tope, Toss, Usual, Wash, Wassail, Wat, Well-oiled, Wet, Winebag, Wino, Wrecked, Zonked

Drip Bore, Dribble, Drop, Gutter, IV, Leak, Seep, Splatter, Stillicide, Trickle, Wimp

Drive(r), Driving, Drive out AA, Actuate, Ambition, Backseat, Banish, Beetle, Ca', Cabby, Campaign, Carman, Charioteer, Chauffeur, Coachee, Coact, Crankshaft, Crew, Crowd, Disk, Dislodge, Dr, Drover, Drum, Economy, Eject, Emboss, Energy, Enforce, Engine, Faze, Ferret, Fire, Fluid, Force, Four-wheel, Front-wheel, Fuel, Goad, Hack, Hammer, Haste, Heard, Helmsman, Herd, Hie, Hoon, Hoosh, Hot-rod, Hoy, Hunt, Hurl, Impel, Impetus, Impinge, Impulse, Jehu, Jockey, Juggernaut, Lash, Libido, Lunge, Mahout, Make, Mall, Motor, Motorman, Offensive, Peg, Penetrate, Piston, Power, Propel, Put, RAC, Rack, Ram, Rebut, Ride, Road, Roadhog, Run, Scorch, Screw, Scud, Shepherd, Shoo, Spank, Spin, Spur, Start, Stroke, Sunday, Sweep, Task-master, Teamster, Tee, Test, Thrust, Toad, Tool, Trot, Truckie, Two-stroke, Urge, Urgence, Wagoner, Wood, Wreak

Drivel Balderdash, Blether(skate), Drip, Drool, Humbug, Nonsense, Pap, Rot, Salivate, Slaver

Drizzle Drow, Haze, Mist, Mizzle, Roke, Scouther, Scowther, Serein, Skiffle, Smir(r), Smur, Spit

Droop(ing) Cernuous, Decline, Flag, Languish, Lill, Limp, Lob, Loll, Lop, Nutate, Oorie, Ourie, Owrie, Peak, Ptosis, ➤ SAG, Slink, Slouch, Weeping, Welk(e), Wilt, Wither

Drop(s), Dropping Acid, Airlift, Apraxia, Bag, Bead, Beres, Blob, Cadence, Calve, Cascade, Cast, Chocolate, Cowpat, Dap, Descent, Deselect, Dink, Drappie, Drib(let), Ease, Ebb, Escarp(ment), Fall, Floor, Flop, Fumet, Gallows, Globule, Gout(te), Guano, Guttate, Instil, Knockout, Land, Minim, Modicum, Muff, Mute, Omit, Pilot, Plonk, Plummet, Plump, Plunge, Plunk, Precepit, Precipice, (Prince) Rupert's, Rain, Scat, Scrap, Shed, Sip, Skat, Spraint, Stilliform, Tass, Taste, Tear, Virga

Drought Dearth, Drouth, Lack, Thirst

Drove(r) Band, Crowd, Flock, Herd, Host, Masses, Overlander, Puncher

Drown(ing) Drook, Drouk, Engulf, Inundate, Noyade, Overcome, Sorrows, Submerge

Drudge(ry) Devil, Dogsbody, Fag, Grind, Hack, Jackal, Johnson, Plod, Scrub, Slave(y), Snake, Sweat, Thraldom, Toil, Trauchle, Treadmill

Drug(ged) Anti-depressant, Bag, Base, Blow, Bolus, Bomber, Boo, Deck, Designer, Dope, Downer, Elixir, Fantasy, Fertility, Fig, Gateway, Hallucinogen, Hard, High, Lifestyle, Line, Load, Mainline, Medicine, Miracle, Nervine, Nobble, Opiate, Painkiller, Paregoric, Parenteral, Pharmaceutics, Pharmacopoeia, Poison, Prophylactic, Psychedelic, Psychodelic, Sedate, Snort, Soft, Spike, Stimulant, Stupefy, Substance, Truth, Upper, Weed, White stuff, Wonder

Drum(mer), Drumming, Drumbeat Arête, Atabal, Barrel, Beatbox, Bodhran, Bongo, Brake, Carousel, Chamade, Conga, Dash-wheel, Devil's tattoo, Dhol, Dr, Drub, Ear, Flam, Kettle, Lambeg, Mridamgam, Mridang(a), Mridangam, Myringa, Naker, Pan, Percussion, Rappel, Rataplan, Reel, Rep, Ridge, Rigger, Roll, Ruff, Ruffle, Salesman, Side, Snare, Steel, Tabla, Tabour, Tabret, Tambourine, Tam-tam, Tap, Tattoo, Thrum, Timbal, Timp(ano), Touk, Tom-tom, Traps, Traveller, Tuck, Tymbal, Tympanist, Tympano, Whim, Work

▷**Drunken** may indicate an anagram

Dry(ing), Drier Air, Anhydrous, Arefaction, Arefy, Arid, Blot, Bone, Brut, Corpse, Crine, Dehydrate, Desiccate, Detox, Drain, Dull, Evaporate, Exsiccator, Firlot, Fork, Harmattan, Hasky,

Hi(r)stie, Humidor, Jejune, Jerk, Khor, Kiln, Mummify, Oast,
➤ PARCH, Prosaic, Reast, Reist, Rizzar, Rizzer, Rizzor, Sciroc,
Scorch, Sear, Sec(co), Seco, Sere, Shrivel, Siccative, Siroc(co),
Sober, Sponge, Steme, Stove, Ted, Thirsty, Thristy, Toasted,
Torrefy, Torrid, Towel, Tribble, Trocken, TT, Unwatery,
Watertight, Welt, Wilt, Win(n), Wipe, Wither, Wizened,
Xeransis, Xerasia, Xero(sis), Xerostomia

Dual Double, Twin, Twofold

Dubious Doubtful, Equivocal, Fishy, Fly-by-night, Hesitant, Iffy,
Improbable, Questionable, Scepsis, Sceptical, Sesey, Sessa,
➤ SHADY, Suspect, Unlikely

▷**Dubious** may indicate an anagram

Duck(ed) Amphibian, Avoid, Blob, Bob, Bum(m)alo, Canard,
➤ COUPLE OF DUCKS, Dead, Dearie, Decoy, Dip, Dodge, Dodo,
Douse, Drook, Drouk, Duk(ker), Enew, Escape, Evade, Heads,
Immerse, Jook, Jouk, Nil, O, Paddling, Palmated, Pekin(g),
Plunge, Poker, Rush, Shun, Sitting, Team, Tunker, Zero

Duct Bile, Canal(iculus), Channel, Conduit, Epididymus, Fistula,
Gland, Lachrymal, Laticifer, Pipe, Tear, Thoracic, Tube, Ureter,
Vas deferens

Due(s) Adequate, Arrearage, Claim, Debt, Deserts, Forinsec,
Geld, Heriot, Just, Lot, Mature, Owing, Reddendo, Rent, Right,
➤ SUITABLE, Thereanent, Toll, Tribute, Worthy

Dug-out Canoe, Shelter, Trench, Trough

Duke(dom) Alva, Clarence, D, Ellington, Fist, Iron, Milan,
Orsino, Peer, Prospero, Rohan, Wellington

Dull(ard), Dullness Anorak, Banal, Besot, Bland, Blear, Blunt,
Boeotian, Cloudy, Deadhead, Dense, Dim, Dinge, Dingy,
Doldrums, Dowf, Dowie, Drab, Drear, Dreich, Dry, Dunce, Fozy,
Grey, Heavy, Hebetate, Ho-hum, Insipid, Jejune, Lacklustre,
Lifeless, Log(y), Lowlight, Mat(t), Matte, Monotonous, Mopish,
Mull, Obtuse, Opacity, Opiate, Ordinary, Overcast, Owlish, Pall,
Pedestrian, Perstringe, Podunk, Prosaic, Prose, Prosy, Rebate,
Rust, Slow, Sottie, Staid, Stodger, Stodgy, Stolid, Stuffy,
Stultify, ➤ STUPID, Sunless, Tame, Tarnish, Tedious, Ticky-tacky,
Toneless, Torpor, Treadmill, Tubby, Vapid, Wonk, Wooden,
Zoid

Dumb(ness) Alalia, Aphonic, Crambo, Hobbididance,
Inarticulate, Mute, Stupid

Dummy Comforter, Copy, Effigy, Mannequin, Mock-up, Model, Pacifier, Table, Waxwork

Dump(s) Abandon, Blue, Core, Dispirited, Doldrums, Empty, Hole, Jettison, Junk, Scrap, Shoot, Store(house), Tip, Unlade, Unload

Dumpling Dim sum, Dough(boy), Gnocchi, Knaidel, Knish, Norfolk, Quenelle, Suet, Won ton

Dune Areg, Bar, Barchan(e), Bark(h)an, Erg, Sandbank, Seif, Star, Whaleback

Dungeon Bastille, Cell, Confine, Donjon, Durance

Dupe Catspaw, Chiaus, Chouse, Cony, Cully, Delude, Geck, Gull, Hoax, Hoodwink, Mug, Pawn, Pigeon, Plover, Sitter, Sucker, Swindle, ► TRICK, Victim

Durable Enduring, Eternal, Eterne, Hardy, Lasting, Permanent, Stout, Tough

Duration Extent, Period, Span

Duress Coercion, Pressure, Restraint

During Amid, Dia-, For, In, Over, Throughout, While, Whilst

Dusk(y) Dark, Dewfall, Dun, Eve, Gloaming, Gloom, Owl-light, Phaeic, Twilight, Umbrose

Dust(y) Arid, Ash, Bo(a)rt, Calima, Clean, Coom, Cosmic, Derris, Devil, Duff, Earth, Fuss, Khaki, Lemel, Limail, Lo(e)ss, Miller, Nebula, Pollen, Pother, Pouder, Poudre, Powder, Pozz(u)olana, Pudder, Rouge, Seed, Shaitan, Slack, Stour, Talc, Volcanic, Wipe

▷**Dusted** may indicate an anagram

Duster Cloth, Feather, Talcum, Torchon

Dutch(man), Dutchwoman Batavian, Boor, Cape, Courage, D(u), Double, Elm, Erasmus, Frow, Kitchen, Knickerbocker, Mynheer, Patron, Sooterkin, Taal, Wife

Dutiful, Duty Active, Ahimsa, Average, Blench, Bond, Charge, Customs, Death, Debt, Devoir, Docile, Drow, Due, Duplicand, End, Excise, Fatigue, Feu, Function, Heriot, Homage, Imposition, Impost, Incumbent, Lastage, Likin, Mission, Mistery, Mystery, Obedient, Obligation, Octroi, Office, Onus, Pia, Point, Pious, Prisage, Rota, Sentry-go, Shift, Stamp, Stint, Tariff, ► TASK, Tax, Toll, Trow, Watch, Zabeta

Dwarf(ism) Achondroplasia, Agate, Alberich, Andvari, Ateleiosis, Bashful, Belittle, Bes, Black, Bonsai, Brown, Doc,

Dopey, Droich, Drow, Durgan, Elf, Gnome, Grumpy, Happy, Hobbit, Homuncule, Hop o' my thumb, Knurl, Laurin, Little man, Man(n)ikin, ➤ MIDGET, Mime, Minikin, Minim, Nanism, Nectabanus, Ni(e)belung, Nurl, Overshadow, Pacolet, Pigmy, Pygmy, Red, Regin, Ront, Rumpelstiltskin, Runt, Skrimp, Sleepy, Sneezy, ➤ STUNT, Tiddler, Titch, Tokoloshe, Tom Thumb, Toy, Troll, Trow, White

Dwindle Decline, Diminish, Fade, Lessen, Peter, Shrink, Wane

Dye(ing), Dyestuff Colour, Embrue, Hue, Imbrue, Imbue, Ingrain, ➤ PIGMENT, ➤ STAIN, Tinct, Tint

▶**Dying** see DIE

Dyke Aboideau, Aboiteau, Bund, Devil's, ➤ DIKE, Gall, Offa's

Dynamic Ballistics, Energetic, Forceful, High-powered, Potent

Dynamite Blast, Explode, Gelignite, TNT, Trotyl

Dynasty Angevin, Bourbon, Capetian, Carolingian, Ch'ing, Chin(g), Chou, Era, Habsburg, Han, Hapsburg, Honan, House(hold), Hyksos, Khan, Manchu, Maurya, Merovingian, Ming, Pahlavi, Ptolemy, Qajar, Q'ing, Rameses, Romanov, Rule, Safavid, Saga, Sassanid, Seleucid, Seljuk, Shang, Sui, Song, Sung, Tai-ping, Tang, Tudor, Wei, Yi, Yuan, Zhou

Ee

E Boat, East, Echo, Energy, English, Spain

Each All, Apiece, Ea, ➤ EVERY, Ilka, Per, Severally

Eager(ly) Agog, Antsy, Ardent, Avid, Beaver, Bore, Earnest, Enthusiastic, Fain, Fervent, Fervid, Frack, Gung-ho, Hot, Intent, ➤ KEEN, Perfervid, Race, Raring, Rath(e), Ready, Roost, Sharp-set, Sore, Spoiling, Thirsty, Toey, Wishing, Yare

Eagle Al(l)erion, American, Aquila, Bald, Bateleur, Berghaan, Erne, Ethon, Gier, Golden, Harpy, Legal, Lettern, Ossifrage

Ear(drum), Ear trouble Ant(i)helix, Attention, Audience, Auricle, Cauliflower, Cochlea, Concha, Deafness, External, Glue, Hearing, Inner, Jenkins, Listen, Lug, Otalgia, Otalgy, Otic, Parotic, Pinna, Tragus, Utricle

Earlier, Early Above, Ago, Ahead, AM, Auld, Betimes, Cockcrow, Daybreak, Ex, Germinal, Incipient, Precocious, Precursor, Prehistoric, Premature, Prevernal, Previous, Primeval, Primordial, Prior, Rear, Rudimentary, Soon, Timely, Tim(e)ous

▷**Early** may indicate belonging to an earl

▷**Early stages of** may indicate first one or two letters of the word(s) following

Earmark Allocate, Bag, Book, Characteristic, ➤ RESERVE, Tag, Target

Earn(er) Achieve, Addle, Breadwinner, Deserve, Gain, Make, Merit, Win

Earnest Ardent, Arle(s)(-penny), Deposit, Fervent, Imprest, Intent, Promise, Serious, Token, Zealous

Earring Drop, Hoop, Keeper, Pendant, Sleeper, Snap, Stud

Earth(y) Antichthon, Art, Capricorn, Clay, Cloam, Cologne, Dirt, Drey, Dust, Eard, Epigene, Foxhole, Friable, Fuller's, Gaea, Gaia, Gault, Ge, Globe, Ground, Horst, Kadi, Lair, Loam, Malm, Mankind, Mantle, Mools, Mould, Mouls, Papa, Pise, Planet, Racy, Rare, Red, Seat, Sett, Sod, ➤ SOIL, Taurus, Telluric, Tellus, Terra, Terrain, Terramara, Terrene, Topsoil, Virgo, Ye(a)rd, Yird

Earthquake Aftershock, Bradyseism, Mercalli, Richter, Seism, Shake, Shock, Temblor

Ease, Easing, Easygoing Alleviate, Carefree, Clear, Clover, Comfort, Content, Defuse, Deregulate, Détente, Facility, Hands down, Informal, Lax, Mellow, Mid(dy), Mitigate, Palliate, Peace, Quiet, Relieve, Reposal, Repose, Soothe

East(erly), Eastward Anglia, Asia, Chevet, E, Eassel, Eassil, Eothen, Eurus, Levant, Orient, Ost, Sunrise

Easter Festival, Island, Pace, Pasch, Pasque

Easy, Easily ABC, Cakewalk, Carefree, Cinch, Cushy, Doddle, Facile, Free, Gift, Glib, Jammy, Lax, Light, Natural, Picnic, Pie, Pushover, Simple, Snotty, Soft, Tolerant, Walk-over, Yare

▷**Easy** may indicate an anagram

Eat(able), Eater, Eating Bite, Bolt, Chop, Consume, Corrode, Edible, Erode, Esculent, Etch, Fare, Feast, ➤ FEED, Fret, Gnaw, Go, Gobble, Graze, Grub, Hog, Munch, Nosh, Nutritive, Omnivore, Partake, Refect, Scoff, Stuff, Sup, Swallow, Take, Taste, Trencherman

Eavesdrop(per) Earwig, Listen, Overhear, Snoop, Tap

Ebb Abate, Decline, Recede, Sink, ➤ WANE

Eccentric(ity) Abnormal, Cam, Card, Character, Crank, Curious, Dag, Deviant, Dingbat, Ditsy, Ditzy, E, Farouche, Fey, Fie, Freak, Geek, Gonzo, Iffish, Irregular, Kinky, Kook(y), Mattoid, Nutcase, Odd(ball), Offbeat, Off-centre, Original, Outré, ➤ PECULIAR, Pixil(l)ated, Queer, Quirky, Quiz, Rake, Raky, Recondite, Rum, Scatty, Screwball, Screwy, Wack(y), Way-out, Weird(o), W(h)acko

▷ **Eccentric** may indicate an anagram

Ecclesiastic Abbé, Clergyman, Clerical, Lector, Secular, Theologian

Echinoderm Asteroidea, Basket-star, Brittle-star, Comatulid, Crinoid, Sea-lily, Sea-egg, Sea-urchin, Starfish

Echo Angel, Answer, Ditto, E, Imitate, Iterate, Rebound, Repeat, Repercussion, Reply, Resonant, ➤ RESOUND, Respeak, Reverb(erate), Ring, Rote

Eclipse Annular, Block, Cloud, Deliquium, Hide, Lunar, Obscure, Occultation, Outmatch, Outweigh, Overshadow, Penumbra, Solar, Total, Transcend

Economic(s), Economise Budget, Conserve, Eke, Husband, Pinch, Retrench, Scrimp, Skimp, Spare, Sparing, ➤ STINT

Economy, Economic(al), Economics Agronomy, Black, Careful, Cliometrics, Conversation, Frugal, Market, Neat, Parsimony, Retrenchment, Shoestring, Thrift

Ecstasy, Ecstatic Bliss, Delight, Dove, E, Exultant, Joy, Lyrical, Rapture, Sent, Trance, Transport

Eden Bliss, Fall, Heaven, Paradise, PM, Utopia

Edge, Edging Advantage, Arris, Border, Brim, Brink, Brittle, Brown, Burr, Chamfer, Coaming, Cutting, Dag, Deckle, End, Flange, Flounce, Frill, Fringe, Furbelow, Gunnel, Gunwale, Hem, Hone, Inch, Kerb, Leading, Leech, Limb(ate), Limbus, Limit, Lip, List, Lute, Marge(nt), Margin, Nosing, Orle, Parapet, Periphery, Picot, Pikadell, Piping, Rand, Rim, Rund, Rymme, Selvage, Selvedge, Sidle, Skirt, Strand, Trim, Tyre, Verge, Wear

▶ **Edible** see EAT(ABLE)

Edict Ban, Bull, Decree, Decretal, Extravagantes, Fatwa, Interim, Irade, Nantes, Notice, Pragmatic, Proclamation, Ukase

Edit(or), Editorial Abridge, Article, City, Cut, Emend, Dele, Expurgate, Garble, Leader, Recense, Redact, Revise, Seaman

▷**Edited** may indicate an anagram

Edition Aldine, Ed, Extra, Hexapla(r), Issue, Limited, Number, Omnibus, Variorium, Version

Educate(d) Baboo, Babu, Enlighten, Evolué, Informed, Instruct, Learned, Noursle, Nousell, Nousle, Nurture, Nuzzle, Polymath, Preppy, Scholarly, School, ➤ TEACH, Train, Yuppie

Education(alist) Adult, B.Ed, Classical, Didactics, Heurism, Learning, Mainstream, Montessori, Pedagogue, Pestalozzi, Piarist, Primary, Schooling, Teacher, Tertiary, Upbringing

Edward Confessor, Ed, Elder, Lear, Martyr, Ned, Ted

Eel Conger, Electric, Elver, Hagfish, Lamprey, Launce, Moray, Olm, Sand(ling)

Efface Cancel, Delete, Dislimn, ➤ ERASE, Expunge, Obliterate

Effect(s), Effective(ness), Effectual Achieve, Acting, Auger, Bags, Belongings, Bit, Causal, Competent, Consequence, Domino, Doppler, Efficacious, Enact, End, Estate, Functional, Fungibles, Gear, Goods, Greenhouse, Home, Impact, Implement(al), Impression, Knock-on, Moire, Neat, Nisi, Operant, Outcome, Personal, Phi, Position, Potent, Promulgate, Repercussion, ➤ RESULT, Ripple, Side, Sound, Special, Spectrum, Spin-off, Striking, Tableau, Telling, Upshot, Viable, Virtual, Work

Effervescence, Effervescent Bubbling, Ebullient, Fizz

▷**Effervescent** may indicate an anagram

Efficiency, Efficient Able, Capable, Competent, Despatch, Ergonomics, Productivity, Smart, Streamlined, Strong

Effigy Figure, Guy, Idol, Image, Statua, Statue

Effluence, Effluent, Effluvia Air, Aura, Billabong, Discharge, Fume, Gas, Halitus, Miasma, Odour, Outflow, Outrush

Effort Achievement, Attempt, Best, Conatus, Drive, Essay, Exertion, Fit, Herculean, Labour, Molimen, Nisus, Rally, Spurt, Stab, Strain, Struggle, ➤ TRY, Work, Yo

Effrontery Audacity, Brass, Cheek, Face, Gall, Neck, Nerve, Temerity

Effuse, Effusion, Effusive Emanate, Exuberant, Exude, Gush, Lyric, Ode, Outburst, Prattle, Rhapsody, Screed, Spill

Eg As, Example

Egg(s) Abet, Benedict, Berry, Bomb, Caviar(e), Chalaza, Cleidode, Clutch, Cockney, Collop, Coral, Curate's, Darning, Easter, Edge, Fabergé, Fetus, Flyblow, Foetus, Free-range, Glair(e), Goad, Goog, Graine, Hoy, Incite, Instigate, Layings, Mine, Nit, Oocyte, Oophoron, Ova, Ovum, Prairie oyster, Press, Raun, Roe, Scotch, Seed, Spat, Spawn, Spur(ne), Tar(re), Tooth, Treadle, Urge, Yelk, Yolk

Egghead Don, Highbrow, Intellectual, Mensa, Pedant

Ego(ism) Che, Conceit, I, Narcissism, Not-I, Pride, Self, Solipsism, Vanity

Egypt(ian), Egyptologist Arab, Cairene, Carter, Cheops, Chephren, Copt(ic), ET, Goshen, Imhetop, Nasser, Nefertiti, Nilote, Nitrian, Osiris, Ptolemy, Rameses, Syene, Wafd

Eight(h), Eighth day Acht, Byte, Crew, Cube, Nundine, Octa, Octad, Octal, Octastrophic, Octave, Octet, Ogdoad, Okta, Ottava, Ure

Either Also, Both, O(u)ther, Such

Ejaculate Blurt, Discharge, Emit, Exclaim

Eject Bounce, Disgorge, Dismiss, Emit, Erupt, Expel, Oust, Propel, Spew, Spit, Spue, Vent

Eke Augment, Eche, Enlarge, Husband, Supplement

Elaborate Detail, Develop, Enlarge, Florid, Intricate, Ornate

Elan Dash, Drive, Esprit, ➤ FLAIR, Gusto, Lotus, Spirit, Vigour

Elastic(ity) Adaptable, Buoyant, Dopplerite, Elater, Flexible, Give, Resilient, Rubber, Spandex®, Springy, Stretchy, Tone, Tonus

Elate(d), Elation Cheer, Euphoric, Exalt, Exhilarate, Gladden, Hault, Ruff(e), Uplift

Elbow, Elbow tip Akimbo, Ancon, Angle, Bender, Cubital, Hustle, Joint, Jostle, Kimbo, Noop, Nudge, Olecranon, Tennis

Elder(ly), Eldest Ancestor, Ancient, Bourtree, Chief, Classis, Eigne, Geriatric, Guru, Kaumatua, OAP, Presbyter, ➤ SENIOR, Sire, Susanna, Wallwort

Elect(ed), Election(eer), Electoral Choice, Choose, Chosen, Eatanswill, Elite, Gerrymander, Hustings, In, Israelite, Khaki, Opt, Pick, PR, Primary, Psephology, Rectorial, Return, Select, Stump

Electricity Galvanism, HT, Juice, Power, Static

Electrify Astonish, Galvanise, Startle, Stir, Thrill

Elegance, Elegant Artistic, Bijou, Chic, Classy, Debonair, Fancy, Finesse, Gainly, Galant, Grace, Luxurious, Polished, Refined, Ritzy, ➤ SMART, Soigné(e), Swish, Tall, Urbane

Element(s), Elementary Abcee, Abecedarian, Absey, Barebones, ➤ COMPONENT, Detail, Earth, ➤ ESSENCE, Factor, Feature, Fire, Inchoate, Primary, Principle, Rare Earth, Simple, Terra, Trace, Water, Weather

Elephant African, Indian, Jumbo, Mammoth, Mastodon, Oliphant, Pachyderm, Rogue, Tusker, White

Elevate(d), Elevation, Elevator Agger, Attitude, Cheer, Eminence, Ennoble, Heighten, Hoist, Jack, Lift, Promote, ➤ RAISE, Random, Relievo, Ridge, Rise, Sublimate, Up(lift)

Eleven Elf, Legs, Side, Team, XI

Eligible Available, Catch, Fit, Nubile, Parti, Qualified, Worthy

Eliminate, Elimination Cull, Delete, Discard, Exclude, Execute, Extirpate, Liquidate, Omit, Preclude, Purge, Rid, Zap

Elite Best, Choice, Crack, ➤ CREAM, Elect, Flower, Meritocracy, Ton, U, Zaibatsu

Elm Slippery, Wich, Wych

Elongate Extend, Lengthen, Protract, Stretch

Eloquence, Eloquent Articulate, Demosthenic, Facundity, Fluent, Honey-tongued, Oracy, Rhetoric, Vocal

Else(where) Absent, Alibi, Aliunde, Other

Elude, Elusive Avoid, Dodge, Escape, ➤ EVADE, Evasive, Foil, Intangible, Jink, Slippy, Subt(i)le, Will o' the wisp

Emaciated, Emaciation Atrophy, Erasmus, Gaunt, Haggard, Lean, Skinny, Sweeny, Tabid, Thin, Wanthriven, Wasted

Emancipate, Emancipation Deliver, Forisfamiliate, Free, ➤ LIBERATE, Manumission, Uhuru

Embankment Bund, Causeway, Dam, Dyke, Earthwork, Levee, Mattress, Mound, Rampart, Remblai, Stopbank

Embargo ➤ BAN, Blockade, Edict, Restraint

Embark Begin, Board, Enter, Inship, Launch, Sail

Embarrass(ed), Embarrassment Abash, Disconcert, Mess, Pose, Predicament, Shame, Sheepish, Squirming, Straitened

▷ **Embarrassed** may indicate an anagram

Embassy Consulate, Embassade, Legation, Mission

Embellish(ed), Embellishment Adorn, Beautify, Bedeck, Deck, Decorate, Embroider, Enrich, Garnish, Garniture, ➤ ORNAMENT, Ornate

Ember(s) Ash, Cinder, Clinker, Gleed

Emblem(atic) Badge, Bear, Colophon, Daffodil, Ichthys, Impresa, Insignia, Kikumon, Leek, Lis, Maple leaf, Oak, Rose, Roundel, Shamrock, Sign, Spear-thistle, ➤ SYMBOL, Tau-cross, Thistle, Token, Totem(ic), Triskelion, Wheel

Emboss(ed) Adorn, Chase, Cloqué, Engrave, Pounce

Embrace(d) Accolade, Arm, Canoodle, Clasp, Clinch, Clip, Coll, Complect, Comprise, Cuddle, Embosom, Encircle, Enclasp, Enclose, Enfold, Envelop, Espouse, Fold, Grab, Hug, Include, Kiss, Lasso, Neck, Press, Twine, Welcome, Wrap

▷ **Embraces, Embracing** may indicate a hidden word

Embroider(y) Appliqué, Braid, Brede, Couching, Crewel-work, Cross-stitch, Cutwork, Embellish, Exaggerate, Fag(g)oting, Fancywork, Featherstitch, Gros point, Handiwork, Lace(t), Needlepoint, Needlework, Orfray, Ornament, Orphrey, Orris, Petit point, Pinwork, Purl, Sampler, Sew, Smocking, Stitch, Stumpwork, Tent

Embryo(nic) Blastocyst, Blastula, Fo(e)tus, Gastrula, Germ, Mesoblast, Origin, Rudiment, Undeveloped

Emend Adjust, Alter, Edit, Reform

Emerge(ncy), Emerging Anadyomene, Arise, Craunch, Crise, Crisis, Crunch, Debouch, Emanate, Erupt, Exigency, Issue, Last-ditch, Need, Outcrop, Pinch, Spring, Stand-by, Strait

▷ **Emerge from** may indicate an anagram or a hidden word

Eminence, Eminent Altitude, Cardinal, Distinguished, Grand, Height, Hill, Light, Lion, Lofty, Luminary, Noble, ➤ NOTABLE, Prominence, Renown, Repute, Stature, Tor, ➤ VIP

Emission, Emit Discharge, Emanate, Give, Issue, Utter

Emolument Income, Perk, Remuneration, Salary, Stipend, Tip, Wages

Emotion(al) Anger, Anoesis, Breast, Chord, Ecstasy, Excitable, Feeling, Freak-out, Hysteria, Joy, Limbic, Passion, Reins, Roar, Sensibility, Sensitive, Sentiment, Spirit, Transport, Weepy

Empathy Rapport, Rapprochement, Sympathy

Emperor Agramant(e), Akbar, Akihito, Antoninus, Augustus, Babur, Barbarossa, Bonaparte, Caligula, Caracalla,

Charlemagne, Claudius, Commodus, Constantine, Diocletian, Domitian, Ferdinand, Gaius, Genghis Khan, Gratian, Hadrian, Heraclius, Hirohito, Jimmu, Justinian, Maximilian, Menelik, Ming, Mogul, Montezuma, Napoleon, Nero, Nerva, Otho, Otto, Peter the Great, Pu-yi, Severus, Shah Jahan, Theodore, Theodosius, Tiberius, Titus, Trajan, Valens, Valentinian, Valerian, Vespasian, Vitellius

Emphasize, Emphatic Accent, Bold, Dramatise, Forcible, Forzando, Hendiadys, Italic, Marcato, Positive, Sforzando, ➤ STRESS, Underscore, Vehement

Empire Assyria, British, Byzantine, Domain, Empery, Kingdom, Ottoman, Realm, Reich, Roman

Employ(ment) Business, Calling, Engage, Hire, Occupy, Pay, Practice, Pursuit, Use, Using, Utilise, Vocation

Employee(s) Factotum, Hand, Help, Minion, Payroll, Personnel, Servant, Staff, Staffer, Worker

Employer Baas, Boss, Master, Padrone, User

▷**Employs** may indicate an anagram

Empress Eugenie, Josephine, Messalina, Sultana, Tsarina

Empty Addle, Bare, Barren, Blank, Buzz, Clear, Deplete, Devoid, Disembowel, Drain, Exhaust, Expel, Futile, Gut, Inane, Jejune, Lave, Null, Pump, Shallow, Teem, Toom, Tume, Unoccupied, Vacant, Vacate, Vacuous, Vain, ➤ VOID

▷**Empty** may indicate an 'o' in the word or an anagram

Emulate Ape, Copy, Envy, Equal, Imitate, Match

Enable Authorise, Empower, Potentiate, Qualify, Sanction

Enamel(led), Enamel work Aumail, Champlevé, Cloisonné, Della-robbia, Dentine, Fabergé, Ganion, Lacquer, Polish, Porcelain, Schwarzlot, Shippo, Smalto, Stoved, Vitreous

Encampment Bivouac, Douar, Dowar, Duar, Laager, Laer, Settlement

Encase(d), Encasement Box, Crate, Emboîtement, Encapsulate, Enclose, Obtect

Enchant(ed), Enchantment Captivate, Charm, Delight, Gramary(e), Incantation, Magic, Necromancy, Rapt, Sorcery, Spellbind, Thrill

Enchanter, Enchantress Archimage, Archimago, Armida, Comus, Circe, Fairy, Lorelei, Magician, Medea, Mermaid, Prospero, Reim-kennar, Sorcerer, Vivien, Witch

Encircle(d) Enclose, Encompass, Enlace, Entrold, Gird, Inorb, Introld, Orbit, Pale, Ring, ➤ SURROUND

Enclose(d), Enclosing, Enclosure Bawn, Beset, Boma, Box, Cage, Carol, Carrel, Case, Common, Compound, Corral, Court, Embale, Embower, Enceinte, Encircle, Enclave, Enshrine, Fence, Fold, Garth, Haw, Hem, Henge, Hope, Impound, In, Incapsulate, Insert, Interclude, Lairage, Pale, Peel, Pele, Pen(t), Pin, Pinfold, Playpen, Plenum, Rail, Rath, Recluse, Ree(d), Ring, Run, Seal, Sekos, Sept, Seraglio, Serail, Several, Sin bin, Steeld, Stell, Stockade, Sty, ➤ SURROUND, Tine, Vibarium, Ward, Wrap, Yard

Encompass Bathe, Begird, Beset, Environ, Include, Surround

Encounter Battle, Brush, Combat, Contend, Cope, Face, Hit, Incur, Interview, ➤ MEET, Rencontre, Ruffle, Skirmish

Encourage(ment), Encouraging Abet, Acco(u)rage, Alley-oop, Attaboy, Bolster, Boost, Cheer, Cohortative, Commend, Dangle, Egg, Embolden, Exhort, Fillip, Fire, Fortify, Foster, Fuel, Gee, Hearten, Heigh, Help, Hortatory, Incite, Nourish, Pat, Patronise, Prod, Push, Reassure, Root, Support, Tally-ho, Uplift, Urge, Yo

Encroach(ment) Impinge, Infringe, Intrude, Invade, Overlap, Overstep, Poach, Trespass, Usurp

Encumber, Encumbrance Burden, Clog, Deadwood, Dependent, ➤ HANDICAP, Impede, Load, Obstruct, Saddle

End(ing) Abolish, Abut, Aim, Ambition, Amen, Anus, Arse, Big, Bitter, Bourn(e), Butt, Cease, Climax, Close, Closure, Cloture, Coda, Conclude, Crust, Curtain, Cut off, Death, Decease, Denouement, Desinence, Destroy, Determine, Dissolve, Domino, Effect, Envoi, Envoy, Epilogue, Exigent, Expire, Extremity, Fatal, Fattrels, Final(e), Fine, Finis, ➤ FINISH, Finite, Grave, Heel, Ish, Izzard, Izzet, Kill, Kybosh, Last, Loose, Mill, Nirvana, No side, Ort, Period, Peter, Point, Purpose, Quench, Receiving, Remnant, Rescind, Result, Roach, Scotch, Scrag, Shank, Slaughter, Sopite, Split, Sticky, Stub, Surcease, Swansong, Tag, Tail, Tailpiece, Telic, Telos, Term, Terminal, Terminate, Terminus, Thrum, Tip, Toe, Ultimate, Up, Upshot, Z

Endeavour Aim, Effort, Enterprise, Strive, Struggle, Try, Venture

Endless Continuous, Ecaudate, Eternal, Eterne, Infinite, Interminable, Perpetual, Undated

▷ **Endlessly** may indicate a last letter missing

Endorse(ment) Adopt, Affirm, Approve, Assurance, Back, Confirmation, Initial, Okay, Oke, Ratify, Rubber stamp, Sanction, Second, Sign, ➤ SUPPORT, Underwrite, Visa

Endow(ment) Assign, Bequeath, Bestow, Bless, Cha(u)ntry, Dotation, Enrich, Foundation, Gift, Leave, Patrimony, Vest

Endure(d), Endurance, Enduring Bear, Brook, Dree, Have, Hold, ➤ LAST, Livelong, Lump, Patience, Perseverance, Pluck, Ride, Stamina, Stand, Stay, Stout, Sustain, Thole, Tolerance, Undergo, Wear

Enemy Adversary, Antagonist, Boer, Devil, Fifth column, Foe(n), Fone, Opponent, Public, Time

Energetic, Energise, Energy Active, Amp, Animation, Arduous, Cathexis, Chakra, Chi, Dash, Drive, Dynamic, Dynamo, E, Enthalpy, Entropy, EV, Fermi, Fireball, Force, Fructan, Gism, Go, Hartree, Input, Instress, Internal, Horme, ➤ JET, Jism, Jissom, Joie de vivre, Joule, Kinetic, Kundalini, Libido, Luminous, Magnon, Moxie, Nuclear, Orgone, Pep, Phonon, Potency, Potential, ➤ POWER, Powerhouse, QI, Quantum, Rad, Radiant, Radiatory, Rydberg, Sappy, Solar, Steam, Trans-uranic, Verve, Vigour, Vim, Vital, Wave, Zing, Zip

Enforce(ment) Administer, Coerce, Control, Exact, Implement, Impose

Engage(d), Engagement, Engaging Absorb, Accept, Appointment, Attach, Bespoken, Betrothal, Bind, Book, Busy, Contract, Date, Embark, Employ, Engross, Enlist, Enmesh, Enter, Gear, Gig, Hire, Hold, Interest, Interlock, Lock, Mesh, Met, Occupy, Pledge, Promise, Prosecute, Reserve, Residency, Skirmish, Sponsal, Sponsion, Spousal, Trip, Wage, Winsome

▷ **Engagement** may indicate a battle

Engine, Engine part Beam, Bricole, Carburettor, Catapult, Diesel, Donkey, Dynamo, Fan-jet, Fire, Ion, Jet, Lean-burn, Locomotive, Machine, Mangonel, ➤ MOTOR, Nacelle, Outboard, Plasma, Pulsejet, Radial, Ramjet, Reaction, Rocket, Rotary, Scramjet, Search, Steam, Tank, Testudo, Traction, Turbine, Turbofan, Turbojet, Turboprop, Two-stroke, V, Vernier, Wankel

Engineer(ing), Engineers AEU, Arrange, Brunel, De Lessops, Greaser, Heinkel, Junkers, Manoeuvre, Marconi, Marine, McAdam, Mastermind, Operator, Organise, Planner,

Repairman, Sapper, Scheme, Siemens, Stage, Stephenson, Telford, Wangle, Wankel, Watt, Whittle

England Albany, Albion, Blighty, John Bull, Merrie

English(man) Anglican, Brit, E, Eng, Estuary, John Bull, King's, Limey, Oxford, Pidgin, Pom(my), Pommie, Pongo, Queen's, Sassenach, Saxon, Shopkeeper, Standard, Southron

Engrave(r), Engraving Aquatint, Blake, Carve, Cerotype, Chalcography, Chase, Cut, Dry-point, Durer, Enchase, Etch, Glyptic, Glyptograph, Hogarth, Impress, Inciser, Inscribe, Intagliate, Lapidary, Mezzotint, Niello, Photoglyptic, Plate, Scrimshandy, Scrimshaw, Steel, Stillet, Stipple, Stylet, Stylography, Xylographer

Engross(ed) Absorb, Engage, Enwrap, Immerse, Monopolise, ➤ OCCUPY, Preoccupy, Prepossess, Rapt, Sink, Writ large

Enhance Augment, Embellish, Exalt, Heighten, Intensify

Enigma(tic) Charade, Conundrum, Dilemma, Gioconda, Mystery, Oracle, Poser, Problem, ➤ PUZZLE, Quandary, Question, Rebus, Riddle, Secret, Sphinxlike, Teaser

Enjoy(able), Enjoyment Apolaustic, Appreciate, Ball, Brook, Delectation, Fruition, Glee, Groove, Gusto, Have, Lekker, Like, Own, Possess, Relish, Ripping, Savour, Taste, Wallow

Enlarge(ment), Enlarger Accrue, Acromegaly, Add, Aneurism, Aneurysm, Augment, Blow-up, Diagraph, Dilate, Exostosis, Expand, Expatiate, Explain, Increase, ➤ MAGNIFY, Piece, Ream, Rebore, Sensationalize, Swell, Telescope, Tumefy, Varicosity

Enlighten(ment) Awareness, Edify, Educate, Explain, Illumine, Instruct, Nirvana, Revelation

Enlist Attest, Conscript, Draft, Engage, Enrol, Induct, Join, Levy, Prest, Recruit, Roster, Volunteer

Enliven(ed) Animate, Arouse, Brighten, Cheer, Comfort, Exhilarate, Ginger, Invigorate, Merry, Pep, Refresh, Warm

Enmity Animosity, Aversion, Hatred, Malice, Nee(d)le, Rancour

Ennoble Dub, Elevate, Exalt, Honour, Raise

Enormous Colossal, Exorbitant, Googol, Huge, Humongous, Humungous, ➤ IMMENSE, Jumbo, Mammoth, Mega, Vast

Enough Adequate, ➤ AMPLE, Anow, Basta, Belay, Enow, Fill, Geyan, Nuff, Pax, Plenty, Qs, Sate, Satis, Suffice, Sufficient, Via

Enquire, Enquiring, Enquiry Ask, Check, Curious, Eh, Inquire, Organon, Request, Scan, See, Trial

Enrage(d) ➤ INCENSE, Inflame, Infuriate, Livid, Madden, Wild

Enrich Adorn, Endow, Enhance, Fortify, Fructify, Oxygenate

Enrol(ment) Attest, Empanel, Enlist, Enter, Incept, ➤ JOIN, List, Matriculate, Muster, Register

Ensign Ancient, Badge, Banner, Duster, ➤ FLAG, Gonfalon, Officer, Pennon, Red, White

Enslave(ment) Bondage, Captivate, Chain, Yoke

Ensue Follow, Result, Succeed, Transpire

Entangle(ment) Ball, Elf, Embroil, Encumber, Ensnarl, Entrail, Fankle, Implicate, ➤ KNOT, Mat, Ravel, Retiarius, Trammel

Enter Admit, Broach, Come, Enrol, Infiltrate, Ingo, Insert, Invade, Lodge, Log, Penetrate, Pierce, Record, Submit, Table

Enterprise, Enterprising Adventure, Ambition, Aunter, Dash, Emprise, Free, Goey, Go-getter, Gumption, Industry, Plan, Private, Public, Push, Spirit, Stunt, Venture

Entertain(er), Entertaining, Entertainment Acrobat, Afterpiece, Amphitryon, Amuse, Balladeer, Beguile, Busk, Cater, Cheer, Circus, Comedian, Comic, Conjure, Consider, Cottabus, Cuddy, Divert, Divertissement, ENSA, Extravaganza, Fete, Fleshpots, Floorshow, Foy, Fun, Gaff, Gala, Gaudy, Harbour, Have, Hospitality, Host(ess), Interest, Interlude, Intermezzo, Karaoke, Lauder, Light, Masque, Minstrel, Olio, Panto, Pap, Peepshow, Piece, Pierrot, Regale, Review, Revue, Rodeo, Serenade, Showbiz, Snake-charmer, Striptease, Table, Tamasha, Tattoo, Treat, Variety, Vaudeville

Enthuse, Enthusiasm, Enthusiast(ic) Ardour, Buff, Bug, Cat, Cheerleader, Devotee, Ebullience, Ecstatic, Fiend, Fire, Flame, Freak, Furor(e), Get-up-and-go, Gung-ho, Gusto, Hearty, Hype, Into, Keen, Lyrical, Mad, Mania, Muso, Oomph, Outpour, Overboard, Passion, Perfervid, Rah-rah, Raring, Rave, Rhapsodise, Sold, Spirit, Verve, Warmth, Whole-hearted, Zealot, Zest

Entice(ment), Enticing Allure, Angle, Cajole, Carrot, Decoy, Lure, Persuade, Seductive, ➤ TEMPT, Tole, Toll

Entire(ly), Entirety Absolute, All, Complete, Intact, Integral, In toto, Lot, Purely, Systemic, Thorough, Total, ➤ WHOLE

Entity Being, Body, Existence, Holon, Tao, Tensor, Thing

Entrail(s) Bowels, Giblets, Gralloch, Guts, Ha(r)slet, Humbles, Lights, Numbles, Offal, Tripe, Umbles, Viscera

Entrance(d), Entrant, Entry Access, Adit, Anteroom, Arch, Atrium, Avernus, Bewitch, Charm, Contestant, Door, Eye, Fascinate, Foyer, Gate, Ghat, Hypnotise, Ingress, Inlet, Jaws, Mesmerise, Pend, Porch, Portal, Postern, Propylaeum, Propylon, Reception, Record, Registration, Starter, Stem, Spellbound, Stoa, Stoma, Stulm

Entreat(y) Appeal, Ask, Beg, Beseech, Flagitate, Impetrate, ► IMPLORE, Orison, Petition, Plead, Pray, Precatory, Prevail, Prig, Rogation, Solicit, Sue, Supplicate

Entrepreneur Businessman, Wheeler-dealer

► **Entry** see ENTRANCE

Entwine Complect, Impleach, Intervolve, Lace, Twist, Weave

Enumerate, Enumeration Catalogue, Count, List, Tell

Envelop(e) Corolla, Corona, Cover(ing), Enclose, Entire, Invest, Involucre, Muffle, Perianth, Sachet, Serosa, Smother, Surround, Swathe

Environment, Environmental(ist) Ambience, Entourage, Green, Habitat, Milieu, Setting, Sphere, Surroundings

Envoy Agent, Diplomat, Hermes, Legate, Plenipotentiary

Epic Aeneid, Ben Hur, Beowulf, Calliope, Colossal, Dunciad, Edda, Epopee, Gilgamesh, Homeric, Iliad, Kalevala, Lusiad(s), Mahabharata, Nibelungenlied, Odyssey, Ramayana, Saga

Epicure(an) Apicius, Connoisseur, Gastronome, Glutton, ► GOURMAND, Gourmet, Hedonist, Sybarite

Epidemic Pandemic, Pestilence, Plague, Prevalent, Rampant

Epilogue Appendix, Coda, Postscript

Episode, Episodic Chapter, Incident, Page, Picaresque, Scene

Epistle(s) Lesson, Letter, Missive, Pastoral

Epitome, Epitomise Abridge, Abstract, Digest, Image, Model, Summary, Typify

Epoch Age, Era, Holocene, Miocene, Ogilocene, Palaeocene, Period, Pleistocene, Pl(e)iocene

Equable, Equably Calm, Just, Smooth, Tranquil

Equal(ly), Equality Alike, Ana, As, Balanced, Commensurate, Compeer, Egal(ity), Emulate, Equinox, Equiparate, Equity, Even, Even-steven, Fifty-fifty, For, Identical, Identity, Is, Iso-, Isocracy,

Equate → Erupt(ion) 196

Level, Level-pegging, Make, Match, Par, ➤ PEER, Peregal, Rise, Rival, ➤ SO, Square

Equate, Equation Balance, Differential, Dirac, Identity, Parametric, Quadratic, Reduce, Relate, Simultaneous

Equilibrium Balance, Composure, Homeostasis, Isostasy, Poise, Stasis, Tautomerism

Equip(age), Equipment Accoutrement, Adorn, Apparatus, Apparel, Appliance, Array, Attire, Carriage, Deck, Dight, Expertise, ➤ FURNISH, Gear, Get-up, Graith, Kit, Material, Matériel, Muniments, Outfit, Retinue, Rig, Stock, Stuff, Tack(le), Tool, Turn-out

Equivalent Correspondent, Equal, Same, Tantamount

Equivocate Flannel, Lie, Palter, Prevaricate, Quibble, Tergiversate, Weasel

Era Age, Archaean, C(a)enozoic, Christian, Common, Cretaceous, Decade, Dynasty, Epoch, Hadean, Hegira, Hej(i)ra, Hijra, Jurassic, Lias, Mesozoic, Period, Precambrian, Proterozoic

Eradicate, Erase Abolish, Delete, Demolish, Destroy, Efface, Expunge, Extirp, Obliterate, Purge, Root, Scratch, Uproot

Erect(ing), Erection Build, Construct(ion), Elevate, Hard-on, Perpendicular, Priapism, Prick, Rear, Upright, Vertical

Ergo Argal, Hence, Therefore

Erode, Erosion Corrasion, Denude, Destroy, Deteriorate, Etch, Fret, Wash, Wear, Yardang

Eros, Erotic(a) Amatory, Amorino, Amorous, Aphrodisiac, Carnal, Cupid, Lascivious, Philtre, Prurient, Salacious, Steamy

Err(or) Aliasing, Anachronism, Bish, Blip, Blooper, Blunder, Boner, Bug, Clanger, Comedy, Corrigendum, Fault, Glaring, Human, Lapse, Lapsus, Literal, Misgo, Misprint, Misprise, Misprize, ➤ MISTAKE, Out, Rove, Sin, Slip, Solecism, Stray, Trip, Typo, Typographical

Errand Chore, Commission, Message, Mission, Sleeveless, Task

Erratic Haywire, Temperamental, Vagary, Vagrant, Wayward

Erroneous False, Inaccurate, Mistaken, Non-sequitur

Erudite, Erudition Academic, Learned, Wisdom

Erupt(ion), Erupture Belch, Brash, Burst, Eject, Emit, ➤ EXPLODE, Fumarole, Hives, Lichen, Mal(l)ander, Mallender, Outbreak, Outburst, Papilla, Pustule, Rash

Escape(e), Escapade Abscond, Avoid, Bolt, Bolthole, Breakout, Caper, Eject, Elope, Elude, Elusion, Esc, Evade, Exit, Flee, Flight, Frolic, Gaolbreak, Hole, Hoot, Houdini, Hout, Lam, Leakage, Leg-it, Levant, Loop(-hole), Meuse, Mews, Muse, Outlet, Prank, Refuge, Runaway, Scarper, Seep(age), Shave, Slip, Vent

Escort Accompany, Attend, Bodyguard, Chaperone, Comitatus, Conduct, Convoy, Cortege, Corvette, Date, Destroyer, Entourage, Frigate, Gallant, Gigolo, Guide, Lead, Outrider, Protector, Retinue, See, Squire, Take, Tend, Usher, Walker

Esoteric Abstruse, Orphic, Rarefied, Recondite, Secret

Especial(ly) Chiefly, Esp, Espec, Outstanding, Particular

Espionage Industrial, Spying, Surveillance

Esprit Insight, Spirit, Understanding, Wit

Essay Article, Attempt, Critique, Disquisition, Dissertation, Endeavour, Paper, Stab, Thesis, Tractate, Treatise, Try

Essayist Addison, Bacon, Columnist, Elia, Ellis, Emerson, Hazlitt, Holmes, Hunt, Huxley, Lamb, Locke, Montaigne, Pater, Prolusion, Ruskin, Scribe, Steele, ➤ WRITER

Essence Alma, Atman, Attar, Aura, Being, Core, Element, Entia, Esse, Extract, Fizzen, Flavouring, Foison, Gist, Heart, Hom(e)ousian, Inbeing, Inscape, Kernel, Marrow, Mirbane, Myrbane, Nub, Nutshell, Ottar, Otto, Perfume, Per-se, Pith, Quiddity, Ratafia, Soul, Ylang-ylang

Essential(ly) Basic, Central, Crucial, Entia, Fundamental, Imperative, Indispensable, Inherent, Integral, Intrinsic, Key, Lifeblood, Linch-pin, Marrow, Material, Must, Necessary, Need, Nitty-gritty, Nuts and bolts, Per-se, Prana, Prerequisite, Quintessence, Radical, Requisite, Vital, Whatness

Establish(ed) Abide, Anchor, Ascertain, Base, Build, Create, Enact, Endemic, Ensconce, Fix, ➤ FOUND, Haft, Instal(l), Instate, Institute, Inveterate, Ordain, Pitch, Pre-set, Prove, Raise, Root(ed), Set, Stable, Standing, Trad, Trite, Valorise, Verify

Establishment Building, Business, CE, Church, Co, Concern, Engrain, Evince, Hacienda, Institution, Lodge, Salon, School, Seat, System

Estate Allod(ium), Alod, Assets, Commons, Demesne, Domain, Dominant, Dowry, Fazenda, Fee-simple, Fee-tail, Fen, First, Fourth, General, Hacienda, Hagh, Haugh, Having, Hay,

Housing, Industrial, Land-living, Latifundium, Legitim, Life, Manor, Messuage, Odal, Personality, Plantation, Press, ➤ PROPERTY, Real, Runrig, Situation, Spiritual, Standing, Talooka, Taluk(a), Temporal, Thanage, Trading, Udal

Esteem(ed), Estimable Account, Admiration, Appreciation, Count, Have, Honour, Izzat, Los, Precious, Prestige, Price, Pride, Prize, Rate, ➤ REGARD, Respect, Store, Value, Venerate, Wonder, Worthy

➤**Estimable** see ESTEEM

Estimate, Estimation Appraise, Assess, Calculate, Carat, Conceit, Cost, Esteem, Extrapolation, Forecast, Gauge, Guess, Guess(timate), Opinion, Projection, Quotation, Rate, Rating, Reckon, Regard, Sight, Value, Weigh

Etch(ing) Aquafortis, Aquatint(a), Bite, ➤ ENGRAVE, Incise, Inscribe

Eternal, Eternity Ageless, Endless, Eviternal, Ewigkeit, Forever, Immortal, Infinity, Never-ending, Perdurable, Perpetual, Tarnal, Timeless

Ether Atmosphere, Ch'i, Gas, Sky, Yang, Yin

Ethereal Airy, Delicate, Fragile, Heavenly, Nymph

Ethic(al), Ethics Deontics, Marcionite, Moral, Principles

Ethiopia(n) African, Amharic, Asmara, Cushitic, Geez, Kabele, Kebele

Etiquette Code, Conduct, ➤ MANNERS, Propriety, Protocol, Ps and Qs, Punctilio

Eucalyptus Bloodwood, Coolabah, Gum-tree, Ironbark, Mallee, Marri, Morrell, Sallee, Stringybark, Tewart, Tooart, Tuart, Wandoo

Euphoria, Euphoric Cock-a-hoop, Elation, High, Jubilation, Rapture, Rush

Europe(an) Balt, Bohunk, Catalan, Community, Continent, Croat, E, Faringee, Faringhi, Feringhee, Fleming, Hungarian, Hunky, Japhetic, Lapp, Lithuanian, Palagi, Polack, Ruthene, Ruthenian, Serb, Slavonian, Slovene, Topi-Wallah, Transleithan, Tyrolean, Vlach, Yugoslav

Evacuate, Evacuation Excrete, Expel, Getter, Planuria, Planury, Scramble, Stercorate, Stool, Vent, Void, Withdraw

Evade, Evasion, Evasive Ambages, Avoid, Cop-out, Coy, Dodge, Duck, Elude, Escape, Fence, Fudge, Hedge, Loophole,

Parry, Prevaricate, Quibble, Quillet, Scrimshank, Shifty, Shirk, Shuffling, Sidestep, Skive, Skrimshank, Stall, Subterfuge, Tergiversate, Waive, Weasel, Whiffler

Evaluate, Evaluation Appraise, Assess, Estimate, Gauge, Rate, Review, Waid(e), Weigh

Evangelical, Evangelist Converter, Crusader, Fisher, Gospeller, Happy-clappy, Jesus freak, John, Luke, Marist, Mark, Matthew, Moody, Morisonian, Peculiar, Preacher, Revivalist, Sim(eonite), Stundist, Wild

Evaporate, Evaporation Condense, Dehydrate, Desorb, Exhale, Steam, Steme, Ullage, Vaporise

Eve(n), Evening Albe(e), Albeit, All, Average, Balanced, Clean, Drawn, Dusk, Een, Ene, Equable, Equal, Erev, Fair, Flush, Iron, Level, Meet, Nightfall, Pair, Par, Plain, Plane, Plateau, Quits, Rib, Smooth, Soirée, Subfusc, Subfusk, Sunset, Tib(b)s, Toss-up, Twilight, Vesperal, Vespertinal, Vigil, Yester, Yet

Event Case, Circumstance, Discus, Encaenia, Episode, Feat, Field, Gymkhana, Happening, Heat, Incident, Landmark, Leg, Media, Milestone, Occasion, Occurrence, Ongoing, Outcome, Pass, Regatta, Result, Three-ring circus, Track

Eventual(ly), Eventuality Case, Contingent, Finally, Future, In time, Nd

Ever Always, Ay(e), Constantly, Eternal, Eviternity

Evergreen Abies, Ageless, Arbutus, Cembra, Cypress, Gaultheria, Ivy, Myrtle, Olearia, Periwinkle, Pinaster, Privet, Thuja, Thuya, Washington, Winterberry

Every(one), Everything All, Complete, Each, Ilk(a), Sum, The works, Tout, Tout le monde, Universal, Varsal

Everyday Informal, Mundane, Natural, Ordinary, Plain

Everywhere Omnipresent, Passim, Rife, Throughout, Ubiquity

Evidence, Evident Adminicle, Apparent, Argument, Axiomatic, Circumstantial, Clear, Confessed, Distinct, Document, Flagrant, Indicate, Internal, Manifest, Obvious, Overt, ➤ PATENT, Plain, Premise, Proof, Record, Sign, Surrebuttal, Testimony, Understandable

Evil Ahriman, Alastor, Amiss, Badmash, Bale, Beelzebub, Budmash, Corrupt, Depraved, Eale, Guilty, Harm, Hydra, Ill, Iniquity, Malefic, Mare, Mischief, Necessary, Night, Perfidious, Rakshas(a), Shrewd, Sin, ➤ SINISTER, Turpitude, Vice, Wicked

Evince Disclose, Exhibit, Indicate, ➤ MANIFEST, Show

Evolution Countermarch, Development, Growth, Holism, Lamarck, Moner(on), Phylogeny, Turning

▷**Evolution** may indicate an anagram

Ex Former, Late, Quondam, Ten

Exacerbate Aggravate, Embitter, Exasperate, Irritate, Needle

Exact(ing), Exactitude, Exactly Accurate, Authentic, Careful, Dead, Definite, Due, Elicit, Estreat, Even, Exigent, Extort, Fine, Formal, It, Jump, Literal, Literatim, Mathematical, Meticulous, Nice(ty), Pat, Point-device, ➤ PRECISE, Require, Slap-bang, Spang, Specific, Spot-on, Strict, T, Verbatim

Exaggerate(d), Exaggeration Agonistic, Amplify, Boast, Brag, Camp, Colour, Distend, Dramatise, ➤ EMBROIDER, Goliathise, Hyperbole, Inflate, Magnify, Overdo, Overpaint, Overplay, Overrate, Over-the-top, Overstate, Stretch, Theatrical

Exalt(ed), Exaltation Attitudes, Deify, Dignify, Elation, Enhance, Ennoble, Erect, Extol, Glorify, High, Jubilance, Larks, Lofty, ➤ PRAISE, Raise, Rapture, Sublime

Exam(ine), Examinee, Examiner, Examination A-level, Analyse, Analyst, Audit, Autopsy, Baccalauréat, Biopsy, Case, Check-up, Collate, Comb, Consideration, Cross-question, CSE, Deposal, Depose, Dissect, Entrance, Explore, Eyeball, GCE, GCSE, Grade(s), Greats, Gulf, Hearing, Inspect, Inter, Interrogate, Introspection, Jury, Local, Mark, Matriculation, Medical, Mocks, Moderator, Mods, Mug, O-level, Once-over, Oral, Ordeal, Overhaul, Palp(ate), Paper, Peruse, Physical, Post-mortem, Prelim, Probe, Pry, Psychoanalyse, Pump, ➤ QUESTION, Quiz, Ransack, Recce, Reconnaissance, Review, Sayer, Scan, Schools, Scrutineer, Scrutinise, Search, Seek, Sift, Sit, Smalls, Sus(s), Test, Trial, Tripos, Try, Vet, Viva

Example Byword, Epitome, ➤ FOR EXAMPLE, Foretaste, Illustration, Instance, Lead, Lesson, Model, Paradigm, Paragon, ➤ PATTERN, Praxis, Precedent, Prototype, Say, Shining, Showpiece, Specimen, Standard, Touchstone, Type, Typify

Excavate, Excavation, Excavator Burrow, Catacomb, Crater, Delf, Delph, ➤ DIG, Dike, Ditch, Dredge, Hollow, JCB, Mine, Pioneer, Pioner, Quarry, Shaft, Sink, Sondage, Stope, Well

Excel(lence), Excellency, Excellent A1, Admirable, Beat, Beaut, Better, Blinder, Boffo, Bonzer, Boss, Bravo, Brill, Bully, Capital, Champion, Cheese, Choice, Class(y), Corking, Crack,

Crackerjack, Crucial, Daisy, Def, Dic(k)ty, Dilly, Dominate,
Elegant, Exemplary, Fab, Fantastic, Five-star, Great, HE, High,
Humdinger, Inimitable, Jake, Jammy, Matchless, Mean, Mega-,
Merit, Noble, Outdo, Overdo, Paragon, Prime, Pure, Rad, Rare,
Rattling, Ring, Ripping, ➤ SHINE, Spanking, Spiffing, Stellar,
Stonking, Stupendous, Sublime, Superb, Super-duper, Superior,
Supreme, Swell, Terrific, Tip-top, Top flight, Top-hole,
Topnotch, Topping, Virtue, Wal(l)y, War, Way-out, Wicked,
Worth

Exceptional Abnormal, Anomaly, Egregious, Especial,
Extraordinary, Rare, Ripsnorter, Singular, Special, Uncommon,
Zinger

Excess(ive), Excessively All-fired, Basinful, Exorbitant,
Extortionate, Extravagant, Flood, Fulsome, Glut, Hard,
Inordinate, ➤ LAVISH, Mountain, Nimiety, OD, Old, OTT,
Outrage, Over, Overage, Overblown, Overcome, Overdose,
Overkill, Overmuch, Overspill, Overcome, Plethora,
Preponderance, Profuse, Salt, Satiety, Spate, Spilth, Steep,
Superabundant, Superfluity, Surfeit, Surplus, Troppo, Ultra,
Undue, Unequal, Woundily

Exchange Baltic, Bandy, Barter, Bourse, Cambist, Catallactic,
Change, Chop, Commute, Contango, Convert, Cope, Corn,
Enallage, Excambion, Foreign, Inosculate, Interplay, Ion,
Labour, Logroll, ➤ MARKET, Mart, ➤ PBX, Paraphrase, Post,
Rally, Recourse, Rialto, Royal, Scorse, Scourse, Stock, Swap,
Switch, Swop, Tolsel, Tolsey, Tolzey, ➤ TRADE, Traffic,
Trophallaxis, Truck

Excite(d), Excitable, Excitement, Exciting Ablaze,
Abuzz, Aerate, Agog, Amove, Animate, Aphrodisiac, Arouse,
Athrill, Atwitter, Awaken, Brouhaha, Buck-fever, Climatic,
Combustible, Commotion, Delirium, Electrify, Emove, Enthuse,
Erethism, Feisty, Fever, Fire, Flap, Frantic, Frenzy, Frisson,
Furore, Fuss, Galvanise, Gas, Headiness, Heat, Hectic, Het,
Hey-go-mad, Hilarity, Hobson-Jobson, Hoopla, Hothead,
Hyped, Hyper, Hysterical, Impel, Incite, Inebriate, Inflame,
Intoxicate, Jimjams, Kick, Kindle, Metastable, Must, Neurotic,
Oestrus, Orgasm, Overheat, Overwrought, Panic, Passion,
Pride, Provoke, Racy, Radge, Red-hot, Rile, Roil, ➤ ROUSE,
Ruff(e), Rut, Send, Spin, Spur, Startle, Stimulate, Stir(e),

Suscitate, Tetany, Tew, Thrill, Titillate, Trickle, Turn-on, Twitter, Upraise, Waken, Whee, Whoopee, Yahoo, Yerk, Yippee, Yoicks

▷ **Excite(d)** may indicate an anagram

Exclaim, Exclamation Ahem, Begorra, Blurt, Bo, Ceas(e), Crikey, Criv(v)ens, Dammit, Ecphonesis, Eina, Ejaculate, Eureka, Expletive, Fen(s), Good-now, Haith, Heigh-ho, Hem, Hosanna, Inshallah, Interjection, Oops, Protest, Pshaw, Whoops, Yippee, Zounds

Exclude, Excluding, Exclusion Ban, Bar, Block, Debar, Disbar, Eliminate, Ex, Except, Excommunicate, Omit, Ostracise

Excursion Airing, Cruise, Dart, Digression, Jaunt, Outing, Road, Sally, Sashay, Sortie, Tour, Trip

Excusable, Excuse Absolve, Alibi, Amnesty, Condone, Evasion, Exempt, Exonerate, Forgive, Mitigate, Occasion, Out, Overlook, Palliate, ➤ PARDON, Pretext, Release, Venial, Viable, Whitewash

Execute(d), Executioner, Executive, Executor Accomplish, Administrate, Behead, Discharge, Finish, Fry, Gar(r)otte, Guardian, Hang, Headsman, Implement, Ketch, Kill, Koko, Lynch, Management, Noyade, Official, Perform, Pierrepoint, Politburo, Top, Trustee

Exempt(ion) Dispensation, Exclude, Free, Immune, Impunity, Indemnity, Quarter, Spare

Exercise(s) Aerobics, Apply, Cal(l)isthenics, Callanetics®, Chi kung, Cloze, Constitutional, Drill, Employ, Enure, Eurhythmics, Exert, Floor, Gradus, Inure, Isometrics, Kata, Lesson, Limber, Medan, Op, Operation, PE, Ply, Practice, Practise, Press-up, PT, Push-up, Qigong, Shintaido, Sit-up, Solfeggi(o), Step (aerobics), Tai chi (ch'uan), Thema, Theme, Thesis, Train, Use, Warm-up, Wield, Work, Wôrk-out, Xyst(us), Yomp

▷ **Exercise(d)** may indicate an anagram

Exert(ion) Conatus, ➤ EFFORT, Exercise, Labour, Operate, Strain, Strive, Struggle, Trouble, Wield

Exhaust(ed), Exhausting, Exhaustion, Exhaustive All-in, Beaten, Burn, Burn-out, Bushed, Consume, Deadbeat, Debility, Deplete, Detailed, Done, Drain, Effete, Emission, Empty, End, Fatigue, Frazzle, Gruelling, Heat, Jet-lagged, Jet-stream, Jiggered, Mate, Milk, Out, Poop, Rag, Rundown, Shatter, Shot, Spend, Spent, Stonkered, Tire, Use, Washed-up, Wasted, Waygone, ➤ WEARY, Wind, Worn, Zonked

Exhibit(ion), Exhibitioner Circus, Concours, Demo, Demonstrate, Demy, Diorama, Discover, Display, Evince, Expo, Expose, Fair, Hang, Indicate, ➤ MANIFEST, Olympia, Pageant, Panopticon, Parade, Present, Retrospective, Salon, Scene, Show(piece), Viewing

Exigency, Exigent Emergency, Pressing, Taxing, Urgent, Vital

Exile Adam, Babylon, Banish, Deport, Emigré, Eve, Expatriate, Exul, Galut(h), Ostracise, Outlaw, Relegate, Tax, Wretch

Exist(ence), Existing Be(ing), Corporeity, Dwell, Enhypostasia, Entelechy, Esse, Extant, Identity, Life, Live, Ontology, Perseity, Solipsism, Substantial, Ubiety

Exit Débouché, Door, Egress, Gate, Leave, Outlet

Exodus Book, Departure, Flight, Hegira, Hejira

Exorbitant Excessive, Expensive, Steep, Tall, Undue

Exotic Alien, Ethnic, Foreign, Strange, Outlandish

Expand, Expanse, Expansion Amplify, Boom, Develop, Diastole, Dilate, Distend, Ectasis, Elaborate, ➤ ENLARGE, Escalate, Grow, Increase, Magnify, Ocean, Snowball, Spread, Stretch, Swell, Wax, Wire-draw

Expatiate Amplify, Descant, Dwell, Enlarge, Perorate

Expect(ant), Expectation, Expected, Expecting Agog, Anticipate, Ask, Await, Due, Foresee, Gravid, Hope, Lippen, Look, Natural, Par, Pip, Pregnant, Presume, Prospect, Require, ➤ SUPPOSE, Tendance, Think, Thought, Usual, Ween

Expedient Advisable, Artifice, Contrivance, Fend, Make-do, Makeshift, Measure, Politic, Resort, Resource, Shift, Stopgap, Suitable, Wise

Expedite, Expedition Advance, Alacrity, Anabasis, Celerity, Crusade, Dispatch, Excursion, Field trip, Hasten, Hurry, Kon-tiki, Pilgrimage, Post-haste, Safari, Speed, Trek, Trip, Voyage

Expel Amove, Dispossess, Egest, Evacuate, Evict, Exile, Exorcize, Hoof, Oust, Out(cast), Void

Expend(iture) Budget, Consume, Cost, Dues, Oncost, Outgo(ing), Outlay, Poll, Squander, Tithe, Toll, Use

Expense(s) Charge, Cost, Exes, Fee, Law, Oncost, Outgoing, Outlay, Overhead, Price, Sumptuary

Expensive Chargeful, Costly, Dear, Executive, Salt, Steep, Upmarket, Valuable

Experience(d) Accomplished, A posteriori, Assay, Blasé, Discovery, Empiric, Encounter, Expert, ➤ FEEL, Felt, Freak-out, Gust, Hands-on, Have, Incur, Know, Learn, Live, Mature, Meet, Mneme, Old hand, Pass, Plumb, Seasoned, See, Senior, Sense, Sensory, Stager, Stand, Street-smart, Streetwise, Taste, Transference, Trial, Trip, Trocinium, Try, Undergo, Versed, Work

Experiment(al) Attempt, Avant-garde, Empirical, Essay, Peirastic, Pilot, Sample, Taste, Tentative, ➤ TRIAL, Try, Venture

Expert(ise) Accomplished, Ace, Adept, Adroit, Arch, Authority, Boffin, Buff, Cambist, Cocker, Cognoscente, Connoisseur, Crack, Dab(ster), Dan, Deft, Don, Egghead, Fundi, Gourmet, Gun, Hotshot, Karateka, Know-all, Know-how, Luminary, Maestro, Masterly, Maven, Mavin, Meister, Nark, Oner, Oneyer, Oneyre, Peritus, Practised, Pro, Proficient, Pundit, Ringer, Savvy, Science, Skill(y), Sly, Specialist, Technique, Technocrat, Ulema, Used, Whiz

Expire(d), Expiry Blow, Collapse, Croak, ➤ DIE, End, Exhale, Invalid, Ish, Lapse, Neese, Pant, Sneeze, Terminate

Explain Account, Annotate, Clarify, Conster, Construe, Decline, Define, Describe, Elucidate, Expose, Expound, Extenuate, Gloss, Gloze, Justify, Parabolize, Salve, Solve, Upknit

Explanation, Explanatory Apology, Commentary, Exegesis, Exegetic, Exposition, Farse, Gloss, Gloze, Hypothesis, Key, Note, Preface, Reading, Rigmarole, Solution, Theory

Expletive Arrah, Darn, Exclamation, Oath, Ruddy, Sapperment

Explicit Clean-cut, Clear, Definite, Express, Frank, Outspoken, ➤ PRECISE, Specific

Explode Backfire, Burst, Cramp, Debunk, Detonate, Erupt, ➤ EXPLOSION, Pop, Snake

Explore(r), Exploration Amerigo, Amundsen, Baffin, Balboa, Bandeirante, Banks, Barents, Bering, Boone, Burton, Cabot, Cartier, Chart, Columbus, Cook, Cortes, Da Gama, Dampier, Darwin, De Soto, Dias, Diaz, Discover, Dredge, Eric, Eriksson, Examine, Feel, Frobisher, Fuchs, Humboldt, Investigate, Livingstone, Magellan, Map, Marco Polo, Mungo Park, Nansen, Navigator, Pathfinder, Peary, Pioneer, Potholer, Probe, Przewalski, Rale(i)gh, Research, Rhodes, Ross, Scott, Scout, Search, Shackleton, Spaceship, Speke, Stanley, Sturt, Tasman, Vancouver, Vasco da Gama, Vespucci

Explosion, Explosive Backfire, Bang, Blast, Cap, Chug,
Cordite, Crump, Fireball, Firecracker, Firedamp, Firework,
Fulminant, Gasohol, Gelatine, Gelignite, Grenade, Guncotton,
Gunpowder, Jelly, Landmine, Megaton, Mine, Nitroglycerine,
Outburst, Payload, Petar(d), Petre, Plastic, Plastique, Pow,
Propellant, SAM, Semtex®, Thunderflash, Tonite, TNT,
Volcanic, Warhead

▷ **Explosive** may indicate an anagram

Exponent Advocate, Example, Index, Interpreter, Logarithm

Expose(d), Exposure Air, Anagogic, Bare, Blot, Debag,
Debunk, Denude, Desert, Disclose, Endanger, En prisé, Exhibit,
Flashing, Indecent, Insolate, Moon, Nude, Object, Open, Out,
Over, Propale, Reveal, Snapshot, Streak, Strip, Subject, Sun,
Time, Unmask, Windswept

Expound(er) Discourse, Discuss, Exegete, Explain, Open,
Prelict, Red, Scribe, Ulema

Express(ed), Expression Air, APT, Aspect, Breathe,
Cacophemism, Cliché, Conceive, Concetto, Couch,
Countenance, Declare, Denote, Embodiment, Epithet, Explicit,
Face, Fargo, Formulate, Good-luck, Gup, Hang-dog, Idiom,
Locution, Manifest, Metonym, Mien, Mot (juste), Neologism,
Non-stop, Orient, Paraphrase, Phrase, Pleonasm, Pony, Precise,
Pronto, Put, Quep, Register, Say(ne), Show, Soulful, ▶ SPEAK,
State, Strain, Succus, Term, Token, Tone, Topos, Utterance,
Vent, ▶ VOICE

Expressionless Blank, Deadpan, Impassive, Inscrutable,
Po(ker)-faced, Vacant, Wooden

Expulsion Discharge, Eccrisis, Ejection, Eviction, Exile, Sacking,
Synaeresis

Extemporise Ad lib, Improvise, Pong

Extend(ed), Extension Aspread, Augment, Cremaster,
Draw, Eke, Elapse, Elongate, Enlarge, Escalate, Expand, Exsert,
Fermata, Grow, Increase, Length, Long, Long-range, Long-stay,
Long-term, Offer, Outgrowth, Overbite, Overlap, Porrect,
Proffer, Prolong, Propagate, Protract, Reach, Retrochoir, Span,
Spread, Steso, ▶ STRETCH, Substantial, Widen

Extensive, Extent Ambit, Area, Capacious, Catch-all,
Compass, Comprehensive, Distance, Large, Length, Limit,
▶ MAGNITUDE, Panoramic, Range, Reach, Scale, Size, Spacious,
Sweeping, Wide, Widespread

Exterior Aspect, Crust, Derm, Facade, Outer, ➤ OUTSIDE, Shell, Surface, Veneer

External Exoteric, Exterior, Extraneous, Foreign, Outer

Extinguish Douse, Dout, Dowse, Extirpate, Obscure, Quash, Quell, Quench, Slake, Snuff, Stifle, Suppress

Extra Accessory, Additament, Addition(al), Additive, Adjunct, And, Annexe, Attachment, Bisque, Bonus, By(e), Debauchery, Encore, Etcetera, Further, Gash, Lagniappe, Left-over, Leg bye, Make-weight, More, Nimiety, Odd, Optional, Out, Over, Perk, Plus, Plusage, Reserve, Ripieno, ➤ SPARE, Spilth, Staffage, Sundry, Super, Supernumerary, Supplementary, Suppletive, Surplus, Trop, Undue, Walking-gentleman, Walking-lady, Wide, Woundy

Extract(ion), Extractor Bleed, Breeding, Catechu, Clip, Corkscrew, Decoction, Descent, Distil, Draw, Educe, Elicit, Essence, Excerpt, Extort, Gist, Gobbet, Insulin, Parentage, Passage, Pick, Piece, Pry, Quintessence, Smelt, Suck, Summary, Tap, Trie, Try, Vanilla, Winkle, Worm, Wring

Extraordinary Amazing, Humdinger, Important, Phenomenal, Preternatural, Rare, Singular, Startling, Strange, Unusual

Extravagance, Extravagant, Extravaganza Excessive, Fancy, Feerie, Heroic, High-flown, Hyperbole, Lavish, Luxury, Outré, Prodigal, Profuse, Rampant, Reckless, Riotise, Splash, Splurge, Squander, Sumptious, Superfluous, Waste

Extreme(ly), Extremist Acute, Almighty, Butt, Desperate, Die-hard, Drastic, Edge, Exceptional, Farthermost, Gross, In spades, ➤ INTENSE, Mega-, Opposite, Parlous, Pretty, Radical, Too, Tremendous, Ultimate, Ultra, Utmost, Utter, ➤ VERY, Vitally, Wing

▷**Extreme** may indicate a first or last letter

Exuberance, Exuberant Brio, Copious, Ebullient, Effusive, Gusto, Hearty, Lavish, Mad, Profuse, Rambustious, Skippy, Streamered

Exult(ant) Crow, Elated, ➤ GLOAT, Glorify, Jubilant, Paeonic, Rejoice, Triumphant, Whoop

Eye(s), Eye-ball, Eye-piece Evil, Glass, Goggles, Iris, Jack, Keek, Klieg, Lamp, Lazy, Lens, Magic, Mincepie, Mind's, Naked, ➤ OBSERVE, Ocellar, Ogle, Optic, Orb, Peeper, PI, Pupil, Regard, Retina, Roving, Sight, Spy, Uvea, Watch, Weather, Windows

Eyesore Blot, Disfigurement, Sty(e)

Eye trouble Cataract, Glaucoma, Iritis, Leucoma, Nystagmus, Presbyopia, Retinitis, Stigmatism, Strabismus, Trachoma, Wall-eye

Ff

F Fahrenheit, Fellow, Feminine, Fluorine, Following, Force, Foxtrot

Fable(s) Aesop, Allegory, Apologue, Exemplum, Fiction, Hitopadesa, La Fontaine, Legend, Marchen, Milesian, Myth, Panchatantra, Parable, Romance, Tale

Fabric ➤ CLOTH, Framework

Fabricate, Fabrication Artefact, Concoct, Construct, Contrive, Cook, Fake, Figment, Forge, ➤ INVENT, Lie, Porky, Trump, Weave, Web

Fabulous, Fabulous beast Chimera, Cockatrice, Eldorado, Fictitious, Fung, Gear, Incredible, Jabberwock(y), Legendary, Magic, Manticore, Merman, Mythical, Orc, Phoenix, Roc, Romantic, Sphinx, Unicorn, Unreal, Wyvern

Face, Facing Abide, Affront, Ashlar, Ashler, Aspect, Audacity, Brave, Brazen, Caboched, Cabochon, Cabossed, Cheek, Chiv(v)y, Coal, Countenance, Culet, Dalle, Dare, Dartle, Deadpan, Dial, Eek, Elevation, Encounter, Facade, Fat, Favour, Features, Fineer, Fortune, ➤ FRONT, Girn, Gonium, Grouf, Grouf, Groue, Gurn, Hatchet, Head-on, Jib, Kisser, Lining, Look, Lore, Mascaron, Meet, Metope, Moe, Mug, Mush, Opposite, Outstare, Outward, Pan, Paper tiger, Phisnomy, Phiz(og), Physiognomy, Poker, Puss, Revet, Revetment, Roughcast, Rud, Rybat, Side, Snoot, Socle, Stucco, Type, Veneer, Vis(age), Visnomy, Withstand, Zocco(lo)

Facetious Frivolous, Jocular, Waggish, Witty

Facile Able, Adept, Complaisant, Ductile, Easy, Fluent, Glib

Facilitate, Facility Amenity, Assist, Benefit, Capability, ➤ EASE, Expedite, Fluency, Gift, ISO, Knack, Skill

Fact(s), Factual Actual, Case, Correct, Data, Datum, Detail, Info, Literal, Mainor, Nay, Really, Truism, Truth, Veridical, Yes

Faction Bloc, Cabal, Camp, Caucus, Clique, Contingent, Junto, Schism, Sect, Tendency, Wing

Factor Agent, Aliquot, Broker, Cause, Co-efficient, Common, ➤ COMPONENT, Divisor, Edaphic, Element, Feel-good, Intrinsic, Load, Modulus, Representative, Rh, Rhesus, Risk, Steward, Wind chill

Factory Cannery, Gasworks, Glassworks, Hacienda, Maquiladora, Mill, Plant, Refinery, Sawmill, Steelworks, Sweatshop, Tinworks, Works, Workshop

Faculty Aptitude, Arts, Capacity, Department, Ear, Ease, Indult, Knack, Power, School, Sense, Speech, ➤ TALENT, Teachers, Wits

Fad(dish) Crank, Craze, Cult, Fashion, Foible, Ismy, Thing, Vogue, Whim

Fade(d), Fading Blanch, Die, Diminuendo, Dinge, Elapsion, Etiolate, Evanescent, Fall, Filemot, Lessen, Mancando, Pale, Passé, Perdendo(si), Peter, Smorzando, Smorzato, Stonewashed, Vade, Vanish, Wallow, Wilt, Wither

Fag Chore, Cigarette, Drag, Drudge, Fatigue, Gasper, Homosexual, Menial, Quean, Reefer, Snout, Tire, Toil, Weary

Fail(ing), Failure Anile, Blemish, Blow, Bomb, Bummer, Cark, ➤ COLLAPSE, Conk, Crash, Cropper, Debacle, Decline, Default, Defect, Demerit, Die, Dog, Dry, Dud, Fault, Feal, Fiasco, Flivver, Flop, Flow, Flunk, Fold, Founder, Frost, Glitch, Gutser, Infraction, Lapse, Lose, Malfunction, Manqué, Miss-, Miscarry, Miss, Muff, Nerd, No-no, Omit, Oversight, Pip, Plough, Pluck, Refer, Refusal, Shambles, Short circuit, Short(coming), Slippage, Smash, Spin, Stumer, Turkey, Vice, Wash-out, Weakness, White elephant, Wipeout

Faint(ness) Black-out, Conk, Darkle, Dim, Dizzy, Dwalm, Fade, Lassitude, Pale, Stanck, Swarf, Swarve, Swelt, Swerf, Swerve, Swoon, Swound, Syncope, Unclear, Wan, Whitish

Fair A(e)fald, Aefauld, Aefwld, Barnet, Bartholomew, Bazaar, Beauteous, Belle, Blond, Bon(n)ie, Bonny, Brigg, Decent, Donnybrook, Equal, Equitable, Evenhanded, Exhibition, ➤ FESTIVAL, Feeing-market, Fine, Funfair, Gaff, Gey, Goose, Gwyn, Hiring, Honest, Hopping, Isle, ➤ JUST, Kermess, Kermis, Kirmess, Market, Mart, Mediocre, Mela, Mop, Nundinal, Objective, OK, Paddington, Passable, Play, Pro rata, Rosamond,

Sabrina, Square, Statute, Straight, Tavistock, Tidy, Tolerable, Tow-headed, Trade, Tryst, Unbias(s)ed, Vanity, Wake, Widdicombe

Fairly Clearly, Enough, Evenly, Midway, Moderately, Pari passu, Pretty, Properly, Quite, Ratherish

Fairy Banshee, Befana, Cobweb, Dobbie, Dobby, Elf(in), Fay, Gloriana, Hob, Hop o' my thumb, Leprechaun, Lilian, Mab, Morgan le Fay, Morgane(tta), Moth, Nis, Peri, Pigwidgin, Pigwiggen, Pisky, Pixie, Pouf, Puck, Punce, Sandman, Spirit, Sprite, Sugar-plum, Tink(erbell), Titania, Tooth, Urchin-shows

Faith(ful) Accurate, Achates, Belief, Constant, Creed, Devoted, Doctrine, Faix, Fay, Feal, Fegs, Fideism, Fiducial, Haith, Implicit, Islam, Lay, Loyal, Plerophory, Puritanism, Quaker, Religion, Shema, Solifidian, Staunch, Strict, Troth, ➤ TRUE, True-blue, Trust, Truth, Umma(h)

Fake(r), Faking Bodgie, Bogus, Copy, Counterfeit, Duffer, Ersatz, False, Fold, Fraud, Fudge, Imitation, Imposter, Impostor, Paste, Phoney, Postiche, Pretend, Sham, Spurious, Trucage, Truquage, Truqueur, Unreal

Falcon Gentle, Hawk, Hobby, Kestrel, Lanner(et), Merlin, Nyas, Peregrine, Prairie, Saker, Sakeret, Sparrow-hawk, Stallion, Staniel, Stannel, Stanyel, Tassel-gentle, Tassell-gent, Tercel-gentle

Fall(s), Fallen, Falling Abate, Accrue, Angel, Arches, Astart, Autumn, Boyorna, Cadence, Cascade, Cataract, Chute, Collapse, Crash, Cropper, Cross press, Declension, Decrease, Degenerate, Descent, Dip, Domino effect, Douse, Downswing, Dowse, ➤ DROP, Ebb, Firn, Flop, Flump, Folding press, Free, Grabble, Gutser, Gutzer, Horseshoe, Idaho, Iguaçu, Incidence, Kabalega, Kaieteur, Lag, Landslide, Lapse, Lin(n), Niagara, Oct(ober), Owen, Perish, Plonk, Plummet, Plump, Plunge, Prolapse, Purl(er), Rain, Reaction, Relapse, Ruin, Sheet, Sin, Sleet, Snow, Spill, Sutherland, Tailor, Takakkau, Topple, Toss, Trip, Tugela, Tumble, Victoria, Voluntary, Wipeout, Yosemite

Fallacious, Fallacy Elench(us), Error, Idolum, Illogical, Illusion, Pathetic, Sophism, Unsound

▷**Falling** may indicate an anagram or a word backwards

False, Falsify Adulterate, Bastard, Bodgie, Bogus, Braide, Canard, Cavil, Charlatan, Cook, Deceitful, Disloyal, Dissemble, Doctor, Fake, Feigned, Fiddle, Forge, Illusory, Knave, Lying,

Meretricious, Mock, Perjury, Pinchbeck, Postiche, Pretence, Pseudo, Roorback, Sham, Specious, Spoof, Spurious, Treacherous, Two-faced, Untrue

Fame, Famous Bruit, Eminent, Glitterati, Gloire, Glory, History, Humour, Kudos, Legendary, Luminous, Name, Noted, Notorious, Prestige, Reclamé, Renown, Repute, Rumour, Spur, Stardom, Word

Familiar(ise), Familiarity Accustom, Acquaint, Assuefaction, Au fait, Auld, Chummy, Comrade, Conversant, Crony, Dear, Demon, Easy, Free, Friend, Habitual, Homely, Homey, Incubus, Intimate, Known, Liberty, Maty, Old, Old-hat, Privy, Python, Used, Versed

Family Ancestry, Bairn-team, Blood, Breed, Clan, Class, Cognate, Consanguine, Descent, Dynasty, Extended, House(hold), Issue, Kin, Kind, Line, Mafia, Medici, Name, Nuclear, Orange, People, Phratry, Progeny, Quiverful, Race, Sept, Sib(b), Sibship, Stem, Stirps, Strain, Taffy, Talbot, Tribe

Famine Dearth, Lack, Scarcity

▷**Famished** may indicate an 'o' in the middle of a word

Fan(s), Fan-like Alligator, Admirer, Aficionado, Alluvial, Arouse, Bajada, Blow, Cat, Clapper, Claque, Colmar, Cone, Cool, Cuscus, Devotee, Diadrom, Dryer, Enthusiast, Extractor, Fiend, Flabellum, Following, Groupie, Hepcat, Khuskhus, Outspread, Partisan, Punka(h), Rhipidate, Ringsider, Sail, Spread, Supporter, Tail, Tifosi, Ventilate, Votary, Voteen, Washingtonia, Wing, Winnow, Zealot, Zelant

▷**Fan** may indicate an anagram

Fanatic(al) Bigot, Devotee, Energumen, Enthusiastic, Extremist, Fiend, Frenetic, Glutton, Mad, Maniac, Nut, Partisan, Phrenetic, Picard, Rabid, Santon, Ultra, Wowser, Zealot

Fancy, Fanciful Caprice, Chim(a)era, Conceit, Concetto, Crotchet, Daydream, Dream, Dudish, Elaborate, Eagle, Fantasy, Fit, Flam, Florid, Frothy, Guess, Hallo, Idea(te), Idolon, ➤ IMAGINE, Inclination, Lacy, Liking, Maya, Mind, My, Nap, Notion, Ornamental, Ornate, Picture, Predilection, Rococo, Suppose, Thought, Vagary, Visionary, Ween, Whigmaleerie, Whigmaleery, Whim(sy)

▷**Fancy** may indicate an anagram

Fanfare Flourish, Sennet, Show, Tantara, Trump, Tucket

Fantastic, Fantasy Absurd, Antic, Bizarre, Caprice, Chimera, Cockaigne, Cockayne, Escapism, Fab, Fanciful, Grotesque, Hallucination, Kickshaw(s), Lucio, Myth, Outré, Phantasmagoria, Queer, Romance, Unreal, Untrue, ➤ WHIM, Whimsical, Wild

Far Apogean, Away, Distal, Distant, Extreme, Outlying, Remote, Thether, Thither

Fare Apex, Charge, Cheer, Commons, Do, Eat, ➤ FOOD, Go, Passage, Passenger, Rate, Table, Traveller

Farewell Adieu, Adios, Aloha, Apopemptic, Bye, Cheerio, Departure, Godspeed, ➤ GOODBYE, Leave, Prosper, Sayonara, Send off, So long, Toodle-oo, Toodle-pip, Totsiens, Vale, Valediction

Farm(ing), Farmhouse Agronomy, Arable, Bowery, Cold Comfort, Collective, Croft, Cultivate, Dairy, Deep-litter, Emmerdale, Estancia, Extensive, Factory, Fat, Fish(ery), Funny, Geoponical, Grange, Hacienda, Health, Home, Homestead, Husbandry, Intensive, Kibbutz, Kolkhoz, Land, Ley, Loaf, Location, Mains, Mas, No-tillage, Onstead, Orley, Pen, Poultry, Ranch, Rent, Sewage, Shamba, Smallholding, Sovkhoz, Station, Stead(ing), Sted(d), Stedde, Steed, Stock, Subsistence, Tank, Till, Toon, Toun, Town, Wick, Wind

Farmer Boer, Campesino, Carl, Cockatoo, Cocky, Collins Street, Colon, Crofter, Estanciero, Gebur, George, Giles, Hick, Macdonald, Metayer, Nester, NFU, Peasant, Pitt Street, Ryot, Share-cropper, Sodbuster, Squatter, Tenant, Tiller, Whiteboy, Yeoman, Zeminda(r)

Farmhand Cadet, Cottar, Cotter, Cottier, Ditcher, Hand, He(a)rdsman, Hind, Ploughman, Redneck, Rouseabout, Roustabout, Shearer

▶**Farmhouse** see FARM

Farthing Brass, F, Fadge, Har(r)ington, Mite, Q, Quadragesimal, Rag

Fascinate, Fascinating Allure, Attract, Bewitch, ➤ CHARM, Dare, Enchant, Engross, Enthral(l), Fetching, Inthral, Intrigue, Kill, Mesmeric, Rivet, Siren, Witch

Fascist Blackshirt, Blue shirt, Brownshirt, Dictator, Falange, Falangist, Iron Guard, Lictor, Nazi, Neo-nazi, NF, Rexist, Sinarchist, Sinarquist

Fashion(able), Fashioned Aguise, A la (mode), Bristol, Build, Chic, Construct, Convention, Corinthian, Craze, Create, Cult, Custom, Cut, Design, Directoire, Elegant, Entail, Fad, Feat, Feign, Forge, Form, Genteel, Go, Hew, Hip, In, Invent, Kitsch, Look, ► MAKE, Manière, Manners, Mode, Mondain(e), Mould, Newgate, Pink, Preppy, Rage, Rate, Sc, Shape, Smart, Smith, Snappy, Snazzy, Stile, Stylar, Style, Swish, Tailor, Ton, Ton(e)y, ► TREND(Y), Turn, Twig, Vogue, Way, Wear, With-it, Work, Wrought

Fast(er) Abstain, Apace, Ashura, Breakneck, Citigrade, Clem, Daring, Double-quick, Elaphine, Express, Fizzer, Fleet, Immobile, Lent, Lightning, Loyal, Maigre, Meteoric, Moharram, Muharram, Muharrem, Pac(e)y, Posthaste, Presto, Pronto, Quadragesimal, Quick, Raffish, Raking, Ramadan, Ramadhan, Rash, Spanking, Speedy, Stretta, Stretto, Stuck, Supersonic, Swift, Tachyon, Thick, Tisha b'Av, Whistle-stop, Yarer, Yom Kippur

Fasten(er), Fastening Anchor, Attach, Bar, Belay, Bind, Bolt, Buckle, Button, Chain, Clamp, Clasp, Clinch, Clip, Cramp, Dead-eye, Diamond-hitch, Espagnolette, Eye-bolt, Frog, Gammon, Hasp, Hesp, Hook, Lace, Latch, Lock, Moor, Morse, Nail, Netsuke, Padlock, Parral, Pectoral, Pin, Preen, Reeve, Rivet, Rope, Rove, Seal, ► SECURE, Shut, Spar, Sprig, Staple, Tach(e), Tag, Tassel, Tether, Tintack, Toggle, Velcro®, Wedge, Zip

Fat(s), Fatten, Fatty Adipic, Bard, Batten, Battle, Blubber, Butter, Calipash, Chubby, Corpulent, Dripping, Embonpoint, Endomorph, Flab, Flesh, Grease, Gross, Lanolin, Lard, Love handles, Margarine, Obese, Oil, Plump, Podgy, Polyunsaturated, Portly, Puppy, Rich, Rolypoly, Rotund, Saturated, Seam(e), Shortening, Stearic, Suet, Tallow, Tomalley, Tub, Unsaturated

Fatal(ism), Fate(ful), Fated Apnoea, Atropos, Cavel, Chance, Clotho, Deadly, Death, Decuma, Destiny, Doom, End, Fay, Fell, Joss, Karma, Kismet, Lachesis, Lethal, Lot, Meant, Moira, Mortal, Mortiferous, Nemesis, Norn(a), Parca, Pernicious, Predestination, Portion, Skuld, Urd, Verdande, Waterloo, Weird

Father(ly) Abba, Abbot, Abuna, Adopt, Apostolic, Bapu, Begetter, Breadwinner, Brown, City, Curé, Dad, Engender, Founding, Fr, Generator, Genitor, Getter, Governor, Male, Pa,

Padre, Papa, Pappy, Parent, Paterfamilias, Pater(nal), Patriarch, Père, Pop(pa), Popper, Priest, Rev, Sire, Stud, Thames, Tiber, William

Fathom Depth, Delve, Dig, F, Plumb, Plummet, Understand

Fatigue Battle, Exhaust, Fag, Jade, Jet lag, ME, Neurosthenia, Overdo, Tire, Weariness, Weary

Fault(y) Arraign, Bad, Beam, Blame(worthy), Blunder, Bug, Cacology, Carp, Culpable, Defect, Demerit, Dip, Drop-out, Duff, ➤ ERROR, Failing, Flaw, Frailty, Gall, Glitch, Henpeck, Imperfect, Literal, Massif, ➤ MISTAKE, Nag, Nibble, Niggle, Nit-pick, Out, Outcrop, Overthrust, Peccadillo, Rate, Reprehend, Rift, Rupes Recta, San Andreas, Sclaff, Short, Slip, Strike, Trap, Vice

Faux pas Blunder, Boner, Gaffe, Leglen-girth, Solecism

Favour(able), Favoured, Favourite Advance, Advantage(ous), Aggrace, Agraste, Alder-liefest, Approval, Back, Befriend, Behalf, Benign, Bless, Boon, Bribe, Cert, Chosen, Cockade, Curry, Darling, Ex gratia, Fancy, Favodian, Grace, Gratify, Graste, Gree, Hackle, Hot, In, Indulge, Kickback, Minion, Odour, Particular, Peat, Persona grata, Pet, Pettle, Popular, ➤ PREFER, Promising, Propitious, Resemble, Rib(b)and, Roseate, Rose-knot, Rosette, Smile, Toast, Token

Fawn(er), Fawning Adulate, Bambi, Beige, Blandish, Brown-nose, Crawl, Creep, Cringe, Deer, Ecru, Flatter, Fleech, Grovel, Ko(w)tow, Lickspittle, Obsequious, Servile, Smarm, Smoo(d)ge, Subservient, Sycophant, Tasar, Toady, Truckle, Tussah, Tusseh, Tusser, Tussore

Fear Angst, Apprehension, Awe, Bugbear, Claustrophobia, Cold sweat, Crap, Cyberphobia, Dismay, Doubt, Drad, Dread, Foreboding, ➤ FOR FEAR, Fright, Funk, Hang-up, Horror, Kenophobia, Mysophobia, Nyctophobia, Ochlophobia, ➤ PHOBIA, Redoubt, Revere, Taphephobia, Taphophobia, Terror, Trepidation, Willies

Fearful Afraid, Cowardly, Dire, Horrific, Nervous, Pavid, Rad, Redoubtable, Timorous, Tremulous, Windy

Fearless Bold, Brave, Courageous, Gallant, Impavid, Intrepid

Feast Adonia, Agape, Assumption, Banquet, Barmecide, Beano, Belshazzar's, Blow-out, Candlemas, Carousal, Celebration, Dine, Do, Double, Eat, Encaenia, Epiphany, Epulation, Festival, Fleshpots, Fool's, Gaudeamus, Gaudy, Hallowmas, Hockey,

Hogmanay, Holy Innocents, Id-al-Adha, Id-al-Fitr, Immaculate Conception, Isodia, Junket, Kai-kai, Lady Day, Lamb-ale, Lammas, Luau, Martinmas, Michaelmas, Movable, Noel, Passover, Pentecost, Pig, Potlatch, Purim, Regale, Revel, Roodmas, Seder, Shindig, Spread, Succoth, Sukkot(h), Tabernacles, Tuck-in, Wayzgoose, Weeks, Yule, Zagmuk

Feat Achievement, Deed, Effort, Exploit, Gambado, Stunt, Trick

Feather(ed), Feathers Alula, Barbicel, Boa, Braccate, Cock, Contour, Covert, Crissum, Down, Duster, Filoplume, Fledged, Fletch, Flight, Gemmule, Hackle, Harl, Hatchet, Herl, Lure, Macaroni, Oar, Ostrich, Pen(na), Pin, Pinna, Pith, Plumage, Plume, Plumule, Pteryla, Ptilosis, ➤ QUILL, Rectrix, Remex, Remiges, Rocket-tail, Saddle-hackle, Scapular, Scapus, Semiplume, Sickle, Standard, Stipa, Swansdown, Tectrix, Tertial, Vibrissa, White, Wing covert

Feature(s) Amenity, Appurtenance, Article, Aspect, Attribute, Brow, Character, Chin, Depict, Eye, Eyebrow, Face, Figure, Hallmark, Highlight, Item, Jizz, Landmark, Lineament, Neotery, Nose, Nucleus, Overfold, Phiz(og), Physiognomy, Spandrel, Star, Temple, Trait, Underlip

Federal, Federation Alliance, Axis, Bund, Commonwealth, Interstate, League, Statal, Union

Fee Charge, Corkage, Dues, Duty, Faldage, Fine, Hire, Honorarium, Mortuary, Mouter, Multure, Obvention, Pay, Premium, Refresher, Retainer, Sub, Transfer, Tribute

Feeble Banal, Characterless, Daidling, Debile, Decrepit, Droob, Effete, Feckless, Flaccid, Footling, Fragile, Geld, Ineffective, Infirm, Jessie, Namby-pamby, Pale, Puny, Sickly, Slender, Slight, Tailor, Tame, Thin, Tootle, Wallydrag, Wallydraigle, Washy, Wastrel, Weak, Weak-kneed, Weak-minded, Weed, Weedy, Wersh, Wet, Wimpish, Worn

Feed(er), Feeding Battle, Bib, Browse, Cake, Cater, Cibation, Clover, Dine, Drip, ➤ EAT, ➤ EMPLOYED, Fatten, Fire, Fishmeal, Fodder, Food, Gavage, Graze, Hay, Lunch, Meal, Nourish, Paid, Pecten, Provender, Refect, Repast, Sate, Soil, Stoke, Stooge, Stover, Sustain, Tire, Tractor, Wean

Feel, Feeling(s) Aesthesia, Affettuoso, Atmosphere, Compassion, Darshan, ➤ EMOTION, Empathy, Empfindung, Euphoria, ➤ EXPERIENCE, Fellow, Finger, Flaw, Frisk, Grope, Groundswell, Handle, Heart, Heartstrings, Hunch, Intuit, Knock,

Know, Palp, Passible, Passion, Pity, Premonition, Presentiment, Probe, Realise, Sensate, Sensation, ➤ SENSE, Sensitive, Sentiment, Spirit, Tactual, Touch, Turn, Undercurrent, Vehemence, Vibes, Zeal

▶**Feet** see FOOT

Feign Act, Affect, Colour, Fake, Malinger, Mime, Mock, ➤ PRETEND, Sham, Simulate

Fel(d)spar Adularia, Albite, Anorthite, Gneiss, Hyalophane, Moonstone, Orthoclase, Petuntse, Petuntze, Plagioclase, Sun-stone

▶**Feline** see CAT

Fell Axe, Chop, Cruel, Deadly, Dire, Dread, Fierce, Hew, Hide, Hill, Inhuman, Knock-down, KO, Lit, Log, Moor, Pelt, Poleaxe, Ruthless, Sca, Shap, Skittle

Fellow(ship) Academic, Associate, Bawcock, Birkie, Bloke, Bo, Bro, Buffer, Carlot, Cat, Chal, Chap, Chi, China, Cock, Cod(ger), Collaborator, Co-mate, Communion, Companion, Comrade, Confrère, Cove, Cully, Cuss, Dandy, Dean, Dog, Don, Dude, Equal, F, Fogey, Fop, Gadgie, Gadje, Gaudgie, Gauje, Gink, Guy, Joe, Joker, Josser, Lad, Like, M, Mall, Man, Mate, Member, Mister, Mun, Partner, Peer, Professor, Rival, Sister, Sociate, Sodality, Swab, Twin, Waghalter, Wallah

Felt Bat(t), Drugget, Knew, Met, Numdah, Numnah, Pannose, Roofing, Sensed, Tactile, Underlay, Velour

Female (bodies), Feminine, Feminist Anima, Bint, Bit, Dame, Distaff, Doe, F, Filly, Girl, Harem, Hen, Her, Kermes, Lady, Libber, Maiden, Pen, Petticoated, Riot girl, Sakti, Shakti, She, Sheila, Shidder, Soft, Spindle, Thelytoky, -trix, ➤ WOMAN, Yin

▷**Female, Feminine** may indicate an -ess ending

Fence(r), Fencing (position) Bar, Barrier, Botte, Carte, Dogleg, Enclose, Epee, Flanconade, Foils, Fraise, Haha, Hay, Hedge, Hurdle, Iaido, Imbrocate, Kendo, Link, Mensur, Netting, Obstacle, Oxer, Pale, Paling, Palisade, Passado, Pen, Picket, Quart(e), Quinte, Raddle, Rail, Rasper, Receiver, Reset, Ring, Scrimure, Seconde, Sept(um), Septime, Singlestick, Sixte, Stacket, Stockade, Stramac, Stramazon, Sunk, Swordplay, Tac-au-tac, Trellis, Virginia, Wattle, Wear, Weir, Wire

Fend(er) Buffer, Bumper, Cowcatcher, Curb, Mudguard, Parry, Provide, Resist, Skid, Ward, Wing

Fennel Finoc(c)hio, Finnochio, Herb, Love-in-a-mist, Narthex, Ragged lady

Ferment(ation) Barm, Enzym(e), Leaven, Mowburn, Protease, Ptyalin, Seethe, Solera, Stum, Trypsin, Turn, Vinify, Working, Ye(a)st, Zyme, Zymosis, Zymurgy

Fern Acrogenous, Archegonial, Bracken, Brake, Pteridology

Ferry(man) Charon, Convey, Hovercraft, Passage, Plier, Roll-on, RORO, Sealink, Shuttle, Traject, Tranect

Fertile, Fertility (symbol) Battle, Fat, Fecund, Fruitful, Linga, Priapus, Productive, Prolific, Rhiannon, Rich, Uberous

Fertilise(r), Fertilisation Ammonia, Auxin, Bee, Bone-ash, Bone-earth, Bone-meal, Caliche, Caprify, Compost, Fishmeal, Guano, Heterosis, Humogen, Humus, In-vitro, IVF, Kainite, Manure, Marl, Nitrate, Nitre, Pearl-ash, Phosphate, Pollen, Potash, Self, Sham, Stamen, Superphosphate, Top dressing

Fervent, Fervid, Fervour Ardent, Burning, Earnest, Heat, Hwyl, Intense, Keen, Passionate, White-hot, Zeal, Zeloso

Festival, Festive, Festivity Ale, Anniversary, Beano, Carnival, Celebration, Commemoration, Convivial, Corroboree, En fête, ➤ FAIR, Feast, Fete, Fiesta, ➤ GALA, Gaudy, Hogmanay, ➤ HOLIDAY, Play, Revel, Slugfest, Tide, Transfiguration, Wake

Fete Bazaar, Champetre, Entertain, ➤ FESTIVITY, Gala, Honour, Tattoo

Fetish Charm, Compulsion, Idol, Ju-ju, Obeah, Obi(a), Talisman, Totem, Voodoo

Fetter Basil, Bilboes, Chain, Gyve, Hamshackle, Hopple, Iron, Leg-iron, Manacle, Shackle

Feud Affray, Clash, Feoff, Fief, Quarrel, Strife, ➤ VENDETTA

Fever(ish) Ague, Brain, Cabin, Childbed, Dengue, Enteric, Ferment, Frenetic, Glandular, Heatstroke, Hectic, Jungle, Malaria, Marsh, Milk, Parrot, Passion, Pyretic, Rheumatic, Scarlatina, Scarlet, Spring, Sunstroke, Swine, Trench, Typhoid, Yellow(jack)

Few(er) Handful, Infrequent, ➤ LESS, Limited, Scarce, Some, Wheen

Fiancé(e) Betrothed, Intended, Promised

Fiasco Bomb, Debacle, Disaster, Failure, Flask, Flop, Lash-up, Wash-out

Fibre, Fibrous Acrylic, Backbone, Bast, Coir, Constitution, Filament, Flax, Hair, Hemp, Ixtle, Jute, Natural, Oakum, Pita, Raffia, Rami, Rhea, Roughage, Sisal, Slub(b), Staple, Strand, Tow, Wood pulp

Fickle(ness) Capricious, Change, False, Inconstant, Light, Mutable, Protean, Shifty, Varying, Volatile

Fiction(al), Fictitious Bogus, Cyberpunk, Fable, Fabrication, Pap, Phoney, Romance, Science, Splatterpunk, ➤ STORY

Fiddle(r), Fiddling Amati, Bow, Calling-crab, Cello, Cheat, Crab, Cremona, Crowd, Crouth, Crowd, Crwth, Fidget, Fix, Gju, Ground, Gu(e), Jerrymander, Kit, Launder, Nero, Peculate, Petty, Potter, Racket, Rebec(k), Rig, Rote, Sarangi, Saw, Sawah, Scam, Scrape, Second, Scrapegut, Spiel, Strad, Sultana, ➤ TAMPER, Tinker, Trifle, Tweedle(-dee), Twiddle, Viola, ➤ VIOLIN, Wangle

Fidget(y) Fantad, Fanteeg, Fantigue, Fantod, Fike, Fuss, Fyke, Hirsle, Hotch, Jimjams, Jittery, Niggle, Trifle, Twiddle, Twitch, Uneasy

Field(er), Fields(man) Aalu, Aaru, Abroad, Aceldama, Aerodrome, Area, Arena, Arish, Arpent, Arrish, Campestral, Campestrian, Catch, Champ(s), Close, Cover, Domain, Electromagnetic, Elysian, Entry, Fid, Flodden, Flying, Forte, Fylde, Glebe, Grid(iron), Gully, Hop-yard, Killing, Land, Lare, Lay, Lea(-rig), Ley, Line, Long-off, Long-on, Longstop, Lords, Magnetic, Mead(ow), Mid-on, Mid-off, Mine, Oil, Padang, Paddock, Paddy, Parrock, Pasture, Pitch, Playing, Point, Province, Runners, Salting, Sawah, Scarecrow, Scope, Scout, Shamba, Shortstop, Silly, Slip, Sphere, Stage, Territory, Tract, Unified, World

▷**Field** may indicate cricket

Field marshal Allenby, Bulow, French, Haig, Ironside, Kesselring, Kitchener, Montgomery, Roberts, Robertson, Rommel, Slim, Wavell

Fiend Barbason, Demon, ➤ DEVIL, Enthusiast, Flibbertigibbet, Fraterretto, Hellhound, Hobbididance, Mahn, Modo, Obidicut, Smulkin, Succubus

Fierce(ly) Billyo, Breem, Breme, Cruel, Draconic, Dragon, Grim, Hard-fought, Ogreish, Rampant, Renfierst, ➤ SAVAGE, Severe, Tigrish, Violent, Wild, Wood, Wud

Fiery Ardent, Argand, Aries, Con fuoco, Dry, Fervent, Hot, Igneous, Leo, Mettlesome, Phlogiston, Sagittarius, Salamander, Zealous

Fiesta Festival, Fete, Gala, Holiday

Fifth Column, Diapente, Hemiol(i)a, Nones, Quint, Sesquialtera

Fig Bania, Benjamin-tree, Caprifig, Fico, Figo, Footra, Fouter, Foutra, Foutre, Hottentot, Moreton Bay, Sycamore, Sycomore, Syncomium, Trifle

Fight(er), Fighting Affray, Alpino, Altercate, Barney, ► BATTLE, Bicker, Bout, Box, Brave, Brawl, Bruiser, Bush-whack, Campaign, Chindit, Combat, Conflict, Contest, Crusader, Defender, Dog, Duel, Encounter, Fence, Fisticuffs, Fray, Freedom, Free-for-all, Gladiator, Grap(p)le, Gunslinger, Gurkha, Hurricane, Lapith, Marine, Med(d)le, Medley, Mêlée, Mercenary, MIG, Mill, Partisan, Pellmell, PLO, Press, Pugilist, Pugnacity, Repugn, Resist, Ring, Ruck, Ruction, Rumble, Savate, Scrap, Scrimmage, Scuffle, Shine, Skirmish, Slam, Soldier, Spar, Spitfire, Squabble, Strife, Struggle, sumo, Swordsman, Tar, Toreador, Tussle, Umbrella, War(-dog), War-horse, War-man, Warrior, Wrestle

Figure(s), Figurine Arabic, Aumail, Bas-relief, Body, Build, Caryatid, Cast, Cinque, Cipher, Cone, Cube, Cypher, Decahedron, Digit, Écorché, Effigy, Eight, Ellipse, Enneagon, ► FORM, Fusil, Girth, Graph, Hour-glass, Icon, Idol, Ikon, Image, Insect, Intaglio, Integer, Lay, Motif, Nonagon, Number, Numeral, Numeric, Octagon, Octahedron, Outline, Parallelogram, Pentacle, Polygon, Prism, Puppet, Pyramid, Reckon, Repetend, See, ► SHAPE, Simplex, Statistics, Statue(tte), Telamon, Tetragon, Torus, Triangle, Triskelion, Waxwork

Figure of speech Allegory, Analogy, Antimask, Antimasque, Antimetabole, Antithesis, Asyndeton, Catachresis, Chiasmus, Deixis, Diallage, Ellipsis, Euphemism, Hypallage, Hyperbaton, Hyperbole, Hysteron proteron, Irony, Litotes, Meiosis, Metalepsis, Metaphor, Metonymy, Oxymoron, Paral(e)ipsis, Prosopoea, Simile, Syllepsis, Synecdoche, Taxeme, Tmesis, Trope, Zeugma

Filament Barbule, Byssus, Cirrus, Fibre, Fimbria, Floss, Gossamer, Hair, Hypha, Mycor(r)hiza, Myofibril, Paraphysis, Protonema, ► THREAD

File, Filing(s) Abrade, Archive, Batch, Binary, Box, Burr, Clyfaker, Coffle, Croc(odile), Crosscut, Data set, Disc, Disk, Dossier, Enter, Floatcut, Generation, Index, Indian, Line, Nail, Pigeon-hole, Pollute, Quannet, ▸ README, Rank, Rasp, Rat-tail, Riffler, Risp, Row, Scalprum, Scratch, Single, String, Swarf, Text, Tickler, TIF(F)

Filibuster Freebooter, Hinder, Obstruct, Run on, Stonewall

Fill(er), Filling Anaplerosis, Balaam, Banoffee, Banoffi, Beaumontag(u)e, Beaumontique, Billow, Bloat, Brick-nog, Brim, Bump, Centre, Charge, Cram, Gather, Gorge, Heart, Imbue, Impregnate, Inlay, Jampack, Line, Mastic, Occupy, Pabulous, Packing, Permeate, Plug, Repletive, Salpicon, Sate, Satisfy, Shim, Stack, Stock, Stocking, Stopping, ▸ STUFF, Tales, Teem, Ullage

Fillet(s) Anadem, Annulet, Band, Bandeau, Bandelet, Bone, Cloisonné, Flaunching, Fret, Goujons, Grenadine, Headband, Infula, Label, Lemniscus, List(el), Mitre, Moulding, Reglet, Regula, Ribbon, Rollmop, Slice, Snood, Sphendone, Stria, Striga, Taeniate, Tape, Teniate, Tournedos, Vitta

Film(s), Filmy, Filming Acetate, Biopic, Blockbuster, Bollywood, Buddy, Caul, Cel, Cine, Cinerama®, Cliffhanger, Cling, Clip, Deepie, Dew, Diorama, Docudrama, Documentary, Dust, Epic, ET, Exposure, Feature, Fiche, Flick, Floaty, Footage, Gigi, Gossamer, Hammer, Haze, Hollywood, Horror, Kell, Lacquer, Layer, Loid, Mask, Membrane, Microfiche, Mist, Montage, Newsreel, Noir, Oater, Outtake, Panchromatic, Patina, Pellicle, Photo, Plaque, Prequel, Psycho, Quickie, Reel, Release, Rush, Scale, Screen, Scum, Short, Shot, Silent, Skin, Skin flick, Slick, Slo-mo, Snuff, Spaghetti western, Splatter, Studio, Talkie, Tear-jerker, Trailer, Two-shot, Ultrafiche, Video, Video-nasty, Web, Weepie, Weepy, Western

Filter(ing) Clarify, Dialysis, Leach, Percolate, Perk, Seep, Sieve, ▸ SIFT, Skylight, Strain

Filth(y) Addle, Augean, Bilge, Colluvies, Crock, Crud, Defile, Dirt, Dung, Foul, Grime, Lucre, Mire, Muck, Obscene, Pythogenic, Refuse, Slime, Smut(ch), Soil, Squalor, Stercoral, Yuck

Final(e), Finalise Absolute, Closing, Coda, Conclusive, Decider, End, Eventual, Extreme, Last, Net(t), Peremptory, Sew up, Swansong, Ultimate, Utter

Finance, Financial, Financier Ad crumenan, Angel, Back, Banian, Banker, Bankroll, Banyan, Cambism, Chrematistic, Exchequer, Fiscal, Gnome, Grubstake, Monetary, Revenue, Sponsor, Subsidise, Treasurer, Underwrite

Finch Bird, Brambling, Bunting, Canary, Charm, Chewink, Crossbill, Darwin's, Fringillid, Linnet, Marsh-robin, Peter, Serin, Siskin, Spink, Twite

Find(ing) Ascertain, Detect, Discover(y), Get, Hit, Inquest, ➤ LOCATE, Meet, Provide, Rumble, Trace, Trouvaille, Verdict

Fine, Fine words Amerce, Arts, Assess, Beau(t), Bender, Boss, Brandy, Brave, Braw, Champion, Dainty, Dandy, End, Eriach, Eric(k), Estreat, F, Fair, Famous, Forfeit, Godly, Good(ly), Gossamer, Gradely, Grand, Hair, Hairline, Handsome, Heriot, Hunkydory, Immense, Issue, Keen, Log, Mulct, Nifty, Niminy-piminy, Noble, OK, Oke, ➤ PENALTY, Precise, Pure, Relief, Sconce, Safe, Sheer, Sicker, Slender, Spanking, Subtle, Summery, Super, Tax, Ticket(t)y-boo, Tiptop, Topping, Waly, Wally

Finery Braws, Fallal, Frills, Frippery, Gaudery, Ornament, Trinket, Wally, Warpaint

Finger, Fingernail Dactyl, Digit, Fork, Handle, Index, Lunula, Medius, Name, Nip, Piggy, Pinky, Pointer, Prepollex, Pusher, Ring(man), Shop, Talaunt, Talon, Tot, Trigger, White

Fingerprint Dabs, Dactylogram, Genetic, Loop, Whorl

Finis, Finish(ed), Finishing touch Arch, Close, Coating, Coda, Complete, ➤ CONCLUDE, Crown, Die, Dish, Do, Dope, Dress, ➤ END, Epiphenomena, Exact, Full, Kibosh, Lacquer, Neat, Outgo, Discharge, Dismiss, Exact, Full, Perfect, Photo, Refine, Ripe, Round, Settle, Shot, Spitcher, Surface, Terminate, Through, Up (tie), Veneer, Wind-up

Finn(ish) Esth, Huck(leberry), Karelian, Mickey, Mordvin, Suomic, Udmurt, Votyak

Fire(side) Accend, Agni, Animate, Ardour, Arson, Arouse, Atar, Axe, Bake, Bale, Barbecue, Barrage, Beacon, Behram, Blaze, Boot, Brand, Brazier, Brush, Burn, Bush, Chassé, Corposant, Delope, Discharge, Dismiss, Elan, Element, Embolden, Ena, Energy, Enfilade, Enkindle, Enthuse, Flak, Flame, Furnace, Greek, Gun, Hearth, Hob, Ignite, Inferno, Ingle, Inspire, Kentish, Kiln, Kindle, Launch, Light, Lowe, Pop, Prime, Prometheus, Pull, Rapid, Red cock, Sack, St Anthony's, St Elmo's, Scorch, Shell,

Shoot, Smudge, Spark, Spunk, Stoke, Stove, Strafe, Tracer, Wake, Wisp, Zeal

▶**Firearm** see GUN

Fire-break Epaulement, Greenstrip

Fireplace Chimney, Grate, Hearth, Hob, Ingle, Loop-hole, Range

Fireproof Abednego, Asbestos, Incombustible, Inflammable, Meshach, Salamander, Shadrach, Uralite

Firewood Billet, Faggot, Knitch, Tinder

Firework(s) Banger, Bengal-light, Bunger, Cherry bomb, Cracker, Devil, Fisgig, Fizgig, Fountain, Gerbe, Girandole, Iron sand, Jumping Jack, Maroon, Pastille, Peeoy, Petard, Pinwheel, Pioy(e), Pyrotechnics, Realgar, Rocket, Roman candle, Serpent, Skyrocket, Sparkler, Squib, Tantrum, Throwdown, Tourbill(i)on, Volcano, Wheel, Whizzbang

Firm Adamant, Agency, Binding, Business, Collected, Compact, Company, Concern, Concrete, Constant, Crisp, Decided, Determined, Duro, Faithful, Fast, Fixed, Hard, Inc, Oaky, Obdurate, Obstinate, ▶ RESOLUTE, Sclerotal, Secure, Set, Siccar, Sicker, ▶ SOLID, Stable, Stalwart, Staunch, Ste(a)dfast, Steady, Steely, Steeve, Stern, Stieve, Stiff, Strict, Sturdy, Tight, Tough, Well-knit

First Ab initio, Alpha, Arch, Archetype, Best, Calends, Champion, Chief, Earliest, E(a)rst, Foremost, Former, Front, Head, I, Ideal, Imprimis, Initial, 1st, Kalends, Led, Maiden, No 1, One, Opener, Or, Original, Pioneer, Pole, Premier, Prima, Primal, Prime, Primo, Principal, Prototype, Rudimentary, Senior, Starters, Top, Victor, Yama

First class, First rate A1, Crack, Prime, Supreme, Tiptop, Top(notch)

First man Adam, Ask, Premier, President, Yama

▶**First rate** see FIRST CLASS

First woman Embla, Eve, Pandora, Premier

Firth Estuary, Forth, Inlet, Moray, Tay

Fish(ing) Angle, Angler, Bob, Cast, Catch, Chowder, Coarse, Cran, Creel, Dredge, Dry-fly, Episcate, Fly, Flying, Fry, Gefilte, Goujons, Guddle, Halieutics, Haul, Ledger, Mess, Net, Otterboard, Overnet, Pilot, Piscine, Roe, Sashimi, Shoal, Snigger, Sniggle, Spin, Spot, Trawl, Troll, Tub, White

Fisher(man) Ahab, Andrew, Angler, Black cat, Caper, High-liner, Liner, Pedro, Peter, Piscator, Rodster, Sharesman, Walton

▶ **Fisherwoman** see FISHSELLER

Fishseller, Fisherwoman Fishwife, Molly Malone, Ripp(i)er, Shawley, Shawlie

Fissure Chasm, Cleft, Crack, Crevasse, Crevice, Gap, Grike, Gryke, Lode, Rent, Sand-crack, Scam, Vallecula, Vein, Zygon

Fist Clench, Dukes, Hand, Join-hand, Neaf(fe), Neif, Neive, Nief, Nieve, Pud, Punch, Thump

Fit(s), Fitting(s), Fitness Able, Access, Adapt, Ague, Appointment, Appropriate, Apropos, Apt, Bout, Canto, Capable, Condign, Congruous, Convulsion, Decent, Decorous, Dod, Dove-tail, Due, Eligible, Ensconce, Epilepsy, Equip, Expedient, Fairing, Fiddle, Furnishing, Gee, Germane, Hale, Hang, Health, Huff, Hysterics, In-form, Just, Lune, Mate, Meet, Mood, Nest, Paroxysm, Pertinent, Prepared, ▶ PROPER, Ready, Rig, Rind, Ripe, Rynd, Seemly, Seizure, Set, Sit, Sort, Sound, Spasm, Spell, Start, Suit(able), Tantrum, Throe, Turn, Up to, Well, Worthy, Wrath

▷ **Fit(ting)** may indicate a 't'

Five(s) Cinque, Mashie, Pallone, Pedro, Pentad, Quinary, Quintet, Sextan, Towns, V

Fix(ed), Fixer, Fixative Affeer, Anchor, Appoint, ▶ ARRANGE, Assess, Assign, Attach, Bind, Brand, Cement, Clamp, Clew, Clue, Constant, Cure, Decide, Destine, Determine, Do, Embed, Engrain, Establish, Fast, Firm, Fit, Freeze, Hold, Immutable, Imprint, Ingrain, Jag, Jam, Locate, Lodge, Nail, Name, Narcotic, Nobble, Orientate, Peg, Persistent, Pin, Point, Repair, Resolute, Rig, Rigid, Rivet, Rut, Screw, Seat, Seize, Set, Settle, Shoo, Skewer, Splice, Staple, Step, Tie, Weld

Fixture Attachment, Event, Match, Permanence, Unit

Fizz(ed), Fizzy Buck's, Effervesce, Gas, Hiss, Pop, Sherbet, Sod, Soda

Flabbergast(ed) Amaze, Astound, Floor, Thunderstruck

Flabby Flaccid, Lank, Lax, Limp, Pendulous, Saggy

Flag(gy), Flags Acorus, Ancient, Ashlar, Banderol, Banner, Black, Blue Peter, Bunting, Burgee, Chequered, Colour(s),

Decline, Droop, Duster, Ensign, Fail, Falter, Fane, Fanion, Gladdon, Gonfalon, Hail, Hoist, Iris, Jack, Jade, Jolly Roger, Kerbstone, Languish, Lis, Old Glory, Orris, Pave(ment), Pennant, Pennon, Peter, Pin, Rag, Red, Red Duster, Red Ensign, Sag, Semaphore, Sink, Slab(stone), Slack, Standard, Stars and bars, Stars and stripes, Streamer, Tire, Tricolour, Union (Jack), Vane, Waif, Whift, White (ensign), Wilt, Wither

Flagon Bottle, Carafe, Jug, Stoop, Stoup, Vessel

Flagrant Egregious, Glaring, Heinous, Patent, Wanton

Flail Beat, Drub, Swingle, Threshel

Flair Art, Bent, Elan, Gift, Knack, Panache, Style, ➤ TALENT

Flake Chip, Flame, Flaught, Flaw, Floccule, Flocculus, Fragment, Peel, Scale, Smut, Snow

Flamboyant Baroque, Brilliant, Florid, Garish, Grandiose, Ornate, Ostentatious, Paz(z)azz, Piz(z)azz, Swash-buckler

Flame, Flaming Ardent, Blaze, Fire, Flake, Flambé, Flammule, Glow, Kindle, Leman, Lover, Lowe, Oxyacetylene, Sweetheart

Flank(s) Accompany, Anta, Flange, Flitch, Ilia, Lisk, Loin, Side, Spur

Flannel Blather, Canton, Cloth, Soft-soap, Waffle, Zephyr

Flap(ped), Flapper, Flapping Aileron, Alar, Alarm(ist), Bate, Beat, Bird, Bobbysoxer, Bustle, Chit, Dither, Elevon, Epiglottis, Flag, Flaught, Flutter, Fly, Fuss, Giglet, Hover, ➤ IN A FLAP, Labrum, Lapel, Loma, Lug, Panic, Spin, Spoiler, Tab, Tag, Tailboard, Tailgate, Tiswas, To-do, Tongue, Wave, Whisk

Flare(d), Flare up Bell, Fishtail, Flame, Flanch, Flaunch, Godet, Magnesium, Scene, Signal, Spread, Spunk, Ver(e)y, Widen

Flash(y), Flasher Flare, Flaught, Fulgid, Garish, Gaudy, Gleam, Glisten, Glitzy, Instant, Lairy, Levin, Lightning, Loud, Mo, Raffish, Ribbon, Roary, Scintillation, Second, Sequin, Showy, Snazzy, Spark, Streak, Strobe, Swank(e)y, Tick, Trice, Twinkle, Vivid, Wire

▷**Flashing** may indicate an anagram

Flask Ampulla, Aryballos, Bottle, Canteen, Carafe, Costrel, Cucurbit, Dewar, Erlenmeyer, Fiasco, Flacket, Flacon, Florence, Goatskin, Hip, Lekythos, Matrass, Mick(e)y, Reform, Retort, Thermos®, Vacuum, Vial

Flat(s), Flatten(ed), Flattener Apartment, Bachelor, Bald, Banal, Beat, Blow-out, Bulldoze, Callow, Compress, Condominium, Dead, Demolish, Dress, Dull, Even, Feeble, Flew, Floor, Flue, Fool, Granny, Horizontal, Insipid, Ironed, Jacent, Key, KO, Law, Level, Lifeless, Llano, Marsh, Monotonous, Nitwit, Oblate, Pad, Pancake, Pedestrian, Penthouse, Pied-à-terre, Plain, Plane, Plat, Plateau, Prone, Prostrate, Recumbent, Rooms, Scenery, Smooth, Spread-edged, Squash, Studio, Tableland, Tame, Tasteless, Tenement, True, Vapid

Flatter(ing), Flatterer, Flattery Adulate, Beslaver, Blandish, Blarney, Bootlick, Butter, Cajole, Candied, Carn(e)y, Claw(back), Complimentary, Fawn, Flannel, Flummery, Fulsome, Honey, Imitation, Lip-salve, Moody, Palp, Poodle-faker, Puffery, Sawder, Smarm, Soap, Soother, Spaniel, Stroke, Sugar, Sweet talk, Sycophant, Taffy, Toady, Treacle, Unction, Wheedle

Flatulence Belch, Borborygmus, Burp, Carminative, Colic, Gas, Wind

Flaunt Brandish, Flourish, Gibe, Parade, Skyre, Strout, Strut, Wave

Flavour(ed), Flavouring Absinth(e), Alecost, Anethole, Angostura, Anise, Aniseed, Aroma, Bold, Borage, Bouquet garni, Clove, Coriander, Cumin, Dill, Essence, Fenugreek, Flor, Garni, Marinate, Mint, Orgeat, Quark, Race, Ratafia, Relish, Sair, Sassafras, Tack, Tang, Tarragon, ➤ TASTE, Tincture, Twang, Vanilla

Flaw Blemish, Brack, Bug, Chip, Crack, Defect, Fallacy, ➤ FAULT, Gall, Hamartia, Imperfection, Kink, Lophole, Rima, Spot, Taint, Tear, Thief, Windshake

Flax(en) Aleseed, Blonde, Codilla, Harden, Hards, Herden, Herl, Hurden, Line, Linseed, Lint, Linum, Mill-mountain, Poi, Tow

Flea Aphaniptera, Chigger, Chigoe, Chigre, Daphnid, Hopper, Itch-mite, Lop, Pulex, Sand, Water

Flee Abscond, Bolt, Decamp, Escape, Eschew, Fly, Lam, Loup, Run, Scapa, Scarper, Scram

Fleece, Fleecy Bleed, Coat, Despoil, Flocculent, Golden, Lambskin, Lanose, Pash(i)m, Pashmina, Plot, Pluck, Rifte, Ring, Rob, Rook, Shave, Shear, Sheepskin, Skin, ➤ SWINDLE, Toison

Fleet(ing) Armada, Brief, Camilla, Ephemeral, Evanescent, Fast, Flit, Flota, Flotilla, Fugacious, Fugitive, Hasty, Hollow,

Lightfoot, Navy, Pacy, Passing, Prison, Spry, Street, Transient, Velocipede

Flesh(y) Beefy, Body, Carneous, Carrion, Corporeal, Corpulent, Creatic, Digastric, Finish, Gum, Hypersarcoma, Joint, Longpig, Lush, Meat, Mons, Muscle, Pulp, Sarcous, Spare tyre, Tissue

Flex(ible), Flexibility Adaptable, Bend(y), Elastic, Genu, Limber, Lissom(e), Lithe, Pliant, ➤ RESILIENT, Rubbery, Squeezy, Tensile, Tonus, Wieldy, Willing, Wiry

▷**Flexible, Flexuous** may indicate an anagram

Flick(er), Flicks Bioscope, Cinema, Fillip, Film, Flip, Flirt, Flutter, Glimmer, Gutter, Movie, Movy, Snap, Snow, Switch, Talkie, Twinkle, Waver

Flier Airman, Alcock, Amy, Aviator, Blimp, Brown, Crow, Daedalus, Erk, Fur, George, Gotha, Handout, Icarus, Leaflet, Lindbergh, Pilot, ➤ RAF, Scotsman, Spec, Speedy

▷**Flier** may indicate a bird

Flight(y) Backfisch, Birdbrain, Bolt, Bubble-headed, Capricious, Charter, Dart, Departure, Escalier, Escape, Exaltation, Exodus, Fast, Fickle, Flaught, Flibbertigibbet, Flip, Flock, Flyby, Fugue, Giddy, Grese, Grise, Guy, Hegira, Hejira, Hejra, Hellicat, Hijra, Lam, Milk-run, Open-jaw, Pair, R(a)iser, Redeye, Ro(a)ding, Rode, Rout, Skein, Sortie, Stairs, ➤ STAMPEDE, Steps, Swarm, Tower, Trap, Vol(age), Volatile, Volley, Whisky-frisky, Wing

▷**Flighty** may indicate an anagram

Flimsy Finespun, Gimcrack, Gossamer, Jimcrack, Sleazy, Sleezy, Tenuous, Thin, Weak, Wispy

Flinch Blench, Cringe, Funk, Quail, Recoil, Shrink, Shudder, Start, Wince

Fling Dance, Flounce, Highland, Hurl, Pitch, Shy, Slat, Slug, Slump, Spanghew, Spree, Throw, ➤ TOSS

Flint Chert, Firestone, Granite, Hag-stone, Hornstone, Pirate, Rock, Silex, Microlith, Mischmetal, Silica, Stone, Touchstone

Flip(pant), Flipping Airy, Bally, Brash, Cocky, Flick, Frivolous, Impudent, Jerk, Nog, Pert, Purl, Sassy, Saucy, Toss, Turn

Flirt(ing), Flirtatious Bill, Buaya, Carve, Chippy, Cockteaser, Come-hither, Come-on, Coquet(te), Dalliance, Demivierge, Footsie, Gallivant, Heart-breaker, Mash, Minx, Neck, Philander(er), Prick-teaser, Rig, Toy, Trifle, Vamp, Wow

Float(er), Floating Balsa, Bob, Buoy, Caisson, Carley, Clanger, Drift, Fleet, Flutterboard, Levitate, Lifebuoy, Milk, Neuston, Oropesa, Outrigger, Planula, Pontoon, Pram, Quill, Raft, Ride, Sail, Skim, Sponson, Trimmer, Vacillate, Waft, Waggler, Waterwings

Flock(s) Assemble, Bevy, Charm, Chirm, Company, Congregation, Drove, Flight, Fold, Forgather, Gaggle, Gather, Gregatim, Herd, Mob, Rally, Sedge, Sord, Spring, Trip, Tuft, Vulgar, Wing, Wisp, Wool

Flog(ger), Flogging Beat, Birch, Breech, Cane, Cat, Exert, Flay, Hawk, Hide, Knout, Lace, Lambast, Larrup, Lash, Lather, Lick, Orbilius, Rope's end, Scourge, Sell, Strap, Tat, ➤ THRASH, Thwack, Tout, Vapulate, Welt, Whip

Flood Bore, Cataclysm, Deluge, Deucalion, Diluvium, Dump, Eger, Flash, Freshet, Gush, Inundate, Irrigate, Noachic, Overflow, Overwhelm, Pour, Rage, Smurf, Spate, Speat, Swamp, Tide, ➤ TORRENT, Undam

Floor(ing) Area, Astound, Baffle, Chess, Deck, Dev(v)el, Down, Entresol, Etage, Fell, Flags(tone), Flatten, Flight, Gravel, Kayo, KO, Parquet, Piano nobile, Planch, Platform, Puncheon, Screed, Stage, Story, Stump, Tessella, Tessera, Thill, Woodblock

Flop Belly-landing, Bomb, Collapse, Dud, Failure, Fizzer, Fosbury, Lollop, Mare's-nest, Misgo, Phut, Plump, Purler, Washout, Whap, Whitewash

Florid Coloratura, Cultism, Flamboyant, Fresh, Gongorism, High, Red, Rococo, Rubicund, Ruddy, Taffeta

Flotsam Detritus, Driftwood, Flotage, Waift, Waveson, Weft

Flounce Falbala, Frill, Furbelow, Huff, Prance, Ruffle, Sashay, Toss

Flounder Blunder, Fluke, Reel, Slosh, Struggle, Stumble, Tolter, Toss, Wallow

Flour Cassava, Couscous(ou), Cribble, Crible, Farina, Graham, Gram, Kouskous, Meal, Middlings, Pinole, Powder, Red-dog, Wheatmeal, Wholegrain, Wholemeal, Wholewheat

Flourish(ed), Flourishing Blague, Bless, Bloom, Blossom, Boast, Brandish, Bravura, Burgeon, Cadenza, Epiphonema, Fanfare, Fiorita, Fl, Flare, Grow, Kicking, Melisma, Mort, Palmy, Paraph, Prosper, Rubric, Scroll, Swash, Tantara, Thrive, Tucket, Veronica, Vigorous, Wampish, Wave, Welfare

Flow(ing) Abound, Afflux, Cantabile, Cash, Current, Cursive, Cusec, Distil, Ebb, Emanate, Estrang(h)elo, Fleet, Fluent, Fluid, Flush, Flux, Freeform, Gush, Knickpoint, Laminar, Liquid, Loose-bodied, Nappe, Nickpoint, Obsequent, Onrush, Ooze, Popple, Pour, Purl, Rail(e), Rayle, Rill, Rin, Run, Scapa, Seamless, Setter, Slur, Spate, Stream, Streamline, Teem, Tidal, Torrent

Flower (part), Flowering, Flowers, Flower bed Best, Bloom, Bloosme, Blossom, Boutonniere, Buttonhole, Cream, Develop, Efflorescence, Elite, Inflorescence, Knot, Nosegay, Parterre, Plant, Prime, ➤ RIVER, Spray, Stalked, Stream, Wreath

▷ **Flower** may indicate a river

Flu Asian, Grippe, Lurgi, Yuppie

Fluctuate(r), Fluctuation Ambivalence, Balance, Seiche, Trimmer, Unsteady, Vacillate, Vary, Waver

Flue Chimney, Duct, Funnel, Pipe, Tewel, Uptake, Vent

Fluent(ly) Eloquent, Facile, Flowing, Glib, Liquid, Oracy, Verbose, Voluble

Fluff(y) Bungle, Dowl(e), Down, Dust, Feathery, Flocculent, Floss, Flue, Fug, Fuzz, Girl, Lint, Muff, Noil, Oose, Ooze, Thistledown

Fluid Amniotic, Anasarca, Ascites, Broo, Chyle, Cisterna, Colostrum, Condy's, Enema, Fixative, Fl, Humour, Juice, ➤ LIQUID, Lymph, Mucus, Oedema, Perilymph, Plasma, Sap, Serum, Shifting, Succus, Synovia, Vitreum, Vril, Water

▷ **Fluid** may indicate an anagram

Fluke Accident, Anchor, Chance, Fan, Flounder, Ga(u)nch, Grapnel, Killock, Liver, Lobe, Redia, Scratch

Flush(ed) Affluent, Beat, Even, Ferret, Florid, Flow, Gild, Hectic, Hot, Level, Red, Rolling, Rose, Royal, Rud, Scour, Sluice, Spaniel, Start, Straight, Sypher, Thrill, Tierce, Vigour, Wash

Fluster Befuddle, Confuse, Disconcert, Faze, Flap, Rattle, Shake

Flute (player) Bellows-maker, Bohm, Channel, Claribel(la), Crimp, Fife, Fipple, Flageolet, Glass, Glyph, Groove, Marsyas, Nose, Ocarina, Piccolo, Pipe, Poogye(e), Quena, Shakuhachi, Sulcus, Thisbe, Tibia, Toot, Transverse, Whistle

Flutter Bat, Bet, Fan, Fibrillate, Flacker, Flaffer, Flaught, Flichter, Flicker, Flitter, Fly, ➤ GAMBLE, Hover, Palpitate, Play, Pulse, Sensation, Twitter, Waft, Winnow

Fly(ing), Flies Abscond, Agaric, Airborne, Alert, Astute, Aviation, Awake, A-wing, Bolt, Cab, Carriage, Cock-a-bondy, ➤ CUNNING, Decamp, Doctor, Dry, Escape, Fiacre, Flee, Flit, Glide, Hackle, Hedge-hop, Hop, Hurtle, Laputan, March brown, Murragh, Opening, Palmer, Para, Pilot, Rapid, Saucer, Scotsman, Scud, Smart, Soar, Speed, Spinner, Tear, Volatic, Volitate, Wide-awake, Wily, Wing, Yogic, Zipper

Fly-catcher Attercop, Cobweb, Darlingtonia, Dionaea, King-bird, Phoebe, Spider, Tanrec, Tyrant

Foam(ing) Barm, Bubble, Froth, Lather, Mousse, Oasis®, Polystyrene, Ream, Scum, Seethe, Spindrift, Spooming, Spume, Sud(s), Surf, Yeast, Yest

Focal, Focus Centre, Converge, Fix, Hinge, Hub, Narrow, Pinpoint, Point, Spotlight, Train

Fodder Alfalfa, Browsing, Buckwheat, Cannon, Clover, Eatage, Ensilage, Foon, Forage, Gama-grass, Grama, Guar, Hay, Lucerne, Oats, Pasture, Provender, Rye-grass, Sainfoin, Silage, Stover

Foe Contender, ➤ ENEMY, Opponent, Rival

Fog Aerosol, Brume, Cloud, Damp, Fret, Haar, Miasm(a), Mist, Murk, Obscure, Pea-soup(er), Roke, Sea-fret, Sea-haar, Smog, Smoke, Soup, Thick, Vapour, Yorkshire

Foil(ed) Ba(u)lk, Chaff, Cross, Dupe, Epée, Fleurette, Frustrate, Lametta, Leaf, Offset, Paillon, Pip, Scotch, Silver, Stooge, Stump, Thwart, Touché

Fold(ed), Folder, Folding Close, Collapse, Concertina, Corrugate, Crease, Crimp, Crinkle, Fan, Frill, Furl, Gather, Jack-knife, Monocline, Nappe, Pintuck, ➤ PLEAT, Ply, Ruck(le), Sheep-pen, Syncline, Tuck, Wrap

Foliage Coma, Finial, Frond, Greenery, Leafage

Follow(er), Following Adhere, After, Agree, Anthony, Attend(ant), Believer, Clientele, Consequence, Copy, Dangle, Disciple, Dog, Echo, Ensew, Ensue, Entourage, Epigon(e), Equipage, F, Fan, Groupie, Heel(er), Henchman, Hereon, Hunt, Man, Merry men, Muggletonian, Myrmidon, Neist, Next, Obey, Pan, Post, Pursue, Rake, Road, Run, Satellite, School, Secundum, Seewing, Segue, Sequel, Seriation, Shadow, Sheep, Sidekick, Stag, Stalk, Stear, Steer, Subsequent, Succeed, Sue, Suivez, Supervene, Tag, Tail, Tantony, Trace, Track, Trail, Train, Use, Vocation, Votary

▷**Follower** 'a follower' may indicate B

Folly Antic, Bêtise, Idiocy, Idiotcy, Imprudence, Lunacy, Mistake, Moria, Unwisdom, Vanity

Fond(ness) Amatory, Ardour, Dote, Keen, Loving, Partial, Tender, Tendre

Fondle Canoodle, Caress, Dandle, Grope, Hug, Nurse, Pet, Snuggle

Food Aliment, Ambrosia, Board, Broth, Bully, Burger, Cate, Cheer, Cheese, Chop, Chow, Collation, Comestible, Commons, Course, ► DISH, Eats, Fare, Fodder, Forage, Fuel, Grub, Keep, Manna, Meat, Nosh, Nourishment, Pasta, Provender, Provision, Scoff, Snack, Staple, Stodge, Table, Tack, Takeaway, Trimmings, Tuck(er), Viand, Victuals, Waffle

Fool(hardy), Foolish(ness) April, Berk, Buffoon, Chump, Clot, Clown, Cockeyed, Coxcomb, Delude, Dummy, Dunce, Flannel(led), Folly, Gaby, Gaga, Git, Goat, Goon, Goose, Gubbins, Gull, Halfwit, Idiotic, Imbecile, Inane, Jest, Joke, Kid, Lark, Mislead, Moron, Muggins, Ni(n)compoop, Ninny, Senseless, Soft, Sot, ► STUPID, Trifle, Zany

Foot(ing), Footwork, Feet Anap(a)est, Athlete's, Base, Choliamb, Choriamb, Club, Dactyl, Dance, Hoof, Iamb(us), Infantry, Pad, Paeon, Paw, Podium, Shanks's pony, Standing, Tarsus, Terms, Tootsie, Tread, Trench, Trochee, Trotter

Football(er) Back, Barbarian, Ba'spiel, Camp, Centre, Fantasy, FIFA, Flanker(back), Gaelic, Goalie, Gridder, Keeper, Kicker, Libero, Lineman, Lock, Midfield, Pack, Pele, Pigskin, RU, Rugby, Rugger, Rules, Safety, Soccer(oos), Sport, Striker, Sweeper, Table, Total, Touch(back), Wing

Footman Attendant, Flunkey, Lackey, Pedestrian, Pompey, Yellowplush

Footprint Ichnite, Ichnolite, Pad, Prick, Pug, Seal, Slot, Trace, Track, Vestige

Footwear Gumboot, ► SHOE, Slipper, Sock, Spats, Stocking

Fop(pish) Apery, Barbermonger, Beau, Buck, Cat, Coxcomb, Dandy, Dude, Exquisite, Fallal, Fantastico, Finical, La-di-da, Macaroni, Monarcho, Muscadin, Popinjay, Skipjack, Toff

For Ayes, Because, Concerning, Cos, Pro, Since, To

Forage Alfalfa, Fodder, Graze, Greenfeed, Lucern(e), Pickeer, Prog, Raid, Rummage, Sainfoin, Search

Forbear(ance), Forbearing Abstain, Clement, Endure, Indulgent, Lenience, Lineage, Longanimity, Mercy, Pardon, Parent, Patient, Quarter, ➤ REFRAIN, Suffer, Tolerant, Withhold

Forbid(den), Forbidding Ban, Bar, City, Denied, Don't, Dour, Enjoin, For(e)speak, Gaunt, Grim, Haram, Hostile, Loury, NL, Prohibit, Stern, Taboo, Tabu, Tapu, Tref(a), Verboten, Veto

Force(d), Forceful, Forces, Forcible Agency, Army, Bludgeon, Body, Brigade, Bring, Brunt, Bulldoze, Centrifugal, Coerce, Commando, Compel, Constrain, Cram, Detachment, Domineer, Dragoon, Drive, Duress(e), Emphatic, Energetic, Expeditionary, Fire brigade, Frogmarch, Gendarmerie, Host, Impetus, Impress, Inertial, Juggernaut, Kinetic, Labour, Legion, Life, Make, Manpower, Muscle, Oblige, Od, Personnel, Police, Posse, Potent, Press(gang), Pressure, Prise, Pull, Railroad, Rape, Ravish, Reave, Require, SAS, Steam(roller), ➤ STRESS, Strong-arm, Subject, TA, Task, Thrust, Torque, Troops, Vehement, Vigorous, Violence, Vim, Vital, Vociferous, Wrench, Wrest, Wring, Zap

▷ **Force(d)** may indicate an anagram

▶ **Forebear** see FORBEAR

Foreboding Anxiety, Augury, Cloudage, Croak, Feeling, Freet, ➤ OMEN, Ominous, Presage, Presentiment, Sinister, Zoomantic

Forecast(er), Forecasting Augury, Auspice, Divine, Extrapolation, Horoscope, Metcast, Perm, Precurse, Predict, Presage, Prescience, Prognosis, Prognosticate, Prophesy, Rainbird, Shipping, Soothsay, Spae, Tip, Weather

Forehead Brow, Front(let), Glabella(r), Sincipitum, Temple

Foreign(er) Alien, Arab, Auslander, Barbarian, Easterling, Eleanor, Ethnic, Exclave, Exotic, External, Extraneous, Extrinsic, Forane, Forinsecal, Forren, Fraim, Fremit, Gaijin, German, Gringo, Gweilo, Malihini, Metic, Moit, Mote, Outlander, Outside, Oversea, Peregrine, Remote, ➤ STRANGE, Stranger, Taipan, Tramontane, Uitlander, Unfamiliar, Wog

Foreman Baas, Boss, Bosun, Chancellor, Gaffer, Ganger, Manager, Overseer, Steward, Superintendent, Topsman

Foremost First, Front, Leading, Prime, Primary, Supreme, Van

▷ **Foremost** may indicate first letters of words following

Forerunner Augury, Harbinger, Herald, Messenger, Omen, Pioneer, Precursor, Trailer, Vaunt-courier

Foreshadow Adumbrate, Augur, Bode, Forebode, Hint, Portend, Prefigure, Presage, Type

Foresight Ganesa, Prescience, Prophecy, Prospect, Providence, Prudence, Taish, Vision

Forest Arden, Ashdown, Black, Bush, Caatinga, Charnwood, Chase, Cloud, Dean, Epping, Gallery, Gapo, Glade, Greenwood, Igapo, Jungle, Monte, Nandi, Nemoral, New, Savernake, Selva, Sherwood, Taiga, Urman, Virgin, ➤ WOOD

Foretaste Antepast, Antipasto, Appetiser, Pregustation, Prelibation, Sample, Trailer

Foretell(ing), Forewarn Augur, Bode, Caution, Divine, Fatidic, Forecast, Portend, Predict, Premonish, Presage, Prognosticate, Prophecy, Soothsay, Spae

Forethought Anticipation, Caution, Prometheus, Provision, Prudence

Forever Always, Amber, Ay(e), Eternal, Evermore, Keeps

▶**Forewarn** see FORETELL

Foreword Introduction, Preamble, Preface, Proem, Prologue

For example Eg, Say, Vg, ZB

Forfeit Deodand, Fine, Forgo, ➤ PENALTY, Relinquish, Rue-bargain, Sconce

Forge(d), Forger(y) Blacksmith, Copy, Counterfeit, Drop, Dud, Fabricate, Fashion, Foundry, Hammer, Heater, Horseshoe, Ireland, Lauder, Mint, Paper-hanger, Pigott, Progress, Smith(y), Smithery, Spurious, Stiff, Stithy, Stumer, Tilt, Trucage, Truquage, Utter, Valley, Vermeer, Vulcan

Forget(ful), Forget-me-not Amnesia, Dry, Fluff, Lethe, Myosotis, Neglect, Oblivious, Omit, Overlook

Forgive(ness), Forgiving Absolution, Amnesty, Clement, Condone, Merciful, Overlook, Pardon, Placable, Remission, Remittal

Forgo(ne) Abstain, Expected, Refrain, Renounce, Waive

Fork(ed) Bifurcate, Biramous, Branch, Caudine, Cleft, Crotch, Divaricate, Forficate, Fourchette, Grain, Graip, Morton's, Osmeterium, Prong, Runcible, Tine, Toaster, Tormentor, Tormentum, Trident, Trifid, Tuner, Tuning, Y

Form(s) Alumni, Bench, Bumf, Cast, Ceremonial, Class, Constitute, Coupon, Create, Document, Experience, Fashion, Feature, Fig, ➤ FIGURE, Formula, Game, Gestalt, Hare, Image,

Keto, Mode, Mood, Mould, Order, Originate, ➤ OUT OF FORM,
Protocol, Questionnaire, Redia, Remove, Rite, Ritual, Schedule,
Shape, Shell, Stage, Stamp, State, Structure, Style, Symmetry,
Version

Formal Conventional, Dry, Exact, Fit, Literal, Methodic, Official,
Pedantic, Precise, Prim, Routine, Set, Starched, Stiff, Stodgy,
Tails

Formality Ceremony, Ice, Pedantry, Protocol, Punctilio, Starch

Formation Battalion, Configuration, Diapyesis, Echelon,
Eocene, Fours, Growth, Line, Manufacture, Origin, Pattern,
Phalanx, Prophase, Riss, Wedge

▷**Former** may indicate something that forms

Former(ly) Ance, Auld, Before, Ci-devant, Earlier, Ere-now,
Erst(while), Ex, Late, Maker, Matrix, Old, Once, One-time, Past,
Previous, Prior, Pristine, Quondam, Sometime, Then, Umquhile,
Whilom

Formidable Alarming, Armipotent, Battleaxe, Fearful,
Forbidding, Gorgon, Powerful, Shrewd, Stoor, Stour, Stowre,
Sture, Tiger

▷**Form of, Forming** may indicate an anagram

Formula(te) Define, Devise, Doctrine, Equation, Frame,
Invent, Lurry, Paternoster, Protocol, Prescription, ➤ RECIPE, Rite,
Ritual

Fort(ification), Fortress Acropolis, Alamo, Bastille,
Battlement, Blockhouse, Burg, Casbah, Castle, Citadel,
Earthwork, Fastness, Fieldwork, Garrison, Haven, Kasba(h),
Keep, La(a)ger, Pa(h), Peel, Rampart, Ravelin, Redoubt, Salient,
Stronghold, Tower

Forthright Candid, Direct, Frank, Prompt

Fortify Arm, Augment, Brace, Casemate, Embattle, Lace,
Munify, Steel, ➤ STRENGTHEN

Fortitude Endurance, Grit, Mettle, Patience, Pluck, ➤ STAMINA

Fortunate Auspicious, Blessed, Blest, Happy, ➤ LUCKY,
Providential, Well

Fortune (teller), Fortune-telling Auspicious, Bonanza,
Bumby, Cartomancy, Chaldee, Cha(u)nce, Destiny,
Dukkeripen, Fame, Fate, Felicity, Genethliac, Geomancy, Hap,
Hydromancy, I Ching, Lot, Luck, Mint, Motser, Motza, Oracle,
Packet, Palmist, Peripety, Pile, Prescience, Pyromancy, Sibyl,

Soothsayer, Sortilege, Spaewife, Success, Taroc, Tarok, Tarot, Tyche, Wealth, Windfall

Forum Arena, Assembly, Debate, Platform, Tribunal

Forward(s) Accede, Advanced, Ahead, Along, Arch, Assertive, Assuming, Bright, Early, Flanker, Forrad, Forrit, Forth, Fresh, Future, Hasten, Hooker, Immodest, Impudent, Insolent, Lock, Malapert, On(wards), Pack, Pert, Petulant, Porrect, Precocious, ➤ PROGRESS, Promote, Prop, Readdress, Redirect, Scrum, Send, Stem, To(ward), Van, Wing

Fossil(ise), Fossils Derived, Fogy, Index, Petrifaction, Relics, Reliquiae, Remanié, Taphonomy, Trace

Foster (child, mother), Fostering Adopt, Cherish, Da(u)lt, Develop, Feed, Forment, Further, Harbour, Incubation, Metapelet, Metaplot, Nourish, Nourse(l), Noursle, Nousell, Nurse, Nurture, Nuzzle, ➤ REAR

Foul, Foul-smelling Base, Beray, Besmirch, Besmutch, Bewray, Bungle, ➤ DEFILE, Dreggy, Drevill, Enseam, Evil, Feculent, Gross, Hassle, Hing, Mephitic, Mud, Noisome, Olid, Osmeterium, Professional, Putid, Putrid, ➤ RANK, Reekie, Rotten, Sewage, Soiled, Squalid, Stagnant, Stain, Stapelia, Technical, Unclean, Unfair, Vile, Violation, Virose

▷**Foul** may indicate an anagram

Found (in) Among, Base, Bed, Bottom, Build, Cast, Emong, Endow, ➤ ESTABLISH, Eureka, Institute, Introduce, Met, Occur, Plant, Recovered, Rest, Start, Table

Foundation(s) Base, Bedrock, Cribwork, Establishment, Footing, Girdle, Grillage, Ground, Groundwork, Hard-core, Infrastructure, Institution, Matrix, Pile, Roadbed, Rockefeller, Scholarship, Stays, Substrata, Substructure, Trackbed, Underlie, Underlinen

▷**Foundations** may indicate last letters

Founder Author, Crumple, Fail, Inventor, Iron-master, Miscarry, Oecist, Oekist, Patriarch, Perish, Settle, Sink, Stumble

Fountain Acadine, Aganippe, Bubbler, Castalian, Cause, Conduit, Drinking, Fauwara, Forts, Gerbe, Head, Hippocrene, Jet, Pant, Pirene, Salmacis, Scuttlebutt, Soda, Spring, Trevi, Youth

Four(some) Cater, Georges, Horsemen, IV, Mess, Quartet, Quaternary, Quaternion, Reel, Tessara, Tessera, Tetrad, Tetralogy, Tiddy, Warp

Fourth Deltaic, Estate, Fardel, Forpet, Forpit, July, Quartet, Quaternary, Quintan, Sesquitertia, Tritone

Fowl Barnyard, Biddy, Boiler, Brahma, Brissle-cock, Burrow-duck, Capon, Chicken, Chittagong, Cob, Cock, Coot, Duck, Ember, Gallinaceous, Gallinule, Game, Guinea, Hamburg(h), ➤ HEN, Houdan, Jungle, Kora, Leghorn, Moorhen, Partridge, Pheasant, Pintado, Poultry, Quail, Rooster, Rumkin, Rumpy, Solan, Spatchcock, Spitchcock, Sultan, Sussex, Teal, Turkey, Wyandotte

Fox(y) Alopecoid, Arctic, Baffle, Blue, Charley, Charlie, Corsac, Cunning, Desert, Fennec, Fool, Friend, Fur, Grey, Kit, Lowrie(-tod), Outwit, Pug, Puzzle, Quaker, Red, Reynard, Rommel, Russel, Silver, Skulk, ➤ SLY (BOOTS), Swift, Tod, Uffa, Uneatable, Vixen, White, Zerda, Zoril(le), Zorro

Fracas Brawl, Dispute, Mêlée, Prawle, Riot, Rumpus, Shindig, Uproar

Fraction Complex, Improper, Ligroin, Mantissa, Part, Piece, Proper, Scrap, Simple, Some, Vulgar

Fracture Break, Colles, Comminuted, Compound, Crack, Fault, Fissure, Greenstick, Hairline, Impacted, Pott's, Rupture, Split, Stress

Fragile Brittle, Crisp, Delicate, Frail, Frangible, Nesh, Slender, Tender, Vulnerable, Weak

Fragment(s) Atom, Bit, Bla(u)d, Brash, Breccia, Brockram, Cantlet, Clastic, Crumb, End, Flinder, Fritter, Frust, Graile, Lapilli, Mammock, Morceau, Morsel, Ort, ➤ PARTICLE, Piece, Potshard, Potsherd, Relic, Rubble, Scrap, Segment, Shard, Shatter, Sheave, Shiver, Shrapnel, Skerrick, Sliver, Smithereens, Smithers, Snatch, Splinter

▷**Fragment of** may indicate a hidden word

Fragrance, Fragrant Aromatic, Attar, Bouquet, Conima, Nosy, Odour, Olent, ➤ PERFUME, Pot-pourri, Redolent, ➤ SCENT, Sent, Spicy, Suaveolent

Frail Brittle, Creaky, Delicate, Feeble, Flimsy, ➤ FRAGILE, Puny, Slight, Slimsy, Weak

Frame(work) Angle, Body, Build, Cage, Case, Casement, Casing, Chassis, Cold, Cradle, Fabric, Form, Gantry, Lattice, Louvre, Pergola, Rack, Scaffold, Setting, Skeleton, ➤ STRUCTURE, Zimmer®

Franchise Charter, Contract, Liberty, Privilege, Right, Suffrage, Vote, Warrant

Frank(ish) Blunt, ➤ CANDID, Direct, Easy, Free, Free-spoken, Honest, Ingenuous, Man-to-man, Merovingian, Natural, Open, Outspoken, Postage, Postmark, Ripuarian, Salian, Sincere, Stamp, Straight, Sty, Upfront

Frantic Demoniac, Deranged, Distraught, Frenzied, Hectic, Mad, Overwrought, Phrenetic, Rabid, Violent, Whirl(ing)

▷**Frantic** may indicate an anagram

Fraternise, Fraternity Affiliate, Brotherhood, Burschenschaft, Consort, Elk, Fellowship, Lodge, Mingle, Moose, Order

Fraud(ulent) Barratry, Bobol, Bubble, Charlatan, Cheat, Chisel, Collusion, Covin, Cronk, Deceit, Diddle, Do, Fineer, Gyp, Humbug, Hypocrite, ➤ IMPOSTOR, Imposture, Jiggery-pokery, Jobbery, Liar, Peculator, Piltdown, Pious, Pseud(o), Put-up, Ringer, Rip-off, Roguery, Rort, Scam, South Sea Bubble, Stellionate, Supercherie, Swindle, Swiz(z), Swizzle, Tartuffe, Trick

Fray(ed) Bagarre, Brawl, Contest, Feaze, Frazzle, Fret, Fridge, Ravel, Riot, Scrimmage

Freak Cantrip, Caprice, Chimera, Control, Deviant, Geek, Sport, Teras, Whim, Whimsy

Free(d), Freely Acquit, Assoil, Buckshee, Candid, Canny, Church, Clear, Cuffo, Dead-head, Deregulate, Devoid, Disburden, Disburthen, Disengage, Eleutherian, Emancipate, Enfranchise, Enlarge, Excuse, Exeem, Exeme, Exempt, Exonerate, Extricate, Familiar, Footloose, Frank, French, Gratis, House, Idle, Immune, Independent, Kick, Large, Lavish, Lax, Leisure, Let, Liberate, Loose, Manumit, Open, Parole, Pro bono, Quit(e), Range, Ransom, Redeem, ➤ RELEASE, Relieve, Rescue, Reskew, Rick, Rid, Sciolto, Solute, Spring, Stald, Stall, Trade, Unlock, Unmew, Unmuzzle, Unshackle, Unsnarl, Untie, Vacant, Verse, Voluntary

▷**Free** may indicate an anagram

Freedom Abandon, Autonomy, Breadth, Carte blanche, Eleutherian, Exemption, Fear, Fling, Four, Immunity, Impunity, Latitude, Liberty, Licence, Play, Releasement, Speech, Uhuru, UNITA, Want, Worship

Freehold(er) Enfeoff, Franklin, Frank tenement, Seisin, Udal(ler), Yeoman

▷**Freely** may indicate an anagram

Freemason(ry), Freemason's son Craft, Lewis, Lodge, Moose, Templar

Freeze(r), Freezing Alcarrazo, Benumb, Congeal, Cool, Cryogenic, Eutectic, Freon®, Frost, Harden, Ice, Lyophilize, Nip, Numb, Paralyse, Regelate, Riss, Stiffen

Freight Cargo, Carriage, Fraught, Goods, Load

French(man), Frenchwoman Alsatian, Basque, Breton, Crapaud, Creole, Dawn, Frog, Gallic(e), Gaston, Gaul, Gombo, Grisette, Gumbo, Huguenot, Joual, M, Mamselle, Marianne, Midi, Mounseer, Neo-Latin, Norman, Parleyvoo, René, Rhemish, Savoyard

Frenzied, Frenzy Amok, Berserk, Corybantic, Deliration, Delirium, Demoniac, Enrage, Enrapt, Euhoe, Euoi, Evoe, Fit, Fury, Hectic, Hysteric, Lune, Maenad, Mania, Must, Nympholepsy, Oestrus, Phrenetic, Rage

Frequency, Frequent(er), Frequently Attend, Audio, Channel, Common, Constant, Familiar, Formant, FR, Fresnel, Habitué, Hang-out, Haunt, Hertz, High, Incidence, Megahertz, Often, Penetration, Pulsatance, Radio, Recurrent, Spectrum, Superhigh, Thick

Fresh(en), Freshness Aurorean, Brash, Caller, Chilly, Clean, Crisp, Dewy, Entire, Forward, Green, Hot, Insolent, Lively, Maiden, New, Novel, Quick, Rebite, Recent, Roral, Roric, Rorid, Smart, Span-new, Spick, Sweet, Tangy, Uncured, Verdure, Vernal, Virent

Fret(ful) Chafe, Filigree, Fray, Grate, Grecque, Haze, Impatient, Irritate, Ornament, Peevish, Repine, Rile, Ripple, Roil, Rub, Tetchy, Tracery, Whittle, Worry

Friar(s) Augustinian, Austin, Bacon, Barefoot, Black, Brother, Bungay, Capuchin, Carmelite, Conventual, Cordelier, Crutched, Curtal, Dervish, Dominican, Fra(ter), Franciscan, Frate, Jacobin, Laurence, Limiter, Lymiter, Minim, Minorite, ➤ MONK,

Observant, Observantine, Predicant, Recollect, Recollet, Rush, Tuck, White

Friction Attrition, Conflict, Dissent, Drag, Rift, Rub, Stridulation, Tribology, Tripsis, Wear, Xerotripsis

Friend(ly), Friends Ally, Alter ego, Ami(cable), Amigo, Benign, Bosom, Bud(dy), China, Chum, Cobber, Companion, Confidant, Comrade, Cordial, Crony, Damon, Familiar, Gossip, Intimate, Mate, Pal, Pen, Quaker, Sidekick, Sociable, Sport, Steady

Friendliness, Friendship Amity, Bonhomie, Camaraderie, Contesseration, Entente, Platonic, Sodality

Fright(en), Frightened, Frightful Afear, Affear(e), Agrise, Agrize, Agryze, Alarm, Aroint, Aroynt, Ashake, Chilling, Cow, Dare, Daunt, Deter, Eek, Eerie, Faceache, Fear(some), Flay, Fleg, Fleme, Fley, Flush, Gallow, Gally, Ghast, Gliff, Glift, Grim, Grisly, Hairy, Horrid, Horrific, Intimidate, Ordeal, Panic, Scar, ➤ SCARE, Scarre, Scaur, Schrecklich, Sight, Skear, Skeer, Skrik, Spook, Stage, Startle, Terrible, Terrify, Terror, Tirrit, Unco, Windy

Frill Armil, Armilla, Bavolet, Falbala, Furbelow, Jabot, Ornament, Papillote, Ruche, Ruff(le), Tucker, Valance

▷ **Frilly** may indicate an anagram

Fringe(d) Bang, Border, Bullion, Ciliated, Ciliolate, Edge, Fall, Fimbria, Frisette, Laciniate, Loma, Lunatic, Macramé, Macrami, Pelmet, Peripheral, Robin, Ruff, Run, Thrum, Toupee, Toupit, Tzitzith, Valance, Verge, Zizith

Frisk(y) Caper, Cavort, Curvet, Fisk, Flimp, Frolic, Gambol, Search, Skip, Wanton

Fritter Batter, Beignet, Dribble, Dwindle, Fragment, Fribble, Pakora, Potter, Puf(f)taloon, Squander, Waste

Frivolous Butterfly, Empty(-headed), Featherbrain, Flighty, Flippant, Frothy, Futile, Giddy, Idle, Inane, Light, Lightweight, Playboy, Skittish, Trifling, Trivial

Frog Anoura, Anura, Batrachia(n), Braid, Bullfrog, Depression, Fourchette, Frenchman, Frush, Goliath, Hairy, Hyla, Marsupial, Mounseer, Nic, Nototrema, Paddock, Paradoxical, Peeper, Pelobatid, Platanna, Puddock, Puttock, Rana, Ranidae, Tree, Wood, Xenopus

Frolic(some) Bender, Bust(er), Cabriole, Caper, Disport, Escapade, ➤ FRISK(Y), Fun, Galravage, Galravitch, Gambol,

Gammock, Gil(l)ravage, Jink, Kittenish, Lark, Play, Prank, Rag, Rand, Rig, Romp, Scamper, Skylark, Splore, Sport, Spree, Tittup, Wanton

From A, Against, Ex, For, Frae, Off, Thrae

Front(al), Frontman Antependium, Anterior, Bow, Brass, Brow, Cold, Cover, Dead, Dickey, Dicky, Facade, Face, Fore(head), Foreground, Groof, Grouf, Head, Home, Metope, National, Newscaster, Occluded, Paravant, People's, Plastron, Polar, Popular, Pose, Pro, Prom, Prow, Sector, Sinciput, Stationary, Tabula, Van, Vaward, Warm, Western

Frost(ing), Frosty Alcorza, Chill, Cranreuch, Cryo-, Freon®, Frigid, Frore(n), Frorne, Glacé, Ground, Hoar, Hore, Ice, Icing, Jack, Mat, Rime, White

Froth(y) Barm, Bubble, Cuckoospit, Despumate, Foam, Frogspit, Gas, Head, Lather, Off-scum, Ream, Saponin, Scum, Seethe, Shallow, Spoom, Spoon, Spume, Sud, Yeasty, Yest

Frugal Meagre, Parsimonious, Provident, Prudent, Scant, Skimpy, Spare, Spartan, Thrifty

Fruit(ing), Fruit tree, Fruity Achene, Ackee, Akene, Allocarpy, Apothecium, Autocarp, Bacciform, Berry, Caryopsis, Clingstone, Coccus, Compot(e), Confect, Conserve, Cremocarp, Crop, Cypsela, Dessert, Drupe, Eater, Encarpus, Etaerio, Follicle, Forbidden, Freestone, Fritter, Harvest, Issue, Key, Nut, Orchard, Pomace, Poof, Product(ion), Pseudocarp, Punicaceae, Raisin, Rath(e)ripe, Regma(ta), Rennet, Replum, Result, Return, Rich, Schizocarp, Seed, Soft, Sorosis, Stoneless, Succade, Syconium, Syncarp, Utricle, Valve, Xylocarp, Yield

Fruitful(ness) Calathus, Ephraim, Fat, Fecund, Feracious, Fertile, Productive, Prolific, Uberty, Worthwhile

Frustrate Baffle, Ba(u)lk, Beat, Blight, Bugger, Check, Confound, Dash, Discomfit, Dish, Foil, Hogtie, Outwit, Scotch, Stymie, Thwart

Fry, Fried Blot, Brit, Fricassee, Fritter, Frizzle, Parr, Sauté, Small, Spawn, Whippersnapper, Whitebait

Fuddle(d) Drunk, Fluster, Fuzzle, Maudlin, Ta(i)vert, Tosticated, Woozy

▷ **Fuddle(d)** may indicate an anagram

Fudge Cook, Doctor, Dodge, Drivel, Evade, Fiddlesticks, Nonsense, Rot, Stop-press

Fuel Anthracite, Argol, Astatki, Avgas, Biodiesel, Biogas, Briquet(te), Bunker, Butane, Candle-coal, Cannel, Coal, Coke, Derv, Diesel, Eilding, Eldin(g), Faggot, Fire(wood), Fossil, Gasohol, Gasoline, Haxamine, Hydrazine, Hydyne, Kerosene, Kerosine, Kindling, Knitch, Lignite, Mox, Napalm, Naphtha, Nuclear, Paraffin, Peat, Propane, Propellant, Stoke, Triptane, Yealdon

Fugitive Absconder, Ephemeral, Escapee, Fleeting, Hideaway, Lot, Outlaw, Refugee, Runaway, Runner, Transient

Fulfil(ment) Accomplish, Complete, Fruition, Honour, Meet, Pass, Realise, ➤ SATISFY, Steed

Full(ness), Fully Abrim, Ample, Arrant, Bouffant, Capacity, Chock-a-block, Chocker, Complete, Copious, Embonpoint, Engorged, Entire, Fat, Fed, Fou, Frontal, German, High, Hoatching, Hotch, Mill, Plein, Plenary, Plenitude, Pleroma, Plethora, Replete, Rich, Sated, Satiated, Thorough, Toss, Turgid, Turgor, Ullage, Up, Wau(l)k, Wholly

Fulminate, Fulmination Detonate, Explode, Levin, Lightning, Rail, Renounce, Thunder

Fumble Blunder, Faff, Grope, Misfield, Muff

Fume(s) Bluster, Gas, Halitus, Nidor, Rage, Reech, Reek, Settle, Smoke, Stum, Vapours

Fun(ny), Funny bone Amusing, Antic, Boat, Buffo, Caper, Clownery, Comedy, Comic(al), Delight, Droll, Frolic, Gammock, Giocoso, Gig, Glaik, Guy, Hilarity, Humerus, Humorous, Hysterical, Jest, Jouisance, Jouysaunce, Killing, Lark, Pleasure, Priceless, Rag, Rich, Rummy, Scream, Sidesplitting, Skylark, Sport, Surjection, Weird(o), Yell

Function(al) Act, Antilog, Arccos, Arcsine, Arctan, Ceremony, Cosec, Cosh, Cotangent, Coth, Discriminant, Dynamic, Exponential, Gibbs, Hamilton(ian), Helmholtz, Hyperbolic, Integrand, Inverse, Job, Logarithm, ➤ OPERATE, Periodic, Quadric, Quantical, Role, Run, Sech, Service, Sine, Sinh, Ste(a)d, Step, Surjection, Tan(h), Tick, Use, Wave, ➤ WORK

Fund(s) Bank, Bankroll, Barrel, Capital, Consolidated, Emendals, Endow, Evergreen, Fisc, Fisk, Gild, Index, Jackpot, Kitty, Pool, Pork-barrel, Prebend, Purse, Sinking, Slush, Sou-sou, Stabilisation, Stock, Subsidise, Treasury, Trust, War chest

Fundamental(ist) Basic(s), Bedrock, Cardinal, Essence, Grass-roots, Hamas, Nitty-gritty, Organic, Prime, Principle, Radical, Rudimentary, Ultimate

Funeral, Funereal Charnel, Cortege, Dismal, Exequy, Feral, Obit, Obsequy, Sad-coloured, Solemn, Tangi

Fungicide Biphenyl, Bordeaux mixture, Captan, Diphenyl, Ferbam, Menadione, Thiram, Zineb

Fungoid, Fungus Apothecium, Asci(us), Asomycete, Barm, Basidium, Gall, Gill, Hypha, Imperfect, Lichen, Mildew, Mould, Mushroom, Mycelium, Mycetes, Mycology, Oidium, Pest, Pileum, Pore, Prototroph, Rust, Saprophyte, Scab, Smut, Stipe, Thalline, Thallophyte, Toadstool, Uredine, Yeast, Zygospore

Funnel Buchner, Chimney, Choana, Flue, Hopper, Infundibulum, Smokestack, Stack, Stovepipe, Tun-dish

Fur Astrakhan, Beaver(skin), Boa, Broadtail, Budge, Calabre, Caracul, Castor, Chinchilla, Crimmer, Ermelin, Ermine, Fitchew, Flix, Flue, Galyac, Galyak, Genet, Kolinsky, Krimmer, Lettice, Minever, Miniver, Mink, Mouton, Musquash, Ocelot, Otter, Pashm, Pean, Pekan, Roskyn, Sable, Sealskin, Sea-otter, Stole, Tincture, Tippet, Vair(e), Victorine, Wolverine, Zorino

Furl Fold, Roll, Stow, Wrap

Furnace Arc, Athanor, Blast, Bloomery, Bosh, Calcar, Cockle, Cremator, Cupola, Destructor, Devil, Finery, Firebox, Forge, Glory-hole, Kiln, Lear, Lehr, Lime-kiln, Oast, Oon, Oven, Producer, Reverberatory, Scaldino

Furnish(ing) Appoint, Array, Deck, Decorate, Endow, Endue, Equip, Feed, Fledge, Gird, Lend, Produce, Provision, Soft, Stock, Supply, Tabaret, Upholster

Furniture Biedermeier, Chattels, Chippendale, Encoignure, Escritoire, Flatpack, Hepplewhite, Insight, Lumber, Moveable, Sheraton, Sideboard, Sticks, Stoutherie, Tire, Unit, Whatnot

Furrow(ed) Crease, Feer, Feerin(g), Furr, Groove, Gutter, Plough, Pucker, Rill(e), Rugose, Rut, Stria, Sulcus, Vallecula, Wrinkle

Further(more), Furthest Additional, Advance, Again, Aid, Also, Besides, Deeper, Else, Expedite, Extra, Extend, Extreme, Fresh, Infra, Longer, Mo(e), Mow, Other, Promote, Serve, Speed, Then

Furtive(ly) Clandestine, Cunning, Secret, Sly, Sneaky, Stealthy, Stowlins, Stownlins

Fury, Furies, Furious Acharné, Agitato, Alecto, ➤ ANGER, Apoplexy, Atropos, Avenger, Eriny(e)s, Eumenides, Exasperation, Frantic, Frenzied, Furor, Incensed, ➤ IRE, Livid, Maenad, Megaera, Rabid, Rage, Savage, Tisiphone, Virago, Wood, Wrath, Yond

Fuse(d), Fusion Anchylosis, Ankylosis, Blend, Coalesce, Cohere, Colliquate, Conflate, Encaustic, Endosmosis, Flow, Flux, Match, Merge, Merit, Nuclear, Portfire, Proximity, Rigelation, Run, Saucisson, Slow-match, Syncretism, Syngamy, Tokamak, Unite

Fuss(y) Ado, Agitation, Anile, Ballyho, Bobsie-die, Bother, Br(o)uhaha, Bustle, Carfuffle, Chichi, Coil, Commotion, Complain, Cosset, Create, Cu(r)fuffle, Dust, Faff, Fantad, Fantod, Fiddle-faddle, Finical, Finikin, Hairsplitter, Hoohah, Hoopla, Mither, Niggle, Nit-pick, Old-womanish, Overnice, Palaver, Particular, Perjink, Pernickety, Picky, Pother, Precise, Prejink, Primp, Prissy, Racket, Razzmatazz, Rout, Song, Song and dance, Spoffish, Spoffy, Spruce, Stashie, Stickler, ➤ STIR, Stishie, Stooshie, Stushie, Tamasha, To-do, Tracasserie

Futile Empty, Feckless, Idle, Inept, No-go, Nugatory, Null, Otiose, Pointless, Sleeveless, Stultified, Trivial, ➤ VAIN

Future, Futurist Again, Be-all, Coming, Demain, Hence, Horoscope, Later, Long-range, Offing, Ovist, Prospect, To-be, Tomorrow

Gg

Gad(about), Gadzooks Gallivant, Lud, Rover, Sbuddikins, Sdeath, Traipse, Trape(s), Viretot

Gadget Appliance, Artifice, Device, Dingbat, Dingus, Doodad, Doodah, Doofer, Doohickey, Gismo, Gizmo, Gubbins, Hickey, Jimjam, Notion, Possum, Utility, Widget

Gag Brank, Choke, Estoppel, Joke, Pong, Prank, Silence(r), Smother, Wheeze

Gain(s), Gained Acquire, Appreciate, Attain, Avail, Boot, Bunce, Carry, Catch, Chevisance, Clean-up, Derive, Earn, Edge, Fruit, ➤ GET, Good, Gravy, Land, Lucre, Obtain, Plus, Profit, Purchase, Rake-off, Reap, Thrift, Use, Velvet, Wan, Win, Windfall, Winnings

Gait Bearing, Canter, Pace, Piaffer, Rack, Trot

Galaxy Heaven, Magellanic cloud, Milky Way, Radio, Seyfert, Spiral, Stars

Gale Backfielder, Peal, Ripsnorter, Sea turn, Snorter, Squall, Storm, Tempest, Winder

Gallant(ry) Admirer, Amorist, Beau, Blade, Buck, Cavalier, Chevalier, Cicisbeo, Courtliness, Lover, Prow, Romeo, Sigisbeo, Spark, Valiance

Gallery Accademia, Amphitheatre, Arcade, Belvedere, Catacomb, Cupola, Gods, Hayward, Hermitage, Loft, Loggia, Louvre, Mine, Minstrel, National, Prado, Press, Rogues', Shooting, Stranger's, Tate, Uffizi, Veranda(h), Whispering

Galley Bireme, Bucentaur, Caboose, Drake, Galliot, Kitchen, Lymphad, Penteconter, Proof

Gallows Dule-tree, Gibbet, Nub, Tree, Tyburn, Tyburn-tree, Woodie

Gambit Manoeuvre, Ploy, Stratagem

Gamble(r), Gambling (place) Back, Bet, Casino, Chance, Dice(-play), Flutter, Mise, Pari-mutuel, Parlay, Piker, Policy, Punter, Raffle, Risk, Roulette, Spec, Speculate, Speculator, Sweep(stake), Throw(ster), Tinhorn, Tombola, Tontine, Two-up, ➤ WAGER

Game(s) Battledore, Cards, Chemin de fer, Computer, Decider, Doubles, Fair, Foursome, Frame, Gallant, Gammy, Gerrymander, Gleek, Gutsy, Handicap, Highland, Intrepid, Isthmian, Jeu, Kill, Laik, ➤ LAME, Match, Nemean, Olympic, On, Palm, Pam, Paralympic, Parlour, PE, Play, Plaything, Preference, Pythian, Rubber, Singles, Slam, Sport, Square, Tie-break, Video, Vie, Wall, Willing, Word

Game, Game birds Bag, Fowl, Grouse, Guan, Hare, Meat, Partridge, Pheasant, Prairie chicken, Ptarmigan, Quail, ➤ QUARRY, Rype(r), Snipe, Spatchcock, Woodcock

Gang Band(itti), Bing, Canaille, Chain, Coffle, Core, Crew, Crue, Elk, Go, Horde, Mob, Nest, Outfit, Pack, Posse, Press, Push, Ratpack, Tribulation, Troop, Yardie

Gangster Bandit, Capone, Crook, Hatchet-man, Highbinder, Hood, Mafioso, Ochlocrat, Skollie, Skolly, Yakuza, Yardie

▶**Gaol(er)** see JAIL(ER)

Gap Breach, Chasm, Chink, Credibility, Day, Embrasure, F-hole, Flaw, Fontanel(le), Generation, Hair-space, Hiatus, Hole, Interlude, Interstice, Lacunae, Loophole, Opening, Pass, Rest, Shard, Sherd, Slap, ➤ SPACE, Spark, Street, Synapse

Garb Apparel, Costume, Gear, Gere, Guise, Ihram, Invest, Leotard, Raiment, Toilet

Garbage Bunkum, Junk, Refuse, Rubbish, Trash

▷**Garble** may indicate an anagram

Garden(ing), Gardens Arbour, Area, Babylon(ian), Bear, Beer, Botanic, Cottage, Covent, Dig, Eden, Floriculture, Gethsemane, Hanging, Hesperides, Hoe, Kew, Kitchen, Knot, Lyceum, Paradise, Pleasance, Plot, Rockery, Roof, Tea, Topiary, Tuileries, Vauxhall, Zoological

Gardener Adam, Capability Brown, Jekyll, Landscape, Mary, Nurseryman

Garland Anadem, Anthology, Chaplet, Coronal, Crants, Festoon, Lei, Stemma, Toran(a), Vallar(y), Wreath

Garment Cerements, Clout, Foundation, Habiliment, Habit, Hand-me-down, Lingerie, Rail, Step-in, Togs, Vestment, Vesture, Weed, Woolly

Garnish Adorn, Attach, Crouton, Decorate, Gremolata, Lard, Parsley, Sippet, Staffage

Gas(sy) Air, Blah(-blah), Blather, Blether, Chat, Chrom(at)osphere, Emanation, Flatulence, Flatus, Flocculus, Flue, Gabnash, Halitus, Hot-air, Ideal, Inert, Jaw, Lurgi, Noble, Orotund, Perfect, Petrol, Poison, Prate, Propellant, Rare, ➤ TALK, Therm, Vapour, Waffle, ➤ WIND, Yackety-yak

Gash Incise, Rift, Score, Scotch, ➤ SLASH

Gasp(ing) Anhelation, Apn(o)ea, Chink, Exhale, Kink, Oh, Pant, Puff, Singult, Sob

Gast(e)ropod Cowrie, Cowry, Euthyneura, Glaucus, Harp-shell, Limpet, Mollusc, Murex, Nerita, Nerite, Nudibranch,

Gate(s) → Gene(tics)

Opisthobranch, Ormer, Periwinkle, Purpura, Sea-ear, Sea-hare, Slug, Snail, Spindle-shell, Stromb, Whelk

Gate(s), Gateway Alley, Brandenburg, Caisson, Crowd, Decuman, Entry, Erpingham, Golden, Head, Kissing, Lych, Menin, Nor, Pearly, Portal, Portcullis, Postern, Propylaeum, Propylon, Pylon, Starting, Toran(a), Torii, Traitor's, Turnstile, Wicket, Yate, Yet(t)

▷**Gateshead** may indicate 'g'

Gather(ed), Gathering Amass, Assemble, Bee, Braemar, Cluster, Collate, ➤ COLLECT, Colloquium, Concourse, Conglomerate, Congregate, Conventicle, Corral, Corroboree, Crop, Crowd, Cull, Eve, Fest, Function, Gabfest, Galaxy, Glean, Glomerate, Harvest, Hootenanny, Hotchpot, Hui, Husking, In, Infer, Jamboree, Kommers, Lek, Lirk, Love-in, Pleat, Plica, Plissé, Pucker, Raft, Rake, Reef, Reunion, Round-up, Rout, Ruche, Ruff(le), Salon, Shindig, Shir(r), Shoal, Shovel, Singsong, Social, Spree, Take, Tuck, Vindemiate, Vintage, Wappensc(h)aw

Gauche Awkward, Clumsy, Farouche, Graceless

Gaudy Criant, Fantoosh, Flash, Garish, Glitz(y), Meretricious, Tacky, Tinsel

Gauge Alidad(e), Anemometer, ➤ ASSESS, Bourdon, Broad, Calibre, Denier, Etalon, Estimate, Evaluate, Feeler, Judge, Loading, Manometer, Marigraph, Measure, Meter, Narrow, Ombrometer, Oncometer, Pressure, Rate, Scantle, Size, Standard, Strain, Tape, Tonometer, Tram, Tread, Udometer

Gaunt Haggard, Lancaster, Lean, Randletree, Rannletree, Rannletree, Rantletree, Rawbone, ➤ THIN, Wasted

Gauze, Gauzy Gas mantle, Gossamer, Muslin, Sheer, Tiffany

Gear(ing) Attire, Bags, Bevel, Clobber, Dérailleur, Differential, Draw, Duds, Engrenage, Fab, Finery, Granny, Harness, Helical, Hypoid, Involute, Kit, Lay-shaft, Mesh, Neutral, Overdrive, Ratio, Rig, Rudder, Sun and planet, Synchromesh, ➤ TACKLE, Top, Trim, Worm(-wheel)

Geld(ing) Castrate, Lib, Neuter, Spado

Gem Baguette, Boule, Brilliant, Briolette, Cabochon, Cachalong, Diamante, ➤ JEWEL, Ligure, Marquise, Scarab, Scarabaeoid, Solitaire, Sparkler, Stone

Gene(tics) Allele, Allelomorph, Anticodon, Codon, Creation, Disomic, Episome, Exon, Factor, Genome, Hereditary,

Heterogamy, Intron, Mendel, Muton, Operon, Selfish, Terminator

Genealogist, Genealogy Armory, Family, Heraldry, Line, Pedigree, Seannachie, Seannachy, Sennachie, Whakapapa

General Ataman, Broad, C in C, Common, Communal, Current, Diadochi, Eclectic, Ecumenical, Election, Gen, GOC, Inspector, Main, Omnify, Overall, Overhead, Prevailing, Regulus, Rife, Strategist, ➤ UNIVERSAL, Vague, Wide

Generate, Generation, Generator Abiogenetic, Age, Beat, Beget, Breeder, Charger, Create, Dynamo, Epigon, Father, Fuel-cell, House, Kipp, Lost, Magneto, Olds, Sire, Spawn, Stallion, Van de Graaff, Yield

Generosity, Generous Bounty, Charitable, Free-handed, Handsome, Kind, Largess(e), ➤ LAVISH, Liberal, Magnanimous, Munificent, Noble(-minded), Open, Open-handed, Open-hearted, Philanthropic, Plump, Profuse, Sporting

▶**Genetic** see GENE

Genial(ity) Affable, Amiable, Benign, Bluff, Bonhomie, Human, Mellow

Genius Agathodaimon, Daemon, Einstein, Engine, Flash, Inspiration, Ka, Michaelangelo, Numen, Prodigy

Gentle Amenable, Amenage, Bland, Clement, Delicate, Gradual, Grub, Light, Maggot, Mansuete, Mild, Tame, Tender

Gentry County, Landed, Quality, Squir(e)age

Genuflexion Bend, Curts(e)y, Kowtow, Salaam

Genuine Authentic, Bona-fide, Dinkum, Dinky-di, Echt, Frank, Heartfelt, Intrinsic, Jonnock, Kosher, Legit(imate), Nain, Pucka, Pukka, Pure, Pusser, ➤ REAL, Real McCoy, Right, Simon-Pure, Sincere, Square, Sterling, True, Veritable

Germ Bacteria, Bug, Klebsiella, Seed, Spirilla, Strep, Virus, Zyme

German(y) Angle, Bavarian, Boche, Frank, Fritz, G, Goth, Habsburg, Hans, Hapsburg, Herr, Hun, Jerry, Jute, Kaiser, Kraut, Prussian, Salic, Saxon, Teuton(ic), Visigoth

Gesticulate, Gesticulation, Gesture(s) Beck(on), Ch(e)ironomy, Mime, Motion, Salute, ➤ SIGN, Signal, Token

Get, Get by, Get On Acquire, Advance, Aggravate, Annoy, Attain, Become, Brat, Bring, Capture, Cop, Cope, Derive, Fet(ch), Fette, Gain, Gee, Learn, Make, Manage, Milk, Net, Noy,

➤ OBTAIN, Peeve, Procure, Progress, Reach, Realise, Rile, Roil, Secure, See, Sire, Twig, Understand, Win

▷ **Getting** may indicate an anagram

Getting better Convalescing, Improving, Lysis

Ghastly Gash, Grim, Hideous, Lurid, Macabre, Pallid, Welladay, White

Ghost(ly) Acheri, Apparition, Apport, Caddy, Chthonic, Duende, Duppy, Eerie, Eery, Fantasm, Fetch, Gytrash, Haunt, Hint, Jumbie, Jumby, Larva(e), Lemur, Malmag, No'canny, Paraclete, Pepper's, Phantasm(agoria), Phantom, Revenant, Sampford, Shade, Shadow, Spectre, ➤ SPIRIT, Spook, Trace, Truepenny, Umbra, Vision, Visitant, Waff, Wraith

Giant(ess) Brobdingnagian, Colossus, Eten, Ettin, Géant, Gigantic, Grim, Jotun(n), Jumbo, Mammoth, Monster, Oak, Ogre, Pope, Red, Titan, Troll, Utgard, Yowie

Gibberish Claptrap, Double Dutch, Greek, Jargon

Gibe Barb, Brocard, Chaff, Fleer, Glike, Jeer, Jibe, Shy, Slant

Gift(s), Gifted Ability, Alms, Aptitude, Bef(f)ana, Bequest, Blessing, Blest, Bonbon, Bonsel(l)a, Boon, Bounty, Charism(a), Congiary, Corban, Covermount, Cumshaw, Dash, Deodate, ➤ DONATION, Etrenne, Fairing, Flair, Foy, Freebie, Gab, Garnish, Godsend, Grant, Han(d)sel, Handout, Hogmanay, Indian, Knack, Koha, Kula, Lagniappe, Largesse, Legacy, Manna, Ne'erday, Nuzzer, Offering, Parting, Potlatch, ➤ PRESENT, Presentation, Prezzie, Propine, Reward, Sop, Talent, Tongues, Windfall

Gigantic Atlantean, Briarean, Colossal, Goliath, ➤ HUGE, Immense, Mammoth, Rounceval, Titan

Giggle Cackle, Ha, Simper, Snigger, Snicker, Tehee, Titter

Gild(ed), Gilding Checklaton, Embellish, Enhance, Inaurate, Ormolu, S(c)hecklaton, Vermeil

Gill(s) Beard, Branchia, Cart, Ctenidium, Jill, Noggin, Spiracle

Gimmick Doodad, Doodah, Hype, Ploy, Ruse, Stunt

Gin Bathtub, Geneva, Genever, Hollands, Juniper, Lubra, Max, Noose, Old Tom, Ruin, Schiedam, Schnapp(s), Sloe, Snare, Springe, Toil, Trap, Trepan, Twankay

Gingerbread D(o)um-palm, Lebkuchen, Parkin, Parliament(-cake)

▶**Gipsy** see GYPSY

Girder Beam, Binder, I-beam, Loincloth, Spar

Girdle Baldric, Cestus, Chastity, Cincture, Cingulum, Corset, Hippolyte, Hoop, Mitre, Sash, Surcingle, Surround

Girl(s) Backfisch, Ball, Bimbo, Bint, Bird, Bit, Bobby-dazzler, Bohemian, Broad, Burd, Call, Charlie, Chit, Chorus, Coed, Colleen, Crumpet, Cutey, Cutie, Deb, Demoiselle, Dish, Doll, Dollybird, Essex, Filly, Flapper, Fluff, Fraulein, Frippet, Gaiety, Gal, Geisha, Gibson, Gouge, Grisette, Hen, Hoiden, Hoyden, Hussy, Judy, Kimmer, Land, Lass(ock), Maid(en), May, Miss(y), Moppet, Nymph(et), Peach, Popsy, Puss, Quean, Queyn, Senorita, Sheila, Shi(c)ksa, Sis(s), Tabby, Trull, Wench

▷ **Girl** may indicate a female name

Gist Essence, Kernel, ➤ NUB, Pith, Substance

Give, Give up, Giving Abandon, Abstain, Accord, Administer, Afford, Award, Bend, Bestow, Buckle, Cede, Confiscate, Dative, Dispense, Dole, ➤ DONATE, Duck, Elasticity, Enable, Forswear, Gie, Impart, Jack, Largition, Render, Resign, Sacrifice, Sag, Spring, Stop, Tip, Vacate, Yeve

Give out Bestow, Dispense, Emit, Exude, Peter

Glacier Aletsch, Crevasse, Drumline, Fox, Franz-Josef, Iceberg, Ice-cap, Icefall, Moraine, Muir, Riss, Serac, Tasman

Glad(ly), Gladden Cheer, Fain, ➤ HAPPY, Lief, Willing

Glamour(ise), Glamorous Charm, Glitter(ati), Glitz, Halo, It, Prestige, SA, Spell

Glance Blink, Browse, Coup d'oeil, Dekko, Glimpse, Oeillade, Once-over, Peek, ➤ PEEP, Ray, Ricochet, Scan, Shufti, Shufty, Skellie, Skelly, Snick, Squint, Vision

Gland Crypt, Goitre, Vesicle

Glare, Glaring Astare, Blare, Dazzle, Flagrant, Garish, Gleam, Glower, Holophotal, Iceblink, Lour, Low(e), Shine, Vivid, Whally

Glass(es), Glassware, Glassy Amen, Ampul(la), Aneroid, Barometer, Bifocals, Brimmer, Bumper, Burning, Cheval, Cloche, Copita, Coupe, Cupping, Dark, Euphon, Field, Flute, Frigger, Frit, Glare, Goblet, Goggles, Granny, Ground, Horn-rims, Humpen, Hyaline, Jar, Jigger, Lens, Liqueur, Liquid, Lorgnette, Loupe, Lozen(ge), Magma, Magnifying, Metal, Mica, Middy, Mirror, Monocle, Opera, Optical, Pane, Parison, Pebble, Peeper, Pele, Pele's hair, Pince-nez, Pon(e)y, Prunt, Psyche, Quarrel-pane, Quarry, Roemer, Rummer, Schooner, Seam,

Seidel, Sleever, Slide, Snifter, Specs, Stein, Stemware, Stone, Supernaculum, Telescope, Trifocals, Tumbler, Varifocals, Vernal, Vitreous

Glass-house Conservatory, Orangery

Gleam(ing) Blink, Flash, Glint, Glitter, Gloss, Leme, Light, Ray, Relucent, Sheen, Shimmer, ➤ SHINE

Glee Exuberance, Joy, Mirth, Song

Glide(away), Glider, Gliding Aquaplane, Coast, Elapse, Float, Illapse, Lapse, Luge, Microlight, Portamento, Sail, Sailplane, Sashay, Scorrendo, Scrieve, Skate, Ski, Skim, Sleek, Slide, Slip, Swim, Volplane

Glimpse Aperçu, Flash, Glance, Glisk, Stime, Styme, Waff, Whiff

Glint Flash, Shimmer, ➤ SPARKLE, Trace, Twinkle

Glisten(ing) Ganoid, Glint, Sheen, Shimmer, ➤ SHINE, Sparkle

Glitter(ing) Clinquant, Garish, Gemmeous, Paillon, Sequin, Spang(le), Sparkle, Tinsel

Gloat(ing) Crow, Drool, Enjoy, Exult, Schadenfreude

Globe, Globule Ball, Bead, Celestial, Drop, Earth, Orb, Shot, Sphear, Sphere

Gloom(y) Atrabilious, Blues, Cheerless, Cimmerian, Cloud, Crepuscular, Damp, Dark, ➤ DESPAIR, Dingy, Disconsolate, Dismal, Dool(e), Drab, Drear, Drumly, Dump(s), Dyspeptic, Funereal, Glum, Grey, Louring, Mirk, Misery, Mopish, Morne, Morose, Murk, Obscurity, Overcast, Sable, Sad, Saturnine, Sepulchral, Solemn, ➤ SOMBRE, Stygian, Tenebrous

Glorification, Glorify Aggrandise, Apotheosis, Avatar, Bless, ➤ EXALT, Halo, Laud, Lionise, Praise, Splendour

Glorious, Gloria, Glory Chorale, Grand, Halo, Hosanna, Ichabod, Kudos, Lustre, Magnificent, Nimbus, Sublime

Gloss(y) Enamel, Gild, Glacé, Japan, Lustre, Patina, ➤ POLISH, Postillate, Sheen, Sleek, Slick, Slide, Slur, Veneer, Whitewash

Glove Boxing, Cestus, Dannock, Gage, Gauntlet, Kid, Mitten, Oven, Velvet

Glow(ing) Aflame, Aura, Bloom, Burn, Candescence, Flush, Foxfire, Gleam, Halation, Incandescence, Lambent, Luculent, Luminesce, Lustre, Phosphorescence, Radiant, Shine, Translucent, ➤ WARMTH

Glue(y) Araldite®, Bee, Cement, Colloidal, Gelatin(e), Ichthyocolla, Isinglass, Paste, Propolis, Size, Spetch

Glum Dour, Livery, Lugubrious, Moody, Morose, Ron, Sombre

Glut Choke, Gorge, Sate, Satiate, Saturate, Surfeit

Glutton(ous), Gluttony Bellygod, Carcajou, Cormorant, Edacity, Gannet, Gorb, Gourmand, Gulosity, Gutsy, Lurcher, Pig, Ratel, Scoffer, Sin, Trencherman, Trimalchio, Wolverine

Gnat Culex, Culicidae, Midge, Mosquito

Gnaw(ing) Corrode, Erode, Fret, Lagomorph, Rodent

Gnome Adage, Bank-man, Chad, Cobalt, Financier, Kobold, Motto, Proverb, Saw, Sprite

Go, Going (after, for, off, on, up, etc) Advance, Afoot, Anabasis, Animation, Assail, Attempt, Bash, Bing, Brio, Choof, Clamber, Continuance, Depart, Die, Do, Energy, Fare, Gae, Gang, Gee, Green, Hamba, Hark, Hence, Hie, Imshi, Imshy, Ish, ► LEAVE, March, Match, Off, Path, Pep, Perpetual, Ply, Quit, Raik, Repair, Resort, Resume, Run, Scat, Scram, Segue, Shoo, Skedaddle, Snick-up, Sour, Spank, Stab, Success, Transitory, Trine, Try, Turn, Vam(o)ose, Verve, Via, Viable, Wend, Work, Yead, Yede, Yeed, Zap, Zing, Zip

Goad Ankus, Brod, Gad, Incite, ► NEEDLE, Prod, Spur, Stimulate, Stimulus, Taunt

Goal Ambition, Basket, Bourn(e), Destination, Dream, Drop, End, Field, Grail, Mission, Own, Score, Target, Ultima Thule

Goat(-like) Angora, Billy, Buck, Caprine, Cashmere, Hircine, Ibex, Kashmir, Kid, Markhor, Nan(ny)

Gobble Bolt, Devour, Gorge, Gulp, Slubber, Wolf

Go-between Broker, Factor, Intermediate, Link, Mediate, Middleman, Pandarus, Pander, Shuttle

Goblin Bargaist, Barg(h)est, Bodach, Bogey, Bogle, Bogy, Bucca, Croquemitaine, Empusa, Erl-king, Genie, Gnome, Gremlin, Knocker, Kobold, Lutin, Nis(se), Phooka, Phynnodderree, Pooka, Pouke, Puca, Pug, Red-cap, Red-cowl, Shellycoat, ► SPRITE, Troll, Trow

God(s) Achelous, Aesir, Aitu, All-father, As, Avatar, Cabiri, D, Delian, Deva, Dieu, Divine, Gad, Gallery, Gracious, Hughie, Lar, Light, Maker, Numen, Pantheon, Penates, Principle, Satyr, Supreme Being, Tin, Truth, Unknown, Vanir, Zombie

Goddess(es) Divine, Eumenides, Grace, Graeae, Graiae, Horae, Houri, Norn, Parcae, Valkyrie, Walkyrie

Godless Agnostic, Atheistic, Atheous, Impious, Profane

▷**Going wrong** may indicate an anagram

Gold(en) Age, Amber, Apple, Ass, Au, Auriferous, Bough, Bull, Bullion, California, Doubloon, Dutch, Eagle, Electron, Electrum, Emerods, Filigree, Fleece, Fool's, Gate, Handshake, Hind, Horde, Horn, Ingot, Leaf, Lingot, Moidore, Mosaic, Muck, Nugget, Oaker, Obang, Ochre, Ophir, Or, Oreide, Ormolu, Oroide, Pistole, Placer, Pyrites, Red, Reef, Rolled, Silence, Sol, Standard, Stubborn, Talmi, Tolosa, Treasury, White, Yellow

Gold-digger Forty-niner, Prospector

Golfer Alliss, Braid, Cotton, Faldo, Hogan, Pivoter, Rees, Roundsman, Seve, Snead, Teer, Trevino, Wolstenholme, Yipper

Gone Ago, Defunct, Napoo, Out, Past, Ygo(e), Yod

▷**Gone off** may indicate an anagram

Good(ness), Goody-goody Agathodaimon, Angelic, Bad, Bein, Benefit, Bon, Bonzer, Bosker, Blesses, Bounty, Brod, Budgeree, Canny, Castor, Coo, Cool, Dab, Dow, Enid, Estimable, Fantabulous, First-class, G, Gear, Gosh, Guid, Humdinger, Lois, Lor, Nobility, ➤ NO GOOD, Pi, Plum, Proper, Purler, Rectitude, Riddance, Right, Rum, Salutary, Samaritan, Sanctity, Slap-up, Smashing, Spiffing, St, Suitable, Tollol, Topping, Valid, Virtue, Virtuous, Weal, Welfare, Whacko, Wholesome, Worthy

Goodbye Addio, Adieu, Adios, Aloha, Arrivederci, Cheerio, Ciao, Farewell, Sayonara, Tata, Toodle-oo, Toodle-pip, Vale

Goods Brown, Cargo, Durables, Fancy, Flotsam, Freight, Gear, Line, Property, Wares, White

Goodwill Amity, Bonhom(m)ie, Favour, Gree

Goose Anserine, Barnacle, Brent, Canada, Daftie, Ember, Gander, Gannet, Greylag, Grope, Hawaiian, Idiot, Juggins, Magpie, Nene, Quink, Roger, Silly, Simpleton, Skein, Snow, Solan, Strasbourg, Stubble, Team, Wav(e)y, Wawa, Whitehead

Goosefoot Allgood, Amarantaceae, Beet, Blite, Fat-hen, Mercury, Orache, Saltbush

Gorge(s) Abyss, Barranca, Barranco, Canyon, Chasm, Cheddar, Cleft, Couloir, Cram, Defile, Donga, Flume, Gap, Ghyll, Glut, Grand Canyon, Grand Coulee, Gulch, Khor, Kloof, Lin(n), Nala, Nalla(h), Nulla(h), Olduvai, Overeat, Pass, Ravine, Staw, ➤ STUFF, Throat, Tire, Tums, Valley, Yosemite

Gorgeous Grand, Splendid, Superb

▶ **Gorilla** see MONKEY

Gosh Begad, Begorra, Blimey, Cor, Gadzooks, Gee, Gum, Lor, My, Odsbobs, Odso

Gossip Ana(s), Aunt, Backbite, Cackle, Cat, Causerie, Chat, Chin, Chitchat, Clash, Claver, Cleck, Clish-clash, Clishmaclaver, Confab, Crack, Dirt, Flibbertigibbet, Gab(nash), Gabfest, Gas, Jaw, Loose-tongued, Maundrel, Natter, Noise, Pal, Prattle, Quidnunc, Rumour, Scandal(monger), Schmooze, Scuttlebutt, Shmoose, Shmooze, Talk(er), Tattle, Tittle(-tattle), Twattle, Yatter

Gourmand, Gourmet Apicius, ▶ EPICURE, Gastronome, Gastrosopher, Lickerish, Table, Trencherman, Ventripotent

Govern(or), Government Administer, Alderman, Autocrat, Bencher, Cabinet, Caretaker, Coalition, Command, Condiminium, Congress, Constitution, Dominate, Federal, G, Gov, Gubernator, Helm, Inspector, Kremlin, Legate, Petticoat, Power, Raj, Regency, Regime(n), Reign, ▶ RULE, Senate, Steer, Sway, Whitehall

Governess Duenna, Eyre, Fraulein, Griffin, Mademoiselle, Prism, Vicereine

Grab Annexe, Bag, Clutch, Cly, Collar, Glaum, Grapnel, Hold, Holt, Rap, Seise, Seize, ▶ SNATCH, Swipe

Grace(s), Graceful Aglaia, Amnesty, Anna, Beauty, Become, Benediction, Blessing, Charis(ma), Charites, Charity, Darling, Dr, Elegance, Euphrosyne, Fluent, Gainly, Genteel, Genty, Godliness, Mense, Mercy, Mordent, Omnium, Ornament, Sacrament, Streamlined, Style, Thalia, Thanks, Willowy

Gracious Benign, By George, Charismatic, Generous, Good, Handsome, Hend, Merciful, Polite

Grade, Gradient Analyse, Angle, Assort, Class(ify), Dan, Degree, Echelon, Gon, Hierarchy, Inclination, Kyu, Lapse, Measure, Order, Rank, Score, Seed, Slope, Standard, Status

Graduate, Graduation Alumnus, BA, Bachelor, Calibrate, Capping, Incept, Laureateship, Licentiate, LlB, MA, Master, Nuance, Optime, Ovate

Graft Anaplasty, Autoplasty, Boodle, Bribery, Bud, Dub, Enarch, Enrace, Heteroplasty, Imp, Implant, Inarch, Inoculate, Payola, Pomato, Racket, Scion, Shoot, Slip, Transplant, Ympe

Grain(y) Bajra, Bajree, Bajri, Bear, Bere, Boll, Bran, Cereal, Corn, Couscous, Crop, Curn, Curn(e)y, Cuscus, D(o)urra, Extine, Frumentation, Gr, Graddan, Granule, Groats, Grumose, Intine, Kaoliang, Knaveship, Malt, Mashlam, Mashlin, Mashloch, Mashlum, Maslin, Mealie, Millet, Milo, Minim, Mongcorn, Oats, Pickle, Pinole, Pollen, Polynology, Popcorn, Puckle, Rabi, Raggee, Ragi, Raggy, Rhy, Rye, Sand, Scruple, Seed, Semsem, Sorghum, Tola, Touch, Wheat, Wholemeal

Grand Canyon, Epical, Flugel, G, Gorgeous, Guignol, High-faluting, Hotel, Imposing, La(h)-di-da(h), Lordly, Magnificent, Majestic, Palatial, Piano(forte), Pompous, Regal, Splendid, Stately, Stoor, Stour, Stowre, Sture, Sublime, Swell, Tour

Granite Aberdeen, Chinastone, Greisen, Luxul(l)ianite, Luxulyanite, NH, Pegmatite, Protogine

Grant(ed) Accord, Aid, Award, Bestow, Bounty, Bursary, Carta, Cary, Charta, Charter, Concession, ➤ CONFER, Cy, Datum, Endow, Exhibition, Feoff, Lend, Let, Munich, Patent, President, Send, Sop, Subsidy, Subvention, Vouchsafe, Yeven, Yield

Grape(s) Botros, Botryoid, Hyacinth, Noble rot, Racemose, Raisin, Rape, Sour, Sultana, Uva, Vino

Graph(ic) Bar, Chart, Contour, Diagram, Histogram, Ogive, Picturesque, Pie (chart), Profile, Sonogram, Table, Vivid

Grapple Clinch, Close, Hook, Lock, Struggle, Wrestle

Grasp(ing) Apprehend, Catch, Clat, Claut, ➤ CLUTCH, Compass, Comprehend, Fathom, Get, Grab, Grapple, Greedy, Grip(e), Hent, Hug, Prehend, Prehensile, Raptorial, Realise, Rumble, Sense, Snap, Snatch, Twig, Uptak(e)

Grass(land), Grass roots, Grassy Agrostology, Bang, Bhang, Blade, Bush, Divot, Fog, Foggage, Ganja, Glume, Glumella, Green(sward), Hassock, Hay, Haycock, Hemp, High veld, ➤ INFORM, Knoll, Laund, Lawn, Machair, Mary Jane, Mead, Moor, Nark, Palet, Pasturage, Pot, Rat, Rat on, Rough, Rumble(r), Savanna(h), Scraw, Shop, Sing, Sinsemilla, Sneak(er), Snitch, Snout, Sourveld, Split, Squeal, Stool-pigeon, Sward, Swath(e), Tath, Tea, Tuffet, Turf, Tussac, Tussock, Veld(t), Windlestraw, Yard

Grasshopper Cicada, Cricket, Katydid, Locust

Grate(r), Grating Abrade, Burr, Cancelli, Chirk, Crepitus, ➤ FRET, Graticule, Grid, Grill, Guichet, Guttural, Hack, Hearth,

Heck, Hoarse, Ingle, Jar, Portcullis, Rasp, Risp, Rub, Ruling, Scrannel, ➤ SCRAPE, Scrat, Shred, Siver, Strident, Syver

Gratuitous, Gratuity Baksheesh, Beer-money, Bonsella, Bonus, Bounty, Cumshaw, Free, Glove-money, Gratis, Tip

Grave(yard) Accent, Arlington, Bass, Bier, Burial, Charnel, Chase, Darga, Demure, Dust, God's acre, Heavy, Heinous, Important, Ingroove, Kistvaen, Kurgan, Mound, Passage, Pit, Sad, Saturnine, Serious, Sober, Sombre, Speos, Staid, Stern, Tomb, Watery

Gravel(ly) Calculus, Channel, Glareous, Grail(e), Grit, Hoggin(g), Murram, Nonplus, Shingle

Gravity Barycentric, G, Geotaxis, Geotropism, Magnitude, Mascon, Specific, Weight

➤**Gray** see GREY

Grease, Greasy Bribe, Creesh, Dope, Dubbing, Elaeolite, Elbow, Enseam, Glit, Lanolin, Lard, Seam(e), Shearer, Sheep-shearer, Smarm, Suint, Unctuous

Great(er), Greatest Ali, Astronomical, Bully, Extreme, Gran(d), Gt, Guns, Helluva, Immortal, Important, Lion, Macro, Main, Major, Mickle, Much, Muckle, OS, Super, Superb, Swingeing, Tall, Titan(ic), Tremendous, Unco, Utmost, Vast, Zenith

Greed(y) Avarice, Avid, Bulimia, Bulimy, Cupidity, Edacious, Esurient, Gannet, Gare, Gulosity, Killcrop, Lickerish, Mercenary, Piggery, Pleonexia, Rapacity, Selfish, Solan, Voracity, Wolfish

Greek(s) Achaean, Achaian, Aeolic, Aonian, Arcadia, Argive, Athenian, Attic, Cadmean, Cleruch, Corinthian, Cretan, Delphian, Demotic, Ding, Dorian, Doric, Eoka, Eolic, Ephebe, Evzone, Fanariot, Gr, Helladic, Hellene, Hellenic, Hoplite, Ionian, Italiot(e), Javan, Katharevousa, Klepht, Koine, Lapith, Linear B, Locrian, Lucian, Macedonia, Pelasgic, Phanariot, Romaic, Samiot, Seminole, Spartan, Stagirite, Sybarite, Tean, Teian, Theban, Thessal(on)ian, Thracian, Typto, Uniat

Green(ery) Apple, Bottle, Callow, Celadon, Cerulein, Chartreuse, Chlorophyll, Chrome, Common, Copper, Crown, Eau de nil, Eco-, Ecofriendly, Emerald, Emerande, Envious, Erin, Fingers, Foliage, Forest, Fundie, Fundy, Glaucous, Goddess, Gretna, Immature, Inexpert, Jade, Lawn, Leafage, Lime, Lincoln, Loden, Lovat, Moss, Naive, New, Nile, Olive, Pea, Peridot, Pistachio, Putting, Raw, Realo, Reseda, Rifle, Rink, Sage,

Scheele's, Sludge, Sward, Teal, Tender, Tyro, Unfledged, Uninitiated, Unripe, Uranite, Verdant, Verdigris, Verdure, Vert, Vir(id)escent

Greens Broccoli, Cabbage, Calabrese, Sprout, Vegetable(s)

Greet(ing) Accost, Banzai, Benedicite, Ciao, Hail, Hallo, Handshake, Heil, Herald, Hi, High-five, Hiya, How, Howsit, Jambo, Kia ora, Kiss, Respects, Salaam, Salute, Salve, Shalom, Shalom aleichem, Sorry, Tena Koe, Wave, ➤ WELCOME, Wotcher, Yo

▶**Gremlin** see GOBLIN

Grey, Gray Argent, Ashen, Ashy, Battleship, Charcoal, Cinereous, Dapple, Dorian, Dove, Drab, Glaucous, Gloomy, Gr, Gridelin, Grise, Grisy, Grizzled, Gunmetal, Hoary, Hore, Iron, Leaden, Mouse-coloured, Pearl, Putty, Slaty, Steel

Greyhound Grew, Longtail, Ocean, Saluki, Sapling, Whippet

Grid(dle), Gridiron Bar, Barbecue, Brandreth, Cattle, Dot matrix, Grate, Graticule, Grating, Network, Reseau, Reticle, Roo-bar, Tava(h), Tawa, Windscale

Grief, Grievance, Grieve, Grievous Axe, Bemoan, Bitter, Complaint, Condole, Cry, Dear(e), Deere, Distress, Dole, Dolour, Gram(e), Gravamen, Heartbreak, Hone, Illy, Io, ➤ MISERY, Monody, O(c)hone, Pain, Pathetic, Plaint, Rue, Sorrow, Teen, Tene, Tragic, Wayment, Weeping, Woe, Wrong

Grill(ing), Grille Braai, Brander, Broil, Carbonado, Crisp, Devil, Gridiron, Inquisition, Interrogate, Kebab, Mixed, Pump, Question, Rack, Reja, Yakimona

Grim Dire, Dour, Gaunt, Glum, Gurly, Hard, Stern

▷**Grim** may indicate an anagram

Grimace Face, Girn, Moe, Mop, Moue, Mouth, Mow, Murgeon, Pout

Grime(s), Grimy Colly, Dirt, Peter, Reechie, Reechy, Soil, Sweep

Grin Fleer, Girn, Risus, Simper, Smirk, Sneer

Grind(ing), Grinder Bray, Bruxism, Chew, Crunch, ➤ CRUSH, Droil, Gnash, Grate, Graunch, Grit, Kern, Kibble, Levigate, Mano, Mill, Mince, Molar, Muller, Pug, Pulverise, Slog, Stamp, Triturate

Grip(ping), Gripper Ascendeur, Bite, Chuck, Clam, Clamp, Clip, Clutch, Craple, Embrace, Enthral, Get, Grapple, ➤ GRASP,

Haft, Hairpin, Handhold, Hend, Hold, Hug, Kirby®, Lewis, Obsess, Pincer, Pinion, Prehensile, Purchase, Raven, Rhine, Sally, Sipe, Strain, Streigne, Valise, Vice, Walise, Wrestle

Gripe(s) Colic, Complain, Ditch, Grasp, Griffin, Ileus, Pain, Tormina

Grit(ty) Blinding, Clench, Gnash, Granular, Grate, Guts, Pluck, Resolution, Sabulose, Sand, Shingle, Swarf

Groin Gnarr, Inguinal, Lisk

▷ **Groom** may indicate an anagram

Groove(d), Groovy Bezel, Canal, Cannelure, Chamfer, Channel, Chase, Clevis, Coulisse, Croze, Dièdre, Exarate, Fissure, Flute, Fuller, Furr, Furrow, Glyph, Gouge, Kerf, Key-seat, Keyway, Oche, Pod, Rabbet, Race(way), Raggle, Rebate, Rif(f)le, Rigol(l), Rout, ➤ RUT, Scrobe, Sipe, Slot, Sulcus, Throat, Track, Trough, Vallecula

Grope(r) Feel, Fumble, Grabble, Hapuka, Ripe, Scrabble

Gross All-up, Coarse, Complete, Crass, Dense, Earthy, Flagrant, Frankish, Gr, Material, Obese, Outsize, Overweight, Pre-tax, Rank, Ribald, Rough, Stupid, Whole

▷ **Gross** may indicate an anagram

Grotesque Antic, Bizarre, Fantastic, Fright, Gargoyle, Magot, Outlandish, Rabelaisian, Rococo

Ground(s) Arena, Astroturf, Basis, Bottom, Breeding, Campus, Cause, Common, Criterion, Crushed, Deck, Dregs, Eard, Earth, Epig(a)eal, Epig(a)ean, Epig(a)eous, Footing, Grated, Grist, Grouts, Lees, Leeway, Lek, Lords, Lot, Marl, Mealed, Occasion, Oval, Parade, Pitch, Plat, Plot, Policy, Proving, Quad, ➤ REASON, Recreation, Réseau, Ring, Sediment, Slade, Soil, Solum, Stadium, Terra, Terrain, Tract, Turf, Udal, Venue, Waste(land), Yard, Yird

▷ **Ground** may indicate an anagram

Group Band, Batch, Beatles, Bee, Bevy, Bloc(k), Body, Camp, Cartel, Category, Cell, Circle, Class(is), Clique, Cluster, Colony, Commune, Community, Congregation, Consort(ium), Contingent, Coterie, Crew, Ensemble, Faction, Genus, Guild, In-crowd, League, Order, Outfit, Panel, Party, Peer, Platoon, Ring, School, Sector, Seminar, Series, Set, Several, Society, Sort, Sub-order, Syndicate, Tribe, Trio, Umbrella, Unit

Grouse Blackcock, Bleat, Caper(caillie), Capercailzie, Covey, Gorcock, Greyhen, Gripe, Growl, Grumble, Hazel-hen, Heath-cock, Heath-hen, Jeremiad, Moan, Moorcock, Moorfowl, Moor-pout, Muir-poot, Muir-pout, Mutter, Natter, Peeve, Pintail, Prairie-hen, Ptarmigan, Resent, Rype(r), Snarl, Spruce, Twelfth, Wheenge, W(h)inge, Willow

Grove Academy, Arboretum, Bosk, Bosquet, Copse, Glade, Hurst, Lyceum, Nemoral, Orchard, Orchat, Silva, Tope

Grow(ing), Grow out, Growth Accrete, Accrue, Acromegaly, Adenoma, Aggrandisement, Angioma, Apophysis, Arborescence, Auxesis, Bedeguar, Boom, Braird, Breer, Burgeon, Car(b)uncle, Cholelith, Chondroma, Compensatory, Condyloma, Crescendo, Crop, Culture, Cyst, Ectopia, Edema, Ellagic, Enate, Enchondroma, Enlarge, Epinasty, Epitaxy, Excrescence, Exostosis, Expansion, Fibroid, Flor, Flourish, Flush, Gain, Gall, Germinate, Get, Goitre, Hepatocele, Hummie, Hyponasty, Increase, Knur(r), Lichen, Lipoma, Mushroom, Myoma, Nur(r), Oedema, Oncology, Osselet, Osteoma, Polyp, Proleg, Proliferate, Rampant, Scirrhus, Septal, Snowball, Spavin, ➤ SPROUT, Stipule, Sympodial, Tariff, Thrive, Tylosis, Vegetable, Wart, Wax, Wox

▷**Grow(n)** may indicate an anagram

Growl(ing) Fremescent, Gnar, Groin, Grr, Gurl, Roar(e), Roin, Royne, Snar(l)

Grub(by) Assart, Bardy, Caddis, Caterpillar, Cheer, Chow, Chrysalis, Dig, Eats, Fare, Fodder, ➤ FOOD, Gentle, Groo-groo, Gru-gru, Larva, Leatherjacket, Mawk, Mess, Nosh, Palmerworm, Peck, Pupa, Root(le), Rout, Rowt, Sap, Slave, Stub, Tired, Wireworm, Witchetty, Worm

Gruesome Ghastly, Grisly, Grooly, Horror, Macaberesque, Macabre, ➤ MORBID, Sick

Grumble Beef, Bellyache, Bitch, Bleat, Chunter, Croak, Girn, Gripe, Grizzle, Groin, Growl, Moan, Murmur, Mutter, Nark, Natter, Repine, Rumble, Whinge, Yammer

Grump(y) Attercap, Bearish, Cross, Ettercap, Grouchy, Moody, Sore-headed, Surly

Grunt Groin, Grumph, Humph, Oink, Pigfish, Ugh, Wheugh

Guarantee Assure, Avouch, Certify, Ensure, Gage, Hallmark, Insure, Mainprise, Money-back, Pignerate, Pignorate,

➤ PLEDGE, Plight, Seal, Secure, Sponsion, Surety,
➤ VOUCH(SAFE), Warrandice, Warrant(y)

Guard(ed), Guards Beefeaters, Blues, Bouncer, Cordon,
Custodian, Duenna, Escort, Fender, Hedge, Home, Jailer, Keep,
Look out, Patrol, Picket, ➤ PROTECT, Rail, Secure, Sentinel,
Sentry, Shield, SS, Vigilante, Visor, Ward, Watch (and ward),
Watchdog, Watchman, Yeoman

Guardian Altair, Argus, Curator, Custodian, Custos, Dragon,
Gemini, Granthi, Hafiz, Janus, Julius, Miminger, Templar,
Trustee, Tutelar(y), Warder, Watchdog, Xerxes

Gue(r)rilla Bushwhacker, Chetnik, Contra, ETA, Fedayee,
Gook, Khmer Rouge, Komitaji, Maquis, Mujahadeen,
Mujaheddin, Mujahedeen, Mujahed(d)in, Mujahideen,
Partisan, Terrorist, Tupamaro, Urban, Viet cong, Zapata

Guess Aim, Aread, Arede, Arreede, Conjecture, Divine, Estimate,
Harp, Hazard, Imagine, Infer, Level, Mor(r)a, Mull, Shot,
Speculate, Suppose, Surmise, Theorise

Guest(s) Caller, Company, Parasite, Paying, PG, Symbion(t),
Symphile, Synoecete, Visitant, ➤ VISITOR, Xenial

Guidance, Guide(line) Advice, Baedeker, Bradshaw,
Cicerone, Clue, Conduct, Counsel, Courier, Director(y),
➤ ESCORT, Index, Inspire, Itinerary, Key, Landmark, Mark, Map,
Mentor, Model, Navigate, Nose, Pilot, Pointer, Ranger,
Reference, Rudder, Shepherd, Sign, Sixer, Steer, Template,
Train, Waymark

Guild Artel, Basoche, Company, Gyeld, Hanse, Hoastman,
League, Society, Tong, Union

Guillotine Closure, Louisiette, Maiden, Marianne

Guilt(y) Angst, Blame, Cognovit, Flagitious, Nocent, Peccavi,
Remorse, Wicked

Guitar(ist) Acoustic, Axe(man), Bottleneck, Cithern, Cittern,
Dobro®, Fender®, Gittern, Hawaiian, Humbucker, Lute,
Plankspanker, Samisen, Sancho, Sanko, Shamisen, Sitar,
Spanish, Steel, Uke, Ukulele

Gulf Aden, Aqaba, Bay, Bothnia, California, Cambay,
Carpentaria, Chasm, Chihli, Darien, Exmouth, Fonseca, Hauraki,
Honduras, Lepanto, Lingayen, Lion, Mannar, Martaban, Maw,
Mexico, Persian, Queen Maud, Saronic, Sidra, Spencer, Tonkin,
Trieste, Tunis

Gull(s) Bonxie, Cheat, Cob(b), Cod, Cozen, Dupe, Fool, Geck, Graucous, Hoodwink, Laridae, Larus, Maw, Mew, Pickmaw, Pigeon, Queer, Rook, Scaury, Scourie, Scowrie, Sea-cob, Sea-mew, Sell, Simp, Skua, Sucker, Tern, Tystie, Xema

Gullet Crop, Enterate, Maw, Throat, Weasand-pipe

Gully Couloir, Donga, Geo, Gio, Goe, Grough, Gulch, Pit, Rake, Ravine, Sloot, Sluit, Wadi

Gulp Bolt, Draught, Gollop, Quaff, Slug, Sob, ➤ SWALLOW, Swipe, Wolf

Gum (tree) Acacia, Acajou, Acaroid, Agar, Algin, Angico, Arabic, Arabin, Arar, Arctic, Asafoetida, Bablah, Balata, Balm, Bandoline, Bdellium, Benjamin, Benzoin, Bloodwood, Boot, Bubble, Cerasin, Chicle, Chuddy, Chutty, Coolabah, Courbaril, Dextrin(e), Dragon's-blood, Ee-by, Eucalyptus, Frankincense, Galbanum, Gamboge, Gingival, ➤ GLUE, Goat's-thorn, Gosh, Guar, Ironbark, Karri, Kauri, La(b)danum, Lac, Lentisk, Mastic(h), Mucilage, Myrrh, Nicotine, Olibanum, Opopanax, Oshac, Sagapenum, Sarcocolla, Scribbly, Size, Sleep, Spearmint, Spirit, Sterculia, Stringybark, Sugar, Tacamahac, Tragacanth, Tupelo, Xanthan

Gun(fire), Guns Bombard, Broadside, Cannonade, Fieldpiece, Heater, Hired, Metal, Ordnance, Piece, Rev, Rod, Shooter, Tool

Gunner, Gunner's assistant Arquebusier, Arsenal, Artillerist, Cannoneer, Cannonier, Culverineer, Gr, Matross, RA

Gunpowder Charcoal, Saucisse, Saucisson

Gurgle Clunk, Gollar, Goller, Guggle, Ruckle, Squelch

Gush(ing) Blether, Effusive, ➤ FLOOD, Flow, Jet, Outpour, Rail, Regurgitate, Scaturient, Spirt, Spout, Spurt, Too-too

Gust Blast, Blore, Flaught, Flaw, Flurry, Puff, Sar, Waff

Gut(s), Gutty Archenteron, Balls, Beer, Bowel(s), Chitterlings, Cloaca, Disembowel, Duodenum, Draw, Enteral, Enteron, Entrails, Gill, Ileum, Insides, Kyle, Mesenteron, Omentum, Omental, Remake, Sack, Sand, Snell, Stamina, Staying-power, Strip, Thairm, Tripe, Ventriculus, Viscera

Gutta-percha Jelutong, Pontianac, Pontianak

Gutter(ing) Channel, Conduit, Cullis, Grip, Kennel, Rhone, Rigol(l), Roan, Rone, Sough, Spout, Strand, Sweal, Sweel

Guy Backstay, Bo, Burgess, Chaff, Clewline, Decamp, Deride, Effigy, Fall, Fawkes, Fellow, Gink, Josh, Mannering, Parody, Rib, Rope, Scarecrow, Stay, Tease, Vang, Wise

Gym(nasium), Gymnast(ic) Acrobat, Akhara, Arena, Dojo, Jungle, Lyceum, Palaestra, PE, PT, Rhythmic, Sokol, Tumbler

Gypsum Alabaster, Gesso, Plaster, Satin-stone, Selenite

Gypsy Bohemian, Cagot, Caird, Caqueux, Chai, Chal, Chi, Collibert, Esmeralda, Faw, Gipsen, Gitano, Hayraddin, Lavengro, Meg, Rom(any), Rye, Scholar, Tinker, Tsigane, Vagabond, Wanderer, Zigan, Zigeuner, Zincala, Zincalo, Zingaro

Gyrate Revolve, Rotate, ➤ SPIN, Twirl

Hh

H Ache, Aitch, Aspirate, Height, Hospital, Hotel, Hydrant, Hydrogen

Habit(s), Habitual, Habituate, Habitué Accustom, Addiction, Apparel, Assuetude, Bent, Chronic, Clothes, Coat, Consuetude, Custom, Dress, Ephod, Frequenter, Garb, Inure, Inveterate, Motley, Mufti, Nature, Outfit, Practice, Raiment, Regular, Riding, Robe, Routine, Scapular, Schema, Season, Set, Soutane, Suit, Surplice, Toge, Trait, Usual, Way, Won, Wont

Habitat Element, Environment, Haunt, Home, Locality, Station

Hack Chip, Chop, Cough, Cut, Drudge, Garble, Gash, Ghost, Grub-street, Hag, Hash, Hedge-writer, Heel, Hew, Horse, Mangle, Mutilate, Nag, Notch, Pad, Paper-strainer, Penny-a-liner, Pot-boiler, Rosinante, Spurn, Tadpole, Taper, Tussis, Unseam

Hackneyed Banal, Cab, Cliché, Corny, Percoct, Stale, Threadbare, Tired, Trite

Haddock Arbroath smokie, Finnan, Whitefish

Hades Dis, Hell, Orcus, Pit, Tartarus

Hag(-like) Anile, Beldame, Besom, Carlin(e), Crone, Harpy, Harridan, Hell-cat, Hex, Rudas, Runnion, Trot, Witch

Haggard Drawn, ➤ GAUNT, Pale, Rider

Haggle Argue, Badger, ➤ BARGAIN, Barter, Chaffer, Dicker, Horse-trade, Niffer, Palter, Prig

Hail(er) Acclaim, Ahoy, Ave, Bull-horn, Cheer, Fusillade, Graupel, Greet, Hi, Ho, Megaphone, Salue, Salute, Shower, Signal, Skoal, Skol, Sola, Stentor, Storm, Whoa-ho-ho

Hair(like), Hairy, Hair condition/cut/style Afro, Bang, Barnet, Beard, Bob, Bouffant, Braid, Bristle, Bun, Bunches, Capillary, Chignon, Coiffure, Cowlick, Crew-cut, DA, Dreadlocks, Fringe, Fur, Lock, Mane, Mohican, Mop, Pageboy, Perm(anent), Pigtail, Plait, Pompadour, Ponytail, Shingle, Shock, Sideburns, Switch, Thatch, Tonsure, Topknot, Tress, Wig

Hairdresser Barber, Coiffeur, Comb, Crimper, Friseur, Marcel, Salon, Stylist, Trichologist

Hairless Bald, Callow, Glabrate, Glabrous, Irate

Hairpiece Merkin, Strand, Toupee, Wig

Halcyon Calm, Kingfisher, Mild

Half, Halved Bifid, Demi, Dimidiate, Divide, Hemi, Moiety, Semi, Share, Split, Stand-off, Term

Half-wit Changeling, Mome, Simpleton, ➤ STUPID

Hall Anteroom, Atrium, Auditorium, Aula, Basilica, Carnegie, Chamber, Citadel, City, Dance, Dotheboys, Festival, Foyer, Liberty, Lobby, Music, Odeon, Palais, Passage, Salle, Saloon, Tammany, Town, Vestibule, Wildfell

➤**Hallo** see HELLO

Hallucinate, Hallucination, Hallucinogen Autoscopy, Fantasy, Freak, Illusion, Image, Mirage, Psychedelic

Halo Antheolion, Areola, Aura, Aureola, Corona, Gloria, Gloriole, Mandorla, Nimbus, Rim, Vesica

Halt(er) Arrest, Block, Brake, Bridle, Cavesson, Cease, Check, Game, Hackamore, Heave-to, Hilch, Lame(d), Limp, Noose, Prorogue, Rope, Stall, Standstill, ➤ STOP, Stopover, Toho, Whoa

Ham(s) Amateur, Barnstormer, Flitch, Gammon, Haunch, Hock, Hoke, Hough, Hunker, Jambon, Jay, Nates, Overact, Overplay, Parma, Prat, Prosciutto, Tiro, Westphalian, York

Hamlet Aldea, Auburn, Cigar, Dane, Dorp, Hero, Kraal, Stead, Thorp(e), Vill(age), Wick

Hammer(ed), Hammerhead Ballpeen, Ballpein, Beetle, Bully, Bush, Celt, Claw, Flatten, Fuller, Gavel, Hack, Incuse,

Kevel, Knap, Madge, Mall(et), Malleate, Martel, Maul,
Mjol(l)nir, Nevel, Pane, Pean, Peen, Pein, Pene, Percussion,
Piledriver, Plessor, Plexor, Rawhide, Shingle, Sledge, Strike,
Tenderizer, Tilt, Trip, Umbre, Water

▷**Hammered** may indicate an anagram

▷**Hammy** may indicate an anagram

Hamper Basket, Cabin, Cramp, Cumber, Delay, Encumber,
Entrammel, Hamstring, Handicap, Hobble, Hog-tie, Obstruct,
Pad, Pannier, Restrict, Rub, Shackle, Tangle, Trammel, Tuck

Hand(s), Hand down, Hand-like, Handwriting
Assist(ance), Bananas, Bequeath, Charge, Clap(ping), Club,
Clutch, Copperplate, Court, Crew, Cursive, Deal, Deck, Deliver,
Devolve, Dukes, Dummy, Fin, Fist, Flipper, Flush, Free, Glad,
Graphology, Help, Helping, Impart, L, Man, Manual, Mitt(en),
Operative, Pad, Part, Pass, Paw, Post, Pud, R, Script, Signature,
Span, Straight, Text, Upper, Whip, Worker

Handbag Caba(s), Grip, Indispensable, Pochette, Purse,
Reticule, Valise

Handbook Baedeker, Companion, Enchiridion, Guide,
Manual, Vade-mecum

Handcuff(s) Bracelet, Darbies, Irons, Manacle, Mittens,
Nippers, Snaps

Handicap Burden, Encumber, Hamper, Impede, Impost, Lame,
Liability, ➤ OBSTACLE, Off, Restrict, Weigh(t), Welter-race

Handkerchief, Hanky Bandan(n)a, Clout, Kleenex®,
Napkin, Nose-rag, Orarium, Tissue, Wipe(r)

Handle(d) Ansate, Bail, Bale, Bitstock, Brake, Broomstick,
Cope, Crank, Dead man's, Deal, Doorknob, Dudgeon, Ear, Feel,
Finger, Forename, Gaum, Gorm, Grip, Haft, Helve, Hilt, Hold,
Knob, Knub, Lug, ➤ MANAGE, Manipulate, Manubrium, Maul,
Name, Nib, Palp, Paw, Pommel, Process, Rounce, Shaft, Snath,
Snead, Sneath, Sned, Staff, Staghorn, Stale, Steal(e), Steel, Steil,
Stele, Stilt, Stock, Tiller, Title, To-name, Touch, Treat, Use,
Whipstock, Wield, Withe

Hand-out Alms, Charity, Dole, Gift, Release, Sample

Handsome Adonis, Apollo, Bonny, Brave, Comely, Dishy,
Featuous, Gracious, Liberal

▶**Handwriting** see HAND

Handy(man) Accessible, Close, Convenient, Deft,
Dext(e)rous, Digit, Factotum, Jack(-of-all-trades), Near, Nigh,
Palmate, Palmist, Ready, Skilful, Spartan, Useful

Hang, Hanger, Hanging(s) Append, Arras, Aweigh, Chick,
Chik, Dangle, Darn, Depend, Dewitt, Dossal, Dossel, Dosser,
Drape, Droop, Execute, Frontal, Gobelin, Hinge, Hoove,
Hove(r), Kakemono, Kilt, Lobed, Loll, Lop, Lynch, Mooch,
Noose, Nub, Pend(ant), Sag, Scenery, Scrag, Set, Sit, Sling,
Suspend, Suspercollate, Swing, Tapestry, Tapet, Tapis, Toran(a)

Hanger-on Bur, Lackey, Leech, Limpet, Liripoop, Parasite,
Satellite, Sycophant, Toady

Hangman, Hangmen Bull, Calcraft, Dennis, Derrick,
Gregory, Ketch, Marwood, Nubbing-cove, Pierrepoint

Hangover Canopy, Cornice, Crapulence, Drape, DT's, Head,
Hot coppers, Katzenjammer, Mistletoe, Tester

Hanker(ing) Desire, Envy, Hunger, Itch, Long, Yearn, Yen

Haphazard Casual, Chance, Higgledy-piggledy, Promiscuous,
➤ RANDOM, Rough and tumble, Slapdash, Willy-nilly

Happen(ing), Happen to Afoot, Be, Befall, Befortune,
Betide, Come, Event(uate), Fall-out, ➤ OCCUR, Pan, Pass, Prove,
Thing, Tide, Transpire, Worth

Happiness, Happy Apposite, Ave, Beatific, Beatitude, Blessed,
Bliss, Bonny, Carefree, Cheery, Chuffed, Cock-a-hoop, Dwarf,
Ecstatic, Elated, Eud(a)emony, Felicity, Felix, Fortunate,
Glad(some), Gleeful, Golden, Goshen, Gruntled, Halcyon,
Half-cut, Hedonism, Jovial, Joy, Larry, Light-hearted, Merry,
Opportune, Radiant, Rapture, Sandboy, Seal, Seel, Sele, Serene,
Sunny, Tipsy, Trigger, Warrior

Harangue Declaim, Diatribe, Lecture, Oration, Perorate,
Philippic, Sermon, Speech, Spruik, Tirade

Harass(ed) Afflict, Annoy, Badger, Bait, Beleaguer, Bother,
Chivvy, Distract, Dun, Gall, Hassle, Heckle, Hector, Hound,
Irritate, Persecute, Pester, Plague, Press, Vex

Harbour Anchorage, Basin, Brest, Cherish, Dock, Entertain,
Herd, Hide, Marina, Mulberry, Pearl, PLA, Port, Quay, Reset,
➤ SHELTER, Watemata

Hard(en), Hardness Abstruse, Adamant(ine), Bony, Brittle,
Bronze, Cake, Calcify, Callous, Cast-iron, Crusty, Difficult, Dour,
Ebonite, Endure, Enure, Firm, Flint(y), Geal, Granite, Gruelling,

H, HH, Horny, Inure, Iron(y), Knotty, Metallic, Moh, Nails, Obdurate, Osseous, Ossify, Permafrost, Petrify, Raw, Rugged, Ruthless, Set, Severe, Solid, Sore, Steel(y), Steep, Stern, Stoic, Stony, Teak, Temper, Tough, Wooden

Hardship Affliction, Grief, Mill, Mishap, Penance, Privation, Rigour, Trial, Trouble

Hardy Brave, Manful, Oliver, Ollie, Rugged, Sturdy, Thomas

Hare Arctic, Belgian, Doe, Down, Electric, Jugged, Leporine, Malkin, Scut, Snowshoe

Harm(ed), Harmful Aggrieve, Bane, Blight, Deleterious, Detriment, Evil, Hurt, Inimical, Injury, Insidious, Maleficent, Malignant, Maltreat, Mischief, Noxious, Pernicious, Sinister, Spoil, Wroken, Wrong

Harmless Benign, Canny, Drudge, Informidable, Innocent, Innocuous, Innoxious, Inoffensive

Harmonious, Harmonise, Harmony Agree(ment), Alan, Assort, Atone, Attune, Balanced, Blend, Chord, Concent, Concentus, Concert, Concinnity, Concord, Congruous, Consonant, Consort, Correspondence, Counterpoint, Descant, Diapason, Diatessaron, Doo-wop, Euphony, Eur(h)ythmy, Faburden, Feng-shui, Jibe, Melody, Musical, Solidarity, Symmetry, Sympathy, Sync, Thorough-bass, Tone, Tune, Unanimity, Unison

Harness(maker) Breeching, Bridle, Cinch, Equipage, Frenum, Gear, Girth, Hitch, Inspan, Lorimer, Loriner, Pad-tree, Partnership, Tack(le), Throat-stop, Trace, Yoke

Harp(sichord) Aeolian, Clairschach, Clarsach, Clavier, Drone, Dwell, Irish, Lyre, Nebel, Trigon, Virginal, Welsh, Zither

Harridan Hag, Harpy, Shrew, Xantippe, Zantippe, Zentippe

Harry Aggravate, Badger, Bother, Champion, Chase, Chivvy, Coppernose, Dragoon, Flash, Fret, Hal, Hassle, Hector, Herry, Houdini, Hound, Lauder, Lime, Maraud, Molest, Nag, Pester, Plague, Rag, Reave, Reive, Rieve, Rile, Tate, Tchick, Torment

▷**Harry** may indicate an anagram

Harsh(ness) Acerbic, Austere, Barbaric, Brassy, Cruel, Desolate, Discordant, Draconian, Glary, Grating, Gravelly, Grim, Gruff, Guttural, Hard, Inclement, Raucle, Raucous, Raw,

Rigour, Rude, Scabrid, Screechy, ➤ SEVERE, Sharp, Spartan, Stark, Stern, Stoor, Stour, Stowre, Strict, Strident

Hart Deer, Spade, Spay, Spay(a)d, Venison

Harvest(er), Harvest home Combine, Crop, Cull, Fruit, ➤ GATHER, Hairst, Hawkey, Hay(sel), Hockey, Horkey, In(ning), Ingather, Kirn, Lease, Nutting, Pick, Produce, Rabi, Random, Reap, Shock, Spatlese, Tattie-howking, Thresh, Vendage, Vendange

Hash(ish) Bungle, Charas, Discuss, Garble, Garboil, Hachis, Lobscouse, Mince, Pi(e), Ragout

▷**Hashed** may indicate an anagram

Haste(n), Hastening, Hastily, Hasty Cursory, Despatch, Express, Festinately, Fly, Hare, Headlong, Hie, Hotfoot, ➤ HURRY, Impetuous, Precipitant, Race, Ramstam, Rash, Rush, Scuttle, Speed, Spur, Stringendo, Sudden, Tear, Tilt

Hat Brass, Chapeau, Christie, Christy, Claque, Cloche, Cocked, Headdress, Head-rig, Lid

Hatch(ment), Hatching Achievement, Altricial, Booby, Breed, Brood, Cleck, Clutch, Companion, Concoct, Cover, Devise, Eclosion, Emerge, Escape, Incubate, Set, Trap-door

▷**Hatching** may indicate an anagram

Hate(ful), Hatred Abhor, Abominable, Abominate, Anims, Aversion, Bugbear, Detest, Enmity, Haterent, Loathe, Misogyny, Odium, Phobia, Racism, Resent, Spite, Ug(h), Vitriol

Haughty Aloof, Aristocratic, Arrogant, Disdainful, Fastuous, High, Hogen-mogen, Hoity-toity, Hye, Imperious, Lofty, Paughty, ➤ PROUD, Scornful, Sniffy, Upstage

Haul(ier) Bag, Bouse, Bowse, Brail, Carry, Cart, Catch, Drag, Heave, Hove, Kedge, Loot, Plunder, Pull, Rug, Sally, Scoop, Snig, Touse, Touze, Tow(se), Towze, Transporter, Winch, Yank

Haunt(s) Catchy, Den, Dive, Frequent, Ghost, Hang-out, Honky-tonk, Houf(f), Howf(f), Obsess, Purlieu, Resort, Spot

Have, Having Bear, Bouse, Ha(e), Han, Hoax, Hold, Of, ➤ OWN, Possess, Sell

Haven Asylum, Harbour, Hithe, Hythe, Oasis, Port, Refuge, Refugium, Retreat, Shelter, Tax

Havoc Desolation, Devastation, Hell, Ravage, Waste

▷**Havoc** may indicate an anagram

Hawk(er), Hawkish Accipitrine, Badger, Bastard, Buzzard, Cast, Cheapjack, Cry, Eagle, Elanet, Eyas, Falcon, Gerfalcon, Goshawk, Hardliner, Harrier, Hobby, Kestrel, Kite, Lammergeier, Lanner(et), Marsh, Monger, Nyas, Osprey, Passage, Pearly, Pedlar, Peddle, Peregrine, Ringtail, Sell, Slab, Soar(e), Sparrow, Spiv, Tallyman, Tassel, Tercel(et), Trant(er), Warlike

Hawthorn Albespine, Albespyne, May(flower), Quickset

Hay, Hey Antic, Cock, Contra-dance, Fodder, Goaf, Hi, Kemple, Math, Mow, Pleach, Salt, Stack, Straw, Windrow

Hazard(ous) Breakneck, Bunker, Chance, Danger, Dare, Die, Dye, Game, Gremlin, Guess, Imperil, In-off, Jeopardy, Main, Nice, Occupational, Peril, Play, Pothole, Queasy, ➤ RISK, Stake, Trap, Venture, Vigia, Wage

Haze, Hazy Blear, Cloud, Filmy, Fog, ➤ MIST, Mock, Muzzy, Nebulous, Smog, Tease

▷ **Haze** may indicate an anagram

Head(s), Heading, Headman, Heady Apex, Beachy, Bean, Behead, Bill, Block, Bonce, Boss, Brain, Brow, But(t), Cape, Capo, Captain, Caudillo, Chief, Coarb, Coconut, Coma, Commander, Conk, Cop, Coppin, Costard, Crest, Crisis, Crown, Crumpet, Director, Dome, Each, Ear, Figure, Flamborough, Foam, Froth, Hoe, Jowl, Knob, Knowledge-box, Lead(er), Lid, Lizard, Loaf, Loo, Lore, Manager, Mayor, Maz(z)ard, Mull, Nab, Nana, Napper, Ness, Nob, Noddle, Noggin, Noll, Noup, Nowl, Nut, Obverse, Occiput, Onion, Pate, Pater(familias), Patriarch, Point, Poll, Pow, Prefect, President, Principal, Promontory, Provost, Ras, Ream, Scalp, Sconce, Short, Sinciput, Skull, Source, Squeers, Superior, Tete, Throne, Tight, Title, Toilet, Top, Topic

▷ **Head** may indicate the first letter of a word

Headdress, Head cover Ampyx, Balaclava, Bandeau, Bas(i)net, Bonnet, Burnous(e), Busby, Calotte, Chaplet, Circlet, Comb, Cor(o)net, Cowl, Coxcomb, Crownet, Curch, Doek, Dopatta, Dupatta, Fascinator, Fontange, Hat(tock), Helm(et), Juliet cap, Kaffiyeh, Kuffiyeh, Kufiah, Kufiya(h), Kell, Kerchief, Mantilla, Mitre, Mobcap, Modius, Mortarboard, Nubia, Periwig, Pill-box, Plug-hat, Porrenger, Porringer, Romal, Sakkos, Skullcap, Sphendome, Taj, Tarbush, Tiara, Tower, Tulban, Turban, War bonnet, Wig, Wimple

Headland Bill, Cape, Head-rig, Hoe, Hogh, Morro, Naze, Ness, Noup, Promontory, Ras, Ross, Scaw, Skaw

Headline Banner, Caption, Frown, Scare-head, Screamer, Streamer, Title

Headlong Breakneck, Pell-mell, Precipitate, Ramstam, Reckless, Steep, Sudden, Tantivy, Tearaway

▶**Headman** see HEAD

Headphone(s) Cans, Earpiece, Walkman®

Headquarters Base, Command, Depot, Pentagon, Station

▷**Heads** may indicate a lavatory

Headstrong Obstinate, Rash, Stubborn, Unruly, Wayward

Headway Advancement, Headroom, Progress

Heal(ing) Aesculapian, Balsam, Chiropractic, Cicatrise, Cleanse, Cure, Esculapian, G(u)arish, Hele, Knit, Mend, Olosis, Osteopathy, Restore, Sain, Salve, Sanitory, Therapeutic

Healer Asa, Doctor, Homeopath, Naturopath, Osteopath, Sangoma, Shaman, Time

Health(y) Bracing, Chin-chin, Doer, Fit, Flourishing, Gesundheit, Hail, Hale, Hartie-hale, Heart, Holism, Kia-ora, L'chaim, Lustique, Lusty, Medicaid, Medicare, Pink, Prosit, Robust, Salubrious, Sane, Slainte, Sound, Toast, Tope, Valetudinarian, Vigour, Well, WHO, Wholesome

Heap(ed) Acervate, Agglomerate, Amass, Bing, Bulk, Car, Clamp, Cock, Congeries, Cumulus, Drift, Hog, Jalopy, Lot, Pile, Rick(le), Ruck, Scrap, Slag, Stash, Toorie

Hear(ing) Acoustic, Attend, Audience, Audile, Avizandum, Captain's mast, Catch, Clairaudience, Dirdum, Ear, Harken, Learn, List(en), Oyer, Oyez, Panel

▷**Hear(say)** may indicate a word sounding like one given

Hearsay Account, Gossip, Report, Rumour, Surmise

Heart(en), Heartily, Hearty, Heart-shaped AB, Agood, Auricle, Backslapping, Beater, Bluff, Bosom, Bradycardia, Cant, Cardiac, Centre, Cheer, Cockles, Columella, Cordate, Cordial, Core, Crossed, Courage, Daddock, Embolden, Essence, Gist, H, Hale, Herz, Inmost, Jarta, Kernel, Lepid, Memoriter, Mesial, Mid(st), Nub, Nucleus, Obcordate, Purple, Robust, Root, Sacred, Sailor, Seafarer, Seaman, Sinoatrial, Staunch, Tachycardia, Tar, Ticker, Yarta, Yarto

Hearth Cupel, Fireside, Home, Ingle

Heartless Callous, Cored, Cruel, Three-suited

Heat(ed), Heater, Heating Anneal, Ardour, Atomic, Barrage, Brazier, Calcine, Caloric, Calorifier, Central, Chafe, Convector, Dudgeon, Element, Eliminator, Etna, Excite, Ferment, Fever, Fire, Fluster, Fug, Furnace, Het, Hyperthermia, Hypocaust, Immersion, Incalescence, J, Kindle, Latent, Lust, Normalise, Oestrus, Prelim, Prickly, Q, Radiant, Radiator, Render, Rut, Salt, Scald, Sizzle, Space, Specific, Spice, Stew, Storage, Stove, Tind, Tine, Torrefy, Underfloor, Warming-pan, Warmth, White

Heathen Ethnic, Gentile, Infidel, Litholatrous, Pagan, Pa(i)nim, Paynim, Philistine, Primitive, Profane

▷**Heating** may indicate an anagram

Heave(d) Cast, Fling, Heeze, Hoist, Hump, Hurl, Popple, Retch, Shy, Sigh, Vomit

▷**Heave** may indicate 'discard'

Heaven(s), Heavenly Air, Aloft, Ama, Ambrosial, Asgard, Bliss, Celestial, Celia, Divine, Ecstasy, Elysian, Elysium, Empyrean, Ethereal, Fiddler's Green, Firmament, Hereafter, Himmel, Holy, Leal, Lift, Mackerel, Olympus, Paradise, Pole, Seventh, Shangri-la, Sion, Sky, Supernal, Svarga, Swarga, Swerga, Tur-na-n'og, Uranian, Welkin, Zion

Heavy(weight), Heavily, Heaviness Ali, Dutch, Elephantine, Embonpoint, Endomorph, Grave, Hefty, Last, Leaden, Onerous, Osmium, Pesante, Ponderous, Sad, Scelerate, Stout, Upse(e), Weighty, Wicked

Heckle Badger, Gibe, Harass, Needle, Spruik

Hedge, Hedging Box, Bullfinch, Enclosure, Equivocate, Haw, Hay, Lay off, Meuse, Mews, Muse, Pleach, Privet, Quickset, Raddle, Sepiment, Shield, Stonewall, Thicket

Hedgehog Gymnure, Hérisson, Tenrec, Tiggywinkle, Urchin

Heed(ed), Heedful Attend, Listen, ▶ MIND, Notice, Observe, Rear, Reck, Regard(ant), Respect, Rought, Tent

Heedless Careless, Incautious, Rash, Scapegrace, Scatterbrain

Heel Cad, Calcaneum, Cant, Careen, Cuban, Dogbolt, Foot, French, Kitten, List, Louse, Rogue, Seel, Spike, Stacked, Stiletto, Tilt, Wedge

Height(en), Heights Abraham, Altitude, Cairngorm, Ceiling, Dimension, Elevation, Embroider, Eminence, Enhance, Golan,

H, Hill, Hypsometry, Level, Might, Peak, Procerity, Stature, Stud, Sum, ➤ SUMMIT, Tor

Heir Alienee, Claimant, Coparcener, Dauphin, Devisee, Eigne, Institute, Intitule, Legatee, Parcener, Scion, Sprig, Tanist

▷ **Held by** may indicate a hidden word

Hell(ish) Abaddon, Ades, Agony, Amenthes, Annw(yf)n, Avernus, Below, Chthonic, Dis, Erebus, Furnace, Gehenna, Hades, Heck, Inferno, Malebolge, Naraka, Orcus, Pandemonium, Perditious, Pit, Sheol, Stygian, Tartar(ean), Tartarus, Tophet, Torment

Hello, Hallo, Hullo Aloha, Chin-chin, Ciao, Dumela, Hi, Ho(a), Howdy, Howzit, Yoo-hoo

Helmet Armet, Balaclava, Basinet, Beaver, Burganet, Burgonet, Cask, Casque, Comb, Crash, Galea, Heaume, Knapscal, Knapscull, Knapskull, Montero, Mor(r)ion, Nasal, Pickelhaube, Pith, Plumed, Pot, Salade, Sal(l)et, Shako, Skid-lid, Topee, Topi

Help(er), Helping, Helpful Abet, Accomplice, Adjuvant, Advantage, Aid(ance), Aidant, Aide, Alleviate, Ally, ➤ ASSIST, Avail, Back, Benefit, Befriend, Bestead, Boon, Brownie, Char(woman), Coadjutor, Complice, Daily, Dollop, Dose, Forward, Further(some), Go, Hand, Hint, Instrumental, Leg-up, Maid, Mayday, Obliging, Order, Patronage, Ration, Recourse, Relieve, Servant, Serve, Slice, SOS, Stead, Sted, Subserve, Subvention, Succour, Taste, Therapeutic, Use

Helpless(ness) Anomie, Feeble, Impotent, Paralytic

Hen Biddy, Fowl

Hence Apage, Avaunt, Ergo, Go, Hinc, So, Therefore, Thus

Herald(ic), Heraldry Abatement, Argent, Armory, Azure, Bars, Bend, Bendwise, Blazonry, Bloody Hand, Bluemantle, Bordure, Caboched, Chevron, Chief, Cicerone, Cinquefoil, Clarenc(i)eux, Compone, Compony, Couchant, Counter-passant, Coue, Couped, Coward, Crier, Difference, Displayed, Dormant, Endorse, Erased, Fecial, Fess(e), Fetial, File, Flory, Forerunner, Gardant, Garter, Golp(e), Gules, Hauriant, Hermes, Issuant, Lionel, Lodged, Lyon, Martlet, Messenger, Mullet, Naiant, Naissant, Nascent, Nombril, Norroy, Opinicus, Or, Ordinary, Pale, Pallet, Paly, Passant, Pile, Portcullis, Potant, Precursor, Proclaim, Purpure, Pursuivant, Quartering, Rampant, Red Hand, Regardant, Roundel, Roundle, Sable, Salient, Scarp, Sea lion, Segreant, Sejant, Statant, Stentor, Subordinary,

Trangle, Tressure, Trick, Trippant, Trundle, Umbrated, Urinant, Usher, Verdoy, Vert, Vol(ant), Vorant, Yale

Herb(s) Garnish, Oleraceous, Paterson's curse, Weed

Herbicide Agent Orange, Atrazine, Defoliant, Picloram

Herd(er), Herdsman Band, Corral, Drive, Drover, Flock, Gang, Mob, Pod, Raggle-taggle, Round-up, Shepherd, Vaquero

Here Adsum, Hi, Hic, Hither, Local, Now, Present

Hereditary, Heredity Ancestry, Blood, Breeding, Codon, Eugenics, Genetics, Id(ant), Idioplasm, Mendelism

▷**Herein** may indicate a hidden word

Heresy, Heretic(al) Agnoitae, Albi, Albigensian, Apostasy, Arian, Bogomil, Bugger, Cathar, Docete, Dulcinist, Eudoxian, Giaour, Heresearch, Heterodoxy, Lollard, Montanism, Nestorian, Nonconformist, Origen, Patarin(e), Pelagius, Phrygian, Racovian, Rebel, Unitarian, Zendik

Hermaphrodite Androgengus, Gynandromorph, Monochinous, Monoecious

Hermit(age) Anchoret, Anchorite, Ascetic, Ashram(a), Augustinian, Austin, Cell, Cloister, Crab, Eremite, Grandmontine, Marabout, Monk, Museum, Nitrian, Peter, Recluse, Retreat, Sannyasi, Solitary, Troglodyte

Hero(ic) Brave, Champ(ion), Demigod, Eponym, Everyman, Folk, God, Goody, Great, Ideal, Idol, Noble, Priestess, Principal, Resolute, Revere, Sheik, Tragic, Valiant

Heroine Andromeda, Ariadne, Candida, Darling, Hedda, Imogen, Isolde, Juliet, Leda, Leonora, Manon, Mimi, Nana, Norma, Pamela, Star, Tess, Una

Herring Bloater, Brisling, Caller, Kipper, Red, Rollmop, Sild, Silt

Hesitate, Hesitation Balance, Boggle, Cunctation, Delay, Demur, Dicker, Dither, Doubtful, Falter, Halting, Haver, Haw, Mammer, ➤ PAUSE, Qualm, Scruple, Shillyshally, Shrink, Stagger, Stammer, Swither, Tarrow, Teeter, Tentative, Um, Ur, Vacillate, Wait, Waver

Hew Ax, Chop, Cut, Hack, Sever

▶**Hey** see HAY

Hiatus Caesura, Gap, Hernia, Interregnum, Lacuna, Lull

Hibernate, Hibernating Estivate, Latitant, Sleep, Winter

Hiccup Glitch, Singultus, Snag, Spasm, Yex

Hidden Buried, Covert, De(a)rn, Doggo, Hooded, Latent, Obscure, Occult, Pentimento, Recondite, Screened, Shuttered, Sly, Ulterior, Unseen, Veiled, Wrapped

▷**Hidden** may indicate a concealed word

Hide, Hiding Abscond, Befog, Bield(y), Box-calf, Burrow, Cache, Camouflage, Ceroon, Coat, ➤ CONCEAL, Cordwain, Couch, Cour, Crop, Curtain, Doggo, Earth, Eclipse, Encave, Ensconce, Enshroud, Envelop, Epidermis, Fell, Flaught, Flay, Harbour, Heal, Heel, Hele, Hell, Incave, Inter, Kip, Kipskin, Lair, Leather, Mask, Nebris, ➤ OBSCURE, Parfleche, Pell, Pelt, Plank, Plant, Robe, Saffian, Screen, Secrete, Shadow, Shellac(k), Skin, Spetch, Stash, Strap-oil, Tappice, Thong, Thrashing, Trove, Veil, Wallop, Whang, Wrap

Hideous(ness) Deform(ed), Enormity, Gash, Grotesque, Horrible, Odious, Ugly, Ugsome

High(er), Highly, Highness Alt(a), Altesse, Altissimo, Apogee, Atop, Brent, Climax, Doped, Drugged, E-la, Elation, Elevated, Eminent, Exalted, Excelsior, Frequency, Gamy, Haut(e), Intoxicated, Lofty, Mind-blowing, Orthian, Prime, Rancid, Ripe, School, Senior, Sent, Shrill, So, Steep, Stenchy, Stoned, String-out, Strong, Superior, Swollen, Tall, Tension, Tipsy, Top-lofty, Topmost, Treble, Up(per), Very, Wired

▷**High** may indicate an anagram

Highbrow Brain, Egghead, Intelligentsia, Long-hair

Highest Best, Climax, Ne plus ultra, Supreme

Highland(er), Highlands Blue-bonnet, Blue-cap, Cameron, Cat(h)eran, Down, Dun(n)iewassal, Duniwassal, Gael, Kiltie, Plaid(man), Redshank, Riff, Scot, Seaforth, Shire, Teuchter

▶**High-pitched** see HIGH

Highway Alaska, Alcan, Autobahn, Autopista, Autostrada, Flyover, Freeway, Interstate, Motorway, Overpass, Pass, Thoroughfare, Tightrope

Highwayman, Highway robber(y) Bandit, Bandolero, Duval, Footpad, Gilderoy, Jack Sheppard, Latrocinium, MacHeath, Scamp, Skyjacker, Toby, Turpin

Hike(r) Backpack, Bushbash, Bushwalk, Raise, Rambler, Ramp, Rise, Traipse, Tramp, Trape(s), Upraise

Hill(ock), Hills, Hillside Barrow, Beacon, Ben, Berg, Brae, Bunker, Butte, Crest, Dun(e), Eminence, Fell, Gradient, Height,

Hummock, Incline, Inselberg, Knap, Knoll, Koppie, Low, Mound, Rand, Range, Scaur, Stoss, Toft, Toot, Tump

Hilt Basket, Coquille, Haft, Handle, Hasp, Shaft

Hind(most) Back, Deer, Lag, Rear

Hinder, Hindrance Back, Bar, Block, Check, Counteract, Cumber, Debar, ➤ DELAY, Deter, Hamper, Harass, Holdback, Impeach, Impede, Obstacle, Posterior, Rear, Rein, Remora, Rump, Shackle, Slow, Stunt, Taigle, Thwart, Trammel

Hindu Arya Samaj, Babu, Bania(n), Banyan, Brahman, Brahmin, Dalit, Gentoo, Gurkha, Harijan, Jaina, Kshatriya, Maharishi, Pundit, Rajpoot, Rajput, Rama, Sad(d)hu, Saiva, S(h)akta, Sankhya, Shaiva, Sheik(h), Shudra, Sudra, Swami, Trimurti, Untouchable, Urdu, Vais(h)ya, Varna, Vedanta

Hinge Butt, Cardinal, Cross-garnet, Garnet, Gemel, Gimmer, Joint, Knee, Pivot

▷**Hinge(s)** may indicate a word reversal

Hint Allude, Clew, Clue, Cue, Element, Gleam, Hunch, Imply, Inkle, Inkling, Innuendo, Insinuate, Intimate, Key, Mint, Nuance, Office, Overtone, Pointer, Preview, Scintilla, Shadow, Soupçon, ➤ SUGGEST, Tang, Tip, Touch, Trace, Trick, Wind, Wink, Wisp, Word, Wrinkle

▷**Hint** may indicate a first letter

Hip(pie), Hippy, Hips Cafard, Cheer, Coxa(l), Drop-out, Huck(le), Hucklebone, Hunkers, Informed, Ischium, Sciatic

Hire(d), Hiring Affreightment, Charter, Engage, Fee, Freightage, Job, Lease, Merc(enary), Never-never, Rent, Shape-up, Ticca, Wage

▷**His** may indicate greetings

Hiss Boo, Fizzle, Goose, Hish, Sibilant, Siffle, Sizzle, Swish

Historian Acton, Adams, Antiquary, Archivist, Arrian, Asellio, Bede, Biographer, Bryant, Buckle, Camden, Carlyle, Chronicler, Etain, Froude, Gibbon, Gildas, Green, Griot, Herodotus, Knickerbocker, Livy, Macaulay, Oman, Pliny, Plutarch, Ponsonby, Renan, Roper, Sallust, Strachey, Suetonius, Tacitus, Thiers, Thucydides, Toynbee, Trevelyan, Wells, Xenophon

History, Historical Account, Anamnesis, Annal, Bunk, Case, Chronicle, Clio, Epoch(a), Ere-now, Ever, Heritage, Legend, Life, Mesolithic, Natural, Ontogency, Past, Record

Hit Bang, Bash, Baste, Bat, Bean, Belt, Blip, Blockbuster, Bloop, Blow, Bludgeon, Bolo, Bonk, Bunt, Clobber, Clock, Clout, Club, Collide, Cuff, Dot, Flail, Flick, Flip, Foul, Fourpenny-one, Fungo, Get, Hay, Head-butt, Home(-thrust), Impact, Knock, Lam, Magpie, Mug, Pandy, Pepper, Polt, Prang, Ram, Score, Sensation, Six, Skier, Sky, Slam, Slap, Slosh, Smash(eroo), Smit(e), Sock, Spank, Stoush, Straik, Stricken, Strike, Strook, Struck, ➤ SUCCESS, Swat, Switch, Thwack, Tip, Tonk, Touché, Venewe, Venue, Wallop, Wing, Ythundered, Zap, Zonk

Hitch Catch, Contretemps, Edge, Espouse, Hike, Hirsle, Hoi(c)k, Hotch, Jerk, Lorry-hop, Rub, Sheepshank, Sheet bend, Shrug, Snag, Technical, Thumb

Hoard(ing) Accumulate, Amass, Bill, Cache, Coffer, Eke, Heap, Hoord, Husband, Hutch, Mucker, Plant, Pose, Save, Sciurine, Snudge, Squirrel, Stash, Stock, Store, Treasure

Hoarse(ness) Croupy, Frog, Grating, Gruff, Husky, Raucous, Roar(er), Roopit, Roopy, Throaty

Hoax Bam, Canard, Cod, Do, Doff, Fub, Fun, Gag, Gammon, Gull, Hum, Huntie-gowk, Kid, Leg-pull, Piltdown, Sell, Skit, Spoof, String, Stuff, ➤ TRICK

Hobble, Hobbling Game, Hamshackle, Hilch, Hitch, Lame, Limp, Pastern, Picket, Spancel, Stagger, Tether

Hobby Avocation, Fad, Falcon, Interest, Pastance, ➤ PASTIME, Predator, Pursuit, Recreation, Scrimshaw

Hock Cambrel, Dip, Gambrel, Gambril, Gammon, Ham, Heel, Hough, Hypothecate, Pawn, Pledge, Rhenish, Wine

Hoe Claut, Dutch, Grub, Jembe, Nab, Pecker, Rake, Weed

Hog Babiroussa, Babirussa, Boar, Glutton, Guttle, Peccary, Pig, Porker, Shoat, Shott

Hoist Boom, Bouse, Crane, Davit, Derrick, Gin, Heft, Hills, Jack, Lewis, Lift, Raise, Shearlegs, Shears, Sheerlegs, Sheers, Sway, Teagle, Trice, Whip-and-derry, Wince, Winch, Windas, Windlass

Hold(er), Holding, Hold back, up, etc Absorb, Anchor, Belay, Believe, Boston crab, Canister, Cease, Cement, Cinch, Clamp, Clasp, Cling, Clutch, Contain, Delay, Detain, Display, Dog, Embrace, Engross, Er, Fast, Fistful, Frog, Full nelson, Garter, ➤ GRASP, Grip, Half-nelson, Hammerlock, Handle, Have, Headlock, Heft, Heist, Hinder, Hitch, Ho(a), Hoy, Hug, Impedance, Impede, Impediment, Incumbent, Intern, Keep, Keepnet, Lease, Maintain, Nelson, Own, Port, Proffer, Rack,

Reserve, Rivet, Rob, Save, Scissors, Shelve, Shore, Sleeve, Sostenuto, Stand, Suspend, Tenancy, Tenement, Tenure, Toehold, Tripod, Wristlock, Zarf

Hole(d), Holey Albatross, Antrum, Beam, Birdie, Black, Cave, Cavity, Coalsack, Crater, Cubby, Dell, Den, Dene, Dog-leg, Dreamhole, Dugout, Eagle, Earth, Eye(let), Finger, Foramen, Funk, Gap, Geat, Gutta, Hag(g), Hideout, Lill, Loop, Loup, Maar, Moulin, Nineteenth, Oillet, ➤ OPENING, Orifice, Perforate, Pierce, Pigeon, Pinprick, Pit, Pocket, Pore, Port, Pot, Priest's, Punctuate, Puncture, Scupper, Scuttle, Slot, Snag, Soakaway, Socket, Spandrel, Stead, Stew, Stop, Stove, Swallow, Tear, Trema, Vent, Voided, Watering, Wookey

Holiday(s) Bank, Benjo, Break, Childermas, ➤ FESTIVAL, Ferial, Festa, Fete, Fiesta, Furlough, Gala, Half(term), High, Laik, Leasure, Leave, Leisure, Long, Minibreak, Outing, Packaged, Pink-eye, Playtime, Recess, Repose, Rest, Roman, Seaside, Shabuoth, Shavuot, Stay, Sunday, Trip, ➤ VAC(ATION), Villegiatura, Wake(s), Whitsun

Hollow Alveary, Antar, Antre, Armpit, Boss, Bowl, Cave(rn), Cavity, Chasm, Cirque, Comb(e), Concave, Coomb, Crater, Cup(mark), Dean, Dell, Delve, Den(e), Dent, Dimple, Dingle, Dip, Dish(ing), Empty, Grot(to), Hole, How, Igloo, Incavo, Insincere, Keck(sy), Kex, Mortise, Niche, Orbita, Pan, Pit, Punt, Rut, Scoop, Sinus, Sleepy, Slot, Slough, Socket, Trough

Holy(man), Holiness Adytum, Alliance, Blessed, ➤ DIVINE, Godly, Grail, Halidom, Helga, Hery, Khalif, Loch, Mountain, Orders, Pious, Sacred, Sacrosanct, Sad(d)hu, Saintly, Sanctitude, Sannyasi(n), Santon, Sekos, Sepulchre, Shrine, Starets, Staretz, SV, Tirthankara, War

Holy Books, Holy writing Adigranth, Atharvaveda, Bible, Gemara, Granth, Hadith, Koran, Mishnah, NT, OT, Pia, Purana, Rigveda, Sama-Veda, ➤ SCRIPTURE, Shaster, Shastra, Smriti, Sura(h), Tanach, Writ

Holy building, Holy place Chapel, Church, Kaaba, Penetralia, Synagogue, Temenos, Temple

Homage Bow, Cense, Honour, Kneel, Obeisance, Tribute

Home Abode, Base, Blighty, Burrow, Cheshire, Chez, Clinic, Domal, Domicile, Earth, Eventide, Fireside, Gaff, Goal, Habitat, Harvest, Heame, Hearth, Heme, Hospice, House, Lair, Libken,

Mobile, Montacute, Nest, Pad, Plas Newydd, Remand, Rest, Stately, Villa

Homespun Plain, Raploch, Russet, Simple

Homicide Chance-medley, Killing, Manslaughter

Homily Lecture, Pi, Postil, Prone, Sermon

▷**Homing** may indicate coming back

Honest(y) Aboveboard, Afauld, Afawld, Candour, Clean, Genuine, Incorruptible, Injun, Jake, Legitimate, Lunaria, Lunary, Open-faced, Penny, Probity, Rectitude, Reputable, Righteous, Round, Sincere, Square, Squareshooter, Straight, Trojan, ➤ TRUE(PENNY), Upright, Upstanding

Honey Comb, Flattery, Hybla, Hymettus, Mel, Melliferous, Nectar, Peach, Popsy-wopsy, Sis, Sugar, Sweetheart, Sweetie

Honeysuckle Lonicera, Woodbind, Woodbine

Honorary, Honour(able), Honours, Honorific Accolade, Ace, Birthday, Blue, CBE, Commemorate, Credit, Dan, Elate, Emeritus, Ennoble, ➤ ESTEEM, Ethic, Face-card, Fame, Fete, Grace, Greats, Glory, Homage, Insignia, Invest, King, Knave, Knight, Kudos, Laudation, Laurels, MBE, Mention, OBE, Pundonor, Queen, Remember, Repute, Respect, Revere, Reward, Ten, Tenace, Titular, Tripos, Venerate, Worship

Hood(ed) Almuce, Amaut, Amice, Amowt, Apache, Balaclava, Bashlik, Biggin, Blindfold, Calash, Calèche, Calyptra, Capeline, Capuccio, Capuche, Chaperon(e), Coif, Cope, Cowl, Cucullate(d), Gangster, Jacobin, Kennel, Liripipe, Liripoop, Mantle, Mazarine, Pixie, Robin, Rowdy, Trot-cosey, Trot-cozy

Hook(ed), Hooker Addict, Adunc, Aduncous, Barb(icel), Becket, Butcher's, Cant(dog), Catch, Chape, Claw, Cleek, Clip, Corvus, Crampon, Cromb, Crome, Crook, Crotchet, Cup, Drail, Fish, Gaff, Grapnel, Hamate, Hamose, Hamulus, Heel, Hitch, Inveigle, Kype, Meat, Pot, Prostitute, Snell, Sniggle, Tala(u)nt, Tenaculum, Tenter, Tie, Trip, Uncus, Wanton

Hooligan Apache, Casual, Desperado, Droog, Hobbledehoy, Keelie, Larrikin, Lout, Ned, Rough(neck), Ruffian, Skollie, Skolly, Tearaway, Ted, Tough, Tsotsi, Yahoo, Yob(bo)

Hoop Bail, Band, Circle, Farthingale, Garth, Gird, Girr, Hula®, O, ➤ RING, Tire, Trochus

Hoot(er) Deride, Honk, Madge, Nose, Owl, Riot, Screech-owl, Siren, Ululate

Hop(per) An(o)ura, Ball, Bin, Cuscus, Dance, Flight, Jeté, Jump, Kangaroo, Leap, Lilt, Opium, Pogo, Saltate, Scotch, Skip, Tremié, Vine

Hope(ful) Anticipate, Aspirant, Contender, Daydream, Desire, Dream, Esperance, Evelyn, Expectancy, Forlorn, Gleam, Pipe-dream, Promising, Roseate, Rosy, Sanguine, Trust, Valley, White, Wish

Hopeless(ness), Hopeless quest Abattu, Anomie, Anomy, Black, Buckley's chance, Despair, Despondent, Forlorn, Goner, Perdu, Pessimist

Horizon Artificial, Event, Scope, Sea-line, Skyline

Horn(y) Advancer, Amalthea, Antenna(e), Baleen, Basset, Brass, Bez, Bugle, Cape, Ceratoid, Cor, Cornet, Cornett, Cornopean, Cornu(a), Cornucopia, Cromorna, Cromorne, Cusp, Dilemma, Flugel-horn, French, Frog, Golden, Gore, Hooter, ➤ HORNBLOWER, Hunting, Ivory, Keratin, Klaxon, Lur, Morsing, Mot, Oliphant, Periostracum, Plenty, Post, Powder, Pryse, Shofar, Shophor, Spongin, Tenderling, Trey, Trez, Trumpet, Waldhorn

Horrible, Horror Aw(e)some, Brat, Dire, Dread(ful), Execrable, Ghastly, Grisly, Gruesome, Hideous, Odious, Shock, Terror, Ugh

Horrid, Horrific, Horrify(ing) Dire, Dismay, Dreadful, Frightful, Ghastly, Gothic, Grim, Grisly, H, Loathy, Odious, Spiteful, Ugly

Hors d'oeuvres Antipasto, Canapé, Carpaccio, Ceviche, Hoummos, Houmus, Hummus, Mez(z)e, Pâté, Smorgasbord, Zak(o)uski

Horse Breaker, Buck(jumper), Cavalry, Centaur, Cert, Chestnut, Coacher, Crib, Cut, Cutting, Daisy-cutter, Dark, Dobbin, Doer, Draught, Drier, Entire, Equine, Ganger, Gee, GG, H, ➤ HEROIN, High, Hobby, Incitatus, Knight, Livery, Mount, Nag, Neddy, Outsider, Pacer, Pantomime, Pegasus, Perissodactyl, Pliohippus, Pommel, Quarter, Remount, Ride, Rocking, Saddle(r), Scag, Sense, Shoo-in, Span, Stumer, Trestle, Trojan, Troop, Trot(ter), Vaulting, Wooden, Xanthos, Xanthus

Horse complaint, Horse disease Bogspavin, Curb, Dourine, Equinia, Eweneck, Farcy, Fives, Frush, Glanders, Gourdy, Head staggers, Heaves, Hippiatric, Malander, Megrims, Mooneye, N(a)agana, Poll-evil, Quittor, Quittor, Ringbone,

Sallenders, Scratches, Seedy-toe, Spavie, Spavin, Strangles, Stringhalt, Surra, Sween(e)y, Thorough-pin, Thrush, Vives, Windgall, Wire-heel, Yellows

Horseman Ataman, Caballero, Cavalry, Centaur, Conquest, Cossack, Cowboy, Death, Dragman, Famine, Farrier, Hobbler, Hussar, Knight, Lancer, Nessus, Ostler, Parthian, Picador, Pricker, Quadrille, Revere, ➤ RIDER, Slaughter, Spahi, Stradiot, Tracer

Horseplay Caper, Polo, Rag, Rant, Romp

Horseshoe(-shaped) Henge, Hippocrepian, King-crab, Lunette, Manilla, Oxbow, Plate

Hose Chausses, Fishnet, Galligaskins, Gaskins, Lisle, Netherstock(ing), Nylons, Panty, Sock, Stockings, Tights, Trunk, Tube

Hospitable, Hospitality Convivial, Entertainment, Euxine, Lucullan, Open house, Philoxenia, Social, Xenial

Hospital Ambulance, Asylum, Barts, Base, Bedlam, Clinic, Cottage, Day, ENT, Field, Guys, H, Home, Hospice, Imaret, Karitane, Lazaretto, Leprosarium, Leprosery, Lock, Loony bin, MASH, Mental, Nosocomial, Pest-house, Polyclinic, San, Scutari, Sick bay, Spital, Spittle, Teaching, UCH

Host(ess) Amphitryon, Army, Barmecide, Chatelaine, Compere, Crowd, Definitive, Emcee, Entertainer, Hirsel, Hotelier, Innkeeper, Laban, Landlady, Landlord, Legend, Legion, Lion-hunter, Lot, Mass, Mavin, MC, Publican, Quickly, Swarm, Taverner, Throng, Trimalchio

Hostile, Hostility Adverse, Aggressive, Alien, Animus, Bellicose, Bitter, Currish, Diatribe, Feud, Hating, Icy, Ill, Ill-will, Inimical, Inveterate, Oppugnant, Unfriendly, Vitriolic, War

Hot (tempered) Ardent, Breem, Breme, Cajun, Calid, Candent, Dog days, Enthusiastic, Facula, Fervid, Feverish, Fuggy, Gospeller, In, Incandescent, Irascible, Lewd, Mustard, Pepper, Piping, Potato, Randy, Red, Roaster, Scorcher, Sizzling, Spicy, Stewy, Stifling, Stolen, Sweltering, Sweltry, Tabasco®, Thermidor, Torrid, Toustie, Tropical, Zealful

Hotchpotch Bricolage, Farrago, Mish-mash, Powsowdy, Welter

Hotel Bo(a)tel, Flophouse, Gasthaus, Gasthof, H, Hilton, Hydro, Inn, Motel, Parador, Posada, Ritz, Roadhouse, Savoy, Tavern

Hothead(ed) Impetuous, Rash, Spitfire, Volcano

Hot-house Conservatory, Nursery, Orangery, Vinery

Hound(s) Afghan, Basset, Beagle, Bellman, Brach, Cad, Canine, Cry, ► DOG, Entry, Harass, Harrier, Hen-harrier, Javel, Kennet, Lyam, Lym(e), Mute, Otter, Pack, Pursue, Rache, Ranter, Reporter, Saluki, Talbot, True, Tufter

Hour(s) Canonical, H, Holy, Hr, Complin(e), Elder's, Happy, None(s), Orthros, Prime, Rush, Sext, Small, Terce, Tide, Time, Undern, Vespers, Visiting, Witching, Zero

House(s), Household(er) Abode, Astrology, Audience, Auditorium, Bingo, Chalet, Chamber, Chateau, Chez, Commons, Convent, Council, Custom(s), Discount, Disorderly, Domicile, Dwelling, Dynasty, Establishment, Firm, Habitat, Halfway, Heartbreak, Hearth, Ho, Home, Inn, Lords, Lot(t)o, Maison(ette), Manor, Mansion, Meeting, Ménage, Opera, Orange, Parliament, Plantagenet, Prefab, Ranch, Residence, Rough, Safe, Semi, Shanty, Stuart, Town, Trinity, Upper, Villa, Windsor, York

Housing Case, Crankcase, Shabrack, Shelter, Slum, Tenement

Hovel Cru(i)ve, Den, Pigsty, Shack, Shanty

However As, But, Leastwise, Sed, Still, Though, Yet

Howl(er) Banshee, Bawl, Bay, Bloop, Clanger, Hue, Mycetes, Ululate, Wow, Yawl, Yowl

Hub Boss, Centre, Focus, Hob, Nave, Pivot, Tee

Hubbub Charivari, Chirm, Coil, Din, Level-coil, Palaver, Racket, Row, Stir

Huckster Hawker, Kidd(i)er, Pedlar

Huddle Cringe, Gather, Hunch, Ruck, Shrink

Hue Colour, Dye, Outcry, Proscription, Steven, Tincture, Tinge, Utis

Huff Dudgeon, Hector, Pant, Pet, Pique, Strunt, Umbrage, Vex

Huge (number) Astronomical, Brobdingnag, Colossal, Enorm(ous), Gargantuan, Giant, ► GIGANTIC, Gillion, Ginormous, Humongous, Humungous, Immane, Immense, Leviathan, Lulu, Mega-, Milliard, Octillion, Socking, Titanian, Tremendous, Whacking

Hull Bottom, Framework, Husk, Inboard, Monocoque, Pod, Sheal, Sheel, Shell, Shiel, Shill

►**Hullo** see HELLO

Hum(ming) Bombilate, Bombinate, Bum, Chirm, Drone, Lilt, Moan, Murmur, Nos(e)y, Pong, Rank, Reek, Sowf(f), Stink, Stir, Whir(r), Zing

Human(e), Humanist, Humanity Anthropoid, Bang, Colet, Earthling, Erasmus, Incarnate, Kindness, Mandom, Merciful, Mortal, Philanthropic, Species, Sympathy, Ubuntu

Humble Abase, Abash, Afflict, Baseborn, Degrade, Demean, Demiss(ly), Lower, Lowly, Mean, ➤ MEEK, Modest, Obscure, Poor, Rude, Small, Truckle

Humbug Berley, Blarney, Blague, Burley, Claptrap, Con, Delude, Flam, Flummery, Fraud, Fudge, Gaff, Gammon, Gas, Guff, Gum, Hoax, Hoodwink, Hookey-walker, Kibosh, Liar, Maw-worm, Nonsense, Shenanigan, Wind

Humdrum Banal, Bourgeois, Monotonous, Mundane, Ordinary, Prosaic, Tedious

Humiliate, Humiliation, Humility Abase, Abash, Baseness, Degrade, Disbench, Eating crow, Fast, Indignity, Mortify, Put-down, ➤ SHAME, Skeleton, Take-down, Wither

Humorist Cartoonist, Comedian, Jester, Leacock, Lear, Punster, Twain, Wodehouse

Humour, Humorous Aqueous, Bile, Caprice, Cardinal, Chaff, Coax, Cocker, Coddle, Cosher, Cuiter, Cuittle, Daut, Dawt, Dry, Facetious, Fun, Gallows, Ichor, Indulge, Irony, Jocose, Jocular, Juice, Kidney, Levity, Light, ➤ MOOD, Observe, Pamper, Phlegm, Pun, Pythonesque, Ribaldry, Serum, Temper, Trim, Vein, Vitreum, Wetness, Whim, Wit

Hump(ed) Boy, Bulge, Dorts, Dowager's, Gibbose, Gibbous, Hog, Huff, Hummock, Hunch, Pip, Ramp, Tussock

▶**Humpback** see HUNCHBACK

Humus Compost, Leafmould, Moder, Mor, Mull

Hunch, Hunchback Camel, Chum, Crookback, Intuition, Kyphosis, Premonition, Quasimodo, Roundback, Urchin

Hundred(s) Burnham, C, Cantred, Cantref, Cent, Centum, Century, Chiltern, Commot, Desborough, Host, ➤ IN A HUNDRED, Northstead, Shire, Stoke, Ton, Wapentake

Hungarian, Hungary Bohunk, Csardas, Magyar, Nagy, Szekely, Tzigane, Ugric, Vogul

Hunger, Hungry Appestat, Appetite, Bulimia, Bulimy, Clem, ➤ CRAVE, Desire, Edacity, Empty, Esurient, Famine, Famish, Fast,

Hanker, Hunter, Pant, Peckish, Rapacious, Raven, Ravin, Sharp-set, Unfed, Yaup

▷**Hungry** may indicate an 'o' in another word

Hunt(er), Hunting, Huntress, Huntsman Chasseur, Dog, Drag, Gun, Hound, Lurcher, Nimrod, Predator, Pursue, Quest, Quorn, Ride, Run, Scavenge(r), ➤ SEARCH, Seek, Stalk, Trap, Venerer, ➤ WATCH, Whipper-in, Woodman, Yager

Hunting-call Rechate, Recheat, Tally-ho, View-halloo

Hurdle(r) Barrier, Doll, Fence, Flake, Gate, Hemery, Raddle, Sticks, Wattle

Hurl(ing) Camogie, Cast, Dash, ➤ FLING, Heave, Put(t), Throw, ➤ TOSS

Hurry Belt, Bustle, Chivvy, Chop-chop, Dart, Dash, Drive, Festinate, Fisk, Frisk, Gad, Giddap, Giddup, Hadaway, Hare, Haste, Hie, Hightail, Mosey, Post-haste, Press, Push, Race, ➤ RUSH, Scamper, Scoot, Scramble, Scur(ry), Scutter, Scuttle, Skelter, Skurry, Spank, Speed, Streak, Tear

Hurt(ful) Abuse, Ache, Ake, Bruise, Damage, De(a)re, Disservice, Harrow, Hit, ➤ INJURE, Lesion, Maim, Nocent, Nocuous, Noxious, Noyous, Pain, Pang, Prick(le), Scaith, Wring

Husband(ry), Husbands Add, Baron, Darby, Ear, Eche, Economy, Eke, Ere, Farm, Georgic, Goodman, Groom, H, Hubby, Ideal, Man, Mate, Partner, Polyandry, Retrench, Save, Scrape, Scrimp, Spouse, Squirrel, ➤ STORE, Tillage

Husk(s), Husky Acerose, Bran, Draff, Ear, Eskimo, Hoarse, Hull, Malemute, Seed, Sheal, Shuck

Hustle(r) Frogmarch, Jostle, Pro, Push, Railroad, Shoulder, Shove, Skelp

Hut(s) Banda, Booth, Bothie, Bothy, Bustee, Cabin, Chalet, Choltry, Gunyah, Hogan, Humpy, Igloo, Mia-mia, Nissen, Pondok(kie), Quonset®, Rancheria, Rancho, Rondavel, Shack, Shanty, Sheal(ing), Shebang, Shed, Shiel(ing), Skeo, Skio, Succah, Sukkah, Tilt, Tolsel, Tolsey, Tolzey, Wan(n)igan, Wi(c)kiup, Wigwam, Wil(t)ja, Wurley

Hybrid Bigener, Bois-brûlé, Catalo, Centaur, Chamois, Chichi, Citrange, Cross, Dso, Funnel, Geep, Graft, Interbred, Jomo, Jumart, Lurcher, Mameluco, Mermaid, Merman, Metis, Mongrel, Mule, Mutation, Ox(s)lip, Percolin, Plumcot, Pomato, Ringed, Tangelo, Tiglon, Tigon, Topaz, Ugli, Zho(mo)

▷**Hybrid** may indicate an anagram

Hydrocarbon Acetylene, Aldrin, Alkane, Alkene, Alkyl, Alkyne, Amylene, Arene, Asphaltite, Benzene, Butadiene, Butane, Butene, Camphane, Camphene, Carotene, Cetane, Cubane, Cyclohexane, Cyclopropane, Decane, Diene, Dioxin, Diphenyl, Ethane, Gutta, Halon, Hatchettite, Heptane, Hexane, Hexene, Hexyl(ene), Isobutane, Isoprene, Ligroin, Limonene, Mesitylene, Naphtha, Naphthalene, Nonane, Octane, Olefine, Paraffin, Pentane, Pentene, Pentylene, Phenanthrene, Phene, Picene, Polyene, Propane, Pyrene, Retene, Squalene, Stilbene, Styrene, Terpene, Toluene, Triptane, Wax, Xylene, Xylol

Hydrogen Deut(er)on, Diplon, Ethene, H, Protium, Tritium

Hyena Aard-wolf, Earthwolf, Strand-wolf, Tiger-wolf

Hymn(s) Anthem, Benedictine, Bhajan, Canticle, Carol, Cathisma, Choral(e), Coronach, Dies Irae, Dithyramb, Doxology, Gloria, Hallel, Introit(us), Ithyphallic, Lay, Magnificat, Mantra, Marseillaise, Nunc dimittis, Ode, P(a)ean, Psalm, Recessional, Rigveda, Sanctus, Sequence, Stabat mater, Sticheron, Tantum ergo, Te deum, Trisagion, Troparion, Veda

Hymnographer, Hymnologist David, Faber, Heber, Moody, Neale, Parry, Sankey, Watts

Hypnosis, Hypnotise, Hypnotic, Hypnotism Braidism, Chloral, Codeine, Entrance, Magnetic, Mesmerism, Svengali

Hypocrisy, Hypocrite, Hypocritical Archimago, Bigot, Byends, Cant, Carper, Chadband, Deceit, Dissembler, Heep, Holy Willie, Humbug, Mucker, Nitouche, Pecksniff, Pharisaic, Pharisee, Prig, Sepulchre, Tartuf(f)e, Two-faced, Whited sepulchre

Hypothetical Biophor, Gluon, Graviton, Suppositious, Virtual

Hysteria, Hysteric(al) Conniption, Delirium, Frenzy, Meemie, Mother

I A, Ch, Cham, Che, Dotted, Ego, Ich, Indeed, India, Iodine, Italy, J, Je, Me, Self

Ice(d), Ice cream, Icing, Icy Álcorza, Arctic, Berg, Black, Camphor, Cassata, Cone, Cool, Cornet, Coupe, Cream, Crystal, Diamonds, Drift, Dry, Floe, Frappé, Frazil, Freeze, Frigid, Frore, Frosting, Frosty, Gelato, Gelid, Gems, Glacé, Glacial, Glacier, Glare, Granita, Graupel, Hailstone, Hok(e)y-pok(e)y, Knickerbocker glory, Kulfi, Lolly, Marzipan, Neapolitan, Pack, Pancake, Pingo, Polar, Rime, Rink, Royal, Serac, Sconce, Shelf, Sherbet, Slider, Slob, Sludge, Sorbet, Spumone, Spumoni, Sugar, Topping, Tortoni, Tutti-frutti, Verglas, Wafer, Water, Wintry

Iceberg Calf, Floe, Growler

▶**Ice-cream** see ICE

Idea(s) Archetype, Brainwave, Clou, Clue, Conceit, Concept, Fancy, Germ, Hunch, Idolum, Idée fixe, Image, Inkling, Inspiration, Interpretation, light, ▶ NOTION, Obsession, Plan, Plank, Rationale, Recept, Theory, Thought, Zeitgeist

Ideal(ise) Abstract, A1, Dream, Eden, Goal, Halo, Hero, Model, Monist, Nirvana, Notional, Paragon, Pattern, ▶ PERFECT, Siddhi, Sidha, Sublimate, Utopian, Vision

Identical Alike, Clone, Congruent, Same, Selfsame, Verbatim

Identification, Identify Credentials, Diagnosis, Differentiate, Discern, Document, Dog-tag, Earmark, Empathy, Espy, Finger(print), ID, Label, Mark, Password, Pin, Place, Recognise, Reg(g)o, Spot, Swan-upping, Verify

Identity Appearance, Corporate, Credentials, Equalness, Likeness, Oneness, Seity, Self

Idiom Argot, Cant, Expression, Jargon, Language, Pahlavi, Parlance, Pehlevi, Syri(a)cism, Syrism

Idiot(ic), Idiocy Congenital, Dingbat, Fool, Goose, Imbecile, Inane, Moron, Natural, Nerk, Nidget, Oaf, Ouph(e), ▶ STUPID (PERSON), Tony, Twit, Zany

Idle(ness), Idler Bum, Deadbeat, Dilly-dally, Drone, Fester, Flaneur, Frivolous, Groundless, Indolent, Inert, Lackadaisical, Layabout, Laze, Lazy, Lead-swinger, Lie, Loaf, Lollop, Lounge, Mooch, Ride, Shiftless, Sloth, Sluggard, Spiv, Stock-still, Stooge, Tarry, Truant, Vain, Vegetate, Waste

Idol(ise) Adore, Adulate, Baal(im), Baphomet, Bel, Crush, Fetich(e), Fetish, God, Hero, Icon, Image, Joss, Juggernaut, Lion, Mammet, Manito, Manitou, Matinee, Maumet, Mawmet,

Molech, Moloch, Mommet, Mumbo-jumbo, Swami,
Teraph(im), Termagant, Vision, Wood, Worship

Idyll(ic) Arcady, Eclogue, Pastoral, Peneian

Ignite, Ignition Coil, Flare, Kindle, Lightning, Spark, Starter

Ignominious, Ignominy Base, Dishonour, Fiasco, Infamous,
Scandal, ➤ SHAME

Ignorance, Ignorant Analphabet, Anan, Artless, Clueless,
Darkness, Green, Hick, Illiterate, Inerudite, Ingram, Ingrum,
Inscient, Lewd, Lumpen, Misken, Nescience, Night, Oik,
Philistine, Purblind, Red-neck, Unaware, Uneducated,
Unlettered, Unread, Unschooled, Untold, Unversed, Unwist

Ignore Ba(u)lk, Blink, Bypass, Connive, Cut, Discount,
Disregard, Forget, Neglect, Omit, Overlook, Pass, Snub

Ill Adverse, All-overish, Bad, Bilious, Cronk, Evil, Income,
Off-colour, Poorly, Queer, Sea-sick, ➤ SICK, Unweal, Unwell,
Valetudinarian, Wog, Wrong

▷**Ill** may indicate an anagram

Ill-bred Churlish, Plebeian, Uncouth, Unmannerly

▷**Ill-composed** may indicate an anagram

Illegal, Illicit Adulterine, Black, Breach, Bootleg, Furtive,
Ill-gotten, Misbegotten, Shonky, Unlawful

Illegitimate Bastard, By-blow, Come-o'-will, Fitz, Irregular,
Natural, Scarp, Spurious

Ill-feeling, Ill-humour Bad blood, Bile, Curt, Dudgeon,
Glum, Hate, Miff, Peevish, Pique, Rheumatic

▶**Illicit** see ILLEGAL

Ill-mannered, Ill-natured Attercop, Crabby, Ethercap,
Ettercap, Guttersnipe, Huffy, Stingy, Sullen, Ugly, Unkind

Illness Aids, Ailment, Attack, Autism, Brucellosis, Complaint,
Croup, Diabetes, Disease, DS, Dwalm, Dwaum, Dyscrasia,
Eclampsia, Grippe, Hangover, Hypochondria, ME, Malady,
Scarlatina, Sickness, Toxaemia, Urosis, Weed, Weid, Wog

▶**Ill-tempered** see ILL-MANNERED

Illuminate(d), Illumination Brighten, Clarify,
Cul-de-lampe, Decorate, Enlighten, Floodlit, Lamplight,
Langley, Light, Limn, Miniate, Nernst, Pixel, Radiate, Rushlight

Illusion, Illusory Air, Apparition, Barmecide, Deception,
Fallacy, Fancy, Fantasy, Hallucination, Ignis-fatuus, Mare's-nest,
Maya, Mirage, Optical, Phantom, Specious, Will o'the wisp

Illustrate, Illustration, Illustrator Case, Centrefold, Collotype, Demonstrate, Drawing, Eg, Elucidate, Epitomise, Exemplify, Explain, Figure, Frontispiece, Grangerize, Graphic, Half-tone, Illume, Illumin(at)e, Instance, Instantiate, Limner, Plate, Show, Sidelight, Spotlight, Tenniel, Vignette

Ill-will Animosity, Enmity, Grudge, Hostility, Malice, Spite

Image(s) Blip, Discus, Effigy, Eidetic, Eidolon, Eikon, Graven, Hologram, Icon, Iconograph, Idol, Invultuation, Joss, Latent, Likeness, Matte, Mirror, Photogram, Photograph, Pic(ture), Pixel(l)ated, Pixil(l)ated, Poetic, Profile, Recept, Scintigram, Simulacrum, Spectrum, Spitting, Stereotype, Symbol, Teraph(im), Tiki, Totem, Virtual

Imaginary, Imaginative, Imagine(d) Assume, Believe, Cloud-cuckoo-land, Conceive, Conjure, Cyborg, Dystopia, Envisage, Faery, Faine, Fancy, Feign, Fictional, Fictitious, Fictor, Figment, Figure, Hallucinate, Hobbit, Ideate, Invent, Oz, Picture, Poetical, Prefigure, Recapture, Replicant, Scotch mist, ➤ SUPPOSE, Surmise, Think, Visualise, Whangam

▷**Imbecile** may indicate an anagram

Imbibe Absorb, Drink, Lap, Quaff, Suck, Swallow

Imitate, Imitation, Imitator Act, Ape, Copy(cat), Counterfeit, Dud, Echo, Echopraxia, Emulate, Epigon(e), Ersatz, Fake, False, Faux, Marinist, Me-too, Mime, Mimetic, Mimic(ry), Mockery, Monkey, Parody, Parrot, Paste, Pastiche, Pinchbeck, Potichomania, Rip-off, Sham, Simulate, Stumer, Take-off, Travesty

Immaculate Conception, Flawless, Lily-white, Perfect, Pristine, Spotless, Virgin

Immature(ly), Immaturity Callow, Crude, Embryo, Ergate(s), Green, Inchoate, Larval, Neotenic, Pubera, Pupa, Raw, Sophomoric, Tender, Unbaked, Unripe, Young

▷**Immature** may indicate a word incompleted

Immediate(ly) At once, Direct, First-time, Forthwith, Imminent, Incontinent, Instantaneous, Near, ➤ NOW, Outright, Present, Pronto, Right-off, Short-term, Slapbang, Spontaneous, Stat, Straight, Straight off, Sudden, Then

Immense Brobdingnag, Cosmic, Enormous, ➤ GIGANTIC, Huge, Vast

Immerse Baptise, Demerge, Demerse, Drench, Emplonge, Enew, Engage, Plunge, Soak, Steep

Immobility, Immobilize Cataplexy, Catatonia, Hog-tie, Inertia, Pinion, Rigidity, Tether

Immodest Brash, Brazen, Forward, Indelicate, Unchaste

Immoral(ity) Corrupt, Dissolute, Evil, Lax, Libertine, Licentious, Nefarious, Peccable, Reprobate, Turpitude, Unsavoury, Wanton

Immortal(ity) Agelong, Amarant(h), Amritattva, Athanasy, ▶ DIVINE, Enoch, Eternal, Famous, Godlike, Memory, Sin, Struldbrug, Timeless, Undying

Immune, Immunisation, Immunise(r), Immunity Anamnestic, Anergy, Cree, Diplomatic, Free, Inoculate, Klendusic, Properdin, Serum, Vaccine

Imp(ish) Devilet, Elf, Flibbertigibbet, Gamin(e), Hobgoblin, Limb, Lincoln, Litherly, Nickum, Nis(se), Puck, Rascal, Sprite

Impact Bearing, Bump, Clash, Collision, Feeze, Impinge, Jar, Jolt, Pack, Percuss, Pow, Slam, Souse, Wham

Impartial Candid, Detached, Equitable, Even-handed, Fair, Just, Neutral, Unbiased

Impassable, Impasse Deadlock, Dilemma, Invious, Jam, Snooker, Stalemate, Zugzwang

Impatience, Impatient Chafing, Chut, Dysphoria, Fiddle-de-dee, Fiddlesticks, Fidgety, Fretful, Hasty, Irritable, Och, Peevish, Peremptory, Petulant, Pish, Tilly-fally, Till(e)y-vall(e)y, Tut

Impedance, Impede, Impediment Burr, Clog, Dam, Encumber, Halt, Hamstring, Handicap, ▶ HINDER, Let, Log, Obstacle, Obstruct, Reactance, Rub, Shackle, Snag, Stammer, Tongue-tie, Trammel, Veto, Z

Imperative Dire, Jussive, Mood, Need-be, Pressing, Vital

Imperfect(ion) Aplasia, Aplastic, Blotch, Defect, Deficient, Faculty, Flawed, Half-pie, Kink, Lame, Poor, Rough, Second

Imperial(ist), Imperious Beard, Commanding, Haughty, Majestic, Masterful, Mint, Peremptory, Regal, Rhodes, Royal

Imperishable Eternal, Immortal, Indestructible

Impersonal Abstract, Cold, Detached, Inhuman

Impersonate, Impersonation Amphitryon, Ape, As, Imitate, Impression, Mimic, Pose

Impertinence, Impertinent Crust, Flip(pant), Fresh, Impudent, Irrelevant, Rude, Sass, Sauce

Impetuous, Impetuosity Birr, Brash, Bullheaded, Elan, ➤ HASTY, Headstrong, Heady, Hothead, Impulsive, Rash, Tearaway, Vehement, Violent

Impetus Birr, Drift, Incentive, Momentum, Propulsion, Slancio

Implant(ation) AID, Embed, Engraft, Enroot, Graft, Inset, Instil, Sow

Implement Agent, Flail, Fork, Hacksaw, Harrow, Hayfork, Muller, Pin, Pitchfork, Plectrum, Plough, Rest, Ripple, Seed drill, Spatula, Squeegee, Tongs, ➤ TOOL, Toothpick, Utensil

Implicate, Implication Accuse, Concern, Connotation, Embroil, Incriminate, Innuendo, ➤ INVOLVE, Overtone

Imply, Implied Hint, Insinuate, Involve, Predicate, Signify, ➤ SUGGEST, Tacit

Importance, Important (person) Big, Big cheese, Calibre, Cardinal, Central, Cheese, Cob, Core, Cornerstone, Critical, Crucial, Crux, Eminent, Epochal, Grave, Gravitas, Greatness, Heavy, Honcho, Hotshot, Huzoor, Key, Macher, Magnitude, Main, Major, Material, Matters, Mighty, Milestone, Moment(ous), Nabob, Nib, Note, Numero uno, Personage, Pivotal, Pot, Prime, Principal, Salient, Seminal, Serious, Something, Special, Status, Stress, Substantive, Urgent, VIP, Weight, Weighty

Importune, Importunate Beg, Coax, Flagitate, Press(ing), Prig, Solicit, Urgent

Impose, Imposing, Imposition Allocate, Assess, August, Burden, Charge, Diktat, Dread, Enforce, Enjoin, Epic, Fine, Flam, Foist, Fraud, Grand(iose), Hidage, Homeric, Hum, Impot, Inflict, Kid, Levy, Lumber, Majestic, Obtrude, Pensum, Pole, Scot, Sponge, Statuesque, Sublime, Whillywhaw

Impossible Hopeless, Incorrigible, Insoluble, Insurmountable, No-no, Unacceptable

Imposter, Impostor Bunyup, Charlatan, Disaster, ➤ FAKE, Fraud, Idol, Pretender, Sham, Triumph, Warbeck

Impotent Barren, Helpless, Spado, Sterile, Weak

Impoverish(ed) Bankrupt, Bare, Beggar, Exhaust, Straiten

Impractical Absurd, Academic, Chim(a)era, Idealist, Laputan, Not on, Other-worldly, Quixotic, Useless

Imprecise Approximate, Inaccurate, Indeterminate, Loose, Nebulous, Rough, Sloppy, Vague

Impregnate Conceive, Imbue, Inseminate, Milt, Permeate

Impress(ive), Impression(able), Impressionist Astonish, Awe, Effect, Feel(ing), Imprint, Pliable, Powerful, Press(gang), Print, Proof, Stamp, Strike, Watermark

Imprison(ment) Cape, Confine, Constrain, Custody, Durance, Immure, Incarcerate, Intern, Jail, Quad, Quod, Time

Impromptu Ad lib, Extempore, Improvised, Offhand, Spontaneous, Sudden, Unrehearsed

Improper, Impropriety Abnormal, Blue, Demirep, False, Indecent, Indecorum, Outré, Prurient, Solecism, Undue, Unmeet, Unseemly, Untoward

▷**Improperly** may indicate an anagram

Improve(ment), Improver, Improving Advance, Ameliorate, Beet, Benefit, Bete, Break, Buck, Cap, Chasten, Conditioner, Détente, Didactic, Ease, Edify, Embellish, Emend, Enhance, Enrich, Eugenic, Euthenics, File, Gentrify, Kaizen, Meliorate, Mend, Potentiate, Promote, Rally, Refine, Reform, Resipiscence, Retouch, Slim, Surpass, Tart, Tatt, Titivate, Top, Touch-up, Turn round, Uptrend, Upturn

Improvise(d), Improvisation Adlib, Break, Devise, Extemporise, Invent, Knock-up, Lash-up, Noodle, Ride, Scratch, Sudden, Vamp, Wing

Impudence, Impudent Audacious, Backchat, Bardy, Bold, Brash, Brassy, Brazen, Cheeky, Cool, Crust, Effrontery, Forward, Gall, Gallus, Impertinent, Insolent, Jackanapes, Lip, Neck, ► NERVE, Pert, Sass(y), Sauce, Saucy, Temerity, Whippersnapper, Yankie

Impulse, Impulsive Compelling, Conatus, Dictate, Drive, Efferent, Headlong, Horme, Ideopraxist, Impetus, Instigation, ► INSTINCT, Madcap, Nisus, Premature, Premotion, Send, Signal, Snap, Spontaneous, Tendency, Thrust, Tic, Urge, Whim

Impure, Impurity Adulterated, Donor, Faints, Feints, Indecent, Lees, Lewd, Regulus, Scum, Unclean

In A, Amid, Chic, Home, Hostel, I', Inn, Intil, Occupying, Pop(ular), Pub, Trendy, Within

Inaccurate Distorted, Erroneous, Faulty, Imprecise, Inexact, Out, Rough, Slipshod

Inactive, Inaction, Inactivity Acedia, Cabbage, Comatose, Dead, Dormant, Extinct, Fallow, Hibernate, Idle, Inert, Moratorium, Passive, Quiescent, Rusty, Sluggish, Torpid, Veg(etate)

Inadequate Derisory, Feeble, Inapt, Inferior, Pathetic, Poor, Ropy, Thin

▷**In a flap** may indicate an anagram

Inane Empty, Fatuous, Foolish, Imbecile, Silly, Vacant

Inappropriate Amiss, Infelicitous, Malapropos, Off-key, Unapt, Unbecoming, Undue, Unsuitable, Untoward

Inaugurate Han(d)sel, Initiate, Install, Introduce

Inauspicious Adverse, Ominous, Sinister

▷**In a whirl** may indicate an anagram

▷**In a word** may indicate two clue words linked to form one

Inborn, Inbred Inherent, Innate, Native, Selfed, Sib

Incandescent Alight, Bright, Brilliant, Excited

Incantation Charm, Magic, Mantra, Spell

Incendiary Arsonist, Firebug, Fire-lighter, Napalm

Incense(d), Incenser Anger, Aroma, Elemi, Enfelon, Enrage, Homage, Hot, ➤ INFLAME, Joss-stick, Navicula, Onycha, Outrage, Pastil(le), Provoke, Thurible, Thus, Vex, Wrathful

Incentive Carrot, Fillip, Impetus, Motive, Spur, Stimulus

Inch Ait, Edge, Isle, Sidle, Uncial

Incident(al) Affair, Baur, Bawr, Carry-on, Chance, Circumstance, Episode, Event, Facultative, Negligible, Occasion, Occurrent, Page, Scene

Incinerate, Incinerator Burn, Combust, Cremate

Incise, Incision, Incisive(ness) Bite, Cut, Engrave, Mordant, Phlebotomy, Slit, Surgical, Tracheotomy, Trenchant

Incite(ment) Abet, Drive, Egg, Fillip, Hortative, Hoy, Inflame, Instigate, Kindle, Motivate, Prod, Prompt, Provoke, Put, Rouse, Sa sa, Set, Sic(k), Sool, ➤ SPUR, Sting, Tar, Urge

Incline(d), Inclination Acclivity, Angle, Aslope, Atilt, Bank, Batter, Bent, Bias, Bow, Clinamen, Declivity, Dip, Disposed, Drift, Enclitic, Glacis, ➤ GRADIENT, Grain, Hade, Heel, Hill, Kant, Kip, Lean, Liking, List, Maw, Minded, Nod, On, Partial, Peck, Penchant, Prone, Propensity, Rake, Ramp, Ready, Rollway, Set, Shelve, Slant, ➤ SLOPE, Steep, Steeve, Stomach, Supine, Tend, Tilt, Tip, Trend, Upgrade, Velleity, Verge, Weathering, Will

Include(d) Add, Bracket, Compass, Comprise, Connotate, Contain, Cover, Embody, Embrace, Enclose, Involve, Therein

Incognito Anonymous, Disguised, Faceless, Secret, Unnamed

Income Annuity, Disposable, Dividend, Earned, Entry, Living, Meal-ticket, Milch cow, Penny-rent, Prebend, Primitiae, Proceeds, Rent, Rent-roll, Returns, Revenue, Salary, Stipend, Unearned, Wages

Incomparable Supreme, Unequalled, Unmatched

Incompatible, Incompatibility Contradictory, Dyspathy, Inconsistent, Mismatched, Unsuited

Incompetent Bungler, Deadhead, Helpless, Ill, Inefficient, Inept, Palooka, Unable, Unfit

Incomplete Cagmag, Catalectic, Deficient, Inchoate, Lacking, Partial, Pendent, Rough, Unfinished

▷**In confusion** may indicate an anagram

Incongruous, Incongruity Absurd, Discordant, Irish, Ironic, Sharawadgi, Sharawaggi

Inconsiderate High-handed, Petty, Presumptuous, Roughshod, Thoughtless, Unkind

Inconsistency, Inconsistent Alien, Anacoluthon, Anomaly, Contradictory, Discrepant, Oxymoronic, Paradoxical, Variance

Inconvenience, Inconvenient Awkward, Bother, Discommode, Fleabite, Incommodious, ➤ TROUBLE

Incorporate(d), Incorporation Absorb, Embody, Inc, Integrate, Introgression, Join, Merge, Subsume

Incorrect Catachresis, False, Improper, Naughty

Incorruptible Honest, Immortal, Pure, Sea-green

Increase, Increasing Accelerando, Accelerate, Accession, Accrue, Add, Aggrandise, Amplify, Appreciate, Approve, Augment, Auxetic, Bolster, Bulge, Crescendo, Crescent, Crescive, Deepen, Dilate, Double, Ech(e), Eech, Eik, Eke, Enhance, Enlarge, Escalate, ➤ EXPAND, Explosion, Greaten, ➤ GROW, Heighten, Ich, Increment, Interbreed, Jack, Jack up, Magnify, Mark up, Mount, Multiply, Plus, Proliferate, Propagate, Redshift, Reflation, Regrate, Rise, Snowball, Swell, Up, Upswing, Wax

Incredible Amazing, Cockamamie, Extraordinary, Fantastic, Steep, Stey, Tall

Incredulity, Incredulous Distrust, Suspicion, Thunderstruck

Incriminate Accuse, Implicate, Inculpate

Incumbent Lying, Obligatory, Occupier, Official

Incursion Foray, Inroad, Invasion, Raid, Razzia

Indecent Bare, Blue, Free, Immodest, Immoral, Improper, Lewd, Obscene, Racy, Scurril(e), Unproper, Unseem(ly)

Indecision, Indecisive Demur, Dithery, Doubt, Hamlet, Hung jury, Suspense, Swither, Weakkneed

Indecorous Graceless, Immodest, Outré, Unbecoming

Indefinite(ly) A, An, Any, Evermore, Hazy, Nth, Some, Undecided, Vague

Indelicate Broad, Coarse, Improper, Vulgar, Warm

Indent(ed), Indentation Apprentice, Contract, Crenellate, Dancetty, Dimple, Impress, Niche, Notch, Order, Subentire

Independence, Independent Autocephalous, Autogenous, Autonomy, Crossbencher, Detached, Extraneous, Free(dom), Free-lance, I, Liberty, Maverick, Mugwump, Perseity, Self-sufficient, Separate, Separatist, Swaraj, UDI, Udal, Uhuru

Indestructible Enduring, Impenetrable, Inextirpable

Index Alidad(e), Catalogue, Dial, Dow Jones, Exponent, Finger, Fist, Footsie, Forefinger, Gazetteer, Hang Seng, Kwic, Nikkei, Price, Refractive, ➤ REGISTER, Table, Thumb, UV

India(n) Adivisi, Ayah, Baboo, Babu, Bharat(i), Canarese, Chin, Dard, Dravidian, File, Gond(wanaland), Gujarati, Harijan, Harsha, Hindu, Ink, Jain, Jat, Jemadar, Kanarese, Kannada, Khalsa, Kisan, Kolarian, Kshatriyas, Lepcha, Ma(h)ratta, Maratha, Mazhbi, Mofussil, Mogul, Munda, Munshi, Nagari, Nair, Nasik, Nation, Nayar, Ocean, Oriya, Pali, Parsee, Parsi, Peshwa, Prakrit, Punjabi, Sanskrit, Sepoy, Shri, Sikh, Sind(h), Sowar, Summer, Swadeshi, Tamil, Telegu, Vakeel, Vakil

Indicate, Indication, Indicative, Indicator Adumbrate, Allude, Argue, Cite, Clue, Cursor, ➤ DENOTE, Design, Desine, Dial, Endeixis, Evidence, Evince, Gesture, Gnomon, Litmus, Manifest, Mean, Mood, Nod, Notation, Pinpoint, Point, Portend, Proof, Ray, Register, Remarque, Representative, Reveal,. ➤ SIGN, Signify, Specify, Symptom, Tip, Token, Trace, Trait, Winker

Indifference, Indifferent Adiaphoron, Aloof, Apathetic, Apathy, Blasé, Blithe, Callous, Cold, Cool(th), Dead, Detached, Disdain, Incurious, Insouciant, Jack easy, Mediocre, Neutral,

Nonchalant, Perfunctory, Phlegm, Pococurante, So-so, Stoical, Supine, Tepid, Unconcerned

Indignant, Indignation Anger, Annoyed, Incensed, Irate, Resentful, Wrathful

Indigo Anil, Blue, Bunting, Carmine, Indole, Isatin(e)

Indirect Back-handed, By(e), Devious, Implicit, Mediate, Oblique, Remote, Roundabout, Sidelong, Zig-zag

Indiscreet, Indiscretion Folly, Gaffe, Imprudence, Indelicate, Injudicious, Loose cannon, Rash, Unguarded

Indiscriminate Haphazard, Random, Scattershot, Sweeping

Indispensable Basic, Essential, King-pin, Necessary, Vital

Indispose(d), Indisposition Adverse, Disincline, Ill, Incapacitate, Sick, Unwell

Indistinct Ambiguous, Bleary, Blur, Bumble, Bummle, Faint, Fuzzy, Hazy, Pale, Sfumato, ➤ VAGUE

▷**In distress** may indicate an anagram

Indite Compose, Pen, Write

Individual(ist), Individuality Being, Discrete, Free spirit, Haecceity, Gemma, Identity, Ka, Libertarian, Loner, Man, Man-jack, One-to-one, Particular, Person, Poll, Respective, Separate, Single, Singular, Solo, Soul, Special, Unit, Zoon

Indomitable Brave, Dauntless, Invincible

Indubitably Certainly, Certes, Manifestly, Surely

Induce Bribe, Cause, Coax, Draw, Encourage, Get, Inveigle, Lead, Motivate, ➤ PERSUADE, Prevail, Suborn, Tempt

Induct(ion), Inductance Epagoge, Henry, Inaugurate, Initiate, Install, L, Logic, Prelude, Remanence

Indulge(nce), Indulgent Absolution, Binge, Coddle, Drink, Favour, Gratify, Humour, Luxuriate, Oblige, Pamper, Pander, Pardon, Pet, Pettle, Please, ➤ SATISFY, Splurge, Spoil, Spoonfeed, Surfeit, Tolerant, Venery, Voluptuous, Wallow

Industrial, Industrious, Industry Appliance, Application, Business, Busy, Cottage, Deedy, Diligence, Eident, Energetic, Labour, Ocnus, Ruhr, Service, Technical, Tourism, Zaibatsu

▶**Inebriate** see INTOXICATE

Ineffective, Ineffectual Clumsy, Deadhead, Drippy, Droob, Dud, Empty, Fainéant, Fruitless, Futile, Idle, Ill, Impotent, Mickey Mouse, Neutralised, Powerless, Resty, Sterile, Toothless, ➤ USELESS, Void, Weak, Wet

Inefficient Clumsy, Incompetent, Lame, Shiftless, Slack

Inept Absurd, Anorak, Farouche, Nerd, Otaku, Sad sack, Schlimazel, Unskilled, Wet

Inert(ia) Catatonia, Comatose, Dead, Dull, Excipient, Inactive, Leaden, Mollusc, Neon, Oblomovism, Potato, Sluggish, Stagnant, Stagnation, Thowless, Torpid

Inevitable, Inevitably Automatic, Certain, Fateful, Inexorable, Needs, Perforce, TINA, Unavoidable

Inexact(itude) Cretism, Incorrect, Terminological, Wrong

Inexpedient Impolitic, Imprudent, Unwise

Inexpensive Bargain, Cheap, Dirt-cheap

Inexperience(d), Inexpert Amateur, Callow, Colt, Crude, Fresh, ➤ GREEN, Ham, Ingénue, Jejune, Raw, Rookie, Rude, Tender, Unseasoned, Unversed, Youthful

Inexplicable Magical, Mysterious, Paranormal, Unaccountable

Infamous, Infamy Base, Ignominious, Notorious, Opprobrium, Shameful, Villainy

Infant Babe, Baby, Innocent, Lamb, Minor, Oral, Rug rat

Infantry(man) Buff, Foot, Grunt, Jaeger, Phalanx, Pultan, Pulto(o)n, Pultun, ➤ SOLDIER, Tercio, Turco

▷**Infantry** may refer to babies

Infatuate(d), Infatuation Assot, Besot, Crush, Enamoured, Engou(e)ment, Entêté, Fanatic, Foolish, Lovesick, ➤ OBSESSION, Rave, Turn

Infect(ed), Infecting, Infection, Infectious Angina, Anthrax, Catching, Catchy, Cholera, Communicable, Contagious, Contaminate, Corrupt, Cowpox, Diseased, Fester, Gonorrhoea, Herpes, Listeria, Lockjaw, Overrun, Poison, Polio(myelitis), ➤ POLLUTE, Ringworm, Roup, Salmonella, Septic, Shingles, Taint, Tetanus, Thrush, Tinea, Typhoid, Typhus, Virulent, Whitlow

Infer(ence) Conclude, Deduce, Divine, Educe, Extrapolate, Generalise, Guess, Illation, Imply, Judge, Surmise

▷**Infer** may indicate 'fer' around another word

Inferior Base, Cheap-jack, Cheesy, Degenerate, Dog, Gimcrack, Grody, Grub-street, Indifferent, Infra, Jerkwater, Less, Lo-fi, Low-grade, Lower, Minor, Naff, Nether, One-horse, Ornery, Paravail, Petty, Poor, Rop(e)y, Schlock, Second, Second-best, Shlock, Shoddy, Sprew, Sprue, Subjacent,

Subordinate, Substandard, Surat, Tatty, Tinpot, Trashy, Underneath, Untermensch, Waste, Worse

Infest(ed), Infestation Beset, Blight, Dog, Hoatching, Overrun, ➤ PLAGUE, Swarm, Torment

Infidel Atheist, Caffre, Heathen, Heretic, Kafir, Pagan, Saracen

Infiltrate Encroach, Enter, Instil, Intrude, Pervade

Infirm Decrepit, Doddery, Feeble, Lame, Shaky

▷**Infirm** may indicate 'co' around another word

Inflame(d), Inflammable, Inflammation Afire, Anger, ➤ AROUSE, Bloodshot, Bubonic, Catarrh, Coryza, Enamoured, Enchafe, Enfire, Enkindle, Fever, Fire, Gleet, Ignite, Incense, Infection, Ire, Napalm, Naphtha, Phlogistic, ➤ RED, Stimulate, Swelling, Touchwood

Inflate(d), Inflation Aerate, Aggrandise, Bloat, Bombastic, Dilate, Distend, Distent, Increase, Pneumatic, Pump, Remonetise, RPI, Spiral, Stagnation, Swell

Inflexible, Inflexibility Adamant(ine), Byzantine, Doctrinaire, Hard-ass, Hard-liner, Iron, Obstinate, Ossified, Relentless, Resolute, Rigid, Rigour, Set, Stubborn

Inflict(ion) Force, Give, Impose, Subject, Trouble, Visit, Wreak

Inflorescence Bostryx, Catkin, Ci(n)cinnus, Drepanium, Glomerule, Panicle, Pleiochasium, Raceme, Umbel

Influence(d), Influential Act, Affect, After, Backstairs, Charm, Clout, Credit, Determine, Drag, Earwig, Embracery, Eminence grise, Factor, Force, Govern, Hold, Impact, Impress, Incubus, Inspire, Interfere, Lead, Leverage, Lobby, Mastery, Militate, Mogul, Octopus, Operation, Power, Pressure, Prestige, ➤ PULL, Push, Reach, Rust, Say, Seminal, Significant, Star, Star-blasting, Stimulus, Suggest, Svengali, Sway, Swing, Telegony, Undue, Will, Work, Wull

Inform(ation), Informed, Informer Acquaint, Advise, Agitprop, Apprise, Au fait, Aware, Beagle, Bit, Burst, Canary, Ceefax®, Clype, Contact, Datum, Delate, Dob(ber), Dope, Education, Facts, Feedback, Fink, Fisgig, Fiz(z)gig, Gen, Genome, Grapevine, Grass, Griff, Gunsel, Hep, Input, Inside, Instruct, Izvesti(y)a, Light, Lowdown, Media, Moiser, Nark, Nepit, Nit, Nose, Occasion, Peach, Pem(m)ican, Poop, Prestel®, Prime, Propaganda, Prospectus, Rat, Read-out, Revelation, Rheme, Rumble, Shelf, Shop, Sidelight, Sing, Sneak, Snitch,

Squeak, Squeal, Stag, Stoolie, Stool-pigeon, Supergrass, Sycophant, Tell, Tidings, Tip-off, Up, Whistle(-blower), Wire

Informal Casual, Intimate, Irregular, Outgoing, Unofficial

Infuriate Anger, Bemad, Bepester, Enrage, Exasperate, Incense, Madden, Pester, Provoke

Ingenious, Ingenuity Adept, Adroit, Art, Artificial, Clever, Cunning, Cute, Inventive, Natty, Neat, Resourceful, Smart, Subtle, Wit

Ingenuous Artless, Candid, Green, Innocent, Naive, Open

Ingot Bar, Billet, Bullion, Lingot, Sycee

Ingratiate, Ingratiating Butter, Court, Flatter, Greasy, Smarm(y)

Ingredient(s) Additive, Admixture, Basis, Content, Element, Factor, Formula, Makings, Staple

Inhabit(ants) Affect, Children, Denizen, Dweller, Inholder, Inmate, Live, Native, Occupant, People, Resident

Inhale, Inhalation Aspirate, Breath(e), Draw, Gas, Inspire, Sniff, Snort, Snuff, Take

Inherit(ance), Inherited, Inheritor Accede, Birthright, Congenital, Gene, Genom, Heirloom, Inborn, Legacy, Legitim, Meek, Patrimony, Portion, Succeed

Inhibit(ing), Inhibition Captopril, Chalone, Chalonic, Deter, Enalapril, Forbid, Hang-up, Restrain, Suppress

Initial Acronym, First, Letter, Monogram, Paraph, Prelim(inary), Primary, Rubric

▷**Initially** may indicate first letters

Initiate(d), Initiation, Initiative Begin, Bejesuit, Blood, Bora, Bring, Ceremony, Debut, Enter, Enterprise, Epopt, Esoteric, Gumption, Induct, Instigate, Instruct, ➤ LAUNCH, Nous, Spark, ➤ START

Inject(or), Injection Booster, Enema, Epidural, Hypo, Implant, Innerve, Inoculation, Instil, Introduce, Jab, Mainline, Pop, Reheat, Serum, Shoot, Skin-pop, Syringe, Venipuncture

Injunction Command, Embargo, Mandate, Mareva, Writ

Injure(d), Injury, Injurious, Injustice ABH, Abuse, Aggrieve, Bale, Bled, Bruise, Contrecoup, Damage, De(a)re, Frostbite, Gash, GBH, Harm, ➤ HURT, Ill-turn, Impair, Iniquity, Lesion, Malign, Mar, Mayhem, Mistreat, Mutilate, Nobble, Nocuous, Noxal, Nuisance, Oppression, Outrage, Packet, Paire,

Prejudice, Rifle, RSI, Scaith, Scath(e), Scotch, Sore, Sprain, Tene, Tort, Trauma, Umbrage, Whiplash, Wound, Wrong

▶**Injury** see AFTER INJURY

Ink(y) Black, Cyan, Indian, Invisible, Marking, Sepia, Stained

Inlaid, Inlay(er) Boulle, Buhl, Damascene, Emblemata, Empaestic, Enamel, Enchase, Incrust, Intarsia, Intarsio, Marquetrie, Marquetry, Piqué, Set, Tarsia, Veneer

Inlet Arm, Bay, Cove, Creek, Entry, Fiord, Firth, Fjord, Fleet, Geo, Gio, Gusset, Infall, Sullom Voe, Table Bay, Wash

▷**Inlet** may indicate 'let' around another word

Inn(keeper) Albergo, Alehouse, Auberge, Barnard's, Boniface, Caravanserai, Coaching, Gray's, Halfway-house, Host, Hostelry, House, Hotel, Imaret, In, Inner Temple, Khan, Ladin(ity), Law, Licensee, Lincoln's, Lodging, Luckie, Lucky, Middle Temple, Padrone, Parador, Patron, Porterhouse, Posada, Posthouse, Pothouse, Publican, Roadhouse, Ryokan, Serai, Tabard, Tavern(er), Victualler

▷**Inn** may refer to the law

Innards Entrails, Giblets, Gizzard, Guts, Harigals, Harslet, Haslet, Rein, Viscera

▶**Innkeeper** see INN

Innocent Absolved, Angelic, Arcadian, Babe, Blameless, Canny, Chaste, Cherub, Childlike, Clean, Doddypoll, Dodipoll, Dove, Encyclical, Green, Idyllic, Ingenue, Lamb, Lily-white, Maiden, Naive, Opsimath, Pope, ➤ PURE, Sackless, Seely, Simple, St, White

Inoperative Futile, Nugatory, Silent, Void

Inordinate Excessive, Irregular, Undue

▷**Inordinately** may indicate an anagram

In place of For, Qua, Vice, With

Inquest Debriefing, Hearing, Inquiry, Investigation

Inquire, Inquiring, Inquiry Ask, Demand, Investigation, Nose, Organon, Probe, Query, Question, See, Speer, Speir

Inquisition, Inquisitive, Iniquisitor Curious, Interrogation, Meddlesome, Nosy, Prying, Rubberneck, Snooper, Stickybeak, Torquemada

▷**In revolt, In revolution** may indicate an anagram

Insane, Insanity Absurd, Batty, Crazy, Deranged, Loco, Mad, Manic, Paranoia, Pellagra, Psycho, Schizo

Inscribe(d), Inscription Chisel, Colophon, Dedicate, Emblazon, Engrave, Enter, Epigraph, Epitaph, Graffiti, Hic jacet, Hierograph, Lapidary, Legend, Lettering, Writ

Insect(s) Borer, Bug, Creepy-crawly, Entomic, Girdler, Gogga, Hexapod, Instar, Nonentity, Non-person, Nymph, Pupa, Wog, Xylophage

Insectivore Agoura, Desman, Donaea, Drosera, Hedgehog, Jacamar, Nepenthaceae, Tanrec, Tenrec(idae), Venus flytrap, Zalambdodont

Insecure Infirm, ➤ LOOSE, Precarious, Shaky, Unsafe, Unstable, Unsteady, Vulnerable

Insert(ion), Inset Cue, Empiecement, Enchase, Enter, Entry, Foist, Fudge, Godet, Gore, Graft, Gusset, Immit, Imp, Implant, Inject, Inlay, Input, Interject, Interpolate, Interpose, Intersperse, Introduce, Intromit, Mitre, Pin, Sandwich

Inside(r) Content, Core, Entrails, Gaol, Heart, Indoors, Interior, Internal, Interne, Inward, Inwith, Mole, Tum, ➤ WITHIN

Insignia Armour, Arms, Badger, Charge, Chevron, Mark, Regalia, Ribbon, Roundel, Tab

Insignificant (person) Dandiprat, Fico, Flea-bite, Fractional, Gnat, Inconsiderable, Insect, Minimus, Miniscule, Minnow, Nebbich, Nobody, Nominal, Nonentity, One-eyed, Petit, Petty, Pipsqueak, Quat, Scoot, Scout, Scrub, Shrimp, Slight, Small-time, Squirt, Squit, Trifling, Trivial, Two-bit, Unimportant, Venial, Whippersnapper

Insincere Affected, Artificial, Barmecide, Cant, Double, Empty, Factitious, Faithless, False, Glib, Hollow, Janus-faced, Mealy-mouthed, Pseudo, Shallow, Synthetic

Insipid Banal, Blab, Bland, Fade, Flat, Insulse, Jejune, Lash, Mawkish, Shilpit, Tame, Tasteless, Vapid, Weak, Wearish

Insist(ent) Assert, Demand, Dogmatic, Exact, ➤ STIPULATE, Stress, Swear, Threap, Threep, Urge

Insolence, Insolent Audacity, Bardy, Brassy, Cheek, Contumely, Effrontery, Gum, Hubris, Hybris, Impudence, Lip, Rude, Snash, Stroppy, Wanton

Insolvent Bankrupt, Broke, Destitute, Penniless

Inspect(ion), Inspector Alnage(r), Auditor, Comb, Conner, Examine, Government, Investigator, Jerque, Keeker, Muster,

Once-over, Peep, Perlustrate, Proveditor, Rag-fair, Recce, Review, Scrutinise, Survey, Test, Vet, Vidimus, Visitation

Inspiration, Inspire(d), Inspiring Actuate, Afflatus, Aerate, Aganippe, Animate, Brainstorm, Brainwave, Breath(e), Castalian, Elate, Exalt, Flash, Draw, Fire, Hearten, Hunch, Idea, Illuminate, Impulse, Induce, Inflatus, Infuse, Move, Muse, Pegasus, Prompt, Prophetic, Satori, Sniff(le), Stimulus, Taghairm, Theopneust(y), Uplift, Vatic

Install(ation) Enchase, Enthrone, Inaugurate, Induction, Infrastructure, Invest, Put (in)

Instalment Episode, Fascicle, Heft, Livraison, Never-never, Part, Serial, Tranche

Instance, Instant As, Case, Example, Flash, Jiffy, Moment, Present, Say, Shake, Spur, Tick, Trice, Twinkling, Urgent

Instead (of) Deputy, For, Lieu, Locum, Vice

Instigate Arouse, Foment, Impel, Incite, Prompt, Spur

Instinct(ive) Automatic, Flair, Herd, Id, Impulse, Inbred, Innate, Intuition, Nature, Nose, Talent, Tendency, Visceral

Institute, Institution Academy, Activate, Asylum, Bank, Begin, Bring, Charity, College, Erect, Found(ation), I, Inaugurate, MORI, Orphanage, Poorhouse, Raise, Redbrick, Retraict, Retrait(e), Retreat, Smithsonian, Start, University, Women's, Workhouse

Instruct(ed), Instruction, Instructor Advice, Apprenticeship, Brief, Catechism, Clinic, Coach, Course, Didactic, Direct(ive), Document, Edify, Educate, Ground(ing), Inform, Lesson, Manual, Notify, Order, Percept, Recipe, Rubric, Swami, ➤ TEACH, Train, Tutelage, Tutorial, Up

Instrument(al) Act, Agent, Dupe, Helpful, Mean(s), ➤ MUSICAL INSTRUMENT, Organ(ic), ➤ RESPONSIBLE, ➤ TOOL, ➤ UTENSIL

Insubordinate Contumacious, Faction, Mutinous, Rebel, Refractory

Insubstantial Airy, Brief, Flimsy, Frothy, Illusory, Jackstraw, Slight, Thin, Wispy, Ye(a)sty

Insult(ing) Abuse, Affront, Aspersion, Barb, Contumely, Cut, Dyslogistic, Embarrass, Facer, Fig, Lese-majesty, Mud, Mud-pie, Offend, Opprobrious, Skit, Slagging, Slight, Slur, Snub, Trauma, Uncomplimentary, Verbal, Yenta, Yente

Insurance, Insure(r) Abandonee, Cover, Fire, Guarantee, Hedge, Indemnity, Knock-for-knock, Life, Lloyds, Medicare, Mutual, National, Policy, Reversion, Security, Underwrite

Insurgent, Insurrection Cade, Mutiny, Outbreak, Rebel, Revolt, Sedition

Intact Complete, Entire, Inviolate, Unused, Whole

Integrate(d) Amalgamate, Assimilate, Combine, Fuse, Harmonious, Mainstream, Merge

Integrity Honesty, Principle, Rectitude, Strength, Uprightness, Whole

Intellect(ual) Academic, Aptitude, Brain, Cerebral, Dianoetic, Egghead, Far-out, Genius, Intelligent, Intelligentsia, Luminary, Mastermind, Titan, -ist, Learned, Mental(ity), Mind, Noesis, Noetic, Noology, Nous, Profound, Reason

Intelligence, Intelligent Advice, Boss, Brains, Bright, CIA, Discerning, Dope, Eggmass, Esprit, G, Grey matter, GRU, Info, Ingenious, IQ, Knowledgeable, Machiavellian, MI, Mossad, Mother wit, News, Pate, Pointy-headed, Rational, Sconce, Sense, Shrewd, Spetsnaz, Spetznaz, Tidings, Wit

Intend(ed), Intending Allot, Contemplate, Design, Destine, Ettle, Fiancé(e), Going, ➤ MEAN, Meditate, Propose, Purpose

Intense, Intensify, Intensity Acute, Aggravate, Ardent, Earnest, Enhance, Emotional, Escalate, Excess, Extreme, Fervent, Keen, Might, Profound, Redouble, Sharpen, Vehement, Vivid

Intent, Intention(al) A dessein, Animus, Deliberate, Dole, Earnest, Hellbent, Manifesto, Mens rea, Mind, Purpose, Rapt, Resolute, Set, Studious, Systematic, Thought, Witting, Yrapt

Interaction Enantiodromia, Solvation

Intercede, Intercession Mediate, Negotiate, Plead, Prayer

Interdict Ban, Forbid, Prohibit, Taboo

Interest(ed), Interesting Amusive, APR, Attention, Behalf, Benefit, Clou, Compound, Concern, Contango, Coupon, Dividend, Engage, Engross, Fad, Fee-simple, Fee-tail, Grab, Hot, Import, Income, Int(o), Intrigue, Line, Part, Partisan, Percentage, Readable, Respect, Revenue, Scene, Share, Side, Simple, Spice, Stake, Topical, Usage, Usance, Usure, Usury, Vested, Vigorish, Warm

Interfere(r), Interference Busybody, Clutter, Disrupt, Hamper, Hinder, Intrude, Mar, ➤ MEDDLE, Molest, Officious, Pry, Shash, Static, Tamper, Teratogen

Interim Break, Meanwhile, Temporary

Interior Backblocks, Cyclorama, Domestic, Innards, Innate, Inner, Inside, Outback, Plain, Up-country, Vitals

Interject(ion) Ahem, Begorra(h), Haith, Hoo-oo, Interpolate, Lumme, Nation, Sese(y), Sessa, 'Sheart, 'Slid, Tarnation, Tush

Interlace Mingle, Weave, Wreathe

Interloper Gate-crasher, Intruder, Trespasser

Interlude Antimask, Antimasque, Divertimento, Entr'acte, Interruption, Kyogen, Lunch-hour, Meantime, Pause, Verset

Intermediary, Intermediate Agent, Bardo, Comprador(e), Go-between, Instar, Mean, Medial, Mesne, Mezzanine, Middle-of-the-road, Middleman

Intermission Apyrexia, Break, Interval, Pause, Recess

Intermittent Broken, Fitful, Periodic, Random, Spasmic, Spasmodic, Sporadic

Intern(e) Confine, Doctor, Impound, Restrict, Trainee

Internal Domestic, Inner, Internecine, Inward, Within

International Cap, Cosmopolitan, Lion, UN, Universal

Interpret(er) Conster, Construe, Decipher, Decode, Dragoman, Exegete, Explain, Exponent, Expositor, Expound, Hermeneutist, Jehovist, Prophet, Read, Rede, Render, Represent, Spokesman, ➤ TRANSLATE, Ulema

Interpretation Anagoge, Anagogy, Construction, Copenhagen, Eisegesis, Exegesis, Exegete, Gematria, Gloss(ary), Gospel, Halacha(h), Halakah, Hermeneutics, Midrash, Portray, Reading, Rede, Rendition, Targum, Translation

Interrogate, Interrogation Catechism, Debrief(ing), Enquire, Examine, Grill, Pump, ➤ QUESTION, Quiz

Interrupt(ion), Interrupter Ahem, Blip, Break, Butt, Chequer, Chip in, Disturb, Entr'acte, Heckle, Hiatus, Intercept, Interfere, Interpellate, Interpolate, Interpose, Interregnum, Intrusion, Pause, Portage, Rheotome, Stop, Suspend

Intersect(ion) Carfax, Carfox, Chiasm(a), Cross, Crunode, Cut, Decussate, Divide, Groin, Metacentre, Orthocentre, Trace

Intersperse Dot, Interpose, Scatter, Sprinkle

Intertwine Braid, Knit, Lace, Plait, Splice, Twist, Writhe

Interval Between, Break, Breather, Class, Closed, Comma, Diesis, Distance, Duodecimo, Entr'acte, Fifth, Gap, Half-time, Hiatus, Hourly, Interim, Interlude, Interregnum, Interspace, Interstice, Meantime, Meanwhile, Ninth, Octave, Ottava, Pycnon, Respite, Rest, Schisma, Semitone, Sixth, Space, Span, Spell, Wait

Intervene, Intervention Agency, Arbitrate, Interfere, Interjacent, Interrupt, Mediate, Mesne, Theurgy, Up

Interview Audience, Audition, Conference, Examine, Hearing, Oral, Press conference, See, Vox pop

Interweave, Interwoven Entwine, Interlace, Monogram, Plait, Plash, Pleach, Raddle, Wreathed

Intestine(s) Bowel, Chit(ter)lings, Duodenum, Entrails, Guts, Harigals, Innards, Jejunum, Mesenteron, Omenta, Rectum, Splanchnic, Thairm, Viscera

Intimacy, Intimate(ly) Achates, Boon, Bosom, Communion, Connote, Familiar, Friend, Inmost, Innuendo, Intrigue, Nearness, Opine, Pack, Private, Signal, Special, Thick, Throng, Warm, Well

Intimidate, Intimidating Browbeat, Bulldoze, Bully, Cow, Daunt, Dragon, Hector, Psych, Threaten, Unnerve

Intolerable, Intolerant Allergic, Bigotry, Excessive, Illiberal, Impossible, Ombrophobe, Self-righteous

Intone, Intonation Cadence

Intractable Disobedient, Kittle, Mulish, Obdurate, Perverse, Surly, Unruly, Wilful

Intransigent Adamant, Inflexible, Rigid, Uncompromising

Intrepid Aweless, Bold, Brave, Dauntless, Doughty, Firm, ► RESOLUTE, Valiant

Intricate Complex, Daedal(ian), Daedale, Dedal, Gordian, Intrince, Involute, Knotty, Pernickety, Tricky, Vitruvian

Intrigue(r), Intriguing Affaire, Artifice, Brigue, Cabal, Camarilla, Cloak and dagger, Collogue, Conspiracy, Fascinate, Hotbed, Ignatian, Jesuit, Jobbery, Liaison, Machinate, Plot, Politic, Rat, ► SCHEME, Strategy, Traffic, Trinketer

▷**Intrinsically** may indicate something within a word

Introduce(r), Introduction, Introductory Acquaint, Anacrusis, Curtain-raiser, Emcee, Enseam, Exordial, Foreword, Immit, Import, Induct, Initiate, Inject, Insert, Instil(l), Intercalate,

Interpolate, Introit, Isagogic, Lead-in, Opening, Plant, Preamble, Preface, Preliminary, Prelude, Prelusory, Preparatory, Present, Proem, Prolegomena, Prolegomenon, Prologue, Proponent, Referral, Start, Usher

▷**Introduction** may indicate a first letter

▷**In trouble** may indicate an anagram

Intrude(r), Intrusion, Intrusive Abate, Aggress, Annoy, Bother, Burglar, ➤ ENCROACH, Gatecrash, Interloper, Invade, Meddle, Nosey, Porlocking, Presume, Raid, Sorn, Trespass

Intuition Belief, ESP, Hunch, Insight, Instinct, Noumenon, Premonition, Seat-of-the-pants, Telepathy

▷**In two words** may indicate a word to be split

Inundate, Inundation Flood, Overflow, Overwhelm, Submerge, Swamp

Inure Acclimatise, Accustom, Harden, Season, Steel

Invade(r), Invasion Angle, Attack, Attila, Dane, Descent, Encroach, Hacker, Hengist, Horsa, Hun, Infest, Inroad, Intruder, Jute, Lombard, Martian, Norman, Norsemen, Ostrogoth, Overrun, Permeate, Raid, Trespass, Vandal

Invalid(ate), Invalidation Bad, Bogus, Bunbury, Cancel, Chronic, Clinic, Defunct, Diriment, Erroneous, Expired, False, Inauthentic, Inform, Inoperative, Irritate, Lapsed, Nugatory, Null, Nullify, Refute, Shut-in, Terminate, Vitiate, Void

Invaluable Essential, Excellent, Precious, Useful

Invariable, Invariably Always, Constant, Eternal, Habitual, Perpetual, Steady, Uniform

Invective Abuse, Billingsgate, Diatribe, Philippic, Reproach, Ribaldry, Tirade

Invent(ion), Inventive Adroit, Babe, Baby, Brainchild, Chimera, Coin, Contrive, ➤ CREATE, Daedal, Design, Device, Fabricate, Fain, Feign, Figment, Imaginary, Improvise, Ingenuity, Mint, Originate, Patent, Resourceful, Synectics, Wit

Inventor Archimedes, Arkwright, Artificer, Author, Babbage, Baird, Bell, Biro, Boys, Bramah, Cartwright, Celsius, Coiner, Creator, Crompton, Daedalus, Edison, Engineer, Galileo, Geiger, Hansom, Marconi, Maxim, Minié, Mint-master, Morse, Nernst, Newcomen, Nobel, Patentee, Savery, Tesla, Torricelli, Tull, Watt, Wheatstone

Inventory Account, Index, Itemise, List, Register, Stock

Inversion, Invert(ed) Capsize, Chiasmus, Entropion, Entropium, Opposite, Overset, Reverse, Turn, Upset

Invertebrate Spineless

Invest(or), Investment Ambient, Angel, Beleaguer, Besiege, Bet, Blockade, Blue-chip, Capitalist, Dignify, Embark, Enclothe, Endow, Enrobe, Flutter, Gilt, Girt, Holding, Infeft, Install, On, Pannicle, Parlay, Place, Portfolio, Put, Ring, Robe, Share, Siege, Sink, Spec, Stake, Stock, Tessa, Trust, Venture

▷**Invest** may indicate one word surrounding another

Investigate, Investigator, Investigation Canvass, Case, CID, Delve, Examine, Explore, Fed, Fieldwork, Hunt, Inquest, Inquirendo, Inquiry, Inquisition, McCarthyism, Nose, Organon, Organum, Probe, Pry, Quester, Rapporteur, Research, Scan, Scrutinise, Search, Sleuth, Snoop, Study, Suss, T-man, Tec, Test, Track, Try, Zetetic

Inveterate Chronic, Dyed-in-the-wool, Habitual, Hardened

Invidious Harmful, Hostile, Malign

Invigorate, Invigorating, Invigoration Analeptic, Brace, Brisk, Cheer, Elixir, Energise, Enliven, Fortify, Insinew, Pep, Refresh, Renew, Stimulate, Tonic, Vital

Invincible Almighty, Brave, Stalwart, Valiant

Invisible Hidden, Imageless, Infra-red, Secret, Tusche, Unseen

Invite, Invitation Ask, Attract, Bid, Call, Card, Overture, ➤ REQUEST, Solicit, Stiffie, Summons, Tempt, Woo

Invocation, Invoke Appeal, Call, Conjure, Curse, Entreat, Epiclesis, Solicit

Invoice Account, Bill, Itemise, Manifest, Pro forma

Involve(d), Involvement Commitment, Complicate, Complicit, Concern, Embroil, Engage, Entail, Envelop, Imbroglio, Immerse, ➤ IMPLICATE, Include, Intricate, Meet, Necessitate, Tangle

▷**Involved** may indicate an anagram

Inward(s) Afferent, Homefelt, Introrse, Mental, Private, Varus, Within

Iota Atom, Jot, Subscript, Whit

IOU Cedula, Market, PN, Vowels

Iranian Babist, Kurd, Mede, Parsee

Irascible Choleric, Crusty, Fiery, Peevish, Snappy, Tetchy

Irate Angry, Cross, Infuriated, Wrathful

Ire Anger, Cholera, Fury, Rage, Wrath

Iridescence, Iridescent Chatoyant, Opaline, Reflet, Shimmering, Shot, Water-gall

Iris Areola, Eye, Flag, Fleur-de-lis, Gladdon, Ixia, Lily, Lis, Orris, Rainbow, Sedge, Seg, Sunbow

Irish(man) Bark, Boy, Bog-trotter, Celt(ic), Clan-na-gael, Defender, Dermot, Dubliner, Eamon(n), Eirann, Erse, Fenian, Gaeltacht, Goidel, Greek, Keltic, Kern(e), Mick(e)(y), Milesian, Mulligan, Ogamic, Orange(man), Ostmen, Paddy(-whack), Partholon, Pat(rick), Rapparee, Redshank, Reilly, Riley, Rory, Sean, Shoneen, Teague, Ultonian

Iron(s), Ironwork(s) Airn, Angle, Carron, Cautery, Chains, Chalybeate, Chancellor, Channel, Climbing, Coquimbite, Cramp(on), Crampon, Crimp, Cross, Curling, Curtain, Delta, Derringer, Dogs, Fayalite, Fe, Ferredoxin, Fetter, Fiddley, Flip-dog, Gem, Golfclub, Goose, Grappling, Grim, Grozing, ► GUN, Gyve, Horse, Ingot, Kamacite, Laterite, Maiden, Marcasite, Mars, Martensite, Mashie, Mashy, Pig, ► PRESS, Pro-metal, Rabble, Rations, Rod, Sad, Smoother, Soft, Soldering, Spiegeleisen, Steam, Stirrup, Strong, Taconite, Taggers, Terne, Tin terne, Waffle, Wedge, Wrought

Ironic, Irony Antiphrasis, Asteism, Dramatic, Meiosis, Metal, Ridicule, Sarcasm, Satire, Socratic, Tongue-in-cheek, Tragic, Trope, Wry

►**Ironwork(s)** see IRON

Irrational Absurd, Brute, Delirious, Foolish, Illogical, Superstitious, Surd, Wild

Irregular(ity) Abnormal, Anomaly, A salti, Asymmetric, Bashi-bazouk, Blotchy, Crazy, Erratic, Evection, Fitful, Flawed, Formless, Guerilla, Heteroclitic, Incondite, Inordinate, Kink, Occasional, Orthotone, Para-military, Partisan, Patchy, Random, Scalene, Sebundy, Solecism, Sporadic, TA, Uneven, Unsteady, Variable, Wayward, Zigzag

▷**Irregular** may indicate an anagram

Irrelevant Digression, Gratuitous, Immaterial, Inept

Irreproachable Blameless, Spotless, Stainless

Irresistible Almighty, Endearing, Inevitable, Mesmeric, Overwhelming

Irresolute, Irresolution Doubtful, Hesitant, Timid, Unsure

Irresponsible Capricious, Feckless, Flighty, Slap-happy, Strawen, Trigger-happy, Wanton, Wildcat

Irreverent Disrespectful, Impious, Profane

Irrigate, Irrigation Colonic, Enema, Flood, Water

Irritable, Irritability, Irritant, Irritate(d), Irritation Acerbate, Anger, Annoy, Blister, Bug, Chafe, Chauff, Chippy, Crabby, Cross-grained, Crosspatch, Crotchety, Crusty, Dod, Dyspeptic, Eat, Edgy, Enchafe, Erethism, Ewk, Exasperate, Fantod, Feverish, Fiery, Fleabite, Frabbit, Fractious, Fraught, Gall, Get, Goad, Grate, Gravel, Heck, Intertrigo, Irk, Itch, Jangle, Livery, Mardy, Narky, Needle, Nettle, Niggly, Ornery, Peevish, Pesky, Pet, Petulance, Pinprick, Pique, Provoke, Rag'd, Ragde, Rankle, Rasp, Rattle, Ratty, Rile, Roil, Rub, Ruffle, Savin(e), Scratchy, Shirty, Snappy, Snit, Splenetic, Sting, Tease, Techy, Testy, Tetchy, Thorn, Tickle, Toey, Touchy, Uptight, ➤ VEX

▷**Irritated** may indicate an anagram

Islam(ic) Crescent, Druse, Druz(e), Kurd(ish), Senus(si), Sheriat, Shia(h), Shiite, Wah(h)abi

Island, Isle(t) Ait, Archipelago, Atoll, Cay, Desert, Eyot, Floating, I, Inch, Is, Key, Lagoon, Mainland, Refuge, Traffic

Isn't Aint, Nis, Nys

Isolate(d) Ancress, Backwater, Cut off, Enclave, Enisle, In vacuo, Incommunicado, Inisle, Island, Lone, Maroon, Pocket, Quarantine, Sea-girt, Seclude, Secret, Segregate, Separate, Sequester, Solitary, Sporadic, Stray

Isotope Actinon, Deuterium, Muonium, Protium, Strontium-90, Thoron, Tritium

Issue(s) Come, Crux, Debouch, Denouement, Derive, Disclose, Dispense, Edition, Effluence, Egress, ➤ EMANATE, Emerge, Emit, Exit, Exodus, Family, Fiduciary, Flotation, Gush, Ish, Litter, Number, Offspring, Outflow, Part, Proof, Publish, Result, Rights, Sally, Seed, Son, Spawn, Spring, Stream, Subject, Topic, Turn, Utter

Isthmus Darien, Karelian, Kra, Neck, Panama

It A, Chic, Hep, Id, Italian, Oomph, SA, 't, Vermouth

Italian, Italy Alpini, Ausonia, Bolognese, Calabrian, Chian, Dago, Ding, Este, Etnean, Etrurian, Etruscan, Eyeti(e), Eytie, Faliscan, Florentine, Genoese, Ghibelline, Guelf, Guelph, Hesperia, Irredentist, It, Latian, Latin, Lombard, Medici, Moro,

Oscan, Paduan, Patarin(e), Roman, Sabine, Samnite, Sicel, Sikel, Sienese, Signor(i), Spag, Tuscan, Umbrian, Venetian, Vermouth, Volscian, Wop

Itch(ing), itchiness Annoy, Cacoethes, Dhobi, Prickle, Prurience, Prurigo, Pruritis, Psora, Scabies, Scrapie, Seven-year, Tickle, ➤ URGE

Item(ise) Also, Article, Bulletin, Detail, Entry, Flash, List, Number, Piece, Point, Spot, Too, Topic

Itinerant, Itinerary Ambulant, Didakai, Didakei, Did(d)icoy, Gipsy, Gypsy, Journey, Log, Pedlar, Peripatetic, Pie-powder, Roadman, Roamer, Romany, Rootless, Route, Stroller, Traveller

Ivory (tower) Bone, Dentine, Distant, Eburnean, Impractical, Incisor, Key, Solitude, Teeth, Tusk, Vegetable

Ivy Aralia, Boston, Bush, Creeper, Grape, Hedera, Helix, Poison

Jj

Jab(ber) Chatter, Foin, Gabble, Immunologist, Inject, Jaw, Jook, Nudge, Poke, Prattle, Prod, Proke, Punch, Puncture, Sook, Sputter, Stab, Venepuncture, Yak

Jack(s) AB, Apple, Ass, Ball, Boot, Bowl(s), Boy, Card, Cheap, Deckhand, Dibs(tones), Flag, Frost, Hoist, Honour, Horner, Idle, J, Jock, Ketch, Kitty, Knave, London, Mark, Matlow, Mistress, Nob, Noddy, Pilot, Point, Pot, Pur, Rabbit, Raise, Ripper, Robinson, Russell, Sailor, Salt, Sprat, Steeple, Sticker, Straw, Tar, Tee, Tradesman, Turnspit, Union, Wood

Jacket Acton, Anorak, Barbour®, Battle, Bed, Blazer, Bolero, Bomber, Bumfreezer, Cagoul(e), Cardigan, Casing, ➤ COAT, Dinner, Dolman, Donkey, Dust-cover, Dustwrapper, Flak, Hacking, Jerkin, Kagool, Life, Lumber, Mae West, Matinée, Mess, Monkey, Norfolk, Parka, Pea, Potato, Reefer, Shell, Slip-cover, Smoking, Spencer, Sports, Tabard, Tunic, Tux(edo), Tweed, Waistcoat, Windbreaker®, Windcheater, Windjammer, Wrapper

Jackknife Dive, Fold, Jockteleg, Pike

Jade(d) Axe-stone, Cloy, Crock, Exhaust, Fatigue, Greenstone, Hack, Hag, Horse, Hussy, Limmer, Minx, Nag, Nephrite, Sate, Screw, Slut, Stale, Tired, Trite, Weary, Yu(-stone)

Jag(ged) Barbed, Cart, Drinking, Erose, Gimp, Injection, Laciniate, Ragde, Ragged, Serrate, Snag, Spree, Spur, Tooth

Jaguar Car, Caracal, Cat, E-type, Ounce, Tiger

Jail(er) Adam, Alcatraz, Bedford, Bin, Can, Clink, Cooler, Gaol, Hoosegow, Imprison, Incarcerate, Jug, Keeper, Lockup, Marshalsea, Newgate, Nick, Pen, Pokey, ➤ PRISON, Screw, Shop, Strangeways, Turnkey, Warder

Jailbird Con, Lag, Lifer, Trusty

Jalopy Banger, Boneshaker, Buggy, Car, Crate, Heap, Stock-car

Jam(my) Block, Choke, Clog, Confiture, Crush, Cushy, Dilemma, Gridlock, Hold-up, Jeelie, Jeely, Lock, Log, Plight, ➤ PREDICAMENT, Preserve, Press, Quince, Seize, Snarl-up, Spot, Squeeze, Stick, Tailback, Traffic, Vice, Vise, Wedge

Jamb Doorpost, Durn, Sconcheon, Scontion, Scuncheon, Upright

Jane Austen, Calamity, Eyre, Seymour, Shore, Sian

Jangle Clank, Clapperclaw, Clash, Rattle, Wrangle

Japan(ese), Japanese drama Ainu, Burakumin, Daimio, Eta, Geisha, Genro, Gloss, Haiku, Heian, Hondo, Honshu, Issei, Kabuki, Kami, Kana, Kirimon, Lacquer, Mandarin, Mikado, Mousmé, Mousmee, Nippon, Nisei, No(h), Resin, Sansei, Satsuma, Shinto, Shogun, Togo, Tycoon, Yamato

Jar(ring) Albarello, Amphora, Bell, Canopus, Churr, Clash, Crock, Cruet, Din, Dolium, Enrough, Gallipot, Grate, Greybeard, Gride, Grind, Gryde, Humidor, Hydria, ➤ JOLT, Kalpis, Kang, Kilner®, Leyden, Mason, Off-key, Olla, Pint, Pithos, Pot(iche), Rasp, Shelta, Shock, Stamnos, Start, Stean, Steen, Stein, Tankard, Tinaja, Turn, Vessel, Water-monkey

Jargon Argot, Baragouin, Beach-la-mar, Buzzword, Cant, Chinook, Eurobabble, Eurospeak, Gobbledegook, Gobbledygook, Jive, Kennick, Legalese, Lingo, Lingoa geral, Lingua franca, Mumbo-jumbo, Newspeak, Parlance, Patois, Patter, Shelta, Shoptalk, ➤ SLANG, Technospeak, Vernacular

Jaundice(d) Cynical, Icterus, Prejudiced, Sallow, Yellow

Jaunt Journey, Outing, Sally, Stroll, Swan, Trip

Jaunty Airy, Akimbo, Chipper, Debonair, Perky, Rakish

▷**Jaunty** may indicate an anagram

Javelin Dart, Gavelock, Harpoon, Jereed, Jerid, Pile, Pilum, Spear

Jaw(s), Jawbone Blab, Chaft, Chap, Chat, Chaw, Cheek, Chide, Chin, Entry, Glass, Gnathite, Gonion, Jobe, Lantern, Mandible, Maxilla, Mesial, Muzzle, Mylohyoid, Natter, Opisthognathous, Overshot, Phossy, Pi, Premaxillary, Prognathous, Ramus, Shark, Stylet, Underhung, Undershot, Wapper-jaw, Ya(c)kety-Ya(c)k

Jazz(er), Jazzman Acid, Barber, Barrelhouse, Bebop, Blues, Boogie, Boogie-woogie, Bop, Cat, Cool, Dixieland, Enliven, Gig, Gutbucket, Hipster, Jive, Latin, Lick, Mainstream, Modern, Progressive, Ragtime, Riff, Scat, Skiffle, Stomp, Swinger, Trad, Traditional

Jealous(y) Envious, Green(-eyed), Grudging, Zelotypia

Jeer(ing) Barrack, Belittle, Birl, Boo, Burl, Digs, Fleer, Flout, Gird, Hoot, Jape, Jibe, ➤ MOCK, Rail, Razz, Ridicule, Scoff, Sneer, Taunt

Jehovah God, Lord, Yahve(h), Yahwe(h)

Jelly Agar(-agar), Aspic, Brawn, Calf's foot, Chaudfroid, Comb, ➤ EXPLOSIVE, Flummery, Gel, Isinglass, Jam, Medusa, Mineral, Mould, Napalm, Petroleum, Royal, Vaseline®

▷**Jelly** may indicate an anagram

Jellyfish Aurelia, Box, Cnidaria, Medusa, Portuguese man-of-war, Sea-wasp, Sea-blubber, Sea-nettle

Jenny Ass, Lind, Mule, Spinner, Spinster, Wren

Jeopardise, Jeopardy Danger, Expose, Hazard, Peril, Risk

Jerk(ily), Jerking, Jerks Aerobics, A salti, Bob, Braid, Cant, Diddle, Ebrillade, Flirt, Flounce, Gym(nastics), Hike, Hitch, Hoi(c)k, Jut, Kant, PE, Peck, Physical, Saccade, Shove, Spasm, Start, Surge, Sydenham's chorea, Tic, Toss(en), Tweak, ➤ TWITCH, Wrench, Yank

Jerry, Jerry-built Boche, Flimsy, Fritz, Hun, Kraut, Mouse, Po(t)

Jersey(s) Cow, Frock, Gansey, Guernsey, Kine, Lily, Maillot, Polo, Roll-neck, Singlet, ➤ SWEATER, Sweatshirt, Yellow, Zephyr

Jest(er), Jesting Badinage, Barm, Buffoon, Clown, Cod, Comic, Droll, Jape, Joker, Josh, Miller, Motley, Patch, Quip, Raillery, Ribaldry, Rigoletto, Sport, Toy, Wag, Wit, Yorick

Jesus ➤ CHRIST, Emmanuel, IHS, INRI, Jabers, Lord

Jet Airbus®, Aircraft, Beadblast, Black, Burner, Chirt, Douche, Fountain, Geat, Harrier, Jumbo, Plane, Pump, Soffione, Spirt, Spout, Spray, Spurt, Squirt, Stream, Turbine, Turbo, Vapour

Jettison Discard, Dump, Flotsam, Jetsam, Lagan, Ligan

Jew(ish), Jews Ashkenazi, Chas(s)id, Diaspora, Essene, Falasha, Has(s)id, Hebrew, Kahal, Karaite, Levite, Lubavitch, Maccabee, Mitnag(g)ed, Pharisee, Sadducee, Semite, Sephardim, Shemite, Shtetl, Tobit, Wandering, Yid(dish)

Jewel(ler), Jewellery Agate, Almandine, Artwear, Beryl, Bijouterie, Brilliant, Chrysoprase, Cloisonné, Cornelian, Costume, Diamond, Earbob, Ear-drop, Emerald, Ewe-lamb, Fabergé, Ferron(n)ière, Finery, Garnet, ➤ GEM, Girandole, Gracchi, Jade, Lherzolite, Marcasite, Navette, Olivine, Opal, Parure, Paste, Pavé, Pearl, Pendant, Peridot, Rivière, Rubin(e), Ruby, Sapphire, Sard, Scarab, Smaragd, Solitaire, Stone, Sunburst, Tom, Tomfoolery, Topaz, Torc, Treasure

Jib Ba(u)lk, Boggle, ➤ DEMUR, Face, Foresail, Genoa, Milk, Reest, Reist, Stay-sail

Jibe Bob, Correspond, Fling, ➤ JEER, Mock, Sarcasm, Slant, Taunt

Jig(gle) Bob, Bounce, Dance, Fling, Frisk, Hornpipe, Jog, Juggle

Jilt Discard, Reject, Shed, Throw-over

Jingle(r) Clerihew, Clink, Ditty, Doggerel, Rhyme, Tambourine, Tinkle

Jinx Curse, Hex, Jonah, Kibosh, Spoil, Voodoo, Whammy

Jitter(s), Jittery Coggly, DT, Fidgets, Funk, Jumpy, Nervous, Willies

▷**Jitter(s)** may indicate an anagram

Job Appointment, Berth, Career, Chore, Comforter, Crib, Darg, Errand, Gig, Homer, Inside, Metier, Oratorio, Patient, Pensum, Plum, Position, Post, Problem, Put-up, Sinecure, Spot, Steady, ➤ TASK, Ticket, Trotter, Undertaking, Work

▷**Job** may indicate the biblical character

Jockey Carr, Cheat, Diddle, Jostle, Jump, Lester, Manoeuvre, Rider, Steve, Swindle, Trick, Video, Winter

▷**Jockey** may indicate an anagram

Jocose, Jocular, Jocund Cheerful, Debonair, Facete, Facetious, Jesting, Lepid, Scurril(e), Waggish

Joe(y), Joseph Addison, Dogsbody, GI, Kangaroo, Pal, Roo, Sloppy, Stalin, Surface, Trey

Jog(gle), Jog-trot Arouse, Canter, Dunch, Dunsh, Heich-how, Heigh-ho, Hod, Jiggle, Jolt, Jostle, Mosey, Nudge, Prompt, Ranke, Remind, Run, Shake, Shog, Tickle, Trot, Whig

Join(er), Joined Accompany, Add, Annex, Associate, Attach, Combine, Connect, ► COUPLE, Dovetail, Engraft, Enlist, Enrol, Enter, Fuse, Glue, Graft, Include, Link, Marry, Meet, Merge, Mix, Rivet, Seam, Solder, Splice, Staple, Tenon, Unite, Wed, Weld, Yoke

Joint(ed) Ankle, Bar, Butt, Carpus, Chine, Clip, Co, Cuit, Cut, Dive, Dovetail, Elbow, Entrecôte, Fish, Haunch, Heel, Hinge, Hip, Hough, Huck, J, Joggle, Jolly, Junction, Knee, Knuckle, Loin, Marijuana, Meat, Mitre, Mortise, Mutton, Phalange, Phalanx, Rack, Reefer, Ribroast, Roast, Saddle, Scarf, Seam, Shoulder, Silverside, Sirloin, Splice, Stifle, Strip, T, Tarsus, T-bone, Tenon, Together, Toggle, Tongue and groove, Topside, Undercut, Universal, Weld, Wrist

Joist Bar, Beam, Dormant, Groundsill, I-beam, Rib, Sleeper, Solive, String

Joke(r), Joke-book Banter, Bar, Booby-trap, Card, Chaff, Chestnut, ► CLOWN, Cod, Comedian, Comic, Crack, Cut-up, Farceur, Farceuse, Fool, Fun, Funster, Gab, Gag, Glike, Guy, Have-on, Hazer, Hoax, Hum, Humorist, Jape, Jest, Jig, Lark, Legpull, Merry-andrew, Merryman, One-liner, Practical, Prank(ster), Pun, Punchline, Quip, Sally, Scherzo, Sick, Skylark, Squib, Standing, Wag, Wheeze, Wisecrack, Wild, Wit

Jollity, Jolly 'Arryish, Bally, Convivial, Cordial, Do, Festive, Galoot, Gaucie, Gaucy, Gawcy, Gawsy, Gay, Hilarious, Jocose, Jovial, Marine, Mirth, Rag, RM, Roger, Sandboy, Tar, Very

Jolt Bump, Jar, Jig-a jig, Jostle, Jounce, Shake, Shog, Start

►**Joseph** see JOE

Josh Chaff, Kid, Rib, Tease

Jostle Barge, Bump, Compete, Elbow, Hustle, Push, Shoulder, ► SHOVE

Journal Daily, Daybook, Diary, Gazette, Hansard, Lancet, Log, Organ, Paper, Periodical, Pictorial, Punch, Rag, Record, Trade

Journalism, Journalist Columnist, Contributor, Diarist, Ed, Fleet St, (GA) Sala, Freelance, Hack, Hackette, Lobby,

Northcliffe, NUJ, Pepys, Press(man), Reporter, Reviewer, Scribe, Stead, Stringer, Wireman, ➤ WRITER

Journey Circuit, Cruise, Errand, Expedition, Eyre, Foray, Hadj, Jaunce, Jaunse, Jaunt, Mush, Odyssey, Passage, Periegesis, Ply, Raik, Rake, Red-eye, Ride, Run, Sentimental, Tour, Travel, Trek, Walkabout

Journeyman Artisan, Commuter, Craftsman, Sterne, Yeoman

Joust Tilt, Tournament, Tourney

Jovial Bacchic, Festive, Genial, Jolly

Joy(ful), Joyous Blithe, ➤ DELIGHT, Dream, Ecstasy, Elation, Exulting, Fain, Felicity, Festal, Frabjous, Glad, Glee, Gloat, Hah, Hey, Jubilant, Nirvana, Rapture, Schadenfreude, Sele, Tra-la, Transport, Treat, Yippee

Jubilant, Jubilation, Jubilee Celebration, Cock-a-hoop, Diamond, Ecstatic, Elated, Holiday, Joy, Triumphant

Judas Double-crosser, Traitor, Tree

Judder Put-put, Shake, Vibrate

Judge(ment), Judges Adjudicator, Arbiter, Assess, Assize, Calculate, Connoisseur, Consider, Coroner, Court, Critic(ise), Decide, Dempster, Estimate, Evaluate, Gauge, Guess, Hearing, Honour, Interlocutor, J, Justice, Opinion, Puisne, Reckon(ing), Recorder, Ref(eree), Regard, Sentence, Sheriff, Sober, Solomon, Suppose, Think, Touch, Try, Umpire, Verdict, Wig, Wisdom, Worship

Judicious Critical, Discreet, Politic, Rational, Sage, Sensible, Shrewd, Sound

Jug Amphora, Bird, Blackjack, Can, Cooler, Cream(er), Crock, Ewer, Gaol, Gotch, Pitcher, Pound, Pourer, Pourie, ➤ PRISON, Quad, Quod, Shop, Stir, Toby

Juice, Juicy Bacca, Cassareep, Cassaripe, Cremor, Current, Fluid, Fruity, Gastric, Hypocist, Ichor, La(b)danum, Laser, Latex, Lush, Must, Oil, Pancreatic, Perry, Rare, Sap, Soma, Spanish, Succulent, Succ(o)us, Thridace, Vril, Zest

Jumble Chaos, Conglomeration, Farrago, Garble, Huddle, Jabble, Lumber, Mass, Medley, Mingle-mangle, Mish-mash, Mixter-maxter, Mixture, Pastiche, Raffle, Ragbag, Scramble, Shuffle, Wuzzle

▷**Jumbled** may indicate an anagram

Jumbo Aircraft, Elephant, Jet, Large-scale, Mammoth, OS

Jump(er), Jumping, Jumpy Assemble, Axel, Bate, Batterie, Boomer, Bound, Bungee, Bungy, Caper, Capriole, Cicada, Cicata, Crew-neck, Cricket, Croupade, Desultory, Entrechat, Euro, Eventer, Flea, Fosbury flop, Gansey, Gazump, Gelande (sprung), Guernsey, Halma, Hurdle, Impala, Itchy, Jersey, Joey, Kangaroo, Katydid, Knight, Lammie, Lammy, Leap(frog), Lep, Lope, Lutz, Nervous, Nervy, Parachute, Pogo, Polo-neck, Pounce, Prance, Prank, Pronking, Quantum, Quersprung, Salchow, Saltatory, Saltigrade, Saltus, Scissors, Scoup, Scowp, Skipjack, ➤ SPRING, Start, Sweater, Trampoline, Triple, Turtle-neck, Vau(l)t, Water, Western roll

Junction Abutment, Alloyed, Box, Bregma, Carfax, Clover-leaf, Connection, Crewe, Crossroads, Intersection, Joint, Josephson, Knitting, Meeting, Point, Raphe, Spaghetti, Suture, T, Union

Jungle Asphalt, Blackboard, Boondocks, Bush, Concrete, Forest

Junior Cadet, Dogsbody, Fils, Petty, Scion, Sub(ordinate), Underling, Younger

Junk Bric-a-brac, Jettison, Litter, Lorcha, Lumber, Refuse, Ship, Tatt, Trash

▷**Junk** may indicate an anagram

Junket(ing) Beano, Creel, Custard, Feast, Picnic, Rennet, Spree

Jurisdiction Authority, Bailiwick, Domain, Province, Soke(n)

Juror(s), Jury Assize, Dicast, Grand, Hung, Inquest, Judges, Mickleton, Old Fury, Pais, Panel, Petit, Petty, Sail, Tales, Tribunal, Venire, Venue

Just(ice) Alcalde, All, Aristides, Astraea, Balanced, Condign, Cupar, Deserved, Equity, Fair, Honest, Impartial, J, Jasper, Jeddart, Jethart, Jurat, Mere, Nemesis, Newly, Nice, Only, Piso, Poetic, Provost, Puisne, Recent, Right(ful), Rightness, Shallow, Silence, Sommer, Themis, Tilt, Upright

Justifiable, Justification, Justify Apology, Autotelic, Avenge, Aver, Avowry, Clear, Darraign(e), Darrain(e), Darrayn, Defend, Deraign, Excusable, Explain, Grounds, Rationale, Vindicate, Warrant

Jut Beetle, Bulge, Overhang, Project, Protrude, Sail

Juvenile Childish, Teenage(r), Yonkers, Young, Younkers

Kk

K Kelvin, Kilo, King, Kirkpatrick

Kangaroo Bettong, Bongary, Boomer, Bounder, Cus-cus, Diprotodont, Euro, Forester, Joey, Macropodidae, Nototherium, Old man, Potoroo, Rat, Steamer, Tree, Troop, Wallaby, Wallaroo

Karate Kung Fu, Wushu

Karma Destiny, Fate, Predestination

Kebab Cevapcici, Gyro, Satay, Sate, Shashli(c)k, Souvlakia

Keel Bottom, Carina, Centreboard, Faint, Fin, List, Overturn, Skeg(g)

Keen(ness), Keener Acid, Acute, Agog, Aspiring, Argute, Astute, Athirst, Avid, Aygre, Bemoan, Bewail, Breem, Breme, Cheap, Coronach, Dash, Devotee, Dirge, Eager, Elegy, Enthusiastic, Fanatical, Fell, Greet, Grieve, Hone, Howl, Into, Lament, Mourn, Mustard, Mute, Narrow, Ochone, Ohone, Peachy, Perceant, Persant, Raring, Razor, Red-hot, Rhapsodic, Sharp, Shrewd, Shrill, Snell, Thirsting, Threnodic, Thrillant, Trenchant, Ululate, Wail, Whet, Zeal(ous)

Keep(er), Keeping Ames, Armature, Austringer, Castellan, Castle, Celebrate, Chatelain(e), Citadel, Conceal, Conserve, Curator, Custodian, Custody, Depositary, Depository, Detain, Donjon, Finder, Fort, Gaoler, Goalie, Guardian, Have, Hoard, ➤ HOLD, Maintain, Nab, Net, Observe, Ostreger, Pickle, Preserve, Retain, Stet, Stock, Store, Stow, Support, Sustain, Tower, Withhold

Keg Barrel, Cask, Tub, Tun, Vat

Kennel(s) Guard, Home, House, Shelter

Kerb Edge, Gutter, Roadside

Kernel Copra, Core, Grain, Nucleus, Praline, Prawlin

Kestrel Bird, Hawk, Keelie, Stallion, Staniel, Stannel

Kettle Boiler, Cauldron, Dixie, Dixy, Drum, Fanny, Pot, Turpin

Key(hole) A, Ait, Ash, B, C, Cay, Clue, D, E, Essential, F, Flat, Function, G, Ignition, Important, Inch, Index, Islet, Ivory, Linchpin, Major, Minor, Note, Opener, Shift, Signature, Skeleton, Yale®

Keyboard Azerty, Console, Digitorium, DVORAK, Manual, Martenot, Piano, Pianola®, Qwerty, Spinet

Kick(ing) Back-heel, Boot, Buzz, Corner, Dribble, Drop, Fling, Fly, Frog, Garryowen, Goal, Hack, Hoof, Lash, Penalty, Pause, Pile, Punt, Recalcitrate, Recoil, Recoyle, Savate, Scissors, Sixpence, Speculator, Spur, Spurn, Squib, Tanner, Thrill, Toe, Vigour, Wince, Yerk, Zip

Kid(s) Arab, Befool, Billy, Brood, Cheverel, Chevrette, Child, Chit, Con, Delude, Goat, Hoax, Hocus, Hoodwink, Hum, Joke, Leather, Misguide, Nipper, Offspring, Pretend, Rag, Rib, Spoof, Suede, Sundance, ▶ TEASE, Tot, Trick, Whiz(z), Wiz

Kidnap Abduct, Hijack, Plagium, Snatch, Spirit, Steal

Kill(er), Killing Assassin, Behead, Butcher, Carnage, Croak, Crucify, Cull, Despatch, Destroy, Euthanasia, Execute, Exterminate, Garotte, Gun, Hatchet man, Hilarious, Homicide, Ice, Knacker, Liquidate, Lynch, Mortify, Murder, Serial, Predator, Quell, Sacrifice, Slaughter, Slay(er), Slew, Smite, Thagi, Thug(gee), Top, Toreador, Veto, Waste, Zap

Kilt Drape, Filabeg, Fustanella, Plaid, Tartan

Kin(sman) Ally, Family, Kith, Like, Nearest, Relation

Kind(ly) Akin, Amiable, Avuncular, Benefic, Benevolent, Benign, Boon, Breed, Brood, Brotherly, Category, Class, Clement, Considerate, Favourable, Gender, Generic, Generous, Genre, Gentle, Genus, Good, Humane, Ilk, Kidney, Kin, Lenient, Manner, Modal, Nature, Sisterly, ▶ SORT, Species, Strain, Strene, Trine, Type, Understanding, Variety, Well-disposed, Ylke

Kindle, Kindling Accend, Fire, Ignite, Incense, Incite, Inflame, ▶ LIGHT, Litter, Lunt, Stimulate, Teend, Tind, Tine

King(s), Kingly Apple, Ard-ri(gh), Butcher, Cobra, Cotton, English, Erl, Evil, GR, Hellen, Highness, Inca, Kong, Laius, Lionheart, Majesty, Monarch, Pearly, Peleus, Penguin, Peishwa(h), Peshwa, Pharaoh, Potentate, R, Ransom, Re, Reigner, Rex, Rial, Royalet, Ruler, Ryal, Sailor, Seven, Shah, Shilling, Sigismund, Sisyphus, Sovereign, Stork, Sweyn Forkbeard

Kingdom, Kingship Animal, Aragon, Barataria, Bhutan, Bohemia, Brunel, Dominion, Edom, Elam, Fife, Heptarchy, Jordan, Lydia, Mercia, Meroe, Mineral, Moab, Navarre, Nepal, Noricum, Parthia, Pontic, Realm, Reign, Royalty, Sphere, Throne, Tonga, Vegetable, Wessex, World

Kink(y) Bent, Buckle, Crapy, Enmeshed, Flaw, Gasp, Knurl, Null, Nurl, Odd, Perm, Perverted, Quirk, Twist, Wavy

▷ **Kink(y)** may indicate an anagram

Kip(per) Cure, Dosser, Doze, Limey, Nap, ➤ SLEEPER, Smoke

Kiss(er), Kissing Buss, Butterfly, Caress, Contrecoup, Cross, French, Lip, Neck, Osculate, Pax(-board), Pax-brede, Peck, Pet, Plonker, Pree, Salue, Salute, Smack(er), Smooch, Smouch, Snog, Spoon, Thimble, X, Yap

Kitchen Caboose, Cookhouse, Cuisine, Galley, Scullery, Soup

Kitty Ante, Cat, Fisher, Float, Fund, Jackpot, Pool, Pot, Tronc

Knack Art, Flair, Forte, Gift, Hang, Instinct, ➤ TALENT, Trick

Knead Massage, Mould, Pug, Pummel, Work

Kneel(er) Defer, Genuflect, Hassock, Kowtow, Truckle

Knicker(bocker), Knickers Bloomers, Culottes, Directoire, Irving, Panties, Plus-fours, Shorts, Trousers

Knick-knack Bagatelle, Bibelot, Bric-a-brac, Gewgaw, Pretty(-pretty), Quip, Smytrie, Toy, Trangam, Trifle, Victoriana

Knife Anelace, Barlow, Barong, Bistoury, Blade, Bolo, Bolster, Bowie, Carver, Catling, Chakra, Clasp, Cleaver, Couteau, Cradle, Cuttle, Cutto(e), Da(h), Dagger, Fleam, Flick, Gull(e)y, Hunting, Jockteleg, Kard, Kukri, Lance(t), Machete, Matchet, Palette, Panga, Parang, Pocket, Scalpel, Sheath, Shiv, Simi, Slash, Snee, Snickersnee, Spade, Stab, Stanley, Steak, Switchblade, Tranchet

Knight Bayard, Black, Carpet, Cavalier, Chevalier, Companion, Crusader, Douceper, Douzeper, Dub, Equites, Errant, Gallant, Garter, Hospitaller, KB, KBE, KG, Malta, Medjidie, N, Noble, Samurai, Sir, Templar, Teutonic, Trencher, White

Knit(ting), Knitwear Contract, Crochet, Entwine, Hosiery, Mesh, Porosis, Purl, Seam, Set, Stockinet, Weave, Wrinkle

Knob(by) Berry, Boll, Boss, Botoné, Bottony, Bouton, Bur(r), Cam, Caput, Cascabel, Croche, Handle, Hill, Inion, Knur(r), Node, Noop, Pellet, Pommel, Protuberance, Pulvinar, Snib, Snub, Snuff, Stud, Torose, Tuber, Tuner

Knock (down, off, out) Bang, Beaut, Biff, Blow, Bonk, Bump, Ca(a), Chap, Clash, Clour, Collide, Con, Criticise, Daud, Dawd, Degrade, Denigrate, Deride, Dev(v)el, Ding, Dinnyhauser, Etherise, Eyeful, Floor, Grace-stroke, ➤ HIT, Innings, KO, Lowse, Lowsit, Mickey Finn, Pan, Pink, Quietus,

Rap, Rat-tat, Skittle, Spat, Steal, Stop, Strike, Stun(ner), Tap, Technical, Thump, Tonk, Wow

Knot(ted), Knotty Apollo, Baff, Bend, Blackwell hitch, Bow, Bowline, Burl, Bur(r), Carrick-bend, Cat's paw, Clinch, Clove hitch, Cluster, Crochet, Englishman's, Entangle, Figure of eight, Fisherman's (bend), French, Gnar, ➤ GNARL, Gordian, Granny, Half-hitch, Harness hitch, Hawser-bend, Herculean, Hitch, Interlace, Knag, Knap, Knar, Knur(r), Loop, Love(r's), Macramé, Macrami, Magnus hitch, Matthew Walker, Mouse, Nirl, Node, Nowed, Nub, Nur(r), Overhand, Picot, Problem, Prusik, Quipu, Reef, Rosette, Seizing, Sheepshank, Sheetbend, Sleave, Slip, Slub, Spurr(e)y, Stevedore's, Surgeon's, Sword, Tangle, Tat, Thumb, Tie, Timberhitch, Truelove, Tubercle, Turk's head, Wale, Wall, Windsor

Know(how), Knowing, Knowledge(able), Known Acquaintance, Autodidactic, Aware, Cognition, Compleat, Comprehend, Cred, Epistemics, Erudite, Expertise, Famous, Fly, Gnosis, Gnostic, Have, Hep, Hip, Info, Information, Insight, Intentional, Intuition, Jnana, Ken, Kith, Kydst, Lare, Light, Lore, Mindful, Omniscience, On, Pansophy, Party, Polymath, Positivism, Privity, Recherché, ➤ RECOGNISE, Sapient, Savvy, Science, Scilicet, Sciolism, Shrewd, Smattering, Understand(ing), Up, Versed, Wat(e), Weet(e), Well-informed, Well-read, Wise, Wist, Wit, Wot

LI

L Latitude, League, Learner, Left, Length, Liberal, Lima, Litre, Long, Luxembourg, Pound

Label Band, Book-plate, Brand, Designer, Docket, File, Mark, Own, Seal, Sticker, Style, Tab, Tag, Tally, Ticket, Trace

Laboratory Lab, Language, Skylab, Space-lab, Studio, Workshop

Labour(er), Laboured, Laborious Arduous, Begar, Birth, Carl, Casual, Chirl, Chore, Coolie, Corvée, Cottager, Cottar, Culchie, Dataller, Dwell, Gandy-dancer, Ganger, Gibeonite,

Grecian, Grind, Hard, Hercules, Hodge, Ida, Job, Journeyman, Kanaka, Katorga, Leaden, Manpower, Moil, Navvy, Okie, Operose, Pain, Peon, Pioneer, Prole, Redneck, Roll, Roustabout, Rouster, Sisyphean, Slave, Stint, Strive, Sudra, Sweated, Task, ➤ TOIL(SOME), Toss, Travail, Uphill, Vineyard, ➤ WORK(ER), Workmen

Labyrinth Daedalus, Maze, Mizmaze, Warren, Web

▷ **Labyrinthine** may indicate an anagram

Lace, Lacy Alençon, Babiche, Beat, Bobbin, Bourdon, Brussels, Chantilly, Cluny, Colbertine, Dash, Dentelle, Duchesse, Filet, Galloon, Guipure, Honiton, Inweave, Irish, Jabot, Lash, Macramé, Malines, Mechlin, Mignonette, Mode, Net, Orris, Pearlin, Picot, Pillow, Point, Reseau, Reticella, Ricrac, Rosaline, Shoestring, Shoe-tie, Spike, Tat(ting), Thrash, Torchon, Trim, Trol(le)y, Valenciennes, Venise, Weave, Welt, Window-bar

Lack(ing), Lacks Absence, Aplasia, Bereft, Dearth, Famine, Ha'n't, Manqué, Minus, ➤ NEED, Poverty, Privation, Remiss, Sans, Shortfall, Shy, Void, Want

Lackey Boots, Flunkey, Moth, Page, Poodle

Lacquer Coromandel, Enamel, Japan, Shellac, ➤ VARNISH

Lad Boy(o), Bucko, Callan(t), Chield, Geit, Gyte, Knight, Loonie, Nipper, Shaver, Stableman, Tad, Whipper-snapper

Ladder(y) Accommodation, Bucket, Companion, Companionway, Etrier, Jack, Jacob's, Pompier, Potence, Rope, Run, Salmon, Scalado, Scalar, Scaling, Stie, Sty, Trap, Turntable

Ladle Bail, Dipper, Scoop

Lady Baroness, Bevy, Bountiful, Burd, Dame, Dark, Don(n)a, Duenna, Female, Frau, Frow, Gemma, Godiva, Hen, Khanum, Luck, Maam, Madam(e), Memsahib, Nicotine, Peeress, Senora, Signora, Tea, Windermere

▷ **Lady** may indicate an '-ess' ending

▷ **Ladybird** may indicate a female of a bird family

Lair Couch, Den, Earth, Haunt, Hideaway, Kennel, Lodge, Warren

Lake(s) Alkali, Basin, Bayou, Carmine, Chott, Crater, Crimson, Finger, L, Lacustrine, Lagoon, Lagune, ➤ LOCH, Lochan, Lough, Madder, Mead, Mere, Nyanza, Ox-bow, Poets, Pool, Red, Reservoir, Salt, Shott, Tarn, Vlei

Lamb(skin) Baa, Barometz, Budge, Bummer, Cade, Canterbury, Caracul, Cosset, Ean(ling), Elia, Innocent, Keb, Larry, Noisette, Paschal, Persian, Rack, Shearling, Target, Yean(ling)

Lame(ness) Accloy, Claude, Cripple, Crock, Game, Gammy, Gimp(y), Halt, Hamstring, Hirple, Hors de combat, Maim, Main, Spavined, Springhalt, Stringhalt, Weak

Lament(able), Lamentation, Lamenter Bemoan, Bewail, Beweep, Complain, Croon, Cry, Dirge, Dumka, Elegy, Funest, Jeremiad, Jeremiah, Keen, Meane, Mein, Mene, Moon, Mourn, Ochone, Paltry, Piteous, Plain, Repine, Sorry, Threne, Threnody, Ululate, ➤ WAIL, Welladay, Wel(l)away, Yammer

Lamina(te) Film, Flake, Folium, Formica®, Lamella, Layer, Plate, Scale, Table

Lamp(s) Aldis, Anglepoise, Arc, Argand, Bowat, Bowet, Buat, Cru(i)sie, Crusy, Davy, Eye, Eyne, Fluorescent, Geordie, Hurricane, Incandescent, Lantern, Lava, Lucigen, Mercury vapour, Neon, Nernst, Nightlight, Padella, Quartz, Scamper, Signal, Sodium, Spirit, Standard, Stride, Stroboscope, Tilley, Torchier(e), Tungsten, Uplight(er), Veilleuse, Xenon

Lampoon Caricature, Parody, Pasquil, Pasquin(ade), Satire, Skit, Squib

Lance Dart, Harpoon, Morne, Pesade, Pike, Prisade, Prisado, Rejôn, Spear, Speisade, Thermic

Land(ed) Acreage, Alight, Alluvion, Bag, Beach, Country, Croft, Demain, Demesne, Disbark, Disembark, Ditch, Dock, Earth, Estate, Fallow, Farren, Fee, Feod, Feoff, Feud, Fief, Freeboard, Gair, Glebe, Ground, Hide, Holding, Holm, Horst, Innings, Isthmus, Kingdom, Lea, Leal, Ley, Light, Maidan, Manor, Mortmain, Nation, Never-never, Nod, No man's, Odal, Onshore, Oxgang, Oxgate, Panhandle, Parcel, Pasture, Peninsula, Piste, Plot, Polder, Promised, Property, Purlieu, Realm, Realty, Reservation, Settle, Spit, Terra(e), Terrain, Territory, Tie, Touchdown, Udal, Unship, Ure, Van Diemen's, Veld(t)

Landing (craft, stair, system) Autoflare, Forced, Gha(u)t, Halfpace, LEM, Module, Pancake, Pier, Quay, Soft, Solar, Splashdown, Three-point, Touchdown, Undercarriage

Landlord, Land owner Absentee, Balt, Boniface, Copyholder, Fiar, Franklin, Herself, Host, Innkeeper, Junker,

Laird, Lessor, Letter, Patron, Proprietor, Publican, Rachman, Rentier, Squattocracy, Squire

Landscape Karst, Paysage, Picture, Saikei, Scene

Landslide, Landfall Avalanche, Earthfall, Eboulement, Lahar, Scree

Lane Boreen, Bus, Corridor, Crawler, Drury, Express, Fast, Fetter, Gut, Loan, Lois, Loke, Memory, Mincing, Passage, Petticoat, Pudding, Ruelle, Sea-road, Twitten, Twitting, Vennel, Wynd

Language(s) Argot, Artificial, Assembly, Auxiliary, Basic, Body, Cant, Dialect, Georgian, Humanities, Idioglossia, Idiom, Inclusive, Jargon, Lingo, Lingua franca, Macaroni, Neo, Newspeak, Object, Parlance, Pidgin, Pragmatics, Procedural, Programming, Prose, Rhetoric, Semitic, Sign, ➤ SPEECH, Style, Symbolic, Target, Technobabble, Telegraphese, Tone, ➤ TONGUE, Verbiage, Vernacular, Vocabulary, Words

Languid, Languish Die, Divine, Droop, Feeble, Flagging, Listless, Lukewarm, Lydia, Melancholy, Quail, Torpid, Wilt

Lanky Beanpole, Gangly, Gawky, Spindleshanks, Windlestraw

Lantern Aristotle's, Bowat, Bowet, Buat, Bull's eye, Chinese, Dark(e)y, Epidiascope, Episcope, Glim, Jaw, Lanthorn, Magic, Sconce, Stereopticon, Storm

Lap Gremial, Leg, Lick, Lip, Luxury, Override, Pace, Sypher

Lapse Drop, Error, Expire, Fa', Fall, Nod, Sliding, Trip

Large(ness), Largest Ample, Astronomical, Big, Boomer, Buster, Colossus, Commodious, Decuman, Enormous, Epical, Gargantuan, ➤ GIGANTIC, Ginormous, Great, Grit, Gross, Hefty, Helluva, Huge, Hulking, Humdinger, Humongous, Humungous, Kingsize, L, Lunker, Macrocephaly, Massive, Maximin, Maximum, Plethora, Prodigious, Rounceval, Rouncival, Skookum, Slew, Slue, Sollicker, Spanking, Stonker, Stout, Swingeing, Tidy, Titanic, Vast, Voluminous, Whopping

Largess Alms, Charity, Frumentation

Lark Adventure, Aunter, Caper, Dido, Dunstable, Exaltation, Fool, Giggle, Guy, Laverock, Mud, Pipit, Prank

Larva Army-worm, Axolotl, Bagworm, Bloodworm, Bot(t), Budworm, Caddice, Caddis, Cankerworm, Caterpillar, Chigger, Chigoe, Doodlebug, Grub, Jigger, Jointworm, Leather-jacket, Maggot, Mealworm, Measle, Muckworm, Naiad, Nauplius,

Ox-bot, Planula, Pluteus, Shade, Silkworm, Tadpole, Wireworm, Witchetty, Woodworm, Zoea

Lascivious(ness) Crude, Goaty, Horny, Lewd, Lubric, Paphian, Satyric, Sotadic, Tentigo

Lash(ed), Lashings Cat, Cilium, Firk, Flagellum, Frap, Gammon, Knout, Mastigophora, Oodles, Oup, Quirt, Riem, Rope's end, Scourge, Secure, Sjambok, Stripe, Swinge, Tether, Thong, Trice, Whang, ➤ WHIP

Lass(ie) Damsel, Maid, Quean, Queyn, Quin(i)e

Lasso Lariat, Reata, Rope

Last(ing) Abide, Abye, Aftermost, ➤ AT LAST, Boot-tree, Bottom, Chronic, Dernier, Dure, Endurance, Endure, Extend, Extreme, ➤ FINAL, Hinder, Latest, Linger, Live, Long-life, Model, Nightcap, Outstay, Perdure, Permanent, Perpetuate, Persist, Spin, Stable, Stay, Supper, Survive, Swan-song, Thiller, Thule, Tree, Trump, Ult(imate), Ultimo, Utmost, Wear, Weight, Whipper-in, Z

Last word(s) Amen, Envoi, Farewell, Ultimatum, Zythum

Latch Bar, Clicket, Clink, Espagnolette, Lock, Sneck

Late(r), Latest After(wards), Afterthought, Behindhand, Chit-chat, Dead, Ex, Former, Gen, Infra, Lag, Lamented, New(s), Overdue, Past, Recent, Sine, Slow, Stop-press, Syne, Tardive, Tardy, Trendy, Umquhile

Latent Concealed, Delitescent, Dormant, Maieutic, Potential

Lateral Askant, Edgeways, Sideways

Lathe Capstan, Mandrel, Mandril, Turret

Lather Flap, Foam, Froth, Sapples, Suds, Tan

Latin(ist) Criollo, Dago, Dog, Erasmus, Eyeti, Greaseball, Humanity, Italiot, L, Low, Neapolitan, Pig, Romanic, Romish, Scattermouch, Spic, Vulgar, Wop

Latitude Breadth, Celestial, Free hand, Horse, L, Leeway, Liberty, Licence, Meridian, Parallel, Play, Roaring forties, Scope, Tropic, Width

Latrine Ablutions, Bog, Cloaca, Furphy, Garderobe, Loo, Privy, Rear

Lattice Bravais, Clathrate, Espalier, Grille, Treillage, Trellis

Laugh(ing), Laughable, Laughter Belly, Cachinnate, Cackle, Chortle, Chuckle, Cod, Corpse, Democritus, Deride, Derision, Fit, Fou rire, Gelastic, Giggle, Goster, Guffaw, Ha,

He-he, Ho-ho, Homeric, Hoot, Horse, Hout, Howl, Irrision, Lauch, Leuch, Levity, ➤ MIRTH, Mock, Nicker, Peal, Present, Riancy, Riant, Rich, Rident, Ridicule, Risus, Scream, Snigger, Snirt(le), Snort, Tehee, Titter, Yo(c)k

Launch(ing) Begin, Blast-off, Catapult, Chuck, Fire, Float, Hurl, Initiate, Lift-off, Pioneer, Presentation, Release, Shipway, Slipway, Unstock, Upsend, VTO

Launder, Laundry Bagwash, Clean, Lav, Steamie, Tramp, Transfer, Wash, Washhouse, Whites

Laurel(s) Aucuba, Bay, Camphor, Daphne, Kalmia, Kudos, Pichurim, Sassafras, Spicebush, Spurge, Stan, Sweet-bay

Lava Aa, Bomb, Coulee, Cysticercus, Dacite, Lahar, Lapilli, Magma, Nuée ardente, Pahoehoe, Palagonite, Pitchstone, Pumice, Pyroclast, Scoria, Tephra, Toadstone

Lavatory Ajax, Can, Carsey, Carzey, Cludgie, Comfort station, Convenience, Cottage, Dike, Dunnakin, Dunny, Dyke, Elsan®, Facilities, Forica, Furphey, Gents, Jakes, Jane, John, Kars(e)y, Karzy, K(h)azi, Kleinhuisie, Ladies, Lat(rine), Loo, Necessary, Netty, Office, Outhouse, Privy, Rear(s), Reredorter, Shithouse, Shouse, Siege, Throne, Thunderbox, Toot, Tout, Urinal, Washroom, WC

Lavish Barmecidal, Copious, Excessive, Exuberant, Flush, Free, Fulsome, Generous, Lucullan, Lush, Prodigal, Shower, Sumptuous, Wanton, Waste

Law Act, Agrarian, Anti-trust, Ass, Avogadro's, Bar, Barratry, ➤ BILL, Bonar, Boyle's, Bragg's, Brewster's, Brocard, Byelaw, Cain, Canon, Capitulary, Case, Chancery, Charles's, Civil, Code, Common, Constitution, Corn, Coulomb's, Cupar, Curie's, Cy pres, Dalton's, Dead-letter, Decree, De Morgan's, Dharma, Dictate, Digest, Din, Edict, Einstein's, Enact, Fundamental, Gresham's, Grimm's, Halifax, Henry's, Homestead, Hooke's, Hubble's, Hume's, International, Irade, Joule's, Jura, Jure, Jus, Kain, Kepler's, Lay, Lien, Lor(d), Losh, Lydford, Lynch, Martial, Mendel's, Military, Mosaic, Murphy's, Natural, Newton's, Ohm's, Oral, Ordinance, Parkinson's, Pass, Periodic, Planck's, Plebiscite, Poor, Principle, Public, Roman, Rubric, Rule, Salic, Salique, Sharia(h), Sheria(t), Snell's, Sod's, ➤ STATUTE, Sunna, Table, Talmud, Tenet, Thorah, Torah, Tort, Tradition, Ulema, Unwritten, Use, Verner's, Vigilante

Lawmaker, Lawman, Lawyer Alfaqui, Attorney, AV, Barrack room, Barrister, Bencher, BL, Bluebottle, Bramble, Bush, Coke, Counsel, DA, Defence, Doge, Draco, Enactor, Fiscal, Greenbag, Grotius, Hammurabi, Jurisconsult, Jurist, Legist, Mooktar, Moses, MP, Mufti, Mukhtar, Nomothete, Notary, Penang, Pettifoggers, Rabbi, Shirra, Shyster, Silk, Solicitor, Spenlow, Stratopause, Talmudist, Templar

Lawn Cloth, Grass, Green, Linen, Sward, Turf

Lawsuit Case, Cause, Plea, Trover

▶**Lawyer(s), Lawman** see LAWMAKER

▷**Lax** may indicate an anagram

Lax(ity) Freedom, Inexact, Laissez-aller, Latitude, Loose, Remiss, ➤ SLACK, Wide

Lay(ing), Layman, Laic, Laid Air, Aria, Ballad, Bed, Bet, Blow, Chant, Ditty, Drop, Earthly, Egg, Embed, Fit, Impose, Lied, Lodge, Man, Minstrel, Oat, Oblate, Ode, Outsider, Oviparous, Oviposit, Parabolanus, Secular, Set, Sirvente, ➤ SONG, Sypher, Tertiary, Tribal, Wager, Warp

Layer(s) Ancona, Appleton, Battery, Cave, Caliche, Cladding, Coating, Crust, D, Depletion, E, Ectoplasm, Ectosarc, Epiblast, Epilimnion, Epithelium, Erathem, Exine, Exocarp, Film, Flake, Ganoin, Gossan, Gozzan, Granum, Heaviside, ➤ HEN, Kennelly(-Heaviside), Kerf, Lamella, Lamina, Lap, Leghorn, Lie, Malpighian, Media, Miocene, Ozone, Pan, Patina, Paviour, Photosphere, Ply, Retina, Scale, Sclerite, Screed, Skin, Sliver, Spathic, Stratify, Stratum, Substratum, Tabular, Tapetum, Tier, Tremie, Trophoblast, Trophoderm, Varve, Vein, Velamen

Lay-off Dismiss, Hedge, Redundance

Lay-out Ante, Design, Fell, Format, Map, Mise, Pattern, Spend, Straucht, Straught, Streak, Streek, Stretch

Laze, Laziness, Lazy (person) Bed-presser, Bummer, Cabbage, Faineant, Hallian, Hallion, Hallyon, Indolent, Inert, Lackadaisical, Languid, Layabout, Lie-abed, Lig(ger), Lime, Lither, Loaf, Lotus-eater, Lusk, Sloth, Slouch, Slug(-a-bed), Sluggard, Susan, Sweer, Sweir, Workshy

▷**Lazily** may indicate an anagram

Lead(er), Leading, Leadership Ag(h)a, Ahead, Akela, Article, Atabeg, Atabek, Ayatollah, Bab, Bluey, Cable, Cade, Calif, Caliph, Capitano, Capo, Captain, Castro, Caudillo,

Centre, Cheer, Chieftain, Chin, CO, Condottiere, Conducive, Conduct, Coryphaeus, Demagogue, Dictator, Duce, Dux, Editorial, Escort, Ethnarch, Extension, Figurehead, Floor, Frontrunner, Fu(e)hrer, Gaffer, Garibaldi, Gerent, Graphite, Guide(r), Halter, Hand, Headman, Headmost, Headnote, Hegemony, Hero, Hetman, Honcho, Idi, Imam, Imaum, Jason, Jump, King, Ksar, Leam, Livid, Loss, Lost, Lyam, Mahatma, Mahdi, Main, Market, Marshal, Massicot, Mayor, No 1, Nomarch, Nose, Numero uno, Pacemaker, Pacesetter, Padishah, Pb, Pilot, Pioneer, Pit, Plummet, PM, Precentor, Premier(e), President, Rebbe, Rebecca, Red, Role, Ruler, Sachem, Sagamore, Saturn, Scudler, Sharif, Sheik(h), Sixer, Skipper, Skudler, Soul, Spearhead, Staple, Star, Sultan, Taoiseach, Tribune, Up, Usher, Vaivode, Van(guard), Va(u)nt, Vaunt-courier, Voivode, Waivode, Warlord, White, Whitechapel, Wulfenite

▷ **Lead(s), Leaders** may indicate first letters of words

Leaf(y), Leaves Acanthus, Acrospire, Amphigastrium, Amplexicaul, Betel, Blade, Bract, Carpel, Cataphyll, Cladode, Consent, Corolla, Costate, Cotyledon, Drop, Duff, Fig, Finial, Foil, Foliage, Foliar, Folio(se), Folium, Frond, Glume, Gold, Holiday, Induviae, Jugum, K(h)at, Megaphyll, Needle, Nervate, Out, P, Pad, Page, Phyllid, Phyllome, Qat, Repair, Riffle, Rosula, Scale, Sclerophyll, Secede, Sepal, Siri(h), Skip, Spathe, Stipule, Tea, TTL, Valve, Vert, Withdraw

Leaflet At(t)ap, Bill, Bracteole, Circular, Dodger, Fly-sheet, Foliolose, Handbill, Pinna, Pinnula, Prophyll, Stipel, ➤ TRACT

League Alliance, Band, Bund, Compact, Delian, Entente, Federation, Gueux, Guild, Hanse(atic), Holy, Ivy, Land, Major, Parasang, Primrose, Redheaded, Rugby, Super, Union, Zollverein, Zupa

Leak(y) Bilge, Drip, Escape, Extravasate, Gizzen, Holed, Holey, Ooze, Pee, Porous, Seepage, Sype, Trickle, Wee, Weep

Lean(ing) Abut, Barren, Batter, Bend, Careen, Carneous, Carnose, Griskin, Heel, ➤ INCLINE, Lie, Lig(ge), Minceur, Propend, Rake, Rely, Rest, Scraggy, Scrawny, Skinny, Spare, Stoop, Taste, Tend, Tilt, Tip, Walty

Leap(ing), Leapt Assemblé, Bound, Brise, Cabriole, Caper, Capriole, Cavort, Clear, Croupade, Curvet, Echappé, Entrechat, Falcade, Fishdive, Frisk, Gambado, Gambol, Jeté, Jump, Loup,

Learn(ed) → Lecture(r)

322

Luppen, Over, Pronk, Quantum, Sally, Salto, Somersa(u)lt, Somerset, ➤ SPRING, Transilient, Vault, Volte

Learn(ed), Learner, Learning Beginner, Blue, Bluestocking, Chela, Con, Discover, Distance, Doctor, Don, Erudite, Gather, Get, Glean, Hear, Instrumental, Kond, L, Lear(e), Leir, Lere, Literate, Literati, Literato, Lucubrate, Master, Memorise, Mirza, Mug up, ➤ NOVICE, Pandit, Programmed, Pundit, Pupil, Rookie, Savant, Scan, Scholar, See, Starter, Student, ➤ STUDY, Tiro, Trainee, Tutee, Tyro, Wise

Learning Culture, Discipline, Erudition, Insight, Lore, Opsimathy, Rep, Wit

Lease(-holder) Charter, Farm, Feu, Gavel, Hire, Let, ➤ RENT, Set(t), Tack, Tacksman

Leash Lead, Lyam, Lym(e), Slip, Three, Trash, Triplet

Leather(y) Bouilli, Bouilly, Box-calf, Buckskin, Buff, Cabretta, Calf, Capeskin, Chamois, Checklaton, Cheverel, Chevrette, Cordovan, Cordwain, Corium, Cowhide, Crispin, Cuir(-bouilli), Deacon, Deerskin, Diphthera, Dogskin, Durant, Hide, Hog-skin, Horsehide, Kid, Kip(-skin), Lamp, Levant, Marocain, Maroquin, Mocha, Morocco, Nap(p)a, Ooze, Oxhide, Patent, Pigskin, Rand, Rawhide, Rexine®, Riem(pie), Roan, Rough-out, Russia, Saffian, Shagreen, Shammy, Sharkskin, Shecklaton, Sheepskin, Skiver, Spetch, Split, Strand, Strap, Suede, Tan, Upper, Wallop, Whitleather, Yuft

Leave(r), Leavings Abandon, Abiturient, Abscond, Absit, Absquatulate, Acquittal, Adieu, Bequeath, Blessing, Bug, Compassionate, Congé, Congee, Decamp, Depart, Desert, Devisal, Devise, Ditch, Exeat, Exit, Exodus, Forego, Forgo, Forsake, French, Furlough, Garlandage, ➤ GO, Inspan, Ish, Legate, Licence, Maroon, Mizzle, Omit, Orts, Pace, Park, Part, ➤ PERMISSION, Permit, ➤ QUIT, Residue, Resign, Sabbatical, Scapa, Scat, Scram, Shore, Sick, Skedaddle, Skidoo®, Strand, Vacate, Vade, Vamo(o)se

Leaven Barm, Ferment, Yeast

Lecher(ous), Lechery Gate, Goaty, Lascivious, Libertine, Lickerish, Lustful, Profligate, Rake, Roué, Salaciousness, Satirisk, Satyr, Silen, Wolf

Lecture(r), Lectures, Lecturing Address, Aristotelian, Creed, Curtain, Dissert(ator), Don, Earful, Erasmus, Expound, Homily, Hulsean, Jaw, Jawbation, Jobe, L, Lector, Prelect, Prone,

Rate, Read(er), Rede, Reith, Sententious, ➤ SERMON, Spout, Talk, Teacher, Teach-in, Wigging, Yaff

Ledge Altar, Berm, Channel, Fillet, Linch, Misericord(e), Scarcement, Settle, ➤ SHELF

Ledger Book, Purchase, Register

Left(-handed), Left-hander, Left-winger Balance, Bolshy, Corrie-fisted, Hie, High, L, Laeotropic, Laevorotation, Larboard, Links, Lorn, Near, Other, Over, Pink, Port, Quit, Rad, Red, Relic, Residuum, Resigned, Sinister, Soc(ialist), Southpaw, Thin, Titoism, Trot, Verso, Vo, Went, West, Wind, Yet

Leg(s), Leggings, Leggy, Leg-wear Antigropelo(e)s, Bandy, Breeches, Cabriole, Cannon, Chaparajos, Chaparejos, Chaps, Crural, Crus, Dib, Drumstick, Fine, Gaiter, Galligaskins, Gam(b), Gamash, Gambado, Garter, Gaskin, Gigot, Gramash, Gramosh, Haunch, Jamb, Limb, Long, Member, Myriapod, Oleo, On(side), Peg, Peraeopod, Periopod, Pestle, Pin, Podite, Proleg, Puttees, Pylon, Relay, Section, Shanks, Shanks's pony, Shaps, Shin, Short, Spats, Spatterdash, Spindleshanks, Square, Stage, Stump, Thigh, Tights

Legacy Bequest, Dowry, Entail, Heirloom

Legal(ism), Legally, Legitimate Bencher, Forensic, Halacha, Halaka(h), Halakha, Lawful, Licit, Nomism, Scienter

Legend Arthurian, Caption, Edda, Fable, Folklore, Motto, Myth, Saga, Story

▷ **Legend** may indicate leg-end, (e.g. foot, talus)

Legible Clear, Lucid, Plain

Legion(ary), Legionnaire Alauda, Army, British, Cohort, Countless, Deserter, Foreign, Geste, Honour, ➤ HOST, Maniple, Many, Throng, Zillions

Legislate, Legislator, Legislature Assemblyman, Decemvir, Decree, MP, Nomothete, Oireachtas, Persian

Legume Bean, Guar, Lentil, Pea, Pod, Pulse

Leisure(ly) Adagio, Ease, Liberty, Moderato, Otium, Respite, Rest, Vacation

Lemon Answer, Cedrate, Citron, Citrus, Yellow

Lemur Angwantibo, Aye-aye, Babacoote, Bush-baby, Colugo, Galago, Half-ape, Indri(s), Loris, Macaco, Malmag, Mongoose, ➤ MONKEY, Potto, Ringtail, Sifaka, Tana, Tarsier

Lend Advance, Loan, Prest, Vaunce

Length(y), Lengthen(ing), Lengthwise Archine, Arsheen, Arshin(e), Aune, Cable, Chain, Cubit, Distance, Eke, Ell, ► ELONGATE, Endways, Epenthetic, Expand, Extensive, Foot, Furlong, Inch, Ley, Mile, Nail, Passus, Perch, Piece, Plethron, Pole, Prolix, Prolong, Protract, Reach, Remen, Rod, Rope, Slow, Span, Stadium, Toise, Vara, Verbose, Yard

Lenient Clement, Exurable, Lax, Mild, Permissive, Tolerant

Lens Achromatic, Anamorphic, Anastigmat, Bifocal, Contact, Cornea, Crookes, Crown, Crystalline, Dielectric, Diopter, Dioptre, Diverging, Electron, Eye, Eyeglass, Eye-piece, Fish-eye, Gravitational, Hard, Lentil, Macro, Magnetic, Metallic, Mirror, Optic, Pantoscope, Soft, Stanhope, Sunglass, Telephoto, Toric, Trifocal, Wide-angle, Zoom

Leopard Clouded, Leap, Libbard, Ounce, Panther, Pard, Snow, Spots

Lesbian Bull dyke, Crunchie, Diesel, Dike, Dyke, Homophile, Lipstick, Sapphist, Tribade

Lesion Cut, Gash, Scar, Serpiginous, Sore

Less(en), Lesser, Lessening Abate, Aliament, Bate, Contract, Decline, Deplete, Derogate, Dilute, ► DWINDLE, Extenuate, Fewer, Junior, Littler, Minus, Reduce, Relax, Remission, Under

Lesson Example, Lear(e), Lection, Leir, Lere, Moral, Object, Period, Sermon, Tutorial

Let (go, off, out), Letting Allow, Cap, Charter, Conacre, Displode, Divulge, Enable, Entitle, Explode, Hire, Impediment, Indulge, Lease, Litten, Loot(en), Luit(en), Lutten, Obstacle, Obstruct, ► PERMIT, Rent, Reprieve, Sett, Unhand, Warrant

Lethal Deadly, Fatal, Fell, Mortal

Lethargic, Lethargy Accidie, Apathy, Coma, Drowsy, Hebetude, Inertia, Lassitude, Passive, Sleepy, Sluggish, Stupor, Supine, Torpid

Letter(s) Ache, Aerogam, Aesc, Airgraph, Aleph, Alif, Alpha, Bayer, Begging, Beta, Beth, Block, Breve, Capital, Capon, Chain, Cheth, Chi, Circular, Col, Collins, Consonant, Cue, Cuneiform, Dead, Delta, Digamma, Digraph, Dominical, Edh, Ef(f), Emma, Encyclical, Ep(isemon), Epistle, Epsilon, Eta, Eth, Fan, Favour, French, Gamma, Gimel, He, Heth, Initial, Iota, Izzard, Kaph, Kappa, Koppa, Labda, Lambda, Lamed(h), Landlady, Landlord, Lessee, Lessor, Literal, Mail, Mail-shot, Majuscule, Mem, Memo,

Missive, Monogram, Mu, Note, Notelet, Nu, Nun, Og(h)am,
Omega, Omicron, Pastoral, Patent, Phi, Pi, Plosive, Poison-pen,
Polyphone, Postbag, Psi, Rho, Rom, Runestave, Sad(h)e,
Samian, Sampi, San, Scarlet, Screed, Screwtape, Script, See,
Shin, Sigma, Sign, Sin, Sort, Swash, Tau, Tav, Taw, Teth, Theta,
Thorn, Toc, Typo, Uncial, Upsilon, Vau, Vav, Versal, Vowel,
Waw, Wen, Xi, Yod(h), Yogh, Ypsilon, Zed, Zeta

Lettuce Chicon, Corn-salad, Cos, Iceberg, Lactuca, Lamb's,
Lollo rosso, Romaine, Salad, Thridace

Level(ler) A, Abney, Abreast, Aclinic, Aim, Base, Break even,
Champaign, Countersink, Degree, Dumpy, Echelon, Equal,
➤ EVEN, Extent, Flat, Flush, Grade, O, Par, Plane, Plat(eau),
Point, Race, Rank, Rase, Raze, Savanna, Spirit, Split, ➤ SQUARE,
Stratum, Strew, Strickle, Tier, Trophic, Water

Lever(age) Backfall, Bell-crank, Crampon, Crowbar, Dues,
Gear, Handspike, Jemmy, Joystick, Key, Landsturm, Peav(e)y,
Prise, Prize, Pry, Purchase, Tappet, Tiller, Treadle, Tremolo arm,
Trigger, Typebar

Levy Impose, Imposition, Leave, Militia, Octroi, Raise, Scutage,
Talliate, Tax, Tithe

Lewd(ness) Bawdy, Blue, Impure, Libidinous, Lubricity,
Obscene, Priapism, Prurient, Silen(us), Unclean

Lexicographer, Lexicon Compiler, Craigie, Drudge,
Etymologist, Florio, Fowler, Grove, Johnson(ian), Larousse,
Liddell, Murray, OED, Thesaurus, Vocabulist, Webster,
Words-man

Liability, Liable Anme, Apt, Debt, Incur, Limited, Open,
Prone, Subject, Susceptible

Liaison Affair, Contact, Link

Libel(lous) Defamatory, Malign, Slander, Smear, Sully, Vilify

Liberal(ity) Abundant, Adullamites, Ample, Besant,
Bounteous, Bountiful, Breadth, Bright, Broad, Free(hander),
Free-hearted, ➤ GENEROUS, Giver, Grey, Grimond, Handsome,
Indulgent, L, Largesse, Lavish, Octobrist, Open, ➤ PROFUSE,
Rad(ical), Samuelite, Simonite, Steel, Tolerant, Trivium,
Unstinted, Verlig, Verligte, Whig

Liberate(d), Liberation, Liberator Bolivar, Deliver,
Emancipate, Fatah, ➤ FREE, Inkatha, Intolerant, Messiah, PLO,
Release, Save, Sucre, Unfetter, UNITA, Women's

Liberty Bail, Discretion, Franchise, Freedom, Hall, Mill, Sauce

Library Bibliothecary, BL, Bodleian, Bookmobile, Cottonian, Harleian, Laurentian, Lending, Mazarin, Public, Radcliffe, Reference, Tauchnitz

Licence, License Abandon, Allow, Authorisation, Carnet, Charter, Dispensation, Driving, Enable, Exequatur, Fling, Franchise, Free(dom), Gale, Imprimatur, Indult, ➤ LATITUDE, Let, Passport, ➤ PERMIT, Poetic, Pratique, Provisional, Rope, Slang, Special

Lichen Apothecia, Archil, Corkir, Crotal, Crottle, Epiphyte, Epiphytic, Graphis, Korkir, Lecanora, Litmus, Orchel, Orchil(la), Orcine, Orseille, Parella, Parelle, Parella, Roccella, Rock tripe, Stone-rag, Stone-raw, Tree-moss, Usnea, Wartwort

Lick(ing) Bat, Beat, Deer, Lambent, Lap, Leather, Salt, Slake, Speed, Whip

Lid Cover, Hat, Kid, Maximum, Opercula, Screwtop, Twist-off

Lie(s), Liar, Lying Abed, Accubation, Accumbent, Ananias, Bam, Bare-faced, Bask, Billy, Bounce(r), Braide, Cau(l)ker, Cellier, Clipe, Clype, Contour, Couchant, Cracker, Cram(mer), Cretism, Cumbent, Deception, Decubitous, Decumbent, Direct, Doggo, Fable, False(r), Falsehood, Falsify, Falsity, Fib, Figment, Flam, Gag, Gonk, Incumbent, Invention, Inveracity, Kip, Lair, Leasing, Lee(ar), Lig(ge), Lurk, Mythomania, Obreption, Oner, Perjury, Plumper, Porky, Porky (pie), Procumbent, Prone, Prostrate, Pseudologia, Recline, Recumbent, Repent, Reptant, Ride, Romance(r), Sham, Sleep, Strapper, Stretcher, Supine, Tale, Tappice, Tar(r)adiddle, Thumper, Tissue, Try, Untruth, Whid, White, Whopper, Yanker

Lieutenant Flag, Loot, Lt, No 1, Sub(altern)

Life Age, Animation, Being, Bio, Biog(raphy), Brio, Clerihew, Esse, Existence, Good, Heart, Plasma, Span, Spirit, Still, Subsistence, Time, Vita, Zoe

Lifeless(ness) Abiosis, Algidity, Amort, Arid, Azoic, Barren, Cauldrife, ➤ DEAD, Dull, Flat, Inanimate, Inert, Log, Mineral, Possum, Sterile, Stonen, Wooden

Lift(ed), Lifter, Lifting Arayse, Arsis, Attollent, Bone, Cable-car, Camel, Chair, Cly, Copy, Crane, Davit, Dead, Dumb waiter, Elate, Elevator, Enhance, Extol, Filch, Fillip, Heave, Heeze, Heezie, Heft, Heist, Hitch, Hoise, Hoist, Hove, Jack, Jigger, Kleptomania, Leaven, Lefte, Lever, Lewis, Nab, Nap,

Paternoster, Pilfer, Pulley, ➤ RAISE, Ride, Scoop, Ski, Sky, Snatch, Steal, T-bar, Thumb, Up, Winch, Windlass

Light(en), Lighting, Lights Aerate, Airy, Albedo, Ale, Alow, Amber, Ancient, Ans(wer), Arc, Aurora, Beacon, Beam, Bengal, Bezel, Bleach, Brake, Bulb, Candle, Casement, Chiaroscuro, Cierge, Clue, Courtesy, Day, Dewali, Direct, Diwali, Eddystone, Electrolier, Ethereal, Fairy, Fall, Fan, Fantastic, Fastnet, Fill, Fire, Flambeau, Flame, Flare, Flicker, Flippant, Flit(t), Flood, Fog (lamp), Frothy, Fuffy, Gleam, Glim(mer), Glow, Gossamer, Green, Guiding, Hazard, Head, Ignite, Illum(in)e, Incandescence, Indirect, Inner, Irradiate, Junior, Kindle, Klieg, Lamp, Land, Lantern, Lanthorn, Laser, Leading, Leerie, Lime, Link, Loadstar, Lodestar, Lucarne, Lucigen, Luminaire, Lumine, Luminescence, Luminous, Lustre, Lux, Match, Mercurial, Mithra(s), Moon, Naphtha, Neon, Nit, Northern, Od(yl), Optics, Pale, Pane, Phosphorescence, Phot, Photon, Pilot, Portable, Red, Riding, Rocket, Rush, Sea-dog, Search, Shy, Spill, Spot, Spry, Strip, Strobe, Subtle, Sun, Svelte, Tail, Taper, Taps, Tind, Tine, Torch, Torchère, Touchpaper, Traffic, Trivial, Ultraviolet, Unchaste, Unoppressive, UV, Ver(e)y, Vesta, Window, Zodiacal

▷ **Light** may indicate an anagram

Lighter Barge, Birlinn, Casco, Gas-poker, Keel, Linstock, Lunt, Match, Pontoon, Pra(a)m, Spill, Taper

Lighthouse Beacon, Caisson, Eddystone, Fanal, Fastnet, Phare, Pharos, Signal

Lightning Ball, Catequil, Eclair, Enfouldered, Forked, Fulmination, Levin, Sheet, Thunderbolt, Wildfire, Zigzag

Like(ness), Liking As, Broo, Care, Corpse, Dig, Duplicate, Effigy, Eg, Egal, Enjoy, Equal, Fancy, Fellow, Lich, Palate, Parallel, Peas, Penchant, Please, Predilection, Semblant, Shine, Similar, Simile, Sort, Speaking, Tiki

Likely Apt, Fair, Odds-on, On, Plausible, Possible, Probable, Probit, Prone

Lily African, Agapanthus, Aloe, Amaryllis, Annunciation, Arum, Asphodel, Aspidistra, Belladonna, Calla, Camas(h), Camass, Canada, Candock, Chincherinchee, Colchicum, Corn, Dale, Day, Easter, Elaine, Fawn, Fleur de lys, Fritillary, Galtonia, Hemerocallis, Herb-paris, Jacob's, Kniphofia, Laguna, Lent, Leopard, Lote, Lotus, Madonna, Martagon, Nelumbo,

Nenuphar, Nerine, Nuphar, Padma, Plantain, Quamash, Regal, Sarsa, Scilla, Sego, Smilax, Solomon's seal, Spider, Star of Bethlehem, Stone, Sword, Tiger, Trillium, Tritoma, Turk's cap, Victoria, Water, Yucca, Zephyr

Limb Arm, Bough, Branch, Crural, Exapod, Flipper, Hindleg, Imp, Leg, Leg-end, Member, Proleg, Ramus, Scion, Shin, Spald, Spall, Spaul(d), Wing

Lime Bass(wood), Beton, Calc, Lind(en), Malm, Mortar, Slaked, Soda, Teil, Tilia, Trap, Viscum, Whitewash

Limit(ation), Limited, Limiting Ambit, Bind, Border, Bound, Bourn(e), Brink, Cap, Ceiling, Circumscribe, Climax, Compass, Confine, Deadline, Define, Demark, Determine, Earshot, Edge, End, Entail, Esoteric, ➤ EXTENT, Extreme, Finite, Frontier, Gate, Goal, Impound, Insular, Limes, Lynchet, March, Mete, Nth, Outedge, Pale, Parameter, Perimeter, Periphery, Predetermine, Qualify, Range, Rate-cap, Ration, Reservation, Restrict, Rim, Roof, Scant, Shoestring, Sky, Speed, Stint, String, Tail(lie), Tailye, Term(inus), Tether, Three-mile, Threshold, Thule, Tie, Time, Tropic, Utmost, Utter, Verge

▷ **Limit** may indicate 'surrounding'

Limp Claudication, Dot, Droopy, Flabby, Flaccid, Flimsy, Floppy, Hobble, Hop, Lifeless, Spancel, Tangle

Line(d), Lines, Lining Abreast, Agate, Agonic, Allan, ➤ ANCESTRY, Anent, Angle, Apothem, Arew, Assembly, Axis, Bar, Battle, Baulk, Becket, Bikini, Bluebell, Bombast, Bottom, Boundary, BR, Brail, Branch, Bread, Bush, Canal, Casing, Ceil, Ceriph, Chord, Ciel, Column, Contour, Cord(on), Course, Crease, Crowsfoot, Curve, Cushion, Dancette, Date, Datum, Delay, Descent, Diagonal, Diameter, Distaff, Dotted, Dress, Dynasty, Earing, E-la-mi, Encase, Equator, Faint, Fall(s), Fault, Feint, Fess(e), Fettle, File, Finishing, Firing, Firn, Flex, Frontier, Frost, Furr(ow), Gimp, Giron, Graph, Gridiron, Gyron, Gyron, Hachure, Hard, Hatching, Hawser, Heptameter, Hexameter, Hockey, Hot, House, Impot, Inbounds, Incase, Intima, Isallobar, Isobar, Isobath, Isoclude, Isogloss, Isogonal, Isohel, Isohyet, Isotherm, Knittle, L, Lane, Lap, Lariat, Latitude, Lead, Leash, Le(d)ger, Ley, Lie, Ling, LMS, Load, Log, Longitude, Lubber, Lye, Macron, Maginot, Main, Mark, Marriage, Mason-Dixon, Median, Meridian, Mesal, Monorail, Noose, Norsel, Northern, Oche, Octastichon, Ode, Og(h)am, Omentum, Onedin,

Ordinate, Painter, Parallel, Parameter, Party, Paternoster, Path, Pencil, Phalanx, Picket, Pinstripe, Plimsoll, Plumb, Poetastery, Police, Popping-crease, Poverty, Product(ion), Profession, Queue, Race, Radial, Radius, Rail, Rank, Raster, Ratlin(e), Ratling, Rattlin, Ray, Retinue, Rew, Rhumb, Ripcord, Rope, Route, Row, Rule, Ry, Score, Script, Secant, Serif, Seriph, Siding, Siegfried, Slur, Soft, Solidus, Spectral, Spunyarn, SR, Staff, Stance, Stanza, Starting, Static, Stave, Stean, Steen, Stein, Stem, Stich(os), Stock, Streak, Striate, String, Tangent, Teagle, Terminator, Thread, Throwaway, Timber, Trade, Transoceanic, Transversal, Trimeter, Tropic, Trunk, Tudor, Variety, Verse, Virgule, Wad, Wallace's, Washing, Water(shed), Widow, Wire, Wrinkle

Linen Amice, Amis, Barb, Bed, Byssus, Cambric, Crash, Damask, Dornick, Dowlas, Ecru, Harn, Lawn, Lint, Napery, Percale, Seersucker, Sendal, Silesia, Toile

Liner Artist, Bin-bag, RMS, Ship, Sleeve, Steamer, Steen, Titanic

Linger Dawdle, Dwell, Hang, Hove(r), Lag, ➤ LOITER, Straggle, Tarry, Tie

Linguist(ics) Glottic, Philological, Phonemics, Polyglot, Semantics, Stylistics, Taxeme

Link(ing), Links Associate, Between, Bond, Bridge, Chain, Cleek, Colligate, Concatenation, Copula, Couple, Desmid, Drag, Ess, Flambeau, Hookup, Hotline, Incatenation, Interface, Internet, Intertwine, Karabiner, Krab, Liaise, Machair, Missing, Nexus, Pons, Preposition, Relate, Tead(e), ➤ TIE, Tie-in, Tie-line, Torch, Unite, Yoke

Lion(ess) Androcles, Aphid, Chindit, Elsa, Glitterati, Hero, Leo, Maned, Nemean, Opinicus, Personage, Pride, Simba

Lip(py), Lips Cheek, Fat, Fipple, Flews, Helmet, Jib, Labellum, Labiate, Labret, Labrum, Ligula, Muffle, ➤ RIM, Rubies, Sass, Sauce, Slack-jaw, Submentum

Liqueur, Liquor Ale, Bree, Brew, Broo, Broth, Chasse, Chicha, Creature, Elixir, Feni, Fenny, Fustian, Hooch, Jungle juice, Kaoliang, Lager, Lap, Malt, Mastic, Metheglin, Mickey Finn, Ooze, Potation, Rakee, Raki, Rotgut, Rum, Samshoo, Schnapps, Shypoo, Skink, Stingo, Stock, Stout, Strunt, Stuff, Supermaculum, Tape, Taplash, Tequila, Tiff, White lightning, Wine

Liquid(ate), Liquidity, Liquids, Liquefaction Acetal, Amortise, Annihilate, Apprize, Bittern, Bouillon, Bromine, Cash,

Court-bouillon, Creosol, Decoction, Dope, Eluate, Erase,
Ethanol, Ether, Eucalyptol, Fluid, Fural, Furfural, Jaw, Lye, Mess,
Minim, Pipe, Potion, Protoplasm, Ptisan, Serum, Solution,
Solvent, Syrup, Titre, Tuberculin, Ullage, Whey

▷**List** may indicate 'listen'

List(s), Listing Active, Agenda, Antibarbarus, Appendix,
Army, Atilt, Barocco, Barrace, Bead-roll, Canon, Cant,
Catalog(ue), Categorise, Catelog, Civil, Class, Entry, Enumerate,
Glossary, Hark, Hearken, Heel, Honours, Index, Inventory,
Itemise, Lean, Leet, Line-up, Mailing, Navy, Notitia, Panel,
Register, Repertoire, Roll, Roon, Roster, Rota, Rund, Schedule,
Short, Sick, Slate, Slope, Strip, Syllabus (of Errors), Table, Tariff,
Ticket, Tilt, Timetable, Tip, Transfer, Waiting, Waybill

Listen(er) Attend, Auditor, Auscultate, Ear, Eavesdropper,
Gobemouche, Hark, ➤ HEED, Lithe, Lug, Monitor, Oyez,
Wire-tap

▷**Listen to** may indicate a word sounding like another

Listless(ness) Abulia, Accidie, Acedia, Apathetic, Atony,
Dawney, Indolent, Lackadaisical, Languor, Mooning, Mope,
Mopus, Sloth, Thowless, Torpor, Waff

▷**Lit** may indicate an anagram

Literary Academic, Bas bleu, Booksie, Erudite, Lettered

Literature Belles lettres, Corpus, Fiction, Gongorism, Midrash,
Page, Picaresque, Prose, Responsa, Wisdom

Litter Bed, Brancard, Brood, Cacolet, Cubs, Debris, Doolie,
Emu-bob, Farrow, Jampan, Kago, Kajawah, Kindle, Mahmal,
Nest, Norimon, Palankeen, Palanquin, Palkee, Palki, Pup,
➤ REFUSE, Scrap, Sedan, Stretcher, Team

Little Brief, Chota, Curn, Dorrit, Drib, Drop, Fewtrils, Insect,
Iota, John, Jot, Leet, Lilliputian, Limited, Lite, Lyte, Mini,
Miniscule, Minnow, Minuscule, ➤ MINUTE, Modicum,
Morceau, Nell, Paltry, Paucity, Petite, Pink, Scant, Scut, Shade,
Shoestring, Shred, Shrimp, Slight, Sma', ➤ SMALL, Smattering,
Smidge(o)n, Smidgin, Some, Soupçon, Spot, Tad, Tich, Tine,
Titch, Touch, Tyne, Vestige, Wee, Weedy, Whit, Women

Live(d), Liveliness, Lively, Lives Active, Alert, Allegro,
Animated, Animation, Animato, AV, Awake, Be, Breezy, Brio,
Brisk, Cant(y), Cheery, Chipper, Chirpy, Cohabit, Con moto,
Crouse, Durante vita, ➤ DWELL, Ebullient, Entrain, Exist, Feisty,
Frisky, Gay, Giocoso, Hang-out, Hard, Is, Jazz, Kedge, Lad, Lead,

Mercurial, Merry, Outgo, Pacey, Peart, Pep, Piert, Quicksilver, Rackety, Racy, Reside, Rousing, Saut, Scherzo, Skittish, Spiritoso, Sprack, Spry, Spunky, Vibrant, Vital, Vitality, ➤ VOLATILE, Zappy, Zoe

▶**Livelihood** see LIVING

Living Advowson, Benefice, Biont, Bread, Canonry, Crust, Glebe, Inquiline, Lodging, Quick, Resident, Simony, Subsistence, Symbiotic, Vicarage, Vital

Lizard Evet, Gila monster, Lounge, Reptile, Sauria, Scincoid, Seps, Slow-worm

Load(ed), Loader Accommodation, Affluent, Ballast, Boot-strap, Burden, Cargo, Charge, Cobblers, Dead weight, Dope, Drunk, Fardel, Fother, Freight, Fulham, Full, Gestant, Heap, Input, Jag, Lade, Lard, Last, Live, Onus, Pack, Pay, Prime, Rich, Seam, Shipment, Some, Surcharge, ➤ TIGHT, Tod, Weight, Wharfinger

Loaf(er), Loaves Baguette, Baton, Bloomer, Bludge, Brick, Bum, Bu(r)ster, Cad, Cob, Coburg, Cottage, Farmhouse, Hawm, Hoe-cake, Idle, ➤ LAZE, Long tin, Lusk, Manchet, Miche, Mouch, Pan(h)agia, Roll, Roti, Shewbread, Showbread, Slosh, Split tin, Sugar, Tin, Vantage, Yob

Loan(s) Advance, Balloon, Benevolence, Bottomry, Bridging, Debenture, Imprest, Lane, Mutuum, Omnium, Out, Prest, Respondentia, Roll-over, Start-up, Sub

Loathe, Loathing, Loathsome Abhor(rent), Abominate, Carrion, Detest, Hate, Nauseate, Scunner, Ug(h)

Lobby Demo, Entry, Foyer, Gun, Hall, Press, Urge

Lobster Cock, Crawfish, Crayfish, Crustacean, Decapoda, Langouste, Norway, Pot, Scampo, Spiny, Thermidor, Tomalley

Local(ity) Area, Endemic, Home, Inn, Landlord, Native, Near, Nearby, Neighbourhood, Number, Parochial, Pub, Regional, Resident, Tavern, Topical, Vicinal

▷**Local** may indicate a dialect word

Locate Connect, Find, Fix, Lay, Pinpoint, Plant, Site, Spot

Location Address, Milieu, Place, Recess, Site, Situation, Sofar, Ubiety, Website, Zone

Loch, Lough Ashie, Awe, Derg, Earn, Eil, Erne, Etive, Fine, Gare, Garten, Holy, Hourn, Katrine, ➤ LAKE, Larne, Leven, Linnhe,

Lomond, Long, Moidart, Morar, More, Nakeel, Neagh, Ness, Rannoch, Ryan, Shiel, Strangford, Tay, Torridon

Lock(er), Locks, Lock up Bar, Bolt, Canal, Chubb®, Clinch, Combination, Cowlick, Curlicue, Davy Jones, Deadbolt, Detent, Drop, Fastener, Foretop, Gate, Haffet, Haffit, Handcuff, Hasp, Intern, Key, Latch, Lazaretto, Mortise, Percussion, Quiff, Ragbolt, Ringlet, Sasse, Scalp, Scissors, ➤ SECURE, Sluice, Snap, Spring, Strand, Tag, Talon, Time, Trap, Tress, Tuft, Villus, Ward, Wheel, Wrestle, Yale®

Locomotive Banker, Bogie, Bul(l)gine, Engine, Iron horse, Mobile, Rocket, Steamer, Train

Locust, Locust tree Anime, Carob, Cicada, Hopper, Nymph, Robinia, Seventeen-year, Voetganger

Lodge(r) Billet, Board(er), Box, Cosher, Deposit, Dig, Doss, Entertain, Freemason, Grange, Guest, Harbour, Host, Inmate, Layer, Lie, Masonic, Nest, Orange, Parasite, PG, Quarter, Rancho, Room(er), Stay, Storehouse, Stow, Tenant, Tepee, Wigwam

Lodging(s) Abode, B and B, Chummage, Dharms(h)ala, Digs, Dosshouse, Ferm, Grange, Grove, Hostel, Inquiline, Kip, Minshuku, Pad, Pension, Pied-à-terre, Quarters, Resiant, Rooms, Singleen, YHA

Loft(iness), Lofty Aerial, Airy, Arrogant, Attic, Celsitude, Chip, Garret, Grand, Haymow, High, Jube, Lordly, Magniloquent, Noble, Rarefied, Rigging, Rood, Roost, Tallat, Tallet, Tallot

Log Billet, Black box, Cabin, Chock, Diarise, Diary, Hack, Mantissa, Nap(i)erian, Neper, Patent, ➤ RECORD, Stock, Yule

Logic(al) Alethic, Aristotelian, Chop, Dialectic(s), Doxastic, Epistemics, Modal, Organon, Ramism, Rational(e), Reason, Sequacious, Sorites, Symbolic, Trivium

Loiter(ing) Dally, Dare, Dawdle, Dilatory, Dilly-dally, Idle, Lag, Lallygag, Leng, Lime, ➤ LINGER, Mooch, Mouch, Potter, Saunter, Scamp, Suss, Tarry

London(er) 'Arry, Big Smoke, Cockaigne, Cockney, Co(c)kayne, East-ender, Flat-cap, Jack, Roseland, Smoke, Town, Troynovant, Wen

Lone(r), Lonely Remote, Rogue, Secluded, Sole, Solitary, Unked, Unket, Unkid

Long(er), Longing, Longs Ache, Aitch, Ake, Appetent, Aspire, Brame, Covet, Desire, Die, Earn, Erne, Far, Greed, Green, Grein, ➤ HANKER, Huey, Hunger, Island, Itch, L, Lanky, Large, Lengthy, Longa, Lust, Macron, Miss, More, ➤ NO LONGER, Nostalgia, Option, Pant, Parsec, ➤ PINE, Prolix, Side, Sigh, Tall, Thirst, Trews, Weary, Wish, Wist, Yearn, Yen

Longitude Celestial, Meridian

Longshoreman Hobbler, Hoveller, Wharfinger

Loo Ajax, Bog, Can, Chapel, Dike, Game, Gents, Jakes, John, Privy, Toilet

Look Air, Aspect, Behold, Belgard, Bonne-mine, Busk, Butcher's, Clock, Close-up, Crane, Daggers, Decko, Deek, Dekko, Ecce, Ecco, Expression, Eye, Face, Facies, Gander, Gawp, Gaze, Geek, Glance, Glare, Gledge, Glimpse, Goggle, Grin, Hallo, Hangdog, Hey, Iliad, Inspect, La, Lo, Mien, New, Ogle, Peek, Peep, Prospect, Ray, Recce, Refer, ➤ REGARD, Scan, Scrutinise, Search, See, Seek, Shade, Shufti, Shufty, Spy, Squint, Squiz, Toot, V, Vista

Look-out (man) Cockatoo, Crow's nest, Huer, Mirador, Sangar, Sentry, Sungar, Toot(er), Watch, Watchtower

▷**Look silly** may indicate an anagram

Loom Beamer, Dobby, Emerge, Impend, Jacquard, Lathe, Menace, Picker, Temple, Threaten, Tower

Loop(ed), Loophole, Loopy Becket, Bight, Billabong, Bouclé, Carriage, Chink, Closed, Coil, Eyelet, Eyesplice, Fake, Frog, Frontlet, Grom(m)et, Grummet, Hank, Henie's, Hysteresis, Infinite, Kink, Knop, Lasket, Lug, Noose, Oillet, Parral, Parrel, Pearl(-edge), Picot, Purl, Staple, Stirrup, Terry, Toe, Twist

Loose(n), Loose woman Absolve, Abstrict, Afloat, Anonyma, Baggage, Bail, Besom, Bike, Chippie, Chippy, Cocotte, Demi-mondaine, Demirep, Desultory, Dissolute, Dissolve, Doxy, Draggletail, Dratchell, Drazel, Emit, Flirt-gill, Floosie, Floozie, Floozy, Floppy, Franion, Free, Gangling, Gay, Hussy, Insecure, Jade, Jezebel, Lax, Loast, Mob, Mort, Pinnace, Profligate, Quail, Ramp, ➤ RELAX, Sandy, Scrubber, Slag, Slapper, Streel, Tart, Tramp, Trull, Unhasp, Unhitch, Unlace, Unpin, Unreined, Unscrew, Untie, Vague, Wappend, Whore

Loot Boodle, Booty, Cragh, Creach, Foray, Haul, Mainour, Peel, Pluck, ➤ PLUNDER, Ransack, Rape, Reave, Rieve, Rob, Sack, Smug, Spoils, Spoliate, Swag, Treasure, Waif

Lop Behead, Clop, Curtail, Detruncate, Droop, Shroud, Sned, Trash

Lord(s), Lordship Adonai, Arrogant, Boss, Byron, Dieu, Domineer, Dominical, Duc, Earl, Elgin, Gad, God, Haw-haw, Herr, Imperious, Jim, Justice, Kami, Kitchener, Landgrave, Law, Ld, Liege, Lonsdale, Losh, Lud, Misrule, Mynheer, Naik, Oda Nobunaga, Omrah, Ordinary, Ormazd, Ormuzd, Peer, Seigneur, Seignior, Shaftesbury, Sire, Spiritual, Taverner, Temporal, Tuan, Ullin

Lore Cab(b)ala, Edda, Lair, Lare, Riem, Upanis(h)ad

Lorry Artic(ulated), Camion, Crummy, Drag, Flatbed, Juggernaut, Low-loader, Rig, Tipper, Tonner, ➤ TRUCK, Wagon

Lose(r) Also-ran, Decrease, Drop, Elude, Forfeit, Leese, Misère, Mislay, Misplace, Nowhere, Tank, Throw, Tine(r), Tyne, Underdog, Unsuccessful, Waste, Weeper

Loss, Lost Anosmia, Aphesis, Aphonia, Apocope, Apraxia, Astray, Attainder, Boohai, Chord, Cost, Dead, Decrease, Depreciation, Detriment, Disadvantage, Elision, Extinction, Foredamned, Forfeited, Forgotten, Forlorn, Gone, Lore, Lorn, Lurch, Missing, Omission, Outage, Pentimento, Perdition, Perdu, Perished, Preoccupied, Privation, Psilosis, Tine, Tinsel, Tint, Toll, Traik, Tribes, Tyne(d), Ullage, Unredeemed, Wastage, Wasted, Will, Wull

▷**Lost** may indicate an anagram or an obsolete word

Lot(s) Abundant, Amount, Aret(t), Badly, Batch, Boatload, Caboodle, Cavel, Chance, Deal, Dole, Doom, Due, ➤ FATE, Fortune, Hantle, Hap, Heaps, Horde, Host, Item, Job, Kevel, Kismet, Lashings, Legion, Luck, Manifold, Many, Mass, Moh, Moira, Mony, Mort, Myriad, Oceans, Omnibus, Oodles, Pack, Parcel, Plenitude, Plenty, Portion, Power, Purim, Raft, Scads, Set, Sight, Slather, Slew, Slue, Sortilege, Stack, Sum, Tall order, Tons, Vole, Wagonload, Weird

Lothario Lady-killer, Libertine, Rake, Womaniser

Lotion After-shave, Blackwash, Calamine, Collyrium, Cream, Humectant, Suntan, Unguent, Wash

Lottery, Lotto Bingo, Cavel, Draw, Gamble, Pakapoo, Pools, Punchboard, Raffle, Rollover, Scratchcard, Sweepstake, Tombola

Loud(ness), Loudly Bel, Big, Blaring, Booming, Brassy, Decibel, F, FF, Flashy, Forte, Fracas, Garish, Gaudy, Glaring,

Hammerklavier, High, Lumpkin, Noisy, Orotund, Raucous, Roarie, Siren, Sone, Stentor(ian), Strident, Tarty, Vociferous, Vulgar

Loudspeaker Action, Boanerges, Bullhorn, Hailer, Megaphone, Stentor, Subwoofer, Tannoy®, Tweeter, Woofer

Lounge Daiker, Da(c)ker, Departure, Hawm, Idle, Laze, Lizard, Loll, Lollop, Parlour, Slouch, Sun, Transit

Louse (up), Lousy, Lice Acrawl, Argulus, Bolix, Bollocks, Chat, Cootie, Crab, Crummy, Head, Isopod(a), Kutu, Nit, Oniscus, Pedicular, Phthiriasis, Psocoptera, Psylla, Slater, Snot, Sowbug, Sucking, Vermin

Lout Clod(hopper), Coof, Cuif, Hallian, Hallion, Hallyon, Hick, Hob, Hobbledehoy, Hooligan, Hoon, Jack, Jake, Keelie, Lager, Larrikin, Lob(lolly), Loord, Lubber, Lumpkin, Oaf, Oik, Rube, Swad, Tout, Yahoo, Yob(bo)

Love(r) Abelard, Adore, Adulator, Affection, Agape, Aloha, Amant, Amateur, Ami(e), Amoret, Amoroso, Amour, Antony, Ardour, Ariadne, Aucassin, Beau, Bidie-in, Blob, Calf, Care, Casanova, Chamberer, Cicisbeo, Concubine, Coquet, Court, Courtly, Cupboard, Cupid, Dotard, Dote, Doxy, Duck(s), Ducky, Dulcinea, Eloise, Eloper, Emotion, Enamorado, Eros, Fan, Flame, Frauendienst, Free, Goose-egg, Idolise, Inamorata, Inamorato, Isolde, Jo, Lad, Leman, Like, Lochinvar, Loe, Loo, Lurve, Nihility, Nil, Nothing, Nought, O, Pairs, Paramour, Pash, Passion, Philander, Platonic, Protestant, Psychodelic, Puppy, Revere, Romance, Romeo, Spooner, Stale, Storge, Suitor, Swain, Thisbe, Toyboy, Troilus, True, Turtle(-dove), Valentine, Venus, Virtu, Zeal, Zero

Lovely Adorable, Belle, Dishy, Dreamy, Nasty

Love-making ➤ INTERCOURSE, Kama Sutra, Sex, Snog

Low(est), Low-cut, Lower(ing) Abase, Abate, Abysmal, Amort, Area, Avail(e), Avale, B, Basal, Base(-born), Bass(o), Beneath, Cartoonist, Cheap, Church, Condescend, Contralto, Cow, Croon, Crude, Darken, Debase, Décolleté, Degrade, Demean, Demit, Demote, Depress, Devalue, Dim, Dip, Dispirited, Doldrums, Drawdown, Drop, Early, Embase, Flat, Foot, Frown, Gazunder, Glare, Guernsey, Gurly, Hedge, Humble, Ignoble, Imbase, Inferior, Jersey, Laigh, Lallan, Law, Mass, Mean, Menial, Moo, Mopus, Morose, Nadir, Net, Nether, Nett, Ostinato, Paravail, Plebeianise, Profound, Prole, Relegate,

Ribald, Rock-bottom, Sad, Scoundrel, Scowl, Shabby, Short, Soft, Stoop, Subordinate, Sudra, Undermost, Vail, Vulgar, Weak, Wretched

▷**Lower** may refer to cattle

Loyal(ty) Adherence, Allegiant, Brick, Dependable, Faithful, Fast, Fidelity, Gungho, Leal, Patriotic, Stalwart, Staunch, ➤ TRUE, Trusty

Lozenge Cachou, Catechu, Fusil, Jujube, Mascle, Pastille, Pill, Rhomb, Rustre, Tablet, Troche

Lubricant, Lubricate Carap-oil, Coolant, Derv, Grease, Oil, Unguent, Wool-oil

Lucid Bright, Clear, Perspicuous, Sane

Lucifer Devil, Match, Proud

Luck(y) Amulet, Auspicious, Beginner's, Bonanza, Break, Caduac, Cess, Chance, Charmed, Chaunce, Daikoku, Dip, Fate, Fluke, ➤ FORTUNE, Godsend, Hap, Heather, Hit, Jam(my), Joss, Lady, Lot, Mascot, Mozzle, Prosit, Providential, Pudding-bag, Purple patch, Seal, Seel, Sele, Serendipity, Sess, Sonsie, Sonsy, Star(s), Streak, Success, Talisman, Tinny, Tough, Turn-up, Windfall

Ludicrous Absurd, Bathetic, Bathos, Farcical, Inane, Irish, Jest, Laughable, Risible

Luggage Bags, Carryon, Cases, Dunnage, Hand, Kit, Petara, Traps, Trunk

Lull, Lullaby Berceuse, Calm, Cradlesong, Hushaby, Respite, Rock, Sitzkreig, Soothe, Sopite

Lumber(ing) Clump, Galumph, Jumble, Pawn, Ponderous, Raffle, Saddle, Scamble, Timber

Luminance, Luminous, Luminosity Aglow, Arc, Glow, Ignis-fatuus, L, Light, Nit, Phosphorescent, Sea-dog, Wildfire, Will o' the wisp

Lump(y) Aggregate, Bubo, Bud, Bulge, Bur(r), Caruncle, Chuck, Clat, Claut, Clod, Clot, Cob, Combine, Da(u)d, Dallop, Dollop, Enhydros, Epulis, Flocculate, Ganglion, Geode, Gnarl, Gob(bet), Goiter, Goitre, Grape, Hunch, Hunk, Inium, Knarl, Knob, Knub, Knur(r), Knurl, Lob, Lunch, Malleolus, Mote, Mott, Myxoma, Neuroma, Nibble, Nirl, Node, Nodule, Nodulus, Nub, Nubble, Nugget, Nur(r), Nurl, Osteophyte, Plook, Plouk,

Quinsy, Raguly, Sarcoma, Scybalum, Sitfast, Slub, Strophiole, Tragus, Tuber(cle), Wart, Wodge

Lunacy, Lunatic Bedlam, Dementia, Demonomania, Folly, Insanity, Mad(ness), Psychosis

▷**Lunatic** may indicate an anagram

Lunch(time) Dejeune, Déjeuner, L, Nacket, Nuncheon, Packed, Piece, Ploughman, Pm, Tiffin, Working

Lung(s) Bellows, Coalminer's, Farmer's, Iron, Lights, Pulmo, Pulmonary, Soul

Lunge Breenge, Breinge, Dive, Stab, Thrust, Venue

Lurch Reel, Stoit, Stumble, Swee

Lure Bait, Bribe, Carrot, Decoy, Entice, Horn, Inveigle, Jig, Judas, Roper, Spinner, Stale, Temptation, Tice, Tole, Toll, Train, Trepan

Lurk(ing) Dare, Latitant, Skulk, Slink, Snoke, Snook, Snowk

Lush Drunk, Fertile, Green, Juicy, Lydian, Sot, Tosspot, Verdant

Lust(ful), Lusty Cama, Concupiscence, Corflambo, Desire, Eros, Frack, Greed, Kama, Lech(ery), Lewd, Megalomania, Obidicut, Randy, Rank, Raunchy, Salacious, Venereous

Lustre, Lustrous Brilliance, Census, Galena, Gaum, Gilt, Gloss, Gorm, Inaurate, Lead-glance, Pentad, Reflet, Satiny, Schiller, ➤ SHEEN, Water

Lute, Lutist Amphion, Chitarrone, Cither, Dichord, Orpharion, Pandora, Theorbo, Vielle

Luxuriant, Luxuriate, Luxurious, Luxury (lover) Bask, Clover, Cockaigne, Cockayne, Copious, Deluxe, Dolce vita, Extravagant, Fleshpots, Lavish, Lucullan, Lush, Mollitious, Ornate, Pie, Plush, Posh, Rank, ➤ RICH, Ritzy, Sumptuous, Sybarite, Wallow

▶**Lying** see LIE

Lyre Cithern, Harp, Psaltery, Testudo

Lyric(al), Lyricist, Lyrist Cavalier, Dit(t), Epode, Gilbert, Melic, Ode, Orphean, Paean, Pean, Poem, Rhapsodic, Song

Mm

M Married, Member, Metre, Mike, Mile, Thousand

Macabre Gothic, Grotesque, Sick

Machine(ry) Apparat(us), Appliance, Automaton, Bathing, Calender, Centrifuge, ➤ DEVICE, Engine, Fax, Fruit, Gin, Heck, Instrument, Jawbreaker, Lathe, Life-support, Loom, Moulinet, Mule, Nintendo®, Plant, Press, Processor, Robot, Slot, Spinning jenny, Throstle, Turbine, Turing, Vending, Virtual, Washing

Mackintosh Burberry®, Mac, Mino, Oilskin, Slicker, Waterproof

Mad(den), Madman, Madness Angry, Balmy, Bananas, Barking, Barmy, Bedlam, Besotted, Bonkers, Crackbrained, Crackpot, Crazy, Cuckoo, Cupcake, Delirious, Dement, Distract, Dotty, Enrage, Fay, Fey, Folie, Folly, Frantic, Frenetic(al), Fruitcake, Furioso, Fury, Gelt, Gyte, Harpic, Hatter, Idiotic, Insane, Insanie, Insanity, Into, Irritate, Kook, Loco, Lunatic, Lycanthropy, Madbrained, Maenad, Mania, Mental, Meshug(g)a, Midsummer, Mullah, Psycho, Rabid, Raving, Redwood, Redwud, Scatty, Screwy, Short-witted, Starkers, Tonto, Touched, Troppo, Unhinged, Wood, Wowf, Wrath, Wud, Xenomania, Yond, Zany

▷**Mad(den)** may indicate an anagram

▷**Madly** may indicate an anagram

Madonna Lady, Lily, Mary, Pietà, Virgin

Mafia Camorra, Capo, Cosa nostra, Godfather, Mob, Ndrangheta, Omerta

Magazine Arsenal, Clip, Colliers, Cornhill, Cosmopolitan, Digizine, Economist, Field, Girlie, Glossy, Granta, Lady, Lancet, Listener, Magnet, Organ, Periodical, Pictorial, Playboy, Pulp, Punch, She, Slick, Spectator, Store, Strand, Tatler, Time, Vogue, Warehouse, Weekly, Yoof

Magic(al), Magician Art, Black, Charm, Conjury, Diablerie, Diablery, Enchanting, Faust, Genie, Goetic, Goety, Gramary(e), Houdini, Illusionist, Incantation, Math, Medea, Merlin, Mojo, Moly, Morgan le Fay, Necromancer, Powwow, Prospero,

Rhombus, Sorcery, Spell, Speller, Supernatural, Talisman, Voodoo, White, Wizard

Magistracy, Magistrate Aedile, Amman, Amtman, Archon, Avoyer, Bailie, Bailiff, Bailli(e), Burgess, Burgomaster, Cadi, Censor, Consul, Corregidor, Demiurge, Doge(ate), Edile, Effendi, Ephor, Field cornet, Finer, Foud, Gonfalonier, JP, Judiciary, Jurat, Kotwal, Landamman(n), Landdrost, Maire, Mayor, Mittimus, Novus homo, Podesta, Portreeve, Pr(a)efect, Pr(a)etor, Prior, Proconsul, Propraetor, Provost, Qadi, Quaestor, Recorder, Reeve, Shereef, Sherif, Stad(t)holder, Stipendiary, Syndic, Tribune, Worship

Magnate Baron, Bigwig, Industrialist, Mogul, Tycoon, VIP

Magnet(ic), Magnetism Attraction, Charisma, Field, Gauss, Horseshoe, It, Loadstone, Lodestone, Maxwell, Od, Oersted, Permanent, Polar, Pole, Pole piece, Poloidal, Pull, Solenoid, Terrella, Tesla, Tole

Magnificence, Magnificent Gorgeous, Grandeur, Imperial, Laurentian, Lordly, Noble, Pride, Regal, Royal, Splendid, State, Superb

Magnifier, Magnify(ing) Aggrandise, Augment, Binocle, ➤ ENLARGE, Exaggerate, Increase, Loupe, Microscope, Teinoscope, Telescope

Magnolia An(n)ona, Beaver-tree, Champac, Champak, Mississippi, Sweet bay, Umbrella-tree, Yulan

Magpie Bell, Bird, Chatterer, Madge, Mag, Margaret, Outer, Pica, Piet, Pyat, Pyet, Pyot

Maid(en) Abigail, Aia, Amah, Biddy, Bonibell, Bonne, Bonnibell, Chamber, Chloe, Clothes-horse, Damosel, Dell, Dey, First, Girl, Guillotine, Ignis-fatuus, Imago, Inaugural, Io, Iras, Iron, Lorelei, M, Marian, May, Miss, Nymph, Opening, Over, Pucelle, Rhine, Skivvy, Soubrette, Suivante, Thestylis, Tirewoman, Tweeny, Valkyrie, Virgin, Wench

Mail Air, ➤ ARMOUR, Byrnie, Cataphract, Chain, Da(w)k, E(lectronic), Express, Fan, Habergeon, Hate, Hauberk, Helm, Junk, Letter, Panoply, Pony express, Post, Ring, Send, Snail, Spam, Surface, Tuille(tte), Voice

Main(s) Brine, Briny, ➤ CENTRAL, Chief, Cockfight, Conduit, Essential, Foremost, Generally, Grid, Gross, Head, ➤ KEY, Lead(ing), Palmary, Predominant, Prime, Principal, Ring, ➤ SEA, Sheer, Spanish, Staple, Water

Maintain, Maintenance Alimony, Allege, Ap(p)anage, Argue, Assert, Aver, Avouch, Avow, Claim, Contend, Continue, Defend, Escot, Insist, Preserve, Run, Sustain, Upbear, Uphold, Upkeep

Maize Corn, Hominy, Indian, Mealie, Popcorn, Samp

Majestic, Majesty August, Britannic, Dignity, Eagle, Grandeur, Imperial, Maestoso, Olympian, Regal, SM, Sovereign, Stately, Sublime, Tuanku

Major (domo) Drum, ➤ IMPORTANT, PM, Seneschal, Senior, Sergeant, Star, Trumpet, Wig

Majority Absolute, Age, Body, Eighteen, Latchkey, Maturity, Most, Preponderance, Silent, Working

Make(r), Make do, Making Amass, Brand, Coerce, Coin, Compel, Compulse, Concoct, Creant, Create, Devise, Earn, Execute, Fabricate, Factive, Fashion, Faute de mieux, Fet(t), Forge, Form, Gar(re), God, Halfpenny, Mak(e), Manage, Prepare, Production, Reach, Render, Shape, Sort

▷**Make** may indicate an anagram

Make believe Fantasy, Fictitious, Pretend, Pseudo

Make up Ad lib, Compose, Concealer, Constitution, Cosmetics, Gaud, Gawd, Gene, Identikit®, Kohl, Liner, Lipstick, Maquillage, Mascara, Metabolism, Paint, Pancake, Powder, Reconcile, Rouge, Slap, Tidivate, Titivate, Toiletry, White-face

Male Arrhenotoky, Buck, Bull, Dog, Ephebe, Ephebus, Gent, Hob, John Doe, Macho, Mansize, Masculine, Ram, Rogue, Spear(side), Stag, Stamened, Telamon, Tom

Malfunction Glitch, Hiccup

Malice, Malicious Bitchy, Catty, Cruel, Despiteous, Envy, Malevolent, Malign, Narquois, Schadenfreude, Serpent, Snide, Spite, Spleen, Venom, Virulent

Malign(ant), Malignity Asperse, Backbite, Baleful, Defame, Denigrate, Gall, Harm, Hate-rent, Hatred, Libel, Sinister, Slander, Spiteful, Swart(h)y, Toxin, Vicious, Vilify, Vilipend, Viperous, Virulent

Malleable Clay, Ductile, Fictile, Pliable

▷**Malleable** may indicate an anagram

Mallet Beetle, Club, Hammer, Mace, Maul, Stick

Mammal Animal

Mammoth Epic, Gigantic, Huge, Jumbo, Mastodon, Whopping, Woolly

Man(kind) Ask(r), Best, Betty, Bimana(l), Biped, Bloke, Bo, Boy, Cad, Cairn, Calf, Castle, Cat, Chal, Chap, Checker, Chequer, Chiel, Cockey, Cod, Crew, Cro-Magnon, Cuffin, Cully, Dog, Don, Draught, Dude, Essex, Family, Family, Fella, Feller, Fellow, Folsom, Friday, G, Gayomart, Gent, Grimaldi, Guy, He, Heidelberg, Himbo, Hombre, Hominid, Homme, Homo, Inner, IOM, Isle, Jack, Java, Joe (Bloggs), Joe Blow, John(nie), John Doe, Josser, Lollipop, M, Male, Microcosm, Mister, Mon, Mr, Mun, Neanderthal, Oreopithecus, Ou, Paleolithic, Party, Pawn, Peking, Person, Piece, Piltdown, Pin, Pithecanthropus, Raff, Remittance, Renaissance, Rhodesian, Rook, Servant, Servitor, Ship, Sinanthropus, Sodor, Soldier, Solo, Staff, Stag, Straw, Third, Thursday, Twelfth, Tyke, Type, Valet, Vir, Wight

Manage(r), Manageable, Management, Managing Administer, Amildar, Attain, Aumil, Behave, Boss, Chief, Conduct, Contrive, Control, Cope, Darogha, Direct, Docile, Exec(utive), Fare, Find, Govern, Grieve, Handle, Honcho, IC, Impresario, Intendant, Logistical, MacReady, Maitre d('hotel), Manipulate, Manoeuvre, Proctor, Procurator, Regisseur, Rig, Roadie, ➤ RUN, Scrape, Shift, Steward, Succeed, Suit, Superintend, Tawie, Tractable, Treatment, Trustee, Wangle, Wield(y), Yare

Mandate Authority, Decree, Fiat, Order

Mangle Agrise, Butcher, Distort, Garble, Hack, Hackle, Haggle, Wring(er)

▷**Mangle** may indicate an anagram

Mania Cacoethes, Craze, Frenzy, Passion, Rage

Manifesto Plank, Platform, Policy, Pronunciamento

Manipulate, Manipulative, Manipulator Chiropractor, Control, Cook, Demagogic, Diddle, Fashion, Gerrymander, Handle, Jerrymander, Juggle, Logodaedalus, Osteopath, Ply, Rig, Tweeze, Use, Wangle, ➤ WIELD

▷**Manipulate** may indicate an anagram

Manner(ism), Mannerly, Manners Accent, A la, Appearance, Attitude, Bedside, Behaved, Behaviour, Bon ton, Breeding, Carriage, Conduct, Couth, Crew, Custom, Deportment, Ethos, Etiquette, Farand, Farrand, Farrant, Habit,

How, Mien, Mode, Morality, Mores, Of, Ostent, Panache, Politesse, Presentation, P's & Q's, Quirk, Rate, Sort, Style, Thew(s), Thewe(s), Trick, Urbanity, Way, Wise

Manoeuvre(s) Campaign, Castle, Engineer, Exercise, Faena, Fianchetto, Fork, Gambit, Heimlich, Hot-dog, Jink(s), Jockey, Manipulate, Op(eration), Pesade, Ploy, Ruse, Skewer, Use, U-turn, Valsalva, Wheelie, Whipstall, Wile, Zigzag

▷**Manoeuvre** may indicate an anagram

Manor (house) Area, Demain, Demesne, Estate, Hall, Vill(a)

Mantle Asthenosphere, Authority, Burnous(e), Capote, Caracalla, Dolman, Elijah, Gas, Pall, Pallium, Paludament, Pelisse, Rochet, Sima, Toga, Tunic, Veil

Manual Blue collar, Bradshaw, Cambist, Console, Enchiridion, Guide, Hand, Handbook, How-to, Portolan(o), Positif

Manure Compost, Dressing, Dung, Fertiliser, Guano, Hen-pen, Lime, Muck, Sha(i)rn, Tath

Manuscript(s) Codex, Codicology, Folio, Hand, Holograph, Longhand, MS, Opisthograph, Palimpsest, Papyrus, Parchment, Script, Scroll, Scrowl(e)(s), Vellum

▷**Manx** may indicate a last letter missing

Many C, CD, Countless, D, Hantle, Herd, Horde, Host, L, Lot, M, Manifold, Mony, Multi(tude), Myriad, Scad, Sight, Stacks, Tons, Umpteen

▷**Many** may indicate the use of a Roman numeral letter

Map(ping) Atlas, Card, Cartogram, Chart, Chorography, Cognitive, Contour, Face, Genetic, Inset, Key, Loxodromic, Mappemond, OS, Plan, Plot, Relief, Sea-card, Sea-chart, Topography, Weather

Maple Acer, Mazer, Norway, Plane, Sugar, Sycamore, Syrup

Map-maker Cartographer, OS, Speed

Marble(s), Marbling Agate, All(e)y, Arch, Bonce, Bonduc, Bool, Boondoggle, Bowl, Chequer, Devil's, Dump, Elgin, Humite, Knicker, Languedoc, Marl, Marmoreal, Mottle, Nero-antico, Nicker, Onychite, Paragon, Parian, Petworth, Plonker, Plunker, Purbeck, Rance, Ringer, Ring-taw, Sanity, Scagliola, Taw, Variegate

March(ing) Abut, Adjoin, Advance, Anabasis, Border(er), Borderland, Dead, Defile, Demo, Etape, File, Footslog, Forced, Freedom, Fringe, Galumph, Go, Goosestep, Hunger, Ides,

Jarrow, Lide, Limes, Lockstep, Meare, Music, ➤ PARADE, Progress, Protest, Quick, Route, Slow time, Step, Strunt, Strut, Trio, Tromp, Wedding, Yomp

Marge, Margin(al) Annotate, Border, Brim, Brink, Curb, Edge, Hair's breadth, Lean, Limit, Littoral, Neck, Nose, Profit, Rand, Repand, ➤ RIM, Selvedge, Sideline, Tail, Term

Marijuana Alfalfa, Dagga, Gage, Ganja, Grass, Greens, Hay, Herb, Jive, Kaif, Kef, Kif, Leaf, Locoweed, Mary-Jane, Pot, Roach, Rope, Shit, Sinsemilla, Splay, Spliff, Tea, Toke

Mariner AB, Ancient, MN, RM, Sailor, Salt, Seafarer, Tar

Mark(ed) Accent, Antony, Apostrophe, Asterisk, Badge, Bethumb, Birth, Blaze, Blot, Brand, Bruise, Bull, Butt, Cachet, Caract, Caret, Caste, Cedilla, Chatter, Chequer, Cicatrix, Clout, Colon, Comma, Coronis, Crease, Dash, Denote, Dent, Diacritic, Diaeresis, Dieresis, Distinction, DM, Ensign, Enstamp, Exclamation, Expression, Feer, Fleck, Glyph, Gospel, Hacek, Hash, Hatch, Heed, High water, Hyphen, Impress(ion), Indicium, Ink, Inscribe, Insignia, Kite, Kumkum, Lentigo, Line, Ling, Logo, Low water, M, Macron, MB, Merk, Mottle, NB, Notal, Note, Notice, Obelisk, Observe, Oche, Paraph, Period, Pilcrow, Pit, Plage, Pling, Point, Popinjay, Port wine, Presa, Punctuation, Record, Reference, Roundel, Scar, Score, See, Sigil, Sign, Smit, Smut, Speck, Splodge, Splotch, Stain, Stencil, Stigma(ta), Strawberry, Stress, Stretch, Sucker, Symbol, Target, Tatow, Tattoo, Tee, Theta, Thread, Tick, Tika, Tittle, Token, Touchmark, Trace, Track, Trout, Tug(h)ra, Twain, Umlaut, Ure, Victim, Wand, Watch, Weal, Welt

Market (day), Market place Agora, Alcaiceria, Baltic, Bazaar, Bear, Billingsgate, Borgo, Bull, Buyer's, Capital, Change, Common, Denet, Dragon, EC, Emporium, Errand, Exchange, Fair, Flea, Forum, Grey, Kerb, Lloyds, Mandi, Mart, Mercat, Nundine, Outlet, Piazza, Sale, Seller's, Shop, Sook, Souk, Stance, Staple, Stock, Tattersall's, Test, Third, Trade, Tron, Tryst, Vent, Wall Street

Maroon Brown, Castaway, Enisle, Firework, Inisle, Isolate, Strand

Marriage ➤ ALLIANCE, Bed, Beenah, Bigamy, Bridal, Coemption, Confarreation, Conjugal, Connubial, Digamy, Endogamy, Espousal, Exogamy, Gandharva, Genial, Hetaerism, Hetairism, Hymeneal, Jugal, Ketubah, Knot, Levirate, Match,

Mating, Matrilocal, Matrimony, Mésalliance, Monandry, Monogamy, Morganatic, Noose, Nuptial, Pantagamy, Punalua, Sacrament, Shidduch, Tie, ➤ UNION, Wedding, Wedlock

Marrow Courgette, Friend, Gist, Medulla, Myeloid, Pith, Pumpkin, Squash, Vegetable

Marry, Married Ally, Amate, Buckle, Cleek(it), Confarreate, Couple, Coverture, Espouse, Feme covert, Forsooth, Hitch, Join, Knit, M, Mate, Matron, Memsahib, Pair, Pardie, Quotha, Splice, Tie, Troggs, Troth, Unite, W, Wed, Wive

Marsh(y) Bayou, Bog, Chott, Corcass, Emys, Everglade, Fen, Hackney, Maremma, Merse, Mire, Morass, Ngaio, Paludal, Plashy, Pontine, Pripet, Quagmire, Romney, Salina, Salt, Shott, Slade, Slough, Sog, Spew, Spue, Swale, Swamp, Taiga, Terai, Vlei, Wetlands

Marshal Arrange, Array, Commander, Earp, Foch, French, Hickok, MacMahon, Muster, Neil, Ney, Order, Pétain, Provost, Shepherd, Tedder, Usher

Marsupial Metatheria, Theria

Martial (arts) Bellicose, Budo, Capoeira, Capuera, Chopsocky, Dojo, Iai-do, Judo, Ju-jitsu, Karate, Kung Fu, Militant, Ninjutsu, Shintaido, Tae kwon do, T'ai chi (chuan), Warlike, Wushu

Martyr(dom), Martyrs Alban, Alphege, Colosseum, Donatist, Justin, Latimer, MM, Passional, Persecute, Sebastian, Stephen, Suffer, Tolpuddle, Wishart

Marvel(lous) Epatant, Fab, Marl, Miracle, Mirific, Phenomenon, Prodigious, Superb, Super-duper, Terrific, Wonder

Marx(ism), Marxist Aspheterism, Chico, Comintern, Commie, Groucho, Gummo, Harpo, Karl, Menshevik

Mary Bloody, Celeste, Madonna, Moll, Morison, Tum(my), Typhoid, Virgin

Masculine, Masculinity He, He-man, Linga(m), M, Machismo, Macho, Male, Manly, Virile

Mash(er) Beau, Beetle, Brew, Lady-killer, Pap, Pestle, Pound, Sour, Squash

Mask(ed) Camouflage, Cloak, Cokuloris, Death, Disguise, Dissemble, Domino, Larvated, Life, Loo, Loup, Mascaron,

Matte, Persona, Respirator, Screen, Semblance, Stalking-horse, Stocking, Template, Visor, Vizard

Mass(es) Aggregate, Agnus dei, Anniversary, Banket, Bezoar, Bike, Body, Bulk, Cake, Chaos, Clot, Congeries, Conglomeration, Consecration, Core, Crith, Critical, Crowd, Demos, Density, Flake, Flysch, Folk, Geepound, Great, Herd, High, Horde, Hulk, Jud, Kermesse, Kermis, Kilo(gram), Kirmess, Low, Lump, M, Majority, Missa, Mop, Nest, Phalanx, Pile, Plumb, Pontifical, Populace, Raft, Requiem, Ruck, Salamon, Salmon, Scrum, Sea, Serac, Service, Shock, Sicilian, Size, Slub, Slug, Stack, Stroma, Sursum corda, Te Igitur, Tektite, Trental, Vesper, Volume, Wad, Weight, Welter

Massacre Amritsar, Blood-bath, Butcher, Carnage, Glencoe, Havock, Manchester, Peterloo, Pogrom, Purge, Scullabogue, Scupper, September, Sicilian vespers, Slaughter, Slay

Massage, Masseur Anmo, Chafer, Do-in, Effleurage, ➤ KNEAD, Malax, Palp, Petrissage, Physio, Rolf(ing), Rubber, Shampoo, Shiatsu, Swedish, Tapotement, Thai, Tripsis, Tui na

Massive Big, Bull, Colossal, Heavy, Herculean, Huge, Monumental, Strong, Titan

Mast(ed) Acorn, Crosstree, Hounds, Jigger, Jury, Mizzen, Pannage, Pole, Racahout, Royal, Ship-rigged, Spar, Top-gallant

Master(ly) Artful, Baalebos, Baas, Beak, Beat, Boss, Buddha, Bwana, Careers, Checkmate, Conquer, Control, Dan, Dominate, Dominie, Employer, Enslave, Exarch, Expert, Gov, Herr, Himself, Learn, Lord, MA, Maestro, Mas(s), Massa, Mes(s), Nkosi, Ollamh, Ollav, Oner, Oppress, Original, Overcome, Overpower, Overseer, Pedant, Rabboni, Seigneur, Seignior, Sir(e), Skipper, ➤ SUBDUE, Subjugate, Superate, Surmount, Swami, Tame, Thakin, Towkay, Tuan, Usher, Vanquish, Virtuoso

Mat(ted), Matting Bast, Coaster, Doily, Dojo, Doyley, Felt, Inlace, Pad, Paunch, Plat, Rug, ➤ TANGLE, Tat(ami), Tatty, Taut, Tawt, Tomentose, Welcome, Zarf

Match(ed) Agree, Alliance, Amate, Balance, Besort, Bonspiel, Bout, Carousel, Compare, Congreve, Contest, Cope, Correspond, Counterpane, Doubles, Emulate, Engagement, Equal(ise), Equate, Even, Exhibition, Fellow, Fit, Fixture, Four-ball, Friction, Friendly, Fusee, Fuzee, Game, Go, International, Joust, Light, Locofoco, Lucifer, Main, Marrow, Marry, Meet, Mouse, Needle, Pair(s), Paragon, Parti, Pit,

Promethean, Reproduce, Return, Rival, Roland, Rubber, Safety, Singles, Slanging, Slow, Spunk, Striker, Suit, Sync, ➤ TALLY, Team, Test, Tie, Twin, Union, Vesta, Vesuvian, Wedding

Mate, Mating Achates, Adam, Amigo, Amplexus, Bedfellow, Bo, Breed, Buddy, Buffer, Butty, Chess, China, Chum, Cobber, Comrade, Consort, Crony, Cully, Digger, Eve, Feare, Feer, Fellow, Fere, Fiere, Fool's, Husband, Maik, Make, Marrow, Marry, Match, Mister, Oldster, Oppo, ➤ PAIR, Pal, Paragon, Partner, Pheer(e), Pirrauru, Scholar's, Serve, Sex, Skaines, Smothered, Soul, ➤ SPOUSE, Tea, Wack, Wife, Wus(s)

Material Agalmatolite, Aggregate, Agitprop, Apt, Armure, Blastema, Bole, Byssus, Ciré, ➤ CLOTH, Cob, Compo, Copy, Corporeal, Data, Documentation, Earthy, ➤ FABRIC, Factual, Fettling, Fines, Fuel, Germane, Hylic, Metal, Papier-maché, Pertinent, Physical, Plasterboard, Positive, Relevant, Skirting, Stuff, Substance, Tangible, Textile, Thingy, Wattle and daub

Mathematician Optime, Wrangler

Mathematics, Maths Algebra, Arithmetic, Arsmetrick, Calculus, Geometry, Logarithms, Mechanics, Numbers, Trig

Matter Alluvium, Bioblast, Biogen, Body, Concern, Consequence, Dark, Empyema, Epithelium, Gear, Gluon, Go, Grey, Hyle, Impost(h)ume, Issue, Mass, Material, Molecule, Phlegm, Pith, Point, Positron, Protoplasm, Pulp, Pus, Quark, Reck, Reke, Scum, Shebang, Signify, Subject, ➤ SUBSTANCE, Thing, Topic, Tousle, Touzle, Ylem

Mattress Bed(ding), Biscuit, Foam, Futon, Lilo®, Pallet, Palliasse, Tick

Mature, Maturity Adult, Age, Blossom, Bold, Concoct, Develop, Mellow, Metaplasis, Puberty, Ripe(n), Rounded, Seasoned, Upgrow(n)

Maul Hammer, Manhandle, Paw, Rough

Maximum All-out, Full, Highest, Most, Peak, Utmost

May Blossom, Can, Hawthorn, Merry, Might, Month, Mote, Quickthorn, Shall, Whitethorn

Maybe Happen, Mebbe, Perchance, Perhaps, Possibly

▷**May become** may indicate an anagram

Mayor Alcaide, Burgomaster, Casterbridge, Councilman, Porteeve, Provost, Whittington

Maze Labyrinth, Meander, Warren, Wilderness

MC Compere, Host, Ringmaster

Mead(ow) Flood, Grass, Haugh, Inch, Lea(se), Ley, Meath(e), ➤ PASTURE, Runnymede, Saeter, Salting, Water

Meagre Bare, Exiguous, Measly, Paltry, Pittance, Scant, Scrannel, Scranny, Skimpy, Skinny, Spare, Stingy, Thin

Meal(s) Barium, Board, Breakfast, Brunch, Buffet, Cassava, Cereal, Cholent, Chota-hazri, Collation, Cornflour, Cottoncake, Cou-cou, Cribble, Dejeune(r), Dinner, Drammock, Ervalenta, Fare, Farina, Flour, Food, Grits, Grout, Hangi, Lock, Lunch, Mandioc, Mandioc(c)a, Mani(h)oc, Melder, Meltith, Mensal, Mess, Mush, No-cake, Nosh, Nuncheon, Obento, Piece, Plate, Poi, Polenta, Porridge, Prandial, Prix fixe, Rac(c)ahout, Refection, Repast, Revalenta, Rijst(t)afel, Salep, Scambling, Scoff, Seder, Smorgasbord, Snack, Spread, Square, Supper, Takeaway, Tea, Tiffin, Tightener, Twalhours, Undern

Mean, Meaning, Meant Aim, Average, Base, Betoken, Caitiff, Connotation, Curmudgeon, Denotate, Denote, Design, Dirty, Drift, Essence, Ettle, Feck, Footy, Foul, Gist, Golden, Hang, Harmonic, Humble, Hunks, Ignoble, Illiberal, Imply, Import, Inferior, Intend, Intermediate, Low, Mang(e)y, Marrow, Medium, Mesquin, Method, Mid, Miserly, Narrow, Near, Nothing, One-horse, Ornery, Paltry, Petty, Pinch-penny, Pith, Point, Purport, ➤ PURPOSE, Ratfink, Revenue, Roinish, Roynish, Scall, Scrub, Scurvy, Semanteme, Semantic(s), Sememe, Sense, Shabby, Signify, Slight, Small, Sneaky, Snot, Sordid, Sparing, Spell, Stingy, Stink(ard), Stinty, Substance, Symbol, Thin, Threepenny, Tightwad, Two-bit, Value, Whoreson

Means Agency, Dint, Income, Media, Method, Mode, Opulence, Organ, Resources, Staple, Substance, Tactics, Ways

Measure(d), Measuring, Measurement Acre, Alnage, Anemometer, Aneroid, Angstrom, Anker, Ardeb, Are, Arpent, Arshin(e), As, Astrolabe, Aune, Barleycorn, Barrel, Barren, Bath, Bathometer, Bel, Boll, Bovate, Breadth, Burette, Bushel, By(e)law, Cab, Calibre, Cal(l)iper, Candela, Caneh, Carat, Centimetre, Chain, Chopin, Clove, Comb(e), Coomb, Cor, Cord, Coss, Coulomb, Crackdown, Cran, Crore, Cubage, Cubit, Cumec, Cusec, ➤ DANCE, Decalitre, Decibel, Denier, Depth, Diameter, ➤ DIMENSION, Distance, Dose, Double, Dram, Drastic, Electrometer, Ell, Em, En, Entropy, Epha(h), Erg, Ergometer, Etalon, Fat, Fathom, Fermi, Firkin, Firlot, Foot,

Furlong, Ga(u)ge, Gallon, Gavotte, Geodesy, Gill, Grain, Groma, Hanap, Height, Hide, Hin, Hogshead, Homer, Hydrometer, Hygrometer, Inch, Jigger, Joule, Kelvin, Kilerg, Kilogray, Kilometre, Koss, Lambert, Last, Lay, Lea, League(r), Lento, Ley, Liang, Ligne, Limit, Line, Lippie, Lippy, Liquid, Log, Loure, Lug, Lysimeter, Manometer, Maze, Mease, Metage, Mete(r), Metre, Micrometer, Mil, Mile, Millimetre, Modius, Mole, Morgan, Mott, Mu, Muid, Nail, Nipperkin, Noggin, Odometer, Of, Omer, Optic®, Oxgang, Pace, Parsec, Pascal, Peck, Perch, Photometer, Pint, Plumb, Pole, Pood, Pottle, Precaution, Prophylactic, Puncheon, Quart(er), Quickstep, Radius, Ream, Reau, Resistance, Riddle, Rod, Romer, Rood, Rope, Ruler, Run(d)let, Scale, Share, Shot, ➤ SIZE, Sleever, Sound, Span, Spondee, Stade, Stadia, Standard, Statute, Step, Steradian, Strike, Survey, Tape(-line), Tappet-hen, Telemeter, Tesla, Therm, Thou, Tierce, Titration, Toise, Token, Tot, Unit, Vara, Verst, Virgate, Volt, Warp, Waywiser, Weighbridge, Wey, Winchester, Yard, Yardstick

Meat(s) Bacon, Bard, Beef, Biltong, Brawn, Burger, Cabob, Carbonado, Carrion, Charcuterie, Chop, Collop, Confit, Croquette, Cut, Devon, Edgebone, Entrecote, Escalope, Essence, Fanny Adams, Fleishig, Fleishik, Flesh, Flitch, Force, Galantine, Gigot, Gobbet, Gosht, Griskin, Ham, Haslet, Jerky, Joint, Junk, Kabab, Kabob, Kebab, Kebob, Lamb, Loin, Luncheon, Mart, Mince, Mutton, Noisette, Offal, Olive, Pastrami, Piccata, Pith, Pork, Rillettes, Roast, Saddle, Sasatie, Satay, Schnitzel, Scran, Scrapple, Sey, Shashlik, Shishkebab, Sirloin, Spam®, Spare rib, Spatchcock, Steak, Tenderloin, Tongue, Veal, Venison, Vifda, Virgate, Vivda, Weiner schnitzel, Wurst

Mechanic(s) Apron-man, Artificer, Artisan, Banausic, Engineer, Fitter, Fundi, Hand, Journeyman, Kinematics, Kinetics, Operative, Statics, Technician

Mechanical, Mechanism Action, Apparatus, Auto, Banausic, Derailleur, Escapement, Gimmal, Instrument, Machinery, Movement, Organical, Pulley, Pushback, Servo, Trippet, Works

Medal(lion)(s) Award, Bar, Bronze, Decoration, Dickin, DSM, GC, George, Gold, Gong, Gorget, MM, Numismatic, Pan(h)agia, Purple Heart, Putty, Roundel, Silver, Touchpiece, VC, Vernicle

Mediate, Mediator ACAS, Arbitrate, Inercede, Interpose, Intervene, Liaison, Muti, Referee, Thirdsman, Trouble-shooter

Medical, Medicament, Medication, Medicine (chest) Alternative, Anodyne, Antacid, Antibiotic, Antidote, Antisepsis, Antiseptic, Arnica, Bi, Bismuth, Charm, Chiropody, Clinician, Complementary, Cordial, Corpsman, Cubeb, Curative, Defensive, Diapente, Dose, Drops, ➤ DRUG, Electuary, Elixir, Empirics, Enema, Excipient, Fall-trank, Febrifuge, Forensic, Galen, Galenism, Gutta, Herb, Herbal, Holistic, Hom(o)eopathy, Iatric(al), Industrial, Inro, Iodine, Iron, Laxative, Leechcraft, Lotion, Magnesia, Menthol, Mishmi, Mixture, Muti, Nephritic, Nervine, Nostrum, Nux vomica, Officinal, Oporice, Orthopoedics, Osteopath, Panacea, Paregoric, Patent, Pharmacy, Physic, Physical, Pill, Placebo, Potion, Poultice, Preparation, Preventive, Psionic, Psychiatry, Quinine, Radiology, Relaxative, ➤ REMEDY, Salve, Sanative, Senna, Serology, Simple, Specific, Steel, Stomachic, Stupe, Suppository, Syrup, Tablet, Tar-water, Tisane, Tonic, Trade, Treatment, Troche, Valerian, Veronal

Medieval Archaic, Feudal, Gothic, Med, Old, Trecento

Meditate, Meditation, Meditator Brood, Chew, Cogitate, Muse, Mystic, Ponder, Reflect, Reverie, Revery, Ruminate, Transcendental, Vipassana, Weigh, Zazen

Medium Agency, Average, Clairvoyant, Element, Ether, Even, Happy, Home, Intermediary, M, Magilp, Mean, Megilp, Midway, Milieu, Oils, Organ, Ouija, Press, Radio, Regular, Shaman, Spiritist, Spiritualist, Television, Telly, TV, Vehicle

Medley Charivari, Collection, Gallimaufry, Jumble, Macedoine, Melange, Mix, Pastiche, Patchwork, Pi(e), Pot-pourri, Quodlibet, Ragbag, Salad, Salmagundi, Series

▷**Medley** may indicate an anagram

Meek Docile, Griselda, Humble, Milquetoast, Patient, Tame

Meet(ing), Meeting place Abide, Abutment, AGM, Appointment, Apropos, Assemble, Assembly, Assignation, Audience, Baraza, Bosberaad, Camporee, Caucus, Chapterhouse, Chautauqua, Clash, Conclave, Concourse, Concur, Confluence, Confrontation, Congress, Connivance, Contact, Conterminous, Convene, Convent(icle), Convention, Converge, Conversazione, Convocation, Correspond, Cybercafé, Defray, Demo, EGM, Encounter, Ends, Face, Find,

Fit, For(e)gather, Forum, Fulfil, Gemot, Giron, Gorsedd, Guild, Gyeld, Gymkhana, Gyron, Howf(f), Hunt, Hustings, Indaba, Infall, Interface, Interview, Join, Junction, Korero, Liaise, Marae, Moot, Obviate, Occlusion, Occur, Oppose, Pay, Plenary, Plenum, Pnyx, Pow-wow, Prosper, Quadrivial, Quorate, Quorum, Races, Rally, Rencontre, Rencounter, Rendezvous, Reunion, Sabbat(h), Satisfy, Seance, See, Seminar, Session, Sit, Social, Suitable, Summit, Symposium, Synastry, Synaxis, Synod, Tackle, Tryst, Venue, Vestry, Wapinshaw, Wardmote, Workshop

Mellow Genial, Mature, Ripe, Smooth

Melody, Melodious Air, Arioso, Cabaletta, Cantabile, Cantilena, Cantus, Conductus, Counterpoint, Descant, Dulcet, Euphonic, Fading, Musical, Orphean, Plainsong, Ranz-des-vaches, Strain, Theme, Tunable, ➤ TUNE(FUL)

Melon(like) Cantaloup(e), Cas(s)aba, Gourd, Honeydew, Mango, Musk, Nar(r)as, Ogen, Pepo, Persian, Rock

Melt(ed), Melting Ablate, Colliquate, ➤ DISSOLVE, Eutectic, Eutexia, Flux, Found, Fusil(e), Liquescent, Liquid, Run, Smectic, Syntexis, Thaw, Touch

Member Adherent, Arm, Branch, Bro(ther), Chin, Confrère, Cornice, Crossbeam, Crypto, Direction, Felibre, Fellow, Forearm, Forelimb, Gremial, Insider, Leg, Limb, Longeron, M, MBE, Montant, MP, Organ, Part, Partisan, Private

Membrane, Membranous Caul, Film, Hymen, Pellicle, Rim, Scarious, Tela, Tissue, Velum, Web

Memento, Memoir Keepsake, Locket, Relic, Remembrancer, Souvenir, Token, Trophy

Memo(randum) Bordereau, Cahier, Chit, IOU, Jot, Jurat, Minute, Note, Notepad, ➤ REMINDER

Memorable, Memorise, Memory Bubble, Con, Core, Echoic, Engram(ma), Flash (bulb), Get, Iconic, Immortal, Learn, Memoriter, Mind, Mneme, Mnemonic, Mnemosyne, Notable, Photographic, RAM, Recall, ➤ REMEMBER, Retention, Retrospection, ROM, Ro(a)te, Samskara, Short-term, Souvenir, Sovenance, Virtual

Memorial Cenotaph, Cromlech, Ebenezer, Gravestone, Hatchment, Marker, Monument, Mount Rushmore, Obelisk, Plaque, Relic, Statue, Tomb, Trophy

Menace, Menacing Danger, Endanger, Foreboding, Minatory, Peril, Pest, Threat(en)

Mend Beet, Bete, Bushel, Cobble, Correct, Darn, Fix, Heal, Improved, Patch, Piece, Recover, Remedy, ➤ REPAIR, Set, Sew, Solder, Trouble-shoot

Menial Drudge, Drug, Eta, Fag, Flunkey, Lowly, Scullion, Servile, Toady, Underling

▷**Mental** may indicate the chin

Mention(ed) Allusion, Bename, Benempt, Broach, Bynempt, Citation, Hint, Name, Notice, Quote, Refer, Speech, State, Suggest, Touch

Menu Card, Carte, Carte du jour, Cascading, Fare, List, Table d'hôte, Tariff

Mercenary Arnaout, Condottiere, Freelance, Greedy, Hack, Hessian, Hireling, Landsknecht, Legionnaire, Pindaree, Pindari, Rutter, Sordid, Spoilsman, Venal, Wildgeese

Merchandise Cargo, Goods, Line, Produce, Ware(s)

Merchant(man) Abudah, Antonio, Broker, Bun(n)ia, Burgher, Chandler, Chap, Crare, Crayer, Dealer, Factor, Flota, Hoastman, Importer, Jobber, Magnate, Marcantant, Mercer, Monger, Négociant, Pedlar, Polo, Retailer, Shipper, Speed, Stapler, Trader, Vintner, Wholesaler

Merciful, Mercy Amnesty, Charity, Clement, Compassionate, Grace, Humane, Kind, Kyrie, Lenient, Miserere, Misericord(e), Pacable, Pity, Quarter, Ruth, Sparing

Merciless Cruel, Hard, Hard-hearted, Inclement, Pitiless

Mere(ly) Allenarly, Bare, Common, Lake, Pond, Pool, Pure, Sheer, Tarn, Very

Merge(r), Merging Amalgamate, Blend, Coalesce, Consolidate, Die, Fusion, Incorporate, Interflow, Meld, Melt, Mingle, Syncretism, Unify, Unite

Merit(ed) CL, Condign, Deserve, Due, Earn, Found, Rate, Virtue, Worth(iness)

Mess(y) Balls-up, Bedraggled, Boss, Botch, Canteen, Caudle, Chaos, Clutter, Cock-up, Failure, Farrago, Fiasco, Flub, Garboil, Glop, G(l)oop, Guddle, Gunge, Gunk, Gun-room, Hash, Horlicks, Hotch-potch, Hugger-mugger, Imbroglio, Lash-up, Louse, Mash, Meal, Mismanage, Mix, Mixter-maxter, Modge, Muck, Muff, Muss, Mux, Pi(e), Piss-up, Plight, Pollute, Pottage, Screw-up, Scungy, Shambles, Shambolic, Shemozzle, Sight, Slaister, Smudge, Snafu, Soss, Sty, Sully, Untidy, Whoopsie

Message(s) Aerogram, Bull, Bulletin, Cable, Contraplex, Dépêche, Despatch, Dispatch, Errand, Flame, Missive, News, Note, Pager, Posting, Postscript, Radiogram, Rumour, Signal, Slogan, SOS, Subtext, Telegram, Telephone, Telex, Tidings, Wire, ➤ WORD

Messenger Angel, Apostle, Azrael, Caddie, Caddy, Chaprassi, Chuprassy, Courier, Culver, Despatch-rider, Emissary, Envoy, Gaga, Gillie Whitefoot, Hatta, Herald, Hermes, Internuncio, Iris, Ladas, Mercury, Nuncio, Peon, Post, Pursuivant, Runner, Send

Messiah Christ, Emmanuel, Immanuel, Mahdi, Mashiach, Saviour, Son of man

Metal(lic) Aglet, Aiglet, Aiguillette, Base, Bell, Billon, Brassy, Death, Filler, Foil, Gib, Heavy, Hot, Ingot, Jangling, Mineral, Noble, Ore, Precious, Protore, Regulus, Speiss, Sprue, Taggers, Terbic, Tole, Type

▷**Metamorphosing** may indicate an anagram

Metaphor Conceit, Figure, Image, Kenning, Mixed, Symbol, Trope, Tropical

Meteor(ite) Achondrite, Aerolite, Aerosiderite, Bolide, Chondrite, Comet, Drake, Fireball, Germinid, Leonid, Perseid, Siderite, Siderolite, Star(dust), Stony

Method(ical) Art, Billings, Formula, Gram's, Line, Manner, Mode, Modus, Modus operandi, Monte Carlo, Montessori, Neat, Orderly, Painstaking, Ploy, Procedure, Process, Stanislavski, ➤ SYSTEM, Tactics, Technique, Way

Metre Alexandrine, Amphibrach, Amphimacer, Anapaest, Antispast, Arsis, Cadence, Choliamb, Choree, Choriamb, Common, Galliambic, Iambic, M, Prosody, Rhythm, Scansion, Scazon, Spondee, Strophe, Trochee

Microphone Bug, Crystal, Mike, Radio, Throat

Mid Amongst

Midday Meridian, N, Noon

Middle, Middling Active, Basion, Centre, Core, Crown, Enteron, Eye, Girth, Heart, Loins, Median, Mediocre, Meridian, Meseraic, Mesial, Mesne, Meso, Midriff, Moderate, Noon, Passive, Turn, Twixt, Wa(i)st

Middleman Broker, Comprador(e), Diaphragm, Interlocutor, Intermediary, Jobber, Median, Navel, Regrater, Regrator

Midget Dwarf, Homunculus, Lilliputian, Pygmy, Shrimp

Might(iness), Mighty Force, Main, Mote, Nibs, Potence, ➤ POWER, Prowess, Puissant, Should, Strength

Migrate, Migration, Migratory Colonise, Diapedesis, Diaspora, Drift, Eelfare, Exodus, Fleet, Run, Tre(c)k

Mild(ly) Balmy, Benign, Bland, Clement, Euphemism, Genial, Gentle, Lenient, Litotes, Mansuete, Meek, ➤ MODERATE, Pacific, Patient, Sarcenet, Sars(e)net, Temperate

Mile(s) Coverdale, Geographical, Li, Milliary, Nautical, Roman, Royal, Soldier, Square, Standish

Militant Activist, Aggressive, Hezbollah, Hizbollah, Hizbullah, Hostile, Ireton, Martial

Military Battailous, Commando, Hawkish, Landwehr, Mameluke, Martial, Presidio, Soldatesque, West Point

Militia Guard, Minuteman, Reserve, Trainband, Yeomanry

Milk(er), Milky Acidophilus, Beestings, Bland, Bleed, Bonny-clabber, Bristol, Casein, Colostrum, Condensed, Creamer, Crud, Curd, Emulge, Evaporated, Exploit, Galactic, Glacier, Goat's, Jib, Kephir, Kephir, K(o)umiss, Lactation, Lacteal, Latex, Madzoon, Magnesia, Matzoon, Mess, Opaline, Pinta, Posset, Sap, Shedder, Skim(med), Soya, Squeeze, Strippings, Stroke, Suckle, UHT, Whig, Yaourt, Yogh(o)urt

Mill(ing), Mills Aswarm, Barker's, Economist, Grind(er), Hayley, Kibble, Knurl, Melder, Molar, Nurl, Post, Press, Pug, Quern, Reave, Rob, Rolling, Satanic, Scutcher, Smock, Stamp, Strip, Surge, Thou, Tower, Water, Works

Mime, Mimic(ry) Ape, Batesian, Copycat, Farce, Imitate, Impersonate, Mina, Mullerian, Mummer, Sturnine

Mind(er) Aide, Beware, Brain, Genius, Handler, ➤ HEED, Herd, Id, Intellect, Psyche, Psychogenic, Resent, Sensorium, Tabula rasa, Tend, Thinker, Wit, Woundwort

Mine Acoustic, Bomb, Bonanza, Burrow, Camouflet, Claymore, Colliery, Dane-hole, Dig(gings), Egg, Eldorado, Excavate, Explosive, Fougade, Fougasse, Gallery, Gob, Golconda, Gopher, Grass, Land, Limpet, Magnetic, Nostromo, Open-cast, Ophir, Pit, Placer, Prospect, Sap, Set(t), Show, Sonic, Stannary, Stope, Strike, Undercut, Wheal, Win, Workings

Miner, Mine-worker, Mine-working Butty-gang, Collier, Cutter, Digger, Forty-niner, Geordie, Leaf, Molly Maguire, NUM, Oncost(man), Pitman, Shot-firer, Stall, Tributer, UDM

Mineral Azurite, Cystolith, Dolomitic, Endomorph, Idiomorphic, Macle, Paramorph, Perimorph, Pseudomorph, YAG

Mingle Blend, Consort, Interfuse, Mell, ➤ MIX, Participate, Socialise, Unite

Minimise, Minimum (range) Bare, Downplay, Fewest, Least, Neap, Shoestring, Stime, Threshold, Undervalue

▷**Minimum of** may indicate the first letter

Minister Ambassador, Attend, Buckle-beggar, Chancellor, Chaplain, Cleric, Coarb, Commissar, Deacon, Dewan, Diplomat, Divine, Dominee, Dominie, D(i)wan, Envoy, Mas(s)john, Mes(s)john, Moderator, Nurse, Officiant, Padre, Parson, Peshwa, Preacher, Predikant, Presbyter, Rector, Secretary, Seraskier, ➤ SERVE, Stickit, Tend, Visier, Vizier

Ministry Defence, Department, Dept, DoE, MOD, MOT, Orders, Service

Minor(ity) Child, Comprimario, Ethnic, Faction, Few, Infant, Junior, Less, Minutia, Nonage, One-horse, Petty, Pupillage, Slight, Trivial, Ward

Mint Aim, Bugle-weed, Catnip, Coin, Ettle, Fortune, Herb, Horse, Humbug, Labiate, Monarda, Monetise, Nep, New, Penny-royal, Polo®, Poly, Selfheal, Stamp, Strike, Unused, Utter

Minute(s), Minutiae Acta, Alto, Degree, Detailed, Diatom, Entry, Infinitesimal, Little, Micron, Mo, Mu, Nano-, Resume, Small, Teen(t)sy, Teeny, Tine, Tiny, Trivia, Tyne, Wee

Miracle Cana, Marvel, Merel(l), Meril, Morris, Mystery, Phenomenon, Thaumaturgic, Theurgy, Wonder

Mirror(ed) Alasnam, Busybody, Cambuscan, Catoptric, Cheval, Coelostat, Conde, Enantiomorph, Glass, Image, Imitate, Lao, Merlin, Pierglass, Psyche, Rearview, ➤ REFLECT, Reynard, Sign, Specular, Speculum, Stone, Vulcan, Wing

▷**Misalliance** may indicate an anagram

Miscellaneous, Miscellany Assortment, Chow, Collectanea, Diverse, Misc, Olio, Omnium-gatherum, Potpourri, Raft, Ragbag, Sundry, Various

Mischief(-maker), Mischievous Ate, Bale, Bane, Cantrip, Cloots, Devilment, Diablerie, Dido, Disservice, Gremlin, Harm, Hellery, Hellion, Hob, Imp, Injury, Jinks, Larrikin, Malicho, Mallecho, Nickum, Owl-spiegle, Pestilent, Pickle, Prank,

Puckish, Rascal, Scally(wag), Scamp, Scapegrace, Shenanigans, Spriteful, Tricksy, Wag, Wicked

Misconception Delusion, Idol(on), Idolum, Misunderstanding

▷**Misdelivered** may indicate an anagram

Miser(ly) Carl, Cheapskate, Cheese-parer, Close, Curmudgeon, Gare, Grasping, Harpagon, Hunks, Marner, Meanie, Mingy, Pennyfather, Pinch-commons, Puckfist, Runt, Scrape-good, Scrape-penny, Screw, Scrimping, Scrooge, Skinflint, Snudge, Storer, Tightwad, Timon

Miserable, Misery Abject, Bale, Distress, Dole, Forlorn, Gloom, Grief, Hell, Joyless, Lousy, Perdition, Sorry, Sourpuss, Tragic, Triste, ➤ UNHAPPY, Woe(begone), Wretched

Misfortune Accident, Affliction, Bale, Calamity, Curse, Disaster, Distress, Dole, Hex, Ill, Reverse, Rewth, Ruth, Wroath

▷**Misguided** may indicate an anagram

Mislead(ing) Blind, Cover-up, Deceive, Delude, Dupe, Equivocate, Fallacious, False, Gag, Red herring, Runaround

▷**Misled** may indicate an anagram

Mismanage Blunder, Bungle, Muddle

Misprint Error, Literal, Slip, Typo

Misrepresent(ation) Abuse, Belie, Calumny, Caricature, Colour, Distort, Falsify, Garble, Lie, Slander, Traduce

Miss(ing) Abord, Avoid, Colleen, Desiderate, Dodge, Drib, Err(or), Fail, Forego, Gal, ➤ GIRL, Kumari, Lack, Lass, Link, Lose, Mademoiselle, Maid, Maiden, Mile, Muff(et), Neglect, Negligence, Omit, Otis, Overlook, Senorita, Skip, Spinster, Unmeet, Wanting

▷**Miss** may refer to Missouri

Missile Air-to-air, Ammo, Anti-ballistic, Arrow, Artillery, Atlas, Ball, Ballistic, Blue streak, Bolas, Bomb, Boomerang, Brickbat, Bullet, Cruise, Dart, Dingbat, Doodlebug, Dum-dum, Exocet®, Fléchette, Grenade, Harpoon, ICBM, Interceptor, Jired, Kiley, Kyley, Kylie, Maverick, Minuteman, MIRV, Missive, Onion, Patriot, Pellet, Pershing, Polaris, Poseidon, Quarrel, Rocket, SAM, Scud, Shell, Shot, Side-winder, Smart bomb, Snowball, Spear, SSM, Standoff, Styx, Surface to air, Surface to surface, Thor, Titan, Torpedo, Tracer, Trident, UAM, Warhead

Mission(ary) Aidan, Alamo, Antioch, Apostle, Assignment, Bethel, Caravan, Charge, Delegation, Embassage, Embassy,

Errand, Evangelist, Iona, Legation, Livingstone, LMS, Message, NASA, Op, Paul, Quest, Reclaimer, Task, Vocation

Mist(y) Blur, Brume, Cloud, Dew, Drow, Fog, Haar, Haze, Hoar, Miasma, Moch, Nebular, Niflheim, Rack, Roke, Scotch, Sfumato, Smir(r), Smog, Smur, Vapour

Mistake(n) Bish, Bloomer, Blooper, Blunder, Boner, Booboo, Boss, Botch, Clanger, Clinker, Confound, Deluded, Erratum, Error, Fault, Floater, Flub, Fluff, Gaffe, Goof, Howler, Incorrect, Lapse, Malapropism, Miss, Muff, Nod, Oversight, Plonker, Pratfall, ➤ SLIP, Slip-up, Solecism, Stumer, Trip, Typo

▷**Mistake(n)** may indicate an anagram

Mistress Amie, Aspasia, Canary-bird, Chatelaine, Concubine, Courtesan, Goodwife, Herself, Hussif, Inamorata, Instructress, Lady, Leman, Maintenon, Montespan, Mrs, Natural, Paramour, Stepney, Teacher, Wardrobe, Wife

Mistrust Doubt, Gaingiving, Suspect, Suspicion

Misunderstand(ing) Disagreement, Discord, Mistake

Misuse Abuse, Defalcate, Malappropriate, Malapropism, Maltreat, Perversion, Torment

Mix(ed), Mixture, Mix-up Alloy, Amalgam, Associate, Assortment, Attemper, Balderdash, Bigener, Bland, Blend, Blunge, Brew, Card, Caudle, Chow, Cocktail, Co-meddle, Compo, Compound, Conglomerate, Consort, Cross, Disperse, Dolly, Drammock, Embroil, Emulsion, Farrago, Garble, Grill, Griqua, Heather, Hobnob, Hotchpotch, Hybrid, Imbroglio, Interlace, Intermingle, Jumble, Lace, Lard, Linctus, Load, Macedoine, Matisse, Meddle, Medley, Melange, Mell, Meng(e), Ment, Mess, Mestizo, Ming(le), Miscellaneous, Miscellany, Mishmash, Mong, Motley, Muddle, Muss(e), Neapolitan, Octaroon, Octoroon, Olio, Olla, Pi(e), Potin, Pouswowdie, Powsowdy, Praiseach, Promiscuous, Raggle-taggle, Ragtag, Salad, Scramble, Stew, Stir, Temper, Through-other, Yblent

▷**Mixed** may indicate an anagram

Moan(ing) Beef, Bleat, Groan, Hone, Keen, ➤ LAMENT, Meane, Plangent, Sough, Wail, W(h)inge

Mob(ster) Army, Assail, Canaille, Crew, Crowd, Gang, Herd, Hoi-polloi, Hoodlum, Lynch, Ochlocrat, Press, Rabble, Raft, Ragtag, Riff-raff, Rout, Scar-face

Mobile, Mobilise, Mobility Donna, Fluid, Movable, Plastic, Rally, Thin, Upward(ly), Vagile, Vertical

Mock(ery), Mocking Ape, Banter, Chaff, Chyack, Cod, Cynical, Deride, Derisory, Dor, Ersatz, False, Farce, Fleer, Flout, Gab, Geck, Gibe, Guy, Imitation, Irony, Irrisory, ➤ JEER, Jibe, Lampoon, Mimic, Narquois, Paste, Pillorise, Rail(lery), Ridicule, Sacrilege, Sardonic, Satirise, Scout, Sham, Simulate, Slag, Travesty, Wry

Mode Convention, Fashion, Form, Manner, Rate, Step, Style, Ton

Model(ler) Archetype, Bozzetto, Cast, Copy, Diorama, Doll, Dummy, Ecorché, Effigy, Epitome, Example, Exemplar, Fictor, Figure, Figurine, Icon, Ideal, Image, Instar, Jig, Last, Layman, Manakin, Manikin, Mannequin, Maquette, Mock-up, ➤ MOULD, Norm, Original, Orrery, Parade, Paragon, Pattern, Pilot, Pose(r), Posture-maker, Prototype, Replica, Sedulous, Sitter, Specimen, Standard, Superwaif, T, Template, Templet, Terrella, Toy, Type, Typify, Waif, Waxwork

▷**Model(s)** may indicate an anagram

Moderate(ly), Moderation Abate, Allay, Alleviate, Average, Centre, Chasten, Continent, Diminish, Discretion, Ease, Gentle, Girondist, Ho, Lessen, Lukewarm, Measure, Medium, Menshevik, Mezzo, Middling, Mild, Mitigate, OK, Politique, Reason(able), Slake, So-so, Temper(ate), Tolerant, Tone, Via media, Wet

Modern(ise) AD, Aggiornamento, Contemporary, Fresh, Latter(-day), Neonomian, Neoterical, ➤ NEW, Present-day, Progressive, Recent, Swinger, Update

Modest(y) Aidos, Blaise, Chaste, Decent, Demure, Humble, Ladylike, Maidenly, Mim, Mussorgsky, Propriety, Prudish, Pudency, Pure, Reserved, Shame, Shy, Unpretending, Unpretentious, Verecund

Modifiable, Modification, Modify Adapt, Alter, Backpedal, Change, Enhance, Extenuate, H, Leaven, Plastic, Qualify, Retrofit, Soup, Streamline, Temper, Vary

Moist(en), Moisture Baste, Bedew, Damp, Dank, De(a)w, Humect, Latch, Love-in-a-mist, Madefy, Mesarch, Nigella, Sponge, Wet

▷**Moither** may indicate an anagram

Molecular, Molecule Atom, Gram, Iota, Quark

Mollusc(s) Bivalve, Malacology, ➤ SHELLFISH, Slug, Snail, Spat, Univalve, Veliger

Moment(s), Momentous Bit, Flash, Import, Instant, Jiffy, ➤ MINUTE, Mo, Nonce, Pun(c)to, Sands, Sec, Shake, Stound, Stownd, Tick, Time, Trice, Twinkling, Weighty, Wink

Momentum Impetus, L, Speed, Thrust

Monarch(y) Autocrat, Butterfly, Crown, Emperor, HM, Karling, King, Potentate, Queen, Raine, Reign, Ruler, Tsar

Monastery Abbey, Abthane, Charterhouse, Chartreuse, Cloister, Community, Gompa, Hospice, Lamaserai, Lamasery, Laura, Priory, Vihara, Wat

Monastic Abthane, Celibate, Holy, Monkish, Oblate, Secluded

Monetary, Money Ackers, Akkas, Allowance, Annat, Ante, Assignat, Banco, Batta, Blood, Blunt, Boodle, Bottle, Brass, Bread, Cabbage, Capital, Cash, Change, Chink, ➤ COIN, Collateral, Conscience, Currency, Danger, Dib(s), Dingbat, Dosh, Dust, Easy, Even, Fat, Fee, Float, Folding, Fonds, Fund, Funny, Gelt, Gilt, Gold, Grant, Gravy, Greens, Hoot, Hot, Hush, Ingots, Investment, Kale, Key, L, Lolly, Loot, Lucre, M, Mammon, Maundy, Mazuma, Means, Mint, Moola(h), Needful, Nest-egg, Note, Numismatic, Nummary, Oaker, Ochre, Offertory, Oof, Outlay, P, Packet, Peanuts, Pecuniary, Pelf, Pin, Plastic, Plum, Pocket, Posh, Prize, Proceeds, Profit, Protection, Purse, Ready, Rebate, Resources, Revenue, Rhino, Rowdy, Salt(s), Scratch, Scrip, Seed, Shin-plaster, Ship, Siller, Silver, Smart, Soap, Spondulicks, Stake, Sterling, Stuff, Sugar, Sum, Table, Takings, Tin, Tranche, Viaticum, Wad, Wealth, Wonga

Monitor Detect, Goanna, Iguana, Lizard, Observe, Prefect, Record, Track, Warship, Watchdog, Worral, Worrel

Monk(s) Abbot, Archimandrite, Augustinian, Austin, Basilian, Bede, Beghard, Benedictine, Bernardine, Bethlehemite, Black, Bonze, Brother, Bruno, Caedmon, Caloyer, Carthusian, Celestine, Cellarist, Cenobite, Coenobite, Cowl, Dan, Dervish, Dom, Dominican, Friar, General, Hermit, Hesychast, Hildebrand, Ignorantine, Jacobin, Jacobite, Jerome, Lama, Mendel, Norbertine, Oblate, Olivetan, Order, Prior, Rakehell, Rasputin, Recluse, Recollect, Roshi, Salesian, Savonarola, Sub-prior, Talapoin, Theatine, Thelonius, Thomas à Kempis, Trappist, Votary

Monkey Anger, Ape, Catar(r)hine, Grease, Kippage, Meddle, Powder, Rage, Ram, Simian, Tamper, Trip-hammer, Troop, Tup, Wrath

Monologue Patter, Rap, Recitation, Soliloquy, Speech

Monopolise, Monopoly Appalto, Bloc, Cartel, Corner, Engross, Octroi, Régie, Trust

▷ **Monsoon** may indicate weekend (Mon soon)

Monster, Monstrous Alecto, Asmodeus, Bandersnatch, Behemoth, Bunyip, Caliban, Cerberus, Cete, Chim(a)era, Cockatrice, Colossal, Cyclops, Deform, Div, Dragon, Echidna, Enormous, Erebus, Erl-king, Eten, Ettin, Fiend, Fire-drake, Frankenstein, Freak, Geryon, Ghost, Giant, Gila, Golem, Gorgon, Green-eyed, Grendel, Harpy, Huge, Hydra, Jabberwock, Kraken, Lamia, Leviathan, Mastodon, Medusa, Minotaur, Moloch, Nessie, Nicker, Nightmare, Ogre, Ogr(e)ish, Orc, Outrageous, Pongo, Satyral, Scylla, Shadow, Simorg, Simurg(h), Siren, Skull, Snark, Spectre, Sphinx, Spook, Stegodon, Stegosaur, Succubus, Teras, Teratoid, Troll, Unnatural, Vampire, Vast, Wendego, Wendigo, Wer(e)wolf, Wyvern, Yowie

Month(ly) Ab, Abib, Adar, April, Asadha, Asvina, August, Bhadrapada, Brumaire, Bul, Cheshvan, Chislev, December, Dhu-al-Hijjah, Dhu-al-Qadah, Elul, February, Floreal, Frimaire, Fructidor, Germinal, Hes(h)van, Iy(y)ar, January, July, Jumada, June, Jysaitha, Kartuka, Kisleu, Kislev, Lide, Lunar, Magha, March, Margasirsa, May, Messidor, Mo, Moharram, Moon, Muharram, Muharrem, Nisan, Nivose, November, October, Periodical, Phalguna, Pluviose, Prairial, Rabia, Rajab, Ramadan, Safar, Saphar, September, S(h)ebat, Sha(a)ban, Shawwal, Sivan, Solar, Tammuz, Tebeth, Thermidor, Tisri, Vaisakha, Veadar, Vendemiaire, Ventose

Monument Ancient, Arch, Archive, Cenotaph, Column, Cromlech, Dolmen, Henge, Megalith, Memorial, Menhir, National, Pantheon, Pyramid, Stele(ne), Stone, Stonehenge, Stupa, Talayot, Tombstone, Trilith, Trilithon, Urn

Mood(y) Active, Anger, Atmosphere, Attitude, Capricious, Dudgeon, Enallage, Fit, Glum, Grammar, Humour, Hump, Imperative, Morale, Optative, Passive, Peat, Pet, Revivalist, Sankey, Spleen, Subjunctive, Temper, Tid, Tone, Tune, Vein, Vinegar, Whim

Moon(light), Moony Aah, Alignak, Aningan, Apogee, Artemis, Astarte, Callisto, Cheese, Cynthia, Diana, Epact, Eye, Flit, Full, Ganymede, Gibbous, Glimmer, Grimaldi, Harvest, Hecate, Hunter's, Hyperion, Inconstant, Juliet, Leda, Lucina, Luna(r), Mani, Mascon, McFarlane's Buat, Month, Mope, Nocturne, Octant, Paddy's lantern, Paraselene, Pasiphaë, Phoebe, Proteus, Raker, Satellite, Selene, Set, Shot, Sickle, Sideline, Silvery, Sonata, Stargaze, Stone, Syzygy, Thebe, Thoth, Titan, Triton, Umbriel, Wander

Mop(ping) Dwile, Flibbertigibbet, Girn, Glib, Shag, Squeegee, Squilgee, Swab, Swob, Thatch, ➤ WIPE

Moral(ity), Morals Apologue, Deontic, Ethic(al), Ethos, Everyman, Fable, High-minded, Integrity, Precept, Principled, Puritanic, Righteous, Tag, Upright, Virtuous

Morale Ego, Mood, Spirit, Zeal

Morbid(ity) Anasarca, Ascites, Cachaemia, Dropsy, Ectopia, Ghoul(ish), Gruesome, Pathological, Plethora, Prurient, Religiose, Sick, Sombre

More Additional, Else, Extra, Increase, Less, Mae, Merrier, Mo(e), ➤ NO MORE, Over, Piu, Plus, Stump, Utopia

Morning Ack-emma, Am, Antemeridian, Dawn, Daybreak, Early, Matin(al), Morrow

Morose Acid, Boody, Churlish, Cynical, Gloomy, Glum, Grum, Moody, Sour-eyed, Sullen, Surly

Morsel Bit, Bite, Bouche, Canape, Crumb, Dainty, Morceau, Ort, Scrap, Sippet, Sop, Tidbit, Titbit

Mortal(ity) Averr(h)oism, Being, Deathly, ➤ FATAL, Grave, Human, Lethal, Yama

Mortgage(e) Balloon, Bond, Cedula, Debt, Dip, Encumbrance, Endowment, Hypothecator, Loan, Pledge, Wadset(t)

Mosaic Buhl, Cosmati, Inlay, Intarsia, Musive, Pietra dura, Screen, Terrazzo, Tessella(te), Tessera

➤**Moslem** see MUSLIM

Mosque Dome of the Rock, El Aqsa, Jami, Masjid, Medina

Moss(y) Acrogen, Agate, Bryology, Carrag(h)een, Ceylon, Club, Fog, Fontinalis, Hag(g), Hypnum, Iceland, Irish, Lecanoram, Lichen, Litmus, Long, Lycopod, Marsh, Musci,

Muscoid, Parella, Peat, Polytrichum, Reindeer, Rose, Scale, Selaginella, Spanish, Sphagnum, Staghorn, Usnea, Wolf's claw

Most Largest, Major, Maxi(mum), Optimum

Moth(s) Imago, Lepidoptera, Woodborer

Mother Bearer, Church, Cognate, Cosset, Courage, Dam(e), Dregs, Ean, Earth, Eve, Generatrix, Genetrix, Goose, Hubbard, Lees, Ma, Machree, Mam(a), Mamma, Mater, Maya, Minnie, Mom, Multipara, Mum, Native, Nature, Nourish, Parity, Pourer, Reverend, Shipton, Superior, Surrogate, Wit

▷**Mother** may indicate a lepidopterist (moth-er)

Motion Early day, Gesture, Harmonic, Impulse, Kinetic, Move, Offer, Perpetual, PL, Proper, Proposal, Rack and pinion, Rider, Slow, Spasm

Motionless Doggo, Frozen, Immobile, Quiescent, Stagnant, Stasis, Still, Stock-still

Motive, Motivate, Motivation Actuate, Cause, Ideal, Impel, Incentive, Intention, Mainspring, Mobile, Object, ➤ PURPOSE, Spur, Ulterior

Motor(boat) Auto, Car, Dynamo, Engine, Hot rod, Inboard, Induction, Jato, Linear, Outboard, Scooter, Thruster, Turbine

Motorway Autobahn, Autopista, Autoput, Autoroute, Autostrada, Expressway, M(1)

Motto Device, Epigraph, Gnome, Impresa, Imprese, Impress(e), Legend, Maxim, Mot, Poesy, Posy, Saw

Mould(ed), Moulding, Mouldy Accolade, Architrave, Archivolt, Astragal, Baguette, Beading, Bend, Black, Bread, Briquet(te), Cabling, Casement, Cast(ing), Chessel, Chill, Cornice, Coving, Cyma, Dariole, Die, Dripstone, Echinus, Egg and dart, Flong, ➤ FORM, Foughty, Fungus, Fust, Gadroon, Godroon, Hood-mould, Hore, Humus, Injection, Matrix, Mildew, Model, Mool, Mucid, Must, Noble rot, Ogee, Ovolo, Palmette, Papier-mâché, Phycomycete, Pig, Plasm(a), Plastic, Plat, Prototype, Prunt, Reglet, Rot, Rust, Sandbox, Scotia, Shape, Smut, Soil, Stringcourse, Tailor, Talon, Template, Templet, Timbale, Tondino, Torus, Water table

Mound Agger, Bank, Barp, Barrow, Berm, Cone, Dike, Dun, Embankment, Heap, Hog, Kurgan, Mogul, Monticule, Mote, Motte, Orb, Pile, Pingo, Pome, Rampart, Rampire, Tuffet

Mount(ed), Mounting, Mountain (peak) ➤ ALP(INE), Aspiring, Back, Barp, Ben, Berg, Board, Breast, Butter, Chain, Charger, ➤ CLIMB, Colt, Cordillera, Cradle, Dew, Display, Djebel, Dolly, Escalade, Frame, Hinge, Horse, Jebel, Massif, Monture, Mt, Nunatak, Orography, Orology, Passe-partout, Pike, Pile, Pin, Pownie, Quad, Ride, Saddlehorse, Scalado, Scale, Set, Soar, Stage, ➤ STEED, Stie, Strideways, Tel, Tier, Tor, Turret, Upgo, Volcano

Mountaineer(ing) Abseil, Alpinist, Arnaut, Climber, Hunt, Sherpa, Smythe, Upleader

Mourn(er), Mournful, Mourning Adonia, Black, Dirge, Dole, Elegiac, Grieve, Grone, Hatchment, Keen, Lament, Niobe, Omer, Ovel, Plangent, Saulie, Shivah, Shloshim, Sorrow, Tangi, Threnetic, Threnodial, Weeds, Weep, Willow

Mouse(like), Mousy Black eye, Deer, Dun(nart), Flitter, Harvest, Honey, Icon, Jumping, Meadow, Muridae, Murine, Pocket, Rodent, Shiner, Shrew, Vermin, Waltzer

Mouth(piece) Aboral, Bazoo, Beak, Buccal, Cakehole, Chapper, Check, Crater, Debouchure, Delta, Embouchure, Estuary, Fipple, Gab, Gam, Gills, Gob, Gum, Hard, Kisser, Labret, Lawyer, Lip, Manubrium, Maw, Neb, Orifex, Orifice, Os, Oscule, Ostium, Outfall, Port, Potato trap, Speaker, Spokesman, Spout, Stoma, Swazzle, Swozzle, Teat, Trap, Uvula

Move(d), Mover, Movable, Moving Act, Actuate, Affect, Andante, Astir, Budge, Carry, Catapult, Chattel, Coast, Counter-measure, Coup, Decant, Démarche, Displace, Disturb, Ease, Eddy, Edge, Evoke, False, Flit, Fluctuate, Forge, Frogmarch, Gambit, Gee, Go, Gravitate, Haulier, Hustle, Inch, Instigate, Jee, Jink, Kedge, Kinetic, Link, Mill, Mobile, Mosey, Motivate, Nip, Opening, Overcome, Pan, Poignant, Proceed, Progress, Prompt, Propel, Qui(t)ch, Quicken, Rearrange, Redeploy, Relocate, Remuage, Retrocede, Roll, Rouse, Roust, Scoot, Scramble, Scuttle, Sell, Shift, Shog, Shoo, Shunt, Sidle, Skelp, Slide, Soulful, Spank, Steal, Steer, Step, Stir, Styre, Tack, Tactic, Taxi, Transfer, Translate, Translocate, Transplant, Transport, Troll, Trundle, Turn, Unstep, Up, Upsticks, Vacillate, Vagile, Veronica, Volt(e), Wag, Wapper, Whirry, Whish, Whisk, Whiz, Wuther, Yank, Zoom, Zwischenzug

Movement Action, Allegro, Allemande, Almain, Andantino, Antic, Bandwagon, Cadence, Cell, Chartism, Course, Crusade,

Dadaism, Diaspora, Diastole, Ecumenical, Enlightenment, Eoka, Eurhythmics, Expressionism, Feint, Fianchetto, Fris(ka), Gait, Geneva, Gesture, Groundswell, Indraught, Intermezzo, Jor, Kata, Kinesis, Kin(a)esthetic, Kinetic, Larghetto, Largo, Lassu, Ligne, Manoeuvre, Nastic, Naziism, New Wave, Nihilism, Operation, Orchesis, Oxford, Parallax, Pase, Passade, Piaffer, Pincer, Play, Poule, Poulette, Procession, Progress, Punk, REM, Romantic, Rondo, Scherzo, Sinn Fein, Stir(e), Swadeshi, Taxis, Telekinesis, Tide, Trend, ➤ UNITA, Verismo, Veronica, Wheel, Zionism

Mow(er), Mowing Aftermath, Cut, Grimace, Lattermath, Math, Rawing, Rawn, Rowan, Rowen, Rowing, Scytheman, Shear, Sickle, Tass, Trim

MP Backbencher, Commoner, Gendarme, Member, Provost, Redcap, Retread, Snowdrop, Stannator, Statist, TD

Much Abundant, Far, Glut, Great, Lots, Mickle, Scad, Sore, Viel

Muck (up), Mucky Bungle, Dirt, Dung, Island, Leep, Manure, Midden, Mire, Rot, Soil, Sordid, Spoil, Stercoral

Mud(dy) Adobe, Clabber, Clart, Clay, Cutcha, Dirt, Dubs, Fango, Glaur, Gutter, Kacha, Lahar, Lairy, Limous, ➤ MIRE, Moya, Ooze, Peloid, Pise, Riley, Roily, Salse, Slab, Slake, Sleech, Slime, Slob, Slough, Sludge, Slur(ry), Slush, Turbid

Muddle Befog, Bemuse, Botch, Cock up, Confuse, Disorder, Embrangle, Fluster, Gump, Mash, Mêlée, Mess, Mix, Mull, Pickle, Puddle, Shemozzle, Stupefy, Tangle

▷**Muddled** may indicate an anagram

Muffle(d), Muffler Damp, Envelop, Hollow, Mob(b)le, Mute, Scarf, Silencer, Sourdine, Stifle

Mug(ger), Muggy Assault, Attack, Bash, Beaker, Bock, Can, Club, Con, Croc(odile), Cup, Dial, Dupe, Enghalskrug, Face, Fool, Footpad, Gob, Humid, Idiot, Latron, Learn, Mou, Noggin, Pan, Pot, Puss, Rob, Roll, Sandbag, Sap, Sconce, Simpleton, Steamer, Stein, Sucker, Swot, Tankard, Tass, Thief, Thug(gee), Tinnie, Tinny, Toby, Trap, Ugly, Visage, Yap

Mule Ass, Bab(o)uche, Barren, Donkey, Funnel, Hybrid, Mocassin, Moccasin, Moyl(e), Muffin, Muil, Rake, Shoe, Slipper, Sumpter

Multiple, Multiplied, Multiplier, Multiply Augment, Breed, Double, ➤ INCREASE, Modulus, Populate, Product, Proliferate, Propagate, Severalfold

Multitude Army, Crowd, Hirsel, Horde, Host, Legion, Populace, Shoal, Sight, Throng, Zillion

Mumble Grumble, Moop, Moup, Mouth, Mump, Mushmouth, Mutter, Royne, Slur

Munch Champ, Chew, Chomp, Scranch

Mundane Banal, Common, Earthly, Nondescript, Ordinary, Prosaic, Quotidian, Secular, Trite, Workaday, Worldly

Munition(s) Arms, Artillery, Matériel, Ordnance

Murder(er), Murderess, Murderous Aram, Assassin, Blue, Bluebeard, Bravo, Burke, Butcher, Butler, Cain, Cathedral, Crackhalter, Crippen, Cutthroat, Do in, Eliminate, Filicide, First degree, Fratricide, Genocide, Hare, Hitman, Homicide, Internecine, ► KILL, Liquidate, Locusta, Made man, Massacre, Matricide, Modo, Parricide, Patricide, Poison, Red, Regicide, Ripper, Ritual, Ritz, Second degree, Sikes, Slaughter, Slay, Strangle(r), Take out, Thagi, Throttle, Thug(gee), Whodun(n)it

Murk(y) Black, Dirk(e), Gloom, Obscure, Rookish, Stygian

Muscle, Muscular Athletic, Beef(y), Bowr, Brawn, Clout, Creature, Force, Intrinsic, Involuntary, Mesomorph, Might, Motor, Mouse, Myalgia, ► POWER, Sinew, Tendon, Thew

Muse(s), Muse's home, Musing Aglaia, Aonia(n), Attic, Calliope, Clio, Cogitate, Consider, Erato, Euphrosyne, Euterpe, Helicon, Inspiration, IX, Melpomene, Nine, Nonet, Pensée, Pierides, Poly(hy)mnia, Ponder, ► REFLECT, Ruminate, Study, Teian, Terpsichore, Thalia, Tragic, Urania, Wonder

Museum Ashmolean, BM, British, Fitzwilliam, Gallery, Guggenheim, Hermitage, Louvre, Metropolitan, Parnassus, Prado, Repository, Smithsonian, Tate, Uffizi, VA, V and A

Mushroom Agaric, Blewits, Burgeon, Button, Cep, Champignon, Darning, Enoki, Expand, Fly agaric, ► FUNGUS, Gyromitra, Horse, Hypha(l), Ink-cap, Magic, Matsutake, Meadow, Morel, Oyster, Parasol, Penny-bun, Porcino, Russula, Sacred, Scotch bonnet, Shaggymane, Shiitake, Sickener, Spread, Start-up, Straw, Truffle, Upstart, Velvet shank, Waxcap

Music Air, Ala(a)p, Alapa, Albumblatt, Aleatory, Allegro, Allemande, Anacrustic, Andante, Antiphony, Arabesque, Art, Bagatelle, Ballade, Berceuse, Bluette, Bour(r)ee, Cadenza, Canon, Cantata, Cantilena, Chant, Chorale, Cliff, Coloratura, Concerto, Concertstuck, Contrapuntal, Coranoch, Coronach, Divertimento, Duet, Enigma, Entracte, Euterpe, Facade, Fanfare,

Fantasia, Fioritura, Fugato, Fugue, Funk(y), Galant, Gat, Grandioso, Humoresque, Incidental, Intermezzo, Introit, Jam session, Jhala, Jor, Landler, Largo, Lydian, Madrigal, Maggiore, Mantra, Marcato, March, Martellato, Melisma, Melody, Meno, Modality, Morceau, Motet, Nocturne, Nonet, Notation, Note, Numbers, Obbligato, Opus, Oratorio, Organum, Orphean, Parlando, Partita, Passacaglia, Passion, Pastiche, Pastorale, Pecking, Phase, Piece, Plainsong, Polyhymnia, Polyphony, Postlude, Pralltriller, Prelude, Progressional, Prom, Psalmody, Pycnon, Quartet, Quintet, Quodlibet, Raga, Ragini, Rastrum, Redowa, Requiem, Rhapsody, Rhythm, Ricercar(e), Riff, Ritornello, Romanza, Rondeau, Rondino, Rondo, Roots(y), Rosalia, Roulade, Sanctus, Saraband, Scherzo, Score, Seguidilla, Septimole, Serenade, Serenata, Setting, Sextet, Sheet, Sinfonietta, Solmisation, Son, Sonata, Strain, Suite, Symphony, Tala, Tambourin, Thema, Toccata, Toccatella, Toccatina, Tonal, Trio, Truth, Tune, Twelve-tone, Verset, Voluntary

Musical Arcadian, Azione, Brigadoon, Cats, Chess, Euphonic, Evergreen, Evita, Gigi, Grease, Hair, Harmonious, Kabuki, Kismet, Lyric, Mame, Melodic, Oliver, Opera, Operetta, Orphean, Revue, Showboat

Musical instrument Accordion, Alpenhorn, Angklung, Antara, Archlute, Aulos, Autoharp®, Ax(e), Bagpipe, Balalaika, Bandoneon, Bandore, Bandura, Banjo, Baryton(e), Baryulele, Bassoon, Bazooka, Bombardon, Bouzouki, Bullroarer, Calliope, Canorous, Celesta, Celeste, Cello, Cembalo, Chalumeau, Charango, Chikara, Chitarrone, Chordophone, Cimbalom, Cithara, Citole, Cittern, Clairschach, Clarinet, Clarion, Clarsach, Clave(cin), Clavicembalo, Clavichord, Clavier, Cobza, Concertina, Console, Contrabasso(on), Contrafagotto, Cor anglais, Cornemuse, Cornet(t), Cornetto, Corno, Cornpipe, Cromorna, Cromorne, Crumhorn, Cr(o)wd, Crwth, Cymbal, Decachord, Dichord, Didgeridoo, Drum, Dulcian, Dulcimer, Euph(on)ium), Fagotto, Fife, Flageolet, Flexatone, Flugel(horn), Flute, Flutina, French horn, Gamelan, Gemshorn, Gittern, Glass harmonica, Glockenspiel, Gong, Gramophone, Gu(e), Guarneri, Guimbard, Guiro, Guitar, Gusla, Gusle, Gusli, Gutbucket, Harmonica, Harmoniphon(e), Harmonium, Harp, Harpsichord, Hautbois, Hautboy, Heckelphone, Helicon, High-hat, Horn, Humstrum, Hurdy-gurdy, Idiophone, Jew's harp, Kalimba,

Musician(s) → Muslim (ritual)

Kanoon, Kantela, Kantele, Kazoo, Kent-bugle, Kettledrum, Key-bugle, Kit, Kithara, Klavier, Kora, Koto, Krummhorn, Langsp(i)el, Lure, Lute, Lyra-viol, Lyre, Lyricon, Mandola, Mandolin(e), Manzello, Maraca, Marimba, Martenot, Mbira, Mellophone, Melodeon, Melodica, Metallophone, Mirliton, Monochord, Moog®, Mouth-harp, Naker, Nebel, Nickelodeon, Oboe, Ocarina, Ondes Martenot, Ophicleide, Orchestrion, Organ, Orpharion, Orpheoreon, Ottavino, Oud, Pandora, Pandore, Pandura, Panharmonicon, Pan pipes, Pantachord, Pantaleon, Pastorale, Penny-whistle, Phonofiddle, Phorminx, Physharmonica, Piano, Piccolo, Pipa, Polyphon(e), Poogye(e), Posaune, Psaltery, Quena, Racket(t), Rate, Rebec(k), Recorder, Reed, Regal, Ribibe, Rote, Sackbut, Sambuca, Samisen, Sancho, Sang, Sanko, Sansa, Santir, Santour, Santur, Sarangi, Sarod, Sarrusophone, Saxhorn, Saxophone, Saxtuba, Saz, Seraphine, Serpent, Shakuhachi, Shalm(e), Shawm, Sitar, Sittar, Slughorn(e), Snare-drum, Sopranino, Sousaphone, Spinet(te), Squeeze-box, Sticcado, Sticcato, Stock and horn, Stockhorn, Stradivarius, Straduarius, Stylophone®, Surbahar, Symphonium, Syrinx, Tabla, Tabor, Tambour(ine), Tamb(o)ura, Tamburin, Tenoroon, Theorbo, Theremin, Thumb piano, Tibia, Timbrel, Triangle, Trigon, Tromba-marina, Trombone, Trompette, Trumpet, Trump-marine, Tuba, Tympany, Uke(lele), Veena, Vibraphone, Vielle, Vihuela, Vina, Viol(a), Violin(cello), Virginal, Vocalion, Washboard, Xylophone, Xylorimba, Zambomba, Zampogna, Zanze, Zel, Zeze, Zinke, Zither, Zuf(f)olo

Musician(s), Musicologist Accompanist, Arion, Arist, Brain, Chanter, Combo, ➤ COMPOSER, Conductor, Crowder, Ensemble, Executant, Flautist, Gate, Grove, Guslar, Handel, Jazzer, Jazzman, Joplin, Mahler, Mariachi, Menuhin, Minstrel, Muso, Orphean, Pianist, Rapper, Reed(s)man, Répétiteur, Rubinstein, Sideman, Spohr, String, Tortelier, Trouvère, Violinist, Wait

Musket Brown Bess, Caliver, Carabine, Eyas, Flintlock, Fusil, Hawk, Nyas, Queen's-arm, Weapon

Muslim (ritual), Moslem Alaouite, Ali, Almohad(e), Balochi, Baluchi, Berber, Caliph, Dato, Dervish, Fatimid, Ghazi, Hadji, Hafiz, Hajji, Iranian, Islamic, Ismaili, Karmathian, Khotbah, Khotbeh, Khutbah, Mahometan, Mogul, Moor, Morisco, Moro,

Mufti, Mus(s)ulman, Mutazilite, Nawab, Paynim, Pomak, Said, Saracen, Say(y)id, Senussi, Shafiite, Shia(h), Shiite, Sofi, Sonnite, Sufi, Sulu, Sunna, Sunni(te), Turk, Wahabee, Wahabi(te)

Must(y) Amok, Essential, Foughty, Froughy, Frowsty, Frowy, Funky, Fust, Man, Maun(na), Mote, Mould, Mucid, Mun, Need(s)-be, Shall, Should, Stum, Wine

▷ **Must** may indicate an anagram

Mustard Charlock, Cress, English, Erysimum, French, Nitrogen, Praiseach, Runch, Sauce-alone, Senvy

▷ **Mutation** may indicate an anagram

Mute(d) Deaden, Dumb, Noiseless, Silent, Sordino, Sordo, Sourdine, Stifle

Mutilate(d), Mutilation Castrate, Concise, Deface, Dismember, Distort, Garble, Hamble, Injure, Maim, Mangle, Mayhem, Obtruncate, Riglin, Tear

▷ **Mutilate(d)** may indicate an anagram

Mutineer, Mutiny Bounty, Caine, Curragh, Indian, Insurrection, Nore, Pandy, ➤ REVOLT, Rising, Sepoy

Mutter(ing) Chunter, Fremescent, Mumble, Mump, Murmur, Mussitate, Rhubarb, Roin, Royne, Rumble, Witter

Muzzle Decorticate, Gag, Jaw, Mouth, Restrain, Snout

Mysterious, Mystery Abdabs, Abdals, Acroamatic, Arcane, Arcanum, Cabbala, Craft, Cryptic, Dark, Deep, Eleusinian, Enigma, Esoteric, Grocer, Incarnation, Miracle, Numinous, Occult, Original sin, Orphic, Riddle, ➤ SECRET, Telestic, Trinity, UFO, Uncanny

▷ **Mysterious(ly)** may indicate an anagram

Mystic (word), Mystical Abraxas, Agnostic, Cab(e)iri, Epopt, Fakir, Familist, Hesychast, Mahatma, Occultist, Rasputin, Secret, Seer, Sofi, Sufi, Swami, Theosophy, Transcendental

Mystify Baffle, Bamboozle, Bewilder, Metagrabolise, Metagrobolise, Puzzle

Myth(ology), Mythical (beast) Allegory, Centaur, Cockatrice, Euhemerism, Fable, Fantasy, Fictitious, Folklore, Garuda, Geryon, Griffin, Impundulu, Kylin, Legend, Lore, Otnit, Pantheon, Pegasus, Selkie, Speewah, Sphinx, Unicorn, Urban, Wivern, Wyvern, Yale

Nn

N Name, Nitrogen, Noon, North, November

Nadir Bottom, Depths, Dregs, Minimum

Nag(ging) Badger, Bidet, Brimstone, Callet, Cap, Captious, Complain, Fret, Fuss, Harangue, Harp, Henpeck, Horse, Jade, Jaw, Keffel, Peck, Pester, Plague, Rosinante, Rouncy, ➤ SCOLD, Tit, Yaff

Nail(ed) Brad, Brod, Catch, Clinker, Clout, Fasten, Hob, Keratin, Onyx, Pin, Rivet, Sisera, Sparable, Sparrow-bill, Spick, Spike, Sprig, Staple, Stub, Stud, Tack(et), Talon, Tenterhook, Thumb, Tingle, Toe, Unguis

Naive(té) Artless, Green, Guileless, Ingenuous, Innocence, Open, Simplistic, Unsophisticated, Wide-eyed

Naked Adamical, Artless, Bare, Blunt, Buff, Clear, Cuerpo, Defenceless, Encuerpo, Exposed, Gymno-, Nuddy, Nude, Querpo, Raw, Scud, Simple, Stark(ers), Uncovered

Name(d), Names Agnomen, Alias, Appellation, Appoint, Baptise, Byline, Call, Celeb(rity), Cite, Cleep, Clepe, Cognomen, Designate, Dinges, Dingus, Dit, Dub, Epithet, Eponym, Exonym, Handle, Hete, Hight, Identify, Identity, Label, Marque, Mention, Metronymic, Moni(c)ker, Nom, Nemn, Nom, Nomen(clature), Noun, Patronymic, Pennant, Personage, Proprietary, Pseudonym, Quote, Red(d), Repute, Sign, Signature, Sir, Specify, Street, Substantive, Tag, Term, ➤ TITLE, Titular, Titule, Trade, Trivial

Nap(py) Bonaparte, Diaper, Doze, Drowse, Fluff, Frieze(d), Fuzz, Kip, Moze, Oose, Ooze, Oozy, Put(t), Shag, Siesta, ➤ SLEEP, Slumber, Snooze, Tease, Teasel, Teaze, Tipsy, Tuft

Napkin Cloth, Diaper, Doily, Sanitary, Serviette

Narcotic Ava, B(h)ang, Benj, Charas, Churrus, Coca, Codeine, Datura, Dope, ➤ DRUG, Heroin, Hop, Laudanum, Mandrake, Marijuana, Meconium, Morphia, Opiate, Pituri, Sedative

Narrate, Narration, Narrative, Narrator Allegory, Anecdote, Cantata, Describe, Diegesis, Fable, History, Periplus, Plot, Raconteur, Récit, Recite, Recount, Saga, Scheherazade, Splatterpunk, Story, Tell

Narrow(ing), Narrow-minded Alf, Bigoted, Borné, Constringe, Cramp, Ensiform, Grundy(ism), Hidebound, Illiberal, Insular, Kyle, Limited, Meagre, Nary, One-idead, Parochial, Phimosis, Pinch, Prudish, Puritan, Scant, Shrink, Slender, Slit, Specialise, Squeak, Stenosed, Strait, Suburban, Verkramp, Waist

Nastiness, Nasty Disagreeable, Drevill, Filth, Fink, Ghastly, Lemon, Lo(a)th, Malign(ant), Noxious, Obscene, Odious, Offensive, Ribby, Sordid, Vile

Nation, National(ist) Anthem, Baathist, Casement, Chetnik, Country, Cuban, Debt, Eta, Federal, Folk, Grand, Indian, IRA, Jingoist, Land, Mexican, Pamyat, Patriot, ➤ PEOPLE, Polonia, Race, Risorgimento, Scottish, Subject, Swadeshi, United, Wafd, Yemini, Young Ireland, Zionist

Native(s) Abo(rigin), Aborigine, African, Amerind, Annamese, Arab, Ascian, Australian, Autochthon, Aztec, Basuto, Belonging, Bengali, Boy, Cairene, Carib, Carioca, Chaldean, Citizen, Colchester, Conch, Creole, Criollo, Domestic, Dyak, Edo, Enchorial, Eskimo, Fleming, Genuine, Habitual, Inborn, Indigene, Indigenous, Inhabitant, Intuitive, Kaffir, Libyan, Local, Malay, Maori, Micronesian, Moroccan, Norwegian, Oyster, Polack, Portuguese, Son, Spaniard, Te(i)an, Thai, Tibetan, Uzbeg, Uzbek, Whitstable, Yugoslav

Natural(ly) Artless, Ass, Easy, Genuine, Homely, Idiot, Illegitimate, Inborn, Inbred, Indigenous, Ingenerate, Inherent, Innate, Moron, Native, Nidget, Nitwit, Nude, Ordinary, Organic, Prat, Real, Sincere, True, Untaught

Nature Adam, Character, Disposition, Esse(nce), Ethos, Inscape, Mould, Quintessence, Second, SN, Temperament

Naught Cypher, Failure, Nil, Nothing, Zero

Naughty Bad, Girly, Improper, Light, Marietta, Rascal, Remiss, Spright, Sprite, Wayward

Nausea, Nauseous Disgust, Fulsome, Malaise, Queasy, Sickness, Squeamish, Wamble, Wambly

Nave Aisle, Apse, Centre, Hub, Nef

Navigate, Navigator Albuquerque, Bougainville, Cabot, Cartier, Columbus, Control, Da Gama, Dias, Direct, Franklin, Frobisher, Gilbert, Hartog, Haul, Henry, Hudson, Keel, Magellan, Navvy, Orienteer, Pilot, Sail, Star-read, ➤ STEER

Navy, Naval AB, Armada, Blue, Fleet, French, Maritime, Merchant, N, Red, RN, Wren

Near(est), Nearby, Nearly, Nearness About, Adjacent, All-but, Almost, Anigh, Approach, Approximate, Beside, By, Close, Cy pres, Degree, Even, Ewest, Forby, Gain, Handy, Hither, Imminent, Inby(e), Mean, Miserly, Neist, Next, Nie, Niggardly, Nigh, Outby, Propinquity, Proximity, Short-range, Stingy, To, Warm, Well-nigh

Neat(ly) Bandbox, Cattle, Clean-cut, Clever, Dainty, Dapper, Deft, Dink(y), Doddy, Donsie, Elegant, Feat(e)ous, Featuous, Gayal, Genty, Gyal, Intact, Jemmy, Jimpy, Nett, Ninepence, Orderly, Ox(en), Preppy, Pretty, Rother, Shipshape, Short, Smug, Snod, Spruce, Straight, ➤ TIDY, Trig, Trim, Unwatered

Necessary, Necessarily Bog, Cash, De rigueur, ➤ ESSENTIAL, Estovers, Important, Indispensable, Intrinsic, Money, Needful, Ought, Perforce, Requisite, Vital, Wherewithal

Necessitate, Necessity Ananke, Compel, Constrain, Emergency, Entail, Exigent, Fate, Indigence, Must, Need, Need-be, Oblige, Perforce, Require, Requisite

Neck(ed) Bottle, Brass, Canoodle, Cervical, Cervix, Channel, Col, Crag, Craig, Crop, Embrace, Gall, Gorgerin, Halse, Hawse, Inarm, Inclip, Isthmus, Kiss, Mash, Nape, Pet, Polo, Rubber, Scrag, Scruff, Smooch, Snog, Strait, Swan, Swire, Theorbo, Torticollis, Trachelate, Vee

▷ **Necking** may indicate one word around another

Necklace Anodyne, Chain, Choker, Collar, Corals, Pearls, Rope, Sautoir, String, Torc, Torque

Neckline Boat, Collar, Cowl, Crew, Décolletage, Plunging, Sweetheart, Turtle, Vee

Neckwear Ascot, Barcelona, Boa, Bow, Collar, Cravat, Fur, Steenkirk, Stock, Tie

Nectar Ambrosia, Amrita, Honey, Mead

Need(ed), Needy Call, Demand, Desiderata, Egence, Egency, Exigency, Gap, Gerundive, Impecunious, Indigent, ➤ LACK, Mister, Pressing, PRN, Require, Strait, Strapped, Want

Needle Acerose, Acicular, Aciform, Between, Bodkin, Darning, Dip, Goad, Hype, Hypodermic, Icicle, Inoculate, Leucotome, Magnetic, Miff, Monolith, Neeld, Neele, Obelisk, Pinnacle,

Pointer, Prick, R(h)aphis, Sew, Sharp, Spicule, Spike, Spine,
Stylus, Tattoo, Tease, Thorn, Wire

Needlework Baste, Crewel, Embroidery, Mola, Patchwork,
Rivière, Sampler, Tapestry, Tattoo

Negation, Negative Anion, Apophatic, Cathode, Denial,
Enantiosis, Ne, No, Non, Nope, Nullify, Photograph, Refusal,
Resinous, Unresponsive, Veto, Yin

Neglect(ed), Neglectful, Negligence, Negligent
Careless, Casual, Cinderella, Cuff, Default, Dereliction,
Disregard, Disuse, Failure, Forget, Forlorn, Heedless,
Inattention, Incivism, Laches, Malpractice, Misprision,
Omission, Oversight, Pass, Pass-up, ➤ REMISS, Shirk, Slight,
Slipshod, Undone

▷**Neglected** may indicate an anagram

Negligee Déshabillé, Manteau, Mob, Nightgown, Robe

Negotiate, Negotiator Arbitrate, Arrange, Bargain, Clear,
Confer, Deal, Diplomat, Intermediary, Liaise, Manoeuvre,
Mediator, Parley, Trade, Transact, Treat(y), Weather

Neigh Bray, Hinny, Nicker, Whicker, Whinny

Neighbour(ly), Neighbouring, Neighbours Abut(ter),
Alongside, Amicable, Bor, Border, But, Friendly, Joneses,
Nearby, Next-door

Neighbourhood Area, Community, District, Environs,
Locality, Precinct, Vicinage, Vicinity

Nerve(s), Nervous (centre), Nervure, Nervy Abdabs,
Accessory, Acoustic, Afferent, Aflutter, Afraid, Axon, Bottle,
Bouton, Chord, Chutzpah, Collywobbles, Column,
Commissure, Courage, Cranial, Depressor, Edgy, Excitor, Facial,
Gall, Ganglion, Grit, Guts, Habdabs, High, Highly-strung, Hyp,
Impudence, Jitters, Jittery, Mid-rib, Motor, Myelon, Neck,
Nidus, Optic, Pavid, Rad, Radial, Restless, Sangfroid, Sauce,
Sciatic, Screaming abdabs, Sensory, Shaky, Solar plexus, Spunk,
Steel, Strung-up, Synapse, Tense, Tizzy, Toey, Tongue-tied,
Trembler, Tremulous, Trochlear, Twitchy, Ulnar, Vagus,
Vapours, Windy, Yips

▷**Nervously** may indicate an anagram

Nest Aerie, Aery, Aiery, Ayrie, Bike, Bink, Brood, Byke, Cabinet,
Cage, Caliology, Clutch, Dray, Drey, Eyrie, Eyry, Lodge, Nid,
Nide, Nidify, Nidus, Sett, Termitarium, Wurley

Nestle Burrow, Cose, Cuddle, Nuzzle, Snug(gle)

Net(ting), Nets, Network BR, Bunt, Cast, Catch, Caul, Clear, Cobweb, Crinoline, Drift, Earn, Eel-set, Enmesh, Filet, Final, Fish, Flew, Flue, Fyke, Gill, ► GRID, Hammock, JANET, Kiddle, Lace, LAN, Land, Lattice, Leap, Line, Linin, Mains, Maze, ► MESH, Mosquito, Old boys', Plexus, Portal system, Pout, Purse-seine, Reseau, Rete, Retiary, Reticle, Reticulate, Reticulum, Safety, Sagene, Screen, Sean, Seine, Set(t), Snood, System, Tela, Telex, Toil, Trammel, Trap, Trawl, Tulle, Tunnel, Usenet, WAN, Web, Wire

Nettle(rash) Anger, Annoy, Day, Dead, Hemp, Hives, Horse, Irritate, Labiate, Nark, Pellitory, Pique, Ramee, Rami, Ramie, Rile, Ruffle, Sting, Urtica(ceae), Urticaria

Neuter Castrate, Gib, Impartial, Neutral, Sexless, Spay

Neutral(ise) Alkalify, Buffer zone, Counteract, Grey, Impartial, Inactive, Schwa, Sheva, Shiva, Unbiased

Never(more) Nary, Nathemo(re), No more

Nevertheless Algate, Anyhow, But, However, Still, Yet

▷**New** may indicate an anagram

New(s), News agency Bulletin, Copy, Coranto, Dope, Euphobia, Evangel, Flash, Forest, Fresh, Fudge, Gen, Green, Griff, Info, Innovation, Intelligence, Item, Kerygma, Latest, Mint, Modern, N, Novel, Oil(s), Original, PA, Paragraph, Pastures, Pristine, Propaganda, Recent, Report, Reuter, Scoop, Span, Tass, Teletext®, Tidings, Ultramodern, Unco, Word

Newcomer Dog, Freshman, Griffin, Immigrant, Jackaroo, Jackeroo, Jillaroo, Johnny-come-lately, Novice, Parvenu, Pilgrim, Settler, Tenderfoot, Upstart

Newsman, News-reader Announcer, Editor, Journalist, Press, Reporter, Sub, Sysop

Newspaper Blat(t), Broadsheet, Courier, Daily, Express, Fanzine, Feuilleton, Freesheet, Gazette, Guardian, Herald, Journal, Jupiter, Le Monde, Mercury, National, Organ, Patent inside, Patent outside, Post, Pravda, Press, Print, Rag, Red-top, Sheet, Spoiler, Squeak, Sun, Tabloid, Today

Newt(s) Ask(er), Eft, Evet, Swift, Triton, Urodela

New Zealand(ers) Aotearoa, Enzed, Kiwis, Maori, Moriori, Pakeha, Pig Island, Shagroon

Next Adjacent, Adjoining, After, Alongside, Beside, Following, Immediate, Later, Nearest, Neist, Proximate, Proximo, Sine, Subsequent, Syne

Nib J, Pen, Point, Tip

Nibble Bite, Brouse, Browse, Byte, Crop, Eat, Gnaw, Knap(ple), Moop, Moup, Munch, Nag, Nepit, Nosh, Peck, Pick, Snack

Nice(ty) Accurate, Amene, Appealing, Dainty, Fastidious, Fine, Finical, Genteel, Lepid, Ninepence, Pat, Pleasant, Precise, Quaint, Rare, Refined, Subtil(e), Subtle, Sweet, T

Niche Alcove, Almehrahb, Almery, Ambry, Apse, Aumbry, Awmrie, Awmry, Columbarium, Cranny, Exedra, Fenestella, Mihrab, Recess, Slot

Nick(ed) Appropriate, Arrest, Bin, Blag, Can, Chip, Cly, Colin, Copshop, Cut, Denay, Dent, Deny, ➤ DEVIL, Erose, Groove, Hoosegow, Kitty, Knock, Nab, Nap, Nim, Nock, Notch, Pinch, Pook, Pouk, Prison, Scratch, ➤ STEAL, Steek, Swan-upping, Swipe, Thieve, Wirricow, Worricow, Worrycow

Nickname Alias, Byname, Byword, Cognomen, So(u)briquet

Night(s), Nightfall Acronychal, Arabian, Darkmans, Guest, Guy Fawkes, Leila, Nacht, Nicka-nan, Nutcrack, Nyx, Stag, Twelfth, Twilight, Walpurgis, Watch

Night-cap Biggin, Cocoa, Nip, Pirnie, Sundowner

Nightingale Bulbul, Florence, Jugger, Lind, Philomel, Scutari, Swedish, Watch

Nightmare, Nightmarish Cacod(a)emon, Ephialtes, Incubus, Kafkaesque, Oneirodynia, Phantasmagoria

Nightshade Belladonna, Bittersweet, Circaea, Dwale, Henbane, Morel, Solanum

Nil Nothing, Nought, Zero

Nimble Active, ➤ AGILE, Alert, Deft, Deliver, Fleet, Light, Lissom(e), Lithe, Quiver, Springe, Spry, Supple, Swack, Wan(d)le, Wannel, Wight, Ya(u)ld

Nip(per) Bite, Check, Chela, Chill, Claw, Dram, Gook, Jap, Lad, Lop, Nep, Nirl, Peck, Pincers, Pinch, Pook, Scotch, Sneap, Susan, Taste, Tot, Tweak, Urchin, Vice, Vise

Nipple Dug, Mastoid, Pap, Teat

No Aikona, Denial, Na(e), Nah, Negative, Nix, Nope, Nyet, O, Refusal

Nob(by) Grandee, Parage, Prince, Swell, Toff

▷**Nobbled** may indicate an anagram

Noble(man), Nobility Adeline, Aristocrat, Atheling, Baron(et), Bart, Boyar, Bt, Childe, Count, County, Daimio, Dom, Don, Doucepere, Douzeper(s), Duc, Duke, Earl, Eorl, Ethel, Eupatrid, Fine, Gent, Glorious, Graf, Grandee, Grandeur, Great, Heroic, Hidalgo, Highborn, Jarl, Junker, King, Landgrave, Lord, Manly, Margrave, Marquis, Palatine, Patrician, Peer, Rank, Seigneur, Seignior, Sheik(h), Stately, Thane, Thegn, Titled, Toiseach, Toisech, Vavasour, Vicomte, Vidame, Viscount

Nobody Gnatling, Jack-straw, Nebbish, Nemo, None, Nonentity, Nyaff, Pooter, Quat, Schlepp, Scoot, Shlep

Nod(ding) Agree, Assent, Beck(on), Bob, Browse, Catnap, Cernuous, Doze, Mandarin, Nutant, Somnolent

Node, Nodular, Nodule Boss, Enhydros, Geode, Knot, Lump, Lymph, Milium, Pea-iron, Ranvier, Swelling, Thorn

Noise, Noisy Babel, Bedlam, Blare, Blip, Bobbery, Boing, Boink, Bruit, Cangle, Charm, Clamant, Clamour, Clangour, Clash, Clatter, Clitter, Clutter, Coil, Creak, Deen, Din, Dirdum, Euphonia, Euphony, F, Fuss, Hewgh, Hubbub, Hue, Hum, Hurly-burly, Knocking, Loud, Obstreperous, Ping, Plangent, Quonk, Racket, Report, Roar, Robustious, Rorie, Rort, Row(dow-dow), Rowdedow, Rowdy(dow)(dy), Scream, Screech, Shindig, Shindy, Shreek, Shreik, Shriech, Shriek, Sone, Sonorous, Sound, Stridor, Surface, Tinnitus, Tumult, ➤ UPROAR, VIP, Vociferous, White, Zoom

Nomad(ic) Bedawin, Bedu, Bed(o)uin, Berber, Chal, Edom(ite), Fula(h), Gypsy, Hottentot, Kurd, Kyrgyz, Rom, Rootless, Rover, Saracen, Sarmatian, Strayer, Tsigane, Tsigany, Tuareg, Vagabond, Vagrant, Zigan

Nominate, Nomination Appoint, Baptism, Designate, Elect, Present, ➤ PROPOSE, Slate, Specify, Term

Nonchalance, Nonchalant Blasé, Casual, Cool, Debonair, Jaunty

Non-conformist, Non-conformity Beatnik, Bohemian, Chapel, Deviant, Dissent(er), Dissident, Ebenezer, Heresiarch, Heretic, Maverick, Odd-ball, Outlaw, Pantile, Patarine, Rebel, Recusant, Renegade, Renegate, Sectarian, Wesleyan

None Nada, Nary, Nil, Nought, Zero

Nonentity Cipher, Nebbich, Nebbish(er), Nebish, Nobody, Pipsqueak, Quat

▷**Nonetheless** may indicate an 'o' to be omitted

Nonsense Absurdity, Amphigory, Balderdash, Baloney, Bilge, Blague, Blah, Blarney, Blat(her), Blether, Bollocks, Boloney, Borax, Bosh, Bull, Bulldust, Bullshit, Buncombe, Bunkum, Claptrap, Cobblers, Cock, Cod, Codswallop, Crap, Drivel, Dust, Eyewash, Faddle, Fandangle, Fiddlededee, Fiddle-faddle, Fiddlesticks, Flim-flam, Footling, Fudge, Gaff, Gammon, Get away, Gibberish, Guff, Gum, Hanky-panky, Haver, Hogwash, Hokum, Hooey, Horsefeathers, Humbug, Jabberwocky, Kibosh, Kidstakes, Malark(e)y, Moonshine, My eye, Piffle, Pshaw, Pulp, Rats, Rhubarb, Rigmarole, Rot, Rubbish, Scat, Shenanigans, Shit(e), Squit, Stuff, Tom(foolery), Tommy-rot, Tosh, Trash, Tripe, Tush, Twaddle, Unreason, Waffle

Noodle(s) Capellini, Crispy, Daw, Fool, Head, Laksa, Lokshen, Manicotti, Mee, Moony, Pasta, Sammy, Simpleton

Nook Alcove, Angle, Corner, Cranny, Niche, Recess, Rookery

Noose Fank, Halter, Lanyard, Loop, Necktie, Rope, Rope's end, Snare, Twitch

▶**Nor** see NOT

Norm Canon, Criterion, Rule, Standard

Normal Average, Everyday, Natural, Norm, Ordinary, Par, Perpendicular, Regular, Standard, Usu(al)

North(ern), Northerner Arctic, Boreal, Cispontine, Copperhead, Doughface, Eskimo, Hyperborean, Magnetic, N, Norland, Runic, Septentrion, True, Up

North American (Indian) Brave, Copperskin, Geronimo, Hiawatha, Injun, Mugwump, Papoose, Pocahontas, Red(skin), Sachem, Sagamore, Sannup, Scalper, Sitting Bull, Tribe

Nose, Nosy A(d)jutage, Aquiline, Beak, Bergerac, Boko, Bouquet, Conk, Cromwell, Curious, Desman, Droop, Fink, Gnomon, Grass, Grecian, Honker, Hooter, Index, Informer, Meddle, Muffle, Muzzle, Nark, Neb, Nozzle, Nuzzle, Proboscis, Prying, Pug, Rhinal, Roman, Schnozzle, Shove, Smelly, Sneb, Sniff, Snoot, Snout, Snub, Squeal, Stag, Stickybeak, Toffee

Nostalgia Longing, Retrophilia, Yearning

Not, Nor Dis-, Na(e), Ne, Neither, Never, No, Pas, Polled, Taint

Notable, Notability Conspicuous, Distinguished, Eminent, Especial, Landmark, Large, Lion, Memorable, Signal, Striking, Unco, VIP, Worthy

▷**Not allowed** may indicate a word to be omitted

  Notation Benesh, Entry, Memo, Polish, Positional

  Notch(ed) Crena(l), Crenel, Cut, Dent, Erode, Erose, Gain, Gap, Gimp, Indent, Jag, Kerf, Nick, Nock, Raffle, Sinus, Snick, Tally, Vandyke

  Note(s) A, Accidental, Apostil(le), Apparatus, Arpeggio, Auxiliary, B, Bill(et), Bradbury, Breve, C, Cedula, Chit(ty), Cob, Comment, Conceit, Continental, Cover, Credit, Crotchet, D, Demand, Dig, Dominant, E, E-la, F, Fa(h), Fame, Fiver, Flat, G, Gamut, Gloss(ary), Grace, Greenback, IOU, Item(ise), Jot(tings), Jug(-jug), Key, Kudos, La, Large, Line, Log, Long, Longa, Marginalia, Masora(h), Me, Melisma, Melody, Memo(randum), Mese, Mi, Minim, Minute, ► MONEY, Mordent, Natural, NB, Nete, Neum(e), Oblong, Observe, Octave, Oncer, Ostmark, Outline, Pound, Promissory, Protocol, PS, Quaver, Rag-money, Re, Record, Remark, Renown, Root, Scholion, Semibreve, Semiquaver, Semitone, Sextolet, Sharp, Si, Sick, Sol, Stem, Subdominant, Submediant, Subtonic, Supertonic, Te, Ten(ner), Third, Tierce, Tonic, Treasury, Treble, Ut, Wad

▷**Notes** may indicate the use of letters A-G

  Noteworthy Eminent, Extraordinary, Memorable, Particular, Signal, Special

  Nothing, Nought Cipher, Devoid, Diddlysquat, Emptiness, FA, Gratis, Nada, Naught, Nihil, Niks-nie, Nil, Nix(-nie), Noumenon, Nowt, Nuffin, O, Rap, Rien, Sweet FA, Void, Zero, Zilch, Zip(po)

  Notice(able) Ad(vertisement), Advice, Affiche, Apprise, Attention, Avis(o), Banns, Bill, Blurb, Caveat, Circular, Cognisance, Crit, D, Descry, Discern, Dismissal, Gaum, Get, Gorm, ► HEED, Intimation, Marked, Mensh, Mention, NB, No(t)chel, Obit, Observe, Oyez, Placard, Plaque, Playbill, Poster, Press, Proclamation, Prominent, ► REMARK, Review, See, Si quis, Spot, Sticker, Tent, Whip

  Notify Acquaint, Advise, Apprise, Awarn, Inform, ► TELL

  Notion Conceit, ► CONCEPT, Crotchet, Fancy, Hunch, Idea, Idolum, Inkling, Opinion, Reverie, Vapour, Whim

  Notoriety, Notorious Arrant, Byword, Crying, Egregious, Esclandre, Fame, Flagrant, Infamous, Infamy, Proverbial, Reclame, ► RENOWN, Repute

▶**Nought** see NOTHING

Noun Agent, Aptote, Collective, Common, Count, Gerund, Mass, N, Proper, Substantive, Tetraptote, Verbal

Nourish(ing), Nourishment Aliment, Cherish, Cultivate, Feed, Ingesta, Meat, Nurse, Nurture, Nutrient, Promote, Replenish, Sustenance, Trophic

Novel(ty) Aga-saga, Book, Campus, Change, Different, Dime, Dissimilar, Epistolary, Fad, Fiction, Fresh, Gimmick, Gothic, Innovation, ➤ NEW, Newfangled, Original, Paperback, Picaresque, Pot-boiler, Primeur, Romance, Roman-à-clef, Roman fleuve, Unusual, Whodun(n)it, Yellowback

▷**Novel** may indicate an anagram

▶**Novelist** see WRITER

Novice Acolyte, Apprentice, Beginner, Chela, Colt, Cub, Greenhorn, Griffin, Jackaroo, Jillaroo, Kyu, L, Learner, Neophyte, Patzer, Postulant, Prentice, Rookie, Tenderfoot

Now(adays) AD, Alate, Anymore, Current, Here, Immediate, Instanter, Interim, Nonce, Nunc, Present, Pro tem, This

Nozzle A(d)jutage, Fishtail, Nose, Nose-piece, Rose, Spout, Stroup, Syringe, Tewel, Tuyere, Tweer, Twier, Twire, Twyer(e)

Nuance Gradation, Nicety, Overtone, Shade

Nub Crux, Gist, Knob, Lump, Point

Nuclear, Nucl(e)ide, Nucleus Cadre, Calandria, Centre, Core, Crux, Daughter, Deuteron, Eukaryon, Euratom, Heartlet, Hub, Isomer, Isotone, Karyon, Kernel, Linin, Mushroom, Nuke, Pith, Prokaryon, Triton

▷**Nucleus** may indicate the heart of a word

Nude, Nudism, Nudist, Nudity Adamite, Altogether, Aphylly, Bare, Buff, Eve, Exposed, Gymnosophy, ➤ NAKED, Nuddy, Scud, Stark, Stripped, Undress

Nudge Dunch, Dunsh, Elbow, Jostle, Poke, Prod

Nuisance Bore, Bot, Bugbear, Chiz(z), Drag, Impediment, Inconvenience, Mischief, Pest, Plague, Public, Terror, Trial

Null(ification), Nullify Abate, Cancel, Counteract, Defeasance, Destroy, Diriment, Disarm, Invalid(ate), Negate, Neutralise, Recant, Terminate, Undo, Veto, Void

Numb(ness) Asleep, Blunt, Dead(en), Stun, Stupor, Torpefy, Torpescent, Torpid

Number(s) Abundant, Air, Algebraic, Algorithm, Aliquant, Aliquot, Amiable, Anaesthetic, Antilog, Army, Atomic,

Babylonian, Binary, Box, Calculate, Cardinal, Cetane,
Chromosome, Class, Cocaine, Coefficient, Complex, Concrete,
Constant, Coordination, Count, Cyclic, Decillion, Deficient,
Deficit, Diapason, Digit, Drove, E, Epidural, Ether, Feck,
Frost(bite), Gas, Gobar, Googol, Handful, Hemlock, Host,
Imaginary, Include, Index, Irrational, Lac, Lakh, Legion(s),
Lepton, Local, Mach, Magazine, Magic, Melodic, Milliard,
Minyan, Mixed, Mort, Muckle, Multiple, Multiplex, Multiplicity,
Multitude, Myriadth, No(s), Nonillion, Nth, Num, Numerator,
Numerical, Octillion, Opiate, Opium, Opposite, Opus, Ordinal,
OT, Paginate, Par, Peck, Perfect, Pile, PIN, Plural, Prime,
Quantum, Quorum, Quotient, Random, Rational, Reckon,
Registration, Regulo®, Scads, Serial, Sight, Slew, Slue, Some,
Square, Strangeness, Strength, Surd, Tale, Tell, Totient, Totitive,
Transcendental, Troop, Turn-out, Umpteen, Umpty, Urethane,
Verse, Wave, Whole

▷**Number** may indicate a drug

Numeral(s) Arabic, Chapter, Figure, Ghubar, Gobar, Integer,
Number, Roman

Nun Beguine, Bhikkhuni, Clare, Cluniac, Conceptionist, Dame,
Minim, Minoress, Mother Superior, Pigeon, Poor Clare,
Religeuse, Sister, Top, Vestal, Vowess, Zelator, Zelatrice, Zelatrix

Nun a biblical character, father of Joshua

Nurse(ry) Aia, Alice, Amah, Ayah, Bonne, Caledonia, Care(r),
Cavell, Charge, Cherish, Crèche, Day, Deborah, District, EN,
Flo(rence), Foster, Gamp, Glumdalclitch, Harbour, Karitane,
Mammy, Minister, Mother, Mrs Gamp, Nan(n)a, Nanny,
Nightingale, Nourice, Nourish, Parabolanus, Probationer, RN,
Seminary, SEN, Sister, Staff, Suckle, Tend, VAD, Wet

Nursery(man) Conservatory, Crèche, Garden, Hothouse,
Rhyme, Seedsman, Slope

▷**Nursing** may indicate one word within another

Nut(s), Nutcase, Nutshell, Nut tree, Nutty Acajou,
Acorn, Amygdalus, Aphorism, Arachis, Areca, Arnut, Babassu,
Barcelona, Barmy, Bats, Beech-mast, Betel, Briefly, Butterfly,
Butternut, Cashew, Cob, Cola, Core, Cranium, Cuckoo, En,
Filberd, Filbert, Gelt, Gilbert, Gland, Glans, Godser, Gum, Hazel,
Head, Hickory, Ivory, Kernel, Kola, Lichee, Litchi, Loaf, Lug,
Lunatic, Lychee, Macadamia, Manic, Mast, Monkey, Noodle,
Palmyra, Para, Pate, Pecan, Philippina, Philippine, Philopoena,

Pili, Pine, Pistachio, Praline, Prawlin, Queensland, Shell, Skull, Slack, Sleeve, Wing, Zany, Zealot

Nut Egyptian god, father of Osiris

Nutrient, Nutriment, Nutrition Eutrophy, Food, Ingesta, Protein, Sustenance, Trace element, Trophic

▷ **Nuts** may indicate an anagram

Nymph(et) Aegina, Aegle, Amalthea, Arethusa, Callisto, Calypso, Camenae, Carme, Clytie, Constant, Cymodoce, Daphne, Doris, Dryad, Echo, Egeria, Eurydice, Galatea, Hamadryad, Hesperides, Houri, Hyades, Ida, Insect, Larva, Liberty, Lolita, Maelid, Maia, Maiden, Mermaid, Naiad, Nereid, Oceanid, Oenone, Oread, Pupa, Rusalka, Sabrina, Scylla, Siren, Sylph, Syrinx, Tessa, Tethys, Thetis

Oo

O Blob, Duck, Nought, Omega, Omicron, Oscar, Oxygen, Spangle, Tan, Zero

Oar(s), Oarsmen Blade, Ctene, Eight, Leander, Organ, Paddle, Propel, Rower, Scull, Spoon, Sweep

Oat(meal), Oats Ait, Athole brose, Avena, Brome-grass, Fodder, Grain, Grits, Groats, Gruel, Haver, Loblolly, Parritch, Pilcorn, Pipe, Porridge, Quaker®, Rolled, Wild

Oath Affidavit, Begorrah, Curse, Dang, Demme, Doggone, Drat, Ecod, Egad, Expletive, God-so, Halidom, Hippocratic, Igad, Imprecation, Jabers, Lumme, Lummy, Nouns, Oons, Promise, Sacrament, Sal(a)mon, Sheart, Strewth, Stygian, Swear, Tarnation, Tennis-court, Voir dire, Vow, Zbud

Obedient, Obedience, Obey Bridlewise, Comply, Dutiful, Follow, Hear, Mindful, Obsequious, Observe, Obtemper, Perform, Pliant, Servant, Yielding

Obese, Obesity Bariatrics, Corpulent, Fat, Stout

Object(s), Objection(able), Objective(ness), Objector Ah, Aim, Ambition, Argue, Article, Bar, Beef, Case, Cavil, Challenge, Clinical, Complain(t), Conchy, Conscientious, Cow, Demur, Direct, End, Exception, Fuss, ➤ GOAL, Her, Him,

Object → Observe(d)

Impersonal, Improper, Indifferent, Indirect, Intention, It, Item, Jib, Loathe, Mind, Moral, Niggle, Non-ego, Noumenon, Obnoxious, Offensive, Oppose, Outness, Point, Protest, Question, Quibble, Quiddity, Rebarbative, Recuse, Refuse, Resist, Sake, Scruple, Subject, Sublime, Target, Thing, Tut, Ultimate, Unbiased, Virtu, Wart

▷ **Object** may indicate a grammatical variant

Oblige, Obliging, Obligation, Obligatory
Accommodate, Affable, Behold, Binding, Burden, Charge, Compel, Complaisant, Compliant, Contract, Corvée, Debt, De rigueur, Duty, Easy, Encumbent, Force, Giri, Gratify, Impel, Incumbent, IOU, Mandatory, Must, Necessitate, Obruk, Promise, Sonties, Synallagmatic, Tie, Wattle

Oblique(ly) Askance, Askew, Awry, Cross, Diagonal, Perverse, Separatrix, Skew, Slanting, Solidus, Squint, Virgule

▷ **Oblique** may indicate an anagram

Oblivion, Oblivious Forgetful, Lethe, Limbo, Nirvana, Obscurity

Obnoxious Foul, Horrid, Offensive, Pestilent, Repugnant

Obscene(ly), Obscenity Bawdy, Blue, Fescennine, Gross, Hard-core, Indecent, Lewd, Lubricious, Paw(paw), Porn(o), Salacious, Smut, Vulgar

Obscure, Obscurity Abstruse, Anheires, Becloud, Befog, Blend, Cloud, Cobweb, Conceal, Cover, Darken, Deep, Dim, Disguise, Eclipse, Encrypt, Envelop, Filmy, Fog, Hermetic, Hide, Mantle, Mist, Murk, Nebular, Night, Nubecula, Obfuscate, Opaque, Oracular, Overcloud, Overshade, Overshadow, Recherché, Recondite, Tenebrific, Twilit, Unclear, ➤ VAGUE, Veil, Vele, Wrap

▷ **Obscure(d)** may indicate an anagram

Observance, Observant, Observation Adherence, Alert, Attention, Comment, Custom, Empirical, Espial, Eyeful, Holy, Honour, Lectisternium, ➤ NOTICE, Obiter dicta, Percipient, Recce, Remark, Right, Rite, Ritual, Vising

Observe(d), Observer Behold, Bystander, Celebrate, Commentator, Detect, Espy, Eye, Heed, Keep, Mark, NB, Note, Notice, Obey, Onlooker, Optic, Regard(er), Remark, Rite, Scry, See, Sight, Spectator, Spial, Spot, Spy, Study, Take, Twig, View, Voyeur, Witness

Obsess(ed), Obsession, Obsessive Besot, Bug, Craze, Dominate, Fetish, Fixation, Hang-up, Haunt, Hobbyhorse, Hooked, Idée fixe, Infatuation, Mania, Monomania, Necrophilia, Neurotic, One-track, Preoccupy, Thing

Obsolete, Obsolescent Abandoned, Antique, Archaic, Dated, Dead, Defunct, Disused, Extinct, Latescent, Obs, Outdated, Outworn, Passé

Obstacle Barrage, Barrier, Boyg, Cheval de frise, Chicane, Dam, Drag, Dragon's teeth, Drawback, Gate, Handicap, Hindrance, Hitch, Hurdle, Node, Oxer, Remora, Rock, Sandbank, Snag, Stimie, Stumbling-block, Stymie

Obstinacy, Obstinate Asinine, Buckie, Bullish, Contumacious, Cussed, Dour, Froward, Headstrong, Inflexible, Intractable, Intransigent, Mule, Persistent, Perverse, Pervicacious, Pig-headed, Recalcitrant, Refractory, Restive, Resty, Self-will, Stiff(-necked), Stubborn, Wilful

Obstruct(ion) Bar, Block, Bottleneck, Clog, Crab, Cross, Cumber, Dam, Embolus, Fil(l)ibuster, Hamper, Hedge, Hinder, Hurdle, Ileus, Impede, Let, Obstacle, Snooker, Stall, Stap, Stonewall, Stop, Stymie, Sudd, Thwart, Trammel, Trump

Obtain Achieve, Acquire, Cop, Exist, Gain, Get, Land, Pan, Prevail, Procure, Realise, Secure, Succeed, Wangle, Win

Obvious Apparent, Axiom, Blatant, Brobdingnag, Clear, Distinct, Evident, Flagrant, Frank, Kenspeck(le), Manifest, Marked, Open(ness), Overt, Palpable, Patent, Pikestaff, Plain, Pronounced, Salient, Self-evident, Transparent, Truism, Visible

Occasion Call, Cause, Ceremony, Encheason, Event, Fete, Field day, Nonce, ➤ OPPORTUNITY, Reason, Ride, Tide, Time

Occasional(ly) Casual, Chance, Daimen, Intermittent, Irregular, Motive, Orra, Periodic, Sometimes, Sporadic, While

Occupant, Occupation, Occupy(ing) Absorb, Activity, Avocation, Beset, Business, Busy, Denizen, Embusy, Employ, Engage, Engross, Hold, In, Incumbent, Indwell, Inhabitant, Inmate, Involve, Line, Metier, People, Profession, Pursuit, Resident, Runrig, Sideline, Squat, Stay, Tenancy, Tenant, Tenure, Thrift, Trade, Upon, Use, Vocation, Walk of life

Occur(rence) Arise, Be, Betide, Betime, Case, Event, Fall, Happen, Incident, Instance, Outbreak, Outcrop, Pass, Phenomenon

Ocean(ic), Oceania Abssal, Abundance, Antarctic, Arctic, Atlantic, Blue, Deep, Hadal, Herring-pond, Indian, Melanesia, Micronesia, Pacific, Pelagic, Polynesia, Sea(way), Waves

Octopus Cephalopod, Devilfish, Scuttle, Squid

Odd (person), Oddity Anomaly, Bizarre, Card, Cure, Curio, Droll, Eccentric, Erratic, Gink, Impair, Imparity, Offbeat, Orra, Outré, Paradox, Parity, Peculiar, Queer, Quiz, Random, Rare, Remote, Rum, Screwball, Singular, ➤ STRANGE, Uneven, Unmatched, Unusual, Weird, Whims(e)y

▷ **Odd(s)** may indicate an anagram or the odd letters in words

Odds, Oddments Bits, Carpet, Chance, Gubbins, Handicap, Line, Price, SP, Tails, Variance

Ode Awdl, Dit, Epicede, Epicedium, Epinicion, Epinikion, Genethliacon, Horatian, Hymn, Lay, Lyric, Monody, Paeon, Pindaric, Poem, Sapphic, Song, Stasimon, Threnody, Verse

Odium, Odious Comparison, Disestimation, Disgrace, Foul, Hatred, Heinous, Invidious, Repugnant, Stigma

Odorous, Odour Air, BO, Flavour, Funk, Hum, Opoponax, Perfume, Quality, Redolence, Sanctity, Scent, Smell

▷ **Of** may indicate an anagram

Of course Certainly, Natch, Yes

Off Absent, Agee, Ajee, Away, Discount, Distance, Far, From, High, Inexact, Licence, Odd, Reasty, Reesty, Relache, Start

▷ **Off** may indicate an anagram

▷ **Off-colour** may indicate an anagram

Offence Attack, Crime, Delict, Delinquency, Distaste, Fault, Huff, Hurt, Lapse, Miff, Misprision, Outrage, Peccadillo, Pip, Pique, Piracy, Regrate, Sedition, ➤ SIN, Summary, Trespass, Umbrage

Offend(ed), Offender Affront, Anger, Annoy, Bridles, Culprit, Default, Disoblige, Displease, Distaste, Hip, Huff, Hurt, Hyp, Infringe, Inveigh, Miffy, Miscreant, Nettle, Nonce, Nuisance, Peeve, Provoke, Sin(ner), Stray, Twoccer, Violate, Wrongdoer

Offensive Affront, Aggressive, Alien, Attack, Bombardment, Campaign, Cruel, Embracery, Execrable, Eyesore, Foul, Indelicate, Nasty, Noisome, Obnoxious, Obscene, Peccant, Personal, Push, Putrid, Rank, Repugnant, ➤ RUDE, Scandalous, Scurrilous, Sortie, Storm, Ugly, Unbecoming

Offer(ing) Alms, Altarage, Anaphora, Bid, Bode, Bouchée, Cadeau, Corban, Deodate, Dolly, Epanophora, Extend, Gift, Godfather, Hold, Inferiae, Oblation, Overture, Peddle, Plead, Potla(t)ch, Present, Propine, ➤ PROPOSAL, Propose, Propound, Sacrifice, Shewbread, Shore, S(h)raddha, Stand, Submit, Tender, Volunteer, Votive, Xenium

Offhand Airy, Banana, Brusque, Casual, Cavalier, Curt, Extempore, Impromptu, Indifferent

Office(s) Agency, Box, Branch, Broo, Bucket shop, Bureau, Buroo, Chair, Complin(e), Crown, Dead-letter, Den, Evensong, Foreign, Function, Holy, Home, Job, Left luggage, Mayoralty, Ministry, Mistery, Nocturn, Nones, Obit, Oval, Papacy, Patent, Personnel, Place, Plum, Portfolio, Position, Post, Prelacy, Prime, Regency, Register, Registry, Rite, See, Sinecure, Situation, Terce, Ticket, Tierce, Tol(l)booth, Vespers

Officer(s) Acater, Adjutant, Admiral, Ag(h)a, Agistor, Aide, Bailiff, Beatty, Black Rod, Blimp, Bombardier, Bos(u)n, Brass-hat, Brigadier, Bumbailiff, Capt(ain), Catchpole, Catchpoll, Cater, Centurion, Chamberlain, Chancellor, CIGS, Colonel, Commander, Commodore, Compliance, Constable, Cop(per), Co-pilot, Cornet, Coroner, Counter-round, Cursitor, Datary, Deacon, Decurion, Ensign, Equerry, Exciseman, Exon, Filacer, Flap, Flying, Gallant, Gen(eral), GOC, Group, Gunner, Havildar, Intendant, Janty, Jaunty, Jonty, Jurat, Lictor, Lt, Marshal, Mate, NCO, Number one, Oxon, Petty, Pilot, PO, Posse, Proctor, Provost, Provost-marshal, Purser, Pursuivant, Quartermaster, Returning, Sbirro, Second mate, Serang, Sewer, Sexton, Sheriff, Skipper, SL, SM, Speaker, Staff, Striper, Sub(altern), Sublieutenant, Tindal, Tipstaff, Treasurer, Tribune, Usher, Varlet, Waldgrave, Warden, Wardroom, Warrant, Yeoman

Official(s), Officious Aga, Agent, Amban, Amtman, Atabeg, Atabek, Attaché, Authorised, Beadle, Bossy, Bureaucrat, Catchpole, Censor, Chamberlain, Commissar, Commissioner, Consul, Count, Dean, Ephor, Equerry, Escheater, Executive, ➤ FORMAL, Functionary, Gauleiter, Hayward, Incumbent, Intendant, Jack-in-office, Jobsworth, Keeper, Landdrost, Lictor, Mandarin, Marplot, Marshal, Mayor, MC, Meddlesome, Mirza, Mueddin, Notary, Ombudsman, Palatine, Plenipotentiary, Polemarch, Poohbah, Postmaster, Pragmatic, Proctor,

Procurator, Prog, Proveditor, Staff, Steward, Suit, Timekeeper, Tribune, Valid, Verderer, Verger

Offset Balance, Cancel, Compensate, Counter(act), Counterbalance

Offspring Boy, Burd, Chick, Children, Daughter, Descendant, Family, Fry, Get, Girl, Heir, Procreation, Product, Progeny, Seed, Sient, Son, Spawn

Often Frequent, Habitual, Repeated

▷**Often** may indicate 'of ten'

Oil(y), Oil producer Aj(o)wan, Anele, Anoint, Argan, Attar, Balm, Banana, Bath, Beech-mast, Ben, Benne, Benni, Bergamot, Bittern, Bone, BP, Bribe, Brilliantine, Camphire, Camphor, Carapa, Carron, Castor, Clove, Coal, Coconut, Cod-liver, Copra, Corn, Cotton-seed, Creosote, Croton, Crude, Diesel, Dittany, Essence, Essential, Eucalyptus, Evening primrose, Extra virgin, Fatty, Fixed, Fuel, Fusel, Gingelli, Gingelly, Gingili, Good, Groundnut, Heavy, Kerosene, Kerosine, Lamp, Lavender, Linseed, Lipid, Lubricant, Macassar, Magilp, Megilp, Menthol, Midnight, Mineral, Mirbane, Multigrade, Mustard, Myrbane, Myrrhol, Naphtha, Neat's-foot, Neem, Neroli, Nim, Oint, Oleo, Olive, Ottar, Otto, Palm, Paraffin, Patchouli, Pomade, Poon, Pristane, Rape, Rapeseed, Retinol, Ricinus, Rose, Rosin, Rusa, Safrole, Sassafras, Savin(e), Semsem, Sesame, Shale, Sleek, Slick, Slum, Smalmy, Smarmy, Smeary, Sperm, Spike(nard), Stand, Star-anise, Sunflower, Tall(ow), Tolu, Train, Tung, Turpentine, Unction, Vegetable, Virgin, Vitriol, Volatile, Whale, Wintergreen

Ointment Balm, Basilicon, Boracic, Boric, Cerate, Cream, Nard, Pomade, Pomatum, Salve, Spikenard, Unguent, Vaseline®, Zinc

OK Agree(d), Approve, Authorise, Clearance, Copacetic, Copesettic, Hunky-dory, Initial, Kosher, Right(o), Sanction, Sound, U, Vet

Old(er) Ae(t), Aged, Aine(e), Ancient, Antique, Auld, Bean, Decrepit, Dutch, Fogram, Former, Gaffer, Geriatric, Glory, Gray, Grey, Hills, Hoary, Immemorial, Methusaleh, Moore, Nestor, Nick, O, OAP, Obsolete, Off, Ogygian, One-time, Outworn, Palae-, Passé, Primeval, Rugose, Sen(escent), Senile, Senior, Shot, Stale, Trite, Venerable, Veteran, Victorian(a)

Old-fashioned Aging, Ancient, Antediluvian, Arch(aic), Arriere, Bygone, Corn(y), Dated, Dowdy, Fuddy-duddy, Medieval, No tech, Obsolete, Ogygian, Outmoded, Passé,

Primeval, Quaint, Relic, Retro, Rinky-dink, Schmaltzy, Shot, Square, Steam, Stick-in-the-mud, Traditional, Uncool

Old man, Old woman Anile, Aunty, Bodach, Burd, Cailleach, Crow, Faggot, Fantad, Fantod, Fogey, Fogramite, Fogy, Fussy, Gammer, Geezer, Grannam, Greybeard, Greyhen, Husband, Kangaroo, Luckie, Lucky, Methuselah, Mort, Mzee, OAP, Oom, Presbyte, Trout, Wife, Wight, Woopie, Wrinkly

Omelette Crepe, Foo yong, Foo yung, Frittata, Fu yung, Pancake, Spanish, Tortilla

Omen Abodement, Absit, Augury, Auspice, Foreboding, Forewarning, Freet, Freit, Portent, Presage, Prodrome, Sign, Token, Warning

Ominous Alarming, Baleful, Bodeful, Dire, Dour, Forbidding, Grim, Inauspicious, Oracular, Sinister, Threatening

Omission, Omit Aph(a)eresis, Apocope, Apospory, Apostrophe, Caret, Disregard, Drop, Elide, Elision, Ellipse, Ellipsis, Failure, Haplography, Haplology, Lipography, Loophole, Miss, Neglect, Nonfeasance, Oversight, Paral(e)ipomenon, Senza, Skip

On (it) About, Agreed, An, An't, At, Atop, By, Game, In, Leg, O', Of, Over, Pon, Re, Tipsy, Up(on)

▷ **On** may indicate an anagram

▷ **On board** may indicate chess, draughts, or 'SS' around another word

Once(r) Ance, ➤ AT ONCE, Bradbury, Earst, Erst(while), Ever, Ex, Fore, Former, Jadis, Oner, Onst, Secular, Sole, Sometime, Whilom

One(self) A, Ace, Ae, Alike, An(e), Any, Body, Chosen, Eeny, Ego, Ein, Individual, Integer, Me, Monad, Per se, Single(ton), Singular, Solo, Tane, Un, Unit(y), Unitary, United, Yin, You

One o'clock 1 am, ➤ NNE

Onion(s) Bengi, Bonce, Bulb, Chibol, Chive, Cibol, Cive, Eschalot, Head, Ingan, Jibbons, Leek, Lyonnaise, Moly, Pearl, Ramp, Ramson, Rocambole, Ropes, Scallion, Scilla, Shal(l)ot, Spanish, Spring, Squill, Sybo(e), Sybow

Onlooker Bystander, Kibitzer, Rubberneck, Spectator, Witness

Only Allenarly, Anerly, But, Except, Just, Meer, Merely, Nobbut, Seul, Singly, Sole

Onward Advance, Ahead, Away, Forth, Forward, Progress

Ooze Drip, Exhale, Exude, Gleet, Mud, Percolate, Pteropod(a), Seep, Sew, Sipe, Slime, Slob, Spew, Spue, Sweat

Opaque, Opacity Dense, Dull, Leucoma, Obscure, Obtuse, Onycha, Roil, Thick

Open(er), Opening, Openness Adit, Ajar, Antithesis, Anus, Apert(ure), Apparent, Apse, Bald, Bare, Bat, Bole, Breach, Break, Broach, Buttonhole, Candid, Cardia, Cavity, Chance, Chasm, Chink, Clear, Crevasse, Dehisce, Deploy, Door, Dup, Embrasure, Exordium, Expansive, Eyelet, Fair, Fenestra, Fissure, Fistula, Flue, Fontanel(le), Foramen, Frank, Free, Gambit, Gap, Gaping, Gat, Gate, Give, Glasnost, Glottis, Hagioscope, Hatch, Hatchback, Hiatus, Hilus, ➤ HOLE, Inaugural, Interstice, Intro, Key, Lacy, Lance, Loid, Loophole, Loose, Manhole, Meatus, Mofette, Mouth, Oillet, Orifice, Oscule, Osculum, Ostiole, Ostium, Overture, Patent, Peephole, Pert, Pervious, Pick(lock), Placket, Plughole, Pore, Port(age), Porta, Porthole, Preliminary, Premiere, Prise, Pro-am, Public, Pylorus, Rent, Room, Scuttle, Sesame, Sicilian, Sincere, Slit, Spare, Spirant, Squint, Start, Stoma, Thereout, Touchhole, Trapdoor, Trema, Trou, Truthful, Unbar, Unbolt, Unbutton, Uncork, Undo, Unfurl, Unhasp, Unlatch, Unscrew, Untie, Vent, Vulnerable, Window

Opera Aida, Ariadne, Ballad, Bouffe, Burletta, Comic, ENO, Ernani, Falstaff, Faust, Fedora, Fidelio, Glyndebourne, Grand, Hansel and Gretel, Horse, Idomineo, Iolanthe, Light, Lohengrin, Lulu, Met, Musical, Nabucco, Norma, Oater, Oberon, Onegin, Orfeo, Otello, Parsifal, Pastorale, Patience, Pinafore, Rigoletto, Ruddigore, Savoy, Scala, Seria, Singspiel, Soap, Space, Tell, The Met, Threepenny, Tosca, Turandot, Verismo, Work, Zarzuela

Operate, Operation, Operative Act(ion), Activate, Actuate, Agent, Artisan, Attuition, Caesarean, Campaign, Conduct, Couching, Current, Detective, Exercise, Function, Game, Hobday, Keystroke, Manipulate, Mechanic, Overlord, Practice, Run, Sortie, Strabotomy, Ure, Valid, Work

Operator Agent, Conductor, Dealer, Manipulator, Nabla, Sparks, Surgeon

Opiate, Opium Dope, Drug, Hop, Laudanum, Meconin, Narcotic, Religion, Soporific, Thebaine

Opinion, Opinionative Attitude, Belief, Bet, Consensus, Cri, Dictum, Dogma, Doxy, Entêté, Esteem, Feeling, Guess,

Judgement, Mind, Private, Public, Pulse, Say, Second, Sense, Sentence, Sentiment, Tenet, Utterance, View, Viewpoint, Voice

Opponent(s) Adversary, Antagonist, Anti, E-N, Enemy, E-S, Foe, Gainsayer, N-E, N-W, S-E, S-W, W-N, W-S

Opportune, Opportunist, Opportunity Appropriate, Apropos, Break, Carpetbagger, ➤ CHANCE, Day, Facility, Favourable, Go-go, Heaven-sent, Occasion, Opening, Pat, Room, Seal, Seel, Sele, Snatcher, Tide, Timely, Timous, Window

Oppose(d), Opposing, Opposite, Opposition Against, Agin, Antipathy, Antipodes, Antiscian, Antithesis, Antithetic, Antonym, Argue, At, Au contraire, Averse, Battle, Black, Breast, Colluctation, Combat, Confront, Contradict, Contrary, Converse, Counter, Diametric, Dissent, Distance, E contrario, Face, Foreanent, Fornen(s)t, Hinder, Hostile, Impugn, Inimical, Irene, Militate, Noes, Object, Overthwart, Polar, Reaction, Reluct, Repugn, Resist, Retroact, Reverse, Rival, Shadow, Subtend, Syzygy, Teeth, Terr, Thereagainst, Thwart, Toto caelo, Traverse, V, Versus, Vis-a-vis, Withstand

Oppress(ion), Oppressive Airless, Bind, Burden, Close, Crush, Despotic, Incubus, Jackboot, Onerous, Overpower, Persecute, Ride, Stifling, Sultry, Tyrannise

Opt, Option(al) Alternative, ➤ CHOICE, Choose, Default, Elect, Facultative, Fine, Menu, Pick, Plump, Select, Soft, Voluntary, Votive, Wale, Zero(-zero)

Optimism, Optimist(ic) Chiliast, Expectant, Hopeful, Morale, Pangloss, Pollyanna, Rosy, Sanguine, Upbeat

Or Au, Either, Ere, Gold, Ossia, Otherwise, Sol

Orange An(n)atta, Annatto, Arnotto, Aurora, Bergamot, Bigarade, Blood, Blossom, Chica, Clockwork, Croceate, Flame, Flamingo, Fulvous, Jaffa, Kamala, Kamela, Kamila, Karaka, Mandarin, Mock, Naartje, Nacarat, Nartjie, Navel, Osage, Pig, Roucou, Ruta, Satsuma, Seville, Shaddock, Tangerine, Tenné, Ugli, Ulsterman

Orate, Oration Address, Eloge, Elogium, Elogy, Eulogy, Harangue, Panegyric, Speech

Oratorio, Orator(y) Boanerges, Brompton, Brougham, Cantata, Cicero, Creation, Demosthenes, Diction, Elijah, Hwyl, Isocrates, Morin, Nestor, Prevaricator, Proseucha, Proseuche, Rhetor, Samson, Spellbinder, Stump, Tub-thumper, Windbag

Orbit Apse, Apsis, Circuit, Dump, Eccentric, Ellipse, Eye, Path, Revolution, Stationary

Orchestra(te), Orchestration Ensemble, Gamelan, Hallé, LPO, LSO, Ripieno, Score, Symphony

Orchid Adam and Eve, Adder's mouth, Arethusa, Bee, Bird's nest, Bog, Burnt-tip, Calanthe, Calypso, Cattleya, Coalroot, Cymbidium, Disa, Epidendrum, Fly, Fragrant, Frog, Helleborine, Lady, Lady's slipper, Lady's tresses, Lizard, Man, Marsh, Military, Monkey, Musk, Naked lady, Odontoglossum, Oncidium, Puttyroot, Salep, Slipper, Snakemouth, Swamp pink, Twayblade, Vanda, Vanilla

Ordain Arrange, Command, Decree, Destine, Enact, Induct, Japan, Priest

Ordeal Corsned, Disaster, Preeve, Test, ➤ TRIAL

Order(ed), Orderly, Orders Adjust, Affiliation, Alphabetical, Apollonian, Apple-pie, Arrange, Array, Attendant, Attic, Avast, Bade, Bath, Batman, Battalia, Bed, Behest, Benedictine, Bespoke, Bid, Book, Call, Canon, Category, Caveat, CB, Charter, Cheque, Class, Coherent, Command(ment), Committal, Compensation, Composite, Court, Decorum, Decree, Demand, Dictate, Diktat, Direct(ion), Directive, Dispone, Dominican, Doric, DSO, Edict, Embargo, Enclosed, Enjoin, En règle, Establishment, Fiat, Firman, Form(ation), Franciscan, Fraternity, Freemason, Garnishee, Garter, Ginkgo, Habeas corpus, Hest, Holy, Indent, Injunction, Interdict, Ionic, Irade, Kilter, Kosmos, Language, Mail, Mandamus, Mandate, Marching, Marshal, Masonic, Merit, Methodical, Monastic, Monitor, Neatness, Nunnery, OBE, Official, OM, Orange, Ord, Ordain, Organic, Pecking, Postal, Precedence, Premonstrant, Prescribe, Preservation, Rank, Receiving, Règle, Regular, Restraining, Right, Rule, Ruly, Series, Settle, Shipshape, Short, Side, Standing, State, Statutory, Stop(-loss), Subpoena, Summons, System, Tabulate, Taxis, Tell, Thistle, Tidy, Trim, Ukase, Uniformity, Writ

▷**Ordering** may indicate an anagram

Ordinary Average, Banal, Bog standard, Canton, Chevron, Comely, Common (or garden), Commonplace, Cot(t)ise, Everyday, Fess(e), Flanch, Flange, Folksy, Grassroots, Hackneyed, Mediocre, Middling, Mundane, ➤ NORMAL, O,

OR, Plain, Prosy, Pub, Saltier, Saltire, Simple, Tressure, Trivial, Usual, Workaday, Your

Ore Coin, Element, Mat, Middlings, Mineral, Minestone, Schlich, Seaweed, Slug

Organ(ic), Organs Barrel, Biogenic, Calliope, Carpel, Chord, Claspers, Clave, Console, Cort's, Ctene, Ear, Echo, Feeler, Fin, Fundus, Gill, Glairin, Gonad, Hammond®, Harmonium, House, Imine, Isomere, Kerogen, Kidney, Lien, Liver, Means, Media, Medulla, Melodion, Ministry, Nasal, Natural, Nectary, Newspaper, Palp, Pancreas, Part, Photophore, Pipe, Placenta, Plastid, Portative, Positive, Prothallus, Receptor, Recit, Regal, Relict, Sang, Sense, Serra, Spinneret, Spleen, Stamen, Steam, Swell, Tentacle, Thymus, Tongue, Tonsil, Tool, Tympanum, Uterus, Viscera, Vitals, Voice, Wurlitzer®

Organise(d), Organisation, Organiser Activate, Anatomy, ➤ ARRANGE, Association, Brigade, Caucus, Collect, Comecon, Company, Coordinate, Design, Embody, Entrepreneur, Fascio, Firm, Impresario, Infrastructure, Jaycee, Logistics, Machine, Mafia, Marshal, Mobilise, Orchestrate, Outfit, Personal, Quango, Rally, Regiment, Rosicrucian, Run, Setup, Soroptimist, Stage, Steward, System, Tidy, Together, UN

▷ **Organise(d)** may indicate an anagram

Organism Aerobe, Agamic, Being, Biont, Biotic, Cell, Chimeric, Ciliate, Clade, Coral, Diplont, Ecad, Entity, Epizoon, Germ, Incross, Infauna, Infusoria(n), Lichen, Medusa, Microbe, Moneron, Nekton, Neuston, Pathogen, Phenetics, Plankton, Protist, Protozoan, Saprobe, Streptococcus, Symbiont, Volvox

Orgy Bacchanalia(n), Binge, Bust, Carousal, Dionysian, Feast, Revel, Saturnalia, Spree, Wassail

Orient(al) Adjust, Annamite, Chinoiserie, Dawn, Dayak, E, East(ern), Fu Manchu, Hindu, Levant, Leyton, Malay, Mongolian, Shan, Sunrise, Tatar, Thai, Tibetan, Turk(o)man

Origin(al), Originate, Originating Abo, Adam, Arise, Beginning, Birth, Come, Cradle, Creation, Derive, Editio princeps, Elemental, Emanate, Epicentre, Etymon, Extraction, First, Firsthand, Focus, Found, Generic, Genesis, Genetical, Germ, Grow, Hatch, Incunabula, Innovate, Invent, Master, Mother, Nascence, Natality, New, Novel, Ord, Primal, Primary, Primigenial, Primordial, Pristine, Prototype, Provenance, Rise, Root, Seminal, Source, Spring, Start, Ur, Ylem, Zoism

Ornament(al), Ornamentation Adorn, Anaglyph,
Anthemion, Arabesque, Barbola, Baroque, Barrette, Bead,
Bedeck, Billet, Boss, Bracelet, Broider, Bugle, Bulla, Cartouche,
Chase, Clock, Cockade, Crocket, Curlicue, Decorate,
Decoration, Diamanté, Diglyph, Dog's-tooth, Doodad,
Embellish, Emblem(a), Enrich, Epaulet(te), Epergne, Fallal,
Fandangle, Figuration, Figurine, Filagree, Filigrain, Filigree,
Fleuret, Fleurette, Fleuron, Florid, Fret, Fretwork, Frill, Furbelow,
Furnish, Gadroon, Gaud, Illustrate, Inlay, Knotwork, Labret,
Leglet, Mantling, Millefleurs, Mordent, Moresque, Motif,
Nail-head, Netsuke, Nicknackery, Niello, O, Ovolo, Palmette,
Parure, Pectoral, Picot, Pipe, Pompom, Pounce,
Prettify, Prunt, Rel(l)ish, Rococo, Spangle, Tassel, Tool, Torque,
Torsade, Tracery, Trappings, Trimming, Trinket, Turn

Orthodox Cocker, Conventional, Hardshell, Proper, Sound,
Standard

Oscillate Fluctuate, Librate, Rock, Seiche, Squeg, Swing,
Vibrate, Waver

Osseous Bony, Hard, Skeletal, Spiny

Ostensibly Apparent, External, Seeming

Ostentation, Ostentatious Camp, Display, Dog, Eclat,
Epideictical, Extravagant, Fantoosh, Flamboyant, Flash(y),
Flaunt, Florid, Flourish, Garish, Gaudy, Highfalutin(g), Parade,
Pomp, Pretence, Puff, ➤ SHOW(ING), Side, Splash, Swank,
Tacky, Tulip

Ostracise, Ostracism Banish, Blackball, Boycott, Cut,
Exclude, Exile, Potsherd, Snub, Taboo

Other(wise), Others Additional, Aka, Alia, Alias, Allo-,
Besides, Different, Distinct, Else, Et al, Etc, Excluding, Former,
Further, Rest, Significant

▷**Otherwise** may indicate an anagram

Ought All, Should

Our(selves) Us, We

Oust Depose, Dislodge, Eject, Evict, Expel, Fire, Supplant

·**Out** Absent, Aglee, Agley, Asleep, Aus, Begone, Bowl, Dated, En
ville, Exposed, External, Forth, Haro, Harrow, Hors, Oust, Skittle,
Striking, Stump, Taboo, Uit, Unfashionable, Up, York

▷**Out** may indicate an anagram

Out and out Absolute, Arrant, Sheer, Stark, Teetotal, Thorough, Totally, Utter

Outbreak Epidemic, Eruption, Explosion, Plague, Putsch, Rash, Recrudescence

Outburst Access, Blurt, Bluster, Boutade, Evoe, Explosion, Fit, Flaw, Furore, Fusillade, Gush, Gust, Paroxysm, Passion, Salvo, Storm, Tantrum, Tumult, Volley

Outcast Cagot, Discard, Exile, Exul, Ishmael, Leper, Mesel, Pariah, Rogue

Outcome Aftermath, Consequence, Dénouement, Effect, Emergence, End, Event, ➤ RESULT, Sequel, Upshot

Outcry Bray, ➤ CLAMOUR, Howl, Hue, Protest, Racket, Steven, Uproar, Utas

Outdated Archaic, Dinosaur, Effete, Feudal, Fossil, Obsolete, Outmoded, Passé, Square

Outdoor(s) Alfresco, External, Garden, Open air, Plein-air

Outer External, Extrogenous, Magpie, Top

Outfit(ter) Catsuit, Ensemble, Equipage, Fitout, Furnish, Get-up, Haberdasher, Habit, Kit, Rig, Samfoo, Samfu, Strip, Suit, Team, Trousseau, Weed(s)

Outgoing Egression, Exiting, Extrovert, Open, Retiring

Outgrowth Ala(te), Aril, Bud, Enation, Epiphenomenon, Exostosis, Offshoot, Root-hair, Sequel, Trichome

Outhouse Lean to, Privy, Shed, Skilling, Skipper, Stable

Outing Excursion, Jaunt, Junket, Picnic, Sortie, Spin, Spree, Treat, Trip, Wayzgoose

Outlandish Barbarous, Bizarre, Exotic, Foreign, Peregrine, Rum

Outlaw Allan-a-Dale, Attaint, Badman, Ban, Bandit(ti), Banish, Exile, Fugitive, Hereward, Horn, Proscribe, Robin Hood, Rob Roy, Ronin, Tory, Waive

Outlet Débouché, Egress, Estuary, Exit, Femerell, Market, Opening, Outfall, Sluice, Socket, Tuyere, Tweer, Twier, Twire, Twyer(e), Vent

Outline Adumbration, Aperçu, Circumscribe, Configuration, Contorno, Contour, Delineate, Digest, ➤ DRAFT, Footprint, Layout, Note, Perimeter, Plan, Profile, Relief, Scenario, Schematic, Shape, Silhouette, Skeletal, Skeleton, Sketch, Summary, Syllabus, Synopsis, T(h)alweg, Trace

Outlook Casement, Perspective, Prospect, View, Vista

▷**Out of** may indicate an anagram

▷**Out of sorts** may indicate an anagram

Output Data, Get, Produce, Production, Turnout, Yield

▷**Output** may indicate an anagram

Outrage(ous) Affront, Atrocity, Desecrate, Disgust, Egregious, Enorm(ity), Flagrant, Insult, OTT, Rich, Sacrilege, Scandal, Shocking, Ungodly, Violate

▷**Outrageously** may indicate an anagram

Outright Clean, Complete, Entire, Point-blank, Utter

Outside Ab extra, Crust, Exterior, External, Front, Furth, Hors, Periphery, Rim, Rind, Rine, Surface

Outsider Alien, Bolter, Bounder, Cad, Extern, Extremist, Foreigner, Incomer, Oustiti, Pariah, Ring-in, Stranger, Stumer, Unseeded, Upstart

Outskirts Edge, Fringe, Periphery, Purlieu

Outspoken Bluff, Blunt, Broad, Candid, Explicit, Forthright, Frank, Plain, Rabelaisian, Round, Vocal

Outstanding Ace, Beaut(y), Belter, Billowing, Bulge, Chief, Eminent, Especial, Exceptional, Extant, First, Fugleman, Highlight, Humdinger, Impasto, Jut, Lulu, Marked, Matchless, Oner, Owing, Paragon, Phenomenal, Prince, Prize, Prominent, Promontory, Prosilient, Proud, Relief, Relievo, Salient, Signal, Special, Squarrose, Star, Stellar, Strout, Superb, Tour de force, Unpaid, Unsettled

Outward Efferent, Extern(e), External, Extrinsic, Extrorse, Extrovert, Posticous, Postliminary, Superficial

Outwit Baffle, Best, Circumvent, Dish, Euchre, Fox, Over-reach, ➤ THWART, Trick

Oval Cartouche, Ellipse, Henge, Navette, Ooidal

Oven(-like) Aga®, Calcar, Convection, Cul-de-four, Dutch, Furnace, Haybox, Horn(it)o, Kiln, Lear, Leer, Lehr, Lime kiln, Microwave, Muffle, Oast, Oon, Stove

Over Above, Across, Again, Atop, C, Clear, Done, Finished, Hexad, Left, Maiden, Of, On, Ore, Ort, Owre, Sopra, Spare, Superior, Surplus, Uber, Yon

Overcast Cloudy, Lowering, Sew, Sombre

Overcharge Clip, Extort, Fleece, Gyp, OC, Rack-rent, Rook, Rush, Soak, Sting

Overcome Beat, Bested, Conquer, Convince, Defeat, Kill, Master, Mither, Prevail, Quell, Speechless, Subjugate, Surmount, Vanquish, Win

▷**Overdrawn** may indicate 'red' outside another word

Overdue Behindhand, Belated, Excessive, Late

Overflow Lip, Nappe, Ooze, Redound, Spillage, Surfeit, Teem

Overhang(ing) Beetle, Bulge, ➤ JUT, Project, Shelvy

Overhaul Bump, Catch, Overtake, Recondition, Revision, Service, Strip

Overhead(s) Above, Aloft, Ceiling, Cost, Exes, Hair(s), Headgear, Oncost, Rafter, Upkeep, Zenith

Overhear Catch, Eavesdrop, Tap

Overlap(ping) Correspond, Equitant, Imbricate, Incubous, Kern(e), Limbous, Obvolute, Tace, Tasse

Overlay Ceil, Smother, Stucco, Superimpose, Veneer

Overload Burden, Plaster, Strain, Surcharge, Tax

Overlook Condone, Disregard, Excuse, Forget, Miss, Pretermit, Superintend

Overpower(ing) Crush, Evince, Mighty, Onerous, Oppress, Overwhelm, Subdue, Surmount, Swelter, Whelm

Overrule Abrogate, Disallow, Veto

Overrun Exceed, Extra, Infest, Inundate, Invade, Swarm, Teem

Overseas Abroad, Colonial, Outremer

Oversee(r) Baas, Boss, Captain, Care, Deputy, Direct, Eyebrow, Foreman, Grieve, Handle, Induna, Periscope, Steward, Supercargo, Survey(or)

Overshadow Cloud, Dominate, Eclipse, Obscure, Outclass

Oversight Blunder, Care, Error, Gaffe, Lapse, Neglect

Overstate(ment) Embroider, Exaggerate, Hyperbole

Overt Manifest, Patent, Plain, Public

Overtake Catch, For(e)hent, Lap, Leapfrog, Overget, Overhaul, ➤ PASS, Supersede

Overthrow Dash, Defeat, Demolish, Depose, Down, Labefact(at)ion, Ruin, Smite, Stonker, Subvert, Supplant, Unhorse, Vanquish, Whemmle, Whommle, Whumple, Worst

Overture Advance, Carnival, Egmont, Hebrides, Intro, Leonora, Offer, ➤ OPENING, Prelude, Propose, Sinfonia, Toccata, Toccatella, Toccatina

Overturn(ing) Catastrophe, Quash, Reverse, Tip, Topple, Up(set), Whemmle

Overwhelm(ed), Overwhelming Accablé, Assail, ➤ CRUSH, Inundate, KO, Mind-boggling, Overcome, Scupper, Smother, Submerge, Swamp

Overwork(ed) Fag, Hackneyed, Ornament, Slog, Stale, Supererogation, Tax, Tire, Toil

Owe(d), Owing Attribute, Due, OD

Owl(s) Barn, Barred, Blinker, Boobook, Brown, Bubo, Bunter, Eagle, Elegant, Fish, Glimmergowk, Hawk, Hoo(ter), Horned, Jenny, Little, Long-eared, Longhorn, Madge, Moper, Mopoke, Mopus, Night, Ogle, Parliament, Ruru, Saw-whet, Scops, Screech, Snowy, Strich, Striges, Strigiformes, Tawny, Wood

Own(er), Owning, Ownership Admit, Agnise, Domain, Dominium, Have, Hold, Mortmain, Nain, Of, Possess, Proper, Proprietor, Recognise, Use

Ox(en) Anoa, Aquinas, Aurochs, Banteng, Banting, Bison, Bonas(s)us, Buffalo, Bugle, Bullock, Cat(t)alo, Fee, Gaur, Gayal, Gyal, Kouprey, Mart, Musk, Neat, Ovibos, Rother, Sapi-utan, S(e)ladang, Steare, Steer, Taurus, Ure, Urus, Yak, Yoke, Zebu

▷**Oxtail** may indicate 'x'

Oxygen (and lack of) Anoxia, Epoxy, Liquid, Lox, Loxygen, O

Oyster (bed), Oyster-eater Avicula, Bivalve, Bush, Cul(t)ch, Kentish, Lay, Mollusc, Native, Ostrea, Ostreophage, Pandore, Pearl, Plant, Prairie, Scalp, Scaup, Seed(ling), Spat, Spondyl, Vegetable

Oz Amos, Australia

Ozone Air, Atmosphere, Oxygen

Pp

Pace, Pacemaker Canter, Clip, Cracking, Dog-trot, Easter, Gait, Jog-trot, Lope, Measure, Pari passu, Pioneer, ➤ RATE, Snail's, Spank, Speed, Stroll, Tempo, Tramp, Tread, Trot

Pacific, Pacify Appease, Bromide, Conciliate, Dove, Ease, Irenic, Lull, Mild, Moderate, Ocean, Placid, Quiet, Serene, Soothe, Subdue, Sweeten, Tranquil

Pack(age), Packed, Packing Bale, Blister, Box, Bubble, Bundle, Cards, Compress, Congest, Cram, Crate, Crowd, Cry, Deck, Dense, Dunnage, Embox, Entity, Excelsior, Fardel, Floe, Gasket, Gaskin, Glut, Hamper, Hunt, Kennel, Knapsack, Load, Matilda, Pair, ➤ PARCEL, Pikau, Rout, Rucksack, Set, Shiralee, Steeve, Stow, Suits, Tamp, Tread, Troop, Truss, Wad, Wolf, Wrap

Packet Boat, Bundle, Liner, Mailboat, Mint, Parcel, Roll, Sachet, Steamboat, Wage

Pact Agreement, Alliance, Bargain, Bilateral, Cartel, Contract, Covenant, Locarno, ➤ TREATY, Warsaw

Pad(ding) Batting, Bombast, Brake, Bustle, Compress, Crash, Cushion, Dabber, Dossil, Enswathe, Expand, Falsies, Filler, Flat, Frog, Hassock, Horse, Launch, Leg-guard, Lily, Nag, Numnah, Paw, Ped, Pillow, Pincushion, Plastron, Pledget, Plumper, Pouf(fe), Protract, Pulvillus, Stuff, Sunk, Tablet, Thief, Touch, Tournure, Tylopod, Tympan, Velour(s), Velure, Wad, Wase

Paddle(-foot) Canoe, Dabble, Doggy, Oar, Pinniped, Seal, Side-wheel, Spank, Splash, Wade

Pagan Animist, Atheist, Gentile, Gentoo, Godless, Heathen, Idolater, Infidel, Odinist, Paynim, Saracen

Page(s), Pageboy Bellboy, Bellhop, Bleep, Boy, Buttons, Flyleaf, Folio, Foolscap, Gate-fold, Groom, Haircut, Hornbook, Leaf, Messenger, Moth, Octavo, P, Pane, PP, Quarto, Ream, Recto, Ro, Servant, Sheet, Side, Squire, Tear sheet, Tiger, Title, Varlet, Verso, Web, Yellow

Pageant Cavalcade, Pomp, Spectacle, Tattoo, Triumph

➤**Paid** see PAY

Pain(ful), Pains Ache, Aggrieve, Agony, Ake, Angina, Anguish, Bad, Bale, Bitter, Bore, Bot(t), Bother, Colic, Cramp, Crick, Distress, Dole, Doleur, Dolour, Dool(e), Dysury, Excruciating, Gip, Grief, Gripe, Gyp, Harrow, Heartburn, ➤ HURT, Ill, Kink, Laborious, Mal, Migraine, Misery, Myalgia, Neuralgia, Pang, Persuant, Pest, Prick, Pungent, Rack, Raw, Referred, Sair, Sciatica, Smart, Sore, Sorrow, Sten(d), Sting, Stitch, Stung, Teen(e), Tene, Throe, Torment, Torture, Twinge, Wrench, Wring

▷**Pain** may indicate bread (French)

Painkiller Aminobutene, Analgesic, Bute, Cocaine, Distalgesic, Enkephalin, Meperidine, Metopon, Morphine, Number, Pethidine

Paint(ed), Painting Abstract, Acrylic, Action, Airbrush, Aquarelle, Art autre, Art deco, Artificial, Art nouveau, Bice, Canvas, Cellulose, Chiaroscuro, Clair-obscure, Clobber, Coat, Colour, Cubism, Dadaism, Daub, Dayglo, Decorate, Depict, Diptych, Distemper, Eggshell, Emulsion, Enamel, Fard, Finery, Flemish, Fresco, Genre, Gild, Gloss, Gouache, Grease, Hard-edge, Impasto, Impressionism, Limn, Matt, Miniate, Miniature, Modello, Naive, Nocturne, Oaker, Ochre, Oil, Old Master, Oleo(graph), Op art, Orphism, Paysage, Pict, Picture, Pigment, Pinxit, Plein air, Pointillism(e), Portray, Poster, Post-Impressionism, Primitive, Raddle, Rosemaling, Roughstuff, Scumble, Secco, Sfumato, Sien(n)ese, Stencil, Stereochrome, Stipple, Tablature, Tempera, Tondo, Umber, Umbrian, War

Painter ➤ ARTIST, Colourist, Cubist, Decorator, Gilder, Illusionist, Impressionist, Limner, Miniaturist, Paysagist, Plein-airist, Pre-Raphaelite, Primitive, Sien(n)ese

Pair(ing) Brace, Couple(t), Duad, Duo, Dyad(ic), Fellows, Geminate, Jugate, Link, Match, Mate, Ocrea, Pigeon, Pr, Span, Synapsis, Syndyasmian, Syzygy, Tandem, Thummim, Twa(e), Tway, Two, Urim, Yoke

Pal Ally, Amigo, Bud(dy), China, Chum, Comrade, Crony, Cully, Mate

Palace Alhambra, Basilica, Blenheim, Buckingham, Court, Crystal, Edo, Elysee, Escorial, Escurial, Fontainebleau, Gin, Holyrood, Hotel, Istana, Lambeth, Lateran, Louvre, Mansion, Nonsuch, Palatine, Pitti, Quirinal, Sans Souci, Schloss, Seraglio, Serail, Shushan, Topkapi, Trianon, Tuileries, Valhalla, Vatican, Versailles

Palatable, Palate Dainty, Relish, Roof, Sapid, Savoury, Soft, Taste, Toothsome, Uranic, Uraniscus, Uvula, Velum

Pale, Paling Ashen, Blanch, Bleach, Cere, Dim, Etiolate(d), Fade, ➤ FAINT, Ghostly, Haggard, Insipid, Lily (white), Livid, Mealy, Ox-fence, Pastel, Peelie-wally, Picket, Sallow, Shilpit, Stang, Verge, Wan, Whey-faced, White, Wishy-washy

Palestine, Palestinian Amorite, Gadarene, Intifada, Israel, Pal, PLO, Samaria

Pall Bore, Cloy, Damper, Glut, Mantle, Satiate, Shroud

Pallet Bed, Cot, Couch, Mattress, Tick

Palm Accolade, Areca, Assai, Atap, Babassu, Betel, Buriti, Bussu, Cabbage, Calamus, Coco, Conceal, Coquito, Corozo, Corypha, Date (tree), Doom, Doum, Elaeis, Fan, Feather, Fob, Foist, Hand, Ita, Itching, Ivory, Laurels, Loof, Macahuba, Macaw, Macoya, Nipa, Oil, Palmyra, Peach, Raffia, Raphia, Rat(t)an, Royal, Sabal, Sago, Sugar, Talipat, Talipot, Thenar, Toddy, Triumph, Troelie, Troolie, Trooly, Trophy, Vola, Wax, Wine

Paltry Bald, Cheap, Exiguous, Mean, Measly, Peanuts, Pelting, Petty, Poor, Puny, Scalled, Sorry, Tin(-pot), Tinny, Trashy, Trifling, Two-bit, Vile, Waff, Whiffet

Pamper(ed) Cocker, Coddle, Cosher, Cosset, Cuiter, Feather-bed, Gratify, High-fed, ➤ INDULGE, Mollycoddle, Pet, Spoon-fed

Pamphlet Brochure, Catalogue, Leaflet, Notice, Sheet, Tract

Pan Agree, Auld Hornie, Bainmarie, Balit, Basin, Betel(-pepper), Braincase, Chafer, Dent, Dial, Drip, Goat-god, Goblet, God, Ice-floe, Iron, Karahi, Ladle, Nature-god, Pancheon, Panchion, Patella, Patina, Peter, Poacher, Prospect, Roast, Salt, Search, Skillet, Slag, Slate, Spider, Vessel, Wo(c)k, Work

Pancake Blin(i), Blintz(e), Burrito, Crêpe (suzette), Drop(ped)-scone, Flam(m), Flapjack, Flaune, Flawn, Fraise, Fritter, Froise, Pikelet, Poppadum, Quesadilla, Slapjack, Suzette, Taco, Tortilla, Tostada, Waffle

Pane Glass, Light, Panel, Quarrel, Quarry, Sheet

Panel(ling) Board, Cartouche, Dashboard, Fa(s)cia, Gore, Hatchment, Inset, Instrument, Jury, Mandorla, Mimic, Orb, Patch(board), Rocker, Screen, Skreen, Solar, Stile, Stomacher, Tablet, Valance, Volet, Wainscot

Pang Achage, Ache, Qualm, Spasm, Stab, Twinge, Wrench

Panic Alar(u)m, Amaze, Consternation, Fear, Flap, Flat-spin, Fright, Funk, Guinea-grass, Millet, Raggee, Raggy, Ragi, ➤ SCARE, Scarre, Stampede, Stampedo, Stew, Tailspin, ➤ TERROR

Pannier Basket, Cacolet, Corbeil, Dosser, Skip, Whisker

Panorama, Panoramic Range, Scenery, Veduta, View, Vista

Pant(s) Bags, Breeches, Capri, Cargo, Chaps, Chinos, Culottes, Deck, Dhoti, Drawers, Fatigues, Flaff, Gasp, Gaucho, Harem,

Long johns, Longs, Parachute, Pech, Pedal-pushers, Pegh, Puff, Slacks, Smalls, Stovepipe, Sweat, Throb, Toreador, Trews, Trousers, Wheeze, Yearn

Panther Bagheera, Black, Cat, Cougar, Jaguar, Leopard, Pink

Pantomime Charade, Cheironomy, Dumb-show, Farce, Galanty, Harlequinade, Play

Pantry Buttery, Closet, Larder, Spence, Stillroom

Papal, Papist Catholic, Clementine, Concordat, Guelf, Guelph, Pontifical, RC, Roman, Vatican

Paper(s), Papery Art, Atlas, Ballot, Bible, Bond, Broadsheet, Broadside, Bromide, Brown, Bumf, Bumph, Carbon, Cartridge, Cellophane®, Chad, Cigarette, Command, Confetti, Cream-laid, Cream-wove, Crepe, Crown, Daily, Decorate, Demy, Document, Dossier, Elephant, Emery, Emperor, Essay, Exam, File, Filter, Final, Flock, Folio, Foolscap, FT, Galley, Garnet, Gem, Glass(ine), Graph, Greaseproof, Green, Guardian, India, Jesus, Journal, Kraft, Laid, Linen, Litmus, Manil(l)a, Mirror, MS, Music-demy, News(print), Note, Onion-skin, Order, Page, Papyrus, Parchment, Pickwick, Position, Post, Pot(t), Pravda, Press, Print, Quair, Quarto, Quire, Rag, Ramee, Rami(e), Ream, Retree, Rhea, Rice, Rolling, Royal, Saxe, Scent, Scotsman, Scrip, Sheaf, Sheet, Slipsheet, Sugar, Sun, Tabloid, Taffeta, TES, Test, Thesis, Tiger, Tissue, Toilet, Touch, Tracing, Treatise, Vellum, Voucher, Waste, Wax(ed), Web, White, Wove, Wrapping, Writing

Paper-cutting, Paper-folding Decoupage, Kirigami, Origami, Psaligraphy

Par Average, Equate, Equivalent, ➤ NORMAL, Scratch

Parable Allegory, Fable, Proverb

Parachute, Parachutist Aigrette, Drogue, Float, Jump, Para, Parabrake, Red Devil, Silk, Skyman, Thistledown, Umbrella

Parade (ground) Air, Arcade, Cavalcade, Church, Display, Dress, Drill, Easter, Emu, Flaunt, Gala, Hit, Identification, Procession, Identity, Maidan, March-past, Pageantry, Pomp, Prom(enade), Show, Sick, Ticker tape

Paradise Arcadia, Avalon, Bliss, Eden, Elysium, Garden, Heaven, Lost, Malaguetta, Nirvana, Park, Regained, Shangri-la, Svarga, Swarga, Swerga, ➤ UTOPIA

Paradox(ical) Absurdity, Cantor's, Contradiction, Dilemma, Electra, Gilbertian, Koan, Olber's, Puzzle, Russell's, Zeno's

Paraffin Earthwax, Kerosene, Kerosine, Liquid, Ozocerite, Ozokerite, Photogen(e), Propane

Parallel Analog, Collimate, Corresponding, Equal, Even, Forty-ninth, Like

Paralysis, Paralyse Apoplexy, Cataplexy, Cramp, Curarise, Cycloplegia, Diplegia, Halt, Hemiplegia, Infantile, Monoplegia, Numbness, Palsy, Paraplegia, Paresis, Polio, Quadriplegia, Scram, Shock, Shut, Spastic, Spina bifida, Stun

Parapet (space) Bartisan, Bartizan, Battlement, Brisure, Bulwark, Crenel, Flèche, Machicolation, Merlon, Rampart, Redan, Surtout, Terreplein, Top, Wall

Parasite, Parasitic Biogenous, Biotroph, Bloodsucker, Lackey, Scrounger, Shark, Sponge(r), Sucker, Symphile, Toady, Trencher-friend, Trencher-knight, Vampire

Parcel Allocate, Allot, Aret, Bale, Bundle, Holding, Lot, Package, Packet, Sort, Wrap

Parch(ed) Arid, Bake, Dry, Graddan, Roast, Scorched, Sere, Thirsty, Torrid

Parchment Diploma, Forel, Mezuzah, Papyrus, Pell, Pergameneous, Roll, Roule, Scroll, Sheepskin, Vellum

Pardon(able), Pardoner Absolve, Amnesty, Anan, Assoil, Clear, Condone, Eh, Excuse, ▶ FORGIVE, Grace, Mercy, Qu(a)estor, Release, Remission, Remit, Reprieve, Venial, What

Parent(al) Ancestral, Father, Forebear, Genitor, Maternal, Mother, Paternal, Storge

Parish District, Flock, Kirkto(w)n, Parischan(e), Parishen, Parochin(e), Peculiar, Province, Title

Park(ing) Battery, Brecon Beacons, Business, Common, Dales, Dartmoor, Enclosure, Everglades, Exmoor, Fun, Garage, Green, Grounds, Hyde, Jasper, Kruger, Lake District, Lung, Mansfield, Mungo, Nairobi, Northumberland, Osterley, P, Paradise, Peak District, Pitch, Preserve, Rec, Safari, Sanctuary, Sandown, Science, Sequoia, Serengeti, Snowdonia, Stop, Theme, Valet, Wildlife, Yard, Yellowstone, Yosemite

Parliament Addled, Althing, Barebones, Black, Commons, Congress, Council, Cross-bench, Dail, Diet, Drunken, House, Imperial, Knesset, Lack-learning, Lawless, Legislature, Long,

Lords, Merciless, Mongrel, Reichstag, Rump, St Stephens, Sanhedrin, Seanad, Short, Stormont, Thing, Tynwald, Unicameral, Westminster

Parliamentarian Cabinet, Fairfax, Ireton, Leveller, Member, MP, Roundhead, Whip

Parlour Beauty, Funeral, Lounge, Massage, Salon, Snug

Parody Burlesque, Lampoon, Mock, Piss-take, Satire, Sendup, Skit, Spoof, Travesty

Parrot Amazon, Cockatoo, Conure, Copy, Flint, Green leek, Imitate, Kaka(po), Kea, Lorikeet, Lory, Lovebird, Macaw, Mimic, Nestor, Owl, Parakeet, Paroquet, Poll(y), Popinjay, Psittacine, Quarrion, Repeat, Rosella, Rote, Stri(n)gops, T(o)uraco

Parson Clergyman, Cleric, Minister, Non juror, Pastor, Priest, Rector, Rev, Sky-pilot, Soul-curer, Yorick

Part(ing) Accession, Aliquot, Antimere, Area, Aught, Bulk, Bye, Cameo, Character, Chunk, Component, Constituent, Crack, Cue, Dislink, Diverge, Dole, Element, Episode, Escapement, Farewell, Fascicle, Fork, Fraction, Goodbye, Half, Instalment, Lathe, Lead, Leave, Leg, Lill, Lilt, Lines, List, Member, Parcel, ➤ PIECE, Portion, Proportion, Pt, Quota, Rape, Ratio, Region, Rive, Role, Scena, Scene, Secondo, Section, Sector, Segment, Separate, Sever, Shade, Share, Shed, Sleave, Sle(i)ded, ➤ SOME, Spare, Split, Stator, Sunder, Tithe, Unit, Vaunt, Walk on, Wrench

Partial(ity), Partially Biased, Ex-parte, Fan, Favour, Halflins, Imbalance, Incomplete, One-sided, Predilection, Slightly, Unequal, Weakness

Particle(s) Alpha, Antineutron, Atom, Baryon, Beta, Bit, Boson, Corpuscle, Dander, Delta, Deuteron, Fleck, Fragment, Gemmule, Gluon, Grain, Granule, Ion, J, Jot, Lambda, Lepton, Meson, Mite, Molecule, Muon, Neutrino, Neutron, Parton, Photon, Pion, Platelet, Positron, Prion, Proton, Quark, Radioactivity, Shower, Sigma, Sinter, Smithereen, Speck, Strange, W, Whit, WIMP, Z

Particular Choosy, Dainty, ➤ DETAIL, Endemic, Especial, Essential, Express, Fiky, Fog, Fussy, Item, Itself, London fog, Nice, Niffy-naffy, Own, Pea-souper, Peculiar, Pernickety, Pet, Point, Prim, Proper, ➤ RESPECT, Special, Specific, Stickler, Strict, Stripe

Partisan Adherent, Axe, Biased, Carlist, Champion, Devotee, Factional, Fan, Irregular, Partial, Provo, Sider, Spear, Supporter, Yorkist

Partition(ed) Abjoint, Bail, Barrier, Brattice, Bretasche, Bulkhead, Cloison, Cubicle, Diaphragm, Dissepiment, Division, Hallan, Mediastinum, Parpane, Parpen(d), Parpent, Parpoint, Perpend, Perpent, Replum, ➤ SCREEN, Scriene, Septum, Tabula, Wall, With

Partner(ship) Accomplice, Ally, Associate, Butty, Cahoot(s), Coachfellow, Colleague, Comrade, Confederate, Consort, Couple, Dutch, Escort, E-W, Firm, Gigolo, Mate, N-S, Pal, Pard, Sidekick, Silent, Sleeping, Sparring, Spouse, Stablemate, Stand, Symbiosis

▷**Part of** may indicate a hidden word

Party Acid house, Alliance, Assembly, At-home, Ball, Band, Barbecue, Bash, Beano, Bee, Bloc, Blowout, Body, Bottle, Bunfight, Bust, Camp, Carousal, Carouse, Caucus, Celebration, Clambake, Cocktail, Commando, Communist, Concert, Conservative, Contingent, Cooperative, Coterie, Cult, Democratic, Detail, Ding, Discotheque, Do, Drum, Faction, Fest, Fianna Fáil, Fine Gael, Funfest, Gala, Gang, Garden, Green, Greenback, Hen, Hoedown, Hooley, Hootenanny, Housewarming, Hurricane, Jol(lities), Junket, Junto, Knees-up, L, Labour, Launch, Lib, Liberal, Low heels, Mallemaroking, National, Neck-tie, Octobrist, Opposition, Person, Plaid, Progressive, Prohibition, Pyjama, Rave, Rave-up, Razzle(-dazzle), Reception, Republican, Revel, Ridotto, Rocking, Rort, Rout, SDP, Search, Sect, Set, Shindig, Shine, Shower, Side, Smoker, SNP, Soc(ialist), Social, Social Democratic, Soiree, Spree, Squad(rone), Stag, Symposium, Tea, Third, Thrash, Tory, Treat, Unionist, Whig, Wingding, Working

Pass(ed), Passing, Pass on, Past Ago, Agon, Aorist, Approve, Arise, Before, Behind, Beyond, Botte, Brenner, Brief, By, Bygone, Chine, Chit(ty), Clear, Col, Cote, Cross, Cursory, Death, Defile, Delate, Demise, Die, Disappear, Double, Elapse, Emit, End, Ensue, Ephemeral, Exceed, Exeat, Elapse, Forby, Forgone, Former, Gap, Gate, Gha(u)t, Glencoe, Glide, Go, Gulch, Halse, Hand, Happen, Hause, Impart, Impermanent, In transit, Khyber, Lap, Lead, Migrate, Nek, Notch, Nutmeg, Occur, Oer, OK, Okay, Oke, Omit, Overhaul, Overshoot,

Overtake, Pa, Palm, Participle, Perish, Permeate, Permit, Poll, Poort, Predicament, Proceed, Propagate, Pun(c)to, Qualify, Railcard, Reach, Reeve, Refer, Relay, Retroactive, Retrospect, Senile, Serve, Simplon, Since, Skim, Skip, Skirt, Slap, Sling, Snap, Spend, State, Thermopylae, Thread, Through, Ticket, Tip, Transient, Transilient, Transitory, Transmit, Transude, Travel, Troop, Veronica, Vet, Visa, Visé, Wall, Wayleave, Weather, While, Yesterday, Yesteryear

Passage Adit, Aisle, Alley(way), Alure, Apostrophe, Arcade, Archway, Arterial, Cadenza, Career, Channel, Chute, Citation, Clause, Close, Coda, Conduit, Corridor, Creep, Crossing, Crush, Dead-end, Defile, Drake, Drift, Duct, Eel-fare, Episode, Excerpt, Extract, Fare, Fat, Flat, Flight, Flue, Gallery, Gangway, Gap, Gat, Gate, Gut, Hall, Head, Inlet, Journey, Lane, Lapse, Loan, Lobby, Locus, Meatus, Mona, Movement, Northeast, Northwest, Para(graph), Path, Pend, Phrase, Pore, Portion, Prelude, Prose, Ride, Rite, Route, Sailing, Shaft, Shunt, Slap, Snicket, Strait, Street, Stretta, Stretto, Subway, Sump, Thorough(fare), Tour, Trachea, Trance, Transe, Transit(ion), Travel, Tunnel, Undercast, Unseen, Ureter, Voyage, Way, Windpipe

▷**Passage of arms** may indicate 'sleeve'

Passenger Cad, Commuter, Fare, Pillion, Rider, Slacker, Steerage, Straphanger, Traveller, Voyager, Wayfarer

Passion(ate), Passionately Anger, Appetite, Ardour, Con fuoco, Fervour, Fire, Flame, Frampold, Fury, Gust, Heat, Hot, Hunger, Hwyl, Ileac, Iliac, Intense, Ire, Irish, Kama, Love, Lust, Mania, Obsession, Oestrus, Rage, Stormy, Sultry, Torrid, Violent, Warm, Wax, Wrath, Yen, Zeal

Passive (stage) Apathetic, Dormant, Inert, Pathic, Patient, Pupa, Supine, Yielding

Passport Access, Clearance, Congé(e), Key, Laissez-passer, Nansen, Navicert, Sea-letter, Visa

Password Code, Countersign, Logon, Nayword, Parole, Sesame, Shibboleth, Tessera, Watchword

▶**Past** see PASS

Pasta Agnolotti, Cannelloni, Capelletti, Conchiglie, Durum, Farfal, Farfel, Fedelini, Fettuc(c)ine, Fusilli, Lasagna, Lasagne, Linguini, Macaroni, Manicotti, Noodles, Orzo, Penne, Perciatelli, Ravioli, Rigatoni, Spaghetti, Spaghettina, Tagliarini, Tagliatelle, Tortelli(ni), Vermicelli, Ziti

Paste, Pasty Ashen, Batter, Beat, Botargo, Boule, Bridie, Cerate, Clobber, Cornish, Dentifrice, Dough, Electuary, Fake, Filler, Fondant, Frangipane, Glue, Guarana, Harissa, Knish, Lute, Magma, Marzipan, Masala, Mastic, Miso, Mountant, Pale, Pallid, Putty, Pâté, Patty, Pearl-essence, Pie, Piroshki, Pirozhki, Poonac, Punch, Rhinestone, Slip, Slurry, Spread, Strass, Tahina, Tahini, Tapenade, Taramasalata, Wan

Pastor(al) Arcadia, Bucolic, Curé, Eclogue, Endymion, Idyl(l), Minister, Priest, Rector, Rural, Shepherd, Simple

Pastry Baclava, Baklava, Choux, Croustade, Cruller, Crust, Danish, Dariole, Dough, Eclair, Filo, Flaky, Flan, Millefeuille, Pie, Phyllo, Pie-crust, Profiterole, Puff, Quiche, Samosa, Shortcrust, Strudel, Tart, Turnover, Vol-au-vent

Pasture Alp, Eadish, Eddish, Feed, Fell, Fodder, Grassland, Graze, Herbage, Kar(r)oo, Lair, Lare, Lea, Lease, Leasow(e), Leaze, Ley, Machair, Mead(ow), Pannage, Potrero, Raik, Rake, Soum, Sowm, Tie, Transhume, Tye

▶**Pasty** see PASTE

Patch(y) Bed, Bit, Cabbage, Clout, Cobble, Cooper, Court plaster, Cover, Friar, Fudge, ➤ MEND, Mosaic, Nicotine, Pasty, Piebald, Piece, Plaque, Plaster, Pot, Purple, Solder, Tingle, Tinker, Vamp, Variegated

Path(way) Aisle, Allée, Alley, Arc, Berm, Berme, Boreen, Borstal(l), Bridle, Causeway, Causey, Clickstream, Course, Eclipse, Flight, Gate, Ginnel, Glide, Lane, Ley, Locus, Orbit, Pad, Parabola, Primrose, Ride, Ridgeway, Route, Runway, Sidewalk, Spurway, Stie, Sty(e), Swath(e), Track, Trail, Trajectory, Trod, Walkway, ➤ WAY, Xystus

Pathetic(ally) Doloroso, Drip, Forlorn, Piteous, Poignant, Sad, Touching

Patience Calm, Endurance, Forbearance, Fortitude, Indulgence, Monument, Solitaire, Stoicism, Virtue

Patient(s) Calm, Case, Clinic, Forbearing, Grisel(da), Grisilda, Invalid, Job, Long-suffering, Passive, Resigned, Stoic, Subject, Ward

Patriot(ic), Patriotism Cavour, Chauvinist, DAR, Emmet, Flag-waving, Flamingant, Garibaldi, Hereward, Irredentist, Jingoism, Loyalist, Maquis, Nationalist, Tell

Patrol Armilla, Guard, Outguard, Picket, Piquet, Prowl-car, Scout, Sentinel, Turm

Patron(age), Patronise(d), Patronising Advowson,
Aegis, Auspices, Benefactor, Business, Champion, Client,
Customer, Donator, Egis, Fautor, Maecenas, Nepotic, Protector,
Protégé, Provider, Shopper, ➤ SPONSOR, Stoop, Stoup

Pattern(ed) Argyle, Bird's eye, Blueprint, Check, Clock,
Design, Diaper, Dog's tooth, Draft, Epitome, Example,
Exemplar, Fiddle, Figuration, Format, Fret, Grain, Herringbone,
Holding, Hound's tooth, Matrix, Meander, ➤ MODEL, Mosaic,
Norm, Paisley, Paradigm, Paragon, Pinstripe, Plan, Pompadour,
Precedent, Prototype, Stencil, Symmetry, Syndrome, Tangram,
Template, Tessera, Tracery, Tread, Type, Willow

Pause Break, Breakpoint, Breather, Caesura, Cessation, Cesura,
Comma, Desist, Er, Fermata, Hesitate, Interkinesis, Interval,
Limma, Lull, Pitstop, ➤ RESPITE, Rest, Selah, Stop

Pave(ment), Paving Causeway, Clint, Diaper, Granolith,
Path, Roadside, Set(t), Sidewalk, Travolator, Trottoir

Pawn(shop) Agent, Betel, Chessman, Counter, Derby, Dip,
Gage, Gallery, Hanging, Hock, Hostage, Leaving-shop, Lumber,
Monte-de-piété, Monti di pieta, Pan, Passed, Peacock, Piece,
Pignerate, Pignorate, Pledge, Pop, Security, Siri, Spout,
Tiddlywink, Tool, Wadset, Weed

Pawnbroker, Pawnee Hockshop, Lumber, Moneylender,
Nunky, Sheeny, Uncle, Usurer

Pay(master), Payment, Paid, Pay off, Pay out
Advertise, Amortise, Annat, Annuity, Ante, Arles, Basic, Batta,
Blench, Bonus, Bukshee, Cashier, Cheque, COD, Commute,
Compensate, Consideration, Damage, Defray, Disburse,
Discharge, Dividend, Down, Dub, Emolument, Endow, Escot,
Farm, Fee, Fine, Foot, Fork out, Fund, Gale, Gate, Give,
Grave, Han(d)sel, Hazard, Hire, HP, Imburse, Mail, Meet,
Modus, Overtime, Payola, Pension, Pittance, Pony, Premium,
Primage, Pro, Pro forma, Purser, Quit(-rent), Ransom, Refund,
Remuneration, Rent, Requite, Residual, Respects, Royalty,
Salary, Satisfaction, Scot, Screw, Scutage, Settle, Severance,
Shell, Sick, Sink, Sold(e), ➤ SPEND, Square, Stipend, Strike,
Stump, Sub, Subscribe, Sweetener, Table, Take-home, Tar,
Tender, Token, Tommy, Treasure, Treat, Tribute, Truck, Veer,
Wage

Pea(s) Carling, Chaparral, Chickling, D(h)al, Desert, Dholl, Garbanzo, Goober, Hastings, Legume, Mangetout, Marrowfat, Pigeon, Passiform, Pulse, Rounceval, Split, Sugar

Peace(ful), Peace-keeper, Peace organisation, Peace symbol Ahimsa, Ataraxy, Calm, Ease, Frith, Halcyon, Interceder, Irenic(on), King's, Lee, Lull, Nirvana, Olive, Pacific, Pax, Queen's, Quiet, Repose, Rest, Salem, Serene, Sh, Shalom, Siesta, Still, Tranquil, Truce, UN

Peach Blab, Cling, Clingstone, Dish, Dob, Freestone, Inform, Laetrile, Malakatoone, Melocoto(o)n, Nectarine, Oner, Quandang, Shop, Sneak, Split, Squeak, Stunner, Tattle, Tell, Victorine

Peacock Coxcomb, Dandy, Fop, Junonian, Muster, Paiock(e), Pajock(e), Payock(e), Pavo(ne), Pawn, Pown, Sashay

Peak(y) Acme, Aiguille, Alp, Apex, Ben, Comble, Communism, Crag, Crest, Darien, Drawn, Eiger, Gable, Gannett, Horn, Matterhorn, Mons, ➤ MOUNTAIN, Nib, Nunatak, Optimum, Pale, Pin, Pinnacle, Rainier, Sallow, Snowdon, Spire, Top, Tor, Visor, Widow's, Zenith

Pear Aguacate, Alligator, Anchovy, Anjou, Asian, Avocado, Bartlett, Bergamot, Beurré, Blanquet, Catherine, Carmelite, Colmar, Conference, Cuisse-madame, Jargonelle, Muscadel, Muscatel, Musk, Nelis, Perry, Poperin, Poppering, Poprin, Prickly, Pyrus, Queez-maddam, Seckel, Seckle, Warden, William

Pearl(s), Pearly Barocco, Barock, Baroque, Cultured, Gem, Jewel, Mabe, Margaret, Margaric, Nacrous, Olivet, Orient, Prize, Rope, Seed, String, Sulphur, Unio(n)

Peasant Bonhomme, Boor, Bumpkin, Chouan, Churl, Clodhopper, Contadino, Cossack, Cottar, Cott(i)er, Fellah(s), Fellahin, Hick, Jungli, Kern(e), Kisan, Kulak, M(o)ujik, Muzhik, Raiyat, Roturier, Rustic, Ryot, Swain, Tyrolean, Whiteboy, Yokel

Pebble(s), Pebbly Banket, Calculus, Cobblestone, Dreikanter, Gallet, Gooley, Gravel, Psephism, Pumie, Pumy, Scree, Shingle

Peck Bill, Bushel, Dab, Forpet, Forpit, Gregory, Kiss, Lip, Lippie, Nibble, Tap

Peculiar(ity) Appropriate, Characteristic, Distinct, Eccentric, Especial, Exclusive, Ferly, Funny, Idiosyncratic, Kink, Kooky, Odd, Own, Proper, Queer, Quirk, Singular, ➤ SPECIAL, Specific, Strange, Unusual

▷**Peculiar** may indicate an anagram

Pedal Bike, Chorus, Cycle, Lever, P, Rat-trap, Soft, Treadle, Treddle

Peddle, Pedlar Bodger, Boxwallah, Camelot, Chapman, Cheapjack, Colporteur, Drummer, Duffer, Hawk, Huckster, Jagger, Packman, Peddler, Pether, Sell, Smouch, Smouse(r), Sutler, Tallyman, Tink(er), Yagger

▷**Peddling** may indicate an anagram

Pedestrian Banal, Commonplace, Dull, Ganger, Hack, Hike, Itinerant, Jaywalker, Laborious, Trite, Mundane, Walker

Pedigree(s) Ancestry, Blood, Breeding, Descent, House, Lineage, Phylogeny, Stemma(ta), Stirps, Thoroughbred

Peel(er) Bark, Bobby, Candied, Decorticate, Exfoliate, Flype, Pare, PC, Rind, Rine, Scale, Shell, Skin, ➤ STRIP, Tiff, Zest

▷**Peeled** may indicate outside letter(s) to be removed from a word

Peep(er) Cheep, Cook, Glance, Gledge, Keek, Kook, Lamp, Nose, Peek, Pink, Pry, Squeak, Squint, Spy, Stime, Styme, Voyeur

Peevish(ness) Capernoited, Captious, Crabby, Cross, Doddy, Frabbit, Frampal, Frampold, Franzy, Fretful, Lienal, Moody, Nattered, Petulant, Pindling, Protervity, Shirty, Sour, Teachie, Te(t)chy, Testy

Peg Cheville, Cleat, Cotter-pin, Die, Fix, Freeze, Knag, Leg, Margaret, Nail, Nog, Pin, Piton, Snort, Spigot, Spile, Square, Stenghah, Stinger, Support, Tap, Tee, Thole, Tholepin, Thowel, Toggle, Tot, Woffington

Pelican Alcatras, Bird, Crossing, Golden Hind, LA, Louisiana

Pellet Bolus, Buckshot, Bullet, Pill, Prill, Slug

Pelt Assail, Clod, Fleece, Fur, Hail, Hide, Hie, Lam, Pepper, Random, Shower, Skin, Squail, Stone

Pen Ballpoint, Bamboo, Bic®, Biro®, Cage, Calamus, Cartridge, Confine, Coop, Corral, Crawl, Cru(i)ve, Cub, Data, Enclosure, Fank, Farm, Fold, Fountain, Gladius, Hen, Highlighter, Hoosegow, J, ➤ JAIL, Keddah, Kraal, Lair, Light, Mew, Mure, Piggery, Pound, Quill, Ree, Reed, Ring, Rollerball, Scribe, Stell, Stie, Stir, Sty(e), Stylet, Stylo, Stylograph, Stylus, Swan, Tank, Write

▷**Pen** may indicate a writer

Penal(ize) Cost, Fine, Gate, Handicap, Huff, Mulct, Punitive, Servitude

Penalty Abye, Amende, Cost, Eric, Fine, Forfeit, Han(d)sel, Huff, Pain, Price, Punishment, Sanction, Wide

Pencil Beam, Ca(l)m, Charcoal, Chinagraph®, Crayon, Caum, Draft, Draw, Fusain, Grease, Keelivine, Keelyvine, Lead, Outline, Propelling, Stump, Styptic

Pendant Albert, Chandelier, Drop, Girandole, Laval(l)ière, Necklace, Poffle

Pending Imminent, In fieri, Unresolved, Until

Penetrate, Penetrating, Penetration Acumen, Acuminate, Bite, Bore, Cut, Enpierce, Enter, Imbue, Impale, Incisive, Indent, Indepth, Infiltrate, Insight, Into, Intrant, Lance, Permeate, Pierce, Probe, Sagacious, Shear, Touch, Thrust, X-ray

Penguin Aeroplane, Anana, Auk, Emperor, Fairy, Gentoo, King, Korora, Macaroni, Rock-hopper

Peninsula Arm, Balkan, Cape, Crimea, Florida, Gallipoli, Gower, Iberia(n), Jutland, Labrador, Malay, Neck, Nova Scotia, Otago, Peloponnese, Promontory, Sinai, Spit, Spur, The Lizard, Tasman, Wirral

Penny Bean, Cartwheel, Cent, Copper, D, Dreadful, P, Sen, Sou, Sterling, Stiver, Win(n), Wing

Pension(er) Allowance, Ann(at), Annuitant, Board, Chelsea, Cod, Cor(r)ody, Gratuity, Half-board, Payment, Retire, Serps, Stakeholder, Stipend, Superannuation

People Bods, Body, Chosen, Commons, Demos, Ecology, Enchorial, Folk, Fraim, Gens, Guild, Human, Inhabit, Janata, Kin, Land, Lapith, Lay, Man(kind), Men, Mob, Nair, Nation(s), Nayar, One, Personalities, Phalange, Populace, Public, Punters, Race, Settle, Society, Souls, Tribe, Volk

Pepper Alligator, All-spice, Ava, Bird, Black, Capsicum, Cayenne, Chilli, Condiment, Cubeb, Devil, Dittander, Dittany, Ethiopian, Green, Guinea, Jalapeno, Jamaica, Kava, Malaguetta, Matico, Negro, Paprika, Pelt, Pim(i)ento, Piper, Red, Riddle, Sambal, Spice, Sprinkle, Szechwan, Tabasco®, Yaqona, Yellow

Perceive, Perception, Perceptive Acumen, Albert, Anschauung, Apprehend, Clairvoyance, Clear-eyed, Cryptaesthetic, Descry, Dianoia, Discern, Divine, ESP, Extrasensory, Feel, Insight, Intelligence, Intuit(ion),

Kinaesthesia, Notice, Observe, Pan(a)esthesia, Remark, ➤ SEE, Sense, Sensitive, Sentience, Shrewd, Tact, Taste

Percentage Agio, Commission, Contango, Cut, Proportion, Royalty, Share, Vigorish

Perch(ing) Aerie, Alight, Anabis, Bass, Comber, Eyrie, Fish, Fogash, Gaper, Insessorial, Lug, Perca, Pole, Roost, Ruff(e), Seat, Serranid, ➤ SIT, Zingel

Percussion (cap) Amorce, Idiophone, Impact, Knee, Knock, Thump, Timbrel

Perennial Continual, Enduring, Flower, Livelong, Perpetual, Recurrent

Perfect, Perfection(ist) Absolute, Accomplish, Accurate, Acme, Apple-pie, Bloom, Complete, Consummation, Cross-question, Dead, Develop, Finish, Flawless, Fulfil, Full, Holy, Ideal(ist), Impeccable, Intact, It, Mint, Par, Paragon, Past, Peace, Pedant, Practice, Pure, Refine, Soma, Sound, Spot-on, Stainless, Sublime, Thorough, Three-pricker, Unblemished, Unqualified, Utopian, Utter, Whole, Witeless

Perform(ed), Performer, Performing Achieve, Act(or), Appear, Artist(e), Basoche, Busk, Chansonnier, Discharge, Do, Enact, Entertainer, Execute, Exert, Exhibit, Fancy Dan, Fulfil, Function, Geek, Hand, Headliner, Hersall, Implement, Interlocutor, Majorette, Make, Moke, On, Player, Praxis, Recite, Render, Ripieno, Sword-swallower, Throw, Vaudevillian, Virtuoso

Performance Accomplishment, Achievement, Act, Bravura, Broadcast, Command, Concert, Dare, Deed, Demonstration, Discharge, Entracte, Execution, Gas, Gig, Hierurgy, Holdover, Hootenanny, Matinee, Operation, Perpetration, Première, Recital, Rehearsal, Rendering, Rendition, Repeat, Rigmarole, Scene, Show, Solo, Stunt, Turn

Perfume (box) Aroma, Attar, Bergamot, Cassolette, Chypre, Civet, Cologne, Enfleurage, Fragrance, Frangipani, Incense, Ionone, Lavender (water), Linalool, Myrrh, Opopanax, Orris, Orrisroot, Patchouli, Patchouly, Pomander, Potpourri, Redolence, ➤ SCENT, Terpineol

Perhaps A(i)blins, Belike, Haply, Happen, May(be), Peradventure, Percase, Perchance, Possibly, Relative, Say

▷**Perhaps** may indicate an anagram

Perimeter Boundary, Circuit, Circumference, Limits

Period(ic) AD, Age, Annual, Cambrian, Carboniferous, Chukka, Chukker, Climacteric, Curse, Cycle, Day, Devonian, Diapause, Dot, ➤ DURATION, Eocene, Epoch, Full-stop, Glacial, Grace, Interregnum, Jurassic, Kalpa, Lesson, Liassic, Limit, Meantime, Meanwhile, Mesolithic, Miocene, Monthly, Neolithic, Octave, Olde-worlde, Oligocene, Paleolithic, Phoenix, Quarter, Quarternary, Regency, Rent, Riss, Romantic, Season, Session, Span, Spell, Stage, Stop, Term, Tertiary, Trecento, Triassic, Trimester, Usance

Periodic(al) Comic, Digest, Economist, Etesian, Journal, Liassic, Listener, Mag, New Yorker, Organ, Paper, Phase, Publication, Punch, Rambler, Regency, Review, Spectator, Strand, Stretch, Tatter, Tract

Perish(able), Perished, Perishing Brittle, ➤ DIE, End, Ephemeral, Expire, Fade, Forfair, Fungibles, Icy, Tine, Tint, Transitory, Tyne, Vanish

Perm(anent) Abiding, Durable, Eternal, Everlasting, Fixed, Full-time, Indelible, ➤ LASTING, Marcel, Stable, Standing, Stative, Wave

Permeate Infiltrate, Leaven, Osmosis, Penetrate, Pervade, Seep

Permission, Permit(ted) Allow, Authorise, Carnet, Chop, Clearance, Congé(e), Copyright, Enable, Grant, Lacet, Laisser-passer, Latitude, Leave, Legal, Let, Liberty, Licence, License, Lief, Luit, Nihil obstat, Ok(e), Pace, Pass, Placet, Power, Pratique, Privilege, Sanction, Stamp-note, Suffer, Ticket, Triptyque, Visa, Vouchsafe, Way-leave, Wear

Perpendicular Aplomb, Apothem, Atrip, Cathetus, Erect, Normal, Orthogonal, Plumb, Sheer, Sine, ➤ UPRIGHT, Vertical

Perplex(ed), Perplexity Anan, Baffle, Bamboozle, Beset, Bewilder, Bother, Buffalo, Bumbaze, Cap, Confound, Confuse, Feague, Floor, Flummox, Knotty, Mystify, Nonplus, Out, Puzzle, Quizzical, Stump, Tangle, Tickle, Tostication

Persecute, Persecution Afflict, Annoy, Badger, Crucify, Dragon(n)ades, Harass, Haze, Intolerant, Oppress, Pogrom, Ride, Torture

Persevere, Perseverance Assiduity, Continue, Fortitude, Insist, Patience, Persist, Plug, Stamina, Steadfastness, Stick, Stickability, Tenacity

Persia(n) Babee, Babi, Bahai, Cyrus, Farsi, Iran(ian), Mazdean, Mede, Pahlavi, Parasang, Parsee, Pehlevi, Pushtu, Samanid, Sassanid, Sohrab, Xerxes, Zoroaster

Persist(ence), Persistent Adhere, Assiduity, Chronic, Continual, Diligent, Doggedness, Endure, Importunate, Labour, Longeval, Lusting, Persevere, Press, Sedulous, Sneaking, Stick, Tenacity, Urgent

Person(s), Personal Alter, Being, Bird, Bod(y), Chai, Chal, Chi, Cookie, Entity, Everymen, Figure, Fish, Flesh, Head, Human, Individual, One, Own, Party, Passer-by, Private, Quidam, Selfhood, Sod, Soul, Specimen, Tales

Personage, Personality Anima, Celeb(rity), Character, Charisma, Dignitary, Ego, Grandee, Identity, Noble, Notability, Panjandrum, Presence, Sama, Seity, Sel, Self, Sell, Star, Tycoon

Personified, Personification, Personify Embody, Incarnate, Prosopop(o)eia, Represent

Perspective Attitude, Distance, Point of view, Proportion, View, Vista

Persuade(d), Persuasion, Persuasive Cajole, Coax, Cogent, Conviction, Convince, Disarm, Eloquent, Faith, Feel, Forcible, Geed, Get, Induce, Inveigle, Move, Plausible, ➤ PREVAIL, Religion, Soft sell, Suborn, Truckled, Wheedle, Winning

Pert(ness) Bold, Cocky, Dicacity, Flippant, Forward, Fresh, Impertinent, Insolent, Jackanapes, Minx, Saucy, Tossy

Pertinent Apropos, Apt, Fit, Germane, Relevant, Timely

Perturb(ation) Aerate, Confuse, Dismay, Disturb, Dither, State, Trouble, Upset, Worry

Pervade, Pervasion, Pervasive(ness) Diffuse, Drench, Immanence, Permeate, Saturate

Perverse, Perversion, Pervert(ed) Aberrant, Abnormal, Algolagnia, Awry, Cam(stairy), Camsteary, Camsteerie, Cantankerous, ➤ CONTRARY, Corrupt, Cussed, Deviate, Distort, Donsie, False, Gee, Kam(me), Kinky, Licentious, Misuse, Nonce, Paraphilia, Refractory, Sadist, Sicko, Stubborn, Thrawn, Traduce, Unnatural, Untoward, Uranism, Warp(ed), Wayward, Wilful, Wrest, Wry

▷ **Perverted** may indicate an anagram

Pessimism, Pessimist(ic) Alarmist, Crapehanger, Crepehanger, Cynic, Defeatist, Doomwatch, Doomy, Doubter, Fatalist, Jeremiah, Killjoy, Negative

Pest(er) Badger, Bedbug, Blight, Bot, ➤ BOTHER, Brat, Breese, Bug, Disagreeable, Dim, Earbash, Fly, Fowl, Harass, Irritate, Mither, Mouse, Nag, Nudnik, Nuisance, Nun, Pize, Plague, Rotter, Scourge, Tease, Terror, Thysanoptera, Vermin, Weevil

Pesticide DDT, Derris, Heplachlor, Mouser, Permethrin, Synergist, Warfarin

Pestilence, Pestilent Curse, Epidemic, Evil, Lues, Murrain, Noxious, Pernicious, Plague

Pet Aversion, Cade, Canoodle, Caress, Chou, Coax, Cosset, Dandle, Daut(ie), Dawt(ie), Dod, Dort, Ducky, Favourite, Fondle, Glumps, Hamster, Huff, Hump, Ire, Jarta, Jo, Lallygag, Lapdog, Miff, Mouse, Neck, Pique, Rabbit, Smooch, Snog, Spat, Strum, Sulk(s), Tantrum, Teacher's, Tiff, Tout, Towt, Umbrage, Virtual, Yarta

Petition(er) Appeal, Beg, Boon, Crave, Entreaty, Orison, Plaintiff, Postulant, Prayer, Representation, Round robin, Solicit, Sue, Suit(or), Suppli(c)ant, Vesper

Petrify(ing) Fossilise, Frighten, Lapidescent, Niobe, Numb, Ossify, Scare, Terrify

Petrol(eum) Cetane, Diesel, Esso®, Ethyl, Fuel, Gas, High-octane, Ligroin, Maz(o)ut, Octane, Olein, Rock-tar, Unleaded

Petticoat Balmoral, Basquine, Crinoline, Female, Filabeg, Fil(l)ibeg, Jupon, Kilt, Kirtle, Phil(l)abeg, Phil(l)ibeg, Placket, Sarong, Shift, Underskirt, Wylie-coat

Petty, Pettiness Baubling, Bumbledom, Childish, Little, Mean, Minor, Narrow, Niggling, Nyaff, One-horse, Parvanimity, Picayunish, Pimping, Puisne, Shoestring, Small, Stingy, Tin, Trivial, Two-bit

Petulance, Petulant Fretful, Huff, Moody, Peevish, Perverse, Procacity, Sullen, Toutie, Waspish

Phantom Apparition, Bogey, Bugbear, Eidolon, Idol, Incubus, Maya, Shade, Spectre, Tut, Wraith

Pharmacist ➤ CHEMIST, Dispenser, MPS, Preparator

Phase Cycle, Form, Period, Post-boost, REM, Stage, State, Synchronise

Phenomenon Blip, Effect, Event, Flying saucer, Marvel, Miracle, Mirage, Paranormal, Psi, Synergy

Philanthropist, Philanthropy Altruist, Benefactor, Carnegie, Charity, Coram, Donor, Nobel, Rockefeller, Samaritan, Shaftesbury, Tate, Wilberforce

Philistine, Philistinism Artless, Ashdod, Barbarian, Foe, Gaza, Gath, Gigman, Goliath, Goth, Lowbrow, Vandal

Philosopher, Philosophy Academist, Activism, Ahimsa, Anthrosophy, Antinomianism, Antiochian, Antiochene, Atomist, Attitude, Averr(h)oism, Cartesian, Casuist, Comtism, Cracker-barrel, Cynic, Cyreniac, Deipnosophist, Deontology, Eclectic, Eleatic, Empiricism, Epistemology, Ethics, Existentialism, Gymnosophist, Hobbism, Holist, I Ching, Ideology, -ism, Marxism, Materialism, Megarian, Metaphysician, Monism, Neoplatonism, Neoteric, Nominalist, Occamist, Occam's razor, Ockhamist, Old Moore, Opinion, Peripatetic, Populism, Positivism, Sage, Sceptic, Sensist, Sophist, Stoic, Taoism, Theosophy, Thomist, Transcendentalism, Ultraism, Vedanta, Yoga, Yogi

Phone Bell, Blower, Call, Cellular, Dial, Intercom, Mobile, Ring

Phonetic Oral, Palaeotype, Spoken, Symbol

▷**Phonetically** may indicate a word sounding like another

Phon(e)y Bogus, Charlatan, Counterfeit, Fake, Impostor, Poseur, ➤ SHAM, Specious, Spurious

▷**Phony** may indicate an anagram

Photo(copy), Photograph(ic), Photography, Photo finish Close-up, Composite, Duplicate, Exposure, Film, Flash, Headshot, Hologram, Microdot, Mugshot, Negative, Panel, Picture, Positive, Print, Rotogravure, Sepia, Shoot, Shot, Snap, Still, Take, Topo, Vignette, X-ray

Phrase Buzzword, Catch(word), Cliché, Comma, Expression, Heroic, Laconism, Leitmotiv, Locution, Mantra, Phr, Refrain, Riff, Slogan, Tag, Term

Physic(s) Cryogenics, Culver's, Cure, Dose, Kinematics, Medicine, Nuclear, Nucleonics, Particle, Purge, Remedy, Rheology, Science, Thermodynamics

Physician Allopath, Doctor, Galen, Hakim, Harvey, Hippocrates, Internist, Leech, Linacre, Lister, Medic(o), Mesmer,

Mindererus, Paean, Paracelsus, Practitioner, Quack, Roget, Therapist, Time

Physicist Scientist

Pi, Pious Devotional, Devout, Fraud, Gallio, God-fearing, Godly, Holy, Mid-Victorian, Sanctimonious, Savoury, Smug

Piano Bechstein, Celesta, Celeste, Concert grand, Cottage, Flugel, Forte, Grand, Honkytonk, Keyboard, Overstrung, P, Player, Softly, Steinway, Stride, Upright

Pick(er), Picking, Pick up Break, Choice, ➤ CHOOSE, Cream, Cull, Elite, Flower, Gather, Glean, Hack, Hopper, Mattock, Nap, Nibble, Oakum, Plectrum, Pluck, Plum, Select, Single, Sort, Steal, Strum, Tong, Wale

▷ **Picked** may indicate an anagram

Pickle(r) Achar, Brine, Cabbage, Caper, Chow-chow, Chutney, Corn, Cure, Dilemma, Dill, Eisel, Esile, Gherkin, Girkin, Jam, Kimchi, Marinade, Marinate, Mess, Mull, Olive, Onion, Peculate, Peregrine, Piccalilli, ➤ PLIGHT, Samp(h)ire, Scrape, Souse, Vinegar, Wolly

Pickpocket Adept, Bung, Cly-faker, Cutpurse, Dip, Diver, Fagin, File, Nipper, Wire

Picnic Alfresco, Braaivleis, Clambake, Fun, Outing, Push-over, Spread, Wase-goose, Wayzgoose

Picture(s) Anaglyph, Art, Canvas, Collage, Decoupage, Depict, Describe, Diptych, Drawing, Drypoint, Emblem, Epitome, Etching, Film, Flick, Fresco, Gouache, Graphic, Histogram, Icon, Identikit®, Imagery, Inset, Landscape, Likeness, Lithograph, Montage, Motion, Movie, Movy, Mugshot, Oil, Photo, Pin-up, Pix, Plate, Portrait, Prent, Presentment, Print, Retrate, Scene, Shot, Slide, Snapshot, Stereogram, Stereograph, Still-life, Table(au), Talkie, Transfer, Transparency, Vision

Pie(s) Anna, Banoffee, Battalia, Bridie, Chewet, Cottage, Custard, Easy, Flan, Hash, Humble, Madge, Mess, Pandowdy, Pastry, Pasty, Patty, Périgord, Pica, Piet, Pirog, Pizza, Pyat, Pyet, Pyot, Quiche, Resurrection, Shepherd's, Shoofly, Spoil, Squab, Star(ry)-gazy, Tart, Tarte tatin, Turnover, Tyropitta, Umble, Vol-au-vent, Warden

▷ **Pie** may indicate an anagram

Piece(s) Add, Bishop, Bit, Blot, Cameo, Cannon, Charm, ➤ CHESSMAN, Chip, Chunk, Coin, Companion, Component, Concerto, Crumb, Domino, End, Extract, Flitters, Fragment, Goring, Haet, Hait, Hunk, Item, Join, Mammock, Mite, Money, Morsel, Nip, Novelette, Oddment, Off-cut, Ort, Part, Party, Patch, Pawn, Peso, Pistareen, ➤ PORTION, Recital, Scrap, Section, Set, Shard, Sherd, Slice, Sliver, Sou, Speck, Stub, Swatch, Tait, Tate, Tile, Toccata, Wedge

Pier(s) Anta, Groyne, Jetty, Jutty, Landing, Mole, Plowman, Quay, Slipway, Swiss roll, Wharf

Pierce(d), Piercer, Piercing Accloy, Awl, Broach, Cleave, Dart, Drill, Endart, Fenestrate(d), Gimlet, Gore, Gride, Gryde, Hull, Impale, Jag, Keen, Lance, Lancinate, Lobe, Move, Needle, Penetrate, Perforate, Pike, Poignant, Punch, Puncture, Riddle, Rive, Shrill, Skewer, Slap, Sleeper, Spear, Spike, Spit, Stab, Steek, Stiletto, Sting, Thirl, Thrill(ant)

Pig(s), Pigskin Anthony, Babe, Barrow, Bartholomew, Bland, Boar, Bush, Doll, Elt, Farrow, Fastback, Football, Gadarene, Gilt, Glutton, Gride, Guinea, Gus, Ham, Hog, Ingot, Iron, Kentledge, Kintledge, Landrace, Large black, Large white, Long, Napoleon, Peccary, Policeman, Pork(er), Razorback, Rosser, Runt, Saddleback, Shoat, Shot(e), Slip, Snowball, Sounder, Sow, Squealer, Suid(ae), Tamworth, Tithe, Toe, Warthog, Yelt

Pigeon Archangel, Barb, Bird, Cape, Carrier, Clay, Cropper, Culver, Dove, Fantail, Goura, Gull, Homer, Homing, Horseman, Jacobin, Kuku, Manumea, Nun, Owl, Passenger, Peristeronic, Pouter, Ringdove, Rock(er), Roller, Ront(e), Ruff, Runt, Scandaroon, Solitaire, Spot, Squab, Squealer, Stock-dove, Stool, Talkie-talkee, Tippler, Tumbler, Turbit, Wonga-wonga, Zoozoo

Pigment(ation) Bilirubin, Bistre, Carmine, Carotene, Chlorophyll, Chrome, Cobalt, Colour, Dye, Etiolin, Flavin(e), Gamboge, H(a)emoglobin, Liverspot, Lutein, Madder, Melanin, Naevus, Ochre, Orpiment, Realgar, Sepia, Sienna, Tempera, Tincture, Umber, Viridian

Pike Assegai, Crag, Dory, Fogash, Gar(fish), Ged, Gisarme, Glaive, Hie, Holostei, Javelin, Lance, Luce, Partisan, Pickerel, Ravensbill, Scafell, Snoek, Spear, Speed, Spontoon, Vouge, Walleyed

Pile(d), Piles, Piling Agger, Atomic, Bing, Bomb, Camp-sheathing, Camp-shedding, Camp-sheeting,

Camp-shot, Clamp, Cock, Column, Crowd, Deal, Down, Emerods, Farmers, Fender, Fig, Floccus, Fortune, Hair, Heap, Hept, Historic, Hoard, Load, Lot, Marleys, Mass, Nap, Post, Pyre, Raft, Reactor, Ream(s), Rouleau, Shag, ➤ STACK, Starling, Stilt, Trichome, Upheap, Voltaic, Wealth, Windrow, Wodge

Pilgrim(age) Aske, Childe Harold, Expedition, Fatima, Hadj(i), Hajj(i), Loreto, Lourdes, Mecca, Palmer, Pardoner, Reeve, Scallop-shell, Shrine, Voyage, Yatra

Pill Ball, Bitter, Bolus, Caplet, Capsule, Dex, Doll, Dose, Globule, Lob, Medicine, Number nine, Peel, Pellet, Pilula, Pilule, Placebo, Poison, Protoplasmal, Sleeping, Spansule, Tablet, Troche, Trochisk, Upper

Pillar(ed), Pillars Anta, Apostle, Atlantes, Baluster, Balustrade, Boaz, Canton, Caryatides, Cippus, Columel, Column, Eustyle, Gendarme, Hercules, Herm, Impost, Islam, Jachin, Lat, Man, Modiolus, Monolith, Newel, Obelisk, Pedestal, Peristyle, Pier, Post, Respond, Stalactite, Stalagmite, Stoop, Telamon, Trumeau

Pilot Ace, Airman, Auto(matic), Aviator, Captain, ➤ CONDUCT, Experimental, George, Govern, Guide, Hobbler, Lead, Lodesman, Palinure, Palinurus, Pitt, Prune, Shipman, Steer, Test, Tiphys, Trial, Usher, Wingman

Pimple, Pimply Blackhead, Botch, Gooseflesh, Grog-blossom, Hickey, Horripilation, Papula, Plook, Plouk, Pock, Pustule, Quat, Rumblossom, Rum-bud, Spot, Uredinial, Wen, Whelk, Whitehead, Zit

Pin Bayonet, Belaying, Bolt, Brooch, Cotter, Dowel, Drawing, Drift, Fasten, Fid, Firing, Fix, Gam, Gudgeon, Hairgrip, Hob, Joggle, Kevel, Needle, Nog, Panel, Peg, Pivot, Preen, Rivet, Rolling, Safety, SCART, Scatter, Shear, Skewer, Skittle, Skiver, Spike, Spindle, Split, Staple, Stump, Swivel, Thole, Thumbtack, Tre(e)nail, U-bolt, Woolder

Pinch(ed) Arrest, Bit, Bone, Chack, Constrict, Cramp, Crisis, Emergency, Gaunt, Misappropriate, Nab, Nick, Nim, Nip, Peculate, Peel, Pilfer, Pocket, Pook(it), Prig, Pugil, Raft, Rob, Scrimp, Scrounge, Skimp, Smatch, Snabble, Snaffle, Sneak, Sneap, Sneeshing, Snuff, Squeeze, ➤ STEAL, Swipe, Tate, Tweak, Twinge

Pine(s), Pining Arolla, Bristlecone, Celery, Cembra, Chile, Cone, Conifer, Cypress, Dwine, Droop, Earn, Erne, Fret,

Ground, Hone, Hoop, Huon, Jack, Jeffrey, Kauri, Languish, Languor, Loblolly, Long, Longleaf, Monkey-puzzle, Picea, Pitch, Radiata, Scotch, Scots, Softwood, Spruce, Starve, Stone, Sugar, Tree, Umbrella, Urman, Waste, Yearn

Pink Blush, Carolina, Castory, Clove, Colour, Coral, Dianthus, Emperce, Gillyflower, Knock, Lake, Lychnis, Moss, Oyster, Peak, Perce, Pierce, Pompadour, Pounce, Rose(ate), Salmon, Scallop, Shell, Shocking, Shrimp, Spigelia, Spit, Stab, Tiny

Pin-point Focus, Identify, Isolate, Localise

Pioneer Baird, Bandeirante, Blaze, Boone, Colonist, Emigrant, Explore, Fargo, Fleming, Frontiersman, Harbinger, Innovator, Lead, Marconi, Oecist, Pathfinder, Rochdale, Sandgroper, Spearhead, Settler, Trail-blazer, Trekker, Voortrekker, Wells

▶**Pious** see PI

Pipe(s), Piper, Pipeline, Piping Aorta, Aulos, Balance, Barrel, Blub, Bong, Bubble, Call, Calumet, Cheep, Cherrywood, Chillum, Churchwarden, Clay, Conduit, Corncob, Crane, Cutty, Drain, Dry riser, Duct, Exhaust, Faucet, Fistula, Flue, Flute, Gage, Hod, Hogger, Hooka(h), Hose, Hubble-bubble, Hydrant, Mains, Manifold, Meerschaum, Montre, Nargile, Nargile(h), Narg(h)il(l)y, Oat(en), Oboe, Peace, Pepper, Pibroch, Piccolo, Pied, Pitch, Pule, Quill, Recorder, Ree(d), Rise, Serpent, Siphon, Skirl, Sluice, Soil, Stack, Standpipe, Tibia, Tootle, Trachea, Tube, Tweet, U-bend, Union, Uptake, Waste, Water(-spout), Weasand, Whistle

Piracy, Pirate, Piratical Algerine, Barbarossa, Blackbeard, Boarder, Bootleg, Brigand, Buccaneer, Buccanier, Cateran, Condottier, Conrad, Corsair, Crib, Dampier, Fil(l)ibuster, Flint, Hijack, Hook, Kidd, Lift, Loot, Morgan, Picaro(on), Pickaroon, Plagiarise, Plunder, Rakish, Rover, Sallee-man, Sallee-rover, Sea-king, Sea-rat, Sea-robber, Silver, Smee, Steal, Teach, Viking, Water-rat, Water-thief

Pistol Air, Ancient, Automatic, Barker, Colt®, Dag, Derringer, Gat, ▶ GUN, Hackbut, Horse, Luger®, Pepperbox, Petronel, Revolver, Rod, Shooter, Starter, Starting, Very, Water, Weapon

Pit(ted) Abyss, Alveolus, Antrum, Catch, Cave, Cesspool, Chasm, Cloaca, Colliery, Crater, Den, Depth, Depression, Dungmere, Ensile, Fossa, Fovea, Foxhole, Hangi, Heapstead, Hell, Hole, Hollow, Inferno, Khud, Lacunose, Mark, Match, ▶ MINE, Mosh, Orchestra, Parterre, Pip, Play, Pock, Pock-mark,

Punctate, Putamen, Pyrene, Ravine, Scrobicule, Silo, Soakaway, Solar plexus, Stone, Sump, Tar, Trap, Trou-de-loup

Pitch(ed) Absolute, Asphalt, Atilt, Attune, Bitumen, Coal-tar, Concert, Crease, Diamond, Dive, Ela, Elect, Encamp, Erect, Establish, Fever, Fling, Fork, Ground, Intonation, Key, Labour, Length, Level, Lurch, Maltha, Neume, Patter, Peck, Perfect, Pight, Pin, Plong(e), Plunge, Pop, Resin, Rock, Ruff(e), Scend, Seel, Send, Shape, Sling, Slope, Spiel, Stoit, Tar, Tessitura, Tilt, Tone, Tonemic, Tonus, Tune, Wicket

Pith(y) Ambatch, Aphorism, Apo(ph)thegm, Core, Down, Essence, Gnomic, Hat-plant, Heart, Marrow, Medulla, Moxa, Nucleus, Rag, Succinct, Terse

Pitiless Flint-hearted, Hard, Ruthless

Pity, Piteous, Pitiful Ah, Alack, Alas, Commiseration, ➤ COMPASSION, Mercy, Pathos, Rue, Ruth(ful), Seely, Shame, Sin, Sympathy

Pivot(al) Ax(i)le, Central, Focal, Fulcrum, Gooseneck, Gudgeon, Kingbolt, Revolve, Rotate, Slue, ➤ SWIVEL, Trunnion, Turn, Wheel

Place Aim, Allocate, Berth, Bro, Decimal, Deploy, Deposit, Fix, Habitat, Hither, Howf, Identify, Impose, ➤ IN PLACE OF, Install, Job, Joint, Juxtapose, Lay, Lieu, Locality, Locate, Locus, Pitch, Plat, Plaza, Point, Posit, ➤ POSITION, Put, Realm, Region, Scene, Second, Set, Site, Situate, Situation, Spot, Stead, Sted(e), Stedd(e), Stratify, Town, Vendome

Plagiarise, Plagiarist Copy, Crib, Lift, Pirate, Steal

Plague (spot) Annoy, Bane, Bedevil, Black death, Boil, Bubonic, Burden, Curse, Dog, Dun, Goodyear, Goujeers, Harry, Infestation, Locusts, Lues, Murrain, Murran, Murrin, Murrion, Pest, Pester, Pox, Press, Scourge, Tease, Token, Torture, Try, Vex

Plain(s) Abraham, Artless, Ascetic, Bald, Bare, Blatant, Broad, Candid, Clear, Dowdy, Downright, Dry, Evident, Explicit, Flat, Girondist, Homely, Homespun, Inornate, Llano, Lombardy, Lowland, Manifest, Marathon, Mare, Obvious, Olympia, ➤ ORDINARY, Outspoken, Overt, Pampa(s), Patent, Pikestaff, Prairie, Sailing, Salisbury, Savanna(h), Secco, Sharon, Simple, Sodom, Spoken, Steppe, Tableland, Tundra, Vega, Veldt, Visible

Plaint(ive) Complaint, Dirge, Lagrimoso, Lament, Melancholy, Sad, Whiny

Plan(ned), Planner, Planning Aim, Angle, Arrange, Architect, Blueprint, Budget, Chart, Contrive, Dart, Deliberate, Design, Device, Devise, Diagram, Draft, Drawing, Elevation, Engineer, Format, Hang, Idea, Intent, Lay(out), Map, Marshall, Mastermind, Outline, Pattern, Pipe-dream, Plot, Ploy, Policy, Premeditate, Procedure, Programme, Project, Projet, Proposal, Scenario, Schedule, Scheme, Spec(ification), Stratagem, Strategy, Subterfuge, System, Wheeze

Plane Aero(dyne), Air, ➤ AIRCRAFT, Airliner, Airship, Bandit, Boeing, Bomber, Bus, Camel, Canard, Cartesian, Chenar, Chinar, Comet, Concorde, Crate, Dakota, Datum, Delta-wing, Even, Facet, Fault, Fillester, Fillister, Flat, Glider, Gotha, Hurricane, Icosahedron, Icosahedra, Jack, Jet, Jointer, Jumbo, Level, MIG, Mirage, Mosquito, Moth, Octagon, Platanus, Polygon, Rocket, Router, Shackleton, Shave, Smooth, Sole, Spitfire, Spokeshave, STOL, Surface, Sycamore, Taube, Thrust, Trainer, Tree, Trident, Viscount

Planet(ary) Alphonsine, Ariel, Asteroid, Body, Cabiri, Ceres, Chiron, Constellation, Earth, Eros, Hyleg, Inferior, Jovian, Jupiter, Mars, Mercury, Moon, Neptune, Pluto, Psyche, Quartile, Saturn, Sphere, Starry, Sun, Superior, Terrestrial, Uranus, Venus, Vista, Vulcan, World

Plank Board, Chess, Duckboard, Garboard, Plonk, Sarking, Slab, Spirketting, Straik, Strake, Stringer, Wood

Plant (part) Annual, Anther, Bed, Biennial, Biota, Cultigen, Cultivar, Dibble, Ecad, Embed, Endogen, Enrace, Epiphyte, Establish, Factory, Fix, Growth, Herbarium, Insert, Instil, Inter, Labiate, Land, Machinery, Ornamental, Sere, Shrub, Sow, Succulent, Tree, Weld, Works

Plantation Arboretum, Bosket, Bosquet, Estate, Grove, Hacienda, Pen, Pinetum, Ranch, Tara, Vineyard

Plaster(ed) Bandage, Blotto, Cake, Cataplasm, Clam, Clatch, Compo, Court, Daub, Diachylon, Diachylum, Drunk, Emplastrum, Fresco, Gesso, Grout, Gypsum, Intonaco, Leep, Lit, Mud, Mustard, Oiled, Parge(t), Poultice, Render, Scratch-coat, Screed, Secco, Shellac, Sinapism, Smalm, Smarm, Smear, Sowsed, Staff, Stookie, Stucco, Teer

Plastic Ductile, Fictile, Laminate, Loid, Pliant, Polythene, PVC, Vinyl, Wet-look, Yielding
▷**Plastic** may indicate an anagram

Plate(d), Platelet, Plating Acierage, Ailette, Angle, Anode, Armadillo, Armour, Ashet, Baffle, Baleen, Batten, Brass, Butt, Chape, Chrome, Coat, Copper, Denture, Disc, Dish, Electro, Elytron, Elytrum, Enamel, Fashion, Fine, Fish, Flatware, Foil, Frog, Hot, Illustration, L, Lame, Lamina, Lanx, Mazarine, Nail, Nef, Nickel, Paten, Patina, Petri, Plaque, Platter, Poitrel, Print, Race, Rove, Salamander, Scale, Scute, Scutum, Selling, Sheffield, Shield, Silver, Slab, Soup, Spoiler, Stencil, Stereo(type), Sternite, T, Tablet, Tace, Tasse(l), Terne, Tin(ware), Torsel, Trade, Trencher, Trophy, Vassail, Vessel, Wall, Web, Whirtle

Plateau Altiplano, Deccan, Fjeld, Highland, Highveld, Horst, Kar(r)oo, La Mancha, Langres, Mat(t)o Grosso, Mesa Verde, Meseta, Nilgiris, Ozark, Paramo, Piedmont, Puna, Tableland

Platform Bandstand, Base, Bema, Catwalk, Crane, Dais, Deck, Dolly, Drilling, Estrade, Exedra, Exhedra, Flake, Footpace, Foretop, Gangplank, Gantry, Hustings, Machan, Pallet, Perron, Plank, Podium, Predella, Programme, Pulpit, Raft, Rig, Rostrum, Round-top, Scaffold, Shoe, Soapbox, Sponson, ► STAGE, Stand, Stoep, Tee, Ticket, Top, Tribune, Turntable

Play(ing) Accompany, Active, Amusement, Antic, Caper, Charm, Clearance, Curtain-raiser, Dandle, Drama, Echo, Endgame, Escapade, Everyman, Extended, Fair, Finesse, Frisk, Frolic, Fun, Gamble, Gambol, Game, Holiday, Inside, Interlude, Jam, Jape, Jest, Jeu, Lake, Latitude, Lear, Leeway, Licence, Long, Mask, Masque, Medal, Melodrama, Miracle, Morality, Mummers, Mysteries, Nativity, Nurse, Oberammergau, Parallel, Passion, Perform, Personate, Portray, Prank, Pretend, Recreation, Represent, Riff, Rollick, Romp, Room, Rope, RUR, Saw, Sketch, Sport, Stage, Strain, Stroke, Strum, Tolerance, Tonguing, Toy, Tragedy, Trifle, Twiddle, Vamp, Word

▷**Play** may indicate an anagram

Player(s) Actor, Athlete, Back, Black, Brass, Bugler, Busker, Cast, CD, Centre, Colt, E, East, ENSA, Equity, Fiddle, Flanker, Fullback, Goalie, Half, Hooker, Juke-box, Kest, Linebacker, Lineman, Lion, Lock, Longstop, Lutanist, Lutenist, Man, Midfield, Mid-on, Mime, Musician, N, North, Onside, Participant, Pianola®, Pitcher, Pone, Pro, Prop, Quarterback, Rover, S, Scrape, Scratch, Seed, Shortstop, Side, South,

Stand-off, Stereo, Strolling, Super, Sweeper, Team, Thespian, Troubador, Troupe, Upright, Virtuosi, W, West, White, Wing

Playful Arch, Coy, Frisky, Humorous, Kittenish, Ludic, Merry, Piacevole, Scherzo, Skittish, Sportive

Playwright Aeschylus, Albee, Arden, Ayckbourn, Barrie, Barry, Beaumarchais, Beaumont, Beckett, Behan, Bellow, Bennett, Besier, Bolt, Brecht, Chekhov, Congreve, Corneille, Coward, Dekker, Delaney, ➤ DRAMATIST, Dramaturge, Dramaturgist, Drinkwater, Euripides, Fletcher, Fry, Gems, Genet, Goldoni, Gorky, Harwood, Hay, Ibsen, Jonson, Marlowe, Massinger, Menander, Miller, Molière, Mortimer, O'Casey, Odets, O'Neill, Orton, Osborne, Pinero, Pinter, Pirandello, Priestley, Racine, Rattigan, Scriptwriter, Shaw, Sheridan, Sherry, Simpson, Sophocles, Stoppard, Storey, Strindberg, Synge, Tate, Terence, Thespis, Travers, Vanbrugh, Webster, Wesker, Wilde

Plea Appeal, Claim, Defence, Entreaty, Excuse, Exoration, Orison, Placitum, Prayer, Rebuttal, Rebutter, Rogation, Suit

Plead(er) Answer, Argue, Beg, Entreat, ➤ IMPLORE, Intercede, Litigate, Moot, Vakeel, Vakil

Please(d), Pleasant, Pleasing, Pleasure(-seeker) Aggrate, Agreeable, Alcina, Algolagnia, Amene, Amuse, Arride, Bitte, Braw, Cheerful, Chuffed, Comely, Comfort, Content, Cute, Delice, Delight, Do, Euphonic, Fair, Felicitous, Fit, Flatter, Fun, Genial, Glad, Gladness, Gratify, Hedonism, Jammy, Joy, Kama, Kindly, Lepid, List, Oblige, Piacevole, Primrose path, Prithee, Prythee, Satisfy, Suit, Tasty, Tickle, Treat, Vanity, Voluptuary, Will, Winsome, Wrapped, Xanadu List

Pleat Accordion, Box, Crimp, Fold, French, Frill, Goffer, Gusset, Kick, Knife, Plait, Pranck(e), Prank, Sunburst, Sunray

Pledge Affidavit, Arles, Band, Betroth, Bond, Borrow, Bottomry, Dedicate, Deposit, Earnest(-penny), Engage, Fire, Gage, Guarantee, Hypothecate, Hock, Impignorate, Mortgage, Oath, Pass, Pawn, Pignerate, Pignoration, Plight, Propine, Sacrament, Security, Stake, Surety, Teetotal, Toast, Troth, Undertake, Vow, Wad, Wed

Plentiful, Plenty Abounding, Abundance, Abundant, Ample, Bags, Copious, Copy, Easy, Excess, Foison, Fouth, Ful(l)ness, Fushion, Galore, Goshen, Lashings, Lots, Oodles, Pleroma, Profusion, Quantity, Riches, Rife, Routh, Rowth, Scouth, Scowth, Slue, Sonce, Sonse, Umpteen

▶**Pliers** see PLY

Plimsoll(s) Dap, Gutty, Gym-shoe, Line, Mutton-dummies, Sandshoe, Tacky

Plot(s) Allotment, Babington, Bed, Brew, Carpet, Chart, Cliché, Connive, Conspiracy, Conspire, Covin, Covyne, Engineer, Erf, Erven, Frame-up, Graph, Gunpowder, Imbroglio, Intrigue, Locus, Lot, Machination, Map, Meal-tub, Odograph, Pack, Patch, Plan, Plat, Rye-house, Scenario, ▶ SCHEME, Sect(ion), Shot, Site, Story, Taluk, Terf, Turf, Web

Plough(man), Ploughed Arable, Ard, Arval, Big Dipper, Bull tongue, Chamfer, Charles's wain, Dipper, Disc, Ear, Earth-board, Ere, Fail, Fallow, Farmer, Feer, Flunk, Gadsman, Gang, Great bear, Harrow, Lister, Middlebreaker, Middlebuster, Piers, Pip, Push, Rafter, Rib, Rive, Rove, Scooter, Septentrion(e)s, Sill, Sow, Till(er), Triones

Ploy Brinkmanship, Dodge, Manoeuvre, Stratagem, Strike, Tactic, Wile

Pluck(ing), Plucky Avulse, Bare, Carphology, Cock, Courage, Deplume, Epilate, Evulse, Floccillation, Gallus, Game, ▶ GRIT, Guts, Loot, Mettle, Pick, Pinch, Pip, Pizzicato, Plectron, Plectrum, Ploat, Plot, Plunk, Pook(it), Pouk(it), Pull, Race, Scrappy, Snatch, Spin, Spirit, Spunk, Summon, Tug, Twang, Tweak, Tweeze, Yank

Plug Ad, Banana, Block, Bung, Caulk, Chew, Commercial, Dam, DIN, Dook, Dossil, Dottle, Douk, Fipple, Fother, Hype, Jack, Lam, Operculum, Pessary, Prod, Promote, Publicity, Ram, Recommendation, Spark(ing), Spile, Spiling, Stop(per), Stopple, Strobili, Suppository, Tampion, Tap, Tompion, Tent, Wander, Wedge

Plum Bullace, Cherry, Choice, Damson, Gage, Greengage, Ground, Japanese, Kaki, Mammee-sapota, Marmalade, Maroon, Mirabelle, Mussel, Myrobalan, Naseberry, Persimmon, Proin(e), Pruin(e), Prune, Quetsch, Raisin, Sapodilla, Sebesten, Victoria

Plumage, Plume Aigrette, Crest, Egret, Feather, Hackle, Panache, Preen, Ptilosis, Quill

Plumb(er) Bullet, Dredge, Fathom, Lead(sman), Perpendicular, Plummet, Sheer, Sound, Test, True, Vertical

Plump(er) Bold, Bonnie, Bonny, Buxom, Chubbed, Choose, Chubby, Dumpy, Embonpoint, Endomorph, Fat, Fleshy, Flop, Fubsy, Full, Lie, Opt, Plonk, Plop, Podgy, Portly, Roll-about,

Rotund, Round, Sonsie, Sonsy, Soss, Souse, Squab, Squat, Stout, Swap, Swop, Tidy, Well-fed

Plunder(er) Berob, Booty, Depredate, Despoil, Devastate, Escheat, Fleece, Forage, Freebooter, Gut, Harry, Haul, Herriment, Herryment, Hership, Loot, Maraud, Peel, Pill(age), Privateer, ➤ RANSACK, Rape, Rapparee, Ravine, Reave, Reif, Reive, Rieve, Rifle, Rob, Sack, Scoff, Shave, Skoff, Spoil(s), Spoliate, Sprechery, Spuilzie, Spuly(i)e, Spulzie, Swag

Plunge Demerge, Dive, Douse, Dowse, Duck, Enew, Immerge, Immerse, La(u)nch, Nose-dive, Plummet, Raker, Send, Sink, Souse, Swoop, Thrust

Ply, Plier(s) Bend, Birl, Cab, Exercise, Exert, Gondoliers, Importune, Layer, Practise, Run, Trade, Wield

▷**Plying** may indicate an anagram

PM Addington, Afternoon, Attlee, Autopsy, Bute, Cabinet-maker, Disraeli, Gladstone, Melbourne, Major, Peel, Pitt, Portland, Premier, ➤ PRIME MINISTER, Salisbury, Taoiseach

Pocket Air, Appropriate, Bag, Bin, Cavity, Cly, Cup, Enclave, Fob, Glom, Hideaway, Jenny, Misappropriate, Patch, Placket, Pot, Pouch, Purloin, Purse, Sac, Sky, Slash, Sling, Steal, Take

Pod(s) Babul, Bean, Belly, Carob, Chilli, Dividivi, Gumbo, Lomentum, Neb-neb, Okra, Pipi, Pregnant, Siliqua, Tamarind, Vanilla

Poem(s), Poetry Acrostic, Anthology, Ballad(e), Dit(t), Doggerel, Elegy, Epic(ede), Haiku, Hokku, Lay, Limerick, Metre, Ode, Pastoral, Poesy, Prelude, Quatrain, Rhapsody, Rime, Rondeau, Song, Sonnet, Stanza, Verse

Poet(s) Bard(ling), Cyclic, Elegist, Georgian, Iambist, Imagist, Laureate, Layman, Lyrist, Maker, Meistersinger, Metaphysical, Metrist, Minnesinger, Minstrel, Monodist, Odist, Parnassian, PL, Pleiade, Poetaster, Rhymer, Rhymester, Rhymist, Rymer, Scald, Scop, Skald, Smart, Sonneteer, Spasmodic, Thespis, Tragic, Troubadour, Trouvère, Trouveur

▶**Poetry** see POEM

Point(ed), Pointer, Points Ace, Aim, Antler, Apex, Apogee, Appui, Bar, Barb, Boiling, Breaking, Brownie, Cape, Cardinal, Cash, Centre, Choke, Clou, Clue, Colon, Comma, Cone, Conic, Corner, Cover, Crisis, Crux, Curie, Cusp, Cursor, Cuss, Decimal, Degree, Detail, Direct, Dot, E, Epee, Fang, Feature, Fitch(e), Focal, Focus, Foreland, Freezing, Fulcrum, Germane, Gist,

Gnomon, Hastate, Head, Hinge, Index, Indicate, Indicator, Ippon, Jester, Knub, Lance, Lead, Limit, Lizard, Locate, Locus, Mark, Melting, Metacentre, Moot, N, Nail, Neb, Needle, Ness, Nib, Node, Now, Nub, Obelisk, Opinion, Ord, Particle, Peak, Perigee, Pin, Pinnacle, Place, Power, Pressure, Prong, Prow, Punctilio, Punctual, Ras, S, Saturation, Scribe, Seg(h)ol, Set, Shaft, Show, Shy, Silly, Socket, Sore, Spearhead, Spicate, Spick, Spike, Stage, Star, Sticking, Stiletto, Sting, Strong, Sum, Talking, Taper, Technicality, Tine, ➤ TIP, Tongue, Trig, Triple, Turning, Use, Vane, Vantage, Verge, Verse, Vertex, Vowel, W

Pointless Blunt, Curtana, Flat, Futile, Inane, Inutile, Muticous, Otiose, Stupid, Vain

Poison(er), Poisoning, Poisonous Abron, Atropia, Borgia, Brom(m)ism, Embolism, Envenom, Ergotise, Gila, Hydragyrism, Iodism, Malevolent, Miasma, Mineral, Mycotoxin, Neutron, Noxious, Obeism, Phosphorism, Plumbism, Ptomaine, Py(a)emia, Raphania, Rot, Sapraemia, Saturnism, Septic(aemia), Toxic, Toxicology, Toxin, Trembles, Venefic, Venin, Venom(ous), Viperous, Virous, Virulent

Poke, Poky Bonnet, Broddle, Garget, Itchweed, Jab, Meddle, Mock, Nousle, Nudge, Nuzzle, Ombu, Peg, Pick, Pote, Pouch, Powter, ➤ PRISON, ➤ PROD, Prog, Proke, Punch, Root(le), Rout, Rowt, Stab, Thrust

Polar, Pole Anode, Antarctic, Arctic, Boom, Bowsprit, Caber, Celestial, Crossbar, Extremity, Flagstaff, Geomagnetic, Lug, Magnetic, Mast, N, Nadir, Negative, Nib, North, Po, Polack, Punt, Quant, Range, Rood, S, Shaft, Slav, South, Spar, Sprit, Staff, Starosta, Stilt, Sting, Telegraph, Topmast, Totem, Zenith

▷**Polar** may indicate with a pole

Police(man), Policewoman Bluebottle, Bobby, Busy, CID, Constable, Cop(per), Detective, Flatfoot, Flying Squad, Force, Fuzz, Garda, Gendarme, Gestapo, G-man, Guard, Inspector, Interpol, Keystone, Military, Met(ropolitan), Mountie, Officer, PC, Peeler, Redcap, Riot, Robert, Rozzer, RUC, Secret, Special, Super, Sweeney, The Bill, The Law, Vigilante

Police station Copshop, Lock-up, Watchhouse

Policy Assurance, Ballon d'essai, CAP, Comprehensive, Course, Demesne, Endowment, Expedience, Insurance, Knock for knock, Laisser-faire, Lend-lease, Line, Method, Open-sky, Plank,

Platform, Practice, Programme, Pork-barrel, Revanchism,
Scorched earth, Stop-go, Tack, Tactics, Ticket

Polish(ed), Polisher Beeswax, Black, Blacklead, Bob, Buff,
Bull, Burnish, Chamois, Complaisant, Edit, Elaborate, Elegant,
Emery, Enamel, Finish, French, Furbish, Gentlemanly, Glass,
Gloss, Heelball, Hone, Inland, Lap, Lustre, Nail, Perfect, Planish,
Polite, Refinement, Refurbish, Rottenstone, Rub, Sand,
Sandblast, Sandpaper, Sejm, Sheen, Shellac, Shine, Slick,
Supercalender, Urbane, Veneer, Wax

Polite Civil, Courteous, Genteel, Grandisonian, Mannered,
Suave, Urbane, Well-bred

Politic(al), Politics Apparat, Body, Chartism, Civic,
Diplomacy, Discreet, Expedient, Falange, Leftism, Poujadism,
Public, Radicalism, Rightism, Statecraft, Tactful, Wise

Politician(s) Bright, Carpet-bagger, Catiline, Chesterfield,
Demo(crat), Diehard, Disraeli, Eden, Green, Guelph,
Independent, Ins, Isolationist, Laski, Left, Legislator, Liberal,
MEP, MP, Parnell, Polly, Rad, Rep, Senator, Socialist, Statesman,
Statist, Tadpole, Taper, TD, Tory, Trotsky, Unionist, Veep,
Warhorse, Whig, Wilberforce

Poll Ballot, Bean, Canvass, Count, Cut, Deed, Dod, Election,
Exit, Gallup, Head, Humlie, Hummel, MORI, Nestor, Not(t),
Opinion, Parrot, Pineapple, Pow, Scrutiny, Straw, Votes

▷ **Poll** may indicate a first letter

Pollen, Pollinated Anemophilous, Beebread, Dust, Errhine,
Farina, Fertilised, Witch-meal, Xenia

Pollute(d), Pollutant, Pollution Adulterate, Contaminate,
Defile, Dirty, File, Foul, Impure, Infect, Miasma, Nox, Rainout,
Soil, Soilure, Stain, Sully, Taint, Violate

Pomp(ous) Big, Bombastic, Budge, Ceremonial, Display,
Dogberry, Euphuistic, Fustian, Grandiloquent, Grandiose,
Heavy, Highfalutin(g), High-flown, High-muck-a-muck,
High-sounding, Hogen-mogen, Inflated, Orotund,
Ostentatious, Pageantry, Parade, Pretentious, Solemn,
Splendour, Starchy, State, Stilted, Stuffy, Turgid

Pond(s) Dew, Dub, Hampstead, Lakelet, Pool, Pound, Puddle,
Slough, Stank, Stew, Tank, Turlough, Vivarium, Viver

Ponder(ous) Brood, Cogitate, Contemplate, Deliberate,
Heavy, Laboured, Mull, Muse, Perpend, Poise, Pore, Reflect,
Ruminate, ➤ THINK, Vise, Volve, Weight(y), Wonder

Pontiff, Pontifical, Pontificate Aaron, Aaronic, Antipope, Dogmatise, Papal

Pontoon Blackjack, Bridge, Caisson, Chess, Game, Vingt-et-un

Pony Canuck, Cayuse, Dartmoor, Exmoor, Garran, Garron, Gen(n)et, GG, Griffin, Griffon, Gryfon, Gryphon, Jennet, Mustang, New Forest, Polo, Pownie, Shanks', Sheltie, Shetland, Show, Tangun, Tat(too), Welsh

Pool Backwater, Bank, Bethesda, Billabong, Bogey hole, Cenote, Cess, Collect, Combine, Dub, Dump, Flash, Flow, Jackpot, Kitty, Lido, Lin(n), Meer, Mere, Mickery, Milkvah, Milkveh, Moon, Natatorium, Piscina, Piscine, Plash, Plesh, Plunge, ➤ POND, Reserve, Snooker, Spa, Stank, Sump, Tank, Tarn, Wave

Poor(ly) Bad, Bare, Base, Bijwoner, Breadline, Buckeen, Bywoner, Catchpenny, Conch, Cronk, Destitute, Gritty, Hard-up, Have-nots, Hopeless, Humble, Hungry, Ill(-off), Impecunious, Indigent, Lazarus, Lean, Low, Low-downer, Meagre, Mean, Needy, Obolary, Pauper, Peaky, Poxy, Roinish, Rop(e)y, Roynish, Sad, Scrub, Shabby, Shitty, Sober, Sorry, Sub, Thin, Third-rate, Trashy, Undeserving, Unwell

▷ **Poor** may indicate an anagram

Pop (off), Popper, Popping Bang, Brit, Burst, Cloop, Crease, Die, Father, Fr, Gingerbeer, Hip-hop, Hock, Insert, Lumber, Mineral, Nip, Pater, Pawn, Pledge, Population, Press-stud, Punk, Sherbet, Soda, Splutter, Weasel

▷ **Pop** may indicate an anagram

Pope(s) Adrian, Alexander, Atticus, Boniface, Clement, Dunciad, Eminence, Fish, Great Schism, Gregory, Hildebrand, Holiness, Innocent, Joan, Leo, Papa, Pius, Pontiff, Ruff(e), Schism, Theocrat, Tiara, Urban, Vatican, Vicar of Christ

Poppy Argemone, Bloodroot, California, Chicalote, Coquelicot, Corn, Diacodin, Eschscholtzia, Flanders, Horned, Iceland, Matilija, Mawseed, Opium, Papaver, Ponceau, Prickly, Puccoon, Rhoeadales, Shirley, Tall, Welsh

Popular(ity) Common, Demotic, General, Heyday, Hit, In, Laic, Lay, Mass, Plebeian, Prevalent, Public, Successful, Tipped, Trendy, Vogue

Population, Populace Catchment, Census, Demography, Inhabitants, Malthusian, Mass, Mob, ➤ PEOPLE, Public, Universe

Porcelain Arita, Bamboo, Celadon, Chelsea, China, Coalport, Crackle(ware), Dresden, Eggshell, Famille, Goss, Hard-paste, Hizen, Imari, Jasper, Jasper(ware), Limoges, Lithophane, Minton, Parian, Sèvres, Softpaste, Spode, Sung

Pore Browse, Hole, Hydrathode, Lenticel, Muse, Ostium, Outlet, Ponder, Stoma, Study

Pork Bacon, Boar, Brawn, Chap, Crackling, Flitch, Griskin, Ham, Pancetta, Scrapple, Spare-rib

Porridge Berry, Bird, Brochan, Brose, Busera, Crowdie, Drammach, Drammock, Gaol, Grits, Grouts, Gruel, Hominy, Kasha, Mahewu, Mealie pap, Oaten, Oatmeal, Parritch, Pease-brose, Polenta, Pottage, Praiseach, Sadza, Samp, Sentence, Skilly, Stirabout, Stretch, Sup(p)awn, Time, Ugali

Port(s) Beeswing, Carry, Cinque, Entrepot, Free, Gate, ➤ HARBOUR, Haven, Hithe, Hythe, Larboard, Left, Manner, Mien, Parallel, Tawny, Treaty, Wine

Porter Ale, Bearer, Bellboy, Bummaree, Caddie, Caddy, Cole, Concierge, Coolie, Doorman, Door-keeper, Dvornik, Entire, Ham(m)al, Hamaul, Humper, Janitor, October, Ostiary, Red-cap, Stout

Portion Ann(at), Bit, Deal, Distribute, Dole, Dose, Dotation, Fragment, Helping, Heritage, Hunk, Jointure, ➤ LOT, Modicum, Nutlet, Ounce, ➤ PART, Piece, Ratio, Scantle, Scantling, Section, Segment, Serving, Share, Size, Slice, Something, Tait, Taste, Tate, Tittle, Tranche, Wodge

Portrait(ist) Depiction, Drawing, Eikon, Icon, Ikon, Image, Kit-cat, Lely, Likeness, Painting, Retraitt, Retrate, Sketch, Vignette

Portray(al) Caricature, Depict, Describe, Feature, Image, Limn, Paint, Render, Represent, ➤ SHOW

Pose(r), Poseur Aesthete, Affect(ation), Arabesque, Asana, Ask, Contrapposto, Drape, Lotus, Masquerade, Model, Place, Plastique, Posture, Pretend, Problem, Propound, Pseud, Sit, Stance, Sticker, Tickler

Position Asana, Attitude, Bearing(s), Emplacement, Enfilade, F(o)etal, Foothold, Grade, Instal, Lay, Lie, Location, Locus, Lodg(e)ment, Lotus, Missionary, Mudra, Office, Pass, Peak, Place, Plant, Point, Pole, Post, Seat, Set(ting), Site, Situ, Stance, Standing, Standpoint, Station, Status, Syzygy, Tagmeme, Thesis, Tierce, Viewpoint

Positive, Positivist Absolute, Anode, Assertive, Categorical, ➤ CERTAIN, Comte, Definite, Emphatic, Plus, Print, Sure, Thetic, Upbeat, Yang, Yes

Possess(ed), Possession, Possessive Apostrophe, Asset, Aver, Bedevil, Belonging(s), Demonic, Driven, Energumen, Estate, Have, Haveour, Haviour, Heirloom, His, Hogging, Know, Lares (l) penates, Mad, Obsessed, Occupation, ➤ OWN, Sasine, Seisin, Sprechery, Usucap(t)ion, Vacant, Worth

Possible, Possibility, Possibly Able, Contingency, Feasible, Likely, Maybe, Mayhap, Peradventure, Perchance, Perhaps, Posse, Potential, Prospect, Resort, Viable, Will

▷**Possibly** may indicate an anagram

Post(s) Affix, After, Assign, Bitt, Bollard, Command, Correspondence, Delivery, Finger, Flagpole, Jamb, King, Last, Listening, Log, Mail, Mast, Newel, Observation, Outstation, Pale, Paling, Parcel, Penny, Picket, Pile, Piling, Piquet, Placard, Place, Plant, Plum, Pole, Position, Puncheon, Quoin, Registered, Remit, RM, Seat, Send, Staff, Staging, Stake, Station, Trading, Upright, Vacancy, Winning

Postman, Postmaster, Postwoman Carrier, Courier, Emily, Hill, Messenger, Nasby, Pat, Portionist, Sorter

Postpone(ment) Adjourn, Contango, Defer, Delay, Frist, Long-finger, Moratorium, Mothball, Pigeon-hole, Postdate, Prorogue, Reprieve, Shelve, Stay, Suspend, Withhold

Posture Affectation, Asana, Attitude, Decubitus, Deportment, Mudra, Pose, Pretence, Site, Stance, Vorlage

Pot(s), Potting, Potty Bankroll, Basil, Belly, Cafetière, Cannabis, Casserole, Ca(u)ldron, Ceramic, Chamber, Chanty, Chimney, Cocotte, Crewe, Crock(ery), Crucible, Cruse(t), Delf(t), Dixie, Ewer, Flesh, Gage, Grass, Hash(ish), Helmet, Hemp, In off, Kettle, Kitty, Lobster, Lota(h), Maiolica, Majolica, Marijuana, Marmite, Melting, Ming, Olla, Olpe, Pan, Pat, Pipkin, Planter, Pocket, Poot, ➤ POTTERY, Pout, Prize, Samovar, Shoot, Skillet, Steamer, Skeet, Stomach, Tea, Test, Throw, Trivet, Tureen, Urn

Potato(es) Batata, Chat, Couch, Datura, Duchesse, Fluke, Hashbrowns, Hog, Hole, Hot, Jersey, Kumara, Lyonnaise, Mash, Murphy, Peel-and-eat, Pratie, Praty, Roesti, Seed, Solanum, Stovies, Tatie, Tattie, Teddy, Tuber, Ware, Yam

Potential Action, Capacity, Making(s), Manqué, Possible, Promise, Resting, Scope, Viable

▷**Potentially** may indicate an anagram

Potter Cue, Dabbity, Dacker, Daidle, Daiker, Dibble, Dilly-dally, Dodder, Etruscan, Fettle, Fiddle, Footer, Footle, Fouter, Gamesmanship, Idle, Mess, Minton, Muck, Niggle, One-upmanship, Plouter, Plowter, Spode, Thrower, Tiddle, Tink(er), Troke, Truck, Wedgwood

▷**Potter** may indicate a snooker-player

Pottery Agateware, Bank, Bisque, Celadon, Ceramet, Ceramic, China, Creamware, Crock, Crouch-ware, Dabbity, Delf(t), Encaustic, Etruria, Faience, Flatback, Gombroon, Graniteware, Hollowware, Jomon, Majolica, Ming, Raku, Satsuma, Scroddled, Sgraffito, Slab, Slipware, Smalto, Spode, Spongeware, Stoneware, Sung, Ware, Wedgwood®, Wemyss, Whieldon

Pouch(ed) Bag, Brood, Bum-bag, Bursa, Caecum, Cheek, Cisterna, Codpiece, Diverticulum, Fanny pack, Gill, Jockstrap, Marsupial, Poke, Purse, Sac, Scrip, Scrotum, Spleuchan, Sporran

Pound(er) Ache, As, Bar, Bash, Batter, Beat, Bombard, Bradbury, Bray, Broadpiece, Bruise, Contund, Coop, Drub, Embale, Enclosure, Ezra, Fold, Green, Hammer, Hatter, Imagist, Intern, Iron man, Jail, Kiddle, Kidel, Kin, Knevell, L, Lam, Lb, Lock, Mash, Nevel, Nicker, Oncer, One-er, Oner, Pale, Pen, Penfold, Pestle, Pin, Pindar, Pinfold, Powder, Pulverise, Pun, Quop, Rint, Smacker, Sov(ereign), Stamp, Strum, Thump, Tower, Weight

Pour Birl(e), Bucket, Cascade, Circumfuse, Decant, Diffuse, Flood, Flow, Jaw, Jirble, Libate, Rain, Seil, Shed, Sile, Skink, Spew, Stream, Teem, Turn, Vent, Weep, Well

Poverty Beggary, Dearth, Deprivation, Illth, Indigence, ▶ LACK, Need, Penury, Poortith, Squalor, Want

Powder(ed), Powdery Baking, Boracic, Calamine, Chalk, Cosmetic, Culm, Cuttlefish, Dentifrice, Dust, Explosive, Floury, Gregory, Grind, Kohl, Meal, Pollen, Pounce, Pulver, Rachel, Rochelle, Rouge, Seidlitz, Sherbet, Talc(um), Toner, Tooth

Power(ful), Powers Ability, Able, Arm, Attorney, Authority, Axis, Big, Cham, Charisma, Clairvoyance, Clout, Cogency, Command, Corridor, Cube, Danger, Despotic, Diadem, Dominion, Effective, Eminence, Empathy, Energy, Eon, Exponent, Facility, Faculty, Flower, Force, Hefty, High, Horse,

Hp, Hydroelectric, Hot, Influence, Kilowatt, Log, Logarithm, Mastery, Might, Mogul, Motive, Muscle, Nature, Nth, Od-force, Omnificent, Omnipotent, P, Panjandrum, Posse, Potency, Puissant, Punch, Regime, Sinew, Soup, Stamina, Steam, Stiff, Strength, ➤ **STRONG**, Supercharge, Supreme, Teeth, Telling, Throne, Tycoon, Vigour, Vis, Volt, Vroom, Water, Watt, Wattage, Weight, Wind

Practical, Practicable Active, Doable, Joker, Pragmatic, Realist(ic), Realpolitik, Sensible, Useful, Viable, Virtual

Practice, Practise, Practitioner Abuse, Custom, Do, Drill, Enure, Exercise, General, Group, Habit, Inure, Ism, Keep, Knock-up, Meme, Nets, Operate, Order, Ply, Policy, Praxis, Private, Prosecution, Pursuit, Rehearsal, Rehearse, Restrictive, Rite, Rut, Sharp, Test-run, Trade, Tradition, Train, Trial, Ure, Usage, Use

Prairie IL, Illinois, Llano, Plain, Savanna, Steppe, Tundra, Veldt

Praise(worthy) Acclaim, Adulation, Alleluia, Allow, Anthem, Applause, Belaud, Bless, Blurb, Bouquet, Butter, Carol, Citation, CL, Commend(ation), Compliment, Dulia, Encomium, Envy, Eulogise, Eulogium, Eulogy, Exalt, Extol, Gloria, Glory, Herry, Hery(e), Hosanna, Hype, Incense, Laud, Lip service, Lo(o)s, Meritorious, Panegyric, Rap, Roose, Tribute

Prance Brank, Canary, Caper, Cavort, Galumph, Gambol, Jaunce, Jaunse, Prank(le), Swagger, Tittup, Trounce

Prank(s) Attrap, Bedeck, Bedizen, Caper, Dido, Escapade, Fredaine, Frolic, Gaud, Jape, Lark, Mischief, Rag, Reak, Reik, Rex, Rig, Spoof, Trick, Vagary

Prattle Babble, Blat(her), Chatter, Gab(nash), Gas, Gibber, Gossip, Gup, Lalage, Patter, Yap

Pray(ing) Appeal, Beg, Beseech, Daven, ➤ **ENTREAT**, Impetrate, Intone, Invoke, Kneel, Mantis, Solicit, Wrestle

Prayer (book), Prayers Act, Angelus, Ave (Maria), Bead, Bede, Bene, Breviary, Collect, Common, Cry, Devotion, Eleison, Entreaty, Grace, Hail Mary, Intercession, Invocation, Kaddish, Khotbah, Kol Nidre, Kyrie, Kyrie eleison, Lauds, Litany, Lord's, Mantis, Mat(t)ins, Missal, Novena, Orant, Orarium, Orison, Our Father, Paternoster, Patter, Petition, Phylactery, Placebo, Plea, Requiem, Requiescat, Rogation, Rosary, Secret, Shema, Suffrage

▷**Prayer** may indicate one who begs

Preach(er) Ainger, Boanerges, Devil-dodger, Donne, Ecclesiastes, Exhort, Evangelist, Gospeller, Graham, Holy Roller, Itinerant, Knox, Lecture, Mar-text, Minister, ➤ MORALISE, Patercove, Postillate, Predicant, Predicate, Predikant, Priest, Prophet, Pulpiteer, Rant, Spintext, Spurgeon, Teach

Precaution Care, Guard, Fail-safe, In case, Prophylaxis, Safeguard

Precede(nce), Precedent Antedate, Example, Forego, Forerun, Herald, Pas, Predate, Preface, Priority, Protocol

Precinct(s) Ambit, Area, Banlieue, Close, Courtyard, District, Environs, Peribolos, Region, Temenos, Verge, Vihara

Precious Adored, Chary, Chichi, Costly, Dear, Dearbought, Ewe-lamb, La-di-da, Murr(h)a, Owre, Precise, Rare, Valuable

Precipitate, Precipitation, Precipitous Abrupt, Accelerate, Cause, Deposit, Hailstone, Headlong, Impetuous, Launch, Lees, Pellmell, Pitchfork, Rash, Sca(u)r, Sheer, Shoot, Sleet, Snowflake, Start, ➤ STEEP

Precise(ly), Precisian, Precision Absolute, Accurate, Dry, Exact, Explicit, Minute, Nice(ty), Particular, Perfect, Plumb, Prig, Prim, Punctilious, Spang, Specific, Starchy, Stringent, Tight, Very

Predator(y) Carnivore, Eagle, Fox, Glede, Harpy-eagle, Jackal, Kestrel, Kite, Lycosa, Marauder, Predacious, Puma, Tanrec, Tarantula, Tenrec

Predecessor Ancestor, Forebear, Foregoer

Predicament Box, Dilemma, Embroglio, Hobble, Hole, Jam, Pass, Peril, Pickle, Plight, Quandary, Scrape, Spot

Predict(ion), Predictable, Predictor Augur, Belomancy, Bet, Divination, Forecast, Foreshow, Foretell, Forsay, Horoscope, Nap, Necromancy, Portend, Presage, Previse, Prognosis, Prophecy, Prophesy, Regular, Soothsayer

Pre-eminence, Pre-eminent Arch, Foremost, Palm, Paramount, Primacy, Supreme, Topnotch, Unique

Preface Foreword, Herald, Intro, Preamble, Precede, Proem, Prolegomenon, Usher

Prefer(ence), Preferred Advance, Choose, Elect, Faard, Faurd, Favour, Incline, Lean, Predilect(ion), Prefard, Priority, Proclivity, Promote, Sooner, Stocks, Taste, Will

Pregnancy, Pregnant Big, Clucky, Cyesis, Ectopic, Enceinte, Fertile, Gestation, Gravid(a), Great, Heavy, Knocked-up, Pseudocyesis

Prehistoric Ancient, Azilian, Beakerfolk, Brontosaurus, Cambrian, Clovis, Cro-magnon, Eocene, Folsom, Primeval, Primitive, Pteranodon, Pterodactyl(e), Pterosaur, Saurian, Sinanthropus, Titanosaurus, Trilith(on)

Prejudice(d) Bias, Discrimination, Down, Derry, Illiberal, Impede, Injure, Insular, Intolerance, Partiality, Parti pris, Preoccupy, Prepossession, Racism

Preliminary Draft, Exploration, Heat, Initial, Introductory, Precursory, Previous, Prodrome, Prolusion, Rough, Title-sheet

Prelude Entree, Forerunner, Intrada, Overture, Proem(ial), Ritornell(e), Ritornello

Premature Early, Precocious, Pre(e)mie, Premy, Previous, Slink, Untimely, Untimeous

Premier Chief, Leader, Main, PM, ➤ PRIME MINISTER, Tojo

Premise(s) Assumption, Datum, Epicheirema, Ground, Hypothesis, Inference, Lemma, Postulate, Property, Proposition, Reason

Premium Ap, Bond, Bonus, Discount, Grassum, Pm, Reward, Scarce

Preoccupation, Preoccupied, Preoccupy Absorb, Abstracted, Distrait, Engross, Hang-up, Intent, Obsess, Thing

Prepare(d), Preparation Address, A la, Arrange, Attire, Boun, Bowne, Busk, Calver, Cock, Concoct, Cooper, Countdown, Decoct, Did, Do, Dress, Edit, Forearm, Game, Groom, Ground, Inspan, Key, Lay, Legwork, Lotion, Measure, Mobilise, Parascene, Prime, Procinct, Prothesis, Provide, Psych, ➤ READY, Rehearsal, Ripe, Set, Spadework, Stand-to, Suborn, Train, Truss, Warm-up, Yare

▷**Prepare(d)** may indicate an anagram

Preposterous Absurd, Chimeric, Foolish, Grotesque, Unreasonable

▷**Preposterous** may indicate a word reversed

Prerequisite Condition, Essential, Necessity, Sine qua non

Presbyter(ian) Berean, Blue, Cameronian, Covenanter, Elder, Knox, Macmillanite, Moderator, Sacrarium, Whig(gamore)

Prescribe Appoint, Assign, Dictate, Enjoin, Impose, Ordain, Rule, Set

Prescription Cipher, Decree, Direction, Formula, Medicine, R, Rec, Receipt, Ritual, Specific

Presence Aspect, Bearing, Closeness, Company, Debut, Hereness, Shechinah, Shekinah, Spirit

Present(ed), Presenter, Presently Anchorman, Anon, Assists, Award, Bestow, Bonsela, Boon, Bounty, Box, Cadeau, Congiary, Coram, Current, Debut, Dee-jay, DJ, Deodate, Donate, Dotal, Douceur, Dower, Endew, Endow, Endue, Enow, Etrenne, Existent, Fairing, Feature, Front-man, Gie, ➤ GIFT, Give, Going, Grant, Gratuity, Hand, Here, Hodiernal, Introduce, Inst, Largess(e), Linkman, MC, Mod, Nonce, Now, Nuzzer, Porrect, Potlach, Pr, Produce, Proffer, Pro-tem, Put, Render, Show, Slice, Tip, Today, Vee-jay, Xenium, Yeven

Preserve(d), Preservative, Preserver Bottle, Burnettize, Can, Chill, Confect, Corn, Creosote, Cure, Dehydrate, Dry, Eisel, Embalm, Fixative, Formaldehyde, Formalin, Freeze, Guard, Hair, Hesperides, Jam, Jerk, Keep, Kinin, Kipper, Konfyt, Kyanise, ➤ MAINTAIN, Marmalade, Mummify, Pectin, Peculiar, Piccalilli, Pickle, Pot, Powellise, Salt, Salve, Saut, Souse, Store, Stuff, Tanalized, Tar, Tin, Vinegar, Waterglass

Preside(nt) Chair, Dean, Director, Lead, Moderator, P, Speaker, Superintendent, Supervisor

Press(ed), Pressing, Pressure Acute, Atmospheric, Bar, Bench, Blackmail, Cabinet, Clothes, Coerce, Cram, Crease, Crimp, Critical, Crowd, Crush, Cupboard, Dragoon, Drill, Dun, Duresse, Enslave, Exigent, Force, Fourth estate, Goad, Gutter, Hasten, Head, Heat, Herd, Hie, Hug, Hustle, Hydraulic, Impact, Important, Importune, Inarm, Iron, Jam, Knead, Lie, Lobby, Mangle, Mill, Minerva, Newspapers, Obligate, Onus, PA, Pascal, Peer, Persist, Ply, Printing, Pump, ➤ PUSH, Ram, Record, Recruit, Reporter, Roll, Rush, Screw, Scrum, Serr(e), Sit, Speed, Spur, Squash, Squeeze, Stop, Straint, Stress, Tension, Throng, Throttle, Tourniquet, ➤ URGE, Urgence, Urgency, Vapour, Vice, Wardrobe, Weight, Wring

Prestige, Prestigious Cachet, Credit, Distinguished, Fame, Influence, Kudos, Notable, Status

Presume, Presumably, Presumption, Presumptuous Allege, Arrogant, Audacity, Believe, Bold, Brass, Cocksure,

Cocky, Doubtless, ➤ EXPECT, Familiar, Gall, Impertinent, Insolent, Liberty, Outrecuidance, Pert, Probably, Suppose, Uppish, Whipper-snapper

Pretence, Pretend(er), Pretext Act, Affect(ation), Afflict, Assume, Blind, Bluff, Charade, Charlatan, Claim, Cover, Cram, Dissemble, Dissimulate, Excuse, Feign, Feint, Gondolier, Hokum, Humbug, Hypocrisy, Impostor, Jactitation, Lambert Simnel, Let-on, Make-believe, Malinger, Masquerade, Obreption, Old, Parolles, Perkin Warbeck, Pose, Profess, Pseud(o), Quack, Sham, Simulate, Stale, Stalking-horse, Subterfuge, Suppose, Warbeck, Young

Pretension, Pretentious(ness) Arty, Bombast, Fantoosh, Fustian, Gaudy, Grandiose, High-falutin(g), Kitsch, La-di-da, Orotund, Ostentatious, Overblown, Paraf(f)le, Pompous, Pseud(o), Sciolism, Showy, Snobbish, Squirt, Tat, Tinhorn, Uppity

Pretty Becoming, Chocolate-box, Comely, Cute, Dish, Decorate, Elegant, Fair(ish), Fairway, Inconie, Incony, Keepsaky, Moderately, Pass, Peach, Picturesque, Primp, Quite, Sweet, Twee, Winsome

Prevail(ing) Dominate, Endure, Go, Induce, Persist, Persuade, Predominant, Preponderate, Reign, Triumph, Victor, Win

Prevalent Catholic, Common, Dominant, Endemic, Epidemic, Obtaining, Rife, Widespread

Prevent(ive) Avert, Bar, Debar, Deter, Embar, Estop, Foreclose, Forfend, Help, Impound, Inhibit, Keep, Let, Obstruct, Obviate, Preclude, Prophylactic, Stop, Theriac, Trammel

Previous(ly) Afore, Already, Before, Earlier, Ere(-now), Fore, Former, Hitherto, Once, Prior

Prey Booty, Feed, Kill, Pelt, Plunder, Predate, Proul, Prowl, Quarry, Raven, Ravin(e), Soyle, Spreagh, Victim

Price(d), Price-raising Appraise, Assess, Charge, Consequence, Contango, ➤ COST, Dearth, Due, Evens, Expense, Fee, Fiars, Hire, Limit, List, Market, Packet, Quotation, Quote, Rate, Regrate, Reserve, Song, Starting, Street value, Unit, Upset, Value, Vincent, Weregild, Wergeld, Wergild, Worth, Yardage

Prick(ed), Prickle, Prickly Acanaceous, Accloy, Argemone, Arrect, Bearded, Brakier, Bramble, Brog, Bunya, Cactus, Cloy, Cnicus, Echinate, Goad, Gore, Hedgehog, Hedgepig, Impel,

Inject, Jab, Jook, Juk, Kali, Penis, Pierce, Prod, Puncture, Rubus, Ruellia, Seta, Setose, Smart, Spinate, Stab, Star-thistle, Stimulus, Sting, Tattoo, Tatu, Teasel, Thistle, Thorn, Tingle, Urge

Pride Bombast, Brag, Conceit, Elation, Esprit de corps, Glory, Hauteur, Hubris, Inordinate, Lions, London, Machismo, Plume, Preen, Purge, Triumphalism, Vainglory, Vanity

Priest(ess), Priests Abbot, Becket, Brahmin, Cardinal, Clergyman, Cleric, Curé, Dalai Lama, Druid, Flamen, High, Lama, Mage, Metropolitan, Missionary, Monsignor, Padre, Pastor, Presbyter, Père, Pontiff, Pope, Preacher, Prelate, Prior(ess), Rabbi, Rev, Seminarian, Sky pilot, Vicar

Primacy, Primate Ape, Aye-aye, Bandar, Bigfoot, Biped, Bishop, Bush baby, Cardinal, Ebor, Gibbon, Hanuman, Hominid, Jackanapes, King-kong, Loris, Macaque, Magot, Mammal, Marmoset, ► MONKEY, Orang, Pongid, Potto, Prosimian, Quadruman, Ramapithecus, Rhesus, Sifaka

Prime(r), Primary, Priming Arm, Basic, Bloom, Cardinal, Charging, Chief, Choice, Claircolle, Clearcole, Clerecole, Detonator, Donat, Donet, Election, Enarm, First, Flower, Heyday, Mature, Original, Paramount, Peak, Radical, Remex, Supreme, Thirteen, Tip-top, Totient, Totitive, Valuable, Windac, Windas, Ylem

Prime Minister Asquith, Attlee, Baldwin, Begin, Bute, Canning, Chamberlain, Chatham, Dewan, Disraeli, Diwan, Eden, Grey, Home, Leaderene, North, Peel, Pitt, PM, Premier, Shastri, Tanaiste, Taoiseach, Thatcher, Walpole

Primitive Aborigine, Amoeba, Antediluvian, Arabic, Archaic, Barbaric, Caveman, Crude, Early, Evolué, Fundamental, Naive, Neanderthal, Neolithic, Old, Persian, Pro, Prothyl(e), Protyl(e), Radical, Rudimentary, Savage, Subman, Turkish, Uncivilised, Ur

Prince(ly) Albert, Amir, Black, Caliph, Charming, Crown, Elector, Florizel, Fortinbras, Highness, Igor, Ksar, Merchant, Noble, Potentate, Rajah, Regal, Serene, Sherif, Student

Princess Begum, Di(ana), Infanta, Rani

Principal Arch, Capital, Central, ► CHIEF, Decuman, Especial, First, Foremost, Head, Leading, Main(stay), Major, Mass, Protagonist, Ringleader, Staple, Star

Principle(s), Principled Animistic, Anthropic, Archimedes, Axiom, Basis, Brocard, Canon, Carnot, Code, Criterion, Cui bono, Cy pres, Doctrine, Dogma, Element, Essential, Generale,

Germ, Honourable, Key, Law, Logos, Methodology, Organon, Peter, Platform, Pleasure, Precept, Prescript, Rationale, Reason, Rudiment, Rule, Spirit, Tenet, Theorem, Ticket, Yang, Yin

Print(er), Printing Baskerville, Batik, Calotype, Caxton, Chromo, Cicero, Collotype, Dab, Dot matrix, Elzevir, Engrave, Etching, Fine, Font, Gravure, Impress, Ink-jet, Intaglio, Italic, Laser, Letterpress, Line, Lino-cut, Lithograph, Logotype, Lower-case, Monotype®, Moon, Off-line, Offset, Oleo, Oleograph, Opaline, Plate, Positive, Press, Publish, Report, Reproduction, Rotogravure, Ship, Silk-screen, Small, Splash, Stamp, Stonehand, Strike, Thermal, Typesetter, Whorl, Woodcut

Prior(ity) Abbot, Afore, Antecedent, Earlier, Former, Hitherto, Monk, Overslaugh, Pre-, Precedence, Prefard, Preference, Previous, Privilege, Triage

Prison Alcatraz, Bastille, Bin, Bird, Bridewell, Brig, Brixton, Cage, Can, Cell, Chok(e)y, Clink, Club, College, Confine, Cooler, Coop, Counter, Dartmoor, Dungeon, Durance, Fleet, Fotheringhay, Gaol, Glass-house, Gulag, Hokey, Holloway, Hulk(s), Internment, ➤ JAIL, Jug, Kitty, Limbo, Lock-up, Marshalsea, Maze, Newgate, Nick, Oflag, Open, Pen, Penitentiary, Pentonville, Pit, Poke(y), Pound, Quad, Quod, Reformatory, Roundhouse, Scrubs, Shop, Sing-sing, Slammer, Spandau, Stalag, Stir, Strangeways, Tol(l)booth, Tower, Wandsworth

Prisoner Canary-bird, Captive, Collegian, Collegiate, Con(vict), Detainee, Detenu, Inmate, Internee, Lag, Lifer, Political, POW, Trustee, Trusty, Yardbird, Zek

Private(ly) Ain, Aside, Atkins, Auricular, Buccaneer, Byroom, Clandestine, Close, Closet, Confidential, Enisle(d), Esoteric, Homefelt, Hush-hush, In camera, Individual, Inner, Intimate, Non-com, Own, Personal, Piou-piou, Poilu, Proprietary, Pte, Rank(er), Retired, Sanction, Sapper, Secret, Several, ➤ SOLDIER, Sub rosa, Tommy

Privileg(ed) Birthright, Blest, Charter, Curule, Enviable, Exempt, Favour, Franchise, Freedom, Indulgence, Liberty, Mozarab, Nomenklatura, Octroi, Patent, Prerogative, Pryse, Regale, Regalia, Right, Sac

Privy Apprised, Can, Closet, Intimate, Jakes, John, Loo, Necessary, Reredorter, Secret, Sedge, Siege

Prize(s), Prizewinner Acquest, Apple, Archibald, Assess, Award, Best, Booby, Booker, Bravie, Capture, Champion, Consolation, Creach, Cup, Dux, Efforce, ➤ ESTEEM, Force, Garland, Goncourt, Grice, Honour, Jackpot, Jemmy, Lever, Lot, Money, Nobel, Palm, Pearl, Pewter, Pie, Plum, Plunder, Pot, Pulitzer, Purse, Ram, Reprisal, ➤ REWARD, Scalp, Ship, Spreaghery, Sprechery, Stakes, Tern, Treasure, Trophy, Turner, Value

Pro Aye, Coach, For, Harlot, Moll, Paid, Tramp, Yea, Yes

Probable, Probability Apparent, Belike, Ergodic, Feasible, Likely, Possible

Probe Antenna, Bore, Cassini, Delve, Dredge, Explore, Fathom, Feeler, Fossick, Inquire, Investigate, Pelican, Poke, Pump, ➤ SEARCH, Seeker, Sound, Space, Stylet, Tent, Thrust, Tracer

Problem(s) Acrostic, Boyg, Brainteaser, Crux, Dilemma, Egma, Enigma, Facer, Glitch, Handful, Hang-up, Headache, Hitch, Hurdle, Indaba, Knot(ty), Koan, Miniature, Musive, Net, Nuisance, Obstacle, Pons asinorum, Poser, Quandary, Question, Re, Rebus, Riddle, Rider, Snag, Sorites, Sum, Teaser, Thing, Tickler, Toughie, Tsuris, Yips

Proceed(s), Proceeding, Procedure Acta, Afoot, Algorithm, Continue, Course, Drill, Emanate, Fand, Flow, Fond, Goes, Haul, Issue, MO, Machinery, March, Mechanics, Mine, Modal, Move, On, Pass, Practice, Praxis, Process, Profit, Punctilio, Pursue, Put, Rake, Return, Rite, Routine, Sap, Steps, System, Take, Use, Yead(s), Yede, Yeed

Process(ion) Acromion, Action, Ala, Ambarvalia, Axon, Ben Day, Bessemer, Catalysis, Cortège, Demo, Haber, Handle, Markov, Method, Moharram, Mond, Motorcade, Muharram, Open hearth, Pageant, Parade, Paseo, Photosynthesis, Pipeline, Pomp, Recycle, Series, Skimmington, Solway, Speciation, String, Train, Treat, Trial

Proclaim, Proclamation Announce, Annunciate, Ban, Blaze, Blazon, Boast, Broadsheet, Cry, Edict, Enounce, Enunciate, Herald, Indiction, Kerygma, Oyez, Preconise, Profess, Publish, Ring, Shout, Trumpet, Ukase

Prodigious, Prodigy Abnormal, Amazing, Huge, Immense, Monster, Monument, Mozart, Phenomenal, Portentous, Tremendous, Wonder, Wonderwork, Wunderkind

Produce(r), Producing Afford, Breed, Cause, Create, Crop, Ean, Edit, Effect, Engender, Evoke, Exhibit, Extend, Fruit, Generate, Get, Grow, Impresario, Issue, Kind, Make, Offspring, Onstream, Originate, Output, Propage, Propagand, Raise, Son, Stage, Supply, Teem, Throw, Wares, Whelp, Yield

▷**Produces** may indicate an anagram

Product(ion), Productive(ness), Productivity Actualities, Apport, Artefact, Ashtareth, Ashtaroth, Astarte, Bore, Coefficient, Drama, Fecund, Fertile, Fruit, Genesis, Harvest, Output, Outturn, Prolific, Result, Rich, Show, Speiss, Uberous, Uberty, Waste, Work, Yield

▷**Production** may indicate an anagram

Profane, Profanation, Profanity Coarse, Coprolalia, Desecrate, Impious, Irreverent, Sacrilege, Unholy, Violate

Profess(ed), Professor Absent-minded, Academic, Adjoint, Admit, Asset, Challenger, Claim, Declare, Disney, Emeritus, Higgins, Hodja, Kho(d)ja, Know-all, Ostensible, Own, Practise, Pundit, Regent, Regius, RP, STP

Profession(al) Admission, Assurance, Buppy, Business, Career, Creed, Expert, Métier, Practitioner, Pretence, Pursuit, Regular, Salaried, Skilled, Trade, Vocation, Yuppie

Proficiency, Proficient Adept, Alert, Dan, Expert, Forte, Past master, Practised, Skill, Technique

Profile Analysis, Contour, Half-face, Loral, Outline, Silhouette, Sketch, Statant, T(h)alweg, Vignette

Profit(able), Profiteer, Profits Advantage, Arbitrage, Asset, Avail, Benefit, Boot, Bunce, Cere, Clear, Divi(dend), Economic, Edge, Emoluments, Exploit, Fat, Gain, Graft, Gravy, Grist, Income, Increment, Issue, Jobbery, Juicy, Leech, Lucrative, Makings, Melon, Milch cow, Mileage, Moneymaker, Net, Pay(ing), Perk, Rake-off, Return, Reward, Royalty, Spoils, Use, Usufruct, Utile, Utility, Vail

Profuse, Profusion Abundant, Copious, Excess, Free, Galore, Lavish, Liberal, Lush, Quantity, Rank, Rich, Two-a-penny

Program(ming) language, Programmer Ada, Algol, Applet, BIOS, Basic, Bloatware, Boot, Bot, Cancelbot, CU See Me, Cobol, Columbus, Debugger, Dictionary, Est, Firmware, Fortran, Freeware, Inputter, Java®, Linker, LISP, LOGO, PROLOG, PROM, Package, Pascal, Router, Screensaver, Search engine, Shell, Spreadsheet, Telnet, Utility, Web browser, Web crawler

Programme Agenda, Broadcast, Card, Code, Docusoap, Event, Fly-on-the-wall, Infotainment, Linear, ➤ PDL, Prank, Playbill, Schedule, Scheme, Sked, Soap, Software, Syllabus, System, Telecast, Telethon, Timetable

Progress(ive), Progression ➤ ADVANCE, Afoot, Arithmetic, Avant garde, Course, Fabian, Flow, Forge, Forward, Gain, Geometric, Go, Growth, Headway, Incede, Liberal, Move, Onwards, Paraphonia, Pilgrim's, Prosper, Rack, Rake's, Reformer, Roll, Run, Sequence, Series, Step, Vaunce, Way, Yead, Yede, Yeed

Prohibit(ion), Prohibitionist Ban, Block, Debar, Dry, Embargo, Estop, Forbid, Hinder, Index, Interdict, Noli-me-tangere, Prevent, Pussyfoot, Taboo, Tabu, Veto

Project(ile), Projecting, Projection, Projector Aim, Ammo, Assignment, Astrut, Ball, Ballistic, Beetle, Bullet, Butt, Buttress, Cam, Cast, Catapult, Cinerama®, Cog, Conceive, Console, Discus, Eaves, Enterprise, Episcope, Excrescence, Exsert, Extrapolate, Fet(ter)lock, Flange, Gore, Guess, Hangover, Hoe, Inion, Jut, Kern, Knob, Ledge, Lobe, Lug, Nab, Nose, Outcrop, Outjut, Overhang, Overhead, Oversail, Peters, Pitch, Planetarium, Prickle, Promontory, ➤ PROTRUDE, Proud(er), Rocket, Sail, Salient, Sally, Scheme, Screen, Shelf, Shrapnel, Snag, Snout, Spur, Tang, Tappet, Tenon, Throw, Toe, Tracer, Trippet, Tusk, Umbo, Undertaking

Prolong(ed) Extend, Lengthen, Protract, Sostenuto, Spin, Sustain

Prom(enade) Alameda, Boulevard, Cakewalk, Catwalk, Crush-room, Esplanade, Front, Mall, Parade, Paseo, Pier, Sea-front, Stroll, ➤ WALK

Prominence, Prominent Antitragus, Blatant, Bold, Colliculus, Condyle, Conspicuous, Egregious, Emphasis, Featured, Gonion, Important, Insistent, Manifest, Marked, Salient, Signal, Teat, Toot, Tragus

Promise, Promising Accept, Augur, Avoure, Behest, Behight, Behote, Bode, Coming, Covenant, Engagement, Foretaste, Guarantee, Hecht, Hest, Hete, Hight, IOU, Likely, Manifest, Parole, Pledge, Plight, Pollicitation, Potential, Recognisance,

Recognizance, Rosy, Sign, Sponsor, Swear, Tile, Undertake, Vow, Warranty, Word

Promote(r), Promotion Adman, Advance, ➤ ADVERTISE, Aggrandise, Aid, Assist, Blurb, Boost, Campaign, Dog and pony show, Elevate, Encourage, Foment, Foster, Further, Help, Hype, Increase, Make, Prefer, Promulgate, Provoke, Queen, Rear, Remove, Run, Sell, Sponsor, Spruik, Stage, Step, Tendencious, Tendentious, Upgrade, Uplead, Uprate

Prompt(er), Promptly, Promptness Actuate, Alacrity, Autocue®, Believe, Celerity, Chop-chop, Cue, Egg, Expeditious, Frack, Idiot-board, Immediate, Incite, Inspire, Instigate, Move, Pernicious, Premove, Punctual, Quick, Ready, Speed(y), Spur, Stimulate, Sudden, Tight, Tit(e), Titely, Tyte, Urgent

Prone Apt, Groof, Grouf, Grovel, Liable, Lying, Prostrate, Recumbent, Subject, Susceptible

Pronounce(d), Pronouncement Adjudicate, Affirm, Articulate, Assert, Conspicuous, Clear, Declare, Dictum, Enunciate, Fiat, Marked, Opinion, Palatalise, Pontificate, Recite, Utter, Vocal, Voice, Vote

Proof Apagoge, Argument, Bona fides, Confirmation, Evidence, Firm, Foundry, Galley, Positive, Preif(e), Probate, Pull, Quality, Refutation, Remarque, Resistant, Revision, Secure, Strength, Test, Tight, Token, Trial, Upmake, Validity

Prop Airscrew, Bolster, Buttress, Crutch, Dog-shore, Fulcrum, Leg, Loosehead, Misericord(e), Punch(eon), Rance, Rest, Shore, Sprag, Spur, Staff, Stay, Stemple, Stilt, Stoop, Stoup, Stull, ➤ SUPPORT, Tighthead, Underpin

Propaganda, Propagandist Agitprop, Ballyhoo, Brainwashing, Chevalier, Doctrine, Promotion, Psyop, Pyswar, Publicity, Slogan

Propel(ler) Airscrew, Ca', Drive, Fin, Launch, Leg, Lox, ➤ MOVE, Oar, Paddle, Pedal, Project, Push, Rotor, Row, Screw, Throw

Proper(ly) Ain, Convenance, Correct, Decent, Decorous, Due, En règle, Ethical, ➤ FIT, Genteel, Governessy, Kosher, Noun, Ought, Own, Pakka, Pathan, Prim, Pucka, Pukka, Puritanic, Seemly, Suitable, Tao, Trew, True, Well

Property Assets, Attribute, Aver, Belongings, Chattel, Chose, Contenement, Demesne, Des res, Dowry, Effects, Enclave, Escheat, Escrow, Estate, Fee, Feu, Flavour, Fonds, Freehold,

Goods, Hereditament, Hotchpot, Inertia, Jointure, Leasehold, Living, Means, Paraphernalia, Peculium, Personal, Personalty, Premises, Private, Public, Quale, Quality, Stock, Stolen, Theft, Time-share, Trait, Usucapion, Usucapation

Prophesy, Prophet(ess), Prophetic Amos, Augur, Bab, Balaam, Cassandra, Daniel, Divine, Deborah, Elias, Elijah, Elisha, Ezekiel, Ezra, Fatal, Forecast, Foretell, Hosea, Is, Isa, Is(a)iah, Jeremiah, Joel, Jonah, Mahdi, Major, Malachi, Mani, Mantic, Micah, Minor, Mohammed, Mormon, Moses, Nahum, Nathan, Nostradamus, Obadiah, Ominous, Oracle, Portend, Predictor, Prognosticate, Pythoness, Seer, Sibyl, Zephaniah, Zoroaster

Proportion(ate) Commensurable, Dimension, Portion, Pro rata, Quantity, Quota, Ratio, Reason, Regulate, Relation, Sine, Size, Soum, Sowm

Proposal, Propose Advance, Bid, Bill, Eirenicon, Feeler, Irenicon, Mean, Motion, Move, Nominate, Offer, Overture, Plan, Pop, Proffer, Propound, Recommend, Resolution, Scheme, Slate, Submission, ➤ SUGGEST, Table, Tender, Volunteer, Woot, Would

Proposition Axiom, Corollary, Deal, Disjunction, Ergo, Hypothesis, Lemma, Overture, Porism, Premise, Premiss, Rider, Sorites, Spec, Superaltern, Theorem, Thesis

Proprietor, Propriety Correctitude, Decorum, Etiquette, Grundy, Keeper, Lord, Master, Owner, Patron, Rectitude

Prose, Prosy Haikai, Polyphonic, Saga, Stich, Verbose, Version, Writing

Prosecute, Prosecutor, Prosecution Allege, Avvogadore, Charge, Fiscal, Furtherance, Indict, Practise, Public, Sue, Wage

Prospect(or) Explore, Forty-niner, Fossick, Look-out, Mine, ➤ OUTLOOK, Panorama, Perspective, Pleases, Reefer, Scenery, Search, Sourdough, View, Vista, Visto, Wildcatter

Prosper(ity), Prosperous Blessed, Blossom, Boom, Fair, Flourish, Heyday, Mérimée, Palmy, ➤ SUCCEED, Thee, Thrift, Thrive, Up, Warison, Wealth, Welfare, Well-to-do

Prostitute Brass, Catamite, Chippie, Cocotte, Debase, Dell, Dolly-mop, Doxy, Harlot, Hetaera, Hetaira, Jailbait, Loose woman, Madam, Magdalen(e), Moll, Mutton, Pro, Rent-boy, Rough trade, Scrubber, Slap, Stew, Streetwalker, Strumpet, Tart, Trull, Whore

Protect(ed), Protection, Protector Adonise, Aegis, Arm, Asylum, Auspice, Bastion, Buckler, Chaffron, Chamfrain, Chamfron, Charm, Cherish, Cloche, Coat, Cocoon, Conserve, Cover, Covert, Cromwell, Cushion, Danegeld, Defend, Defilade, Egis, Entrenchment, Escort, Flank, Groundsheet, Guard(ian), Gumshield, Hedge, House, Hurter, Indemnify, Insure, Keep, Kickback, Mac(k)intosh, Mail, Male, Mollycoddle, Mother, Noll, Nosey, Overall, Parados, Patent, Patron, Pomander, Preserve, Safeguard, Sandbag, Save, Screen, Scug, Shadow, Sheathing, Sheeting, Shelter, ► SHIELD, Skug, Splashback, Splashboard, Splasher, Starling, Sunscreen, Tribute, Tutelar, Umbrella, Vaccine, Ward(ship), Weatherboard, Weatherstrip

Protein Alanine, Allergen, Analogon, Antibody, Complement, Conjugated, Gelatin, Haemoglobin, Histone, Incaparina, Leucin(e), Luciferin, Lysin, Meat, Myogen, Mucin, Pepsin(e), Proteose, Prothrombin, Quorn®, Ribosome, Single-cell, Soya, Tempeh

Protest(er) Aver, Avouch, Clamour, Come, Démarche, Demo, Demonstrate, Demur, Deprecate, Dissent, Expostulate, Hartal, Inveigh, Lock-out, Luddite, March, Object, Outcry, Picket, Plea, Refus(e)nik, Remonstrate, Sit-in, Squawk, Squeak, Squeal, Work-to-rule

Protestant Amish, Anabaptist, Anglo, Calvin, Congregationalism, Covenanter, Cranmer, Dissenter, Evangelic, Gospeller, Huguenot, Independent, Lady, Lutheran, Mennonite, Methodist, Moravian, Nonconformist, Oak-boy, Orangeman, Pentecostal, Pietism, Prod, Puritan, Stundist, Swaddler, Wesleyan

Protract(ed) Delay, ► EXTEND, Lengthen, Livelong, Prolong

Proud Arrogant, Boaster, Cocky, Conceited, Dic(k)ty, Elated, Flush, Haughty, Haut, Level, Lordly, Orgulous, Superb, Vain

Prove(d) Apod(e)ictic, Argue, Ascertain, Assay, Attest, Authenticate, Aver, Confirm, Convince, Evince, Justify, ► PROOF, ► SHOW, Substantiate, Test

Proverb Adage, Axiom, Byword, Gnome, Maxim, Paroemia, Saw

▷**Proverbial** may refer to the biblical Proverbs

Provide(d), Provident Afford, Allow, Arrange, Besee, Bring, Cater, Compare, Conditional, Endow, Equip, Far-seeing, Fend,

Find, Furnish, Generate, Give, If, Maintain, Proviso, Purvey, Serve, So, Sobeit, ➤ SUPPLY

Province, Provincial(ism) Area, District, Exclave, Land, Regional, Suburban, Territory, Ulster

Provision(s) Acates, A(p)panage, Board, Fodder, Jointure, Larder, Proggins, Scran, Skran, Stock, Supply, Suttle, Viands, Viaticum, Victuals

Proviso, Provisional Caution, Caveat, Clause, Condition, Interim, IRA, On trial, Reservation, Salvo, Temporary, Tentative

Provocation, Provocative, Provoke Agacant, Alluring, Egg, Elicit, Erotic, Exacerbate, Excite, Flirty, Harass, Incense, Induce, Instigate, Irk, Irritate, Needle, Nettle, Occasion, Pique, Prompt, Raise, Sedition, Spark, Stimulate, Tar, Tease, Vex, Wind up

Prowl(er) Hunt, Lurch, Lurk, Mooch, Prole, Ramble, Roam, Rove, Snoke, Snook, Snowk, Tenebrio, Tom

Proxy Agent, Attorn, Deputy, PP, Regent, Sub, Surrogate, Vicar, Vice

Prude(nce), Prudent, Prudery Bluenose, Canny, Caution, Circumspect, Comstocker, Conservative, Discreet, Discretion, Foresight, Frugal, Grundyism, Metis, Mrs Grundy, Politic, Prig, Prissy, Provident, Sage, Sensible, Sparing, Strait-laced, Strait-lacer, Thrifty, Vice-nelly, Victorian, Ware, Wary, Well-advised, Wise

Prune(r) Bill-hook, Dehorn, Lop, Plum, Proign, Proin(e), Reduce, Reform, Secateur, Sned, Thin, Trim

Pry Ferret, Force, Lever, Meddle, Nose, Paul, Peep, Question, Search, Snoop, Toot

Psalm Anthem, Cantate, Chant, Chorale, Hallel, Hymn, Introit, Jubilate, Metrical, Miserere, Neck-verse, Paean, Proper, Ps, Song, Tone, Tract, Venite

Pseudonym Aka, Alias, Allonym, Anonym, Pen-name, Stage-name

Psychiatrist, Psychologist Adler, Alienist, Clare, Coué, Ellis, Freud, Headshrinker, Jung, Laing, Reich, Shrink, Trick-cyclist

Psychic ESP, Lodge, Medium, Seer, Telekinesis

Psychology, Psychologist Behaviourism, Clinical, Depth, Eysenck, Gestalt, Piaget

Pub Bar, Boozer, Free-house, Gin-palace, Houf(f), House, Howf(f), Inn, Joint, Local, Pothouse, Potshop, Shanty, Tavern, Tiddlywink

Public Apert, Bar, Civil, Common, Demos, General, Inn, Lay, Limelight, National, Open, Overt, Populace, State, Vulgar, World

Publican Ale-keeper, Bung, Host, Landlord, Licensee, Tapster, Taverner

Publication Announcement, Broadsheet, Edition, Exposé, Issue, ➤ JOURNAL, Lady, Mag, Organ, Pictorial, Samizdat, Tabloid, Tatler, Tract, Tribune, Yearbook

Publicist, Publicity Ad(vert), Airing, Ballyhoo, Coverage, Exposure, Flack, Glare, Hype, Leakage, Limelight, Plug, PRO, Promotion, Propaganda, Réclame, Spin-doctor, Splash

Publish(ed), Publisher, Publicise Air, Blaze, Cape, Delator, Desktop, Disclose, Edit, Evulgate, Issue, Noise, OUP, Out, Pirate, Plug, Post, Print(er), Proclaim, Propagate, Release, Run, Vanity, Vent, Ventilate

Pudding Afters, Black, Blancmange, Brown Betty, Cabinet, Charlotte, Christmas, College, Custard, Dessert, Duff, Dumpling, Eve's, Flummery, Fritter, Fromenty, Frumenty, Haggis, Hasty, Milk, Pandowdy, Parfait, Pease, Plum, Popover, Rice, Roly-poly, Sponge, Spotted dick, Stickjaw, Stodge, Suet, Summer, Sundae, Sweet, Tansy, Tapioca, Umbles, Yorkshire, Zabaglione

Puff(ed), Puffer, Puffy Advertise, Blouse, Blow, Blowfish, Blurb, Bouffant, Breath, Chuff, Chug, Drag, Encomist, Eulogy, Exsufflicate, Fag, Flaff, Flatus, Fluffy, Fuff, Globe-fish, Grampus, Gust, Hype, Lunt, Pech, Pegh, Pluffy, Plug, Powder, Recommend, Skiff, Slogan, Steam, Swell, Toke, Waff, Waft, Waif, Whiff, Whiffle

Pull (up) Adduce, Attraction, Crane, Drag, Draw, Force, Haul, Heave, Heeze, Hook, ➤ INFLUENCE, Lug, Mousle, Pluck, Rein, Ring, Rove, Rug, Saccade, Sally, Sole, Soole, Sowl(e), Stop, Tit, Tow, Trice, Tug, Undertow, Yank, Wrest

Pulp Cellulose, Chyme, Chymify, Crush, Flong, Kenaf, Marrow, Mash, Mush, Pap, Paste, Pomace, Pound, Puree, Rot, Rubbish, Squeeze, Squidge

Pulpit(e) Ambo(nes), Lectern, Mimbar, Minbar, Pew, Rostrum, Tent, Tub, Wood

Pulse Alfalfa, Beat, Calavance, Caravance, Chickpea, D(h)al, Dholl, Dicrotic, Garbanzo, Gram, Groundnut, Ictus, Lentil, Lucerne, Pea, Rhythm, Sain(t)foin, Soy beans, Sphygmus, Sync, Systaltic, Systole, Throb

▷**Pummelled** may indicate an anagram

Pump Bellows, Bowser, Centrifugal, Compressor, Cross-question, Drive, Elicit, Filter, Force, Grease-gun, Grill, Heart, Heat, Hydropult, Inflate, Knee-swell, Nodding-donkey, Parish, Piston, Pulsometer, Question, Shoe, Stirrup, Stomach, Suction, Water

Pun Calembour, Clinch, Equivoque, Paragram, Paronomasia, Quibble, Ram

Punch(ed) Biff, Blow, Box, Bradawl, Card, Check, Chop, Clip, Fist(ic), Haymaker, Hit, Hook, Horse, Jab, Key, Knobble, Knubble, KO, Lander, Milk, One-er, Perforate, Planter's, Plug, Poke, Polt, Pommel, Pounce, Prod, Pummel, Rabbit, Roundhouse, Slosh, Sock, Sting(o), Suffolk, Upper-cut, Wap, Wind, Zest

Punctuate, Punctuation (mark) Bracket, Colon, Comma, Emphasize, Interabang, Interrobang, Interrupt, Mark, Semicolon

Puncture(d) Bore, Centesis, Criblé, Cribrate, Deflate, Drill, Flat, Hole, Lumbar, Perforate, Pierce, Prick

Pungency, Pungent Acid, Acrid, Acrolein, Alum, Ammonia, Bite, Bitter, Caustic, Hot, Mordant, Nidorous, Piquant, Poignant, Point, Racy, Salt, Spice, Sting, Tangy, Witty

Punish(ed), Punishing, Punishment Amerce, Baffle, Bastinado, Beat, Birch, Cane, Capital, Cart, Castigate, Chasten, Chastise, Come-uppance, Corporal, Dam(nation), Defrock, Desert(s), Detention, ➤ DISCIPLINE, Fine, Flog, Gate, Gauntlet, Gruel, Hellfire, Horsing, Imposition, Impot, Interdict, Jankers, Keelhaul, Knout, Lambast(e), Lines, Necklace, Nemesis, Pack-drill, Penalise, Penance, Perdition, Picket, Pillory, Pine, Rap, Reprisal, Retribution, Scaffold, Scourge, Sentence, Six of the best, Smack, Smite, Stocks, Strafe, Strap, Strappado, Toco, Toko, Treadmill, Trim, Trounce, Whip

▷**Punish** may indicate an anagram

Punt(er), Punting Antepost, Back, Bet, Gamble, Kent, Kick, Pound, Quant, Turfite

Pupil Abiturient, Apple, Apprentice, Boarder, Cadet, Catechumen, Disciple, Etonian, Eyeball, Follower, Gyte, Junior, L, Monitor, Prefect, Protégé(e), Scholar, Senior, Student, Tutee, Ward

▷**Pupil** may refer to an eye

Puppet(eer) Creature, Doll, Dummy, Fantoccini, Glove, Guignol, Judy, Marionette, Mawmet, Mommet, Pawn, Pinocchio, Punch(inello), Rod, Tool

Purchase, Purchasing Bargain, Buy, Coff, Compulsory, Earn, Emption, Get, Grip, Halliard, Halyard, Hold, Layaway, ➤ LEVERAGE, Louisiana, Parbuckle, Secure, Shop, Toehold

Pure, Purity Absolute, Cando(u)r, Cathy, Chaste, Chiarezza, Clean(ly), Cosher, Fine, Good, Holy, Immaculate, Incorrupt, Innocent, Intemerate, Inviolate, Kathy, Kosher, Lily, Lilywhite, Maidenhood, Me(a)re, Net(t), Pristine, Quintessence, Sanctity, Sheer, Simon, Simple, Sincere, Snow-white, Stainless, True, Unalloyed, Vertue, Virgin, Virtue, White

Purgative, Purge Aloes, Cascara, Castor-oil, Catharsis, Delete, Drastic, Eliminate, Emetic, Erase, Evacuant, Expiate, Ipecacuanha, Laxative, Relaxant, Senna

Purification, Purifier, Purify(ing) Absolve, Bowdlerise, Catharsis, Clay, Clean(se), Depurate, Dialysis, Distil, Edulcorate, Elution, Exalt, Expurgate, Filter, Fine, Gas-lime, Lustre, Lustrum, Refine, Retort, Samskara, Sanctify, Scorify, Scrub, Try

Puritan(ical) Bible belt, Bluenose, Digger(s), Ireton, Ironsides, Pi, Pilgrim, Precisian, Prude, Prynne, Roundhead, Seeker, Traskite, Waldenses, Wowser, Zealot

Purple Amarantin(e), Aubergine, Eminence, Heather, Indigo, Lilac, Magenta, Mulberry, Pansy, Plum, Puce, Royal, Violet

Purpose Advertent, Aim, Avail, Cautel, Design, Ettle, Goal, Here-to, ➤ INTENT, Mean(ing), Meant, Mint, Motive, Object, Plan, Point, Raison d'être, ➤ REASON, Resolution, Resolve, Sake, Telic, Telos, Tenor, Use

Purse Ad crumenam, Bag, Bung, Caba, Clutch, Crease, Crumenal, Fisc, Fisk, Long Melford, Pocket, Prim, Privy, Prize, Pucker, Spleuchan, Sporran, Wallet, Whistle

▷**Pursed** may indicate one word within another

Pursue(r), Pursuit Alecto, Business, Chase, Chivvy, Course, Dog, Follow, Hobby, Hot-trod, Hound, Hunt, Practice, Practise, Proceed, Prosecute, Quest, Scouring, Stalk, Trivial

Push (in) Barge, Birr, Boost, Bunt, Detrude, Drive, Edge, Effort, Elbow, Fire, Horn, Hustle, Impulse, Invaginate, Jostle, Nose, Nudge, Nurdle, Obtrude, Pitchfork, Plod, Ply, Press, Promote, Propel, Railroad, Ram, Sell, ➤ SHOVE, Snoozle, Subtrude, Thrust, Urge

Put (off; on; out; up) Accommodate, Add, Bet, Cup, Daff, Defer, Dish, Do, Don, Douse, Implant, Impose, Incommode, Inn, Lade, Lodge, Lump, Oust, Pit, Place, Plonk, Set, Smore, Station, Stow

Put down Abase, Demean, Disparage, Floor, Humiliate, Land, Write

▷**Put off** may indicate an anagram

Puzzle(r) Acrostic, Baffle, Bemuse, Bewilder, Chinese, Confuse, Conundrum, Crossword, Crux, Egma, Elude, Enigma, Fox, Glaik, Gravel, Intrigue, Jigsaw, Kittle, Logogriph, Mind-bender, Monkey, Mystify, Nonplus, Perplex, Ponder, Pose(r), Rebus, Riddle, Sorites, Sphinx, Stick(l)er, Stump, Tangram, Tickler

Pyramid Cheops, Chephren, Frustum, Stack, Teocalli

Qq

Quack Charlatan, Crocus, Dulcamara, Empiric, Fake, ➤ IMPOSTOR, Katerfelto, Mountebank, Pretender, Saltimbanco

Quagmire Bog, Fen, Imbroglio, Marsh, Morass, Swamp, Wagmoire

Quail Asteria, Bevy, Bird, Blench, Bob-white, Button, Caille, Colin, Flinch, Harlot, Hen, Quake, Shrink, Tremble

Quaint Naive, Odd, Old-world, Picturesque, Strange, Twee, Wham, Whim(sy)

Quake(r), Quaking Aminadab, Broad-brim, Dither, Dodder, Fox, Friend, Fry, Hicksite, Obadiah, Penn, Quail, Seism, Shake(r), Shiver, Trepid, ➤ TREMBLE, Tremor

Qualification, Qualified, Qualify Able, Adapt, Capacitate, Caveat, Competent, Condition, Degree, Diplomatic, Entitle, Graduate, Habilitate, Meet, Pass, Proviso, Restrict, Temper, Versed

Quality Aroma, Attribute, Body, Calibre, Cast, Charisma, Essence, Fabric, Fame, Five-star, Flavour, Grade, Inscape, It, Long suit, Mystique, Premium, Property, Q, Quale, Reception, Sort, Standard, Stature, Substance, Suchness, Thew, Thisness, Timbre, Virgin, Virtu(e), Water, Worth

Quantity ► AMOUNT, Analog(ue), Batch, Bundle, Capacity, Deal, Dose, Feck, Fother, Hundredweight, Intake, Jag, Lock, Lot, Mass, Measure, Melder, Myriad, Nonillion, Number, Ocean(s), Operand, Parameter, Parcel, Peck, Plenty, Posology, Pottle, Qs, Qt, Quire, Quota, Quotient, Ream, Scalar, Slather, Slew, Slue, Sum, Surd, Tret, Vector, Warp, Whips

Quarrel(some) Altercate, Barney, Bate, Bicker, Brawl, Cantankerous, Clash, Contretemps, Difference, Disagree, Dispute, Feisty, Fracas, Fray, Hassle, Pugnacious, Squabble, Tiff, Vendetta, Wrangle

Quarry Chalkpit, Game, Mine, Pit, Prey, Scabble, Scent, Stone pit, Victim

Quarter(ing), Quarters Airt, Barrio, Billet, Canton(ment), Casern(e), Chinatown, Clemency, Close, Coshery, District, Dorm, E, Enclave, Fardel, Focsle, Forpet, Forpit, Fourth, Ghetto, Ham('s), Harbour, Haunch, Latin, Medina, ► MERCY, N, Note, Oda, Pity, Point, Principium, Quadrant, Region, S, Season, Sector, Tail, Trimester, W, Wardroom, Warp

▷**Quarterdeck** may indicate a suit of cards

‣**Quartz** Agate, Amethyst, Buhrstone, Cacholong, Cairngorm, Chalcedony, Citrine, Flint, Jasp(er), Morion, Onyx, Plasma, Prase, Rubasse, Silex, Silica, Smoky, Stishovite, Tiger-eye, Tonalite

Quash Abrogate, Annul, Quell, Recant, Scotch, Subdue, Suppress, Terminate, Void

Quaver Shake, Trill, Vibrate, Warble

Quay Bund, Levee, Wharf

Queasy Delicate, Nauseous, Squeamish

Queen(ly) Alexandra, Anne, Beauty, Bee, Begum, Bess, Boadicea, Boudicca, Card, Cleopatra, Dido, Drag, Ellery, Esther,

Guinevere, Hecuba, Helen, Juno, Maam, Mary, Monarch, Pansy, Pearly, Qu, R, Ranee, Regal, Regina(l), Titania, Victoria, Virgin

Queer(ness) Abnormal, Berdash, Bizarre, Crazy, Cure, Curious, Fey, Fie, Fifish, Gay, Nance, Nancy, ➤ ODD, Outlandish, Peculiar, Pervert, Poorly, Quaint, Rum, Spoil, Uranism, Vert

Quench Assuage, Cool, Extinguish, Satisfy, Slake, Slo(c)ken, Sta(u)nch, Yslake

➤ **Query** see Question

Quest Goal, Graal, Grail, Hunt, Pursuit, Venture

Question(ing), Questionnaire Appose, Ask, Bi-lateral, Catechise, Chin, Contest, Conundrum, Cross-examine, Debrief, Direct, Dispute, Dorothy Dixer, Doubt, Erotema, Eroteme, Erotesis, Examine, Grill, Heckle, Impeach, Impugn, Indirect, Innit, Interpellation, Interrogate, Interview, Koan, Leading, Maieutic, Matter, Oppugn, Pop, Probe, Problem, Pump, Q, Qu, Quare, Quiz, Rapid-fire, Refute, Rhetorical, Riddle, Speer, Speir, Survey, Suspect, Tag, Teaser, Vexed, What, Worksheet

Queue Braid, Breadline, Cercus, Crocodile, Cue, Dog, File, ➤ LINE, Pigtail, Plait, Plat, Tail(back), Track

Quibble(r) Balk, Carp, Carriwitchet, Casuist, Cavil, Chicaner, Dodge, Elenchus, Equivocate, Nitpick, Pedantry, Pettifoggery, Prevaricate, Pun, Quiddity, Quillet, Sophist

Quick(en), Quickening, Quicker, Quickly, Quickness Accelerate, Acumen, Adroit, Agile, Alive, Animate, Breakneck, Brisk, Celerity, Chop-chop, Cito, Deft, Enliven, Existent, Expeditious, Express, Fastness, Hasten, Hie, Hotfoot, Impulsive, Jiffy, Keen, Living, Mercurial, Mistress, Mosso, Nailbed, Nimble, Pdq, Piercing, Post-haste, Prestissimo, Presto, Prompt, Pronto, Rapid, Sharp, Smart, Snappy, Soon, Spry, Streamline, Sudden, Swift, Tout de suite, Trice, Veloce, Vital, Vite

Quid Chaw, Chew, L, Nicker, Plug, Pound, Quo, Sov, Tertium, Tobacco

Quiet(en), Quietly Accoy, Allay, Appease, Barnacle, Calm, Compose, Doggo, Ease, Easeful, Easy, Encalm, Entame, Gag, Grave, Kail, Laconic, Loun(d), Low, Low-profile, Lown(d), Lull, Meek, Muffle, Mute, P, Pacify, Pause, Peace, Piano, QT, Reserved, Sedate, Settle, Sh, Shtoom, Silence, Sober, Soothe, Sotto voce, Still, Subdued, Tace, Tranquil, Whisht, Whist

Quilt(ed), Quilting Comfort(er), Counterpane, Cover, Doona®, Duvet, Echo, Eiderdown, Futon, Kantha, Matel(l)asse, Patchwork, Trapunto

Quip Carriwitchet, Crack, Epigram, Gibe, Jest, Jibe, Joke, Taunt, Zinger

Quirk Concert, Foible, Idiosyncrasy, Irony, Kink, Twist

Quit(s) Abandon, Absolve, Ap(p)ay, Cease, Desert, Even(s), Go, Leave, Meet, Resign, ➤ STOP

Quite Actually, All, Ap(p)ay, Clean, Dead, Enow, Fairly, Fully, Precisely, Real, Right, Sheer, Very

Quiver(ing) Aspen, Quake, Shake, Sheath, The yips, Tremble, Tremolo, Tremor, Tremulate, Trepid, Vibrant, Vibrate

Quiz Bandalore, Catechism, Examine, Interrogate, I-spy, Mastermind, Oddity, Probe, Question, Smoke, Trail, Yo-yo

Quota Proportion, Ration, Share

Quotation, Quote(d) Adduce, Citation, Cite, Co(a)te, Duckfoot, Epigraph, Evens, Extract, Instance, Name, Price, Recite, Reference, Say, Soundbite, Tag, Verbatim, Wordbite

Quotient Intelligence, Kerma, Quaternion, Ratio, Respiratory

Rr

Rabbit Angora, Astrex, Brer, Buck, Bun(ny), Chat, Con(e)y, Cottontail, Daman, Dassie, Doe, Harp, Hyrax, Jack, Klipdas, Marmot, Muff, Nest, Novice, Oarlap, Patzer, Prate, Rattle, Rex, Snowshoe, Tapeti, Terricole, Waffle, Yak, Yap, Yatter

Rabble Canaille, Clamjamphrie, Clanjamfray, Colluvies, Crowd, Doggery, Herd, Hoi-polloi, Horde, Legge, Mob, Raffle, Rag-tag, Rascaille, Rascal, Riff-raff, Rout, Scaff-raff, Shower, Tag, Tagrag

Race(course), Racing, Race meeting Aintree, Ascot, Autocross, Boat, Breed, Bumping, Career, Caucus, Cesarewitch, Chantilly, Chase, Classic, Contest, Country, Course, Current, Cursus, Dash, Derby, Dogs, Doncaster, Drag, Epsom, Event, Fastnet, Flat, Flow, Generation, Ginger, Goodwood, Grand Prix, Handicap, Harness, Human(kind), Hurry, Inca, Indy, Kind, Le Mans, Leat, Leet, Leger, Lick, Lignage, Line(age), Longchamps,

Man, Marathon, Master, Meets, Mile, Motocross, ➤ NATIONAL, Newmarket, Nursery, Oaks, Obstacle, One-horse, Plate, Point-to-point, Pursuit, Rallycross, Rallying, Rapids, Redcar, Regatta, Relay, Rill, Rod, Sack, Selling, St Leger, Scramble, Scratch, Scud, Scurry, Seed, Slalom, Slipstream, Speedway, Sprint, Stakes, Steeplechase, Stem, Stock, Strain, Streak, Sweepstake, Tear, Three-legged, Toe, Torpids, Towcester, Tribe, TT, Turf, Two-horse, Walk-over, Waterway, Wincanton

Racehorse, Racer Eclipse, Filly, Hare, Maiden, Plater, Red Rum, Steeplechaser, Trotter

Rack Bin, Cloud, Cratch, Drier, Flake, Frame, Hack, Hake, Pulley, Roof, Stretcher, Toast, Torment, Torture

Racket(eer) ➤ BAT, Bassoon, Battledore, Bloop, Brattle, Caterwaul, Chirm, Clamour, Crime, Deen, Din, Discord, Earner, ➤ FIDDLE, Gyp, Hubbub, Hustle, ➤ NOISE, Noisiness, Protection, Ramp, Rort, Sokaiya, Stridor, Swindle, Tumult, Uproar, Utis

Radar Angel, AWACS, DEW line, Doppler, Gee, Lidar, Loran, Monopulse, Rebecca-eureka, Shoran, Teleran®

Radiance, Radiant Actinic, Aglow, Aureola, Beamish, Brilliant, Glory, Glow, Happy, Lustre, Refulgent, Sheen

Radiate, Radiating, Radiation, Radiator Actinal, Air-colour, Beam, Bremsstrahlung, Cherenkov, Effuse, Emanate, Fluorescence, Glow, Heater, Infrared, Isohel, Laser, Millirem, Pentact, Photon, Pulsar, Quasar, Rem(s), Rep, Roentgen, ➤ SHINE, Sievert, Spherics, Spoke, Stellate, SU, Sun, Ultra violet, Van Allen

Radical Amyl, Aryl, Bolshevist, Bolshie, Butyl, Ester, Extreme, Fundamental, Innate, Leftist, Methyl, Phenyl, Pink, Propyl, Red, Revolutionary, Root, Rudiment, Trot(sky), Vinyl, Whig

Radio Boom-box, CB, Cellular, Citizen's band, Crystal set, Ether, Gee, Loudspeaker, Marconigraph, Receiver, Reflex, Set, Simplex, Sound, Tranny, Transceiver, Transmitter, Transponder, Walkman®, Wireless

Radioactive, Radioactivity Actinide, Americium, Astatine, Bohrium, Cobalt 60, Emanation, Hot, Nucleonics, Steam, Thorium, Uranite

Raft Balsa, Catamaran, Float, Kontiki, Life, Pontoon

Rafter Barge-couple, Beam, Chevron, Jack, Joist, Ridge, Spar, Timber

Rag(ged), Rags Bait, Bate, Clout, Coral, Deckle, Dud(s), Duddery, Duddie, Duster, Fent, Figleaf, Glad, Guyed, Haze, Kid, Lap(pie), Lapje, Mop, Paper, Red, Remnant, Revel, Rivlins, Roast, Rot, S(c)hmatte, Scold, Scrap, ➤ SHRED, Slate, Slut, Splore, Tat(t), Tatter(demalion), Tatty, Taunt, ➤ TEASE, Tiger, Tongue, Uneven

▷ **Rag(ged)** may indicate an anagram

Rage, Raging ➤ ANGER, Ardour, Bait, Bate, Bayt, Chafe, Conniption, Explode, Fashion, Fierce, Fit, Fiz(z), Fume, Furibund, Furore, Fury, Gibber, Go, Ire, Mode, Paddy(-whack), Passion, Pelt, Pet, Rabid, Ramp, Rant, Road, Snit, Storm, Tear, Temper, Ton, Utis, Wax, Wrath

Raid(er) Assault, Attack, Bodrag, Bust, Camisado, Chappow, Commando, Do, For(r)ay, Imburst, Incursion, Inroad, Inrush, Invade, Jameson, Maraud, March-treason, Mosstrooper, Pict, Pillage, Plunder, Ransel, Razzia, Reive, Sack, Scrump, Skrimp, Skrump, Smash-and-grab, Sortie, Spreagh, Storm, Viking

Rail(er), Railing Abuse, Arm, Arris, Balustrade, Ban, Banister, ➤ BAR, Barre, Barrier, Bird, Conductor, Coot, Corncrake, Criticise, Dado, Fender, Fiddle, Flow, Gush, Insult, Inveigh, Metal, Picture, Plate, Post, Pulpit, Rag, Rate, Rave, Rung, Scold, Slate, Sora, Soree, Spar, Taffrail, Taunt, Towel, Train

Railroad, Railway Amtrak, BR, Bulldoze, Cable, Coerce, Cog, Cremaillière, Dragoon, El, Elevated, Funicular, GWR, Inclined, L, Light, Lines, LMS, LNER, Maglev, Metro, Monorail, Rack, Rack and pinion, Rly, Road, Rollercoaster, Ropeway, ROSCO, Ry, Scenic, SR, Switchback, Telpher-line, Track, Train, Tramline, Tramway, Tube, Underground

Rain(y) Acid, Brash, Deluge, Drizzle, Hyad(e)s, Hyetal, Mistle, Mizzle, Oncome, Onding, Onfall, Pelt, Pluviose, Pluvious, Pour, Precipitation, Right, Roke, Scat, Seil, Serein, Serene, Shell, Shower, Sile, Skiffle, Skit, Smir(r), Smur, Soft, Spat, Spet, Spit, Storm, Thunder-plump, Virga, Weep, Wet

Raise(d), Raising Advance, Aggrade, Attollent, Boost, Build, Cat, Coaming, Cock, Collect, Elate, ➤ ELEVATE, Emboss, Enhance, Ennoble, Erect, Escalate, Exalt, Fledge, Grow, Heave, Heezie, Heft, High, Hike, Hoist, Increase, Jack, Key, Leaven, Lift, Mention, Overcall, Perk, Rear, Regrate, Repoussé, Revie, Rouse, Saleratus, Siege, Sky, Snarl, Sublimate, Upgrade, Weigh

Rake, Rakish Casanova, Comb, Corinthian, Dapper, Dissolute, Enfilade, Jaunty, Lecher, Libertine, Lothario, Raff, Reprobate, Rip, Roué, Scan, Scour, Scowerer, Scratch, Strafe, Swash-buckler, Swinge-buckler, Wagons

Rally, Rallying-point Autocross, Autopoint, Badinage, Banter, Demo, Gather, Jamboree, Meeting, Mobilise, Monte Carlo, Muster, Oriflamme, Persiflage, Recover, Rely, Rest, Risorgimento, Roast, Rouse, Scramble

Ram Aries, Battering, Buck, Bunt, Butter, Corvus, Crash, Drive, Hidder, Hydraulic, Mendes, Pun, Sheep, Stem, Tamp, Tup, Wether

Ramble(r), Rambling Aberrant, Aimless, Digress, Incoherent, Liana, Liane, Rigmarole, Roam, Rove, Rove, Skimble-skamble, Sprawl, Stray, Vagabond, Wander

Ramp Bank, Gradient, Helicline, Incline, Slipway, Slope

▷**Rampant** may indicate an anagram or a reversed word

Rampart Abat(t)is, Brisure, Butt, Defence, Fortification, Parapet, Terreplein, Vallum, Wall

Ranch Bowery, Corral, Farm, Hacienda, Spread

Rancid Frowy, Reast(y), Reest(y), Sour, Turned

Rancour Gall, Hate, Malice, Resentment, Spite

Random Accidental, Aleatoric, Arbitrary, ➤ AT RANDOM, Blind, Casual, Desultory, Fitful, ➤ HAPHAZARD, Harvest, Hit-or-miss, Indiscriminate, Scattershot, Sporadic, Stochastic

▷**Random(ly)** may indicate an anagram

Range(r), Rangy Align, Ambit, Andes, Atlas, AZ, Band, Carry, Cheviot, Compass, Cotswolds, Course, Diapason, Dolomites, Err, ➤ EXTENT, Gamut, Gunshot, Himalayas, Ken(ning), Limit, Line, Long, Massif, ➤ MOUNT, Orbit, Oven, Palette, Point-blank, Purview, Rake, Reach, Register, Repertoire, Roam, Scale, Scope, Sc(o)ur, Selection, Short, Sierra, Sloane, Spectrum, Sphere, Urals, Woomera

Rank(s) Arrant, Begum, Brevet, Caste, Category, Cense, Classify, Cornet, Degree, Dignity, Downright, Earldom, Estate, Etat(s), Grade, Gross, High, Olid, Place, Range, Rate, Rooty, Row, Sergeant, Serried, Sort, ➤ STATION, Status, Taxi, Tier, ➤ TITLE, Utter, Viscount

Ransack Fish, Loot, Pillage, Plunder, Rifle, Ripe, Rob, Rummage

Rant(er), Ranting Bombast, Declaim, Fustian, Ham, Harangue, Rail, Rodomontade, Scold, Spout, Spruik, Stump, Thunder, Tub-thump

Rap(ped) Blame, Censure, Clour, Gangsta, Halfpenny, Knock, Ratatat, Shand, Strike, Swapt, Tack, Tap

Rape Abuse, Assault, Belinda, Cole-seed, Colza, Creach, Creagh, Date, Deflower, Despoil, Gangbang, Hundred, Lock, Lucretia, Navew, Oilseed, Plunder, Stuprate, Thack, Violate

Rapid(ity), Rapidly Chute, Dalle, Express, Fast, Meteoric, Mosso, Presto, Pronto, Quick-fire, Riffle, Sault, Shoot, Speedy, Suckle, Swift, Veloce, Wildfire

Rapport Accord, Affinity, Agreement, Harmony

Rapture, Rapturous Bliss, ➤ DELIGHT, Ecstasy, Elation, Joy, Trance

Rare, Rarity Blue moon, Curio, Earth, Geason, Infrequent, Intemerate, One-off, Rear, Recherché, Scarce, Seeld, Seld(om), Singular, ➤ UNCOMMON, Uncooked, Underdone, Unusual

Rascal(ly) Arrant, Bad hat, Cad, Cullion, Cur, Devil, Gamin, Hallian, Hallion, Hallyon, ➤ KNAVE, Limner, Loon, Low, Rip, Rogue, Scallywag, Scamp, Scapegrace, Schelm, Skeesicks, Skellum, Skelm, Smaik, Spalpeen, Tinker, Toe-rag, Varlet, Varmint, Villain

Rash(er) Acne, Bacon, Brash, Collop, Daredevil, Eruption, Erysipelas, Fast, Foolhardy, Harum-scarum, ➤ HASTY, Headlong, Hives, Hotspur, Impetigo, Impetuous, Imprudent, Impulsive, Lichen, Madbrain, Madcap, Nettle, Outbreak, Overhasty, Precipitate, Reckless, Roseola, Rubella, Sapego, Serpigo, Spots, Thoughtless, Unheeding, Unthinking, Urticaria

Rat(s), Ratty Agouta, Bandicoot, Blackleg, Blackneb, Boodie, Brown, Bug-out, Cane, Cur, Defect, Desert, Fink, Footra, Foutra, Geomyoid, Gym, Heck, Hydromys, Informer, Kangaroo, Maori, Mole, Moon, Norway, Pack, Poppycock, Potoroo, Pshaw, Pup(py), Rice, Rodent, Roland, Rot(ten), Scab, Shirty, Squeal, Stinker, Turncoat, Vole, Water, Whiskers

Rate, Rating Able, Appreciate, Assess, Base, Bit, Castigate, Cess, Classify, Count, Credit, Deserve, Erk, Estimate, Evaluate, Exchange, Grade, Hearty, ISO, MPH, Octane, OS, Pace, Percentage, Rag, Red, Refresh, Reproof, Rocket, Row, Sailor, Scold, ➤ SET, ➤ SPEED, Standing, TAM, Tax, Tempo, Upbraid, Value, Water, Wig, World-scale

Rather Degree, Gey, Instead, Lief, Liever, Loor, More, Prefer, Pretty, Some(what), Sooner

Ratio Albedo, Aspect, Bypass, Compression, Cosine, Fraction, Gyromagnetic, Loss, Neper, Pi, Poisson's, Proportion, PE, Sin(e), Tensor, Trigonometric

Ration(s) Allocate, Apportion, Compo, Dole, Etape, Iron, K, Quota, Restrict, Scran, Share, Size

Rational Dianoetic, Level-headed, Logical, Lucid, Matter-of-fact, Sane, Sensible, Sine, Sober, Tenable

Rattle (box) Chatter, Clack, Clank, Clap, Clatter, Conductor, Death, Demoralise, Disconcert, Gas-bag, Hurtle, Jabber, Jangle, Jar, Natter, Nonplus, Rale, Rap, Reel, Rhonchus, Ruckle, Shake, Sistrum, Tirl, Upset

Ravage Depredation, Desecrate, Despoil, Havoc, Pillage, Prey, Ruin, Sack, Waste

Raven(ous) Black, Corbel, Corbie, Corvine, Croaker, Daw, Grip, Hugin, Munin, Unkindness

Ravine Arroyo, Barranca, Barranco, Canada, Chasm, Chine, Clough, Coulee, Couloir, Dip, Flume, Ghyll, Gorge, Grike, Gulch, Gully, Kedron, Khor, Khud, Kidron, Kloof, Lin(n), Nal(l)a, Nallah, Nulla(h), Pit

Ravish Constuprate, Debauch, Defile, Devour, Rape, Stuprate, Transport, Violate

Raw Brut, Chill, Coarse, Crude, Crudy, Damp, Fresh, Greenhorn, Natural, Recruit, Rude, Uncooked, Wersh

Ray(ed) Actinic, Alpha, Beam, Beta, Canal, Cathode, Cosmic, Delta, Diactine, Dun-cow, Eagle, Electric, Fish, Gamma, Grenz, Guitarfish, Homelyn, Manta, Medullar, Monactine, Polyact, R, Radius, Re, Roentgen, Roker, Röntgen, Sawfish, Sea-devil, Sephen, Shaft, Skate, Stick, Sting, Stingaree, Tetract, Thornback, Torpedo

Reach(ed) Ar(rive), Attain, Boak, Boke, Carry, Come, Get out, Hent, Hit, Key-bugle, Lode, Octave, Peak, Raught, Rax, Retch, Ryke, Seize, Stretch, Touch, Win

React(or), Reaction(ary) Allergy, Answer, Backlash, Backwash, Behave, Blimp, Blowback, Breeder, Bristle, Catalysis, Chain, Convertor, Core, Counterblast, Dibasic, Falange, Fast(-breeder), Feedback, Furnace, Gut, Interplay, Kickback, Knee-jerk, Nuclear, Outcry, Pile, Reciprocate, Recoil,

Repercussion, Respond, Reversible, Rigid, Sensitive, Sprocket, Thermal

▷ **Reactionary** may indicate reversed or an anagram

Read(ing) Bearing, Browse, Decipher, Decode, Exegesis, Grind, Grounden, Haftarah, Haphtarah, Interpret, Learn, Lection, Lesson, Lu, Maftir, Maw, Pericope, Peruse, Pore, Rad, Rennet-bag, Scan, See, Solve, Stomach, ➤ STUDY, Vell, Ycond

Reader ABC, Alidad(e), Bookworm, Editor, Epistoler, Lay, Lector, Primer, Silas Wegg, Taster

Readiest, Readily, Readiness, Ready Alacrity, Alamain, Alert, Amber, Apt, Atrip, Available, Boun, Bound, Brass, Cash, Conditional, Dough, Eager, Early, Eftest, Fettle, Fit, Forward, Game, Go, Keyed, Lolly, Masterman, Money, Predy, Prepared, Present, Prest, Primed, Prompt, Reckoner, Ripe, Set, Soon, Spot, Turnkey, Usable, Willing, Yare

Readymade Bought, Precast, Prepared, Prêt-à-porter, Slops, Stock, Store

Real, Reality, Realities, Really Actual, Bona-fide, Coin, Deed, Dinkum, Dinky-di(e), Earnest, Echt, Ens, Entia, Entity, Essence, ➤ GENUINE, Honest, Indeed, McCoy, McKoy, Naïve, Ontic, Royal, Simon Pure, Sooth, Sterling, Substantial, Tangible, Tennis, Thingliness, True, Verismo, Very, Virtual

Realise, Realisation, Realism, Realistic Achieve, Attain, Attuite, Cash, Embody, Encash, Fetch, Fruition, Fulfil, Learn, Practical, Sell, Sense, Understand

▶ **Realities, Reality** see REAL

Realm Dominion, Field, Kingdom, Land, Region, Special(i)ty, UK

Ream Bore, Foam, Froth, Paper, Rime, Screed

Reap(er) Binder, Crop, Death, Earn, Gather, Glean, Harvest, Scythe, Shear, Sickleman, Solitary, Stibbler

Rear(ing) Aft, Back(side), Baft, Behind, Bring-up, Bunt, Cabré, Derrière, Foster, Haunch, Hind, Loo, Nousell, Nurture, Prat, ➤ RAISE, Serafile, Serrefile, Tonneau

Reason(ing), Reasonable A fortiori, Analytical, Apagoge, A priori, Argue, Argument, Basis, Call, Cause, Colour, Consideration, Deduce, Expostulate, Fair, Ground(s), Ijtihad, Inductive, Intelligent, Logic, Logical, Logistics, Mind, Moderate, Motive, Noesis, Plausible, Petitio principii, Point, Pretext, Pro,

Proof, Purpose, Rational(e), Sanity, Sense, Sensible, Settler,
Syllogism, Synthesis, Think, Why, Wit

Rebate Diminish, Lessen, Refund, Repayment

Rebel(lion), Rebellious Apostate, Beatnik, Bolshy, Boxer,
Cade, Contra, Danton, Diehard, Fifteen, Forty-five, Iconoclast,
Insurgent, Insurrection, IRA, Jacobite, Kick, Luddite, Mutine(er),
Mutiny, Oates, Putsch, Recalcitrant, Recusant, Resist, Revolt,
Rise, Sedition, Straw, Tyler, Warbeck, Zealot

▷**Rebellious** may indicate a word reversed

Rebuff Check, Cold-shoulder, Noser, Quelch, Repulse, Retort,
Rubber, Sneb, Snib, Snub

Rebuke Admonish, Berate, Check, Chide, Earful, Lecture, Neb,
Objurgate, Rap, Razz, Reproof, Reprove, Reprimand,
Rollick, Scold, Slap, Slate, Snub, Strop, Threap, Threep, Tick off,
Trim, Tut, Upbraid, Wig

Recall(ing) Annul, Eidetic, Encore, Evocative, Reclaim,
Recollect, Redolent, Remember, Remind, Reminisce, Repeal,
Retrace, Revoke, Total, Withdraw

▷**Recast** may indicate an anagram

Recede Decline, Ebb, Lessen, Regress, Shrink, Withdraw

Receipt(s) Acknowledge, Chit, Docket, Recipe, Revenue, Take,
Voucher

Receive(d), Receiver Accept, Accoil, Admit, Antenna,
Assignee, Bailee, Dipole, Dish, Donee, Ear, Fence, Get, Grantee,
Greet, Hydrophone, Inherit, Pernancy, Phone, Pocket, Radio,
Reset, Roger, Set, Take, Tap, Transistor

Recent(ly) Alate, Current, Fresh, Hot, Late, Modern, New,
Yesterday, Yestereve, Yesterweek

Receptacle Ash-tray, Basket, Bin, Bowl, Box, Ciborium,
Container, Cyst, Hell-box, Monstrance, Reliquary, Relique,
Sacculus, Spermatheca, Tank, Thalamus, Tidy, Tore, Torus

Reception, Receptive Accoil, At home, Bel-accoyle,
Couchée, Court, Durbar, Greeting, Infare, Kursaal, Levée, Open,
Ovation, Ruelle, Saloon, Sensory, Soirée, Teleasthetic, Welcome

Recess(ion) Alcove, Apse, Bay, Break, Cove, Dinette, Ebb,
Embrasure, Fireplace, Grotto, Inglenook, Interval, ► NICHE,
Nook, Respite, Rest, Withdrawal

▷**Recess** may indicate 'reversed'

▷**Recidivist** may indicate 'reversed'

Recipient Assignee, Beneficiary, Disponee, Grantee, Heir, Legatee, Receiver

Reciprocal, Reciprocate Corresponding, Elastance, Exchange, Inter(act), Mutual, Repay, Return

Recital, Recitation(ist), Recite(r) Ave, Declaim, Diseuse, Enumerate, Litany, Monologue, Parlando, Quote, Reading, Reel, Relate, Rhapsode, Say, Sing, Tell

Reckless(ness) Blindfold, Careless, Catiline, Desperado, Devil-may-care, Gadarene, Harum-scarum, Hasty, Headfirst, Headlong, Hell-bent, Madcap, Perdu(e), Ramstam, Rantipole, ➤ RASH, Slapdash, Temerity, Ton-up, Wanton, Wildcat

▷**Reckless** may indicate an anagram

Reckon(ing) Assess, Calculate, Cast, Census, Computer, Consider, Count, Date, Doomsday, Estimate, Fancy, Figure, Number, Rate, Settlement, Shot, Tab

Reclaim(ed), Reclamation Assart, Empolder, Impolder, Innings, Novalia, Polder, Recover, Redeem, Restore, Swidden, Tame, Thwaite

Recognise(d), Recognition Accept, Acknow(ledge), Admit, Anagnorisis, Appreciate, Ascetic, Cit(ation), Exequatur, Identify, Isolated, Ken, ➤ KNOW, Nod, Oust, Own, Reward, Salute, Scent, Wat, Weet

Recoil Backlash, Bounce, Kick(back), Quail, Rebound, Redound, Repercussion, Resile, Reverberate, Shrink, Shy, Spring, Start

Recollect(ion) Anamnesis, Memory, Pelmanism, Recall, ➤ REMEMBER, Reminisce

▷**Recollection** may indicate an anagram

Recommend(ation) Advise, Advocate, Counsel, Direct, Endorse, Nap, Promote, Rider, Suggest, Testimonial, Tip, Tout

Recompense Cognisance, Deodand, Deserts, Expiate, Guerdon, Pay, Remunerate, Repayment, Requite, Restitution, Reward

Reconcile(d) Adapt, Adjust, Affrended, Atone, Harmonise, Henotic, Make up, Mend

Record(er), Record company, Recording Album, Ampex, Annal(ist), Archive, Bench-mark, Black box, Book, Can, Casebook, CD, Chart, Chronicle, Coat(e), Daybook, Diary, Disc, Document, Dossier, Elpee, EMI, Enter, Entry, EP, Estreat, Ever, File, Film, Flight, Flute, Form, Forty-five, Gram, Hansard, Indie,

Journal, Ledger, List, Log, Logbook, LP, Mark, Memento, Memo(randum), Memorial, Memorise, Meter, Minute, Mono, Notate, Notch, Note, Pass book, Platter, Playback, Pressing, Public, Quote, Register, Release, Roll, Score(board), Seven-inch, Seventy-eight, Single, Tally, Tape, Thirty-three, Trace, Track, Transcript, Twelve-inch, VERA, Vid(eo), Vote, Wax, Write

Recover(y) Amend, Clawback, Comeback, Convalescence, Cure, Dead cat bounce, Lysis, Over, Perk, Rally, Reclaim, Recoup, Redeem, Regain, Repaint, Replevin, Replevy, Repo(ssess), Rescript, Rescue, Resile, ➤ RETRIEVE, Revanche, Salvage, Salve, Upswing

Recruit(s) Attestor, Bezonian, Choco, Conscript, Crimp, Draft, Employ, Engage, Enlist, Enrol, Headhunt, Intake, Muster, Nignog, Nozzer, Rookie, Sprog, Volunteer, Wart, Yobbo

Rectify Adjust, Amend, Dephlegmate, Redress, Regulate, ➤ REMEDY, Right

Recur(rent), Recurring Chronic, Quartan, Quintan, Recrudesce, Repeated, Repetend, Return

▷**Recurrent** may indicate 'reversed'

Red(den), Redness Admiral, Angry, Ashamed, Auburn, Beet, Blush, Bolshevik, Brick, Burgundy, C, Carmine, Cent, Cerise, Cherry, Claret, Commo, Communist, Coral, Corallin(e), Debit, Duster, Embarrassed, Eosin, Eric, Erik, Erythema, Florid, Flush, Geranium, Gory, Gu(les), Guly, Hat, Herring, Indian, Inflamed, Infra, Inner, Lake, Left(y), Lenin, Letter, Magenta, Maoist, Marxist, Murrey, Neaten, Oxblood, Pillar-box, Pompeian, Raddle, Radical, Raw, Realgar, Rhodamine, Rhodopsin, Ridinghood, Roan, Rosaker, Rose, Rot, Rouge, Rubefy, Rubella, Ruby, Russ(e), Russet, Russian, Rust(y), Sanguine, Sard, Setter, Tape, Tidy, Titian, Trot, Trotsky, Turkey, Venetian, Vermilion, Vinaceous, Wine

▷**Red** may indicate an anagram

Redeem, Redemption Cross, Liberate, Mathurin, Ransom, Retrieve, Salvation, Save

▷**Rediscovered** may indicate an anagram

Reduce(r), Reduced, Reduction Abatement, Allay, Alleviate, Attenuate, Beggar, Clip, Commute, Condense, Contract, Cut, Cutback, Damping, Debase, Decimate, Decrease, Decrement, Demote, Deplete, Detract, Devalue, Diminish, Diminuendo, Discount, Downsize, Draw-down,

Epitomise, Grind, ➤ LESSEN, Lite, Markdown, Mitigate, Moderate, Palliate, Pot, Pulp, Put, Remission, Retrench, Rundown, Scant, Shade, Shorten, Shrinkage, Slash, Strain, Taper, Telescope, Thin, Weaken, Write-off

Redundancy, Redundant Frill, Needless, Otiose, Pleonasm, Superfluous, Surplus

Reef Atoll, Barrier, Bombora, Cay, Coral, Fringing, Great Barrier, Key, Knot, Lido, Motu, Sca(u)r, Skerry, Witwatersrand

Reel Bobbin, Dance, Eightsome, Hoolachan, Hoolican, Pirn, Spin, Spool, Stagger, Strathspey, Sway, Swift, Swim, Totter, Wheel, Whirl, Wintle

Refer Advert, Allude, Assign, Cite, Direct, Mention, Pertain, Relate, Renvoi, Renvoy, See, Submit

Referee Arbiter, Commissaire, Mediate, Oddsman, Ref, Umpire, Voucher, Whistler, Zebra

Reference Allusion, Apropos, Character, Coat, Index, Innuendo, Mention, Passion, Quote, Regard, Renvoi, Respect, Retrospect, Testimonial

Refine(d), Refinement, Refiner(y) Alembicate, Attic, Catcracker, Couth, Cultivate, Culture, Distinction, Elaborate, Elegance, Exility, Exquisite, Genteel, Grace, Nice, Nicety, Polish(ed), Polite, Précieuse, Pure, Rare(fy), Recherché, Saltern, Sift, Smelt, Spirituel, Subtilise, Try, U, Urbane, Veneer

Reflect(ing), Reflection, Reflective, Reflector Albedo, Blame, Cat's eye, Cats-eye, Chew, Cogitate, ➤ CONSIDER, Echo, Glass, Glint, Image, Meditate, Mirror, Muse, Ponder, Ruminate, Thought

Reform(er) Amend, Apostle, Bloomer, Calvin, Chastise, Correct, Enrage, Fry, Ghandi, Howard, Improve, Knox, Lollard, Luther, Mend, PR, Progressionist, Protestant, Puritan, Rad(ical), Recast, Reclaim, Reconstruction, Rectify, Regenerate, Ruskin, Transmute

▷ **Reform(ed)** may indicate an anagram

Refrain Abstain, Alay, Avoid, Bob, Burden, Chorus, Desist, Epistrophe, Fa-la, Forbear, Hemistich, Repetend, Ritornello, Rumbelow, Rum(p)ti-iddity, Rum-ti-tum, Spare, Tag, Tirra-lirra, Tirra-lyra, Undersong, Wheel

Refresh(er), Refreshment Air, Bait, Be(a)vers, Cheer, Elevenses, Enliven, Food, Nap, New, Nourishment, Refection,

Reflect, Refocillate, Reinvigorate, Renew, Repast, Restore,
Revive, Seltzer, Shire, Slake, Water

Refuge Abri, Asylum, Bolthole, Dive, Fastness, Funkhole, Girth,
Grith, Harbour, Haven, Hideaway, Hole, Holt, Home, Hospice,
Oasis, Port, Reefer, Resort, Retreat, Sheet-anchor, ➤ SHELTER,
Soil, Stronghold

▷**Refurbished** may indicate an anagram

Refusal, Refuse Bagasse, Ba(u)lk, Bilge, Bin, Black, Bran,
Brash, Breeze, Brock, Bull, Bunkum, Chaff, Clap-trap, Crane,
Crap, Debris, Decline, Deny, Disown, Draff, Drivel, Dross,
Dunder, Dung, Fag-end, Fenks, Finks, Frass, Garbage, Guff,
Husk, Interdict, Jib, Junk, Knub, Lay-stall, Leavings, Litter,
Lumber, Marc, Megass(e), Midden, Mush, Nay(-say), Nill, No,
Nould, Nub, Offal, Off-scum, Orts, Pigwash, Punk, Raffle,
Rape(cake), Rat(s), Rebuff, Red(d), Reest, Regret, Reneg(u)e,
Renig, Rot, ➤ RUBBISH, Ruderal, Scaff, Scrap, Scree, Scum,
Sewage, Shant, Spurn, Sullage, Sweepings, Swill, Tinpot, Tip,
Tosh, Trade, Trash, Tripe, Trumpery, Twaddle, Unsay, Utter,
Wash, Waste

▷**Re-fused** may indicate an anagram

▶**Regal** see ROYAL

Regard(ing) As to, Attention, Care, Consider, ➤ ESTEEM, Eye,
Gaum, Look, Observe, Odour, Pace, Rate, Re, Respect, Revere,
Sake, Steem, Value, Vis-à-vis

Regardless Despite, Heedless, Irrespective, Notwithstanding,
Rash, Uncaring, Willy-nilly

Regiment Black Watch, Buffs, Colour(s), Discipline, Greys,
Ironsides, Lifeguard, Monstrous, Nutcrackers, Organise, RA, RE,
REME, Rifle, Royals, Tercio, Tertia

▷**Regiment** may indicate an anagram

Region Arctogaea, ➤ AREA, Belt, Brittany, Bundu, Camargue,
Chiasma, Climate, Clime, District, E, End, Hinterland, Hundred,
Midi, Offing, Pargana, Part, Pergunnah, Piedmont, Province,
Quart(er), Realm, Refugium, Ruthenia, Sector, Stannery,
Subtopia, Tagma, Territory, Tetrarchate, Tract, Tundra, Umbria,
Vaud, Weald, Zone

Register(ing), Registration Actuarial, Almanac, Annal,
Cadastral, Cadastre, Calendar, Cartulary, Census, Check-in,
Diptych, Enlist, Enrol, Enter, Index, Indicate, Inscribe, Inventory,
Ledger, List, Log, Matricula, Menology, Note, Notitia, Park,

Patent, Read, Record, Reg(g)o, Roll, Roule, Score, Soprano, Terrier, Voice

Regret(ful), Regrettable Alack, Alas, Apologise, Deplore, Deprecate, Ewhow, Forthwink, Ichabod, Lackaday, Lament, Mourn, Otis, Pity, Remorse, Repentance, Repine, ➤ RUE, Ruth, Sorrow, Tragic

Regular(ity), Regularly Clockwork, Constant, Custom, Episodic, Even, Giusto, Goer, Habitual, Habitué, Hourly, Insider, Methodic, Nine-to-five, Normal, Often, Orderly, Orthodox, Patron, Peloria, Periodic, Rhythmic, Routine, Set, Smooth, ➤ STANDARD, Stated, Statutory, Steady, Strict, Symmetric, Uniform, Usual, Yearly

Regulate, Regulation, Regulator Adjust, Appestat, Bye-law, Code, Control, Correction, Curfew, Customary, Direct, Gibberellin, Governor, Guide, Logistics, Metrostyle, Order, Ordinance, Police, Rule, Snail, Square, Standard, Statute, Stickle, Sumptuary, Thermostat, Valve

Rehearsal, Rehearse Drill, Dry-run, Dummy-run, Practice, Practise, Preview, Recite, Repeat, Trial

Reign Era, Govern, Meiji, Prevail, Raine, Realm, Restoration, ➤ RULE

Rein(s) Bearing, Check, Control, Curb, Free, Lumbar, Restrain

Reinforce(ment) Aid, Augment, Bolster, Boost, Brace, Buttress, Cleat, Line, Plash, Pleach, Recruit, Reserve, ➤ STRENGTHEN, Support, Tetrapod, Underline

Reject(ion) Abhor, Abjure, Athetise, Bin, Blackball, Cast, Deny, Dice, Discard, Disclaim, Disdain, Diss, Flout, Frass, Jilt, Kest, Kill, Knock-back, Ostracise, Oust, Outcast, Outtake, Pip, Plough, Rebuff, Recuse, Refuse, Reny, Reprobate, Repudiate, Repulse, Scout, Scrub, Spet, Spin, Spit, ➤ SPURN, Sputum, Thumbs-down, Turndown, Veto

Rejoice, Rejoicing Celebrate, Exult, Festivity, Gaude, Glory, Joy, Maffick, Sing

Rejoin(der), Rejoined Answer, Counter, Relide, Reply, Response, Retort, Reunite

Relate(d), Relation(ship), Relative Account, Affair, Agnate, Akin, Allied, Appertain, Associate, Cognate, Concern, Connection, Connexion, Consanguinity, Cousin, Coz, Eme, Enate, German(e), Granny, Impart, Item, Kin, Link, Love-hate, Mater, Material, Matrix, Narrative, Pertain, Pi, Plutonic,

➤ PROPORTION, Public, Rapport, Ratio, Recite, Recount, Refer(ence), Relevant, Respect(s), Sib(b), Sibling, Sine, Syntax, Tale, Tell, Who

Relax(ation), Relaxant, Relaxed Abate, Atony, Calm, Com(m)odo, Degage, Detente, Diversion, Downbeat, Ease, Easy-going, Flaccid, Laid-back, Leisured, ➤ LOOSEN, Mitigate, Peace, Relent, Relief, Remit, Rest, Slacken, Sleep, Toneless, Unbend, Unknit, Untie, Unwind

▷ **Relaxed** may indicate an anagram

▷ **Relay(ing)** may indicate an anagram

Release Abreact, Announcement, Bail, Catharsis, Clear, Day, Death, Deliver(y), Desorb, Disburden, Discharge, Disclose, Disimprison, Dismiss, Disorb, Emancipate, Enfree, Excuse, Exeem, Exeme, Extricate, Exude, Free, ➤ LIBERATE, Manumit, Moksa, Parole, Quietus, Quittance, Relinquish, Ripcord, Spring, Tre corde, Unconfine, Undo, Unhand, Unloose, Unpen, Unshackle, Untie

Relevance, Relevant Ad rem, Applicable, Apposite, Apropos, Apt, Germane, Material, Pertinent, Point, Valid

▶ **Reliable, Reliance** see RELY

Relic Antique, Ark, Artefact, Fossil, Leftover, Memento, Neolith, Remains, Sangraal, Sangrail, Sangreal, Souvenir, Survival

Relief, Relieve(d) Aid, Air-lift, Allay, Alleviate, Alms, Anodyne, Assistance, Assuage, Bas, Cameo, Cavo-relievo, Comfort, Cure, Détente, Ease(ment), Emboss, Emollient, Free, High, Let-up, Lighten, Mafeking, Palliate, Phew, Pog(e)y, Reassure, Redress, Remedy, Replacement, Repoussé, Reprieve, ➤ RESCUE, Respite, Rid, Spell, Stand-in, Succour, Whew, Woodcut

Religion, Religious (sect) Biblist, Congregant, Creed, Denomination, Devout, Doctrine, Faith, God-squad, Hieratic, Missionary, Missioner, Nun, Opium, Pi, Pietà, Postulant, Progressive, Reformation, Sabbatarian, Sacramentalist, Serious, Sodality, Spike, Theology, Whore, Zealous

Relish(ing) Botargo, Catsup, Chow-chow, Condiment, Enjoy, Flavour, Gentleman's, Gout, Gust(o), Ketchup, Lap(-up), Lust, Opsonium, Palate, Sapid, Sar, Sauce, Savour, Seasoning, Tang, Tooth, Worcester sauce, Zest

Reluctant Averse, Backward, Chary, Circumspect, Grudging, Laith, Loth, Nolition, Renitent, Shy, Unwilling

Rely, Reliance, Reliant, Reliable Addiction, Authentic, Bank, Confidence, Constant, ➤ COUNT, Dependent, Found, Hope, Jeeves, Lean, Loyal, Mensch, Presume, Pukka, Rest, Safe, Secure, Solid, Sound, Sponge, Stand-by, Staunch, Trustworthy, Trusty, Unfailing

Remain(der), Remaining, Remains Abide, Ash(es), Balance, Bide, Continue, Corse, Dreg(s), Dwell, Embers, Estate, Exuviae, Fag-end, Kreng, Last, Late, Lave, Left, Lie, Locorestive, Manet, Nose, Oddment, Orts, Other, Outstand, Relic(ts), Persist, Reliquae, Remnant, Residue, Rest, Ruins, Scourings, Scraps, Stay, Stick, Stub, Surplus, Survive, Tag-end, Talon, Tarry, Wait

Remark Aside, Barb, Bromide, Comment(ary), Descry, Dig, Generalise, Mention, Noise, ➤ NOTE, Notice, Obiter dictum, Observe, Platitude, Reason, Sally, Shot, State

Remarkable, Remarkably Arresting, Beauty, Bodacious, Conspicuous, Egregious, Extraordinary, Heliozoan, Legendary, Lulu, Mirable, Notendum, Noteworthy, Phenomenal, Rattling, ➤ SIGNAL, Singular, Some, Striking, Tall, Unco, Visible

Remedial, Remedy Aid, Antacid, Antibiotic, Antidote, Arnica, Calomel, Corrective, Cortisone, ➤ CURE, Drug, Elixir, Feverfew, Fumitory, Ginseng, Heal, Ipecac, Medicate, Medicine, Nostrum, Palliative, Panacea, Paregoric, Poultice, Repair, Rectify, Redress, Salve, Simple, Specific, Therapeutic, Treatment

Remember(ing), Remembrance Bethink, Commemorate, Con, Mention, Mem, Memorial, Memorise, Mneme, Recall, Recollect, Remind, Reminisce, Retain, Rosemary, Souvenir

▷ **Remember** may indicate RE-member, viz. Sapper

Remind(er) Aftertaste, Aide-memoire, Bookmark, Evocatory, Evoke, Jog, Keepsake, Mark, Memento, Memo, Mnemonic, Mnemotechnic, Monition, Nudge, Phylactery, Prod, Prompt, Souvenir, Token

Remission Abatement, Absolution, Acceptilation, Indulgence, Pardon, Pause

Remnant Butt, End, Fent, Heeltap, Left-over, Odd-come-short, Offcut, Relic, ➤ REMAINDER, Rump, Trace, Vestige

Remorse Angst, Ayenbite, Breast-beating, Compunction, Contrition, Had-i-wist, Pity, ➤ REGRET, Rue, Ruing, Ruth, Sorrow

Remote Aloof, Aphelion, Backveld, Backwater, Backwood, Bullamakanka, Bundu, ➤ DISTANT, Forane, Inapproachable,

Insular, Irrelevant, Jericho, Long(inquity), Out(part), Outback, Scrub, Secluded, Shut-out, Slightest, Surrealistic, Unlikely, Withdrawn

Removal, Remove(d) Abduct, Abstract, Banish, Blot, Circumcision, Clear, Couch, Declassify, Dele(te), Depilate, Depose, Detach, Detract, Dislodge, Dispel, Doff, Efface, Eject, Eloi(g)n, Emend, Eradicate, Erase, Estrange, Evacuate, Evict, Exalt, Excise, Extirpate, Far, Flit, Huff, Nick, Rid, Scratch, Shift, Spirit, Subtract, Supplant, Transfer, Transport, Unseat, Uproot

Render(ing) Construe, Deliver, Do, Gie, Give, Interpretation, Make, Melt, Pebble-dash, Plaster, Provide, Recite, Represent, Restore, Setting, Tallow, Try, Yeve

Rendezvous Date, Meeting, Philippi, Tryst, Venue

Rendition Account, Delivery, Interpretation, Translation

Renegade, Renege Apostate, Default, Defector, Deserter, Rat(ton), Traitor, Turncoat

▷**Renegade** may indicate a word reversal

Renew(al) Instauration, Neogenesis, Palingenesis, Refresh, Replace, Resumption, Retrace, Revival, Urban

Renounce, Renunciation Abandon, Abdicate, Abjure, Abnegate, Disclaim, Disown, For(e)go, For(e)say, Forfeit, Forisfamiliate, Forsake, Forswear, Kenosis, Recede, Relinquish, Renay, Retract, Sacrifice

Renovate, Renovation Instauration, Refurbish, Renew, Repair, Restore, Revamp

Rent Broken, Charge, Cornage, Crack, Cranny, Cuddeehih, Cuddy, Division, Economic, Farm, Fee, Fissure, Gale, Gavel, Ground, ► HIRE, Lease, Let, Mail, Occupy, Quit-rent, Rack, Rip, Rived, Riven, Screed, Slit, Split, Stallage, Tare, Tithe, Tore, Torn, Tythe

Repair(er), Reparation Amend(s), Anaplasty, Botch, Cobble, Damages, Darn, Doctor, Fettle, Fitter, Go, Haro, Harrow, ► MEND, Overhaul, Patch, Recompense, Redress, Refit, Reheel, Remedy, Renew, Repoint, Resort, Restore, Retouch, Satisfaction, Stitch, Ulling, Vamp, Volery

Repartee Backchat, Badinage, Banter, Persiflage, Rejoinder, Retort, Riposte, Wit

Repast Bever, Collection, Food, Meal, Tea, Treat

Repay(ment) Avenge, Compensate, Quit, Refund, Requite, Retaliate, Reward, Satisfaction

Repeat(edly), Repetition, Repetitive Again, Alliteration, Belch, Bis, Burden, Burp, Copy, Ditto(graphy), Duplicate, ► ECHO, Echolalia, Encore, Eruct, Facsimile, Habitual, Harp, Image, Imitate, Iterate, Leit-motiv, Parrot, Passion, Perpetuate, Playback, Recite(r), Redo, Refrain, Regurgitate, Reiterate, Renew, Rep, Repetend, Rerun, Retail, Rote, Same(y), Screed, Tautology, Thrum

Repel(lent) Estrange, Harsh, Offensive, Rebarbative, Reject, Repulse, Revolt, Squalid, Turn-off, Ug(h), Ward

►**Repetition** see REPEAT

Replace(ment), Replaceable, Replacing Change, Deputise, Diadochy, For, Pre-empt, Raincheck, Refill, Replenish, Restore, Stand-in, Substitute, Supersede, Supplant, Surrogate, Taxis, Transform, Transliterate, Understudy

Replete, Repletion Awash, Full, Gorged, Plenitude, Plethora, Sated, Satiation

Replica Clone, Copy, Duplicate, Facsimile, Image, Repetition, Spit

Reply Accept, Answer, Churlish, Duply, Rejoinder, Rescript, Response, Retort, Surrebut, Surrejoin

Report(er) Account, Announce, Bang, Bulletin, Bruit, Clap, Columnist, Comment, Commentator, Correspondent, Court, Cover, Crack, Crump, Cub, Debrief, Disclose, Dispatch, Explosion, Fame, Fireman, Grapevine, Hansard, Hearsay, Jenkins, Journalist, Legman, Libel, News, Newshawk, Newshound, Newsman, Noise, Pop, Pressman, Protocol, Relate, Relay, Repute, Return, Rumour, Sitrep, Sound(bite), State(ment), Stringer, Tale, ► TELL, Thesis, Transcribe, Tripehound, Troop, Update, Whang

▷**Reported** may indicate the sound of a letter or word

Represent(ation), Representative Agent, Ambassador, Caricature, Commercial, Cross-section, Delegate, Depict, Deputation, Describe, Display, Drawing, Drummer, Effigy, Elchee, Eltchi, Emblem, Embody, Emissary, Example, Image, John Bull, Lobby, Map, Mouthpiece, MP, Personate, Personify, Portray, Proportional, Rep, Resemble, Salesman, Senator, Spokesman, Stand-in, Steward, Symbolic, Tableau, Typical

▷**Represented** may indicate an anagram

Reprimand Bounce, Carpet, ➤ CENSURE, Chide, Dressing-down, Earful, Jobe, Lace, Lecture, Rating, Rebuke, Reproof, Rocket, Rollicking, Slate, Strafe, Targe, Tick off, Tongue-lashing, Wig

Reproach Blame, Braid, Byword, Chide, Discredit, Dispraise, Exprobate, Gib, Mispraise, Odium, Opprobrium, Rebuke, Ronyon, Runnion, Scold, Shend, Sloan, Stigma, Taunt, Truant, Upbraid, Upcast, Yshend

Reproduce(r), Reproduction, Reproductive (organ) Clone, Copy, Counterfeit, Depict, Edition, Etch, Eugenics, Megaspore, Mono, Multiply, Oogamy, Parthogenesis, Phon(e)y, Propagate, Refer, Replica, Roneo®, Seminal, Simulate, Stereo

▷ **Reproduce** may indicate an anagram

Reproof, Reprove Admonish, Berate, Chide, Correction, Correption, Lecture, Rate, Rebuff, Rebuke, Scold, Sloan, Tut, Upbraid

Reptile, Reptilian Agamid, Alligarta, Alligator, Base, Basilisk, Caiman, Cayman, Chameleon, Chelonian, Creeper, Crocodile, Diapsid, Dicynodont, Dinosaur, Goanna, Herpetology, Lacertine, Lizard, Mamba, Pteranodon, Pterodactyl, Rhynchocephalian, Sauroid, ➤ SNAKE, Squamata, Synapsid, Tegu(exin), Thecodont, Therapsid, Tortoise, Tuatara, Tuatera, Turtle, Worm

Republic Banana, R, Second, State

Republican Antimonarchist, Democrat, Fenian, Fianna Fail, Girondist, IRA, Iraqi, Leveller, Montagnard, Mugwump, Plato, Red, Sanaculotte, Sansculottic, Sinn Fein, Whig

Repudiate Abjure, Deny, Discard, Disclaim, Disown, Ignore, Recant, Reject, Renounce, Repel

Repugnance, Repugnant Abhorrent, Alien, Disgust, Distaste, Fulsome, Horror, Loathing, Revulsion

Reputable, Reputation, Repute(d) Bubble, Dit, Estimate, Fame, Good, Izzat, Loos, Los, Name, Note, Notoriety, Odour, Opinion, Prestige, Putative, Regard, Renown, Said, Sar, ➤ STANDING, Stink, Trustworthy

Request Adjure, Appeal, Apply, Ask, Desire, Entreaty, Invite, Petition, Plea, Prayer, Solicit

Require(d), Requirement Charge, Crave, De rigueur, Desire, Enjoin, Exact, Expect, Incumbent, Lack, Necessity, Need, Prerequisite

Requisite, Requisition Commandeer, Due, Embargo, Essential, Indent, Necessary, Needful, Order, Press

Rescue Aid, Air-sea, Deliver, Free, Liberate, Ransom, Recover, Recower, Redeem, Regain, Relieve, Reprieve, Retrieve, Salvage, Salvation, ➤ SAVE

Research(er) Boffin, Delve, Dig, Enquiry, Explore, Fieldwork, Investigate, Legwork, Market, Operational, Pioneer, Sus(s)

Resemblance, Resemble, Resembling Affinity, Apatetic, Approach, Assonant, Likeness, Similitude, -oid, -opsis, Replica, Simulate

Resent(ful), Resentment Anger, Bridle, Choler, Cross, Dudgeon, Grudge, Indignation, Ire, Malign, Miff, Pique, Rankle, Smart, Spite, Umbrage

Reservation, Reserve(d), Reservist(s) Aloof, Arrière-pensée, Backlog, Bashful, Book, By, Caveat, Cold, Demiss, Detachment, Distant, Earmark, Engage, Ersatz, Except, Fall-back, Fort Knox, Hold, Husband, Ice, Introvert, Layby, Landwehr, Locum, Nature, Nest-egg, Proviso, Qualification, Reddendum, Res, Rest, Restraint, Retain, Reticence, Retiring, Rez, Salvo, Sanctuary, Save, Scruple, Special, Stand-by, Stand-offishness, Stash, Stock(pile), TA(men), Uncommunicate, Understudy, Warren, Waves, Withhold

Reservoir Basin, Cistern, G(h)ilgai, Gilgie, Repository, Stock, Sump, Tank

Reside(nce), Resident Abode, Address, Amban, Chequers, Commorant, Consulate, Denizen, Dwell, Embassy, Establishment, Expatriate, Exurbanite, Gremial, Guest, Home, Indweller, Inholder, Inmate, Intern, Ledger, Lei(d)ger, Lieger, Lodger, Metic, Pad, Parietal, Resiant, Settle, Sojourn, Stay, Tenant, Villager, Yamen

Residual, Residue Ash, Astatki, Calx, Caput, Chaff, Cinders, Crud, Draff, Dregs, Expellers, Greaves, Leavings, Mazout, Mortuum, Remainder, Remanent, Remnant, Slag, Slurry, Snuff, Vinasse

Resign(ed), Resignation Abandon, Abdicate, Demit, Fatalism, Heigh-ho, Leave, Meek, ➤ QUIT, Reconcile, Stoic, Submit

Resin Amber, Amine, Bakelite®, Balsam, Colophony,
Dam(m)ar, Elemi, Epoxy, Frankincense, Gamboge, Gum,
Hashish, Lac, Mastic, Melamine, Myrrh, Olibanum, Polyester,
Polymer, Rosin, Shellac, Synthetic

Resist Bristle, Buck, Contest, Defy, Face, Fend, Gainstrive,
Impede, Oppose, Redound, Reluct, Stand, ➤ WITHSTAND

Resistance, Resistant, Resistor Barretter, Bleeder,
Ceramal, Cermet, Chetnik, Coccidiostat, Drag, Element,
Friction, Hostile, Immunity, Impediment, Klendusic, Klepht,
Maquis, Maraging, Megohm, Microhm, Obstacle, Ohm,
Passive, Pull, R, Reluctance, Renitent, Resilient, Rheostat,
Satyagraha, Stability, Stand, Stonde, Stubborn, Tough

Resolute, Resolution Analysis, Bold, Cast-iron, Courage,
Decided, Decision, Denouement, Determined, ➤ FIRM,
Fortitude, Granite, Grim, Grit, Hardiness, Insist, Pertinacity,
Promotion, Rede, Resolve, Stable, Stalwart, Staunch, Stout,
Strength, Sturdy, Tenacity, Unbending, Valiant, Willpower

Resolve(d), Resolver Analyse, Calculate, Decide, Declare,
➤ DETERMINE, Deux et machina, Factorise, Fix, Hellbent, Intent,
Nerve, ➤ PURPOSE, Settle, Steadfast, Tenacity, Vow

▷**Resolved** may indicate an anagram

Resort Centre, Dive, Etaples, Expedient, Frame, Frequent,
Haunt, Hove, Hydro, Invoke, Lair, Las Vegas, Last, Morecambe,
Nassau, Pau, Pis aller, Rapallo, Recourse, Resource, Riviera,
Southend, Spa(w), Use

▷**Resort(ing)** may indicate an anagram

Resource(s), Resourceful Assets, Beans, Bottom,
Chevisance, Clever, Faculty, Funds, Gumption, Ingenious,
Input, Inventive, Means, Sharp, Stock-in-trade, ➤ VERSATILE,
Wealth

Respect(ed), Respectable, Respectful Admire, Ahimsa,
Aspect, Behalf, Consider, Decent, Deference, Devoir, Duty,
Esteem, Gigman, Homage, ➤ HONOUR, Kempt, Latria,
Obeisant, Officious, Pace, Particular, Preppy, Prestige, Proper,
Reference, Regard, Relation, Reputable, Revere, S(t)irrah, Sir, U,
Venerate, Wellborn, Well-thought-of, Wise, Worthy

Respirator, Respire, Respiration Artificial, Blow, Breathe,
Exhale, Gasmask, Inhale, Iron lung, Pant, Snorkel

Respond, Response, Responsive Amenable, Answer,
Antiphon, Comeback, Conditioned, Echo, Feedback, Flechman,

Immune, Kyrie, Litany, Nastic, Pavlovian, Photonasty, React(ion), Reflex, Reply, Rheotaxis, Rise, Synapte, Syntonic, Tender, Thigmotropic, Tic, Tropism, Warm

Responsibility, Responsible Answerable, Baby, Blame, Buck, Charge, Culpable, Dependable, Diminished, Duty, Incumbent, Instrumental, Liable, Mea culpa, Onus, Pigeon, Sane, Solid, Trust

Rest (day) Anchor, Balance, Bed, Break, Breather, Calm, Catnap, Depend, Dwell, Ease, Easel, Etc, Feutre, Gite, Halt, Inaction, Jigger, Lave, Lean, Lie, Lie-in, Light, Lodge, Loll, Lound, Nap, Others, Pause, Quiescence, Quiet, Relache, Relax, Rely, Remainder, Repose, Requiem, Respite, Sabbath, Siesta, ➤ SLEEP, Slumber, Spell, Spider, Stopover, Support, Surplus

Restaurant, Restaurateur Automat, Beanery, Bistro, Brasserie, Cabaret, Cafe, Canteen, Chophouse, Commissary, Diner, Eatery, Estaminet, Greasy spoon, Grill, Grub shop, Maxim's, Noshery, Padrone, Rathskeller, Rotisserie, Slap-bang, Takeaway, Taqueria, Taverna, Teahouse, Tearoom, Teashop, Trattoria

Restive, Restless(ness) Chafing, Chorea, Fikish, Free-arm, Itchy, Jactitation, Toey, Unsettled

▷ **Restless** may indicate an anagram

Restoration, Restorative, Restore(d) Cure, Descramble, Heal, Mend, Pentimento, Pick-me-up, Redeem, Redintegrate, Redux, Regenerate, Rehabilitate, Rejuvenate, Remedial, Renew, Repone, Restitute, Revamp, Revive, Stet, Tonic

Restrain(ed), Restraint Abstinence, Ban, Bate, Bit, Bottle, Branks, Bridle, Cage, Chain, Chasten, ➤ CHECK, Cohibit, Compesce, Confinement, Contain, Control, Cramp, Curb, Dam, Decorum, Detent, Dry, Duress, Embargo, Enfetter, Freeze, Halt, Hamshackle, Handcuffs, Harness, Heft, Hinder, Hopple, Impound, Inhibit, Jess, Lid, Low-key, Manacle, Measure, Mince, Moderation, Muzzle, Quiet, Rein, Repress, Restrict, Ritenuto, Shackle, Sober, Sobriety, Squeeze, Stay, Stent, Stint, Straitjacket, Temper, Tether, Tie, Trash

Restrict(ed), Restriction Band, Bar, Bind, Bit, Cage, Catch, Chain, Closet, Condition, Cord, Corset, Cramp, Curb, DORA, Fence, Fold, Gate, Ground, Guard, Hamper, Hidebound, Hobble, Inhibit, Intern, Kennel, Let, ➤ LIMIT, Lock, Mere, Narrow, Net, Nick, Pale, Parochial, Pen, Pent, Pier, Pin,

Result(s) → Retrieve(r)

Pot-bound, Private, Proscribed, Qualify, Regulate, Rein, Rope, Scant, Seal, Section, Selected, Shackle, Snare, Squeeze, Stenopaic, Stint, Stop, Straiten, Tether, Tie

Result(s) Aftermath, Ans(wer), Bring, Causal, Consequence, Effect, Emanate, End, Ensue, Entail, Event, Eventuate, Finding, Fruict, Fruits, Issue, Karmic, Lattermath, ➤ OUTCOME, Outturn, Pan, Proceeds, Quotient, Sequel, Side-effect, Sum, Upshot, Wale

Retain(er), Retains Brief, Contain, Deposit, Fee, Hold, Keep, Panter, Pantler, Reserve, Retinue, Servant

Retaliate, Retaliation Avenge, Counter, Lex talionis, Quit(e), Redress, Repay, Reprisal, Requite, Retort, Talion

Reticence, Reticent Clam, Coy, Dark, Reserve, Restraint, Secretive, Shy, Taciturn

Retinue Company, Cortège, Equipage, Following, Meiney, Meinie, Meiny, Sowarry, Suite

Retire(d), Retirement, Retiring Abed, Aloof, Baccare, Backare, Backpedal, Blate, Bowler-hat, Cede, Coy, Depart, Ebb, Emeritus, Essene, Former, Leave, Lonely, Modest, Mothball, Nun, Outgoing, Pension, Private, Quit, Recede, Recluse, Reserved, Resign, Retract, Retreat, Retrocedent, Roost, Rusticate, Scratch, Shy, Superannuate, Unassertive, Withdraw

▷**Retirement** may indicate 'bed' around another word, or word reversed

Retort Alembic, Comeback, Courteous, Quip, Repartee, ➤ REPLY, Retaliate, Riposte, Still

Retract(ion) Disavow, Epanorthosis, Palinode, Recall, Recant, Renounce, Revoke

Retreat Abbey, Arbour, Ashram(a), Asylum, Backwater, Bower, Bug, Cell, Cloister, Convent, Dacha, Departure, Donjon, Girth, Grith, Hermitage, Hideaway, Hide-out, Hole, Ivory-tower, Lair, Lama(sery), Mew, Monastery, Nest, Nook, Recede, Recoil, Redoubt, Reduit, Refuge, Retire, Retraite, Right-about, Rout, Shelter, Skedaddle, Stronghold, Withdraw

Retribution Come-uppance, Deserts, Nemesis, Revenge, Reward, Utu, Vengeance

Retrieve(r), Retrieval Access, Bird-dog, Field, Gundog, Labrador, Read-out, Recall, Recoup, Recover, Redeem, Rescue, Salvage

Return(s) Agen, Bricole, Census, Comeback, Day, Dividend, Elect, Er, Extradite, Gain, Pay, Profit, Rebate, Rebound, Recur, Redound, Regress, Reject, Render, Rent, Repay, Replace, Reply, Requital, Respond, Restore, Retour, Revenue, Reverse, Revert, Riposte, Takings, Tax, ➤ YIELD

Reveal(ing), Revelation Advertise, Air, Apocalyptic, Bare, Betray, Bewray, Confess, Descry, Disclose, Discover, Discure, ➤ DIVULGE, Epiphany, Exhibit, Explain, Expose, Giveaway, Hierophantic, Impart, Indicate, Ingo, Kythe, Leak, Manifest, Open, Satori, ➤ SHOW, Spill, Tell-tale, Unclose, Uncover, Unfold, Unheal, Unmask, Unveil

Revel(ling), Reveller, Revelry Ariot, Bacchanalia, Bend, Carnival, Carouse, Comus, Corybant, Dionysian, Feast, Gloat, Glory, Joy, Merriment, Orgy, Rant, Rejoice, Riot, Roister, Rollicks, Rout, Saturnalia, Splore, Swig, Upsee, Ups(e)y, Wallow, Wassail, Whoopee

Revenge(ful) Aftergame, Avenge, Commination, Goel, Grenville, Montezuma's, Reprise, Requite, Retaliation, Revanche, Ultion, Utu, Vindictive

Revere(nce) Admire, Awe, Bostonian, Dread, Dulia, Esteem, Hallow, Hery, Homage, ➤ HONOUR, Hyperdulia, Latria, Obeisance, Paul, Respect, Venerate

Reversal, Reverse, Reversing, Reversion Antithesis, Antonym, Arsy-versy, Atavism, Back(slide), Change-over, Chiasmus, Counter(mand), Escheat, Evaginate, Exergue, Flip, Inversion, Misfortune, ➤ OPPOSITE, Overturn, Palindrome, Pile, Regress, Revoke, Rheotropic, Switchback, Tails, Throwback, Transit, Turn, Un-, Undo, U-turn, Verso, Vice versa, Volte-face

Review(er) Appeal, Censor, Critic, Critique, Editor, Feuilleton, Footlights, Inspect, Judicial, Magazine, March-past, Notice, Pan, Recapitulate, Repeat, Revise, Rundown, Spithead, Summary, Survey, Write-up

▷ **Review** may indicate an anagram or a reversed word

Revise(r), Revision Alter, Amend, Correct, Diaskeuast, Edit, Peruse, Reappraise, Reassess, Recense, Reform, Rev, Update

▷ **Revise(d)** may indicate an anagram

Revival, Revive, Revivify, Reviving Araise, Enliven, Gothic, Rally, Reanimate, Reawake(n), Rebirth, Redintegrate, Refresh, Rekindle, Renaissance, Renascent, Renew, Renovate,

Restore, Resurrect, Resuscitate, Risorgimento, Romantic, Rouse, Wake

Revolt(ing), Revolution(ary) Agitator, Anarchist, Apostasy, Bloodless, Bolshevik, Boxer, Cade, Castro, Chartist, Che, Circle, Coup d'etat, Cultural, Cycle, Dervish, Disgust, Enrage, February, Girondin, Glorious, Gyration, Industrial, ➤ IN REVOLT, Insurgent, Insurrection, IRA, Lenin, Marat, Marx, Mutiny, Orbit, Putsch, ➤ REBEL(LION), Reformation, Riot, Robespierre, Roll, Rotation, Sedition, Trot(sky), ➤ UPRISING, Whirl

▷ **Revolutionary** may indicate 'reversed'

Revolve(r), Revolving Carrier, Catherine wheel, Centrifuge, Colt®, Gat, Girandole, Grindstone, ➤ GUN, Gyrate, Iron, Klinostat, Lathe, Maelstrom, Peristrephic, Pistol, Pivot, Roller, Rotate, Rotifer, Rotor, Roundabout, Run, Tone, Turn(stile), Turntable, Turret, Wheel, Whirl(igig), Whirlpool

Reward Albricias, Bonus, Bounty, Compensate, Consideration, Desert, Emolument, Fee, Guerdon, Head money, Meed, Payment, Premium, Price, Prize, Profit, Purse, Recompense, Reguerdon, Remuneration, Requital, Requite, S, Shilling, Wage, War(r)ison

Rhetoric(al) Anaphora, Apophasis, Aureate, Bombast, Chiasmus, Eloquence, Enantiosis, Epistrophe, Erotema, Eroteme, Erotesis, Euphemism, Hendiadys, Oratory, Paral(e)ipsis, Peroration, Pleonasm, Syllepsis, Trivium

Rhyme(r), Rhyming Assonance, Clerihew, Closed couplet, Couplet, Crambo, Cynghanedd, Doggerel, Eye, Feminine, Head, Internal, Masculine, Measure, Nursery, Perfect, Poetry, Rondel, Runic, Sight, Slang, Slant, Tercet, Terza-rima, Thomas, Triple, ➤ VERSE, Virelay

Rhythm(ic) Agoge, Alpha, Asynartete, Backbeat, Beat, Beta, Bo Diddley beat, Breakbeat, Cadence, Circadian, Duple, In-step, Meter, Movement, Oompah, Pyrrhic, Rubato, Sdrucciola, Singsong, Sprung, Swing, Syncopation, Tala, Talea, ➤ TEMPO, Time, Voltinism

Rib(bed), Ribbing, Rib-joint Bar, Chaff, Cod, Costa, Cross-springer, Dutch, Eve, False, Floating, Futtock, Groin, Intercostal, Lierne, Nervate, Nervular, Nervure, Ogive, Persiflage, Rally, Spare, Springer, Sub-Costa, Tease, Tierceron, Tracery, True, Wife

Ribbon Band, Bandeau, Blue, Bow, Braid, Caddis, Caddyss, Cordon, Fattrels, Ferret, Fillet, Grosgrain, Hatband, Infula, Pad, Petersham, Radina, Rein, Soutache, Taenia, Tape, Teniate, Tie, Torsade

Rice Arborio, Basmati, Brown, Elmer, Entertainer, Indian, Kedgeree, Patna, Pilaf, Pilau, Pilaw, Reis, Risotto, Sushi, Twigs, Wild

Rich(es) Abounding, Abundant, Affluent, Amusing, Bonanza, Comic, Copious, Croesus, Dives, Edmund, Edwin, Fat, Feast, Fertile, Flush, Fruity, Full, Golconda, Haves, Heeled, High, Loaded, Lush, Luxurious, Mammon, Moneybags, Moneyed, Nabob, Oberous, ► OPULENT, Plenteous, Plush, Plutocrat, Rolling, Sumptuous, Toff, Vulgarian, ► WEALTHY, Well-heeled, Well-to-do

▷**Rickety** may indicate an anagram

Riddle Boulter, Charade, Colander, Dilemma, Enigma, Koan, Logogriph, Pepper, Perforate, Permeate, Puzzle, Screen, Searce, Search, Sieve, Sift, Siler, Sorites, Strain, Tems(e), Trommel

Ride, Riding Annoy, Bareback, Bestride, Bruise, Canter, Coast, Cycle, District, Division, Drive, Equitation, Field, Hack, Harass, Haute école, Hitchhike, Merry-go-round, Mount, Pick(-a-)back, Piggyback, Postil(l)ion, Rape, Revere's, Roadstead, Rollercoaster, Sit, Spin, Stang, Switchback, Third, Trot, Weather, Welter, Wheelie, White-knuckle

Rider Addendum, Adjunct, Appendage, Attachment, Cavalier, Charioteer, Codicil, Condition, Corollary, Equestrian, Eventer, Godiva, Guidon, Haggard, Horseman, Jockey, Lochinvar, Postil(l)ion, Proviso, PS, Revere, Walkyrie

Ridge Arete, As(ar), Bank, Baulk, Chine, Crease, Crest, Dune, Esker, Hoe, Ledge, Promontory, Wale, Weal, Whorl

Ridicule, Ridiculous Absurd, Badinage, Bathos, Chaff, Cockamamie, Deride, Derisory, Egregious, Foolish, Gibe, Gird, Guy, Haze, Jibe, Josh, Laughable, Ludicrous, Mimic, Mock, Paradox, Pasquin, Pillory, Pish, Pooh-pooh, Raillery, Rich, Roast, Satire, Scoff, Scout, Screwy, Sight, Silly, Skimmington, Taunt, Travesty

Rifle Air, Armalite®, Bone, Browning, Bundook, Burgle, Carbine, Chassepot, Enfield, Enfield musket, Express, Garand, ► GUN, Kalashnikov, Loot, Martini®, Mauser®, Minié, Pilfer, Ransack, Repeater, Rob, Springfield, Winchester®

Rig(ging) Accoutre, Attire, Bermuda, Drilling, Equip, Feer, Gaff, Get-up, Gunter, Hoax, Jack-up, Manipulate, Marconi, Martingale, Outfit, Panoply, Ratline, Ropes, Schooner, Sport, Stack, Swindle, Tackle, Trull

▷ **Rigged** may indicate an anagram

Right(en), Rightness, Rights Appropriate, Befit, Blue-pencil, Civil, Claim, Competence, Conjugal, Conservative, ► CORRECT, Cure, Direct, Divine, Droit, Due, Equity, Ethical, Exactly, Fascist, Fitting, Franchise, Freedom, Germane, Interest, Liberty, Lien, Meet, Moral, Offside, OK, Okay, Prerogative, Priority, Privilege, Proper, R, Rain, Reason, Rectify, Redress, Remedy, Repair, Rt, True

Rigid(ity) Acierated, Catalepsy, Craton, Extreme, Fixed, Formal, Hidebound, Inflexible, Renitent, Set, Slavish, Starch(y), Stern, Stiff, Stretchless, Strict, Stringent, Tense, Turgor

Rigorous, Rigour Accurate, Austere, Cruel, Exact, Firm, Hard, Inclement, Iron-bound, Stern, Strait, Strict, Stringent

▷ **Rile(y)** may indicate an anagram

Rim Atlantic, Border, Chimb, Chime, Edge, Felloe, Felly, Flange, ► LIP, Margin, Strake, Verge

Ring(ed), Ringing, Rings Angelus, Annulus, Arena, Band, Bangle, Bell, Call, Cartel, Change, Chime, Circle, Circlet, Circus, Clang, Clink, Coil, Cordon, Corral, Cycle, Dial, Ding, Disc, Dong, D(o)uar, Echo, Encircle, Encompass, Engagement, Enhalo, Enlace, Environ, Enzone, Eternity, Fairy, Ferrule, Gird(le), Girr, Gloriole, Grom(m)et, Halo, Hob, ► HOOP, Hoop-la, Ideal, Inorb, Inner, Keeper, Key, Knell, Knock-out, Kraal, Link, Loop, Lute, Manacle, Magpie, O, Orb, Outer, Peal, Pen, Phone, Ping, Piston, Prize, Quoit, Resonant, Resound, Round, Rove, Runner, Signet, Snap-link, Sound, Spell, Split, Surround, Swivel, Syndicate, Tang, Tattersall, Thimble, Ting, Tingle, Tink, Tintinnabulate, Toe, Toll, Tore, Torques, Torret, Torus, Vice, Wagnerian, Washer, Wedding, Woggle, Zero

Riot(er), Riotous(ly), Riots Anarchy, Brawl, Clamour, Demo, Deray, Gordon, Hilarious, Hubbub, Luddite, Medley, Melee, Orgy, Pandemonium, Peterloo, Porteous, Profusion, Quorum, Rag, Rebecca, Rebel, Roister, Rout, Rowdy, Ruffianly, Swing, Tumult

▷ **Rioters, Riotous** may indicate an anagram

Rip(ping) Basket, Buller, Cur, Grand, Handful, Horse, Lacerate, Rent, Rep, Splendid, Tear, Tide, Topnotch, To-rend, Unseam

Ripe, Ripen(ing) Auspicious, Full, Mature, Mellow, Rathe, Ready

▷ **Rippling** may indicate an anagram

Rise(r), Rising Advance, Appreciate, Ascend, Assurgent, Bull, Butte, Cause, Easter, Eger, Elevation, Emerge, Emeute, Eminence, Erect, Escalate, Hance, Hauriant, Haurient, Heave, Hike, Hill, Hummock, Hunt's up, Improve, Increase, Insurgent, Intumesce, Jibe, Knap, Knoll, Lark, Levee, Levitate, Lift, Mount, Mutiny, Orient, Peripety, Putsch, Rear, Resurgent, Resurrection, ➤ REVOLT, Saleratus, Scarp, Soar, Stand, Stie, Sty, Surface, Surge, Tor, Tower, Transcend, Up, Upbrast, Upburst, Upgo, Uprest, Upsurge, Upswarm, Upturn, Well

Risk(y) Actuarial, Adventure, Back, Calculated, Chance, Compromise, ➤ DANGER, Daring, Dice, Dicy, Emprise, Endanger, Fear, Gamble, Game, Hairy, Hazard, Imperil, Jeopardy, Liability, Peril, Precarious, Security, Spec, Unsafe, Venture

Rite(s) Asperges, Bora, Ceremony, Exequies, Initiation, Liturgy, Nagmaal, Obsequies, Powwow, Ritual, Sacrament, Sarum use, Superstition, York

Ritual Agadah, Arti, Ceremony, Chanoyu, Customary, Formality, Haggada, Lavabo, Liturgy, Rite, Sacring, Seder, Social, Use

Rival(ry), Rivals Absolute, Acres, Aemule, Compete, Emulate, Emule, Envy, Fo(n)e, ➤ MATCH, Needle, Opponent, Touch, Vie

River Ea, Estuary, Flood, Flower, Fluvial, Ord, Potamic, R, Riverain, Runner, Stream, Tributary, Waterway

Road(side) A, A1, Anchorage, Arterial, Autobahn, Autostrada, Ave(nue), B, Beltway, Boulevard, Burma, Carriageway, Causeway, Cloverleaf, Corduroy, Corniche, Course, Escape, Expressway, Fairway, Feeder, Foss(e) Way, Freeway, Highway, Kerb, Lane, Loan, Loke, Mall, Metal, M1, Motorway, Parkway, Path, Pike, Rd, Relief, Ride, Ring, ➤ ROUTE, Service, Shoulder, Shunpike, Slip, Spur(way), St(reet), Switchback, Thoroughfare, Tobacco, Toby, Trunk, Turning, Turnpike, Underpass, Verge, Via, Way

Roam Extravagate, Peregrinate, Rake, Ramble, Rove, Stray, Wander, Wheel

Roar(ing) Bawl, Bell(ow), Bluster, Boom, Boys, Cry, Forties, Guffaw, Laugh, Roin, Rote, Rout, Royne, Thunder, Tumult, Vroom, Wuther, Zoom

Roast Barbecue, Bake, Baste, Birsle, Brent, Cabob, Cook, Crab, Crown, Decrepitate, Grill, Kabob, Pan, Ridicule, Scathe, Scald, Sear, Slate, Tan, Torrefy

Rob(bed), Robber(y) Abduct, Bandit, Bereave, Brigand, Burgle, Bust, Cateran, Clyde, Dacoit, Daylight, Depredation, Do, Fake, Filch, Fleece, Footpad, Heist, Highjack, Highwayman, Hijack, Hold-up, Hustle, Ladrone, Larceny, Latron, Loot, Pad, Pinch, Piracy, Plunder, Rapine, Reave, Reft, Reive, Rieve, Rifle, Robertsman, Roll, Roy, Rustler, Sack, Screw, Short change, Skinner, Smash and grab, ▶ STEAL, Steaming, Stick-up, Sting, Swindle, Thief, Toby, Turn-over, Turpin

Robe(s) Alb, Amice, Amis, Attrap, Camis, Camus, Cassock, Chimer, Chrisom(-cloth), Christom, Dalmatic, Dolman, ▶ DRESS, Gown, Ihram, Kanzu, Khalat, Khilat, Kill(a)ut, Kimono, Mantle, Parament, Parliament, Pedro, Peplos, Pontificals, Regalia, Rochet, Saccos, Sanbenito, Soutane, Sticharion, Stola, Stole, Talar, Tire, Vestment, Yukata

Robot Android, Automaton, Cyborg, Dalek, Golem, Nanobot, Puppet, RUR, Telechir

Rock(er), Rocking, Rocks, Rocky Ages, Agitate, Astound, Country, Cradle, Heavy metal, Marciano, Punk, Quake, Reggae, Rip-rap, Sally, ▶ SHAKE, Shoogle, Showd, Stun, Sway, Swee, Swing, Ted, Teeter, Totter, Unstable, Unsteady

Rocket Arugula, Booster, Capsule, Carpet, Congreve, Delta, Drake, Dressing down, Engine, Flare, Jato, Onion, Posigrade, Reprimand, Reproof, Retro, SAM, Skylark, Soar, Sounding, Stephenson, Thruster, Tourbillion, Upshoot, V1, Vernier, Warhead, Weld

▷**Rocky** may indicate an anagram

Rod(like), Rods Aaron's, Bar, Barbel(l), Barre, Birch, Caduceus, Cam, Can, Cane, Cue, Cuisenaire, Dipstick, Divining, Dowser, Drain, Firearm, Fisher, Fly, Fuel, Gun, Handspike, Laver, Linchpin, Lug, Moses, Newel, Perch, Pin, Pistol, Piston, Pitman, Pointer, Pole, Pontie, Pontil, Ponty, Puntee, Punty, Raddle, Rood, Shaft, Spindle, Spit, Stair, Staple, Stave, Stay-bolt, Stick, Switch, Tie, Twig, Verge, Virgate, Virgulate, Wand, Withe

Rodent Gnawer, Renegade, Runagate, Vermin

Rogue, Roguish(ness) Arch, Bounder, Charlatan, Chiseller, Drole, Dummerer, Elephant, Espiegle(rie), Ganef, Ganev, Ganof, Gonif, Gonof, Greek, Gypsy, Hempy, Herries, Imp, Knave, Latin, Limmer, Panurge, Picaresque, Picaroon, Poniard, Rapparee, Ra(p)scal(l)ion, Riderhood, Savage, Scamp, Schellum, Schelm, Skellum, Sleeveen, Slip-string, Swindler, Varlet, Villain

Roll(ed), Roller, Roll-call, Rolling, Rolls Absence, Bagel, Bap, Bolt, Bridge, Brioche, Comber, Cop, Court, Croissant, Cylinder, Dandy, Drum, Electoral, Eskimo, Even, Furl, Go, Labour, List, Mangle, Moving, Muster, Opulent, Patent, Piano, Pipe, Platen, Ragman, Record, Reef, Reel, Register, Ren, Revolute, Revolve, Road, Rob, Roster, Rota, Roulade, RR, Rumble, Run, Sausage, Snap, Somersault, Spool, Spring, Sway, Swell, Swiss, Table, Taxi, Temple, Tent, Terrine, Toilet, Tommy, Trill, Trindle, Trundle, Victory, Volume, Wad, Wallow, Wave, Western

▷**Rollicking** may indicate an anagram

Roman Agricola, Agrippa, Candle, Calpurnia, Catholic, Cato, Consul, CR, Crassus, Decemviri, Decurion, Empire, Flavian, Galba, Holiday, Italian, Jebusite, Latin, Maecenas, Papist, Patrician, PR, Quirites, Raetic, RC, Retarius, Rhaetia, Road, Scipio, Seneca, Sulla, Tarquin, Tiberius, Type, Uriconian

Romance, Romantic (talk) Affair, Amorous, Byronic, Casanova, Catalan, Dreamy, Fancy, Fantasise, Fib, Fiction, Gest(e), Gothic, Invention, Ladin(o), Ladinity, Langue d'oc(ian), Langue d'oïl, Langue d'oui, Lie, Neo-Latin, Novelette, Poetic, Quixotic, R(o)uman, Stardust, Tale

▶**Romany** see GYPSY

Roof (edge), Roofing Belfast, Bell, Ceil, Cl(e)ithral, Cover, Curb, Divot, Dome, Drip, Eaves, French, Gable, Gambrel, Hardtop, Hip(ped), Home, Imperial, Jerkin-head, Leads, Mansard, Monopitch, Palate, Pavilion, Pop-top, Porte-cochère, Rigging, Saddle, Shingle, Skirt, Tectiform, Tectum, Teguila, Thatch, Thetch, Tiling, Top, Uraniscus

Room(s), Roomy Anteroom, Apartment, Attic, Ben, Berth, Boudoir, Bower, But, Cabin(et), Camera, Capacity, Casemate, CC, Ceiling, Cell, Cellar, Chamber, Changing, Closet, Commodious, Compartment, Consulting, Cubicle, Cutting, Delivery, Digs, Divan, Dressing, Elbow, End, Extension, Foyer,

Root(ing) → Rough(en) 478

Gap, Garret, Lab, Latitude, Laura, Lavra, Leeway, Library,
Locker, Lodge, Loft, Loo, Lounge, Margin, Oda, Orderly, Oriel,
Pad, Parlour, Powder, Private, Projection, Public, Pump,
Recovery, Recreation, Rest, Robing, Rumpus, Salon, Scope,
Shebang, Single, Snug, Solar, ➤ SPACE, Spence, Still, Strong,
Studio, Study, Suite, Tap, Twin, Utility, Vestry, Waiting, Ward

Root(ing), Roots Cassava, Cheer, Cube, Delve, Dig, Eddo,
Eradicate, Foundation, Ginseng, Grass, Grub, Heritage,
Horseradish, Hurrah, Mandrake, Nuzzle, Poke, Pry, Radish,
Rhizome, Snuzzle, Source, Square, Tap, Taro, Tuber, Tulip,
Turnip, Turpeth, Zedoary

Rope(s) Ba(u)lk, Backstay, Bind, Bobstay, Cable, Cord, Cringle,
Earing, Fall, Foresheet, Forestay, Gantline, Guide, Guy, Halliard,
Halser, Halter, Halyard, Hawser, Headfast, Inhaul, Jump, Ladder,
Lanyard, Lasher, Lasso, Line, Lunge, Mainbrace, Mainsheet,
Marlin(e), Mooring, Noose, Painter, Pastern, Prolonge,
Rawhide, Riata, Rode, Runner, Sally, Seal, Sennit, Sheet, Shroud,
Sinnet, Span, Stay, String, Swifter, Tackle, Tether, Tie,
Tow(line), Trail

Rose(-red), Rosie, Rosy Albertine, Avens, Blooming,
Bourbon, Briar, Brier, Cabbage, Canker, China, Christmas,
Compass, Damask, Dog, Eglantine, England, Floribunda, Geum,
Guelder, Hybrid, Lancaster, Lee, Moss, Multiflora, Musk,
Noisette, Peace, Pink, Promising, Rambler, Red(dish), Rugosa,
Snowball, Sprinkler, Standard, Tea, Tokyo, Tudor, York

Rot(ten), Rotting Addle, Baloney, Bosh, Bosh, Botrytis, Bull,
Caries, Carious, Corrode, Corrupt, Daddock, Decadent,
➤ DECAY, Decompose, Degradable, Dotage, Dry, Eat, Erode,
Fester, Foul, Kibosh, Manky, Mildew, Noble, Nonsense,
Poppycock, Poxy, Punk, Putid, Putrefy, Putrid, Rail, Rancid,
Rank, Rat, Ret, Rust, Sapropel, Septic, Sour, Squish, Twaddle,
Wet

Rotate(r), Rotation Gyrate, Pivot, Pronate, Rabat(te),
Reamer, Revolve, Roll, Selsyn, Trundle, Turn, Wheel, Windmill

▶**Rotten** see ROT

▷**Rotten** may indicate an anagram

Rough(en), Roughly, Roughness About, Approximate,
Asper(ate), Burr, C, Ca, Choppy, Circa, Coarse, Craggy, Crude,
Frampler, Grained, Gross, Gruff, Gurly, Gusty, Hard, Harsh,
Hispid, Hoodlum, Hooligan, Impolite, Imprecise, Incondite,

Inexact, Irregular, Jagged, Karst, Keelie, Kokobeh, Muricate, Push, Ragged, Ramgunshoch, Raspy, Raucle, Rip, Risp, Robust, Row, Rude, Rugged, Rusticate, Rusty, Scabrid, Sea, Shaggy, Sketchy, Some, Spray, Spreathe, Squarrose, Stab, Strong-arm, Swab, Tartar, Tearaway, Ted, Textured, Uncut, Violent, Yahoo

▷**Roughly** may indicate an anagram

Round(ness) About, Ammo, Ball, Beat, Bout, Cartridge, Catch, Circle, Complete, Cycle, Dome, Doorstep, Figure, Full, Global, Hand, Jump-off, Lap, Leg, Milk, O, Oblate, Orb, Patrol, Peri-, Pirouette, Plump, Rev, Ring, Robin, Roly-poly, Rota, Rotund, Route, Routine, Rung, Salvo, Sandwich, Semi-final, Shot, Skirt, Slice, Sphere, Step, Table, Tour, Tubby, U-turn

▷**Round** may indicate a word reversed

Roundabout Ambages, Approximately, Bypass, Carousel, Circuit, Circumambient, Circumbendibus, Circus, Devious, Eddy, ➤ INDIRECT, Peripheral, Rotary, Tortuous, Turntable, Waltzer, Whirligig

Routine Automatic, Drill, Everyday, Grind, Groove, Habitual, Jogtrot, Pattern, Perfunctory, Pipe-clay, Red tape, Rota, Rote, Round, Rut, S(c)htick, Schtik, Treadmill, Workaday

Row(er) Align, Altercation, Arew, Argue, Argument, Bank, Barney, Bedlam, Bow, Cannery, Colonnade, Death, Debate, Din, Dispute, Dust-up, Feud, File, Fireworks, Food, Hullabaloo, Line(-up), Noise, Oar, Paddle, Parade, Pull, Quarrel, Range, Rank, Rew, Rotten, Ruction, Rumpus, Scene, Scull, Series, Set, Shindig, Shindy, Shine, Skid, Spat, Stern, Street, Stroke, Sweep, Terrace, Tier, Tiff, Torpid, Wetbob, Wherryman

Rowdy, Rowdiness Hooligan, Loud, Noisy, Rorty, Rough, Roughhouse, Ruffian, Scourer, Skinhead, Stroppy, Unruly, Uproarious

Royal(ty), Royalist Academy, Angevin, Basilical, Battle, Bourbon, Emigré, Exchange, Fee, Hanoverian, Imperial, Imposing, Inca, Kingly, Majestic, Malignant, Palatine, Payment, Pharaoh, Plantagenet, Prince, Purple, Queenly, Regal, Regis, Regius, Regnal, Sail, Sceptred, Society

Rub(bing), Rubber(y), Rub out Abrade, Buff, Bungie, Bungy, Calk, Caoutchouc, Chafe, Cold, Condom, Corrode, Crepe, Destroy, Ebonite, Efface, Elastic, Embrocate, Emery, Erase, Fawn, Foam, Fray, Fret, Friction, Frottage, Grate, Graze, Grind, Gutta-percha, India, Irritate, Latex, Masseur, Obstacle,

Polish, Safe, Sandpaper, Scour, Scrub, Scuff, Seringa, Sorbo®, Towel, Trace, Ule, Wipe

▷**Rubbed** may indicate an anagram

Rubbish Bull, Bunkum, Clap-trap, Debris, Dre(c)k, Drivel, Fiddlesticks, Garbage, Grot, Grunge, Hogwash, Kak, Landfill, Leavings, Mullock, Nonsense, Phooey, Raffle, ➤ REFUSE, Stuff, Tinpot, Tip, Tom(fool), Tosh, Twaddle

Rude Abusive, Barbaric, Bestial, Bumpkin, Callow, Churlish, Coarse, Discourteous, Elemental, Goustrous, Green, Ill-bred, Impolite, Indecorous, Inficete, Ingram, Ingrum, Insolent, Ocker, Offensive, Peasant, Raw, Risque, Rough, Simple, Surly, Unbred, Uncomplimentary, Uncourtly, Unlettered, Unmannered, Vulgar

▷**Ruffle** may indicate an anagram

Rug Afghan, Bearskin, Carpet, Drugget, Ensi, Flokati, Gabbeh, Hearth, Herez, Heriz, Kelim, K(h)ilim, Kirman, Lap robe, Mat, Maud, Numdah, Oriental, Prayer, Runner, Rya, Scatter, Travelling

Ruin(ed), Ruins Annihilate, Blast, Blight, Carcase, Corrupt, Crash, Crock, Damn, Decay, Defeat, Demolish, Despoil, Destroy, Devastate, Disfigure, Dish, Dogs, Doom, Downcome, Downfall, End, Fordo, Hamstring, Heap, Hell, Insolvent, Inure, Kaput(t), Kibosh, Loss, Mar, Overthrow, Petra, Pot, Puckerood, Ravage, Reck, Relic, Scotch, Scupper, Scuttle, Shatter, Sink, Smash, ➤ SPOIL, Stramash, Subvert, Undo, Unmade, Ur, Violate, Whelm, Woe, Wrack

▷**Ruined** may indicate an anagram

Rule(r), Rules, Ruling Align, Atabeg, Autocrat, Ban, Bey, Britannia, Bylaw, Caesar, Caliph, Canon, Club-law, Code, Condominium, Control, Criterion, Czar, Decree, Despot, Dictator, Doge, Domineer, Dominion, Duce, Dynast, Elector, Emir, Emperor, Empire, Etiquette, Fatwa, Feint, Fetwa, Formation, Formula, Fuhrer, Gerent, Golden, Govern, Ground, Herod, Hierarch, Home, Jackboot, K, Kaiser, Khan, Khedive, King, Law, Lex, Liner, Majority, Maxim, Mede, Method, Mikado, Mir, Mistress, Mogul, Monarchy, Motto, Mpret, Nawab, Negus, Nizam, Norm(a), Oligarchy, Ordinal, Parallel, Pharaoh, Plutocracy, Plumb, Potentate, Precedent, Precept, Prevail, Prince, Principle, Queen, Queensberry, R, Raj(ah), Realm, Rector, Regal, Regent, Reign, Rex, Ring, Rubric, Saladin, Satrap, Shah, Sheik, Sherif, Shogun, Sirdar, Slide, Sophi, Sovereign,

Squire, Standard, Statute, Sultan, Suzerain, Swaraj, Sway, Three, Thumb, Toparch, Tsar, T-square, Tyrant, Wield

Rumble, Rumbling Borborygmus, Brool, Curmurring, Drum-roll, Groan, Growl, Guess, Lumber, Mutter, Rumour, Thunder, Tonneau, Twig

Rumour Breeze, Bruit, Buzz, Canard, Cry, Fame, Furphy, ➤ GOSSIP, Grapevine, Hearsay, Kite, Noise, On-dit, Pig's-whisper, Report, Repute, Say-so, Smear, Talk, Underbreath, Unfounded, Vine, Voice, Whisper, Word

Run(ning), Run away, Run into, Runny, Runs Admin(ister), Arpeggio, Bleed, Bolt, Break, Bunk, Bye, Career, Chase, Coop, Corso, Course, Cresta, Current, Cursive, Cut, Dash, Decamp, Direct, Double, Drive, Escape, Extra, Fartlek, Flee, Flit, Flow, Fly, Follow, Gad, Gallop, Gauntlet, Go, Hare, Haste(n), Hennery, Hie, Idle, Jog, Ladder, Lauf, Leg, Lienteric, Lope, Manage, Marathon, Melt, Mizzle, Molt, Neume, Now, On, On-line, Operate, Pace, Pelt, Ply, Pour, Purulent, R, Race, Renne, Rin, Romp, Roulade, Rounder, Ruck, Scapa, Scamper, Scarper, Schuss, Scud, Scutter, Scuttle, See, Sequence, Shoot, Single, Skate, Skedaddle, Ski, Skid, Skitter, Slalom, Slide, Smuggle, Spew, Split, Spread, Sprint, Sprue, Squitters, Stampede, Straight, Streak, Stream, Taxi, Tear, Tenor, Trickle, Trill, Trot

Runner(s) Atalanta, Bean, Blade, Bow Street, Carpet, Coe, Courser, Deserter, Emu, Field, Geat, Gentleman, Harrier, Internuncio, Leg bye, Legman, Messenger, Miler, Milk, Owler, ➤ RUN(NING), Scarlet, Series, Slipe, Smuggler, Stolon, Stream, Trial

▷ **Running, Runny** may indicate an anagram

Rural Agrarian, Agrestic, Boo(h)ai, Bucolic, Boondocks, Country, Forane, Georgic, Mofussil, Platteland, Praedial, Predial, Redneck, Rustic, Sticks, The Shires, Wops-wops

Rush(ed) Accelerate, Barge, Bolt, Bustle, Career, Charge, Dart, Dash, Expedite, Feese, Fly, Gold, Hare, Hasten, High-tail, ➤ HURRY, Hurtle, Jet, Lance, Leap, Onset, Pellmell, Phase, Plunge, Precipitate, Railroad, Rampa(u)ge, Rash, Reed, Rip, Scamp(er), Scour, Scud, Scurry, Sedge, Spate, Speed, Stampede, Star(r), Streak, Streek, Surge, Swoop, Swoosh, Tear, Thrash, Thresh, Tilt, Torrent, Tule, Zap, Zoom

Russia(n), Russian headman, Russian villagers
Apparatchik, Ataman, Belorussian, Beria, Bolshevik, Boris, Boyar, Byelorussian, Circassian, Cossack, D(o)ukhobor, Dressing, Esth, Igor, Ivan, Kabardian, Kalmuk, Kalmyck, Leather, Lett, Mari, Menshevik, Minimalist, Mir, Muscovy, Octobrist, Osset(e), Red, Romanov, Rus, Russ(niak), Russki, Ruthene, Salad, Serge, Slav, Stakhanovite, SU, Thistle, Udmurt, Uzbeg, Uzbek, Vladimir, Vogul, Yuri, Zyrian

Rust(y) Aeci(di)um, Brown, Corrode, Cor(ro)sive, Erode, Etch, Ferrugo, Iron-stick, Maderise, Oxidise, Rubiginous, Soare, Stem, Teleutospore, Telium, Uredine, Uredo, Verdigris

Rustic Arcady, Bacon, Bor(r)el(l), Bucolic, Bumpkin, Chawbacon, Churl, Clodhopper, Clown, Corydon, Damon, Doric, Forest, Georgic, Hayseed, Hick, Hillbilly, Hind, Hob, Hobbinoll, Hodge, Homespun, Idyl(l), Pastorale, Peasant, Pr(a)edial, Put(t), Rube, Rural, Strephon, Swain, Villager, Villatic, Yokel

▷**Rustic** may indicate an anagram

Rustle(r), Rustling Abactor, Crinkle, Duff, Fissle, Frou-frou, Gully-raker, Poach, Speagh(ery), Sprechery, Steal, Stir, Susurration, Swish, Thief, Whig

Rut Channel, Furrow, Groove, Heat, Routine, Track

Ruthless Brutal, Cruel, Fell, Hard, Hardball

Ss

S Ogee, Saint, Second, Sierra, Society, South, Square

SA It, Lure

Sabotage, Saboteur Destroy, Frame-breaker, Ratten, Spoil, Wrecker

Sack(cloth), Sacking Bag, Bed, Boot, Bounce, Budget, Burlap, Can, Cashier, Chasse, Congé, Congee, Dash, Depredate, Despoil, Discharge, Doss, Fire, Gunny, Havoc, Jute, Knap, Loot, Mailbag, Maraud, Mitten, Pillage, Plunder, Poke, Push, Rapine, Reave, Road, Rob, Sanbenito, Sherris, Sherry, Spoliate, Vandalise

▷**Sacks** may indicate an anagram

Sacrifice Forego, Gambit, Immolate, Lay down, Oblation,
➤ OFFERING, Relinquish, Suttee

Sad(den), Sadly, Sadness Alas, Attrist, Blue, Con dolore,
Dejected, Desolate, Disconsolate, Dismal, Doleful, Dolour,
Downcast, Drear, Dull, Dumpy, Heartache, Lovelorn, Low,
Lugubrious, Mesto, Oh, Plangent, Sorry, Tabanca, Tear-jerker,
Threnody, Tragic, Triste, Tristesse, Unhappy, Wan,
Wo(e)begone

Saddle (bag, girth, pad) Alforja, Aparejo, Arson, Burden,
Cantle, Cinch, Col, Crupper, Demipique, Lumber, Numnah,
Oppress, Pack, Panel, Pigskin, Pilch, Pillion, Seat, Sell(e),
Shabrack, Side, Stock, Tree, Western

▷**Sadly** may indicate an anagram

Safe(ty) Copper-bottomed, Harmless, Impunity, Inviolate,
Night, Peter, Reliable, Roadworthy, Sanctuary, Secure, Sound,
Strong-box, Strongroom, Sure, Worthy

Safeguard Bulwark, Caution, Ensure, Fail-safe, Frithborh, Fuse,
Hedge, Palladium, Protection, Register, Ward

Saga Aga, Chronicle, Edda, Epic, Icelandic, Legend

▷**Said** may indicate 'sounding like'

Sail(s) Bunt, Canvas, Coast, Cloth, Course, Cruise, Fan,
Gaff(-topsail), Genoa, Head, Jib, Jut, Lateen, Leech, Luff, Lug,
Moonraker, Muslin, Navigate, Peak, Ply, Rag, Reef, Rig, Ring-tail,
Royal, Sheet, Spanker, Spencer, Spinnaker, Spritsail, Square,
Staysail, Steer, Studding, Top(-gallant), Yard

Sailor(s) AB, Admiral, Argonaut, Blue-jacket, Boatman,
Boatswain, Bosun, Budd, Commodore, Crew, Deckhand, Drake,
Evans, Gob, Hat, Hearties, Helmsman, Hornblower, Jack, Jaunty,
Lascar, Leadsman, Limey, Lt, Lubber, Mariner, Matelot,
Matlo(w), Middy, MN, Nelson, Noah, Oceaner, OS, Popeye,
Privateer, Rating, RN, Salt, Seabee, Sea-dog, Sea-lord,
➤ SEAMAN, Serang, Sin(d)bad, Submariner, Tar

Saint(ly), Saints Canonise, Canonize, Hagiology, Hallowed,
Latterday, Patron, Pillar, Plaster, Ride, Rishi, Rule, S, SS, St,
Templar

Sake Account, Behalf, Cause, Drink

Salad Caesar, Chef's, Cos, Cress, Cucumber, Days, Endive,
Fennel, Finoc(c)hio, Frisée, Fruit, Greek, Guacamole, Lettuce,

Lovage, Mixture, Niçoise, Purslane, Radicchio, Radish, Rampion, Rocket, Russian, Slaw, Tabbouli, Tomato, Waldorf

▷ **Salad** may indicate an anagram

Salary Emolument, Fee, Hire, Pay, Prebend, Screw, Stipend, ➤ WAGE

➤ **Sale(s)** Auction, Cant, Clearance, Fire, Garage, Market, Outroop, Outrope, Raffle, Retail, Roup, Subhastation, Turnover, Venal, Vendue, Vent, White, Wholesale

Salmon Atlantic, Chinook, Chum, Cock, Coho(e), Grav(ad)lax, Grilse, Kelt, Keta, Par(r), Pink, Redfish, Rock, Smelt, Smolt, Smowt, Sockeye

Salt(s), Salty Attic, Bath, Brackish, Brine, Complex, Cure(d), Deer lick, Double, Enos, Epsom, Halo-, Health, Lake-basin, Liver, Matelot, Piquancy, Powder, Rating, Sailor, Salify, Saut, Sea-dog, Seafarer, Seasoned, Smelling, Water-dog, Wit(ty)

Salutation, Salute Address, Ave, Banzai, Barcoo, Bid, Cap, Cheer, Command, Coupé(e), Curtsey, Embrace, Feu de joie, Fly-past, Genuflect, Greet, Hail, Hallo, Halse, Homage, Honour, Jambo, Kiss, Present, Salaam, Salvo, Sieg Heil, Toast, Tribute, Wassail

Salvage Dredge, Lagan, Ligan, Reclaim, Recover, Recycle, Rescue, Retrieve, Tot

Salve Anele, Anoint, Assuage, Ave, Lanolin(e), Lotion, Ointment, Remedy, Saw, Tolu, Unguent

Same(ness) Ae, Agnatic, Contemporaneous, Do, Egal, Equal, Ib(id), Ibidem, Id, Idem, Identical, Identity, Ilk, Iq, Like, One, Thick(y), Thilk, Uniform, Ylke

Sample Biopsy, Blad, Browse, Example, Foretaste, Handout, Muster, Pattern, Pree, Prospect, Quadrat, Scantling, Specimen, Swatch, Switch, ➤ TASTE, Transect, Try

▷ **Sam Weller** may indicate the use of 'v' for 'w' or vice versa

Sanction Allow, Appro, Approbate, Approof, Approve, Authorise, Bar, Countenance, Endorse, Imprimatur, Mandate, OK, Pass, Pragmatic, Ratify, Sustain

Sanctuary, Sanctum Adytum, Asylum, By-room, Cella, Ch, Church, Frithsoken, Frithstool, Girth, Grith, Holy, Lair, Naos, Oracle, Penetralia, Preserve, Refuge, Sacellum, Sacrarium, ➤ SHELTER, Shrine, Temple

Sandwich Bruschetta, Butty, Club, Croque-monsieur, Cuban, Doorstep, Earl, Hamburger, Island, Open, Roti, Round, Sarney, Sarnie, Smorbrod, Smorgasbord, Smorrebrod, Sub, Submarine, Thumber, Toastie, Triple-decker, Victoria

▷**Sandwich(es)** may indicate a hidden word

Sane, Sanity Compos mentis, Formal, Healthy, Judgement, Rational, Reason, Sensible, Wice

Sanguine Confident, Hopeful, Optimistic, Roseate, Ruddy

Sap Benzoin, Bleed, Cremor, Drain, Enervate, Entrench, Ichor, Juice, Laser, Latex, Lymph, Mine, Mug, Pulque, Ratten, Resin, Roset, Rosin, Rozet, Rozit, Secretion, Soma, Sura, Swot, Undermine, Weaken

Sarcasm, Sarcastic Biting, Cutting, Cynical, Derision, Irony, Mordacious, Mordant, Pungent, Quip, Sarky, Satire, Sharp, Snide, Sting, Wisecrack

Sardonic Cutting, Cynical, Ironical, Scornful

Sash Baldric(k), Band, Belt, Burdash, Cummerbund, Obi, Scarf, Window

Satan Adversary, Apollyon, Arch-enemy, Cram, ➤ DEVIL, Eblis, Lucifer, Shaitan

Satellite Attendant, Communications, Comsat®, Disciple, Early bird, Echo, Explorer, Follower, Geostationary, Henchman, Intelsat, Moon, Mouse, Orbiter, Sputnik, Syncom, Telstar

▶**Satin** see SILK

Satisfaction, Satisfactory, Satisfy(ing) Agree, Ah, Ap(p)ay, Appease, Atone, Change, Compensation, Complacent, ➤ CONTENT, Defrayment, Enough, Feed, Fill, Fulfil, Glut, Gratify, Indulge, Jake, Liking, Meet, OK, Pacation, Palatable, Pay, Please, Propitiate, Qualify, Redress, Repay, Replete, Sate, Satiate, Serve, Settlement, Slake, Square, Suffice, Well

Saturate(d) Drench, Glut, Imbue, Impregnate, Infuse, Permeate, ➤ SOAK, Sodden, Steep, Waterlog

Sauce, Saucy Arch, Baggage, Catchup, Catsup, Cheek, Condiment, Dapper, Dip, Dressing, Gall, Gravy, Impudence, Ketchup, Lip, Malapert, Nerve, Peart, Pert, Relish, Sal, Sass, Sue, Tossy

Sausage(s) Andouillette, Banger, Black pudding, Boerewors, Bologna, Bratwurst, Cervelat, Cheerio, Chipolata, Chorizo,

Cumberland, Devon, Drisheen, Frankfurter, Knackwurst, Knockwurst, Liver(wurst), Mortadella, Pep(p)eroni, Polony, Salami, Sav(eloy), Snag(s), String, White pudding, Wiener(wurst), Wienie, Wurst, Zampone

Savage Barbarian, Boor, Brute, Cruel, Fierce, Grim, Immane, Inhuman, Maul, Sadistic, Truculent, Vitriolic, Wild

Save, Saving(s) Bank, Bar, Besides, But, Capital, Conserve, Deposit, Economy, Except, Hain, Hoard, Husband, ISA, Layby, Keep, Nest egg, Nirlie, Nirly, PEPS, Preserve, Put by, Reclaim, Redeem, Relieve, Reprieve, ► RESCUE, Reskew, Sa', Salt, Salvage, Scrape, Scrimp, Shortcut, Slate club, Spare, Stokvel, Succour, TESSA, Unless

Saw Adage, Aphorism, Apothegm, Back, Band, Beheld, Bucksaw, Buzz, Chain, Circular, Cliché, Compass, Coping, Cross-cut, Crown, Cut, Dictum, Dovetail, Frame, Fret, Gang, Gnome, Grooving, Hack, Jig, Keyhole, Legend, Maxim, Met, Motto, Panel, Paroemia, Pitsaw, Priority, Ribbon, Rip, Sash, Saying, Scroll, Serra, Slogan, Spied, Stadda, Sweep, Tenon, Trepan, Trephine, Whip, Witnessed

Say(ing) Adage, Agrapha, Aphorism, Apophthegm, Apostrophise, Articulate, Axiom, Beatitude, Bromide, Byword, Cant, Catchphrase, Cliché, Declare, Dict(um), Eg, Enunciate, Epigram, Express, Fadaise, Gnome, Impute, Logia, Logion, ► MAXIM, Mean, Mot, Mouth, Observe, Predicate, Pronounce, Proverb, Put, Quip, Recite, Rede, Relate, Remark, Report, Saine, Saw, Sc, Sententia, ► SPEAK, Suppose, Utter, Voice, Word

▷ **Say** may indicate a word sounding like another

Scale, Scaly Ascend, Balance, Beaufort, Brix, Bud, Burnham, Celsius, Centigrade, Chromatic, ► CLIMB, Diatonic, Escalade, Fahrenheit, Flake, Gamme, Gamut, Gauge, Kelvin, Ladder, Lamina, Layer, Leaf, Lepid, Libra, Ligule, Major, Mercalli, Minor, Mohs, Natural, Nominal, Ordinal, Palet, Peel, Pentatonic, Plate, Platform, ► RANGE, Rankine, Réaumur, Regulo, Richter, Scan, Scurf, Shin, Sliding, Submediant, Tegula, Tonal, Tron(e), Vernier

Scan(ning), Scanner CAT, CT, Examine, Helical, OCR, Peruse, PET, Rake, Raster, Scrutinise, SEM, SPET, Survey, Tomography, Ultrasound, Vet

Scandal(ous), Scandalise Belie, Canard, Commesse, Disgrace, Gamy, Hearsay, Muck-raking, Opprobrium, Outrage, Shame, Slander, Stigma, Watergate

Scant(y) Bare, Brief, Exiguous, Ihram, Jejune, Jimp, Poor, Scrimpy, Short, Shy, Slender, Spare, Sparse, Stingy

Scapegoat Butt, Fall-guy, Hazazel, Joe Soap, Patsy, Stooge, Target, Victim, Whipping-boy

Scarce(ly), Scarcity Barely, Dear, Dearth, Famine, Few, Hardly, Ill, Lack, Rare, Scanty, Seldom, Short, Strap, Uncommon, Want

Scarecrow Bogle, Bugaboo, Dudder, Dudsman, Gallibagger, Gallibeggar, Gallicrow, Gallybagger, Gallybeggar, Gallycrow, Malkin, Mawkin, Potato-bogle, Ragman, S(h)ewel, Tattie-bogle

Scarf Babushka, Belcher, Cataract, Comforter, Cravat, Curch, Doek, Dupatta, Fichu, Hai(c)k, Haique, Hyke, Lambrequin, Madras, Mantilla, Muffettee, Muffler, Neckatee, Nightingale, Orarium, Pagri, Palatine, Rail, Rebozo, Sash, Screen, Stole, Tallith, Tippet, Trot-cosy, Trot-cozy, Vexillum

Scatter(ed), Scattering Bestrew, Broadcast, Diaspora, Disject, Dispel, ➤ DISPERSE, Dissipate, Flurr, Litter, Rout, Scail, Skail, Sow, Sparge, Splutter, Sporadic, Spread, Sprinkle, Squander, Straw, Strew

Scavenge(r) Dieb, Forage, Hunt, Hy(a)ena, Jackal, Rake, Ratton, Rotten, Scaffie, Sweeper, Totter

Scene(ry) Arena, Boscage, Coulisse, Decor, Flat(s), Landscape, Locale, Prop, Prospect, Set, Sight, Site, Sketch, Stage, Tableau, Tormenter, Tormentor, Venue, View

Scent Aroma, Attar, Chypre, Cologne, Essence, Fragrance, Frangipani, Fumet(te), Gale, Moschatel, Nose, Odour, Orris, Ottar, Otto, Perfume, Sachet, Smell, Spoor, Vent, Waft, Wind

Sceptic(al) Cynic, Doubter, Incredulous, Infidel, Jaundiced, Nihilistic, Pyrrho(nic), Sadducee

Schedule Agenda, Calendar, Itinerary, Prioritise, Programme, Register, Slot, Table, Timetable

Scheme(r), Scheming Concoct, Conspire, Crafty, Cunning, Dare, Darien, Dart, Decoct, Devisal, Diagram, Dodge, Draft, Gin, Honeytrap, Intrigue, Jezebel, Machiavellian, Machinate, Manoeuvre, Nostrum, ➤ PLAN, Plat, Plot, Project, Purpose, Racket, Ruse, Stratagem, System, Table, Wangle, Wheeze

Scholar Abelard, Academic, Alumni, BA, Bookman, Clergy, Clerk, Commoner, Demy, Disciple, Erasmus, Erudite, Etonian, Exhibitioner, Extern(e), Graduate, Literate, MA, Pauline,

Plutarch, Polymath, Pupil, Rhodes, Sap, Savant, Schoolboy, Soph, ➤ STUDENT, Tom Brown

School Academy, Approved, Boarding, Charm, Choir, Church, Classical, Composite, Comprehensive, Conservative, Conservatoire, Conservatory, Correspondence, Crammer, Cult, Day, Direct grant, Drama, Drill, Driving, Educate, Elementary, Exercise, Finishing, Gam, Grade, Grammar, Grant-aided, Grant-maintained, Group, Gymnasium, Hedge, High, Historical, Honour, Hospital, Hostel, Independent, Infant, Institute, Integrated, Intermediate, Junior, Kindergarten, Lower, Maintained, Middle, Night, Normal, Nursery, Parochial, Pensionnat, Pod, Poly, Prep, Preparatory, Primary, Public, RADA, Reformatory, Residential, Rossall, Rydal, Satanic, Secondary(-modern), Sect, Seminary, Special, State, Style, Summer, Sunday, Teach, Trade, ➤ TRAIN, Tutor, Upper, Whales

Science Anatomy, Anthropology, Art, Atmology, Axiology, Biology, Botany, Chemistry, Dismal, Eth(n)ology, Exact, Geology, Life, Noble, Nomology, Ology, Optics, Pedagogy, Physics, Rocket, Skill, Social, Soil, Sonics, Stinks, Tactics, Technics, Technology

Scoff Belittle, Boo, Chaff, Deride, Dor, Eat, Flout, Food, Gall, Gibe, Gird, Gobble, ➤ JEER, Mock, Rail, Rib, Ridicule, Scaff, Scorn, Sneer, Taunt

Scold(ing) Admonish, Berate, Callet, Catamaran, Chastise, Chide, Clapperclaw, Do, Earful, Flite, Flyte, Fuss, Jaw(bation), Jobation, Lecture, Nag, Objurgate, Philippic, Rant, Rate, ➤ REBUKE, Reprimand, Reprove, Revile, Rouse on, Row, Sas(s)arara, Sis(s)erary, Slang, Slate, Termagant, Tick-off, Tongue-lash, Upbraid, Virago, Wig, Xant(h)ippe, Yaff, Yankie, Yap

Scope Ambit, Diapason, Domain, Elbow-room, Extent, Freedom, Gamut, Ken, Latitude, Leeway, Purview, Range, Remit, Room, Rope, Scouth, Scowth, Size, Sphere

Scorch(er) Adust, Blister, Brasero, ➤ BURN, Char, Destroy, Frizzle, Fry, Parch, Souther, Scowder, Scowther, Sear, Singe, Soar, Speed, Swale, Swayl, Sweal, Sweel, Torrefy, Torrid, Wither

Score Apgar, Bill, Birdie, Bye, Capot, Chase, Conversion, Count, Crena, Debt, Eagle, Etch, Groove, Hail, Honours, Ingroove, Ippon, Law, Make, Music, Net, Notation, Notch, Partitur(a), Peg, Pique, Point, Record, Repique, Rit(t), Rouge, Run, Rut,

Scotch, Scratch, Scribe, Scrive, Set, Single, Spare, Stria, String, Sum, Tablature, ➤ TALLY, Twenty, Vocal, Waza-ari, Win

▷**Scoring** may indicate an anagram

Scorn(ful) Arrogant, Bah, Contempt, Contumely, Deride, Despise, Dis(s), Disdain, Dislike, Flout, Geck, Haughty, Insult, Meprise, Mock, Opprobrium, Putdown, Rebuff, Ridicule, Sarcastic, Sardonic, Sarky, Scoff, Scout, Sdaine, Sdeigne, Sneer, Spurn, Wither

Scotland Alban(y), Albion, Caledonia, Lallans, Lothian, NB, Norland, Scotia

Scoundrel Cur, Knave, Reprobate, Scab, Smaik, Varlet, ➤ VILLAIN

▷**Scour** may indicate an anagram

Scout Akela, Beaver, Bedmaker, Colony, Disdain, Explorer, Flout, Guide, Outrider, Pathfinder, Pickeer, Pioneer, Reconnoitre, Rover, Runner, Scoff, Scorn, Scourer, Scurrier, Sixer, Talent, Tenderfoot, Tonto, Venture

Scrap(s), Scrappy Abandon, Abrogate, ➤ BIT, Cancel, Conflict, Discard, Dump, ➤ FIGHT, Fisticuffs, Fragment, Fray, Iota, Jot, Mélée, Mellay, Morceau, Morsel, Odd, Off-cut, Ort, Ounce, Patch, Piece, Pig's-wash, Rag, Rase, Raze, Remnant, Scarmoge, Scissel, Scissil, Scrub, Set-to, Shard, Sherd, Shred, Skerrick, Skirmish, Snap, Snippet, Spall, Tait, Tate, Tatter, Titbit, Trash, Truculent, Whit

Scrape(r) Abrade, Agar, Bark, Clat, Claw, Comb, Curette, D and C, Escapade, Grate, Graze, Harl, Hoe, Hole, Jar, Kowtow, Lesion, Lute, Predicament, Racloir, Rake, Rasorial, Rasp, Rasure, Raze, Razure, Saw, Scalp, Scart, Scrat(ch), Scroop, Scuff, Shave, Skimp, Skive, Squeegee, Strake, Strigil, Xyster

▷**Scratch(ed)** may indicate an anagram

Scream(er) Bellow, Cariama, Caterwaul, Comedian, Comic, Cry, Eek, Headline, Hern, Kamichi, Laugh, Priceless, Primal, Riot, Scare-line, Screech, Seriema, Shriek, Skirl, Squall, Sutch, Yell

Screen Arras, Backstop, Blind(age), Camouflage, Chancel, Check, Chick, Cinerama®, Cloth, Cornea, Cover, Curtain, Dodger, Eyelid, Fire, Glib, Grille, Hallan, Hide, Hoard, Hoarding, Lattice, Mantelet, Mask, Nonny, Obscure, Organ, Parclose, Partition, Pella, Purdah, Radar, Riddle, Road, Sconce, Scope, ➤ SHADE, Shelter, Shield, Show, Sift, Silver, Small, Smoke, Split,

Sunblock, Televise, Touch, Traverse, Umbrella, VDU, Vet, Windbreak, Windshield

Screw Adam, Allen, Archimedes, Butterfly, Coach, Countersunk, Dungeoner, Extort, Grub, Interrupted, Jailer, Jailor, Lag, Lead, Levelling, Machine, Miser, Monkey-wrench, Niggard, Phillips®, Prop(ellor), Salary, Skinflint, Spiral, Thumb(i)kins, Twist, Vice, Worm

Script Book, Gurmukhi, Hand, Hiragana, Italic, Jawi, Kana, Libretto, Linear A, Linear B, Lines, Lombardic, Miniscule, Nagari, Nastalik, Nastaliq, Ogam, Ronde, Scenario, Screenplay, Writing

Scripture(s), Scriptural version Adi Granth, Agadah, Antilegomena, Avesta, Bible, Gemara, Gematria, Gospel, Granth (Sahib), Guru Granth, Haggada(h), Hermeneutics, Hexapla, Holy book, Holy writ, Koran, K'thibh, Lesson, Lotus Sutra, Mishna(h), OT, Rig-veda, Smriti, Tantra, Targum, Testament, Upanishad, Veda, Vedic, Verse, Vulgate

Scrounge(r) Blag, Bludge(r), Borrow, Bot, Cadge, Forage, Freeload, Layabout, Ligger, Scunge, Sponge

Scrub(ber) Cancel, Chaparral, Cleanse, Dele(te), Gar(r)igue, Loofa(h), Luffa, Masseur, Negate, Pro, Rub, Scour, Tart

▷ **Scrub** may indicate 'delete'

Scrutinise, Scrutiny Check, Docimasy, Examine, Observe, Peruse, Pore, Pry, ➤ SCAN, Study

▷ **Scuffle** may indicate an anagram

Sculpt(ure) Bas-relief, Bronze, Carve, Della-robbia, Figure, Kouros, Mobile, Nude, Pieta, Relievo, Shape, ➤ STATUARY, Topiary

Scum Dregs, Dross, Epistasis, Scorious, Slag, Slime, Spume, Sullage

Scurf, Scurvy Dander, Dandriff, Dandruff, Furfur, Horson, Lepidote, Leprose, Scabrous, Scall, Scorbutic, Whoreson, Yaws, Yaw(e)y

Sea(s) Benthos, Billow, Blue, Brine, Briny, Ditch, Drink, Head, Herring-pond, High, Inland, Main, Mare, ➤ OCEAN, Offing, Offshore, Oggin, Pelagic, Quantity, Seven, Strand, Thalassic, Tide, Water, Zee

Seaman, Seamen AB, Crew, Jack, Lascar, Lubber, Mariner, OD, Ordinary, PO, RN, ➤ SAILOR, Salt, Swabby, Tar

Sear Brand, Burn, Catch, Cauterise, Frizzle, Parch, Scath(e), Scorch, Singe, Wither

Search(ing) Beat, Comb, Dragnet, Examine, Ferret, ➤ FORAGE, Fossick, Frisk, Grope, Home, Hunt, Indagate, Inquire, Jerk, Jerque, Kemb, Manhunt, Perscrutation, Probe, Proll, Prospect, Proul, Prowl, Quest, Rake, Rancel, Ransack, Ransel, Ranzel, Ravel, Ripe, Root, Rootle, Rummage, Scan, Scour, Scur, Sker, Skirr, Snoop, Strip, Thumb, Trace, Zotetic

Season(able), Seasonal, Seasoned, Seasoning Accustom, Age, Aggrace, Autumn, Betimes, Christmas, Close, Condiment, Devil, Dress, Duxelles, Easter, Enure, Etesian, Fall, Fennel, Festive, Flavour, G(h)omasco, Garlic, Growing, Hiems, High, In, Inure, Lent, Marjoram, Master, Mature, Nutmeg, Open, Paprika, Pepper, Powellise, Practised, Ripen, Salt, Sar, Seal, Seel, Sele, Silly, Solstice, Spice, Spring, Summer(y), Tahini, Ticket, Tide, Time, Whit, Winter

Sea-weed Agar, Alga(e), Badderlock, Bladderwort, Fucus, Kelp, Laver, Nori, Nullipore, Oarweed, Ore, Sargasso, Tang, Vraic, Wrack

Seclude, Seclusion Cloister, Incommunicado, Isolate, Maroon, Nook, Privacy, Purdah, Retreat, Secret, Sequester, Solitude

Second(ary), Seconds Abet, Alternative, Another (guess), Appurtenance, Assist, Back(er), Beta, Coming, Comprimario, Deuteragonist, Flash, Friend, Imperfect, Indirect, Inferior, Instant, Jiffy, Latter, Lesser, Minor, Mo(ment), Nature, Other, Pig's-whisper, Runner-up, Sec, Shake, Share, Side(r), Sight, Silver, Split, Subsidiary, Support, Tick, Trice, Twinkling, Wind

Second-hand Hearsay, Reach-me-down, Used

Secrecy, Secret(s), Secretive Apocrypha, Arcana, Arcane, Backstairs, Cabbalistic, Cagey, Clam, Clandestine, Closet, Code, Covert, Cryptic, Dark, Deep, Devious, Esoteric, Hidden, Hole and corner, Hush-hush, Inly, Inmost, Latent, Mysterious, Mystical, Mystique, Oyster, ➤ PRIVATE, Privy, QT, Rune, Shelta, Silent, Sly, State, Stealth, Sub rosa, Trade, Unbeknown, Undercover, Underhand, Unknown, Unre(a)d, Unrevealed, Untold

Secretary Aide, Amanuensis, Chancellor, Chronicler, CIS, Desk, Desse, Famulus, Minuteman, Moonshee, Munshi, Notary, Permanent, Scrive, Social, Stenotyper, Temp

Section, Sector Caesarian, Chapter, Classify, Conic, Cross, Cut, Division, Ellipse, Eyalet, Gan, Hyperbola, Lith, Metamere, Mortice, Movement, Octant, Outlier, Passus, ➤ PIECE, Platoon, Private, Public, Segment, Severy, Slice, Stage, Ungula, Unit, Zone

Secure, Security Anchor, Assurance, Bag, Bail, Band, Bar, Batten, Belay, Bolt, Bond, Calm, Catch, Cement, Chain, Cinch, Clamp, Clasp, Clench, Clinch, Close, Cocoon, Collateral, Consols, Debenture, Engage, Ensure, Equity, Establishment, Fasten, Fastness, Fortify, Gilt, Guarantee, Guy, Immune, Indemnity, Invest(ment), Knot, Lace, Land, Lash, Latch, Lien, Lock, Longs, Mortgage, Nail, National, Obtain, Patte, Pin, Pledge, Pot, Pre-empt, Preference, Protect, Quad, Rope, Rug, ➤ SAFE, Safety, Settle, Snell, Snug, Sound, Stable, Staple, Stock, Strap, Sure(ty), Tack, Take, Tie, Tight, Trap, Warrant, Watertight, Wedge, Win

Sedative Amytal®, Anodyne, Aspirin, Barbitone, Bromide, Chloral, Depressant, Hypnic, Lenitive, Lupulin, Meprobamate, Metopryl, Miltown, Narcotic, Nembutal®, Opiate, Paraldehyde, Pethidine, Phenobarbitone, Premed(ication), Scopolamine, Seconal®, Soothing, Thridace, Veronal

Sediment Alluvium, Chalk, Deposit, Dregs, F(a)eces, Fecula, Foots, Grounds, Lees, Molasse, Placer, Residue, Salt, Sapropel, Silt, Sludge, Terrigenous, Till, Varve, Warp

Seduce(r), Seductive Bewitch, Debauch, Dishonour, Honeyed, Honied, Jape, Lothario, Luring, Mislead, Siren, Tempt

▷ **Seduce** may indicate one word inside another

See(ing) Behold, Bishopric, Consider, Descry, Diocesan, Discern, Episcopal, Eye, Glimpse, Holy, Lo, Notice, Observe, Papal, Perceive, Realise, Spot, Spy, Twig, Understand, Vatican, Vid(e), View, Vision, Voila, Witness

Seed(s), Seedy Achene, Argan, Arilli, Arillode, Ash-key, Bean, Ben, Bere, Bonduc, Cacoon, Caraway, Carvy, Cebadilla, Cevadilla, Chickpea, Coriander, Corn, Cum(m)in, Dragon's teeth, Embryo, Endosperm, Ergot, Favourite, Germ, Grain, Gritty, Issue, Ivory-nut, Kernel, Lomentum, Mangy, Miliary, Nucellous, Nut, Offspring, Ovule, Pea, Pinon, Pip, Poorly, Poppy, Sabadilla, Scuzz, Semen, Seminal, Sesame, Shabby, Silique, Sorus, Sow, Sperm, Spore, Zoosperm

Seek(er) Ask, Beg, Busk, Chase, Court, Endeavour, Pursue, Quest, Scur, Search, Skirr, Solicit, Suitor

Seem(ingly) Appear, Look, Ostensible, Purport, Quasi, Think

Seemly Comely, Decent, Decorous, Fit, Suitable

Seer Eye, Nahum, Observer, Onlooker, Prescience, Prophet, Sage, Sibyl, Soothsayer, Witness, Zoroaster

Segment Antimere, Arthromere, Cut, Division, Gironny, Gyronny, Intron, Lacinate, Lobe, Merome, Merosome, Metamere, Pig, Prothorax, Scliff, Share, Shie, Skliff, Somite, Split, Sternite, Syllable, Tagma, Telson, Urite, Uromere

Segregate, Segregation Apartheid, Exile, Insulate, Intern, ➤ ISOLATE, Jim Crow, Seclude, Separate

Seize, Seizure Angary, Apprehend, Areach, Arrest, Attach(ment), Bag, Bone, Capture, Claw, Cleek, Cly, Collar, Commandeer, Confiscate, Distrain, Distress, For(e)hent, ➤ GRAB, Grip, Hend, Impound, Impress, Maverick, Na(a)m, Nab, Nap, Nim, Poind, Possess, Pot, Raid, Replevy, Rifle, Sequestrate, Smug, Tackle, Wingding

Select(ing), Selection, Selector Assortment, Bla(u)d, Cap, Casting, Choice, Choose, Classy, Cull, Darwinism, Discriminate, Draft, Draw, Eclectic, Edit, Elite, Excerpt, Exclusive, Extract, Favour, Garble, Inside, K, Nap, Natural, Pericope, ➤ PICK, Pot-pourri, Prefer, Recherché, Sample, Seed, Single, Sort, Stream, Tipster, Triage, UCCA

Self Atman, Auto, Character, Ego, Person, Psyche, Seity, Sel, Soul

➤ **Self-defence** see MARTIAL (ARTS)

Self-esteem Amour-propre, Conceit, Confidence, Egoism, Pride

Self-important, Self-indulgent, Self-interested Aristippus, Arrogant, Conceited, Immoderate, Jack-in-office, Licentious, Narcissistic, Pompous, Pragmatic, Profligate, Solipsist, Sybarite

Selfish(ness) Avaricious, Egoist, Greedy, Hedonist, Mean, Solipsism

Self-possession Aplomb, Composure, Cool, Nonchalant

Self-satisfied, Self-satisfaction Complacent, Narcissism, Smug, Tranquil

Sell(er), Selling Apprize, Auction, Barter, Bear, Betray, Catch, Chant, Chaunt, Cope, Dispose, Do, Flog, Go, Hard, Have, Hawk, Hustle, Inertia, Knock down, Market, Menage, Merchant, Peddle, Purvey, Push, Pyramid, Realise, Rep, Retail, Ruse, Simony, Stall-man, Sugging, ➤ TRADE, Vend

Semblance Aspect, Likeness, Sign, Verisimilitude

Senator Antiani, Cicero, Elder, Legislator, Solon

Send, Sent Consign, ➤ DESPATCH, Disperse, Emit, Entrance, Issue, Launch, Order, Post, Rapt, Ship, Transmit, Transport

Send up Chal(l)an, Lampoon, Promote

Senile, Senility Caducity, Dementia, Disoriented, Doddery, Doitit, Dotage, Eild, Eld, Gaga, Nostology, Twichild

Senior Aîné, Doyen, Elder, Father, Grecian, Mayor, Père, Primus, Superior, Upper

Sensation(al) Acolouthite, Anoesis, Aura, Blood, Commotion, Emotion, Empfindung, Feeling, Gas, Lurid, Melodrama, Pyrotechnic, Shock-horror, Shocker, Splash, Stir, Styre, Synaesthesia, Thrill, Tingle, Vibes, Wow, Yellow

Sense, Sensual Acumen, Aura, Carnal, Coherence, Common, Dress, Faculty, Feel, Gross, Gumption, Gustation, Hearing, Horse, Idea, Import, Instinct, Intelligence, Lewd, Meaning, Olfactory, Palate, Rational, Receptor, Rumble-gumption, Rumgumption, Rum(m)el-gumption, Rum(m)le-gumption, Sight, Sixth, Slinky, Smell, Synesis, Taste, Touch, Voluptuary, Voluptuous, Wisdom, Wit

Senseless Absurd, Anosmia, Illogical, Mad, Numb, Stupid, Stupor, Unconscious, Unwise

Sensible Aware, Dianoetic, Prudent, Raisonné, Rational, Sane, Solid, Well-balanced

Sensitive, Sensitivity Alive, Allergic, Delicate, Keen, Passible, Sympathetic, Tactful, Tender, Thin-skinned, Ticklish

Sentence(s) Assize, Bird, Carpet, Clause, Commit, Condemn, Custodial, Death, Decree(t), Deferred, Doom, Fatwah, Indeterminate, Judgement, Life, Matrix, Paragraph, Period(ic), Porridge, Predicate, Rap, Rheme, Rune, Stretch, Suspended, Swy, Tagmene, Verdict, Versicle

Sentiment(al), Sentimentality Byronism, Corn, Cornball, Drip, Feeling, Goo, Govey, Gucky, Gush, Maudlin, Mawkish, Mind, Mush, Opinion, Romantic, Rose-pink, Rosewater,

Saccharin, Schmaltzy, Sloppy, Smoochy, Soppy, Spoony, Tear-jerker, Traveller, Treacly, Twee, View, Weepy, Yucky

Sentry Picket, Sentinel, Vedette, Vidette, Watch

Separate(d), Separation, Separately Abstract, Asunder, Comma, Cull, Cut, Decollate, Decompose, Decouple, Demerge, Detach, Dialyse, Disally, Disconnect, Dissociate, Distance, Distinct, Disunite, Divide, Division, Divorce, Eloi(g)n, Elute, Elutriate, Esloin, Estrange, Filter, Hive, Hyphenate, Insulate, Intervene, Isolate, Laminate, Lease, Legal, Part, Piece, Prescind, Red(d), Scatter, Screen, Sever, Several, Shed, Shore, Shorn, Sift, Sleave, Sle(i)ded, Solitary, Sort, ➤ SPLIT, Stream, Sunder, Sundry, Tems(e), Tmesis, Try, Twin(e), Unclasp, Winnow, Wrench

Sepulchral, Sepulchre Bier, Cenotaph, Charnel, Crypt, Funeral, Monument, Pyramid, Tomb, Vault, Whited

Sequence Agoge, Algorithm, Byte, Chronological, Continuity, Continuum, Fibonacci, Intron, Line, Order, Program(me), Run, Seriatim, Series, Succession, Suit, Suite, Train, Vector

Serene, Serenity Calm, Composed, Placid, Repose, Sangfroid, Sedate, Smooth, ➤ TRANQUIL

Serf(dom) Adscript, Bondman, Ceorl, Churl, Helot, Manred, ➤ SLAVE, Thete, Thrall, Vassal, Velle(i)nage

Sergeant Buzfuz, Cuff, Drill, Havildar, Kite, ➤ NCO, Platoon, RSM, Sarge, SL, SM, Staff, Technical, Troy

Series Chain, Concatenation, Continuum, Course, Cycle, Cyclus, Enfilade, En suite, Episode, Gradation, Harmonic, Homologous, Line, Partwork, ➤ PROGRESSION, Rest, Rubber, Run, Sequence, Ser, Sitcom, String, Succession, Suit, Train, World

Serious(ly) Critical, Earnest, Grave, Gravitas, Important, Major, Momentous, Pensive, Sad, Serpentine, Sober, Solemn, Sombre, Staid, Straight(-faced), Very

Sermon Address, Discourse, Gatha, Homily, Lecture, Preachment, Spital

Serpent(ine) Adder, Anguine, Asp, Aspic(k), Basilisk, Boa, Cockatrice, Dipsas, Firedrake, Nagas, Sea-snake, ➤ SNAKE, Traitor, Viper

Serum Antilymphocyte, Antitoxin, ATS, Fluid, Humoral, Opsonin, Senega

Servant, Server Attendant, Ayah, Batman, Bearer, Bedder, Bedmaker, Boots, Butler, Boy, Caddie, Cook, Daily, Domestic, Dromio, Drudge, Employee, Factotum, Flunkey, Footboy, Footman, Friday, G(h)illie, Gip, Gully, Gyp, Handmaid, Helot, Henchman, Hireling, Jack, Lackey, Maid, Major-domo, Man, Man Friday, Menial, Minion, Myrmidon, Obedient, Page, Pantler, Retainer, Retinue, Scout, Scullion, Servitor, Soubrette, Steward, Tiger, Tweeny, Underling, Valet, Varlet, Vassal, Waiter

Serve, Service Ace, Act, Active, Amenity, Answer, Assist, Attendance, Avail, Benediction, Candlemas, Cannonball, China, Civil, Communion, Community, Complin(e), Credo, Devotional, Dinnerset, Duty, Employ, Evensong, Fault, Fee, Feudal, Forward, ➤ FUNCTION, Help, Helpline, Lip, Litany, Liturgy, Mass, Mat(t)ins, Memorial, Minister, Ministry, Missa, National, Nocturn, Nones, Oblige, Office, Oracle, Overhaul, Pass, Pay, Pottery, Prime, Proper, Public, RAF, Requiem, Rite, Sacrament, Secret, Senior, Sext, Shuttle, Silver, Social, Sue, Tableware, Tea, Vespers, Wait, Watch-night, Worship

▷ **Serviceman** may indicate a churchman

Servile, Servility Abasement, Base, Crawling, Knee, Lickspittle, Menial, Obsequious, Slavish, Slimy, Suck-hole, Sycophantic, Truckle

Session(s) Bout, Meeting, Nightshift, Petty, Quarter, Round, Séance, Sederunt, Settle, Sitting, Term

Setback Checkmate, Hiccup, Jolt, Relapse, Retard, Retreat, Reversal, Scarcement, Sickener, Tes, Vicissitude

Settle(d), Settler, Settlement Adjust, Agree, Alight, Appoint, Arrange, Ascertain, Avenge, Balance, Bed, Bench, Boer, Camp, Clear, Clench, Clinch, Colonial, Colonise, Colony, Compose, Compound, Compromise, Decide, Defray, Determine, Discharge, Dowry, Encamp, Endow, Ensconce, Entail, Establish, Fix, Foot, Foreclose, Gravitate, Guilder, Illegitimate, Jointure, Kibbutz, Land, Ledge, Light, Merino, Mission, Nest, Nestle, Opt, Outpost, Pa(h), Pale, Patroon, Pay, Penal, Perch, Pilgrim, Pioneer, Placate, Planter, Populate, Pueblo, Readjust, Reduction, Reimburse, Remit, Reside, Resolve, Rest, Sate, Satisfaction, Secure, Sedimentary, Sofa, Solve, Square, State, Still, Subside, Township, Vest(ed), Voortrekker

▷ **Settlement** may indicate an anagram

▷ **Settler** may indicate a coin

Seven(th) Ages, Days, Dials, Great Bear, Hebdomad, Hepta-, Hills, Nones, Pleiad(es), S, Sages, Seas, Septenary, Septimal, Sins, Sisters, Sleepers, Stars, Wonders, Zeta

Several Divers, Many, Multiple, Some, Sundry

Severe(ly), Severity Acute, Bad, Chronic, Cruel, Dour, Draconian, Drastic, Eager, Extreme, Grave, Grievous, Gruel(ling), Hard, ➤ HARSH, Ill, Inclement, Morose, Penal, Rhadamanthine, Rigo(u)r, Roundly, Serious, Sharp, Snell(y), Sore, Spartan, Stern, Strict

Sew(ing) Baste, Cope, Embroider, Fell, Machine, Mitre, Overlock, Run, Seam, Seel, Stitch, Tack, Whip

Sewage, Sewer Cesspool, Cloaca, Culvert, Dorcas, ➤ DRAIN, Effluence, Jaw-box, Jaw-hole, Mimi, Needle, Privy, Shore, Soil, Sough, Soughing-tile, Waste

Sex(y) Bed-hopping, Coupling, Erotic, Favours, Female, Gam(ic), Gender, Hump, Incest, Intercourse, Kind, Libidinous, Libido, Lingam, Lumber, Male, Mate, Nookie, Oomph, Oral, Paedophilia, Pederasty, Phat, Priapean, Race, Randy, Raunchy, Rut(ish), Salacious, Screw, Sect, Steamy, Sultry, Teledildonics, Venereal, Venery, VI, Voluptuous

Shabby Base, Buckeen, Dog-eared, Down-at-heel, Fusc(ous), Grotty, Mean, Moth-eaten, Oobit, Oorie, Oubit, Ourie, Outworn, Owrie, Raunch, Scaly, Scruffy, Seedy, Shoddy, Squalid, Tatty, Worn, Woubit

Shackle(s) Bind, Bracelet, Chain, Entrammel, Fetter(lock), Hamper, Irons, Manacle, Restrict, Tie, Trammel, Yoke

Shade(d), Shades, Shading, Shadow, Shady Adumbrate, Arbour, Awning, Blend, Blind, Bongrace, Bowery, Brocken spectre, Buff, Cast, Chiaroscuro, Chroma, Cloche, Cloud, Cross-hatch, Degree, Dis, Dog, Dubious, Eclipse, Eye, Five o'clock, Galanty, Gamp, Ghost, Gradate, Gray, Hachure, Hell, Herbar, Hint, Hue, Inumbrate, Larva, Lee, Mezzotint, Nuance, Opaque, Overtone, Parasol, Phantom, Presence, Ray-Bans®, Satellite, Screen, Shroud, Sienna, Silhouette, Silvan, Skia-, Soften, Spectre, Spirit, Stag, Sunglasses, Swale, Swaly, Tail, Tinge, Tint, Tone, Ugly, Umbra(tile), Umbrage(ous), Underhand, Velamen, Velar(ium), Velum, Visor

Shaft Arbor, Arrow, Barb, Barrow-train, Beam, Capstan, Cardan, Chimney, Column, Crank, Cue, Disselboom, Dolly, Drive, Fil(l), Fust, Incline, Journal, Limber, Loom, Mandrel, Mandril, Moulin,

Parthian, Passage, Pile, Pit, Pitch, Pole, Propellor, Ray, Scape, Scapus, Shank, Snead, Spindle, Staff, Stale, Steal(e), Steel, Stele, Stulm, Sunbeam, Thill, Tige, Trave, Upcast, Winze, Winning

Shaggy Ainu, Comate, Hairy, Hearie, Hirsute, Horrid, Horror, Rough, Rugged, Shock, Shough, Tatty, Untidy

Shake(n), Shakes, Shaky Ague(-fit), Astonish, Brandish, Coggle, Concuss, Dabble, Dick(e)y, Didder, Dither, Dodder, ► DT'S, Feeble, Groggy, Hod, Hotch, Jar, Jiggle, Joggle, Jolt, Jounce, Judder, Jumble, Milk, Mo, Nid-nod, Press flesh, Quake, Quiver, Quooke, Rattle, Rickety, Rickle, ► ROCK, Rouse, Shimmer, Shiver, Shock, Shog, Shoogle, Shudder, Succuss(ation), Tremble, Tremolo, Tremor, Tremulous, Trill(o), Undulate, Vibrate, Vibrato, Wag, Wobble, Wonky

▷ **Shake** may indicate an anagram

Shallow(s) Ebb, Flat, Fleet, Flew, Flue, Justice, Neritic, Shoal, Slight, Superficial

Sham Apocryphal, Bluff, Bogus, Braide, Charade, Counterfeit, Deceit, Fake, ► FALSE, Hoax, Idol, Impostor, Mimic, Mock, Phony, Pinchbeck, Pretence, Pseudo, Repro, Snide, Spurious

Shame(ful), Shame-faced Abash, Aidos, Contempt, Crying, Degrade, Discredit, Disgrace, Dishonour, Embarrass, Fie, Gross, Hangdog, Honi, Humiliate, Ignominy, Infamy, Inglorious, Modesty, Mortify, Pity, Pudor, Pugh, Shend, Sin, Slander, Stain, Stigma, Yshend

Shape(d), Shapely, Shaping Blancmange, Boast, Cast, Contour, Face, Fashion, Figure, Form, Format, Geoid, Gnomon, Headquarters, Hew, Jello, Model, ► MOULD, Ream, Rhomb(us), Scabble, Sculpt, Wrought

Share(d), Shares Allocation, Allotment, Apportion, Blue-chip, Co, Cohabit, Coho(e), Common, Contango, Culter, Cut, Divi(dend), Divide, Divvy, Dole, Dutch, Equity, Finger, Impart, Interest, Kaffir, Kaf(f)ir, Lion's, Market, Moiety, Ordinary, ► PART, Partake, Participate, Plough, Portion, Prebend, Pref(erred), Preference, Pro rata, Quarter, Quota, Ration, Rug, Scrip, Security, Shr, Slice, Snack, Snap, Sock, Split, Stock, Tranche, Whack

Shark Angel, Basking, Beagle, Blue, Bonnethead, Carpet, Cestracion, Cow, Demoiselle, Dog(fish), Hammerhead, Houndfish, Huss, Lemonfish, Loan, Mackerel, Mako, Noah, Nurse, Penny-dog, Plagiostomi, Porbeagle, Requiem,

Rhin(e)odon, Rigg, Sail-fish, Sea-ape, Sharp, Shovelhead, Smoothhound, Squaloid, Swindler, Thrasher, Thresher, Tiger, Tope, Usurer, Whale, Wobbegong, Zygaena

Sharp(er), Sharpen(er), Sharpness Abrupt, Accidental, Acerose, Acidulous, Acrid, Aculeus, Acumen, Acuminate, Acute, Alert, Angular, Arris, Bateless, Becky, Bitter, Brisk, Cacuminous, Cheat, Clear, Coticular, Cutting, Dital, Edge(r), Fine, Gleg, Grind, Hone, Hot, Keen, Kurtosis, Massé, Oilstone, Peracute, Piquant, Poignant, Pronto, Pungent, Razor, Rogue, Rook, Set, Shrewd, Snap, Snell, Sour, Spicate, Strop, Swindler, Tart, Tomium, Vivid, Volable, Whet

Shawl Afghan, Buibui, Cashmere, Chuddah, Chuddar, Dopatta, Dupatta, Fichu, Kaffiyeh, Mantilla, Maud, Paisley, Partlet, Prayer, Serape, Stole, Tallith, Tonnag, Tozie, Tribon, Whittle, Wrap(per), Zephyr

Shed(der), Shedding Autotomy, Barn, Cast, Cho(u)ltry, Coducity, Depot, Discard, Doff, Drop, Effuse, Exuviate, Hangar, Hovel, Hut, Infuse, Lair, Lean-to, Linhay, Linny, Mew, Moult, Pent, Potting, Salmon, Shippen, Shippon, Shuck, Skeo, Skillion, Skio, Slough, Sow, Spend, Spent, Spill, Tilt, Tool

Sheep(ish) Bell(wether), Black, Blate, Coy, Crone, Embarrassed, Ewe, Fank, Flock, Fold, Hangdog, Hidder, Hirsel, Hog(g), Hogget, Jemmy, Jumbuck, Lamb, Lanigerous, Mor(t)ling, Mug, Mutton, Ovine, Ram, Rosella, Shearling, ➤ SHY, Sumph, Teg(g), Theave, Trip, Tup, Wether, Woollyback, Yow(e), Yowie

Sheet(s) Balance, Cere-cloth, Cerement, Charge, Chart, Crime, Cutch, Dope, Expanse, Film, Folio, Foolscap, Heft, Leaf, Membrane, Nappe, Out-hauler, Page, Pot(t), Pour, Proof, Prospectus, Ream, Rope, Sail, Scandal, Shroud, Stern, Stratus, Taggers, Tarpaulin(g), Tear, Tentorium, Terne, Thunder, Time, Web, Winding

Shell(ed), Shellfish Ambulacrum, Ammo, Blitz, Bombard, Camera, Capsid, Carapace, Cartridge, Casing, Chitin, Cochlea, Cover, Dariole, Dop, Framework, Frustule, Hull, Husk, Hyoplastron, Limacel, Lorica, Lyre, Mollusc, Mother-of-pearl, Nacre, Peag, Peak, Pea(s)cod, Periostracum, Pipsqueak, Plastron, Pod, Projectile, Putamen, Sal, Shale, Sheal, Sheel, Shiel, Shill, Shock, Shot, Shrapnel, Shuck, Sial, Smoke-ball,

Spend, Star, Stonk, Straddle, Strafe, Test(a), Valency, Wampum, Whiz(z)bang

▷ **Shelled** may indicate an anagram

Shelter Abri, Anderson, Asylum, Awn, Awning, Belee, Bender, Bield, Blockhouse, Booth, Bunker, Butt, Cab, Carport, Casemate, Cot(e), Cove, Covert, Coverture, Defence, Dripstone, Dug-out, Fall-out, Garage, Gunyah, Harbour, Haven, Hithe, Hospice, Hostel, House, Hovel, Humpy, Hut, Kipsie, Lee, Loun, Lound, Lown, Lownd, Mai mai, Morrison, ➤ REFUGE, Retreat, Roof, Sanctuary, Scog, Sconce, Scoog, Scoug, Scug, Shed, Shiel(ing), Shroud, Skug, Succah, Sukkah, Summerhouse, Tent, Testudo, Tortoise, Tupik, Twigloo, Umbrage, Weather, Wheelhouse, Wi(c)kiup, Wickyup, Wil(t)ja, Windbreak

Shepherd(ess) Abel, Acis, Amaryllis, Amos, Bergère, Bo-peep, Chloe, Clorin, Conduct, Corin, Corydon, Cuddy, Daphnis, Dorcas, Drover, Endymion, Escort, Ettrick, German, Grubbinol, Gyges, Herdsman, Hobbinol, Lindor, Marshal, Menalcas, Padre, Pastor(al), Pastorella, Phebe, Sheepo, Strephon, Tar-box, Thenot, Thyrsis, Tityrus

Sherry Amoroso, Cobbler, Cyprus, Doctor, Fino, Gladstone, Jerez, Manzanilla, Oloroso, Sack, Solera, Whitewash, Xeres

Shield(-shaped) Ablator, Achievement, Aegis, Ancile, Armour, Arms, Bodyguard, Box, Buckler, Canadian, Cartouche, Clypeus, Defend, Escutcheon, Fence, Gobo, Guard, Gyron, Hatchment, Heat, Hielaman, Insulate, Mant(e)let, Pavis(e), Pelta, Protect, Riot, Rondache, Screen, Scute, Scutum, Sternite, Targe(t), Thyroid, Visor

Shift(er), Shifty Amove, Astatic, Blue, Budge, Change, Chemise, Core, Cymar, Devious, Displace, Doppler, Evasive, Expedient, Fend, Graveyard, Hedging, Landslide, Linen, Move, Night, Nighty, Red, Relay, Remove, Ruse, Scorch, Shirt, Shovel, Shunt, Simar(re), Slicker, Slip(pery), Spell, Stagehand, Stint, Tour, Transfer, Tunic, Turn, Vary, Veer, Warp

▷ **Shift(ing)** may indicate an anagram

▷ **Shimmering** may indicate an anagram

Shin Clamber, Climb, Cnemial, Leg, Shank, Skink, Swarm

Shine(r), Shining, Shiny Aglow, Beam, Buff, Burnish, Deneb, Effulge, Excel, Flash, Gleam, Glisten, Gloss, ➤ GLOW, Irradiant, Japan, ➤ LAMP, Leam, Leme, Lucent, Luminous,

Lustre, Mouse, Nitid, Phosphoresce, Polish, Radiator, Relucent, Resplend, Rutilant, Skyre, Sleek, Twinkle, Varnish

▷ **Shiny** may indicate a star

Ship(ping) Boat, Container, Convoy, ▶ DISPATCH, Embark, Export, Her, Hulk, Jolly, Keel, Man, MV, Post, Privateer, Prize, Prow, Raft, Ram, Sail, She, SS, Tall, Tub, Vessel, Weather

Shipshape Apple-pie, Neat, Orderly, Tidy, Trim

Shirt Boiled, Brown, Calypso, Camese, Camise, Chemise, Choli, Cilice, Dasheki, Dashiki, Dick(e)y, Dress, Fiesta, Garibaldi, Grandad, Hair, Hawaiian, Jacky Howe, Kaftan, Kaross, K(h)urta, Nessus, Non-iron, Parka, Partlet, Polo, Red, Safari, Sark, Serk, Shift, Smock, Stuffed, Subucula, T

Shiver(ing), Shivers, Shivery Aguish, Break, Chitter, Crumble, Dash, Dither, Fragile, Frisson, Grew, Grue, Malaria, Oorie, Ourie, Owrie, Quake, Quiver, ▶ SHAKE, Shatter, Shrug, Shudder, Smash, Smither, Smithereens, Splinter, Timbers, Tremble

▷ **Shiver(ed)** may indicate an anagram

Shock(ed), Shocker, Shocking Aghast, Agitate, Appal, Astound, Bombshell, Bunch, Culture, Defibrillate, Disgust, Dreadful, Drop, Earthquake, ECT, Egregious, Fleg, Floccus, Galvanism, Hair, Horrify, Impact, Infamous, Jar, Jolt, Live, Mane, Mop, Outrage, Putrid, Recoil, Revolt, Rick(er), Scandal(ise), Seismic, Shake, Sheaf, Stagger, Start(le), Stun, Trauma, Turn

▷ **Shocked** may indicate an anagram

Shoe(s) Accessory, Bauchle, Brake, Calceate, Calk(er), Calkin, Caulker, Cawker, Skid, Skimmer, Upper, Welt

Shoemaker Blacksmith, Clogger, Cobbler, Cordiner, Cordwainer, Cosier, Cozier, Crispi(a)n, Farrier, Leprechaun, Sachs, Smith, Snob, Soutar, Souter, Sowter, Sutor

Shoot(er), Shooting Ack-ack, Airgun, Arrow, Bine, Bostryx, Braird, Breer, Bud, Bulbil, Catapult, Chit, Cyme, Dart(le), Delope, Discharge, Drib, Elance, Enate, Eradiate, Film, Fire, Germ, Germaine(e), Germen, Germin(ate), Glorious twelfth, ▶ GUN, Gunsel, Head-reach, Hurl, Imp, Layer, Limb, Loose, Offset, Photograph, Pluff, Plug, Poot, Pop, Pot, Pout, Ramulus, Rapids, Ratoon, Riddle, Rod, Rove, Runner, Septembriser, Skeet, Snipe, Spire, Spirt, Spout, Spray, Sprout, Spurt, Spyre, Start, Stole, Stolon, Strafe, Sucker, Tellar, Teller, Tendril, Tiller, Turion, Twelfth, Twig, Udo, Vimen, Wand, Weapon, Wildfowler

Shop(s) Atelier, Arcade, Betray, Boutique, Bucket, Buy, Chain, Charity, Chippy, Closed, Coffee, Co-op, Corner, Dairy, Delicatessen, Denounce, Duddery, Duka, Emporium, Factory, Galleria, Gift, Grass, Inform, Luckenbooth, Machine, Mall, Market, Parlour, Patisserie, Precinct, PX, Retail, RMA, Salon, Shebang, Spaza, Store, Studio, Superette, Supermarket, Thrift, Tuck, Union, Warehouse, Works

Shopkeeper British, Butcher, Chemist, Gombeen-man, Greengrocer, Grocer, Haberdasher, Hosier, Ironmonger, Merchant, Newsagent, Provisioner, Retailer, Stationer

Shore Bank, Beach, Buttress, Coast, Coste, Landfall, Littoral, Offing, Prop, Rivage, Seaboard, Strand, Strandline

Short(en), Shortly Abbreviate, Abridge, Abrupt, Anon, Brief, Brusque, Commons, Concise, Contract, Crisp, Cross, Curt, Curtail, Curtal, Diminish, Drink, Epitomise, Ere-long, Inadequate, Lacking, Laconical, Light, Limited, Low, Mini, Near, Nip, Nutshell, Punch, Reduce, Reef, Scanty, Scarce, Shrift, Shy, Soon, Sparse, Spirit, Squab, Squat, Staccato, Stint, Stocky, Strapped, Stubby, Succinct, Taciturn, Teen(s)y, Terse, Tight, Tot, Wee

Shortage Dearth, Deficit, Drought, Famine, Lack, Need, Paucity, Scarcity, Sparsity, Wantage

Shorts Bermuda, Board, Boxer, Briefs, Culottes, Hot pants, Kaccha, Lederhosen, Plus-fours, Stubbies®, Trunks

Shot(s) Ammo, Approach, Attempt, Backhand, Ball, Barrage, Blank, Blast, Bull, Bullet, Burl, Canna, Cartridge, Case, Chain, Chip, Crack, Dink, Dolly, Dram, Draw, Drop, Dunk, Exhausted, Forehand, Gesse, Glance, Go, Grape, Guess, Hook, Jump, Marksman, Massé, Matte, Mulligan, Noddy, Parthian, Parting, Passing, Pellet, Photo, Pop, Pot, Puff, Rid, Round, Salvo, Scratch, Shy, Silk, Six, Slam-dunk, Slap, Slice, Slug, Sped, Spell, Spent, Square cut, Stab, Still, Throw, Tonic, Tracking, Trial, Try, Turn, Volley, Warning

Shout(er), Shouting Barrack, Bawl, Bellow, Boanerges, Call, Claim, Clamour, Cry, Din, Exclaim, Heckle, Hey, Hoi(cks), Holla, Holla-ho(a), Holler, Hollo, Holloa, Hooch, Hosanna, Howzat, Hue, Rah, Rant, Root, Round, Sa sa, Treat, Trumpet, Vociferate, Whoop, Yell(och), Yippee, Yoohoo

Shovel Backhoe, Dustpan, Hat, Main, Peel, Power, Scoop, Shool, Spade, Steam, Trowel, Van

Show(ing), Shown, Showy Appearance, Bench, Betray,
Burlesque, Cabaret, Circus, Come, Con, Cruft's, Demo(nstrate),
Depict, Diorama, Display, Do, Dressy, Establish, Evince,
➤ EXHIBIT, Expo, Extravaganza, Facade, Fair, Fangled, Farce,
Flamboyant, Flash, Flaunt, Game, Garish, Gaudy, Gay, Give,
Glitz(y), Gloss, Horse, Indicate, Jazzy, Light, Loud, Manifest,
Matinée, Musical, Ostentatious, Pageant, Pantomime, Parade,
Performance, Phen(o), Point, Pomp, Portray, Pretence, Pride,
Project, Prominence, Prove, Pseudery, Puff, Raree, Razzmatazz,
Represent, Reveal, Revue, Road, Rushes, Screen, Sight, Sitcom,
Slang, Soap, Son et lumière, Specious, Spectacle, Splay, Stage,
Stunt, Talk, Tattoo, Tawdry, Telethon, Theatrical, Uncover,
Usher, Vain, Variety, Vaudeville, Veneer, Wear, Wild west
Shower Douche, Exhibitor, Flurry, Hail, Indicant, Indicator,
Meteor, Party, Pelt, Pepper, Precipitation, Rain, Scat, Scouther,
Scowther, Skit, Snow, Spat, Spet, Spit, Splatter, Spray, Sprinkle,
Ticker tape
▷ **Showing, Shown in** may indicate a hidden word
Shred Clout, Filament, Grate, Mammock, Mince, Rag, Screed,
Swarf, Tag, Tatter, Thread, Wisp
Shrewd Acute, Arch, Argute, Artful, Astucious, Astute, Callid,
Canny, Clued-up, Cute, File, Gnostic, Gumptious, Judicious,
Knowing, Pawky, Politic, Sagacious, Sapient(al), Wily, Wise
Shriek Cry, Scream, Shright, Shrike, Shrill, Shritch, Skirl, Yell
Shrine Adytum, Altar, Dagoba, Dargah, Delphi, Fatima,
Feretory, Harem, Holy, Joss house, Kaaba, Marabout, Naos,
Pagoda, Reliquary, Scrine, Scryne, Stupa, Tabernacle, Temple,
Tope, Vimana, Walsingham
Shrink(age), Shrinking, Shrunk Alienist, Blanch, Blench,
Cling, Compress, Contract, Cour, Cower, Creep, Crine, Cringe,
Dare, Decrew, Depreciate, Dread, Dwindle, Flinch, Funk, Less,
Nirl, ➤ PSYCHIATRIST, Quail, Recoil, Reduce, Sanforised, Shrivel,
Shy, Violet, Wince, Wizened
Shrub ➤ BUSH, Plant, Savanna(h), Undergrowth
Shuttle Alternate, Commute, Drawer, Flute, Go-between,
Shoot, Shunt, Space, Tat(t), Weave
Shy Bashful, Blate, Blench, Cast, Catapult, Chary, Coy, Deficient,
Demure, Farouche, Flinch, Funk, Heave, Jerk, Jib, Laithfu', Lob,
Mim, Rear, Recoil, Reserved, Sheepish, Shrinking, Skeigh, Start,
Throw, Timid, Tongue-tied, Toss, Try, Violet, Withdrawn

Sick(en), Sickening, Sickly, Sickness Affection, Ague, Ail, Bad, Bends, Cat, Colic, Chunder, Crapulence, Crook, Delicate, Disorder, Gag, Icky, Ill, Infection, Mal, Mawkish, Morbid, Nauseous, Pale, Peaky, Pestilent, Plague, Queasy, Radiation, Regorge, Repulsive, Retch, Spue, Squeamish, Travel, Twee, Valetudinarian, Virus, Vomit, Wan

Side Abeam, Airs, Beam, Border, Camp, Distaff, Edge, Effect, Eleven, English, Epistle, Facet, Flank, Flip, Gunnel, Hand, Hypotenuse, Iliac, Lateral, Lee(ward), Left, Off, On, OP, Pane, Part, Partisan, Party, Port, Pretension, Profile, Prompt, Rave, Reveal, Right, Rink, Silver, Slip, Spear, Starboard, Swank, ➤ TEAM, Windward, Wing, XI

Sight(ed) Aim, Barleycorn, Bead, Conspectuity, Eye(ful), Eyesore, Glimpse, Ken, Long, Oculated, Prospect, Range, Riflescope, Scene, Scotopia, Second, See, Short, Spectacle, Taish, Vane, ➤ VIEW, Visie, Vision, Vista

Sign, Signing Ampersand, Aquarius, Archer, Aries, Arrow, Auspice, Autograph, Badge, Balance, Beck, Brand, Bull, Bush, Call, Cancer, Capricorn, Caract, Caret, Chevron, Clue, Crab, Cross, Cue, Di(a)eresis, DS, Earmark, Emblem, Endorse, Endoss, Enlist, Evidence, Exit, Fascia, Fish, Gemini, Gesture, Goat, Hallmark, Harbinger, Hex, Hieroglyphic, Hint, Ideogram, Indian, Indicate, Indication, Initial, Inscribe, Ivy-bush, Leo, Libra, Logogram, Nod, Notice, Obelisk, Obelus, Omen, Pisces, Presage, Radical, Ram, Rest, Sagittarius, Sain, Scorpio, Segno, Semeion, Shingle, Show, Sigil, Sigla, Signal, Subscribe, Superscribe, Symbol, Symptom, Syndrome, Tag, Taurus, Tic(k)tac(k), Tilde, Token, Trace, Twins, Umlaut, V, Virgo, Warning, Waymark, Word, Zodiac

Signal(ler) Alarm, Alert, Amber, Assemble, Beacon, Bell, Bleep, Bugle, Buzz, Code, Cone, Cue, Detonator, Distress, Earcon, Flag, Flagman, Flare, Flash, Gantry, Gesticulate, Gong, Griffin, Gun, Harmonic, Heliograph, Heliostat, Herald, Hooter, Icon, Important, Interrupt, Mark, Message, Modem, Morse, NICAM, Notation, Noted, Output, Password, Peter, Pinger, Pip, Radio, Renowned, Reveille, Robot, Salient, Semaphore, Singular, Smoke, SOS, Squawk, Taps, Target, Telegraph, Thumb, Tic(k)-tac(k), Time, Troop, Video, Very, Waff, Waft, Wave

Signature Alla breve, Autograph, By-line, Digital, Hand, John Henry, John Hancock, Key, Mark, Onomastic, Specimen, Time

Significance, Significant Cardinal, Consequence, Emblem, Impact, Important, Indicative, Key, Magnitude, Matter, Meaningful, Moment(ous), Noted, Noteworthy, Paramount, Pith, Pregnant, Salient, Special, Telling

Silence(r), Silent Clam, Clamour, Gag, Hist, Hush, Hushkit, Mim(budget), Muffler, Mum(p), Mute, Omertà, Quench, Quiesce, ► QUIET, Reticence, Shtoom, Shush, Speechless, Still, Sulky, Tace(t), Tacit(urn), Throttle, Wheesh(t)

Silk(y), Silk screen Baratea, Brocade, Bur(r), Chenille, Chiffon, Cocoon, Crape, Crepe, Floss, Georgette, Glossy, Organza, Parachute, Peau de soie, Pongee, Prunella, Prunelle, Raw, Samite, Sars(e)net, Satin, Seric, Shantung, Sleek, Smooth, Spun, Taffeta, Tulle, Velvet

Silly, Silliness Absurd, Brainless, Crass, Cuckoo, Daft, Ditsy, Divvy, Dumb, Fatuous, Folly, Fool, Footling, Frivolous, Goopy, Goosey, Gormless, Idiotic, Imbecile, Inane, Inept, Infield(er), Mid-off, Mid-on, Mopoke, Puerile, Season, Simple, Soft(y), Spoony, ► STUPID, Tripe, Wacky

▷ **Silver** may indicate a coin

Similar(ity) Analog(ue), Analogical, Corresponding, Etc, Equivalent, Homoeonetic, Homogeneous, Homological, Homonym, Kindred, ► LIKE, Parallel, Resemblance, Samey

Simple(r), Simplicity, Simplify, Simply Arcadian, Artless, Austere, Bald, Bare, Basic, Crude, Doddle, Doric, ► EASY, Eath(e), Elegant, ESN, Ethe, Fee, Folksy, Gotham, Green, Herb(alist), Homespun, Idyllic, Incomposite, Inornate, Mere, Naïve(té), Naked, Niaiserie, One-fold, Open and shut, Ordinary, Paraphrase, Pastoral, Peter, Plain, Pleon, Provincial, Pure, Reduce, Rustic, Sapid, Semplice, Sheer, Silly, Simon, Spartan, Stupid, Woollen

Sin(ful) Aberrant, Anger, Avarice, Besetting, Bigamy, Covetousness, Crime, Deadly, Debt, Envy, Err, Evil, Folly, Gluttony, Hamartiology, Harm, Hate, Impious, Lapse, Lust, Misdeed, Misdoing, Mortal, ► OFFENCE, Original, Peccadillo, Piacular, Pride, Scape, Scarlet, Sine, Sloth, Transgress, Trespass, Unrighteous, Venial, Vice, Wicked, Wrath, Wrong

Sincere(ly), Sincerity Bona-fide, Candour, Earnest, Entire, Frank, Genuine, Heartfelt, Honest, Open, Real(ly), True, Verity, Whole-hearted

► **Sinful** see SIN

Sing(ing) Barbershop, Bel canto, Carol, Chant, Cheep, Chorus, Coloratura, Cough, Croon, Crow, Hum, Inform, Intone, Karaoke, La-la, Lilt, Melic, Parlando, Peach, Pen(n)illion, Pipe, Rand, Rant, Rap, Scat, Second(o), Squeal, Tell, Thrum, Trill, Troll, Vocalise, Warble, Yodel

Singer Alto, Bard, Baritone, Bass, Bing, Bird, Canary, Cantatrice, Cantor, Car, Castrato, Chanteuse, Chantor, Chazan, Cher, Chorister, Coloratura, Crooner, Diva, Falsetto, Gleeman, Kettle, Lark, Lauder, Lorelei, Melba, Minstrel, Siren, Songstress, Soprano, Soubrette, Succentor, Tenor, Torch, Treble, Troubador, Vocalist, Voice, Warbler

Single, Singly Ace, Aefa(u)ld, Aefawld, Alone, Azygous, Bachelor, Celibate, Discriminate, EP, Exclusive, Feme sole, Matchless, Monact, Mono, Odd, One-off, Only, Pick, Run, Sole, Solitary, Spinster, Unattached, Uncoupled, Unique, Unwed, Versal, Yin

Singular Curious, Especial, Exceptional, Extraordinary, Ferly, Odd, Once, One, Peculiar, Queer(er), Rare, ➤ UNIQUE, Unusual

Sink(ing), Sunken Basin, Bog, Cower, Delapse, Depress, Descend, Devall, Dip, Down, Drain, Drink, Drop, Drown, Ebb, Flag, Founder, Gravitate, Hole, Immerse, Invest, Jawbox, Lagan, Laigh, Lapse, Ligan, Merger, Pot, Prolapse, Put(t), Relapse, Sag, Scupper, Scuttle, Set, Settle, Shipwreck, Steep-to, Sty, Submerge, Subside, Swag, Swamp

Siren Alarm, Alert, Hooter, Houri, Ligea, Lorelei, Mermaid, Oceanides, Parthenope, Salamander, Teaser, Temptress, Vamp

Sister(s) Anne, Beguine, Minim, ➤ NUN, Nurse, Religeuse, Sib, Sibling, Sis, Sob, Soul, Swallow, Titty, Ursuline, Verse, Weird

Sit(ter), Sitting Bestride, Clutch, Dharna, Duck, Gaper, Model, Perch, Pose, Reign, Roost, Séance, Session, Squat

Site, Siting Area, Camp, Feng shui, Greenfield, Home-page, Location, Lot, Pad, Place, Plot, Rogue, Silo, Spot, Stance

Situation Berth, Cart, Case, Catch, Catch-22, Cliff-hanger, Contretemps, Cow, Dilemma, Galère, Hole, Job, Lie, Lurch, Matrix, Niche, No-win, Office, Plight, Position, Post, Scenario, Set-up, Showdown, Status quo, Strait, Where

Size(able) Amplitude, Area, Bulk, Calibre, Countess, Demy, ➤ EXTENT, Format, Girth, Glair, Glue, Gum, Imperial, Measure, Physique, Pot(t), Princess, Proportion, Tempera, Tidy

Skate(r), Skating Blade, Figure, Fish, In-line, Maid, Mohawk, Rock(er), Roller, Rollerblade®, Runner

Skeleton, Skeletal Anatomy, Atomy, Axial, Bones, Cadaverous, Cadre, Cage, Coenosteum, Corallum, Framework, Key, Ossify, Outline, Scenario, Sclere

Sketch Cameo, Character, Charade, Croquis, Delineate, Diagram, Draft, ➤ DRAW, Ebauche, Esquisse, Illustration, Limn, Line, Maquette, Modello, Outline, Pencilling, Playlet, Pochade, Précis, Profile, Skit, Summary, Thumbnail, Trick, Vignette, Visual

Ski(ing) Aquaplane, Glide, Glissade, Hot-dog, Langlauf, Nordic, Schuss, Super G, Telemark, Vorlage, Wedeln

Skill(ed), Skilful Ability, Able, Ace, Adept, Address, Adroit, Art, Bravura, Canny, Chic, Competence, Craft, Deacon, Deft, Dextrous, Expertise, Facility, Feat, Finesse, Flair, Gleg, Hand, Handicraft, Handy, Hend, Hot, Ingenious, Knack, Know-how, Knowing, Lear(e), Leir, Lere, Masterly, Masterpiece, Mean, Mistery, Mystery, Mystique, Practised, Proficient, Prowess, Quant, Resource, Savvy, Science, Skeely, Sleight, Tactics, Technic, Technique, Touch, Trade, Trick, Versed, Virtuoso

Skin(s) Agnail, Armour, Bark, Basan, Basil, Box-calf, Calf, Callus, Case, Cere, Chevrette, Coat, Cortex, Cuticle, Cutis, Deacon, Derm(a), Dermis, Dewlap, Disbark, Ectoderm, Enderon, Epicarp, Eschar, Excoriate, Exterior, Fell, Film, Flaught, Flay, Flench, Flinch, Hangnail, Hide, Jacket, Kip, Leather, Membrane, Pachyderm, Peau, Peel, Pell, Pellicle, Pelt, Plew, Prepuce, Rack, Rind, Scarskin, Serosa, Shell, Spetch, Strip, Tegument, Veneer

Skin disease, Skin trouble Boil, Cowpox, Dermatitis, Herpes, Hives, Impetigo, Mange, Prurigo, Psoriasis, Rash, Ringworm, Rosacea, Scabies, Scurvy, Verruca, Yaws

Skip(ped), Skipper Boss, Caper, Captain, Cavort, Drakestone, Elater, Frisk, Hesperian, Jump, Jumping-mouse, Lamb, Luppen, Miss, Omit, Patroon, Ricochet, Saury, Scombresox, Spring, Tittup, Trounce(r)

Skull Bregma(ta), Calvaria, Cranium, Head, Malar, Obelion, Occiput, Pannikell, Phrenology, Scalp, Sinciput

Sky(-high) Air, Azure, Blue, Canopy, Carry, E-layer, Element, Empyrean, Ether, Firmament, Heaven, Lift, Loft, Mackerel, Occident, Octa, Welkin

Slab Briquette, Bunk, Cake, Chunk, Dalle, Hawk, Ledger, Metope, Mihrab, Mud, Plank, Slice, Stela, Tab, Tile

Slack(en), Slackness Abate, Careless, Crank, Dilatory, Dross, Ease, Easy-going, Idle, Lax(ity), Loose, Malinger, Nerveless, Relax, Release, Remiss, Shirk, Skive, Slow, Surge, Unscrew, Veer

Slander(ous) Asperse, Backbite, Calumny, Defame, Derogatory, Disparage, Libel, Malediction, Malign, Missay, Mud, Obloquy, Sclaunder, Smear, Traduce, Vilify, Vilipend

Slang Abuse, Argot, Back, Berate, Cant, Colloquial, Ebonics, Flash, Jargon, Lingo, Nadsat, Rhyming, Slate, Zowie

Slant(ing) Angle, Asklent, Atilt, Bevel, Bias, Brae, Cant, Careen, Chamfer, Clinamen, Diagonal, Escarp, Oblique, Prejudice, Slew, ➤ SLOPE, Splay, Talus, Tilt, Virgule

Slash(ed) Chive, Cut, Gash, Jag, Laciniate, Leak, Oblique, Rash, Rast, Reduce, Scorch, Scotch, Separatrix, Slit, Solidus, Wee

Slaughter(house), Slaughterer Abattoir, Bleed, Bloodshed, Butcher, Carnage, Decimate, Hal(l)al, Holocaust, Jhatka, Kill, Mactation, ➤ MASSACRE, Sc(h)ehita(h), Schochet, Scupper, Shambles, Shechita(h), Smite

Slave(ry), Slaves Addict, Aesop, Aida, Androcles, Barracoon, Blackbird, Bond, Bond(s)man, Bondwoman, Boy, Caliban, Contraband, Drudge, Drug, Esne, Galley, Helot, Mameluke, Maroon, Minion, Odali(s)que, Odalisk, Peasant, Pr(a)edial, Rhodope, Serf, Servitude, Spartacus, Terence, Theow, Thersites, Thete, Thrall, Topsy, Vassal, Villein, White, Yoke

Slay(er), Slaying Destroy, Execute, Ghazi, ➤ KILL, Mactation, Murder, Quell, Slaughter, Saul

Sled(ge), Sleigh(-ride) Bob, Dray, Hurdle, Hurly-hacket, Kibitka, Komatik, Lauf, Luge, Polack, Pulk(h)(a), Pung, Skidoo®, Slipe, Stoneboat, Tarboggin, Toboggan, Travois

Sleep(er), Sleepiness, Sleeping, Sleepy Beauty, Bed, Bivouac, Blet, Car, Catnap, Coma, Couchette, Crash, Cross-sill, Cross-tie, Dormant, Dormient, Doss, Doze, Drowse, Gum, Hibernate, Hypnology, Hypnos, Kip, Lethargic, Lie, Morpheus, Nap, Narcolepsy, Nod, Over, Paradoxical, Petal, REM, Repast, Repose, Rest, Rip Van Winkle, Sandman, Shuteye, Skipper, Sloom, Slumber, Snooz(l)e, Somnolent, Sopor(ose), Sownd, Tie, Torpid, Twilight, Wink, Zizz

Sleeve (opening) Arm(hole), Batwing, Bishop's, Bush, Collet, Cover, Dolman, Gigot, Gland, Leg-o'-mutton, Liner, Magyar, Manche, Querpo, Raglan, Sabot, Scye, Slashed

▶ **Sleigh** see SLED

Slender(ness) Asthenic, Ectomorph, Elongate, Exiguity, Exility, Fine, Flimsy, Gracile, Jimp, Leptosome, Loris, Skinny, Slight, Slim, Spindly, Styloid, Svelte, Sylph, Tenuous, Waif

Slice Cantle, Chip, Collop, Cut, Doorstep, Fade, Frustrum, Piece, Rasure, Round, Sector, Segment, Share, Sheave, Shive, Slab, Sliver, Tranche, Wafer, Whang

Slide Chute, Cursor, Diapositive, Drift, Glissando, Hirsle, Ice-run, Illapse, Lantern, Mount, Pulka, Schuss, Skid, Skite, Slip, Slither, Snowboard, Transparency

Slight(ly) Affront, Belittle, Cold shoulder, Cut, Detract, Disparage, Disregard, Facer, Flimsy, Halfway, Insult, Neglect, Nominal, Pet, Petty, Rebuff, Remote, ➤ SLENDER, Slim, Slimsy, Slur, Small, Sneaking, Snub, Subtle, Superficial, Sylphine, Thin, Tiny

Slime, Slimy Glair, Glit, Guck, Gunk, Mother, Muc(o)us, Oily, Ooze, Slake, Sludge, Uliginous

Sling Balista, Catapult, Drink, Fling, Hang, Parbuckle, Prusik, Support, Toss, Trebuchet

Slip(ped), Slipping, Slips Boner, Cutting, Disc, Docket, Drift, EE, Elapse, Elt, Error, Faux pas, Fielder, Form, Freudian, Glide, Glissade, Infielder, Label, Landslide, Lapse, Lath, Mistake, Muff, Nod, Oversight, Petticoat, Prolapse, Quickset, Rejection, Relapse, Run, Scape, Sc(h)edule, Scoot, Set, Shim, Sin, Ski, Skid, Skin, Skite, Slade, Slidder, Slide, Slither, Slive, Spillican, Stumble, Surge, Ticket, Trip, Tunicle, Underskirt, Unleash

Slipper Baboosh, Babouche, Babuche, Calceolate, Carpet, Eel, Mocassin, Moccasin, Moyl, Mule, Pabouche, Pampootie, Pantable, Pantof(f)le, Panton, Pantoufle, Pump, Rullion, Runner, Ski, Sledge, Sneaker, Sock

Slippery Foxy, Glid, Icy, Lubric, Shady, Shifty, Skidpan, Slick
▷**Slipshod** may indicate an anagram

Slit Cut, Cranny, Fent, Fissure, Fitchet, Gash, Loop, Pertus(at)e, Placket, Race, Rit, Scissure, Spare, Speld(er), Vent

Slogan Amandla, Byword, Catchword, Jai Hind, Mot(to), Phrase, Rallying-cry, Slughorn(e), Warcry, Watchword

Slope(s), Sloping Acclivity, Angle, Bahada, Bajada, Bank, Batter, Bevel, Borrow, Borstal(l), Brae, Breast, Chamfer, Cuesta, Declivity, Delve, Diagonal, Fla(u)nch, Glacis, Grade, Gradient, Heel, Hill, Incline, Kant, Lean, Nursery, Oblique, Pent, Periclinal,

Pitch, Rake, Ramp, Rollway, Scarp, Schuss, Scrae, Scree, Shelve, Sideling, Skewback, Slant, Slippery, Slipway, Splay, Steep, Stoss, Talus, Tilt, Verge, Versant, Weather

Sloppily, Sloppy Lagrimoso, Lowse, Madid, Mushy, Remiss, Schmaltzy, Slapdash, Slipshod, Sloven, Slushy, Untidy

▷**Sloppy** may indicate an anagram

Sloth(ful) Accidie, Acedia, Ai, Bradypus, Edentate, Ground, Idle, Inaction, Indolent, Inertia, Lazy, Lie-abed, Megatherium, Sweer(t), Sweir(t), Three-toed

Slough(ing) Cast, Despond, Ecdysis, Eschar, Exuviae, Lerna, Marsh, Morass, Paludine, Shed, Shuck, Swamp

Sloven(ly) Careless, D(r)aggle-tail, Dag(gy), Frowsy, Grobian, Jack-hasty, Slattern, Sleazy, Slipshod, Slummock, Untidy

Slow(ing), Slower, Slowly Adagio, Allargando, Andante, Brady, Brake, Broad, Calando, Crawl, Dawdle, Deliberate, Dilatory, Dull, Dumka, ESN, Flag, Gradual, Inchmeal, Lag, Langram, Larghetto, Largo, Lash, Lassu, Late, Leisurely, Lentando, Lento, Lifeless, Loiter, Meno mosso, Obtuse, Pedentatous, Rall(entando), Rein, Reluctant, Retard, Ribattuta, Ritardando, Ritenuto, Slack, Slug, Sluggish, Snaily, Solid, Stem, Tardigrade, Tardive, Tardy

Slug(s) Ammo, Bêche-de-mer, Blow, Bullet, Cosh, Drink, Limaces, Limax, Mollusc, Nerita, Pellet, Shot, Snail, Trepang

Sluggish Dilatory, Drumble, Idler, Inert, Jacent, Lacklustre, Laesie, Languid, Lazy, Lentor, Lethargic, Lug, Phlegmatic, Saturnine, Sleepy, ► SLOW, Stagnant, Tardy, Torpid, Unalive

Slumber Doze, Drowse, Nap, Nod, Sleep, Sloom, Snooze

Slump Decrease, Depression, Deteriorate, Dip, Flop, Recession, Sink, Slouch

Slur(ring) Defame, Drawl, Innuendo, Opprobrium, Slight, Smear, Synaeresis, Tie

Sly Christopher, Clandestine, Coon, Covert, Cunning, Foxy, Leery, Peery, Reynard, Shifty, Sleeveen, Stealthy, Subtle, Tinker, Tod, Tricky, Weasel, Wily

▷**Slyly** may indicate an anagram

Smack(er) Buss, Cuff, Flavour, Foretaste, Fragrance, Hooker, Kiss, Lander, Lips, Pra(h)u, Relish, Salt, Saut, Skelp, Slap, Slat, Smatch, Smouch, Soupçon, Spank, Spice, Splat, Tack, ► TANG, Taste, Thwack, Tincture, Trace, X, Yawl

Small (thing) Atom, Bantam, Beer, Bittie, Bitty, Denier, Dinky, Drib, Elfin, Few, Fry, Grain, Haet, Ha'it, Half-pint, Handful, Holding, Insect, Ion, Leet, Lilliputian, Limited, Lite, ➤ LITTLE, Lock, Low, Meagre, Measly, Midget, Mignon, Miniature, Minikin, Minute, Mite, Modest, Modicum, Peerie, Peewee, Petit(e), Petty, Pigmy, Pink(ie), Pinky, Pint-size, Pittance, Pocket, Poky, Rap, Reduction, Runt, S, Scattering, Scrump, Scrunt, Scut, Shrimp, Slight, Slim, Smattering, Smidge(o)n, Smidgin, Smithereen, Smout, Soupçon, Sprinkling, Spud, Stim, Stunted, Tad, Thin, Tidd(l)y, Tiny, Titch(y), Tittle, Tot(tie), Totty, Trace, Trivial, Wee, Weedy, Whit

Smart(en), Smartest Ache, Acute, Alec, Astute, Best, Bite, Chic, Classy, Clever, Cute, Dandy, Dapper, Dressy, Elegant, Flash, Flip, Fly, Groom, Kookie, Kooky, Natty, Neat, Nifty, Nip, Nobby, Pac(e)y, Pacy, Posh, Preen, Primp, Prink, Pusser, Raffish, Rattling, Ritzy, Saucy, Slick, Sly, Smoke, Smug, Snappy, Soigné(e), Spiff, Sprauncy, Sprightly, Spruce, Sprush, Spry, Sting, Swagger, Sweat, Swish, Tiddley, Tippy, Titivate, Toff, U

Smash(ed), Smasher, Smashing Atom, Brain, Break, Crush, Demolish, Devastate, Dish, High, Kaput, Kill, Lulu, Shatter, Shiver, Slam, Stave, Super, Terrific, Tight, ➤ WRECK

Smear Assoil, Besmirch, Blur, Cervical, Clam, Daub, Defile, Denigrate, Discredit, Drabble, Enarm, Gaum, Gorm, Lick, Oil, Pay, Plaster, Slairg, Slaister, Slather, Slime, Slubber, Slur, Smalm, Smarm, Smudge, Sully, Teer, Traduce, Wax

Smell(ing), Smelly Aroma, BO, Effluvium, Fetor, F(o)etid, Fug, Gale, Gamy, Graveolent, Guff, Hing, Honk, Hum, Mephitis, Miasm(a), Musk, Niff, Nose, Odour, Olent, Olfact(ory), Osmatic, Perfume, Pong, Ponk, Pooh, Rank, Redolent, Reech, Reek, Sar, Savour, ➤ SCENT, Sniff, Snifty, Snook, Snuff, Steam, Stench, Stifle, Stink, Tang, Whiff

Smile(s), Smiling Agrin, Beam, Cheese, Favour, Gioconda, Grin, Rictus, Self-help, Simper, Smirk

Smoke(r), Smoking, Smoky Blast, Bloat, Censer, Chain, Chillum, ➤ CIGAR(ETTE), Cure, Fog, Fuliginous, Fume, Funk, Gasper, Hemp, Incense, Indian hemp, Inhale, Kiff, Latakia, Lum, Lunt, Manil(l)a, Nicotian, Pother, Pudder, Puff, Reech, Reek, Reest, Roke, Smeech, Smeek, Smoor, Smoulder, Smudge, Snout, Toke, Vapour, Viper, Whiff, Wreath

Smooth(e), Smoother, Smoothly Bland, Brent, Buff, Chamfer, Clean, Clockwork, Dress, Dub, Easy, Even, Fettle, File, Flat, Fluent, Glabrous, Glare, Glassy, Glib, Goose, Iron, Legato, Level, Levigate, Linish, Mellifluous, Oil, Plane, Plaster, Rake, Roll, Rub, Sand(er), Satiny, Scrape, Sleek, Slick, Slickenslide, Slur, Smug, Snod, Sostenuto, Streamlined, Suave, Swimmingly, Terete, Terse, Trim, Urbane

Smother Burke, Choke, Muffle, Oppress, Overlie, Smoor, Smore, Stifle, Suppress

Smug Complacent, Conceited, Goody-two-shoes, Neat, Oily, Pi, Self-satisfied, Trim

Smuggle(d), Smuggler, Smuggling Bootleg, Contraband, Donkey, Fair trade, Gunrunning, Moonshine, Mule, Owler, Rum-runner, Run, Secrete, Steal, Traffic

Smut(ty) Bawdy, Blight, Blue, Brand, Burnt-ear, Coom, Filth, Grime, Racy, Soot, Speck

Snack Bever, Bhelpuri, Bite, Brunch, Butty, Canapé, Chack, Crudités, Elevenses, Entremets, Gorp, Meze, Nacket, Nibble, Nocket, Nooning, Nuncheon, Pie, Popcorn, Rarebit, Refreshment, Samo(o)sa, Sandwich, Savoury, Tapa, Taste, Vada, Voidee, Wada, Zakuska

Snag Catch, Contretemps, Drawback, Hindrance, Hitch, Impediment, Knob, Nog, Obstacle, Remora, Rub, Tear

Snail Brian, Cowrie, Cowry, Dodman, Escargot, Gasteropod, Helix, Hodmandod, Limnaea, Lymnaea, Nautilus, Nerite, Roman, Slow, Slug, Strombus, Unicorn-shell, Univalve, Wallfish, Whelk

Snake Aesculapian, Anguine, Anguis, Apod(e), Berg-adder, Constrictor, Hydra, Joe Blake, Kaa, Meander, Ophidian, Plumber's, Reptile, ➤ SERPENT, Squamata, Thread, Wind, Worm

Snap(per), Snappy, Snap up Autolycus, Bite, Break, Brittle, Camera, Click, Crack, Curt, Edgy, Fillip, Girnie, Glom, Gnash, Hanch, Knacker, Knap, Photo, Photogene, Snack, Snatch, Spell, Still, Tetchy, Vigour

Snare Bait, Benet, Engine, Entrap, Gin, Grin, Hook, Illaqueate, Inveigle, Net, Noose, Rat-trap, Springe, Toil, ➤ TRAP, Trapen, Trepan, Web, Weel, Wire

Snarl(ing) Chide, Complicate, Cynic, Enmesh, Gnar(l), Gnarr, Growl, Grumble, Knar, Knot, Snap, Tangle, Yirr

Sneak Area, Carry-tale, Clipe, Clype, Inform, Lurk, Mumblenews, Nim, Peak, Scunge, Skulk, Slip, Slyboots, Snitch, Snoop, Split, Steal, Stoolie, Tell(-tale)

Sneeze (at), Sneezing Atishoo, Sternutation

Sniff Inhale, Nose, Nursle, Nuzzle, Scent, Smell, Snivel, Snort, Snuffle, Vent, Whiff

Snob(bery), Snobbish Cobbler, Crispin, High-hat, Scab, Side, Snooty, Soutar, Souter, Sowter, Toffee-nose, Vain, Vamp

Snore, Snoring Rhonchus, Rout, Snort, Stertorous, Zz

Snort(er) Drink, Grunt, Nare, Nasal, Roncador, Snore, Toot

Snout Bill, Boko, Cigar, Informer, Muzzle, Nose, Nozzle, Proboscis, Schnozzle, Tinker, Tobacco, Wall

Snub Cut, Diss, Go-by, Lop, Pug, Quelch, Rebuff, Reproof, Retroussé, Short, Slap, Slight, Sloan, Sneap, Snool, Wither

Snuff(le) Asarabacca, Dout, Errhine, Extinguish, Maccaboy, Ptarmic, Pulvil, Rappee, Smother, Snaste, Sneesh(an), Sniff, Snift, Snush, Tobacco, Vent

Snuffbox Mill, Mull

Snug(gle) Burrow, Cose, ➤ COSY, Couthie, Couthy, Croodle, Cubby, Cuddle, Embrace, Lion, Neat, Nestle, Nuzzle, Rug, Snod, Tight, Trim

So Ergo, Hence, Sic(h), Sol, Therefore, Thus, True, Very, Yes

Soak Bate, Bath(e), Beath, Bewet, Bloat, Blot, Buck, Cree, Deluge, Drench, Drink, Drook, Drouk, Drown, Drunk, Duck, Dunk, Embay, Embrue, Fleece, Grog, Imbrue, Infuse, Lush, Macerate, Marinate, Mop, Oncome, Permeate, Rait, Rate, Ret(t), Saturate, Seep, Sipe, Sog, Sop, Souce, Souse, Sows(s)e, Steep, Sype, Thwaite, Toper, Wet

Soap(y) Cake, Carbolic, Flake, Flannel, Flattery, Green, Lather, Metallic, Moody, Saddle, Saponaceous, Saponin, Sawder, Slime, Soft, Suds, Sudser, Sugar

Soar(ing) Ascend, Essorant, Fly, Glide, Rise, Tower, Zoom

Sociable, Sociability Affable, Cameraderie, Chummy, Cosy, Extravert, Folksy, Friendly, Genial, Gregarious

Socialism, Socialist Champagne, Chartist, Dergue, Fabian, Fourierism, ILP, International, Lansbury, Left(y), Marxism, Nihilism, Owen(ist), Owenite, Pinko, Red, Revisionist, Sandinista, Spartacist, Utopian, Webb

Society Affluent, Association, Body, Building, Camorra, Class, Club, College, Company, Co-op, Culture, Dorcas, Elks, Fabian, Fashion, Foresters, Freemans, Freemasons, Friendly, Friends, Glee club, Group, Guilds, Haut monde, High, Institute, Invincibles, Ku-klux-klan, Law, Linnean, Lodge, Mafia, Mau-mau, Oddfellows, Oratory, Order, Permissive, Plural, Pop, Provident, Rotary, S, School, Secret, Soc, Soroptomist, Sorority, Stakeholder, Tammany, Toc H, Ton, Tong, Triad, U

Socket Acetabulum, Alveole, Budget, Gudgeon, Hollow, Hosel, Hot shoe, Jack, Nave, Ouch, Pod, Port, Power-point, Strike

Sod Clump, Delf, Delph, Divot, Gazo(o)n, Mool, Mould, Mouls, Scraw, Sward, Turf

Sofa Canapé, Chesterfield, Couch, Daybed, Divan, Dos-à-dos, Dosi-do, Ottoman, Settee, Squab, Tête-à-tête

Soft(en), Softener, Softening, Softly Amalgam, Anneal, B, BB, Blet, Boodle, Cedilla, Cree, Dim, Doughy, Emolliate, Emollient, Flabby, Gentle, Hooly, Humanise, Lash, Lax, Lenient, Limp, Low, Mease, Mellow, Melt, Mild, Milksop, Mitigate, Modulate, Mollify, Morendo, Mulch, Mush(y), Mute, Neale, Nesh, Option, P, Palliate, Pastel, Piano, Plushy, Porous, Propitiate, Rait, Rate, Relent, Sentimental, Silly, Slack, Squashy, Squidgy, Squishy, Temper, ➤ TENDER, Tone, Velvet, Weak

Soil(ed), Soily Acid, Adscript, Agronomy, Alluvium, Bedraggle, Chemozem, Clay, Defile, Desecrate, Dinge, Dirt(y), Discolour, Earth, Edaphic, Glebe, Grey, Grimy, Ground, Gumbo, Hotbed, Humus, Illuvium, Lair, Land, Latosol, Loam, Loess, Lome, Loss, Mire, Mo(u)ld, Mool, Mud, Peat, Ped, Pedology, Phreatic, Planosol, Podsol, Podzol, Pure, Regar, Regur, Rendzina, Root-ball, Sal, Smudge, Smut, Solonchak, Solonetz, Solum, Soot, Stain, Stonebrash, Sully, Tarnish, Tash, Terrain, Terricolous, Tilth, Udal, Umber

Soldier(s) Alpini, Ant, Anzac, Army, Arna(o)ut, Atkins, ATS, Battalion, Bombardier, Borderer, Brigade, Cadet, Campaigner, Chindit, Cohort, Colonel, Colours, Commando, Confederate, Cornet, Corp(s), Cossack, Doughboy, Draftee, Dragoon, Emmet, Fighter, Foot, Fusilier, GI, Grenadier, Guardsman, Guerilla, Gurkha, Hussar, Inf(antry), Ironside, Irregular, Joe, Lancer, Legionary, Legionnaire, Line, Militiaman, Minuteman, Musketeer, Non-com, OR, Orderly, Paratroop, Partisan, Phalanx, Platoon, Private, Rank(er), Regiment, Regular,

Rifleman, Sabre, Samurai, SAS, Sepoy, Serviceman, Squaddy, Stormtrooper, Subaltern, Terrier, Tommy, Trooper, Troops, Unknown, Vet(eran), Volunteer, Warrior

▷ **Soldiers** may indicate bread for boiled eggs

Sole, Solitaire, Solitary Alone, Anchoret, Anchorite, Clump, Fish, Incommunicado, Lemon, Lonesome, Megrim, Merl, Meunière, Monkish, Only, Pad, Palm, Patience, Pelma, Planta(r), Plantigrade, Platform, Recluse, Scaldfish, Single(ton), Skate, Slip, Smear-dab, Tap, Thenar, Unique, Vibram®, Vola

Solemn Austere, Devout, Earnest, Grave, Gravitas, Owlish, Po-faced, Sacred, Sedate, Serious, Sober, Sobersides

Solicit Accost, Approach, Ask, Attract, Bash, ➤ BEG, Canvass, Cottage, Importun(at)e, Plead, Ply, Speer, Speir, Tout, Woo

Solid(arity), Solidify Cake, Chunky, Clot, Clunky, Compact, Comradeship, Concrete, Cone, Congeal, Consolidate, Cube, Cylinder, Dense, Enneahedron, Firm, Foursquare, Freeze, Frustrum, Fuchsin(e), Gel, Hard, Holosteric, Impervious, Merbromin, Octahedron, Pakka, Petrarchan, Platonic, Polyhedron, Prism, Pucka, Pukka, Robust, Set, Stilbene, Sublimate, Substantial, Tetrahedron, Thick, Unanimous

Solo Aria, Cadenza, Cavatine, Concertante, Lone, Monodrama, Monody, Ombre, One-man, Scena, Variation

▷ **Solution** may indicate an anagram

Solve(d), Solver Assoil, Casuist, Clear, Crack, Decode, Loast, Loose, Read(er), Troubleshoot, Unclew, Unriddle

Solvent Acetaldehyde, Acetone, Alcahest, Aldol, Alkahest, Anisole, Aqua-regia, Banana oil, Cleanser, Decalin, Diluent, Dioxan(e), Eluant, Eluent, Ether, Funded, Furan, Hexane, Ligroin, Megilp, Menstruum, Methanol, Methylal, Naphtha, Paraldehyde, Picoline, Protomic, Pyridine, Sound, Stripper, Terebene, Terpineol, Tetrachloromethane, Thiophen, Toluene, Toluol, Trike, Trilene, Turpentine

Sombre Dark, Drab, Drear, Dull, Gloomy, Grave, Morne, Subfusc, Subfusk, Sullen, Triste

Some Any, Arrow, Ary, Certain, Few, Divers, One, Part, Portion, Quota, These, They, Wheen

▷ **Some** may indicate a hidden word

▷ **Somehow** may indicate an anagram

Sometime(s) Erstwhile, Ex, Former, Occasional, Off and on, Quondam

Son Boy, Disciple, Epigon(e), Fils, Fitz, Lad, Lewis, M(a)c, Offspring, Prodigal, Progeny, Scion

Song Air, Anthem, Aria, Art, Aubade, Ballad, Barcarol(l)e, Berceuse, Blues, Burden, Calypso, Canticle, Carol, Catch, Chanson, Cha(u)nt, Descant, Dirge, Ditty, Flamenco, Folk, Glee, Hillbilly, Hymn, Internationale, Lay, Lied(er), Lilt, Lullaby, Lyric, Madrigal, Marseillaise, Melody, Number, Paean, Psalm, Rap, Rhapsody, Roulade, Roundelay, Rune, Scat, Serenade, Shanty, Siren, Spiritual, Stave, Strain, Strophe, Swan, Taps, Theme, Torch, Trill, Tune, Warble, Yodel

Sonnet Amoret, Italian, Petrarch(i)an, Shakespearean, Shakespearian, Spenserian

Soon(er) Anon, Directly, Erelong, OK, Oklahoma, Presently, Shortly, Tight, Timely, Tite(ly), Tite, Tyte

Soothe, Soothing Accoy, Allay, Anetic, Appease, Assuage, Bucku, Calm, Compose, Demulcent, Emollient, Irenic, Lenitive, Lull, Mellifluous, Mollify, Pacific, Paregoric, Poultice, Quell, Rock

Sophisticate(d) Blasé, Boulevardier, City slicker, Civilised, Cosmopolitan, Couth, Doctor, High-end, Patrician, Polished, Sative, Slicker, Svelte, Urbane, Worldly

▷**Sophoclean** may indicate Greek (alphabet, etc)

Sorcerer, Sorceress, Sorcery Angakok, Ashipu, Circe, Conjury, Diablerie, Hoodoo, Kadaitcha, Kurdaitcha, Lamia, Mage, Magic(ian), Magus, Medea, Merlin, Morgan le Fay, Mother Shipton, Necromancer, Obi, Pishogue, Shaman, Sortilege, Voodoo, Warlock, Witch, Wizard

Sore(ly), Sores Abrasion, Bitter, Blain, Boil, Canker, Chancre, Chap, Chilblain, Cold, Dearnly, Felon, Gall, Impost(h)ume, Ireful, Kibe, Quitter, Quittor, Raw, Rupia(s), Saddle, Sair, Shiver, Sitfast, Surbate, Ulcer(s), Whitlow, Wound

Sorrow(ful) Affliction, Distress, Dole, Dolour, ➤ GRIEF, Lament, Misery, Nepenthe, Penance, Pietà, Remorse, Rue, Triste, Wae, Waugh, Wirra, Woe, Yoop

Sorry Ashamed, Contrite, Miserable, Oops, Penitent, Pitiful, Poor, Regretful, Relent, Wretched

▷**Sorry** may indicate an anagram

▶**Sorts** see OUT OF SORTS

▷**So to speak** may indicate 'sound of'

Soul(ful) Alma, Ame, Anima, Animist, Atman, Ba, Brevity, Deep, Eschatology, Expressive, Heart, Inscape, Larvae, Manes, Person, Psyche, Saul, Shade, Spirit

Sound(ed), Soundness, Sound system Accurate, Acoustic, Audio, Bleep, Blow, Bong, Cacophony, Chime, Chord, Clam, Clang, Clop, Clunk, Dental, Echo, Fast, Fathom, Fettle, Fit, Hale, Harmonics, Healthy, Hearty, Hi-fi, Inlet, Knell, Lucid, Mersey, Milford, Music, Narrow, ➤ NOISE, Onomatopaeia, Oompah, Orthodox, Palatal, Peal, Phone(me), Phonetic, Phonic, Plap, Plink, Plonk, Plop, Plosion, Plumb, Plummet, Plunk, Probe, Quadraphonic(s), Rale, Rational, Real, Ring, Robust, Rumble, Rustle, Safe, Sane, Solid, Sone, Souffle, Sough, Stereo, Strait, Swish, Tannoy®, Thorough, Timbre, Tone, Trig, Trumpet, Twang, Ultrasonic(s), Unharmed, Valid, Voice, Vowel, Well, Whole(some)

Soup Alphabet, Bird's nest, Bisque, Borsch, Bouillabaisse, Bouillon, Broth, Chowder, Cock-a-leekie, Consommé, Gazpacho, Gumbo, Minestrone, Mock turtle, Mulligatawny, Oxtail, Pot(t)age, Pot-au-feu, Primordial, Puree, Ramen, Rubaboo, Sancoche, Skink, Stock, Turtle, Vichyssoise

▷**Soup** may indicate an anagram

Sour(puss) Acerb, Acescent, Acid, Acidulate, Alegar, Bitter, Citric, Crab, Esile, Ferment, Moody, Stingy, ➤ TART, Turn, Verjuice, Vinegarish

Source Authority, Basis, Bottom, Centre, Database, Derivation, Egg, Fons, Font, Fount, Fountain-head, Germ, Head-stream, Mine, Mother, Origin, Parent, Pi, Pion, Provenance, Quarry, Reference, Rise, Root, Seat, Seed, Spring, Springhead, Urn, Well, Wellhead, Wellspring, Ylem

South(ern), Southerner Austral, Dago, Decanal, Decani, Dixieland, Meridian, S

South African Bantu, Caper, Grikwa, Griqua, Hottentot, Kaf(f)ir, SA, Springbok, Swahili, Xhosa, ZA, Zulu

Souvenir Keepsake, Memento, Relic, Remembrance, Scalp, Token, Trophy

Sovereign(ty), Sovereign remedy Anne, Autocrat, Bar, Condominium, Couter, Dominant, ER, Goblin, Haemony, Harlequin, Imperial, Imperium, James, King, L, Liege, Nizam, Pound, Quid, Royalty, Ruler, Shiner, Supreme, Swaraj, Synarchy

Sow(ing) Catchcrop, Elt, Foment, Gilt, Inseminate, Plant, Scatter, Seed, Sprue, Strew, Yelt

Spa Baden, Baden-Baden, Bath, Evian, Harrogate, Hydro, Kurhaus, Kursaal, Leamington, Vichy

Space(d), Spacing Abyss, Acre, Area, Areola, Bay, Bracket, Breathing, Cellule, Concourse, Cubbyhole, Deep, Distal, Distance, Elbow-room, Esplanade, Ether, Expanse, Extent, Footprint, Gap, Glade, Goaf, Gob, Gutter, Hair, Headroom, Inner, Interstice, Lacuna, Lair, Legroom, Logie, Lumen, Lung, Maidan, Metope, Muset, Musit, Orbit, Outer, Quad, ➤ ROOM, Ruelle, Sheets, Spandrel, Spandril, Step, Storage, Tympanum, Ullage, Vacuole, Vacuum, Vast, Vector, Void

Spacecraft, Space agency, Space object, Spaceship, Space station Apollo, Capsule, Explorer, Galileo, Giotto, Lander, LEM, Mariner, MIR, Module, NASA, Orbiter, Pioneer, Probe, Quasar, Salyut, Shuttle, Skylab, Soyuz, Sputnik, Starship, Tardis, Vostok, Voyager

Spade Breastplough, Caschrom, Cas crom, Castrato, Detective, Graft, Loy, Negro, Paddle, Pattle, Pettle, Pick, S, Shovel, Slane, Spit, Suit, Tus(h)kar, Tus(h)ker, Twiscar

Span Age, Arch, Attention, Bestride, Bridge, Chip, Ctesiphon, Extent, Life, Range

Spaniard, Spanish Alguacil, Alguazil, Barrio, Basque, Cab, Caballero, Carlist, Castilian, Catalan, Chicano, Dago, Don, Fly, Grandee, Hidalgo, Hispanic, Jose, Main, Mestizo, Mozarab, Pablo, Señor, Spic(k), Spik

Spar Barytes, Blue John, Boom, Bowsprit, Box, Cauk, Cawk, Fight, Gaff, Iceland, Jib-boom, Mainyard, Martingale, Mast, Nail-head, Outrigger, Rafter, Rail, Ricker, Shearleg, Sheerleg, Snotter, Spathic, Sprit, Steeve, Stile, Triatic, Yard

Spare, Sparing Angular, Cast-off, Dup(licate), Economical, Free, Frugal, Gash, Gaunt, Hain, Lean, Lenten, Other, Pardon, Reserve, Rib, Save, Scant, Slender, Stint, Subseive, Thin

Spark Animate, Arc, Beau, Blade, Bluette, Dandy, Flash, Funk, Ignescent, Kindle, Life, Scintilla, Smoulder, Spunk, Trigger, Zest

Sparkle(r), Sparkling Aerated, Coruscate, Diamanté, Effervesce, Elan, Emicate, Fire, Fizz, Flicker, Frizzante, Glint, Glisten, Glitter, Pétillant, Scintillate, Seltzer, Seltzogene, Spangle, Spritzig, Spumante, Twinkle, Verve, Witty, Zap

Spartan(s) Austere, Basic, Enomoty, Hardy, Helot, Laconian, Lysander, Menelaus, Severe, Valiant

Spasm(odic) Blepharism, Chorea, Clonus, Cramp, Crick, Fit(ful), Hiccup, Hippus, Intermittent, Irregular, ➤ JERK, Kink, Laryngismus, Nystagmus, Paroxysm, Periodical, Start, Tetany, Throe, Tonic, Tonus, Trismus, Twinge, Twitch

▷**Spasmodic** may indicate an anagram

Speak(er), Speaking Address, Articulate, Broach, Chat, Cicero, Collocuter, Communicate, Converse, Coo, Declaim, Dilate, Discourse, Diseur, Dwell, Effable, Elocution, Eloquent, Expatiate, Express, Extemporise, Filibuster, Intercom, Intone, Inveigh, Jabber, Jaw, Lip, Loq, Mang, Mention, Mina, Mike, Mouth, Mouthpiece, Nark, Open, Orate, Orator, Palaver, Parlance, Parley, Pontificate, Prate, Preach, Prelector, Rhetor, ➤ SAY, Sayne, Spout, Spruik, Stump, Talk, Tannoy®, Tongue, Trap, Tweeter, Utter, Voice, Waffle, Witter, Word

Spear Ash, Asparagus, Assagai, Assegai, Dart, Gad, Gavelock, Gig, Gungnir, Hastate, Impale, Javelin, Lance(gay), Launcegaye, Leister, Morris-pike, Partisan, Pierce, Pike, Pilum, Skewer, Spike, Trident, Trisul(a), Waster

Special Ad hoc, Constable, Designer, Distinctive, Extra, Important, Notable, Notanda, Particular, Peculiar, Specific

Specialise, Specialist(s) Authority, Concentrate, Connoisseur, Consultant, ENT, Expert, Illuminati, Maestro, Major, Quant, Recondite, Technician

Specific(ally), Specified, Specify As, Ascribe, Assign, Cure, Define, Detail, Explicit, Itemise, Medicine, Namely, Precise, Remedy, Sp, Special, Stipulate, The, Trivial

Speck(le) Atom, Bit, Dot, Fleck, Floater, Freckle, Muscae volitantes, Particle, Peep(e), Pip, Spreckle, Stud

Spectacle(d), Spectacles, Spectacular Bifocals, Blinks, Colourful, Epic, Escolar, Glasses, Goggles, Optical, Pageant, Pince-nez, Pomp, Preserves, Scene, Show, Sight, Son et lumière, Sunglasses, Tattoo

Spectator(s) Bystander, Dedans, Etagère, Eyer, Gallery, Gate, Groundling, Kibitzer, Observer, Onlooker, Standerby, Witness

Spectral, Spectre Apparition, Boggle, Bogy, Eidolon, Empusa, Ghost, Idola, Iridal, Malmag, Phantasm, Phantom, Phasma, Spirit, Spook, Tarsier, Walking-straw, Wraith

Speculate, Speculative, Speculator Arbitrage, Bear, Better, Bull, Conjecture, Flier, Flyer, Gamble, Guess, Ideology, If, Imagine, Meditate, Notional, Operate, Pinhooker, Shark, Stag, Theoretical, Theorise, Thought, Trade, Wonder

Speech, Speech element Accents, Address, Argot, Articulation, Bunkum, Burr, Delivery, Dialect, Diatribe, Diction, Direct, Dithyramb, English, Eulogy, Free, Gab, Glossolalia, Harangue, Idiolect, Idiom, Indirect, Jargon, Keynote, Lallation, ➤ LANGUAGE, Lingua franca, Litany, Monologue, Morph(eme), Oral, Oration, Parabasis, Parle, Peroration, Phasis, Philippic, Prolog(ue), Reported, Rhetoric, Sandhi, Screed, Sermon, Side, Slang, Soliloquy, Talk, Tirade, Tongue, Vach, Visible, Voice

Speed(ily), Speedy Accelerate, Alacrity, Amain, Amphetamine, Apace, Bat, Belive, Belt, Breakneck, Burn, Celerity, Clip, Dart, Despatch, DIN, Dispatch, Expedite, Fangy, Fast, Fleet, Further, Gait, Gallop, Goer, Gun, Haste, Hie, Hotfoot, Hypersonic, Induce, Knot, Lick, Mach, Merchant, MPH, ➤ PACE, Phase, Pike, Post-haste, Pronto, Race, Rapidity, Rate, RPS, Scorch, Scud, Scurr, Skirr, Soon, Spank, Split, Stringendo, Supersonic, Swift, Tach, Tear, Tempo, V, Velocity, Vroom, Whid, Wing

Spell(ing) Abracadabra, Bewitch, Bout, Cantrip, Charm, Conjuration, Do, Elf-shoot, Enchantment, Entrance, Fit, Go, Gri(s)-gri(s), Hex, Incantation, Innings, Jettatura, Juju, Knur, ➤ MAGIC, Need-fire, Nomic, Orthography, Period, Philter, Philtre, Pinyin, Relieve, Ride, Romaji, Run, Rune, Scat, Shot, Signify, Snap, Snatch, Sorcery, Sp, Spasm, Splinter, Stint, Stretch, Tack, Tour, Trick, Turn, Weird, Whammy, Witchcraft

Spend(ing) Anticipate, Birl, Blue, Boondoggling, Consume, Deplete, Disburse, Exhaust, Fritter, Live, Outlay, Pass, Pay, Splash, Splurge, Ware

Spendthrift Prodigal, Profligate, Profuser, Wastrel

Sphere, Spherical Armillary, Celestial, Discipline, Element, Field, Firmament, Globe, Mound, Orb(it), Planet, Prolate, Province, Realm, Theatre, Wheel

Spice, Spicy Anise, Aniseed, Cardamom, Cinnamon, Clove, Clow, Coriander, Cum(m)in, Dash, Devil, Garam masala, Ginger, Mace, Marjoram, Masala, Myrrh, Nutmeg, Oregano, Paprika, Peppercorn, Pimento, Piquant, Season, Tansy, Tarragon, Taste, Turmeric, Vanilla, Variety

Spider(s) Arachnid, Aranea, Araneida, Attercop, Bird, Cardinal, Cheesemite, Citigrade, Diadem, Epeira, Epeirid, Ethercap, Ettercap, Funnel-web, Harvester, Harvestman, Hunting, Huntsman, Jumping, Mite, Money, Pan, Red, Redback, Rest, Saltigrade, Spinner, Strap, Tarantula, Telary, Trapdoor, Violin, Water, Wolf

Spike(d) Barb, Brod, Calk, Calt(h)rop, Chape, Cloy, Crampon, Ear, Fid, Foil, Gad, Goad, Grama, Herissé, Impale, Lace, Locusta, Marlin(e), Nail, ➤ PIERCE, Point, Pricket, Prong, Puseyite, Rod, Sharp, Shod, Skewer, Spadix, Spear, Spicate, Spicule, Strobiloid, Tang, Thorn, Tine

Spill(age) Divulge, Drop, Fidibus, Jackstraw, Lamplighter, Leakage, Let, Overflow, Overset, Scail, Scale, Shed, Skail, Slop, Stillicide, Taper, Tumble

Spin(ner), Spinning Arachne, Birl, Cribellum, Cut, Dextrorse, DJ, Flat, Flip, Gimp, Googly, Gymp, Gyrate, Gyre, Hurl, Lachesis, Mole, Nun, Peg-top, Pirouette, Precess, Prolong, Purl, Rev(olve), Ride, Rotate, Screw, Sinistrorse, Slide, Spider, Stator, Strobic, Swirl, Swivel, Throstle, Tirl, Toss, Trill, Twirl, Twist, Wheel, Whirl, Work

Spinal (chord), Spine, Spiny Acromion, Aculeus, Areole, Backbone, Barb, Chine, Coccyx, Column, Doorn, Epidural, Muricate, Myelon, Notochord, Ocotillo, Prickle, Quill, Rachial, Ray, R(h)achis, Thorn, Tragacanth

▶ **Spine** see SPINAL

Spirit(ed) Akvavit, Alcohol, Angel, Animation, Aqua vitae, Aquavit, Arak, Ardent, Ariel, Arrack, Blithe, Bogle, Brandy, Bravura, Brio, Cant, Cherub, Courage, Creature, Daemon, Dash, Distillation, Div, Djinn(i), ➤ DRINK, Dryad, Eblis, Elan, Element(al), Emit, Empusa, Entrain, Esprit, Essence, Ethos, Faints, Familiar, Feints, Fetich(e), Fetish, Fettle, Fight, Firewater, Gamy, Geist, Geneva, Genie, Genius, ➤ GHOST, Ghoul, Ginger, Ginn, Gism, Go, Grappa, Gremlin, Grit, Grog, Gumption, Heart, Hollands, Imp, Incubus, Jinn(i), Ka, Kelpie, Kindred, Kobold, Larva, Lemur(e), Liquor, Lively, Loki, Manes, Manito(u), Mare, Metal, Meths, Methyl(ated), Mettle, Mobby, Morale, Nix, Nobody, Numen, Ondine, Panache, Pecker, Pep, Peri, Pernod®, Petrol, Phantom, Pluck(y), Pneuma, Poltergeist, Poteen, Presence, Proof, Psyche, Puck, Python, Racy, Ruin, Rye, Schnapps, Seraph, Shade, Shadow, Short, Spectre, Spright,

Sprite, Spunk, Steam, Surgical, Sylph, Team, Tequila, Ton, Turps, Undine, Verve, Vigour, Vim, Vodka, Voodoo, White, Wili, Wood, Wraith, Zing

Spiritual Aerie, Aery, Coon-song, Ecclesiastic, Ethereous, Eyrie, Eyry, Incorporeal, Negro, Planchette

Spit(ting), Spittle Barbecue, Broach, Chersonese, Dead ringer, Dribble, Drool, Emptysis, Eructate, Expectorate, Fuff, Gob, Golly, Gooby, Grill, Hawk, Impale, Jack, Lookalike, Peninsula, Ras, Ringer, Rotisserie, Saliva, Skewer, Slag, Spade(ful), Spawl, Sputter, Sputum, Tombolo, Yesk, Yex

Spite(ful) Grimalkin, Harridan, Irrespective, Malevolent, Malice, Petty, Pique, Rancour, Spleen, Venom, Waspish

Splash Blash, Blue, Dabble, Dash, Dog, Drip, Feature, Flouse, Fl(o)ush, Gardyloo, Jabble, Ja(u)p, Jirble, Paddle, Plap, Plop, Plowter, Sket, Slosh, Soda, Sozzle, Spairge, Spat(ter), Spectacle, Splat(ch), Splatter, Splodge, Splosh, Splotch, Spray, Spree, Squatter, Swash, Swatter, Water, Wet

Splendid, Splendour Braw, Brilliant, Bully, Capital, Champion, Clinker, Dandy, Eclat, Effulgent, Excellent, Fine, Finery, Gallant, Garish, Glittering, Glorious, Glory, Gorgeous, Grand(eur), Grandiose, Heroic, Lustrous, Noble, Palatial, Panache, Pomp, Proud, Radiant, Rich, Ripping, Stunning, Super(b), Wally

▷ **Spliced** may indicate an anagram

Splinter(s) Flinder, Fragment, Matchwood, Shatter, Shiver, Skelf, Sliver, Spale, Spicula, Spill

Split Axe, Banana, Bifid, Bifurcate, Bisect, Break, Chasm, Chine, Chop, Clint, Clove(n), Crack, Crevasse, Cut, Disjoin, Distrix, ► DIVIDE, Division, Divorce, End, Fissile, Fissure, Grass, Lacerate, Partition, Red(d), Rift(e), Rip, Rive, Ryve, Schism, Scissor, Segregate, Separate, Sever, Share, Skive, Slit, Sliver, Spall, Spalt, Speld, Tattle, Tmesis, Told, Wedge

▷ **Split** may indicate a word to become two; one word inside another; or a connection with Yugoslavia

Spoil(s), Spoilt Addle, Blight, Booty, Botch, Bribe, Coddle, Corrupt, ► DAMAGE, Dampen, Deface, Defect, Deform, Dish, Foul, Hames, Harm, Impair(ed), Indulge, Loot, Maltreat, Mar, Muck, Mutilate, Mux, Pamper, Pet, Pickings, Pie, Plunder, Prize, Queer, Rait, Rate, Ravage, Ret, Rot, Ruin, Scupper, Swag, Taint, Tarnish, Vitiate, Winnings

▷ **Spoil(ed), Spoilt** may indicate an anagram

▷ **Spoken** may indicate the sound of a word or letter

Sponge(r), Spongy Battenburg, Bum, Cadge, Cake, Diact, Free-loader, Lig, Loofa(h), Madeira, Madeleine, Mooch, Mop, Parasite, Scrounge, Sop, Sucker, Swab, Sycophant, Tetract, Tiramisu, Wangle, Wipe, Zoophyte

Sponsor(ship) Aegis, Angel, Backer, Egis, Finance, Godfather, Godparent, Gossip, Guarantor, Lyceum, Patron, Surety

Spontaneous Autonomic, Gratuitous, Immediate, Impromptu, Impulsive, Instant, Intuitive, Natural

Spoof Chouse, Cozenage, Deception, Delusion, Fallacy, ➤ HOAX, Imposture, Ramp, Swindle, Trick

Spoon(ful), Spoon-shaped Apostle, Canoodle, Cochlear, Dollop, Dose, Gibby, Labis, Ladle, Mote, Neck, Rat-tail, Runcible, Scoop, Scud, Server, Spatula, Sucket, Woo, Wooden

Sport(s), Sporting, Sportive Aikido, Amusement, Angling, Aquatics, Autocross, Blood, Bonspiel, Breakaway, Brick, By-form, Contact, Curling, Cyclo-cross, Daff, Dalliance, Dally, Deviant, Drag-racing, Field, Freak, Frisky, Frolic, Fun, ➤ GAME, Gent, Gig, In, Joke, Karate, Kickboxing, Korfball, Laik, Lake, Langlauf, Lark, Merimake, Merry, Morph, Mutagen, Octopush, Orienteering, Pal, Paragliding, Parasailing, Parascending, Paraskiing, Polo, Recreate, Rogue, RU, Shinny, Shinty, Skijoring, Spectator, Speed-skating, Speedway, Squash, Steeplechase, Sumo, Tournament, Tourney, Toy, Trampolining, Water polo, Wear, Weightlifting, Windsurfing, Wrestling

▷ **Sport(s)** may indicate an anagram

Spot(s), Spotted, Spotting, Spotty Ace, Acne, Areola, Areole, Bead, Beauty, Blackhead, Blain, Blemish, Blind, Blip, Blob, Blot, Blotch(ed), Blur, Brind(l)ed, Carbuncle, Caruncle, Cash, Check, Cloud, Colon, Comedo, Corner, Cyst, Dance, Dapple(-bay), Dick, Discern, Discover, Dot, Drop, Eruption, Espy, Eye, Fleck, Floater, Foxed, Freak, Furuncle, G, Gay, High, Hot, Jam, Leaf, Lentago, Location, Loran, Macle, Mackle, Macul(at)e, Mail, Meal, Measly, Microdot, Moil, Mole, Mote, Note, Ocellar, Ocellus, Paca, Papula, Parhelion, Patch, Peep(e), Penalty, Pied, Pimple, Pin, Pip, Place, Pock, Punctuate, Pupil, Pustule, Quat, Radar, Rash, Recognise, Red, Skewbald, Smut, Soft, Speck(le), Speculum, Splodge, Spy, Stigma, Sully, Taint, Touch, Weak, Whelk, Whitehead, X, Zit

Spouse Companion, Consort, F(i)ere, Hubby, Husband, Mate, Oppo, Partner, Pheer, Pirrauru, Wife, Xant(h)ippe

Spout(er) Adjutage, Erupt, Gargoyle, Geyser, Grampus, Gush, Impawn, Jet, Mouth, Nozzle, Orate, Pawn, Pourer, Raile, Rote, Spurt, Stream, Stroup, Talk, Tap, Vent

Sprain(ed) Crick, Reckan, Rick, Stave, Strain, Wrench, Wrick

Spray Aerosol, Aigrette, Atomiser, Buttonhole, Corsage, Egret, Hair, Posy, Rose, Rosula, Shower, Sparge, Spindrift, Splash, Sprent, Sprig, Sprinkle, Spritz, Strinkle, Syringe, Twig

▷**Spray** may indicate an anagram

Spread(ing), Spreader Air, Apply, Banquet, Bestrew, Blow-ing, Branch, Bush, Butter, Carpet, Centre, Contagious, Couch, Coverlet, Coverlid, Deploy, Diffract, Diffuse, Dilate, Disperse, Dissemination, Distribute, Divulge, Drape, Dripping, Elongate, Expand, Extend, Fan, Feast, Flare, Guac(h)amole, Honeycomb, Jam, Lay, Marge, Multiply, Nutter, Oleo, Open, Overgrow, Paste, Perfuse, Pervade, Pâté, Patent, Patulous, Picnic, Propagate, Radiate, Ran, Run, Scale, Set, Sheet, Slather, Smear, Smorgasbord, Sow, Span, Speld, Spelder, Spillover, Splay, Sprawl, Spray, Straw, Stretch, Strew, Suffuse, Teer, Unfold, Unguent, Widen, Wildfire

▷**Spread** may indicate an anagram

Spring(s), Springtime, Springy Arise, Bolt, Bounce, Bound, Box, Bunt, Cabriole, Caper, Capriole, Cavort, Cee, Coil, Dance, Elastic, Eye, Fount(ain), Germinate, Geyser, Grass, Hair, Helix, Hop, Hot, Jump, Leap, Lent, May, Originate, Persephone, Pierian, Pounce, Prance, Primavera, Resilient, Ribbon, Rise, Season, Skip, Snap, Spa, Spang, Spaw, Stem, Sulphur, Thermae, Thermal, Vault, Ware, Waterhole, Well-(head), Whip

▷**Spring(y)** may indicate an anagram

Sprinkle(r) Asperge, Aspergill(um), Bedash, Bedrop, Bescatter, Caster, Dredge, Dust, Hyssop, Lard, Pouncet, Rose, Scatter, Shower, Sow, Spa(i)rge, Spatter, Splash, Spray, Spritz, Strinkle

Sprout Braird, Breer, Bud, Burgeon, Chit, Crop, Eye, Germ(inate), Grow, Pullulate, Shoot, Spire, Tendron, Vegetate

Spruce Dapper, Engelmann, Natty, Neat, Norway, Picea, Pitch-tree, Prink, Shipshape, Sitka, Smart, Spiff, Tidy, Tree, Trim, Tsuga

Spur Accourage, Activate, Calcar(ate), Encourage, Fame, Fire, Goad, Heel, Incite, Limb, Lye, Needle, Prick, Rippon, Rowel, Shoot, Spica, Stimulus, Strut, Stud, Tar, Urge

▷ **Spurious** may indicate an anagram

Spy, Spies Agent, Beagle, Caleb, CIA, Descry, Dicker, Emissary, Fink, Informer, Keeker, Mata Hari, MI, Mole, Mouchard, Nark, Nose, Operative, Pimp, Plant, Pry, Recce, Scout, See, Setter, Shadow, Sinon, Sleeper, Spetsnaz, Spook, Tout, Wait

Squalid, Squalor Abject, Colluvies, Dinge, Dingy, Filth, Frowsy, Grungy, Poverty, Scuzzy, Seedy, Sleazy, Slum(my), Slurb, Sordid

Squall Blast, Blow, Commotion, Cry, Drow, Flaw, Flurry, Gust, Sumatra, Wail, Yell, Yowl

Squander Blow, Blue, Fritter, Frivol, Mucker, Slather, Splash, Splurge, Ware, ➤ WASTE

Square(d), Squares Agree, Anta, Ashlar, Ashler, Bang, Belgrave, Berkeley, Block, Bribe, Chequer, Compone, Compony, Corny, Deal, Dinkum, Even(s), Fair, Fog(e)y, Forty-nine, Fossil, Four, Gobony, Grey, Grosvenor, Leicester, Level, Magic, Meal, Nasik, Neandert(h)aler, Nine, Norma, Old-fashioned, Palm, Passé, Pay, Perfect, Piazza, Place, Plaza, Platz, Quad(rangle), Quadrate, Quarry, Quits, Red, Rood, S, Set(t), Sloane, Solid, Squier, Squire, Straight, T, Tee, Times, Traditionalist, Trafalgar, Unhip

Squash Adpress, Butternut, Conglomerate, Crush, Gourd, Kia-ora, Knead, Marrow, Mash, Oblate, Pattypan, Press, Pulp, Silence, Slay, Slew, Slue, Squidge, Suppress, Torpedo

Squeeze Bleed, Chirt, Coll, Compress, Concertina, Constrict, Cram, Crowd, Crush, Dispunge, Exact, Express, Extort, Hug, Jam, Mangle, Milk, Preace, Press, Sandwich, Sap, Scrooge, Scrouge, Scrowdge, Scruze, Shoehorn, Squash, Squish, Sweat, Thrutch, Wring

Squid Calamari, Calamary, Cephalopod, Ink-fish, Loligo, Mortar, Nautilus, Octopus

▷ **Squiggle** may indicate an anagram

Squint(ing) Boss-eyed, Cast, Cock-eye, Cross-eye, Glance, Gledge, Glee, Gley, Heterophoria, Louche, Proptosis, Skellie, Skelly, Sken, Squin(n)y, Strabism, Swivel-eye, Vergence, Wall-eye

Squire Armiger(o), Beau, Donzel, Escort, Hardcastle, Headlong, Land-owner, Scutiger, Swain, Western

Squirt(er) Chirt, Cockalorum, Douche, Jet, Scoosh, Scoot, Skoosh, Spirt, Spout, Spritz, Urochorda, Wet, Whiffet, Whippersnapper

Stab Bayonet, Crease, Creese, Dag, Effort, Go, Gore, Guess, Jab, Knife, Kreese, Kris, Lancinate, Pang, Pierce, Pink, Poniard, Prick, Prong, Stick, Stiletto, Wound

Stabilise(r), Stability Aileron, Balance, Emulsifier, Even, Maintain, Peg, Permanence, Plateau, Poise, Steady

Stable(s) Augean, Balanced, Byre, Constant, Durable, Firm, Livery, Manger, Mews, Poise, Secure, Solid, Sound, Stall, Static(al), Steadfast, Steady, Stud, Sure

Stack Accumulate, Chimney, Clamp, Cock, End, Funnel, Heap, Lum, ➤ PILE, Rick, Shock, Staddle

Stadium Arena, Ballpark, Bowl, Circus, Circus Maximus, Coliseum, Hippodrome, Velodrome

Staff Alpenstock, Ash-plant, Bato(o)n, Bourdon, Burden, Caduceus, Cane, Crook, Crosier, Cross(e), Crozier, Crutch, Cudgel, Entourage, Equerry, Etat-major, Faculty, Ferula, Ferule, Flagpole, Linstock, Lituus, Mace, Omlah, Personnel, Pike, Pole, Rod, Runic, Sceptre, Skeleton, Stave, Stick, Taiaha, Tapsmen, Thyrsus, Truncheon, Verge, Wand, Workers, Workforce

Stage Act, Anaphase, Apron, Arena, Bema, Boards, Catasta, Chrysalis, Committee, Diligence, Dog-leg, Estrade, Fargo, Fit-up, Grade, Juncture, Key, Landing, Leg, Level, Metaphase, Milestone, Moment, Mount, Oidium, Phase, Phasis, Pier, Pin, Platform, Point, Prophase, PS, Puberty, Report, Rostrum, Scene, Sensorimeter, Sound, Stadium, Step, Stor(e)y, Subimago, Theatre, Thrust, Transition, Trek, Yuga

Stagger(ed) Alternate, Amaze, Astichous, Falter, Floor, Lurch, Recoil, Reel, Rock, Shock, Stoiter, Stot(ter), Stumble, Sway, Teeter, Thunderstruck, Titubate, Tolter, Totter

▷**Staggered** may indicate an anagram

Stain(er) Aniline, Bedye, Besmirch, Blemish, Blot, Blotch, Discolour, Dishonour, Dye, Embrue, Ensanguine, Eosin, Fox, Gram's, Grime, Imbrue, Iodophile, Keel, Maculate, Mail, Meal, Mote, Slur, Smirch, Smit, Soil, Splodge, Splotch, Stigma, Taint, Tarnish, Tinge, Tint, Woad

Stair(case), Stairs Apples, Apples and pears, Caracol(e), Cochlea, Companionway, Escalator, Flight, Perron, Rung, Spiral, Step, Tread, Turnpike, Vice, Wapping

Stake Ante, Bet, Claim, Gage, Holding, Impale, Impone, Interest, Lay, Loggat, Mark, Mise, Paal, Pale, Paling, Palisade, Peel, Peg, Pele, Picket, Pile, Play, Post, Pot, Punt, Rest, Revie, Risk, Spike, Spile, Stang, Stob, Sweep, Tether, Vie, Wager

Stale Aged, Banal, Flat, Fozy, Frowsty, Hackneyed, Handle, Hoary, Mouldy, Musty, Old, Pretext, Rancid, Urine, Worn

▷ **Stale** may indicate an obsolete word

Stalk(s) Bun, Cane, Follow, Funicle, Ha(u)lm, Pedicel, Pedicle, Peduncle, Petiole, Petiolule, Phyllode, Pursue, Scape, Seta, Shaw, Spear, Spire, Stem, Stipe(s), Stride, Strig, Strut, Stubble, Stump, Trail, Yolk

Stall(s) Arrest, Bay, Booth, Box, Bulk, Crib, ➤ DELAY, Floor, Flypitch, Hedge, Kiosk, Loose-box, Orchestra, Pen, Pew, Prebendal, Seat, Shamble, Sideshow, Stand, Stasidion, Temporise, Trap, Traverse, Travis, Trevis(s)

Stamina Endurance, Fibre, Fortitude, Guts, Last, Stay, Steel

Stammer(ing) Hesitate, Hum, Stumble, ➤ STUTTER, Waffle

Stamp(s), Stamped Appel, Cast, Character, Date(r), Die, Enface, Frank, Impress, Imprint, Incuse, Label, Mint, Pane, Penny black, Perfin, Philately, Pintadera, Press(ion), Rubber, Seal, Seebeck, Signet, Spif, Strike, Swage, Tête-bêche, Touch, Trading, Trample, Tromp, Type

Stand(ing), Stand up Apron, Arraign, Attitude, Base, Be, Bear, Bide, Binnacle, Bipod, Bristle, Brook, Caste, Crease, Dais, Degree, Dock, Dree, Easel, Etagère, Face, Foothold, Freeze, Gantry, Gueridon, Hob, Insulator, Last, Lectern, Nef, Odour, One-night, Ovation, Place, Plant, Podium, Pose, Position, Prestige, Promenade, Protest, Rack, Rank, Regent, Remain, Represent, Repute, Rise, Stall, Statant, Station, ➤ STATUS, Stay, Stillage, Stock, Stool, Straddle, Stroddle, Strut, Table, Tantalus, Terrace, ➤ TREAT, Tree, Tripod, Trivet, Upright, Whatnot

Standard(s) Banner, Base, Basic, Benchmark, Bogey, Canon, Classic(al), Cocker, Colour(s), Criterion, Eagle, English, Ethics, Examplar, Example, Exemplar, Flag, Ga(u)ge, Gold, Gonfalon, Labarum, Level, Living, Model, Norm(a), Normal, Numeraire, Old Glory, Par, Parker Morris, Pennon, Principle, Rate, Regular,

Rod, Rose, Routine, ➤ RULE, Staple, Sterling, Stock, Time, Touchstone, Tricolour, Troy, Usual, Valuta, Vexillum, Yardstick

Star(s) Alpha, Aster(isk), Beta(crucis), Binary, Body, Brown dwarf, Carbon, Celebrity, Chamber, Circumpolar, Comet, Constant, Constellation, Cynosure, Dark, Delta, Dwarf, Epsilon, E(s)toile, Evening, Falling, Feature, Film, Fixed, Galaxy, Gamma, Headline, Hero, Hexagram, Lead, Lion, Lode, Meteor(ite), Morning, Movie, Mullet, Neutron, Nova, Pentacle, Pentagram, Personality, Phosphor(us), Pip, Pointer, Principal, Pulsar, Pulsating, Quasar, Radio, Red dwarf, Red giant, Sabaism, Shell, Shine, Shooting, Sidereal, Spangle, Spica, Starn(ie), Stellar, Stern, Sterope, Supergiant, Supernova, Synasty, Theta, Top-liner, Variable, Vedette, White dwarf, Zeta

Stare Eyeball, Fisheye, Gape, Gapeseed, Gawp, Gaze, Goggle, Gorp, Look, Outface, Peer, Rubberneck

Stark Apparent, Austere, Bald, Bare, Gaunt, Harsh, Naked, Nude, Sheer, Stiff, Utterly

Start(ed), Starter Abrade, Abraid, Abray, Activate, Actuate, Begin, Boggle, Broach, Bug, Chance, Commence, Crank, Create, Dart, Ean, Embryo, Face-off, False, Fire, Flinch, Float, Flush, Flying, Found, Gambit, Gan, Genesis, Getaway, Gun, Handicap, Hot-wire, Impetus, Imprimis, Incept(ion), Initiate, Instigate, Institute, Intro, Jerk, Jump, Jump-off, Kick-off, L, Lag, Launch, Lead, Off, Offset, Onset, Ope(n), Ord, Origin, Outset, Preliminary, Prelude, Put-up, Reboot, Resume, Roll, Rouse, Scare, Set off, Shy, Slip, Snail, Spring, Spud, String, Wince

▷ **Start** may indicate an anagram or first letter(s)

Starvation, Starve(d), Starving Anorexia, Anoxic, Cold, Diet, Famish, Perish, Pine, Undernourished

▷ **Starving** may indicate an 'o' in the middle of a word

State(s) Affirm, Alle(d)ge, Aread, Arrede, Assert, Assever, Attest, Aver, Avow, Buffer, Case, Cite, Client, Commonwealth, Condition, Confederate, Country, Declare, Dependency, Emirate, Empire, Federal, Fettle, Flap, Free, Habitus, Humour, Land, Name, Nation, Palatinate, Perak, Plight, Police, Predicament, Predicate, Premise, Pronounce, Protectorate, Puppet, Realm, Reich, Republic, Satellite, Say, Sorry, Standing, Threeness, Union, Welfare

▷ **Stated** may indicate a similar sounding word

Statement Account, Affidavit, Aphorism, Assertion, Attestation, Avowal, Bill, Bulletin, Communiqué, Deposition, Dictum, Diktat, Encyclical, Evidence, Expose, Factoid, Invoice, Jurat, Manifesto, Mission, Outline, Pleading, Press release, Profession, Pronouncement, Proposition, Quotation, Release, Remonstrance, Report, Sentence, Soundbite, Sweeping, Testimony, Truism, Utterance, Verb

Station(s) Action, Berth, Birth, Camp, Caste, CCS, Crewe, Deploy, Depot, Dressing, Euston, Filling, Fire, Garrison, Halt, Hill, Ice, Lay, Location, Marylebone, Outpost, Panic, Pitch, Place, Plant, Point, Police, Polling, Post, Power, Quarter, Rank, Relay, Rowme, Seat, Service, Sit, Space, Stance, Stand, Status, Stond, Tana, Tanna(h), Terminus, Thana(h), Thanna(h), Tracking, Victoria, Waterloo, Waverley, Weather

Statuary, Statue(tte) Acrolith, Bronze, Bust, Colossus, Discobolus, Effigy, Figure, Figurine, Idol, Image, Galatea, Kore, Kouros, Liberty, Memnon, Monument, Oscar, Palladium, Pietà, Sculpture, Sphinx, Stonework, Tanagra, Torso, Xoanon

Staunch Amadou, Leal, Resolute, Steady, Stem, Stout, Styptic, Watertight

Stay(s) Alt, Avast, Bide, Bolster, Cohab(it), Corselet, Corset, Embar, Endure, Fulcrum, Gest, Guy, Hawser, Indwell, Jump, Lie, Lig, Linger, Moratorium, Prop, ➤ REMAIN, Reprieve, Restrain, Settle, Sist, Sleepover, Sojourn, Strut, Sustain, Tarry

Steadfast Constant, Firm, Implacable, Resolute, Sad, Stable

Steady Andantino, Ballast, Beau, Boyfriend, Composer, Constant, Even, Faithful, Firm, Girlfriend, Measured, Regular, Stabilise, Stable, Unswerving

Steak Chateaubriand, Chuck, Fillet, Flitch, Garni, Mignon, Minute, Porterhouse, Rump, Slice, T-bone, Tenderloin, Tournedos

Steal(ing) Abstract, Bag, Bandicoot, Bone, Boost, Cabbage, Cly, Convey, Creep, Crib, Duff, Embezzle, Filch, Glom, Grab, Half-inch, Heist, Kidnap, Knap, Lag, Liberate, Lift, Loot, Mag(g), Mahu, Mill, Naam, Nam, Nap, Nick, Nim, Nip, Nym, Peculate, Pilfer, Pillage, Pinch, Plagiarise, Plunder, Poach, Prig, Proll, Purloin, Ram-raid, Remove, Rifle, Rob, Rustle, Scrump, Skrimp, Smug, Snaffle, Snatch, Sneak, Snitch, Souvenir, Swipe, Take, Theft, Thieve, Tiptoe, TWOC, Whip

Steam(ed), Steamy Boil, Condensation, Fume, Gaseous, Het, Humid, Mist, Porn, Radio, Roke, Sauna, Spout, Vapor, Vapour

Steep Abrupt, Arduous, Brent, Embay, Expensive, Hilly, Krans, Krantz, Kranz, Macerate, Marinade, Marinate, Mask, Precipice, Precipitous, Rapid, Rate, Rait, Ret, Saturate, Scarp, ➤ SHEER, Soak, Sog, Souse, Stey, Stickle

Steer(er), Steering Ackerman, Airt, Buffalo, Bullock, Cann, Castor, Con(n), Cox, Direct, ➤ GUIDE, Helm, Navaid, Navigate, Ox, Pilot, Ply, Rudder, Stot, Whipstaff, Zebu

Stem Alexanders, Arrow, Axial, Bine, Bole, Caudex, Caulicle, Caulome, Check, Cladode, Cladophyll, Confront, Corm, Culm, Dam, Epicotyl, Floricane, Ha(u)lm, Kex, Pedicle, Peduncle, Pin, Rachis, Rhizome, Rise, Sarment, Scapus, Seta, Shaft, Shank, Spring, Stalk, Staunch, Stipe, Stolon, Sympodium, Tail

Step(s) Act, Balancé, Chassé, Choctaw, Corbie, Dance, Démarche, Echelon, Escalate, Flight, Fouetté, Gain, Gait, Goose, Grecian, Greece, Grees(e), Greesing, Grese, Gressing, Griece, Grise, Grize, Halfpace, Lavolt, Measure, Move, Notch, Pace, Pas, Pas de souris, Phase, Pigeon's wing, Raiser, Ratlin(e), Rattlin(e), Rattling, Roundel, Roundle, Rung, Shuffle, Slip, Stage, Stair, Stalk, Stile, Stope, Stride, Toddle, Trap, Tread, Unison, Waddle, Walk, Winder

Sterile, Sterilise(r), Sterility Barren, Dead, Fruitless, Impotent, Infertile, Neuter, Pasteurise, Spay

Stern Aft, Austere, Counter, Dour, Flinty, Grim, Hard, Implacable, Iron, Isaac, Nates, Poop, Rear, Relentless, Rugged, Stark, Strict, Tailpiece

Stew(ed), Stews Bath, Blanquette, Boil, Bouillabaisse, Bouilli, Braise, Bredie, Brothel, Burgoo, Carbonade, Casserole, Cassoulet, Chowder, Coddle, Colcannon, Compot(e), Daube, Flap, Fuss, Goulash, Haricot, Hash, Hell, Hot(ch)pot(ch), Irish, Jug, Lobscouse, Matelote, Mulligan, Navarin, Olla podrida, Osso bucco, Paddy, Paella, Pepperpot, Pot-au-feu, Pot-pourri, Ragout, Ratatouille, Salmi, Sass, Scouse, Seethe, Simmer, Squiffy, Stie, Stove, Stovies, Sty, Succotash, Sweat, Swelter

▷**Stewed** may indicate an anagram

Stick(ing) (out), Sticks, Sticky, Stuck Adhere, Aground, Ash, Attach, Bamboo, Bastinado, Bat, Baton, Bauble, Bayonet, Bludgeon, Bond, Boondocks, Cambrel, Cane, Celery, Cement, Chalk, Clag, Clam(my), Clarty, Clave, Cleave, Cling, Clog, Club,

Cocktail, Cohere, Coinhere, Crab, Crosier, Croze(s), Crozier,
Cue, Distaff, Divining-rod, Dog, Dure, Endure, Fag(g)ot,
Firewood, Flak, Founder, Fuse, Gad(e), Gambrel, Gelatine, Glair,
Glit, Glue, Goad, Goo, Gore, Ground-ash, Gum, Gunge, Gunk,
Harpoon, Hob, Hurley, Immobile, Impale, Inhere, Isinglass, Jab,
Jam, Jut, Kid, Kindling, Kip, Kiri, Knitch, Knobkerrie, Lance,
Lath(i), Lug, Message, Orange, Parasitic, Paste, Penang-lawyer,
Persist, Pierce, Plaster, Pogo, Pole, Posser, Protrude,
Protuberant, Quarterstaff, Rash, Ratten, Rhubarb, Rhythm, Rod,
Ropy, Shillela(g)h, Shooting, Size, Smudge, Spear, Spurtle,
Staff, Stand, Stang, Stob, Stodgy, Swagger, Switch, Swizzle,
Swordstick, Tack(y), Tally, Tar, Thick, Throwing, Truncheon,
Viscid, Viscous, Waddy, Wait, Walking, Wand, Woomera(ng)

Sticker Barnacle, Bur, Glue, Label, Limpet, Poster

Stiff, Stiffen(er), Stiffening, Stiffness Anchylosis,
Angular, Ankylosis, Baleen, Bandoline, Brace, Buckram, Budge,
Corpse, Corpus, Dear, Defunct, Expensive, Formal, Frore('n),
Goner, Gut, Hard, Mort, Petrify, Pokerish, Prim, Ramrod, Rigid,
Rigor, Rigor mortis, Sad, Set, Size, Solid, Starch, Stark, Stay,
Steeve, Stieve, Stilted, Stoor, Stour, Stowre, Sture, Unbending,
Whalebone, Wigan, Wooden

Still Accoy, Airless, Alembic, Assuage, Becalm, Calm, Check,
Current, Doggo, Ene, Even(ness), Howbe, However, Hush, Illicit,
Inactive, Inert, Kill, Languid, Limbec(k), Lull, Motionless,
Nevertheless, Patent, Peaceful, Photograph, Placate, Placid,
Posé, Quiescent, Quiet, Resting, Silent, Snapshot, Soothe,
Stagnant, Static, Stationary, Though, Yet

Stimulant, Stimulate, Stimulus Activate, Adrenaline,
Antigen, Arak, Arouse, Caffeine, Cinder, Coca, Cue, Dart,
Digitalin, Digoxin, Egg, Energise, Evoke, Excitant, Fillip, Fuel,
Galvanize, Ginger, Goad, Hormone, Incite, Innerve, Irritate, Jog,
Key, K(h)at, Kick, Mneme, Motivate, Oestrus, Pep, Philtre,
Pick-me-up, Piquant, Prod, Promote, Provoke, Psych, Qat, Rim,
Roborant, ➤ ROUSE, Rowel, Rub, Sassafras, Sensuous, Spur,
Sting, Stir, Tannin, Tar, Theine, Tickle, Titillate, Tone, Tonic,
Upper, Whet(stone)

Sting(ing) Aculeate, Barb, Bite, Cheat, Cnida, Goad,
Nematocyst, Nettle(tree), Overcharge, Perceant, Piercer,
Poignant, Prick, Pungent, Rile, Scorpion, Sephen, Smart, Spice,
Stang, Stimulus, Surcharge, Tang, Trichocyst, Urent, Urtica

Stingy Cheeseparing, Chintzy, Close, Costive, Hard, Illiberal, Mean, Miserly, Narrow, Near, Nippy, Parsimonious, Snippy, Snudge, Tight-arse, Tight(wad)

▷**Stingy** may indicate something that stings

Stipulate, Stipulation Clause, Condition, Covenant, Insist, Provision, Proviso, Rider, Specify

Stir(red), Stirring Accite, Admix, Ado, Afoot, Agitate, Amo(o)ve, Animate, Annoy, Bother, Bustle, Buzz, Can, Churn, Cooler, Excite, Foment, Furore, Fuss, Gaol, Hectic, Impassion, Incense, Incite, Inflame, Insurrection, Intermix, Jee, Jog, Kitty, Limbo, Live, ► MIX, Move, Noy, Poss, Pother, ► PRISON, Prod, Provoke, Quad, Quatch, Quetch, Quinche, Qui(t)ch, Quod, Rabble, Rear, Roil, Rouse, Roust, Rummage, Rustle, Sod, Steer, Styre, Swizzle, To-do, Upstart, Wake

▷**Stir(red), Stirring** may indicate an anagram

Stitch Bargello, Baste, Blanket, Blind, Buttonhole, Cable, Chain, Couching, Crochet, Embroider, Feather, Fell, Florentine, Garter, Gathering, Herringbone, Insertion, Knit, Lazy daisy, Lock, Moss, Needle, Overlock, Petit point, Rag, Running, Saddle, Satin, Sew, Slip, Spider, Stab, Stay, Steek, Stem, Stockinette, Stocking, Straight, Sutile, Suture, Tack, Tent, Topstitch, Whip

Stock(ed), Stocks, Stocky Aerie, Aery, Blue-chip, Bouillon, Bree, Breech, But(t), Carry, Cattle, Choker, Cippus, Congee, Court-bouillon, Cravat, Debenture, Endomorph, Equip, Fumet, Fund, Graft, Handpiece, He(a)rd, Hilt, Hoosh, Inventory, Kin, Laughing, Line, Little-ease, Omnium, Pigeonhole, Preferred, Pycnic, Race, Ranch, Rep(ertory), Replenish, Reserve, Rolling, Scrip, Seed, Shorts, Soup, Squat, Staple, Steale, Steelbow, Stirp(e)s, ► STORE, Strain, Stubby, Supply, Surplus, Talon, Team, Tie, Utility

Stocking(s) Fishnet, Hogger, Hose, Leather, Moggan, Netherlings, Nylons, Seamless, Sheer, Sock, Spattee, Tights

Stole(n) Bent, Epitrachelion, Hot, Maino(u)r, Manner, Manor, Nam, Orarion, Orarium, Reft, Scarf, Staw, Tippet

Stomach(ic) Abdomen, Abomasum, Accept, Appetite, Belly, Bible, Bingy, Bonnet, Bread-basket, Brook, C(o)eliac, Corporation, Epiploon, Gaster, Gizzard, Gut, Heart, Jejunum, King's-hood, Kite, Kyte, Manyplies, Mary, Maw, Mesaraic, Midriff, Omasum, Paunch, Potbelly, Psalterium, Pylorus, Rennet,

Reticulum, Rumen, Stick, Swagbelly, ➤ SWALLOW, Tripe, Tum, Urite, Vell, Venter, Wame, Wem

Stool Buffet, Coppy, Cracket, Creepie, Cricket, Cucking, Curule, Cutty, Faeces, Hassock, Milking, Piano, Pouf(fe), Seat, Sir-reverence, Step, Stercoral, Sunkie, Taboret, Tripod, Turd

Stop(page), Stopper, Stopping Abort, Arrest, Avast, Bait, Bide, Block, Brake, Buffer, Bung, ➤ CEASE, Cessation, Check, Cheese, Clarabella, Clarino, Clarion, Clog, Close, Colon, Comma, Conclude, Cork, Coupler, Cremo(r)na, Cut, Deactivate, Debar, Demurral, Desist, Deter, Devall, Diaphone, Discontinue, Dit, Dolce, Dot, Embargo, End, Field, Fifteenth, Flue, Flute, Foreclose, Freeze, Gag, Gamba, Gemshorn, Glottal, Gong, Halt, Hartal, Hinder, Hitch, Ho, Hold, Hoy, Intermit, Jam, Kibosh, Let-up, Lill, Lin, Lute, Media, Mutation, Nasard, Oboe, Obturate, Occlude, Oppilate, Organ, Outspan, Pause, Period, Piccolo, Pit, Plug, Point, Poop, Preclude, Prevent, Principal, Prorogue, Punctuate, Quash, Quint, Quit, Racket, Red, Reed, Refrain, Register, Rein, Remain, Request, Scotch, Screw-top, Semi-colon, Sext, Sist, Solo, Spigot, Stall, Stanch, Standstill, Stash, Stasis, Station, Staunch, Stay, Stive, Strike, Subbase, Suppress, Suspend, Tamp(ion), Tenuis, Terminate, Toby, Truck, Voix celeste, When, Whistle, Whoa

Storage, Store(house) Accumulate, Arsenal, Backing, Barn, Bin, Bottle, Bunker, Buttery, Cache, Cell, Cellar, Chain, Clamp, Coop, Cupboard, Cutch, Deli, Dene-hole, Department(al), Depository, Depot, Dime, Discount, Elevator, Emporium, Ensile, Entrepot, Etape, Fund, Garner, Girnal, Glory hole, Go-down, Granary, ➤ HOARD, Hold, House, Humidor, Husband, Hypermarket, Larder, Magazine, Mart, Memory, Mine, Morgue, Mothball, Mow, Multiple, Nest-egg, Off-licence, Pantechnicon, Pantry, Pithos, Provision, Rack(ing), RAM, Repertory, Reposit, ROM, Sector, Shop, Silage, Silo, Spence, Stack, Stash, Stock, Stockroom, Stow, Supermarket, Supply, Tack-room, Tank, Thesaurus, Tithe-barn, Tommy-shop, Warehouse

▶**Storey** see STORY

Storm(y) Ablow, Adad, Assail, Attack, Baguio, Blizzard, Bluster, Buran, Charge, Cyclone, Devil, Dirty, Dust, Enlil, Expugn, Furore, Gale, Gusty, Haboob, Hurricane, Magnetic, Monsoon, Onset, Rage(ful), Raid, Rain, Rampage, Rant, Red spot, Rugged,

Rush, Shaitan, Snorter, Squall, Tea-cup, Tempest, Tornade, Tornado, Tropical, Unruly, Weather, Willy-willy, Zu

▷**Stormy** may indicate an anagram

Story, Storey, Stories Account, Allegory, Anecdote, Apocrypha, Attic, Bar, Basement, Baur, Biog, Chestnut, Clearstory, Clerestory, Cock and bull, Conte, Cover, Decameron, Edda, Epic, Episode, Etage, Exclusive, Fable, Fabliau, Fib, Fiction, Flat, Floor, Gag, Geste, Ghost, Hard-luck, Heptameron, Horror, Idyll, Iliad, Jataka, Lee, Legend, Lie, Marchen, Mezzanine, Myth(os), Mythus, Narrative, Nouvelle, Novel(la), Oratorio, Parable, Pentameron, Plot, Rede, Report, Romance, Rumour, Saga, Scoop, Script, Serial, SF, Shaggy dog, Shocker, Sob, Spiel, Spine-chiller, Splash, Stage, Success, Tale, Tall, Tier, Upper, Version, Yarn

Story-teller Aesop, Fibber, Griot, Liar, Munchausen, Narrator, Raconteur, Shannachie, Tusitala

Stout(ness) Ale, Burly, Chopping, Chubby, Embonpoint, Endomorph, Entire, Fat, Fubsy, Hardy, Humpty-dumpty, Lusty, Manful, Milk, Obese, Overweight, Porter, Portly, Potbelly, Robust, Stalwart, Stalworth, Sta(u)nch, Strong, Stuggy, Sturdy, Substantial, Tall

Stove Baseburner, Break, Calefactor, Cockle, Cooker, Furnace, Gasfire, Oven, Primus®, Potbelly, Range, Salamander

Straggle(r), Straggly Estray, Gad, Meander, Ramble, Rat-tail, Spidery, Sprawl, Stray, Wander

Straight(en), Straightness Align, Bald, Beeline, Correct, Die, Direct, Downright, Dress, Frank, Gain, Het(ero), Honest, Lank, Legit, Level, Normal, Rectilineal, Rectitude, Righten, Sheer, Slap, Tidy, True, Unbowed, Unlay, Upright, Veracious, Virgate

Straightforward Candid, Direct, Easy, Even, Forthright, Honest, Level, Jannock, Plain sailing, Pointblank, Simple

Strain(ed), Strainer, Straining Agonistic, Ancestry, Aria, Breed, Carol, Clarify, Colander, Distend, Drawn, Effort, Exert, Filter, Filtrate, Fit, Fitt(e), Force, Fray, Fytt(e), Intense, Kind, Melody, Milsey, Molimen, Music, Note, Overtask, Passus, Percolate, Pressure, Pull, Rack, Raring, Reck(an), Retch, Rick, Seep, Seil(e), Set, Shear, Sieve, Sift, Sile, Stape, Start, Stock, Streak, Stress, Stretch, Sye, Tamis, Tammy, Tax, Tenesmus, Tense, Tension, Threnody, Try, Vein, Vice, Work, Wrick

Strange(ness), Stranger Alien, Aloof, Amphitryon, Curious, Eerie, Exotic, Foreign, Fraim, Frem(d), Fremit, Frenne, Funny, Guest, Malihini, New, Novel, Odd(ball), Outlandish, Outsider, Quare, Queer, Rum, S, Screwy, Selcouth, Singular, Tea-leaf, Uncanny, Unco, Unked, Unket, Unkid, Unused, Unusual, Weird, Wondrous

▷ **Strange** may indicate an anagram

Strap(ping) Band, Barber, Beat, Bowyangs, Brail, Braw, Breeching, Browband, Crupper, Cuir-bouilli, Curb, Girth, Halter, Harness, Jess, Larrup, Lash, Ligule, Lorate, Lore, Manly, Martingale, Nicky-tam, Pandy, Rand, Rein, Robust, Sling, Spider, Strop, Surcingle, T-bar, Tab, Taws(e), Thong, Throatlash, Throatlatch, Trace, Tump-line, Wallop

Stratagem, Strategist, Strategy Artifice, Coup, Deceit, Device, Dodge, Fetch, Finesse, Fraud, Masterstroke, Maximum, Minimax, Plan, ➤ RUSE, Scheme, Sleight, Tactic(s), Tactician, Trick, Wile

Straw(s), Strawy Balintutal, Boater, Buntal, Chaff, Cheese, Halm, Hat, Haulm, Hay, Insubstantial, Last, Leghorn, Nugae, Oaten, Panama, Parabuntal, Pedal, Stalk, Stramineous, Strammel, Strummel, Stubble, Trifles, Wisp, Ye(a)lm

Stray Abandoned, Chance, Depart, Deviate, Digress, Err, Forwander, Foundling, Maverick, Meander, Misgo, Pye-dog, Ramble, Roam, Sin, Straggle, Street, Traik, Unowned, Waff, Waif, Wander

Streak(ed), Streaker, Streaky Bended, Blue, Brindle, Comet, Flaser, Flash, Fleck, Freak, Hawked, Highlights, Lace, Layer, Leonid, Mark, Merle, Mottle, Race, Run, Schlieren, Seam, Striate, Striga, Strip(e), Vein, Venose, Vibex, Waif, Wake, Wale

Stream Acheron, Beam, Beck, Bourne, Burn, Course, Current, Driblet, Fast, Flow, Flower, Freshet, Gulf, Gush, Headwater, Influent, Jet, Kill, Lade, Lane, Leet, Logan, Pokelogan, Pour, Pow, Rill, River, Rivulet, Rubicon, Run, Runnel, Sike, Streel, Syke, Tide-race, Tributary, Trickle, Watercourse

Street Alley, Ave(nue), Bowery, Broad, Carey, Carnaby, Cato, Causey, Cheapside, Civvy, Close, Corso, Court, Crescent, Downing, Drive, Easy, Fleet, Gate, Grub, Harley, High(way), Lane, Meuse, Mews, One-way, Parade, Paseo, Queer, Road, Side, Sinister, St, Strand, Terrace, Thoroughfare, Threadneedle, Throgmorton, Wall, Wardour, Watling, Way, Whitehall

Strength(en), Strengthening Afforce, Bant, Beef, Brace, Brawn, Build, Confirm, Consolidate, Enable, Energy, Foison, Force, Forte, Fortify, Freshen, Grit, Herculean, Horn, Intensity, Iron, Line, Main, Man, Might, Munite, Muscle, Nerve, ➤ POWER, Prepotence, Pre-stress, Proof, Reinforce, Roborant, Sinew, Spike, Stamina, Steel, Sthenia, ➤ STRONG, Stoutness, Tensile, Thews, Titration, Unity, Vim

Stretch(able), Stretched, Stretcher, Stretching Belt, Brick, Crane, Distend, Draw, Ectasis, Eke, Elastic, Elongate, Expanse, Extend, Extensile, Farthingale, Fib, Frame, Give, Gurney, Lengthen, Litter, Narrows, Outreach, Pallet, Porrect, Procrustes, Prolong, Protend, Pull, Rack, Rax, ➤ REACH, Sentence, Shiner, Spell, Spread, Strain, Taut, Tend, Tense, Tensile, Tenter, Term, Time, Tract, Tractile, Tree, Trolley

Strict Dour, Harsh, Literal, Orthodox, Penal, Puritanical, Rigid, Rigorous, Severe, Spartan, Stern, Strait(-laced)

Stride Gal(l)umph, Leg, Lope, March, Pace, Piano, Stalk, Sten, Straddle, Stroam, Strut, Stump

Strident Brassy, Grinding, Harsh, Raucous, Screech

Strife Bargain, Barrat, Conflict, Contest, Discord, Disharmony, Dissension, Feud, Food, Friction, Ignoble, Scrap(ping)

Strike(r), Striking, Strike out Air, Alight, Annul, Arresting, Attitude, Backhander, Baff, Band, Bang, Bash, Bat, Baton, Batsman, Batter, Beat, Belabour, Better, Biff, Black, Bonanza, Buff, Buffet, Butt, Catch, Cane, Chime, Chip, Clap, Clash, Clatch, Clip, Clock, Clout, Club, Cob, Collide, Coup, Cue, Cuff, Dad, Dent, Dev(v)el, Ding, Dint, Dismantle, Douse, Dowse, Dramatic, Drive, Dush, Eclat, Fet(ch), Fillip, Firk, Fist, Flail, Flog, Frap, Get, Gowf, Hail, Hartal, ➤ HIT, Horn, Hour, Hunger, Ictus, Illision, Impact, Impinge, Impress, Jarp, Jaup, Jole, Joll, Joule, Jowl, Knock, Lam, Lambast, Laser, Lay(-off), Lightning, Match, Notable, Noticeable, Out, Pash, Pat(ter), Peen, Percuss, Picket, Plectrum, Pronounced, Pummel, Punch, Ram, Rap, Remarkable, Salient, Scrub, Shank, Sideswipe, Sitdown, Sit-in, Slam, Slap, Slat, Slog, Slosh, Smack, Smash, Smite, Sock, Souse, Spank, Stayaway, Stop(page), Stub, Swap, Swat, Swinge, Swipe, Swop, Sympathy, Tan, Tat, Thump, Tip, Walk-out, Wallop, Wap, Whack, Whap, Wildcat, Wipe, Wondrous, Zap

String(s), Stringy Band, Beads, Cello, Chalaza, Chanterelle, Cord, Cosmic, Drill, Enfilade, Fiddle, G, Gut, Henequin, Hypate,

Keyed, Lace, Lag, Lichanos, Macramé, Mese, Necklace, Nete,
Nicky-tam, Proviso, Quint, Ripcord, Rope, Second, Series,
Shoe(-tie), Sinewy, Straggle, Strand, Sympathetic, Team,
Tendon, Thairm, Tough, Train, Trite, Viola, Violin

Strip(ped), Stripper, Striptease Airfield, Armband, Band,
Bare, Bark, Batten, Belt, Bereave, Comic, Cote, Defoliate,
Denude, Deprive, Derobe, Despoil, Devest, Disbark, Dismantle,
Dismask, Disrobe, Divest, Drag, Ecorché, Fannel(l), Fiche,
Flaught, Flay, Fleece, Flench, Flense, Flinch, Flounce, Flype,
Gaza, Goujon, Hatband, Infula, Jib, Label, Lardon, Lath, Ledge,
Linter, List, Littoral, Loading, Median, Mobius, Panhandle, Peel,
Pillage, Pluck, Pull, Puttee, Puttie, Rand, Raunch, Raw, Ribbon,
Roon, Royne, Rumble, Rund, Runway, Screed, Scrow, Shear,
Shed, Shuck, Skin, Slat, Slit, Sliver, Spellican, Spilikin, Spill(ikin),
Splat, Splent, Spline, Splint, Splinter, Spoil, Straik, Strake, Strap,
Streak, Strop, Swath, Sweatband, Tack, Tee, Thong, Tirl, Tirr,
Uncase, Undress, Unfrock, Unrig, Unrip, Valance, Zone

Strive, Striving Aim, Aspire, ➤ ATTEMPT, Contend,
Endeavour, Enter, Kemp, Labour, Nisus, Pingle, Press, Strain,
Struggle, Toil, Try, Vie

Stroke Apoplex(y), Backhander, Bat, Blow, Boast, Breast,
Butterfly, Caress, Carom, Chip, Chop, Counterbuff, Coup, Coy,
Crawl, Dash, Dint, Dog(gy)-paddle, Drear(e), Dropshot,
Effleurage, Exhaust, Feat, Flick, Fondle, Forehand, Glance,
Hairline, Hand(er), Ictus, Jenny, Jole, Joll, Joule, Jowl, Knell,
Knock, Lash, Line, Link, Loft, Loser, Oarsman, Oblique, Odd,
Off-drive, Outlash, Palp, Paw, Pot-hook, Pull, Put(t), Reverso,
Roquet, Rub, Scart, Sclaff, Scoop, Seizure, Sixte, Smooth,
Solidus, Strike, Stripe, Sweep, Swipe, Tact, Tittle, Touk, Trait,
Trudgen, Trudgeon, Tuck, Virgule, Wale, Whang

Strong Able, Brawny, Cast-iron, Doughty, Durable, F, Fit,
Forceful, Forcible, Forte, Hale, Hercules, Humming, Husky,
Intense, Mighty, Nappy, Pithy, Pollent, Potent, Powerful,
Pungent, Racy, Rank, Robust, Samson, Solid, Stalwart, Stark,
Steely, ➤ STRENGTH, Sthenic, Stiff, Stout, Str, Strapping,
Sturdy, Substantial, Suit, Tarzan, Thesis, Thickset, Trusty,
Vegete, Vehement, Vigorous, Violent, Well-set, Ya(u)ld

Stronghold Acropolis, Aerie, Bastion, Castle, Citadel, Eyrie,
Fastness, Fortress, Keep, Kremlin, Redoubt, Tower

Structural, Structure Anatomy, Armature, Analysis, Building, Edifice, Erection, Fabric, Fairing, Format(ion), Frame, Ice-apron, Lantern, Mole, Organic, Pediment, Pergola, Physique, Shape, Skeleton, Starling, Syntax, System, Texas, Texture, Trochlea, Undercarriage

Struggle Agon(ise), Agonistes, Buckle, Camp, Chore, Conflict, Contend, Contest, Cope, Debatement, Effort, Endeavour, Fight, Flounder, Grabble, Grapple, Kampf, Labour, Luctation, Mill, Pingle, Rat-race, Scrape, Scrimmage, Scrum, Scrummage, Scuffle, Sprangle, ➤ STRIVE, Toil, Tug, Tussle, Vie, War(sle), Wrestle

▷ **Struggle** may indicate an anagram

Stubborn(ness) Adamant, Bigoted, Contumacious, Cussed, Diehard, Entêté, Hard(-nosed), Hidebound, Intransigent, Inveterate, Moyl(e), Mulish, Mumpsimus, Obdurate, Obstinate, Opinionated, Ornery, Ortus, Pertinacious, Perverse, Recalcitrant, Reesty, Refractory, Rigwiddie, Rigwoodie, Self-willed, Stiff, Tenacious, Thrawn, Wrong-headed

Student(s) Alumnus, Apprentice, Bajan, Bejant, Cadet, Class, Coed, Commoner, Dan, Dig, Disciple, Dresser, Dux, Exhibitioner, Form, Fresher, Freshman, Gownsman, Graduand, Gyte, ➤ LEARNER, Magistrand, Mature, NUS, Opsimath, Ordinand, Oxonian, Plebe, Poll, Preppy, Pupil, Reader, Sap, ➤ SCHOLAR, Self-taught, Semi, Seminar, Shark, Sizar, Sizer, Smug, Softa, Soph(omore), Sophister, Swot, Templar, Tosher, Trainee, Tuft, Tutee, Wrangler, Year

Study, Studied, Studies, Studious Analyse, Bone, Brown, Carol, Classics, Con(ne), Conscious, Consider, Cram, Den, Dig, Etude, Feasibility, Field, Learn, Media, Mug, Mull, Muse, Perusal, Peruse, Pore, Post-doctoral, Probe, Read, Recce, Reconnoitre, Research, Revise, Sanctum, Sap, Scan, Scrutinise, Take, Time and motion, Typto, Voulu, Wonk

Stuff(iness), Stuffing, Stuffy Airless, Canvas, Close, Cloth, Codswallop, Cram, Crap, Dimity, Farce, Feast, Fiddlesticks, Fill, Force, Forcemeat, Frows(t)y, Frowzy, Fug, Gear, Gobble, Gorge, Guff, Havers, Hooey, Horsehair, Lard, Line, Linen, ➤ MATERIAL, Matter, No-meaning, Nonsense, Overeat, Pad, Pang, Panne, Pompous, Ram, Replete, Rot, Sate, Scrap, Sob, Stap, Steeve, Stew, Taxidermy, Trig, Upholster, Wad, Youth

Stumble Blunder, Err, Falter, Flounder, Founder, Lurch, Peck, Snapper, Stoit, Titubate, Trip

Stun(ning), Stunned Astonish, Astound, Awhape, Bludgeon, Concuss, Cosh, Daze, Dazzle, Deafen, Dove, Drop-dead, Glam, KO, Shell-shocked, Shock, Stoun, Stupefy

Stunt(ed) Aerobatics, Confine, Droichy, Dwarf, Feat, Gimmick, Hot-dog, Hype, Jehad, Jihad, Loop, Nirl, Puny, Ront(e), Runt, Ruse, Scroggy, Scrub(by), Scrunt(y), Stub, Trick, Wanthriven

Stupid (person) Airhead, Anserine, Asinine, Ass, Auf, Berk, Besotted, Bete, Blockhead, Bob, Bonehead, Booby, Boodle, Bozo, Brute, Buffer, Buffoon, Bumbo, Burk, Cake, Calf, Changeling, Charlie, Chick, Chump, Clot, Clunk, Cod, Cony, Coof, Coot, Crackpot, Crass, Cretin, Cuckoo, Cuddie, Cuddy, Cully, Daft, Daw, Dense, Dick(e)y, Dickhead, Dill, Dim(wit), Dipstick, Dodkin, Dolt, Donkey, Dote, Dotterel, Dottle, Dottrell, Drongo, Dull(ard), Dumbbell, Dumbo, Dunce, Dunderhead, Dunderpate, Fatuous, Featherbrain, Flat, Flathead, Fog(e)y, Fon, Fool(ish), Gaga, Galah, Geck, Gelt, Git, Goat, Golem, Goof, Goon, Goop, Goose(-cap), Gormless, Gowk, Gross, Gubbins, Gull, Gump, Gunsel, Half-wit, Hammerheaded, Hash, Headbanger, Hoser, Idiot, Ignoramus, Imbecile, Inane, Insensate, Inipient, Jackass, Jay, Jerk, Juggins, Lob, Log, Looby, Loony, Lummox, Meathead, Mindless, Moron, Muggins, Mutt, Nana, Natural, Neddy, Nerd, Nerk, Nidget, Nig-nog, Nincompoop, Nit(wit), Noddy, Noodle, Nurd, Oaf, Obtuse, Ocker, Patch, Pea-brain, Pillock, Pinhead, Plonker, Poon, Poop, Pot-head, Prat, Prune, Put(t), Rook, Sap, Schlemiel, Schlep, Silly, Simon, Simp(leton), Snipe, Softhead, Sot, Spoon, Stock, Stot, Sucker, Thick, Thickhead, Thickie, Thicko, Tony, Torpid, Tosser, Touchstone, Turkey, Turnip, Twerp, Twit, Waldo, Wally, Wiseacre, Woodcock, Wooden(head), Yap, Yo-yo, Zany, Zombie

Sturdy Burly, Dunt, Gid, Hardy, Hefty, Lusty, Stalwart, Staunch, Steeve, Strapping, Strong, Thickset, Turnsick, Vigorous

Style(s), Stylish Adam, A la, Band, Barocco, Barock, Baroque, Burin, Call, Chic, Class, Cultism, Cut, Dapper, Dash, Decor, Decorated, Diction, Dub, Elan, Elegance, Empire, Entitle, Execution, Face, Farand, ➤ FASHION, Finesse, Flamboyant, Flossy, Form(at), Genre, Gnomon, Grace, Hair-do, Hand, Hip, Manner, Mod(e), Modish, New, Nib, Nifty, Old, Panache,

Pattern, Pen, Perm, Phrase, Pistil, Pointel, Port, Preponderant,
Probe, Rakish, Rank, Regency, Rococo, Romanesque, Silk,
Snazzy, Snorty, Spiffy, Swish, Taste, Term, Title, Ton, Tone,
Touch, Tuscan, Uncial, Vogue, Way

Subconscious Inner, Instinctive, Not-I, Subliminal, Suppressed

Subdue(d) Abate, Allay, Chasten, Conquer, Cow, Dominate,
Lick, Low-key, Master, Mate, Mute, ➤ QUELL, Quieten, Reduce,
Refrain, Slow, Sober, Suppress, Tame, Under

Subject(s), Subjection, Subject to Amenable, Art,
Bethrall, Caitive, Case, Citizen, Core, Cow, Enthrall, Gist,
Hobby, Hobby-horse, Inflict, Liable, Liege(man), Matter,
National, On, Overpower, PE, People, Poser, RE, RI, Serf,
Servient, Servitude, Slavery, Sitter, Snool, Submit, Suit,
➤ THEME, Thirl, Thrall, Topic, Under, Vassal

Sublime August, Empyreal, Grand, Great, Lofty, Majestic,
Outstanding, Perfect, Porte, Splendid

Submarine Diver, Nautilus, Polaris, Sub, U-boat, Undersea

▷ **Submarine** may indicate a fish

Submerge(d) Dip, Dive, Drown, Embathe, Engulf, Imbathe,
Lemuria, Overwhelm, Ria, Sink, Take, Whelm

Submissive, Submit Acquiesce, Bow, Capitulate, Comply,
Defer, Docile, Knuckle, Meek, Obedient, Passive, Pathetic, Refer,
Render, Resign, Snool, Stoop, Succumb, Truckle, ➤ YIELD

Subordinate Adjunct, Dependent, Flunky, Inferior, Junior,
Minion, Myrmidon, Offsider, Postpone, Secondary, Servient,
Stooge, Subject, Subservient, Surrender, Under(ling),
Underman, Under-strapper, Vassal

Subscribe(r), Subscription Approve, Assent, Conform,
Due, Pay, Sign(atory), Signature, Undersign, Underwrite

Subsequent(ly) Anon, Consequential, Future, Later, Next,
Postliminary, Since, Then

Subside, Subsidence, Subsidy Abate, Adaw, Aid, Assuage,
Bonus, Diminish, Ebb, Grant, Sink, Sit, Swag

Substance, Substantial Ambergris, Antitoxin, Body,
Cermet, Chalone, Chitin, Colloid, Considerable, Content,
Ectoplasm, Elemi, Essential, Exudate, Fabric, Fixative, Getter,
Gist, Gluten, Gossypol, Gravamen, Hearty, Hefty, Indol,
Inhibitor, Isatin(e), Isomer, Linin, Material, Matter, Meaning,

Meat(y), Mineral, Mole, Orgone, Polymer, Protyl(e), Quid, Reality, Resin, Sense, Solid, Stuff, Sum, Tangible

▶ **Substantial** see SUBSTANCE

Substitute, Substitution Acting, Change, Changeling, Commute, Creamer, Deputy, Emergency, Ersatz, -ette, Euphemism, Exchange, Fill-in, Improvise, Instead, Lieu(tenant), Locum, Makeshift, Pinch-hit, Proxy, Regent, Relieve, Replace, Represent, Reserve, Resolution, Ringer, Stand-in, Stead, Stopgap, Surrogate, Switch, Swop, Understudy, Vicarious

Subterfuge Artifice, Chicane, Evasion, Hole, Ruse, Strategy, Trick

Subtle(ty) Abstruse, Alchemist, Crafty, Fine(spun), Finesse, Ingenious, Nice, Sly, Thin, Wily

Subtract(ion) Deduct, Discount, Take, Tithe, Withdraw

Suburb Environs, Exurbia, Outskirts, Purlieu

Subversion, Subvert Fifth column, Overthrow, Reverse, Sabotage, Sedition, Treasonous, Undermine, Upset

Succeed, Success(ful) Accomplish, Achieve, Arrive, Blockbuster, Boffo, Breakthrough, Contrive, Coup, Eclat, Effective, Efficacious, Fadge, Felicity, Flourish, Follow, Fortune, Gangbuster, Go, Hit, Hotshot, Inherit, Killing, Landslide, Luck, Manage, Masterstroke, Mega, Offcome, Pass, Prevail, Prosper, Purple patch, Reach, Replace, Riot, Score, Seal, Seel, Sele, Socko, Speed, Tanistry, Triumph, Up, Up and coming, Upstart, Vault, Weather, Win, Wow, Wunderkind

Successor Co(m)arb, Deluge, Descendant, Ensuite, Epigon(e), Heir, Incomer, Inheritor, Khalifa, Next, Syen

Succulent Cactus, Echeveria, Juicy, Lush, Rich, Saguaro, Sappy, Spekboom, Tender, Toothy

Suck(er), Sucking Absorb, Aspirator, Ass, Dracula, Drink, Dupe, Fawn, Gnat, Graff, Graft, Gull, Hoove, Lamia, Lamprey, Leech, Liquorice, Mammal, Mouth, Mug, Patsy, Plunger, Shoot, Siphon, Slurp, Smarm, Swig, Sycophant, Toad-eater, Vampire

Sudden(ly) Abrupt, Astart, Astert, Extempore, Ferly, Fleeting, Foudroyant, Hasty, Headlong, Impulsive, Overnight, Rapid, Slap, Sodain, Subitaneous, Swap, Swop, Unexpected

Sue Ask, Beseech, Dun, Entreat, Implead, Implore, Petition, Pray, Process, Prosecute, Woo

Suffer(er), Suffering Abide, Aby(e), Ache, Affliction, Agonise, Auto, ➤ BEAR, Brook, Calvary, Cop, Die, Distress, Dree, Endurance, Endure, Feel, Gethsemane, Golgotha, Grief, Hardship, Have, Incur, Let, Luit, Martyr, Pain, Passible, Passion, Passive, Patible, Patience, Pellagrin, Permit, Pine, Plague, Purgatory, Stand, Stomach, Sustain, Thole, Tolerate, Toll, Torment, Trial, Tribulation, Undergo, Use, Victim

Suffice, Sufficient Adequate, Ample, Basta, Do, Due, Enow, Enough, Satisfy, Serve

Suffocate Asphyxiate, Choke, Smother, Stifle, Strangle, Throttle

Sugar(y), Sugar cane Aldose, Barley, Blood, Brown, Candy, Cane, Caramel, Caster, Cellose, Daddy, Demerara, Dextrose, Flattery, Fructose, Gallise, Glucose, Goo(r), Granulated, Grape, Gur, Heroin, Hexose, Honeydew, Iced, Icing, Inulin, Invert, Lactose, Loaf, Lump, Maltose, Manna, Maple, Money, Muscovado, Palm, Saccharine, Simple, Sis, Sorg(h)o, Sorghum, Sparrow, Spun, Sweet, Trehala(se)

Suggest(ion), Suggestive Advance, Advice, Advise, Connote, Cue, Hint, Idea, Imply, Innuendo, Insinuate, Intimate, Mention, Modicum, Moot, Posit, Prompt, Proposal, Propound, Provocative, Racy, Raise, Recommend, Redolent, Reminiscent, Risqué, Smacks, Soft core, Suspicion, Touch, Trace

Suicide Felo-de-se, Hara-kiri, Hari-kari, Kamikaze, Lemming, Lethal, Sati, Seppuku, Suttee

Suit Action, Adapt, Agree, Answer, Appropriate, Become, Befit, Beho(o)ve, Bequest, Birthday, Cards, Case, Clubs, Conform, Courtship, Diamonds, Dittos, Do, Dress, Etons, Fashion, Fit, G, Garb, Gee, Gree, Hearts, Hit, Jump, Long, Lounge, Major, Mao, Match, Minor, Monkey, Orison, Outcome, Paternity, Petition, Plaint, Plea, Please, Point, Prayer, Process, Pyjama, Quarterdeck, Queme, Romper(s), Safari, Sailor, Salopettes, Satisfy, Serve, Shell, Siren, Spades, Strong, Sunday, Supplicat, Tailleur, Three-piece, Track, Trouser, Trumps, Twin, Two-piece, Uniform, Wet, Zoot

Suitable Apposite, Appropriate, Apt, Becoming, Capable, Congenial, Consonant, Convenance, Convenient, Due, Expedient, ➤ FIT, Keeping, Meet, Opportune, Relevant, Seemly, Worthy

Suite Allemande, Apartment, Chambers, Ensemble, Entourage, Hospitality, Lounge, Nutcracker, Partita, Retinue, Rooms, Serenade, Set, Tail, Three-piece, Train, Two-piece

Suitor Beau, Gallant, Lover, Petitioner, Pretender, Swain

Sulk(y), Sulkiness B(r)oody, Dod, Dort, Gee, Glout(s), Glower, Glum, Grouchy, Grouty, Grumps, Huff, Hump, Jinker, Mope, Mump, Pet, Pique, Pout, Spider, Strunt, Sullen

Sullen Dorty, Dour, Farouche, Glum(pish), Grim, Moody, Peevish, Stunkard, Sulky, Surly

Sully Assoil, Bedye, Besmirch, Blot, Defile, Glaur(y), Smear, Smirch, Soil, Tarnish, Tar-wash

Sultry Humid, Sexy, Smouldering, Steamy, Tropical

Sum(s), Sum up Add(end), Aggregate, All, Amount, Bomb, Encapsulate, Foot, Number, Perorate, ➤ QUANTITY, Re-cap, Refund, Solidum, Total, Vector

Summarize, Summary Abridge, Abstract, Aperçu, Bird's eye, Brief, Compendium, Condense, Conspectus, Digest, Docket, Epitome, Gist, Instant, Minute, Offhand, Outline, Overview, Precis, Recap, Resume, Résumé, Round-up, Syllabus, Synopsis, Tabloid, Tabulate, Tabulation, Wrap-up

Summer(time) Aestival, BST, Computer, Estival, Indian, Lintel, Luke, Prime, Solstice, St Luke's, St Martin's, Totter

Summit Acme, Acri-, Apex, Brow, Climax, Conference, ➤ CREST, Crown, Height, Hillcrest, Jole, Peak, Pike, Pinnacle, Spire, Vertex, Vertical, Yalta

Summon(s) Accite, Arrière-ban, Azan, Beck(on), Call, Cist, Cital, Citation, Command, Convene, Drum, Evoke, Garnishment, Gong, Hail, Invocation, Muster, Order, Page, Post, Preconise, Rechate, Recheat, Reveille, Signal, Sist, Ticket, Warn, Warrant, Whoop, Writ

Sun(-god), Sunlight, Sunny, Sunshine Amen-Ra, Amon-Ra, Apollo, Aten, Bright, Cheer, Day(star), Dry, Earthshine, Glory, Heater, Helio(s), Helius, Horus, Mean, Midnight, New Mexico, Parhelion, Phoebean, Photosphere, Ra, Radiant, Rays, Re, Rising, Shamash, Sol(ar), Soleil, Sonne, Surya, Svastika, Swastika, Tabloid, Tan, Titan, UV

Sunder Divide, Divorce, Part, Separate, Sever, Split

▶**Sun-god** see SUN

▶**Sunken** see SINK

Sunshade Awnning, Canopy, Parasol, Umbrella

Sup Dine, Eat, Feast, Sample, Sip, Swallow

Super A1, Arch, Extra, Fab(ulous), Great, Grouse, Ideal, Lulu, Paramount, Superb, Terrific, Tip-top, Tops, Walker-on, Wizard

Superb A1, Fine, Grand, Majestic, Splendid, Top-notch

Supercilious Aloof, Arrogant, Bashaw, Cavalier, Haughty, Lordly, Snide, Sniffy, Snooty, Snotty, Snouty, Superior

Superficial Cosmetic, Cursenary, Cursory, Exterior, Facile, Glib, Outside, Outward, Overlying, Perfunctory, Shallow, Sketchy, Skindeep, Smattering, Veneer

▷**Superficial(ly)** may indicate a word outside another

Superfluous, Superfluity De trop, Extra, Lake, Mountain, Needless, Otiose, Redundant, Spare, Unnecessary

Superhuman Bionic, Herculean, Heroic, Supernatural

Superintend(ent) Boss, Director, Foreman, Guide, Janitor, Oversee(r), Preside, Sewer, Surveillant, Warden, Zanjero

Superior(ity) Abbess, Abeigh, Above, Advantage, Aloof, Atop, Better, Choice, Condescending, Custos, De luxe, Dinger, Eminent, Excellent, Exceptional, Finer, Herrenvolk, Liege, Mastery, Nob, Over, Paramount, Predominance, Prestige, Pretentious, Superordinate, Supremacy, Swell, Top(-loftical), Transcendent(al), U, Udal, Upper(most), Uppish, Upstage

Superlative Best, Exaggerated, Peerless, Supreme, Utmost

Supernatural Divine, Eerie, Fey, Fie, Fly, Gothic, Mana, Paranormal, Sharp, Siddhi, Unearthly

Supernumerary Additional, Corollary, Extra, Mute, Orra

Supersede Replace, Stellenbosch, Supplant

Supervise(d), Supervision, Supervisor Administer, Chaperone, Check, Direct, Engineer, Foreman, Grieve, Handle, Honcho, Invigilate, Manager, Officiate, Overman, Oversee(r), Probation, Shopwalker, Targe, Under, Walla(h)

Supper Dinner, ➤ DRINK(ER), Hawkey, Hockey, Horkey, Last, Meal, Nagmaal, Repast, Soirée

Supplant Displace, Exchange, Replace, Substitute, Supersede

Supple Compliant, Leish, Limber, Lissom(e), ➤ LITHE, Loose, Loose-limbed, Pliable, Souple, Wan(d)le, Wannel, Whippy

Supplement(ary) Addend(um), Addition, And, Annex(e), Appendix, Auxiliary, Colour, Eche, Eke, Extra, Paralipomena, Postscript, Relay, Ripienist, Ripieno, Weighting

Supplier, Supplies, Supply Accommodate, Advance, Afford, Cache, Cater, Commissariat, Contribute, Crop, Endue, Equip, Feed, Fill, Find, Fit, Foison, Fund, Furnish, Give, Grist, Heel, Holp(en), Indue, Issue, Lend, Lithely, Mains, Materiel, Plenish, Ply, ➤ PROVIDE, Provision, Purvey, RASC, Retailer, Serve, Source, Stake, Stock, ➤ STORE, Vintner, Yield

Support(er), Supporting Abet, Adherent, Advocate, Aficionado, Aid, Ally, Ancillary, Andiron, Anta, Arch, Arm, Assistant, Axle, Back-up, Back(bone), Baluster, Bankroll, Banister, Barrack, Barre, Base, Batten, Beam, Bear, Belt, Bier, Bolster, Boom, Bra, Brace, Bracket, Brassiere, Breadwinner, Bridge, Buttress, Chair, Champion, Clientele, Column, Confirm, Console, Cornerstone, Cross-beam, Crutch, Dado, Easel, Encourage, Endorse, Endow, Espouse, Fan, Favour, Fid, Finance, Flying buttress, Fly-rail, Footrest, Footstool, For, Gamb, Gantry, Garter, Girder, Headrest, Help, Henchman, Impost, Income, Jack, Jockstrap, Joist, Keep, Kingpost, Knee, Lectern, Leg, Lifebelt, Lifebuoy, Lobby, Loyalist, Mainstay, Maintain, Makefast, Miserere, Misericord(e), -nik, Nourish, Partisan, Partners, Patronage, Pedestal, Pier, Pillar, Pin, Plinth, Poppet, Post, Potent, Prop, Proponent, PTA, Pylon, Raft, Reinforce, Relieve, Respond, Rest, Rind, Rod, Root, Royalist, Samaritan, Sanction, Sawhorse, Second, Shore, Skeg, Skeleton, Skid, Sleeper, Sling, Socle, Solidarity, Splat, Splint, Sponson, Sprag, Spud, Staddle, Staff, Staging, Stalwart, Stanchion, Stay, Steady, Step, Stirrup, Stool, Stringer, Strut, Subscribe, Subsidy, Succour, Summer, Suspender, Sustain, Tee, Tendril, Third, Tie, Tige, Torsel, Trestle, Tripod, Trivet, Truss, Underlay, Underpin, Understand, Uphold, Upkeep, Viva, Waterwings, Zealot

Suppose(d), Supposition An, Assume, Believe, Expect, Guess, Hypothetical, Idea, If, Imagine, Imply, Opine, Presume, Putative, Sepad, Theory

Suppress(ion) Abolish, Adaw, Burke, Cancel, Censor, Clampdown, Crush, Ecthlipsis, Elide, Elision, Gleichschaltung, Mob(b)le, Quash, Quell, Quench, Restrain, Silence, Smother, Squash, Stifle, Submerge, Subreption

Supreme, Supremacy, Supremo Baaskap, Caudillo, Consummate, Kronos, Leader, Napoleon, Overlord, Paramount, Peerless, Regnant, Sovereign, Sublime, Sudder, Top, Utmost

Sure(ly) Assured, Ay, Bound, Cert(ain), Confident, Definite, Doubtless, Firm, Know, Pardi(e), Pardy, Perdie, Positive, Poz, Safe, Secure, Shoo-in, Sicker, Syker, Uh-huh, Yes

Surety Bail, Guarantee, Mainprise, Security, Sponsional

Surface Appear, Area, Arise, Camber, Day, Dermal, Dermis, Emerge, Epigene, Exterior, External, Face, Facet, Flock, Macadam, Meniscus, Outcrop, Outward, Patina, Pave, Plane, Reveal, Rise, Salband, Side, Skin, Soffit, Superficies, Tar-seal, Tarmac®, Texture, Top, Toroid

Surfeit(ed) Blasé, Cloy, Excess, Glut, Overcloy, Plethora, Satiate, Stall, Staw

Surge Billow, Boom, Drive, Gush, Onrush, Seethe, Sway, Swell

Surgeon Abernethy, BCh, BS, CHB, CM, Doctor, Lister, Medic, Operator, Orthopod, Plastic, Sawbones, Tang, Vet(erinary)

Surgery Facelift, Keyhole, Knife, Laparotomy, Medicine, Op, Open-heart, Osteoplasty, Plastic, Prosthetics

Surly Bluff, Cantankerous, Chough, Chuffy, Churl(ish), Crusty, Cynic, Glum, Gruff, Grum, Grumpy, Rough, Sullen, Truculent

Surpass Bang, Beat, Best, Cap, Ding, Eclipse, Efface, Exceed, Excel, Outdo, Outgun, Out-Herod, Outshine, Outstrip, Overtop, Transcend

Surplus Excess, Extra, Glut, Lake, Mountain, Out-over, Over, Overcome, Remainder, Rest, Spare, Surfeit

Surprise(d), Surprising Alert, Amaze, Ambush, Astonish, Bewilder, Blimey, Bombshell, Caramba, Catch, Confound, Coo, Cor, Crikey, Criminé, Cripes, Dear, Eye-opener, Gadso, Gee, Gemini, Gobsmacked, Golly, Gordon Bennett, Gosh, Ha, Hah, Hallo, Hech, Heh, Hello, Ho, Jeepers, Jeez(e), Lawks, Lordy, Lummy, Marry, Musha, My, Och, Odso, Oops, Open-mouthed, Overtake, Pop-eyed, Really, Shock, Singular, Spot, Stagger, Startle, Strewth, Stun, Sudden, Treat, Turn-up, Uh, Whew, Whoops, Wonderment, Wow, Wrongfoot, Yikes, Yow, Zowie

Surrender Capitulate, Cave-in, Cession, Enfeoff, Fall, Forfeit, Handover, Hulled, Recreant, Release, Relinquish, Submit, Succumb, Waive, ➤ YIELD

Surround(ed), Surrounding(s) Ambient, Architrave, Background, Bathe, Bego, Beset, Bundwall, Circumvallate, Circumvent, Compass, Doughnutting, Ecology, Embail, Encase, ➤ ENCIRCLE, Enclave, Enclose, Encompass, Enfold, Environ,

Enwrap, Fence, Gherao, Gird, Hedge, Impale, Invest, Mid, Orb, Orle, Outflank, Outside, Perimeter, Setting, Wall

Surveillance, Survey(ing), Surveyor Behold, Cadastre, Case, Conspectus, Domesday, Doomwatch, Espial, Examination, Eye, Geodesy, Groma, Look-see, Once-over, Ordnance, Poll, Recce, Reconnaissance, Regard, Review, Scan, Scrutiny, Stakeout, Straw poll, Supervision, Terrier, Theodolite, Triangulate, Vigil, Watch

Survival, Survive, Surviving, Survivor Cope, Endure, Extant, Hibakusha, Last, Leftover, Outlast, Outlive, Persist, Relic(t), Ride, Weather

Suspect, Suspicion, Suspicious Askance, Breath, Dodgy, Doubt, Dubious, Fishy, Grain, Guess, Hint, Hunch, Jalouse, Jealous, Leery, Misdeem, Misdoubt, Misgiving, Mistrust, Modicum, Notion, Paranoia, Queer, Scent, Smatch, Soupçon, Thought, Tinge, Whiff

▷ **Suspect, Suspicious** may indicate an anagram

Suspend(ed), Suspense, Suspension Abate, Abeyance, Adjourn, Cliffhanger, Colloid, Dangle, Defer, Delay, Freeze, Ground, ► HANG, Hydraulic, Intermit, Mist, Moratorium, Nailbiter, Pensile, Poise, Prorogue, Reprieve, Respite, Rusticate, Sideline, Sol, Swing, Tenterhooks, Truce, Withhold

▷ **Suspended** may indicate 'ice' (on ice) at the end of a down light

Sustain(ed), Sustaining, Sustenance Abide, Aliment, Bear, Constant, Depend, Endure, Food, Keep, Last, Maintain, Nutriment, Pedal, Prolong, Sostenuto, Succour, Support

Suture Lambda, Pterion, Stitch

Swab Dossil, Dry, Mop, Pledget, Scour, Sponge, Stupe, Tampon, Tompon, Squeegee, Wipe

Swagger(er), Swaggering Birkie, Bluster, Boast, Brag, Bragadisme, Bravado, Bucko, Cock, Crow, Jaunty, Matamore, Nounce, Panache, Pra(u)nce, Roll, Roist, Rollick, Roul, Royster, Ruffle, Side, Strive, Swank, Swash(-buckler)

Swallow(able), Swallowing Barn, Bird, Bolt, Consume, Devour, Down, Drink, Eat, Endue, Engulf, Esculent, Glug, Gobble, Gulp, Incept, Ingest, Ingulf, Ingurgitate, Itys, Lap, Martin, Martlet, Progne, Quaff, Shift, Sister, Slug, Stomach, Swig, Take

Swamp(y) Bog, Bunyip, Cowal, Deluge, Dismal, Drown, Engulf, Everglade, Flood, Inundate, Lentic, Lerna, Lerne, Loblolly, Mar(i)sh, Morass, Muskeg, Overrun, Overwhelm, Paludal, Quagmire, Slash, Slough, Sudd, Vlei, Vly

▷ **Swap(ped)** may indicate an anagram

Swarm(ing) Abound, Alive, Bike, Bink, Byke, Cast, Cloud, Crowd, Flood, Geminid, Host, Hotter, Infest, Pullulate, Rife, Shin, Shoal, Throng

Sway(ing) Careen, Carry, Command, Diadrom, Domain, Dominion, Flap, Fluctuate, Govern, Hegemony, Influence, Lilt, Oscillate, Prevail, Reel, Reign, Rock, Roll, Rule, Shog, Shoogle, Swag, Swale, Swee, Swing(e), Teeter, Titter, Totter, Vacillate

Swear(ing), Swear word Attest, Avow, Coprolalia, Curse, Cuss, Depose, Execrate, Jurant, Juratory, Oath, Pledge, Plight, Rail, Sessa, Tarnal, Tarnation, Verify, Vow

Sweat(ing), Sweaty Apocrine, Clammy, Diaphoresis, Excrete, Exude, Forswatt, Glow, Hidrosis, Lather, Ooze, Osmidrosis, ► PERSPIRE, Secretion, Slave, Stew, Sudament, Sudamina, Sudate, Swelter

Sweater Argyle, Circassian, Circassienne, Cowichan, Fair Isle, Guernsey, Jersey, Polo, Pullover, Roll-neck, Siwash, Skivvy, Slip-on, Slop-pouch, Sloppy Joe, Woolly

Sweep(er), Sweeping(s) Besom, Broad, Broom, Brush, Chimney, Clean, Curve, Debris, Detritus, Expanse, Extensive, Lash, Lottery, Net, Oars, Range, Scud, Sling, Snowball, Soop, Stroke, Surge, Swathe, Vacuum, Waft, Wide

Sweet(s), Sweetener, Sweetmeat Adeline, Afters, Bombe, Bonbon, Bonus, Brandyball, Bribe, Bull's eye, Burnt-almonds, Butterscotch, Candy, Candyfloss, Caramel, Charming, Choc(olate), Cloying, Comfit, Confect(ion), Confetti, Confit, Conserve, Crème, Cute, Dessert, Dolce, Dolly, Douce(t), Dragée, Dulcet, Flummery, Fondant, Fool, Fragrant, Fresh, Fudge, Glycerin, Gob-stopper, Goody, Gum(drop), Hal(a)vah, Halva, Honey(ed), Humbug, Ice, Jelly baby, Jelly bean, Jube, Jujube, Kiss, Lavender, Licorice, Liquorice, Lollipop, Lolly, Lozenge, Luscious, Marshmallow, Marzipan, Melodious, Mint, Mousse, Muscavado, Nectared, Noisette, Nonpareil, Nougat, Pastille, Pea, Peardrop, Pet, Pie, Praline, Pud(ding), Redolent, Rock, Seventeen, Sillabub, Sixteen, Soot(e), Sop, Sorbet, Spice,

Split, Stickjaw, Sucrose, Sugar, Syllabub, Syrupy, Tablet, Taffy, Tart, Toffee, Torte, Trifle, Truffle, Twee, Uses, William, Winsome

Sweetheart Amoret, Amour, Beau, Dona(h), Dowsabel(l), Doxy, Dulcinea, Flame, Follower, Honey(bunch), Honeybun, Jarta, Jo(e), Lass, Leman, Lover, Masher, Neaera, Peat, Romeo, Steady, Toots(y), True-love, Valentine, Yarta, Yarto

Swell(ing) Ague-cake, Aneurysm, Bag, Bellying, Berry, Billow, Blab, Blister, Bloat, Blow, Boil, Boll, Bolster, Botch, Braw, Bubo, Bulb, Bulge, Bump, Bunion, Cat, Chancre, Chilblain, Cratches, Cyst, Dandy, Diapason, Dilate, ➤ DISTEND, Dom, Don, Eger, Enhance, Excellent, Farcy-bud, Frog, Gall, Gathering, Gent, Goiter, Goitre, Gout, Grandee, Ground, Heave, Heighten, Hove, Increase, Inflate, Intumesce, Kibe, L, Lump, Macaroni, Mouse, Nodule, OK, Onco-, Plim, Plump, Protrude, Proud, Rise, Roil, Sea, Strout, Stye, Surge, Toff, Tuber(cle), Tumour, Tympany, Upsurge, Venter, Wallow, Warble, Wen, Whelk

▷ **Swelling** may indicate a word reversed

Swerve, Swerving Bias, Broach, Careen, Deflect, Deviate, Lean, Sheer, Shy, Stray, Swing, Warp, Wheel

Swift(ly) Apace, Bird, Dean, Dromond, Fleet, Flock, Hasty, Martlet, Newt, Nimble, Presto, Prompt, Quick, ➤ RAPID, Slick, Spanking, Velocipede, Wight

▷ **Swilling** may indicate an anagram

Swim(ming) Bathe, Bogey, Bogie, Crawl, Dip, Float, Naiant, Natatorial, Paddle, Reel, Run, Skinny-dip, Soom, Synchro(nized), Trudgen, Whirl

▷ **Swim** may indicate an anagram

▷ **Swimmer** may indicate a fish

Swindle(r) Beat, Bunco, Cajole, Champerty, ➤ CHEAT, Con, Defraud, Diddle, Do, Escroc, Fiddle, Finagle, Fleece, Fraud, Gazump, Gip, Graft, Grifter, Gyp, Hocus, Hustler, Leg, Leger, Mulct, Nobble, Peter Funk, Plant, Racket, Ramp, Rig, Rogue, Scam, Sell, Shark, Sharper, Shicer, Shyster, Skin, Sting, Stitch-up, Suck, Swiz(z), Trick, Twist, Two-time

Swing(er), Swinging Colt, Dangle, Flail, Hang, Hep, Kip(p), Lilt, Metronome, Mod, Music, Oscillate, Pendulate, Pendulum, Rock, Rope, Shoogie, Shuggy, Slew, Swale, Sway, Swee, Swerve, Swey, Swipe, Trapeze, Vibratile, Voop, Wave, Wheel, Whirl, Yaw

▷**Swirling** may indicate an anagram

Switch Birch, Change, Convert, Dimmer, Dip, Exchange, Hairpiece, Knife, Replace, Retama, Rocker, Rod, Scutch, Thyristor, Time, Toggle, Trip, Twig, Twine, Wave, Zap

Swivel Caster, Pivot, Root, Rotate, Spin, Terret, Territ, Torret, Turret, Wedein

Swollen Blown, Bollen, Bulbous, Full, Gourdy, Gouty, Incrassate, Nodose, Puffy, Tumid, Turgescent, Turgid, Varicose, Ventricose, Vesiculate

Swoon Blackout, Collapse, Dwa(l)m, Dwaum, Faint

▶**Swop** see SWAP

Sword(-like), Swordplay Anelace, Anlace, Bilbo, Blade, Brand, Brandiron, Broad(sword), Claymore, Cutlass, Damascene, Damocles, Dirk, Ensate, Ensiform, Epée, Espada, Estoc, Excalibur, Foil, Gleave, Glorious, Hanger, Joyeuse, Kendo, Kris, Kukri, Morglay, Rapier, Sabre, Samurai, Scimitar, Semita(u)r, Shabble, Shamshir, Sharp, Sigh, Simi, Skene-dhu, Spadroon, Spirtle, Spit, Steel, Toledo, Tulwar, Whinyard

Sycophant Brown-nose, Claqueur, Crawler, Creeper, Fawner, Lickspittle, Parasite, Toad-eater, Toady, Yesman

Syllable(s) Acatalectic, Anacrusis, Aretinian, Om, Tonic

Syllabus Program(me), Prospectus, Résumé, Summary, Table

Symbol(ic), Symbols, Symbolism, Symbolist Agma, Allegory, Ampersand, Ankh, Asterisk, Cachet, Caret, Cedilla, Character, Chord, Cipher, Clef, Colon, Decadent, Del, Diesis, Dingbat, Eagle, Emblem, Equal, Hash, Hieroglyph, Icon, Ideogram, Index, Logo(gram), Mark, Metaphor, Minus, Moral, Motif, Mystical, Nominal, Notation, Obelus, Pentacle, Phonetic, Pi, Plus, Rose, Rune, Segno, Semicolon, Shamrock, Sign, Slur, Status, Swastika, Tag, Talisman, Thistle, Tiki, Tilde, Token, Totem, Trademark, Triskele, Type

Symmetric(al), Symmetry Balance, Digonal, Diphycercal, Even, Harmony, Isobilateral, Radial, Regular

Sympathetic, Sympathise(r), Sympathy Approval, Commiserate, Compassion, Condole(nce), Condone, Congenial, Crypto, Empathy, Fellow-traveller, Humane, Par, Pity, Rapport, Ruth, Side, Vicarious

Symphony Concert, Eroica, Fifth, Jupiter, Manfred, Music, New World, Opus, Pastoral, Sinfonia, Unfinished

Symptom(s) Epiphenomenon, Feature, Indicia, Merycism, Mimesis, Prodrome, Semiotic, Sign, Syndrome, Token, Trait, Withdrawal

Syncopated, Syncopation Abridged, Breakbeat, Revamp, Zoppa, Zoppo

Syndrome Adams-Stokes, Asperger's, Carpal tunnel, Characteristic, China, Chronic fatigue, Cushing's, Down's, Empty nest, Fragile X, Hutchinson-Gilford, Jerusalem, Korsakoff's, Locked-in, Marfan, ME, Menières, Munchhausen's, Nonne's, Pattern, Postviral, Premenstrual, Reiter's, Reye's, Sezary, Sjogren's, Stevens-Johnson, Stockholm, Stokes-Adams, Temperomandibular, TMJ, Tourette's, Toxic shock, Turner's, Wag the Dog, Wernicke-Korsakoff, Wobbler

Synopsis Abstract, Blurb, Conspectus, Digest, Outline, Résumé, Schema, ➤ SUMMARY

Synthetic Ersatz, Fake, False, Mock, Polyamide, Spencerian

Syringe(s) Douche, Flutes, Harpoon, Hypo, Needle, Reeds, Spray, Squirt, Wash

Syrup Cassis, Corn, Flattery, Grenadine, Linctus, Maple, Molasses, Orgeat, Rob, Sugar, Treacle

System(atic) ABO, Binary, Braille, Code, Cosmos, Course, Decimal, Dewey (Decimal), Economy, Eocene, Establishment, Feudal, Harvard, Life-support, Limbic, Linear, Madras, ➤ METHOD, Metric, Nervous, Network, Nicam, Notation, Octal, Order, Organon, Process, Regime, Regular, Root, Scientific, SI, Solar, Sonar, Structure, Studio, Ternary, Theory, Tommy, Universe

Tt

Table(-like) Altar, Board, Bradshaw, Breakfast, Calendar, ➤ CHART, Console, Counter, Desk, Diagram, Dinner, Dressing, Drop-leaf, Food, Gateleg, Glacier, Graph, Green-cloth, High, Index, Key, League, ➤ LIST, Mahogany, Matrix, Mensa(l), Mesa,

Occasional, Pembroke, Periodic, Piecrust, Pier, Plane, Platen, Pool, Pythagoras, Reckoner, Refectory, Roll, Round, Slab, Spoon, Stall, Stone, Te(a)poy, Tea, Tide, Times, Trestle, Trolley, Twelve, Washstand, Water, Workbench

Tablet Abacus, Album, Aspirin, Caplet, Eugebine, Medallion, Opisthograph, Osculatory, Ostracon, Ostrakon, ➤ PAD, ➤ PILL, Plaque, Slate, Stele, Stone, Tombstone, Torah, Triglyph, Triptych, Troche, Trochisk, Ugarit

Taboo, Tabu Ban(ned), Bar, Blackball, Forbidden, No-no

Tack Baste, Beat, Brass, Cinch, Clubhaul, Cobble, Gybe, Leg, Martingale, Nail, Saddlery, Salt-horse, ➤ SEW, Sprig, Stirrup, Veer, White-seam, Yaw, Zigzag

Tackle Accost, Approach, Attempt, Beard, Bobstay, Burton, Claucht, Claught, Clevis, Collar, Dead-eye, Garnet, Gear, Haliard, Halyard, Harness, Jury-rig, Rig, Rigging, Scrag

Tact, Tactful Delicacy, Diplomacy, Diplomatic, Discreet, Discretion, Politic, Savoir-faire

Tactic(s) Audible, Hardball, Manoeuvre, Masterstroke, Plan, Ploy, Salami, Shock, ➤ STRATEGY, Strong-arm

Tactless(ness) Blundering, Brash, Crass, Gaffe, Gauche, Indelicate

Tail, Tailpiece ➤ APPENDAGE, Bob, Brush, Caudal, Coda, Colophon, Cue, Dock, Fan, Fee, ➤ FOLLOW, Fud, Liripoop, Parson's nose, Pole, Pope's nose, PS, Queue, Seat, Scut, Stag, Stern, Telson, ➤ TIP, Train, Women

Tailor(ed) Bespoke, Bushel, Cabbager, Couturier, Cutter, Darzi, Durzi, Epicene, Feeble, Nine, Outfitter, Pick-the-louse, Pricklouse, Sartor, Seamster, Snip, Starveling, Style, Whipcat, Whipstitch

▷**Tailor** may indicate an anagram

Taint(ed) Besmirch, Blemish, Fly-blown, High, Infect, Leper, Off, Poison, ➤ SPOIL, Stain, Stigma, Trace, Unwholesome

Take(n), Take in, Taking(s), Take over Absorb, ➤ ACCEPT, Adopt, Assume, Attract, Bag, Beg, Bone, Borrow, Bottle, ➤ CAPTURE, Catch, Cop, Coup, Detract, Dishy, Exact, Expropriate, Get, Grab, Haul, Hent, House, Howe, Huff, Incept, Ingest, Mess, Nick, Occupy, Pocket, Quote, R, Rec, Receipt, Receive, Recipe, Rob, Seise, Sequester, Ship, Smitten,

Snatch, Sneak, ➤ STEAL, Stomach, Subsume, Swallow, Sweet, Swipe, Toll, Trump, Turnover, Usurp, Wan, Winsome, Wrest

▷**Taken up** may indicate reversed

Tale(s) Allegory, Blood, Conte, Decameron, Edda, Fable, Fabliau, Fairy, Fiction, Gag, Geste, Hadith, Iliad, Jataka, Jeremiad, Legend, Lie, Mabinogion, Maise, Ma(i)ze, Marchen, Narrative, Odyssey, Rede, Saga, Score, Sinbad, Spiel, ➤ STORY, Tradition, Travellers', Weird

Talent(ed) Accomplishment, Aptitude, Bent, Dower, Faculty, Flair, Genius, Gift, Knack, Nous, Prodigy, Schtick, Strong point, Versatile, Virtuoso, W(h)iz(z), Whiz-kid

Talk, Talker, Talks Ana, Articulate, Babble, Blab, Blat, Blether-skate, Cant, Chat, Chinwag, Chirp, Commune, Confer, Converse, Coo, Cross, Descant, Dialog(ue), Diatribe, Dilate, Discourse, Diseur, Dissert, Earbash, Earful, Express, Froth, Gab, Gabble, Gabnash, Gas, Gibber, Gossip, Guff, Harp, Imparl, Jabber, Jargon, Jaw, Jazz, Lip, Mang, Maunder, Mince, Monologue, Nashgab, Noise, Palaver, Parlance, Parley, Patter, Pawaw, Pep, Pidgin, Pillow, Pitch, Potter, Powwow, Prate, Prattle, Prose, Ramble, Rap, Regmarole, Rote, SALT, Shop, Slang(-whang), Small, Soliloquy, ➤ SPEAK, Spiel, Spout, Sweet, Table, Turkey, Twaddle, Twitter, Up(s), Utter, Vocal, Waffle, Witter, Wrangle, Yabber, Yack, Yak, Yammer, Yap, Yalta, Yatter

Talkative Chatty, Fluent, Gabby, Garrulous, Gash, Glib, Loquacious, Vocular, Voluble

Tall Etiolated, Exaggerated, Hie, High, Hye, Lanky, Lathy, Leggy, Lofty, Long, Procerity, Randle-tree, Tangle, Taunt, Tower, Towery

Tally ➤ AGREE, Census, Correspond, Count, Match, Nickstick, Notch, Record, ➤ SCORE, Stick, Stock, Tab, Tag

Tame Amenage, Break, Docile, Domesticate, Mansuete, Meek, Mild, Safe, Snool, Subdue

Tamper(ing) Bishop, Cook, Doctor, Fake, Fiddle, Meddle, Medicate, Monkey, Nobble, Phreaking

Tan(ned), Tanned skin, Tanning Adust, Bablah, Babul, Bark, Basil, Beige, Bisque, Bronze, ➤ BROWN, Catechu, Insolate, Lambast, Leather, Neb-neb, Paste, Pipi, Puer, Pure, Spank, Sun, Tenné, Umber, Valonea, Val(l)onia, Ybet

Tangle Alga, Badderlock, Burble, Dulse, Embroil, Entwine, Fank, Fankle, Heap, Implication, Ket, ➤ KNOT, Labyrinth, Laminaria,

Lutin, Mat, Mix, Nest, Oarweed, Ore, Pleach, Perplex, ➤ RAVEL, Sea-girdle, Seaweed, Skean, Skein, Snarl, Taigle, Taut(it), Tawt, Thicket, Varec

▷**Tangled** may indicate an anagram

Tank Amphibian, Aquarium, Centurion, Cesspool, Challenger, Chieftain, Cistern, Feedhead, Float, Flotation, Gasholder, Header, Keir, Ker, Panzer, Pod, ➤ RESERVOIR, Ripple, Septic, Sherman, Sponson, Sump, Think, Tiger, Vat, Vivarium

Tantalise Entice, Tease, Tempt, Torture

Tantrum Paddy, Pet, Rage, Scene, Tirrivee, Tirrivie

Tap(ping), Taps Accolade, Blip, Broach, Bug, Cock, Drum, Faucet, Flick, Hack, Mixer, Paracentesis, Pat, Patter, Percuss, Petcock, ➤ RAP, Spigot, Stopcock, Tack, Tat, Tit

Tape DAT, ➤ DRINK, Ferret, Finish, Incle, Inkle, Insulating, Magnetic, Masking, Measure, Metal, Passe, Passe-partout, Perforated, Punched, Record, Red, Scotch, Sticky, Ticker, Video

Taper(ed), Tapering Diminish, Fastigiate, Featheredge, Fusiform, Lanceolate, Narrow, Nose, Subulate, Tail

Tapestry Alentous, Arras(ene), Bayeux, Bergamot, Crewel-work, Dosser, Gobelin, Hanging, Oudenarde, Tapet

Target ➤ AIM, Blank, Butt, Cockshy, End, Hit, Home, Hub, Inner, Magpie, Mark, Motty, ➤ OBJECT, Outer, Pelta, Pin, Prey, Prick, Quintain, Sitter, Tee, Victim

Tarry Bide, Dally, Leng, ➤ LINGER, Stay, Sticky

Tartar Argal, Argol, Beeswing, Crust, Hell, Plaque, Rough, Scale, Tam(b)erlane, Zenocrate

Task Assignment, Aufgabe, ➤ CHORE, Duty, Errand, Exercise, Fag, Imposition, Mission, Ordeal, Stint, Thankless, Vulgus

Taste(ful), Tasty Acquired, Aesthetic, Appetite, Degust, Delibate, Discrimination, ➤ EAT, Fashion, Flavour, Form, Gout, Gust, Hint, Lick, Palate, Penchant, Pica, Pree, Refinement, Relish, ➤ SAMPLE, Sapor, Sar, Savour, S(c)hme(c)k, Sip, Smack, Smatch, Snack, Stomach, Soupçon, Succulent, Tang, Titbit, Toothsome, ➤ TRY, Vertu, Virtu

Tasteless Appal, Fade, Flat, Insipid, Stale, Vapid, Vulgar, Watery, Wearish, Wersh

Tattle(r) Blab, Chatter, ➤ GOSSIP, Prate, Rumour, Sneak, Snitch, Totanus, Willet

Taunt Dig, Fling, Gibe, Gird, ➤ JEER, Rag, Ridicule, Twight, Twit

Tavern Bar, Bodega, Bousing-ken, Bush, Fonda, ➤ INN, Kiddleywink, Kneipe, Mermaid, Mitre, Mughouse, Pothouse, Shebeen, Taphouse

Tawdry Catchpenny, ➤ CHEAP, Flashy, Gaudy, Sleazy, Tatty

Tax(ing), Taxation ACT, Aid, Agist, Alms-fee, Assess, Capitation, Cense, Cess, ➤ CHARGE, Corporation, Council, Custom, Danegeld, Direct, Duty, Energy, EPT, Escot, Escuage, Exact, Excise, Exercise, Geld, Gift, Head, Impose, Imposition, Impost, Impute, Indirect, Inheritance, IR, Land, Levy, Lot, Octroi, Operose, Overwork, PAYE, Poll, Poundage, Primage, Property, Proportional, PT, Purchase, Rate, Road, Scat(t), Scot (and lot), Scutage, Sess, SET, Skat, Stent, Task, Teind, Tithe, Toilsome, Toll, Tonnage, Tribute, Try, VAT, Wattle, Wealth, Weary, White rent, Window, Withholding

Tax-collector, Taxman Amildar, Cheater, Exciseman, Farmer, Gabeller, Inspector, IR(S), Publican, Stento(u)r, Tithe-proctor, Tollman, Undertaker, Zemindar

Tea Afternoon, Brew, Brick, Cambric, Cha, Chirping-cup, Cream, Cuppa, High, K(h)at, Kitchen, Leaves, Marijuana, Orange pekoe, Pot, Qat, Russian, Switchel, Tay, Thea, Theophylline

Teach(er), Teaching (material), Teachings Adjoint, Agrege, Apostle, Beale, BEd, Buss, ➤ COACH, Con(ne), Didactic, Doctrine, Dogma, Dominie, Dressage, Edify, ➤ EDUCATE, Explain, Faculty, Froebel, Gospel, Governess, Guru, Head, Inculcate, Indoctrinate, Inform, Instil, Instruct, Ism, Lair, Lear(e), Lecturer, Leir, Lere, Maam, Magister, Marker, Marm, Master, Mentor, Miss, Mistress, Molla(h), Monitor, Mufti, Mullah, Munshi, PT, Pedagogue, Pedant, Pr(a)efect, Preceptor, Prof, Rabbi, Rebbe, Rhetor, Scholastic, Schoolman, Scribe, Show, Sir, Socrates, Sophist, Staff, Sunna, Supply, Swami, Tantra, Train(er), Tutelage, Tutor, Usher

Team Colts, Crew, Dream, Ecurie, Eleven, Equipe, Fifteen, Outfit, Oxen, Panel, Possibles, Relay, Scrub, ➤ SIDE, Span, Squad, Squadron, Staff, Troupe, Turnout, Unicorn, United, XI

Tear(s), Tearable, Tearful, Tearing Beano, Claw, Crocodile, Drop, Eye-drop, Eye-water, Greeting, Hurry, Lacerate, Laniary, Pelt, Ranch, Rash, Reave, ➤ REND, Rheum, Rip, Rive, Rume, Screed, Shred, Snag, Split, Spree, Tire, Wet, Worry, Wrench, Wrest

Tease, Teasing Arch, Backcomb, Badinage, Bait, Banter, Chap, Chiack, Chip, Cod, Grig, Guy, Hank, Imp, Ironic, Itch, Josh, Kemb, Kid, Mag, Nark, Persiflage, ➤ RAG, Raillery, Rally, Razz, Rib, Rot, Strip, ➤ TANTALISE, Torment(or), Twit

Teat Dug, Dummy, Mamilla, Mastoid, Nipple, Pap, Soother, Tit

Technical, Technician, Technique Adept, Alexander, Artisan, Brushwork, College, Delphi, Execution, Kiwi, Manner, ➤ METHOD, Operative, Salami, Science

Tedium, Tedious Boring, Chore, Deadly, Drag, Dreich, Dull, Ennui, Heaviness, Long, Longspun, Monotony, Operose, Prosy, Soul-destroying, ➤ TIRING, Wearisome, Yawn

Teem(ing) Abound, Bustling, Empty, Great, Pullulate, Swarm

Teenager Adolescent, Bobbysoxer, Junior, Juvenile, Minor, Mod, Rocker, Sharpie

▶**Teeth** see TOOTH

Teetotal(ler) Abdar, Blue Ribbon, Nephalist, Rechabite, Temperate, TT, Water-drinker, Wowser

Telegram, Telegraph Bush, Cable, Ems, Grapevine, Greetings, Message, Moccasin, Telex, Wire

Telephone Ameche, ATLAS, Bell, Blower, BT, Call, Cellphone, Centrex, Cordless, Dial, GRACE, Handset, Horn, Intercom, Line, Mercury, Pdq, Ring, STD, Touch-tone, Vodafone®, Wire

Telescope Altazimuth, Binocle, Cassegrain(ian), Collimator, Coudé, Finder, Galilean, Glass, Gregorian, Heliometer, Hubble, Intussuscept, Newtonian, Palomar, Radio, Reflector, Refractor, Schmidt, Shorten, Spyglass, Stadia, Terrestrial, Tube

Television, Telly Box, Digital, Diorama, Goggle box, ITV, MAC, PAL, RTE, Set, Small screen, Tube, ➤ TV, Video

Tell Acquaint, Announce, Apprise, Beads, Blab, Clipe, Clype, Direct, ➤ DISCLOSE, Divulge, Grass, Impart, Inform, ➤ NARRATE, Noise, Notify, Number, Recite, Recount, Relate, Report, Retail, Rumour, Sneak, Snitch, Spin, Teach, William

Temper, Temperate Abstinent, Allay, Anneal, Assuage, Attune, Balmy, Bile, Blood, Calm, Choler, Continent, Dander, Delay, Ease, Fireworks, Flaky, Irish, Leaven, ➤ MILD, Mitigate, Moderate, Modify, ➤ MOOD, Neal, Paddy, Pet, Rage, Season, Sober, Soften, Spitfire, Spleen, Strop, Tantrum, Techy, Teen, Teetotal, Tetchy, Tiff, Tone, Trim, Tune

Temperament(al) Bent, Blood, Crasis, Disposition, Kidney, Mettle, Moody, ➤ NATURE, Over-sensitive, Prima donna

Temperature Absolute, Celsius, Centigrade, Chambré, Curie, Fahrenheit, Fever, Flashpoint, Heat, Heterothermal, Hyperthermia, Kelvin, Regulo, Room, T, Weed, Weid

Temple, Temple gate Capitol, Chapel, Church, Delphi, Delubrum, Ephesus, Fane, Gurdwara, Heroon, Inner, Masjid, Middle, Mosque, Museum, Naos, Pagod(a), Pantheon, Parthenon, ➤ SHRINE, Shul(n), Teocalli, Teopan, Torii, Vihara, Wat

Temporary Acting, Caretaker, Cutcha, Ephemeral, Hobjob, Interim, Kutcha, Locum, Makeshift, Pro tem, Provisional, Short-term, Stopgap, Temp, Transient, Transitional

Tempt(ation), Tempting, Tempter, Temptress Allure, Apple, Bait, Beguile, Beset, Dalilah, Decoy, Delilah, ➤ ENTICE, Eve, Groundbait, Impulse, Lure, Providence, Satan, Seduce, Siren, Snare, Tantalise, Tice, Test, Trial

Ten Commandments, Decad, Iota, Tera-, Tribes, X

Tenacious, Tenacity Clayey, Determined, Dogged, Fast, Guts, Hold, Intransigent, Persevering, Persistent, Resolute, Retentive, Sticky

Tenancy, Tenant(s) Censuarius, Cosherer, Cottar, Cotter, Cottier, Dreng, Feuar, Feudatory, Homage, Ingo, Inhabit, Leaseholder, Lessee, ➤ LODGER, Metayer, Occupier, Rentaller, Renter, Shorthold, Sitting, Socager, Socman, Sokeman, Suckener, Tacksman, Valvassor, Vassal, Vavasour, Visit

Tend Care, Dress, Herd, Incline, Lean, Liable, Nurse, Prone, Run, Shepherd, Verge

Tendency Apt, Bent, Bias, Conatus, Drift, Import, Militant, Penchant, Proclivity, Propensity, Trend

Tender(iser), Tenderly, Tenderness Affettuoso, Amoroso, Bid, Bill, Coin, Con amore, Crank, Ding(h)y, Dingey, Fond, Frail, Gentle, Green, Humane, Jolly-boat, Legal, Nesh, Nurse, ➤ OFFER, Papain, Pinnace, Prefer, Present, Proffer, Proposal, Quotation, Red Cross, Sair, Shepherd, ➤ SOFT, Sore, SRN, Submit, Sympathy, Tendre

Tendon Achilles, Aponeurosis, Hamstring, Leader, Paxwax, Sinew, String, Vinculum, Whiteleather

Tenor Course, ➤ DRIFT, Effect, Gigli, Gist, Purport, Singer, T, Timbre, Trial, Vein

Tense Aor, Aorist, Case, Clench, Drawn, Edgy, Electric, Essive, Imperfect, Keyed up, Mood(y), Nervy, Overstrung, Past, Perfect, Pluperfect, Preterite, Rigid, Stiff, Stressed(-out), Strict, T, ➤ TAUT, Uptight

Tension Isometrics, Isotonic, Nerviness, Premenstrual, ➤ STRAIN, Stress, Stretch, Surface, Tone, Yips

Tent Bell, Bivvy, Cabana, Douar, Duar, Kedar, Kibitka, Marquee, Oxygen, Pavilion, Probe, Ridge, Shamiana(h), Shamiyanah, Shelter, Tabernacle, Teepee, Tepee, Tipi, Top, Topek, Trailer, Tupek, Tupik, Wigwam, Y(o)urt

Term(s), Terminal, Termly Anode, Buffer, Cathode, Coast, Coste, Designate, Desinant, Distal, ➤ EPITHET, Euphemism, Expression, Final, Gnomon, Goal, Half, Hilary, Inkhorn, Lent, Michaelmas, ➤ PERIOD, Sabbatical, Semester, Session, Stint, Stretch, Trimester, Trimestrial, Trinity, ➤ WORD

Terminate, Termination, Terminus Abort, Axe, Conclude, Depot, Desinent, Earth, ➤ END, Expiry, ➤ FINISH, Goal, Liquidate, Naricorn, Railhead, Suffix

Terrace Barbette, Beach, Bench, Linch, Lynchet, Perron, Shelf, Stoep, Tarras, Undercliff, Veranda(h)

Terrible, Terribly Awful, Deadly, Fell, Frightful, Ghastly, Horrible, Much, Odious, Very

Terrific, Terrified, Terrify Affright, Aghast, Agrise, Agrize, Agryze, Appal, Awe, Enorm, Fear, Fine, Fley, Gast, Helluva, Huge, Overawe, ➤ PETRIFY, Scare, Superb, Unman, Yippee

Territory Abthane, Ap(p)anage, Colony, Domain, Dominion, Duchy, Emirate, Enclave, Exclave, Goa, Lebensraum, Manor, Margravate, No-man's-land, Northern, Nunavut, Panhandle, Principate, Protectorate, Province, Realm, ➤ REGION, Sphere, Sultanate, Ter(r), Trust, Yukon

Test(er), Testing Acid, Alpha, Ames, Appro, Assay, Audition, Bench, Bender, Beta, Breathalyser®, Candle, Canopy, Check, Chi-square, Cloze, Conn(er), Coomb's, Criterion, Crucial, Crucible, Crunch, Dick, Driving, Dummy-run, Examine, Exercise, Experiment, Field, International, Litmus, Means, MOT, Mug, Neckverse, Objective, Oral, ➤ ORDEAL, Pale, Pap, Patch, Paternity, Performance, Personality, PH, Pilot, Pree, Preeve, Preve, Probe, Projective, Proof, Prove, Pyx, Quiz, Rally, Reagent,

Rorschach, SAT, Screen, Showdown, Shroff, Significance, Sixpence, Skin, Smear, Sound, Tempt, Touch, Touchstone, Trier, Trior, Try, Viva

Testament Bible, Heptateuch, Hexateuch, New, Old, Pentateuch, Scripture, Septuagint, Tanach, Targum, Will

Testicle(s) Ballocks, Balls, Bollocks, Bollix, Cojones, Gool(e)y, Goolie, Knackers, Monorchid, Nuts, Ridgel, Ridgil, Rig(gald), Rocks, Stone

Testify, Testimonial, Testimony Character, Chit, Declare, Depone, Deposition, ➤ EVIDENCE, Rap, Scroll, Viva voce, Witness

Tether Cord, Endurance, Noose, Picket, Seal, Stringhalt, ➤ TIE

Text(s), Textbook ABC, Body, Brahmana, Codex, Donat, Ennage, Harmony, Libretto, Mandaean, Mezuzah, Octapla, Op-cit, Philology, Plain, Pyramid, Quran, Responsa, Rubric, S(h)astra, Script, Shema, ➤ SUBJECT, Sutra, Tefillin, Tephillin, Tetrapla, Thesis, Topic, Tripitaka, Typography, Upanis(h)ad, Variorium, Vulgate, Zohar

Thank(s), Thankful, Thanksgiving Appreciate, Collins, Deo gratias, Gloria, Grace, Gramercy, Grateful, Gratitude, Kaddish, Mercy, Roofer

Thatch(er), Thatching At(t)ap, Hair, Heard, Hear(i)e, Hele, Hell, Mane, PM, Reed, Straw, Thack, Theek, Wig

▷ **Thaw** may indicate 'ice' to be removed from a word

Theatre, Theatrical(ity) Abbey, Adelphi, Broadway, Camp, Cinema, Coliseum, Criterion, Drama, Everyman, Field, Gaff, Gaiety, Globe, Grand Guignol, Haymarket, Hippodrome, Histrionic, House, Kabuki, La Scala, Legitimate, Lyceum, Mermaid, National, Noh, Odeon, Odeum, OUDS, Palladium, Panache, Playhouse, Political, Rep(ertory), Shaftesbury, Sheldonian, Shop, Stage, Stoll, Straw-hat, Street, Touring, Vic, Windmill, Zarzuela

Theft Appropriation, Burglary, Heist, Kinchinlay, Larceny, Maino(u)r, Manner, Pilfery, Plunder, Ram-raid, Robbery, Stealth, Stouth(rief), Touch

Theme Crab canon, Donnée, Fugue, Idea, Leitmotiv, Lemma, Lemmata, ➤ MELODY, Motif, Peg, Question, ➤ SUBJECT, Text, Topic, Topos

Theologian, Theologist, Theology Abelard, Aquinas, Calvin, Christology, Colet, DD, Divine, Erastus, Eschatology, Eusebius, Exegetics, Hase, Irenics, Jansen, Kierkegaard, Knox, Mullah, Newman, Niebuhr, Origen, Paley, Pelagius, Pusey, Rabbi, Religious, Schoolman, Softa, STP, Tertullian, Ulema

Theorem, Theoretical, Theorist, Theory Academic, Binomial, Chaos, Dependency, Dictum, Domino, Dow, Einstein, Guess, Holism, Hypothesis, Ideal, Ideology, Ism(y), Kinetic, Lemma, Notion, Probability, Proof, Pure, Pythagoras, Quantity, Quantum, Relativity, Steady state, System

Therapeutic, Therapy Aversion, Behaviour, Cognitive, Curative, Electric shock, Gene, Gestalt, Group, Occupational, Osteopathy, Physical, Primal, Radiation, Radio, Reflexology, Reichian, Reiki, Relaxation, Rolfing, Sanatory, Scientology®, SHEN, Shiatsu, Shiatzu, Shock, Speech

Thermometer Aethrioscope, Centesimal, Glass, Pyrometer, Wet and dry bulb

Thick(en), Thickening, Thickener, Thickness, Thickset Abundant, Algin, Burly, Bushy, Callosity, Callus, Clavate, Cloddy, Cruddle, Curdle, Dense, Dextrin(e), Dumose, Engross, Grist, Grume, Guar, Gum, Hyperostosis, Incrassate, Inspissate, Kuzu, Liaison, Panada, Roux, Sclerosis, ➤ SOLID, Soupy, Squat, Stumpy, ➤ STUPID, Thieves, This, Thixotropic, Waulk, Wooden, Xantham

Thicket Bosk, Brake, Brush, Cane-brake, Chamisal, Coppice, Copse, Dead-finish, Greve, Grove, Macchie, Maquis, Queach, Reedrand, Reedrond, Salicetum, Shola

Thief, Thieves, Thievish Autolycus, Blood, Chummy, Coon, Corsair, Cutpurse, Filcher, Flood, Footpad, Freebooter, Heist, Hotter, Ice-man, Jackdaw, Kiddy, Larcener, Light-fingered, Looter, Mag, Nip(per), Pad, Pilferer, Pirate, Plagiarist, Poacher, Prig, Raffles, ➤ ROBBER, Rustler, Shark, Shop-lifter, Sneak, Taffy, Taker, Tea-leaf, Thick

Thin(ner) Acetone, Bald, Bony, Cull, Dilute, Emaciated, Enseam, Fine, Fine-drawn, Flimsy, Gaunt, Hair('s-)breadth, Inseam, Lanky, Lean, Puny, Rangy, Rare, Rarefied, Reedy, Scant, Scraggy, Scrawny, Sheer, Sieve, Skeletal, Skimpy, Skinking, Slender, Slim, Slimline, Slink, ➤ SPARE, Sparse, Spindly, Stilty, Stringy, Subtle, Taper, Tenuous, Turps, Wafer, Washy, Waste, Watch, Water(y), ➤ WEAK, Weedy, Wiry, Wispy, Wraith

Thing(s) Alia, Article, Chattel, Chose, Doodah, Doofer, Entia, Fetish, Fixation, It, Item, Jingbang, Job, Material, Matter, ➤ OBJECT, Obsession, Paraphernalia, Phobia, Res, Tool, Whatnot

Thingummy Dingbat, Dinges, Doodah, Doofer, Doohickey, Gubbins, Whatsit, Yoke

Think(er), Thinking Associate, Believe, Brain, Brood, Casuistry, Cogitate, Consider, Contemplant, ➤ CONTEMPLATE, Deem, Deliberate, Descartes, Dianoetic, Esteem, Fancy, Fear, Ghesse, Gnostic, Guess, Hegel, Hold, ➤ IMAGINE, Judge, Lateral, Meditate, Mentation, Muse, Opine, Pensive, Philosopher, Phrontistery, Ponder, Pore, Presume, Rational, Reckon, Reflect, Reminisce, Ruminate, Trow, Ween

Third, Third rate Bronze, C, Eroica, Gamma, Gooseberry, Interval, Mediant, Picardy, Quartan, Tertius, Tierce, Trisect

Thirst(y) ➤ CRAVE, Dives, Drought, Drouth, Dry, Hydropic, Nadors, Pant, Polydipsia, Thrist

Thirteen Baker's dozen, Long dozen, Riddle, Unlucky

Thistle Canada, Carduus, Carline, Cnicus, Echinops, Musk, Safflower, Sow, Star, Thrissel, Thristle

Thomas Aquinas, Arnold, Christadelphian, De Quincey, Didymus, Doubting, Dylan, Erastus, Hardy, Loco, Parr, Rhymer, Tompion, True, Turbulent

Thorn(y) Acantha, Bael, Bel, Bhel, Bramble, Briar, Coyotillo, Doom, Edh, Eth, Irritation, Jerusalem, Mahonia, Mayflower, Nabk, Nebbuk, Nebe(c)k, ➤ NEEDLE, Prickle, Slae, Spine, Spinescent, Spinulate, Trial, Wagn'bietjie, Ye, Zare(e)ba, Zariba, Zeriba

Thorough(ly) A fond, Complete, Even-down, Firm, Fully, Ingrained, Inly, Out, Out and out, Painstaking, Pakka, Pucka, Pukka, Ripe, Sound, Strict, Total, Tout à fait, Up

Thought(ful), Thoughtfulness Avisandum, Broody, Cerebration, Cogitation, Concept, Considerate, Contemplation, Dianoetic, Idea, Innate, Kind, Maieutic, Mind, Musing, Opinion, Pensée, Pensive, Philosophy, Reflection, Rumination

Thoughtless Blindfold, Careless, Heedless, Inconsiderate, Pillock, ➤ RASH, Remiss, Reckless, Scatter-brained, Vacant

Thousand(s) Chiliad, Gorilla, K, Lac, Lakh, M, Millenary, Millennium, Plum, Toman

Thrash(ing) ► BEAT, Belabour, Belt, Bepelt, Binge, Bless, Cane, Dress, Drub, Flail, Flog, Jole, Joll, Joule, Jowl, Lace, Laldie, Laldy, Lambast, Larrup, Lather, Leather, Lick, Marmelise, Paste, Ploat, Quilt, Slog, Smoke, Strap-oil, Swat, Targe, Towel, Trim, Trounce, Whale, Whap

Thread, Threadlike Ariadne, Bottom, Buttress, Chalaza, Chromosome, Clew, Clue, Cord, Eel-worm, End, Fibre, Filament, File, Filiform, Filose, Gossamer, Heddle, Ixtle, Lace, Lap, Lingel, Lingle, Link, Lisle, Lurex®, Meander, Organzine, Pearlin(g), Pick, Ravel, Reeve, Sacred, Seton, ► STRAND, Suture, Tassel, Tendril, Theme, Thrid, Thrum, Trace, Tram, Trundle, Tussore, Twine, Warp, Weft, Wick, ► WIND, Wisp, Worm

Threat(en), Threatened, Threatening Baleful, Blackmail, Bluster, Coerce, Comminate, Face, Fatwa, Fraught, Greenmail, Greymail, Hazard, Impend, Imperil, Loom, ► MENACE, Minacious, Minatory, Omen, Overcast, Overhang, Parlous, Peril, Portent, Ramp, Shore, Strongarm, Ugly, Veiled, Warning

Three, Threefold, Three-wheeler, Thrice Graces, Har, Harpies, Jafenhar, Leash, Muses, Musketeers, Pairial, Pair-royal, Prial, T.i.d, Ter, Tern, Terzetta, Thrice, Thridi, Tid, Tierce, Tray, Trey, Triad, Tricar, Triennial, Trifid, Trigon, Trilogy, Trinal, Trine, Trinity, Trio, Triple, Triptote, Troika

Threshold Cill, Doorstep, Limen, Liminal, Sill, Verge

► **Thrice** see THREE

Thrift(y) Economy, Frugal, Husbandry, Oeconomy, Sea-grass, Sea-pink, Virtue

Thrill(er), Thrilling Atingle, Delight, Dindle, Dinnle, Dirl, Dread, Emotive, ► ENCHANT, Excite, Film noir, Frisson, Gas, Jag, Kick, Perceant, Plangent, Pulsate, Pulse, Quiver, Sensation, Thirl, Tingling, Tremor, Vibrant, Whodunit

Thrive Batten, Blossom, Boom, Do, Fl, ► FLOURISH, Flower, Grow, Mushroom, ► PROSPER, Succeed, Thee

Throat(y) Craw, Crop, Deep, Dewlap, Fauces, Gorge, Gular, Gullet, Guttural, Jugular, Maw, Pereion, Pharynx, Prunella, Quailpipe, Roopit, Roopy, Strep, Swallet, Thrapple, Thropple, Throttle, Weasand, Wesand, Whistle, Windpipe

Throb(bing) Beat, Palpitate, Pant, Pit-a-pat, Pulsate, Quop, Stang, Tingle, Vibrato

▷**Throbbing** may indicate an anagram

Throne Bed-of-justice, Cathedra, Episcopal, Gadi, Rule, Seat, See, Siege, Tribune

Throttle ➤ CHOKE, Gar(r)otte, Gun, Mug, Scrag, Silence, Stifle, Strangle, Strangulate, We(a)sand

Through, Throughout Along, Ana, By, Dia-, During, Everywhere, Over, Passim, Per, Pr, Sempre, Sic passim, To, Trans, Via, Yont

▶**Throw(n)** see TOSS

Throw-out, Throw-up Bin, Cast-off, Chunder, Egesta, Jettison, Puke, Spew, Squirt, Squit

Thrust, Thruster Aventre, Bear, Boost, Botte, Burn, Detrude, Dig, Drive, Elbow, Exert, Extrude, Foin, ➤ FORCE, Hay, Impulse, Job, Lunge, Obtrude, Oust, Pass, Passado, Peg, Perk, Pitchfork, Poke, Potch(e), Pote, Probe, Propel, Pun, Punto, ➤ PUSH, Put, Remise, Repost, Run, Shove, Sock, Sorn, Stap, Stick, Stoccado, Stoccata, Stock, Stuck, Thrutch, Tilt, Tuck

Thug(s) Goon(da), Gorilla, Gurrier, Hoodlum, Loord, Ninja, Ockers, Phansigar, Roughneck, SS, Strangler, Ted, Tityre-tu, Tsotsi

Thump(ing) Blow, Bonk, Cob, Crump, Drub, Dub, Hammer, Knevell, Knock, Nevel, Oner, Paik, ➤ POUND, Pummel, Slam, Slosh, Swat, Swingeing, Thud, Tund

Thunder(ing), Thunderstorm Bolt, Boom, Clap, Donnerwetter, Foudroyant, Foulder, Fulminate, Intonate, Lei-king, Pil(l)an, Raiden, ➤ ROAR, Rumble, Summanus, Tempest, Thor, Tonant

Thwart Baffle, Balk, ➤ CROSS, Dish, Foil, Frustrate, Hamstring, Hogtie, Obstruct, Outwit, Pip, Prevent, Scotch, Snooker, Spike, Spite, Stonker, Stymie, Transverse

Tick, Tick off Acarida, Acarus, Beat, ➤ CHIDE, Click, Cr, ➤ CREDIT, Deer, HP, Idle, Instant, Jar, Ked, Mattress, Mile, Mo, Moment, Ricinulei, Second, Strap, Worm

Ticket(s) Billet, Bone, Brief, Carnet, Complimentary, Coupon, Docket, Dream, Label, Meal, Parking, Pass, Pass-out, Platform, Raincheck, Return, Season, Single, Stub, Supersaver, ➤ TAG, Tempest, Tessera(l), Tyburn

Tickle, Ticklish Amuse, Delicate, Divert, Excite, Gratify, Gump, ► ITCH, Kittle, Queasy, Thrill, Titilate

Tide, Tidal Current, Drift, Eagre, Easter, Eger, Estuary, Flood, High, Low, Marigram, Neap, Roost, Sea, Seiche, Slack water, Spring, Trend, Wave

Tidy Comb, Considerable, Curry, Fair, Fettle, Kempt, Large, Neat, ► ORDER, Pachyderm, Predy, Preen, Primp, Red(d), Slick, Snug, Sort, Spruce, Trim

Tie, Tying Ascot, Attach, Barcelona, Berth, Bind, Black, ► BOND, Bootlace, Bow, Bowyang, Cable, Cope, Cravat, Cup, Dead-heat, Drag, Draw, Frap, Halter, Handicap, Harness, Holdfast, Kipper, ► KNOT, Lash, Level, Ligament, Ligate, Ligature, Link, Marry, Match, Moor, Oblige, Obstriction, Oop, Oup, Overlay, Raffia, Restrain, Rod, Scarf, School, Score draw, Shackle, Shoelace, Shoestring, Sleeper, Slur, Solitaire, Soubise, Splice, Stake, Strap, String, Tether, Trice, Truss, Unite, White

Tiff Bicker, Contretemps, Difference, Dispute, Feed, Feud, Huff, Miff, Skirmish, Spat, Squabble

Tiger Bengal, ► CAT, Clemenceau, Demoiselle, Lily, Machairodont, Machairodus, Margay, Paper, Sabre-tooth, Smilodon, Tasmanian, Woods

Tight(en), Tightness, Tights Boozy, Bosky, Brace, Close(-hauled), Constriction, Cote-hardie, ► DRUNK, Fishnet, Fleshings, High, Hose, Jam, Leggings, Lit, Loaded, Maillot, Mean, Merry, Niggardly, Oiled, Pang, Phimosis, Pickled, Pinch(penny), Plastered, Prompt, Proof, Rigour, Snug, Squiffy, Stenosis, ► STINGY, Strict, Stringent, Swift, Swig, Taut, Tense, Tipsy, Trig, Woozy

Tile(d), Tiles Antefix, Arris, Azulejo, Dalle, Derby, Encaustic, ► HAT, Imbrex, Imbricate, Lid, Ostracon, Ostrakon, Peever, Quarrel, Quarry, Rag(g), Rooftop, Sclate, Shingle, Slat, ► SLATE, Tegula, Tessella, Tessera, Titfer, Topper, Wall, Wally

Till Cashbox, Checkout, Coffer, Ear, Eulenspiegel, Farm, Hasta, Hoe, Husband, Lob, Peter, ► PLOUGH, Set, Unto

Tilt Awning, Bank, Camber, Cant, Cock, Dip, Heel, Hut, Joust, Just, ► LIST, Quintain, Rock, Tip, Unbalance

Timber Apron, Batten, Beam, Chess, Cross-tree, Cruck, Elmwood, Flitch, Four-by-two, Greenheart, Intertie, Iroko, Ironwood, Joist, Knee, Ligger, Lintel, Log, Lumber, Purlin(e), Putlock, Putlog, Rib, Rung, Sandalwood, Sapele, Satinwood,

Scantling, Shook, Skeg, Softwood, Souari, Stemson, Stere, Sternson, Straddle, Stull, Summer, Transom, Wale, ➤ WOOD, Yang

Time(s), Timer Access, Agoge, Apparent, Bird, BST, Chronic, Chronometer, Chronon, Clock, Closing, Connect, Core, Counter, Date, Day, Decade, Dimension, Double, Duple, Duration, Early, Eastern, Egg-glass, Enemy, Eon, Epoch, Equinox, Era, Extra, Father, Forelock, Free, Gest, Healer, Hour, Hourglass, Hr, Idle, Injury, Innings, Instant, Interlude, Jiff, Juncture, Kalpa, Lead, Lean, Leisure, Life, Lighting-up, Lilac, Mean, Menopause, Metronome, Multiple, Nonce, Nones, Occasion, Oft, ➤ ON TIME, Part, Period, Pinger, Porridge, Post, Prime, Quality, Question, Quick, Reaction, Real, Reaper, Seal, ➤ SEASON, Seel, Serial, Session, Shelf-life, Sidereal, Sight, Sith(e), Solar, Space, Span, Spare, Spell, Spin, Split, Standard, Stoppage, Stopwatch, Stound, Stownd, Stretch, Summer, Sundown, Sythe, T, Tem, Tempo, Tempore, Tense, Thief, Thunderer, Tick, Tid, Tide, Triple, Two-four, Universal, Usance, While, X, Yonks, Zero

Time-keeper Ben, Clock, Hourglass, Ref, Sand-glass, Sundial, Ticker, Tompion, Watch

Timely Appropriate, Apropos, Happy, Opportune, Pat, Prompt

Timetable Bradshaw, ➤ CHART, Schedule

Timid, Timorous Afraid, Aspen, Bashful, Blate, Chicken, Cowardly, Eerie, Eery, Faint-hearted, Fearful, Hare, Hen-hearted, Milquetoast, Mous(e)y, Mouse, Pavid, Pigeon-hearted, Pusillanimous, Quaking, ➤ SHY, Shrinking, Skeary, Sook, Yellow

Tin(ned), Tinfoil, Tinny Argentine, Britannia metal, Can, Cash, Debe, Dixie, Maconochie, ➤ MONEY, Moola(h), Ochre, Plate, Rhino, Sn, Stannary, Stannic, Tain, Tole

Tincture Arnica, Bufo, Chroma, Elixir, Fur, Infusion, Laudanum, Metal, Or, Sericon, Sol, Spice, Taint, Tenné, Vert

Tinder Amadou, Faggot, Fuel, Funk, Punk, Spark, Spunk, Touchwood

Tingle, Tingling Dinnle, Dirl, Paraesthesia, Prickle, Thrill, Throb, Tinkle

Tinker Bell, Caird, Coster, Didicoy, Didikoi, ➤ FIDDLE, Gypsy, Mender, Pedlar, Potter, Prig, Putter, Repair, Sly, Snout, Tamper, Tramp, Traveller

Tiny Atto-, Baby, Diddy, Dwarf, Ha'it, Infinitesimal, Itsy-bitsy, Lilliputian, Minikin, Minim, Mite, Negligible, Petite, Small, Smidgeon, Teeny, Tim, Tine, Toy, Wee

Tip, Tipping Apex, Arrowhead, Asparagus, Backshish, Baksheesh, Batta, Beer-money, Cant, Cert, Chape, Counsel, Coup, Cowp, Crown, Cue, Cumshaw, Douceur, Dump, Extremity, Fee, Felt, Ferrule, Filter, Forecast, Glans, Gratuity, Heel, ➤ HINT, Hunch, Inkle, Iridise, Largess(e), List, Mess, Nap, Noop, Ord, Perk, Perquisite, Point, Pointer, Pour, Previse, Suggestion, Summit, Tag, Tail, Tilt, Toom, Touch, Tronc, Vail, Vales, Whisper, Wrinkle

Tipsy Bleary, Boozy, Bosky, ➤ DRUNK, Elevated, Moony, Nappy, Oiled, On, Rocky, Screwed, Slewed, Slued, Squiffy, Wet

▷ **Tipsy** may indicate an anagram

Tirade Diatribe, Invective, Jobation, Laisse, Philippic, Rand, Rant, Screed, Slang

Tire(d), Tiredness, Tiring All-in, Beat, Bore, Bushed, Caparison, Dress, Drowsy, ➤ EXHAUST, Fag, Fatigue, Flag, Fordid, Fordod, Forjeskit, Frazzle, Gruel, Irk, Jade, Lassitude, Limp, ME, Poop, Puggled, ➤ ROBE, Rubber, Sap, Shagged, Sicken, Sleepy, Sleepy, Swinkt, Tax, Tedious, Wabbit, Wappend, Weary, Wrecked

▶ **Tiro** see TYRO

Tissue Adenoid, Adhesion, Aerenchyma, Aponeurosis, Archesporium, Callus, Cartilage, Cementum, Chalaza, Cheloid, Chlorenchyma, Coenosarc, Collagen, Collenchyma, Commissure, Connective, Cortex, Diploe, Epimysium, Epineurium, Epithelium, Eschar, Fabric, Fascia, Flesh, Gamgee, Gauze, Gleba, Glia, Gum, Heteroplasia, Histogen, Histoid, Infarct, Keloid, Lamina, Lies, Ligament, Luteal, Medulla, ➤ MEMBRANE, Meristem, Mesophyll, Mole, Myelin(e), Myocardium, Neuroglia, Nucellus, Pack, Pannus, Paper, Papilla, Parenchyma, Perimysium, Perinephrium, Perineurium, Perisperm, Phellogen, Phloem, Pith, Plerome, Polyarch, Primordium, Prothallis, Pterygium, Pulp, Radula, Sarcenet, Sars(e)net, Scar, Sclerenchyma, Sequestrum, Sinew, Somatopleure, Stereome, Stroma, Submucosa, Suet, Tarsus, Tela, Tendon, Tonsil, Tunica, Vascular, Velum, Web, Xylem

Tit, Tit-bit(s) Analecta, Currie, Curry, Delicacy, Dug, Nag, Nipple, Pap, Quarry, Sample, Scrap, Snack, Teat, Tug, Twitch, Zakuska

Titan(ic), Titaness Atlas, Colossus, Cronos, Enormous, Giant, Huge, Hyperion, Kronos, Leviathan, Liner, Oceanus, Phoebe, Prometheus, Rhea, Themis, Vast

Title Abbe, Ag(h)a, Appellative, Baroness, Baronet, Bart, Calif, Caliph, Caption, Charta, Claim, Conveyance, Count(ess), Courtesy, Credit, Dan, Datin, Dauphin, Dayan, Deeds, Devi, Dom, Don, Dowager, Dub, Duchess, Duke, Earl, Effendi, Epithet, Esquire, Excellency, Frau(lein), Handle, Header, Heading, Headline, Hon, Interest, Kalif, Kaliph, King, Lady, Lala, Lemma, ➤ LIEN, Lord, Marchesa, Marchese, Marquess, Marquis, Masthead, Memsahib, Meneer, Milord, Mr(s), Name, Nomen, Padishah, Peerage, Pir, Polemarch, Prefix, Prince(ss), Queen, ➤ RANK, Reb, ➤ RIGHT, Rubric, Sahib, Sama, San, Sayid, Senhor(a), Señor(a), Shri, Sir, Son, Sowbhagyawati, Sri, Torrens, Tycoon, V

To(wards) At, Beside, Inby, Onto, Shet, Shut, Till

Toad(y) Bootlicker, Bufo, Bumsucker, Cane, Clawback, Crawler, Fawn, Frog, Horned, Jackal, Jenkins, Knot, Lackey, Lickspittle, Midwife, Minion, Natterjack, Nototrema, Paddock, Parasite, Pipa, Placebo, Platanna, Puddock, Sook, Spade-foot, Surinam, Sycophant, Tuft-hunter, Xenopus, Yesman

Toadstool Amanita, Death-cap, Death-cup, ➤ FUNGUS, Grisette, Paddock-stool, Parrot, Sulphur tuft

Toast Bacchus, Bell, Birsle, Brindisi, ➤ BROWN, Bruschetta, Bumper, Cheers, Chin-chin, Crostini, Crouton, French, Gesundheit, Grace-cup, Grill, Health, Iechyd da, Kiaora, L'chaim, Lechayim, Loyal, Melba, Pledge, Propose, Prosit, Round, Scouther, Scowder, Scowther, Sentiment, Sippet, Skoal, Slainte, Soldier, Sunbathe, Zwieback

Tobacco, Tobacco-field Alfalfa, Bacchi, Baccy, Bird's eye, Broadleaf, Burley, Canaster, Capa, Caporal, Cavendish, Chew, Dottle, Honeydew, Killikinnick, Kinnikinick, Latakia, Mundungus, Nailrod, Navy-cut, Negro-head, Nicotine, Niggerhead, Perique, Pigtail, Plug, Quid, Régie, Returns, Shag, Sneesh, Snout, Snuff, Stripleaf, Turkish, Twist, Vega, Virginia, Weed

Today Hodiernal, Now, Present

Toddle(r) → Ton   568

Toddle(r) Baim, Gangrel, Mite, Tot, Totter, Trot, Waddle

Toe Dactyl, Digit, Hallux, Hammer, Piggy, Pinky, Pointe, Poulaine, Prehallux, Tootsie

Toffee Butterscotch, Caramel, Cracknel, Gundy, Hard-bake, Hokey-pokey, Humbug, Tom-trot

Together Among, At-one, Atone, Attone, Gathered, Infere, ► JOINT, Pari-passu, Sam, Unison, Wed, Y, Yfere, Ysame

Toil(s) Drudge, Fag, Industry, ► LABOUR, Mesh, Net, Seine, Sisyphus, Sweat, Swink, Tela, Tew, Trap, Travail, Tug, Web, Wrest, ► WORK, Yacker, Yakka, Yakker

Toilet Can, Coiffure, John, Lat(rine), Lavatory, Loo, Pot, Powder room, WC

Token Buck, Counter, Coupon, Disc, Double-axe, Emblem, Gift, Indication, ► MEMENTO, Nominal, Portend, Seal, Sign, Signal, Symbol, Symptom, Tessera, Valentine

Tolerable Acceptable, Bearable, Mediocre, Passable, So-so

Tolerance, Tolerant, Tolerate(d) Abear, Abide, ► ALLOW, Bear, Brook, Endure, Hack, Had, Latitude, ► LENIENT, Lump, Mercy, Permit, Stand, Stick, Stomach, Studden, Suffer, Support, Thole, Wear

Toll Chime, Customs, Due, Duty, Excise, Joll, Joule, Jowl, Octroi, Pierage, Pike, Pontage, Rates, ► RING, Scavage, Streetage, Tariff, Tax

Tom(my) Atkins, Bell, Bowling, Bread, Brown, ► CAT, Collins, Edgar, Gib, Grub, Gun, He-cat, Had, Jerry, Jones, Mog(gy), Nosh, Peeping, Private, Pte, Puss, Ram-cat, Sawyer, Snout, Soldier, Stout, Thos, Thumb, Tiddler, Tucker

Tomato Beef(steak), Cherry, Husk, Love-apple, Plum, Strawberry, Tamarillo, Wolf's peach

Tomb(stone) Burial, Catacomb, Catafalque, Cenotaph, Cist, Coffin, Dargah, Durgah, Grave, Hypogeum, Kistvaen, Marmoreal, Mastaba, Mausoleum, Megalithic, Monument, Pyramid, ► SEPULCHRE, Sepulture, Serdab, Shrine, Speos, Tholos, Tholus, Through-stone, Treasury, Vault

Tomboy Gamine, Gilpey, Gilpy, Hoyden, Ladette, Ramp, Romp

Tomorrow Future, Manana, Morrow

Ton C, Chic, Hundred, T

Tone, Tonality Brace, Fifth, Harmonic, Inflection, Key, Klang, Ninth, Partial, Qualify, ➤ SOUND, Strain, Temper, Tenor, Timbre, Trite, Whole

Tongue Brogue, Burr, Chape, Clack, Clapper, Doab, Final, Forked, Glossa, Glossolalia, Jinglet, ➤ LANGUAGE, Languet(te), Lap, Ligula, Lill, Lingo, Lingulate, Mother, Organ, Radula, Ranine, Rasp, Red rag, Spit, Tab, Voice

Tonic Bracer, C(h)amomile, Doh, Key, Mease, Medicinal, Mishmee, Mishmi, Oporice, Pick-me-up, Quassia, Refresher, Roborant, Sarsaparilla, Solfa

▷**Tonic** may indicate a musical note

Too Als(o), Besides, Eke, Excessive, Item, Likewise, Moreover, Oer, Over, Overly, Plus, Troppo

Tool Adze, Auger, Awl, Ax(e), Beetle, Bevel, Billhook, Bit, Broach, Brog, Bur(r), Burin, Calipers, Catspaw, Chisel, Clippers, Dibber, Dibble, Die, Dolly, Drawknife, Elsin, Eolith, Facer, Fid, File, Float, Former, Fraise, Froe, Frow, Gad, Gimlet, Graver, Hammer, Hardy, Hob, Hoe, ➤ IMPLEMENT, ➤ INSTRUMENT, Iron, Jemmy, Jointer, Laster, Loom, Lute, Marlin(e)spike, Muller, Outsiders, Pattle, Pawn, Penis, Percussion, Pestle, Pick, Picklock, Pitchfork, Piton, Plane, Pliers, Plunger, Pricker, Property, Punch, Puncheon, Rabble, Rasp, Ripple, Router, Sander, Saw, Scalpel, Scissors, Scraper, Screwdriver, Sickle, Slater, Spanner, Spirit-level, Spokeshave, Strickle, Strike, Strimmer®, Swage, Swingle, Swipple, Triblet, Trowel, Tweezers, Twibill, Upright, Wrench

Tooth(ed), Toothy, Teeth Bicuspid, Bit, Buck, Bunodont, Canine, Carnassial, Chactodon, Cog, Crena(te), Ctenoid, Cusp, Dentin(e), Dentures, Egg, Eye, Fang, Gam, Gat, Gnashers, Grinder, Heterodont, Incisor, Ivory, Joggle, Laniary, Milk, Molar, Nipper, Odontoid, Pawl, Pearly gates, Pectinate, Peristome, Phang, Plate, Pre-molar, Prong, Ratch, Scissor, Secodont, Sectorial, Serration, Set, Snaggle, Sprocket, Sweet, Trophi, Tush, Tusk, Uncinus, Upper, Wallies, Wang, Wiper, Wisdom, Zalambdodont

Top (drawer; hole; line; notcher), Topmost, Topper Ace, Acme, A1, Apex, Apical, Altissimo, Behead, Best, Better, Big, Blouse, Blouson, Brow, Bustier, Cap, Capstone, Ceiling, Coma, Cop, Coping, Corking, ➤ CREST, Crista, Crown, Culmen, Decollate, Diabolo, Dog, Dome, Drawer, Elite, Execute, Finial,

Gentry, Gyroscope, Hard, Hat, ➤ HEAD, Height, Hummer, Imperial, Lid, Nun, One-er, Optimate, Orb, ➤ PEAK, Peerie, Peery, Peg, Peplos, Peplus, Pinnacle, Pitch, Replenish, Ridge, Roof, Sawyer, Secret, Shaw, Shirt, Skim, Slay, Star, Summit, Superb, Supreme, Supremo, Surface, Tambour, Targa, Teetotum, Texas, Tile, Trash, T-shirt, Up(most), Uppermost, V, Vertex

▷**Top** may indicate first letter

Topic(al) Head, Item, Motion, Subject, Text, ➤ THEME

Topping Grand, Icing, Meringue, Pepperoni, Piecrust, Streusel

Topple Oust, Overbalance, Overturn, Tip, Upend, ➤ UPSET

Topsy-turvy Careen, Cockeyed, Inverted, Summerset, Tapsalteerie, Tapsleteerie

Torch Brand, Cresset, Flambeau, Lamp, Lampad, Link, Plasma, Tead(e), Wisp

Toreador Escamillo, Matador, Picador, Torero

Torment(ed), Tormentor Agony, Anguish, Bait, Ballyrag, Bedevil, Butt, Cruciate, Crucify, Curse, Distress, Excruciate, Frab, Grill, Harass, Hell, Martyrdom, Molest, Nag, Nettle, Pang, Pine, Plague, ➤ RACK, Sadist, Tantalise

Torpedo Bangalore, Bomb, Ray, Weapon

Torpid, Torpor Comatose, Dormant, Languid, Lethargic, Sluggish, Slumbering

Torrid Amphiscian, Hot, Sultry, Tropical

Tortoise Chelonia, Emydes, Emys, Galapagos, Hic(c)atee, Kurma, Pancake, Snapping-turtle, Terrapin, Testudo, Timothy, Turtle

Tortoiseshell Epiplastra, Hawksbill, Testudo

▷**Tortuous** may indicate an anagram

Torture, Torture chamber, Torture instrument Agonise, Auto-da-fé, Bastinade, Bastinado, Boot, Bootikin, Catasta, Crucify, Engine, Excruciate, Flageolet, Fry, Gadge, Gyp, Iron maiden, Knee-cap, Naraka, Persecute, Pilliwinks, Pine, Pinniewinkle, Pinnywinkle, ➤ RACK, Sadism, Scaphism, Scarpines, Scavenger, Strappado, Tantalise, Thumbscrew, Tumbrel, Tumbril, Water, Wheel, Wrack

▷**Tortured** may indicate an anagram

Toss, Throw(n) Abject, Bandy, Bounce, Buck, Bung, Buttock, Cant, Canvass, Cast, Catapult, ➤ CHUCK, Crabs, Cross-buttock,

Dad, Daud, Deal, Disconcert, Elance, Estrapade, Falcade, ► FLING, Flip, Flump, Flutter, Flying (head)-mare, Gollum, Haunch, Heave, Hipt, Hoy, ► HURL, Jact(it)ation, Jaculation, Jeff, Jump, Lance, Lob, Loft, Pash, Pitch, Purl, Round-arm, Seamer, Shy, Slat, Sling, Unhorse, Unseat, Upcast

Tot Add, Babe, Bairn, ► CHILD, Dop, Dram, Infant, Mite, Nightcap, Nip(per), Nipperkin, Slug, Snifter, Snort, Tad

Total, Toto Absolute, Aggregate, All(-out), Amount, Balance, Be-all, ► COMPLETE, Entire, Gross, Lot, Sum, Tale, Tally, Unqualified, Utter, Whole

Totter Abacus, Daddle, Daidle, Didakai, Didakei, Didicoi, Did(d)icoy, Halt, Ragman, Rock, ► STAGGER, Swag, Sway, Topple, Waver

Touch(ed), Touching, Touchy Accolade, Adjoin, Anent, Badass, Barmy, Cadge, Captious, Carambole, Caress, Carom, Common, Concern, Connivent, Contact, Contiguous, Emove, ► FEEL, Finger, Finishing, Flick, Fondle, Haptic, Huffy, ► IN TOUCH, J'adoube, Liaison, Libant, Loan, Loco, Midas, Miffy, Nie, Nigh, Nudge, Pathetic, Potty, Re, Sense, Skiff, Soft, Sore, Spice, ► SPOT, Tactile, Tactual, Tag, Tap, Taste, Tat, Tickle, Tig, Tinderbox, Trace, Trait, Vestige

Touchstone Basanite, Criterion, Norm, Standard

Tough(en) Adamantine, Anneal, Apache, Arduous, Ballsy, Burly, ► HARD, Hard-boiled, Hardy, Heavy duty, He-man, Hood, Husky, Indurate, Knotty, Leathern, Leathery, Nut, Pesky, Rambo, Rigwiddie, Rigwoodie, Roughneck, Sinewy, Spartan, Steely, Stiff, Sturdy, Teuch, Thewed, Tityre-tu, Virile

Tour(er), Tourist Barnstorm, Circuit, Cook's, Emmet, Excursion, Grand, Grockle, GT, Holiday-maker, Itinerate, ► JOURNEY, Lionise, Mystery, Outing, Posting, Roadie, Rubberneck, Safari, ► TRAVEL, Trip(per), Viator, Whistle-stop

Tournament Basho, Carousel, Drive, Event, Joust, Just, Plate, Pro-am, Round robin, Royal, Tilt, Tourney, Wimbledon

Tow(ing) Button, Fibre, ► HAUL, Pull, ► ROPE, Skijoring, Stupe, Track

►**Towards** see TO

Towel Dry, Jack, Nappy, Roller, Rub, Sanitary, Tea, Terry, Turkish

Tower Atalaya, Babel, Barbican, Bastille, Bastion, Belfry, Bell, Bloody, Brattice, Brettice, Brogh, Campanile, Conning, Control, Cooling, Donjon, Dungeon, Edifice, Eiffel, Fortress, Garret, Ivory, Keep, Leaning, Loom, Maiden, Martello, Minar(et), Monument, Mooring, Mouse, Nurhag, Overtop, Peel, Pinnacle, Pound, Pylon, Rear, Rise, Sail, Sears, Shot, Silo, Ski-lift, Spire, Stealth, Steeple, ➤ TURRET, Tête-de-pont, Tractor, Tugboat, Victoria, Water, Ziggurat

Town, Township Boom, Borgo, Borough, Bourg, Burg(h), City, Conurbation, County, Deme, Dormitory, Dorp, Favella, Ghost, Ham(let), Market, Municipal, Nasik, One-horse, Podunk, Pueblo, Satellite, Shanty, Tp, Twin, Urban, Wick

Townee, Townsman Cad, Cit(izen), Dude, Freeman, Oppidan, Philister, Resident

Toxic, Toxin Abrin, Antigen, Botulin, Coumarin, Curare, Deadly, Dioxan, Eclampsia, Lethal, Muscarine, Phenol, Phenothiazine, Psoralen, Sepsis, Serology, Venin, Venomous

Toy Bauble, Bull-roarer, Cockhorse, Dally, Dandle, Doll, Executive, Faddle, Finger, Flirt, Frisbee®, Gewgaw, Golly, Gonk, Kaleidoscope, Kickshaw, Knack, Pantine, Peashooter, Plaything, Praxinoscope, Rattle, Skipjack, Taste, Teddy, Thaumatrope, ➤ TRIFLE, Trinket, Tu(r)ndun, Whirligig, Yoyo

Trace Atom, Cast, Derive, Describe, Draft, Dreg, Draw, Echo, Footprint, Ghost, ➤ HINT, Mark, Outline, Relic, Relict, Remnant, Scintilla, Semblance, Sign, Smack, Soupçon, Strap, ➤ TOUCH, Track, Vestige, Whit

Track(er), Tracking, Trackman Aintree, B-road, Band, Caterpillar®, Circuit, Course, DOVAP, Dog, Ecliptic, El, Fast, Fettler, Footing, Gaudy dancer, Hunt, Ichnite, Ichnolite, Lane, Line, Loipe, Loopline, Monitor, Monza, ➤ PATH, Persue, Piste, Pug, Pursue, Race, Raceway, Rail, Railway, Rake, Ridgeway, Route, Run, Rut, Siding, Sign, Slot, Sonar, Speedway, Spoor, Tan, ➤ TRAIL, Trajectory, Tram, Tread, Trode, Tug(boat), Wake, Way

Tract(able), Tracts Area, Belt, Bench, Clime, Common, Dene, Enclave, Flysheet, Lande, Leaflet, Monte, Moor, ➤ PAMPHLET, Prairie, Province, Purlieu, Pusey, Region, Taluk, Tawie, Terrain, Wold

Trade(r), Tradesman, Trading Arb(itrageur), Banian, Banyan, Bargain, Barter, Burgher, Business, Cabotage, Calling,

Carriage, Chaffer, Chandler, Chapman, Cheapjack, Coaster,
➤ COMMERCE, Coster, Costermonger, Crare, Crayer, Deal(er),
Errand, Exchange, Factor, Free, Handle, Hosier, Hot, Importer,
Indiaman, Industry, Insider, Ironmonger, Jobber, Line,
Merchant, Métier, Middleman, Mister, Monger, Outfitter, Ply,
Rag, Retailer, Scalp, Sell, Simony, Slave, Stationer, Sutler,
➤ SWAP, Traffic, Trant, Truck, Union, Vend, Wholesaler, Wind

Trademark Brand, Chop, Idiograph, Label, Logo

Tradition(s), Traditional(ist) Ancestral, Classical,
Convention, Custom(ary), Hadith, Heritage, Legend, Lore,
Misoneist, Old guard, Old-school, Pharisee, Pompier, Practice,
Purist, Time-honoured, Trad, Tralaticious, Tralatitious

Traffic, Traffic pattern Barter, Broke, Cabotage,
Clover-leaf, Commerce, Contraflow, Deal, Negotiate, Passage,
Run, Smuggle, Trade, Truck, Vehicular

Tragedian, Tragedy, Tragic Aeschylus, Buskin, Calamity,
Cenci, Corneille, Dire, ➤ DRAMA, Euripides, Macready,
Melpomene, Oedipean, Oresteia, Otway, Pathetic, Seneca,
Sophoclean, Thespian, Thespis

Trail(er), Trailing Abature, Bedraggle, Caravan, Creep,
Drag, Draggle, Follow, Ipomaea, Lag, Liana, Liane, Nature,
Oregon, Path, Persue, Preview, Promo(tion), Pursue, Repent,
Runway, Scent, Shadow, Sign, Sleuth, Slot, Spoor, Stream,
Streel, Trace, ➤ TRACK, Trade, Traipse, Trape, Trauchle, Trayne,
Troad, Vapour, Vine, Virga, Wake

Train(er), Training Advanced, APT, BR, Breed, Caravan,
Cavalcade, Coach, Commuter, Condition, Cortège, Diesel,
Direct, Discipline, Dressage, Drill, Drive, Educate, Entourage,
Enure, Eurostar®, Exercise, Fartlek, Flier, Freightliner®, Fuse,
Gear, Ghan, Ghost, Gravy, Grounding, GWS, Handle(r),
Instruct, Intercity®, Interval, Journey, Link, LMS, LNER,
Loco, Lunge, Maglev, Mailcar, Mentor, Nurture, Nuzzle, Pack,
Paddy, PE, Potty, Practise, ➤ PREPARE, Procession, PT, Puffer,
Puff-puff, Queue, Rattler, Rehearse, Retinue, Roadwork, Rocket,
Ry, Sack, ➤ SCHOOL, Series, Sloid, Sloyd, Sowarry, Special, SR,
Steer, String, Suite, Tail, ➤ TEACH, Tire, Track shoe, Trail, Tube,
Wagon

▷**Train(ed)** may indicate an anagram

Traitor Betrayer, Casement, Dobber-in, Joyce, Judas,
Nid(d)ering, Nid(d)erling, Nithing, Proditor, Quisling,

Renegade, Reptile, Tarpeian, Traditor, Treachetour, Turncoat, Viper, Wallydraigle, Weasel

▷**Trammel** may indicate an anagram

Tramp, Trample Bog-trotter, Bum, Caird, Clochard, Clump, Derelict, Dero, Dingbat, Dosser, Estragon, Footslog, Freighter, Gadling, Gook, Hike, Hobo, Knight of the road, Overrun, Override, Pad, Piker, Plod, Poach, Potch(e), Rover, Scorn, Ship, Splodge, Sundowner, Swagman, ➤ TINKER, Toe-rag(ger), Track, Traipse, Tread, Trek, Trog, Tromp, Truant, Trudge, Tub, Vagabond, Vagrant, Weary Willie

Trance Catalepsy, Cataplexy, Goa, Narcolepsy

Tranquil(lity) Ataraxy, Calm, Composure, Hàlcyon, Lee, Quietude, Sedate, ➤ SERENE

Tranquillise(r) Appease, Ataraxic, Ataractic, ➤ CALM, Diazepam, Downer, Hypnone, Hypnotic, Librium®, Nervine, Nitrazepam, Oxazepam, Placate, Satisfy, Soothe, Still, Valium®

Transcend(ent), Transcendental(ist) Excel, Mystic, Overtop, Surpass, Thoreau

Transfer Alien, Alienate, ➤ ASSIGN, Attorn, Calk, Cede, Communize, Consign, Convey(ance), Crosstalk, Decal, Demise, Devolve, Download, Exchange, Explant, Mancipation, Metathesis, Mortmain, On-lend, Pass, Reassign, Redeploy, Remit, Remove, Repot, Second, Settlement, Uproot, Virement

▷**Transferred** may indicate an anagram

Transform(ation), Transformer Alter, Balun, Change, Lorentz, Metamorphism, Metamorphose, Metamorphosis, Metaplasia, Metastasis, Morphing, Permute, Rectifier, Sea change, Tinct, Toupee, Transmogrify, Wig

▷**Transform(ed)** may indicate an anagram

Transgress(ion) Encroach, Err, Infringe, Offend, Overstep, Peccancy, ➤ SIN, Violate

Transient, Transit(ion), Transitory Brief, Ephemeral, Fleeting, Fly-by-night, Fugacious, Hobo, Metabasis, Passage, Passing, Provisional, Seque, T, Temporary

Translate, Translation, Translator Calque, Crib, Construe, Convert, Coverdale, Explain, Free, Horse, Interpret, Key, Linguist, Metaphrase, Paraphrase, Pinyin, Polyglot, Reduce, Render, Rendition, Rhemist, Targum, Tr, Transcribe, Transform, Trot, Unseen, Version(al), Vulgate, Wycliffe

▷**Translate(d)** may indicate an anagram

Transmit(ter), Transmitted, Transmission Air, Band, Beacon, ➤ BROADCAST, Carry, CB, Communicate, Consign, Contagion, Convection, Convey, Forward, Gearbox, Gene, Heredity, Impart, Intelsat, Manual, Microphone, Modem, Nicol, Permittivity, Propagate, Racon, Radiate, Radio, Receiver, Simulcast, Sonabuoy, Tappet, Telecast, Telegony, Telemetry, Teleprinter, Televise, Telex, Tiros, Traduce, Traject, Tralaticious, Tralatitious, UART, Uplink, Upload, Walkie-talkie

Transparent, Transparency Adularia, Clear, Crystal(line), Diaphanous, Dioptric, Glassy, Glazed, Hyaloid, Iolite, Leno, Limpid, Lucid, Luminous, Patent, Pellucid, Sheer, Slide, Tiffany

Transport(ed), Transporter, Transportation Argo, Bear, Bike, Broomstick, BRS, Bus, Cargo, Carract, ➤ CARRY, Cart, Charm, Convey, Delight, Ecstasy, Eloin, Enrapt, Enravish, Entrain, Esloin, Estro, Freight, Haul(age), Helicopter, Jerrican, Joy, Kurvey, Maglev, Monorail, Palanquin, Pantechnicon, Public, Put, Rape, Rapine, Rapture, Roadster, Shuttle, Ship, Sledge, Supersonic, Tote, Trap, Tuktuk, Waft, Wheels, Wireway

Transpose, Transposition Anagram, Commute, Convert, Invert, Metathesis, Shift, Spoonerism, Switch, Tr

▷**Transposed** may indicate an anagram

Trap(s), Trapdoor, Trappings Ambush, ➤ BAGGAGE, Bags, Belongings, Booby, Buckboard, Bunker, Carriage, Catch, Clapnet, Corner, Cru(i)ve, Deadfall, Decoy, Dogcart, Eelset, Emergent, Ensnare, Entrain, Fall, Fit-up, Fly, Flypaper, Frame-up, Fyke, Gig, Gin, Gob, Grin, Hatch, Jinri(c)ksha(w), Keddah, Kettle, Kheda, Kiddle, Kidel, Kipe, Kisser, Knur(r), Lime, ➤ LUGGAGE, Lure, Mesh, Mouth, Net, Nur(r), Paraphernalia, Pitfall, Plant, Pot, Poverty, Putcheon, Putcher, Quicksand, Radar, Regalia, Sand, Scruto, ➤ SNARE, Speed, Spell, Spider, Springe, Stake-net, Stench, Sting, Tangle, Toil, Tonga, Trou-de-loup, U, U-bend, Vampire, Web, Weel, Weir, Wire

Trash(y) Bosh, Deface, Dre(c)k, Garbage, Junk, Kitsch, Pulp, ➤ RUBBISH, Schlock, Scum, Tinpot, Vandalise, Worthless

Travel(ler), Travelling Backpack, Bagman, Commercial, Commute, Crustie, Crusty, Drive, Drummer, Fare, Fellow, Fly, Fogg, Gipsen, Gipsy, Gitano, Globe-trotter, Go, Gulliver, Gypsy, Hike, Interrail, Itinerant, Journey, Long-haul, Marco Polo, Meve, Migrant, Motor, Move, Mush, Nomad, Passepartout,

Peregrination, Peripatetic, Pilgrim, Ply, Polo, Range, Rep, Ride, Rom(any), Rove, Safari, Sail, Salesman, Samaritan, ➤ TOUR, Trek, Tripper, Tsigane, Viator, Voyage, Wayfarer, Wend, Wildfire, Zigan

Travesty Burlesque, Charade, Distortion, Parody, Show, Skit

Tray Antler, Carrier, Case, Charger, Coaster, Gallery, Joe, Lazy Susan, Plateau, ➤ SALVER, Tea, Trencher, Voider

Treacherous, Treachery Deceit, Delilah, Fickle, Ganelon, Guile, Insidious, Knife, Medism, Perfidious, Punic, Quicksands, Serpentine, Sleeky, Snaky, Trahison, Traitor, ➤ TREASON, Two-faced, Viper

Tread Clamp, Clump, Dance, Pad, Step, Stramp, Track, Trample

Treason Betrayal, Insurrection, Lèse-majesté, Lese-majesty, Perduellion, Sedition, ➤ TREACHERY

Treasure(r), Treasury Banker, Bursar, Cache, Camerlengo, Camerlingo, Cherish, Chest, Cimelia, Coffer, Ewe-lamb, Exchequer, Fisc(al), Fisk, Godolphin, Golden, Heritage, Hoard, Montana, Palgrave, ➤ PRIZE, Procurator, Purser, Relic, Riches, Steward, Thesaurus, Trove

Treat, Treatment Action, Acupuncture, Allopathy, Antidote, Aromatherapy, Beano, Besee, Capitulate, Care, Chemotherapy, Condition, Course, Cupping, Cure, Deal, Detox(ification), Dialysis, Do, ➤ DOCTOR, Dose, Dress, Dutch, Entertain, Facial, Fango, Figuration, Foment, Handle, Holistic, Homeopathy, Hydrotherapy, Kenny, Manage, Medicate, Naturopathy, Negotiate, Osteopathy, ➤ OUTING, Pasteur, Pedicure, Physic, Pie, Process, Psychoanalysis, Psychotherapy, Radiotherapy, Shout, Shrift, Smile, ➤ STAND, Tablet, Therapy, Titbit, Traction, Usance, Use, Vet

▷**Treated** may indicate an anagram

Treatise Almagest, Commentary, Didache, Discourse, Monograph, Pandect, Summa, Tract(ate), Upanishad, Vedanta

Treaty Agreement, Alliance, Assiento, Concordat, Covenant, Entente, Lateran, Maastricht, ➤ PACT, Protocol, Utrecht

Treble Castrato, Choirboy, Chorist(er), Pairial, Soprano, ➤ TRIPLE, Triune

Tree Actor, ➤ ANCESTRY, Axle, Beam, Boom, Bottle, Conifer, Corner, Deciduous, Decision, Dendrology, Descent, Family,

Fault, Fringe, Gallows, Grove, Hang, Hardwood, Jesse, Nurse, Pedigree, Pole, Sawyer, Shoe, Softwood, Staddle, Summer, Timber, Tyburn, ➤ WOOD

Tremble, Trembling, Tremor Aftershock, Butterfly, Dither, Dodder, Hotter, Judder, Palpitate, Quail, Quake, Quaver, Quiver, Seismal, ➤ SHAKE, Shiver, Shock, Shudder, Stound, Temblor, Trepid, Twitchy, Vibrate, Vibration, Vibratiuncle, Vibrato, Wobble, Wuther, Yips

Tremendous Big, Enormous, Howling, Immense, Marvellous

▶**Tremor** see TREMBLE

Trench(er) Boyau, Cunette, Cuvette, Delf, Delph, Dike(r), ➤ DITCH, Dyke(r), Encroach, Fleet, Foss(e), Foxhole, Fur(r), Furrow, Grip, Gullet, Gutter, Leat, Line, Mariana, Moat, Oceanic, Outwork, Rill, Rille, Ring-dyke, Salient, Sap, Shott, Slit, Sod, Sondage

Trend(y) Bent, Bias, Chic, Climate, Drift, Fashion, Hep, In, Mainstream, Newfangled, Pop, Posey, Rage, Style, Swim, Tendency, Tendenz, Tenor, Tide, Tonnish

Trespass(ing) Encroach, Errant, Hack, Impinge, Infringe, Offend, Peccancy, Sin, Trench, Wrong

Trial Adversity, Affliction, Appro, Approbation, Approval, Assize, Attempt, Bane, Bernoulli, Bout, Corsned, Cross, Court-martial, Cow, Dock, Essay, ➤ EXPERIMENT, Field, Fitting, Hearing, Nuremberg, Pilot, Pree, Ordeal, Probation, Proof, Rehearsal, Scramble, Taste

Triangle(d), Triangular Acute, Bermuda, Cosec, Deltoid, Equilateral, Eternal, Gair, Golden, Gore, Gyronny, Isosceles, Obtuse, Pascal's, Pedimental, Pyramid, Rack, Right-angled, Scalene, Similar, Trigon, Tromino, Warning

Tribe, Tribal, Tribesmen Clan(nish), Dynasty, Family, Nation, ➤ RACE

Tribune, Tribunal Aeropagus, Bema, Bench, ➤ COURT, Divan, Forum, Hague, Industrial, Leader, Platform, Rienzi, Rota, Star-chamber

Tributary Affluent, Bogan, Branch, Creek, Fork

Tribute Cain, Citation, Commemoration, Compliment, Deodate, ➤ DUE, Epitaph, Festschrift, Gavel, Heriot, Homage, Kain, Memento, Ode, Panegyric, Peter's pence, ➤ PRAISE, Rome-penny, Scat(t), Tax, Toast, Wreath, Wroth

Trick(s), Trickery, Trickster, Tricky Antic, Art, Artifice, Attrap, Bamboozle, Begunk, Book, Bunco, Bunko, Cantrip, Capot, Catch, Cheat, Chicane(ry), Chouse, Claptrap, Cog, Confidence, Coyote, Crook, Davenport, Deception, Deck, Delicate, Delude, Device, DO, ➤ DODGE, Dupe, Elf, Fard, Fetch, Fiddle, Finesse, Flam, Flim-flam, Fob, Fox, Fraud, Fun, Game, Gaud, Gleek, Glike, Guile, Hoax, Hocus(-pocus), Hoodwink, Hum, Illude, Illusion, Jockey, John, Kittle, Knack, Lark, Mislead, Monkey, Nap, Palter, Parlour, Pass, Pawk, Pleasantry, Prank, Prestige, Put-on, Ramp, Raven, Reak, Reik, Rex, Rig, Ruse, Scam, Sell, Set-up, Shanghai, Shenanigan, Shifty, Shill, Skite, Skul(l)duggery, Skylark, Sleight, Slight, Spoof, Stall, Stint, Subterfuge, Three-card, Ticklish, Trap, Trump, Turn, Underplot, Vole, Wangle, Wheeze, Wile, Wrinkle

▷**Trick** may indicate an anagram

Trifle(s), Trifling Bagatelle, Banal, Bibelot, Birdseed, Bit, Cent, Chickenfeed, Coquette, Dabble, Dalliance, ➤ DALLY, Denier, Do, Doit, Faddle, Falderal, Fallal, Fewtril, Fiddle, Fig, Flamfew, Fleabite, Flirt, Folderol, Fool, Footle, Fribble, Frippery, Fritter, Frivol, Gewgaw, Idle, Iota, Kickshaw, Knick-knack, Mite, Nothing, Palter, Peanuts, Peddle, Peppercorn, Petty, Philander, Piddle, Piffle, Pin, Pingle, Pittance, Play, Potty, Quiddity, Quiddle, Slight, Smatter, Song, Sport, Stiver, Straw, Sundry, Tiddle, Toy, Trinket, Trivia, Whit

Trigger Detent, Hair, Instigate, Pawl, Precipitate, Start

Trill(ed), Triller, Trilling Burr, Churr, Hirrient, Quaver, Ribattuta, Roll, Staphyle, Trim, Twitter, Warble

Trim(mer), Trimming Ballast, Bleed, Braid, Bray, Chipper, Clip, Dapper, Dinky, Dress, Ermine, Face, Fettle, File, Froufrou, Garnish, Garniture, Gimp, Guimpe, Macramé, Macrami, Marabou, Neat, Net(t), Ornament, Pare, Pipe, Plight, Posh, Preen, Pruin(e), Prune, Robin, Ruche, Sax, Sett, Shipshape, Smirk, Smug, Sned, Snod, ➤ SPRUCE, Straddle, Stroddle, Stylist, Svelte, ➤ TIDY, Time-server, Torsade, Trick, Wig

Trinket Bauble, Bibelot, Bijou(terie), Charm, Fallal, Nicknack, Toy, Trankum

Trip(per) Cruise, Dance, Day, Ego, Errand, ➤ FALL, Field, Flight, Flip, Guilt, Head, High, Journey, Junket, Kilt, Link, Outing, Power, Ride, Round, Run, Sail, Sashay, Spin, Spurn, ➤ STUMBLE, Tour, Trek, Voyage

▷**Trip** may indicate an anagram

Triple, Triplet Codon, Hemiol(i)a, Sdrucciola, Ternal, Tiercet, Treble, Trifecta, Trilling, Trin(e), Tripling

Trite Banal, Boilerplate, Corny, Hackneyed, Hoary, Novelettish, Rinky-dink, Stale, Stock, Time-worn

Triumph(ant) Cock-a-hoop, Codille, Cowabunga, Crow, Exult, Glory, Impostor, Killing, Oho, Olé, Ovation, Palm, Victorious, ➤ WIN

Trivia(l) Adiaphoron, Bagatelle, Balaam, Bald, ➤ BANAL, Frippery, Frothy, Futile, Idle, Light, Minutiae, Nitpicking, Paltry, Pap, Peppercorn, Pettifoggery, Petty, Picayune, Piffling, Shallow, Small, Small beer, Small fry, Snippety, Squirt, Squit, Toy(s)

Trolley Brute, Cart, Dolly, Gurney, Shopping, Tea, Truck, Trundler

▶**Trollop** see LOOSE WOMAN

Troop(s), Trooper Band, BEF, Brigade, Company, Depot, Detachment, Guard, Horde, Midianite, Militia, Pultan, Pulton, Pultoon, Pultun, SAS, School, Sowar, State, Storm, Tp, Turm(e)

Trophy Adward, Ashes, ➤ AWARD, Belt, Cup, Emmy, Memento, Palm, ➤ PRIZE, Scalp, Schneider, Spoils, Tourist, TT

Trot(ter), Trot out Air, Crib, Crubeen, Job, Jog, Passage, Pettitoes, Piaffe, Pony, Ranke, Red(-shirt), Rising, Tootsie

Trouble(s), Troublemaker, Troublesome Ache, Ado, Affliction, Aggro, Agitate, Ail, Alarm, Annoy, Bale, Barrat, ➤ BOTHER, Brickle, Burden, Care, Coil, Concern, Debate, Disaster, Disquiet, Distress, Disturb, Dog, Dolour, Eat, Exercise, Fash, Firebrand, Gram(e), Grief, Harass, Harry, Hassle, Hatter, Heat, Heist, Hellion, Hot water, Howdyedo, Inconvenience, ➤ IN TROUBLE, Jam, Mess, Moil, Molest, Noy, Perturb, Pester, Plague, Poke, Reck, Rub, Shake, Soup, Spiny, Stir, Storm, Sturt, Tartar, Teen, Teething, Thorny, Tine, Toil, Trial, Turn-up, Tyne, Unsettle, Vex, ➤ WORRY

▷**Troublesome** may indicate an anagram

Trough Back, Bed, Bucket, Buddle, Channel, Chute, Culvert, Graben, Hod, Hutch, Manger, Stock, Straik, Strake, Syncline, Troffer, Tundish, Tye

Trousers Bags, Bell-bottoms, Bloomers, Capri pants, Churidars, Clam-diggers, Continuations, Cords, Corduroys, Cossacks,

Trout → Trust(y) 580

Culottes, Daks, Drainpipe, Drawers, Ducks, Eel-skins, Flannels, Flares, Galligaskins, Gaskins, Gauchos, Hipsters, Inexpressibles, Innominables, Jeans, Jodhpurs, Kaccha, Lederhosen, Longs, Loons, Moleskins, Oxford bags, Palazzos, Pantaloons, Pants, Pedal pushers, Pegtops, Plus-fours, Reach-me-downs, Salopettes, Shalwar, Ski pants, Slacks, Strides, Strossers, Sweatpants, Trews, Trouse, Unmentionables, Unutterables, Utterless

Trout Aurora, Brook, Brown, Bull, Coral, Finnac(k), Finnock, Fish, Gillaroo, Herling, Hirling, Peal, Peel, Phinnock, Pogies, Quintet, Rainbow, Sewen, Sewin, Speckled, Splake, Steelhead, Togue, Whiting

Truant Absentee, AWOL, Dodge, Hooky, Kip, Miche, Mitch, Mooch, Mouch, Wag

Truce Armistice, Barley, Ceasefire, Fainites, Fains, Interlude, Pax, Stillstand, Treague, Treaty

Truck Bakkie, Bogie, Business, Cattle, Cocopan, Dealings, Dolly, Dumper, Forklift, Haul, Journey, ► LORRY, Low-loader, Pallet, Pick-up, Tipper, Trolley, Ute, Utility, Van

Trudge Footslog, Jog, Lumber, Pad, Plod, Stodge, Stramp, Taigle, Traipse, Trash, Trog, Vamp

True Accurate, Actual, Apodictic, Constant, Correct, Exact, Factual, Faithful, Genuine, Honest, Indubitable, Leal, Literal, Loyal, Platitude, Plumb, Pure, Real, Realistic, Sooth, Very

Truly Certes, Fegs, Forsooth, Indeed, Verily, Yea

Trump(er), Trumpet(er) Agami, Alchemy, Alchymy, Bach, Blare, Blast, Bray, Buccina, Bugle(r), Call, Card, Clarion, Conch, Cornet, Corona, Crow, Daffodil, Elephant, Fanfare, Hallali, Honours, ► HORN, Invent, Jew's, Last, Lituus, Lur(e), Lurist, Manille, Marine, Megaphone, ► NO TRUMP, Proclaim, Ram's-horn, Resurrect, Ruff, Salpingian, Salpinx, Satchmo, Sennet, Shofar, Shophar, Slug-horn, Surpass, Tantara, Tantarara, Tar(at)antara, Theodomas, Tiddy, Triton, Triumph

Trunk(s) Aorta(l), A-road, Bole, Body, Box, Bulk, But(t), Carcase, Chest, Coffer, Hose, Imperial, Log, Peduncle, Pollard, Portmanteau, Portmantle, Proboscis, Ricker, Road, Saratoga, Shorts, STD, Stock, Stud, Synangium, Torso, Valise, Wardrobe

Trust(y), Trusting, Trustworthy Affy, Authentic, Belief, Care, Cartel, Charge, Combine, Confide, Credit, Dependable, Discretionary, ► FAITH, Fiduciary, Gullible, Honest, Hope,

Investment, Leal, Lippen, Loyal, National, NT, Reliable, Reliance, Rely, Repose, Reputable, Staunch, Tick, Trojan, Trow, True, Trump, Unit

Truth(ful), Truism Accuracy, Alethic, Axiom, Bromide, Cliché, Cold turkey, Dharma, Dialectic, ➤ FACT, Facticity, Forsooth, Gospel, Home, Honesty, Idea(l), Naked, Pravda, Reality, Sooth, Veridical, Verity

Try(ing) Aim, Approof, Assay, Attempt, Audition, Bash, Bid, Birl, Burden, Burl, Conative, Contend, Crack, Effort, Empiric(utic), ➤ ENDEAVOUR, Essay, Examine, Experiment, Fand, Fish, Fling, Foretaste, Go, Harass, Hard, Hear, Importunate, Irk, Offer, Ordalium, Practise, Pree, Prieve, ➤ SAMPLE, Seek, Shot, Sip, Stab, Strain, Strive, Taste, Tax, Tempt, Test, Touchdown, Whirl

Tub, Tubbiness, Tub-thumper Ash-leach, Back, Bath, Boanerges, Bran, Corf, Cowl, Dan, Diogenes, Endomorph, Firkin, Keeve, Kid, Kieve, Kit, Pin, Podge, Pudge, Pulpit, Tun, Vat, Wash

Tube Arteriole, Artery, Barrel, Blowpipe, Bronchus, Burette, Calamus, Cannula, Capillary, Casing, Catheter, Cathode-ray, Conduit, Crookes, Digitron, Diode, Discharge, Duct, Electron, Eustachian, Fallopian, Fistule, Grommet, Hose, Inner, Kinescope, Macaroni, Matrass, Metro, Nixie, Oval, Oviduct, Pentode, Pilot-static, ➤ PIPE, Pipette, Pitot, Pneumatic, Pollen, Promethean, Salpinx, Saucisse, Saucisson, Schnorkel, Sieve, Siphon, Sleeve, Snorkel, Spaghetti, Speaking, Spout, Staple, Static, Swallet, Teletron, Television, Test, Tetrode, Tile, Torpedo, Trachea, Trocar, Trunk, Tunnel, Tuppenny, U, Ureter, Urethra, Vacuum, Vas, Vein, Vena, Venturi, Video

Tuber(s) Arnut, Arracacha, Bulb, Chufa, Coc(c)o, Dasheen, Earth-nut, Eddoes, Mashua, Oca, Potato, Salep, Taproot, Taro, Yam

Tuberculosis Consumption, Crewels, Cruel(l)s, Decline, Lupus, Phthisis, Scrofula

Tuck Dart, Friar, Gather, Grub, Kilt, Pin, Pleat, Scran

Tuft(ed) Amentum, Beard, C(a)espitose, Candlewick, Catkin, Cluster, Coma, Comb, Cowlick, Crest, Dollop, Flaught, Floccus, Goatee, Hassock, Pappus, Penicillate, Quiff, Scopate, Shola, Tait, Tassel, Toorie, Toupee, Tourie, Tussock, Tuzz, Whisk

Tug Drag, Haul, Jerk, Lug, Pug, ➤ PULL, Rive, Ship, Sole, Soole, Sowl(e), Tit, Tow, Towboat, Yank

Tumble, Tumbler Acrobat, Cartwheel, Drier, Fall, ➤ GLASS, Pitch, Popple, Purl, Realise, Spill, Stumble, Topple, Trip, Twig, Voltigeur, Welter

▷**Tumble** may indicate an anagram

Tumour Enchondroma, ➤ GROWTH, Metastasis, Neoplasm, -oma, Oncology, Scirrhous, Wolf

Tumult Brattle, Brawl, Coil, Deray, Ferment, Fracas, Hirdy-girdy, Hubbub, Reird, Riot, ➤ ROAR, Romage, Rore, Stoor, Stour, Stowre, Stramash, Tew, ➤ UPROAR

Tune(s), Tuneful, Tuner Adjust, Air, Aria, Canorous, Carillon, Catch, Choral, Dump, Etude, Fork, Harmony, Hornpipe, Jingle, Key, Maggot, Measure, Melisma, ➤ MELODY, Old Hundred, ➤ OUT OF TUNE, Peg, Port, Potpourri, Raga, Rant, Ranz-des-vaches, Signature, Snatch, Song, Spring, Strain, Sweet, Syntonise, Temper, Theme, Tone, Tweak

Tungstate, Tungsten Scheelite, W, Wolfram

Tunic Ao dai, Caftan, Chiton, Choroid, Cote-hardie, Dalmatic, Dashiki, Gymslip, Hauberk, Kabaya, Kaftan, Kameez, K(h)urta, ➤ SINGLET, Tabard, Toga

Tunnel Bore, Channel, Condie, Countermine, Culvert, Cundy, Gallery, Head, Mine, Qanat, Simplon, Stope, Subway, Syrinx, Tube, Underpass, Wind, Wormhole

Turban Bandanna, Hat, Mitral, Pagri, Puggaree, Puggery, Puggree, Sash, Scarf

Turbulence, Turbulent Becket, Bellicose, Buller, Factious, Fierce, Rapids, Stormy

▷**Turbulent** may indicate an anagram

Turf Caespitose, Clod, Divot, Earth, Fail, Feal, Flaught, ➤ GRASS, Greensward, Peat, Screw, ➤ SOD, Sward

Turk(ish) Anatolian, Bashaw, Bashkir, Bey, Bimbashi, Bostangi, Byzantine, Caimac(am), Crescent, Effendi, Gregory, Horse(tail), Irade, Kajamak, Kazak(h), Kurd, Mameluke, Mutessarif(at), Omar, Osman(li), Ottamite, Ottoman, Ottomite, Rayah, Scanderbeg, Selim, Seljuk(ian), Seraskier, Spahi, Tatar, Timariot, Usak, Uzbeg, Uzbek, Yakut

Turkey, Turkey-like Anatolia, Brush, Bubbly(-jock), Curassow, Eyalet, Flop, Gobbler, Norfolk, Sultanate, Talegalla, TR, Trabzon, Vulturn

Turmoil Chaos, Din, Ferment, Stoor, Stour, Tornado, Tracasserie, Tumult, ➤ UPROAR, Welter

▷ **Turn(ing)** may indicate an anagram

Turn(ing), Turned away, Turned up, Turns Act, Addle, Advert, Antrorse, Avert, Bank, Become, Bend, Bump, Careen, Cartwheel, Cast, Change, Char(e), Chore, Christiana, Christie, Christy, Churn, Cock, Coil, Crank(le), Cuff, Curd(le), Curve, Defect, Deflect, Detour, Deviate, Dig, Digress, Divert, Ear, Earn, Elbow, Evert, Fadge, Flip, Go, Hairpin, Handbrake, Head-off, Hie, High, Hinge, Hup, Influence, Innings, Invert, Jar, Jink, Keel, Kick, Lot, Luff, Mohawk, Number, Obvert, Parallel, Parry, Penchant, Pivot, Plough, Pronate, Prove, PTO, Quarter, Rebut, Refer, Refract, Retroflex, Retroussé, Retrovert, Rev, Revolt, Ride, Riffle, Rocker, Roll, Root, ➤ ROTATE, Rote, Roulade, Rout, Routine, Screw, Sheer, ➤ SHOT, Shout, Sicken, Slew, Slue, Solstice, Sour, ➤ SPELL, Spin, Spot, Sprain, Star, Start, Step, Swash, Swing, Swivel, Telemark, Three-point, Throw, Tiptilt, Tirl, Transpose, Trend, Trick, Turtle, Twiddle, Twist, U, Uey, Up, Veer, Versed, Version, Vertigo, Volta, Volte-face, Wap, Warp, Wend, Went, ➤ WHEEL, Whelm, Whirl, Whorl, Wimple, Wind, Wrest, Zigzag

Turn-coat Apostate, Cato, Defector, Quisling, Rat, Renegade, Tergiversate, Traitor

Turner Axle, Lana, Lathe, Painter, Pivot, Rose-engine, Spanner, Worm, Wrench

Turnip(-shaped) Bagie, Baggy, Hunter, Napiform, Navew, Neep, Rutabaga, ➤ STUPID PERSON, Swede, Tumshie

Turn over Capsize, Careen, Flip, Inversion, Production, PTO, Somersault, TO, Up-end

Turret(ed) Barmkin, Bartisan, Garret, Louver, Louvre, Pepperbox, Sponson, ➤ TOWER, Turriculate

Turtle, Turtle head Bale, Calipash, Calipee, Chelone, Green, Hawksbill, Inverted, Leatherback, Loggerhead, Matamata, Mossback, Mud, Musk, Ridley, Snapper, Soft-shelled, Stinkpot, Terrapin, Thalassian

Tusk Gam, Horn, Ivory, Tooth, Tush

Tussle Giust, Joust, Mêlée, Scrimmage, Scrum, Scuffle, Skirmish, Touse, Touze, Towse, Towze, Tuilyie, Wrestle

Tutor Abbé, Aristotle, Ascham, Bear, ➤ COACH, Crammer, Don, Instruct, Leader, Preceptor, Répétiteur, Supervisor, Teacher

TV Baird, Box, Cable, Digital, Idiot-box, Lime Grove, Monitor, PAL, SECAM, Sky, Tele, Telly, Tube, Video

Twaddle Blether, Drivel, Rot, Slipslop, Tripe

Tweak Pluck, Twiddle, Twist, Twitch

Twelfth, Twelve Apostles, Dozen, Epiphany, Glorious, Grouse, Midday, Midnight, N, Night, Noon, Ternion, Twal

▶**Twice** see TWO

Twig(s) Besom, Birch, Cotton, Cow, Dig, Grasp, Kow, Osier, Realise, Reis, Rice, Rumble, Sarment, See, Sprig, Sticklac, Switch, Understand, Wand, Wattle, Wicker, Withe

Twilight Cockshut, Crepuscular, Demi-jour, Dusk, Gloam(ing), Gotterdämmerung

Twin(s) Asvins, Castor, Coetaneous, Didymus, Dioscuri, Ditokous, Dizygotic, Double, Fraternal, Gemel, Identical, Isogeny, Kindred, Macle, Monozygotic, Pigeon-pair, Pollux, Siamese, Tweedledee, Tweedledum

Twine Braid, Coil, Cord, Inosculate, Packthread, Sisal, Snake, String, Twist, Wreathe

Twinkle, Twinkling Glimmer, Glint, Mo(ment), ➤ SPARKLE, Starnie, Trice

▷**Twirling** may indicate an anagram

Twist(ed), Twister, Twisting, Twisty Askant, Askew, Becurl, Bought, Card-sharper, Chisel, Coil, Contort, Convolution, Crinkle, Crisp, Cue, Curl(icue), Cyclone, Deform, Detort, Distort, ➤ DODGE, Garrot, Helix, Kink, Mat, Oliver, Plait, Quirk, Raddle, Ravel, Rick, Rogue, Rotate, Rove, Skew, Slew, Slub(b), Slue, Snarl, Spin, Spiral, Sprain, Squiggle, Squirm, Swivel, Tendril, Torc, Tornado, Torque, Torsade, Torsion, Tortile, Turn, Tweak, Twiddle, Twine, Twirl, Warp, Wind, Wreathe, Wrench, Wrest, Wriggle, Wring, Writhe, Wry, Zigzag

▷**Twisted, Twisting** may indicate an anagram

Twit, Twitter Chaff, Cherup, Chirrup, Dotterel, Gear(e), Giber, ➤ JEER, Stupid, Taunt, Warble

Twitch(ing), Twitchy Athetosis, Clonic, Grass, Jerk, Life-blood, Start, Subsultive, Tic, Tig, Tit, Tweak, Twinge, Vellicate, Yips

Two(some), Twice Bice, Bis, Bisp, Both, Brace, Couple(t), Deuce, Double, Duad, Dual, Duet, Duo, Dyad, ➤ PAIR, Swy, Tête-à-tête, Twain, Twins, Twister

Tycoon Baron, Magnate, Plutocrat, Shogun

Type(s) A, Agate, Aldine, Antimony, Antique, B, Balaam, Baskerville, Black-letter, Body, Bold face, Bourgeois, Braille, Brand, Brevier, Brilliant, Canon, Category, Character, Chase, Cicero, Clarendon, Class, Columbian, Cut, Egyptian, Elite, Elzevir, Em, Emblem, Emerald, English, Face, Font, Form(e), Fount, Fraktur, Fudge, Gem, Genre, Gent, Gothic, Hair, Ilk, Image, Key, Kidney, Kind, Ligature, Minion, Modern, Moon, Mould, Non-pareil, Norm, Old style, Old-face, Paragon, Pattern, Pearl, Peculiar, Pi, Pica, Pie, Point, Primer, Print, Quad(rat), Roman, Ronde, Ruby, Sanserif, Semibold, Serif, ➤ SORT, Sp, Species, Stanhope, Style, Times, Tissue, Version

▷ **Type of** may indicate an anagram

Typical Average, Characteristic, Classic, Normal, Representative, Standard, Symbolic, True-bred, Usual

Tyrant, Tyranny, Tyrannical Absolutism, Autocrat, Caligula, Despot, Dictator, Drawcansir, Gelon, Herod, Lordly, Nero, Oppressor, Pharaoh, Sardanapalus, Satrap, Stalin, Totalitarian, Tsar, Yoke

Tyre Balloon, Cross-ply, Michelin, Pericles, Radial, Recap, Remould, Retread, Sidewall, Slick, Snow, Spare, Tread, Tubeless, Whitewall

Tyro Beginner, Ham, ➤ NOVICE, Rabbit, Rookie, Rooky, Starter

Uu

Ugly Cow, Customer, Eyesore, Foul, Gorgon, Gruesome, Hideous, Homely, Huckery, Loth, Mean, Ominous, Plain

Ulcer(ous) Abscess, Aphtha, Canker, Chancroid, Decubitus, Duodenal, Gastric, Helcoid, Noma, Peptic, Phagedaena, Rodent, Rupia, Sore, Wolf

Ulster NI, Overcoat, Raincoat, Ulad

Ultimate Absolute, Basic, Deterrent, Eventual, Final, Furthest, Last, Maximum, So, Supreme, Thule

Umbrage Offence, Pique, Resentment, Shade

Umbrella(-shaped) Bumbershoot, Chatta, Gamp, Gingham, Gloria, Mush(room), Parasol, Sunshade, Tee

Umpire Arb(iter), Byrlawman, Daysman, Decider, Judge, Oddjobman, Odd(s)man, Overseer, Referee, Rule, Stickler, Thirdsman

Unable Can't, Incapable

Unacceptable Non-U, Not on, Out, Stigmatic

Unaccompanied A cappella, Alone, High-lone, Secco, Single, Solo, Solus

Unaffected Artless, Genuine, Homely, Natural, Plain, Sincere, Unattached

Unanswerable Erotema, Irrefragable, Irrefutable

Unattractive Drac(k), Lemon, Plain, Plug-ugly, Rebarbative, Seamy, Ugly

▷**Unauthentic** may indicate an anagram

Unavail(able), Unavailing Bootless, Futile, Ineluctable, Lost, No use, Off, Vain

Unaware Heedless, Ignorant, Incognisant, Innocent

Unbalanced Asymmetric, Deranged, Doolalli, Doolally, Loco, Lopsided, Uneven

Unbecoming, Unbefitting Improper, Infra dig, Shabby, Unfitting, Unseemly, Unsuitable, Unworthy

Unbelievable, Unbeliever Agnostic, Atheist, Cassandra, Doubter, Giaour, Heathen, Incredible, Infidel, Pagan, Painim, Paynim, Sceptic, Tall, Zendik

Unbiased Fair, Impartial, Just, Neutral, Objective, Unattainted

Unbreakable Infrangible, Inviolate

Unbridled Fancy free, Footloose, Lawless, Uncurbed, Unrestricted, Unshackled, Untramelled

Uncanny Eerie, Eldritch, Extraordinary, Geason, Rum, Spooky, Weird

Uncertain(ty) Blate, Broken, Chancy, Chary, Contingent, Delicate, Dicey, Dither, Doubtful, Dubiety, Hesitant, Iffy, Indeterminate, Indistinct, Irresolute, Peradventure, Queasy, Risky, Slippery, Tentative, Vor

▷**Uncertain** may indicate an anagram

Unchangeable, Unchanged, Unchanging As is, Enduring, Eternal, Idempotent, Immutable, Monotonous, Stable

Unchaste Corrupt, Immodest, Immoral, Impure, Lewd, Wanton

Uncivil(ised) Barbaric, Benighted, Boondocks, Discourteous, Disrespectful, Giant-rude, Heathen, Impolite, Military, Rude, Rudesby

Uncle Abbas, Afrikaner, Arly, Bob, Dutch, Eme, Nunky, Oom, Pawnbroker, Pop-shop, Remus, Sam, Tio, Tom, Usurer, Vanya

Unclean Defiled, Dirty, Impure, Obscene, Ordure, Squalid, Tabu, T(e)refa(h)

Unclear Ambitty, Hazy, Nebulous, Obscure

Uncommon Rare, Strange, Unusual

▷**Uncommon(ly)** may indicate an anagram

Uncompromising Hardshell, Intransigent, Rigid, Strict, Ultra

Unconcerned Bland, Careless, Casual, Cold, Indifferent, Insouciant, Nonchalant, Strange

Unconditional Absolute, Free, Pure

Unconnected Asyndetic, Detached, Disjointed, Off-line

Unconscious(ness) Asleep, Catalepsy, Cold, Comatose, Instinctive, Non-ego, Subliminal, Trance, Under

Uncontrolled Atactic, Free, Incontinent, Loose, Wild

Unconventional Beatnik, Bohemian, Drop-out, Eccentric, Gonzo, Heretic, Heterodox, Informal, Irregular, Offbeat, Original, Outlandish, Outré, Raffish, Unorthodox

▷**Unconventional** may indicate an anagram

Uncouth(ness) Backwoodsman, Bear, Crude, Gothic, Inelegant, Rube, Rude, Rugged, Uncivil

Uncover(ed) Bare, Disclose, Expose, Inoperculate, Open, Peel, Reveal, Shave, Shill, Shuck, Uncap

Unction, Unctuous(ness) Anele, Balm, Chrism, Extreme, Ointment, Oleaginous, Ooze, Smarm, Soapy

Uncultivated, Uncultured Artless, Bundu, Fallow, Ignorant, Philistine, Rude, Tramontane, Wild

Undecided Doubtful, Non-committal, Pending, Open-ended, Pendulous, Uncertain, Wavering

Under Aneath, Below, Beneath, Hypnotized, Sotto, Sub-, Unconscious

Undercoat Base, Primer

Undercover Espionage, Secret, Veiled

▶**Undergarment** see UNDERWEAR

Undergo Bear, Dree, Endure, Sustain

Undergraduate Fresher, L, Pup, Sizar, Sophomore, Student, Subsizar

Underground (group) Basement, Catacomb, Cellar, Hell, Hypogaeous, Irgun, Kiva, Macchie, Maquis, Mattamore, Metro, Phreatic, Pict, Plutonia, Pothole, Secret, Souterrain, Subsoil, Subterranean, Subway, Tube

Undergrowth Brush, Chaparral, Firth, Frith, Scrub

Underhand Dirty, Haunch, Insidious, Lob, Oblique, Secret, Sinister, Sly, Sneaky, Surreptitious

Underline Emphasise, Insist

Underling Bottle-washer, Cog, Inferior, Jack, Menial, Munchkin, Subordinate

Undermine Erode, Fossick, Sap, Subvert, Tunnel, Weaken

Understand(able), Understanding Accept, Acumen, Agreement, Apprehend, Capeesh, Clear, Comprehend, Conceive, Concept, Cotton-on, Deal, Dig, Enlighten, Entente, Exoteric, Fathom, Follow, Gather, Gauge, Gaum, Gorm, Grasp, Have, Head, Heels, Insight, Ken, Kind, Knowhow, Learn, Omniscient, Pact, Rapport, Rapprochement, Realise, Savey, Savvy, See, Sole, Substance, Tolerance, Tumble, Twig, Uptak(e), Wisdom, Wit

Understatement Litotes, M(e)iosis

Understood Implicit, OK, Perspicuous, Roger, Tacit, Unspoken

Understudy Deputy, Double, Stand-in, Sub

Undertake, Undertaking Attempt, Contract, Covenant, Enterprise, Guarantee, Pledge, Promise, Scheme, Shoulder, Warranty

Undertaker Entrepreneur, Mortician, Obligor, Sponsor, Upholder

Underwear Balbriggan, Bloomers, Bodice, Body, Bra(ssiere), Briefs, Broekies, Camiknickers, Camisole, Chemise, Combs, Dainties, Frillies, Girdle, Innerwear, Jump, Linen, Lingerie, Linings, Long Johns, Pantalets, Pantaloons, Panties, Petticoat, Scanties, Semmit, Slip, Smalls, Stays, Step-ins, Subucula, Suspenders, Tanga, Teddy, Thermal, Underdaks, Undergarments, Underpants, Undershirt, Underthings, Undies, Unmentionables, Vest, Wyliecoat, Y-fronts®

Underworld Chthonic, Criminal, Hell, Lowlife, Mafia, Shades, Tartar(e), Tartarus, Tartary

Underwrite, Underwritten Assure, Endorse, Guarantee, Insure, Lloyds, PS

Undeveloped Backward, Depauperate, Green, Inchoate, Latent, Ridgel, Ridgil, Ridgling, Rig, Riggald, Riglin(g), Rudimentary, Seminal

Undo(ing) Annul, Defeat, Destroy, Downfall, Dup, Poop, Poupe, Release, Ruin, Unravel

Undone Arrears, Left, Postponed, Ran, Ruined

Undoubtedly Certes, Positively, Sure

Undress(ed) Bare, Disrobe, En cuerpo, Expose, Négligé, Nude, Nue, Peel, Querpo, Raw, Rough, Self-faced, Spar, Strip, Unapparelled

Undulate, Undulating Billow, Nebule, Ripple, Roll, Wave

▷**Unduly** may indicate an anagram

Unearth(ly) Astral, Dig, Discover, Disentomb, Exhumate, Indagate

Unease, Uneasiness, Uneasy Angst, Anxious, Creeps, Inquietude, Itchy, Malaise, Restive, Shy, Tense, The willies, Uptight, Windy, Womble-cropped

Unemployed, Unemployment Drone, Idle, Latent, Lay-off, Redundant

Unending Chronic, Eternal, Lasting, Sempiternal

Unequal(led) Aniso-, Disparate, Non(e)such, Scalene, Unjust

Unerring Dead, Exact, Precise

Uneven(ness) Accident, Blotchy, Bumpy, Irregular, Jaggy, Patchy, Ragged, Scratchy

▷**Unevenly** may indicate an anagram

Unexpected(ly) Abrupt, Accidental, Adventitious, Fortuitous, Inopinate, Snap, Sodain(e), Sudden, Turn-up, Unawares, Unwary

Unfair Bias(s)ed, Crook, Dirty, Inclement, Invidious, Mean, Partial

Unfaithful Disloyal, Godless, Infidel, Traitor

Unfashionable Cube, Dowdy, Passe, Square

▷**Unfashionable** may indicate 'in' to be removed

Unfavourable Adverse, Ill, Poor, Untoward

Unfeeling Adamant, Callous, Cold, Cruel, Dead, Hard, Inhuman(e), Insensate, Robotic

Unfinished Crude, Inchoate, Raw, Scabble, Scapple, Stickit

Unfit(ting) Disabled, Faulty, Ill, Impair, Inept, Outré, Tref(a), Unable

▷**Unfit** may indicate an anagram

Unfold Deploy, Display, Divulge, Evolve, Interpret, Open, Relate, Spread

Unfortunate(ly) Accursed, Alack, Alas, Hapless, Ill-starred, Luckless, Shameless, Unlucky

Unfriendly Aloof, Antagonistic, Asocial, Chill(y), Cold, Fraim, Fremd, Fremit, Hostile, Icy, Remote, Surly

Unfruitful Abortive, Barren, Sterile

Ungainly Awkward, Gawkish, Uncouth, Weedy

Ungracious Cold, Offhand, Rough, Rude

Unguent Nard, Pomade, Salve

Ungulate Antelope, Dinoceras, Eland, Equidae, Hoofed, Moose, Rhino, Ruminantia, Takin, Tapir, Tylopoda

Unhappily, Unhappy, Unhappiness Blue, Depressed, Disconsolate, Dismal, Doleful, Down-hearted, Downcast, Dysphoria, Glumpish, Love-lorn, Lovesick, Miserable, Sad, Sore, Tearful, Unlief, Upset

▷**Unhappily** may indicate an anagram

Unhealthy Bad, Clinic, Diseased, Epinosic, Insalubrious, Morbid, Noxious, Peaky, Prurient, Sickly

Uniform Abolla, Battledress, Consistent, Dress, Equable, Equal, Even, Flat, Forage-cap, Homogeneous, Identical, Khaki, Kit, Livery, Regimentals, Regular, Rig, Robe, Same, Sole, Standard, Steady, Strip, Unvaried

Unimaginative Banausic, Literalistic, Pedestrian, Pooter

Unimportant Cog, Fiddling, Footling, Frivolous, Idle, Immaterial, Inconsequent, Inconsiderable, Insignificant, MacGuffin, Makeweight, Minnow, Minutiae, Negligible, Nugatory, Peripheral, Petty, Small-time, Trifling, Trivia(l)

Uninhabited Bundu, Deserted, Lonely

Uninspired Humdrum, Pedestrian, Pompier, Tame

Uninterested, Uninteresting Apathetic, Bland, Dreary, Dry, Dull, Incurious, Nondescript

Uninterrupted Constant, Incessant, Running, Steady

Union(ist) Affiance, Allegiance, Alliance, Association, Bed, Benelux, Bond, Combination, Concert, Craft, Credit, Diphthong, Economic, Enosis, Ensemble, Equity, EU, European, Federal, Federation, Fusion, Group, Guild, Heterogamy, Industrial, Liaison, Link-up, Marriage, Match, Merger, Nuptials, NUM, NUR, NUS, NUT, Pearl, RU, Rugby, Samiti, Sex, Sherman, Solidarity, Splice, Sponsal, Student, Soviet, Synthesis, Teamsters, ➤ TRADE UNION, TU, U, UNISON, USDAW, Uxorial, Wedding, Wedlock, Wield

Unique(ness) Alone, A-per-se, Hacceity, Inimitable, Lone, Matchless, Nonesuch, Nonpareil, Nonsuch, Only, One-off, Peerless, Rare, Singular, Sole, Sui generis

Unit Ace, Amp, Angstrom, Bar, Barn, Baud, Becquerel, Bit, Byte, Cadre, Candela, Cell, Chaldron, Corps, Coulomb, Cusec, Dalton, Daraf, Darcy, Debye, Degree, Denier, Derived, DIN, Detachment, Dioptre, Division, Dol, Dyne, Echelon, Electron, Element, Em, En, Energid, Ensuite, Erg, Farad, Fermi, Flight, Fresnel, Gal, Gauss, GeV, Gigabit, Gilbert, Gram, Gray, Henry, Hertz, Hide, Ion, Item, Joule, K, Kelvin, Kilerg, Kilowatt, Lambert, Last, League, Lumen, Lux, Magneton, Man-hour, Maxwell, Measure, Megabyte, Megahertz, Megaton, Megawatt, Metre, Mho, Micron, Mil, Module, Mole, Monad, Morgan, Morgen, Morpheme, Neper, Nepit, Nest, Newton, Nit, Octa, Oersted, Ohm, Okta, Organ, Parasang, Pascal, Pennyweight, Phoneme, Phot, Pixel, Poise, Poundal, Ploughgate, Probit, Protoplast, RA, Radian, Rem, Remen, Rep, Ro(e)ntgen, Rutherford, Sabin, Second, Semeion, SI, Siemens, Sievert, Singleton, Slug, Sone, Stoke(s), Syllable, TA, Tagmeme, Tesla, Therm, Tog, Token, Torr, Vanity, Var, Volt, Watt, Weber, Wing, Yrneh

Unite(d) Accrete, Bind, Coalesce, Combine, Concordant, Connate, Connect, Consolidate, Consubstantiate, Covalent, Fay, Federal, Federate, Fuse, Gene, Injoint, Join, Kingdom, Knit, Lap, Link, Marry, Meint, Meng, Ment, Merge, Meynt, Ming, Nations, Oop, Oup, Siamese, Solid, States, Tie, ➤ WED, Weld, Yoke

Unity Harmony, One, Solidarity, Sympathy, Togetherness

Universal, Universe All, Catholic, Cosmos, Creation, Ecumenic(al), Emma, General, Global, Infinite, Macrocosm, Maddala, Microcosm, Sphere, U, World(wide)

University Academe, Academy, Alma mater, Aston, Berkeley, Bonn, Brown, Campus, Civic, College, Columbia, Cornell, Exeter, Gown, Harvard, Ivy League, Open, OU, Oxbridge, Pennsylvania, Princeton, Reading, Redbrick, St Andrews, Sorbonne, Varsity, Yale

Unjust(ified) Groundless, Inequity, Iniquitous, Invalid, Tyrannical

Unknown Agnostic, Anon, A.N.Other, Hidden, Ign, Incog(nito), N, Nobody, Noumenon, Occult, Quantity, Secret, Soldier, Strange, Symbolic, Tertium quid, Warrior, X, Y

Unless Nisi, Save, Without

Unlike(ly) Difform, Disparate, Dubious, Improbable, Inauspicious, Long shot, Outsider, Remote, Tall, Unlich

Unlimited Almighty, Boundless, Indefinite, Measureless, Nth, Universal, Vast

Unload Disburden, Discharge, Drop, Dump, Jettison, Land

Unlucky Donsie, Hapless, Ill(-starred), Inauspicious, Infaust, Jonah, Misfallen, S(c)hlimazel, Stiff, Thirteen, Untoward, Wanchancie, Wanchancy

Unmarried Bachelor, Common-law, Single, Spinster

Unmentionable(s) Bra, Foul, ➤ UNDERWEAR, Undies

Unmindful Heedless, Oblivious

Unmistakable Clear, Manifest, Plain

Unnatural Abnormal, Affected, Cataphysical, Contrived, Eerie, Flat, Geep, Irregular, Strange

▷**Unnaturally** may indicate an anagram

Unnecessary Extra, Gash, Gratuitous, Needless, Otiose, Redundant, Superfluous

Unobserved Backstage, Sly, Unseen

Unoccupied Empty, Idle, Vacant, Void

Unoriginal Banal, Copy, Derivative, Imitation, Plagiarised, Slavish

Unorthodox Heretic, Heterodox, Maverick, Off-the-wall, Unconventional

Unpaid Amateur, Brevet, Hon(orary), Voluntary

Unperturbed Bland, Calm, Serene

Unpleasant, Unpleasant person Creep, God-awful, Grim, Grotty, Horrible, Icky, Invidious, Nasty, Obnoxious, Odious, Offensive, Painful, Pejorative, Rebarbative, Shady, Shitty, Shocker, Sticky, Toerag, Wart

Unpredictable Aleatory, Dicy, Erratic, Maverick, Wild card

Unprepared Ad lib, Extempore, Impromptu, Unready

Unprincipled Amoral, Dishonest, Irregular, Reprobate

Unproductive Arid, Atokal, Atokous, Barren, Dead-head, Eild, Fallow, Futile, Lean, Poor, Shy, Sterile, Yeld, Yell

Unprofitable Bootless, Fruitless, Lean, Thankless

Unprotected Exposed, Nude, Vulnerable

Unqualified Absolute, Entire, Outright, Profound, Pure, Quack, Sheer, Straight, Thorough, Total, Utter

Unquestionably, Unquestioning Absolute, Certain, Doubtless, Implicit

Unravel Construe, Disentangle, Feaze, Fray, Solve

Unreal(istic) Eidetic, En l'air, Escapist, Fake, Fancied, Illusory, Mirage, Oneiric, Phantom, Phon(e)y, Pseudo, Romantic, Sham, Spurious

Unreasonable, Unreasoning Absurd, Bigot, Extreme, Illogical, Irrational, Misguided, Perverse, Rabid

Unrecognised Incognito, Inconnu, Invalid, Thankless, Unsung

Unrefined Coarse, Common, Crude, Earthy, Gur, Rude, Vul(g), Vulgar

Unrelenting Implacable, Remorseless, Severe, Stern

Unreliable Dodgy, Erratic, Fickle, Flighty, Fly-by-night, Shonky, Unstable, Wankle, Wonky

Unresponsive Cold, Frigid, Nastic, Rigor

Unrestrained Free, Hearty, Homeric, Immoderate, Incontinent, Lax, Lowsit, Rampant, Wanton, Wild

Unruly Anarchic, Bodgie, Buckie, Camstairy, Camsteary, Camsteerie, Exception, Lawless, Obstreperous, Ragd(e), Raged, Ragged, Rampageous, Rattlebag, Riotous, Tartar, Turbulent, Turk, Wanton, Wayward

▷**Unruly** may indicate an anagram

Unsafe Deathtrap, Fishy, Insecure, Perilous, Precarious, Vulnerable

Unsatisfactory, Unsatisfying Bad, Lame, Lousy, Meagre, Rocky, Thin, Wanting

Unseasonable, Unseasoned Green, Murken, Raw, Untimely

Unseemly Coarse, Improper, Indecent, Indign, Untoward

Unselfish Altruist, Generous

Unsettled Homeless, Hunky, Indecisive, Nervous, Outstanding, Queasy, Restive

▷**Unsettled** may indicate an anagram

Unsightly Hideous, Repulsive, Ugly

Unskilled Awkward, Dilutee, Gauche, Green, Inexpert, Rude

Unsophisticated Alf, Boondocks, Boonies, Bushie, Direct, Faux-naif, Hillbilly, Homebred, Homespun, Inurbane, Jaap, Jay, Naive, Rube

Unsound Barmy, Infirm, Invalid, Shaky, Wildcat, Wonky

▷**Unsound** may indicate an anagram

Unspeakable Dreadful, Ineffable, Nefandous

Unspoiled, Unspoilt Innocent, Natural, Perfect, Pristine, Pure

Unstable, Unsteady Anomic, Astatic, Bockedy, Casual, Crank, Crank(y), Dicky, Erratic, Fluidal, Groggy, Infirm, Insecure, Labile, Rickety, Shifty, Slippy, Tickle, Tottery, Totty, Variable, Wambling, Wankle, Wobbly

▶**Unsteady** see UNSTABLE

▷**Unstuck** may indicate an anagram

Unsubstantial Aeriform, Airy, Flimsy, Paltry, Shadowy, Slight, Thin, Yeasty

Unsuccessful Abortive, Futile, Manqué, Vain

Unsuitable Impair, Improper, Inapt, Incongruous, Inexpedient, Malapropos, Unfit

Untidy Daggy, Dowd(y), Frowzy, Litterbug, Ragged, Scruff(y), Slipshod, Slovenly, Tatty

▷**Untidy** may indicate an anagram

Untie Free, Undo, Unlace

Untold Secret, Umpteen, Unred, Unread, Vast

Untouchable Burakumin, Dalit, Harijan, Immune, Sealed

▷**Untrained** may indicate 'BR' to be removed

Untrue, Untruth Apocryphal, Eccentric, Faithless, False(hood), Lie, Prefabrication, Unleal

Untrustworthy Dishonest, Fickle, Shifty, Sleeky, Tricky

Unused, Unusable Impracticable, New, Over, Wasted

Unusual(ly) Abnormal, Atypical, Extra(ordinary), Freak, New, Novel, Odd, Particular, Rare, Remarkable, Singular, Special, ► STRANGE, Unique, Untypical, Unwonted

▷**Unusual** may indicate an anagram

Unvarying Constant, Eternal, Stable, Static, Uniform

Unwanted De trop, Exile, Gooseberry, Nimby, Outcast, Sorn

Unwelcome, Unwelcoming Frosty, (Persona) Non grata, Icy, Lulu, Obtrusive

Unwell Ailing, Crook, Dicky, Ill, Impure, Poorly, Seedy, Toxic

Unwholesome Miasmous, Morbid, Noxious

Unwilling(ness) Averse, Disinclined, Intestate, Loth, Nolition, Nolo, Perforce, Reluctant

Unwind Relax, Straighten, Unreave, Unreeve

▷**Unwind** may indicate an anagram

Unwise Foolish, Ill-advised, Impolitic, Imprudent, Inexpedient, Injudicious

Unworthy Below, Beneath, Indign, Inferior

Unyielding Adamant, Eild, Firm, Inexorable, Intransigent, Obdurate, Rigid, Steely, Stubborn, Tough

Up(on), Upper, Uppish A, Afoot, Antidepressant, Arrogant, Astir, Astray, Astride, Cloud-kissing, Euphoric, Heavenward, Hep, Horsed, Incitant, Off, On, Primo, Range, Ride, Riding, Skyward, Speed, ► UPPER CLASS, Vamp, Ventral

Upbraid Abuse, Rebuke, Reproach, Reprove, Scold, Twit

Update Renew, Report

Upheaval Cataclysm, Eruption, Seismic, Stir

▷**Upheld** may indicate 'up' in another word

Uphill Arduous, Borstal, Sisyphean

Upholstery Lampas, Moquette, Trim

Uplift Boost, Edify, Elate, Elevation, Exalt, Hoist, Levitation, Sky

Upper class, Upper crust Aristocrat, County, Crachach, Nobility, Patrician, Posh, Sial, Top-hat, Tweedy, U

Upright(s), Uprightness Aclinic, Anend, Apeak, Apeek, Aplomb, Arrect, Erect, Goalpost, Honest, Jamb, Joanna, Merlon, Mullion, Orthograde, Perpendicular, Piano, Pilaster(s), Post, Rectitude, Roman, Splat, Stanchion, Stares, Stile, Stud, Vertical, Virtuous

Uprising Incline, Intifada, Rebellion, Revolt, Tumulus

Uproar(ious) Ballyhoo, Bedlam, Blatancy, Brouhaha, Charivari, Clamour, Collieshangie, Commotion, Cry, Din, Dirdam, Dirdum, Durdum, Emeute, Ferment, Flaw, Fracas, Furore, Garboil, Hell, Hoopla, Hubbub(oo), Hullabaloo, Hurly(-burly), Katzenjammer, Noise, Noyes, Outcry, Pandemonium, Racket, Raird, Reird, Riotous, Ruckus, Roister, Romage, Rowdedow, Rowdydow(dy), Ruction, Rumpus, Stramash, Turmoil, Whoobub

Uproot Eradicate, Evict, Outweed, Supplant, Weed

Upset(ting) Aggrieve, Alarm, Bother, Capsize, Catastrophe, Choked, Coup, Cowp, Crank, Derange, Dip, Discomboberate, Discombobulate, Discomfit, Discomfort, Discommode, Disconcert, Dismay, Disquiet, Distraught, Disturb, Dod, Eat, Fuss, Inversion, Keel, Miff, Nauseative, Offend, Overthrow, Overturn, Perturb, Pip, Pother, Purl, Rattle, Rile, Ruffle, Rumple, Sad, Seel, Shake, Sore, Spill, Tapsalteerie, Tip, Topple, Trauma, Undo

▷**Upset** may indicate an anagram; a word upside down; or 'tes'

Upshot Outcome, Result, Sequel

Upside down Inverted, Resupinate, Tapsie-teerie, Topsy-turvy

▷**Upstart** may indicate 'u'

Up to Till, Until

Up-to-date Abreast, Contemporary, Current, Mod, New-fashioned, Right-on, State-of-the-art, Swinging, Topical, Trendy

Upwards Acclivious, Aloft, Antrorse, Cabré

Urban Civic, Megalopolis, Municipal, Town

Urbane Civil, Debonair, Townly

Urchin Arab, Brat, Crinoid, Crossfish, Cystoid, Echinoidea, Echinus, Gamin, Gutty, Heart, Mudlark, Nipper, Ragamuffin,

Sand-dollar, Sea-egg, Spatangoidea, Spatangus, Street-arab, Township

Urge, Urgent Admonish, Ca, Coax, Constrain, Crying, Dire, Drive, Egg, Enjoin, Exhort, Exigent, Goad, Hard, Hie, Hoick, Hunger, Hurry, Id, Impel, Impulse, Incense, Incite, Insist(ent), Instance, Instigate, Itch, Kick, Libido, Nag, Peremptory, Persuade, Press(ing), Prod, Push, Set on, Spur, Strong, Wanderlust, Whig, Yen

▷**Urgent** may indicate 'Ur-gent', viz. Iraqi

Urinal Bog, John, Jordan, ➤ LAVATORY, Loo, Pissoir

Urinate, Urine Chamber-lye, Emiction, Enuresis, Lant, Leak, Micturition, Pee, Piddle, Piss, Slash, Stale, Strangury, Tiddle, Widdle

Urn(s) Cinerarium, Ewer, Grecian, Olla, Ossuary, Samovar, Storied, Vase

Us 's, UK, Uns, We

Usage, Use(d), Utilise Application, Apply, Avail, Boot, Consume, Custom, Deploy, Dow, ➤ EMPLOY, Ex, Exercise, Exert, Exploit, Flesh, Habit, Hand-me-down, Inured, Manner, Ply, Practice, Sarum, Spent, Sport, Tradition, Treat, Ure, Wield, With, Wont

Useful Asset, Availing, Commodity, Dow, Expedient, Invaluable

Useless Base, Bung, Cumber, Dead-wood, Dud, Empty, Futile, Gewgaw, Idle, Inane, Ineffective, Lame, Lemon, Otiose, Plug, Sculpin, Sterile, Swap, US, Vain, Void, Wet

Usher Black Rod, Chobdar, Commissionaire, Conduct(or), Doorman, Escort, Herald, Huissier, Macer, Rod, Show, Steward

Usual Common, Customary, Habit(ual), Natural, Normal, Ordinary, Rule, Solito, Typical, Wont

Usurer, Usury Gombeen, Loanshark, Moneylender, Note-shaver, Shark, Uncle

Utensil(s) Chopsticks, Colander, Cookware, Corer, Fish-kettle, Fork, Gadget, Implement, Instrument, Knife, Mandolin(e), Ricer, Skillet, Spatula, Spoon, Things, Tool, Zester

▶**Utilise** see USE

Utilitarian Benthamite, Mill, Practical, Useful

Utility Elec(tricity), Gas, Water

Utmost Best, Extreme, Farthest, Maximum

Utopia(n) Adland, Cloud-cuckoo-land, Ideal, Pantisocracy, Paradise, Perfect, Shangri-la

Utter(ance), Uttered, Utterly Absolute, Accent, Agrapha, Agraphon, Arrant, Cry, Dead, Deliver, Dictum, Dog, Downright, Ejaculate, Enunciate, Express, Extreme, Glossolalia, Issue, Judgement, Lenes, Lenis, Most, Oracle, Pass, Phonate, Pronounce, Pure, Quo(th), Rank, Rattle, Remark, Saw, ➤ SAY, Sheer, Stark, State, Syllable, Tell, Vend, Vent, Very, Voice

Vv

V Anti, Bomb, Del, Five, Nabla, See, Sign, Verb, Verse, Versus, Victor(y), Volt, Volume

Vacancy, Vacant Blank, Empty, Glassy, Hole, Hollow, Inane, Place, Space, Vacuum

Vacation Holiday, Leave, Outing, Recess, Trip, Voidance

Vaccination, Vaccine Antigen, Cure, HIB, Jenner, Sabin, Salk, Serum, Subunit

Vacuum Blank, Cleaner, Dewar, Emptiness, Magnetron, Nothing, Plenum, Thermos®, Void

Vagabond Bergie, Gadling, ➤ GYPSY, Hobo, Landlo(u)per, Rapparee, Romany, Rover, Runagate, Tramp

Vague(ness) Amorphous, Bleary, Blur, Confused, Dim, Equivocal, Hazy, Ill-headed, Indeterminate, Indistinct, Loose, Mist, Nebulous, Shadowy, Woolly-minded

▷**Vaguely** may indicate an anagram

Vain Bootless, Coxcomb, Coxcomical, Egoistic, Empty, Fruitless, ➤ FUTILE, Hollow, Idle, Proud, Strutting, Useless, Vogie

Valet Aid, Andrew, Jeames, Jeeves, Man, Passepartout, Servant, Skip-kennel

Valiant Brave, Doughty, Resolute, Stalwart, Wight

Valid(ate) Confirm, Establish, Just, Legal, Sound

Valley Clough, Comb(e), Coomb, Cwm, Dale, Dean, Defile, Dell, Den, Dene, Dingle, Dip, Ghyll, Glen, Hollow, Ravine, Ria, Rift, Silicon, Tempe, Vale

Valour Bravery, Courage, Heroism, Merit, Prowess

Valuable, Valuation, Value Appraise, Appreciate, Apprize, Assess(ment), Asset, Bargain, Calibrate, Checksum, Cherish, Cop, Cost, CIF, Equity, Esteem, Estimate, Face, Intrinsic, Limit, Market, Modulus, Nominal, Nuisance, Omnium, Ph, Place, Precious, Price, Prize, Prys, Quartile, Rarity, Rate, Rating, Regard, Respect, Salt, Sentimental, Set, Steem, Stent, Store, Surrender, Taonga, Treasure, Valuta, ► WORTH

Valve Air, Ball, Bicuspid, Bleed, Butterfly, Check, Clack, Cock, Dynatron, Flip-flop, Gate, Magnetron, Mitral, Non-return, Pentode, Petcock, Piston, Poppet, Puppet, Resnatron, Safety, Seacock, Semilunar, Shut-off, Sleeve, Sluice, Stopcock, Tap, Tetrode, Thermionic, Throttle, Thyratron, Triode, Ventil, Vibroton

Vampire Bat, Dracula, False, Ghoul, Lamia, Lilith, Pontianak

Van(guard) Advance, Box-car, Brake, Camper, Cart, Dormobile®, Forefront, Foremost, Front, Head, Kombi®, Lead, Leader(s), Lorry, Loudspeaker, Panel, Pantechnicon, Removal, Spearhead, Truck, Wagon, Ute

Vandal(ise), Vandalism Desecrate, Hooligan, Hun, Loot, Pillage, Ravage, Rough, Sab(oteur), Sack, Saracen, Skinhead, Slash, Trash

Vanish(ed) Cease, Disappear, Disperse, Dissolve, Evanesce(nt), Evaporate, Extinct, Faint(ed), Mizzle, Slope, Unbe

Vanity Amour-propre, Arrogance, Ego, Esteem, Futility, Pomp, Pretension, Pride, Self-esteem

Vaporise, Vapour Boil, Cloud, Fog, Fume, Halitus, Iodine, Miasma, Mist, Reek, Roke, ► STEAM, Steme, Water

Variable Amphoteric, Cepheid, Diverse, Fickle, Fluctuating, Inconstant, Omniform, Parametric, Protean, Twistor, Versatile

►**Variance, Variant, Variation** see VARY

►**Varied, Variety** see VARY

▷**Varied** may indicate an anagram

Variegate(d) Dappled, Flecked, Fretted, Motley, Mottle, Pied, Rainbow, Skewbald, Tissue

▷**Variety of** may indicate an anagram

Various Divers(e), Manifold, Multifarious, Several, Sundry

Varnish(ing) Arar, Bee-glue, Copal, Cowdie-gum, Dam(m)ar, Desert, Dope, Dragon's-blood, Glair, Japan, Lacquer, Lentisk,

Nail, Nibs, Resin, Shellac, Spirit, Tung-oil, Tung-tree, Vernis martin, Vernissage

Vary(ing), Variable, Variance, Variant, Variation, Varied, Variety Ablaut, Alter, Assortment, Breed, Brew, Change, Chequered, Colour, Contrapuntal, Counterpoint, Discrepancy, Diversity, Enigma, Form, Iid, Inconsistent, Line, Medley, Mix, Morph, Multifarious, Multiplicity, Mutable, Nuance, Olio, Remedy, Smorgasbord, Sort, Species, Spice, Sport, Stirps, Strain, Timeserver, Tolerance, Var, Versiform, Version, VI, Wane, Wax, X, Y, Z

Vase Bronteum, Canopus, Diota, Hydria, Jardiniere, Kalpis, Lecythus, Lekythos, Murr(h)a, Portland, Pot, Potiche, Stamnos, Urn, Vessel

Vast(ness) Big, Cosmic, Enormous, Epic, Extensive, Huge(ous), Immense, Mighty, Ocean, Prodigious

Vat Back, Barrel, Blunger, Chessel, Copper, Cowl, Cuvee, Fat, Girnel, Keir, Kier, Tank, Tub, Tun

Vault(ed), Vaulting Arch, Barrel, Cavern, Cellar, Chamber, Clear, Cross, Crypt, Cul-de-four, Cupola, Dome, Dungeon, Fan, Firmament, Fornicate, Groin, Hypogeum, Jump, Kiva, Leap(frog), Lierne, Palm, Pend, Pendentive, Pole, Rib, Safe, Sepulchre, Severy, Shade, Souterrain, Tomb, Wagon, Weem

▷**Vault** may indicate an anagram

Veer Bag, Boxhaul, Broach, Deviate, Gybe, Swerve, Tack, Turn, Wear, Yaw

Vegetable(s) Castock, Colcannon, Coulis, Crout, Custock, Flora, Greens, Inert, Legume(n), Macedoine, Mirepoix, Olitory, Plant, Pottage, Primavera, Pulse, Ratatouille, Root, Sabji, Salad, Sauce, Sauerkraut, Triffid

Vegetarian Herbivore, Meatless, Vegan, Veggie

Vegetate, Vegetator, Vegetation Alga, Flora, Greenery, Herb, Maquis, Quadrat, Scrub, Stagnate

Vehemence, Vehement(ly) Amain, Ardent, Fervid, Frenzy, Heat, Hot, Intense, Violent

Vehicle Channel, Conveyance, Landau, Machine, Means, Medium, Transporter

Veil Burk(h)a, Calyptra, Chad(d)ar, Chador, Chuddah, Chuddar, Cover, Curtain, Envelop, Hejab, Hijab, Humeral, Kalyptra,

Kiss-me, Lambrequin, Mantilla, Mist, Obscure, Purdah, Scene, Veale, Volet, Weeper, Wimple, Yashmak

Vein Artery, Basilic, Coronary, Costa, Epithermal, Fahlband, Gate, Innominate, Jugular, Ledge, Lode, Mainline, Media, Midrib, Mood, Nervure, Percurrent, Portal, Postcava, Precava, Pulmonary, Rake, Rib, Saphena, Sectorial, Stockwork, Stringer, Style, Varicose, Varix, Vena, Venule

Velocity Muzzle, Radial, Rate, Speed, Terminal, V

Veneer Facade, Gloss, Varnish

Venerate, Veneration Adore, Awe, Douleia, Dulia, Hallow, Homage, Idolise, Latria, Revere, Worship

Vengeance, Vengeful Erinyes, Reprisal, Ultion, Vindictive, Wannion, Wrack, Wreak

Venom(ous) Poison, Rancour, Spite, Toxic, Virus

Vent Aperture, Belch, Chimney, Emit, Express, Fumarole, Issue, Ostiole, Outlet, Solfatara, Spiracle, Undercast, Wreak

Ventilate, Ventilator Air, Air-brick, Air-hole, Discuss, Express, Louvre, Plenum, Shaft, Voice, Winze

Venture(d) Ante, Chance, Dare, Daur, Durst, Flutter, Foray, Handsel, Hazard, Opine, Presume, Promotion, Risk, Spec, Throw

Venue Bout, Locale, Place, Tryst, Visne

Venus Cohog, Cytherean, Hesper(us), Love, Lucifer, Morning-star, Primavera, Quahog, Rokeby, Vesper

Veracity, Veracious Accurate, Factual, Sincere, Truth(ful)

Veranda(h) Balcony, Gallery, Lanai, Patio, Porch, Sleep-out, Stoep, Stoop, Terrace

Verb(al) Active, Auxiliary, Conative, Copula, Infinitive, Intransitive, Irregular, Passive, Phrasal, Preterite, Stative, Transitive, Vb, Word-of-mouth

Verbose, Verbosity Padding, Prolix, Talkative, Wordy

Verdict Decision, Judg(e)ment, Open, Opinion, Pronouncement, Resolution, Ruling

Verge Border, Brink, ➤ EDGE, Hard shoulder, Incline, Rim

Verify Affirm, Ascertain, Check, Crosscheck, Prove, Validate

Vermin(ous) Lice, Mice, Ratty, ➤ RODENT, Scum

Vernacular Common, Dialect, Idiom, Jargon, Lingo, Native, Patois

Versatile Adaptable, All-rounder, Flexible, Handy, Protean, Resourceful

Verse(s), Versed Alcaics, Alexandrine, Amphigory, Awdl, Ballad, Beatitude, Blank, Burden, Canto, Cinquain, Comus, Dimiter, Dithyramb, Doggerel, Elegiac, Epic, Epode, Epos, Fit, Free, Gnomic, Haikai, Heroic, Hexameter, Hokku, Huitain, Hymn, Ionic, Jingle, Kyrielle, Laisse, Lyric, Macaronic, Madrigal, Meter, Mock-heroic, Neck, Nonsense, Octave, Pentameter, Poem, Poesy, Prosody, Quatrain, ➤ RHYME, Rhyme-royal, Rime, Rondeau, Rondel, Rubai(yat), Sapphic, Saturnian, Scansion, Sestina, Sixaine, Song, Stanza, Stave, Strain, Strophe, Tercet, Tetrameter, Tiercet, Tract, Triad, Trimeter, Tristich, Up, V, Vers, Versicle, Vers libre

Version Account, Authorised, Cover, Edition, Form, Paraphrase, Rede, Rendering, Rendition, Revision, Translation

Vertical Apeak, Apeek, Atrip, Erect, Lapse, Ordinate, Perpendicular, Plumb, Sheer, Standing, Stemmed, Stile, Upright

Vertigo Dinic, Dizziness, Fainting, Giddiness, Megrim, Nausea, Staggers, Whirling

Very (good, well) A1, Ae, Assai, Awfully, Bonzer, Boshta, Boshter, Dashed, Def, Ever, Extreme(ly), Fell, Frightfully, Gey, Grouse, Heap, Hellova, Helluva, Highly, Jolly, Light, Mighty, Molto, Much, OK, Opt, Precious, Precise, Purler, Real, Self same, So, Sore, Stinking, Très, Utter, V, VG, Way

Vessel Aludel, Amphora, Ampulla, Aorta, Argyle, Ark, Artery, Autoclave, Barge, Bark, Beaker, Bicker, Bin, Blood, ➤ BOAT, Bouget, Bowl, Bucket, Buss, Calabash, Canteen, Carafe, Carboy, Cask, Casserole, Cat, Cauldron, Chalice, Chatty, Coaster, Colander, Container, Copper, Corvette, Cot(t), Cowl, Craft, Crare, Cresset, Crewe, Crock, Crucible, Cruet, Cruiser, Cup, Cupel, Cuvette, Dandy, Decanter, Destroyer, D(h)ow, Dinghy, Dish, Dixie, Dogger, Dredger, Drifter, Etna, Fat, Felucca, Flagon, Flagship, Font, Frigate, Galiot, Galleass, Galleon, Galley, Galliass, Galliot, Gallipot, Goblet, Gourd, Grab, Hydrofoil, Jardinière, Jerrican, Keel, Ketch, Kettle, Laver, Longboat, Mazer, Monteith, Mortar, Noggin, Oiler, Olpe, Pan(cheon), Panchion, Pannikin, Pig, Pinnace, Pitcher, Privateer, Quart, Receptacle, Retort, Round, Saic(k), Saique, Sampan, Sconce, Scoop, She, Shell, ➤ SHIP, Shippo, Skin, Smack, Snow, Steamer, Steen, Stoop, Stoup, Tankard, Tanker, Tappit-hen, Tassie, Tazza,

Terreen, Triaconter, Troopship, Trough, Tub, Tureen, Urn, Utensil, Vas(e), Vat, Vein, Vena, Vial, Wherry, Xebec

Vest Beset, Confer, Gilet, Modesty, Semmit, Singlet, Skivvy, Spencer, Sticharion, String, Undercoat, Waistcoat

Vestibule Anteroom, Atrium, Entry, Exedra, Foyer, Hall, Lobby, Narthex, Porch, Portico, Pronaos, Tambour

Vestment Alb, Chasuble, Cotta, Dalmatic, Ephod, Fannel, Fanon, Garb, ➤ GARMENT, Mantelletta, Omophorion, Pallium, Parament, Ph(a)elonian, Pontificals, Raiment, Rational, Rochet, Rocquet, Sakkos, Sticharion, Stole, Surplice, Tunic(le)

Vet(ting), Veterinary, Vets Check, Doc(tor), Examine, Inspect, OK, Screen, Veteran, Zoiatria, Zootherapy

Veteran BL, Expert, GAR, Master, Old sweat, Old 'un, Oldster, Old-timer, Retread, Seasoned, Soldier, Stager, Stalwart, Stalworth, Vet, War-horse

▷**Veteran** may indicate 'obsolete'

Veto Ban, Debar, Negative, Pocket, Reject, Taboo, Tabu

Vex(ed) Anger, Annoy, Bother, Chagrin, Debate, Fret, Gall, Grieve, Harass, Irritate, Mortify, Pester, Rankle, Rile, Sore, Spite, Tease, Torment, Trouble

Via By, Per, Through

Viable Economic, Going, Healthy, Possible

Vibrate, Vibration(s) Atmosphere, Diadrom, Dinnle, Dirl, Flutter, Fremitus, Hotter, Jar, Judder, Oscillate, Pulse, Quake, Resonance, Seiche, Shimmy, Shudder, Thrill, Throb, Tingle, Tremble, Tremor, Trill, Twinkle, Wag, Whir(r)

Vicar Bray, Elton, Incumbent, Pastoral, Plenarty, Primrose, Rector, Rev(erend), Trimmer

Vice Clamp, Crime, Deputy, Eale, Evil, Greed, Iniquity, Instead, Jaws, Regent, Second (in command), ➤ SIN

Viceroy Khedive, Nawab, Provost, Satrap, Willingdon

Vicinity Area, Environs, Locality, Neighbourhood, Region

Victim Abel, Butt, Casualty, Dupe, Frame, Host, Lay-down, Mark, Martyr, Nebbich, Neb(b)ish, Pathic, Patsy, Prey, Quarry, Sacrifice, Scapegoat

Victor(y) Banzai, Beater, Cadmean, Captor, Champ(ion), Conqueror, Conquest, Epinicion, Epinikion, Flagship, Fool's mate, Gree, Gris, Hugo, Jai, Kobe, Landslide, Lepanto, Ludorum,

Mature, Nike, Palm, Philippi, Pyrrhic, Runaway, Scalp, Signal, Triumph, VE (day), Vee, Vic, Walkover, Win(ner)

Vie Compete, Contend, Emulate, Strive

View(er) Aim, Angle, Aspect, Belief, Bird's eye, Cineaste, Consensus, Consider, Cosmorama, Dekko, Dogma, Doxy, Endoscope, Eye, Facet, Gander, Glimpse, Grandstand, Idea, Introspect, Kaleidoscope, Landscape, Notion, Opinion, Optic®, Outlook, Pan, Panorama, Point, Private, Profile, ➤ PROSPECT, Scan, Scape, Scene(ry), See, Sight, Slant, Specular, Standpoint, Stereoscope, Synop(sis), Tenet, Thanatopsis, Theory, Veduta, Vista, Visto, Watch, Witness, Worm's eye

Viewpoint Attitude, Belvedere, Grandstand, Perspective, Sight

Vigil, Vigilant(e) Awake, Aware, Deathwatch, Eve, Lyke-wake, Wake, Wake-rife, Wary, Watch

Vigorous(ly), Vigour Athletic, Billy-o, Birr, Blooming, Con brio, Drastic, Elan, Emphatic, Energetic, Flame, Forceful, Furioso, Go, Green, Heart(y), Heterosis, Lush, Lustihood, Lusty, P, Pep, Pith, Potency, Punchy, Racy, Rank, Robust, Round, Rude, Spirit, Sprack, Sprag, Sthenic, Stingo, Strength, Strong, Thews, Tireless, Tone, Trenchant, Vegete, Vim, Vitality, Vivid, Zip

▷**Vigorously** may indicate an anagram

Vile Base, Corrupt, Depraved, Dregs, Durance, Earthly, Mean, Offensive, Scurvy, Vicious

Villa Bastide, Chalet, Dacha, House

Village Aldea, Auburn, Burg, Clachan, Dorp, Endship, Global, Gram, Greenwich, Hamlet, Kainga, Kampong, Kraal, Mir, Pueblo, Rancheria, Rancherie, Shtetl, Thorp(e), Vill, Wick

Villain(y) Baddy, Bluebeard, Bravo, Crim(inal), Crime, Dastard, Dog, Heavy, Iago, Knave, Macaire, Miscreant, Mohock, Nefarious, Ogre, Rogue, Scelerat, Scoundrel, Tearaway, Traitor

Vim Go, Vigour, Vitality, Zing

Vindicate, Vindication Absolve, Acquit, Apologia, Avenge, Clear, Compurgation, Darraign(e), Darrain(e), Darrayn, Defend, Deraign, Justify

Vindictive Hostile, Malevolent, Repay(ing), Spiteful

Vinegar Acetic, Alegar, Balsam, Eisel(l), Esile, Oxymel, Tarragon, Wine

Vintage Classic, Crack, Cru, Old, Quality

Viola, Violet African, Alto, Amethyst, Archil, Dame's, Dog, Dog's tooth, Gamba, Gentian, Gridelin, Ianthine, Indole, Ionone, Kiss-me, Mauve, Orchil, Pansy, Parma, Prater, Saintpaulia, Shrinking, Tenor

Violate, Violating, Violation Abuse, Breach, Contravene, Defile, Fract, Infraction, ➤ INFRINGE, March-treason, Outrage, Peccant, Rape, Ravish, Stuprate, Transgress, Trespass

Violence, Violent(ly) Amain, Attentat, Berserk, Brutal, Drastic, Extreme, Fierce, Flagrant, Force, Frenzied, Furious, Heady, Het, High, Hot, Mighty, Onset, Rage, Rampage, Rampant, Rough, Rude, Severe, Slap, Stormy, Ta(r)tar, Tearaway, Thuggery, Tinderbox, Vehement, Vie

➤**Violet** see VIOLA

Violin(ist), Violin-maker, Violin-shaped Alto, Amati, Cremona, Fiddle, Griddle, Guarneri(us), Guarnieri, Kit, Leader, Luthier, Nero, Paganini, Rebeck, Rote, Stradivarius

VIP Bashaw, Bigshot, Bigwig, Brass, Cheese, Cob, Effendi, Envoy, Imago, Magnate, Magnifico, Mugwump, Nabob, Nib, Nob, Pot, Snob, Someone, Swell, Tuft, Tycoon, Worthy

Virago Amazon, Battle-axe, Beldam(e), Harpy, Shrew

Virgin(al), Virginity Celibate, Chaste, Cherry, Intact, Maiden, Maidenhead, Maidenhood, May, New, Pietà, Pucel(l)age, Pucelle, Pure, Queen, Snood, Tarpeia, Vestal

Virile, Virility Energetic, Machismo, Macho, Manly, Red-blooded

Virtue, Virtuous Angelic, Assay-piece, Attribute, Cardinal, Caritas, Charity, Chastity, Continent, Dharma, Efficacy, Ethical, Excellent, Faith, Fortitude, Good, Grace, Hope, Justice, Moral(ity), Patience, Plaster-saint, Prudence, Qua, Say-piece, Temperance, Upright, Worth

Virulent Acrimonious, Deadly, Hostile, Malign, Noxious, Toxic, Vitriolic, Waspish

Viscera Bowels, Entrails, Giblets, Guts, Harigal(d)s, Haslet, Innards, Omentum, Umbles, Vitals

Viscous (liquid), Viscosity Glaireous, Gluey, Gummy, Slab, Sticky, Stoke, Tacky, Tar, Thick

Visible Clear, Conspicuous, Evident, Explicit, Obvious

Vision(ary) Aery, Aisling, Apparition, Bourignian, Double, Dream(er), Emmetropia, Fancy, Idealist, Image, Kef,

Moonshine, Mouse-sight, Mystic, Ocular, Phantasm(a), Phantom, Pholism, Photopia, Romantic, Seeing, Seer, Sight, Stereo, Tunnel, Twenty-twenty

Visit(or) Affliction, Alien, Caller, ET, Event, First-foot, Guest, Habitue, Haunt, Kursaal, See, Sightseer, Stranger, Take

Visor, Vizor Eyeshade, Mesail, Mezail, Umbrel, Umbr(i)ere, Umbril, Vent(ayle)

Vital(ity) Central, Critical, Crucial, Energy, Esprit, Essential, Existent, Foison, Gusto, Indispensable, Key, Kick, Life-blood, Linchpin, Lung, Mites, Momentous, Oomph, Organ, Pizzazz, Salvation, Sap, Viable, Vigour, Zing, Zoetic

Vitriol(ic) Acid, Acrimonious, Biting, Caustic, Mordant

Vituperate Abuse, Berate, Castigate, Censure, Defame, Inveigh, Lash, Rail, Scold

Vivid Bright, Brilliant, Dramatic, Eidectic, Fresh, Graphic, Keen, Live, Pictorial, Picturesque, Sharp, Violent

▶ **Vizor** see VISOR

Vocabulary Idiolect, Idioticon, Jargon, (Kata)kana, Lexicon, Lexis, Meta-language, Nomenclator, Wordbook

Vocation Call, Métier, Mission, Priesthood, Profession, Shop

Vogue Chic, Day, ▶ FASHION, Mode, Rage, Style, Ton

Voice(d) Active, Air, Alto, Ancestral, Contralto, Countertenor, Edh, Emit, Eth, Express, Falsetto, Glottis, Harp, Opinion, Passive, Phonic, Pipe, Presa, Quill, Say, Sonant, Soprano, Speak, Spinto, Sprechstimme, Steven, Syrinx, Tais(c)h, Tenor, Throat, Tone, ▶ TONGUE, Treble, Utter

Voiceless Aphonia, Aphony, Dumb, Edh, Eth, Mute, Silent, Tacit

Void Abyss, Annul, Belch, Defeasance, Defecate, Diriment, Empty, Evacuate, Gap, Hollow, Inane, Invalid, Irritate, Lapse, Nullify, Quash, Space, Vacuum

Volatile Explosive, Latin, Live(ly), Mercurial, Temperamental, Terpene

Volcanic, Volcano Aa, Agglomerate, Amygdale, Andesite, Cone, Conic, Fumarole, Ice, Idocrase, Igneous, Ignimbrite, Mofette, Mud, Obsidian, Plinian, Pumice, Salse, Soffioni, Solfatara, Trass, Tuff

Volley Barrage, Boom, Broadside, Platoon, Salvo, Tirade, Tire

Volume Band, Barrel, Book, Bushel, Capacity, CC, Code(x), Content, Cubage, Gallon, Hin, Loudness, Mass, Ml, Omnibus, Peck, Pint, Quart, Quart(o), Roll, Roul(e), Size, Space, Stere, Tome, Vol

Voluntary, Volunteer Enlist, Fencible, Free, Honorary, Offer, Postlude, Reformado, Spontaneous, Tender, Tennessee, Terrier, TN, Ultroneous, Yeoman

Voluptuary, Voluptuous Carnal, Hedonist, Luscious, Sensual, Sensuous, Sybarite

Vomit(ing) Barf, Boak, Boke, Cascade, Cat, Chunder, Disgorge, Egist, Egurgitate, Emesis, Honk, Keck, Posset, Puke, Ralph, Retch, Rolf, Spew, Upchuck

Voracious, Voracity Bulimia, Edacity, Gluttony, Greed, Ravenous, Serrasalmo

Vote(r), Votes, Voting Aye, Ballot, Block, Card, Casting, Choose, Colonist, Coopt, Cross, Division, Donkey, Fag(g)ot, Floating, Franchise, Informal, Nay, No, Opt, People, Placet, Plebiscite, Plump, Poll, Postal, PR, Referendum, Return, Scrutiny, Side, Straw(-poll), Suffrage, Swinging, Tactical, Theta, Ticket, Transferable, Voice, X, Yea, Yes

Vouch(er), Vouchsafe Accredit, Assure, Attest, Chit, Coupon, Endorse, Gift, Guarantee, Luncheon, Meal-ticket, Receipt, Ticket, Token, Warrant

Vow Behight, Behot(e), Earnest, Ex voto, Hecht, Hest, Nuncupate, ► OATH, Pledge, Plight, Promise, Swear, Troth

Vowel(s) Ablaut, Anaptyxis, Aphesis, Breve, Cardinal, Diphthong, Indeterminate, Monophthong, S(c)hwa, Seg(h)ol, Svarabhakti, Triphthong

Voyage(r) Anson, Course, Cruise, Launch, Passage, Peregrinate, Sinbad, Travel

Vulture Aasvogel, Bird, Buzzard, California (condor), Condor, Culture, Falcon, Gallinazo, Gier, Griffon, Gripe, Grype, Lammergeier, Lammergeyer, Ossifrage, Predator, Turkey, Urubu, Zopilote

Ww

Wad(ding) Batting, Lump, Pad, Pledget, Roll, Swab, Wodge

Wade(r), Wading Antigropelo(e)s, Curlew, Dikkop, Egret, Flamingo, Gallae, Grallatorial, Greenshank, Heron, Ibis, Jacksnipe, Limpkin, Paddle, Phalarope, Plodge, Sarus, Seriema, Shoebill, Splodge, Stilt(bird), Terek, Virginia

Wafer Biscuit, Cracker, Crisp, Gaufer, Gaufre, Gofer, Gopher, Host, Papad, Seal

Waffle Adlib, Blather, Equivocate, Gas, Gaufer, Gaufre, Gofer, Gopher, Hedge, Poppycock, Prate, Rabbit

Wag(gish), Waggle Arch, Card, Comedian, Joker, Lick, Nod, Rogue, Shake, Sway, Wit(snapper), Wobble

Wage(s) Ante, Fee, Hire, Living, Meed, Pay, Practise, Prosecute, Salary, Screw

Wage-earner Breadwinner, Employee, Proletariat(e)

Wager Back, ➤ BET, Gamble, Lay, Pascal's, Stake, Wed

Wagon(er) Ar(a)ba, Aroba, Bootes, Boxcar, Brake, Buckboard, Buggy, Caisson, Carriage, Cart, Cattle truck, Chuck, Cocopan, Conestoga, Corf, Covered, Dray, Flatcar, Fourgon, Gambo, Hopper, Hutch, Low-loader, Mammy, Paddy, Palabra, Patrol, Plaustral, Rave, Reefer, Rubberneck, Shandry, Station, Tartana, Telega, Tender, Trap, Trekker, Truck, Van, Wain

Wail(er) Banshee, Bawl, Blubber, Howl, Keen, Lament, Moan, Skirl, Threnody, Threnos, Ululate, Vagitus, Wah-wah, Yammer

Waist(band) Belt, Cummerbund, Girdlestead, Hour-glass, Middle, Midship, Obi, Sash, Shash, Wasp, Zoster

Waistcoat Gilet, Jerkin, Lorica, MB, Sayon, Vest, Weskit

Wait(er) Abid(e), Ambush, Bide, Butler, Buttle, Commis, Dally, Delay, Expect, Flunkey, Frist, Garçon, Hesitate, Hover, Interval, Khidmutgar, Linger, Lurch, Maitre d', Maitre d'hôtel, Omnibus, Pannier, Pause, Remain, Serve(r), Sommelier, Stay, Steward, Suspense, Taihoa, Tarry, Tend(ance), Tray, Won

Waitress Hebe, Miss, Mousme(e), Nippy, Server

Waive Abandon, Defer, Overlook, Postpone, Relinquish, Renounce

Wake(n) Abrade, Abraid, Abray, Aftermath, Alert, Animate, Arouse, Astern, Deathwatch, Excite, Hereward, Keen, Prod, Rear, ➤ ROUSE, Train, Wash

Walk(er), Walking, Walkabout, Walkway Alameda, Alley, Alure, Amble, Arcade, Birdcage, Cloister, Clump, Constitutional, Dander, Esplanade, EVA, Gait, Gallery, Ghost, Go, Gradient, Hike, Hump, Lambeth, Leg, Lumber, Mall, Mince, Mosey, Pace, Pad, Pasear, Paseo, Passage, Path, Ped, Perambulate, Pergola, Prance, Prom(enade), Rack, Ramble, Rampart, Sashay, Shamble, Sidle, Space, Stalk, Step, Stroll, Strut, Stump, Terrace, Toddle, Tramp, Trash, Travolator, Tread, Trog, Trudge, Turn

Wall Bail, Bailey, Barrier, Berlin, Berm, Cavity, Chinese, Curtain, Dado, Dam, Dike, Dry-stone, Fail-dike, Gable, Great, Hadrian's, Hanging, Head, Immure, Parapet, Parpane, Parpen(d), Parpent, Partition, Party, Perpend, Perpent, Retaining, Revet(ment), Roman, Roughcast, Septum, Side, Street, Tariff, Wa', Wailing

Wallaby Brusher, Dama, Kangaroo, Pademelon, Pad(d)ymelon, Quokka, Tammar

Wall-covering Anaglypta®, Arras, Burlap, Lincrusta, Paper, Tapestry, Tapet

Wallet Billfold, Case, Notecase, Pochette, Purse, Scrip

Wallop Bash, Baste, Batter, Beat, Biff, Clout, Cob, ➤ HIT, Lam, Lounder, Polt, Pound, Slog, Strap, Swinge, Tan, Tat, Trounce

Wallow(ing) Bask, Flounder, Luxuriate, Revel, Roll, Splash, Swelter, Tolter, Volutation, Welter

Walrus Morse, Moustache, Pinniped, Rosmarine, Sea-horse, Tash

Wan Pale, Pallid, Pasty, Sanguine, Sorry

Wander(er), Wandering Bedouin, Berber, Bum, Caird, Delirious, Deviate, Digress, Drift, Errant, Estray, Excursive, Expatiate, Gad(about), Grope, Hobo, Jew, Landloper, Maunder, Meander, Mill, Moon, Nomad(e), Odysseus, Peregrine, Peripatetic, Ramble, Range, Romany, Rove, Rove, Stooge, Straggle, Stray, Stroam, Stroll, Swan, Ta(i)ver, Tramp, Troll, Vagabond, Vagrant, Vague, Waif, Wend, Wheel, Wilder

▷**Wandering** may indicate an anagram

Want(ing), Wants Absence, Conative, Covet, Crave, Dearth, Defect, Deficient, Derth, Desiderata, ➤ DESIRE, Destitution,

Envy, Hardship, Indigent, Itch, Lack, Long, Mental, Need, Penury, Require, Scarceness, Scarcity, Shortfall, Shy, Void, Wish, Yen

Wanton(ness) Bona-roba, Cadgy, Chamber, Cocotte, Deliberate, Demirep, Filly, Flirt-gill, Gammerstang, Giglet, Giglot, Gillflirt, Hussy, Jay, Jezebel, Jillflirt, Lewd, Licentious, Loose, Nice, Protervity, Roué, Slut, Smicker, Sportive, Sybarite, Toyish, Twigger, Unchaste, Wayward

War(fare) Ares, Armageddon, Arms, Attrition, Bate, Battle, Biological, Chemical, Civil, Clash, Cod, Cold, Combat, Conflict, Crimean, Crusade, Emergency, Feud, ▶ FIGHT, Flame, Food, Fray, Germ, Guer(r)illa, Gulf, Hostilities, Hot, Hundred Years', Internecine, Jenkin's Ear, Jihad, Mars, Mexican, Napoleonic, Opium, Peloponnesian, Peninsular, Price, Psychological, Punic, Roses, Seven Years', Six Day, Star, Sword, Trench, Vietnam, World

Warble(r) Carol, Chiff-chaff, Chirl, Fauvette, Peggy, Rel(l)ish, Trill, Vibrate, Yodel, Yodle

Ward (off) Artemus, Averruncate, Care, Casual, Charge, Defend, District, Fend, Guard, Maternity, Nightingale, Oppose, Parry, Protégé, Pupil, Soc, Soken, Vintry, Wear, Weir

Warden Caretaker, Concierge, Constable, Curator, Custodian, Game, Guardian, Keeper, Meter maid, Ranger, Septimus, Spooner, Steward, Traffic

Ware(s) Arretine, Beware, Biscuit, Cameo, Canton, China, Etruria, Faience, Goods, Lustre, Merchandise, Palissy, Samian, Shippo, Truck

Warehouse Data, Depository, Entrepôt, Freight-shed, Go-down, Hong, Store

▶**Warfare** see WAR

Wariness, Wary Ca'canny, Cagey, Careful, Cautel, Caution, Chary, Discreet, Distrust, Guarded, Leery, Mealy-mouthed, Prudent, Sceptical, Vigilant

Warlike Battailous, Bellicose, Gung-ho, Lachlan, Martial, Militant

Warm(er), Warming, Warmth Abask, Admonish, Air, Ardour, Balmy, British, Calefacient, Calid(ity), Chambré, Cordial, Empressement, Enchafe, Fervour, Foment, Genial, Global, Glow, ▶ HEAT, Hot, Incalescent, Kang, Lew, Logic, Loving, Muff, Muggy, Mull, Tepid, Thermal, Toast, Toasty

Warn(ing) Admonish, Alarum, Alert, Amber, Apprise, Beacon, Bleep, Buoy, Caution, Caveat, Cone, Counsel, Document, Early, En garde, Example, Fore, Foretoken, Gardyloo, Garnishment, Harbinger, Heads up, Hoot, Horn, Klaxon, Larum, Lesson, Light, Maroon, Nix, Nota bene, Notice, Omen, Pi-jaw, Premonitory, Portent, Presage, Signal, Tattler, Threat, Tip-off, Token

Warp(ed) Bias, Buckle, Cast, Contort, Distort, Kam, Kedge, Pandation, Time, Twist, Weft

▷**Warped** may indicate an anagram

Warrant Able, Authorise, Caption, Certificate, Detainer, Distress, Guarantee, Justify, Mittimus, Permit, Precept, Royal, Search, Sepad, Swear, Transire, Vouch, Warn

Warrior Achilles, Agamemnon, Ajax, Amazon, Anzac, Brave, Crusader, Eorl, Fighter, Geronimo, Impi, Myrmidon, Nestor, Samurai, Soldier, Tatar, Unknown, Warhorse, Zulu

Warship Battleship, Castle, Cog, Corvette, Cruiser, Destroyer, Drake, Dromon(d), Invincible, Man-o-war, Mine-layer, Monitor, Privateer, Ram

▶**Wary** see WARINESS

Wash(ed), Washer, Washing, Wash out Ablution, Affusion, Alluvion, Bath, Bay(e), Bidet, Bur(r), Calcimine, Circlip, Clean(se), Cradle, D, Dashwheel, Dele(te), Dip, Edulcorate, Elute, Enema, Fen, Flush, Freshen, Gargle, Grommet, Grummet, Irrigate, Kalsomine, Lap, ➤ LAUNDER, Lave, Leather, Lip, Lotion, Marsh, Maundy, Mop, Nipter, Pan, Pigswill, Poss, Purify, Rinse, Scrub, Shampoo, Shim, Sind, Sloosh, Sluice, Soogee, Soojee, Soojey, Squeegie, Sujee, Swab, Synd, Tie, Twin tub, Tye, Wake

Wasp(ish) Bembex, Bink, Bite, Chalcid, Cuckoo-fly, Cynipidae, Cynips, Digger, Fig, Fretful, Gall(-fly), Hornet, Horntail, Hoverfly, Irritable, Marabunta, Mason, Miffy, Muddauber, Paper, Peevish, Pompilid, Potter, Seed, Solitary, Spider, Vespa, Yellow jacket

Wastage, Waste(d), Wasting, Wasteland Atrophy, Blue, Cesspit, Cirrhosis, Consume, Crud, Decay, Desert, Detritus, Devastate, Dilapidate, Dissipate, Dross, Dung, Dwindle, Dwine, Dystrophy, Effluent, Egesta, Emaciate, Erode, Exhaust, Expend, Flue, Fritter, Garbage, Gash, Gob, Gunge, Haggard, Havoc, Hazardous, Knub, Lavish, Loose, Lose, Loss, Misspent, Moor, Muir, Mungo, Nub, Nuclear, Offal, Ordure, Pellagra, Pine, Prodigalise, Radioactive, Ravage, Red tape,

➤ REFUSE, Rubble, Ruderal, Scissel, Scoria, Scrap, Sewage, Slag, Slurry, Spend, Spill, Spoil(age), Squander, Sullage, Tailing, Thin, Ureal, Urine, Vast, Wear, Wilderness

▷**Wasted** may indicate an anagram

Watch(er) Analog(ue), Argus, Await, Bark, Bird-dog, Black, Clock, Coastguard, Digital, Dog, Espy, Fob, Gregory, Guard, Half-hunter, Huer, Hunter, Lo, Look, Morning, Nark, Neighbourhood, Night, Note, Observe, Patrol, Posse, Quartz, Regard, Repeater, Rolex®, Scout, Sentinel, Sentry, Shadow, Spectate, Spotter, Stemwinder, Surveillance, Tend, Ticker, Timepiece, Timer, Tompion, Tout, Turnip, Vedette, ➤ VIGIL, Voyeur, Wait, Wake

Watchman Bellman, Charley, Charlie, Chok(e)y, Cho(w)kidar, Guard, Sentinel, Sentry, Speculator, Tompion, Viewer

Watch-tower Atalaya, Barbican, Beacon, Mirador, Sentry-go

Water(ed), Waters, Watery Adam's ale, Apollinaris, Aq(ua), Aquatic, Aqueous, Barley, Bayou, Bedabble, Broads, Brook, Burn, Canal, Cancer, Chuck, Dew, Dill, Dilute, Dribble, Eau, Ebb, Element, Evian®, Flood, Ford, Gripe, Ground, Hard, Heavy, Holy, Irrigate, Javel(le), Lagoon, Lagune, Lake, Lavender, Light, Lode, Lough, Lymph, Mineral, Moiré, Nappe, Oasis®, Oedema, Pawnee, Pee, Perrier®, Pisces, Polly, Rain, Rate, Rip, Riverine, Rose, Runny, Scorpio, Sea, Seltzer, Sera, Serous, Serum, Shower, Soda, Sodden, Soft, Sound, Souse, Stream, Surface, Territorial, Thin, Toilet, Tonic, Urine, Vichy, Wash(y), Weak, Wee, Whey, White, Wishy-washy

Water-carrier Aqueduct, Bheestie, Bheesty, Bhistee, Bhisti, Bucket, Carafe, Chatty, Furphy, Hose, Hydra, Kirbeh, Pail, Pitcher

Water-course Arroyo, Billabong, Canal, Ditch, Dyke, Falaj, Furrow, Gutter, Khor, Lead, Nala, Nulla, Rean, Rhine, Shott, Spruit, Wadi

Waterfall Angel (Falls), Cataract, Churchill, Chute, Cuquenan, Force, Foss, Kabiwa, Kile, Lasher, Lin(n), Mardel, Mtarazi, Niagara, Overfall, Rapid, Sault, Sutherland, Takakkaw, Tugela, Yosemite

Waterman Aquarius, Bargee, Ferryman, Oarsman

Water-plant Alisma, Aquatic, Cress, Crowfoot, Elodea, Gulfweed, Lace-leaf, Lattice-leaf, Nelumbo, Nenuphar, Nuphar,

Ouvirandra, Pontederia, Quillwort, Reate, Sea-mat, Sedge, Seg, Stratiotes, Urtricularia, Vallisneria

Waterproof, Water-tight Caisson, Caulk, Cofferdam, Dampcourse, Dubbin(g), Groundsheet, Loden, Mac, Mino, Oilers, Oilskin, Pay, Seaworthy, Stank, Sta(u)nch, Waders

Water-sprite Kelpie, Kelpy, Nix(ie), Nixy, Tangie, Undine, Water-nymph

Waterway Aqueduct, Canal, Channel, Culvert, Ditch, Igarapé, Illinois, Intracoastal, Lode, River, Sound, Straight, Suez

Water-wheel Noria, Pelton, Sakia, Saki(y)eh

Wave(d), Waves, Wavy Alpha, Beachcomber, Beam, Beck, Beta, Billow, Bore, Brain, Brandish, Breaker, Carrier, Comber, Complex, Crest, Crime, Crimp, Delta, Dumper, Finger, Flap, Flaunt, Float, Flote, Gesticulate, Gravity, Groundswell, Heat, Internal, Lee, Long, Marcel, Medium, Mexican, New, Perm(anent), Plunger, Primary, Radar, Radiation, Radio, Ripple, Roller, Sea, Secondary, Seiche, Seismic, Shock, Short, Sine, Sky, Snaky, Sound, Spiller, Squiggle, Standing, Stationary, Stream, Surf, Surge, Sway, Tabby, Theta, Tidal, Train, Transverse, Tsunami, Undate, Unde, Undulate, Waffle, Waft, Wag, Waive, Wash, Waw, Whitecap, White-horse, Wigwag

▷**Wave(s)** may indicate an anagram

Waver(ing) Dither, Falter, Flag, Gutter, Hesitate, Oscillate, Stagger, Sway, Swither, Teeter, Vacillate, Waffle, Wet, Wow

Wax(ed), Waxing, Waxy Ambergris, Appal, Bate, Cere, Ceresin, Cerumen, Cobbler's, Cutin, Effuse, Enseam, Gr(e)aves, Grow, Heelball, Honeycomb, Increase, Increscent, Inseam, Ire, Japan, Kiss, Livid, Lost, Lyrical, Mineral, Mummy, Paraffin, Pela, Petroleum, Rage, Seal, Spermaceti, Tallow, Tantrum, Temper, Vegetable, Yielding

Way(s), Wayside Access, Agate, Appian, Autobahn, Avenue, Borstal(l), Bypass, Companion, Course, Crescent, Direction, Door, Draw, E, Each, Entrance, Family, Fashion, Flaminian, Foss(e), Gate, Habit, Hatch, Hedge, High, Hither, How, Lane, Manner, Means, Method, Milky, Mo, Mode, N, Pass, Path, Permanent, Pilgrim's, Procedure, Railroad, Regimen, Ridge, ➤ ROAD, Route, S, Sallypost, St(reet), Style, System, Thoroughfare, Thus, Trace, Trail, Troade, Turnpike, Underpass, Untrodden, Via, W, Wise

Way-out Advanced, Bizarre, Egress, Esoteric, Exit, Exotic, Extreme, Offbeat, Trendy

Wayward Capricious, Disobedient, Errant, Erratic, Loup-the-dyke, Obstreperous, Perverse, Stray, Unruly, Wilful

Weak(er), Weaken(ing), Weakest, Weakness Achilles' heel, Appal, Arsis, Blot, Brittle, Chink, Cripple(d), Debile, Debilitate, Decrease, Delay, Dilute, Disable, Effete, Emasculate, Enervate, Enfeeble, Entender, Fade, Faible, Failing, Faint, Fatigue, Feeble, Fissile, Flag, Flaw, Flimsy, Foible, Fragile, Frailty, Give, Gone, Ham, Helpless, Honeycomb, Impair, Impotence, Infirm, Knock-kneed, Lassitude, Low, Milk and water, Namby-pamby, Pale, Pall, Paresis, Puny, Push-over, Pusillanimous, Reduce, Simp, Slack, Thesis, Thin, Tottery, Unable, Underdog, Undermine, Unnerve, Unstable, Vapid, Vessel, Vulnerability, W, Water(y), Wish(y)-wash(y)

Wealth(y) Abundance, Affluence, Bullion, Croesus, Fat-cat, Fortune, Golconda, Jet-set, Klondike, Klondyke, Loaded, Lolly, Mammon, Means, Mine, Mint, Moneyed, Nabob, Opulence, Ore, Pelf, Plutocrat, Reich, Rich, Ritzy, Solid, Substance, Treasure, Untold, Well-heeled, Well-off, Well-to-do

Weapon Arm, Arsenal, Hoplology, Missile, Munition, Sidearm

Wear(ing), Wear Out Abate, Ablative, Abrade, Attrition, Chafe, Corrade, Corrode, Deteriorate, Detrition, Efface, Erode, Erosion, Fashion, For(e)spend, Fray, Frazzle, Fret, Garb, Impair, In, Pack, Scuff, Sport, Stand, Tedy

▷ **Wear** may indicate the NE (eg Sunderland)

Weariness, Wearisome, Weary Beat, Bejade, Bore, Cloy, Dog-tired, Ennui, Ennuyé, Exhaust, Fag, Fatigate, Fatigue, Harass, Hech, Irk, Jade, Lacklustre, Lassitude, Pall, Puny, Ramfeezle, Sleepy, Spent, Tire, Trash, Try, Tucker, Wabbit, Worn

Weasel Beech-marten, Cane, Delundung, Ermine, Ferret, Glutton, Grison, Kolinsky, Marten, Mink, Mustela, Pekan, Polecat, Stoat, Taira, Tayra, Vermin, Whitrick, Whitterick, Whit(t)ret, Wolverine, Woodshock

Weather, Weather forecast Atmosphere, Cyclone, Discolour, Ecoclimate, Elements, Endure, Met, Sky, Stand, Survive, Tiros, Undergo, Withstand

Weave(r), Weaves, Weaving Arachne, Basket, Cane, Complect, Entwine, Finch, Heald, Heddle, Interlace, Lace, Lease,

Leno, Lion, Loom, Marner, Plain, Raddle, Ripstop, Rya, Shuttle, Sparrow, Spider, Splice, Taha, Texture, Throstle, Tissue, Tweel, Twill, Twine, Wabster, Waggle, Webster, Zigzag

Web(bing), Web-footed, Web-site Aranea, Food, Fourchette, Infomediary, Internet, Mat, Maze, Mesh(work), Offset, Palama, Palmate, Palmiped, Patagium, Pinnatiped, Skein, Snare, Tela, Tissue, Toil, Totipalmate, World Wide

Wed(ding), Wedlock Alliance, Bet, Diamond, Espousal, Golden, Hymen, Join, Knobstick, Link, Marriage, Marry, Mate, Meng(e), Me(i)nt, Meynt, Ming, Nuptials, Pair, Penny, Ruby, Shotgun, Silver, Spousal, ➤ UNION, Unite, White, Y

Wedge Chock, Chunk, Cleat, Cotter, Cuneal, Doorstop, Feather, Forelock, Gagger, Gib, Jack, Jam, Key, Niblick, Prop, Quoin, Scotch, Shim, Sphenic, Stick, Trig, Vomerine, Whipstock

Weed(y) Cigar(ette), Cissy, Colonist, Fag, Hoe, Marijuana, Scal(l)awag, Scallywag, Tobacco

Weedkiller Arsenic, Atrazine, Dalapon, Diquat, Diuron, Herbicide, Paraquat®, Simazine

Week(ly) Hebdomadary, Holy, Orientation, Ouk, Oulk, Passion, Periodical, Sennight

Weep(er), Weepy, Wept Bawl, Blubber, Cry, Grat, Greet, Lachrymose, Lament, Loser, Maudlin, Niobe, Ooze, Pipe, Sob, Wail

Weigh(ing), Weigh down, Weight(y) All-up, Arroba, Artal, As, Atomic, Avoirdupois, Balance, Bantam, Bob, Bulk, Burden, Candy, Cantar, Carat, Catty, Cental, Clove, Consider, Count, Counterpoise, Cruiser, Ct, Dead, Decagram(me), Deliberate, Drail, Dumbbell, Emphasis, Equivalent, Feather, Fother, G, Gerah, Grain, Gram, Heft, Importance, Impost, Incumbent, Journey, Kandy, Kantar, Kerb, Khat, Kin, Kip, Last, Libra, Load, Mark, Massive, Maund, Metage, Mina, Mna, Molecular, Moment, Mouse, Nail, Obol, Öke, Onerous, Oppress, Ounce, Overpoise, Oz, Pease, Perpend, Plummet, Poise, Pood, Pound, Preponderance, Prey, Pud, Pudge, Quintal, Rod, Rotolo, Scruple, Seer, Sinker, Sit, Slang, Stone, Stress, Talent, Tare, Throw, Tical, Tod, Tola, Ton(nage), Tonne, Tophamper, Troy, Unce, Unmoor, Welter, Wey, Wt

Weir Cauld, Dam, Garth, Kiddle, Kidel, Lasher, Pen, Watergate

Weird Bizarre, Curious, Dree, Eerie, Eery, Eldritch, Kookie, Offbeat, Spectral, Strange, Supernatural, Taisch, Uncanny, Zany

Welch, Welsh Abscond, Cheat, Default, Embezzle, Levant, Rat, Reneg(ue), Renig, Skedaddle, Weasel

Welcome, Welcoming Aloha, Ave, Bel-accoyle, Ciao, Embrace, Entertain, Glad-hand, Greet, Haeremai, Halse, Hallo, Hello, Hospitable, How, Hullo, Receive, Reception, Salute

Welfare Advantage, Alms, Benison, Ha(y)le, Heal, Health, Sarvodaya, Weal

Well (done) Artesian, Atweel, Aweel, Bien, Bore(hole), Bravo, Cenote, Development, Dry hole, Euge, Famously, Fine, Fit, Gasser, Good, Gosh, Gusher, Hale, ➤ HEALTHY, Hot, Inkpot, Law, My, Namma hole, Odso, Oh, Oil, Phreatic, Potential, So, Source, Spa, Spring, Sump, Surge, Um, Upflow, Zemzem

Well-being Atweel, Bien-être, Comfort, Euphoria, Euphory, Good, Health, Welfare

Well-known Famous, Illustrious, Notorious, Notour, Prominent

Well-off Affluent, Far, Rich, Wealthy

▶**Welsh** see WELCH

Welshman Briton, Brittonic, Brython, Cake, Cambrian, Celtic, Cog, Cym(ric), Cymry, Dai, Emlyn, Evan, Fluellen, Gareth, Harp, Idris, Ifor, Keltic, P-Celtic, P-Keltic, Rabbit, Rarebit, Rees, Rhys, Sion, Taffy, Tudor, W

West(ern), Westerly Ang mo, Favonian, Hesperian, Mae, Movie, Oater, Occidental, Ponent, Spaghetti, Sunset, W, Wild

▷**West end** may indicate 't' or 'W1'

Wet(ting) Bedabble, Bedraggled, Clammy, Daggle, Damp, Dank, Dew, Dip, Douse, Dowse, Drench, Drip(ping), Drook, Drouk, Embrue, Enuresis, Feeble, Humect, Humid, Hyetal, Imbue, Irrigate, Madefy, Madid, Marshy, Moil, Moist(en), Molly, Namby-pamby, Pee, Rainy, Ret(t), Roral, Roric, Runny, Saturate, Shower, Simp(leton), Sipe, Sluice, ➤ SOAK, Sodden, Sopping, Sour, Steep, Urinate, Wat, Wee, Wimpy, Wringing

Whale(meat), Whaling Baleen, Beaked, Beluga, Blower, Blubber, Blue, Bottlehead, Bottlenose, Bowhead, Cachalot, Calf, Cetacea(n), Cete, Dolphin, Fall, Fin(back), Finner, Gam, Glutton, Grampus, Greenland, Grey, Humpback, Killer, Kreng, Leviathan, Manatee, Minke, Monodon, Mysticeti, Paste, Pilot, Pod, Porpoise, Right, Rorqual, School, Scrag, Sei, Sperm, Thrasher, Toothed, Toothless, White

▷**Whale** may indicate an anagram

What Anan, Eh, How, Pardon, Que, Siccan, That, Which

Whatnot, What's-its-name Dinges, Dingus, Doings, Etagère, Gismo, Jiggamaree, Jiggumbob, Thingamy, Thingumajig, Thingumbob, Thingummy, Timenoguy

Wheat Amelcorn, Blé, Bulg(h)ur, Cracked, Durum, Einkorn, Emmer, Federation, Fromenty, Frumenty, Furme(n)ty, Furmity, Grain, Hard, Mummy, Rivet, Sarrasin, Sarrazin, Seiten, Semolina, Sharps, Spelt, Triticum

Wheedle Banter, Barney, Blandish, Cajole, Coax, Cog, Cuiter, Cuittle, Flatter, Inveigle, Tweedle, Whilly(whaw)

Wheel(er) Balance, Bedel, Bevel, Bogy, Buff(ing), Caster, Castor, Catherine, Circle, Cistern, Crown, Cycle, Daisy, Disc, Driving, Emery, Escape, Felloe, Felly, Ferris, Gear, Helm, Hurl, Idle(r), Kick, Nabob, Nose, Paddle, Pedal, Pelton, Perambulator, Pinion, Pivot, Planet, Potter's, Prayer, Pulley, Ratchet, Roll, Rotate, Roulette, Rowel, Sheave, Spinning, Sprocket, Steering, Trindle, Trolley, Trundle, ➤ TURN, Water, Wire, Worm

Wheelwright Spokesman

Wheeze Asthma, Jape, Joke, Pant, Ploy, Rale, Reak, Reik, Rhonchus, Ruse, Stridor, Trick, Whaisle, Whaizle

Where(abouts) Location, Neighbourhood, Place, Site, Vicinity, Whaur, Whither

Wherewithal Finance, Means, Money, Needful, Resources

Whet(stone) Coticular, Excite, Hone, Sharpen, Stimulate

Whether Conditional, If

Which(ever), Which is Anyway, As, QE, Whatna, Whilk, Who

While Although, As, Interim, Since, Space, Span, Though, Throw, Time, When, Whenas, Yet

Whim(s), Whimsical, Whimsy Bizarre, Caprice, Conceit, Crotchet, Fad, Fancy, Fey, Flisk, Kicksy-wicksy, Kink, Notion, Quaint, Quirk, Tick, Toy, Vagary

Whine, Whinge Cant, Carp, Complain, Cry, Grumble, Kvetch, Mewl, Moan, Peenge, Pule, Snivel, Whimper, Yammer

Whip(ped), Whip out, Whipping Beat, Braid, Bullwhip, Cat, Chastise, Chief, Colt, Crop, Drive, Flagellate, Firk, Flay, Hide, Jambok, Knout, Larrup, ➤ LASH, Limber, Quirt, Rawhide,

Riem, Scourge, Sjambok, Slash, Steal, Swinge, Switch, Taw, Thong, Three-line, Trounce, Welt, Whap

Whirl(ing) Circumgyrate, Dervish, Eddy, Gyrate, ➤ IN A WHIRL, Pivot, Reel, Spin, Swing, Swirl, Vortex, Vortical, Whirry

Whirlpool Eddy, Gulf, Gurge, Maelstrom, Moulin, Swelchie, Vorago, Vortex, Weel, Wiel

Whirlwind Cyclone, Dust devil, Eddy, Tornado, Tourbillion, Typho(o)n, Vortex, Willy-willy

Whisker(s) Beard, Beater, Burnsides, Cat's, Dundreary, Hackle, Hair, Moustache, Mutton-chop, Samuel, Side(-boards), Side-burns, Vibrissa

Whisk(e)y Alcohol, Bond, Bourbon, Canadian, Cape Smoke, Corn, Creature, Fife, Fire-water, Hoo(t)ch, Irish, Malt, Moonshine, Morning, Mountain dew, Nip, Peat-reek, Pot(h)een, Red eye, Rye, Scotch, Usquebaugh

▷ **Whisky** may indicate an anagram

Whisper Breath(e), Bur(r), Hark, Hint, Innuendo, Murmur, Rumour, Round, Rustle, Sigh, Stage, Susurrus, Tittle, Undertone

Whistle(r) Blow, Calliope, Feedback, Hiss, Marmot, Penny, Ping, Pipe, Ref, Siffle(ur), Sowf(f), Sowth, Steam, Stop, Stridor, Swab(ber), Tin, Toot, Tweedle, Tweet, Warbler, Wheeple, Wheugh, Whew, Wolf

White(n), Whitener, Whiteness Agene, Agenise, Alabaster, Albedo, Albescent, Albino, Albumen, Argent, Ashen, Blameless, Blanch, Blanco, Bleach, Buckra, Cam, Calm, Camstone, Candid, Candour, Canescent, Canities, Caucasian, Chinese, Christmas, Cliffs, Collar, Company, Egg, Elephant, Ermine, European, Fang, Fard, Feather, Flag, Flake, Glair, Gwen(da), Gwendolen, Honorary, Hore, House, Innocent, Ivory, Lie, Lily, Livid, Man, Mealy, Opal, Oyster, Pale(face), Pallor, Paper, Pearl, Poor, Pure, Redleg, Russian, Sclerotic, Sheep, Snow(y), Taw, Wan, Wedding

White man Ba(c)kra, Buckra, Caucasian, Gub(bah), Haole, Honkie, Honky, Larney, Mzungu, Occidental, Ofay, Pakeha, Paleface, Redleg, Redneck, WASP

Whole, Wholehearted, Wholeness, Wholly All, Eager, Entire(ty), Fully, Hale, Intact, Integer, Integrity, Largely, Lot, Sum, Systemic, Thoroughly, Total, Unbroken, Uncut

Wholesale(r) Cutprice, En bloc, Engrosser, Jobber, Sweeping

Whoop(er), Whooping cough Alew, Celebrate, Chincough, Crane, Cry, Excite, Kink(cough), Kink-hoast, Pertussis, Swan

Whopper, Whopping Barn, Crammer, Huge, Immense, Jumbo, Lie, Lig, Oner, Out and outer, Scrouger, Slapper, Slockdolager, Soc(k)dalager, Soc(k)dolager, Soc(k)doliger, Soc(k)dologer, Sogdolager, Sogdoliger, Sogdologer, Tale, Taradiddle

Whore Drab, Harlot, Loose woman, Pinnace, Pro, Quail, Road, Strumpet, Tart

Wicked(ness) Atrocity, ➤ BAD, Candle, Criminal, Cru(i)sie, Crusy, Depravity, Devilish, Evil, Goaty, Godless, Heinous, Immoral, Impious, Improbity, Iniquity, Lantern, Nefarious, Night-light, Pravity, Prolate, Routh(ie), Sweeping, Taper, Turpitude, Unholy, Vile

▷ **Wicked** may indicate containing a wick

Wicket Gate, Hatch, Pitch, Square, Sticky, Stool, Stump, Yate

Wide, Widen(ing), Width Abroad, Ample, Bay, Broad, Dilate, Drib, Eclectic, Expand, Extend, Far, Flanch, Flange, Flare, Flaunch, Ga(u)ge, General, Miss, Prevalent, Roomy, Spacious, Spread, Sundry, Sweeping, Vast

Widespread Diffuse, Epidemic, Extensive, General, Pandemic, Panoramic, Prevalent, Prolate, Routh(ie), Sweeping

Widow(ed) Black, Dame, Dowager, Golf, Grass, Jointress, Relict, Sati, Sneerwell, Suttee, Vidual, Viduous, Whydah-bird, Widdy

Wife, Wives Bride, Concubine, Consort, Devi, Dutch, Enid, Feme, Feme covert, Frau, Harem, Harim, Helpmate, Helpmeet, Hen, Kali, Mate, Memsahib, Missis, Missus, Mrs, Partner, Potiphar's, Rib, Seraglio, Spouse, Squaw, Trouble and strife, Ux(or), W

Wig Bagwig, Bob(wig), Brutus, Buzz-wig, Campaign, Carpet, Cauliflower, Caxon, Chevelure, Chide, Cockernony, Dalmahoy, Full-bottomed, Gizz, Gregorian, Hair(piece), Jas(e)y, Jazey, Jiz, Major, Periwig, Peruke, Postiche, Ramil(l)ie(s), Rate, Reprimand, Rug, Scold, Scratch, Sheitel, Spencer, Targe, Tie, Toupee, Toupet, Tour

Wild Aberrant, Agrestal, Barbarous, Berserk, Bundu, Bush, Chimeric, Crazy, Earl, Errant, Erratic, Farouche, Feral, Frantic, Frenetic, Haggard, Hectic, Lawless, Mad(cap), Manic,

Meshugge, Myall, Natural, Rampant, Raver, Riotous, ➤ SAVAGE, Unmanageable, Unruly, Violent, Warrigal, West, Woolly

▷**Wild(ly)** may indicate an anagram

Wile, Wily Art, Artifice, Artful, Astute, Braide, ➤ CUNNING, Deceit, Foxy, Peery, Ruse, Shifty, Shrewd, Slee, ➤ SLY, Spider, Stratagem, Streetwise, Subtle, Trick, Versute, Wide

Wilful Deliberate, Headstrong, Heady, Obstinate, Recalcitrant, Wayward

Will, Willing(ly) Alsoon, Amenable, Bard, Bequeath, Bewildered, Bill(y), Complaisant, Compliant, Conation, Content, Desire, Devise, Fain, Free, Game, Hay, Leave, Legator, Lief, Lieve, Living, Obedient, On, Please, Prone, Purpose, Ready, Receptive, Scarlet, Soon, Spirit, Swan, Testament, Testate, Volition, Voluntary, Volunteer, Way, Wimble

▷**Will** may indicate an anagram

William(s) Bill(y), Conqueror, Occam, Orange, Pear, Rufus, Silent, Sweet, Tell, Tennessee

Willow(ing), Willowy Crack, Lissom(e), Lithe, Osier, Poplar, Pussy, Salix, Sallow, Sauch, Saugh, Supple, Twilly, Weeping, Withy

▶**Wily** see WILE

▷**Wimple** may indicate an anagram

Win(ner), Winning Achieve, ➤ BEAT, Capot, Champion, Conquer, Cup, Cute, Decider, Disarming, Dormie, Dormy, Earn, Endearing, First, Gain, Gammon, Hit, Jackpot, Land, Laureate, Lead, Medallist, Motser, Motza, Nice, Pile, Pot, Prevail, Profit, Purler, Rubicon, Shoo-in, Slam, Snip, Success, Sweet, Take, ➤ TRIUMPH, Up, Vellet, Velvet, Victor(y), Vole, Wrest

Wind(y) Aeolian, Air, Airstream, Anti-trade, Aquilo(n), Auster, Bend, Berg, Bise, Blore, Blow, Bluster, Bora, Boreas, Brass, Breeze, Brickfielder, Burp, Buster, Cape doctor, Chili, Chill, Chinook, Coil, Colic, Corus, Crank, Curl, Cyclone, Downwash, Draught, Draw, Dust devil, Easterly, Etesian, Eurus, Fearful, Firn, Flatulence, Flatus, Flaw, Fo(e)hn, Gale, Gas, Gregale, Gust, Haboob, Harmattan, Heaves, Hurricane, Kamseen, K(h)amsin, Levant(er), Libs, Meander, Mistral, Monsoon, Nervous, Nor(th)wester(ly), Noreast, Norther, Noser, Notus, Pampero, Ponent, Poop, Puna, Purl, Quill, Reeds, Reel, Rip-snorter, Roll, Samiel, Sciroc, Scirocco, Screw, Sea, Second, Serpentine, Simoom, Simoon, Sirocco, Slant, Snake, Snifter, Snorter,

Solano, Solar, Sough, Souther, Spiral, Spool, Squall, Stellar, Sumatra, Tail, Thread, Throw, Tornado, Tourbillon, Trade, Tramontana, Trend, Turn, Twaddle, Twine, Twister, Typhoon, Veer, Ventose, Waffle, Weave, Wester, Whirlblast, White squall, Williwaw, Willy-willy, Winch, Wrap, Wreathe, Wrest

Winding(s) Ambages, Anfractuous, Creeky, Evagation, Link, Sinuous, Spiral, Tortuous, Twisty

Window(s) Bay, Bow, Casement, Catherine-wheel, Companion, Compass, Day, Deadlight, Dormer, Dream-hole, Eye, Eyelids, Fanlight, Fenestella, Fenestra, French, Gable, Garret, Glaze, Guichet, Jalousie, Jesse, Judas, Lancet, Lattice, Launch, Loop-light, Lozen, Lucarne, Lunette, Luthern, Lychnoscope, Marigold, Mezzanine, Mirador, Monial, Mullion, Oculus, Oeil-de-boeuf, Ogive, Orb, Oriel, Ox-eye, Pane, Pede, Picture, Porthole, Quarterlight, Rosace, Rose, Sash, Sexfoil, Spyhole, Storm, Transom, Trellis, Ventana, Weather, Wicket, Windock, Winnock

Window-bar, Window-fastening Astragal, Espagnolette

Wine Anker, Biddy, Bin, Bishop, Blanc, Bombo, Bubbly, Champers, Chateau, Comet, Cup, Cuvée, Dessert, Fortified, Gluhwein, Hippocras, Log-juice, Loll-shraub, Loll-shrob, Mountain, Mull, Must, Negus, Noisy, Oenology, Oenomel, Ordinaire, Piece, Piment, Pipe, Plonk, Plotty, Prisage, Race, Red, Sangaree, Sangria, Sec, Sparkling, Straw, Stum, Supernaculum, Table, Toddy, Tun, Vat, Vermouth, Vin ordinaire, Vin(o), Vinho verde, Vintage, White

Wing(ed), Winger, Wings, Wing-like Aerofoil, Ala(r), Alula, Annexe, Appendage, Arm, Bastard, ➤ BIRD, Branch, Canard, Cellar, Corium, Coulisse, Delta, Dipteral, El(l), Elevon, Elytral, Elytriform, Elytron, Elytrum, Fender, Flap, Flew, Flipper, Forward, Halteres, Hurt, Left, Limb, Parascenia, Parascenium, Patagium, Pennate, Pennon, Pinero, Pinion, Pip, Pterygoid, Putto, Right, Rogallo, Sail, Scent-scale, Segreant, Seraphim, Sweepback, Sweptback, Sweptwing, Swift, Swingwing, Tailplane, Tectrix, Tegmen, Transept, Van, Vol(et), Wound(ed)

▷ **Winger** may indicate a bird

Wink Bat, Condone, Connive, Flicker, Ignore, Instant, Nap, Nictitate, Pink, Twinkle

Winnow Fan, Riddle, Separate, Sift, Van, Wecht

Winter, Wintry Bleak, Brumal, Cold, Dec, Fimbul, Frigid, Frore, Hibernate, Hiemal, Hiems, Hodiernal, Jasmine, Nuclear, Snowy

Wipe (out), Wiping Abolish, Abrogate, Absterge, Amortise, Cancel, Cleanse, Demolish, Destroy, Deterge, Dicht, Dight, Expunge, Hanky, Mop, Nose-rag, Null, Purge, Raze, Sponge, Tersion, Tissue

Wire(s), Wiry Aerial, Barb(ed), Cable, Chicken, Coil, Earth, Filament, Filar, File, Heald, Heddle, High, Lean, Lecher, Live, Marconigram, Mil, Nichrome®, Nipper, Pickpocket, Razor, Sinewy, Snake, Spit, Staple, Stilet, Strand, String, Stylet, Telegram, Thoth, Thread

Wise(acre), Wisdom Advisedly, Athena, Athene, Canny, Depth, Ernie, Gothamite, Hep, Hindsight, Judgement, Learned, Long-headed, Lore, Manner, Mimir, Minerva, Norman, Oracle, Owl, Philosopher, Philosophy, Politic, Polymath, Prajna, Profound, Prudence, Sagacity, Sage, Salomonic, Sapience, Savvy, Shrewd, Sophia, Smartie, Solon, Wice

Wise man Balthazar, Caspar, Heptad, Melchior, Nestor, Sage, Sapient, Seer, Solomon, Swami, Thales, Worldly

Wish(es) Crave, Death, Desiderate, ➤ DESIRE, Hope, List, Long, Pleasure, Precatory, Regards, Velleity, Want, Yearn

Wit(s), Witticism, Witty Acumen, Attic, Badinage, Banter, Brevity, Commonsense, Concetto, Cunning, Dry, Epigram, Esprit, Estimation, Eutrapelia, Eutrapely, Facetious, Fantasy, Hartford, Humour, Imagination, Intelligence, Irony, Jest, Jeu d'esprit, Joke, Marbles, Marinism, Memory, Mind, Mot, Mother, Native, Nous, Pawky, Pun, Repartee, Rogue, Sally, Salt, Saut, Sconce, ➤ SENSE, Shaft, Smart, Videlicet, Viz, Wag, Weet, Wisecrack, Word-play

Witch(craft) Broomstick, Cantrip, Carline, Circe, Coven, Craigfluke, Crone, Cutty Sark, Ensorcell, Galdragon, Glamour, Goety, Gramary(e), Gyre-carlin, Hag, Hecat(e), Hex, Lamia, Magic, Medea, Myal(ism), Night-hag, Obeahism, Obiism, Pythoness, Salem, Selim, Sibyl, Sieve, Sorceress, Speller, Sycorax, Trout, Valkyrie, Vaudoo, Vilia, Voodoo, Weird, Wicca

With And, By, Con, Cum, Hereby, In, Mit, Of, W

Withdraw(al), Withdrawn Abdicate, Alienate, Aloof, Cold turkey, Detach, Disengage, Distrait, Enshell, Evacuate, Inshell, Introvert, Offish, Palinode, Preserve, Recant, Recoil, Repair,

Resile, Reticent, Retire, Retract(ion), Retreat, Revoke, Revulsion, Scratch, Secede, Sequester, Shrink, Shy, Subduct, Unreeve, Unsay

Wither(ed), Withering, Withers Arefy, Atrophy, Burn, Corky, Die, Droop, Dry, Evanish, Fade, Forpine, Googie, Languish, Marcescent, Miff, Nose, Scram, Sere, Shrink, Shrivel, Welk, Welt

▷**With gaucherie** may indicate an anagram

Withhold(ing) Abstain, Conceal, Curt, Deny, Detain, Detinue, Hide, Keep, ► RESERVE, Trover

Within Enclosed, Endo-, Indoors, Inside, Interior, Intra

Without Bar, Beyond, Ex, Lack(ing), Less, Minus, Orb, Outdoors, Outside, Sans, Save, Sen, Senza, Sine, X

▷**Without** may indicate one word surrounding another

▷**Without restraint** may indicate an anagram

Witness Attest, Bystander, Deponent, Depose, Expert, Evidence, Hostile, Jehovah's, Martyr, Material, Muggletonian, Observe, Obtest, Onlooker, Proof, ► SEE, Testament, Teste, Testify, Testimony

►**Witticism** see WIT

Wizard (priest) Archimage, Carpathian, Conjuror, Expert, Gandalf, Hex, Magician, Merlin, Oz, Prospero, Shaman, Sorcerer, Super, Warlock, ► WITCH-DOCTOR

Wobble, Wobbling Chandler's, Coggle, Precess, Quaver, Rock, Shoggle, Shoogle, Totter, Tremble, Trillo, Wag, Waggle, Walty, Waver

Woe(ful) Alack, Alas, Bale, Bane, Distress, Doole, Dule, Ewhow, Gram, Grief, Jeremiad, Lack-a-day, Misery, Pain, Plague, ► SORROW, Tribulation

Wolf(-like) Akela, Assyrian, Cancer, Casanova, Coyote, Cram, Dangler, Earth, Engorge, Fenrir, Fenris, Gorge, Grey, Ise(n)grim, Lobo, Lone, Lothario, Lupine, Luster, Lycanthrope, MI, Michigan, Pack, Prairie, Red, Rip, Rout, Rye, Scoff, Sea, Strand, Tasmanian, Thylacine, Tiger, Timber, Wanderer, Were, Whistler

Woman(hood), Women Anile, Besom, Biddy, Bimbo, Bint, Boiler, Broad, Callet, Chai, Crone, Cummer, Dame, Daughter, Doe, Dona(h), Dorcas, Drab, Eve, F, Fair, ► FEMALE, Feme, Flapper, Floozy, Frail, Frow, Gammer, Gin, Girl, Gyno-, Harpy,

Harridan, Inner, Jade, Lilith, Madam(e), Mademoiselle, Peat, Tottie, Totty, -gyny, Hen, Her, Jane, Lady, Lorette, Mary, Miladi, Milady, Mob, Mort, Ms, Pandora, Pict, Piece, Placket, Popsy, Quean, Queen, Ramp, Rib, Ribibe, Rudas, Runnion, Sabine, Scarlet, She, Skirt, Sort, Squaw, Tail, Tib, Tiring, Tit, Trot, Wahine, Wifie

Wonder(s) Admire, Agape, Amazement, AR, Arkansas, Arrah, Awe, Colossus, Ferly, Grape-seed, Marle, ➤ MARVEL, Meteor, Mirabilia, Miracle, Muse, Nine-day, Phenomenon, Prodigy, Speculate, Stupor, Suppose, Surprise, Wheugh, Whew, Wow

Wonderful(ly) Amazing, Bees' knees, Bitchin(g), Chinless, Ferly, Gee-whiz, Gramercy, Épatant, Fantastic, Far-out, Geason, Glorious, Great, Lal(l)apalooza, Magic, Mirable, Old, Purely, Ripping, Smashing, Sublime

Wood(en), Woodland, Woody Batten, Bavin, Beam, Beaver, Bent, Birnam, Blockboard, Board, Bocage, Boord(e), Boscage, Bowl, Brassie, Bushveld, Caatinga, Cam, Cambium, Carr, Cask, Channel, Chipboard, Chittagong, Clapboard, Conductor, Coppice, Copse, Cord, Coulisse, Dead, Deadpan, Deal, Dingle, Drive, Dunnage, Duramen, Fathom, Fire, Firth, Fish, Forest, Frith, Fruitwood, Funk, Furious, Gambrel, Gantry, Gapó, Gauntree, Green, Grove, Hanger, Hard, Heartwood, Holt, Hurst, Hyle, Igapó, Isle, Joist, Kindling, Kip, Knee, Lath, Log(gat), Lumber, Mad, Matchwood, Mazer, Nemoral, Nemorous, Offcut, Pallet, Pulpwood, Punk, Raddle, Rock, Shaw, Silvan, Slat, Soft, Spinney, Splat, Spline, Splint, Spoon, Stolid, Taiga, Tangle, Three-ply, Timber, Touch, Treen, Trees, Twiggy, Vert, Wald, Wenge, Wild, Xylem, Xyloid

▷ **Wood** may indicate an anagram (in sense of mad)

Woodpecker Bird, Flicker, Hickwall, Picarian, Rainbird, Sapsucker, Saurognathae, Witwall, Woodwale, Yaffle

Woodwind Bassoon, Clarinet, Cornet, Flute, Oboe, Piccolo, Pipe, Recorder, Reed

Wool(len), Woolly Alpaca, Angora, Aran, Beige, Berlin, Botany, Bouclé, Cardi(gan), Cashmere, Clip, Cotton, Dog, Doily, Doyley, Down, Drugget, Duffel, Fadge, Fingering, Fleece, Flock, Fuzz, Glass, Guernsey, Hank, Jaeger, Jersey, Kashmir, Ket, Lanate, Lock, Merino, Mineral, Noil(s), Offsorts, Oo, Pashm, Pelage, Persian, Rock, Say, Shetland, Shoddy, Skein, Slip-on,

Slipe, Slub, Spencer, Staple, Steel, Swansdown, Tammy, Three-ply, Tod, Tricot, Tweed, Vicuna, Virgin, Wire, Yarn

Word(s), Wording, Wordy Buzz, Claptrap, Code, Comment, Dick, Dit(t), Epos, Etymon, Faith, Ghost, Grace, Hard, Heteronym, Hint, ➤ IN A WORD, ➤ IN TWO WORDS, Key, Last, Lexeme, Lexicon, Lexis, Logia, Logos, Lyrics, Mantra, Message, Mot, Neologism, News, Nonce, Nonsense, Noun, Oracle, Order, Palabra, Paragram, Parole, Phrase, Pledge, Portmanteau, Prolix, Promise, Rumour, Saying, Semantics, Signal, Subtitle, Surtitle, Term, Tetragram, Text, Verb, Verbiage, Verbose, Warcry, Weasel, Written

Work(er), Working(-class), Workman(ship) Act(ivate), Ant, Appliqué, Artefact, Artel, Artifact, Artificer, Artisan, Beaver, Bee, Blue-collar, Bohunk, Business, Casual, Char, Chore, Claim, Clock, Coolie, Corvée, Do, Dog, Dogsbody, Drudge, Drug, Earn, Effect, Effort, Ergon, Ergonomics, Em, Eta, Evince, Exercise, Exploit, Factotum, Facture, Fat, Fettler, Field, Fret, ➤ FUNCTION, Fuller, Gel, Go, Graft, Grind, Hand, Harness, Hat, Hobo, Horse, Hunky, Industry, Innards, Job, Journeyman, Labour, Laid, Luddite, Lump, Man, Manipulate, Midinette, Mine, Moil, Moonlight, Movement, Navvy, Neuter, Oeuvre, On, Op, Opera(tion), Operative, Operator, Opus, Ouvrier, Ox, Peasant, Peg, Pensum, Peon, Ply, Potboiler, Practise, Production, Prole(tariat), Pursuit, Red-neck, Rep, Ride, Roughneck, Rouseabout, Roustabout, Run, Satisfactory, Scabble, Serve, Service, Situation, Slogger, Smithy, Social, Staff, Stevedore, Stint, Strive, Sweat, Swink, Take, Tamper, Task, Temp, Tenail(le), Termite, Tew, Tick, Till, Toccata, Toil, Travail, Treatise, Trojan, TU, Tut, Uphill, Walla(h), White-collar

▷**Working** may indicate an anagram

Works, Workshop Atelier, Engine, Factory, Forge, Foundry, Garage, Hacienda, Innards, Lab, Mill, Plant, Shed, Shop, Skylab, Smithy, Studio

World(ly) Carnal, Chthonic, Cosmopolitan, Cosmos, Dream, Earth, Fourth, Ge, Globe, Kingdom, Lay, Mappemond, Microcosm, Mondaine, Mondial, Mundane, Orb, Oyster, Planet, Possible, Secular, Sensual, Society, Sphere, Temporal, Terra, Terrene, Terrestrial, Third, Universe, Vale, Welt

Worm(-like), Worms, Wormy Annelid, Annulata, Apod(e), Apodous, Articulata, Diet, Edge, Helminth, Merosome, Servile, Termite, Vermiform

Worn(-out) Attrite, Bare, Decrepit, Detrition, Effete, Epuisé, Exhausted, Forfairn, Forfoughten, Forjaskit, Forjeskit, Frazzled, Old, On, Passé, Raddled, Rag, Seedy, Shabby, Shot, Spent, Stale, Tired, Traikit, Trite, Used, Weathered, Whacked

Worried, Worrier, Worry Agonise, Annoy, Anxiety, Badger, Bait, Beset, Bother, Care(worn), Cark, Chafe, Concern, Deave, Deeve, Distress, Disturb, Dog, Eat, Exercise, Feeze, Frab, Fret, Fuss, Harass, Harry, Hyp, Inquietude, Knag, Nag, Perturb, Pester, Pheeze, Pheeze, Phese, Pingle, Pium, Rile, Sool, Stew, Tew, Touse, Towse, Trouble, Vex, Wherrit, Worn

▷**Worried** may indicate an anagram

Worse(n) Adversely, Degenerate, Deteriorate, Exacerbate, Impair, Inflame, Pejorate, Regress, War(re), Waur

Worship(per) Adore, Adulation, Angelolatry, Autolatry, Bless, Churchgoer, Cult, Deify, Douleia, Dulia, Epeolatry, Fetish, Glorify, Gurdwara, Idolise, Latria, Lionise, Liturgics, Lordolatry, Mariolatry, Oncer, Orant, Praise, Puja, Revere, Sabaism, Sakta, Service, Shacharis, Shakta, Synaxis, Thiasus, Vaishnava, Venerate, Votary, Wodenism

Worst Beat, Best, Defeat, Get, Nadir, Outdo, Overpower, Pessimum, Rock-bottom, Scum, Severest, Throw, Trounce

Worsted Caddis, Caddyss, Challis, Coburg, Genappe, Lea, Ley, Serge, Shalli, Tamin(e), Whipcord

▷**Worsted** may indicate an anagram

Worth(while), Worthy Admirable, Asset, Be, Cop, Deserving, Eligible, Estimable, Feck, ➤ **MERIT**, Notable, Substance, Tanti, Use, Value, Virtuous, Wealth

Worthless (person) Base, Beggarly, Bodger, Bootless, Bum, Catchpenny, Cheapjack, Crumb, Cypher, Damn, Doit, Dreck, Dross, Fallal, Frippery, Gimcrack, Gingerbread, Gubbins, Jimcrack, Left, Light, Mud, Nugatory, Nyaff, Obol, Orra, Otiose, Paltry, Pin, Poxy, Punk, Raca, Rag, Rap, Rubbishy, Scabby, Scum, Sorry, Straw, Tinhorn, Tinpot, Tinsel, Tittle, Toerag, Trangam, Trashy, Trumpery, Tuppenny, Twat, Two-bit, Twopenny, Useless, Vain, Vile

Wound(ed) Battery, Bite, Bless, Blighty, Bruise, Chagrin, Coiled, Crepance, Cut, Dere, Engore, Ganch, Gash, Gaunch,

Gore, Harm, Hurt, Injury, Lacerate, Lesion, Maim, Molest, Mortify, Offend, Pip, Sabre-cut, Scab, Scar, Scath, Scotch, Scratch, Shoot, Snaked, Snub, Sore, Stab, Sting, Trauma, Twined, Umbrage, Vuln, Vulnerary, Walking, Wing, Wint

Wrangle, Wrangling Argie-bargie, ➤ ARGUE, Altercate, Bandy, Bicker, Brangle, Broil, Dispute, Haggle, Mathematical, Rag, Vitilitigation

Wrap(per), Wrapping, Wrap up Amice, Amis, Bind, Bubble, Bundle, Cellophane®, Cere, Clingfilm, Cloak, Clothe, Cocoon, Conclude, Emboss, Enfold, Enrol(l), Ensheath(e), Envelop(e), Foil, Folio, Furl, Hap, Hem, Kimono, Kraft, Lag, Lap, Mail, Muffle, Negligee, Parcel, Roll, Rug, Shawl, Sheath(e), Stole, Swaddle, Swathe, Tinfoil, Tsutsumu, Velamen, Wap, Wimple

Wreath(e) Adorn, Anadem, Chaplet, Coronal, Crown, Entwine, Festoon, Garland, Laurel, Lei, Torse, Tortile, Twist

Wreck(age), Wrecked, Wrecker Crab, Debris, Demolish, Devastate, Flotsam, Founder, Goner, Hesperus, Hulk, Lagan, Ligan, Luddite, Mutilate, Ruin(ate), Sabotage, Shambles, Shatter, Sink, Smash, Subvert, Torpedo, Trash, Wrack

▷**Wrecked** may indicate an anagram

Wrench Allen, Fit, Jerk, Lug, Mole, Monkey, Pin, Pull, Socket, Spanner, Sprain, Stillson®, Strain, Tear, Twist, Windlass, Wrest

Wrestle(r), Wrestling All-in, Arm, Basho, Clinch, Flying mare, Grapple, Haystacks, Indian, Judo, Milo, Sambo, Stable, Struggle, Sumo, Tag, Tag (team), Tussle, Writhe

Wretch(ed) Blackguard, Blue, Caitiff, Chap-fallen, Cullion, Forlorn, Git, Hapless, Lorn, Measly, Miser, Miserable, Peelgarlic, Pilgarlick, Pipsqueak, Poltroon, Poor, Punk, Rat, Scoundrel, Scroyle, Seely, Snake, Unblest, Wo(e)

▷**Wretched** may indicate an anagram

Wrinkle(d), Wrinkly Clue, Cockle, Corrugate, Crease, Crepy, Crimpy, Crow's-foot, Crumple, Fold, Frounce, Frown, Frumple, Furrow, Gen, Groove, Headline, Hint, Idea, Line, Lirk, Plissé, Pucker, Purse, Ridge, Rimple, Rivel, Rop(e)y, Ruck(le), Rugose, Rumple, Runkle, Seamy, Shrivel, Sulcus, Time-worn, Tip

Writ(s) Capias, Certiorari, Cursitor, Dedimus, Distringas, Elegit, Fieri facias, Filacer, Habeas corpus, Holy, Injunction, Latitat, Law-burrows, Mandamus, Mittimus, Noverint, Praemunire,

Process, Replevin, Scirefacias, Significat, Subpoena, Summons, Supersedeas, Tolt, Venire, Warrant

Write(r), Writing Apocrypha, ➤ AUTHOR, Automatic, Ballpoint, Biographer, Biro®, Bloomsbury Group, Calligraphy, Clerk, Columnist, Creative, Diarist, Dite, ➤ DRAMATIST, Draft, Endorse, Endoss, Engross, Epigrammatise, Epistle, ➤ ESSAYIST, Expatiate, Fist, Form, Formulary, Freelance, Ghost, Graffiti, Graphite, Hack, Hairline, Hand, Hieratic, Hiragana, Indite, Ink, Inkslinger, Inscribe, Join-hand, Jot(tings), Journalese, Journalist, Journo, Kaleyard School, Kana, Leader, Lexigraphy, Lexis, Linear A, Lipogram, Litterateur, Longhand, Lucubrate, Mirror, Ms(s), Nib, Notary, Notate, Novelese, ➤ NOVELIST, Pen, Pencil, Penmanship, Pentel®, Planchette, ➤ POET, Polemic, Pot-hook, Proser, Quill, Roundhand, Sanskrit, Sci-fi, Scratch, Screed, Screeve, Scribe, Scrip(t), Scripture, Scrivener, Secretary, Style, Subscript, Superscribe, Sutra, Syllabary, Tantra, Transcribe, Treatise, Uncial, Wordsmith

▷**Writhing** may indicate an anagram

Wrong Aggrieve, Agley, Amiss, Astray, Awry, Bad, Chout, Delict, Disservice, Err, Fallacious, False, Harm, Ill, Immoral, Improper, Incorrect, Injury, Mischief, Misintelligence, Misled, Mistake(n), Misuse, Nocent, Offbase, Offend, Peccadillo, Perverse, Sin(ful), Tort, Transgress, Unethical, Unright, Unsuitable, Withershins, Wryly, X

▷**Wrong** may indicate an anagram

Wry Askew, Contrary, Devious, Distort, Droll, Grimace, Ironic

Xx

X(-shaped) Buss, By, Chi, Christ, Cross, Decussate, Drawn, Kiss, Ten, Times, Unknown, X-ray

X-ray Angiogram, Cholangiography, Emi-Scanner, Encephalogram, Encephalograph, Fermi, Grenz, Mammogram, Plate, Pyelogram, Radioscopy, Rem, Roentgen, Sciagram, Screening, Skiagram, Tomography, Venogram

Xmas Noel, Yuletide
Xylophone Marimba, Sticcado, Sticcato

Yy

Yacht Britannia, Dragon, Ice, Keelboat, Land, Maxi, Sailboat, Sand
Yachtsman, Yachtsmen Chichester, RYS
Yank(ee) Bet, Carpetbagger, Hitch, Jerk, Jonathan, Lug, Northerner, Pluck, Pull, Rug, Schlep(p), So(o)le, Sowl(e), ➤ TUG, Tweak, Twitch, Wrench, Wrest
▷ **Yank** may indicate an anagram
Yard Area, CID, Close, Court, Farm-toun, Garden, Haw, Hof, Kail, Mast, Measure, Patio, Ree(d), Scotland, Spar, Sprit, Steel, Stick, Stride, Y, Yd
Yarn(s) Abb, Berlin, Bouclé, Caddice, Caddis, Chenille, Clew, Clue, Cop, Cord, Crewel, Fib, Fibroline, Fingering, Genappe, Gimp, Gingham, Guimp(e), Gymp, Homespun, Jaw, Knittle, Knot, Lay, Lea, Ley, Line, Lisle, Lurex®, Marl, Merino, Nylon, Organzine, Orlon®, Ply, Rigmarole, Ripping, Saxony, Sennit, Sinnet, Skein, Story, Strand, Tale, Taradiddle, Thread, Thrid, Thrum(my), Tram, Warp, Weft, Woof, Wool, Worsted, Zephyr
Yawn(ing) Boredom, Chasmy, Fissure, Gant, Gape, Gaunt, Greys, Hiant, Oscitation, Pandiculation, Rictus
Year(ly), Years A, Age, Anno, Annual, Astronomical, Common, Dot, Equinoctial, Financial, Fiscal, Gap, Indiction, Julian, Leap, Light, Lunar, PA, Platonic, Riper, Sabbatical, Sidereal, Solar, Sothic, Summer, Sun, Tax, Time, Towmon(d), Towmont, Twelvemonth
Yearn(ing) Ache, Ake, Aspire, Brame, Burn, Crave, Curdle, Desire, Erne, Greed, Hanker, Hone, ➤ LONG, Nostalgia, Pant, Pine, Sigh
▷ **Yearning** may indicate an anagram
Yeast Barm, Bees, Brewer's, Ferment, Flor, Leaven, Saccharomycete, Torula, Vegemite®

Yellow(ish) Amber, Auburn, Back, Beige, Buff, Canary, Chicken, Chrome, Citrine, Cowardly, Craven, Etiolin, Fallow, Fever, Filemot, Flavin(e), Flaxen, Gamboge, Gold, Icteric, Isabel(le), Jack, Jaundiced, Lemon(y), Mustard, Nankeen, Naples, Oaker, Or(eide), Pages, Peril, Pink, Primrose, River, Saffron, Sallow, Sear, Spineless, Straw, Sulphur, Tawny, Topaz, Tow, Weld, Yolk

Yes Ay(e), Da, Indeed, Ja, Jokol, Nod, OK, Oke, Quite, Sure, Truly, Uh-huh, Wilco, Yea, Yokul, Yup

Yesterday Démodé, Eve, Hesternal, Pridian

Yield(ing) Abandon, Afford, Bend, Bow, Breed, Capitulate, Catch, Cede, Come, Comply, Concede, Crack, Crop, Defer, Dividend, Docile, Ductile, Easy, Elastic, Facile, Flaccid, Flexible, Give, Harvest, Interest, Knuckle, Meek, Meltith, Mess, Output, Pan, Pay, Pliant, Produce, Relent, Render, Return, Sag, Soft, ➤ SUBMIT, Succumb, Surrender, Susceptible, Truckle

Yoke Bow, Cang(ue), Collar, Couple, Harness, Inspan, Jugal, Pair, Span

Yokel Boor, Bumpkin, Chaw(-bacon), Clumperton, Hayseed, Hick, Jake, Jock, Peasant, Rustic

Yon(der) Distant, Further, O'erby, Thae, There, Thether, Thither

York(shire), Yorkshireman Batter, Bowl, Ebor, Pudding, Ridings, Tyke

You One, Sie, Thee, Thou, Usted, Ye

Young (person), Youngster, Youth(ful) Adolescent, Boy, Boyhood, Bub, Ch, Chick, Chicken, Child, Chile, Cockerel, Cockle, Colt, Cub, DJ, Early, Ephebe, Ephebus, Esquire, Flapper, Fledgling, Foetus, Fry, Gigolo, Girl, Hebe, Hobbledehoy, Immature, Imp, Infant, Issue, Junior, Juvenal, Juvenesce, Juvenile, Kid, Kiddo, Kiddy, Kipper, Lad, Lamb, Latter-day, Less, Litter, Little, Minor, Misspent, Mod, Mormon, Nance, Nestling, New, Nipper, Nymph, Plant, Progeny, Protégé(e), Punk, Pup, Sapling, Scent, Scion, Shaver, Skinhead, Slip, Son, Spawn, Sprig, Stripling, Swain, Ted, Teenager, Teens, Teenybopper, Toyboy, Whelp, Whippersnapper

Younger, Youngest Baby, Benjamin, Cadet, Last born, Less, Minimus, Seneca, Wallydrag, Wallydraigle, Yr

Zz

Z Izzard, Izzet, Zambia, Zebra

Zeal(ous) Ardour, Bigotry, Devotion, Eager, Enthusiasm, Evangelic, Fervour, Fire, Perfervid, Study

Zealot Bigot, Devotee, Fan(atic), St Simon, Votary

Zenith Acme, Apogee, Height, Pole, Summit

Zephyr Breeze, Wind

Zeppelin Airship, Balloon, Dirigible

Zero Absolute, Blob, Cipher, Ground, Nil, Nothing, Nought, O, Z

Zest Condiment, Crave, Élan, Gusto, Pep, Piquancy, Relish, Spice, Tang, Zap

Zigzag Crémaillère, Crinkle-crankle, Dancette, Feather-stitch, Indent, Ric-rac, Slalom, Stagger, Tack, Traverse, Yaw

Zinc Blende, Gahnite, Mossy, Sherardise, Spelter, Sphalerite, Tutenag, Tutty, Willemite, Wurtzite, Zn

Zip(per) Dash, Energy, Fastener, Fly, Go, Oomph, Presto, Stingo, Vim, Vivacity, Whirry, Zero

Zodiac(al) Aquarius, Archer, Aries, Bull, Cancer, Capricorn, Counter-glow, Crab, Fish, Gemini, Gegenschein, Goat, Horoscope, Leo, Libra, Lion, Ophiuchus, Pisces, Ram, Sagittarius, Scales, Scorpio(n), Taurus, Twins, Virgin, Virgo, Watercarrier

Zone Anacoustic, Area, Band, Belt, Benioff, Buffer, Canal, Climate, Collision, Convergence, Crumple, Drop, Ecotone, End, Enterprise, Erogenous, Exclusion, F layer, Free, Fresnel, Frigid, Hot, Impact, No-fly, Precinct, ➤ REGION, Rift, Ring, Sahel, Smokeless, Temperate, Time, Torrid, Tundra, Twilight